St. Vincent's Hospital
Library
209
WITHDRAWN

D1419216

DSM-IV Classification: Axes I and II

Axis I

DISORDERS USUALLY FIRST DIAGNOSED IN INFANCY, CHILDHOOD, OR ADOLESCENCE

Mental Retardation
Mild Mental Retardation / Moderate Retardation / Severe Mental Retardation / Profound Mental Retardation

Learning Disorders (Academic Skills Disorders)
Reading Disorder (Developmental Reading Disorder) / Mathematics Disorder (Developmental Arithmetic Disorder) / Disorder of Written Expression (Developmental Expressive Writing Disorder)

Motor Skills Disorder
Developmental Coordination Disorder

Pervasive Developmental Disorders
Autistic Disorder / Rett's Disorder / Childhood Disintegrative Disorder / Asperger's Disorder

Disruptive Behavior and Attention-deficit Disorders
Attention-deficit/Hyperactivity Disorder / Oppositional Defiant Disorder / Conduct Disorder

Feeding and Eating Disorders of Infancy or Early Childhood
Pica / Rumination Disorder / Feeding Disorder of Infancy or Early Childhood

Tic Disorders
Tourette's Disorder / Chronic Motor or Vocal Tic Disorder / Transient Tic Disorder

Communication Disorders
Expressive Language Disorder (Developmental Expressive Language Disorder) / Mixed Receptive/Expressive Language Disorder (Developmental Receptive Language Disorder) / Phonological Disorder (Developmental Articulation Disorder) / Stuttering

Elimination Disorders
Encopresis / Enuresis

Other Disorders of Infancy, Childhood, or Adolescence
Separation Anxiety Disorder / Selective Mutism (Elective Mutism) / Reactive Attachment Disorder of Infancy or Early Childhood / Stereotypic Movement Disorder (Stereotypy/Habit Disorder)

DELIRIUM, DEMENTIA, AMNESTIC AND OTHER COGNITIVE DISORDERS

Deliria
Delirium Due to a General Medical Condition / Substance-induced Delirium / Delirium Due to Multiple Etiologies

Dementias
Dementia of the Alzheimer's Type; With Early Onset: if onset at age 65 or below; With Late Onset: if onset after age 65 / Vascular Dementia / Dementias Due to Other General Medical Conditions / Substance-induced Persisting Dementia / Dementia Due to Multiple Etiologies

Amnestic Disorders
Amnestic Disorder Due to a General Medical Condition / Substance-induced Persisting Amnestic Disorder (refer to specific substance for code)

SUBSTANCE RELATED DISORDERS

Alcohol Use Disorders
Amphetamine (or Related Substance) Use Disorders
Caffeine Use Disorders
Cannabis Use Disorders
Cocaine Use Disorders
Hallucinogen Use Disorders
Inhalant Use Disorders
Nicotine Use Disorders
Opioid Use Disorders
Phencyclidine (or Related Substance) Use Disorders
Sedative, Hypnotic, or Anxiolytic Substance Use Disorders
Polysubstance Use Disorder

SCHIZOPHRENIA AND OTHER PSYCHOTIC DISORDERS

Schizophrenia
Paranoid Type / Disorganized Type / Catatonic Type / Undifferentiated Type / Residual Type

Schizophreniform Disorder
Schizoaffective Disorder
Delusional Disorder
Brief Psychotic Disorder
Shared Psychotic Disorder (Folie à Deux)
Psychotic Disorder Due to a General Medical Condition
with delusions / with hallucinations / Substance-induced Psychotic Disorder

MOOD DISORDERS

Depressive Disorders
Major Depressive Disorder / Dysthymic Disorder

Bipolar Disorders
Bipolar I Disorder / Bipolar II Disorder (Recurrent Major Depressive Episodes with Hypomania) / Cyclothymic Disorder

Mood Disorder Due to a General Medical Condition
Substance-Induced Mood Disorder

ANXIETY DISORDERS

Panic Disorder
Without Agoraphobia / With Agoraphobia

Agoraphobia Without History of Panic Disorder
Specific Phobia (Simple Phobia)
Social Phobia (Social Anxiety Disorder)
Obsessive-Compulsive Disorder
Posttraumatic Stress Disorder
Acute Stress Disorder
Generalized Anxiety Disorder (includes Overanxious Disorder of Childhood)
Anxiety Disorder Due to a General Medical Condition
Substance-Induced Anxiety Disorder

SOMATOFORM DISORDERS

Somatization Disorder
Conversion Disorder
Hypochondriasis
Body Dysmorphic Disorder
Pain Disorder

FACTITIOUS DISORDERS

Factitious Disorder

DISSOCIATIVE DISORDERS

Dissociative Amnesia
Dissociative Fugue
Dissociative Identity Disorder (Multiple Personality Disorder)
Depersonalization Disorder

SEXUAL AND GENDER IDENTITY DISORDERS

Sexual Dysfunctions
Sexual Desire Disorders: Hypoactive Sexual Desire Disorder; Sexual Aversion Disorder / Sexual Arousal Disorders: Female Sexual Arousal Disorder; Male Erectile Disorder / Orgasm Disorders: Female Orgasmic Disorder (Inhibited Female Orgasm); Male Orgasmic Disorder (Inhibited Male Orgasm); Premature Ejaculation / Sexual Pain Disorders: Dyspareunia; Vaginismus / Sexual Dysfunctions Due to a General Medical Condition / Substance-induced Sexual Dysfunction
Paraphilias
Exhibitionism / Fetishism / Frotteurism / Pedophilia / Sexual Masochism / Sexual Sadism / Voyeurism / Transvestic Fetishism
Gender Identity Disorders
Gender Identity Disorder: in Children / in Adolescents and Adults (Transsexualism).

EATING DISORDERS

Anorexia Nervosa
Bulimia Nervosa

SLEEP DISORDERS

Primary Sleep Disorders
Dyssomnias: Primary Insomnia; Primary Hypersomnia; Narcolepsy; Breathing-Related Sleep Disorder; Circadian Rhythm Sleep Disorder (Sleep-Wake Schedule Disorder) / Parasomnias; Nightmare Disorder (Dream Anxiety Disorder); Sleep Terror Disorder; Sleepwalking Disorder / Sleep Disorders Related to Another Mental Disorder
Sleep Disorder Due to a General Medical Condition
Substance-induced Sleep Disorder

IMPULSE CONTROL DISORDERS NOT ELSEWHERE CLASSIFIED

Intermittent Explosive Disorder
Kleptomania
Pyromania
Pathological Gambling
Trichotillomania

ADJUSTMENT DISORDERS

Adjustment Disorder
With Anxiety
With Depressed Mood
With Disturbance of Conduct
With Mixed Disturbance of Emotions and Conduct
With Mixed Anxiety and Depressed Mood

Axis II

PERSONALITY DISORDERS

Paranoid Personality Disorder
Schizoid Personality Disorder
Schizotypal Personality Disorder
Antisocial Personality Disorder
Borderline Personality Disorder
Histrionic Personality Disorder
Narcissistic Personality Disorder
Avoidant Personality Disorder
Dependent Personality Disorder
Obsessive-Compulsive Personality Disorder

OTHER CONDITIONS THAT MAY BE A FOCUS OF CLINICAL ATTENTION

Psychological Factors Affecting Medical Condition
Medication-Induced Movement Disorders
Relational Problems
Relational Problem Related to A Mental Disorder or General Medical Condition / Parent-Child Relational Problem / Partner Relational Problem / Sibling Relational Problem
Problems Related to Abuse or Neglect
Physical Abuse of Child / Sexual Abuse of Child / Neglect of Child / Physical Abuse of Adult / Sexual Abuse of Adult
Additional Conditions That May Be a Focus of Clinical Attention
Bereavement / Borderline Intellectual Functioning / Academic Problem / Occupational Problem / Childhood or Adolescent Antisocial Behavior / Adult Antisocial Behavior / Malingering / Phase of Life Problem / Noncompliance with Treatment for a Mental Disorder / Identity Problem / Religious or Spiritual Problem / Acculturation Problem / Age-Associated Memory Decline

ABNORMAL PSYCHOLOGY

ABNORMAL PSYCHOLOGY

SIXTH EDITION

GERALD C. DAVISON
University of Southern California
JOHN M. NEALE
State University of New York
at Stony Brook

John Wiley & Sons, Inc.
New York • Chichester • Brisbane • Toronto • Singapore

Acquisitions Editor	Karen Dubno
Developmental Editor	Johnna Barto
Marketing Manager	Catharine Faduska
Production Manager	Linda Muriello
Senior Production Editor	Micheline A. Frederick
Manufacturing Manager	Susan Stetzer
Director of Photo Department	Stella Kupferberg
Photo Editors	Elaine Bernstein
	Jennifer Atkins
Photo Assistant	Alissa Mend
Illustration Coordinator	Anna Melhorne
Cover Photo	Marty Loken/Allstock
Preface Photo	Lafayette Photographers

This book was set in 10/12 Palatino by Waldman Graphics, Inc. and printed and bound by Von Hoffman, Inc. The cover was printed by Lehigh Press.

Recognizing the importance of preserving what has been written, it is a policy of John Wiley & Sons, Inc. to have books of enduring value published in the United States printed on acid-free paper, and we exert our best efforts to that end.

Library of Congress Cataloging in Publication Data:

Davison, Gerald C.
Abnormal psychology / Gerald C. Davison, John M. Neale.—6th ed.
p. cm.
Includes bibliographical references and index.

1. Psychology, Pathological. I. Neale, John M., 1943–
II. Title.
[DNLM: 1. Psychopathology. WM 100 D265a 1994]
RC454.D3 1994
616.89—dc20
DNLM/DLC
for Library of Congress

93-24113
CIP

Printed in the United States of America

10 9 8 7 6 5 4 3 2 1

To *Kathleen C. Chambers*
(GCD)

To *Gail* and *Sean*
(JMN)

GERALD C. DAVISON (*right*) is Professor of Psychology at the University of Southern California, where he was also Director of Clinical Training from 1979 to 1984 and Chair of the Department from 1984 to 1990. Previously he was on the psychology faculty at the State University of New York at Stony Brook (1966–1979). He received his B.A. from Harvard and his Ph.D. from Stanford. He is a Fellow of the American Psychological Association and has served on the Executive Committee of the Division of Clinical Psychology, on the Board of Scientific Affairs, on the Committee on Scientific Awards, and on the Council of Representatives. He is also a Charter Fellow of the American Psychological Society, a past president of the Association for the Advancement of Behavior Therapy, and currently Publications Coordinator of that organization. He served two terms on the National Academy of Sciences Committee on Techniques for the Enhancement of Human Performance. In 1988 Davison received an outstanding achievement award from APA's Board of Social and Ethical Responsibility, in 1989 was the recipient of the Albert S. Raubenheimer Distinguished Faculty Award from USC's College of Letters, Arts and Sciences, and in 1993 won the university-wide USC Associates Award for Excellence in Teaching. His book *Clinical Behavior Therapy*, co-authored in 1976 with Marvin Goldfried, is one of two publications that have been recognized as Citation Classics by the Social Sciences Citation Index. He is on the editorial board of *Behavior Therapy, Cognitive Therapy and Research, Journal of Cognitive Psychotherapy*, and *Journal of Psychotherapy Integration*. His current research program focuses on the relationships between cognition and a variety of behavioral and emotional problems. In addition to his teaching and research, he is a practicing clinical psychologist.

JOHN M. NEALE (*left*) is Professor of Psychology at the State University of New York at Stony Brook. He received his B.A. from the University of Toronto and his M.A. and Ph.D. from Vanderbilt University. His internship in clinical psychology was as a Fellow in Medical Psychology at the Langley Porter Neuropsychiatric Institute. In 1975 he was a Visiting Fellow at the Institute of Psychiatry, London, England. In 1974 he won the American Psychological Association's Early Career Award for his research on cognitive processes in schizophrenia. In 1991 he won a Distinguished Scientist Award from the American Psychological Association's Society for a Science of Clinical Psychology. He has been on the editorial boards of several journals and has been associate editor of the *Journal of Abnormal Psychology*. Besides his numerous articles in professional journals, he has published books on the effects of televised violence on children, research methodology, schizophrenia, case studies in abnormal psychology, and psychological influences on health. His major research interests are schizophrenia and the relationship of stress and coping to health.

Preface

In contemporary abnormal psychology there are few hard and fast answers. Indeed, the very way the field should be conceptualized and the kinds of questions that should be asked are hotly debated issues. In this book we have tried to present glimpses of possible answers to two primary questions: *What causes psychopathology?* and *Which treatments are most effective in preventing or reducing psychological suffering?*

Goals of the Book

Our intent is to communicate to students (and faculty as well) our own excitement about our discipline, particularly the puzzles that challenge researchers in their search for the causes of psychopathology and for ways to prevent and ameliorate it. We try to encourage readers to participate with us in a process of discovery as we sift through the evidence on the origins of psychopathology and the effectiveness of specific interventions. We discuss these and other points in our Note to the Student, which instructors might find useful to read and to suggest that students look at also.

Scientific Approach

As in the preceding five editions of this book, we share a strong commitment to a scientific approach but at the same time appreciate the often uncontrollable nature of the subject matter and the importance of clinical findings. It has become commonplace in psychology to recognize the selective nature of perception. Therefore, rather than pretend that we are unbiased, we have tried to alert readers to our assumptions. We encourage readers to think critically and consider the merits of our and others' points of view. We believe we have succeeded in presenting fairly and comprehensively the major alternative conceptualizations in contemporary psychopathology.

Various Paradigms

A recurrent theme in the book is the importance of major points of view or, to use Kuhn's (1962) phrase, paradigms. Our experience in teaching undergraduates has made us very much aware of the importance of making explicit the unspoken assumptions underlying any quest for knowledge. In our handling of the paradigms, we have tried to make their premises clear. Long after specific facts are forgotten, the student should retain a grasp of the basic problems in the field of psychopathology and should understand that the answers one arrives at are, in an important but often subtle way, constrained by the questions one poses and the methods employed to ask those questions. Throughout the book we discuss four major paradigms: *psychoanalytic, learning, cognitive,* and *biological.* When therapy is discussed, we also describe the *humanistic and existential* paradigm.

A related issue is the use of more than one paradigm in studying abnormal psychology. Rather than force an entire field into, for example, a biological paradigm, we argue from the available information that different problems in psychopathology are amenable to analyses within different frameworks. For instance, biological processes must be considered when examining mental retardation and schizophrenia, but for other disorders a cognitive behavioral theory seems the most helpful, and for still others psychoanalytic theories can enhance our understanding. Over the course of our several revisions the importance of a *diathesis-stress approach* has become more and more evident. Emerging data indicate that many, perhaps most, disorders arise from subtle interactions between somatic or psychological predispositions and stressful life events. Our coverage continues to reflect these hypotheses and findings, strengthening our basic position that a diathesis-stress paradigm is necessary for understanding most psychopathologies.

Organization

As in previous editions, treatments of specific disorders are discussed in the chapters reviewing them. The final section, Part Four, on intervention is also retained, however, for we continue to believe that only a separate and extended consideration allows us to explore with the reader the many perplexing and intriguing problems encountered by health professionals who try to prevent or treat mental disorders. Chapter 2, the pivotal chapter devoted to paradigms, lays the foundation for Chapters 6 through 17, which describe the various disorders and give what is known about their etiologies and about treating and preventing them.

Improvements in This Sixth Edition

Preparing this edition has given us an opportunity to strengthen many parts of the book and to include significant new material that has appeared since completion of the Fifth Edition. Those familiar with our earlier efforts will find that our basic orientation has not changed.

DSM-IV

Any abnormal psychology textbook published today must attend to the *Diagnostic and Statistical Manual of Mental Disorders,* and ours is no exception. We are fortunate to have had available to us the March 1993 *DSM-IV Draft Criteria* from the Task Force on DSM-IV of the American Psychiatric Association. As our book goes to press in mid-1993, this version is being reviewed for final approval by the administrative leadership of the American Psychiatric Association. The substantive work has been carried out over the past four years by a distinguished group of mental health professionals (many of them psychologists) and critiqued by hundreds of researchers and practitioners in numerous articles and conferences. Therefore we do not anticipate major changes as the draft criteria work their way toward publication in 1994. To help readers find their way through DSM-IV, we provide a summary table on the front endpapers of the book.

We do not, however, accept DSM-IV uncritically; those responsible for its compilation are themselves aware of our incomplete and evolving understanding of human psychological suffering. Many times throughout the book we comment critically on this diagnostic scheme. As we are pleased to have seen with earlier editions of our book, we hope to make some contribution, along with other colleagues, to the continuing refinement of the manual.

Content Enhancements

We can mention a small sampling of some of the new material included in this Sixth Edition:

- clinical vignettes opening most chapters
- major additions on cultural diversity factors in diagnosis and treatment (throughout the book but especially in Chapters 4 and 20)
- new theory and research on posttraumatic stress disorder (Chapter 6)
- ethical dilemmas in the prevention of suicide (Chapter 9)
- issues in integrating different schools of psychotherapy (Chapter 19)
- in-depth discussion of reliability and validity of various clinical assessment procedures (Chapter 4)
- some surprising findings on how group therapy can help terminally ill cancer patients live longer (Chapter 8)
- the latest findings in theory and research in depression and its treatment (Chapter 9)
- new material on prevention of HIV-infection (Chapter 12)
- the latest on substance abuse and treatment (Chapter 11) and on schizophrenia (Chapter 14)
- discussion of dialectical behavior therapy for borderline personality disorder (Chapter 10)
- new material on rape and child sexual abuse (Chapter 12)
- a proposal for an insanity defense based on multiple personality disorder (Chapter 21)
- new discussions of ego analytic and brief psychodynamic psychotherapies (Chapters 2 and 18)
- some current epistemological issues in psychotherapy integration as expressed in a lively debate between two proponents (Chapter 19)
- integration of Rogerian notions of acceptance in behavioral couples therapy (Chapter 20).

We continue to devote three full chapters to developmental disorders: Chapters 15 and 16 on children and Chapter 17 on psychological problems associated with the aged. Our chapter on aging in our third edition was the first such chapter in a book of this kind, and our current chapter 17 is, we believe, the most comprehensive chapter on this important and still inadequately studied set of topics. Also, we have continued to update Chapter 21 on legal and ethical issues, pleased to know that it has been assigned to law school classes for purposes of providing an accurate and analytical introduction to mental health law.

In general, we present the latest information on the causes and interventions for all the psychopathologies and the issues underlying the ways investigators are going about generating that knowledge.

Acknowledgments

It is a pleasure to acknowledge the contributions of a number of colleagues to the Sixth Edition. Their thoughtful comments have helped us to refine and improve the book.

Survey Respondents

Before we began to develop the Sixth Edition, we surveyed a number of abnormal psychology instructors concerning their classroom experiences with textbooks. Comments and suggestions were offered by the following:

M. Akhtar
Slippery Rock University (PA)

Robert Arndt
Delta College (MI)

S. H. Baron
Kent State University (OH)

David K. Bernhardt
Carleton University (ONT)

Christopher Blodgutt
Buffalo State College (NY)

Robert Bornstein
Gettysburg College (PA)

Melissa M. Brown
Penn State University

Peter Campos
SUNY-Binghamton

Daniel V. Caputo
Queens College (NY)

Caryn L. Carlson
University of Texas at Austin

Salvatore Cullari
Lebanon Valley College (PA)

C. Stuart Dubé II
SUNY-Brockport

Elizabeth Eaken
San Diego State University

Anthony F. Fazio
University of Wisconsin at Milwaukee

Christopher France
Ohio University

William Fremouw
West Virginia University

William Rick Fry
Youngstown State University (OH)

Joseph Giacobbe
Adirondack Community College (NY)

Perilou Goddard
Northern Kentucky University

Ethan Gorenstein
Columbia University

John M. Grossberg
San Diego State University

Rand J. Gruen
New York University

Larry Hall
North Seattle Community College

A. R. Heidemann
West Virginia Wesleyan College

Curt Hileman
Okanagan College (BC)

Douglas Hindman
Eastern Kentucky University

Stephen Hinshaw
UC-Berkeley

Jill Hooley
Harvard University

Ray Huebschmann
Vincennes University (IN)

Chris Koronakos
Western Michigan University

John Kremer
Indiana University-Purdue University at Indianapolis

Marvin L. Kumler
Bowling Green State University (OH)

Richard LaFeming
Suffolk County Community College (NY)

Cindy Marriott
Wayne State University (MI)

Kevin Masters
Ball State University (IN)

Lily D. McNair
SUNY-New Paltz

Donald H. Millikan
San Diego Mesa College

Robin K. Morgan
Indiana University, Southeast

Paul E. Morocco
SUNY-Plattsburgh

Bradley Olsie
Northern Michigan University

Michael Pogue-Geile
University of Pittsburgh

A. L. Porterfield
Oberlin College (OH)

Mary Procidano
Fordham University (NY)

David F. Ricks
University of Cincinnati

Caton Roberts
SUNY-Buffalo

David Rollock
Purdue University (IN)

Patricia Rourke
Grand Valley State University (MI)

Kurt Salzinger
Polytechnic University (NY)

David Santogrossi
Purdue University (IN)

C. E. Sequeira
Ryerson Polytechnical Institute (ONT)

Daniel S. Shaw
University of Pittsburgh

G. Sperrazio
University of San Diego

Cheryl L. Spinweber
University of California at San Diego

M. Strauss
Case Western Reserve University (OH)

Soren Svanum
Indiana University-Purdue University

Purcell Taylor Jr.
University College (OH)

J. D. Thompson
Sheridan College (ONT)

Richard Viken
Indiana University

Richard L. Wessler
Pace University (NY)

Michael Wierzbicki
Marquette University (WI)

Sharon R. Woods
Clarion University (PA)

Melvin Zax
University of Rochester (NY)

Ed Zuckerman
Carnegie-Mellon University (PA).

Expert Reviewers

We also called upon a number of colleagues to critique chapters in their areas of expertise and offer advice to help us update specific chapters. We are grateful to the following:

Edward Carr
SUNY-Stony Brook

Lorraine Collins
University of Washington

Todd Heatherton
Harvard University

Jill M. Hooley
Harvard University

Jan Loney
SUNY-Stony Brook

Steven Lopez
University of California at Los Angeles

Joseph LoPiccolo
University of Missouri

Frank Manis
University of Southern California

Ken Winters
University of Minnesota

Manuscript Reviewers

During the development phase, a number of instructors read and commented on the manuscript:

John T. Ault
Southern Utah University

Heather Banis
Scripps College (California)

Allen E. Bergin
Brigham Young University (Utah)

Ira Bernstein
University of Texas at Arlington

Peggy Brooks
North Adams State College (Massachusetts)

Patricia Crane
University of Texas at San Antonio

Christopher Cronin
Transylvania University (Kentucky)

Anthony Fazio
University of Wisconsin at Milwaukee

Henry F. Gromoll
Millikin University (Illinois)

David A. F. Haaga
American University (District of Columbia)

Brian Hayden
Brown University (Rhode Island)

Kenneth Heller
Indiana University

Kevin Keating
Broward Community College (Florida)

Barry Ledwidge
Simon Fraser University (British Columbia)

Scott Lilienfeld
SUNY-Albany

Janet Matthews
Loyola University of New Orleans

Terrie Moffitt
University of Wisconsin at Madison

W. G. Murdy
Winthrop College (South Carolina)

James Overholser
Case-Western Reserve University (Ohio)

Dimitri Papageorgis
University of British Columbia

Anthony Pinizzotto
Georgetown University (District of Columbia)

James M. Riggio
Oakland Community College (Michigan)

L. E. Roberts
McMaster University (Ontario)

Stephen Royce
University of Portland (Oregon)

Victor L. Ryan
University of Colorado

Paul M. Valliant
Laurentian University (Ontario)

Michael W. Vasey
Ohio State University

Donald Whitehead
Fayetteville Technical College (North Carolina)

Helpful library research and other assistance were provided at the University of Southern California by Ellie Nezami, Chiaan Yen, Natalie Masson, Sandra Navarre, Ralph Vogel, Victoria Bedrosian, and Bonnie Wolkenstein; and at the State University of New York at Stony Brook by Antonis Kofsaftis and Katherine Putnam. Special thanks go to Marian Williams, for drafting and rewriting major portions of Chapters 15 and 16 and to Asher Davison for editorial assistance with the Glossary. We are also grateful to law professors Stephen Morse of the University of Pennsylvania and Elyn Saks of the University of Southern California for helpful suggestions on legal issues in psychopathology and treatment.

We signed on with Wiley 1971 and continued in this revision to enjoy the skills and dedication of our "Wiley family": Karen Dubno, Johnna Barto, Micheline Frederick, Stella Kupferberg, Alissa Mend, Pete Noa, Linda Muriello, Anna Melhorn, Sean Culhane, Neal Sigda, and copy editor, Jennifer Cooke. Special thanks go to Joanne Tinsley, who provided many helpful editing suggestions as we continued our efforts to produce a readable and engaging text without sacrificing scientific accuracy or professional responsibility. Clerical assistance on the References was ably provided by Ann Langerud and Irene Takaragawa, USC.

For putting up with occasional limited accessibility and mood swings, and for always being there for moral support, our loving thanks go to the most important people in our lives—Kathleen Chambers, Eve and Asher Davison (GCD), and Gail and Sean Neale (JMN).

Finally, we have maintained the order of authorship as it was for the first edition, decided by the toss of a coin.

June 1993

Gerald C. Davison
Los Angeles

John M. Neale
Stony Brook

A Note to the Student

Our goals in writing this textbook are not only to present theories and research in psychopathology and intervention but also to convey some of the intellectual excitement that is associated with the search for answers to some of the most puzzling questions facing humankind. A reviewer of an earlier edition once commented that our book sometimes reads like a detective story, for we do more than just state the problem and then its solution. Rather, we try to involve the reader in the search for clues, the follow-up of hunches, and the evaluation of evidence that are part and parcel of the science and art of the field.

There are several features of this book that we hope will make it easier for you to master and enjoy the material, elements designed to make it "user-friendly." Some are common to all textbooks, others particular to our book.

1. Chapter Summaries. Though a summary appears at the end of each chapter, you may find it useful to read it after perusing the overview that opens each chapter. Even if you do not understand all of the summary, you will get some idea of what the chapter is about. Then, when you reread it after completing the chapter itself, your enhanced understanding of it will give you an immediate sense of what you have learned in just one reading of the chapter. If something remains unclear to you in the summary, you have some indication of what you would do well to reread then and there.

2. Heads and Subheads. We have employed a hierarchy of four levels of heads. The first and second levels of heads are listed at the beginning of each chapter to provide a general idea of how the chapter is organized. You might also want to flip through the chapter and note the other subheads as well; this will give you a better idea of how the chapter as a whole is organized.

3. Glossary Terms. When an important term is introduced, it is boldfaced and listed after the chapter summary as a key term. A definition and/or discussion of that term immediately follows its appearance in the text. Of course, the term will probably appear again later in the book, in which case it will not be highlighted in this way. We have provided at the end of the book a glossary that includes all these terms.

4. Focus Boxes. There are many in-depth discussions of interesting topics encased in focus boxes throughout the book. This feature allows us to involve the reader in a sometimes very specialized topic in a way that does not detract from the flow of the regular text. Sometimes a focus box expands on a point in the text; sometimes it deals with an entirely separate but relevant issue. Reading these boxes with care will deepen your understanding of the subject matter. In addition, we urge you not to neglect the footnotes. Oftentimes they reflect our ongoing thinking and preliminary ideas about topics, helping the reader better understand how we're analyzing a question or controversy.

5. Subject and Name Indices. Also in the back of the book is an index of terms and ideas, the subject index, and a listing of names cited as bibliographic sources, the name index. Sometimes you may wish to know where in the book a certain topic, such as depression, has been discussed. You will find in the subject index that depression is mentioned in more than one context, and the page numbers enable you to look up quickly these several discussions, perhaps to compare how it was dealt with in the different contexts. The name index can help you find a particular reference, though sometimes we think that a principal purpose is to enable colleagues to look themselves up quickly to see if they have been cited in someone else's book! (We've certainly been guilty of this "sin.")

6. DSM-IV Table. On the front endpapers of the book is a summary of the new psychiatric nomenclature, DSM-IV. This provides a handy guide to where particular disorders appear in the "official" taxonomy, or classification. You will see, as you read our book, that we make considerable use of DSM-IV, yet in a selective vein. Sometimes we find it better to discuss theory and research on a particular problem in a way that is different from DSM's conceptualization.

7. Study Guide. *A Student Study Guide,* written

by Douglas Hindman, is available to help you read and study the textbook. For each chapter there is a summary of the chapter, a list of key concepts, important study questions, and practice tests to encourage active reading and learning. We believe that it is a very helpful study aid.

8. Supplemental Texts. Finally, there are two separate books that can enrich your understanding. With Thomas Oltmanns we developed a supplemental paperback text, *Case Studies in Abnormal Psychology,* based on our own clinical experience with real patients. We hope it gives an appreciation of the range and nature of abnormal behavior. The response from students has been overwhelmingly positive. The other book, *Readings in Abnormal Psychology,* is a collection of original articles that we edited with Jill Hooley. This volume provides a survey of theoretical and empirical papers that textbook authors and other professionals rely on to find out what researchers are actually doing.

One of the things previous users have liked about our textbook is its readability. We hope you, too, will find it engaging and interesting. From time to time students have written us their comments on the book. Should the spirit move you to do so, you can glean our addresses from the brief biographies that appear next to our pictures at the beginning of the book.

GCD AND JMN

Contents in Brief

Contents

PART ONE INTRODUCTION AND BASIC ISSUES 1

Focus Boxes

PART ONE

Introduction and Basic Issues

c h a p t e r o n e

Introduction: Historical and Scientific Considerations

Slumping in a comfortable leather chair, Ernest H., a thirty-five-year-old city policeman, looked skeptically at his therapist as he struggled to relate a series of problems. His recent inability to maintain an erection when making love to his wife was the immediate reason for his seeking therapy, but after gentle prodding from the therapist, Ernest recounted a host of other difficulties, some of them dating from his childhood but most of them originating during the previous several years.

Ernest's childhood had not been a happy one. His mother, whom he loved dearly, died suddenly when he was only six, and for the next ten years he lived either with his father or with a maternal aunt. His father drank so heavily that he seldom managed to get through any day without some alcohol. Moreover, the man's moods were extremely variable; he had even spent several months in a state hospital with a diagnosis of "manic-depressive psychosis." The father's income was irregular and never enough to pay bills on time or to allow his son and himself to live in any but the most run-down neighborhoods. At times the father was totally incapable of caring for himself, let alone his son. Ernest would then spend weeks, sometimes months, with his aunt in a nearby suburb.

Despite these apparent handicaps, Ernest completed high school and entered the tuition-free city university. He earned his miscellaneous living expenses by waiting tables at a small restaurant. During these college years his psychological problems began to concern him. He often became profoundly depressed, for no apparent reason, and these bouts of sadness were sometimes followed by periods of manic elation. His lack of control over these mood swings troubled him greatly, for he had observed this same pattern in his alcoholic father. He also felt an acute self-consciousness with people who he felt had authority over him—his boss, his professors, and even some of his classmates, with whom he compared himself unfavorably. He was especially sensitive about his clothes, which were old and worn compared with those of his peers: their families had more money than his.

It was on the opening day of classes in his junior year that he first saw his future wife. When the tall, slender young woman moved to her seat with grace and self-assurance, his were not the only eyes that followed her. He spent the rest of that semester watching her from afar, taking care to sit where he could glance over at her without being conspicuous. Then one day, as they and the other students were leaving class, they bumped into each other quite by accident, and her warmth and charm emboldened him to ask her to join him for some coffee. When she said yes, he almost wished she had not.

Amazingly enough, as he saw it, they soon fell in love, and before the end of his senior year they were married. Ernest could never quite believe that his wife, as intelligent a woman as she was beautiful, really cared for him. As the years wore on, his doubts about himself, and about her feelings toward him, would continue to grow.

He hoped to enter law school, and both his grades and law school boards made these plans a possibility, but he decided instead to enter the police academy. His reasons, as he related them to his therapist, had to do with doubts about his intellectual abilities, as well as his increasing uneasiness in situations in which he felt himself being evaluated. Seminars had become unbearable for him in his last year in college, and he had hopes that the badge and uniform of a police officer would give him the instant recognition and respect that he seemed incapable of earning on his own.

To help him get through the academy, his wife quit college at the end of her junior year, against Ernest's pleas, and sought a secretarial job. He felt she was far brighter than he and saw no reason why she should sacrifice her potential to help him make his way in life. But at the same time he recognized the fiscal realities and grudgingly accepted her financial support.

The police academy proved to be even more stressful than college. Ernest's mood swings, although less frequent, still troubled him. And like his father, who was now confined to a state mental hospital, he drank to ease his psychological pain. He felt that his instructors considered him a fool when he had difficulty standing up in front of the class to give an answer that he himself knew was correct. But he made it through the physical, intellectual, and social rigors of the academy, and he was assigned to foot patrol in one of the wealthier sections of the city.

Several years later, when it seemed that life should be getting easier, he found himself in even greater turmoil. Now thirty-two years old, with a fairly secure job that paid reasonably well, he began to think of starting a family. His wife wanted this as well, and it was at this time that his problems with impotence began. He thought at first it was the alcohol—he was drinking at least six ounces of bourbon every night, except when on the swing shift. Soon, though, he began to wonder whether he was actually avoiding the responsibility of having a child, and later he began to doubt that his wife really found him attractive and desirable. The more understanding and patient she was about his sometimes frantic efforts to consummate sex with her, the less "manly" he felt himself to be. He was unable to accept help from his wife, for he did not believe that this was the "right" way to maintain a sexual relationship. The problems in bed spread to other areas of their lives. The less often they made love, the more suspicious he was of his wife, for she had become even more beautiful and vibrant as she entered her thirties. In addition, she had been promoted to the position of administrative assistant at the law firm where she worked. She would mention—perhaps to taunt him—long, martini-filled lunches with her boss at a posh uptown restaurant.

The impetus for his contacting the therapist was an ugly argument with his wife one evening when she came home from work after ten. Ernest had been agitated for several days. To combat his fear that he was losing control, he had consumed almost a full bottle of bourbon each night. By the time his wife walked in the door on that final evening, Ernest was already very drunk, and he attacked her both verbally and physically about her alleged infidelity. In her own anger and fear, she questioned his masculinity in striking a woman and taunted him with the disappointments of their lovemaking. Ernest stormed out of the house, spent the night at a local bar, and the next day somehow pulled himself together enough to seek professional help.

We'll return to Ernest later.

Every day of our lives we try to understand other people. Determining why another person does or feels something is a difficult task. Indeed, we do not always understand why we feel and behave as we do. Acquiring insight into what we consider normal, expected behavior is difficult enough; understanding human behavior beyond the normal range, such as that of the policeman just described, is even more difficult.

This book is concerned with the whole range of abnormality and with the varied explanations for it, both past and present. We face numerous challenges in seeking these explanations. Foremost, we must have a tolerance for ambiguity, an ability to be comfortable with tentative, often conflicting information. Then, of course, we must have the endurance to work with that information, to study and research it. As you will see, the human psyche remains elusive; we know with certainty much less about our field than we might hope. As we approach the study of **psychopathology**, the field concerned with the nature and development of mental disorders, we do well to keep in mind that the subject offers few hard and fast answers. And yet, as will become evident when we discuss our orientation to scientific inquiry, the study of psychopathology is no less worthwhile because of its ambiguities. The kinds of questions asked rather than the specific answers to those questions constitute the very essence of the field.

Another challenge we face in studying abnormal psychology is to remain objective. Our subject matter, human behavior, is so very personal. The pervasiveness and disturbing effects of abnormal behavior intrude on our lives. Who, for example, has not experienced irrational thoughts and feelings? Or who has not known someone, a friend or perhaps a relative, whose behavior was impossible to fathom? If you have, you realize how frustrating and frightening it is to try to understand and help a person suffering psychological difficulties. Although not personally observed by most of us, terrifying instances of unusual behavior are very much in the public eye. Hardly a week passes without a violent act, such as an ax murder or multiple slayings, being reported. The assailant is diagnosed by a police officer or mental health authority as a "mental case" and is found to have had a history of mental instability. Sometimes we learn that the person has previously been confined in a mental hospital.

Our closeness to the subject matter, of course, adds to its intrinsic fascination; undergraduate courses in abnormal psychology are among the most popular in psychology departments and indeed in the entire college curriculum. Familiarity with the subject matter encourages people to study abnormal psychology, but it has one distinct disadvantage. All of us bring to our study preconceived notions of what our subject matter is. We have developed certain ways of thinking and talking about behavior, certain words and concepts that somehow seem to *fit*. For example, we may believe that to study fear is to study the immediate experience of fear, technically known as a phenomenological approach. That is one way of viewing fear, but it is not the only one. As behavioral scientists, we ourselves have to grapple with the difference between what we may *feel* is the appropriate way to talk about human behavior and experience and what may be a more productive way of defining it in order to study and learn about it. Where most people would speak of a "feeling of terror," for example, we might be more inclined to use a phrase such as "fear-response of great magnitude." In doing so we would not be merely playing verbal games. The concepts and verbal labels we use to study abnormal behavior scientifically must be free of the subjective feelings of appropriateness ordinarily attached to certain human phenomena. We may be asking you, then, to adopt frames of reference different from those you are accustomed to, and indeed different from those we ourselves use when we are not wearing our professional hats.

The case study with which this chapter began is open to a wide range of interpretations. No doubt you have some ideas about how Ernest's problems developed, what his primary difficulties are, and perhaps even how you might try to help him. We know of no greater intellectual or emotional challenge than deciding both how to conceptualize the life of a person with psychological problems and how best to treat him or her. At the end of Chapter 2 we will refer back to the case of Ernest H. to illustrate how workers from different theoretical orientations might describe him and try to help him.

Now we turn to a discussion of what we mean by the term *abnormal behavior*. Then we will look briefly at how our view of abnormality has evolved throughout history to the more scientific perspectives of today.

What Is Abnormal Behavior?

One of the more difficult challenges facing those in the field of abnormal psychology is to define **abnormal behavior**. Here we will consider several components that have been proposed. We will see that no single one is adequate, although each has merit and captures some part of what might be the full definition. We will return to this issue after we have examined the components of statistical infrequency, violation of norms, personal distress, disability or dysfunction, and unexpectedness.

Statistical Infrequency

One component of abnormal behavior is that it is *infrequent*. Those who focus on this statistical aspect of abnormal behavior typically measure specific characteristics of people, such as personality traits and ways of behaving and the distribution of these characteristics in the population. One type of population distribution, the **normal curve** (Figure 1.1), depicts the majority of people as being in the middle as far as any particular characteristic is concerned; that is, very few people fall at either extreme. An assertion that a person is normal implies that he or she does not deviate much from the average in a particular trait or behavior pattern.

Statistical infrequency is used explicitly in diagnosing mental retardation. Figure 1.1 gives the normal distribution of intelligence quotient measures in the population. Though a host of measures are used to diagnose mental retardation, low intelligence is a principal criterion in the determination (see page 458). When an individual's intelligence quotient

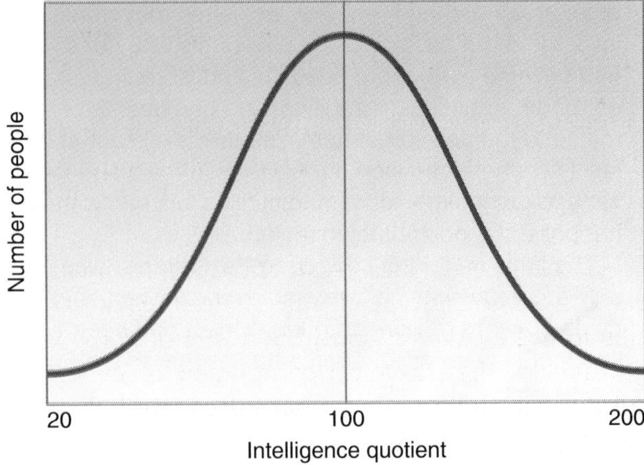

Figure 1.1 The intelligence distribution among adults, illustrating a normal or bell-shaped curve.

Although abnormal behavior is often infrequent, so too is great athletic talent like that of Jackie Joyner-Kersee. Therefore, infrequency is not a sufficient definition of abnormal behavior.

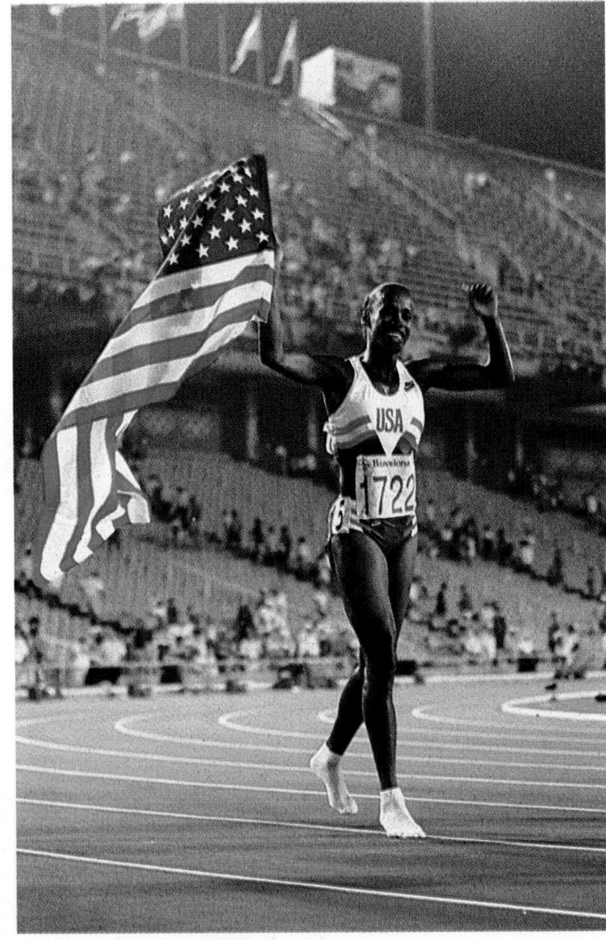

is below 70, intellectual functioning is considered sufficiently subnormal to be designated as mental retardation.

Although much infrequent behavior indeed strikes us as abnormal, in some instances the relationship breaks down. Having great athletic ability is infrequent but not abnormal in the sense implied here. Only certain infrequent behavior, such as being subject to hallucinations or deep depression, falls into the domain considered in this book. Unfortunately, the statistical component gives us no guidance in determining what infrequent behavior psychopathologists should study.

Violation of Norms

Another view is that abnormal behavior is whatever *violates social norms* and threatens or makes anxious those observing it. Again, this component rings true, at least partially. The psychopath's callousness fits the definition, as do the sometimes wild behavior of a manic and the strange antics of a schizophrenic. This component explicitly makes abnormality a relative concept; various forms of unusual behavior can be tolerated, depending on the prevailing cultural norms. But the component is also at once too broad and too narrow. Criminals and prostitutes, who violate social norms, are usually not studied within the domain of abnormal psychology. The highly anxious person, who is generally regarded as a central character in the field of abnormal psychology, would not be noticed by many lay observers.

Also, cultural diversity can affect how people view social norms—what is the norm in one culture may be abnormal in another. This is a subtle issue addressed in many places throughout the book; see especially Chapter 4 (pp. 102–104).

Personal Distress

Abnormality invokes the notion of *personal suffering*. People's behavior is abnormal if it creates great distress and torment in them. Personal distress clearly fits many of the forms of abnormality we consider in this book. People experiencing anxiety disorders and depression truly suffer greatly. But some disorders do not cause distress. The psychopath, for example, treats others coldheartedly and may continually violate the law without experiencing any guilt, remorse, or anxiety whatsoever. Furthermore, all forms of distress—for example, hunger or the pain of childhood—do not seem equally to belong to the field. Another difficulty in using personal discomfort as a defining characteristic is that it is inherently subjective. People decide and report on how much they are suffering. The degrees of their distress are difficult to compare, since their standards for defining their own psychological states can vary greatly.

Attending class in the nude, as this Berkeley student did in 1992, is a clear norm violation but does not necessarily indicate psychopathology.

Personal distress is also part of the definition of abnormal behavior but unlike grief, which is an expected response to losing a loved one, the distress most relevant to psychopathology is not expected given the situation in which it occurs.

Disability or Dysfunction

Another component of abnormal behavior is *disability*, that is, the individual is unable to pursue some goal because of the abnormality. Substance use disorders, for example, are defined principally by how the substance abuse creates social or occupational disability (e.g., poor work performance, serious arguments with spouse). Similarly, a phobia could indicate both distress and disability if, for example, a severe fear of flying prevented someone from taking a job promotion. As with suffering, however, disability applies to some, but not all, disorders. It is not clear, for example, whether transvestism (cross-dressing for sexual pleasure) is necessarily a disability. Most transvestites are married, lead conventional lives, and usually cross-dress in private. Further characteristics that might in some circumstances be considered disabilities—for example, being short if you want to be a professional basketball player—do not fall within the domain of abnormal psychology. As with distress, the absence of a more precise definition of disability does not allow us to determine which disabilities belong and which do not.

Related to the view of disorder as disability, Wakefield (1992) suggests that a central component of illness or disorder is harmful *dysfunction*, that is, a failure of natural functioning of some structure or mechanism in the person that causes harm to the person. For example, phobias are disorders, Wakefield asserts, because people were not "designed" to be afraid of things, ideas, or events that cannot harm them. Thus, while it is normal to be afraid of drowning if one cannot swim, it is phobic and abnormal to be afraid of entering the water if one has swimming skills and if there are not other objective dangers in the water. Wakefield's argument rests heavily on our knowing or at least agreeing on what is normal, on how the human organism is put together, on how we are meant to function. He suggests that only an appeal to notions of natural functioning, what the organism was designed to do, can provide a valid criterion for disorder. Since the validity of this suggestion depends on our knowing what, in fact, is the normal state or internal functioning of the human animal, it may be begging the very question it purports to answer.

Unexpectedness

Another component of the definition of abnormality is that it is *unexpected*. Hunger is an expected response to not eating and thus would be excluded as a state of distress that is relevant to abnormal behavior. In contrast, many forms of abnormal behavior are unexpected responses to environmental stressors. For example, anxiety disorders are diagnosed when the anxiety is out of proportion to the situation, as when people worry continually about their financial situations even though they are well-off.

Over the years some of the categories of abnormal behavior appearing in official diagnostic manuals have changed, but not because any particular definition of abnormal behavior has been adopted. In some cases clinical research has led to the identification of a new syndrome. Infantile autism, for example, did not appear among official psychiatric diagnoses until 1980 even though it was first described in the clinical literature in the 1940s. In other cases, norms and values have shifted. Over the last century, for example, more and more people decided that their psychological problems warranted professional help. With this increased flow of patients, therapists and researchers saw problems that were new to them, and new diagnoses emerged. What we present in a text such as this is a list of conditions that are currently considered abnormal. The disorders in the list will undoubtedly change with time.

Because of the changing nature of the field, it is not possible to offer a simple definition of abnormality that captures it in its entirety. The components of abnormality that we have just presented are partial definitions, but they are not equally applicable to every diagnosis.

Clinicians with various degrees often work together in a team, as in this diagnostic conference.

The Mental Health Professions

The training of **clinicians**, the various professionals authorized to provide psychological services, takes different forms. To be a **clinical psychologist** (the profession of the authors of this textbook) requires a Ph.D. or Psy.D. degree, which entails four to six years of graduate study. Training for the Ph.D. in clinical psychology is much like that for the other specialty fields of psychology—cognitive, physiological, social, developmental, aging—with a heavy emphasis on laboratory work, research designs, statistics, and the empirically based study of human and animal behavior. As with these other fields of psychology, the degree is basically a research degree, and candidates are required to research and write a lengthy dissertation on a specialized topic. In addition, candidates in clinical psychology learn skills in two other areas that distinguish them from other Ph.D. candidates in psychology. First, they learn techniques of assessment and **diagnosis** of mental disorders; that is, they learn the skills necessary to determine that a patient's symptoms or problems indicate a particular disorder. Second, they learn how to practice **psychotherapy**, a primarily verbal means of helping troubled individuals change their thoughts, feelings, and behavior to reduce distress and to achieve greater life satisfaction. Students take courses in which they master specific techniques under close professional supervision; then, during an intensive internship or postdoctoral training, they gradually assume increasing responsibility for the care of patients.

Other clinical graduate programs are more focused on *practice*. These programs offer the relatively new degree of Psy.D. (Doctor of Psychology). The curriculum is generally the same as that available to Ph.D. students, but there is less emphasis on research and more on clinical training. The thinking here is that clinical psychology has advanced to a level of knowledge and certainty that justifies—even requires—intensive training in specific techniques of assessment and therapeutic intervention rather than combining practice with research.[1]

A **psychiatrist** holds an M.D. degree and has had postgraduate training, called a residency, in which he or she has received supervision in diagnosis and psychotherapy. By virtue of the medical degree, and

[1]In fact, only a minority of mental health professionals teach and conduct research in academic and research settings. However, nearly all the empirical work discussed in this book comes from such individuals, who are generally less involved in providing direct mental health services.

in contrast with psychologists, psychiatrists can also continue functioning as physicians—giving physical examinations, diagnosing medical problems, and the like. In actuality, however, the only aspect of medical practice that most psychiatrists engage in is prescribing **psychoactive drugs**, chemical compounds that can change how people feel and think.

There has recently been a lively and sometimes acrimonious debate concerning the merits of allowing clinical psychologists, with suitable training, to prescribe psychoactive drugs. Predictably, such a move is opposed by psychiatrists, for it would represent a clear invasion of their professional turf. Profits are an issue, but so is the question of whether a non-M.D. can learn enough about biochemistry and physiology to monitor the effects of drugs and protect patients from adverse side effects and drug interactions. This debate will undoubtedly continue for some time before any resolution is reached.

A **psychoanalyst** has received specialized training at a psychoanalytic institute; the program usually involves several years of clinical training as well as an in-depth psychoanalysis of the trainee. Although Sigmund Freud held that psychoanalysts do not need medical training, until recently most psychoanalytic institutes required of their graduates an M.D. and a psychiatric residency. Thus, it can take up to ten years of graduate work to become a psychoanalyst.

A **psychiatric social worker** obtains an M.S.W. (Master of Social Work) degree. There are also master's and doctoral programs for **counseling psychologists**, somewhat similar to graduate training in clinical psychology but usually with less emphasis on research.

The term *clinician* is often applied to people who, regardless of professional degree, offer diagnostic and therapeutic services to the public. Thus, clinicians can include Ph.D.'s in clinical or counseling psychology, Psy.D.'s, holders of an M.S.W. degree, and psychiatrists. Or the term can be used for people who do both research and clinical work, such as the authors of this textbook, when they are performing clinical services. A highly diverse group of people can be called **psychopathologists**. These people conduct research into the nature and development of the various disorders that their therapist colleagues try to treat. Psychopathologists may come from any number of disciplines; some are clinical psychologists, but the educational backgrounds of others may range from biochemistry to developmental psychology. What unites them is their commitment to the study of how abnormal behavior develops. Since we still have much to learn about psychopathology, the diversity of backgrounds and interests is an advantage, for it is too soon to be certain in which area major advances will be made.

History of Psychopathology

As psychopathologists, our interest is in the causes of deviant behavior. The search for these causes has gone on for a considerable period of time. Before the age of scientific inquiry, all good and bad manifestations of power beyond the control of humankind—eclipses, earthquakes, storms, fire, serious and disabling disease, the passing of the seasons—were regarded as supernatural. Any behavior seemingly beyond individual control was subject to similar interpretation. The earliest writings of the philosophers, theologians, and physicians who studied the troubled mind found its deviancy to reflect the displeasure of the gods or possession by demons.

Early Demonology

The doctrine that an evil being, such as the devil, may dwell within a person and control his or her mind and body is called **demonology**. The ancient Babylonians had in their religion a specific demon for each disease. Idta was the demon who caused insanity. Examples of demonological thinking can be found in the records of the early Chinese, Egyptians, and Greeks as well. Among the Hebrews, deviancy was attributed to possession of the person by bad spirits, after God in his wrath had withdrawn protection. Christ is reported to have cured a man with an unclean spirit by casting out the devils from within him and hurling them onto a herd of swine (Mark 5:8–13).

Exorcism, the casting out of evil spirits by ritualistic chanting or torture, typically took the form of elaborate prayer rites, noisemaking, forcing the afflicted to drink terrible-tasting brews, and on occasion more extreme measures, such as flogging and starvation, to render the body uninhabitable to the devils.

Somatogenesis

In the fifth century B.C. Hippocrates (460?–377? B.C.), often regarded as the father of modern medicine, separated medicine from religion, magic, and superstition. Operating outside the **Zeitgeist**, or the

The Greek physician Hippocrates held a somatogenic view of abnormal behavior, considering insanity a disease of the brain.

intellectual and emotional orientation of the times, Hippocrates rejected the prevailing Greek belief that the gods sent serious physical diseases and mental disturbances as punishment. He insisted instead that such illnesses had natural causes and hence should be treated like other more common maladies, such as colds and constipation. Hippocrates regarded the brain as the organ of consciousness, of intellectual life and emotion, and it followed that if someone's thinking and behavior were deviant, there was some kind of brain pathology. He is often considered one of the very earliest proponents of **somatogenesis**—the notion that something wrong with the *soma*, or physical body, disturbs thought and action. In contrast, **psychogenesis** is the belief that something is due to psychological origins.

Hippocrates classified mental disorders into three categories: mania, melancholia, and phrenitis or brain fever. Through his teachings the phenomena of abnormal behavior became more clearly the province of physicians than of priests. The treatments Hippocrates suggested were quite different from the earlier exorcistic tortures. For melancholia he prescribed tranquillity, sobriety, care in choosing food and drink, and abstinence from sexual activity. Such a regimen was assumed to have a healthful effect on the brain and the body. Because Hippocrates believed in natural rather than supernatural causes, he depended on his own keen observations and made a valuable contribution as a clinician. Remarkably detailed records describing many of the symptoms now recognized in epilepsy, alcoholic delusion, stroke, and paranoia have come down to us from him.

Hippocrates' physiology was rather crude, however, for he conceived of normal brain functioning, and therefore of mental health, as dependent on a delicate balance among four humors, or fluids of the body, namely, blood, black bile, yellow bile, and phlegm. An imbalance produced disorders. If a person was sluggish and dull, for example, the body supposedly contained a preponderance of phlegm. A preponderance of black bile was the explanation for melancholia; too much yellow bile explained irritability and anxiousness; and too much blood, changeable temperament. Hippocrates' humoral pathology did not withstand later scientific scrutiny. His basic premise, however, that human behavior is markedly affected by bodily structures or substances and that abnormal behavior is produced by some kind of imbalance or even damage, foreshadowed aspects of contemporary thought. In the next seven centuries, Hippocrates' naturalistic approach to disorder was generally accepted by other Greeks as well as by the Romans, who adopted the medicine of the Greeks after their city became the seat of power in the ancient European world.

The Dark Ages and Demonology

In a massive generalization, historians have often suggested that the death of Galen (A.D. 130–200), the second-century Greek who is regarded as the last major physician of the classical era, marked the beginning of the Dark Ages for all medicine and for the treatment and investigation of abnormal behavior in particular. Over several centuries of decay, Greek and Roman civilization ceased to be. The churches gained in influence, and the papacy was soon declared independent of the state and became the important element of unity. Christian monasticism, through its missionary and educational work, replaced classical culture.

The monasteries cared for and nursed the sick, and a few were repositories for the classic Greek medical manuscripts, even though the knowledge within them might not be applied. When monks cared for the mentally disordered, they prayed over them and touched them with relics or they concocted fantastic potions for them to drink in the

The four temperaments, as depicted in this medieval painting, were thought by the followers of Hippocrates to result from excesses of the four humors. Top left: the irritable man. Top right: the melancholic man. Lower left: the sluggish man. Lower right: the changeable man.

waning phase of the moon. The families of the deranged might take them to shrines or sometimes disavowed them out of fear and superstition. Many of the mentally ill roamed the countryside, becoming more and more bedraggled and losing more and more of their faculties.

The Mentally Ill as Witches

During the thirteenth and the next few centuries, a populace that was already suffering from social unrest and recurrent famines and plagues become obsessed with the devil. Witchcraft, now viewed as instigated by the powerful Satan of the heretics, was itself a heresy and denial of God. Faced with inexplicable and frightening occurrences, people tend to seize on whatever explanation is available. The times conspired to heap enormous blame on those regarded as witches, who were persecuted with great zeal.

In 1484 Pope Innocent VIII, in a papal bull, exhorted the clergy of Europe to leave no stone unturned in the search for witches. He sent two Dominican monks to northern Germany as inquisitors. Two years later they issued a comprehensive and explicit manual, *Malleus Maleficarum* (''the witches' hammer''), to guide the witch hunts. This legal and theological document came to be regarded by Catholics and Protestants alike as a textbook on witchcraft. Various signs by which witches could be detected, such as red spots or areas of insensitivity on the skin, supposedly made by the claw of the devil when touching the person to seal a pact, were described. Those accused of witchcraft should be tortured if they did not confess; those convicted and penitent were to be imprisoned for life; and those convicted and unrepentant were to be handed over to the law for execution. The manual specified that a person's sudden loss of reason was a symptom of demonic possession and that burning was the usual method of driving out the supposed demon. Over

In the dunking test, if the woman did not drown, she was thought to be in league with the devil.

the next several centuries hundreds of thousands of women, men, and children are said to have been accused, tortured, and put to death, but records of the period are not reliable.

The first abatement in witch hunting came in Spain in 1610, when the inquisitor Alonso Salazar y Frías concluded that most of the accusations in Logroño, Navarre, had been false. He ordained that accusations must be accompanied by independent evidence, that torture could not be used, and that the property of the convicted would not be confiscated. Thereafter accusations of witchcraft dropped sharply in Spain. In Sweden in 1649 Queen Christina ordered that all prisoners accused of witchcraft be freed except those clearly guilty of murder. In France witchcraft trials declined after an edict was issued by Louis XIV in 1682. The last execution of a witch was in Switzerland in 1782.

For some time the prevailing interpretation has been that all the mentally ill of the later Middle Ages were considered witches (Zilboorg & Henry, 1941). In their confessions the accused sometimes reported having had intercourse with the devil and having flown to sabbats, the secret meetings of their cults. These reports have been interpreted by contemporary writers as delusions or hallucinations and thus are taken to indicate that some witches were psychotic. Moreover, to identify people with the "Devil's mark," areas of insensitivity to pain, professional witch prickers went from town to town sticking pins into the bodies of the accused. Because anesthesia is regarded as a symptom of hysteria (see Chapter 7, page 167), the fact that some "witches" did not respond to the prickings is considered evidence of their madness.

More careful analyses of the witch hunts, however, reveal that although some accused witches were mentally disturbed, many more sane than insane people were tried. The delusionlike confessions were typically obtained during brutal torture; words were put on the lips of the tortured by their accusers and by the beliefs of the times. Indeed, in England, where torture was not allowed, the confessions did not usually contain descriptions indicative of delusions or hallucinations. Similarly, insensitivity to pain has many causes, including organic dysfunctions. More important, there are documented cases of deliberate trickery. Often during pricking, a needle was attached to a hollow shaft so that it did not actually puncture the skin, although to observers it appeared to be penetrating deeply (Schoeneman, 1977; Spanos, 1978).

Evaluations of other sources of information indicate that witchcraft was not the primary interpretation of mental illness. From the thirteenth century onward, as the cities of Europe grew larger, hospitals began to come under secular jurisdiction. Municipal authorities, when they grew powerful, tended to supplement or take over some of the activities of the church, one of these of course being the care of the ill. The foundation deed for the Holy Trinity Hospital in Salisbury, England, dating from the mid-fourteenth century, specified the purposes of the hospital, among them that "mad are kept safe until they are restored of reason." British laws during this period allowed both the dangerously insane and the incompetent to be confined in a hospital. Notably, the people to be confined were not described as being possessed (Allderidge, 1979).

Neugebauer (1979) examined the records from lunacy trials in Britain during the Middle Ages. Beginning in the thirteenth century, these trials were held to determine a person's sanity. The trials were conducted under the Crown's right to protect the mentally impaired, and a judgment of insanity allowed the Crown to become guardian of the lunatic's estate. The defendant's orientation, memory, intellect, daily life, and habits were at issue in the trial. Explanations for strange behavior typically linked it to physical illness or injury or to some emotional shock. In all the cases that Neugebauer examined only *one* referred to demonological possession. The preponderance of evidence, then, indicates that this explanation of mental disturbance was not as dominant during the Middle Ages as had once been thought.

Focus Box 1.1 presents the most famous episode of witchcraft that occurred in America, the Salem incident. It also provides an opportunity to see how different viewpoints play a role in trying to interpret the behavior of the accused witches.

Development of Asylums

Until the end of the Crusades in the fifteenth century, there were very few mental hospitals in Europe. Earlier, however, there were thousands of hospitals for lepers. In the twelfth century, for example, England and Scotland had 220 leprosy hospitals for a population of a million and a half. After the principal Crusades had been waged, leprosy gradually disappeared from Europe, probably because of the break with the eastern sources of the infection. With leprosy no longer of such great social concern, attention seems to have turned to the mad.

Confinement of the mentally ill began in earnest in the fifteenth and sixteenth centuries. The leprosariums were converted to **asylums**, refuges established for the confinement and care of the mentally ill. Many of these asylums took in a mixed lot of disturbed people and beggars. Beggars were regarded as a great social problem at the time. Indeed, in the sixteenth century, Paris had 30,000 beggars in its population of fewer than 100,000 (Foucault, 1965). These institutions had no specific regimen for their inmates other than to get them to work. But during the same period hospitals geared more specifically for the confinement of the mentally ill also appeared. The Priory of St. Mary of Bethlehem was founded in 1243. By 1403 it housed six insane men, and in 1547 Henry VIII handed it over to the city of London, thereafter to be a hospital devoted solely to the confinement of the mentally ill. The conditions in Bethlehem were deplorable. Over the years the word *bedlam*, a contraction and popular name for this hospital, became a descriptive term for a place or scene of wild uproar and confusion. Bethlehem eventually became one of London's great tourist attractions, by the eighteenth century rivaling both Westminster Abbey and the Tower of London. Even as late as the nineteenth century, viewing the violent patients and their antics was considered entertainment, and tickets of admission to Bedlam were sold. Similarly, in the Lunatic's Tower, constructed in Vienna in 1784, patients were confined in the spaces between inner square rooms and the outer walls. There they could be viewed by passersby. The first mental hospital in the United States was founded in Williamsburg, Virginia, in 1773.

It should not be assumed that the inclusion of abnormal behavior within the domain of hospitals and medicine necessarily led to more humane and effective treatment. Benjamin Rush (1745–1813), who began practicing medicine in Philadelphia in 1769 and was also deeply involved in his country's struggle for independence, is considered the father of American psychiatry. He believed that mental disorder was caused by an excess of blood in the brain. Consequently, his favored treatment was to draw from "the insane" great quantities of blood, as much as six quarts over a period of a few months. Little wonder that patients so treated became less agitated; anyone would be weak from the loss of that much blood (Farina, 1976)! Rush entertained another hypothesis, namely, that many "lunatics" could be cured by frightening them. In one such recommended procedure the physician was to convince the patient of his impending death. A New England doctor of the nineteenth century implemented this prescription in an ingenious manner. "On his premises stood a tank of water, into which a patient, packed into a coffin-like box pierced with holes, was lowered. . . . He was kept under water until the bubbles of air ceased to rise, after which he was taken out, rubbed, and revived—if he had not already passed beyond reviving!" (Deutsch, 1949, p. 82).

Moral Treatment

Philippe Pinel (1745–1826) is considered a primary figure in the movement for humanitarian treatment

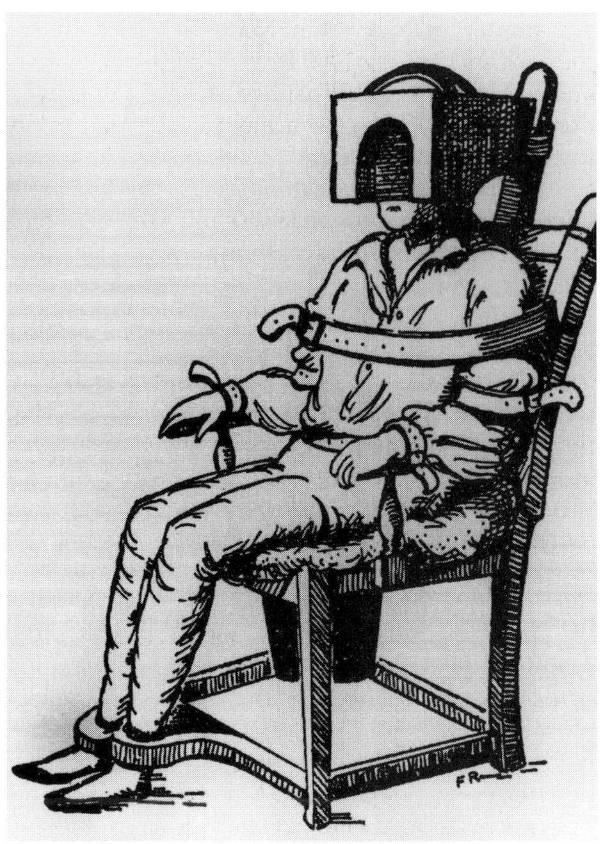

The tranquilizing machine was used by Rush to restrain unmanageable patients.

of those in asylums. In 1793, while the French Revolution raged, he was put in charge of a large asylum in Paris known as La Bicêtre. A historian has written of the conditions at this particular hospital.

> [The patients were] shackled to the walls of their cells, by iron collars which held them flat against the wall and permitted little movement. . . . They could not lie down at night, as a rule. . . . Oftentimes there was a hoop of iron around the waist of the patient and in addition . . . chains on both the hands and the feet. . . . These chains [were] sufficiently long so that the patient could feed himself out of a bowl, the food usually being a mushy gruel—bread soaked in a weak soup. Since little was known about dietetics, [no attention] was paid to the type of diet given the patients. They were presumed to be animals . . . and not to care whether the food was good or bad. (Selling, 1940, p. 54)

Pinel was allowed to remove the chains of the people imprisoned in La Bicêtre and to treat them as sick human beings rather than as beasts. Many who had been completely unmanageable became calm and much easier to handle. Formerly considered dangerous, they strolled through the hospital and grounds with no inclination to create disturbances or to harm anyone. Light and airy rooms replaced their dungeons. Some who had been incarcerated for years were soon restored to health and were eventually discharged from the hospital.

Freeing the patients of their restraints was not the only humanitarian reform advocated by Pinel. Con-

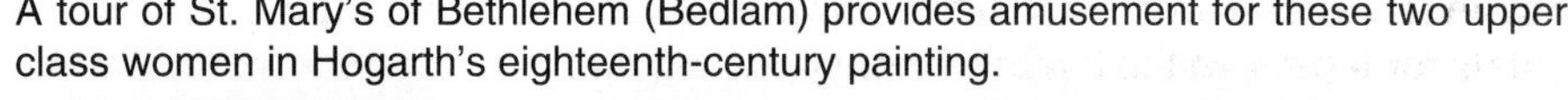

A tour of St. Mary's of Bethlehem (Bedlam) provides amusement for these two upper class women in Hogarth's eighteenth-century painting.

FOCUS

1.1 • The Salem Incident: Witchcraft or Poisoning?

In December 1691 eight girls who lived in or near Salem Village were afflicted with "distempers," which called for medical attention. Physicians, however, could find no cause for their disorderly speech, strange postures and gestures, and convulsive fits. One of the girls was the daughter of the minister, Samuel Parris, another his niece. A neighbor soon took it upon herself to have Parris's Barbados slave, Tituba, concoct a "witch cake" of rye meal and the urine of the afflicted and feed it to a dog to determine whether witchcraft was indicated. Shortly thereafter, in February 1692, the girls accused Tituba and two elderly women of witchcraft, and the three were taken into custody.

Accusations began to spew as well from other residents of the village. The jails of Salem, of surrounding towns, and even of faraway Boston filled with prisoners awaiting trial. By the end of September, nineteen people had been sent to the gallows, and one man had been pressed to death. The convictions were all obtained on the bases of spectral evidence—an apparition of the accused had appeared to the accuser—and the test of touch—an accuser's fit ceased after he or she was touched by the accused. The afflicted girls were present at the trials and often disturbed the proceedings with their violent fits, convulsions, and apparent hallucinations of specters and familiars. (Familiars are spirits, often in animal form, who are believed to act as servants to a witch.)

In January 1693 a superior court convened and received fifty new indictments for witchcraft that had been made by a grand jury. It tried twenty persons, acquitted seventeen, and condemned three, although they were never executed. In May of 1693 Governor Phips ordered a general reprieve; about 150 persons still being held on charges of witchcraft were released, ending the strange episode.

These happenings in Salem have often been presented as an illustration of how the hapless mentally ill of the era were mistreated through the widespread belief that they were possessed, although the accused witches were for the most part persons of good reputation in the community. The accusers are sometimes proposed to have been schizophrenic, on the basis of their hallucinations. But schizophrenia is not likely to occur simultaneously in a group of young women. Or the episode is sometimes seen as an instance of mass hysteria; the witchcraft accusation, once

The Salem witch trials during which many women were accused of witchcraft. The afflictions of the accused witches may have been caused by ergot poisoning.

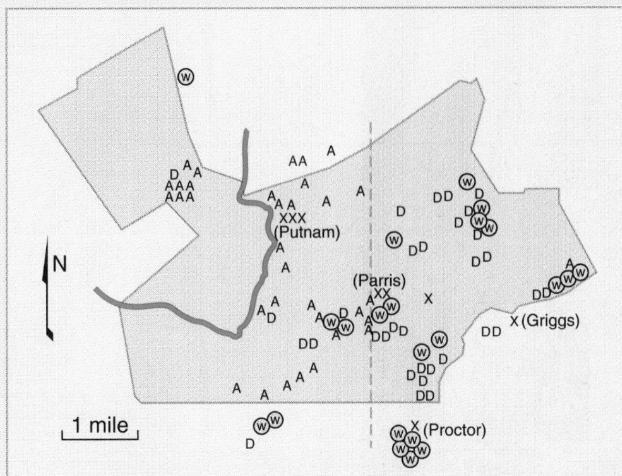

Residence patterns in Salem 1692. The names in parentheses indicate the homes where the "possessed" girls lived. Residents are labeled as follows: X, afflicted girl; W, accused witch; D, defender of an accused witch; and A, accuser. Thirty of the thirty-two adult accusers lived in the western section of the village, and twelve of the fourteen accused witches in the eastern section.

made, mushroomed for some reason. Earlier accusations of witchcraft in Puritan communities of New England had never had such an outcome, however. Caporael (1976) proposed a different theory, that the accusers in Salem were suffering from ergot poisoning.

Ergot, a parasitic fungus, grows on cereal grains, principally rye, and its development is fostered by warm, rainy growing seasons. Several of the alkaloids* of ergot contain lysergic acid, from which LSD is synthesized. Ingestion of food made from flour contaminated with ergot can cause crawling sensations on the skin, tingling in the fingers, vertigo, headache, hallucinations, vomiting, diarrhea, and convulsions. The alkaloids of ergot can also induce delirium and mood changes, such as mania and depression.

Could ergot poisoning account for the events in question? First, the behavior of the initial accusers is indeed similar to the known effects of ergot poisoning. The girls did report having hallucinations; they also vomited, had convulsions, and said that they felt as though they were being choked and pricked with pins. Second, rye was a well-established crop in Salem, and there had been heavy rains in 1691, which would promote the growth of the fungus. Rye was usually harvested in August and threshed in the late autumn. The onset of the girls' strange behavior occurred at about the time they would be beginning to eat food made from the new grain. The accumulating accusations of witchcraft apparently came to an abrupt halt in the following autumn, when a new supply of grain, grown during a dry 1692, became available. After that time the afflictions of the girls and those of others in Salem were not mentioned in accounts of the period.

Why then did only some people feel that their bodies had been possessed? Caporael argues that the western portion of Salem Village, where the ground is lower and the meadows are swampy, would be the most likely source of contaminated grain. The pattern of residence of the young girls and of the other accusers fits this hypothesis; they were more likely to reside in or to eat grain grown in the western fields. Most of the accused witches and their defenders lived in the eastern section of the village.

Caporael has presented a compelling set of arguments for her ergot-poisoning theory. Of course, it remains a theory, but it is interesting to speculate how many witchcraft persecutions throughout the later Middle Ages may have had ergot poisoning as a root cause.

---

*Alkaloids are organic substances that are found for the most part in seed plants, usually not singly but as mixtures of similar alkaloids. They all contain nitrogen and are the active agents that give a number of natural drugs their medicinal and also their toxic properties.

Pinel's freeing the patients at La Bicetre is the event often considered as the beginning of more humanitarian treatment of the insane.

sistent with the egalitarianism of the new French Republic, he believed that the mental patients in his care were essentially normal people who should be approached with compassion and understanding and treated with dignity as individual human beings. Their reason supposedly having left them because of severe personal and social problems, it might be restored to them through comforting counsel and purposeful activity.

We should add here that for all the good Pinel did for the mentally ill, he was not a complete paragon of enlightenment and egalitarianism in his treatment of them. The more humanitarian treatment he reserved for the upper classes; patients of the lower classes were still subjected to terror and coercion as a means of control—a telling commentary on the duplicity of prejudice in the birth of a new government (Szasz, 1974).

After Pinel's revolutionary work in La Bicêtre, the hospitals established in Europe and the United States were for a time relatively small and privately supported. A prominent merchant and Quaker. William Tuke (1732–1822), shocked by the conditions at York Asylum in England, proposed to the Society of Friends that they found their own institution. In 1796 York Retreat was established on a country estate. It provided the mentally ill with a quiet and religious atmosphere in which to live, work, and rest. They discussed their difficulties with attendants, worked in the garden, and took walks through the countryside. In the United States the Friends' Asylum, founded in 1817 in Pennsylvania, and the Hartford Retreat, established in 1824 in Connecticut, were patterned after the York Retreat. A number of other American hospitals were influenced by the sympathetic and attentive treatment provided by Pinel and Tuke. In accordance with this approach, which became known as **moral treatment**, patients had close contact with attendants, who talked and read to them and encouraged them to purposeful activity. Residents were to lead as normal lives as possible and in general take responsibility for themselves within the constraints of their disorders. This moral treatment had to be abandoned in the second half of the nineteenth century, however. The staffs of the large, public mental hospitals being built to take in the many patients for whom the private ones had no room could not provide such individual attention (Bockhoven, 1963). Moreover, these hospitals came to be administered by physicians, who were more interested in the biological aspects of illness and in the physical well-being of mental patients. The money that once paid the salaries of personal attendants now went into equipment and laboratories. See Focus Box 1.2 for an examination of the conditions in today's mental institutions.

Two findings have emerged from a recent review of detailed case records of the York Retreat from 1880 through 1884, conducted by contemporary researchers (Renvoize & Beveridge, 1989). First, drugs were the most common treatment used and included alcohol, cannabis, opium, and chloryl hydrate (knockout drops). Second, the outcomes achieved do not appear very favorable. Less than one-third of the patients were discharged as improved or recovered. Moral treatment may not be all that it has been cracked up to be.

The Beginning of Contemporary Thought

Somatogenesis

After the fall of Greco-Roman civilization, the writings of Galen were the standard source of information about both physical and mental illness. It was not until the Middle Ages that any new facts began to emerge. One development that fostered progress was the discovery by Vesalius that Galen's presentation of human anatomy was incorrect. Galen had presumed that human physiology mirrored the apes he had studied. It took more than one thousand years for autopsy studies of humans—not allowed during his time—to begin to prove that Galen had been wrong. Empirical medical science received another boost from the efforts of the famous English physician Thomas Sydenham (1624–1689). Sydenham was particularly influential in advocating an empirical approach to classification and diagnosis that subsequently influenced those interested in mental disorders.

One of these was a German physician, Wilhelm Griesinger, who insisted that any diagnosis of mental disorder specify a physiological cause, a clear return to the somatogenic views first espoused by Hippocrates. A textbook of psychiatry, written by his well-known follower Emil Kraepelin (1856–1926) and first published in 1883, furnished a classification system to help establish the organic nature of mental illnesses. Kraepelin discerned among mental disorders a tendency for a certain group of symptoms, called a **syndrome**, to appear together regularly enough to be regarded as having an underlying physical cause, much as a particular medical disease and its syndrome may be attributed to a physiological dysfunction. He regarded each mental illness as distinct from all others, having its own genesis, symptoms, course, and outcome. Even though cures had not been worked out, at least the course of the disease could be predicted. Kraepelin proposed that there were two major groups of severe mental diseases: dementia praecox, an early term for schizophrenia, and manic-depressive psychosis. He postulated a chemical imbalance as the cause of schizophrenia and an irregularity in metabolism as the explanation of manic-depressive psychosis. Kraepelin's scheme for classifying these and other mental illnesses became the basis for the present diagnostic categories, which will be described more fully in Chapter 3.

Much was learned about the nervous system in the second half of the nineteenth century but not enough yet to reveal all the expected abnormalities in structure that might underlie mental disorders. Degenerative changes in the brain cells associated with senile and presenile psychoses and some structural pathologies that accompany mental retardation were identified, however. Perhaps the most striking medical success was the discovery of the full nature and origin of syphilis, a venereal disease that had been recognized for several centuries. Since 1798 it had been known that a number of mental patients manifested a syndrome characterized by a steady deterioration of both physical and mental abilities, and that these patients suffered multiple impairments, including delusions of grandeur and progressive paralysis. Soon after these symptoms were recognized, it was realized that these patients never recovered. In 1825 this deterioration in mental and physical health was designated a disease, **general paresis**. Although in 1857 it was established that some patients with paresis had earlier had syphilis, there were many competing theories of the origin of paresis. For example, in attempting to account for the high rate of the disorder among sailors, some supposed that seawater might be the cause. And Griesinger, in trying to explain the higher incidence among men, speculated whether liquor, tobacco, and coffee were implicated. Then in the 1860s and 1870s Louis Pasteur established the **germ theory** of disease that set forth the view that disease is caused by infection of the body by minute organisms. It then became possible to demonstrate the relation between syphilis and general paresis. In 1897 Richard von Krafft-Ebing innoculated paretic patients with matter from syphilitic sores. The patients did not develop syphilis, indicating that they had been infected earlier. Finally, in 1905, the specific microorganism causing syphilis was discovered. A causal link had been established between infection, destruction of certain areas of the brain, and a form of psychopathology. If one type of psychopathology had a biological cause, so could others. Somatogenesis gained credibility, and the search for more biological causes was off and running.

Psychogenesis

The search for somatogenic causes dominated psychiatry until well into the twentieth century, no doubt partly because of the stunning discoveries made about general paresis. But in other parts of western Europe, in the late eighteenth and throughout the nineteenth century, mental illnesses were considered to have an entirely different origin. Var-

FOCUS 1.2 • The Mental Hospital Today

Each year over two million Americans are hospitalized for mental disorders. Deinstitutionalization sweeps in the 1970s greatly reduced the number of patients in mental hospitals, but the problems of the chronic patient have yet to be handled adequately (as we will discuss in more detail in Chapter 21). Treatment in public mental institutions is primarily custodial in nature, and the existence of patients is monotonous and sedentary for the most part.

Mental hospitals in this country today are usually funded either by the federal government or by the state. In fact, the term *state hospital* is taken to mean a *mental* hospital run by the state. They are often old, grim, and somewhat removed from major metropolitan centers. Their costs to society in economic terms are staggering. Some Veterans Administration hospitals and general medical hospitals also contain psychiatric wards.

In addition, there are private mental hospitals. Sheppard and Enoch Pratt near Baltimore, Maryland, and McLean Hospital, in Belmont, Massachusetts, are two of the most famous. The physical facilities and professional care in private hospitals tend to be superior to those of state hospitals for one reason: the private hospitals have more money. The daily costs to patients in these private institutions can exceed $1,000 per day and may still not include individual therapy sessions with a member of the professional staff! Although some patients may have medical insurance, usually with a ninety-day limit, such hospitals are clearly beyond the means of most citizens.

A somewhat specialized mental hospital, sometimes called a prison hospital, is reserved for people who have been arrested and judged unable to stand trial and for those who have been acquitted of a crime by reason of insanity (see page 625). They have not been sent to prison, but armed guards and tight security regiment their lives. Treatment of some kind is supposed to take place during their internment.

Even in the best hospitals, patients usually have precious little contact with psychiatrists or clinical psychologists, an impression confirmed by careful behavioral observations of Paul and his co-workers, who found that most patients had no contact with staff for 80 to 90 percent of their waking hours and that the clinical staff spent less than one-fourth of their working time having contact with patients (Paul, 1987, 1988). Most of a patient's days and evenings are spent either alone or in the company of other patients and of aides, individuals who often have little more than a high school education. As with imprisonment, the overwhelming feeling is of helplessness and depersonalization. Patients sit endless hours in hallways waiting for dining halls to open, for medication to be dispensed, and for consultations with psychologists, social workers, and vocational counselors to begin. Except for the most severely disturbed, patients have access to the various facilities of a hospital, ranging from woodworking shops to swimming pools, from gymnasiums to basket-weaving shops.

Most hospitals require patients to attend group therapy—here a general term indicating only that at least two patients are supposed to relate to each other and to a group leader in a room for a specific period of time. For some patients there are a few sessions alone with a professional therapist. For the most part, however, traditional hospital treatment over the past forty years has been biologically oriented, with these other activities used primarily to occupy the patients' time until drugs have taken effect; the institutional setting itself is used as a way to provide supportive care and to protect and care for patients whose conditions make it virtually impossible for them to look after themselves or render them an unreasonable burden or threat to others (Paul & Menditto, 1992).

One nagging problem is that institutionalization is difficult to reverse once people have resided in mental hospitals for more than a year. We recall asking a patient who had improved markedly over the previous several months why he was reluctant

ious psychogenic points of view, attributing mental disorders to psychological malfunctions, were fashionable in France and Austria. For reasons not clear to us even today, many people in western Europe were at that time subject to hysterical states (in contemporary terms, conversion disorders): they suffered from physical incapacities, such as blindness or paralysis that made no anatomical sense (see page 167).

Franz Anton Mesmer (1734–1815), an Austrian

to be discharged. "Doc," he said earnestly, "it's a jungle out there." Although we cannot entirely disagree with his view, there nonetheless appear to be at least a few advantages to living on the outside. But this man—a veteran and chronic patient with a clinical folder more than two feet thick—had become so accustomed to the restrictions and care of various Veterans Administration hospitals that the prospect of leaving was as frightening to him as the prospect of entering a mental hospital is to those who have never lived in one.

One treatment sometimes applied is **milieu therapy**, in which the entire hospital becomes a "therapeutic community" (e.g., Jones, 1953). All its ongoing activities and all its personnel become part of the treatment program. Milieu therapy appears to be a return to the moral practices of the nineteenth century. Social interaction and group activities are encouraged so that through group pressure the patients are directed toward normal functioning. Patients are treated as responsible human beings rather than as custodial cases (Paul, 1969). They are expected to participate in their own readjustment as well as that of their fellow patients. Open wards allow them considerable freedom. There is some evidence for the efficacy of milieu therapy (e.g., Fairweather, 1964; Greenblatt et al., 1965), the most convincing from a milestone project by Paul and Lentz (1977).

In this ambitious study, Paul and Lentz demonstrated encouraging improvement in chronic, hard-core patients through both milieu and social-learning therapy. A token economy, which reached into many details of the patients' lives, was combined with other behavior therapy interventions tailored to the particular needs of each resident. Described in more detail on pages 558–9, a token economy rewards patients for behaving in a particular way by reinforcing behaviors with tokens that can be exchanged for privileges or other items patients desire. A host of measures were taken on the behavior of both staff and patients over four and a half years of treatment, with a later eighteen-month follow-up on patients who had since been discharged. The social-learning program was markedly more successful than both milieu therapy carried out for a matched group at another unit of the mental health center, and routine hospital management of a second matched group in an older Illinois state hospital.

Since mental hospitals will be needed for the foreseeable future, especially by people who demonstrate time and again that they have difficulty functioning on the outside, Paul's work is of special importance. It suggests specific ways in which the chronic patient can be helped to cope better not only within the hospital but after discharge as well.

Most dormitory rooms at state mental hospitals are bleak and unstimulating.

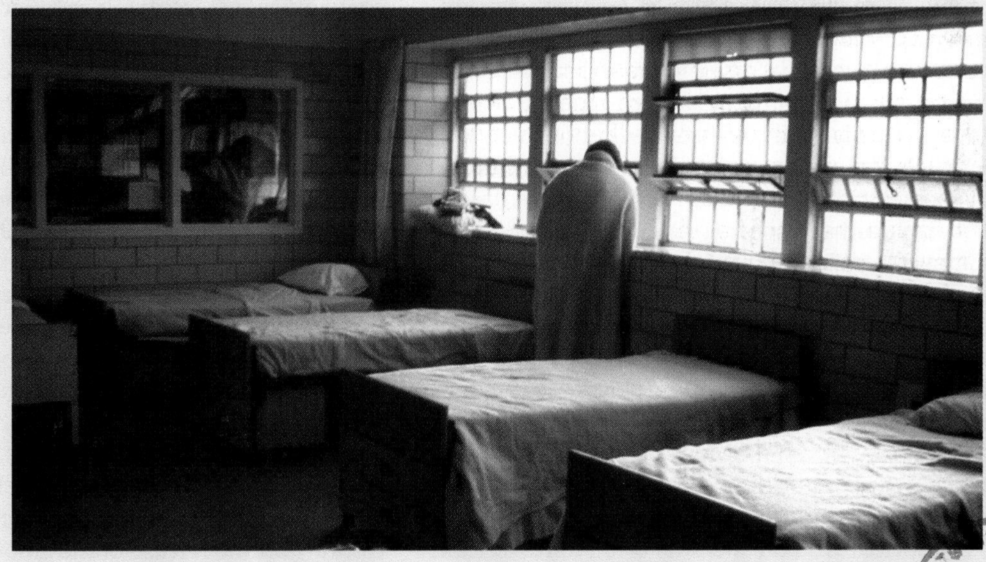

physician practicing in Vienna and Paris in the late eighteenth century, believed that hysterical disorders were caused by a particular distribution of a universal magnetic fluid in the body. Moreover, he felt that one person could influence the fluid of another to bring about a change in the other's behavior. He conducted meetings cloaked in mystery and mysticism, during which afflicted patients sat around a covered *baquet*, or tub, with iron rods protruding through the cover from bottles of various

Mesmer's procedure for transmitting animal magnetism was generally considered a form of hypnosis.

The French psychiatrist, Jean Charcot, lectures on hysteria in this famous painting. Charcot was an important figure in reviving interest in psychogenesis.

chemicals that were beneath. Mesmer would enter a room, clothed in rather outlandish garments, take various rods from the tub, and touch afflicted parts of his patients' bodies. The rods were believed to transmit animal magnetism and adjust the distribution of the universal magnetic fluid, thereby removing the hysterical anesthesias and paralyses. Whatever we may think of what seems today to be a questionable theoretical explanation and procedure, Mesmer apparently helped many people overcome their hysterical problems. The reader may wonder about our discussing Mesmer's work under the rubric of psychogenic causes, since Mesmer regarded the hysterical disorders as strictly physical. Because of the setting in which Mesmer worked with his patients, however, he is generally considered one of the earlier practitioners of modern-day hypnosis, which is discussed in more detail in Chapter 7 (p. 183). The word *mesmerize* is the older term for *hypnotize*. The phenomenon itself, however, was known to the ancients of probably every culture, part of the sorcery and magic of conjurers, fakirs, and faith healers.

Although Mesmer was regarded as a quack by his contemporaries, the study of hypnosis gradually became respectable. A great Parisian neurologist, Jean Martin Charcot (1825–1893), also studied hysterical states, not only anesthesia and paralysis, but blindness, deafness, convulsive attacks, and gaps in memory brought about by hysteria. Charcot initially espoused a somatogenic point of view. One day, however, some of his enterprising students hypnotized a normal woman and suggested to her certain hysterical symptoms. Charcot was deceived into believing that she was an actual hysterical patient. When the students showed him how readily they could remove the symptoms by waking the woman, Charcot changed his mind about hysteria and became interested in nonphysiological interpretations of these very puzzling phenomena. Further psychological theorizing and research were done by Pierre Janet (1859–1947), one of Charcot's pupils. He believed that in hysteria part of the organized system of thoughts, emotions, and sensations broke loose from the rest through a weakness of the nervous system.

In Vienna, toward the end of the century, a physician named Josef Breuer (1842–1925) treated a young woman who had become bedridden with a number of hysterical symptoms. Her legs and right arm and side were paralyzed, her sight and hearing were impaired, and she often had difficulty speaking. She also sometimes went into a dreamlike state or "absence," during which she mumbled to herself, seemingly preoccupied with troubling thoughts. During one treatment session Breuer hypnotized Anna O. and repeated some of her mumbled words. He succeeded in getting her to talk more freely and ultimately with considerable emotion about some very disquieting past events. Upon awakening from these hypnotic sessions, she would frequently feel much better. With Anna O. and other hysterical patients Breuer found that the relief and cure of symptoms seemed to last longer if, under hypnosis, they were able to recall the precipitating event for the symptom and if, furthermore, their original emotion was expressed. Reliving an earlier emotional catastrophe and the release of the emotional tension produced by previously forgotten thoughts about the event was called catharsis. Breuer's method became known as the **cathartic method**. In 1895 one of his colleagues joined him in the publication of *Studies in Hysteria*, a book considered a milestone in abnor-

Josef Breuer, the Austrian physician and physiologist, collaborated with Freud in the early development of psychoanalysis. He treated only Anna O. by the cathartic method he originated. Becoming alarmed by what would later be called her transference and his own countertransference, he described his procedures to a colleague and turned her over to him.

Anna O., actually Bertha Pappenheim, was the patient in the celebrated case that Breuer treated with the cathartic method.

mal psychology. In the next chapter we examine the thinking of Breuer's collaborator, Sigmund Freud.[2]

Science: A Human Enterprise

In space exploration highly sophisticated satellites are sent aloft to make observations. Astronauts have also been catapulted to the moon, where they used their human senses as well as machines to carry out still more observations. It is possible, however, that certain phenomena are missed because our instruments do not have sensing devices capable of recording the presence or absence of such phenomena and because people are not trained to look for them. When the Viking 1 and Viking 2 Mars landers began to forage for life in July and September of 1976, space scientists repeatedly cautioned against concluding that there was no life on Mars just because instruments failed to detect any. Scientists are sophisticated enough by training to know that they are in a bind. Life on another planet can be looked for only with the instruments they themselves have developed, but these devices are limited by their own preconceptions. The tests run on Mars made assumptions about the nature of living matter that may not match what has evolved on this distant planet.

This discussion on outer-space exploration is one way of pointing out that scientific observation is a human endeavor, reflecting both the strengths of human ingenuity and scholarship as well as our intrinsic incapacity to be fully knowledgeable about the nature of our universe. Scientists are able to design instruments to make only the kinds of observations about which they have some initial idea. They realize that certain observations are not being

---

[2]Anna O., the young woman treated by Breuer with the cathartic method, or "talking cure," has become one of the best-known clinical cases in all psychotherapy literature, and as indicated above, the report of this case and four others in 1895 formed the basis of Freud's important later contributions. But historical investigations by Ellenberger (1972) cast serious doubt on the accuracy of Breuer's reporting. Indeed, Anna O.—in reality Bertha Pappenheim, member of a well-to-do Viennese family—was apparently helped only temporarily by Breuer's talking cure! Carl Jung, Freud's renowned colleague, is quoted as saying that, during a conference in 1925, Freud told him that Anna O. had never been cured. Hospital records discovered by Ellenberger confirmed that Anna O. continued to rely on morphine to ease the "hysterical" problems that Breuer is reputed to have removed by catharsis. In fact, evidence suggests that some of her problems were organic, not psychological. It is fascinating and ironic to consider that psychoanalysis traces its roots back to an improperly reported clinical case.

made because our knowledge about the general nature of the universe is limited. Thomas Kuhn, a well-known philosopher of science, put the problem this way: "The decision to employ a particular piece of apparatus and to use it in a particular way carries an assumption that only certain sorts of circumstances will arise" (1962, p. 59). Einstein said "It is the theory which decides what we can observe" (Heisenberg, 1971, p. 63). Robert Pirsig, in *Zen and the Art of Motorcycle Maintenance* (1974), expressed the issue somewhat more poetically: "We take a handful of sand from the endless landscape of awareness around us and call that handful of sand the world" (p. 75).

Subjectivity in Science: The Role of Paradigms

We believe that every effort should be made to study abnormal behavior according to scientific principles. It should be clear at this point, however, that science is *not* a completely objective and certain enterprise. Rather, as we can infer from the comment by Kuhn, subjective factors, as well as limitations in our perspective on the universe, enter into the conduct of scientific inquiry. Central to any application of scientific principles, in Kuhn's view, is the concept of **paradigm**, a conceptual framework or approach within which a scientist works. A paradigm, according to Kuhn, is a set of basic assumptions that outline the particular universe of scientific inquiry, specifying both the kinds of concepts that will be regarded as legitimate as well as methods that may be used to collect and interpret data. A paradigm has profound implications for how scientists operate at any given time, for "[People] whose research is based on shared paradigms are committed to the same rules and standards for scientific practice" (Kuhn, 1962, p. 11). Paradigms specify what problems scientists will investigate and how they will go about the investigation.

Paradigms are an intrinsic part of a science, serving the vital function of indicating the rules to be followed. In perceptual terms a paradigm may be likened to a general set, a tendency to see certain factors and not to see others.

In addition to injecting inevitable biases into the definition and collection of data, a paradigm may also affect the interpretation of facts. In other words, the meaning or import given to data may depend to a considerable extent on a paradigm. We will describe the major paradigms of abnormal psychology in the next chapter.

An Example of Paradigms in Abnormal Psychology

A striking demonstration of the "I'll see it when I believe it" feature of science is provided in an experiment by Langer and Abelson (1974). They were interested in how different theoretical orientations or paradigms might affect the ways in which trained clinicians view the adjustment of a person.

Behavior therapy stems from the behaviorism-learning branch of psychology, which sees as its purpose the observation of overt behavior and which has formulated laws that describe learning. Behavior therapists believe that abnormal behavior is acquired according to the same learning principles as normal behavior and that the very designation of a person as mentally ill reflects a social judgment. In contrast, more traditionally trained clinicians look for the inner conflict supposedly causing disturbed behavior and tend more than behavior therapists to think in terms of mental illness. Langer and Abelson reasoned that behavior therapists might be less swayed by being told that a person was ill than would traditionally trained clinicians. To test this supposition, they conceived the following experiment. A group of behavior therapists and another of traditional clinicians with some training in psychoanalysis (see page 10) were shown a videotape of an interview in progress between two men. Before viewing this videotape, half the subjects in each group were told that the interviewee was a job applicant, the other half that he was a patient. The traditional clinicians who were told that the interviewee was a patient were expected to rate him as more disturbed than those who considered him a job applicant. The ratings of the two groups of behavior therapists were expected to be less affected by the labels and thus to be rather similar.

The videotape shown to all subjects depicted a bearded professor interviewing a young man in his mid-twenties. The interviewee had been recruited through a newspaper advertisement that offered ten dollars to someone who had recently applied for a new job and was willing to be interviewed and videotaped. The fifteen-minute segment chosen from the original interview contained a rambling, autobiographical monologue by the young man in which he described a number of past jobs and dwelt on his conflicts with bureaucrats. His manner was considered by Langer and Abelson to be intense but uncertain; they felt that he could be regarded either as sincere and struggling or as confused and troubled.

A questionnaire measured the clinicians' impressions about the mental health of the interviewee.

When the young interviewee was identified as a job applicant, there were no significant differences in the adjustment ratings given by the traditional clinicians and the behavior therapists. But the patient label, as expected, produced sharp differences (Figure 1.2). When the interviewee was identified as a patient, the traditional clinicians rated him relatively disturbed—significantly more so than did the traditional clinicians who viewed the man as a job applicant. In contrast, the behavior therapists rated the "ill" interviewee as relatively well adjusted, in fact, no less adjusted than the other behavior therapists rated the man they considered a job applicant.

Qualitative evaluations obtained from the clinicians supported their ratings. Whereas the behavior therapists described the man as "realistic," "sincere," and "responsible," regardless of label, the traditional clinicians who viewed him as a patient used phrases such as "tight, defensive person," "conflict over homosexuality," and "impulsivity shows through his rigidity."

Why, in this particular experiment, did the behavior therapists appear to be unbiased? Langer and Abelson explain it this way. The behavioral approach encourages clinicians to concentrate on overt or manifest behavior and to be skeptical about illness that is not readily apparent. Those with such an orientation had the advantage in this particular study because, however the interviewee rambled, his behavior on balance was not overtly disturbed. The traditional therapists on the other hand, had been trained to look beyond what is most obvious in a client. Therefore, when they heard the negative ramblings about bureaucrats, they probably paid too much attention to them and inferred that something was basically wrong with the young man.

Langer and Abelson properly alert readers to the limitations of their experiment, reminding them that a different study—perhaps using an interviewee who is obviously disturbed—might put behavior therapists at a disadvantage. The purpose of the experiment, and this discussion of it, is not to pit one orientation against another but rather *to illustrate how a paradigm can affect perception.* Indeed, psychopathology can be in the eye of the beholder.

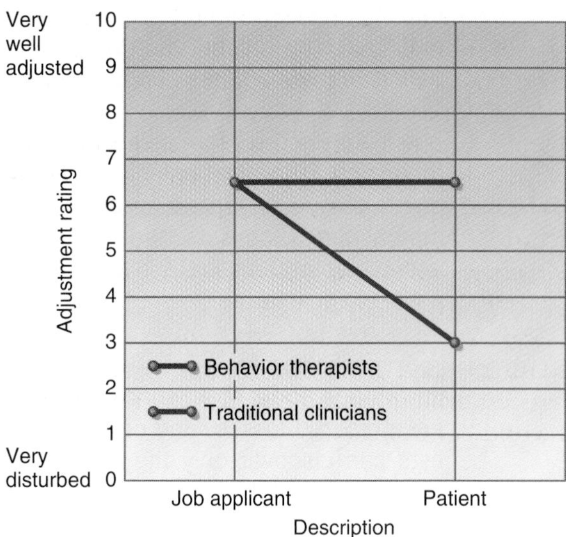

Figure 1.2 The mean adjustment ratings given the interviewee, depending on the investigators' description of him and the diagnosticians' training. Adapted from Langer and Abelson (1974). Copyright 1974 by the APA. Reprinted by permission.

Thus subjective factors in the guise of theoretical persuasions pervade psychology and strongly affect our conception of the nature of abnormal behavior. Scientists, whatever their field, do not resign from the family of human beings when they formulate hypotheses and conduct investigations and controlled research. Perhaps it is especially appropriate for the psychologist-as-scientist to remain aware of this simple, although frequently overlooked, point. With that in mind we will turn in the next chapter to a discussion of the major paradigms of abnormal psychology.

SUMMARY

The study of psychopathology is a search for why people behave, think, and feel in unexpected, sometimes bizarre, and typically self-defeating ways. Much less is known than we would like; this book will focus on the ways in which psychopathologists have been trying to learn the causes of abnormal behavior and what they know about preventing and alleviating it.

Several components of abnormality are discussed: statistical infrequency, violation of societal norms, personal distress, disability or dysfunction, and unexpectedness. Each characteristic tells something about what can be considered abnormal, but conceptions change with time, making it impossible to offer a simple definition that captures abnormality in its entirety.

A history of the field indicates its origins in ancient demonology and crude medical theorizing. Since the beginning of scientific inquiry into abnormal behavior, two major points of view have vied for attention: the somatogenic, which assumes that every mental aberration is caused by a physical malfunction; and the psychogenic, which assumes that the sufferer's body is intact and that difficulties are to be explained in psychological terms.

Scientific inquiry is presented as a special way in which human beings acquire knowledge about their world. In a very important sense people see only what they are prepared to see, and certain phenomena may go undetected because scientists can discover only the things about which they already have some general idea. There is subjectivity in science as there is in everyday perception and problem solving.

KEY TERMS

psychopathology
abnormal behavior
normal curve
clinicians
clinical psychologist
diagnosis
psychotherapy
psychiatrist
psychoactive drugs
psychoanalyst
psychiatric social worker
counseling psychologists
psychopathologists
demonology
exorcism
Zeitgeist
somatogenesis
psychogenesis
asylums
moral treatment
syndrome
general paresis
germ theory [of disease]
milieu therapy
cathartic method
paradigm

c h a p t e r t w o

Current Paradigms in Psychopathology and Therapy

> Paradigms are self-created, wafer-thin barriers against the pain of uncertainty. (Yalom, 1980, p. 26)

In Chapter 1, in summing up our examination of how we have attempted to understand abnormality throughout history, we touched on the importance of paradigms. In this chapter we consider current paradigms of abnormal behavior. A **paradigm**, as we said, is a set of basic assumptions that together define how to conceptualize, study, gather and interpret data, and even think about a particular subject. As you will soon see, several paradigms exist that focus on abnormal behavior. The paradigms we will cover here focus both on understanding the **etiology**, or causes, of abnormal behavior and on therapeutic interventions. In Chapters 18 through 20, we will examine the several paradigms in greater detail for the perspectives they provide in treating abnormal behavior.

In this chapter, we will discuss four paradigms of abnormal psychology: biological, psychoanalytic, learning, and cognitive. In previous editions of this book, we discussed in this chapter as well the humanistic and existential paradigms. In this edition, however, we are reserving our in-depth discussion of these for Chapter 18, where we will examine and compare current approaches to therapy. Our reasoning is that proponents of the humanistic and existential paradigms usually object to thinking in terms of categories of disorder, such as schizophrenia and anxiety disorders, and, in fact, these paradigms are seldom used to analyze how psychological problems develop; rather, they focus more on personal growth, not disorder. Although different in some ways, humanistic and existential approaches share several important features: they emphasize free will; they regard as the most important determinant of behavior a person's phenomenological world, that is, how he or she construes and experiences events; they focus more on the strengths of people rather than on their weaknesses; they are concerned with issues of the meaning of life and how one forges a place in it; and they encourage personal growth and fulfillment rather than relieving psychological distress. Leading figures in these paradigms are Carl Rogers, Abraham Maslow, Viktor Frankl, and Frederic (Fritz) Perls.

Many people go about the study of abnormal psychology without explicitly considering the nature of the paradigm that they have adopted. But, as this chapter will indicate, the choice of a paradigm has some very important consequences for the way abnormal behavior is defined, investigated, and treated. In fact, our discussion of paradigms will lay the groundwork for the in-depth examination of the major categories of disorder and of intervention that makes up the rest of the book.

The Biological Paradigm

The **biological paradigm** of abnormal behavior is a broad theoretical point of view holding that mental disorders are caused by aberrant somatic, or bodily, processes. This paradigm has often been referred to as the **medical** or **disease model**, but that terminology has proved limiting for a number of reasons that we will discuss below. Today's approach to the biological paradigm is considerably broader, focusing primarily on genetic and biochemical factors underlying etiology.

A Disease Approach

As indicated in Chapter 1, the study of abnormal behavior is historically linked to medicine. Many early workers and contemporaries as well have used the model of physical illness as the basis for understanding deviant behavior. Clearly, within the field of abnormal behavior the terminology of medicine is pervasive. As Maher (1966) noted, "[deviant] behavior is termed *pathological* and is classified on the basis of *symptoms*, classification being called *diagnosis*. Processes designed to change behavior are called *therapies* and are [sometimes] applied to patients in mental *hospitals*. If the deviant behavior ceases, the patient is described as *cured*" (p. 22).

The critical assumption of the medical paradigm is that abnormal behavior may be likened to a disease. To determine how a disease model can be applied to abnormal behavior, we must first examine the concept of disease used in medicine. During the Dark Ages a disease was thought to consist simply of observable signs and symptoms, such as a rash and high temperature. As medical science, particularly autopsy studies, became more sophisticated, symptoms were attributed to internal malfunctions. Then, when Louis Pasteur discovered the relation between bacteria and disease and soon thereafter postulated viruses, the germ theory of disease provided a new explanation of pathology. External symptoms were assumed to be produced through infection of the body by minute organisms and viruses. For a time the germ theory was the paradigm of medicine, but it soon became apparent that not all diseases could be explained by the germ theory.

Diabetes, for example, a malfunction of the insulin-secreting cells of the pancreas, cannot be attributed to infection. Nor does it have a single cause. Heart disease provides another example. A multitude of factors—genetic makeup, stress produced by smoking and obesity, and perhaps Type A behavior (see page 206)—are all related to the frequency of heart disease. Is there a single paradigm here? We think not. Because medical diseases themselves vary in their causes and symptoms, asserting that abnormal behavior can be considered a disease clarifies little (see Focus Box 2.1).

Contemporary Approaches to the Biological Paradigm

As our knowledge of bodily functioning has increased, it has become more meaningful to say that a psychological abnormality may be attributed, at least in part, to a disruption in one or more biological processes. There is now a considerable literature, both research and theory, dealing with biological factors relevant to psychopathology. For example, heredity probably predisposes a person, through physiological malfunction, to develop schizophrenia (see Chapter 14). Depression may result from a failure of the usual processes of neural transmission (Chapter 9). Anxiety disorders are considered by some to stem from a defect within the autonomic nervous system that causes a person to be too easily aroused (Chapter 6). Other so-called organic mental diseases can be traced to impairments in structures of the brain (Chapter 17). In each case a type of psychopathology is viewed as caused by the disturbance of some biological process. Those working with this paradigm assume that answers to puzzles of psychopathology will be found by concentrating on somatic, that is, bodily, causes.

In this section, we will look at two areas of research in which the data are particularly interesting, behavior genetics and biochemistry.

Behavior Genetics

When the ovum, the female reproductive cell, is joined by the male's spermatozoon, a zygote, or fertilized egg, is produced. It has forty-six chromosomes, the number characteristic of a human being. Each chromosome is made up of thousands of **genes**. The genes are the carriers of the genetic information (DNA) that is passed from parents to child. Each cell of the human body contains a full complement of chromosomes and genes in its nucleus.

Behavior genetics is the study of individual differences in behavior that are attributable in part to differences in genetic makeup. The total genetic makeup of an individual, consisting of inherited genes, is referred to as the **genotype**. An individual's genotype is the unobservable, physiological genetic constitution, in contrast with the totality of observable characteristics, which is referred to as the **phenotype**. The genotype is fixed at birth, whereas the phenotype changes and is generally viewed as the product of an interaction between the genotype and experience. For example, an individual may be born with the capacity for high intellectual achievement. Whether he or she develops this genetically given potential depends on such environmental factors as upbringing and education. Any measure of intelligence (IQ) is therefore best viewed as an index of the phenotype.

On the basis of the distinction between phenotype and genotype, we realize that various clinical syndromes are disorders of the phenotype. Thus it is not proper to speak of the direct inheritance of schizophrenia or anxiety disorders. At most, only

Behavior genetics studies the degree to which characteristics, like physical resemblance or psychopathology, are shared by family members.

FOCUS 2.1 • Criticisms of the Medical or Disease Model of Abnormal Behavior

Although we have argued that the term *medical model* is not very valuable, it is so widely discussed by psychopathologists and clinicians that an overview of some of its problems is useful. A common criticism is that in examining the abnormal behavior of an individual, the clinician has no independent means of verifying the existence of a disease. In medicine both the symptoms and the factors producing them, that is, the disease process, can often be assessed. It is possible, for example, to determine that an individual has a temperature of 104 degrees. Moreover, the particular germ or microorganism that caused the rise in temperature can also be independently determined, say, by taking a throat culture and analyzing the foreign organisms that are present. When a disease model is applied to abnormal behavior, however, it is often not possible to assess independently both the symptoms and the supposed cause of the symptoms. Certain behaviors or symptoms are categorized as mental illnesses and given names, but then the name of the illness itself is often cited as an explanation for or cause of these same symptoms. For example, a patient who is withdrawn and hallucinating is diagnosed as schizophrenic; however, when we ask why the patient is withdrawn and hallucinating, we are often told that it is because the patient is schizophrenic. Thus the label *schizophrenia* is applied to certain behavior and then in addition is specified as a cause of this same behavior. This is a clear example of circular reasoning, something to be avoided in scientific inquiry.

This criticism of the way mental illnesses are assessed is reasonable, but it is not always entirely applicable. Someone holding a medical or disease model point of view could assert that we may make a diagnosis of schizophrenia based on symptoms, without claiming that these symptoms are produced by the presence of schizophrenia. This diagnostician would propose that although we do not know the cause of the symptoms, future research may uncover the cause(s). For example, some deviant chemical may eventually be located within schizophrenics and be identified as the cause of the disorder. In sum, the more sophisticated practitioner of the disease model may acknowledge that we currently have little information about causes of disorders, but that when such information becomes available, it will, in principle, be possible to assess independently both the symptoms and the etiology, as is the case in medicine.

A second common criticism of applying the

the genotypes for these disorders can be inherited. Whether these genotypes will eventually engender the phenotypic behavior disorder will depend on environment and experience; a predisposition (diathesis) may be inherited, but not the disorder itself.

The two major methods of study in behavior genetics are to compare members of a family and pairs of twins. In the **family method** members of a family can be compared because the average number of genes shared by two blood relatives can be determined. For example, children receive half their genes from one parent and half from the other. Thus, on the average, siblings are identical in 50 percent of their genetic background. In contrast, relatives not as closely related share fewer genes. For example, nephews and nieces share 25 percent of the genetic makeup of an uncle. If a predisposition for a mental disorder can be inherited, a study of the family should reveal a correlation between the number of shared genes and the prevalence of the disorder in relatives. The starting point in such investigations is to collect a sample of individuals who bear the diagnosis in question; these are referred to as **index cases**, or probands. Then relatives are studied to determine the frequency with which the same diagnosis might be applied to them.

In the **twin method** both **monozygotic (MZ) twins**, and **dizygotic (DZ) twins** are compared. MZ, or identical, twins develop from a single fertilized egg and are genetically the same. DZ pairs develop from separate eggs and on the average are only 50 percent alike genetically, actually no more alike than two siblings. MZ twins are always the same sex, but DZ, or fraternal, twins can be either the same sex or opposite in sex. Again, such studies begin with diagnosed cases and then search for the presence of the disorder in the other twin. When the twins are similar diagnostically, they are said to be concordant. To the extent that a predisposition for a mental disorder can be inherited, **concordance** for the disorder should be greater in MZ pairs than in DZ pairs.

medical model to abnormal behavior involves the contention that the symptoms of physical illness are objective whereas the symptoms of mental illness are subjective. This argument, most often associated with Thomas Szasz (1960), holds that so-called mental symptoms are a patient's communications about himself or herself to others. When we call such communications symptoms, Szasz asserts, we are making a judgment within a particular social and cultural context. For example, a patient's belief that he is Christ might lead an observer to make a diagnosis of paranoid schizophrenia. Even in this extreme case, however, the diagnosis depends on whether the observer believes the patient's assertion. If the observer gives credence to the patient's statement, the behavior will clearly not be judged a symptom of mental illness. Although the importance of subjective factors as they enter into the definition of mental illness should not be minimized, distinguishing between mental and physical illness on this basis alone is a questionable procedure.

Finally, many people have alleged that so-called mental illnesses have neither a specific etiology nor a specific set of symptoms and thus do not qualify as diseases (e.g., Milton & Wahler, 1969). Our knowledge of the etiologies of psychopathologies is indeed limited. As we have indicated, however, the fact that these etiologies have not been uncovered as yet does not mean that we should stop looking for them.

Our failure to define specific sets of symptoms for some categories of deviant behavior may be a more damning criticism. Again, however, a person wishing to maintain a medical model for mental illness may counter this criticism with the following line of reasoning. Many medical diseases do *not* have a set of specific symptoms. Paresis is a good example. Before it was discovered to be infectious, there was considerable debate whether the symptoms had a physical cause or whether paresis should be considered a psychological disturbance. Proponents of the psychological view argued that the symptoms were not entirely consistent from one person to another, for some patients suffer depression rather than delusions of grandeur. Therefore they did not consider paresis a medical disease. Although paresis was indeed found to have a single causal agent, the manifestations of its *later* stage may *differ markedly from patient to patient.* Thus even an infectious disease may not necessarily have a homogeneous set of symptoms.

Taken as a whole, the information presented here indicates that the decision to view abnormal behavior as a medical disease is determined partly by subjective factors, and, although the medical model is subject to many potential criticisms, there is a possible rejoinder for each critique.

Although the methodology of the family and twin studies is clear, the data they yield are not always easy to interpret. Let us assume that parents with agoraphobia (a cluster of fears centering on being in open spaces and leaving home) have been found to produce more than the average number of agoraphobic offspring. Does this mean that anxiety disorders are genetically transmitted? Not necessarily. The greater number of anxiety disorders could as well reflect child-rearing practices and the children's adult models.

Consider also a finding of greater concordance for schizophrenia among MZ than among DZ twins. Again, such data do not necessarily implicate heredity, since MZ twins, perhaps because they look so much alike, may be raised in a more similar fashion than are DZs, thus accounting for the greater concordance for schizophrenia among them. There are, however, special but infrequent circumstances that are not subject to the aforementioned problems: a child reared completely apart from its abnormal parents, and MZ twins reared separately from very early infancy. A high frequency of agoraphobia in children reared apart from their agoraphobic parents would offer convincing support for the theory that genetic factors figure in the disorder. Similarly, greater concordance of separately reared MZ twins than of DZ twins would offer compelling evidence that a predisposition for a disorder can be inherited.

Biochemistry in the Nervous System

The nervous system is composed of billions of neurons. Although differing in some respects, each **neuron** has four major parts (Figure 2.1): (1) the cell body; (2) several dendrites, its short and thick extensions; (3) one or more axons, but usually only one, long and thin, extending a considerable distance from the cell body; and (4) terminal buttons on the many end branches of the axon. When a neuron is appropriately stimulated at its cell body (primarily inhibitory messages) or through its dendrites

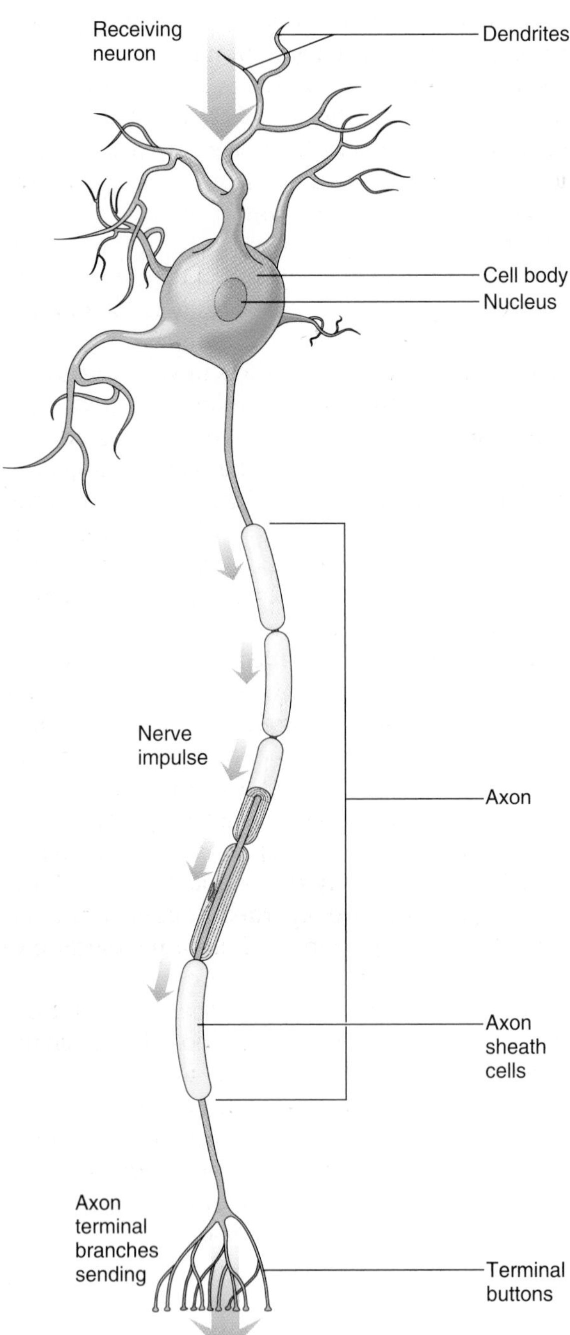

Figure 2.1 The neuron, the basic unit of the nervous system.

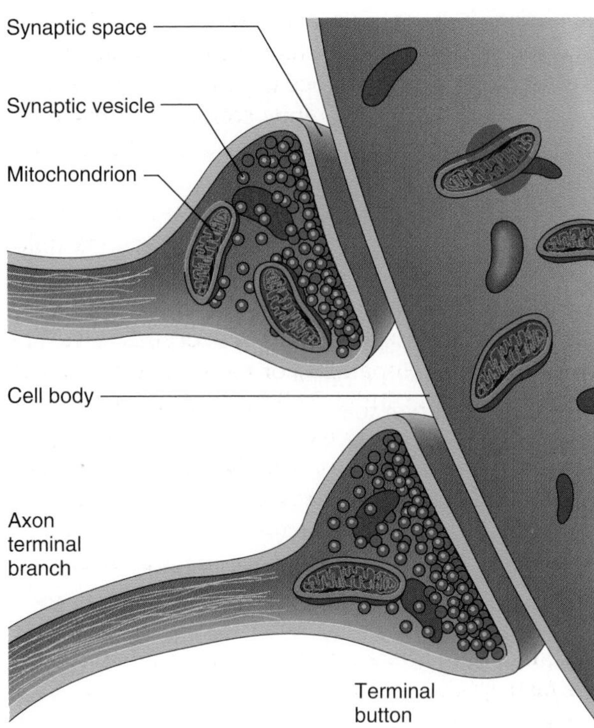

Figure 2.2 A synapse, showing the terminal buttons of two axon branches in close contact with a very small portion of the cell body of another neuron.

(primarily excitatory messages), a **nerve impulse**, which is a change in the electric potential of the cell, travels down the axon to the terminal endings. Between the terminal endings of the sending axon and the receiving neurons there is a small gap, the **synapse** (Figure 2.2).

For a nerve impulse to pass from one neuron to another, it must have a way of bridging the synaptic space. The terminal buttons of each axon contain synaptic vesicles, small structures that are filled with **neurotransmitters**, chemical substances that are important in transferring a nerve impulse from one neuron to another. A neuron synthesizes and stores only one principal neurotransmitter. Neuropeptides (chains of amino acids), which serve as auxiliary neurotransmitters, may be stored in a neuron by themselves, with another neuropeptide, or with a principal neurotransmitter, whose action it supports or modifies. Nerve impulses cause the synaptic vesicles to release their transmitter substances, which flood the synapse and can then stimulate an adjacent neuron. The molecules of a transmitter fit into receptor sites in the postsynaptic neuron and thereby transmit the impulse.

Several principal neurotransmitters have been identified and implicated in psychopathology, including norepinephrine, epinephrine, dopamine, and serotonin. The latter is found in greater quantities in other bodily tissues than in the central nervous system, occurring in large amounts in cells of the mucous membranes of the intestines. Norepinephrine is a neurotransmitter of the peripheral sympathetic nervous system. Another brain transmitter of some importance is gamma-aminobutyric acid (GABA), which inhibits some nerve impulses and is thought to be involved in the anxiety disorders.

To understand the theory and research linking neurotransmitters to the various psychopathologies, we note that these theories usually propose that a given disorder is due to either too much of a particular transmitter (e.g., schizophrenia results from too much dopamine) or too little (e.g., anxiety results from too little GABA). Each of the neurotransmitters is synthesized in the neuron through a series of metabolic steps, usually beginning with an amino acid. Each of the reactions along the way to producing an actual transmitter is catalyzed by an enzyme. Too much or too little of a particular transmitter could result from an error in these metabolic pathways. Similar disturbances in the amounts of specific transmitters could result from alterations in the usual processes by which transmitters are deactivated after being released into the synapse. Generally, when a neurotransmitter has been released into the synapse, not all of it interacts with the receptors. What is left over needs to be cleaned up to restore the synapse to its prior state. Some of this excess transmitter is pumped back into the presynaptic neuron and some is deactivated by enzymes. A failure of either of these processes could result in a neuron firing too easily and thus would be similar to a state of excess transmitter. Finally, the receptors could be at fault. If the receptors on the postsynaptic neuron were too numerous or too easily excited, for example, the result would be akin to having too much transmitter released. Any of these deviant biochemical processes could produce abnormal behavior.

Biological Approaches to Treatment

An important implication of the biological paradigm is that altering bodily functioning may well be effective in treating or even preventing certain abnormalities. Certainly if a deficiency in a particular biochemical substance is found to underlie or contribute to some problem, it makes sense to attempt to correct the imbalance by providing appropriate doses of the deficient chemical. Here there is a clear connection between viewing a disorder as a biological defect and attempting to correct the fault through a biological intervention.

As an example, phenylketonuria (PKU) is a form of mental retardation caused by a genetically determined enzyme deficiency that makes the body unable to metabolize phenylalanine into tyrosine. State laws require routine testing of an infant's blood for excess phenylalanine; if the test is positive, a specific diet low in the amino acid is prescribed. Children otherwise doomed to profound mental deficiency can thereby be brought closer to the normal range of intelligence (Chapter 16). The prevention of some of these ravages is a successful example of an intervention to correct a biological anomaly.

Other biological interventions in widespread use do not necessarily derive from knowledge of what causes a given disorder. Sedatives, such as Valium, can be effective in reducing the tension associated with anxiety disorders. Antidepressant and antipsychotic drugs are in widespread use for disorders such as depression and schizophrenia. Lithium is the most frequently used drug in the treatment of bipolar disorder, and stimulants are often employed in treating children with attention-deficit disorder. For severe cases of obsessive-compulsive disorder that have not responded to conventional therapies, brain surgery is sometimes performed. The controversial electroconvulsive shock treatment (ECT) seems to be useful in alleviating severe depression. None of these somatic therapies is as yet known to be related meaningfully to possible causes of these disorders, but they are regarded as biological treatments. Further, a person can hold a biological theory about the nature of a mental problem, yet recommend psychological intervention. Recall from Chapter 1 that Hippocrates proposed *non*somatic therapies—rest for melancholia, for example—to deal with mental disorders that he considered somatic in origin. Contemporary workers also appreciate that nonbiological interventions can have beneficial effects on the soma (see also Focus Box 8.1, which discusses Cartesian dualism).

The Psychoanalytic Paradigm

Probably the most widespread paradigm in psychopathology and therapy is the **psychoanalytic** or **psychodynamic paradigm**, originally developed by Sigmund Freud (1856–1939). The essence of this paradigm is the assumption that psychopathology results from unconscious conflicts. We will spend considerable time here looking at the significant im-

Sigmund Freud was the founder of the psychoanalytic paradigm proposing both a theory of the causes of mental disorder and devising a new method of therapy.

pact of Freud in the development of this paradigm. However, those who have followed have modified the focus of the paradigm through the years, and we will examine those changes as well.

Classical Psychoanalytic Theory

By classical psychoanalytic theory we mean the original views of Freud. We will describe these in this section and then turn to the later modifications of psychoanalytic theory.

Structure of the Mind

Freud divided the mind, or the psyche, into three principal parts, id, ego, and superego; these are metaphors for specific functions or energies. The **id** is present at birth and is the part of the personality that accounts for all the energy needed to run the psyche. It consists of the basic urges for food, water, elimination, warmth, affection, and sex. Freud, trained as a neurologist, regarded the source of all energy of the id as biological; it is later converted by some means into psychic energy, all of it unconscious, below the level of awareness.

Within the id Freud postulated two basic instincts, Eros and Thanatos. The more important is Eros, which Freud saw as a life-integrating force, principally sexual. The energy of the instinct Eros is called **libido**. Eros, libido, and sexual energy are sometimes indiscriminately equated, but libido and Eros are also occasionally expanded to include all integrative, life-furthering forces, some of which may not be strictly sexual. Thanatos, the death or aggressive instinct, plays a relatively small role in Freudian thinking, and indeed its energy never received a name.

The id seeks immediate gratification and operates on what Freud called the **pleasure principle**. When the id is not satisfied, tension is produced, and the id strives to eliminate this tension as quickly as possible. For example, the infant feels hunger, an aversive drive, and is impelled to move about, sucking, in order to reduce the tension arising from the unsatisfied drive. This behavior, called reflex activity, is one means by which the id obtains gratification; it represents the organism's first interaction with the environment. The other means of obtaining gratification is **primary process**, generating images—in essence, fantasies—of what is desired. The infant who wants mother's milk imagines the mother's breast and thereby obtains some short-term satisfaction of the hunger drive through a wish-fulfilling fantasy.

The second part of the personality, the **ego**, is primarily conscious and begins to develop out of the id during the second six months of life. The task of the ego is to deal with reality. The ego does not employ primary process, for fantasy will not keep the organism alive. Through its planning and decision-making functions, called **secondary process**, the ego realizes that operating on the pleasure principle at all times, as the id would like to do, is not the most effective way of maintaining life. The ego thus operates on the **reality principle** as it mediates between the demands of reality and the immediate gratification desired by the id.

The ego, however, derives all its energy from the id and may be likened to a horseback rider who receives energy from the horse that is being ridden. But a real horseback rider directs the horse with his or her own energy, not depending on that of the horse for thinking, planning, and moving. The ego, on the other hand, derives *all* its energies from the id and yet must direct what it is entirely dependent on for energy.

The **superego**, the third part of the personality, is the carrier of society's moral standards as interpreted by the child's parents. The superego develops through the resolution of the oedipal conflict, to be discussed shortly, and is generally equivalent to what we call conscience. When the id pressures the ego to satisfy its needs, the ego must cope not only with reality constraints but also with the right–wrong moral judgments of the superego. For example, a youngster may judge that it is possible to cheat on a test because the teacher has left the room, but refrains from doing so because of the guilt he or she would feel as a result of being dishonest.

The behavior of the human being, as conceptualized by Freud, is thus a complex interplay of three psychic systems, all vying for the achievement of goals that cannot always be reconciled. The interplay of these forces is referred to as the **psychodynamics** of the personality.

Freud was drawn into studying the mind by his work with Breuer on hypnosis and hysteria (see page 22). The apparently powerful role played by factors of which patients seemed unaware led Freud to postulate that much of our behavior is determined by forces that are inaccessible to awareness. Both the id instincts and many of the superego's activities are not known to the conscious mind. The ego is primarily conscious, for it is the metaphor for the psychic systems that have to do with thinking and planning. But the ego, too, has important unconscious aspects, the **defense mechanisms**, that protect it from anxiety; these will also be discussed shortly. Basically, Freud considered most of the important determinants of behavior to be **unconscious**.

The oral stage is the first of Freud's psychosexual stages. During this stage maximum gratification of id impulses comes from sucking.

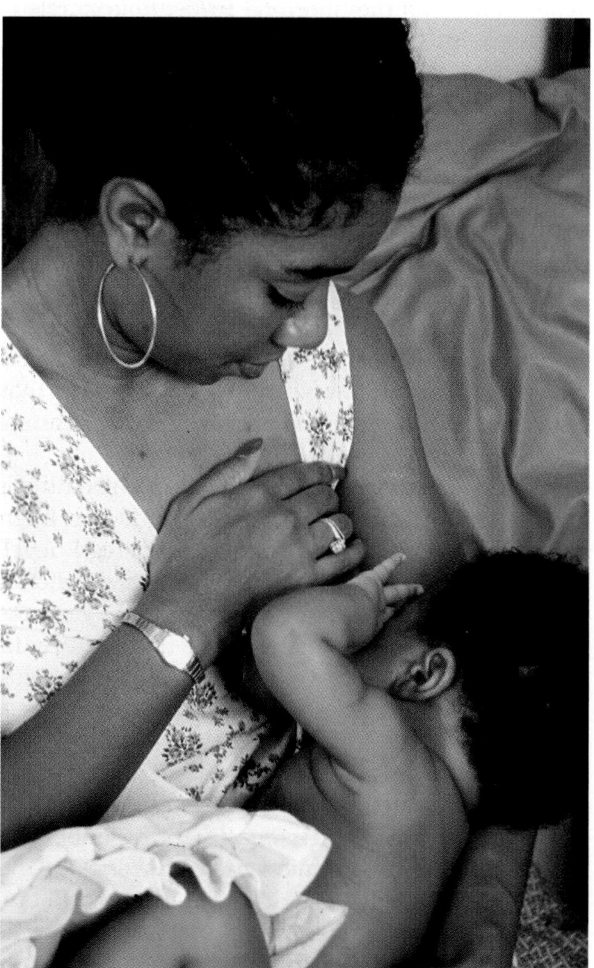

Freud saw the human personality as a closed energy system: at any one time there is a fixed amount of energy in the id to operate the psychic apparatus. The three parts of the personality therefore battle for a share of a specific amount of energy. Moreover, natural scientist that he was, Freud espoused a totally deterministic theory: he saw every bit of behavior, even seemingly trivial slips of the tongue, as having specific causes, many of them unconscious.

Stages of Psychosexual Development

Freud conceived of the personality apparatus as developing through a series of four separate **psychosexual stages**. At each stage a different part of the body is the most sensitive to sexual excitation and therefore the most capable of providing libidinal satisfaction to the id. The **oral stage** is first, during which the infant derives maximum gratification of id impulses from excitation of the sensory endings around the mouth. Sucking and feeding are the principal pleasures. In the second year of life the

During the anal stage the site of pleasure shifts to the anus and toilet training typically begins.

Too much or too little gratification during one of the psychosexual stages may lead to regression to this stage during stress.

child enters the **anal stage**, as enjoyment shifts to the anus and the elimination and retention of feces. In the **phallic stage**, which extends from age three to age five or six, maximum gratification comes from stimulation of the genitalia. Between ages six and twelve the child is in a **latency period**, which is not considered a psychosexual stage. During these years the id impulses do not play a direct role in motivating behavior. The child behaves asexually, although according to Freud's theoretical scheme all behavior is *basically* driven by id impulses. The final and adult stage is the **genital stage**, during which heterosexual interests predominate.

During each stage the growing person must resolve the conflicts between what the id wants and what the environment will provide; how this is accomplished determines basic personality traits that will last throughout the person's life. For example, a person who in the anal stage experiences either excessive or deficient amounts of gratification, depending on the toilet-training regimen, becomes fixated and is likely to regress to this stage when stressed. Such a person would be called an **anal personality**. One type, the anal retentive, is considered stingy and sometimes obsessively clean. These traits appear throughout life but receive the greatest attention in adulthood, when people typically seek the help of psychoanalysts. These traits can, however, be traced back to early events and to the manner in which gratification was provided or denied the child. Freud referred to this freezing of development at an earlier psychosexual stage as **fixation**.

Perhaps the most important crisis of development occurs during the phallic stage, around age four, for then, Freud asserted, the child is overcome with sexual desire for the parent of the opposite sex. Threat of dire punishment from the parent of the same sex may cause the child to repress the entire conflict, pushing it into the unconscious. This desire and repression are referred to as the **Oedipus complex** for the male and the **Electra complex** for the female. The dilemma is usually resolved through increased identification with the parent of the same sex and through the adoption of society's mores, which forbid the child to desire his or her parent. Through the learning of these moral values, the superego develops.

Neurotic Anxiety

Freud proposed two theories of neurotic anxiety, or unrealistic fear. It is important that we describe both here in order to present a clear picture of how Freudian theory evolved. In his first formulation, published in 1895, Freud postulated that neurotic anxiety resulted from the blockage of unconscious impulses. Such impulses are blocked, for example, under conditions of extreme sexual deprivation. When repressed they become susceptible to transformation into neurotic anxiety. In his second theory, proposed in 1926, Freud reversed the relationship between neurotic anxiety and repression. According to the first theory, neurotic anxiety develops through repression of impulses. In the second, anxiety about impulses signals the need for their repression. In a sense, according to the first theory we become anxious because we want things that we do not get; according to the second we are anxious because we fear our wants (Wachtel, 1977). According to the second theory, then, **neurotic anxiety** is the fear of the disastrous consequences that are expected if a previously punished id impulse is allowed expression.

The second theory viewed birth as the prototypic anxiety situation, for the infant is flooded with excitation over which he or she has no control. After the development of the ego in the first year of life, anxiety becomes a signal of impending overstimulation. The person is warned that he or she is in danger of being reduced to an infantile state of helplessness through overstimulation by id impulses and other forces. Anxiety thus plays a functional role, signaling the ego to take action before being overwhelmed.

Two other kinds of anxiety were described by Freud. **Objective** or **realistic anxiety** refers to the ego's reaction to danger in the external world, for example, the anxiety felt when life is in real jeopardy. **Moral anxiety**, experienced by the ego as guilt or shame, is really fear of the punishment that the superego imposes for failure to adhere to standards of moral conduct.

Perhaps because Freud's earlier views held that repression of id impulses would create neurotic anxiety, we often hear that Freudians preach as much gratification of impulses as possible, lest a person become neurotic. But this is not the case. For Freudians the essence of neurotic anxiety is repression. Being unaware of conflicts lies at the core of neurotic anxiety, rather than simply being reluctant, unwilling, or unable to reduce the demands of the id. A celibate Catholic priest and nun, for example, are not considered candidates for neurosis provided that they consciously acknowledge their sexual or aggressive tendencies. Such individuals do not have to act on these felt needs to avoid neurotic anxiety. They must only remain aware of these needs whenever they vie for expression.

Defense Mechanisms

According to Freud and elaborated by his daugher Anna (A. Freud, 1966), the discomfort experienced by the anxious ego can be reduced in several ways. Objective anxiety, rooted in reality, can often be handled by removing or avoiding the danger in the external world or by dealing with it in a rational way. Neurotic anxiety may be handled through an unconscious distortion of reality by means of a defense mechanism. A **defense mechanism** is a strategy, unconsciously utilized, to protect the ego from anxiety. Perhaps the most important is **repression**, which pushes impulses and thoughts unacceptable to the ego into the unconscious. Repression not only prevents awareness but also keeps buried desires from growing up (Wachtel, 1977). By remaining repressed, these infantile memories cannot be corrected by adult experience and therefore retain their original intensity. Another defense mechanism, important in paranoid disorders (see Chapter 14), is **projection**, attributing to external agents characteristics or desires that are possessed by an individual and yet are unacceptable to conscious awareness. For example, a hostile woman may unconsciously find it aversive to regard herself as angry at others and may project her angry feelings onto them; thus she sees others as angry with her. Other defense mechanisms are **displacement**, redirecting emotional responses from a perhaps dangerous object to a substitute, for instance, kicking the cat instead of the boss; **reaction formation**, converting one feeling, such as hate, into its opposite, love; **regression**, retreating to the behavioral patterns of an earlier age; and **rationalization**, inventing a reason for an unreasonable action or attitude.[1]

All these defense mechanisms allow the ego to discharge some id energy while not facing frankly the true nature of the motivation. Because defense mechanisms are more readily observed than other symptoms of a disordered personality, they very often make people aware of their troubled natures and thus provide the impetus for consulting a therapist.

The Question of Child Sexual Abuse

In his early writings and lectures Freud postulated that the cause of his patients' neurotic problems was sexual abuse in childhood, typically rape by the father. His views elicited outrage from his colleagues, yet he persisted until 1897 when, in a letter to his colleague Wilhelm Fleiss, he indicated that he had come to believe that many of his patients' accounts were fantasies. Over the next few years Freud struggled with these competing theories, sometimes favoring one and other times the other. But by 1905 the fantasy theory had clearly won out (Masson, 1984).

This change had a profound impact on the development of psychoanalysis, for it directed the search for the causes of psychopathology away from the environment and toward the patient and his or her fantasies. Furthermore, it was crucial to the "discovery" of the oedipal conflict, a cornerstone of psychoanalytic thought. So important was this emphasis on fantasy that in a letter to Jeffrey Masson, Anna Freud wrote that without it there would have been no psychoanalysis.

What made Freud change his mind? Drawing on unpublished material as well as published documents from which important passages had been removed before publication, Masson (1984) argues that the important factor was the disapproval generated by the sexual abuse theory. Masson shows that Freud was aware of cases of possible child sexual abuse in which there was clear *physical* evidence of the abuse. Clear proof of Masson's claim is lacking, but we can be sure that the reason for Freud's change was not a simple encounter with new evidence. Indeed, contemporary evidence on the frequency of child sexual abuse and its effects indicates that Freud's first theory may have reflected reality more than did his fantasy theory.

---

[1]A psychoanalytic quip defines a rationalization as a *good* reason for an action—but not the *real* reason.

Methodological and Conceptual Problems of Classical Psychoanalytic Theory

Perhaps no investigator of the vagaries of human life has been honored and criticized as much as Freud. During the last years of the nineteenth century and the first years of this century, when he was first espousing his view of infantile sexuality, he was personally vilified. At that time sexuality was little discussed among adults. How scandalous, then, to assert that infants and children were also motivated by sexual drives!

Because of his very great impact in the field it is important to look at some current criticisms of his methodology and concepts. Although we attach considerable significance to case reports compiled by clinicians who are "on the front line," clinical reporting by its very nature presents problems that are extremely difficult to avoid. Freud's theorizing, as well as the thinking of the **neo-Freudians**, those who have accepted his basic framework but with certain modifications, rests primarily on case studies. Like many clinicians, Freud did not take careful notes during his sessions and relied almost completely on recollection. The reliability of his perceptions and recollections is impossible to evaluate. Furthermore, the behavior of a listener affects what a speaker has to say. It is possible that Freud's patients were influenced, at least to some degree, to talk about the childhood events that he was most interested in.

The inferential leaps made by Freud and other psychoanalysts may be difficult to accept without a prior commitment to the point of view. The distinction between observation and interpretation is sometimes blurred. Consider an example from the analyst Main (1958). "The little boy who babbles tenderly to himself as he soaps himself in his bath does so because he has taken into himself his tender soaping mother." What, in fact, is readily observed by the average onlooker is the child bathing himself. To see his mother incorporated in the soapy bath play is to operate at a very high level of inference. The influence of paradigms is once again evident. What we perceive is strongly colored by the paradigm we adopt.

There is considerable disagreement as to whether Freud's theorizing should be considered scientific, for it is difficult to disprove or corroborate. Few of the statements are very explicit. If our view of science requires concepts to to be measurable, and theories testable, much of psychoanalytic thinking cannot be regarded as scientific.

Freud's findings do not have general applicability because his sample of patients was selective and small. Nearly all his patients were from the upper middle class of early twentieth-century Vienna, hardly a representative sampling of human beings. Nonetheless, Freud was prepared to apply his findings to all humankind. In a related vein, after making limited observations, Freud held that a repressed homosexual inclination was the basis for all paranoid disorders. But he never considered, nor for that matter have others who have accepted his point of view, how many paranoids have not had homosexual desires in the past and, indeed, how many people with repressed homosexuality do not develop into paranoids.

Although Freud insisted upon using concepts like id, ego, superego, and the unconscious as metaphors to describe psychic functions, at times these concepts seem reified, that is, they are made into independent, behavior-determining agents whose own actions must still be explained. For example, Freud spoke of "immediate and unheeding satisfaction of the instincts, such as the id demands. . . . The id knows no solicitude about ensuring survival" (1937). Thus the id "demands" immediate satisfaction and "knows" certain things. In spite of occasional reminders in psychoanalytic writings that these concepts are meant as metaphors, or as summary statements of functions, they are sometimes written about as though they had an existence of their own and power to push things around, to think, and to act.

It should be obvious by now that there are many legitimate questions about the validity and usefulness of Freud's work. On the other hand, it would be a serious mistake to minimize his importance in psychopathology or, for that matter, in the intellectual history of Western civilization. Freud was an astute observer of human nature. Moreover, his work has elicited the kind of critical reaction that helps to advance knowledge. He was instrumental in getting people to consider nonbiological explanations for disordered behavior, and his descriptions of abnormal behavior were often exceptionally perceptive. It is impossible to acquire a good grasp of the field of abnormal psychology without some familiarity with his writings.

Neo-Freudian Psychodynamic Perspectives

The significance of Freud's theories and clinical work was widely recognized by his contemporaries.

A number of them, including Carl Jung and Alfred Adler, met with Freud periodically to discuss psychoanalytic theory and therapy. As often happens when a brilliant leader attracts brilliant followers and colleagues, disagreements arose about a number of important general issues, such as the relative importance of id versus ego; of biological instinctual drives versus sociocultural determinants; of how critical the earliest years of life are in contrast with adult experiences; of whether sexual urges are at the core of motives and actions that are themselves not obviously sexual; of unconscious processes versus conscious ones; and of the reflexlike nature of id impulses versus purposive behavior governed primarily by conscious ego deliberations.

To elaborate on some of these themes, we outline the major ideas of three theorists who adapted Freud's ideas in forging approaches of their own. Others who adapted and modified Freud's theories are discussed in Chapter 10 (the object-relations theorists) and Chapter 18 (brief analytic psychotherapy).

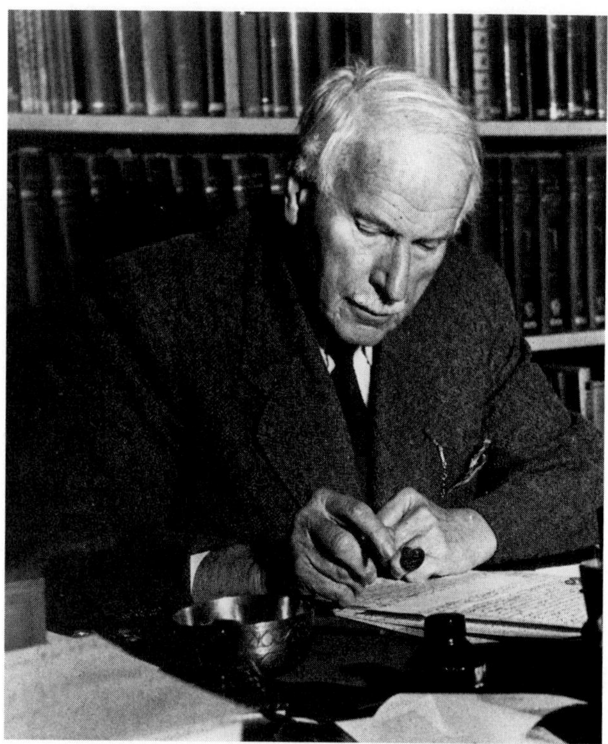

Carl Jung was the founder of analytical psychology, a blending of Freudian and humanistic concepts.

Jung and Analytical Psychology

Carl Gustav Jung (1887–1961), a Swiss psychiatrist, broke with Freud on many issues in 1914, after a seven-year period during which they had an intense correspondence. Jung proposed ideas radically different from Freud's, ultimately establishing **analytical psychology**, a blend of Freudian psychology and humanistic psychology (see page 539). His theory's similarity to humanistic theories comes from Jung's deemphasis of the importance of biological drives as the main determinants of behavior and his use of the concept of self-actualization, a state of fulfillment that occurs when a person balances and gives expression to all aspects of his or her personality.

Jung hypothesized that, in addition to our personal unconscious, which Freud stressed, our **collective unconscious** contains information from the social history of humankind. The collective unconscious is the repository of all the experiences people have had over the centuries and, unlike Freud's unconscious, contains positive and creative forces. He also asserted that each of us has masculine and feminine traits that can be blended to forge a creative personality and held that people have spiritual and religious needs that are as basic as their libidinal ones. Jung also catalogued various personality types, perhaps the most important of which is extraversion versus introversion. In addition, Jung wrote at length on religious symbolism and the meaning of life and as a consequence became quite popular among mystics, novelists, and poets. Finally, whereas Freud regarded current and future behavior as determined primarily by the past, Jung focused on purposiveness, decision making, and goal setting, or what philosophers call *teleology*. To understand people, then, one has to appreciate their dreams and aspirations, not just the effects of their past experiences, as important as those may be (Jung, 1928).

Adler and Individual Psychology

Alfred Adler (1870–1937) was even less dependent on Freud's views of instincts than was Jung, and Freud remaind quite bitter toward the psychiatrist after their relationship ended. Adler, who had been a sickly child in Vienna and had to strive mightily to overcome feelings of inferiority, emphasized striving for superiority, but not in an antisocial sense. Indeed, Adler regarded people as inextricably tied to their society because he believed that fulfillment is found in doing things for the social good. Like Jung, he stressed the importance of working toward goals: and, like Jung, much of his theorizing

Alfred Adler was the founder of individual psychology and well-known for his notion of the inferiority complex.

Eric Erikson emphasized the importance of psychosocial development throughout the life-span. He was more optimistic than Freud about people's continuing capacity for growth.

anticipated later developments in humanistic therapy (Adler, 1924).[2]

One central element in Adler's work was the focus on the individual's *phenomenology*, or **individual psychology**, as the key to understanding that person, an emphasis that also anticipated contemporary developments in cognitive behavior therapy (page 51). Another connection with cognitive behavior therapy is the way Adler worked to help patients change their illogical, mistaken beliefs and expectations: to feel and behave better, one has first to think more rationally. Finally, Adler's interest in growth and in the prevention of problems and the betterment of society influenced the development of child guidance centers and parent education.

Erikson and Psychosocial Stages of Development

Erik Erikson (1902–   ), who had only the equivalent of a high school diploma, is identified as an ego psychologist because he emphasized the formation of ego identity and psychosocial development. Whereas Freud believed that development ended early in life, Erikson's major contribution lies in a field that has come to be called life-span developmental psychology, which has as a central thesis the idea that people continue to change and differentiate through middle age and into their senior years. To get a good sense of the significance of this general viewpoint, consider that "child psychology" used to be synonymous with "developmental psychology." Thanks in large part to Erikson, people now distinguish between the two or, in a more radical vein, even propose that there be only one developmental psychology and that it refers to the entire life span.

Erikson proposed eight **psychosocial stages of development** through which people progress, each of them characterized by a particular challenge or crisis. The resolution of the crisis affects how the individual deals with each subsequent stage (Table 2.1). If an earlier crisis is not adequately handled, says Erikson, the resolution of subsequent ones is hampered.

To illustrate, let us look at the fifth stage, perhaps the most important one, in which Erikson introduces a term for which he is famous, **identity crisis**. This crisis, said to occur between the ages of 12 and 20, reflects the transition from childhood to adulthood, a period when we all create a sense of self,

[2]Indeed, as we read about neo-Freudians like Jung and Adler, we might wonder why they are considered part of the psychoanalytic tradition rather than the humanistic. Perhaps their historical ties to Freud and their close association with him until each broke with "the Master" have colored our perceptions of their theorizing.

Table 2.1 • Erikson's Eight Stages of Psychosocial Development

Stage and Approximate Age Range	*Psychosocial Crisis*	*Major Developments*
Infancy 0–1	Trust vs. mistrust	In the caregiver—baby relationship, the infant develops a sense of trust or mistrust that basic needs such as nourishment, warmth, cleanliness, and physical contact will be provided.
Early Childhood 1–3	Autonomy vs. shame, doubt	Children learn self-control as a means of being self-sufficient, e.g., toilet training, feeding, walking, or developing shame and doubt about their abilities to be autonomous.
Play Age 3–6	Initiative vs. guilt	Children are anxious to investigate adult activities, but may also have feelings of guilt about trying to be independent and daring.
School Age 7–11	Industry vs. inferiority	Children learn about imagination and curiosity, develop learning skills, or develop feelings of inferiority if they fail—or if they think they fail—to master tasks.
Adolescence 12–20	Identity vs. identity confusion	Adolescents try to figure out who they are, how they are unique, if they want to have a meaningful role in society, how they can establish sexual, ethnic, and career identity. Feelings of confusion can arise over these decisions.
Young Adulthood 20–30	Intimacy vs. isolation	The wish to seek companionship and intimacy with a significant other, or avoid relationships and become isolated.
Adulthood 30–65	Generativity vs. stagnation	The need to be productive—for example, to create products, ideas, or children—or to become stagnant.
Mature Age 65+	Integrity vs. despair	A review and effort to make sense of one's life, reflecting on completed goals or doubts and despair about unreached goals and desires.

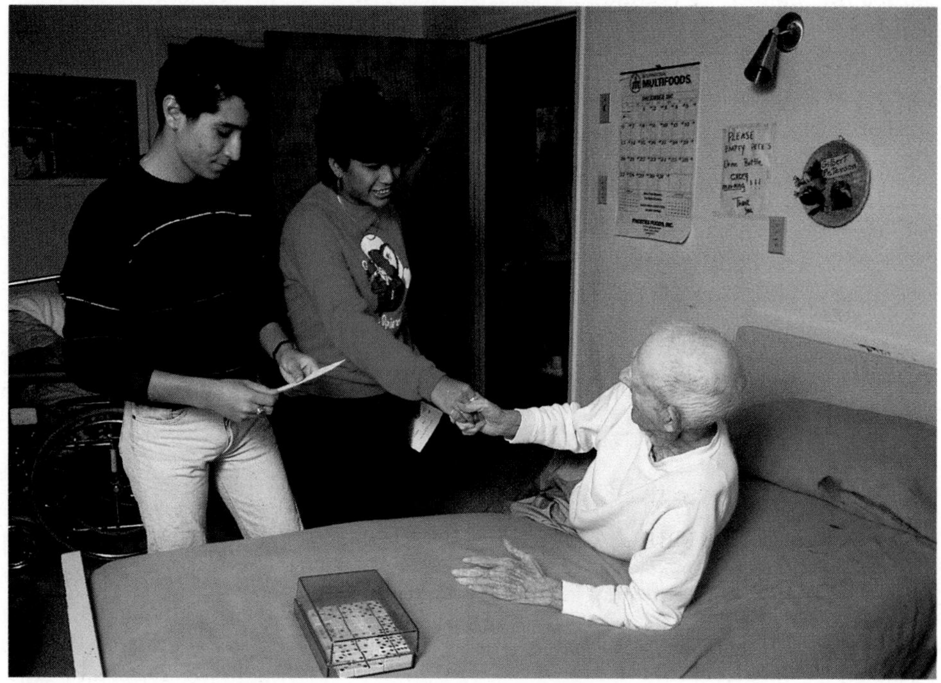

Erikson believed that an identity crisis occurs during adolescence. Volunteer work may help teenagers develop a clearer sense of their identity and what they value in life.

both the kind of psychological beings we are and the kind of lives we plan to forge for ourselves. Although the choice of an occupation, role, or profession is important—physician, lawyer, construction worker, parent, and so on—a person's identity is said to go much deeper. We are concerned with the direction of our lives: what things are going to be important and sought after, what kinds of compromises we are prepared to make to achieve our goals, what kind of people we want to be; in general all the things that go into our sense of self as developing adults who are responsible for ourselves and who are ready to make commitments to goals and to other human beings. It is a tumultuous time, considering that young people are simultaneously trying to come to terms with their sexuality.[3]

Like others who adapted Freud's ideas, Erikson was more optimistic than Freud about people's capacity to change and more positive generally about the nature of existence. The resolution of any psychosocial stage could be reversed, Erikson believed, with appropriate psychotherapy (Erikson, 1959).

Psychoanalytic Therapy

Since Freud's time the body of psychoanalytic thinking has changed in important ways, but all treatments purporting to be psychoanalytic have some basic tenets in common. Classical psychoanalysis is based on Freud's second theory of neurotic anxiety, that it is the reaction of the ego when a previously punished and repressed id impulse presses for expression. The unconscious part of the ego, encountering a situation that reminds it of a repressed conflict from childhood—one usually having to do with sexual or aggressive impulses—is overcome by debilitating tension. Psychoanalytic therapy attempts to remove the earlier repression and to help the patient face the childhood conflict and resolve it in the light of adult reality. The repression, occurring so long ago, has prevented the ego from growing in an adult fashion; the lifting of the repression is supposed to enable this relearning to take place.

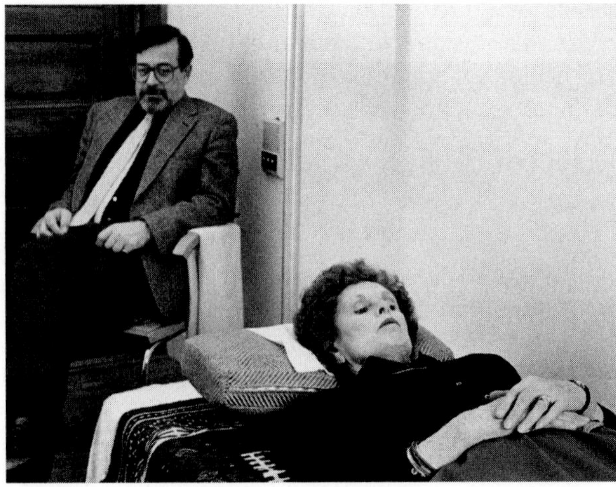

In a typical psychoanalytic therapy session, the patient reclines on a couch and the analyst sits out of the patient's view.

The essence of psychoanalysis has been captured by Paul Wachtel (1977) in the metaphor of the woolly mammoth. Some of these gigantic creatures, frozen alive eons ago, have been recovered so perfectly preserved that their meat can actually be eaten. Neurotic problems were considered by Freud to be the encapsulated residue of conflicts from long ago. Present adult problems are merely reflections or expressions of these frozen intrapsychic conflicts.

> The patient's neurosis is seen as deriving most essentially from his continuing and unsuccessful efforts to deal with internalized residues of his past [the "woolly mammoth"] which, by virtue of being isolated from his adaptive and integrated ego, continue to make primitive demands wholly unresponsive to reality. It is therefore maintained that a fully successful treatment must create conditions whereby these anachronistic inclinations can be experienced consciously and integrated into the ego, so that they can be controlled and modified. (Wachtel, 1977, p. 36)

Analysts employ a number of techniques in their efforts to lift repressions. Perhaps the best known is **free association**. The patient, reclining on a couch, is encouraged to give free rein to his or her thoughts, verbalizing whatever comes to mind, without the censoring ordinarily done in everyday life. It is assumed that the patient can gradually learn this skill, and that defenses built up over many years can eventually be bypassed. **Dream analysis** is another

---

[3]Hall, Lindzey, Loehlin, and Manosevitz (1985) suggest that Erikson's own childhood and adolescence may have contributed to the concept of identity crisis. Erikson was born in Germany of Danish parents who were separated before his birth, and he never knew his biological father. He was raised by a German stepfather who he assumed for years was his actual father. Although he looked Nordic because of his biological father, his mother's Jewish ancestry caused him to be taunted by Jewish peers as a "goy" (an uncomplimentary Yiddish term for a non-Jew) and by non-Jewish age-mates as a Jew (not an easy thing to be in Germany at that time). He felt out of place after high school and, thinking he might want to become an artist, wandered around Europe making sketches. He began to teach in Vienna at age 25, where he met Sigmund Freud and his daughter, Anna. Erikson enrolled in the Vienna Psychoanalytic Institute, where he was analyzed by Anna Freud. Erikson would not be the first psychological theorist whose professional interests and ideas were shaped by his own experiences.

classic analytic technique. Psychoanalytic theory holds that in sleep, ego defenses are relaxed, allowing normally repressed material to enter the sleeper's consciousness. But since this material is extremely threatening, it usually cannot be allowed into consciousness in its actual form. Rather, the repressed material is disguised, and dreams take on heavily symbolic content. For example, a woman concerned about aggressive sexual advances from men may dream of being attacked by savages who throw spears at her: the spears are considered phallic symbols, substituting for an explicit sexual advance.

Analysis of defenses, long a focus of psychoanalysis, is emphasized even more by contemporary psychoanalysts, who are sometimes referred to as **ego analysts**. They dispute the relatively weak role that Freud assigned the ego. Defense mechanisms, as we have seen, are the ego's unconscious tools for warding off a confrontation with anxiety. For instance, a man who appears to have trouble with intimacy may look out the window and change the subject whenever anything touches on closeness during the course of a session. The analyst will attempt at some point to interpret the patient's behavior, pointing out its defensive nature, in hopes of stimulating the patient to acknowledge that he is, in fact, avoiding the topic. Psychoanalytic treatment has in the past extended over several years, with as many as five sessions per week. It is interesting to note, however, that Freud's psychoanalyses seldom lasted longer than six months.

Over the past forty or so years, the ideas and work of neo-Freudians, such as Karen Horney and Harry Stack Sullivan (see page 535), and of ego psychologists/analysts, such as Erik Erikson and Heinz Hartman, have blended into psychoanalytically oriented psychotherapy, sometimes called psychodynamic therapy. This approach, developed in part through the work of Alexander and French (1946), advocates a briefer, more present- and future-oriented analytic therapy, informed by such Freudian concepts as defense mechanisms and unconscious motivation but without relying on the couch and the time-consuming techniques of free association and dream analysis. Such therapy is more active and directive than Freudian therapy, is focused more on present problems and relationships than on childhood conflicts, and is briefer and less intensive.

> The hope of total personality reconstruction is put aside in favor of dealing with more focal and acute problems, but these therapists feel that their work is facilitated by training in and *sensitivity to psychoanalytic principles*. A large part of the work of current psychoanalysts is in these briefer forms of therapy; few practice standard psychoanalysis exclusively. (Korchin, 1976, p. 335, emphasis added)

To our mind, procedural changes do not invariably reflect important theoretical differences. Session frequency and body position matter less than what the patient does with support from the therapist, namely, slowly examining the true sources of tension and unhappiness by a lifting of repression. Psychoanalysis and related therapies are discussed in greater depth in Chapter 18.

Learning Paradigms

The **learning paradigm** is a set of assumptions that abnormal behavior is learned in the same way as other human behavior. Early twentieth-century psychology was dominated not by learning but by structuralism, which held that the proper subject of study was mental functioning and structure. The goal of psychology, then a very new discipline, was to learn more about what goes on in the mind by analyzing the elementary constituents making up its contents. To do this, experimental psychologists such as Wilhelm Wundt (1882–1920), who founded the first formal psychological laboratory and the discipline itself in Leipzig in 1879, and Edward Titchener (1867–1927), whose laboratory was at Cornell University, devised elaborate training procedures to teach subjects to report on the most basic aspects of their experiences while being exposed to stimuli. Through painstaking **introspection**, self-observation of mental processes, subjects attempted to uncover the building blocks of experience and the structure of consciousness. For example, Wundt's subjects listened to a metronome set to click slowly and sometimes to click fast, sometimes sounding only a few times and then many. The subjects looked within themselves and reported that a fast series of clicks made them excited, a slow series relaxed. Just before each click they were conscious of a slight feeling of tension, and afterward, slight relief.

The Rise of Behaviorism

After some years many in the field began to lose faith in the ability of introspection to obtain useful knowledge about people. The problem was that different laboratories using the introspective method were yielding conflicting data; thus it appeared that

John B. Watson, American psychologist, was the major figure in establishing psychology as the study of observable behavior rather than an investigation of subjective experience.

introspection was not clarifying the answers to any questions. This dissatisfaction was brought to a head by John B. Watson (1878–1958), who in 1913 revolutionized psychology with statements such as the following:

> Psychology as the behaviorist views it is a purely objective experimental branch of natural science. Its theoretical goal is the prediction and control of behavior. Introspection forms no essential part of its methods, nor is the scientific value of its data dependent upon the readiness with which they lend themselves to interpretation in terms of consciousness. (p. 158)

To replace introspection, Watson looked to the experimental procedures of the psychologists who were investigating learning in animals. Because of his efforts, the dominant focus of psychology changed to learning rather than thinking. Finding out which stimuli would elicit which directly observable responses was now considered the task of psychology. With such objective stimulus–response information it was hoped that human behavior could be both predicted and controlled. **Behaviorism** can be defined as an approach that focuses on the study of observable behavior rather than consciousness.

Classical Conditioning

With the focus of psychology now on learning, a vast amount of research and theorizing was generated. Two types of learning attracted the research efforts of psychologists. The first type, **classical conditioning**, had originally been discovered quite by accident by the Russian physiologist Ivan Pavlov (1849–1936) at the turn of the century. In his studies of the digestive system, a dog was given meat powder to make it salivate. Before long Pavlov's laboratory assistants became aware that the dog began salivating when it saw the person who fed it, and as the experiment continued, the dog began to salivate even earlier, when it heard the footsteps of its feeder. Pavlov was intrigued by these findings and decided to study the dog's reactions systematically. In the first of many experiments, a bell was rung behind the dog, and then the meat powder was placed in its mouth. After this procedure had been repeated a number of times, the dog began salivating as soon as it heard the bell ring and before meat powder was given.

In this experiment, because the meat powder automatically elicits salivation with no prior learning, the powder is termed an **unconditioned stimulus** (UCS) and the response of salivation an **unconditioned response** (UCR). When the offering of meat powder is preceded several times by a neutral stimulus, the ringing of a bell (Figure 2.3), the sound of the bell alone (the **conditioned stimulus**, CS) is able to elicit the salivary response (the **conditioned response**, CR). In fact, the CR usually differs somewhat from the UCR (e.g., Rescorla, 1988), but these subtleties are beyond the needs of this book. As the number of paired presentations of the bell and the meat powder increases, the number of salivations elicited by the bell increases. **Extinction** refers to what happens to the CR when the repeated soundings of the bell are later *not* followed by meat powder; fewer and fewer salivations are elicited, and the CR gradually disappears.

Ivan P. Pavlov, Russian psychologist and Nobel Laureate, was responsible for extensive research and theory in classical conditioning. His influence is still very strong in Russian psychology.

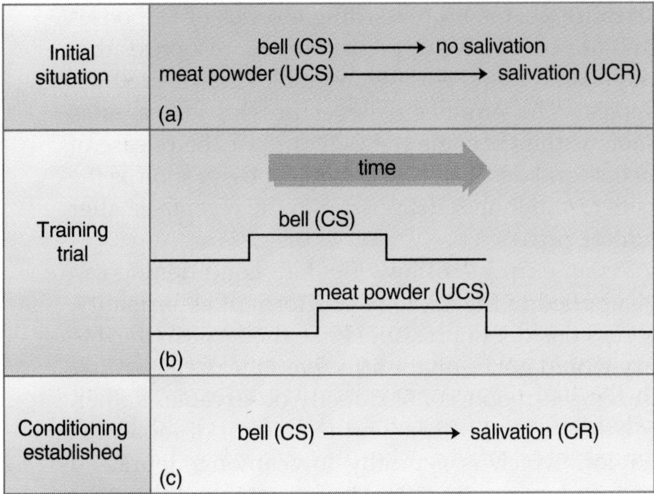

Figure 2.3 The process of classical conditioning. (a) Before learning, the meat powder (UCS) elicits salivation (UCR), but the bell (CS) does not. (b) A training or learning trial consists of presentations of the CS, followed closely by the UCS. (c) Classical conditioning has been accomplished when the previously neutral bell elicits salivation (CR).

Another famous experiment, questionable from an ethical point of view, was conducted by John Watson and Rosalie Rayner (1920). They introduced a white rat to an eleven-month-old boy, Little Albert, who indicated no fear of the animal and appeared to want to play with it. But whenever he reached for the rat, the experimenter made a loud noise (the UCS) by striking a steel bar behind Albert's head, causing him great fright (the UCR). After five such experiences Albert became very frightened (the CR) by the sight of the white rat, even when the steel bar was not struck. The fear initially associated with the loud noise had come to be elicited by the previously neutral stimulus, the white rat (now the CS). This study suggests the possible relationship between classical conditioning and the development of certain emotional disorders, in this instance a phobia.

Operant Conditioning

The second principal type of learning drew primarily on the work of Edward Thorndike (1874–1949), begun in the 1890s. Rather than investigating the association between stimuli as Pavlov did, Thorndike was interested in the effect that consequences have on behavior. He had observed that alley cats, angered by being caged and making furious efforts to escape, would eventually and accidentally hit the latch that freed them. Recaged again and again, they would soon come to touch the latch immediately and purposely. Thorndike formulated what was to become an extremely important principle, the **law of effect**: behavior that is followed by consequences satisfying to the organism will be repeated, and behavior that is followed by noxious or unpleasant consequences will be discouraged. Thus the behavior or response that has consequences serves as an instrument, encouraging or discouraging its own repetition. For this reason, learning that focuses on consequences was first called instrumental learning.

Almost sixty years ago, B. F. Skinner (1904–1990) introduced what is called the operant approach because it studies behavior that operates on the environment. He reformulated the law of effect by shifting the focus from the linking of stimuli and responses—S–R connections—to the relationships between responses and their consequences or contingencies. The distinction is subtle, but it reflects Skinner's contention that stimuli do not so much get connected to responses as they become the occasions for responses to occur if, in the past, they have been reinforced. Thus, Skinner introduced the concept **discriminative stimulus** to refer to external events that, in effect, tell an organism that if it performs a certain behavior, a certain consequence will follow. In this sense, Skinner was an R–R (response–reinforcement) rather than an S–R (stimulus–response) theorist.

B. F. Skinner was responsible for the study of operant behavior and the extension of this approach to education, psychotherapy, and society as a whole.

Renaming the "law of effect" the "principle of reinforcement," Skinner distinguished two types of reinforcement. **Positive reinforcement** refers to the strengthening of a tendency to respond by virtue of the presentation of an event, called a positive reinforcer. For example, a water-deprived pigeon will tend to repeat behaviors (operants) that are followed by the availability of water. **Negative reinforcement** also strengthens a response, but it does so via the *removal* of an event, such as the cessation of electric shock; Skinner called such consequences negative reinforcers. Extrapolating his extensive work with pigeons to complex human behavior (his book *Walden Two* is one of the better known utopian novels, describing an ideal society governed by his principles of reinforcement), Skinner argued that freedom of choice is a myth and that all behavior is determined by the reinforcers provided by the social environment. The goal of Skinner (1953) and the Skinnerians, like that of their mentor, Watson, is the prediction and control of behavior. These experimenters hope that by analyzing behavior in terms of observable responses and reinforcement, they will be able to determine when certain behavior will occur. The information gathered should then help indicate how behavior is acquired, maintained, changed, and eliminated. In the Skinnerian approach, abstract terms and concepts are avoided. For example, references to needs, motivation, and wants are conspicuously absent in Skinnerian writings. To provide an entirely satisfactory account of human behavior, Skinner believed that psychology must restrict its attention to directly observable stimuli and responses and to the effects of reinforcement. Psychologists who hold this view do not, as human beings, deny the existence of inner states of mind and emotion. Rather, they urge that investigators not employ such mediators in trying to develop a science of behavior.

In a prototypical **operant conditioning** experiment a hungry rat might be placed in a box that has a lever located at one end (the well-known Skinner box). The rat will explore its new environment and by chance come close to the lever. The experimenter may then drop a food pellet into the receptacle located near the lever. After a few such rewards the animal will come to spend more and more time in the area around the lever. But now the experimenter may drop a pellet into the receptacle only when the rat happens to touch the lever. After capitalizing on a few chance touches, the rat begins to touch the lever frequently. With lever–touching well established, the experimenter can make the criterion for reward more stringent: the animal must now actually press the lever. Thus the desired operant behavior, lever pressing, is gradually achieved by **shaping**, that is by rewarding a series of responses that are **successive approximations**, responses that more and more closely resemble the desired response. The number of lever presses increases as soon as they become the criterion for the release of pellets and decreases, or extinguishes, as soon as the pellet is no longer dropped into the receptacle after a lever press.

As an example of how operant conditioning can be applied to the etiology of a form of abnormality, let us consider depression. First, the focus of the theory would not be on the affective state itself, because depressed mood is not directly observable. Rather, the theory could focus on the amount of motor behavior, which is typically low among depressed people. Lewinsohn (1974) proposed that depression results from a low level of reinforcement. When the amount of reinforcement decreases, the person emits fewer responses, the amount of reinforcement decreases further, and depression finally results.

Modeling

There is a good deal of current interest in yet a third type of learning, **modeling**. We all learn by watching and imitating others. Experimental work has demonstrated that witnessing someone perform certain activities can increase or decrease diverse kinds of behavior, such as sharing, aggression, and fear. For example, Bandura and Menlove (1968) used a modeling treatment to reduce fear of dogs in children. After witnessing a fearless model engage in various activities with a dog, initially fearful children showed a decided increase in their willingness to approach and handle a dog. Similarly, modeling may be applied to the acquisition of abnormal behavior. Children of parents with phobias or substance abuse problems may acquire similar behavior patterns, in part, through observation.

Mediational Learning Paradigms

Among the learning paradigms, modeling illustrates what is clearly an important issue, namely, the role of mediators in learning and behavior. Consider what happens in the typical modeling experiment. A person watches another do something and immediately shows a change in behavior. No overt responding is necessary for the learning to take place, nor does the observer need to be reinforced. Something is learned before the person makes any observable response. Similar outcomes led some learning theorists of the 1930s and 1940s to infer mediators of various kinds in order to explain overt behavior.

In the most general terms, a **mediational theory of learning** holds that an environmental stimulus does not initiate an overt response directly: rather it does so through some intervening process or **mediator**, such as fear or thinking. This process is conceptualized as an internal response. Without divorcing themselves from behaviorism, mediational learning theorists adopt the paradigmatic position that, under certain conditions, it is both legitimate and important to go beyond observables. Many psychologists who aspire to the status accorded physicists and chemists point out that in these natural sciences ample and effective use is made of supposed entities, like the gluon, that are not directly observed but whose existence is inferred to make sense of existing data and to encourage the search for new data.

Consider the mediational learning analysis of anxiety, as developed by O. Hobart Mowrer (1939) and Neal Miller (1948). In a typical experiment rats were shocked repeatedly in the presence of a neutral stimulus such as the sound of a buzzer. The shock (UCS) produced a UCR of pain, fear, and flight. After several pairings the fear that was naturally produced by the shock came to be produced by the buzzer. The shock could eventually be omitted, and yet the animal would continue to react fearfully to the previously neutral stimulus (CS). In addition, it was shown (e.g., Miller, 1948) that the rat could learn new responses to avoid the CS. The question became how to conceptualize the finding that animals would learn to *avoid* a harmless event. Mowrer (1947) and others suggested that in this, a typical **avoidance conditioning** experiment, two bits of learning were taking place (Figure 2.4): (1) the animal, by means of classical conditioning, learned to fear the CS; and (2) the animal, by means of operant conditioning, learned an overt behavior to remove itself from the CS and thus to reduce the fear. This came to be known as two-factor theory.

Figure 2.4 Schematic representation of Mowrer's account of avoidance learning. The dashed line indicates that the subject is learning to fear the buzzer tone, and the solid line that the subject is learning to avoid the shock.

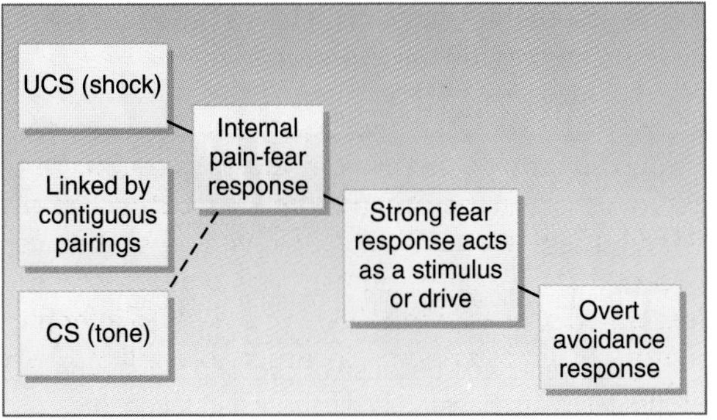

The essential features of this theorizing are that fear or anxiety can be conceived of both as an internal response, which can be learned as observable responses are learned, and an internal state, which can mediate avoidance behavior. Anxiety, then, becomes amenable to the same kind of experimental analysis employed in the investigation of observable behavior. Mowrer and Miller speak of "mediating fear-responses" to point up their assumption that such responses, although inferred, are much the same as overt responses. The knowledge gleaned about overt behavior can therefore, it is hoped, be transferred to the study of mental and emotional life. For instance, if we know that repetition of an overt response without reinforcement leads to the extinction of the response, we can predict that repeated evocation of a fear-response while withholding the expected pain or punishment will reduce the fear. This is no trivial prediction, and, as indicated below, treatments based on such reasoning have helped to reduce many irrational fears.

Applying Learning Points of View to Deviant Behavior

The crucial assumption of behavioral and learning approaches is that abnormal behavior is learned in the same manner as most other human behavior. This view minimizes the importance of biological factors, and focuses instead on elucidating the learning processes that supposedly make behavior maladaptive. The gap between normal and abnormal behavior is reduced, since both are viewed within the same general framework; thus a bridge is forged between general experimental psychology and the field of abnormal psychology. Moreover, according to many who have adopted a learning paradigm, abnormality is a *relativistic* concept: labeling someone or some behavior abnormal is inextricably linked to a particular social or cultural context.

One very important advantage of applying a learning view in psychopathology is the increased precision of observation. Stimuli must be accurately observed and controlled; the magnitude and rate of responses, and their latency, the rapidity with which they are made, are measured and recorded; and relationships among stimuli, responses, and outcomes are carefully noted. Unobservable processes, such as fear and thought, must be linked to observable behavior.

Criticisms of the Learning Paradigm

Although we view these and other features of learning approaches to deviant behavior as very advantageous, it is difficult to persuade those not already committed to the paradigm that it is adequate. The learning paradigm of abnormal behavior is in much the same position as the biological paradigm. Just as many pertinent biological malfunctions have not been uncovered, abnormality has not yet been convincingly traced to particular learning experiences. Consider how difficult it would be to show that depression results from a particular reinforcement history. A person would have to be continually observed over a period of years while his or her behavior was recorded and occurrences of reinforcement noted. Similarly if identical twins reared by their natural parents become schizophrenic later in life, the clinician holding a learning view will usually assert that they had similar reinforcement histories. When fraternal twins are raised at home and only one becomes schizophrenic, the learning explanation is that their reinforcement histories were different. Such explanations are as circular and as unsatisfactory as the psychoanalyst's inference of unconscious processes, a practice deplored by behaviorists, and with good reason. Neither hypothesis explains anything, nor does either encourage the search for new data.

One more point needs to be made here. Although adopting a learning explanation of abnormal behavior has clearly led to many treatment innovations (see the following section on behavior therapy), the effectiveness of these treatments does not mean that the particular deviant behavior was learned in the first place. The fact that a treatment based on learning principles is effective in changing behavior does not show that the behavior was itself learned in a similar way. For example, if the mood of depressed persons is elevated by providing them with rewards for increased activity, this fact cannot be considered evidence that the depression and apathy were initially produced by an absence of rewards (Rimland, 1964).

Behavior Therapy

A number of therapeutic techniques have been developed as an outgrowth of the learning paradigms. The terms **behavior therapy** and **behavior modification** are applied to these techniques because they were initially asserted to be based on the experimentally tested laws of learning formulated by the behaviorists.

Because in mediation theory anxiety is assumed to be classically conditioned, an effective way to

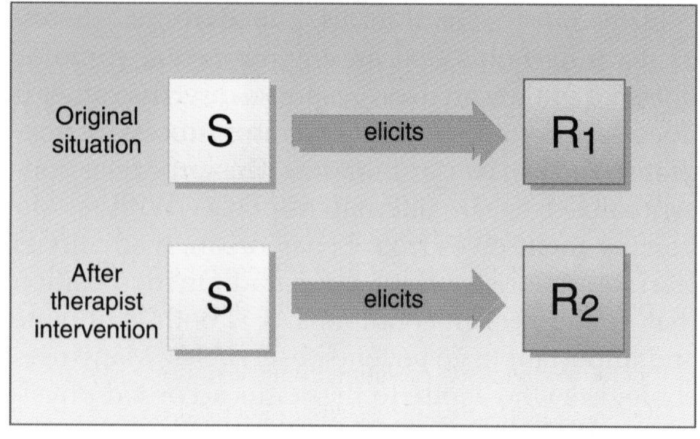

Figure 2.5 Schematic diagram of counterconditioning, whereby an original response (R_1) to a given stimulus (S) is eliminated by evoking a new response (R_2) to the same stimulus.

eliminate fear is to associate the conditioned stimulus with a nonfearful response. Referred to as **counterconditioning**, this principle of behavior change holds that a response (R_1) to a given stimulus (S) can be eliminated by eliciting a new response (R_2) in the presence of that stimulus, as diagramed in Figure 2.5. For example, if a child is afraid (R_1) of a harmless animal (S), the therapist might attempt to elicit a playful reaction (R_2) in the presence of the animal. This counterconditioning, or substitution of a response (R_2), can eliminate R_1.

The counterconditioning principle played a central role in the innovative thinking of Joseph Wolpe (1958), who devised a set of behavior therapy techniques that he asserts are effective for the reasons just stated. The most widely used technique is **systematic desensitization**. A person who suffers from anxiety works with the therapist to compile a list of feared situations, starting with those that arouse minimal anxiety and progressing to those that are the most frightening. He or she is also taught to relax deeply. Then, step-by-step, while relaxed, the person imagines the graded series of anxiety-provoking situations. The relaxation tends to inhibit any anxiety that might otherwise be elicited by the imagined scenes. The fearful person becomes able to tolerate increasingly more difficult imagined situations as he or she climbs the hierarchy over a number of therapy sessions. This technique is useful in reducing a wide variety of fears.

The thirty-five-year-old substitute mail carrier who consulted us had dropped out of college sixteen years ago because of crippling fears of being criticized. Earlier, his disability had taken the form of extreme tension when faced with tests and speaking up in class. When we saw him, he was debilitated by fears of criticism in general and of evaluations of his mail sorting in particular. As a consequence, his everyday activities were severely constricted and, though highly intelligent, he had apparently settled for an occupation that did not promise self-fulfillment.

After the client agreed that a reduction in his unrealistic fears would be beneficial, he was taught over several sessions to relax all the muscles of his body while in a reclining chair. We then created for him a list of anxiety-provoking scenes.

You are saying "Good morning" to your boss.

You are standing in front of your sorting bin in the post office, and your supervisor asks why you are so slow.

You are only halfway through your route, and it is already 2:00 P.M.

As you are delivering Mrs. Mackenzie's mail, she opens her screen door and complains about how late you are.

Your wife criticizes you for bringing home the wrong kind of bread.

The officer at the bridge toll gate appears impatient as you fumble in your pocket for the correct change.

These and other scenes were arranged in an *anxiety hierarchy*, from least to most fear-evoking. Desensitization proper began with the client instructed first to relax deeply as he had been taught. Then he was to imagine the easiest item, remaining as relaxed as possible. When he had learned to confront this image without becoming anxious, he went on to the next scene, and so on. After ten sessions the man was able to imagine the most distressing scene in the hierarchy without feeling anxious and gradually his tension in real life became markedly less.

Though outcomes of single cases do not prove anything, this early case of one of the authors just happened to turn out exceptionally well. Freed of his social evaluative anxieties, this client went on to finish college, then earned a Ph.D., and is now a tenured professor. Would that all our clients fared as well.[4]

Relaxation training is the first step in systematic desensitization. Once clients master relaxation, they begin to imagine scenes from the anxiety hierarchy.

Other behavioral techniques include **assertion training**, which encourages people to speak up and react openly when with others, expressing both their positive and negative feelings. In **aversive conditioning**, a stimulus attractive to the patient is paired with an unpleasant event, such as shock to the fingertips, in hopes of endowing it with negative properties. Aversive techniques, somewhat controversial, as might be imagined, have been employed to reduce the socially inappropriate attraction that objects have for some people, such as the irresistible appeal a woman's boots may have for a fetishist.

Several behavioral procedures derive from operant conditioning. For example, children who misbehave in classrooms can be systematically rewarded by the teacher for their socially acceptable behavior, whereas their undesirable behavior is ignored and thus eventually extinguished. The **token economy**, a program established in mental hospitals to encourage severely disturbed patients to behave more appropriately, is an operant treatment. Explicit rules are set up for obtaining rewards in the form of tokens or other moneylike scrip. At predetermined intervals patients can trade in their tokens for specific reinforcers, such as a visit to the canteen or a more desirable sleeping arrangement.

Modeling has also been used in therapeutic interventions. Bandura, Blanchard, and Ritter (1969) were able to help people reduce their phobias of nonpoisonous snakes by having them view both live and filmed close and successful confrontations between people and snakes. In an analogous fashion, some behavior therapists use **role-playing** in the consulting room. They demonstrate to patients patterns of behaving that might prove more effective than those the patients usually engage in, and then have the patients practice them. Lazarus (1971), in his **behavior rehearsal** procedures, demonstrates

[4]Unreferenced case reports such as this one have been drawn from our own clinical files. Identifying features are changed to protect the confidentiality of the individual.

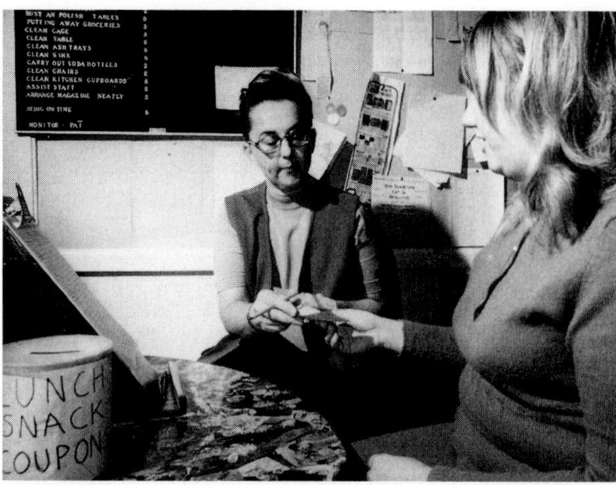

In a token economy, changes in patients' behavior are reinforced with chips which can later be exchanged for specific reinforcers.

exemplary ways of handling a situation and then encourages patients to imitate them during the therapy session. For example, a student who does not know how to ask a professor for an extension on a term paper would watch the therapist portray a potentially effective way of making the request. The clinician would then help the student practice the new skill in a similar role-playing situation.

The Cognitive Paradigm

Cognition is a term that groups together the mental processes of perceiving, recognizing, conceiving, judging, and reasoning. The **cognitive paradigm** focuses on how people (and animals as well!) *structure* their experiences, how they make sense of them, transforming environmental stimuli into information that is usable.

The Basics of Cognitive Theory

At any given moment we are bombarded by far more stimuli than we can possibly respond to. How do we filter this overwhelming input, put it into words or images, form hypotheses, and arrive at a perception of what is out there? Cognitive psychologists consider the learning process to be much more complex than passively forming new stimulus–response associations. Even classical conditioning, for example, is viewed by cognitive psychologists as an active process by which organisms learn about relationships among events rather than an automatic stamping in of associations between stimuli (Rescorla, 1988). Moreover, cognitive psychologists regard the learner as aware and actively interpreting a situation in the light of what has been acquired in the past, as imposing a perceptual funnel on experience, so to speak. The learner fits new information into an organized network of already accumulated knowledge, often referred to as a **schema** (Neisser, 1976). New information may fit the schema or, if not, the learner reorganizes the schema to fit the information. The cognitive approach may remind the reader of our earlier discussions of paradigms in science; that is, scientific paradigms are very similar in function to a cognitive schema for they act as filters to our experience of the world.

Contemporary experimental psychology is very much concerned with cognition. The following situation illustrates how a schema, or cognitive set, may alter the way in which information is processed and remembered.

> The man stood before the mirror and combed his hair. He checked his face carefully for any places he might have missed shaving and then put on the conservative tie he had decided to wear. At breakfast, he studied the newspaper carefully and, over coffee, discussed the possibility of buying a new washing machine with his wife. Then he made several phone calls. As he was leaving the house he thought about the fact that his children would probably want to go to that private camp again this summer. When the car didn't start, he got out, slammed the door and walked down to the bus stop in a very angry mood. Now he would be late. (Bransford & Johnson, 1973, p. 415)

Now read the excerpt again, but add the word "unemployed" before the word "man." Now read it a third time, substituting "stockbroker" for "man." Notice how differently you understand the passage. Ask yourself what parts of the newspaper these men read. If this query had been posed on a questionnaire, you might have answered "the want ads" for the unemployed man and "the financial pages" for the stockbroker. Actually, the passage does not specify which part of the paper was read. Your answers would have been wrong, but in each instance the error would have been a meaningful, predictable one.

Cognitive psychologists have until recently paid little systematic attention to how their research findings bear on psychopathology or how they might help generate effective therapies. Now cognitive explanations appear more and more often in the search for the causes of abnormality and for new methods of intervention. A widely held view of depression, for example, places the blame on a cognitive set, namely the individual's overriding sense of hopelessness (see page 234). Many who are depressed may believe themselves to have no important effect on their surroundings, regardless of what they do. Their destiny seems to them to be out of their hands and they expect their future to be negative. If depression does develop through a sense of hopelessness, this could have implications for how clinicians treat the disorder.

Some clinicians assert that cognitive theorizing is nothing more than a mediational stimulus–response analysis of behavior (e.g., Wolpe, 1980), similar to the historically important contributions of Mowrer and Miller. We disagree. A cognitive explanation of behavior is *fundamentally different* from a mediational stimulus–response analysis. The mediational researcher asserts that an environmental stimulus automatically evokes an internal mediational response, which is subject to the same reinforcement principles as are overt responses. The cognitive researcher, in contrast, does not conceptualize perception or thinking as a "little" response. Rather, this worker focuses on how people actively interpret environmental stimuli and how these transformed stimuli affect behavior. Reinforcement plays a minor role in the theorizing of cognitive psychologists (Davison, 1980).

Criticisms of the Cognitive Paradigm

Although the cognitive paradigm is currently the most common among psychologists, some criticisms should be noted. The concepts (e.g., schema) are somewhat slippery and not always well-defined. Furthermore, cognitive explanations of psychopathology do not always explain much. To say that depression results from a negative schema tells us that depressives think gloomy thoughts. But everyone knows that such a pattern of thinking is actually part of the diagnosis of depression. What is distinctive in the cognitive paradigm is that the thoughts are given causal status, that is, the thoughts are regarded as causing the other features of the disorder, for example, sadness. Left unanswered, however, is the question of where the negative schema came from in the first place. Cognitive explanations of psychopathology tend to focus on current determinants of disorder and not its historical antecedents. As a consequence, they have as yet shed little light on the etiology of mental disorders.

Cognitive Behavior Therapy

The cognitive point of view has gained widespread attention in behavior therapy. Generally speaking, cognitively oriented behavior therapists attempt to change the thinking processes of their patients in order to influence their emotions and behavior. The following is an early example of **cognitive restructuring**, a procedure that attempts to alter the manner in which clients think about life so that they change their overt behavior and emotions (Davison, 1966).

A man had been diagnosed as paranoid schizophrenic, primarily because of his complaints of "pressure points" on his forehead and other parts of his body. He believed that these pressure points were signals from outside forces helping him to make decisions. These paranoid delusions had been resistant to drug treatment and other psychotherapeutic approaches. The therapist, in examining the man's case history, hypothesized that the patient became very anxious and tense when he had to make a decision, that his anxiety took the form of muscular tension in certain bodily parts, and that the patient misconstrued the tension as pressure points, signals from helpful spirits. Both patient and therapist agreed to explore the possibility that the pressure points were in fact part of a tension reaction to specific situations. For this purpose the therapist decided to teach the man deep-muscle relaxation, with the hope that relaxation would enable him to control his tensions, including the pressure points.

But it was also important to have the man question his delusional system. So in the first session the therapist asked the patient to extend his right arm, clench his fist, and bend his wrist downward so as to bring the fist toward the inside of the forearm. The intent was to produce a feeling of tension in his forearm; this is precisely what happened, and the man noted that the feeling was quite similar to his pressure points.

Extensive relaxation training enabled the client to begin to control his anxiety in various situations within the hospital and at the same time to reduce the intensity of the pressure points. As he gained control over his feelings, he gradually came to refer to his pressure points as "sensations," and his conversation in general began to lose its earlier paranoid flavor.

The relaxation training apparently allowed the patient to test a nonparanoid hypothesis about his pressure points, to see it confirmed, and thereby to shake off a belief about these sensations that had contributed to his paranoia.

A somewhat different approach to cognitive therapy stems from the ideas of the prominent cognitive therapist Albert Ellis (1962), who holds that mal-

Albert Ellis, a cognitive behavior therapist, has focused on the role of irrational beliefs as causes of abnormal behavior.

adaptive feelings and activity are caused by **irrational beliefs**. Through mistaken assumptions people place excessive demands on themselves and others. A man who believes that he must always be perfect in everything he does feels terrible whenever he makes a mistake. A woman may think, "I should be able to win the love and approval of everyone," and then exhaust herself trying to please others. Ellis and his followers, the proponents of so-called **rational-emotive therapy**, help their patients challenge such assumptions and teach them to substitute ideas like, "Although it would be terrific never to make a mistake, that doesn't mean I *have* to be without fault."

Aaron Beck developed a cognitive therapy for the cognitive biases of depressed people.

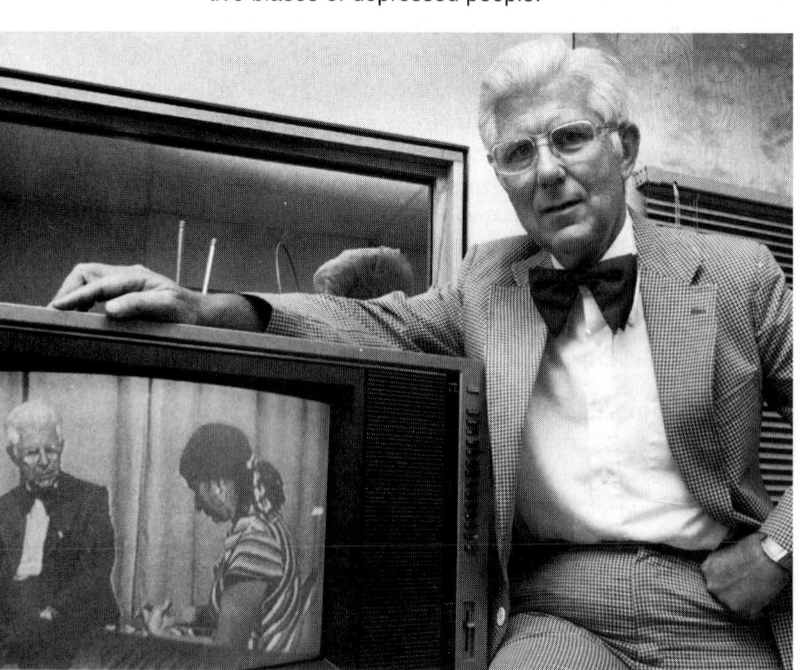

Another leading cognitive therapist is the psychiatrist Aaron Beck (1967, 1976), whose theorizing and research on depression we examine in detail in Chapters 9 and 19. For now it is sufficient to note that Beck's cognitive focus is on how people distort experience. For example, many depressed individuals selectively abstract from a complex event those features that will maintain their gloomy perspective on life, for example, when a person ignores all the positive occurrences on a given day and focuses exclusively on negative happenings. Beck's therapy tries to persuade patients to change their opinions of themselves and the way in which they interpret life events. When a depressed person exhibits selective abstraction during a therapy session, for example, the therapist would offer counterexamples, pointing out how the client had overlooked favorable features of a complex set of events.

Learning Paradigms and Cognitive Paradigms

Is the cognitive point of view basically different and separate from the learning paradigm? Much of what we have just said suggests that it is. But the growing field of cognitive behavior therapy gives us pause, for here workers study the complex interplay of beliefs, expectations, perceptions, and attitudes on the one hand and overt behavior on the other. For example, Albert Bandura (1977), a leading advocate of changing behavior through cognitive means, argues that different therapies produce improvement by increasing people's sense of **self-efficacy**, a belief that they can achieve desired goals (see page 574). *But*, at the same time, he argues that changing behavior through behavioral techniques is the most powerful way to enhance self-efficacy. People like Ellis, by way of contrast, emphasize direct alteration of cognitions through argument, persuasion, Socratic dialogue, and the like to bring about improvements in emotion and behavior. Complicating matters still further, Ellis and his followers also place considerable importance on homework assignments requiring clients to behave in ways in which they were formerly unable to behave, having been hindered by negative thoughts. Indeed, therapists identified with cognitive behavior therapy work at both the cognitive and behavioral levels, and most of those who use cognitive concepts and try to change beliefs with verbal means also use behavioral procedures to alter behavior directly.

This issue is reflected in the terminology employed to refer to people like Beck and Ellis. Are they *cognitive therapists* or cognitive *behavior* therapists? For the most part we will use the latter term because it denotes both that the therapist regards cognitions as major determinants of emotion and behavior and that he or she maintains the focus on overt behavior that has always characterized behavior therapy. Nonetheless, it is important for the reader to know that Beck, even though he assigns many behavioral tasks as part of his therapy, is usually referred to as the founder of cognitive therapy (CT), and that Ellis's rational-emotive therapy (RET) is often spoken of as something separate from behavior therapy.

Whatever their differences in theory and practice, behavior therapists and cognitive therapists are alike in allying themselves philosophically with their colleagues in experimental psychology. For this reason these approaches are regarded by some (e.g., Davison & Goldfried, 1973; Goldfried & Davison, 1976) not as a set of techniques but rather as a particular epistemological stance, one that demands rigorous standards of proof. Specific techniques, it is assumed, will be revised as new research uncovers better ways of altering and preventing abnormality. The implications of this emphasis on experimental research and methodology will become clearer when behavior therapy and cognitive therapy are discussed in depth in Chapter 19.

Consequences of Adopting a Paradigm

The student of abnormal behavior who adopts a particular paradigm necessarily makes a prior decision concerning what kinds of data will be collected and how they will be interpreted. Thus he or she may very well ignore possibilities and overlook other information in advancing what seems to be the most probable explanation. A behaviorist is prone to attribute the high prevalence of schizophrenia in lower-class groups to the paucity of social rewards that these people have received, the assumption being that normal development requires a certain amount and patterning of reinforcement. A biologically oriented theorist will be quick to remind the behaviorist of the many deprived people who do *not* become schizophrenic. The behaviorist will undoubtedly counter with the argument that those who do not become schizophrenic had different reinforcement histories. The biologically oriented theorist will reply that such *post hoc*, or after-the-fact, statements can always be made.

Our biological theorist may suggest that certain biochemical factors that predispose both to schizophrenia and to deficiencies in the intellectual skills necessary to maintain occupational status account for the observed correlation between social class and schizophrenia. The behaviorist will be entirely justified in reminding the biological theorist that these alleged factors have yet to be found, to which the biological theorist might rightfully answer, "Yes, but I'm placing my bets that they are there, and if I adopt *your* behavioral paradigm, I may not look for them." To which the learning theorist may with justification reply, "Yes, but *your* assumption regarding biochemical factors makes it less likely that you will look for and uncover the subtle reinforcement factors that in all likelihood account for both the presence and the absence of schizophrenia."

The fact that our two colleagues are in a sense correct and in another sense incorrect is both exasperating and exciting. They are both correct in asserting that certain data are more likely to be found through work done within a particular paradigm. But they are incorrect to become unduly agitated that each and every social scientist is not assuming that one and the same factor will ultimately be found crucial in the development of all mental disorders. Abnormal behavior is much too diverse to be explained or treated adequately by any one of the current paradigms. As we subsequently examine various categories of psychopathology, we will find substantial differences in the extent to which biological and learning paradigms are applicable. As for future discoveries, it is probably for the best that psychologists do *not* agree on which paradigm is the best. We know far too little to make hard-and-fast decisions on the exclusive superiority of any one paradigm, and there is enough important work to go around. We will often see, too, that a plausible way of looking at the data is to assume multiple causation. A particular disorder may very well develop through an interaction of biological defects and environmental factors, a view we turn to next.

Diathesis–Stress: A Proposed Paradigm

A paradigm that is more general than the ones we have previously discussed is called **diathesis–**

stress. It links biological, psychological, and environmental factors and is not limited to one particular school of thought, such as learning, cognitive, or psychodynamic. This paradigm focuses on the interaction between a predisposition toward disease—the diathesis—and environmental, or life, disturbances—the stress. Diathesis refers most precisely to a constitutional predisposition toward illness, but the term may be extended to any characteristic of a person that increases his or her chance of developing a disorder. In the realm of biology, for example, a number of problems considered in later chapters appear to have a genetically transmitted diathesis. That is, having a close relative with the disorder and therefore sharing to some degree his or her genetic endowment increases a person's risk for the disorder. Although the precise nature of these genetic diatheses is currently unknown (i.e., we don't know exactly what is inherited that makes one person more likely than another to develop schizophrenia), it is clear that a biological predisposition is an important component of many psychopathologies. On a psychological level, for example, the cognitive set already mentioned, the chronic feeling of hopelessness sometimes found in the depressed, may be considered a diathesis for depression.

Possessing the diathesis for a disorder increases a person's chance of developing it but does not, by any means, guarantee that a disorder will develop. The stress part of diathesis–stress is meant to account for how a diathesis may be translated into an actual disorder. Generally speaking, in this context stress refers to some noxious or unpleasant environmental stimulus that can be either biological or psychological.[5] Examples of the former include oxygen deprivation at birth or poor nutrition during childhood, both leading to some form of brain dysfunction. Psychological stressors include both major traumatic events (e.g., rape, death of a spouse) and more mundane happenings that many of us experience (e.g., not achieving goals we have set for ourselves).

The key point of the diathesis–stress model is that both diathesis and stress are necessary in the development of disorders. Some people, for example, have inherited a biological predisposition that places them at high risk for schizophrenia (see Chapter 14). Given a certain amount of stress, they stand a good chance of becoming schizophrenic. Other people, those at low genetic risk, are not likely to develop schizophrenia, regardless of how difficult their lives are.

Different Perspectives on a Clinical Problem

It will now be useful to recall the case of the policeman with which this book began. The information provided is open to a number of interpretations, depending on the paradigm adopted. For instance, if you hold a biological point of view, you will be attentive to the similarity between the man's alternately manic and depressed states and the cyclical swings of mood suffered by his father. You probably are mindful of the research (to be reviewed in Chapter 9) that suggests a genetic factor in mood disorders. You do not, however, discount environmental contributions to his problems, but you hypothesize that some inherited, probably biochemical, defect predisposes him to break down under stress. After all, not everyone who experiences a difficult childhood and adolescence develops the kinds of problems Ernest H. has. For treatment you may prescribe lithium carbonate, a drug that is generally helpful in reducing the magnitude of mood swings in manic-depression.

Now suppose that you are committed to a cognitive-behavioral perspective, which encourages you to analyze human behavior in terms of reinforcement patterns as well as cognitive variables. You may focus on Ernest's self-consciousness at college, which seems related to the fact that, compared with his fellow students, he grew up with few advantages. Economic insecurity and hardship may have made him unduly sensitive to criticism and rejection. Moreover, he regards his wife as warm and charming, pointing up his own perceived lack of social skills. Alcohol has been his escape from such tensions. But heavy drinking, coupled with persistent doubt about his own worth as a human being, has interfered with sexual functioning, worsening an already deteriorating marital relationship. As a behavior therapist, you may employ systematic desensitization. You teach Ernest to relax deeply as he imagines a hierarchy of situations in which he is being evaluated by others. Or you may decide on rational-emotive therapy to convince Ernest that he need not obtain universal approval for every undertaking. Or, given Ernest's deficiency in social skills, you may choose behavior rehearsal to teach him how to function effectively in social situations

[5]*Stress* actually refers to the individual's reaction to a *stressor*, the environmental event that causes stress. For this reason one should probably call this paradigm the diathesis–stress*or* paradigm, but we shall adopt the former term because of its general acceptance among psychopathologists. This distinction is discussed more fully in Chapter 8 (page 191).

in which he has had little experience. His sexual problems might be breached via a Masters and Johnson therapy program of undemanding but increasingly more intimate sexual encounters with his wife. Indeed, more than one of the strategies might be followed.

A psychoanalytic point of view will cast Ernest H. in yet another light. Believing that events in early childhood are of great importance in later patterns of adjustment, you may hypothesize that Ernest has blamed his father for his mother's early death. Such strong anger at the father has been repressed, but Ernest has not been able to regard him as a competent, worthwhile adult and to identify with him. Fixation at the oedipal stage of psychosexual development may have made Ernest anxious about authority and kept him from functioning as an adult male. For treatment you may choose dream analysis and free association to help Ernest lift his repressions and deal openly and consciously with his hitherto buried anger toward his father.

Eclecticism in Psychotherapy: Practice Makes Imperfect

A final word is needed about paradigms and the activities of therapists. From our presentation of treatment approaches, it may appear that they are practices of separate, nonoverlapping schools of therapy. The impression may have been conveyed that a behavior therapist would never listen to a client's report of a dream, nor would a psychoanalyst be caught dead prescribing assertion training to a patient. Such suppositions could not be further from the truth. Most therapists subscribe to **eclecticism**, employing ideas and techniques from a variety of schools (Garfield & Kurtz, 1974). Therapists often behave in ways that are not entirely consistent with the theories they hold. For years, practicing behavior therapists have listened empathically to clients, trying to make out their perspectives on events, on the assumption that this understanding would help them plan a better program for changing troublesome behavior. Behavioral theories do not prescribe such a procedure, but on the basis of clinical experience, and perhaps through their own humanity, behavior therapists have realized that empathic listening helps them establish rapport, determine what is really bothering the client, and plan a sensible therapy program. By the same token, Freud himself is said to have been more directive and done far more to change immediate behavior than would be concluded from his writings alone. A vivid example of this is found in one of Freud's earliest cases as described in Breuer and Freud's *Studies in Hysteria.* Yalom (1980) paraphrased this study and argued that all effective therapists use "throw-ins" and "off the record extras":

> In 1892, Sigmund Freud successfully treated Fraulein Elisabeth von R., a young woman who was suffering from psychogenic difficulties in walking. Freud explained his therapeutic success solely by his technique of abreaction, of de-repressing certain noxious wishes and thoughts. However, in studying Freud's notes, one is struck by the vast number of his other therapeutic activities. For example, he sent Elisabeth to visit her sister's grave and to pay a call upon a young man whom she found attractive. He demonstrated a "friendly interest in her present circumstances" by interacting with the family in the patient's behalf: he interviewed the patient's mother and "begged" her to provide open channels of communication with the patient and to permit the patient to unburden her mind periodically. Having learned from the mother that Elisabeth had no possibility of marrying her dead sister's husband, he conveyed that information to his patient. He helped untangle the family financial tangle. At other times Freud urged Elisabeth to face with calmness the fact that the future, for everyone, is inevitably uncertain. He repeatedly consoled her by assuring her that she was not responsible for unwanted feelings, and pointed out that her degree of guilt and remorse for these feelings was powerful evidence of her high moral character. Finally, after the termination of therapy, Freud, hearing that Elisabeth was going to a private dance, procured an invitation so he could watch her "whirl past in a lively dance." One cannot help but wonder what really helped Fraulein von R. Freud's extras, I have no doubt, constituted powerful interventions; to exclude them from theory is to court error. (p. 4)

Especially today psychoanalysts are paying more attention to overt behavior and the relieving of symptoms than analytic theory would lead them to do. Some contemporary writers, like Paul Wachtel (see page 588), even propose that analysts employ behavior therapy techniques, openly acknowledging that behavior therapy has something to offer in the alleviation of behavior pathology.

These are weighty issues; the final section of this textbook will give them the attention they need and deserve. The reader should be aware of this complexity at the beginning, however, in order to better appreciate the intricacies and realities of psychotherapy.

SUMMARY

Several major paradigms, or points of view, are current in the study of psychopathology and therapy. The *biological* paradigm assumes that psychopathology is caused by an organic defect. Previous discussions of this point of view have taken the form of arguments, pro and con, about a medical, or disease, model. But an examination of the meaning of the term *medical model* reveals that it is actually too vague about etiology to enjoy the status of a formal model of psychopathology. The medical model does have one implication—that psychopathology may be attributed to biological malfunctions and defects. Therefore, we have proposed instead the biological paradigm. Biological therapies attempt to rectify the specific organic defects underlying disorders or to alleviate symptoms of disorders that have not been traced to such defects.

Another paradigm derives from the work of Sigmund Freud. The *psychoanalytic* point of view directs our attention to repressions and other unconscious processes that are traceable to early childhood conflicts. Whereas present-day ego analysts who are part of this tradition place greater emphasis on conscious ego functions, the psychoanalytic paradigm has generally searched the unconscious and early life of the patient for the causes of abnormality. Therapeutic interventions based on psychoanalytic theory usually attempt to lift repressions so that the patient can examine the infantile and unfounded nature of his or her fears.

Behavioral, or *learning*, paradigms suggest that aberrant behavior has developed through classical conditioning, operant conditioning, or modeling. Investigators who believe that abnormal behavior may have been learned share a commitment to examine carefully all situations affecting behavior, as well as to define concepts carefully. Behavior therapists try to apply learning principles to the direct alteration of overt behavior, thought, and emotion. Less attention is paid to the historical causes of abnormal behavior than to what maintains it, such as the reward and punishment contingencies encouraging problematic response patterns.

More recently, *cognitive* theorists have argued that certain schemata and irrational interpretations are major factors in abnormality. In both practice and theory, the cognitive paradigm has usually blended with the behavioral in an approach to intervention that is referred to as cognitive-behavioral.

The *diathesis–stress* paradigm integrates several of the previous points of view. People are assumed to be disposed to react inadequately to environmental stressors. The diathesis may be biological, as appears to be the case in schizophrenia, or it may be extended to the psychological, for example, the chronic sense of hopelessness that appears to contribute to depression.

The most important implication of paradigms is that they determine where and how investigators look for answers. Paradigms necessarily limit perceptions of the world, for investigators will interpret data differently according to their points of view. In our opinion it is fortunate that workers are not all operating within the same paradigm, for at this point too little is known about psychopathology and its treatment to settle on any one of them. Indeed, most clinicians are eclectic in their approach to intervention, employing techniques that are outside their paradigm but that seem useful in dealing with the complexities of human psychological problems.

KEY TERMS

paradigm
etiology
biological paradigm
medical (disease) model
genes
behavior genetics
genotype
phenotype
family method
index cases (probands)
twin method
monozygotic (MZ) twins
dizygotic (DZ) twins
concordance
neuron
nerve impulse
synapse
neurotransmitters
psychoanalytic (psychodynamic) paradigm
id
libido
pleasure principle
primary process
ego
secondary process
reality principle
superego
psychodynamics
defense mechanism
unconscious
psychosexual stages
oral stage
anal stage
phallic stage
latency period
genital stage
anal personality
fixation
Oedipus complex
Electra complex
neurotic anxiety
objective (realistic) anxiety
moral anxiety
defense mechanisms
repression
projection
displacement
reaction formation
regression
rationalization
neo-Freudians
analytical psychology
collective unconscious
individual psychology
psychosocial stages of development
identity crisis
free association
dream analysis
analysis of defenses
ego analysts
learning paradigm
introspection
behaviorism
classical conditioning
unconditioned stimulus
unconditioned response
conditioned stimulus
conditioned response
extinction
law of effect
discriminative stimulus
positive reinforcement
negative reinforcement
operant conditioning
shaping
successive approximations
modeling
mediational theory of learning
mediators
avoidance conditioning
behavior therapy
behavior modification
counterconditioning
systematic desensitization
assertion training
aversive conditioning
token economy
role-playing
behavior rehearsal
cognition
cognitive paradigm
schema
cognitive restructuring
irrational beliefs
rational-emotive therapy
self-efficacy
diathesis–stress
eclecticism

chapter three

Classification and Diagnosis

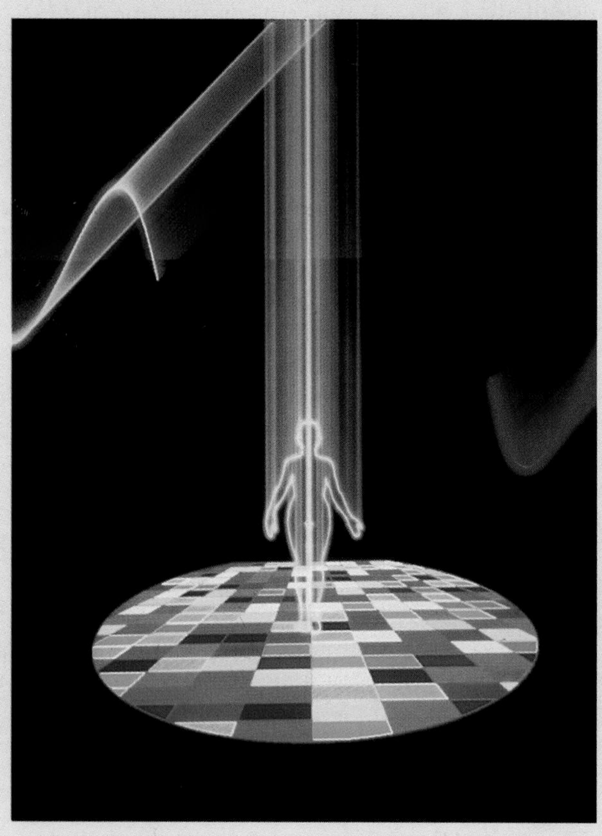

Alex, a forty-five-year-old construction worker, was picked up by the police after he sexually molested a woman early one evening on a crowded city street. He had been drinking in a bar since leaving work two hours earlier and was quite inebriated when arrested. It turned out that he had drunk a six-pack of beer at breakfast, then another two six-packs during lunch. This had been his pattern for the past four years, following the death of his five-year-old daughter in a hit-and-run accident in front of the modest tract house where he lived with his wife of eleven years. A heavy drinker since early adolescence, as well as the member of a neighborhood gang known for its brutal attacks on rival gangs and its other antisocial activities, Alex's occupational history was irregular at best. His current job was obtained only through the influence of an uncle who had been trying for many years to help his errant nephew overcome both his earlier criminal history and his alcoholism. Even before the death of their child, the marriage had been marked by incessant conflicts and mutual recriminations, with Alex ending each argument by physically abusing his wife, sometimes to the point that she had to go to a hospital emergency room for her injuries. Since their daughter's tragic death, the marital situation had deteriorated still further, and it was a source of puzzlement to their few friends why they even stayed together. Alex's wife was thought by family members to be harboring the unrealistic belief that she could get her husband to change both his alcohol abuse and his aggressive and other antisocial behavior. While he was not as physically aggressive outside the home as he had been as a teenager, he enjoyed shoplifting, was often late with his rent, and, in general, showed little concern for basic social mores and no tendency to be considerate of others. The years of alcohol abuse had taken their toll, and a diagnosis of liver damage had been made two years earlier. When Alex sobered up in the "tank" the morning following his arrest, he realized that he would probably lose his job and perhaps this time also his wife, but he did not seem to care.

This case could be described in any number of ways, depending on the paradigm and theoretical preference of the clinician who has to deal with Alex. Diagnosis is a critical aspect of the field of abnormal psychology. It is essential that professionals be able to communicate accurately with one another about the types of cases they are treating or studying. Only in recent years, however, has diagnosis been accorded the attention it deserves. In this chapter we focus on the current, official diagnostic system widely employed by mental health professionals, the **Diagnostic and Statistical Manual of Mental Disorders, Fourth Edition**, commonly referred to as **DSM-IV**. It is published by the American Psychiatric Association and has an interesting history, which we will examine.

By the end of the nineteenth century, medicine had progressed far beyond its practice during the Middle Ages, when the common technique of bloodletting was at least part of the treatment of virtually all physical problems. It was gradually recognized that different illnesses required different treatments. Diagnostic procedures were improved, diseases classified, and applicable remedies administered. Impressed by the successes that new diagnostic procedures had achieved in the field of medicine, investigators of abnormal behavior also sought to develop classification schemes. Moreover, advances in other sciences, such as botany and chemistry, had followed the development of classification systems, reinforcing hope that similar efforts in the field of abnormal behavior might bring progress.

But during the nineteenth century, and indeed into the twentieth as well, there had been great inconsistency in the classification of abnormal behavior. By the end of the nineteenth century, the diversity of classifications was recognized as a serious problem that impeded communication among people in the field. In Paris in 1889, the Congress of Mental Science adopted a single classification system, but it was never widely used. Earlier, in Great Britain in 1882, the Statistical Committee of the Royal Medico-Psychological Association had produced a classification scheme that, even though revised several times, was never adopted by the members. In the United States, in 1886, the Association of Medical Superintendents of American Institutions for the Insane, a forerunner of the American Psychiatric Association, adopted a somewhat revised version of the British system. Then in 1913 this group accepted a new classification incorporating some of Emil Kraepelin's ideas (p. 19). But again, consistency did not emerge. The New York State Commission on Lunacy, for example, insisted on retaining its own system (Kendell, 1975).

Nor have more contemporary efforts at achieving uniformity of classification been totally successful. In 1939 the World Health Organization (WHO) added mental disorders to the *International List of Causes of Death*. In 1948 the list was expanded to become the *International Statistical Classification of Diseases, Injuries, and Causes of Death (ICD)*, a comprehensive listing of all diseases, including a classification of abnormal behavior. Although this nomenclature was unanimously adopted at a WHO conference, the mental disorders section failed to be widely accepted. In the United States, for example, even though American psychiatrists had a prominent role in the WHO effort, the American Psychiatric Association published its own *Diagnostic and Statistical Manual* (DSM) in 1952.

In 1969 the WHO published a new classification system, which was more widely accepted. A second version of the American Psychiatric Association's DSM (DSM-II, 1968) was similar to the WHO system, and in Great Britain a glossary of definitions was produced to accompany it (General Register Office, 1968). But true consensus still eluded the field. The WHO classifications were simply a listing of diagnostic categories; the actual behavior or symptoms that are the basis for the diagnoses were not specified. DSM-II and the British Glossary provided this crucial information, but the symptoms listed by each were not always similar. Therefore actual diagnostic practices still varied widely. In 1980 the American Psychiatric Association published an extensively revised diagnostic manual—DSM-III. A somewhat revised version, DSM-IIIR, appeared in 1987.

In 1988 the American Psychiatric Association appointed a task force, chaired by Allen Frances, to begin work on DSM-IV. Working groups were established to review sections of DSM-IIIR, prepare literature reviews, analyze previously collected data, and collect new data if needed. Perhaps the most important feature of the process was a change in the way in which diagnostic criteria could be altered: "Decisions must be substantiated by explicit statements of rationale and by the systematic review of empirical data" (Frances et al., 1990). In previous versions of the DSM the reasons for diagnostic changes were not always explicit, so the evidence that led to them was never exposed to public scrutiny.

Some controversy surrounding the new effort surfaced immediately. To some (e.g., Zimmerman, 1988) it appeared that diagnostic revisions had outpaced any real gains in knowledge. However, the main reason that work on DSM-IV followed the publication of DSM-IIIR so quickly was the expected publication of the tenth version of the *International Classification of Diseases* (ICD-10) in 1993. Many inconsistencies had emerged between the ICD and the DSM, and it was desirable to resolve as many of them as possible.[1]

In 1991, the American Psychiatric Association published what they called the DSM-IV options book. For each diagnosis it spelled out problems and possible solutions for them. As we finish this edition of our text, the work of the committees on specific diagnoses has been completed and their reports submitted to the task force. A draft of DSM-IV became available in March of 1993 and is the basis of the information we will present.

In this chapter the major DSM-IV categories are given in brief summary. We then examine criticisms of classification in general and of the DSM in particular. In the next chapter we consider the assessment procedures that provide the data on which diagnostic decisions are based.

The Diagnostic System of the American Psychiatric Association (DSM-IV)

The Axes

A number of major innovations distinguish the third edition and subsequent versions of the DSM. Perhaps the most sweeping change is the use of **multiaxial classification**; each individual is to be rated on five separate dimensions, or axes (Table 3.1). The multiaxial system, by requiring judgments to be made on each of the five axes, forces the diagnostician to consider a broad range of information. Axis I includes all categories except for the personality disorders, which make up axis II. Thus axes I and II constitute the classification of abnormal behavior. Axes I and II were separated to ensure that the possible presence of long-term disturbances is considered when attention is directed to the current one. For example, a person who is now a heroin addict would be diagnosed on axis I as having a substance related disorder; he or she might also

[1]Attempting to iron out differences between American and international diagnostic practices raises the issue of the effects of culture on psychopathology. For example, are diagnostic criteria formulated in industrialized societies applicable in developing countries? Evidence on the issue is rather meager, but for the two disorders that have been most thoroughly studied (schizophrenia and depression), it appears that the core symptoms are similar cross-culturally. There are, however, some differences; for example, guilt is a frequent symptom of depression in Western society, but an infrequent symptom in Japan and Iran (Draguns, 1989).

have a long-standing antisocial personality disorder, which would be noted on axis II.

Although the remaining three axes are not needed to make the actual diagnosis, their inclusion in the DSM indicates recognition that factors other than a person's symptoms should be considered in an assessment. On axis III the clinician indicates any general medical conditions believed to be relevant to the mental disorder in question. In some individuals a physical disorder, a neurological dysfunction, for example, may be the cause of the abnormal behavior, whereas in others it may be an important factor in their overall condition, for example, diabetes in a child with a conduct disorder. Axis IV codes psychosocial and environmental problems that the person has been experiencing and that may be contributing to the disorder. These include occupational problems, economic problems, interpersonal difficulties with family members, and a variety of problems in other life areas. Finally, on axis V, the clinician indicates the person's current level of adaptive functioning. Life areas to be considered are social relationships, occupational functioning, and use of leisure time. Ratings of current functioning are supposed to give information about the need for treatment. Table 3.2 shows how the case of Alex, with which we opened this chapter, would look in DSM-IV terms.

Table 3.1 • DSM-IV Multiaxial Classification System[a]

Axis I	*Axis II*	*Axis III*
Clinical syndromes: Disorders Usually First Diagnosed in Infancy, Childhood, or Adolescence Delirium, Dementia, Amnestic and other Cognitive Disorders Substance Related Disorders Schizophrenia and Other Psychotic Disorders Mood Disorders Anxiety Disorders Somatoform Disorders Factitious Disorder Dissociative Disorders Sexual and Gender Identity Disorders Eating Disorders Sleep Disorders Impulse Control Disorders Not Elsewhere Classified Adjustment Disorders	Personality Disorders: paranoid, schizoid, schizotypal, antisocial, borderline, histrionic, narcissistic, avoidant, dependent, obsessive-compulsive	General Medical Conditions

Axis IV
Psychosocial and Environmental Problems

Check:

_____ Problems with primary support group (Childhood, Adult, Parent-Child. Specify: ____________
_____ Problems related to the social environment. Specify: ____________
_____ Educational problem. Specify: ____________
_____ Occupational problem. Specify: ____________
_____ Housing problem. Specify: ____________
_____ Economic problem. Specify: ____________
_____ Problems with access to health care services. Specify: ____________
_____ Problems related to interaction with the legal system/crime. Specify: ____________
_____ Other psychosocial problem. Specify: ____________

Table 3.1 *Continued*

Axis V

Global Assessment of Functioning Scale (GAF Scale)

Consider psychological, social, and occupational functioning on a hypothetical continuum of mental health/illness. Do not include impairment in functioning due to physical (or environmental) limitations.

Code	
100–91	Superior functioning in a wide range of activities, life's problems never seem to get out of hand, is sought out by others because of his many positive qualities. No symptoms.
90–81	Absent or minimal symptoms (e.g., mild anxiety before an exam), good functioning in all areas, interested and involved in a wide range of activities, socially effective, generally satisfied with life, no more than everyday problems or concerns (e.g., an occasional argument with family members).
80–71	If symptoms are present, they are transient and expectable reactions to psychosocial stressors (e.g., difficulty concentrating after family argument); no more than slight impairment in social, occupational, or school functioning (e.g., temporarily falling behind in school work).
70–61	Some mild symptoms (e.g., depressed mood and mild insomnia) OR some difficulty in social, occupational, or school functioning (e.g., occasional truancy, or theft within the household), but generally functioning pretty well, has some meaningful interpersonal relationships.
60–51	Moderate symptoms (e.g., flat affect and circumstantial speech, occasional panic attacks) OR moderate difficulty in social, occupational, or school functioning (e.g., no friends, unable to keep a job).
50–41	Serious symptoms (e.g., suicidal ideation, severe obsessional rituals, frequent shoplifting) OR any serious impairment in social, occupational or school functioning (e.g., no friends, unable to keep a job).
40–31	Some impairment in reality testing or communication (e.g., speech is at times illogical, obscure, or irrelevant) OR major impairment in several areas, such as work or school, family relations, judgment, thinking, or mood (e.g., depressed man avoids friends, neglects family, and is unable to work; child frequently beats up younger children, is defiant at home, and is failing at school).
30–21	Behavior is considerably influenced by delusions or hallucinations OR serious impairment in communication or judgment (e.g., sometimes incoherent, acts grossly inappropriately, suicidal preoccupation) OR inability to function in almost all areas (e.g., stays in bed all day; no job, home, or friends).
20–11	Some danger of hurting self or others (e.g., suicide attempts without clear expectation of death, frequently violent, manic excitement) OR occasionally fails to maintain minimal personal hygiene (e.g., smears feces) OR gross impairment in communication (e.g., largely incoherent or mute).
10–1	Persistent danger of severely hurting self or others (e.g., recurrent violence) OR persistent inability to maintain minimal personal hygiene OR serious suicidal act with clear expectation of death.
0	Inadequate information.

Note: Reprinted with permission from the Draft Criteria of DSM-IV, 1993 American Psychiatric Association.

[a]This listing is generally selective rather than complete. A more comprehensive listing of DSM-IV categories is given on the front endpapers of this book.

Table 3.2 • Example of a DSM-IV Multiaxial Diagnosis

Axis I:	Alcohol Dependence
Axis II:	Antisocial Personality
Axis III:	Cirrhosis
Axis IV:	Psychosocial and Environmental Problems: Arrest, Death of a Child
Axis V:	Level of current functioning: 42

Diagnostic Categories

In this section we provide a brief description of the major diagnostic categories of axes I and II. A general overview of the entire DSM appears on the front and back endpapers of the book for quick reference.

Disorders Usually First Diagnosed in Infancy, Childhood, or Adolescence

Within this broad-ranging category are the intellectual, emotional, and physical disorders that usually begin in infancy, childhood, or adolescence. Some of the problems described are *separation anxiety disorders; conduct disorders; attention deficit/hyperactivity disorder; mental retardation; pervasive developmental disorder* (*infantile autism*); and *learning disorders*, which cover delays in the acquisition of speech, reading, arithmetic, and writing skills. These disorders are discussed in Chapters 15 and 16.

Substance Related Disorders

Here the ingestion of various substances—alcohol, opiates, cocaine, amphetamines, and so on—has changed behavior enough to impair social or occupational functioning. The individual may become unable to control or discontinue ingestion of the substance and may develop withdrawal symptoms if he or she stops using it. These substances may also cause or contribute to the development of other Axis I disorders such as those of mood or anxiety. These disorders are examined in Chapter 11.

Schizophrenia and Other Psychotic Disorders

For individuals with *schizophrenic disorders* self-care, social relations, and ability to work have deteriorated. Their language and communication are disordered, and they may shift from one subject to another only obliquely related or even completely unrelated. They commonly experience delusions, such as believing that thoughts not their own have been placed in their heads; in addition, they are plagued by hallucinations, in particular, hearing voices that come from outside themselves. Their emotions are blunted, flattened, or inappropriate, and they have lost contact with the world and with others. These serious mental disorders are discussed in Chapter 14.

The most obvious symptoms of people with *delusional disorders* are their delusions of being persecuted. The diagnosis can also be applied to extreme and unjustified jealousy, as when a spouse becomes convinced, without reasonable cause, that his or her partner is unfaithful. DSM-IV distinguishes delusional disorders from *schizophrenia, paranoid type*, by noting that in schizophrenia, delusions tend to be more bizarre and fragmented; the person also has hallucinations and is generally more disturbed. Delusional disorders are discussed in Chapter 14.

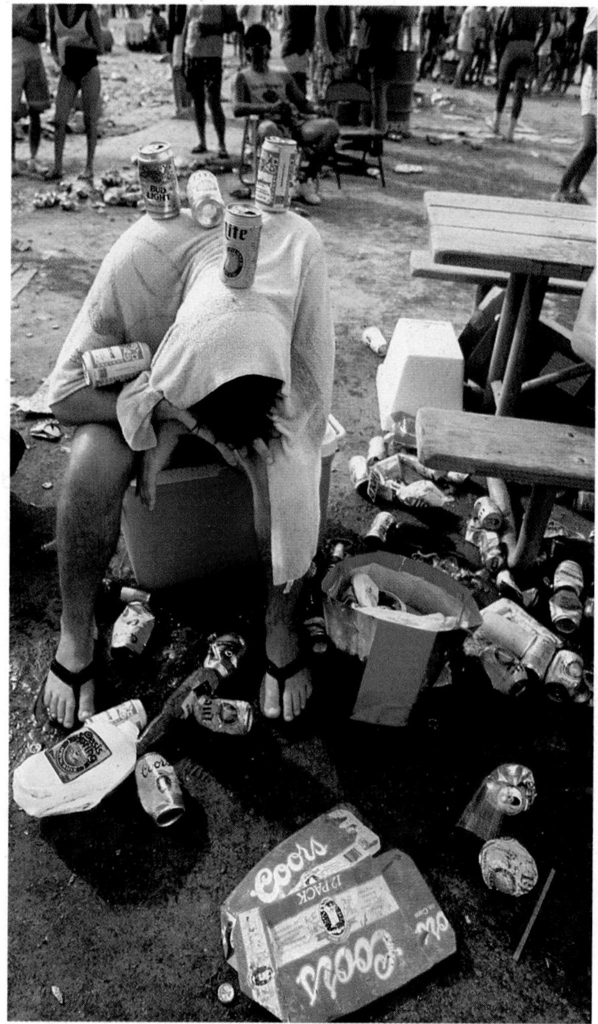

Alcohol is the most frequently abused substance.

Mood Disorders

In *major depressive disorder* the person is deeply sad and discouraged and is also likely to lose weight and energy and to have suicidal thoughts and feelings of self-reproach. The person suffering *mania* may be described as exceedingly euphoric, irritable, more active than usual, distractable, and possessed of unrealistically great self-esteem. *Bipolar disorder* is diagnosed if the person experiences episodes of mania or of both mania and depression. The disorders of mood are surveyed in Chapter 9.

Anxiety Disorders

Anxiety disorders are those that have some form of anxiety as the central disturbance. Individuals with a *phobia* fear an object or situation so intensely that they must avoid it, even though they know that

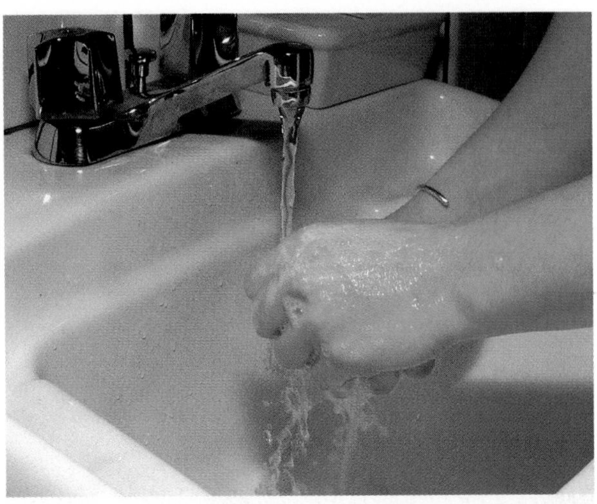

Fear of contamination and excessive handwashing are frequent in obsessive-compulsive disorder.

their fear is unwarranted and unreasonable and disrupts their lives. In *panic disorder* the person is subject to sudden but brief attacks of intense apprehension, so upsetting that he or she is likely to tremble and shake, feel dizzy, and have trouble breathing. Panic disorder may also be accompanied by *agoraphobia,* in which case the person is also fearful of leaving familiar surroundings. The anxiety of *generalized anxiety disorder* is pervasive and persistent. Individuals are jumpy and may have a lump in the throat and a pounding heart. They worry constantly and feel generally on edge. A person with *obsessive-compulsive disorder* is subject to persistent obsessions or compulsions. Obsessions are recurrent thoughts, ideas, and images that uncontrollably dominate a person's consciousness. A compulsion is an urge to perform a stereotyped act with the seeming but usually impossible purpose of warding off an impending feared situation. Attempts to resist a compulsion create so much tension that the individual usually yields.

The anxiety and numbness suffered in the aftermath of a very traumatic event is called *posttraumatic stress disorder.* Individuals have painful, intrusive recollections by day and bad dreams at night. They find it difficult to concentrate, and feel detached from others and ongoing affairs. *Acute stress disorder* is like posttraumatic stress disorder but the symptoms do not last as long. The anxiety disorders are reviewed in Chapter 6.

Somatoform Disorders

The physical symptoms of somatoform disorders have no known physiological cause but seem to serve a psychological purpose. Persons with *somatization disorder*, or Briquet's syndrome, have a long history of multiple physical complaints for which they have taken medicine or consulted doctors. In *conversion disorder* the person reports the loss of motor or sensory function, such as a paralysis, an anesthesia, or blindness. Individuals with *pain disorder* suffer from severe and prolonged pain. *Hypochondriasis* is the misinterpretation of minor physical sensations as serious illness. People with *body dysmorphic disorder* are preoccupied with an imagined defect in their appearance. These disorders are covered in Chapter 7.

Dissociative Disorders

Psychological dissociation is a sudden alteration in consciousness affecting memory and identity. Persons with *dissociative amnesia* may forget their whole past or more selectively lose memory for a particular time period. With *dissociative fugue* the individual suddenly and unexpectedly travels to a new locale, starts a new life, and is amnesic for his or her previous identity. The person with *multiple personality (dissociative identity disorder)* possesses two or more distinct personalities, each complex and dominant one at a time. *Depersonalization disorder* is a severe and disruptive feeling of self-estrangement or unreality. These disorders are examined in Chapter 7.

Sexual and Gender Identity Disorders

The sexual disorders section of DSM-IV lists three principal subcategories. In *paraphilias* the sources of sexual gratification—as in exhibitionism, voyeurism, sadism, and masochism—are unconventional. Persons with *sexual dysfunctions* are unable to complete the usual sexual response cycle. Inability to maintain an erection, premature ejaculation, and inhibition of orgasms are examples of their problems. People with *gender identity* disorders feel extreme discomfort with their anatomical sex and identify themselves as members of the opposite sex. These disorders are studied in Chapters 12 and 13.

Sleep Disorders

Two major subcategories of sleep disorders are distinguished. In the *dyssomnias,* sleep is disturbed in amount (e.g., not being able to maintain sleep or sleeping too much), quality (not feeling rested after sleep), or timing (e.g., inability to sleep during conventional sleep times). In the *parasomnias,* an unusual event occurs during sleep (e.g., nightmares, sleepwalking).

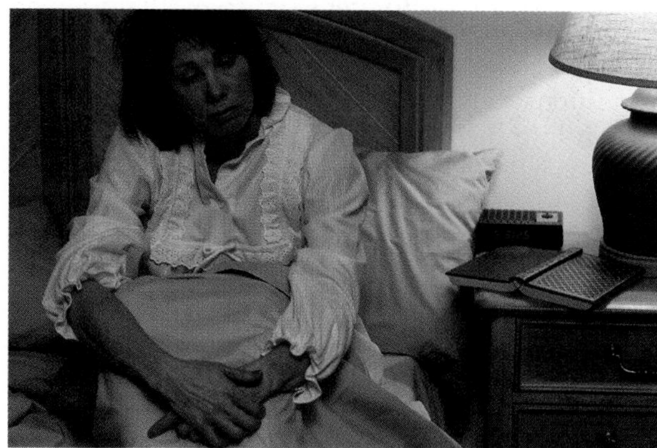

Not being able to sleep, technically termed a dyssomnia, is one type of sleep disorder.

Eating Disorders

In *anorexia nervosa* the person avoids eating and becomes emaciated, often because of an intense fear of becoming fat. In *bulimia nervosa,* there are frequent episodes of binge eating coupled with compensatory activities such as self-induced vomiting and heavy use of laxatives. These disorders are discussed in Chapter 15.

Factitious Disorder

This diagnosis is applied to people who intentionally produce or complain of either physical or psychological symptoms, apparently because of a psychological need to assume the role of a sick person.

Adjustment Disorders

This diagnosis refers to the development of emotional or behavioral symptoms following the occurrence of a major life stressor. However, the symptoms that ensue do not meet diagnostic criteria for any axis I diagnosis.

Impulse Control Disorders

This category includes a number of conditions where the person's behavior is inappropriate and seemingly out of control. For example, in *intermittent explosive disorder* the person has episodes of violent behavior that result in destruction of property or injury to another person. In *kleptomania* the person steals repeatedly but not for the monetary value of the object or to use it. In *pyromania,* the person purposefully sets fires and derives pleasure from doing so. In *pathological gambling* the person is preoccupied with gambling, is unable to stop, and gambles as a way to escape from problems.

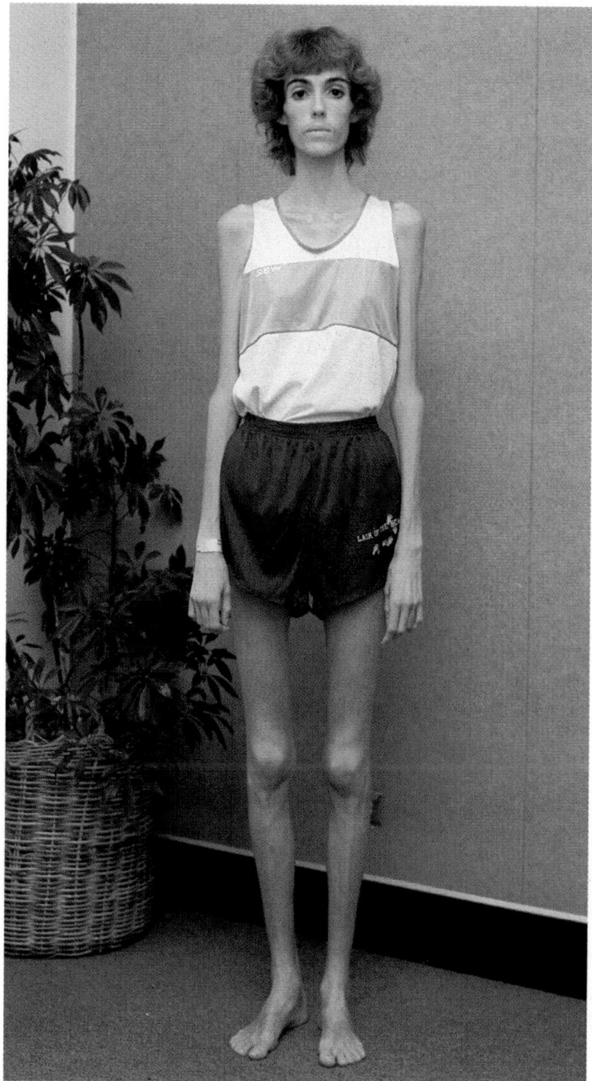

Anorexia, involving severe weight loss and extreme fear of becoming fat, is one of the eating disorders.

Personality Disorders

Personality disorders are defined as ''inflexible and maladaptive'' patterns of behavior. They are listed on axis II. Ten distinct personality disorders make up the category. In *schizoid personality disorder,* for example, the person is aloof, has few friends, and is indifferent to praise and criticism. The individual with a *narcissistic personality* has an overblown sense of self-importance, fantasizes about great successes, requires constant attention, and is likely to exploit others. The *antisocial personality* surfaced before the age of fifteen, through truancy, running away from home, delinquency, and general belligerence. In adulthood he or she is indifferent about holding a job, being a responsible mate or parent, planning ahead for the future and even for tomorrow, and staying on the right side of the law. Also called psychopaths, antisocial personalities do not feel guilt or shame for transgressing social mores. Chapter 10 covers the personality disorders and examines psychopathy in particular.

Other Conditions That May Be a Focus of Clinical Attention

This all-encompassing category is for conditions that are not regarded as mental disorders per se but still may be a focus of attention or treatment. Essentially, the category seems to exist so that anyone entering the mental health system can be categorized, even in the absence of a formally designated mental disorder. If an individual's medical illness appears to be caused, in part, or exacerbated by a psychological condition, the diagnosis is *psychological factors affecting physical condition.* Referred to previously as psychophysiological or psychosomatic disorders, these conditions are reviewed in detail in Chapter 8. Among the other diagnoses are the following:

academic problem

antisocial behavior

malingering

marital problem

relational problem (e.g., with sibling or spouse)

occupational problem

physical or sexual abuse

uncomplicated bereavement

In this context it is interesting to recall our discussion of the difficulties of defining mental disorder (pages 6–9). Can these life difficulties really be readily distinguished from mental disorders?

Many of these conditions will not be covered in this book, although malingering will be discussed in Chapter 7, therapy for marital problems will be presented in Chapter 20, and physical and sexual abuse are covered in Chapters 7 and 12.

Delirium, Dementia, Amnestic, and Other Cognitive Disorders

In addition to the axis I conditions already described, DSM-III and DSM-IIIR contained sections on organic mental disorders. The implication of this organizational structure was that the other axis I conditions did not have a biological basis. Yet, research into the biological bases of many axis I diagnoses has yielded evidence favoring the presence of important biological causes. To remedy this situation, DSM-IV has dropped the organic mental disorders section and replaced it, in part, with the label that is the title of this section.

Delirium is a clouding of consciousness, wandering attention, and an incoherent stream of thought. It may be caused by several medical conditions as well as substance abuse. **Dementia**, a deterioration of mental capacities, especially memory, is associated with Alzheimer's Disease, stroke, several other medical conditions, and substance abuse. Delirium and dementia will be discussed in detail in Chapter 17 because they are often associated with aging. Amnestic syndrome, an impairment in memory when there is no delirium or dementia, will be considered in Chapter 11, because it is often linked to alcohol abuse.

In its brain disorders section, DSM-III and III-R also had a number of diagnoses that were almost

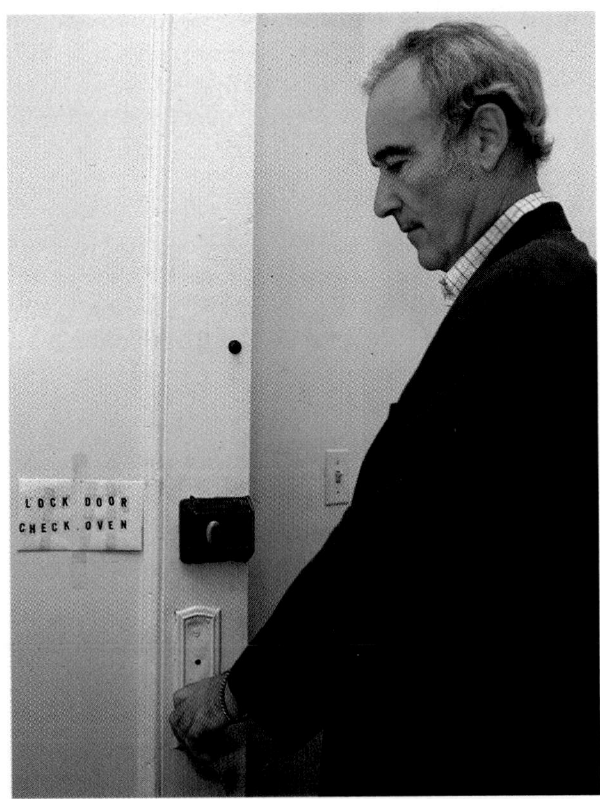

Memory loss, especially for recent events, is the most critical symptom of Alzheimer's disease and other dementias.

identical symptomatically to axis I disorders already described. Organic delusional syndrome was behaviorally the same as delusional (paranoid) disorder; organic mood syndrome the same as major depression; organic anxiety syndrome the same as anxiety disorders; and organic personality syndrome identical to personality disorders. The difference between the pairs of diagnoses was not the symptoms, but the cause. Each brain disorder had a presumed biological cause. For example, organic delusional syndrome could be caused by amphetamine abuse, brain lesions, and temporal lobe epilepsy. Organic mood syndrome could result from disturbances of the endocrine glands (as in hyperthyroidism or abnormal secretions of cortisone), viral illnesses, and stroke. Organic anxiety syndrome could be caused by endocrine disturbances as well as the use of stimulants, such as caffeine and cocaine. Organic personality syndrome was said to result from brain tumors or other injuries to the brain.

These diagnoses are no longer found in DSM-IV. Instead, each Axis I diagnosis includes a provision for indicating that it is due to a general medical condition or substance abuse. For example, a mood disorder caused by endocrine dysfunction would be placed in the mood disorders section but listed as due to a specific medical problem.

Two important implications arise. First, clinicians must be extremely careful to determine whether, for example, a depressed person is suffering from a medical problem or substance abuse. The use of a treatment that does not deal with the biological underpinnings of such a depression would be doomed to fail. Second, the fact that biological factors *can* cause disordered behavior is grist for the mill of the biological paradigm. Perhaps many of the disorders we discuss will, one day, be shown to be best construed within the biological or the diathesis–stress paradigms. But for now, the etiology of the disorders that are our central concern remain elusive, and no single paradigm has gained ascendancy.

Issues in the Classification of Abnormal Behavior

This review of the major categories of abnormal behavior was brief, for they will be examined in more detail throughout this text. On the basis of this overview, however, we will examine here the usefulness of the system as it exists today. Two major lines of criticism can be distinguished. One group of critics asserts that classification per se is irrelevant to the field of abnormal behavior. The second group of critics finds specific deficiencies in the way diagnoses are made.

The Relevance of Classification Per Se

Those opposed to any attempt to classify argue that whenever we do so we lose information and hence overlook some of the uniqueness of the person being studied. In evaluating this claim, recall our earlier discussions of paradigms and their effect on how we glean information about our world. It appears to be in the nature of humankind to categorize whenever we perceive and think about anything. Those who argue against classification per se therefore overlook the inevitability of classification and categorization in human thought.

Consider the simple example of casting dice. Any of the numbers one through six may come up on a given toss of a single die. Let us suppose, however, that we classify each outcome as odd or even. Whenever a one, three, or five comes up on a roll, we call out "odd," and whenever a two, four, or six appears, we say "even." A person listening to our calls will not know whether the call "odd" refers to a one, three, or five, or whether "even" refers to a two, four, or six. In classification, some information must inevitably be lost.

What matters, however, is whether the information lost is *relevant*, which in turn depends on the purposes of the classification system. Any classification is designed to group together objects having a common property and to ignore differences in the objects that are not relevant to the purposes at hand. If our intention is merely to count odd and even rolls, it is irrelevant whether a die comes up one, three, or five or two, four, or six. In judging abnormal behavior, however, we cannot so easily decide what is wheat and what is chaff, for the relevant and irrelevant dimensions of abnormal behavior are uncertain. Thus when we do classify, we may be grouping people together on rather trivial bases while ignoring their extremely important differences.

Classification may also stigmatize a person. Consider how you might be affected by being told, for example, that you are a schizophrenic. You might become guarded and suspicious lest someone recognize your disorder. Or you might be chronically on edge, fearing the onset of another "attack." Furthermore, the fact that you are a "former mental patient" could have a great impact on your life. Friends and loved ones now treat you differently, and employment may be difficult to obtain.

There is little doubt that diagnosis can have such negative consequences. It is clear from the existing research that the general public holds a very negative view of mental patients, and that patients and their families believe that such stigmatizing effects are common (Rabkin, 1974; Wahl & Harrman, 1989). Documenting the actual negative consequences of diagnosis, however, has been difficult. Gove and Fain (1973), for example, followed up a large sample of patients one year after discharge from a hospital. The former patients were interviewed about jobs, social relationships, and outside activities. The patients' descriptions of how they were functioning now and had in the past were not very different. Thus, although we must recognize and be on guard against the possible social stigma of a diagnosis, the problem may not be as serious as generally believed.

Assuming that various types of abnormal behavior do differ from one another, it is essential to classify them, for these differences may constitute keys to the causes and treatments of the various deviant behaviors. For example, a form of mental retardation, phenylketonuria, is attributed to a deficiency in the metabolism of the protein phenylalanine, resulting in the release of incomplete metabolites that injure the brain (see pages 467–68). A diet drastically reduced in phenylalanine prevents some of this injury. As Mendels (1970) has noted, however,

> had we taken 100, or even 1000, people with mental deficiency and placed them all on the phenylalanine-free diet, the response would have been insignificant and the diet would have been discarded as a treatment. It was first necessary to recognize a subtype of mental deficiency [retardation], phenylketonuria, and then subject the value of a phenylalanine-free diet to investigation in this specific population, for whom it has been shown to have value in preventing the development of mental deficiency. (p. 35)

Forming categories may thus further knowledge, for once a category is formed, additional information may be ascertained about it. Even though the category is only an asserted and not a proven entity, it may still be heuristically[2] useful in that it facilitates the acquisition of new information. Only after a diagnostic category has been formed can people who fit its definition be studied in hopes of uncovering factors that were responsible for the development of their problems and of devising treatments that may help them.

Criticisms of Actual Diagnostic Practice

More specific criticisms are commonly made of psychiatric classification, the principal ones concerning whether discrete diagnostic categories are justifiable and whether or not the diagnostic categories are reliable and valid. These criticisms were frequently leveled at DSM-I and DSM-II. At the close of this section we will see how subsequent editions of the DSM have come to grips with them.

Discrete Entity versus Continuum

The DSM represents a **categorical classification** or a yes–no approach to classification. Is the patient schizophrenic or not? It may be argued that this type of classification, because it postulates discrete diagnostic entities, does not allow the continuity between normal and abnormal behavior to be taken into consideration. Those who advance the continuity argument hold that abnormal and normal behavior differ only in intensity or degree, not in kind and therefore discrete diagnostic categories foster a false impression of discontinuity.

In contrast, in **dimensional classification**, the entities or objects being classified must be ranked on a quantitative dimension (e.g., a 1 to 10 scale of anxiety where 1 represents minimal and 10 extreme). Classification would be accomplished by assessing patients on the relevant dimensions and perhaps plotting the location of the patient in a system of coordinates defined by his or her score on each dimension. A dimensional system can, in fact, subsume a categorical one by specifying a cutting point or threshold on one of the quantitative dimensions. This is a potential advantage of the dimensional approach.

Clearly, a dimensional system can be applied to most of the symptoms that constitute the diagnoses of the DSM—anxiety, depression, and the many personality traits that are included in the personality disorders. These are to be found in different people in different degrees and thus do not seem to fit well with the DSM categorical model. DSM-IV offers a provisional dimensional classification of the personality disorders.

The choice between a categorical and a dimensional system of classification, however, is not as simple as it might first seem. Let us consider hypertension (high blood pressure), a topic discussed at

[2] *Heuristic* is a central word and concept in science. It comes from the Greek *heuriskein*, "to discover or find," and is defined in *Webster's* as serving to guide, discover, or reveal, and more specifically as valuable for stimulating or conducting empirical research. The frequent use of this word and its derivatives underlines the importance scientists place on ideas in generating new knowledge.

length in Chapter 8. Blood-pressure measurements clearly fit a dimensional approach, yet it has proved useful to categorize certain people as having high blood pressure in order to research its causes and possible treatments. A similar situation could exist for the DSM categories. Even though anxiety is a dimensional variable, it could prove useful to create a diagnostic category for those people whose anxiety is extreme. There is inevitably a certain arbitrariness to such a categorization (where exactly should the cutoff be?), but it could prove to be fruitful nonetheless.

It is also possible that a variable that on the surface appears dimensional actually represents an underlying categorical or off–on process. This is a complex argument, but some of its flavor can be appreciated by considering a hypothetical single-gene cause for hypertension. The actual observed blood pressure might result from a complex interplay between the gene (off or on) and a variety of environmental influences—diet, weight, smoking, stress, and so on. Observed blood pressure is a dimensional variable, but hypertension results principally from the operation of the single off–on gene, which is a categorical variable. Given that we can observe only the surface variable, how can we tell whether there might be an underlying categorical process? Although well beyond the scope of this book, complex mathematical procedures are being developed to test such questions; their answers are likely to be most interesting (e.g., Meehl, 1986).

The Issue of Reliability

The extent to which a classification system, or a test or measurement of any kind, produces the same scientific observation each time it is applied is the measure of its **reliability**. A general way to think about reliability is to note that all measurement involves a certain degree of error. The type of measurement error considered here is viewed as a random process. It is not like using a 12-inch ruler that is actually 12½ inches long—which would be confusing enough—but more like using a flexible, elastic-like ruler, whose actual length changes every time we use it! In the most general terms, we try to create reliable assessment procedures in order to keep measurement error to a minimum.

Interrater reliability refers to the extent to which two judges agree about an event. For example, suppose you want to know if a child suspected of being conduct disordered is aggressive with his or her peers. You could decide to observe the child playing with classmates during recess. To make your observational data reliable, you would want to have at least two people watch the child at play and make independent judgments about the level of aggression. The extent to which the raters agree would be an index of interrater reliability.

Clearly, for a classification system to be useful, those applying it must be able to agree on what is and what is not an instance of a particular category.[3] Thus reliability becomes a primary requisite for judging any classification system. Reliability was not acceptable prior to DSM-III, mainly because the criteria for making a diagnosis were not presented clearly (Ward et al., 1962). As we'll see below, reliability for most current diagnostic categories is good.

The Issue of Validity

Whether or not accurate statements and predictions can be made about a category once it has been formed is the test of its **validity**. We should state at the outset that validity bears a particular relation to reliability; the less reliable a category is, the more difficult it is to make valid statements about that category. If the reliability of diagnosis is not entirely adequate, we can expect that its validity will not be either.

A diagnosis can have three kinds of validity: etiological, concurrent, and predictive. For a diagnosis to have **etiological validity**, the same causal factors must be found in the people who constitute the diagnostic group. Consider, for example, the supposition that bipolar disorder is, in part, genetically determined. According to this theory, people with episodes of both depression and mania must have a family tree that contains other bipolars. As we shall see in Chapter 9, evidence that supports this theory has been collected, giving this diagnostic category some etiological validity.

A diagnosis has **concurrent validity** if other symptoms or disordered processes not part of the diagnosis itself are discovered to be characteristic of those diagnosed. Finding that most people with schizophrenia have difficulty in personal relationships is an example. **Predictive validity** refers to similar future behavior on the part of the disorder or patients suffering from it. The disorder may have a specific prognosis, or outcome; that is, whether recovery is highly likely or whether continuing problems can be expected depends on the diagnos-

[3]These two components of reliability—agreeing on who is a member of a class and who is not—are referred to as *sensitivity* and *specificity*, respectively. Sensitivity refers to agreement regarding the presence of a specific diagnosis; specificity refers to agreement concerning the absence of a diagnosis.

tic category being considered. Or members of the diagnostic group may be expected to respond in a similar way to a particular treatment. Bipolar patients, for example, tend to respond well to a drug called lithium carbonate. The fact that this drug does not work well for people in most other diagnostic classes supports the predictive validity of the bipolar diagnosis. We have organized this book around the major DSM diagnostic categories because we believe that they indeed possess some validity. Certain categories have greater validity than others, however; these differences will become apparent as we discuss each diagnostic classification.

DSM and Criticisms of Diagnosis

Beginning with DSM-III and DSM-IIIR the diagnostic categories were devised to be more reliable and valid than their predecessors. Each diagnostic category in axes I and II was described much more extensively than had been the case in DSM-II. First there is a description of essential features, then of associated features. Given next are statements, drawn from the research literature, about age of onset, course, degree of impairment and complications, predisposing factors, prevalence and sex ratio, familial pattern, and differential diagnosis. Finally, specific *diagnostic criteria* for the category are spelled out in a more precise fashion—these are the symptoms and other facts that must be present to justify the diagnosis—and the clinical symptoms that constitute a diagnosis are defined in a glossary. Table 3.3 compares the descriptions of a manic episode given in DSM-II with the diagnostic criteria given in DSM-IV. Clearly the bases for making diagnoses are decidedly more detailed and concrete in DSM-IV.

Table 3.3 • Description of Manic Disorder in DSM-II versus DSM-IV

DSM-II (APA, 1968, p. 36)

Manic-depressive illness, manic type. This disorder consists exclusively of manic episodes. These episodes are characterized by excessive elation, irritability, talkativeness, flight of ideas, and accelerated speech and motor activity. Brief periods of depression sometimes occur, but they are never true depressive episodes.

DSM-IV (APA, 1993 draft)

Diagnostic Criteria for a Manic Episode

A. A distinct period of abnormally and persistently elevated, expansive, or irritable mood.
B. During the period of mood disturbance, at least three of the following symptoms have persisted (four if the mood is only irritable) and have been present to a significant degree:
   (1) Inflated self-esteem or grandiosity
   (2) decreased need for sleep, e.g., feels rested after only three hours of sleep
   (3) more talkative than usual or pressure to keep talking
   (4) flight of ideas or subjective experience that thoughts are racing
   (5) distractibility, i.e., attention too easily drawn to unimportant or irrelevant external stimuli
   (6) increase in goal-directed activity (either socially, at work or school, or sexually) or psychomotor agitation
   (7) excessive involvement in pleasurable activities which have a high potential for painful consequences, e.g., the person engages in unrestrained buying sprees, sexual indiscretions, or foolish business investments
C. Mood disturbance sufficiently severe to cause marked impairment in occupational functioning or in usual social activities or relationships with others, or to necessitate hospitalization to prevent harm to self or others.

Note: DSM-IV material reprinted with permission from the DSM-IV Draft Criteria, 1993, American Psychiatric Association.

The explicitness of the DSM criteria can be expected to reduce the descriptive inadequacies that were the major source of diagnostic unreliability. Results of field testing of DSM-III were reported in the manual itself and are shown in Table 3.4. As can be seen, the reliabilities vary but are quite acceptable for most of the major categories. There is no reason to expect that reliabilities will decline in DSM-IV, although the data are not yet available. Progress has also been made in dealing with the second largest source of diagnostic unreliability, inconsistency on the part of the diagnostician. The use of standardized, reliably scored interviews, discussed in the following chapter, greatly reduces this problem.

Thus far the description of the DSM has been in positive terms. The attainment of adequate diagnostic reliability is a considerable achievement, but problems remain. It is unclear, for example, whether the rules for making diagnostic decisions are ideal. Examining Table 3.3, we see that for patients to be diagnosed as suffering from mania, they must have three symptoms from a list of seven, or four if their mood is irritable. But the reason for requiring three symptoms rather than two or five is unknown (see Finn, 1982). Furthermore, the reliability of axes I and II may not always be as high in everyday usage, for

Table 3.4 • Reliabilities for Major Diagnostic Categories Achieved in Field Trials with DSM-III[a]

Diagnostic Category	*Reliability[b]*
Disorders Usually First Evident in Infancy, Childhood, or Adolescence	.65
Organic Mental Disorders	.79
Substance Use Disorders	.86
Schizophrenic Disorders	.81
Paranoid Disorders	.66
Affective Disorders	.69
Anxiety Disorders	.63
Somatoform Disorders	.54
Dissociative Disorders	.80
Psychosexual Disorders	.92
Psychological Factors Affecting Physical Condition	.62
Personality Disorders	.56

[a]The data shown are from phase I of the field trial. The number of patients was 339.

[b]These reliabilities use a statistic called kappa, which reflects the percent agreement corrected for chance agreements.

diagnosticians may not adhere as precisely to the criteria as do those whose work is being scrutinized in formal studies. And although the improved reliability of the DSM *may* lead to more validity, there is no guarantee that it will. The diagnoses made according to it may not reveal anything useful about the patients. Moreover, subjective factors still play a role in evaluations made according to DSM-IV. Consider again the criteria for manic syndrome in Table 3.3. What exactly does it mean to say that the elevated mood must be abnormally and persistently elevated? Or what level of involvement in activities with high potential for painful consequences is excessive? As another example, on axis V the clinician must judge the patient's level of current functioning. The clinician determines what, for the patient, is adaptive and how his or her behavior compares with that of an average person. Such a judgment sets the stage for cultural biases to creep in, as well as the clinician's own personal ideas of what the average person *should* be doing at a given stage of life and in particular circumstances (Taylor, 1983).

Finally, not all the DSM classification changes seem positive. The learning disorders—of reading, arithmetic, and writing—really cover the waterfront! Should a problem such as difficulty in learning arithmetic be considered a psychiatric disorder? By expanding its coverage, the DSM seems to have made too many childhood problems into psychiatric disorders, without good justification for doing so.

In sum, although we regard the DSM as promising, it is far from perfect. Throughout this book, as we present the literature on various disorders, there will be further opportunities to describe both the strengths and weaknesses of this effort of health professionals to categorize mental disorders and to consider how DSM-IV may deal with some of the problems that still exist. What is most heartening about the DSM, however, is that its attempts to be explicit about the rules for diagnosis will make it easier to detect problems in the diagnostic system. We can expect more changes and refinements over the next several years.

SUMMARY

The recent editions of the *Diagnostic and Statistical Manual of Mental Disorders*, published by the American Psychiatric Association, reflect the efforts by mental health professionals to categorize the various psychopathologies. A novel feature is their multiaxial organization; every time a diagnosis is made, the clinician must describe the patient's condition according to each of five axes, or dimensions. Axes I and II make up the mental disorders per se; on axis III are listed any physical disorders believed to bear on the mental disorder in question; axis IV is used to indicate the psychosocial and environmental problems that the person has been experiencing; and axis V rates the person's current level of adaptive functioning. A multiaxial diagnosis is believed to provide a more adequate and useful description of the patient's mental disorder.

Both general and specific issues in the classification of abnormality were discussed. Because recent versions of the DSM are far more concrete and descriptive than DSM-II, diagnoses based on them are more reliable. Validity, however, remains an open question. It is too soon to know whether more useful knowledge about psychopathology, its prevention and treatment, will be gained though widespread use of DSM-IV.

KEY TERMS

multiaxial classification
delirium
dementia
categorical classification
dimensional classification
reliability
validity
etiological validity
concurrent validity
predictive validity

c h a p t e r f o u r

Clinical Assessment Procedures

> . . . consider the assessment of a young child brought to a clinic by his mother with the complaint that he is excessively demanding, unruly, stubborn, spoiled, and immature. Assume, also, that this boy is of average intelligence and has no gross organic problems. Even the first tentative hypotheses about the child depend on the interpreter's theoretical approach. A Freudian might be alert to the child's behavior as a sign of weak ego strength and ambivalence toward the mother related to basic problems in handling impulses, or perhaps as a reflection of the mother's own unconscious neurotic conflicts. An Adlerian would attend to rivalry between the boy and his siblings, or to his inferiority complex and compensatory strivings. The Rogerian might think about self-realization, growth crises, and problems with the ego ideal, and an Erikson disciple might entertain hypotheses about identity crises and autonomy. . . . A behaviorist would abstain from all speculations about the psychodynamic meanings of the problem behaviors. Instead, he would define the observable behavioral referents of the described problems and seek to assess the stimulus conditions that seem to affect and maintain them in the child's current life.
>
> For each "school" of personality there is a different orientation and focus. The hypotheses and expectations of the investigator are not merely private views: they affect not only what he looks for but also what he finds, both in research and in psychotherapy. (Mischel, 1968, p. 3)

The account with which this book began, that of the policeman with drinking and marital problems, allowed no opportunity to find out why he was behaving as he was. We did not learn more about him by any of the means commonly available to clinicians—interviews, tests, and a variety of other procedures for assessing behavior. Though sometimes given different names, such as "the psychiatric interview" or "psychologicals," all clinical assessment procedures are more or less formal ways of finding out what is wrong with a person, what may have caused a problem or problems, and what steps may be taken to improve the individual's condition. Some of these procedures are also used to evaluate the effects of therapeutic interventions.

In this chapter, we exam both biological and psychological assessment techniques and then conclude with a look at an important issue that affects all assessment, that is, the question of whether, in the long run, behavior is consistent or variable. We also discuss a sometimes neglected aspect of assessment, the role of cultural diversity and clinician bias.

Throughout the discussion, it will be clear that reliability and validity, two concepts first addressed in the discussion of diagnosis in Chapter 3, play a key role in assessment as well. Thus, we begin the chapter with a brief overview of these two concepts.

Reliability and Validity in Assessment

The issues of reliability and validity are extremely complex; there are several kinds of each, and an entire subfield of psychology—psychometrics—exists primarily for their study. We provide here a brief and general overview that should be sufficient for critically examining the wide diversity of clinical assessment procedures.

In the most general sense, **reliability** refers to consistency of measurement. **Interrater reliability**, discussed in the preceding chapter, refers to the degree to which two independent observers or judges agree. To take an example from baseball, the third-base umpire may or may not agree with the home-

Reliability is an essential property of all assessment procedures. One means of determining reliability is to find if different judges agree, as happens when two umpires witness the same event in a baseball game.

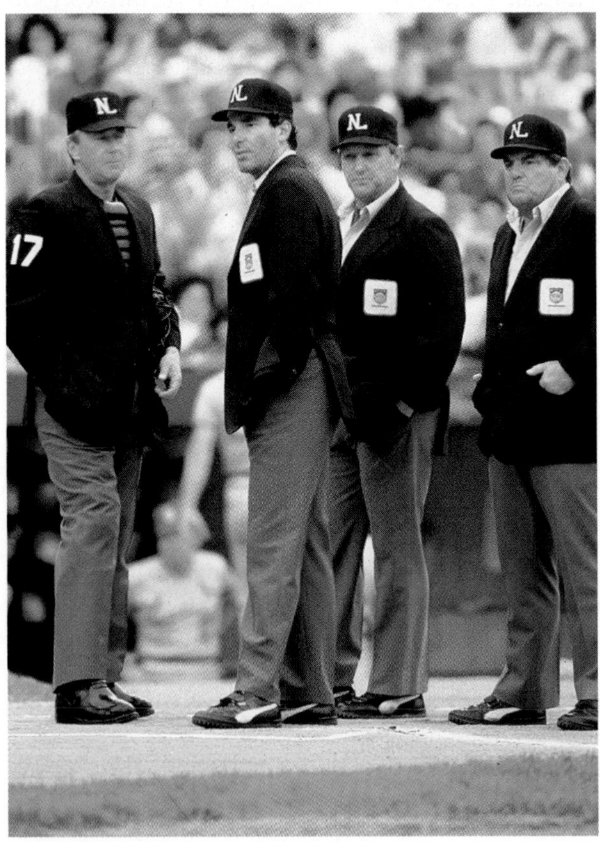

plate umpire as to whether a line drive down the left field line is fair or foul. **Test-retest reliability** measures the extent to which people being observed twice or taking the same test twice, perhaps several weeks or months apart, score in generally the same way. This kind of reliability makes sense, of course, only when our theory assumes that people will not change appreciably between testings on the variable being measured. A prime example is an intelligence test (see p. 91). Sometimes psychologists use two forms of the same test rather than give the same test twice, perhaps when there is concern that people will remember their answers from the first test-taking and merely try to be consistent. This situation enables the tester to determine **alternate-form reliability**. Finally, **split-half reliability** can be computed from a single administration of a test. The test is divided into two halves, and the two sections are regarded essentially as responses from separate assessment sessions. Of course, steps have to be taken to ensure that the items on each half are comparable. If, for example, items in an achievement test become progressively more difficult from begining to end, it would not make sense to compare the first part with the second part of the test; rather, even-numbered items versus odd might provide a more reasonable basis for comparison.

In each of the types of reliability described, a **correlation**, a measure of how closely two variables are related (see page 116), is calculated between raters or sets of items. The higher the correlation, the better the reliability. This is so because the larger the measurement error, the smaller the correlation.

We turn now to **validity**, the extent to which an assessment procedure is measuring what we intend it to measure. For example, does a paper-and-pencil questionnaire believed to measure anxiety really do so? **Concurrent** (sometimes also called **descriptive**) **validity** concerns the extent to which scores on an assessment instrument correlate with another measure of a psychological feature that has been assessed at approximately the same point in time. An example would be whether the score on our anxiety questionnaire identifies people who have been designated as being highly anxious when observed interacting with others in a laboratory situation. **Predictive validity** is similar to concurrent, except that the measure with which it is to be compared is not available until some time in the future. For example, does our anxiety questionnaire administered at the beginning of a college semester predict who will do poorly on final exams?

Finally, perhaps the most subtle and interesting form of validity is **construct validity**, which subsumes concurrent and predictive validity. This kind of validity refers to the place of our anxiety questionnaire within a theoretical framework and can be understood only in the context of that framework. For example, suppose that our hypothesis is that highly anxious college students will do poorly only on those final examinations that are in fields related to the occupations of their fathers or mothers, and that the reason for this expectation is our belief that children are especially worried about disappointing their parents by not doing well in something in which the parent is expert. The assessment of construct validity here might involve separating students' grades in courses that do and that do not relate to their respective parents' work, and then looking to see if the negative correlations are higher between anxiety and grades on the target courses than on courses unrelated to the parents' occupations. We can readily see that the analyses performed depend on what our theory tells us to look for. If the pattern of relationships that emerges is generally what the theory predicts, then we have not only provided construct validation for the questionnaire but also support for the underlying theory. Thus, construct validation is an important part of theory testing and is understandable only within the context of a theory.

Most of the assessment techniques that follow have acceptable reliability, but their validities are sometimes wanting.

Biological Assessment

For many years, researchers and clinicians have attempted to observe directly or make inferences about the functioning of the brain and other parts of the nervous system in their efforts to understand both normal and abnormal psychological functioning. (See Focus Box 4.1) Recall from Chapters 2 and 3 that throughout history people interested in psychopathology have assumed, quite reasonably, that some malfunctions of the psyche are likely to be due to, or at least reflected in, malfunctions of the soma. We turn now to contemporary work in biological assessment.

"Seeing" the Brain

As many behavioral problems can be brought on by brain abnormalities, neurological tests such as checking the reflexes, examining the retina for any indication of blood vessel damage, and evaluating

FOCUS

Focus 4.1 • Structure and Function of the Human Brain

The brain is located within the protective coating of the skull and is enveloped with three layers of nonneural tissue, membranes referred to as **meninges**. The three membranes are the outer, tough, dura mater, the intermediate, weblike arachnoid, and the inner, soft pia mater. Viewed from the top, the brain is divided by a midline fissure into two mirror-image **cerebral hemispheres**; together they constitute most of the cerebrum. The major connection between the two hemispheres is a band of nerve fibers called the **corpus callosum**. Figure 4.a shows the surface of one of the cerebral hemispheres. The upper, side, and some of the lower surfaces of the hemispheres constitute the **cerebral cortex**. The cortex consists of six layers of tightly packed neuron cell bodies with many short, unsheathed interconnecting processes. These neurons, estimated to be 10 to 15 billion in number, make up a thin outer covering, the so-called gray matter of the brain. The cortex is vastly convoluted; the ridges are called **gyri** and the depressions between them **sulci** or fissures. Deep fissures divide the cerebral hemispheres into several distinct areas, called lobes. The **frontal lobe** lies in front of the central sulcus; the **parietal lobe** is behind it and above the lateral sulcus; the **temporal lobe** is located below the lateral sulcus; and the **occipital lobe** lies behind the parietal and temporal lobes. Different functions tend to be localized in particular areas of the lobes—vision in the occipital; discrimination of sounds in the temporal; reasoning and other higher mental processes, plus the regulation of fine voluntary movement, in the frontal; initiation of movements of the skeletal musculature in a band in front of the central sulcus; in a brand behind this sulcus, receipt of sensations of touch, pressure, pain, temperature, and body position from skin, muscles, tendons, and joints.

The two hemispheres of the brain have different functions. The left hemisphere, which generally controls the right half of the body by a crossing over of motor and sensory fibers, is usually dominant; it is responsible for speech and, according to some neuropsychologists, for analytical thinking in right-handed people and in a fair number of left-handed people as well. The right hemisphere controls the left side of the body, discerns spatial relations and patterns, and is involved in emotion and intuition. But analytical thinking cannot be located exclusively in the left hemisphere or intuitive and even creative thinking in the right; the two hemispheres communicate with each other constantly via the corpus callosum. Localization of apparently different modes of thought is probably not as clear-cut as some would have us believe.

If the brain is sliced in half, separating the two cerebral hemispheres (Figure 4.b), additional important features can be seen. The gray matter of the cerebral cortex does not extend throughout the interior of the brain. Much of the interior is **white matter** and is made up of large tracts or bundles of myelinated (sheathed) fibers that connect cell bodies in the cortex with those in the spinal cord and in other centers lower in the brain. These centers are additional pockets of gray matter, referred to as *nuclei*. The nuclei serve both as way stations, connecting tracts from the cortex with other ascending and descending tracts, and as integrating motor and sensory control centers. Some cortical cells project their long fibers or axons to motor neurons in the spinal cord, but others project them only as far as these clusters of interconnecting neuron cell bodies. Four masses are deep within each hemisphere, called collectively the basal ganglia. Deep within the brain too

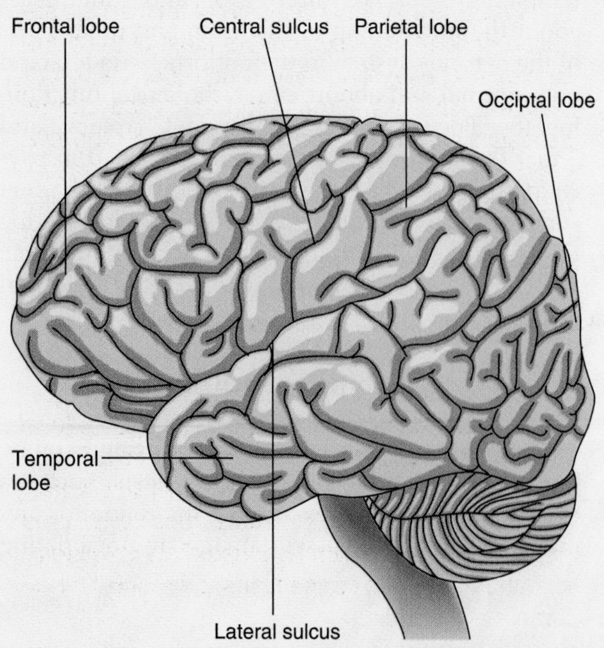

FIGURE 4.a (left) Surface of the left cerebral hemisphere, indicating the lobes and the two principal fissures of the cortex.

FIGURE 4.b (right) Slice of brain through the medial plane, showing the internal structures.

are cavities, called *ventricles*, which are continuous with the central canal of the spinal cord and which are filled with cerebrospinal fluid.

In Figure 4.b are shown four important functional areas or structures.

1. The **diencephalon**, connected in front with the hemispheres and behind with the midbrain, contains the *thalamus* and the **hypothalamus**, which consist of groups of nuclei. The thalamus is a relay station for all sensory pathways except the olfactory. The nuclei making up the thalamus receive nearly all impulses arriving from the different sensory areas of the body before passing them on to the cerebrum, where they are interpreted as conscious sensations. The hypothalamus is the highest center of integration for many visceral processes. Its nuclei regulate metabolism, temperature, water balance, sweating, blood pressure, sleeping, and appetite.
2. The **midbrain** is a mass of nerve fiber tracts connecting the cerebral cortex with the pons, the medulla oblongata, the cerebellum, and the spinal cord.
3. The **brain stem** is made up of the **pons** and **medulla oblongata** and functions primarily as a neural relay station. The pons contains tracts that connect the cerebellum with the spinal cord and the cerebellum with motor areas of the cerebrum. The medulla oblongata serves as the main line of traffic for tracts ascending from the spinal cord and descending from the higher centers of the brain. At the bottom of the medulla, many of the motor fibers cross to the opposite side. The medulla also contains nuclei that maintain the regular life rhythms of the heartbeat, of the rising and falling diaphragm, and of the constricting and dilating blood vessels. In the core of the brain stem is the *reticular formation*, sometimes called the reticular activating system because of the important role that it plays in arousal and in the maintenance of alertness. The tracts of the pons and medulla send in fibers to connect with the profusely interconnected cells of the reticular formation, which in turn send fibers to the cortex, the basal ganglia, the hypothalamus, the septal area, and the cerebellum.
4. The **cerebellum**, like the cerebrum, is made up for the most part of two deeply convoluted hemispheres with an exterior cortex of gray matter and an interior of white tracts. The cerebellum receives sensory nerves from the vestibular apparatus of the ear and from muscles, tendons, and joints. The information received and integrated relates to balance and posture and equilibrium and to the smooth coordination of the body when in motion.

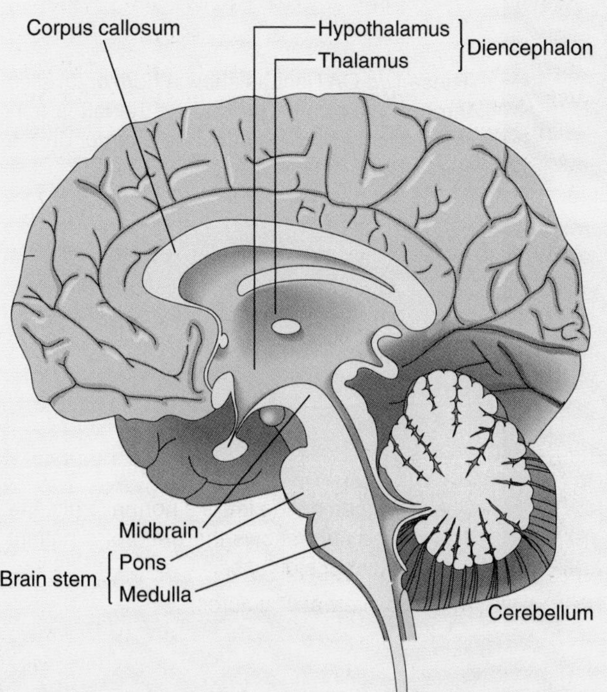

A fifth important part of the brain, not shown in Figure 4.b, is the **limbic system**, structures that are continuous with one another in the lower cerebrum, and that developed earlier than did the mammalian cerebral cortex. The limbic system controls the visceral and physical expressions of emotion—quickened heartbeat and respiration, trembling, sweating, and alterations in facial expressions—and the expression of appetitive and other primary drives—hunger, thirst, mating, defense, attack, and flight. This system is made up of cortex that is phylogenetically older than the so-called neocortex, which covers most of the hemispheres. The juxallocortex, which consists of four or five layers of neurons, surrounds the corpus callosum and the underlying thalamus. The cingulate gyrus stretching about the corpus callosum is an important structure made up of this juxallocortex. The allocortex, with only three layers of neurons, makes up the cortex of the septal area, which is anterior to the thalamus; the long, tubelike hippocampus, which stretches from the septal area into the temporal lobe; and the part of the lower temporal lobe that surrounds the under portions of the hippocampus and the amygdala (one of the basal ganglia), which is embedded in its tip. The amygdala and the septal area itself, which also consists of nuclei, are sometimes considered part of the limbic systm because of their anatomical and functional connections to its other structures.

motor coordination and perception are useful procedures in diagnosing brain dysfunction.

Computerized axial tomography, the **CAT scan**, and positron emission tomography, the **PET scan**, are recent advances in assessing brain abnormalities. In the CAT scan a moving beam of X rays passes into a horizontal cross section of the patient's brain, scanning it through 360 degrees. The moving X-ray detector on the other side measures the amount of radioactivity that penetrates; it thus detects subtle differences in tissue density. The computer uses the information to construct a two-dimensional, detailed image of the cross section, giving it optimal contrasts. Then the patient's head is moved, and the machine scans another cross section of the brain. The resulting images can show the enlargement of ventricles, which signals degeneration of tissue and the locations of tumors and blood clots.

In PET scanning, a more expensive and invasive procedure, a substance used by the brain is "labeled" with a short-lived radioactive isotope and injected into the bloodstream. The radioactive molecules of the substance emit a particle called a positron, which quickly collides with an electron. A pair of high-energy light particles shoot out from the skull in opposite directions and are detected by the scanner. The computer analyzes millions of such recordings and converts them into a motion picture of the functioning brain in horizontal cross section, projected onto a television screen. The images are in color; fuzzy spots of lighter and warmer colors are areas in which metabolic rates for the substance are higher. Moving visual images of the working brain can indicate sites of epileptic seizures, brain cancers, strokes, and trauma from head injuries, as well as the distribution of psychoactive drugs in the brain. The PET scanner is also being used to study possible abnormal biological processes underlying disorders (see Chapter 14, p. 406).

Newly developed computer-based devices for seeing into the living brain include **nuclear magnetic response imaging (NMR)** also known as MRIs, which is superior to CAT scans because it produces pictures of higher quality and does not rely on even the small amount of radiation that CAT (and PET) requires. In NMR the person is placed inside a large circular magnet that causes the hydrogen atoms in the body to move. When the magnetic force is turned off, the atoms return to their original positions and thereby produce an electromagnetic signal. These signals are then read by the computer and translated into black-and-white pictures of brain tissue. The implications of this technique are enormous. For example, it may allow us to specify the origin of different abnormalities.

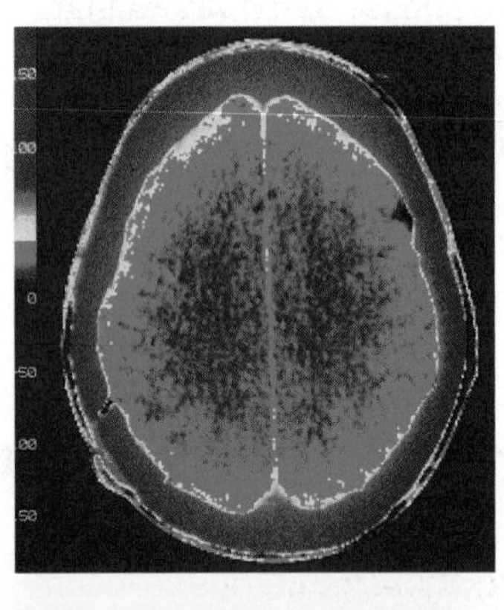

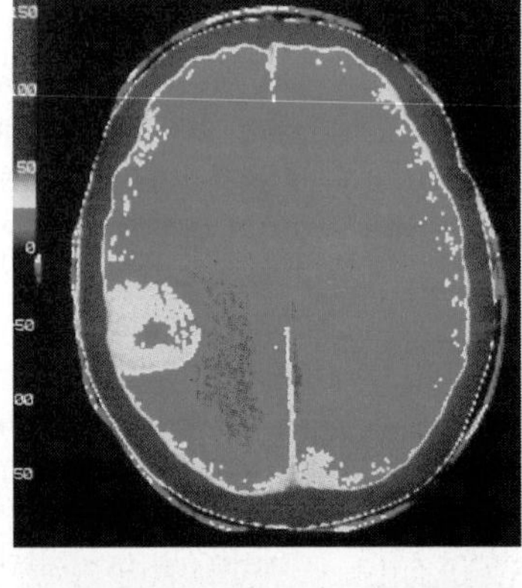

These two CAT scans show a horizontal slice through the brain. The one on the left is normal while that on the right has a tumor on the right side.

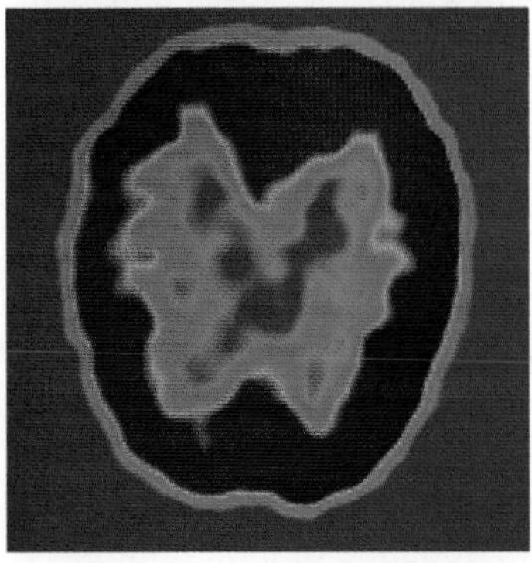

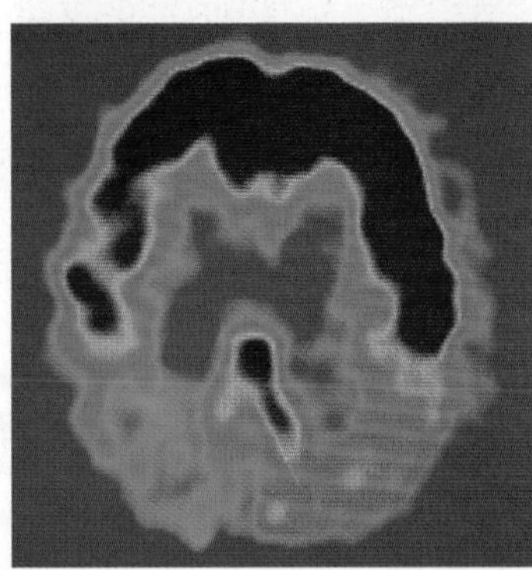

The PET scan on the left is a normal brain; the one on the right shows the brain of a patient with Alzheimer's disease.

All these tools provide startling "pictures" of internal organs and permit the gathering of information about living tissue, including the brain. Clinicians and researchers in many disciplines are currently using these techniques both to discover previously undetectable tumors and other organic problems and to conduct inquiries into the neural bases of thought, emotion, and behavior.

Neuropsychological Assessment

It is important to note here a distinction between neurologists and neuropsychologists, even though both specialists are concerned with the study of the central nervous system. A **neurologist** is a physician who specializes in medical diseases that affect the nervous system, such as muscular dystrophy or cerebral palsy. A **neuropsychologist** is a psychologist who studies how dysfunctions of the brain affect the way we think, feel, and behave. As the term implies, a neuropsychologist is trained as a psychologist and, as such, is interested in behavior, but with a focus on the way abnormalities of the brain affect behavior in deleterious ways. Both kinds of specialists contribute much to each other as they work in different ways to learn how the nervous system functions and how to ameliorate problems caused by disease or injury to the brain.

We might reasonably assume that neurologists and physicians, with the help of such procedures and technological devices, can observe the brain and its functions more or less directly and thus assess brain abnormalities. Many brain abnormalities and injuries, however, involve alterations in structure so subtle or slight in extent that they have thus far eluded direct physical examination.

Because the way in which the person functions is the problem—what he or she does, says, thinks, or feels—a number of tests assessing behavioral disturbances that are caused by organic brain dysfunctions have been developed by neuropsychologists. The literature on these tests is extensive and, as with most areas of psychology, so too, is the disagreement about them. The weight of the evidence, however, does seem to indicate that psychological tests have some validity in the assessment of brain damage, and they are often used in conjunction with the brain-scanning techniques just described. They are accordingly called **neuropsychological tests**. One of these tests is Reitan's modification of a battery or group of tests previously developed by Halstead. The concept of using a battery of tests, each tapping different functions, is critical, for only by studying a person's pattern of performance can an investigator adequately judge whether the person is brain-damaged. But the Halstead–Reitan battery can do even more than this: it can sometimes help to locate the area of the brain that has been affected. Four of the tests included in the Halsted–Reitan group are as follows:

1. **Tactile Performance Test—Time.** While blindfolded, the subject tries to fit various shaped blocks into spaces of a form board, first using the preferred hand, then the other, and finally both. The purpose is to measure the person's motor-speed response to the unfamiliar.
2. **Tactile Performance Test—Memory.** After completing the timed test, the subject is asked to draw the form board from memory, showing the blocks in their proper location. Both this and the time test are sensitive to damage in the right parietal lobe.

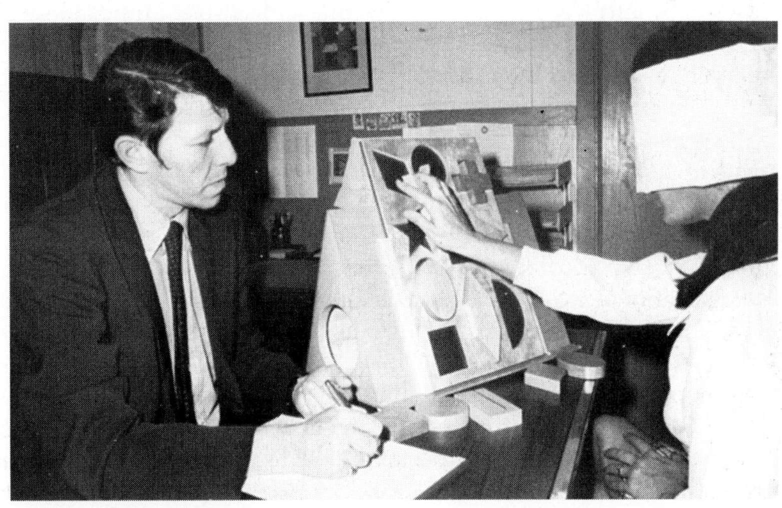

Neuropsychological tests assess various performance deficits in the hope of detecting a specific area of neural malfunction. Shown here is the tactile performance test.

3. **Category Test.** The subject, seeing an image on a screen that suggests one of the numbers between one and four, presses a button to show which number he or she thinks it is. A bell indicates that the choice is correct, a buzzer that it is incorrect. The subject must keep track of these images and signals in order to figure out the rules for making the correct choices. This test measures problem-solving, especially the ability to abstract a principle from a nonverbal array of events. Impaired performance reflects damage to either the left or right frontal lobes.
4. **Speech Sounds Perception Test.** Subjects listen to a series of nonsense words, each comprised of two consonants with a long "e" sound in the middle. They then select the "word" they heard from a set of alternatives. This test measures left-hemisphere function, especially temporal and parietal areas.

The Luria–Nebraska battery (Golden, Hammeke & Purisch, 1978), based on the work of the Russian psychologist Aleksandr Luria (1902–1977), is also in widespread use (Adams, 1980; Kane, Parsons, & Goldstein, 1985; Spiers, 1982). A battery of 269 items makes up 11 sections to determine basic and complex motor skills, rhythm and pitch abilities, tactile and kinesthetic skills, verbal and spatial skills, receptive speech ability, expressive speech ability, writing, reading, arithmetic skills, memory, and intellectual processes. The pattern of scores on these sections, as well as on the 32 items found to be the most discriminating and indicative of overall impairment, helps reveal damage to the frontal, temporal, sensorimotor, or parietal-occipital area of the right or left hemisphere.

The Luria–Nebraska battery can be administered in two and a half hours, and research demonstrates that this test can be scored in a highly reliable manner (Maruish, Sawicki, Franzen, & Golden, 1984; Moses & Schefft, 1984). The Luria–Nebraska is also believed to pick up effects of brain damage that are not (yet) detectable by neurological examination; such deficits are in the cognitive domain rather than in the sensorimotor (on which neurological assessments focus) (Moses, 1983). A particular advantage of the Luria–Nebraska tests is that one can control for educational level so that a less-educated person will not receive a lower score solely because of limited educational experience (Brickman, McManus, Grapentine, & Alessi, 1984). Finally, a children's version (Golden, 1981), for ages 8 to 12, has also been found useful in diagnosing brain damage and in evaluating the educational strengths and weaknesses of children, a very important consideration indeed (Sweet, Carr, Rossini, & Kasper, 1986).

The Children's Luria-Nebraska test is an assessment of possible brain dysfunction or damage. This child is taking a subtest.

A Cautionary Note

There is no one-to-one relationship between a score on a given neuropsychological test or a finding on a PET or CAT scan, on the one hand, and psychological dysfunction, on the other. This is especially so with chronic brain damage known or suspected to have been present for some years before the assessment is conducted. The reasons for these sometimes loose relationships have to do with such factors as how the person has, over time, reacted to and coped with the losses brought about by the brain damage. And the success of efforts to cope have, in turn, to do with the social environment in which the individual has lived—for example, how understanding parents and associates have been, how well the school system has provided for the special educational needs of the individual. Therefore, in addition to the imperfect nature of the assessment instruments themselves and our incomplete understanding of how the brain actually functions, workers must consider these experiential factors that operate over time to contribute to the clinical picture.

A final caution to neuropsychological assessors is that they must recognize the simple, yet often unappreciated, fact that in attempting to understand the neurocognitive consequences of any brain-injuring event, one must understand the abilities that the patient has brought to that event (Boll, 1985). This straightforward truth brings to mind the story of the man who, recovering from an accident that has broken all the fingers in both hands, earnestly asks the surgeon whether he will be able to play the piano when his wounds heal. "Yes, I'm sure you will," says the doctor reassuringly. "That's wonderful," exclaims the man, "because I don't even know how to play the piano *now*!"

Physiological Measurement

A number of procedures are used for assessing physiological aspects of behavior. The discipline of **psychophysiology** is concerned with the bodily changes that accompany psychological events or that are associated with a person's psychological characteristics (Grings & Dawson, 1978). For example, we know that the skin conductance of most people increases markedly under conditions of psychological stress.

Experimenters have studied such changes, as well as heart rate, tension in the muscles, blood flow in various parts of the body, and brain waves, while subjects are afraid, depressed, asleep, imagining, solving problems, and so on. Special attention has been paid to the *patterning* of such responses, as when heart rate increases while skin conductance remains constant.

The activities of the autonomic nervous system (see Focus Box 4.2) are frequently assessed by electrical and chemical measurements and analyses in attempts to understand the nature of emotion. One important measure is heart rate. Each heartbeat generates spreading changes in electrical potential, which can be recorded by an electrocardiograph or on a suitably tuned polygraph and graphically depicted in an **electrocardiogram**. Electrodes are usually placed on the chest and lead to an instrument for measuring electric currents. The deflections of this instrument may be seen as waves on an oscilloscope, or a pen recorder may register the waves on a continuously moving roll of graph paper. Both types of recordings are called electrocardiograms. Also available is the cardiotachometer, a device that measures the precise elapsed time between two heartbeats and then instantaneously provides the heart rate on a beat-to-beat basis. This technological advance is especially important for experimental psychologists, who are typically interested in bodily changes that occur over short periods of time in response to rapidly shifting circumstances. Generally a fast heart rate is taken to indicate increased arousal.

A second measure is **electrodermal responding**, or skin conductance, previously referred to as the **galvanic skin response (GSR)**. Anxiety, fear, anger, and other emotions increase sweat gland activity. The electrophysiological processes in the cells of these glands change the electric conductance of the skin as well as produce sweat. It is typically measured by determining the current that flows through the skin when a known small voltage derived from an external source is passed between two electrodes on the hand. This current also shows a pronounced increase after activation of the sweat glands. Since the sweat glands are activated by the sympathetic nervous system, increased sweat-gland activity indicates sympathetic autonomic excitation and is often taken as a measure of anxiety.

Advances in technology allow researchers to track such things as blood pressure *in vivo* as the person goes about his or her normal business. The subject wears a portable device that records blood pressure automatically every few minutes. Combined with self-reports recorded by the subject in a specially designed diary, van Egeren and Madarasmi (1987) were able to study how people's thoughts and moods co-vary with increases in blood pressure, data of great interest to psychologically oriented researchers in hypertension (see Chapter 8).

A more complete picture of the human being is obtained by assessing physiological functioning along with overt behavior and cognitive activity. If experimenters wonder whether showing schizophrenic patients pictures of their mothers is stressful, they can, in addition to asking the patients how they feel about looking at the pictures, measure their heart rate and electrodermal activity. Psychophysiological measuring procedures, which are constantly being improved, are relatively unobtrusive. Once the person has adapted to having electrodes pasted on the arm, for example, measurement of heart rate does not interfere with many experimental tasks, such as listening to a story or solving a mathematical problem.

Inasmuch as psychophysiology employs highly sophisticated electronic machinery and many psychologists aspire to be as scientific as possible, psychologists sometimes believe uncritically in these apparently objective assessment devices without appreciating their real limitations and complications. Many of the measurements, however, do not

4.2 • The Autonomic Nervous System

The mammalian nervous system can be divided into two relatively separate functional parts: the **somatic** (or voluntary) **nervous system** and the **autonomic** (or involuntary) **nervous system (ANS)**. Because the autonomic nervous system is especially important in the study of emotional behavior, it will be useful to review its principal characteristics and the ways in which its activity can be monitored.

Skeletal muscles, such as those that move our limbs, are innervated, or stimulated, by the voluntary nervous system. Much of our behavior, however, is dependent on a nervous system that operates generally without our awareness and has traditionally been viewed as beyond voluntary control, hence the term autonomic. Research on biofeedback has shown, though, that the ANS is under greater voluntary control than previously believed (see p. 577). The autonomic nervous system innervates the endocrine glands, the heart, and the smooth muscles that are found in the walls of the blood vessels, stomach, intestines, kidneys, and other organs. This nervous system is itself divided into two parts, the **sympathetic** and **parasympathetic nervous systems** (Figure 4.c), which work sometimes in opposition to each other, sometimes in unison. The sympathetic portion of the ANS, when energized, accelerates the heartbeat, dilates the pupils, inhibits intestinal activity, and initiates other smooth muscle and glandular responses that prepare the organism for sudden activity and stress. Indeed, some physiologists view the sympathetic nervous system as primarily excitatory, whereas the other division, the parasympathetic, is viewed as responsible for maintenance functions and more quiescent behavior, such as deceleration of the heartbeat, constriction of the pupils, and acceleration of intestinal contractions. Division of activities is not quite so clearcut, however, for the parasympathetic system may be active during situations of stress. Animals, and human beings, to their consternation, may urinate and defecate involuntarily when extremely frightened.

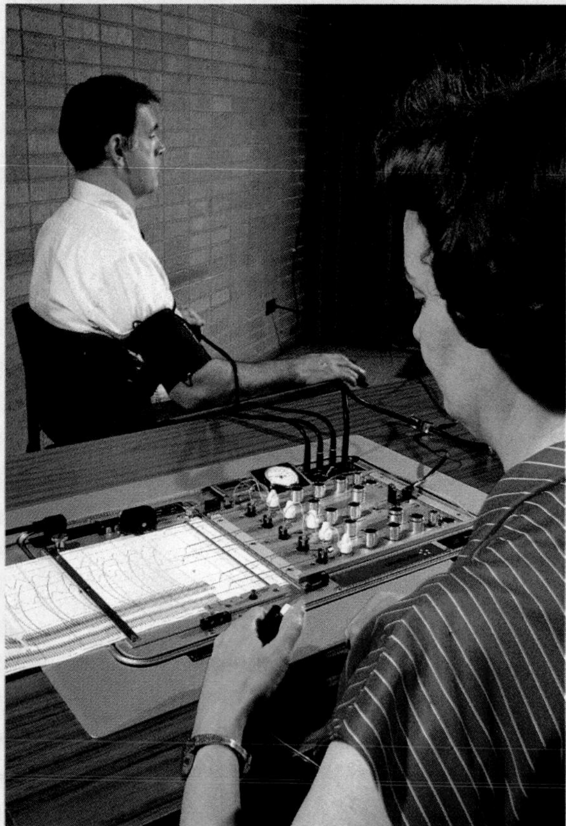

A polygraph is used to assess various features of the functioning of the automatic nervous system.

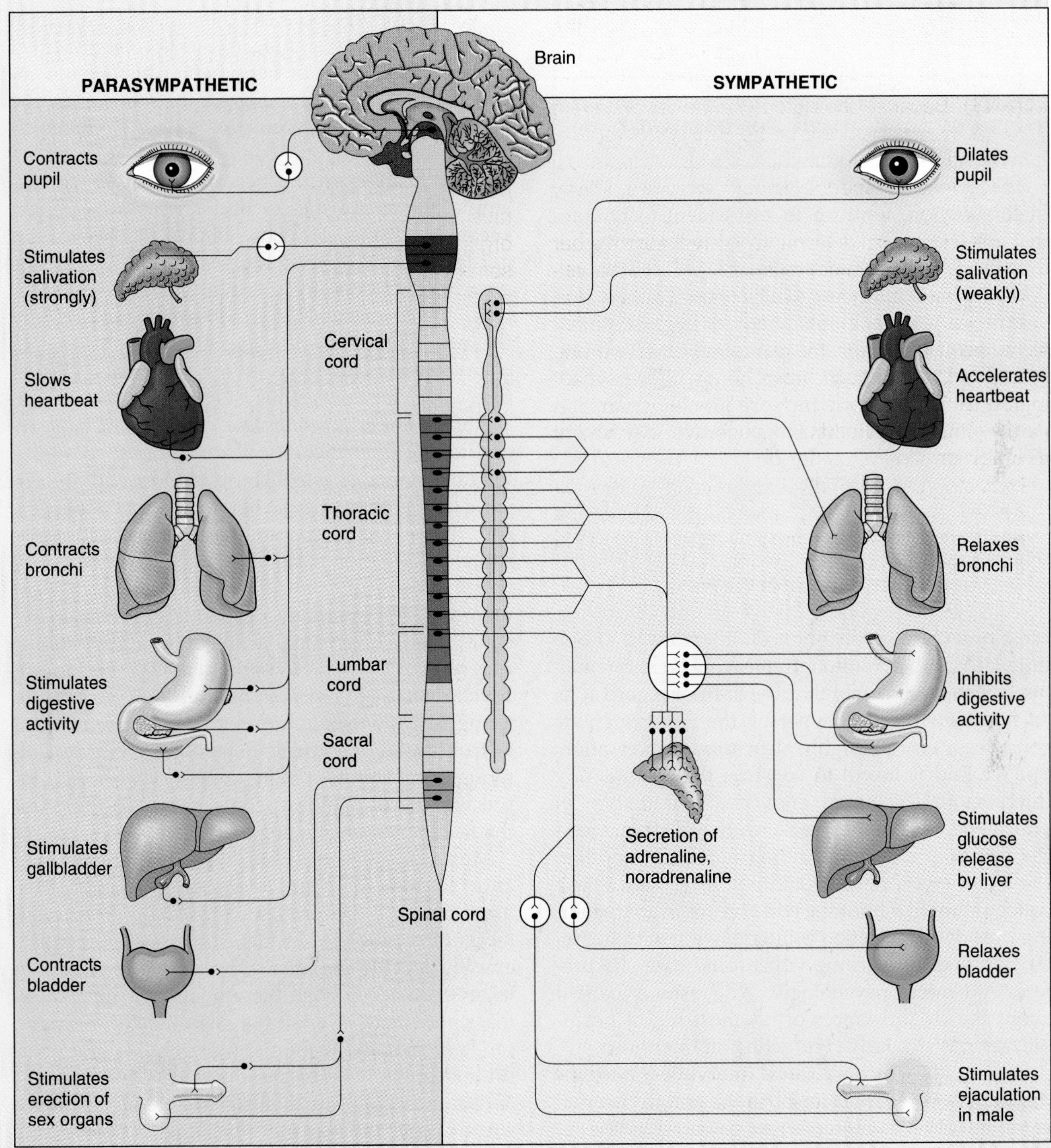
PARASYMPATHETIC
Brain
SYMPATHETIC
Contracts pupil
Stimulates salivation (strongly)
Slows heartbeat
Contracts bronchi
Stimulates digestive activity
Stimulates gallbladder
Contracts bladder
Stimulates erection of sex organs
Cervical cord
Thoracic cord
Lumbar cord
Sacral cord
Spinal cord
Dilates pupil
Stimulates salivation (weakly)
Accelerates heartbeat
Relaxes bronchi
Inhibits digestive activity
Secretion of adrenaline, noradrenaline
Stimulates glucose release by liver
Relaxes bladder
Stimulates ejaculation in male

Figure 4.c The autonomic nervous system

differentiate clearly among emotional states. Blood pressure, for example, increases with a variety of emotions, not just with anxiety. Special care must also be taken to ensure a proper setting for taking measurements so that the data collected are meaningful.

Psychological Assessment

In this section, we turn to assessment techniques that are designed to determine psychological, rather than biological, malfunctioning. We will see that beyond the basic interview, which is used almost universally in various guises, many of the assessment techniques stem from the paradigms that we discussed in Chapter 2. Included here will be psychological tests, many of which are psychodynamic in nature, and behavioral and cognitive assessment techniques.

Clinical Interviews

Most of us have probably been interviewed at one time or another, although the conversation may have been so informal that we did not regard it as an interview. To the layperson the word *interview* connotes a formal, highly structured conversation, but we find it useful to construe the term as any interpersonal encounter, conversational in style, in which one person, the interviewer, uses language as the principal means of finding out about another, the interviewee. Thus a Gallup pollster who asks a college student whom she will vote for in an upcoming presidential election is interviewing with the restricted goal of learning which candidate she prefers. A clinical psychologist who asks a patient about the circumstances of his most recent hospitalization is similarly conducting an interview.

One way in which a **clinical interview** is perhaps different from a casual conversation and from a poll is the attention the interviewer pays to *how* the respondent answers questions—or does not answer them. For example, if a client is recounting her marital conflicts, the clinician will generally be attentive to any emotion accompanying her comments. If the woman does not seem upset about a difficult situation, her answers will probably be interpreted differently than if she were to cry while relating her story.

The paradigm within which an interviewer operates influences the type of information sought and obtained. A psychoanalytically trained clinician can be expected to inquire about the person's childhood history. He or she is also likely to remain skeptical of verbal reports because the analytic paradigm holds that the most significant aspects of a disturbed or normal person's developmental history are repressed into the unconscious. By the same token, the behaviorally oriented clinician is likely to focus on current environmental conditions that can be related to changes in the person's behavior, for example, the circumstances under which the person becomes anxious. Thus the clinical interview does not follow a prescribed course, but varies with the paradigm adopted by the interviewer. Like scientists, clinical interviewers in some measure find only the information that they look for.

Great skill is necessary to carry out good clinical interviews, for they are conducted with people who are often under considerable stress. Clinicians, regardless of their theoretical orientations, recognize the importance of establishing rapport with the client. The interviewer must obtain the trust of the person; it is naive to assume that a client will easily reveal information to another, even to an authority figure with the title "Dr." Furthermore, even a client who sincerely, perhaps desperately, wants to recount intensely personal problems to a professional may not be able to do so without assistance. Indeed, psychodynamic clinicians assume that people entering therapy usually are not even aware of what is truly bothering them. Behavioral clinicians, although concentrating more on observables, also appreciate the difficulties people have in sorting out the factors responsible for their distress.

Most clinicians empathize with their clients in an effort to draw them out, to encourage them to elaborate on their concerns, and to examine different facets of a problem. In fact, humanistic therapists employ specific empathy techniques (see page 539) in order to accomplish these goals. A simple summary statement of what the client has been saying can help sustain the momentum of talk about painful and possibly embarrassing events and feelings, and an accepting attitude toward personal disclosures dispels the fear that revealing terrible secrets to another human being will have disastrous consequences.

The interview can be a source of considerable information to the clinician; its importance in abnormal psychology and psychiatry is unquestionable. Whether the information gleaned can always be depended on is not so clear, however. Clinicians often tend to overlook *situational* factors of the interview that may exert strong influences on what the patient says or does. Consider, for a moment, how a teenager is likely to resond to the question, "How often have you used illegal drugs?" when it is asked by a young, informally dressed psychologist and again when it is asked by a sixty-year-old psychologist in a business suit.

Interviews vary in the degree to which they are structured. In practice, most clinicians probably operate from only the vaguest outlines. Exactly *how* information is collected is left largely up to the particular interviewer. Through years of clinical experience and both teaching and learning from students and colleagues, each clinician develops ways of asking questions with which he or she is comfortable and that seem to extract the information that will be of maximum benefit to the client. Thus, to the extent that an interview is unstructured, the interviewer must rely on intuition and general experience. As a consequence, reliability for clinical interviews is probably low. And because the overwhelming majority of clinical interviews are conducted within confidential relationships, it is not possible to establish their validity.

However, we must look at the broader picture here to avoid a judgment that may be too harsh. Both reliability and validity may indeed be low for a single clinical interview that is conducted in an unstructured fashion. But clinicians usually do more than one interview with a given patient, and hence a self-corrective process is probably at work. To wit, the clinician may regard as valid what a patient said in the first interview, but then at the sixth may recognize it to have been incorrect or only partially correct.

At times mental health professionals need to collect standardized information, particularly for making diagnostic judgments on operational criteria. To meet that need, investigators have developed structured interviews, such as the Schedule for Affective Disorders and Schizophrenia (Spitzer & Endicott, 1978), which was devised to provide a standard set of questions to elicit the information needed for DSM-III diagnoses. The Structured Clinical Interview for DSM-IIIR (SCID) (Spitzer & Williams, 1985) was later used by many because its questions allowed the best fit to revised diagnostic criteria. The SCID is a branching interview (the client's resonse determines the next question), with detailed instructions to the interviewer concerning when to probe in detail and when to go on to questions about another diagnosis. Most symptoms are rated on a three-point scale of severity with instructions in the interview schedule for directly translating the symptom ratings into diagnoses. The initial questions pertaining to obsessive-compulsive disorder (discussed in Chapter 6) are presented in Figure 4.1. The interviewer begins by asking about obsessions. If the responses elicit a rating of 1 (absent), the interviewer turns to questions about compulsions. If the patient's responses again elicit a rating of 1, the interviewer is instructed to go to the question for generalized anxiety disorder. On the other hand, if positive responses are elicited, the interviewer continues with further questions about obsessive-compulsive disorder. Like its predecessor, the Schedule for Affective Disorders and Schizophrenia (Spitzer & Endicott, 1978), the SCID is an important tool for collecting information to make diagnoses. Indeed, the use of structured interviews is clearly a major factor in the improvement of diagnostic reliability that we described in Chapter 3. We can expect newer structured diagnostic interviews to reflect the changes in DSM-IV.

Psychological Tests

Psychological tests are standardized procedures designed to measure a subject's performance on a particular task or to assess his or her personality. These tests structure still further the process of assessment. The same test is administered to many people at different times, and the responses collected are analyzed to indicate how certain kinds of people tend to respond. Statistical norms for the test can thereby be established as soon as the data collected are extensive enough. This process is called **standardization**. The responses of a particular patient can then be compared with the statistical norms. We will examine the three basic types of psychological tests: projective personality tests, self-report personality inventories, and tests of intelligence.

Projective Personality Tests

A **projective test** is a psychological assessment device in which a set of standard stimuli, ambiguous enough to allow variation in responses, is presented to the individual. The assumption here is that because the stimulus materials are unstructured, the patient's responses will be determined primarily by unconscious processes and will reveal his or her true attitudes, motivations, and modes of behavior; this is referred to as the **projective hypothesis**. This technique is clearly out of the psychoanalytic mold. The **Rorschach Inkblot Test** and the **Thematic Apperception Test** are perhaps the best known projective techniques. In the Rorschach test the subject is

Figure 4.1 Sample item from the SCID

Obsessive-Compulsive Disorder Criteria	Rating Scale	*Interview*
Obsessions:		
(1) Recurrent, persistent ideas, thoughts, impulses, or images that are experienced as intrusive, unwanted, and senseless or repugnant (at least initially).	? 1 2 3	I would like to ask you if you have ever been bothered by thoughts that kept coming back to you even when you tried not to have them?
(2) The individual attempts to ignore or suppress them or to neutralize them with some other thought or action.	? 1 2 3	IF YES: DISTINGUISH FROM BROODING ABOUT PROBLEMS (SUCH AS HAVING A PANIC ATTACK) OR ANXIOUS RUMINATION ABOUT REALISTIC DANGERS: What were they?
(3) The individual recognizes that they are the product of his or her own mind and not imposed from without (as in thought insertion).	? 1 2 3 1 → GO TO COMPULSIONS 3 → DESCRIBE OBSESSIONS	(What about awful thoughts, or thoughts that didn't make any sense to you—like actually hurting someone even though you didn't want to, or being contaminated by germs or dirt?)
Compulsions:		
(1) Repetitive, purposeful and intentional behavior that is performed according to certain rules or in a stereotyped fashion.	? 1 2 3	Was there anything that you had to do over and over again and couldn't resist doing, like washing your hands again and again, or checking something several times to make sure you'd done it right?
(2) The behavior is not an end in itself, but is designed to neutralize or prevent extreme discomfort or some dreaded event or situation. However, either the activity is not connected in a realistic way with what it is designed to neutralize or prevent or it is clearly excessive.	? 1 2 3 1 → GO TO GENERAL ANXIETY DISORDERS SECTION 3 → DESCRIBE COMPULSIONS	IF YES: What did you have to do? (What were you afraid would happen if you didn't do it?) (How many times did you have to ____? How much time did you spend each day ____?)
	Key to rating scale ? = Inadequate information 1 = Absent or false 2 = Subthreshold 3 = Threshold or true	

Source: Reprinted by permission of New York State Psychiatric Institute Biometrics Research Division.

During a ride in the country with his two children, Hermann Rorschach (1884–1922), Swiss psychiatrist, noticed that what they saw in the clouds reflected their personalities. From this observation came the famous inkblot test.

shown ten inkblots, one at a time, and asked to tell what figures or objects he or she sees in each of them. Half the inkblots are in black, white, and shades of gray, two add red splotches, and three are in pastel colors. If a patient reports seeing eyes on the Rorschach, for example, the projective hypothesis might be that the patient is experiencing paranoia.

In the Thematic Apperception Test (TAT), the examinee is shown a series of black-and-white pictures one by one and asked to tell a story related to each. For example, if a patient, seeing a picture of a prepubescent girl looking at nattily attired mannequins in a store window, tells a story that contains angry references to the girl's parents, the clinician may, through the projective hypothesis, infer that the patient harbors resentment toward his or her mother and father.

The assumption for clinicians using projective tests is that the respondent would be either unable or unwilling to express his or her true feelings if asked directly. Psychoanalytically oriented clinicians tend to favor such tests, a tendency that is consistent with the psychoanalytic assumption that people defend against unpleasant thoughts and feelings by repressing them into the unconscious. In order to bypass the defense mechanism of repression (see page 37) and get to the basic causes of distress, the real purposes of a test are best left unclear. Indeed, this has to be the case, for psychoanalytic theory asserts that the factors of greatest importance are unconscious.

In the Rorschach test, the client is shown a series of inkblots and is asked what he or she sees in each of them.

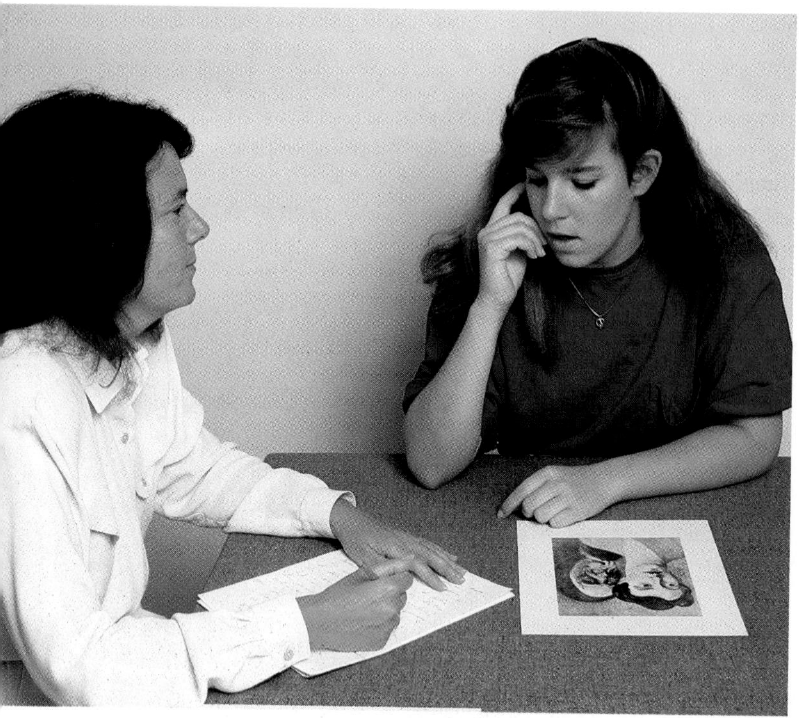

A client relates a story in response to one of the cards from the Thematic Apperception Test. Like the Rorschach, this projective test is designed to reveal unconscious conflicts and concerns.

The use of the projective hypothesis is not limited to formal tests such as these. A psychoanalytically oriented colleague of ours uses it to form hypotheses about the client during the very first meeting. He sees clients in an office that contains a wide variety and large number of places to sit. When he brings a person into this office for the first time, he makes it a point not to tell the client where to sit. The therapist's belief is that he can learn something useful about the new client from the choice of seating. Being less psychoanalytic in approach, we rejected this tactic outright—until one day one of us had a new client who entered the office and, before being shown where to sit, strode resolutely to the author's desk chair! As it turned out, this person was highly resistant to being in therapy and made continual efforts to dominate and control the early sessions.

The preceding discussion of projective tests reflects how they were conceptualized and used originally, that is, as a stimulus to fantasy that was assumed to bypass ego defenses. The person's responses were viewed as *symbolic* of internal dynamics, for example, judging a man to have homosexual interests on the basis of his seeing buttocks in the Rorschach inkblots (Chapman & Chapman, 1969). Other use of the Rorschach concentrates more on the *form* of the person's responses (Exner, 1978). The test is considered more as a perceptual-cognitive task, and the person's responses now are viewed as a sample of how they perceptually and cognitively organize real-life situations (Exner, 1986). For example, Erdberg and Exner (1984) conclude from the literature that respondents who express a great deal of human movement in their Rorschach responses tend to use inner resources when coping with their needs, whereas those whose Rorschach responses can be characterized as involving color are more likely to seek interaction with the environment. Rorschach himself suggested this approach in his original manual, *Psychodiagnostics: A Diagnostic Test Based on Perception* (1921), but he died only eight months after publishing his ten inkblots, and his immediate followers devised other methods of interpreting the test.

Though many, perhaps most, clinical practitioners still rely on the projective hypothesis in analyzing Rorschach responses, Exner's work is increasingly recognized as having adequate psychometric properties—at least with respect to reliability of scoring—and is attracting a good deal of favorable attention from academic researchers (Shontz & Green, 1992).

In the sixth edition of her classic book on psychological testing, Anastasi's (1990) overall evaluation of projective tests, including the Rorschach, TAT, and other devices, reveals several advantages and disadvantages (far more of the latter than of the former):

1. **Establishing rapport.** Because they are intrinsically interesting, even entertaining, projective tests can be useful for breaking the ice.
2. **Faking.** Because the purposes of these instruments are not obvious and because most clients cannot tell what kinds of answers would present them in a positive versus a negative light, it might seem at first blush that they are less susceptible to faking. This may be true to some extent, but research suggests that people can alter their Rorschach responses so as to create a more favorable impression (Masling, 1960). Other projective tests have also been shown to be vulnerable to such deliberate efforts at self-presentation.
3. **Examiner and situational variables.** The basic assumption of these tests downplays the role of situational variables—it is assumed that unconscious needs and fears are more powerful than such factors as the personality of the tester or the relationship between examiner and examinee. Research suggests, however, that "warm"

versus "cold" examiners obtain different Rorschach responses (Masling, 1960). Such findings sensitize us to the role of situational factors and imply some limits on the basic projective hypothesis. Furthermore, the scoring of these tests is so complex and inferential that it may not be possible to compare the test results from different examiners. The "implication is that interpretation of scores is often as projective for the examiner as the test stimuli are for the examinee" (p. 614). That is, the examiner's interpretation of the projective responses may, in fact, tell us more about the examinee's theoretical perspective, hypotheses, and personal preferences than it does about the examinee's personality.

4. **Norms.** Unlike the personality inventories and intelligence tests described next, norms for projective tests are virtually nonexistent, though Exner (1986) and his associates have been trying to correct that deficiency for the Rorschach. In the absence of norms, the clinician must rely on his or her clinical experience, with all the potential errors arising from bias and memory distortion associated with this frame of reference.
5. **Reliability.** Reliabilities with certain scoring systems for the Rorschach and the TAT range from acceptable to poor.
6. **Validity.** The news here is even more negative, which should come as no surprise given that low reliability sets limits on validity. Most efforts at validation are too flawed methodologically to allow sound conclusions. In some studies, for example, the examiner had available other information about the respondent that could have facilitated a diagnosis—a judgment that was to have been made on the basis of test responses alone. Other research suggests that people are subject to prior stereotypes, as in the aforementioned study by Chapman and Chapman (1969). Additional challenges to validity come from research showing that productivity, or sheer number of verbal responses given by a subject, a parameter given major diagnostic significance by some Rorschach users, has been found to be correlated with age, educational level, and intellectual level and also to vary among examiners (e.g., Lostof, 1953; Masling, 1960). Such findings suggest that response productivity, which may itself be a major determinant of many of the common Rorschach scores, is influenced by factors extraneous to the personality variables assumed to be measured by the Rorschach.

In light of the limited evidence on the validity of many of these instruments, why does their use continue in clinical settings? Anastasi makes the following suggestion:

> The effectively functioning clinical psychologist engages in a continuing sequence of hypothesis generation and hypothesis testing about the individual case. Each item of information—whether it be an event recorded in the case history, a comment by the client, or a test score—suggests a hypothesis . . . that will either be confirmed or refuted as other facts are gathered. Such hypotheses themselves indicate the direction of further lines of inquiry. It should be borne in mind that even highly reliable tests with well-established validity do not yield sufficiently precise results for individual diagnosis. Hence, it is understandable that clinicians as a group tend to be more receptive than other psychologists to psychometrically crude instruments, which may nevertheless provide a rich harvest of leads for further exploration. (1990, p. 480)

We see here the heuristic role that test scores can play, that is, these scores can generate ideas for the clinician or investigator. Important as well in what Anastasi says is that psychometric data, based on the analysis of group trends, fall short of enabling clinicians to make unequivocal statements about an individual case. Of course, the down-side risk is that the use of poorly validated assessment instruments can lead the clinician into dead ends or to repeated errors within the constraints of a given paradigm.

Personality Inventories

In a **personality inventory**, an examinee is asked to complete a self-report questionnaire indicating whether statements assessing habitual tendencies apply to him or her. Typically, these inventories meet the general requirements of test construction and standardization. It is therefore rare for a personality inventory to lack reliability. Validity, however, still presents a problem, especially if the personality inventory has been designed to reveal unconscious conflicts and the like. Some personality inventories have been constructed with more specific purposes in mind. Perhaps the best known of these is the **Minnesota Multiphasic Personality Inventory (MMPI)**, which was developed in the early 1940s by Hathaway and McKinley (1943) and was revised in 1989 (Butcher et al., 1989). It is intended to be an inexpensive means of detecting psychopathology and is called multiphasic because it was designed to detect a number of psychiatric problems. Over the years, the MMPI has been widely used to screen large groups of people for whom clinical interviews are not feasible.

In developing the test, the investigators relied on factual information. First, many clinicians provided statements that they considered indicative of various mental problems. Second, these items were rated as self-descriptive or not by patients already diagnosed as having particular disorders and by a large group of individuals considered normal. Items that served to discriminate among the patients were retained: that is, items were selected if patients in one clinical group responded to them more often in a certain way than did those in other groups. With additional refinements, sets of these items were established as scales for determining whether or not a respondent should be diagnosed in a particular way. If the individual answered a large number of the items in a scale in the same way as had a certain diagnostic group, his or her behavior was expected to resemble that of the particular diagnostic group. The scales of the instrument, in fact, related reasonably well to psychiatric diagnoses, although the original MMPI began to relate less well as the psychiatric classification system changed in DSM; for example, Winters, Weintraub, and Neale (1981) found that the MMPI did very poorly in predicting the DSM-III diagnosis of schizophrenia.

The revised MMPI-2 (Butcher et al., 1989) has several noteworthy changes designed to improve its validity and acceptability. The original sample fifty years ago lacked representation of racial minorities such as African-Americans and Native Americans, restricting its standardization sample to white men and women, essentially rural Minnesotans. The new version was standardized with a much larger sample that is more similar to 1980 U.S. census figures. A number of items containing allusions to sexual adjustment, bowel and bladder functions, and excessive religiosity have been removed because they were judged in some testing contexts to be needlessly intrusive and objectionable. Sexist wording has been eliminated along with outmoded idioms. Several new items have been added that deal with substance abuse, Type A behavior (see page 206), eating disorders, and interpersonal relationships. MMPI-2 is otherwise quite similar to the original, having the same format, yielding the same scale scores and profiles (Ben-Porath & Butcher, 1989; Graham, 1988), and in general providing continuity with the vast literature already existing on the original MMPI (Graham, 1990). Early research on the new instrument demonstrates good test-retest and split-half reliability (Butcher et al., 1989) and also suggests adequate concurrent validity with criteria such as behavioral ratings by spouses and symptom ratings by psychiatrists and psychologists (Graham, 1988). Items similar to those on the various scales are presented in Table 4.1.

There are several commercial MMPI computerized services that score the test and provide narratives about the respondent. Of course the validity and usefulness of the printout is only as good as the program, which in turn is only as good as the competency and experience of the psychologist who wrote it. Figure 4.2 shows a hypothetical profile. These profiles can be used in conjunction with a therapist's evaluation to help diagnose a client.

We may well wonder whether answers that would designate the subject as normal might not be easy to fake. A superficial knowledge of contemporary abnormal psychology would alert even a seriously disturbed person to the fact that, in order to be regarded as normal, he or she must not admit to worrying a great deal about germs on doorknobs. In fact, there is evidence that these tests *can* be "psyched out." In most testing circumstances, however, people do not *want* to falsify their responses, for they want to be helped. Moreover, the test designers have included as part of the MMPI several so-called validity scales designed to detect deliberately faked responses (see Table 4.1). In one of these, the lie scale, a series of statements sets a trap for the person who is trying to look too good. An item on the lie scale might, say, "I read the newspaper editorials every night." The assumption is that few people would be able to endorse such a statement honestly. Thus persons who endorse a large number of the statements in the lie scale might well be attempting to present themselves in a particularly good light. Their scores on other scales are usually viewed with more than the usual skepticism.

Intelligence Tests

Alfred Binet, a French psychologist, originally constructed mental tests to help the Parisian school board predict which children were in need of special schooling. Intelligence testing has since developed into one of the largest psychological industries. An **intelligence test**, sometimes referred to as an **aptitude test**, is a standardized means of assessing a person's current mental ability. The Scholastic Aptitude Test, the Graduate Record Examination, and individually administered tests such as the Wechs-

Table 4.1 • Typical Clinical Interpretations of Items Similar to Those on the MMPI-2.

Scale[a]	*Sample Item*	*Interpretation*
? (cannot say)	This is merely the number of items left unanswered or marked both true and false.	A high score indicates evasiveness, reading difficulties, or other problems that could invalidate the results of the test. A very high score could also suggest severe depression or obsessional tendencies.
L (Lie)	I approve of every person I meet. (True)	Person is trying to look good, to present self as someone with an ideal personality.
F (Infrequency)	Everything tastes sweet. (True)	Person is trying to look abnormal, perhaps to ensure getting special attention from the clinician.
K (Correction)	Things couldn't be going any better for me. (True)	Person is guarded, defensive in taking the test, wishes to avoid appearing incompetent or poorly adjusted.
1. Hs (Hypochondriasis)	I am seldom aware of tingling feelings in my body. (False)	Person is overly sensitive to and concerned about bodily sensations as signs of possible physical illness.
2. D (Depression)	Life usually feels worthwhile to me. (False)	Person is discouraged, pessimistic, sad, self-deprecating, feeling inadequate.
3. Hy (Hysteria)	My muscles often twitch for no apparent reason. (True)	Person has somatic complaints unlikely to be due to physical problems; also tends to be demanding and histrionic.
4. Pd (Psychopathy)	I don't care about what people think of me. (True)	Person expresses little concern for social mores, is irresponsible, has only superficial relationships.
5. Mf (Masculinity–Femininity)	I like taking care of plants and flowers. (True, female)	Person shows traditional gender characteristics, e.g., men with high scores tend to be artistic and sensitive; women with high scores tend to be rebellious and assertive.
6. Pa (Paranoia)	If they were not afraid of being caught, most people would lie and cheat. (True)	Person tends to misinterpret the motives of others, is suspicious and jealous, vengeful and brooding.
7. Pt (Psychasthenia)	I am not as competent as most other people I know. (True)	Person is overanxious, full of self-doubts, moralistic, and generally obsessive-compulsive.
8. Sc (Schizophrenia)	I sometimes smell things others don't sense. (True)	Person has bizarre sensory experiences and beliefs, is socially seclusive.
9. Ma (Hypomania)	Sometimes I have a strong impulse to do something that others will find appalling. (True)	Person has overly ambitious aspirations and can be hyperactive, impatient, and irritable.
10. Si (Social Introversion)	Rather than spend time alone, I prefer to be around other people. (False)	Person is very modest and shy, preferring solitary activities.

[a]The first four scales assess the validity of the test; the numbered scales are the clinical or content scales.
Source: Hathaway, S. R., and Mckinley, J.C. (1943). Reused 1989 Butcher et al.

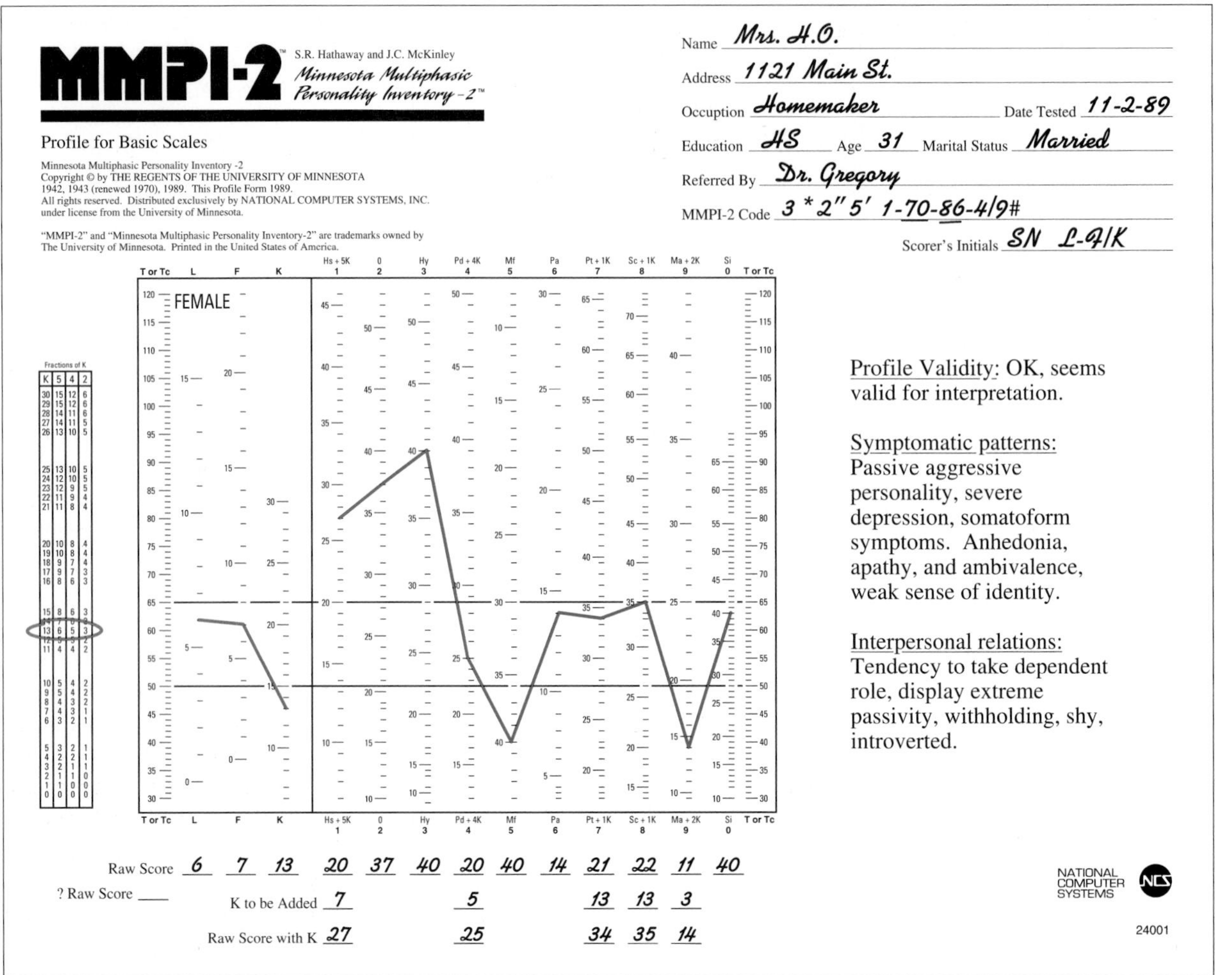

MMPI-2™ S.R. Hathaway and J.C. McKinley
Minnesota Multiphasic Personality Inventory-2™

Profile for Basic Scales

Minnesota Multiphasic Personality Inventory-2
Copyright © by THE REGENTS OF THE UNIVERSITY OF MINNESOTA 1942, 1943 (renewed 1970), 1989. This Profile Form 1989.
All rights reserved. Distributed exclusively by NATIONAL COMPUTER SYSTEMS, INC. under license from the University of Minnesota.

"MMPI-2" and "Minnesota Multiphasic Personality Inventory-2" are trademarks owned by The University of Minnesota. Printed in the United States of America.

Name *Mrs. H.O.*
Address *1121 Main St.*
Occupation *Homemaker* Date Tested *11-2-89*
Education *HS* Age *31* Marital Status *Married*
Referred By *Dr. Gregory*
MMPI-2 Code *3 * 2" 5' 1-70-86-4/9#*
Scorer's Initials *SN L-F/K*

FEMALE

	L	F	K	Hs+5K 1	D 2	Hy 3	Pd+4K 4	Mf 5	Pa 6	Pt+1K 7	Sc+1K 8	Ma+2K 9	Si 0
Raw Score	6	7	13	20	37	40	20	40	14	21	22	11	40
K to be Added				7			5			13	13	3	
Raw Score with K				27			25			34	35	14	

? Raw Score ____

Profile Validity: OK, seems valid for interpretation.

Symptomatic patterns: Passive aggressive personality, severe depression, somatoform symptoms. Anhedonia, apathy, and ambivalence, weak sense of identity.

Interpersonal relations: Tendency to take dependent role, display extreme passivity, withholding, shy, introverted.

NATIONAL COMPUTER SYSTEMS

24001

Figure 4.2 Hypothetical MMPI-2 Profile

ler Adult Intelligence Scale and the Stanford–Binet, are all based on the assumption that a detailed sample of an individual's current intellectual functioning can predict how well he or she will perform in school.

These tests have other uses as well: in conjunction with achievement tests, to diagnose learning disabilities and to identify areas of strengths and weaknesses for academic planning; to identify intellectually gifted children so that appropriate instruction can be provided them in school; and as part of neuropsychological evaluations, for example, periodically testing a person believed to be suffering from a degenerative dementia so that deterioration of mental ability can be followed over time. Indeed, the Wechsler Adult Intelligence Scale (WAIS) is often used as part of a neuropychological test battery, an area of assessment discussed earlier in this chapter. A Spanish-language version of the WAIS has been available for almost thirty years (Wechsler, 1968) and can be useful in assessing the intellectual functioning of people from Hispanic cultures (Gomey, Piedmont, & Fleming, 1992; Lopez & Romero, 1988; Lopez & Taussig, 1991). Further discussion of IQ tests can be found in Chapter 16, where their role in diagnosing mental retardation is examined.

In general, these tests have very good test-retest and split-half reliability. Concurrent validity is also strong. For example, the fourth edition of the Stanford–Binet, published in 1986, readily distinguishes among intellectually gifted, learning disabled, and mentally retarded individuals (Thorndike et al., 1986). Similar data are available on the revised version of the Wechsler Scale (e.g., Matarazzo, 1972). However, predictive validities of these scales are more problematic, a seeming irony considering that the original Stanford–Binet was designed to predict future performance.

Indeed, it is important to keep in mind that, strictly speaking, the tests measure only what a psychologist considers intelligence to be. The tasks and items on an IQ test are, after all, invented by psychologists—they did not come down to us inscribed on stone tablets. In addition, factors other than what we think of as pure intelligence play an important

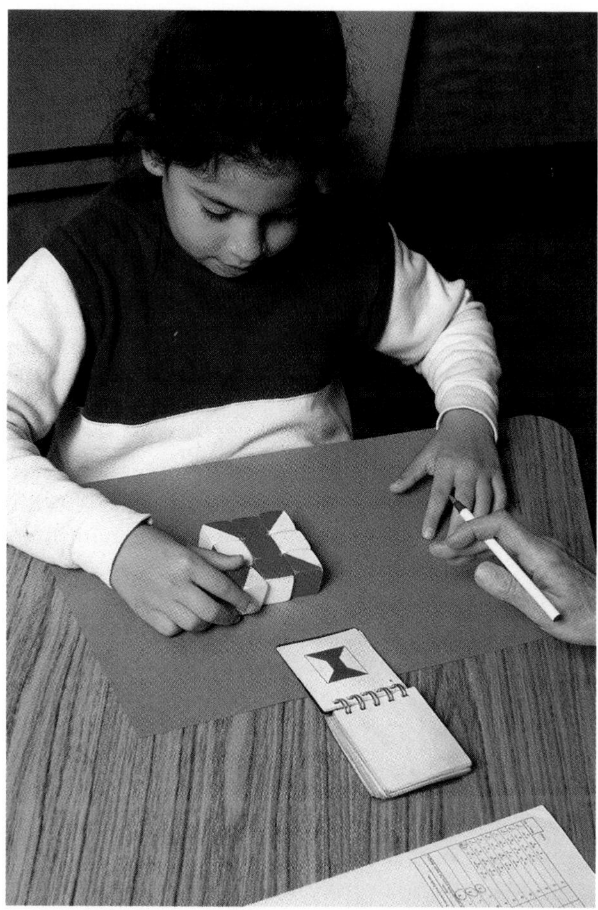

In the Block Design subtest of the Wechsler IQ test the blocks are to be arranged to match the design in the examiner's booklet.

role in how people will do in school, for example, family and personal circumstances, motivation to do well, and the difficulty of the curriculum one selects or is placed in. Though the correlations between IQ scores and school performance are statistically significant (see p. 118), in technical terms IQ tests explain only a small part of the variance in school performance: much more is unexplained by IQ or aptitude test scores than is explained. Finally, if and when there are major changes in our school systems, we can expect analogous changes in our definition and assessment of intelligence. Some important cross-cultural issues are considered later in this chapter (p. 102).

Behavioral and Cognitive Assessment

As part of the continuing development of behavioral and cognitive approaches to the study of psychopathology and treatment, interest has been growing in assessment procedures that are different from the Rorschach inkblot test, the TAT, and the MMPI. In Chapter 2, learning researchers and behaviorists were described as being interested in situational determinants of behavior, that is, in the environmental conditions that precede and follow certain responses. In addition, with the growing interest in cognitive explanations, we can expect the assessments made by behavioral clinicians to include self-reports as well; but, as we shall see, interpretations of self-reports within a cognitive-behavioral framework differ from those in more traditional assessment.

Traditional assessment concentrates on measuring underlying personality structures and traits, such as obsessiveness, paranoia, coldness, aggressiveness, and so on. "A chief aim of the trait approach is to infer the underlying personality structure of individuals and to compare persons and groups on trait dimensions" (Mischel, 1968, pp. 5–6).

Behavioral and cognitively oriented clinicians, on the other hand, are concerned with four sets of variables, sometimes referred to by the acronym SORC (Kanfer & Phillips, 1970). The *S* stands for stimuli, the environmental situations that precede the problem. For instance, the clinician will try to ascertain which situations tend to elicit anxiety. The *O* stands for organismic, referring to both physiological and psychological factors assumed to be operating "under the skin." Perhaps the client's fatigue is caused in part by excessive use of alcohol, or by a cognitive tendency toward self-deprecation with such statements as "I never do anything right, so what's the point in trying?" The *R* refers to overt responses, which probably receive the most attention from behavioral clinicians. They must determine what behavior is problematic, its frequency, intensity, and form. For example, a client might say that she is forgetful and procrastinates. Does she mean that she does not return phone calls, comes late for appointments, or both? Finally, *C* refers to consequent variables, events that appear to be reinforcing or punishing the behavior in question. When the client avoids a feared situation, does his spouse offer sympathy and excuses, thereby unwittingly keeping the person from facing up to his fears?

SORC factors are those that a behavioral clinician attempts to specify for a particular client. It might be mentioned in passing that *O* variables are understandably underplayed by Skinnerians; similarly, *C* variables receive less attention from cognitively oriented behavior therapists than do *O* variables.

The information necessary for a behavioral or cognitive assessment is gathered by several methods, including direct observation of behavior in real life as well as in contrived settings, interviews and self-report measures, and various other methods of cognitive assessment.

Direct Observation of Behavior

It is not surprising that behavior therapists have paid considerable attention to careful observation of overt behavior in a variety of settings, but it should not be assumed that they simply go out and *observe*. Like other scientists, they try to fit events into a framework consistent with their point of view. This excerpt from a case report by Gerald Patterson and his colleagues (1969), describing an interaction between a boy named Kevin and his mother, father, and sister Freida, serves as the first part of an example.

> Kevin goes up to father's chair and stands alongside it. Father puts his arms around Kevin's shoulders. Kevin says to mother as Freida looks at Kevin, "Can I go out and play after supper?" Mother does not reply. Kevin raises his voice and repeats the question. Mother says "You don't have to yell; I can hear you." Father says "How many times have I told you not to yell at your mother?" Kevin scratches a bruise on his arm while mother tells Freida to get started on the dishes, which Freida does. Kevin continues to rub and scratch his arm while mother and daughter are working at the kitchen sink. (p. 21)

Behavioral assessment often involves direct observation of behavior as in this case where the observer is behind a one-way mirror.

This informal description could probably be provided by any observer. But in formal **behavioral observation**, the observer divides the uninterrupted sequence of behavior into various parts and applies terms that make sense within a learning framework. "Kevin begins the exchange by asking a routine question in a normal tone of voice. This ordinary behavior, however, is not reinforced by the mother's attention; for she does not reply. Because she does not reply, the normal behavior of Kevin ceases and he yells his question. The mother expresses disapproval—punishing her son—by telling him that he does not have to yell. And this punishment is supported by the father's reminding Kevin that he should not yell at his mother." This behavioral rendition acknowledges the consequences of ignoring a child's question. At some point the behavior therapist will undoubtedly advise the parents to attend to Kevin's requests when expressed in an ordinary tone of voice, lest he begin yelling. This example indicates an important aspect of behavioral assessment, namely, its link to *intervention*. The behavioral clinician's way of conceptualizing a situation typically implies a way to change it.

It is difficult to observe most behavior as it actually takes place, and little control can be exercised over where and when it may occur. For this reason many therapists contrive artificial situations in their consulting rooms or in a laboratory so that they can observe how a client or a family acts under certain conditions. For example, Barkley (1981) had a mother and her hyperactive child spend time together in a laboratory living room, complete with sofas and television set. The mother was given a list of tasks for the child to complete, such as picking up toys or doing arithmetic problems. Observers behind a one-way mirror watched the proceedings and coded the child's reactions to the mother's efforts to control as well as the mother's reactions to the child's compliant or noncompliant responses. These behavioral assessment procedures yielded data that could be used to measure the effects of treatment. For example, Barkley and Cunningham (1979) showed that hyperactive children who were being treated with methylphenidate (Ritalin) were more obedient to their mothers, who, in turn, were more positive in their reactions to their children—as compared with children who had been given placebo medications. Such behavioral observations can facilitate the study of complex interactions between parent and child.

Behavioral observations can also be made by significant others in the client's natural environment. For example, the Conners Teacher Rating Scale (Conners, 1969) enables teachers to provide reliable behavioral assessment data on children in classrooms, and the Achenbach Child Behavior Checklist (Achenbach & Edelbrook, 1983) has either parents or teachers rate children's behavior.

Most of the research just described is conducted within an operant framework that employs no inferential concepts. But behavioral assessment techniques can also be applied within a framework that makes use of mediators. For instance, Gordon Paul (1966) was interested in assessing the anxiety of public speakers. He decided to count the frequency of behaviors indicative of this emotional state. One of his principal measures, the Timed Behavioral Checklist for Performance Anxiety, is shown in Figure 4.3. Subjects were asked to deliver a speech in front of a group, some members of which were raters trained to consider the subject's behavior every thirty seconds and to record the presence or absence of twenty specific behaviors. By summing the scores, Paul arrived at a behavioral index of anxiety. This study is one example of how observations of overt behavior have been used to infer the presence of an internal state.

In Paul's study people other than the speaker made the observations. For several years behavior therapists and researchers have also asked individuals to observe their own behavior, to keep track of various categories of response. This approach is called **self-monitoring**. An early application of self-monitoring was used in research to reduce smoking. Subjects were provided with booklets in which they recorded the time each cigarette was lighted at baseline, before treatment had been introduced, during treatment, and after.

Although some research indicates that self-monitoring can provide accurate measurement of such behavior, considerable research indicates that behavior may be altered by the very fact that it is being self-monitored (Haynes & Horn, 1982). **Reactivity** of behavior is the phenomenon of its changing

Figure 4.3 Paul's (1966) Timed Behavioral Checklist for Performance Anxiety

Behavior Observed	*Time Period*								
	1	*2*	*3*	*4*	*5*	*6*	*7*	*8*	Σ
1. Paces									
2. Sways									
3. Shuffles feet									
4. Knees tremble									
5. Extraneous arm and hand movement (swings, scratches, toys, etc.)									
6. Arms rigid									
7. Hands restrained (in pockets, behind back, clasped)									
8. Hand tremors									
9. No eye contact									
10. Face muscles tense (drawn, tics, grimaces)									
11. Face "deadpan"									
12. Face pale									
13. Face flushed (blushes)									
14. Moistens lips									
15. Swallows									
16. Clears throat									
17. Breathes heavily									
18. Perspires (face, hands, armpits)									
19. Voice quivers									
20. Speech blocks or stammers									

because it is being observed. Generally speaking, desirable behavior, such as engaging in social conversation, often increases in frequency when self-monitored (Nelson, Lipinski, & Black, 1976), whereas behavior the subject wishes to reduce, like cigarette smoking, diminishes (McFall & Hammen, 1971). Such findings suggest that therapeutic interventions can take advantage of the reactivity that is an outcome of self-monitoring.

Interviews and Self-Report Measures

For all their interest in direct observation of behavior, behavioral clinicians still rely very heavily on the interview to assess the needs of their clients. Like other clinicians, they make every effort to establish good rapport, creating an atmosphere of trust and caring that encourages clients to reveal aspects of their lives that they may not have shown any other person—what London (1964) poetically called "secrets of the heart." Within this trusting relationship the behavior therapist's job is to determine, by skillful questioning and careful observation of the client's emotional reactions during the interview, the SORC factors—already mentioned—the situations in which the problematic behavior occurs, the internal conditions mediating the influence of the environment, the particular patterns of behavior causing distress, and the events that may help to maintain the problem. Some behaviorally oriented clinicians conduct an initial interview with the goal of writing an intake report such as the one shown in Figure 4.4. In its situational focus, its concern with specific details of thought, emotion, and behavior, and its focus on how assessment is linked to possible interventions, such an interview and intake report can be distinguished from those in nonbehavioral clinical settings.

Behavior therapists also make use of self-report inventories. For example, McFall and Lillesand (1971) employed a Conflict Resolution Inventory containing thirty-five items that focus on the ability of the respondent to refuse unreasonable requests. Each item describes a specific situation in which a person is asked for something unreasonable. For example, "You are in the thick of studying for exams when a person you know slightly comes into your room and says, 'I'm tired of studying, mind if I come in and take a break for a while?' " Subjects are asked to indicate the likelihood that they would refuse such a request and how comfortable they would be in doing so. Responses to this self-report inventory have been found to be correlated with a variety of direct observational data in research on social skills (Frisch & Higgins, 1986). This and similar inventories can be used by clinicians and have helped behavioral researchers measure the outcome of clinical interventions as well.

Specialized Approaches to Cognitive Assessment

When patients are asked about their thoughts in interviews and self-report inventories, they have to reflect backward in time and provide a retrospective and rather general report of their thoughts in certain situations. "When someone criticizes you in class, what thoughts go through your mind?" is a question a client might be asked in an interview or on a paper-and-pencil inventory. Perhaps the most widely employed cognitive assessment methods are self-report questionnaires that tap a wide range of cognitions, such as fear of negative evaluation, tendency to think irrationally, and making negative inferences about life experience.

As with behavioral assessment, a key feature of contemporary approaches in cognitive assessment is that the development of methods is determined primarily by theory and data as well as by the purposes of the assessment. For example, much research on depression is concerned with cognition—both the things that people tell themselves and of which they are generally conscious as well as the underlying schemata (see p. 231) or attitudes that can be inferred from their behavior and verbal reports. As we shall examine in greater detail in Chapter 9, Aaron Beck (1967) holds that depression is caused primarily by negative ideas that people have about themselves, their world, and their future; for example, that they are not worth much and that things are never going to get better. These pessimistic attitudes, or schemata, bias the way in which they interpret events around them to the extent that a misstep that might be taken in stride by a nondepressed person is construed by a depressed individual as compelling evidence of his or her ineptitude and worthlessness. Researchers in cognitive assessment set themselves the task of trying to identify these different kinds of cognitions, obtaining their ideas both from the clinical reports of practitioners who have firsthand experience with depressed patients as well as from controlled research that adheres to the methodological principles discussed in the next chapter.

For example, to assess depressive attitudes, Weissman and Beck (1978) devised the Dysfunctional Attitude Scale (DAS), containing items such as "People will probably think less of me if I make a mistake." Researchers have shown that one can differentiate between depressed and nondepressed people on the basis of their scores on this scale and that scores decrease (that is, improve) after inter-

Figure 4.4 Behaviorally Oriented Intake Report; Goldfried, M. R., and Davison, G. C. (1976). Reprinted by permission of Holt, Rinehart and Winston.

Name: BRIAN, James (fictitious name)
Class: Senior

Age: 22 Sex: Male
Date of interview: March 26, 1993
Therapist: John Doe

1. Behavior during interview and physical description:
James is a clean-shaven, long-haired young man who appeared for the intake interview in well-coordinated eastern college garb: jeans, open shirt, and tennis shoes. He came across as shy and soft-spoken, with occasional minor speech blocks. Although uneasy during most of the session, he nonetheless spoke freely and candidly.

2. Presenting problem:
(a) Nature of problem: Anxiety in public-speaking situations and in other situations in which he is being evaluated by others.
(b) Historical setting events: James was born in France and arrived in this country seven years ago, at which time he experienced both social and language problems. His social contacts had been minimal until he entered college; there a socially aggressive friend helped him to break out of his shell. James describes his father as an overly critical perfectionist who would, on occasion, rip up his son's homework if it fell short of the mark. His mother he pictures as a controlling, overly affectionate person who always shows concern about his welfare. His younger brother, who has always been a good student, is continually thrown up to James by his parents as being far better than he.
(c) Current situational determinants: Interaction with his parents, examinations, family gatherings, participation in classes, initial social contacts.
(d) Relevant organismic variables: The client appears to be approaching a number of situations with certain irrational expectations, primarily unrealistic strivings for perfection and an overwhelming desire to receive approval from others. He is not taking any medication at this time except as indicated under 10 below.
(e) Dimensions of problem: The client's anxiety about social relationships and evaluations of himself is long-standing and occurs in a wide variety of day-to-day situations.
(f) Consequences of problem: His chronic level of anxiety resulted in an ulcer operation at the age of 15. In addition, he has developed a skin rash on his hands and arms, apparently from excessive perspiration. He reports that his nervousness at one time caused him to stutter, but this problem appears to have diminished in recent years. His anxiety when taking examinations has typically interfered with his ability to perform well.

3. Other problems:
(a) Assertiveness: Although obviously a shy and timid individual, James says that lack of assertiveness is no longer a problem with him. At one time in the past, his friends would take advantage of him, but he claims that this is no longer the case. His statements should be followed up, for it is unclear what he means by assertiveness.
(b) Forgetfulness: The client reports that he frequently misses appointments, misplaces items, locks himself out of his room, and is generally absentminded.

4. Personal assets:
The client is fairly bright and comes across as a warm, friendly, and sensitive individual.

5. Targets for modification:
Unrealistic self-statements about how he should fare in social evaluative situations; possible behavioral deficits associated with unassertiveness; and forgetfulness.

6. Recommended treatment:
It appears that relaxation training would be a good way to begin, especially in light of the client's high level of anxiety. Treatment should then undertake the restructuring of his unrealistic expectations. Behavior rehearsal is a possibility. The best strategy for dealing with forgetfulness is unclear as yet.

7. Motivation for treatment:
High.

8. Prognosis:
Good.

9. Priority for treatment:
High.

10. Expectancies:
On occasion, especially when going out on a date, James takes a tranquilizer (Valium, 10 mg) to calm himself down. He wants to get away from this and feels that he needs to learn to cope with his anxieties by himself. It would appear that he will be receptive to whatever treatment plan we finally decide on, especially if the emphasis is on self-control of anxiety.

11. Other comments:
Considering the brief time available between now and the end of the semester, between-session homework assignments are of particular importance.

ventions that relieve depression. Furthermore, the DAS relates well to other aspects of cognition in ways consistent with Beck's theory. For example, it correlates with an instrument called the Cognitive Bias Questionnaire (Krantz & Hammen, 1979), which measures the ways in which depressed patients distort information. These and other instruments, most of them self-report questionnaires, both help to test Beck's theory of depression and are validated when certain patterns of scores arise, as when a sample of depressed patients manifests higher levels of cognitive distortion than do controls (construct validity). An accumulating body of data is helping to establish both the validity and reliability of these instruments (Segal & Shaw, 1988).

However, replies of subjects to questions asked by interviewers and inventories about their thoughts in certain past situations may well be different from what they would report were they able to do so in the immediate circumstance. Moreover, cognitive-behavioral clinicians such as Albert Ellis and Aaron Beck make predictions about the kinds of thoughts troubled people will have under very specific conditions. Researchers have been working on ways to enable subjects to tap into their immediate and ongoing thought processes when confronted with particular circumstances (cf. Parks & Hollon, 1988). Can we show, for example, that a socially anxious person does in fact, as Ellis would predict, view criticism from others as catastrophic, whereas someone who is not socially insecure does not?

The Articulated Thoughts in Simulated Situations (ATSS) method of Davison and his associates (Davison, Robins, & Johnson, 1983) is an example of research assessing immediate thoughts. In this procedure a subject pretends that he or she is a participant in a situation, such as listening to a teaching assistant criticize a term paper. Presented on audiotape, the scene pauses every ten or fifteen seconds. During the ensuing thirty seconds of silence, the subject talks aloud about whatever is going through his or her mind in reaction to the words just heard. Then the audiotaped scene continues, stopping after a few moments so that the subject can articulate his or her thoughts another time. One taped scene in which the subject overhears two pretend acquaintances criticizing him or her includes the following segments.

> **First acquaintance:** He certainly did make a fool of himself over what he said about religion. I just find that kind of opinion very close-minded and unaware. You have to be blind to the facts of the universe to believe that. [Thirty-second pause for subject's response.]
>
> **Second acquaintance:** What really bugs me is the way he expresses himself. He never seems to stop and think, but just blurts out the first thing that comes into his head. [Thirty-second pause.]

Subjects readily become involved in the pretend situations, regarding them as credible and realistic. The following cognitive patterns have emerged from a few of the studies conducted thus far.

1. Socially anxious therapy patients articulated thoughts of greater irrationality than did nonanxious control subjects (Bates, Campbell, & Burgess, 1990; Davison & Zighelboim, 1987).
2. Recent ex-smokers who would relapse within three months showed a greater tendency to think of smoking without prompting (Haaga, 1987), as well as having fewer negative expectations for smoking than did those who would still be abstinent three months later (Haaga, 1988a).
3. Men with borderline hypertension achieved significant reductions in anger as expressed in their articulated thoughts and experienced decreases in their blood pressure and heart rate following a program of relaxation training and medical information about diet and exercise. Most significantly, these two kinds of decreases were positively correlated, that is, the less angry subjects' thinking became, the lower their blood pressure became—consistent with research that links anger with hypertension (Davison, Williams, et al., 1991; see also Chapter 8, p. 202).
4. In an experiment that directly compared ATSS data with overt behavior, Davison, Haaga, et al., (1991) found that articulated thoughts of positive self-efficacy were inversely related to behaviorally indexed speech anxiety, that is, the more anxiously subjects behaved on a timed behavioral checklist measure of public-speaking anxiety, the less capable they felt themselves to be while articulating thoughts in a stressful, simulated speech-giving situation.

This pattern of results indicates that the method ferrets out people's thinking about both inherently bothersome and "objectively" innocuous situations.

Other cognitive assessment methods have also proved useful. For example, thought listing has the person write down his or her thoughts prior to or following an event of interest, such as entering a room to talk to a stranger, as a way to determine the cognitive components of social anxiety (Cacioppo, Glass, & Merluzzi, 1979). Different procedures may be more or less useful under different circumstances. For example, open-ended techniques like the ATSS just described may be preferable when investigators know relatively little and want to get general ideas of the cognitive terrain, whereas more focused techniques, such as questionnaires, may be better—and are certainly more easily scored—when there is more prior knowledge about the cognitions of interest (Haaga, 1988b). So far the various cognitive assessment techniques correlate poorly with each other (Clark, 1988), but this is perhaps to be expected, given their different formats and the elusive nature of human thought.

The interest in cognitive assessment has recently brought cognitive-behavioral clinicians into contact with literature in experimental cognitive psychology, the branch of psychological research concerned with how people transform environmental input into usable information, how they think and plan, remember and anticipate. In addition to self-talk research, workers have developed assessment tools for inferring the existence of a number of cognitive structures, particularly schemata (Bartlett, 1932). A simple example of a schema would be the idea we carry around in our heads of what a face is—a configuration having two eyes, a nose, a mouth, and two ears. We are able to identify an object as a face, even when its configuration has much that is unusual about it.

Experimental cognitive psychologists have used the schema concept in understanding memory phenomena (see page 50). Clinical researchers have built on this experimental research and infer schemata from distortions in memory. For example, Nelson and Craighead (1977) wanted to test whether depressives encounter their world with a failure schema as posited by Beck. They gave groups of depressed and nondepressed students a task on which they were rewarded or punished 30 percent or 70 percent of the time. In the 70 percent reward condition, the depressed subjects recalled having been reinforced less often than was actually the case. By the same token, in the 30 percent punishment condition, depressed students recalled having received more punishment. These differences in memory are explained in terms of a schema, or cognitive set. For example, the depressed subject believes something like "I am not competent." In this sense a schema is equivalent to a basic, underlying assumption that people have about themselves and their world and that affects the way they perceive, conceptualize, feel, and act.

Reliability and Validity of Behavioral and Cognitive Assessment

Allusions to reliability and validity were made throughout the overview of behavioral and cogni-

Cognitive assessment focuses on the person's perception of a situation, realizing that the same event can be perceived differently. For example, moving could be regarded as very stressful or seen in a positive light.

tive assessment. Because many of these procedures developed from empirical research, often in laboratory settings, it is to be expected that workers have been sensitive to whether, for example, behavioral raters agreed with each other when observing subjects (e.g., Paul, 1966), or whether coders of think-aloud data achieved satisfactory levels of agreement (Davison et al., 1983). We can thus assume reliability. With respect to validity, most of the focus in behavioral and cognitive assessment is on construct validity, because experimental research typically involves the testing of hypotheses. Thus, the Davison et al. (1991) finding that decreases in anger on the ATSS were correlated with decreases in blood pressure, both contributed to the construct validity of the articulated thoughts procedure and corroborated the hypothesis about the relationship between anger and hypertension.

The Assessment of Anxiety: In Pursuit of an Elusive Construct

Many issues in assessment can be appreciated by considering efforts to measure anxiety, one of the most prevalent emotions and one of great interest to psychopathologists and therapists. They have generally relied on three modes of measurement: self-report questionnaires, observations of overt behavior, and physiological measurements.

Allowing people to describe the phenomena of their emotions in their own terms, as in clinical interviews, provides useful information about the one individual interviewed; but this strategy alone makes it difficult to compare the experiences of a number of people and, even more important, to quantify what they say. Researchers have therefore devised various self-report questionnaires that attempt to direct the individual's impressions into standardized terms. The following are some sample items from the Taylor Manifest Anxiety Scale (Taylor, 1953), which consists of fifty items drawn from the MMPI.

I work under a great deal of strain.	**True**	False
I am usually calm and not easily upset.	True	**False**
I sweat very easily even on cool days.	**True**	False
I always have enough energy when faced with difficulty.	True	**False**
My sleep is restless and disturbed.	**True**	False

An anxious person would tend to underline the true and false responses as indicated. The test is scored by summing the number of "anxious" responses. This score is then assumed to represent the person's general level of anxiety.

A second means of assessing anxiety is to observe overt behavior for reactions and movements that are believed to reflect the internal emotional state—trembling, perspiring, nail biting, fleeing from a situation. As indicated earlier (p. 95), observers trained to administer Paul's (1966) Timed Behavioral Checklist for Performance Anxiety time-sampled the overt behavior of subjects in a stressful

Anxiety, as could be evoked by public speaking, is assessed by self-reports, direct observation, and physiological measurement.

situation, recording instances of twenty indexes of anxiety whenever they were observed.

Physiological measurements of activities of the autonomic nervous system and the output of certain endocrine glands also indicate levels of anxiety. The availability of these measurements has encouraged researchers to define anxiety in physiological terms. The situation in which physiological measurements are taken is very important, however. What would be revealed, for example, if recording electrodes were attached to a woman who is about to have sexual relations? Both before and during sexual activity the heartbeat is very likely to be faster, blood pressure higher, perspiration greater, and breathing more rapid, all physiological responses that are generally regarded as indicators of sexual excitement as well as of anxiety. But why would we not conclude that our female subject is, indeed, anxious as she contemplates sexual intercourse? As we shall see in Chapter 13, many people are debilitated by fear in sexual situations. How can an investigator distinguish rapid breathing that reflects sexual excitement from rapid breathing that reflects anxiety? Part of the answer necessarily lies in observations made concurrently. If at the time physiological measures are taken the female subject convincingly reports that she is looking forward to what is to come, and if she ultimately derives great enjoyment from her sexual partner, we would almost certainly choose to interpret her rapid breathing and other physiological responses as indicating sexual arousal. The situation and her self-report of it must be taken into consideration.

Not only are the physiological indicators of anxiety evident in other emotional states, but the many measures of anxiety have been found time and again *not* to correlate well with one another (see Martin, 1961; Lang, 1969). In a stressful situation such as being threatened with painful electric shock, many people report being very nervous, but their heart rates may be lower rather than elevated. An individual taking an important examination for which he or she is ill-prepared may deny feeling anxious and yet be observed trembling. Moreover, if people are asked to report on their awareness of various symptoms of anxiety, such as a feeling of tightness in the neck, avoidance of social gatherings, and worrying, their self-reports tend to cluster into one of three fairly independent groups—somatic, behavioral, and cognitive (Lehrer & Woolfolk, 1982). Thus the anxiety reported by people appears to be made up of one of three relatively separate components. One person may have bodily indicators, such as muscle tension and acid stomach, and yet not experience cognitive signs, such as ruminating about an alarming event.

On a more general level many workers regard the concept of anxiety as a useful one for organizing and interrelating data from numerous sources. Maher (1966) and Lang (1969), for example, consider anxiety to be a hypothetical construct, a convenient fiction or inferred state that mediates between a threatening situation and the observed behavior of an organism. They also assume that the construct is multifaceted or multidimensional and that each facet is not necessarily evoked by a given stressful situation or always expressed to the same degree, another explanation for the low intercorrelations among measures of anxiety.

As a scientific construct, anxiety must be tied to observables, the conditions that produce it and the effects that follow its induction. For this very reason Skinner (1953), as we indicated earlier (see page 46), argued that mediators are not essential in accounting for behavior. Because the construct of anxiety is linked to stimuli and responses, why not dispense with it and talk only of observables? Furthermore, might not the inference of an internal state lead us to believe that an adequate explanation has been found and thereby discourage the search for ways to predict and control behavior?

These are cogent objections, and they have forced workers to exercise great care in their use of the anxiety construct. As will be noted in Chapter 5, investigators who employ mediators such as anxiety do so in hope of better organizing their data and of generating hypotheses. We seldom find experimental psychologists speaking about anxiety without being able at any time to explain how and why they infer that the emotional state exists.

Finally, certain experiments would not be undertaken or could not be explained without inferring the mediating state. To illustrate, let us consider a classic experiment reviewed by Rescorla and Solomon (1967). Dogs were taught to avoid a stimulus (CS) by pairing it repeatedly with a painful shock (UCS). Then they were totally paralyzed with injections of curare, a drug that prevents movement of the skeletal muscles. One group of animals, while paralyzed, was repeatedly presented with the CS, but shock did not accompany it. In Pavlovian, classical conditioning terms, these would be considered attempts to extinguish the conditioned response. Did these animals learn, while paralyzed and unable to move, that the CS was in fact no longer followed by shock? Phrased another way, did the previously learned fear of the CS undergo any extinction? The answer was obtained on a subsequent day when the dogs in this group had completely recovered from the curare and were confronted with the CS. The unshocked presentations of the CS a day or two earlier had indeed reduced avoidance behavior, even though no overt response could have occurred during the curare paralysis. The control animals, who had not been confronted with the CS while paralyzed, did not show a reduction in avoidance behavior.

How do we account for such remarkable findings? Rescorla and Solomon deem it necessary, and legitimate, to infer a mediating anxiety that was lessened when the dogs were presented with the CS while paralyzed with curare. Clearly something was being unlearned during the time that the dogs could not respond by avoiding the CS. By positing a mediating anxiety, we can make sense of these findings and relate them to a wealth of other theory and research. The experiment just described indicates that anxiety, or fear, can be useful as an explanatory device. Nonetheless, the anxiety construct poses continual difficulties for those who employ it.

Cultural Diversity and Clinical Assessment

If a diagnostician is trying to understand a seemingly abnormal behavior in a member of a minority group—an African-American or Hispanic, for example—will he or she best serve the mental health interests of that patient by attending to cultural factors that may distinguish the patient from the majority culture in which he or she lives? If, for instance, the clinician is assessing an Asian-American man who is very emotionally withdrawn, should the clinician consider that lower levels of emotional expressiveness in men are positively sanctioned among Asian-Americans as compared with the culture that predominates in the U.S. at this time? In so doing, will the clinician thereby tend to *normalize* this behavior, that is, not believe that it reflects an emotional disorder, whereas if the same behavior were found in a white male of the same age, the clinician might find it unusual enough to be judged abnormal?

Assessment of Hispanics

A review by Malgady, Rogler, and Constantino (1989) discusses cultural and linguistic biases in the mental health evaluation of Hispanics. Biases have been found when clinicians use established tests and instruments with non-English-speaking clients, such as Mexican-Americans. For example, a patient's emotional problems can be underestimated because of the way an interpreter translates between the English-speaking clinician and the Spanish-speaking patient (Sabin, 1975). Different cultural norms can also set the stage for misjudgments. The belief that evil spirits can possess a person is not, in the Puerto Rican culture, a sign of schizophrenia, rather it is consistent with the spiritualism prevalent in Puerto Rico, whereby people are believed to be surrounded by invisible spirits (Rogler & Hollingshead, 1985). Other difficulties arise because Hispanics may disclose less about themselves to non-Hispanic white clinicians than do Anglo patients (Levine & Padilla, 1980); and Hispanics not fluent

Assessment must take the person's cultural background into account. Believing in possession by spirit is common in some cultures and thus should not always be taken to mean that the believer is psychotic.

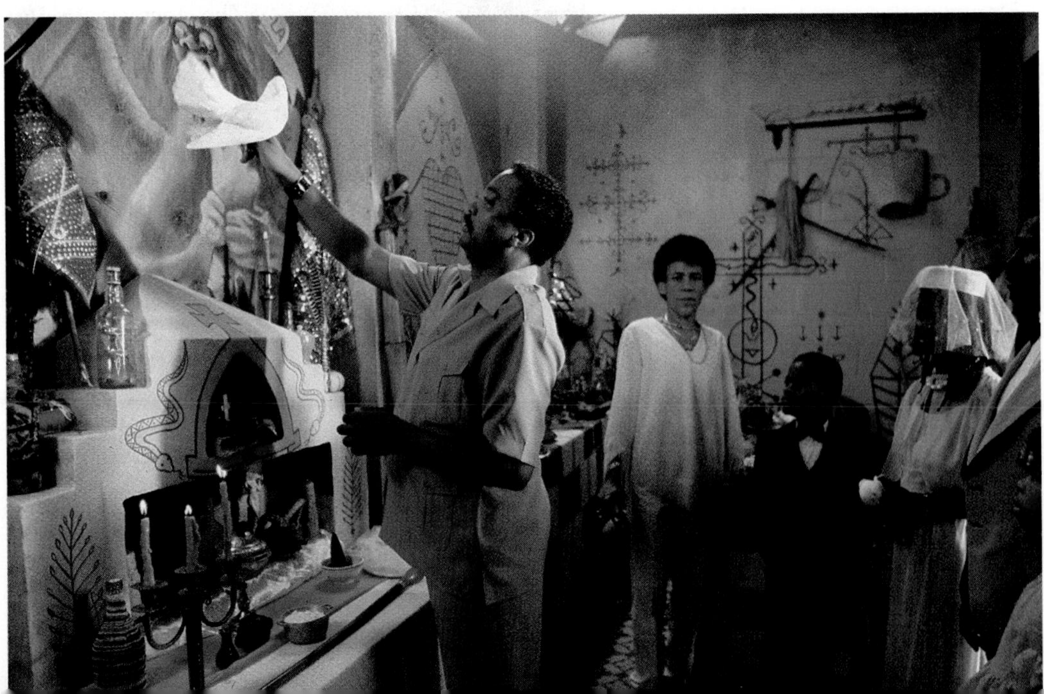

in English can become even less so under stressful circumstances (Peck, 1974).[1] In addition, the very term *Hispanic* subsumes several differing cultures, for example, Mexican-American, Cuban, Puerto Rican, Central or South American. While Malgrady et al.'s conclusions have not gone unchallenged (Lopez, 1988), they do alert the mental health establishment to be sensitive to biases in diagnostic practices that might compromise efforts to provide scientifically justifiable clinical services to members of Hispanic minority groups.

Assessment of Native Americans

Greater cultural sensitivity is warranted also in assessing Native Americans, as can be seen by the following quotation from a classic book on intelligence written by Lewis Terman, the Stanford psychologist who adapted the original Binet scale early in this century.

> [After examining two Portuguese brothers] Their dullness seems to be racial or at least inherent in the family stocks from which they come. . . . The writer predicts that when [racial differences in mental abilities among Mexican, American Indian, and Afro-American individuals are investigated] there will be discovered enormously significant racial differences in general intelligence, differences which cannot be wiped out by any scheme of mental culture.
>
> Children of this group should be segregated in special classes and be given instruction which is concrete and practical. They cannot master abstraction, but they can often be made efficient workers, able to look out for themselves. There is no possibility at present of convincing society that they should not be allowed to reproduce, although from a eugenic point of view they constitute a grave problem because of their unusually prolific breeding. (Terman, 1916, p. 92)

The field has come quite a distance since those blatantly racist times, but, as recently pointed out by Dauphinais and King (1992), most approaches to Native Americans and native Alaskans have been ethnocentric and unappreciative of their particular cultures and life circumstances. Examples are legion. O'Conner (1989) suggests that some Native American children lack interest in the individualistic, competitive nature of an IQ test because of the cooperative, group-oriented values instilled by their culture. Their performance on such a test may therefore underestimate their intellectual abilities. Furthermore, as with other minority groups who are overrepresented in the lower socioeconomic classes, interpretation of IQ test scores should be informed by the conditions in which they have grown up; Dauphinais and King (1992) caution that professionals should not assume that below-average test performance means that such children are unable to learn (National Commission on Testing and Public Policy, 1990).

Although, as noted earlier in this chapter, the samples on which the MMPI-2 was developed were more representative than was the case with the original MMPI, only 77 Native Americans were included (Butcher et al., 1989), and they were all from a single tribe, which overlooks differences among Native American tribes. Furthermore, no validation studies with Native Americans have been conducted, even though the MMPI is the most frequently used psychological assessment technique with them (Manson, Walker, & Kivlahan, 1987). The situation is similarly problematic for other psychological tests, such as the Rorschach and the TAT (Dauphinais & King, 1992). Studies are in progress at the National Center for American Indian and Alaska Native Mental Health Research to study the applicability of various psychological assessment techniques to these populations.

Assessment of African-Americans

Many questions of bias in assessment and clinical judgment were addressed in the work of Lopez and his associates (Lopez, 1989). The answers are far from clear. In an initial study, Lopez and Hernandez (1986) cast doubt on the idea that including cultural differences in one's diagnostic work necessarily contributes to an accurate and helpful diagnosis. They surveyed a large sample of mental health practitioners in California and found that clinicians sometimes *minimized* the seriousness of a patient's problems by attributing them to a subcultural norm. For example, one clinician reported attaching less psychopathological significance to an African-American woman's hallucinations because of his own belief that hallucinations are more prevalent among African-Americans than among whites. As a result, the clinician did not consider a diagnosis of schizophrenia, a decision that may not have been in the woman's best interests. The thrust of this study

[1]Most Americans seldom encounter a situation in which they have to try to express themselves in a second language. They have difficulty enough using computer-based translators or tourist phrase books in order to find out where to catch a bus in a foreign city. Imagine how much more daunting it is to have to respond in a second language to highly personal questions from a clinician.

is that by being mindful of cultural differences—and believing that what is abnormal in one culture may be normal in another—clinicians can err on the side of minimizing problems and hence reduce the chances of providing appropriate professional intervention. Thus efforts to avoid discrimination against minority groups by underpathologizing may not help minority patients.

On the other hand, clinicians can also overpathologize, which is another kind of diagnostic bias. For example, Blake (1973) found that clinicians were more likely to diagnose a patient as schizophrenic if a case summary referred to the person as African-American than if the person were described as white. In a hospital-based study with actual patients, Simon et al. (1973) found that African-Americans were overdiagnosed as schizophrenic and underdiagnosed as mood disordered. Mukherjee et al. (1983) reported similar findings for Hispanic patients. In an analogous fashion, Luepnitz, Randolph, & Gutsch (1982) discovered that, based on identical symptoms, alcoholism was more likely to be diagnosed in a lower-class African-American patient than in a middle-class white patient. (Actually, in this study, alcoholism *should* have been diagnosed in all the patients, so the findings are best seen as underpathologizing in a patient from a majority group.) Both underpathologizing and overpathologizing biased judgments are found as well when patients are women, old, from lower socioeconomic classes, and mentally retarded (Lopez, 1989).

Considering Culture in Clinical Assessment

Lopez extended his study of diagnostic bias by examining eleven widely used diagnostic criteria and interview schedules for schizophrenia, affective disorders, and personality disorders (Lopez & Nunez, 1987). Included in these measures were several already mentioned or to be discussed later in this book: the DSM-III (American Psychiatric Association, 1980), the Research Diagnostic Criteria (Spitzer, Endicott, & Robins, 1977), the Diagnostic Interview Schedule (Robins, Helzer, Croughan, & Ratliff, 1981), and the Schedule for Affective Disorders and Schizophrenia (SADS; Spitzer & Endicott, 1978). If a client's cultural background is considered when making diagnoses, cultural factors will begin to appear in standard diagnostic instruments. If so, this inclusion may be seen as a reflection of the mental health establishment's sensitivity to cultural differences in psychopathology. Furthermore, if cultural factors are found in widely used instruments, the cognitive activities of clinicians are likely to be shaped or informed by a consideration of cultural factors in psychopathology.

The results of the Lopez and Nunez study indicate very minimal mention of cultural variables. The DSM-III, for example, contained only one cultural reference for the three groups of disorder (DSM-IV pays considerably more attention to cultural diversity.) Overall, although eight of the eleven instruments studied did consider culture, they referred to it very infrequently, revealing an insensitivity to cultural differences in psychopathology.

Lopez's research challenges clinicians who would include cultural factors in diagnoses of minority patients. If clinicians are sensitive to cultural differences, then they might well interpret a given behavior that is not typical of the general culture as a result of a cultural difference and therefore not a sign of psychopathology—a minimizing bias. If, on the other hand, as Lopez and Hernandez suggest, clinicians recognize that such an attribution may discourage them from justifiably attributing a behavior to psychopathology, then they should overlook, or at least downplay, the significance of cultural factors when diagnosing a minority client lest they fail to attribute an unusual behavior to a mental disorder and, in so doing, deny necessary care to the client.

The Consistency and Variability of Behavior

In this last section, we address a critical question that is relevant in any assessment of behavior; that is, is behavior consistent or variable over time? In other words, do we possess personality traits that operate in the same way in a variety of situations, or do we behave differently, depending on the situation? This question has prompted much debate and research, and it is of concern in any careful consideration of how to assess people and their problems in clinical settings.

Walter Mischel, in *Personality and Assessment* (1968), argued that personality traits are not important determinants of behavior. Trait theorists believe that human beings can be described as having a certain amount of a characteristic, such as stinginess or obsessiveness, and that their behavior in a variety of situations can be predicted reasonably well by the degree to which they possess this characteristic. This position implies that people will behave fairly consistently in a variety of situations—

The work of the prominent psychologist, Walter Mischel, stimulated the current debate concerning whether traits or situations are the most powerful determinants of behavior.

a highly aggressive person, for example, will be more aggressive than someone low in aggression at home, at work, and at play. After reviewing the evidence bearing on this question, Mischel concluded that the behavior of people is often not very consistent from situation to situation.

Not surprisingly, Mischel's attack on trait theory elicited a heated debate in the literature. For example, the psychodynamic theorist Paul Wachtel (1977) argued that Mischel ignored current psychoanalytic thinking, which does not entirely overlook the way behavior varies across different situations. Moreover, Wachtel argued, the behavior of individuals whom clinicians tend to encounter may indeed be predictable on the basis of some underlying trait or disposition. Clinical problems may, in fact, be associated with a rigidity or inflexibility to changing conditions. On the other hand, it has been suggested that people at the other extreme, those who shift with the wind, may also be subject to emotional disorder. That is, some forms of disorder may be connected to overdependence on the environment as a guide to behavior. To be totally at the mercy of one's surroundings, like a rudderless ship, would seem to pose as many problems as being insensitive to varying environmental demands (Phares, 1979).

Wachtel also suggested that people tend to perceive certain kinds of situations in a particular fashion; the perception in effect renders objectively different situations equivalent in their own eyes. For example, a person who might be described as paranoid sees threats in seemingly innocuous situations. Insensitivity to circumstances is not his or her problem; rather this person perceives a great many situations as containing threats. In addition, people can *elicit* certain kinds of reactions from their surroundings. The paranoid individual may not only perceive people as threatening but may make them so by attacking them first. In effect, he or she transforms different situations into similar and dangerous ones. As a result the paranoid's own behavior varies little.

Wachtel proposed also that a personality disposition can affect the kinds of situations an individual selects or constructs for himself or herself. (This view was espoused by Gordon Allport, 1937, a famous Harvard personality psychologist whose work on traits underlies much of the current debate. Contrary to what some situationalists allege, Allport did not ignore the role of the environment in his theorizing about personality traits; cf. Zuroff, 1986.) A generally optimistic person, for example, may seek out situations that confirm his or her positive outlook, which in turn strengthens the trait tendency to find or to construct similar sanguine situations in the future. There is a constantly reciprocating interaction, then, with personality traits influencing situations one is in, and situations in turn influencing personality. "Consistency over extended periods of time . . . may be the product of extended histories of choosing situations conducive to one's attitudes, traits, and dispositions" (Snyder, 1983, p. 510). Interestingly enough, Wachtel's psychodynamic speculations are consistent with social psychological research, including that of Bandura (1982), Mischel himself (1977), Snyder (1983), and Emmons and Diener (1986).

Wachtel went on to argue that the studies Mischel cited were generally done with normals, whose behavior is probably more flexible than that of patients. As mentioned, one of the hallmarks of mental disorder may be rigidity and inflexibility, which is another way of saying that behavior is consistent in a variety of situations. Therefore, by studying basically normal people, Mischel may have concluded that people are more variable than he might had he studied patients.

Mischel (1973) replied to some of his critics by suggesting that social-learning theory can indeed incorporate certain personality variables in a more systematic fashion than was made clear in his original pronouncements in 1968. He suggested a set of primarily cognitive "person variables." The expectancy of affecting or not affecting the environment may, for example, be a major factor determining behavior and allowing its prediction.

In the course of the debate touched off by Mischel's important book, other psychologists suggested that his original position was too extreme. Block (1971) challenged Mischel's conclusions regarding the inconsistency of behavior. In examining the studies Mischel used to support his claim, Block found that most of them had serious flaws. Evidence of consistency and stability of behavior was reported by Epstein (1979), who also criticized the studies used by Mischel to buttress the situationist position. Those studies, noted Epstein, looked only at small bits of behavior, a strategy as inappropriate as it would be to measure IQ by looking at a person's score on a single item. More appropriate is an *averaging* of behavior from a range of situations. In the studies he conducted, Epstein collected and averaged data on a number of occasions and was able to demonstrate marked consistency in behavior. Indeed Allport's original views on the importance of global traits in understanding complex human behavior are enjoying a revival of interest as more data are collected that support the importance of personality dispositions (Funder, 1991).

Bandura (1986) has proposed that the heavy reliance of trait theorists on self-report questionnaires colors their conclusions because people may selectively perceive themselves as consistent and respond accordingly on these questionnaires. The questionnaires probe for typical behavior in poorly specified situations, for example, "Do you tend to lose your temper when you get angry?" On the other hand, if people are observed in a variety of different situations, their actual behavior will show itself to be much more diverse and sensitive to environmental differences—a conclusion that can be drawn from a vast literature in social and personality psychology.

An intriguing possibility is that the culture fosters a trait orientation to understanding behavior. Most of us grew up with the idea that people can be characterized as nice, good-humored, just, rotten, and so forth. It may also be the case that most of us *value* consistency in our and others' behavior even when, alas, that consistency leads us to conclude that little good is to be expected from a given individual because we judge that person to be lazy or mean. A belief in traits conveys predictability and perhaps also control: if Joe is a good guy, then we can rely on him no matter what; and if Jake is a jerk, then that too can be relied on and planned around, even if we wish he were a different sort of person.

Bandura (1986) went on to assert that Epstein and other trait theorists neglect the *functionality* of performing behavior X in situation Y, that is, whether it pays off to act a certain way in a particular situation. As a social behaviorist, Bandura focuses more than do trait theorists on the situational determinants of behavior, especially the reinforcements anticipated by the individual. "Aggressive acts by delinquents towards parish priests and rival gang members will correlate poorly, however much averaging one does" (p. 10).

Of course some situations call forth the same behavior from virtually *all* individuals; a situationalist perspective can thus sometimes lead to a traitlike prediction. For example, most people at a beach on a hot summer day are likely to wear few clothes and to swim; and most people in a library are likely to read and to speak only in hushed tones. All well and good, but a complete analysis of behavior would have to include a prediction of whether a given individual would read at the beach, daydream about the beach while sitting in a library, or even be in such a situation at all (Anastasi, 1990)! What is emerging from this sometimes contentious literature on traits versus behavioral variability is an appreciation for the way personality factors *interact* with different environments, a paradigmatic perspective that overlaps considerably with the diathesis–stress viewpoint that marks our own study of psychopathology.

SUMMARY

Clinicians rely on several modes of assessment in trying to find out how best to describe a patient, in their search for the reasons a patient is troubled, and in designing effective treatments. However clinicians and researchers go about gathering such information, they must be concerned with both reliability and validity, the former referring to whether measurement is consistent and replicable, the latter, whether our assessments are tapping into what we want to be measuring. The many assessment procedures described in this chapter vary greatly in their reliability and validity. Regardless of how unstructured an assessment method may appear, it inevitably reflects the paradigm of the investigator; our earlier discussion of scientific paradigms in Chapter 2 is important to bear in mind when considering how information is gathered in the clinical context.

Two main approaches to assessment are examined: biological and psychological. Biological assessments include sophisticated, computer-controlled imaging techniques, such as CAT scans, that allow us to actually see various structures of the living brain; neuropsychological tests, such as the Halstead–Reitan, that base inferences of brain defects on variations in responses to psychological tests; and physiological measurements, such as heart rate and skin conductance.

Psychological assessments include clinical interviews, structured or relatively unstructured conversations in which the clinician probes the patient for information about his or her problems; psychological tests, which range from the presentation of ambiguous stimuli, as in the Rorschach and the Thematic Apperception Test, to empirically derived self-report questionnaires like the Minnesota Multiphasic Personality Inventory; and intelligence tests, which evaluate a person's intellectual ability and predict how well he or she will do in future academic situations.

Newer approaches to clinical assessment are found in behavioral and cognitive assessment, which is more situationally oriented than most of the preceding techniques. Information is gathered on four sets of factors: situational determinants, organismic variables, responses, and the consequences of behavior. Whereas traditional assessment seeks to understand people in terms of general traits or personality structure, behavioral and cognitive assessment is concerned more with how people act, feel, and think in particular situations. Specificity is the hallmark of cognitive and behavioral assessment, the assumption being that by operating within this framework it is possible to gather more useful information about people.

Another characteristic is its close links to therapy: the validity of an assessment is asserted to depend in large measure on its utility in helping us decide on and design therapeutic interventions. Behavioral and cognitive assessment approaches include: direct observation of behavior either in natural surroundings or in contrived settings; interviews and self-report measures that are situational in their focus; and specialized cognitive assessment procedures that attempt to uncover beliefs, attitudes, and thinking patterns thought to be important in theories of psychopathology and therapy. The assessment of anxiety reflects the complexities of conceptualizing and measuring a construct that is as important in psychopathology as it is difficult to measure.

Cultural and racial factors play a role in clinical assessment. Minority clients may react differently from whites to assessment techniques developed on the basis of research with white populations. Clinicians can have biases when evaluating minority patients, which can lead to minimizing or overdiagnosing a patient's psychopathology. These questions are important for both scientific and ethical reasons.

The stability of human behavior across situations is highly controversial. The issue has for years been of both theoretical and practical interest to psychologists. Now, with the development of behavioral models of psychopathology and treatment, it has assumed special importance. The answers are far from in, but it appears prudent to say that behavior across situations is probably more variable than was once thought by traditional personality theorists and also more stable than many of those working in the learning paradigm believe.

KEY TERMS

reliability
interrater reliability
test-retest reliability
alternate-form reliability
split-half reliability
correlation
validity
concurrent (descriptive) validity
predictive validity
construct validity
meninges
cerebral hemispheres
corpus callosum
cerebral cortex
gyri
frontal lobe
parietal lobe
temporal lobe
occipital lobe
white matter
diencephalon
hypothalamus
midbrain
brain stem
pons
medulla oblongata
cerebellum
limbic system
CAT scan
PET scan
nuclear magnetic response imaging (NMR)
neurologist
neuropsychologist
neuropsychological tests
psychophysiology
electrocardiogram
electrodermal responding
galvanic skin response (GSR)
somatic nervous system
autonomic nervous system (ANS)
sympathetic nervous system
parasympathetic nervous system
clinical interview
psychological tests
standardization
projective test
projective hypothesis
Rorschach Inkblot Test
Thematic Apperception Test
personality inventory
Minnesota Multiphasic Personality Inventory (MMPI)
intelligence test
aptitude test
behavioral observation
self-monitoring
reactivity [of behavior]

c h a p t e r   f i v e

Research Methods in the Study of Abnormal Behavior

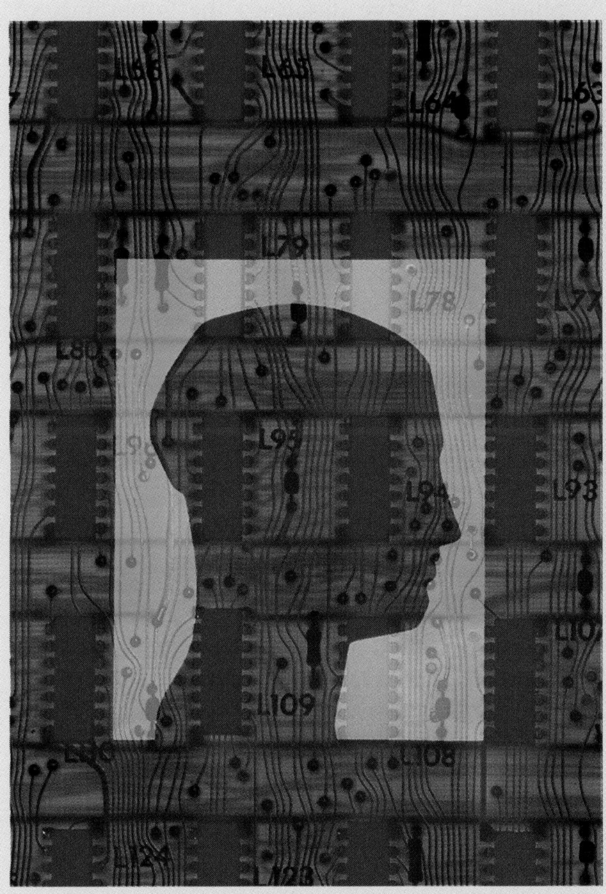

From our discussion of different ways of conceptualizing and treating abnormal behavior and of problems in its classification and assessment, it should be clear that there is less than total agreement on how abnormal behavior ought to be studied. Our approach to the field is based on the belief that more progress will be made through scientific research than armchair speculation. Abnormal behavior, as we have already noted, has been the subject of theorizing for centuries; this is a field with a high ratio of speculation to data. Because facts are hard to come by, it is important to discuss in some detail the research methods that are applied in contemporary psychopathology.

Science and Scientific Methods

In Chapter 1 we described the important role that subjective factors play in the collection and interpretation of data, indeed, in the very definition of what constitutes an observation. Although we often read in college textbooks of "the scientific method," there is actually no one science or scientific method. The word **science** comes from the Latin *scire*, "to know." In current practice, science is the pursuit of systematized knowledge through observation. Thus, the term refers to a method of systematic acquisition and evaluation of information and to a goal, the development of general theories that explain the information. It is always important for scientific observations and explanations to be testable (open to systematic probes) and reliable. We'll look briefly at the criteria of testability and reliability and then in more depth at the kingpin of it all, theory. After that, we will examine the major research methods used in studying abnormal psychology.

Testability and Falsifiability

A scientific approach requires first that propositions and ideas be stated in a clear and precise way. Only then can scientific claims be exposed to systematic probes and tests, any one of which could negate the scientist's expectations about what will be found. Statements, theories, and assertions, regardless of how plausible they may seem, must be testable in the public arena and be subject to disproof. This is the essence of **falsifiability**. The attitude of the scientist must be a doubting one. It is not enough to assert, for example, that particular traumatic experiences during childhood may cause psychological maladjustment in adulthood. This is no more than a possibility or proposition. According to a scientific point of view, such a hypothesis must be amenable to systematic testing that could show it to be false.

Reliability

Closely related to testability is the need for each observation forming a scientific body of knowledge to be reliable. We have discussed the importance of reliability as it relates to diagnosis and assessment. It is equally important in the research process. Whatever is observed must occur under prescribed circumstances not once but repeatedly. An event must be reproducible under the circumstances stated, anywhere, anytime. If the event cannot be reproduced, scientists become wary of the legitimacy of the original observation.

The Role of Theory

A **theory** is a set of propositions meant to explain a class of phenomena. A primary goal of science is to advance theories to account for data, often by proposing cause–effect relationships. The results of empirical research allow the adequacy of theories to be evaluated. Theories themselves can also play an important role in guiding research by suggesting that certain additional data be collected. More specifically, a theory permits the generation of hypotheses that are tested in research. For example, using a diathesis–stress theory of schizophrenia, researchers could derive specific hypotheses concerning the types of stress that are involved and then gather data to see if they are indeed present. Theories themselves exist within paradigms (Chapter 2). For example, a theory that assumes that phobias are a displacement of repressed conflicts would be nested with the psychodynamic paradigm.

The generation of a theory is perhaps the most challenging part of the scientific enterprise—and one of the least understood. It is sometimes asserted, for example, that a scientist formulates a theory simply by considering data that have been previously collected and then deciding, in a rather straightforward fashion, that a given way of thinking about the data is the most economical and useful.

Although some theory building follows this course, not all does. Aspects too seldom mentioned are the *creativity* of the act and the *excitement* of finding a novel way to conceptualize things. A theory sometimes seems to leap from the scientist's head in a wonderful moment of insight. New ideas suddenly occur and connections previously overlooked are suddenly grasped. What formerly seemed obscure or meaningless makes a new kind of sense within the framework of the new theory.

In formulating a theory—and theories are *constructions* of scientists—scientists must often make use of theoretical concepts, unobservable states or processes that are inferred from observable data. Although theoretical concepts can often be inferred from observable data, they go beyond what can actually be seen or measured. Several advantages may thus be gained. First, theoretical concepts often bridge spatiotemporal relations. For example, in early physics it was noted that a magnet placed close to some iron filings would cause some of the filings to move toward it. How does one piece of metal influence another over the spatial distance? The inferred concept of magnetic fields proved to be very useful in accounting for this phenomenon. Similarly, in abnormal psychology we may want to bridge temporal gaps with theoretical concepts. If a child has had a particularly frightening experience and his or her behavior is changed for a lengthy period of time, we need to explain how the earlier event exerts an influence over subsequent behavior. The unobservable and inferred concept of *acquired fear* has been very helpful in this regard.

Theoretical concepts may also be used to summarize already observed relationships. Let us take a classic example proposed by a philosopher of science, Carl Hempel (1958). An early observer of nature has been studying what happens to various objects as they are placed in water. He or she formulates some lawlike generalizations, such as "Wood floats in water, iron sinks." In addition to the fact that a large number of such generalizations would be needed to describe exhaustively the behavior of all objects placed in liquids, exceptions to the generalizations are likely. Iron in a particular shape (boatlike) floats on water, and a waterlogged piece of wood sinks. The solution is to propose a theoretical term, in this case *specific gravity*—the ratio of the weight of an object to its volume—that can both fine-tune descriptions of what will and will not float and allow errorless statements to be made. With this theoretical term we can now readily predict what will happen to *any* body placed in *any* liquid. If the specific gravity of the object is less than that of the liquid displaced, the object will float.

Let us now examine a similar and familiar example closer to the field of psychopathology. We may observe that people who are taking an examination, who expect a momentary electric shock, or who are arguing with a companion all have sweaty palms, trembling hands, and a fast heartbeat. If we ask them how they feel, they all report that they are tense. The relationships can be depicted as shown in Figure 5.1*a*. We could also say that all the situations have made these individuals anxious, and that anxiety has in turn caused the reported tension, the sweaty palms, the faster heartbeat, and the trembling hands. Figure 5.1*b* shows anxiety as a theoretical concept explaining what has been observed. The

A theoretical concept like acquired fear is useful in accounting for the fact that some earlier experience can have an effect on current behavior.

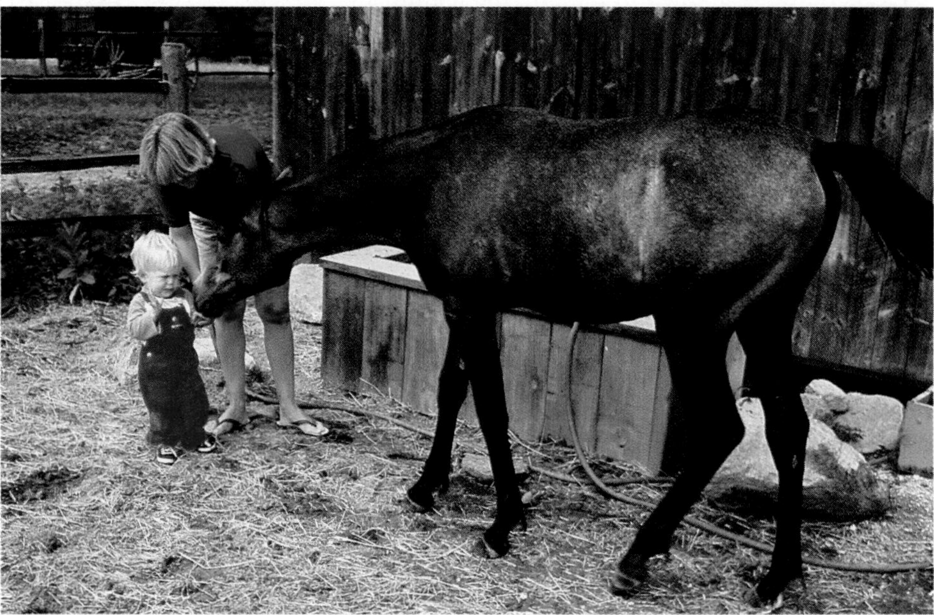

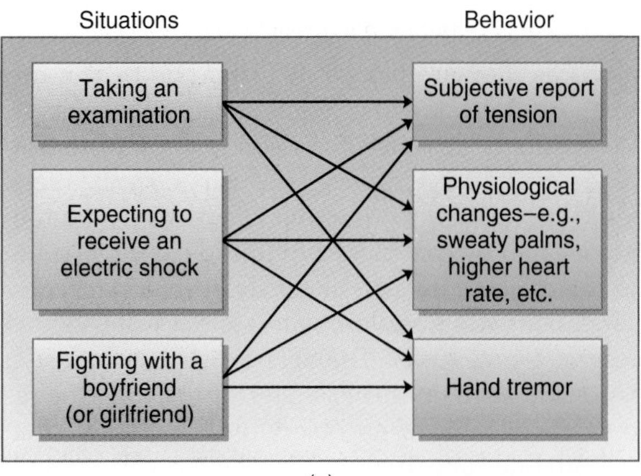

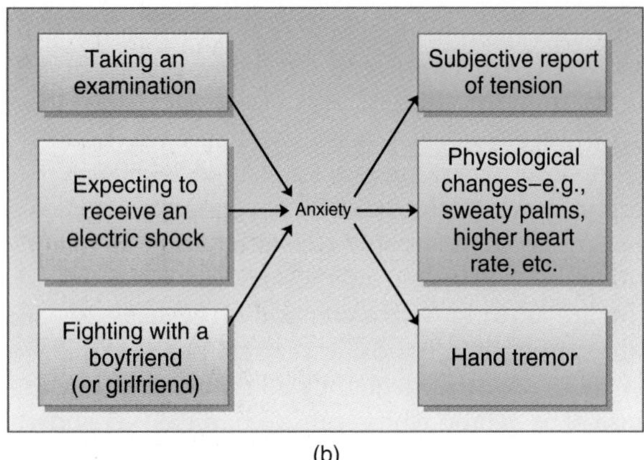

Figure 5.1 An illustration of the advantages of using anxiety as a theoretical concept. The arrows in part (b) are fewer and more readily understood. After Miller in Koch (1959).

first figure is much more complex than the second, in which the theoretical concept of anxiety becomes a mediator of the relationships.

With these advantages in mind, we must consider the criteria to be applied in judging the legitimacy of a theoretical concept. One earlier school of thought, the operationist, proposed that each concept take as its meaning a single observable and measurable operation. In this way each theoretical concept would be nothing more than one particular measurable event. For example, anxiety might be identified as *nothing more* than scoring 50 on an anxiety questionnaire. It was soon clear, however, that this approach deprived theoretical concepts of their greatest advantage. If each theoretical concept is *operationalized* in only one way, its generality is lost. If the theoretical concept of learning, for instance, is identified as a *single* operation or effect that can be measured, such as how often a rat presses a bar, other behavior, such as a child performing arithmetic problems or a college student studying this book, cannot also be called learning, and attempts to relate the different phenomena to one another might be discouraged. The early operationistic point of view quickly gave way to the more flexible position that a theoretical concept can be defined by *sets* of operations or effects. In this way the concept may be linked to several different measurements, each of which taps a different facet of the concept. For example, in Figure 5.1*b* a subjective report of tension, physiological changes, and hand tremor are a set of operations defining anxiety.

The Research Methods of Abnormal Psychology

All empirical research entails the collection of observable data. Sometimes research remains at a purely descriptive level, but often researchers observe several events and try to determine how they are associated or related. In the field of abnormal psychology, for example, there is a large descriptive literature concerning the typical symptoms of people who have been diagnosed as having particular disorders. These symptoms can then be related to other characteristics, such as gender or social class: for example, attention-deficit disorder is more common in boys than in girls. But science demands more than descriptions of relationships. We often want to understand the *causes* of the relationships we have observed. For example, we want to know *why* attention-deficit disorder is found more often in boys than in girls.

In this section we describe the most commonly used research methods in the study of abnormal behavior: the case study; epidemiological research; the correlational method; and the experiment, with groups or single subjects and mixed designs. The methods vary in the degree to which they permit the collection of adequate descriptive data and the extent to which they allow causal relationships to be inferred.

The Case Study

The most familiar and time-honored method of observing others is to study them one at a time and record detailed information about them. A clinician prepares a **case study** by collecting historical and biographical information on a single individual, often including experiences in therapy. A comprehensive case study would cover family history and background, medical history, educational background, jobs held, marital history, and details concerning development, adjustment, personality, the life course, and the current situation. Important to bear in mind, though, is the role of the clinician's paradigm in determining the kinds of information actually collected and reported in a case study. To take but one example, case studies of psychoanalytically oriented clinicians contain more information about the client's early childhood and conflicts with parents than reports made by behaviorally oriented practitioners.

Case studies from practicing clinicians may lack the degree of control and objectivity of research using other methods, but these descriptive histories have played an important role in the study of abnormal behavior. Specifically, the case study has been used in the following ways: (1) to provide a detailed description of a rare or unusual phenomenon and of important, often novel, methods or procedures of interviewing, diagnosis, and treatment; (2) to disconfirm allegedly universal aspects of a particular theoretical proposition; and (3) to generate hypotheses that can be tested through controlled research (Lazarus & Davison, 1971).

Providing Detailed Description

Because it deals with a single individual, the case study can examine a person in much more detail than is typical of other research methods. In a famous case history of multiple personality reported in 1954, Thigpen and Cleckley described a patient, Eve White, who assumed at various times three very distinct personalities. Their description of the case required an entire book, *The Three Faces of Eve*. The following brief summary emphasizes the moments in which new personalities emerged and what the separate selves knew of one another.

Eve White had been seen in psychotherapy for several months because she was experiencing severe headaches accompanied by blackouts. Her therapist described her as a retiring and gently conventional figure. One day during the course of an interview, however, she changed abruptly and in a surprising way.

> As if seized by sudden pain, she put both hands to her head. After a tense moment of silence, both hands dropped. There was a quick, reckless smile, and, in a bright voice that sparkled, she said, "Hi there, Doc!" The demure and constrained posture of Eve White had melted into buoyant repose. . . . This new and apparently carefree girl spoke casually of Eve White and her problems, always using she or her in every-reference, always respecting the strict bounds of a separate identity. . . . When asked her name, she immediately replied, "Oh, I'm Eve Black." (p. 137)

After this rather startling revelation, Eve was observed over a period of fourteen months in a series of interviews that ran to almost a hundred hours. A very important part of Eve White's therapy was to help her learn about Eve Black, her other infectiously exuberant self, who added seductive and expensive clothing to her wardrobe and lived unremembered episodes of her life. During this period still a third personality, Jane, emerged while Eve White was recollecting an early incident in which she had been painfully scalded by water from a washpot.

Jane, who from then on knew all that happened to the two Eves, although they did not share in her existence, was "far more mature, more vivid, more boldly capable, and more interesting than Eve White. She also developed a deep and revering affection for the first Eve, who was considered somewhat of a ninny by Eve Black. Jane, however, knew nothing of Eve White's earlier life, except as she learned of it through Eve's memories.

Some eleven months later, in a calamitous session, with all three personalities present at different times, Eve Black emerged and reminisced for a moment about the many good times she had had in the past but then remarked that she did not seem to have real fun anymore. She began to sob, the only time Dr. Thigpen had seen her in tears. She told him that she wanted him to have her red dress to remember her by. All expression left her face and her eyes closed. Eve White opened them. When Jane was summoned a few minutes later, she soon realized that there was no longer any Eve White either and began to experience a terrifying lost event. "No, no. . . .! Oh no, Mother. . . . I can't. . . . Don't make me do it," she cried. Jane, who earlier had known nothing of Eve's childhood, was five years old and at her grandmother's funeral. Her mother was holding her high off the floor and above the coffin and saying that she must touch her grandmother's face. As she felt her hand leave the clammy cheek, the young woman screamed so piercingly that Dr. Cleckley came running from his office across the hall.

The two physicians were not certain who confronted them. In the searing intensity of the remembered moment, a new personality had been welded. Their transformed patient did not at first feel herself as apart, and as sharply distinct a person, as had the two Eves and Jane, although she knew a great deal about all of them. When her initial bewilderment lessened, she tended to identify herself with Jane. But the identification was not sure or complete, and she mourned the absence of the two Eves, as though they were lost sisters. This new person decided to call herself Mrs. Evelyn White.

Chris Sizemore was the woman who was the subject of the famous "three faces of Eve" case. She subsequently claimed to actually have had twenty-one separate personalities.

The case of Eve White, Eve Black, Jane, and eventually Evelyn constitutes a valuable classic in the literature because it is one of only a few detailed accounts of a rare phenomenon, multiple personality. Moreover, in addition to illustrating the phenomenon itself, the original report of Thigpen and Cleckley provides valuable details about the interview procedures that they followed, and it sheds light on the way in which the woman's behavior may have developed and how the treatment progressed in this one case of multiple personality.

However, the validity of the information gathered in a case study is sometimes questionable. Chris Sizemore's book *I'm Eve* (Sizemore & Pittillo, 1977) indicates the incompleteness of Thigpen and Cleckley's case study. This woman—the real Eve White—claims that following her period of therapy with them her personality continued to fragment. In all, twenty-one separate and distinct strangers came to inhabit her body at one time or another. Contrary to Thigpen and Cleckley's report, Sizemore maintains that nine of them existed before Eve Black ever appeared. One set of personalities—they usually came in threes—would weaken and fade, to be replaced by others. Eventually her personality changes were so constant and numerous that she might become her three persons in rapid switches resembling the flipping of television channels. The debilitating round robin of transformations and the fierce battle for dominance among her selves filled her entire life. After resolving what she hopes was her last trio, by realizing finally that her alternate personalities were true aspects of herself rather than strangers from without, Chris Sizemore decided to reveal her story as a means of minimizing the past.

Disconfirming Evidence

Case histories can provide especially telling instances that negate an assumed universal relationship or law. Consider, for example, the proposition that episodes of depression are *always* preceded by an increase in life stress. Finding even a single case in which this is not true would negate the theory and, at the least, force it to be changed to assert that only *some* episodes of depression are triggered by stress.

The case study fares less well in providing evidence *in favor of* a particular theory or proposition. In the presentation of a case study, the means for confirming one hypothesis and ruling out alternative hypotheses are usually absent. To illustrate this lack of validity, let us consider a clinician who has developed a new treatment for depression, tries it out on a client, and observes that the depression lifts after six weeks of the therapy. Although it would be tempting to conclude that the therapy worked, such a conclusion cannot be drawn because any of several other factors could also have produced the change. A stressful situation in the patient's life may have resolved itself, or perhaps (and there is evidence for this) episodes of depression are naturally time-limited. Thus, there are several plausible rival hypotheses that could account for the clinical improvement. The data yielded by the case study do not allow us to determine the true cause of the change.

Generating Hypotheses

Although the case study may not play much of a role in confirming hypotheses, it does play a unique and important role in generating them. Through exposure to the life histories of a great number of patients, clinicians gain experience in understanding and interpreting them. Eventually they may notice similarities of circumstances and outcomes and formulate important hypotheses that could not have been uncovered in a more controlled investigation. For example, in his clinical work with disturbed children, Kanner (1943) noticed that some of them showed a similar constellation of symptoms, including failure to develop language and extreme isolation from other people. He therefore proposed the existence of a new diagnosis—infantile autism—which was subsequently confirmed by larger scale research and eventually found its way into the DSM (see Chapter 16).

In summary, the case study is an excellent way of examining the behavior of a single individual in great detail and in generating hypotheses that can later be evaluated by controlled research. Thus it is useful in clinical settings, where the focus is on just one person. In the fields of clinical and personality psychology, some investigators argue that the essence of psychological studies always lies in the unique characteristics of an individual (e.g., Allport, 1961). The case history is an ideal method of study in such an individualistic or **idiographic** context. But in a **nomothetic** context, when general, universal laws are sought to explain phenomena, the case study is of limited usefulness. Information collected on a single person may *not* reveal principles that are characteristic of people in general. Furthermore, the case study is unable to provide satisfactory evidence concerning cause–effect relationships.

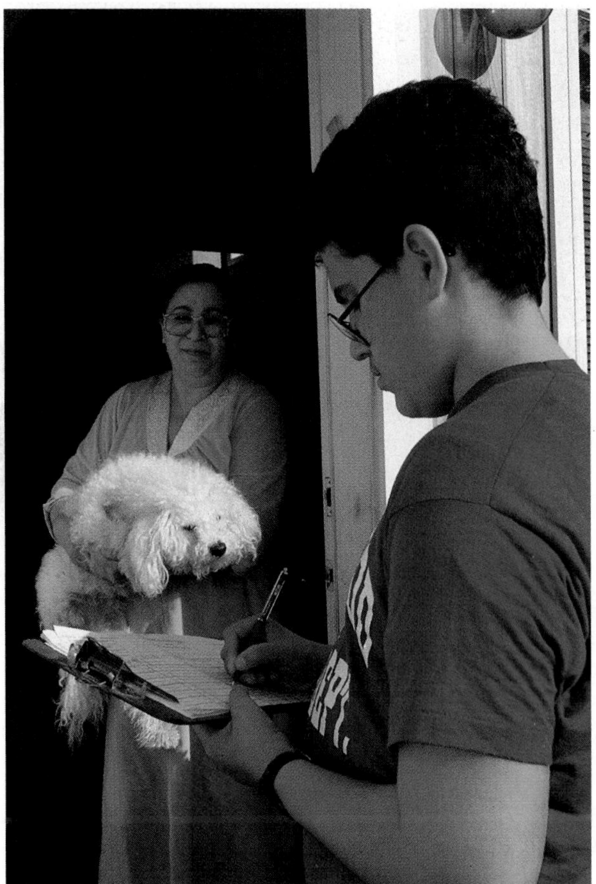

In some epidemiological research, interviewers go to homes in a community to determine the rates of different disorders.

Epidemiological Research

Epidemiology is the study of the frequency and distribution of a disorder in a population. In epidemiological research, data are gathered about the rates of disorder and its possible correlates in a large sample or population. Some key terms in epidemiological research include the following:

prevalence, the proportion of a population that has the disorder being studied at a given point or period of time;

incidence, the number of new cases of a disorder that occur in some period, usually a year;

risk factor, a condition or variable that, if present, increases the likelihood of developing the disorder being studied.

In psychopathology, knowledge of rates of various diagnoses is important for planning health care facilities. Such information has been collected in a significant large-scale study conducted in three cities—Baltimore, St. Louis, and New Haven (Myers et al., 1984). In each city a careful plan was developed for sampling residents and interviewing them using a specially constructed interview to formulate diagnoses. More than three thousand people were interviewed at each site. Some data from this study are displayed in Table 5.1. The table presents what are called **lifetime prevalence rates**, the proportion of the sample that had ever experienced a disorder up to the time of the interview. We will make use of the Myers data throughout this book.

Epidemiological research can also contribute to understanding the causes of illness. A classic example comes from a study by an early epidemiologist, John Snow. During an outbreak of cholera in London, Snow was able to determine how the disease had spread and, finally, how to stop it. As he examined cases, he learned that most victims drank water from one source, the Broad Street pump. He then hypothesized that cholera was transmitted by contaminated water. He investigated further and showed that rates of the disease were higher in London than in upstream communities, where the water was cleaner. Numerous contemporary examples also attest to the importance of epidemiological research in understanding disease. As we will see in Chapter 8, the various risk factors for heart disease (e.g., smoking, high cholesterol) were discovered in large-scale studies comparing rates of disease in persons with and without the risk factor.

In psychopathology there is no example of epidemiological research providing a convincing etiological theory of any diagnostic category. Nevertheless, useful data have been gathered in epidemiological investigations. Depression, for example, is more prevalent in women than in men. Understanding this relationship may provide clues to the cause of the disorder. Schizophrenia is much more frequent in the lowest social class. Again, if the cause of this relationship were known, it might provide clues to the etiology of the disorder. Epidemiological research may thus provide empirical results that offer avenues to search for causes.

The Correlational Method

The **correlational method** establishes whether there is a relationship between or among two or more variables. Numerous examples can be drawn from everyday life. Income correlates positively with the number of luxuries purchased: the higher the income, the more luxuries purchased. Height tends to be positively correlated with weight: taller people are usually heavier. This second relationship, that between height and weight, is by no means perfect, for many individuals are overweight, or too fat for their height, and underweight, or too thin for their height.

The correlational method is often employed in epidemiological research as well as in other studies that use smaller samples. Correlational studies address questions of the form "Are variable *X* and variable *Y* associated in some way so that they vary together (co-relate)?" In other words, questions are asked concerning relationships; for example, "Is schizophrenia related to social class?" or "Are scores obtained on college examinations related to anxiety?"

Measuring Correlation

The first step in determining a correlation is to obtain pairs of observations of the variables in question, such as height and weight, on each member in a group of subjects (Table 5.2). Once such pairs of observations are obtained, the strength of the rela-

Table 5.1 • Lifetime Prevalence of Several DSM-III Diagnoses

Diagnosis	*New Haven*	*Baltimore*	*St. Louis*
Alcohol Abuse/Dependence	11.5%	13.7%	15.7%
Schizophrenia	1.9%	1.6%	1.0%
Manic Episode	1.1%	0.6%	1.1%
Major Depressive Episode	6.7%	3.7%	5.5%
Phobia	7.8%	23.3%	9.4%
Panic Disorder	1.4%	1.4%	1.5%
Obsessive-Compulsive	2.6%	3.0%	1.9%
Somatization	0.1%	0.1%	0.1%
Anorexia	0.0%	0.1%	0.1%
Antisocial Personality	2.1%	2.6%	3.3%

Source: After Myers et al., 1984.

tionship between the two sets of observations can be determined. The most prevalent means of measuring such a relationship was devised by Karl Pearson and is referred to as the Pearson product-moment **correlation coefficient**, denoted by the symbol r. This statistic may take any value between -1.00 and $+1.00$ and measures both the magnitude and the direction of a relationship. The higher the absolute value of r, the larger or stronger the relationship between the two variables. An r of either $+1.00$ or -1.00 indicates the highest possible or perfect relationship, whereas an r of .00 indicates that the variables are unrelated. If the sign of r is positive, the two variables are said to be *positively related*. In other words, as the values for variable X increase, those for variable Y also tend to increase. Conversely, when the sign of r is negative, variables are said to be *negatively related*: as values for one variable increase, those for the other tend to decrease. The correlation between height and weight, based on the data in Table 5.2 is $+.88$, indicating a very strong positive relationship: as height increases so does weight.

Table 5.2 • Data for Determining a Correlation[a]

Individuals	*Height*	*Weight, pounds*
John	5′10″	170
Asher	5′10″	140
Eve	5′4″	112
Gail	5′3″	105
Jerry	5′10″	177
Gayla	5′2″	100
Steve	5′8″	145
Margy	5′5″	128
Gert	5′6″	143
Sean	5′10″	140
Kathleen	5′4″	116

[a]For these figures $r = +.88$

Plotting a relationship graphically often provides a better feel for it. Figure 5.2 presents diagrams of positive and negative correlations as well as unrelated variables. In the diagrams each point corresponds to two values determined for the given subject, the value of variable X and that of variable Y.

Figure 5.2 Scatter diagrams showing various degrees of correlational relationship.

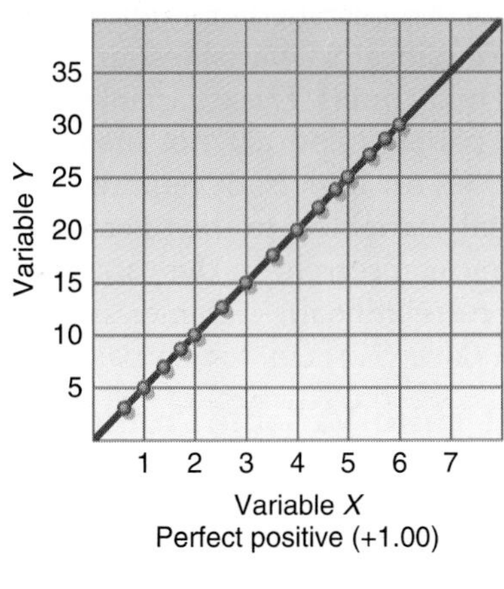

Perfect positive (+1.00)

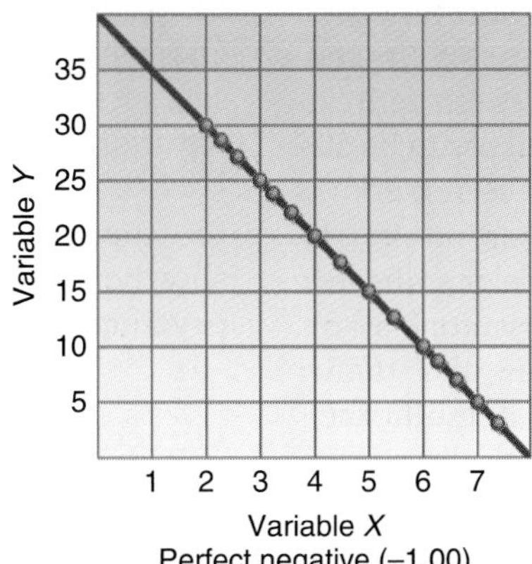

Perfect negative (–1.00)

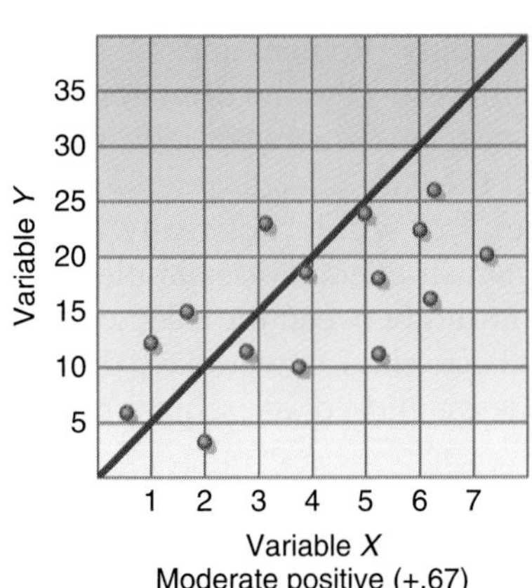

Moderate positive (+.67)

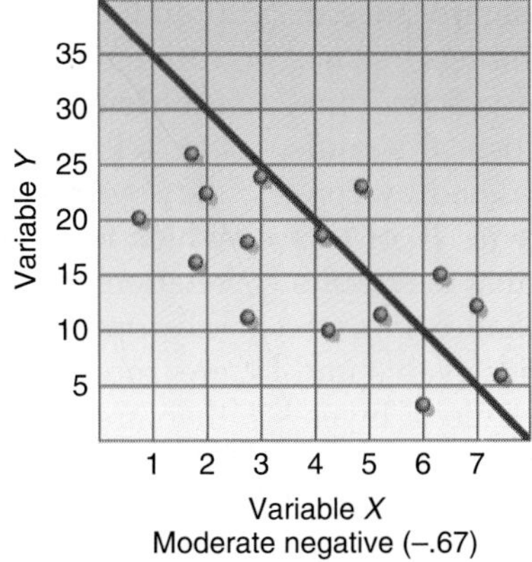

Moderate negative (–.67)

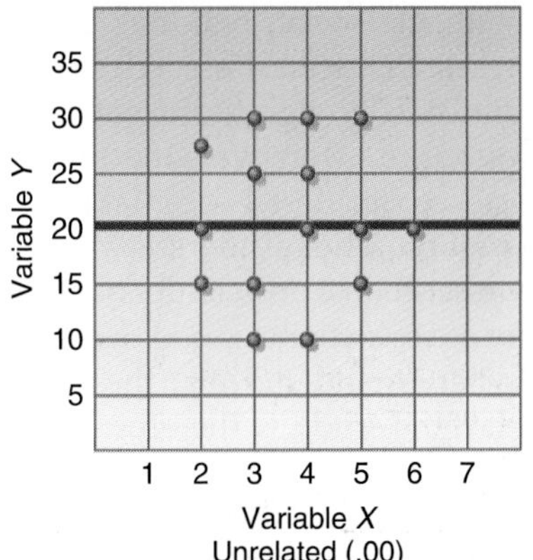

Unrelated (.00)

In perfect relationships all the points fall on a straight line; if we know the value of only one of the variables for an individual, we can state with certainty the value of the other variable. Similarly, when the correlation is relatively large, there is only a small degree of scatter about the line of perfect correlation. The values tend to scatter increasingly and become dispersed as the correlations become lower. When the correlation reaches .00, knowledge of a person's score on one variable tells us nothing about his or her score on the other.

Statistical Significance

Thus far we have established that the magnitude of a correlation coefficient tells us the strength of a relationship between two variables. But scientists demand a more rigorous evaluation of the importance of correlations and use the concept of statistical significance for this purpose. Essentially, **statistical significance** refers to the likelihood that the results of an investigation are due to chance. A statistically significant correlation is one that is *not* likely to have occurred by chance.

Traditionally in psychological research, a correlation is considered statistically significant if the likelihood is five or less in one hundred that it is a chance finding. This level of significance is called the .05 level, commonly written as $p < .05$. In general, as the size of the correlation coefficient increases, the result is more and more likely to be statistically significant. For example, a correlation of .80 is more likely to be significant than one of .40. Whether a correlation attains statistical significance also depends on the number of observations made. The greater the number of observations, the smaller r needs to be in order to reach statistical significance. Thus a correlation of $r = .30$ is statistically significant when the number of observations is large, for example, .300, although it would not be significant if only 20 observations were made.

Statistical significance should not be confused with the social, real-life, or clinical significance of research results. Research can yield findings that are statistically significant yet devoid of practical importance. Moreover, the level of statistical significance considered acceptable is determined by convention. Thus if there is a probability of .10 or less rather than a probability of .05 or less that the results of a correlational study occurred by chance, it is nowhere mandated that these are chance events and that the study is therefore totally worthless. Investigators may decide that, given the nature of a particular study, these results are quite encouraging and should not be disregarded. Then they must convince their colleagues that these findings are indeed valid. In this sense, science is a game of persuasion.

Applications to Psychopathology

The correlational method is widely used in the field of abnormal psychology. Whenever we compare people given one diagnosis with those given another or with normal people, the study is correlational. For example, two diagnostic groups may be compared to see how much stress members of each experienced before the onset of their disorders. Or, normal people and people with an anxiety disorder may be compared on their physiological reactivity to a stressor administered in the laboratory.

Often such investigations are not recognized as correlational, perhaps because—as is often so in experiments—subjects come to a laboratory for testing, or data are analyzed by comparing the average scores of the groups on each test or measure. But the logic of such studies is correlational: the correlation between two variables—having an anxiety disorder or not and the average score of each group on the physiological measure—is what is being examined. Variables such as having an anxiety disorder or not are called **classificatory variables**. In this case, the anxiety disorders were already present before the subjects performed the laboratory task. Other examples of classificatory variables are age, sex, social class, and body build. These variables are naturally occurring patterns and are not manipulated by the researcher, an important requirement for the experimental variables to be discussed shortly. Therefore, most research on the causes of psychopathology is correlational.

Directionality and Third-Variable Problems

The correlational method, although often employed in abnormal psychology, has a critical drawback. It does not allow us to determine cause–effect relationships because of two major problems of interpretation, the directionality problem and the third-variable problem. With respect to the **directionality problem**, a sizable correlation between two variables tells us only that they are related or tend to covary with each other, but we do not really know which is cause and which effect. For example, correlations have been found between the diagnosis of schizophrenia and social class; lower-class people are more frequently diagnosed as schizophrenic than are middle- and upper-class people. One possible explanation is that the stresses of living in the lower social classes produce the behavior that is subsequently labeled schizophrenic. But a second and perhaps equally plausible hypothesis has been advanced: it may be that the disorganized behavior patterns of schizophrenic individuals cause them to lose their jobs and thus to become impoverished. The problem of directionality is present in many correlational research designs, hence the often-cited dictum "Correlation does not imply causation."

The directionality problem is best addressed by using a longitudinal design in which variables of interest are studied before a disorder has developed. In this way, the hypothesized cause can be measured before the effect. For example, the most desirable way of collecting information about the development of schizophrenia would be to select a large sample of babies and follow them for the twenty to forty-five years that are the period of risk for the onset of schizophrenia. But such a method would be prohibitively expensive, for only about one individual in one hundred eventually becomes schizophrenic. The yield of data from such a simple longitudinal study would be small indeed. The **high-risk method** overcomes this problem; only individuals with greater than average risk of becoming schizophrenic in adulthood are selected for study. In most current research using this methodology, individuals who have a schizophrenic parent are selected for study; a schizophrenic parent increases a person's risk for developing schizophrenia. The high-risk method is also used to study several other disorders, and we will examine these findings in subsequent chapters.

Although correlation does not imply causation, determining whether or not two variables correlate may allow for the *disconfirmation* of certain causal hypotheses. That is, *causation does imply correlation.* For example, if an investigator has asserted that cigarette smoking causes lung cancer, he or she implies that lung cancer and cigarette smoking will be positively correlated. Studies of the two variables must show this positive correlation, or the theory will be disproved.

As for the **third-variable problem**, it may be that neither of the two variables studied in the correlation produces the other. Rather, some as yet unspecified variable or process may be responsible for the correlation. Consider the following example, which points out an obvious third variable.

> One regularly finds a high positive correlation between the number of churches in a city and the number of crimes committed in that city. That is, the more churches a city has, the more crimes are committed in it. Does this mean that religion fosters crime or does it mean that crime fosters religion? It means neither. The relationship is due to a particular third variable—population. The higher the population of a particular community, the greater . . . the number of churches and . . . the frequency of criminal activity. (Neale & Liebert, 1980, p. 109)

In psychopathology research there are numerous examples of third variables. For instance, biochemical differences between schizophrenics and normals have frequently been reported. These differences could reflect different diets or the fact that the patients are taking medication for their condition—the differences do not reveal anything telling about the nature of schizophrenia. Are there any solutions to the third-variable problem? In general, the answer is yes, although the solutions are only partially satisfactory and do not permit unambiguous causal inferences to be made from correlational data.[1]

We have already noted that facts about the causes of abnormal behavior are hard to come by. The issues we have just discussed are major reasons for this state of affairs. The psychopathologist is forced to make heavy use of the correlational method because diagnosis, a classificatory variable, is best suited to this strategy. But the relationships discovered between diagnosis and other variables are then clouded by the third-variable and directionality problems. Searching for the causes of the various psychopathologies will continue to be a challenging enterprise.

The Experiment

The factors causing the associations and relationships revealed by correlational research cannot, as we have seen, be determined with absolute certainty. The **experiment** is generally considered to be the most powerful tool for determining causal relationships between events. It involves the manipulation of an independent variable, the measurement of a dependent variable, and the random assignment of subjects to the different conditions being investigated. In the field of psychopathology, it is most often used to evaluate the effects of therapies. As an introduction to the basic components of experimental research, let us consider here the major aspects of the design and results of a study of how expressing emotions about past traumatic events is related to health (Pennebaker, Kielcolt-Glaser, & Glaser, 1988). Fifty undergraduates participated in a six-week study, one part of which required them to come to a laboratory for four consecutive days. Half the subjects were required, on each of the four days, to write a short essay about

---

[1]A readable presentation of the techniques to handle directionality and third variables can be found in Neale and Liebert's *Science and Behavior* (1986).

a past traumatic event. They were instructed as follows:

> During each of the four writing days, I want you to write about the most traumatic and upsetting experiences of your entire life. You can write on different topics each day or on the same topic for all four days. The important thing is that you write about your deepest thoughts and feelings. Ideally, whatever you write about should deal with an event or experience that you have not talked with others about in detail.

The remaining students also came to the laboratory each day but wrote essays describing such things as their daily activities, a recent social event, the shoes they were wearing, and their plans for the rest of the day. Information about how often the participating undergraduates used the university health center was available for the fifteen-week period before the study began and for the six weeks after it had begun. These data are shown in Figure 5.3. As can be seen, members of the two groups had visited the health center about equally prior to the experiment. After writing the essays, however, the number of visits declined for students who wrote about traumas and increased for the remaining students. (This increase may have been due to seasonal variation in rates of visits to the health center. The second measure of number of visits was taken in February, just before midterm exams.) From these data the investigators concluded that expressing emotions has a beneficial effect on health.

Basic Features of Experimental Design

The foregoing example illustrates many of the basic features of an experiment. The researcher typically begins with an **experimental hypothesis**, what he or she assumes will happen when a particular variable is manipulated. Pennebaker et al. hypothesized that expressing emotion about a past event would improve health. Second, the investigator chooses an **independent variable** that can be manipulated, that is, some factor that will be under the control of the experimenter. In the case of the Pennebaker et al. study, some students wrote about past traumatic events and others about mundane happenings. Third, the researcher arranges for the measurement of a **dependent variable**, which is expected to depend on or vary with manipulations of the independent variable. The dependent variable in this study was the number of visits to the health center. When differences between groups are found to be a function of variations in the independent variable, the researcher is said to have produced an **experimental effect**.

Figure 5.3 Health center illness visits for the periods before and during the experiment. After Pennebaker *et al.* (1987).

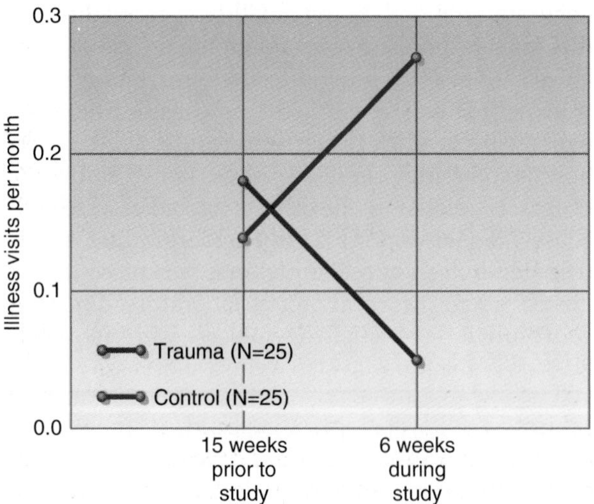

Internal Validity

An important feature of any experimental design is the inclusion of at least one **control group** which does not receive the experimental treatment (the independent variable). A control group is necessary if the effects in an experiment are to be attributed to the manipulation of the independent variable. In the Pennebaker et al. study the control group wrote about mundane happenings. The data from the control group provide a standard against which the effects of expressing emotion can be compared.

To illustrate this point with another example, consider a study of the effectiveness of a particular therapy in modifying some form of abnormal behavior. Let us assume that persons with poor self-concepts undergo therapy to remedy their condition. At the end of six months the patients are reassessed, and it is found that their self-concepts have improved compared with what they were at the beginning of the study. Unfortunately, if there is no control group against which to compare the improvement, such an investigation would not produce internally valid data. The improvement in self-concept from the beginning of the treatment to the end could have been brought about by several factors in addition to or instead of the treatment employed. For example, it may be that certain environmental events occurring within the six months produced the improvement. Or people with a poor self-concept may acquire better feelings about themselves with the mere passage of time.

Variables such as these are often called **confounds**; their effects are so intermixed that they cannot be measured separately and, like the third variables in correlational studies, they make the results difficult or impossible to interpret. These confounds, and others described in this chapter, are unfortunately widespread in research on the effects of psychotherapy, as is documented often throughout this book. Studies in which the effect obtained cannot be attributed with confidence to the independent variable are called *internally invalid* studies. In contrast, research has **internal validity** when the effect can be confidently attributed to the manipulation of the independent variable.

In the example just outlined, internal validity could improve by the inclusion of a control group. Such a group might consist of individuals with poor self-concepts who do *not* receive the therapeutic treatment. Changes in the self-concepts of these control subjects would constitute a standard against which the effects of the independent variable could be assessed. If a change in self-concept is brought about by particular environmental events, quite beyond any therapeutic intervention, the experimental group receiving the treatment and the control group receiving no treatment are equally likely to be affected. On the other hand, if after six months the self-concepts of the treated group have improved more than those of the untreated control group, we can be relatively confident that this difference is, in fact, attributable to the treatment.

The inclusion of a control group, however, does not ensure internal validity. To illustrate, let us consider another study of therapy, this time the treatment of two hospital wards of psychiatric patients. An investigator may decide to select one ward to receive an experimental treatment and another ward as a control. When the researcher later compares the frequencies of deviant behavior in these two groups, he or she will want to attribute any differences between them to the fact that patients in one ward received treatment and those in the other did not. But the researcher cannot legitimately draw this inference, for there is a competing hypothesis that cannot be disproved—that even before treatment the patients who happened to receive therapy might have had a lower level of deviant behavior than the patients who became the control group. The principle of experimental design disregarded in this defective study is that of **random assignment**, a technique that ensures that every subject in the research has an equal chance of being assigned to any of the groups. For example, in a two-group experiment a coin can be tossed for each subject. If the coin turns up heads, the subject is assigned to one group; if tails, he or she is assigned to the other. This procedure minimizes the likelihood that differences between the groups after treatment will reflect pretreatment differences in the samples rather than true experimental effects. Random assignment was employed in the Pennebaker experiment.

Even with both a control group and random assignment, the results of the research may still be invalid. An additional source of error is the potential biasing influence of the experimenter or observers. As Rosenthal (1966) suggested, the expectancies of an experimenter about the outcome of a study may conspire to produce results favorable to the initial hypothesis, an outcome that has become known as the **Rosenthal effect**. The researcher might, for example, subtly manipulate the subject to give expected and desired responses. Although the pervasiveness of these effects has been questioned (Barber & Silver, 1968; Kent et al., 1974), experimenters must remain on guard lest their results be influenced by their own expectations. To avoid biases of this type, many studies apply the **double-blind procedure**. For example, in an investigation comparing the psychological effects of two drugs, the person dispensing the pills is kept ignorant (i.e., blind) about their actual content, and the subject is also not informed about the treatment he or she is receiving. With such controls the behavior observed during the course of the treatment is probably not influenced by biasing.

Earlier, we briefly defined the term *experimental effect*, but we have yet to learn how to decide that an effect is important. To evaluate the importance of experimental results, as with correlations, researchers determine their statistical significance, the logic being the same as with correlations.

External Validity

The extent to which the results of any particular piece of research can be generalized beyond the immediate experiment is the measure of their **external validity**. For example, if investigators have demonstrated that a particular treatment helps a group of patients, they will undoubtedly want to determine whether this treatment will be effective in ministering to other patients, at other times, and in other places. Pennebaker et al. would hope that their findings generalize to other instances of emotional expression (e.g., confiding to a close friend), to other situations, and to people other than those who participated in the experiment.

The external validity of the results of a psychological experiment is extremely difficult to determine. For example, there is the reactivity of observed behavior: merely knowing that one is a subject in a psychological experiment often alters behavior, and thus results are produced in the laboratory that may not automatically be produced in the natural environment. In many instances results obtained from investigations with laboratory animals such as rats have been generalized to human beings. Such generalizations are hazardous, since there are enormous differences between *Homo sapiens* and *Rattus norvegicus*. Researchers must be continually alert to the extent to which they claim generalization for findings, for there are, in fact, no entirely adequate ways of dealing with the questions of external validity. The best that can be done is to perform similar studies in new settings with new participants so that the limitations, or the generality, of a finding can be determined.

Analogue Experiments

The experimental method is judged to be the most telling way to determine cause–effect relationships. The effectiveness of treatments for psychopathology is usually evaluated by the experimental method, for it has proved a powerful tool for determining whether a therapy reduces suffering. As you may well have surmised, however, the method has in fact been little used by those seeking the causes of abnormal behavior. Suppose that a researcher has hypothesized that a child's emotionally charged, overdependent relationship with his or her mother causes schizophrenia. An experimental test of this hypothesis would require assigning infants randomly to either of two groups of mothers! The mothers in one group would undergo an extensive training program to ensure that they would be able to create a highly emotional atmosphere and foster overdependence in children. The mothers in the second group would be trained not to create such a relationship with the children under their care. The researcher would then wait until the subjects in each group reached adulthood and determine how many of them had become schizophrenic. Obviously, such an experimental design already contains insurmountable practical problems. But practical issues are hardly the principal ones that must concern us. Consider the ethics of such an experiment. Would the potential scientific gain of proving that an overdependent relationship with a person's mother brings on schizophrenia outweigh the suffering that would surely be imposed on some of the participants? In almost any person's view it would not. (Ethical issues are considered in greater detail in Chapter 21.)

In an effort to take advantage of the power of the experimental method, research on the causes of abnormal behavior has sometimes taken the format of an **analogue experiment**. Investigators attempt to bring a *related* phenomenon, that is, an analogue, into the laboratory for more intensive study. In this way, internally valid results can be obtained, although the problem of external validity may be accentuated. In one type of analogue study, behavior is rendered temporarily abnormal through experimental manipulations. For example, lactate infusion can elicit a panic attack, hypnotic suggestion can produce blindness, and threats to self-esteem can increase anxiety and depression. If pathology can be experimentally induced by any one of these manipulations, the same process, existing in the natural environment, might well be a cause of the disorder. The key to interpreting such studies lies in the validity of the independent variable as a reflection of some true environmental experience and of the dependent variable as an analogue of a clinical problem. Is a stressor encountered in the laboratory fundamentally similar to one that occurs in the natural environment? Are transient increases in anxiety or depression reasonable analogues of their clinical

Harlow's famous analog research examined the effects of early separation from the mother on infant monkeys. Even a cloth surrogate mother is better than isolation for preventing subsequent emotional distress and depression.

counterparts? Results of such experiments must be interpreted with great caution and generalized with care, but they do provide valuable hypotheses about the origins of psychopathology.

In another type of analogue study, subjects are selected because they are considered similar to patients given certain diagnoses. A large amount of research, for example, has been conducted with college students who were selected for study because they scored high on a paper-and-pencil measure of anxiety or depression. The question here is whether these anxious or depressed students are adequate analogues for those with an anxiety disorder or major depression. Some research bearing on this issue will be discussed in Chapter 9.

Whether experiments are regarded as analogues depends not on the experiment itself but rather on the use to which it is put. We can very readily study avoidance behavior in a white rat. The data collected from such studies are not analogue data if we limit our discussion to the behavior of rats. They become analogue data only when we draw implications from them and apply them to other domains, such as anxiety in human beings.

Some of the animal experiments we examine in later chapters are analogue in nature, with their results being generalized to human beings (e.g., see Chapter 9, page 234). It is important to keep in mind that we are arguing by analogy when, for example, we attempt to relate stress reactions of white rats to anxiety in people. At the same time, however, we do not agree with those who regard such analogue research as totally and intrinsically worthless for the study of human behavior. Although human beings and other mammals differ on many important dimensions, it does not follow that principles of behavior derived from animal research are necessarily irrelevant to human behavior.

Single-Subject Experimental Research

Experiments do not always have to be conducted on groups of people. In this section we shall consider **single-subject experimental designs** in which one subject is studied and experiences a manipulated variable.

The strategy of relying on a single subject appears to violate many of the principles of research design that we have discussed. As with the case study, there is no control group to act as a check on a single subject. Moreover, generalization is difficult because the findings may relate to a unique aspect of the one individual whose behavior we have explored. Hence the study of a single individual would appear unlikely to yield any findings that could possess the slightest degree of internal or external validity. But, as we shall see, the experimental study of a single subject *can* be an effective research technique for certain purposes (Hersen & Barlow, 1976).

A method developed by Tate and Baroff (1966) for reducing the self-injurious behavior of a nine-year-old boy, Sam, serves as an example. The child, who had been diagnosed as psychotic, engaged in a wide range of self-injurious behavior, such as banging his head against the floors and walls, slapping his face with his hands, punching his face and head with his fists, hitting his shoulder with his chin, and kicking himself. Despite his self-injurious behavior, Sam was not entirely antisocial. In fact, he obviously enjoyed contact with other people and would cling to them, wrap his arms around them, and sit in their laps. This affectionate behavior gave the investigators the idea for an experimental treatment.[2]

The study ran for twenty days. For a period of time on each of the first five days, the frequency of Sam's self-injurious actions was observed and recorded. Then on each of the next five days the two adult experimenters accompanied Sam on a short walk around the campus, during which they talked to him and held his hands continuously. The adults responded to each of Sam's self-injurious actions by immediately jerking their hands away from him and not touching him again until three seconds after such activity had ceased. The frequency of the self-injurious acts was again recorded. As part of the experiment, the schedule was then systematically reversed. For the next five days there were no walks, and Sam's self-afflicting behavior was again merely observed. Then for the last five days the experimenters reinstated their experimental procedure. The dramatic reduction in undesirable behavior induced by the treatment is shown in Figure 5.4. The design of such experiments, usually referred to as a **reversal design** or **ABAB design** requires that some aspect of the subject's behavior be carefully measured during a given time period, the baseline (A); during a period when a treatment is introduced (B); during a reinstatement of the conditions that pre-

[2]The use of the adjective *experimental* in this context prompts us to distinguish between two different meanings of the word. As applied to the research methods that have been discussed, the adjective refers to the manipulation of a variable that allows conclusions of a cause–effect relationship to be drawn. But here the word refers to a treatment whose effects are unknown or only poorly understood. Thus an experimental drug is one about which we know relatively little; however, such a drug might well be used in a correlational design or reported in a case study.

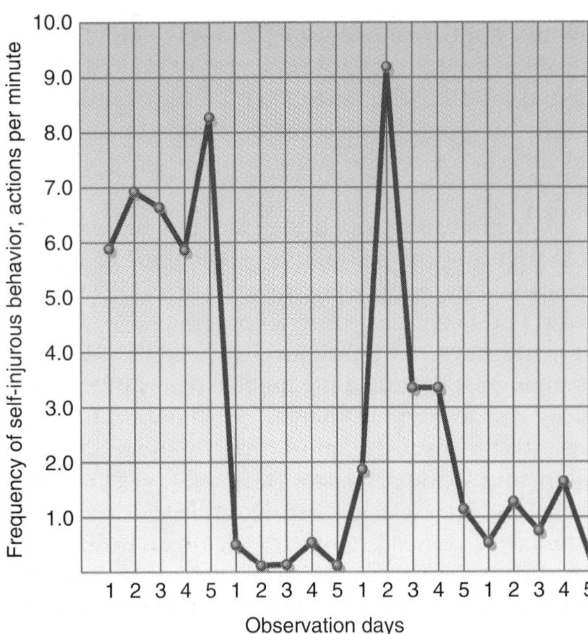

Figure 5.4 Effects of a treatment for self-injurious behavior in an experiment with an ABAB single-subject design. Note the rapid shifts in frequency of problem behavior as treatment is introduced (b), withdrawn (a), and finally reinstated (b). Adapted from Tate and Baroff (1966).

vailed in the baseline period (A); and finally during a reintroduction of the experimental manipulation (B). If behavior in the experimental period is different from that in the baseline period, reverses when the experimentally manipulated conditions are reversed, and re-reverses when the treatment is again introduced, there is little doubt that the manipulation, rather than chance or uncontrolled factors, has produced the change.

The reversal technique cannot always be employed, however, for the initial state of a subject may not be recoverable, as when treatment aims to produce enduring change, the goal of all therapeutic interventions. Moreover, in studies of therapeutic procedures, reinstating the original condition of the subject or patient would generally be considered an unethical practice. Most therapists would be extremely unwilling to act in any way that might bring back the very behavior for which a client has sought help, merely to prove that a particular treatment was indeed the effective agent in changing the behavior. Fortunately, there are other single-subject experimental designs that avoid these problems.

As indicated earlier, even though an experiment with a single subject can demonstrate an effect, generalization is not usually possible. The fact that a treatment works for a single subject does not necessarily imply that the treatment will be universally effective. If the search for more widely applicable treatment is the major focus of an investigation, the single-subject design has a serious drawback. However, it may well help investigators to decide whether large-scale research with groups is warranted.

Mixed Designs

The experimental and correlational research techniques can be combined in what is called a mixed design. In a **mixed design**, subjects who can be divided into two or more discrete and typically nonoverlapping populations are assigned as groups to each experimental condition. The two different types of populations, for example, schizophrenics and phobics, constitute a classificatory variable. That is, the variables schizophrenia and phobia were neither manipulated nor created by the investigator, and they can only be correlated with the manipulated conditions, which are true experimental variables.

To illustrate how a mixed design is applied, consider an investigation of the effectiveness of three types of therapy (the experimental variable) on psychiatric patients who were divided into two groups on the basis of the severity of their illnesses (the classificatory variable). The question was whether the effectiveness of the treatments varied with the severity of illness. The hypothetical outcome of such a study is presented in Figure 5.5. Figure 5.5*b* shows the results obtained when the patients were divided into two groups on the basis of the severity of their problems. Figure 5.5*a* illustrates the unfortunate

Figure 5.5 Effects of three treatments on patients whose symptoms vary in degree of severity. In (a), when the severity of the illness is not known and the patients are grouped together, treatment number 3 appears to be best. In (b), the same data as in (a) are reanalyzed, dividing patients by severity. Now, treatment 3 is no longer best for any patients.

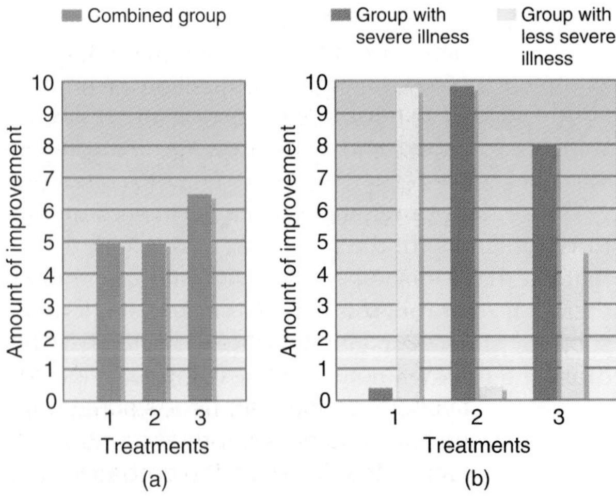

conclusions that would be drawn were the patients not divided into those with severe and those with less severe illnesses. When all patients were grouped together, treatment 3 produced the greatest amount of improvement. Therefore, if no information about differential characteristics of the patients is available, treatment 3 would be preferred. When the severity of the patients' difficulties is considered, however, treatment 3 would no longer be the therapy of choice for *any* of the patients. Rather, as seen in Figure 5.5*b*, treatment 1 would be selected for those with less severe illness and treatment 2 for patients with more severe illness. Thus a mixed design can identify which treatment applies best to which group of subjects.

In interpreting the results of mixed designs, we must be continually aware of the fact that one of the variables (severity of illness in our example) is not manipulated. Therefore the problems we have previously noted in interpreting correlations are to be found in interpreting the results of mixed designs as well.

Yet the inclusion of a manipulated variable, particularly one with multiple levels, does offer some advantages. Consider a study (Neale, 1971) in which schizophrenics and control subjects were administered an information-processing task of four different levels of complexity. The subjects were briefly presented with visual displays containing one, four, eight, or twelve alphabetic characters. Their task was to search the display and tell the experimenter whether it contained a *T* or an *F*. The results of this investigation showed that schizophrenics differed from control subjects whenever the two groups saw more than one letter. The schizophrenics' performance was poorer than the control subjects' in one, but not all, of the conditions. A differential deficit is more informative than a simple deficit on a single task. Maher (1974) explains why:

> With the hypothesis that bulls are characterized by a desire to break Royal Worcester china, we stock a shop exclusively with that item, turn the bulls loose, and watch the ensuing destruction. Our hypothesis is duly confirmed—especially if our control group is composed of mice. (p. 2)

Maher goes on to point out that "just as bulls tend to break any kind of china, patient populations tend to do poorly at many tasks." In other words, the demonstration of a simple deficit provides little specific information, because the poor performance could be caused by any number of factors. A differential deficit, however, allows certain plausible rival hypotheses to be ruled out. The equality of performances of schizophrenics and control subjects when only a single letter was presented makes it unlikely that the schizophrenics' difficulties with larger displays could be attributed to a general failure to comprehend the task. If the schizophrenic subjects had been unable to understand the task or comply with the experimenter's instructions, they would not have done as well as control subjects in determining whether a single letter was a *T* or an *F*.

Our survey of the major research methods of abnormal psychology is now complete. It should be apparent that there is no perfect method that will easily reveal the secrets of psychopathology and therapy. Our task in subsequent chapters will be to attempt to synthesize the information yielded by investigations conducted with varying methodologies and to apply these results to advance knowledge.

SUMMARY

Science represents an agreed-upon problem-solving enterprise, with specific procedures for gathering and interpreting data in order to build a systematic body of knowledge. The position taken in this book is that scientific statements must have the following characteristics: they must be testable in the public arena; they must be subject to falsification, they must derive from reliable observations; and, although they may contain references to unobservable processes, the concepts inferred must be linked to observable and measurable events or outcomes.

It is important to consider the various methods that scientists employ to collect data and arrive at conclusions. Clinical case studies serve unique and important functions in psychopathology, such as allowing rare phenomena to be studied intensively in all their complexity. Case studies also encourage the formulation of hypotheses that can be tested later through controlled research. Epidemiological research gathers information about the prevalence of disorders and about risk factors that increase the probability of a disorder.

Correlational methods are the most important means of conducting research in abnormal psychology, for diagnoses are classificatory and not experimentally manipulated variables. In correlational studies, statistical procedures allow us to determine the extent to which two or more variables correlate or co-vary. Conclusions drawn from nearly all correlational studies cannot legitimately be interpreted in cause–effect terms, however, although there is great temptation to do so.

The experimental method entails the manipulation of independent variables and the careful measurement of their effects on dependent variables. An experiment usually begins with a hypothesis to be tested, that manipulation of one variable will cause another to change in a specific way. Subjects are generally assigned to one of at least two groups: an experimental group, which experiences the manipulation of the independent variable, and a control group, which does not. If differences between the experimental and control groups are observed on the dependent variable, we can conclude that the independent variable did have an effect. Since it is important to ensure that experimental and control subjects do not differ from one another before the introduction of the independent variable, they are assigned randomly to groups. Experimenters must guard against bias by keeping themselves unaware of what group a given subject is in, experimental or control. If these conditions are met, the experiment has internal validity. The external validity of the findings, whether they can be generalized to situations and people not studied within the experiment, can be assessed only by performing similar experiments in the actual domain of interest with new subjects.

Single-subject experimental designs that expose one subject to different treatments over a period of time can provide internally valid results, although the generality of conclusions is typically limited. Mixed designs are combinations of experimental and correlational methods. For example, two different kinds of patients (the classificatory variable) may be exposed to various treatments (the experimental variable).

A science is only as good as its methodology. Thus students of abnormal psychology must appreciate the rules that social scientists abide by if they are to adequately evaluate the research and theories that form the subject matter of the remainder of this book.

KEY TERMS

science
falsifiability
theory
case study
idiographic
nomothetic
epidemiology
prevalence
incidence
risk factor
lifetime prevalence rates
correlational method
correlation coefficient
statistical significance
classificatory variables
directionality problem
high-risk method
third-variable problem
experiment
experimental hypothesis
independent variable
dependent variable
experimental effect
control group
confounds
internal validity
random assignment
Rosenthal effect
double-blind procedure
external validity
analogue experiment
single-subject experimental design
reversal (ABAB) design
mixed design

PART TWO

Psychological Disorders

c h a p t e r s i x

Anxiety Disorders

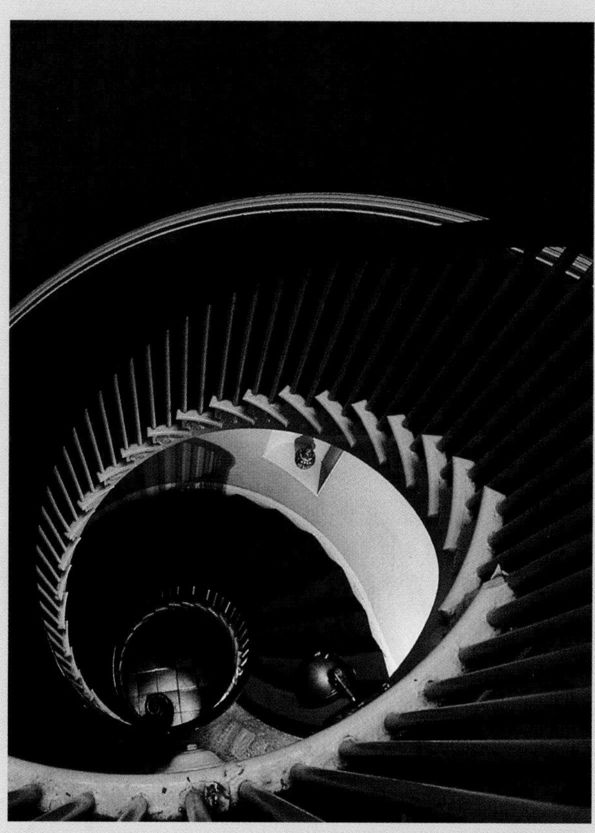

> How would you like to be a tame, somewhat shy and unaggressive little boy of nine, somewhat shorter and thinner than average, and find yourself put three times a week, every Monday, Wednesday, and Friday, as regularly and inexorably as the sun sets and the sky darkens and the globe turns black and dead and spooky with no warm promise that anyone anywhere ever will awaken again, into the somber, iron custody of someone named Forgione, older, broader, and much larger than yourself, a dreadful, powerful, broad-shouldered man who is hairy, hard-muscled, and barrel-chested and wears immaculate tight white or navy-blue T-shirts that seem as firm and unpitying as the figure of flesh and bone they encase like a mold, whose ferocious, dark eyes you never had courage enough to meet and whose assistant's name you did not ask or were not able to remember, and who did not seem to like you or approve of you? He could do whatever he wanted to you. He could do whatever he wanted to me. (Heller, 1966, p. 236)

This excerpt from Joseph Heller's second novel, *Something Happened*, portrays the terrified helplessness of a nine-year-old boy who has to interact every other school day with a burly gym teacher. As described by his equally fearful father, the youngster has an overwhelming anxiety about his gym class, a situation into which he is forced and from which he cannot escape, a situation that makes demands on him that he feels utterly unable to meet. Once again a gifted novelist captures the phenomenology—the direct experience—of an important human emotion in a way that speaks vividly to each of us.

There is, perhaps, no other single topic in abnormal psychology that touches so many of us as **anxiety**, that unpleasant feeling of fear and apprehension. This emotional state can occur in many psychopathologies and is a principal aspect of the disorders considered in this chapter. Furthermore, anxiety plays an important role in the study of the psychology of normal people, for very few of us go through even a week of our lives without experiencing some measure of what we would all agree is the emotion called anxiety or fear. But the briefer periods of anxiety that beset the normal individual are hardly comparable in intensity or duration, nor are they as debilitating, as those suffered by someone with an anxiety disorder.

The specific disorders considered in this chapter and the next were for a considerable period regarded as forms of **neuroses**, a large group of nonpsychotic disorders characterized by unrealistic anxiety and other associated problems. They were conceptualized through Freud's clinical work with his patients, and thus the diagnostic category of neuroses was inextricably bound up with psychoanalytic theory. In DSM-II, the behavior encompassed by the forms of neuroses varied greatly—the fear and avoidance of phobia, the irresistible urge to perform certain acts over and over again found in compulsiveness, the paralyses and other "neurological" symptoms of conversion hysteria. How could such diverse problems be grouped into a single category? Although the observed symptoms differ, all neurotic conditions were assumed, according to the psychoanalytic theory of neuroses, to reflect an underlying problem with repressed anxiety.

Over the years many psychopathologists questioned the viability of the concept of neuroses because it had become so all-encompassing as to be meaningless as a diagnostic category. Furthermore, there simply were no data to support the assumption that all patients labeled neurotic shared some common problem or set of symptoms.[1] In DSM-IV the old categories of neuroses are distributed into several new, more distinct diagnostic classes: anxiety disorders, the topic of this chapter, and somatoform disorders and dissociative disorders, both of which are covered in Chapter 7.

In all likelihood, many people will continue to use the term *neurosis* as a broad descriptive label when discussing disordered behavior presumed to be due to underlying anxiety—indeed the term is part of our everyday vocabulary and appears throughout this book. The important point to remember is that when a precise diagnosis is called for, the term falls short. Thus, in this chapter and the next, our presentation will be organized according to the newer diagnostic categories.

Anxiety disorders are diagnosed when subjectively experienced feelings of anxiety are clearly present. DSM-IV proposes six principal categories: phobias, panic disorder, generalized anxiety disorder, obsessive-compulsive disorder, posttraumatic stress disorder, and acute stress disorder. Often someone with one anxiety disorder also meets the diagnostic criteria for another disorder. This situation is called **comorbidity**. Comorbidity among anx-

---

[1]In many ways, the term *neurosis* serves as a nice counter to another broad-based term, *psychosis*, that is part of our everyday vocabulary and was prominent in DSM-II. Certain diagnoses in DSM-IV—schizophrenic and paranoid disorders, and some mood disorders—are recognized as psychoses, although they are not generally grouped as such. Individuals with a psychosis typically suffer extreme mental unrest and have lost contact with reality. Their hallucinations and delusions—false perceptions and misguided beliefs that are a jumble of distortions and impossibilities but are firmly accepted by them—so engulf them that they are often unable to meet even the most ordinary demands of life.

iety disorders arises for two reasons. First, symptoms of the various disorders in this category are not entirely specific. For example, somatic signs of anxiety (e.g., sweating, fast heart rate) are among the diagnostic criteria for panic disorder, generalized anxiety disorder, and posttraumatic stress disorder. Second, current ideas about the pathogenic processes that give rise to various anxiety disorders also have been applied to more than one disorder. For example, feeling that you can't control the stressors you encounter has been proposed as relevant to both phobias and generalized anxiety disorder. Therefore, comorbidity could reflect the operation of these common mechanisms. As yet, theories of anxiety disorders tend to focus exclusively on a single disorder. The development of theories that take comorbidity into account is a challenge for the future.

We turn now to an examination of the defining characteristics, theories of etiology, and therapies for each of the anxiety disorders.

Phobias

Psyhopathologists define a **phobia** as a disrupting, fear-mediated avoidance, out of proportion to the danger posed by a particular object or situation and, indeed, recognized by the sufferer as groundless. For example, when people are extremely fearful of heights, closed spaces, snakes, or spiders, provided there is no objective danger and their distress is sufficient to disrupt their lives, the label *phobia* is likely to be applied to their avoidance and fear.[2]

Over the years complex terms have been formulated to name these unwarrented avoidance patterns. In each instance the suffix *phobia* is preceded by a Greek word for the feared object or situation. The suffix is derived from the name of the Greek god Phobos, who frightened his enemies. Some of the more familiar terms are *claustrophobia*, fear of closed spaces; *agoraphobia*, fear of public places; and *acrophobia*, fear of heights. More exotic fears have also been given Greek-derived names, for example, *ergasiophobia*, fear of writing; *pnigophobia*, fear of choking; *taphephobia*, fear of being buried alive, and, believe it or not, *Anglophobia*, fear of England. All too often the impression is conveyed that we understand how a particular problem originated or even how to treat it merely because we have an authoritative-sounding name for it. However, nothing could be further from the truth. As with so much else in the field of abnormal psychology, there are more theories and jargon pertaining to phobias than there are firm findings.

Phobias are relatively common in the general population. An extensive survey found a rate of 5.9 phobias per 100 people, with women having a substantially higher rate, 8.0, than men, 3.4 (Myeers et al., 1984). Many specific fears do not cause enough hardship to compel an individual to seek treatment. For example, if a person with an intense fear of snakes lives in a metropolitan area, he or she will probably have little direct contact with the feared object and may therefore not believe that anything is seriously wrong. The term phobia usually implies subjective distress or social/occupational impairment due to the anxiety.

It is interesting to note that psychologists tend to focus on different aspects of phobias depending on the paradigm they have adopted. Psychoanalysts, for example, focus on the *content* of the phobia. They see great significance in the phobic object as a symbol of an important unconscious fear. In a celebrated case reported by Freud, Little Hans was afraid of encountering horses if he went outside (see Focus Box 6.1). Freud paid particular attention to Hans's reference to the "black things around horses' mouths and the things in front of their eyes." The horse was regarded as representing the father, who had a moustache and wore eyeglasses. Freud theorized that fear of the father had become transformed into fear of horses, which were then avoided by Hans. Countless other such examples might be cited; the principal point is that psychoanalysts believe that the content of phobias has important symbolic value. Behaviorists, on the other hand, tend to ignore the content of the phobia and focus instead on its *function*; for them, fear of snakes and fear of heights are equivalent in the means by which they are acquired, in how they might be changed, and so on.

With that in mind, let us look now at three types of phobias: specific phobias, agoraphobia, and social phobias.

Specific Phobias

Specific phobias are unwarranted fears caused by the presence or anticipation of a specific object or situation. The most common sources of these phobias are animals (e.g., dogs, snakes, insects), heights, closed spaces, air travel, and blood and injections. Only 3 percent of all phobics have specific phobias. The majority of these phobias occur in women, and

[2]Phobias of childhood will be discussed in Chapter 15.

FOCUS 6.1 • Little Hans

A classic case of phobia, reported by Freud in 1909, was that of a five-year-old boy, Little Hans, who was afraid of horses and thus would not venture out of his home. The importance of this case is attested to by many psychoanalytic scholars. Ernest Jones, Freud's famous biographer, calls it "the brilliant success of child analysis" (1955, p. 289); and Glover, a respected scholar, terms it "a remarkable achievement . . . [constituting] one of the most valued records in psychoanalytic archives" (1956, p. 76).

Freud's analysis of Little Hans was based on information reported in letters written to Freud by the boy's father; Freud actually saw the child only once. Two years before the development of his phobia, when he was three, Hans was reported to have "a quite peculiarly lively interest in the part of his body which he used to describe as his widdler." When he was three and a half his mother caught him with his hand on his penis and threatened to have it cut off if he continued "doing that." At age four and a half, while on summer vacation, Hans is described as having tried to "seduce" his mother. As his mother was powdering around his penis one day, taking care not to touch it, Hans said, "Why don't you put your finger there?" His mother answered, "Because that would be piggish." Hans replied, "What's that? Piggish? Why?" Mother: "Because it's not proper." Hans, laughing: "But it's great fun." These events were taken by Freud as proof that Hans had strong sexual urges, that they were directed toward his mother, and that they were repressed for fear of castration. According to Freud's first theory of anxiety (see page 36), this sexual privation would ultimately be transformed into neurotic anxiety.

The first signs of the phobia appeared about six months later while Hans was out for a walk with his nursemaid. After a horse-drawn van had tipped over, he began crying, saying that he wanted to return home to "coax" (caress) with his mother. Later he indicated that he was afraid to go out because a horse might bite him, and he soon elaborated on his fears by referring to "black things around horses' mouths and the things in front of their eyes."

Freud considered this series of events to reflect Hans's oedipal desire to have his father out of the way so that he could possess his mother. His sexual excitement for his mother was converted into anxiety because he feared that he would be punished. Hans's father was considered the initial source of his son's fear, but the fear was then transposed to a symbol for his father—horses. The black muzzles and blinders on horses were viewed as symbolic representations of the father's moustache and eyeglasses. Thus, by fearing horses, Hans was said to have succeeded unconsciously in avoiding the fear of castration by his father—even though it was the *mother* who had threatened this punishment—while at the same time arranging to spend more time at home with his principal love object, his mother.

There are many other details in the case study, which occupies 140 pages in Freud's *Collected Papers.* In our brief account we have attempted to convey the flavor of the theorizing. We agree with Wolpe and Rachman (1960) that Freud made large inferential leaps from the data of the case. First, the evidence for Hans's wanting sexual contact with his mother is minimal, making it debatable that Hans wanted to possess his mother sexually and replace his father. Second, there is little evidence that Hans hated or feared his father, and in the original case report it is stated that Hans directly denied any symbolic connection between horses and his father. This denial was interpreted as evidence for the connection, however. Third, there is no evidence, or any reason to believe, that intense sexual excitement was somehow translated into anxiety. Indeed, the fact that Hans became afraid of horses after being frightened by an accident involving a horse may be more parsimoniously explained by the classical conditioning model, although this interpretation has its own problems (see page 135).

they very often begin in early childhood (Marks & Gelder, 1967). Specific phobias may not be a homogeneous category, however. Ost (1987) found that age of onset differed across four major groupings of phobias: animal phobias develop earliest, around age seven; blood phobias develop around age nine; dental phobias tend to begin around age twelve; and claustrophobia, around age twenty.

Fear and avoidance of heights is classified as a specific phobia. Other specific phobias include fears of animals, injections, and enclosed spaces.

Agoraphobia

A complicated syndrome, **agoraphobia** (from the Greek *agora*, "place of assembly", "marketplace") is a cluster of fears centering around public places and being unable to escape or find help should the individual suddenly become incapacitated. Fears of shopping, encountering crowds, and traveling are often a part of agoraphobia. From a patient's point of view, agoraphobia is surely very distressing. Consider how limiting it must be to be afraid of leaving the house. Perhaps for this reason agoraphobia is the most common phobia seen in the clinic, constituting roughly 60 percent of all phobias examined. It is more commonly diagnosed in women, a fact that we examine in more detail in Focus Box 6.2. The majority of sufferers develop their problems in adolescence and early adulthood. The disorder often begins with recurrent panic attacks. Numerous other symptoms are also evident,

A crowd is one of the situations likely to be very distressing to a person with agoraphobia. The agoraphobic is often afraid of having a panic attack in a public place.

FOCUS 6.2 • Sex Roles and Agoraphobia

In numerous surveys more women than men are found to be agoraphobic (Brehony & Geller, 1981). Even allowing for the possibility that women may admit to such problems more readily than men, the numbers still indicate that most agoraphobics are women. Why?

In recent years, as part of women's liberation and appreciation of how women have been and are still being stereotyped, agoraphobia has been explained in terms of traditional sex roles. Consider the following. Clinical descriptions of agoraphobics employ such words as passive, shy, and dependent, descriptors traditionally applied to women (Bem, 1974; Broverman et al., 1970). It may be, as Fodor (1978) suggests, that being agoraphobic is in part a logical, although exaggerated, extension of the stereotyped female role. Until recently, and still in many segments of American and other societies, it has been more acceptable for a woman than for a man to be housebound. Any indications that men might be housebound would be more readily criticized, hence encouraging their continuing forays into the outside world and giving them opportunities to extinguish fears of leaving their homes.

Sex-role models in some media still support the female stereotype. A task force of the National Organization for Women determined from a study of children's readers that female characters in them are usually portrayed as helpless, home-oriented, passive, dependent, fearful, and incompetent compared with males (Brehony & Geller, 1981). As these stereotypes change, there should be corresponding shifts in the male–female sex ratio of agoraphobics.

including tension, dizziness, minor checking compulsions—seeing that the screen door is latched, no intruder is under the bed, the iron is off—rumination, fear of going mad, and especially depression. One study found that 93 percent of a sample of agoraphobics also reported fears of heights and enclosed spaces such as subways and elevators (Buglass et al., 1977). But many agoraphobics have good days when they can move about with relative ease. Being with a trusted companion can also help them leave the house. Psychophysiological responses confirm the clinical impression that agoraphobics are subject to a rather diffuse, nonspecific anxiety. Recordings taken of their autonomic activity usually show high levels of arousal, even when they are supposedly relaxing (Marks, 1969).

In DSM-IV, agoraphobia can be diagnosed as occurring with or without a history of panic disorder. As will be seen below, one view of agoraphobia is that in some people it develops from panic attacks, which are sometimes found in the histories of agoraphobics. We have elected to discuss agoraphobia in this section on phobias for two reasons: first, much of the clinical and research literature addresses it in these terms; second, as will be obvious in our discussion of panic disorder, questions still remain as to the true nature of the relationship between agoraphobia and panic disorder.

Social Phobias

A **social phobia**, sometimes referred to as social anxiety disorder, is a persistent, irrational fear generally linked to the presence of other people. It can be an extremely debilitating condition. The phobic individual usually tries to avoid a particular situation in which he or she might be evaluated and reveal signs of anxiousness or behave in an embarrassing way. Speaking or performing in public, eating in public, using public lavatories, or virtually any other activity that might be carried out in the presence of others, can elicit extreme anxiety.

Social phobias are fairly common, with a lifetime prevalence of 2 percent (Myers et al., 1984); and, though perhaps not of clinical proportions, many people experience significant discomfort in social situations (Zimbardo, 1977). Unlike other phobias, which occur in women more frequently than in men, social phobia occurs about equally in the two sexes. Social phobia has a high comorbidity rate with other disorders and is often found in conjunction with generalized anxiety disorder, specific phobias, panic disorder, and avoidant and compulsive personality disorders (Turner et al., 1990). As might be expected, onset is generally during adolescence, when social awareness and interaction with others are assuming much more importance in a person's life.

Etiology of Phobias

As is true for virtually all the disorders discussed in this book, proposals for the causes of phobias have been made by adherents of the psychoanalytic, behavioral, cognitive, and biological paradigms.

Psychoanalytic Theories of Phobias

Freud was the first to attempt to account systematically for the development of phobic behavior. According to Freud, phobias are a defense against the anxiety produced by repressed id impulses. This anxiety is displaced from the feared id impulse and moved to an object or situation that has some symbolic connection to it. These objects or situations—for example, elevators or closed spaces—then become the phobic stimuli. By avoiding them, the person is able to avoid dealing with repressed conflicts. As discussed in Chapter 2 (page 37), the phobia is the ego's way of warding off a confrontation with the real problem, a repressed childhood conflict.

Another psychoanalytic theory of phobias has been proposed by Arieti (1979). According to him, the repression is of a particular interpersonal problem of childhood rather than of an id impulse. Arieti theorizes that as children, phobics first lived through a period of innocence during which they trusted the people around them to protect them from danger. But then these children came to fear that adults, usually the parents, were not reliable. This mistrust, or generalized fear of others, was something they could not live with; in order to be able to trust people again, they unconsciously transformed this fear of others into a fear of impersonal objects or situations. The phobia supposedly surfaces when, in adulthood, the person undergoes some sort of stress. As is true of most psychoanalytic theorizing, evidence in support of these views is restricted to conclusions drawn from clinical case reports.

Behavioral Theories of Phobias

The primary assumption of all behavioral accounts of phobias is that such reactions are learned. But the exact learning mechanisms and what is actually learned in the development of a phobia are viewed differently depending on the behavioral theory. We will look at three: avoidance conditioning, modeling, and operant conditioning.

The Avoidance Conditioning Model Historically, Watson and Rayner's (1920) demonstration of the apparent conditioning of a fear or phobia in Little Albert (see page 45) is considered the model of how a phobia may be acquired. Learning theorists have elaborated on the case by asserting that the classically conditioned fear of an objectively harmless stimulus forms the basis of an operant avoidance response. This formulation, based on the two-factor theory originally proposed by Mowrer (1947), holds that phobias develop from two related sets of learning (see page 47). (1) Via classical conditioning a person can learn to fear a neutral stimulus (the CS) if it is paired with an intrinsically painful or frightening event (the UCS). (2) Then the person can learn to reduce this conditioned fear by escaping from or avoiding the CS. This second kind of learning is assumed to be operant conditioning; the response is maintained by its reinforcing consequences.

For a phobia to develop the fear must become generalized. That is, one must come to fear and avoid not only the specific stimulus that was paired with a UCS but a class of stimuli (e.g., heights in general rather than a particular tall building). Research on conditioned fears provides a mechanism by which the fear can become generalized. Riccio, Richardson, and Ebner (1984), for example, showed that with the passage of time following aversive conditioning, fear responses became greater to stimuli similar to (but not identical with) the CS. Apparently specific aspects of the CS are forgotten, leading to overgeneralized responding.

Some clinical phobias fit the avoidance conditioning model rather well. For example, a phobia of a specific object has sometimes been reported to have developed after a particularly painful experience with that object. Some people become intensely afraid of driving an automobile after a serious accident, or of descending stairs after a bad fall. Other phobias apparently originate in similar fashion.

The patient was a forty-five-year-old female physician who came for treatment of a long-standing fear of birds. At first proclaiming that there was never a time she was unafraid of them, she recalled, under questioning from the clinician, that the first time she became frightened of a bird was when she was about five years old. She had been playing by herself in the screened-in back porch of her family's tenement apartment when she was startled by the snarling sound of an alley cat who had just pounced on a pigeon. The bird managed to get away but was injured. In pain and disoriented, it flew against the screening of the porch several times in its fruitless efforts to escape from the cat. The patient did not understand why the pigeon continued to strike against the screen and for a while was afraid that it would break through and attack her. Her screams seemed to frighten the bird still more, and after what seemed an eternity but was probably less than half a minute, the bird fell helplessly to the ground, where the cat jumped on it again and eventually killed and ate it, much to the horror of the already terrified child. From that day on, the patient's fear of birds generalized even to caged canaries and to the whole killed chickens her grandmother would bring home from the butcher shop.

A problem exists in the application of an avoidance conditioning model for all phobias. The fact that Little Albert's fear and certain clinical phobias such as that presented in the case study were acquired through conditioning can *not* be taken as evidence that *all* fears and phobias are acquired by this means. Rather, the evidence demonstrates only the *possibility* that some fears *may* be acquired in this particular way. Indeed, other clinical reports suggest that phobias may develop *without* prior frightening experience. Many individuals with severe fears of snakes, germs, airplanes, and heights tell clinicians that they have had no particularly unpleasant experiences with any of these objects or situations (Ost, 1987). In a systematic study Keuthen (1980) found that half of a sample of phobics could recall no upsetting experience in the feared situation. Such accounts are called **retrospective reports**, that is, reports made by people looking back into their past, sometimes for many, many years. Since memory of long-ago events is often distorted, such reports must be viewed with some skepticism. The fact that many phobics cannot recall traumatic experiences with their now-feared objects may indeed be distortions of memory. Accounts of traumatic episodes may be questioned on the same grounds. In addition, many people who have had a harrowing automobile accident or a bad fall down stairs do *not* become phobic to automobiles or stairs. Thus the avoidance conditioning model cannot account for the acquisition of all phobias.

Furthermore, attempts to replicate Watson and Rayner's experiment and demonstrate again the acquisition of fear via classical conditioning have for the most part *not* been successful (e.g., English, 1929). In fact, there is very little experimental evidence to support the contention that human beings can be classically conditioned to fear neutral stimuli even when such stimuli are paired repeatedly with primary aversive stimuli, such as electric shock (e.g., Davison, 1968b; Dawson, Schell, & Banis, 1986). Ethical considerations have of course restrained most researchers from employing highly aversive stimuli with human beings, but considerable evidence indicates that fear is extinguished rather quickly when the CS is presented a few times without the reinforcement of moderate levels of shock (Bridger & Mandel, 1965; Wickens, Allen, Hill, 1963). Finally, it is also unclear whether the model itself is an accurate portrayal of a phobia. The essence of phobic behavior is the fear and avoidance elicited by the CS. However, in the avoidance learning literature, an animal's fear of the CS quickly declines, and it has proved difficult (perhaps impossible) to train an animal to avoid a CS (Mineka, 1985).

In sum, the data we have reviewed suggest that not all phobias are learned through avoidance conditioning. Such a process *may* be involved in the etiology of some phobias, but other processes must also be implicated in their development (see Focus Box 6.3).

Modeling Phobic responses may also be learned through imitating the reactions of others. As we have previously noted (see page 46), a wide range of behavior, including emotional responses, may be learned by witnessing a model. The learning of phobic reactions by observing others is generally referred to as **vicarious conditioning**. In one study Bandura and Rosenthal (1966) arranged for subjects to watch another person, the model (a confederate of the experimenter), in an aversive conditioning situation. The model was hooked up to an impressive-looking array of electrical apparatus. Upon hearing a buzzer, the model withdrew his hand rapidly from the arm of the chair and feigned pain. The physiological responses of the subjects witnessing this behavior were recorded. After the subjects had watched the model "suffer" a number of times, they showed an increased frequency of emotional responses when the buzzer sounded. The subjects began to react emotionally to a harmless stimulus even though they had had no direct contact with a noxious event.

Vicarious learning may also be accomplished through verbal instructions. That is, phobic reactions can be learned through another's description of what might happen as well as by observing another's fear. As an example from everyday life, a mother may repeatedly warn her child not to engage in some activity lest dire consequences ensue. (We should not assume, however, that such learning is necessarily a product of conditioning.)

The clearest demonstration of the potential importance of observational learning comes from a study by Mineka and her colleagues (1984). Adolescent rhesus monkeys were reared with parents who had an intense fear of snakes. During the observational learning sessions, the offspring saw their parents interact fearfully with real and toy snakes as well as nonfearfully with neutral objects. After six sessions, the fear of the adolescent monkeys was indistinguishable from that of the parents. A three-month follow-up showed that the fear was durable.

In an ingenious follow-up study related to the preparedness theory, Cook and Mineka (1989) studied four groups of rhesus monkeys, each of which saw a different videotape. The tapes were created by splicing so that a monkey exhibiting intense fear appeared to be responding to different stimuli: a toy snake, a toy crocodile, flowers, or a toy rabbit. Only the monkeys exposed to the tapes showing the toy snake or crocodile acquired fear to the object shown, again demonstrating that not every stimulus is capable of becoming a source of acquired fear.

As with classical conditioning, however, vicarious learning experiments fail to provide a complete model for all phobias. First, phobics who seek treatment do not often report that they became frightened after witnessing someone else's distress. Second, many people have been exposed to the bad experiences of others but have not themselves developed phobias.

Mineka's research has shown that when monkeys observe another monkey display fear of a snake, they also acquire the fear. Observational learning may therefore play a role in the etiology of phobias.

Operant Conditioning Related to the two-factor theory of avoidance conditioning, whereby avoidance is negatively reinforced by the reduction of fear, phobic reactions may also be learned or maintained by positive reinforcement. For example, a daughter who wants to stay close to a parent may invent excuses so that she does not have to attend school. If the mother or father gives in to these excuses, the child is directly rewarded by being allowed to stay home with the adult. In this instance fear is not mentioned as a mediator. The child avoids school simply because it produces favorable results.

Although some phobias may develop because of the payoff provided by the environment, the fact that the lives of many phobics become severely limited through their compelling need to avoid harmless situations limits the general plausibility of the theory.

Cognitive Theories in Fears and Phobias

A good deal of research indicates that emotions can influence cognitions and vice versa. The interactions between emotions and cognitive processes could therefore be relevant to both the etiology and maintenance of phobias. For example, phobic individuals seem to be tuned in to the stimuli that elicit their fears. In one study demonstrating this phenomenon (Burgess et al. 1981), phobic and normal subjects participated in a dichotic listening task that required them to shadow (repeat aloud) a message presented to one ear and, at the same time, to indicate when either neutral or phobia-related words were presented to either ear. The researchers found that the subjects typically did not perceive the material presented to the unattended ear (the one subjects were not shadowing). However, the phobic subjects detected more of the phobia-related words than did the normal subjects when they were presented to the unattended ear.

Similarly, Beck and Emery (1985) have proposed that socially anxious people operate within a "vulnerability schema." They are continually concerned with danger and harm and with what unpleasant events might befall them in the future.

Tomarken, Mineka, and Cook (1989) have demonstrated a cognitive bias in phobics. Subjects high and low in fears of snakes or spiders participated in a study in which they were shown a series of fear-relevant (e.g., a hissing snake) or fear-irrelevant (e.g., flowers) slides followed by one of three outcomes—a brief electric shock, a tone, or nothing. After viewing the slides, subjects were asked to estimate the degree of association between each type of

6.3 • Avoidance Conditioning and Preparedness

The avoidance conditioning view of phobias might be more valid if it were modified to take into account the fact that certain neutral stimuli may be more likely than others to become classically conditioned stimuli. Seligman (1971) suggested that phobias may well reflect classical conditioning, but only to stimuli to which an organism is physiologically predisposed to be sensitive. Accordingly, classical conditioning experiments that show quick extinction of fear may have used CSs that the organism was really not prepared to learn to associate with UCSs.

An example from the research on **preparedness**, a supposed biological predisposition to associate particular stimuli readily with the unconditioned stimulus, may make this notion clearer. Garcia and his associates (Garcia, McGowan, & Green, 1972) found that rats could learn to avoid the taste of a given food if they became nauseated following its ingestion—even if the nausea did not begin for many hours. In contrast, they could not be aversively conditioned to the *sight* of food if they were nauseated in its presence but had not actually tasted it. Similarly, rats could readily learn to avoid a light paired with shock (a common experimental finding), but they could not learn to avoid taste paired with shock. Thus, as seen in Figure 6.A, gustatory sensations and illness (taste–nausea) are readily associated, as are visual and tactile modalities (light–shock). But visual stimuli and illness (sight of food–nausea) and gustatory and tactile sensations (taste–shock) are not.

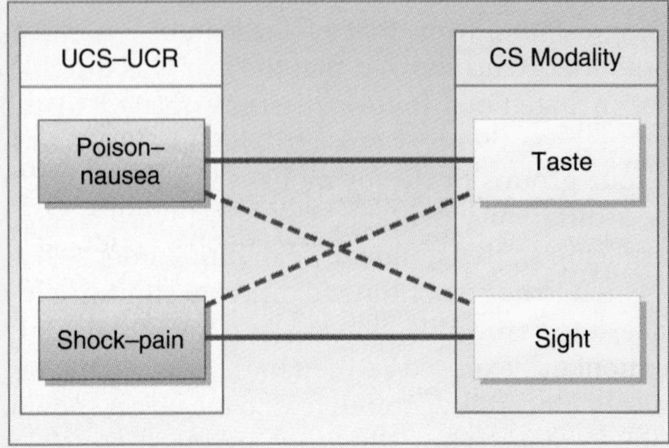

Figure 6.A The organism may be prepared through innate sensitivity to learn certain associations but not be prepared to learn others. Solid lines indicate easily made associations; dashed lines connect classes of stimuli that are difficult to associate.

Seligman provided a personal illustration of the operation of this process.

> Sauce Béarnaise is an egg-thickened, tarragon-flavored concoction, and it used to be my favorite sauce. It now tastes awful to me. This happened several years ago. . . . After eating filet mignon with Sauce Béarnaise, I became violently ill and spent most of the night vomiting. The next time I had Sauce Béarnaise, I couldn't bear the taste of it. At the time I had no ready way to account for the change, although it seemed to fit a classical conditioning paradigm: CS (sauce) paired with US (illness) and UR (vomiting) yields CR (nauseating taste). [Although I learned that flu had caused the nausea and others with me did not get sick . . .] I

slide and each outcome (e.g., on what percentage of trials was the flower followed by a shock?) In actuality, the degree of association between each type of slide and each outcome was the same, 33 percent. Nonetheless, the high-fear subjects markedly overestimated the association between fear slides and shock. The researchers concluded that the phobic subjects were processing information in a way that would be expected to maintain or enhance fear.

In a review of the research concerning memory biases in both anxious and depressed individuals, Mineka (1992) found that depressed subjects showed a bias toward recalling information that is consistent with their mood state (that is, they tend to recall negative events from the past). Anxious subjects show no such tendency; in fact, in one study (Watts, Trezise, & Sharrock, 1986) phobics showed poor recall and recognition of the anxiety-inducing stimuli. At first, these data may seem inconsistent with the hypervigilance of phobics for the source of their anxiety. But another interpretation is possible. Perhaps, even though vigilant for stimuli related to could not later inhibit my aversion. (Seligman & Hager, 1972, p. 8)

This and related research prompted Seligman to hypothesize that some associations, and thereby phobias, are easily learned by human beings and are not readily extinguished. Marks (1969), in a related observation, pointed to the fact that human beings tend to be afraid only of certain types of objects and events. People may have phobias of dogs, cats, and snakes—but few lamb phobics have been encountered. It is even more remarkable how few people phobically avoid electrical outlets, which do present certain dangers under specified circumstances.

Partial support for the hypothesis that certain fears are easily learned comes from a conditioning study in which different types of stimuli were used as the CS (Öhman, Erixon, & Löftberg, 1975). All subjects viewed three sets of pictures varying in content—snakes, houses, and faces. Half the participants received a shock (UCS) immediately after viewing each slide of snakes. The remainder received shocks after viewing slides either of houses or of faces. The galvanic skin response (GSR) served as the CR and was analyzed for both the conditioning trials and for a subsequent extinction series. During the conditioning part of the study, the GSRs of the groups of participants receiving shocks after viewing slides of any of the three classes of stimuli were about the same. During extinction, however, the CR to the slides of houses or faces quickly diminished, whereas the CR to slides of snakes remained strong. Thus the CR was more durably associated with the sight of snakes, which are a fairly common elicitor of clinical phobias.

Note, however, that in the Öhman et al. study, as well as in subsequent research, the CR to the prepared stimulus was not more easily acquired or of greater magnitude; rather, it extinguished more slowly. Furthermore, as pointed out by McNally (1987), it is not clear that mild shocks actually arouse fear. McNally also argued that the similarities between prepared learning and phobias have been overstated. Specific phobias, for example, are actually fairly easy to extinguish, given the right treatment. (The reason they persist without treatment is that the phobic avoids the feared stimulus.) Thus, the preparedness hypothesis does not make avoidance conditioning a comprehensive and well-supported model of phobias. It has, however, provided a means of addressing the fact that the stimuli that are feared by phobics are not random.

The preparedness concept was used to control attacks by coyotes on sheep. Poisoned sheep carcasses were left for the coyotes, who then developed an aversion to sheep and sought other food.

their fears, once encountered, the stimuli are quickly avoided rather than fully processed. This would result in an absence of the memory bias seen in depressives and would also be an excellent avoidance mechanism for promoting the maintenance of the phobia.

Furthermore, socially anxious people are more concerned about evaluation than are those not socially anxious (Goldfried, Padawer, & Robins, 1984); they are also more aware of the image they present to others (Bates, 1990; Fenigstein, Scheier, & Buss, 1975; Fenigstein, 1979).

Supportive evidence for these notions comes from the study by Davison and Zighelboim (1987) mentioned in Chapter 4. The thoughts of two groups of subjects were compared—by the Articulated Thoughts During Simulated Situations method—as they role-played participation in both a neutral situation and one in which they were being sharply criticized. One group of subjects were volunteers from an introductory psychology course, and the others were undergraduates referred from the student counseling center and identified as shy, withdrawn, and socially anxious. The thoughts articulated by the socially anxious subjects in both the stressful and neutral situations were more negative than those of the control subjects.

Here are examples of some of the thoughts expressed by socially anxious subjects as they imagined themselves being criticized:

> I've been rejected by these people. I have this very depressed feeling, a feeling of rejection. There is no place to turn to now. There is no way to eliminate that feeling I have inside.
>
> I think I am boring when I talk to people. I often think I should not talk at all.
>
> I should maybe not be so argumentative and maybe let things drop even if I don't like the way they are . . . like if I am not happy with the situation. Just for the sake of everybody else, to keep everybody else happy, I should let things go at times. [These thoughts reflect the belief that one must be loved and approved of by everyone.]

Other recent research on self-statements also finds more negative thoughts and anxious self-preoccupation among the socially anxious (e.g., Bates, 1990; Glass & Arnkoff, 1989; Schwartz & Garamoni, 1989), for example, having more pessimistic expectations and evaluating their own behavior more negatively than people who are not socially anxious.

Social Skills Deficits in Social Phobias

Another model focused on social phobia considers inappropriate behavior or a lack of social skills as the cause of social anxiety. According to this view, the individual has not learned how to behave so that he or she feels comfortable with others, or the person repeatedly commits faux pas, is awkward and socially inept, and is often criticized by social companions. Support for this model comes from findings that socially anxious people are indeed rated as being low in social skills (Twentyman & McFall, 1975) and that the timing and placement of their responses in a social interaction are impaired (Fischetti, Curran, & Wessberg, 1977).

One of the difficulties in conducting research on social anxiety is that social anxiety may actually be a *group* of problems rather than a single one (Goldfried, Greenberg, & Marmar, 1990; Heimberg, Dodge, & Becker, 1987). The terminology varies among the many studies and reports: Is social anxiety the same as social phobia? When we discuss personality disorders (Chapter 10), we describe the concept of avoidant personality disorder, which overlaps considerably with social anxiety and social phobia. Consider also that some people who are socially anxious avoid or run from social situations, whereas others engage in what analysts term *counterphobic behavior*, forcing themselves into these situations in spite of their debilitating anxiety. Is the phobic simply more anxious about social situations than the person who does not avoid? Research does not tell us. Moreover, the exact source of the fear can vary: some people fear criticism from the opposite sex only; others shrink with fright from speaking in front of groups regardless of the gender mix of the audience; and still others speak with ease in front of many but are very anxious in small social gatherings. Furthermore, some people are concerned about urinating in public restrooms or writing a check in front of others. Perhaps *evaluation phobia* or *embarrassment phobia* would be more appropriate terms than social phobia. There are indications in the treatment literature that considering subtypes of social phobias may enhance the effectiveness of therapeutic interventions by tailoring treatment to those factors underlying a person's social fears (Jerremalm, Jansson, & Ost, 1986; Ost, Jerremalm, & Johansson, 1981).

Biological Factors Predisposing to the Development of Phobias

The theories we have previously described look largely to the environment for the cause and maintenance of phobias. But why do some people acquire unrealistic fears whereas others do not, given similar opportunities for learning? Perhaps those who are adversely affected by stress have a biological malfunction (a diathesis) that somehow predisposes them to develop a phobia following a particular stressful event. Two areas of research seem promosing: the autonomic nervous system and genetic factors.

Autonomic Nervous System One way in which people may react differently to certain environmental situations is the ease with which their autonomic nervous systems become aroused. Lacey (1967) has referred to a dimension of autonomic activity that he calls stability–lability. Labile or jumpy individuals are those whose autonomic systems are readily aroused by a wide range of stimuli. Clearly, because of the extent to which the autonomic nervous system is involved in fear and hence in phobic behavior, a dimension such as **autonomic lability** would assume considerable importance. Since there is reason to believe that autonomic lability is to some degree genetically determined (Gabbay, 1992; Lacey, 1967), the heredity of individuals may very well have a significant role in the development of phobias.

Genetic Factors Several studies have questioned whether a genetic or innate factor is involved in anxiety disorders, although most have not been directly concerned with whether such a factor is implicated in the formation of phobias per se. In a family study of anxiety disorders, Harris and her co-workers (1983) found that the first-degree relatives of individuals with agoraphobia were at greater risk for it or one of the other anxiety disorders than were the first-degree relatives of nonanxious control subjects. Noyes et al. (1986) also found that relatives of agoraphobics were at higher than usual risk for both agoraphobia and panic disorder. Similarly, Torgersen (1983) found more concordance for agoraphobia in identical twins than in fraternal twins.

These data do not unequivocally implicate innate factors, however. Although close relatives share genes, they also have considerable opportunity to observe and influence one another. The fact that a son and his father are both afraid of heights may indicate not a genetic component but rather direct modeling of the son's behavior after that of his father (or both factors could be involved). In sum, although there is some reason to believe that genetic factors may be involved in the etiology of phobias, there has as yet been no clear-cut demonstration of the extent to which they may be important.

Therapies for Phobias

Many people suffer, sometimes quietly, with their phobias. In fact, some people who could be diagnosed as phobic by a clinician do not regard themselves as having a problem that merits attention. A decision to seek treatment often arises when a change in the person's occupational situation requires exposure that had for years been avoided or minimized.

A thirty-five-year-old industrial engineer consulted us for treatment of his fear of flying in airplanes when a promotion required him to travel frequently. This professional recognition was a result of his having worked with distinction for several years in his firm at a job that kept him at his desk. Family trips were always by car or train, and those close to him worked around his debilitating fear of getting on an airplane. Imagine his mixed feelings at being informed that his excellence was to be rewarded by the promotion! His ambition and self-respect—and encouragement from family and friends—goaded him into seeking assistance, which fortunately we were able to provide in the form of systematic desensitization.

Throughout the book, after reviewing theories about the causes of the various disorders, we will briefly describe the principal therapies for them. The treatment sections of Chapter 2 were meant to furnish the reader with a context for understanding these discussions of therapy. An in-depth study and evaluation of therapy is reserved for the final section of the book. Here we will look briefly at a number of therapeutic approaches used to treat phobias.

Psychoanalytic Approaches

Just as psychoanalytic theory has many derivations, so, too, does psychoanalytic therapy. In general, however, all psychoanalytic treatments of phobias attempt to uncover the repressed conflicts that are assumed to underlie the extreme fear and avoidance characteristic of these disorders. Because the phobia itself is regarded as symptomatic of underlying conflicts, it is not dealt with directly. Indeed, direct attempts to reduce phobic avoidance are contraindicated, because the phobia is assumed to protect the person from repressed conflicts that are too painful to confront.

In treating agoraphobia, for example, a psychoanalyst typically focuses on a presumed repressed conflict between an overanxious attachment to the patient's mother or father and desires for independence. Discussion would involve recognition of the pathogenic belief that if the person leaves home and becomes independent, he or she will not survive (Weiss & Sampson, 1986). The analyst uses the various techniques that have been developed within the psychoanalytic tradition in various combinations to help lift the repression. During free association (see page 42) the analyst listens carefully to what the patient mentions in connection with any references to the phobia. The analyst also attempts to discover clues to the repressed origins of the phobia in the manifest content of dreams. Exactly what the analyst believes these repressed origins to be depends, of course, on the particular psychoanalytic theory held. An orthodox analyst will look for sexual conflicts, whereas an analyst holding to Arieti's interpersonal theory will encourage patients to examine their generalized fear of other people.

Contemporary ego analysts focus less on historical insights; instead they encourage the patient to confront the phobia, even though they continue to view it as an outgrowth of an earlier problem. Alexander and French in their classic book, *Psychoanalytic Therapy* (1946), spoke of the "corrective emotional experience" in therapy, by which they meant the patient's confrontation with what is so desperately feared. They observed that "Freud himself came to the conclusion that in the treatment of some cases, phobias for example, a time arrives when the analyst must encourage the patient to engage in those activities he avoided in the past" (p. 39). Wachtel (1977) even more boldly recommended that analysts employ the fear reduction techniques of behavior therapists, such as systematic desensitization.

Other analytically oriented workers also recognize the importance of another behaviorally oriented technique—exposure to what is feared—although they usually tend to regard any subsequent improvement as only symptomatic and not a resolution of the underlying conflict that was assumed to have produced the phobia in the first place (Wolitzky & Eagle, 1990).

Behavioral Approaches

A widely used behavioral treatment for phobias is systematic desensitization (see p. 48 and 556) (Wolpe, 1958). The phobic individual imagines a series of increasingly frightening scenes while in a state of deep relaxation. Clinical and experimental evidence indicates that this technique is effective in eliminating or at least reducing phobias (Wilson & O'Leary, 1980). Some behavior therapists have, over the years, come to recognize the importance of exposure to real-life phobic situations, sometimes during the period in which a patient is being desensitized in imagination, sometimes instead of the imagery-based procedure. Indeed, evidence is beginning to accumulate on the long-term effectiveness of treating agoraphobics by graded exposures to real-life crowds and public places (Craske, Rapee, & Barlow, 1992; Emmelkamp, 1986; Munby & Johnston, 1980).

One of the most impressive clinical research programs on the treatment of agoraphobia comes from David Barlow's Center for Stress and Anxiety Disorders at the State University of New York at Albany. In this program phobic women—nearly all their patients are women—participate with their spouses or with significant others in group meetings during which encouragement and exhortation are given for exposure *between* therapy sessions. Gradual forays away from the home are nurtured by the nonphobic participants and then discussed at the weekly group meetings. With twelve group meetings plus a few follow-up sessions, outcomes of this approach are very positive (Barlow & Waddell, 1985), though many of those who begin such exposure therapies drop out and some of those who improve relapse (Craske et al., 1992). Related work by Barlow on panic disorder is described later.

A focus on the lack of social skills among some social phobics—not knowing what to do or to say in social situations—has led some workers to encourage patients to role-play or rehearse in the consulting room how they might handle interpersonal encounters. Several studies attest to the effectiveness of such an approach (e.g., Mattick, Peters, & Clarke, 1989). As pointed out recently by Turner, Beidel, and Townsley (1992), such practice may also expose the timorous person, even when there is no social-skills deficit, to anxiety-provoking cues so that, through real-life exposure, extinction of fear takes place. This is but one of countless examples where a particular therapeutic technique can work for more than one reason.

Modeling is another technique in which fearful clients can be exposed to either filmed or live demonstrations of other people interacting fearlessly with the phobic object. **Flooding** is a therapeutic technique in which the client is exposed to the source of the phobia at full intensity. The extreme discomfort that is an inevitable part of this procedure has tended to discourage therapists from em-

David Barlow, Director of the Center for Stress and Anxiety Disorders at the State University of New York, Albany.

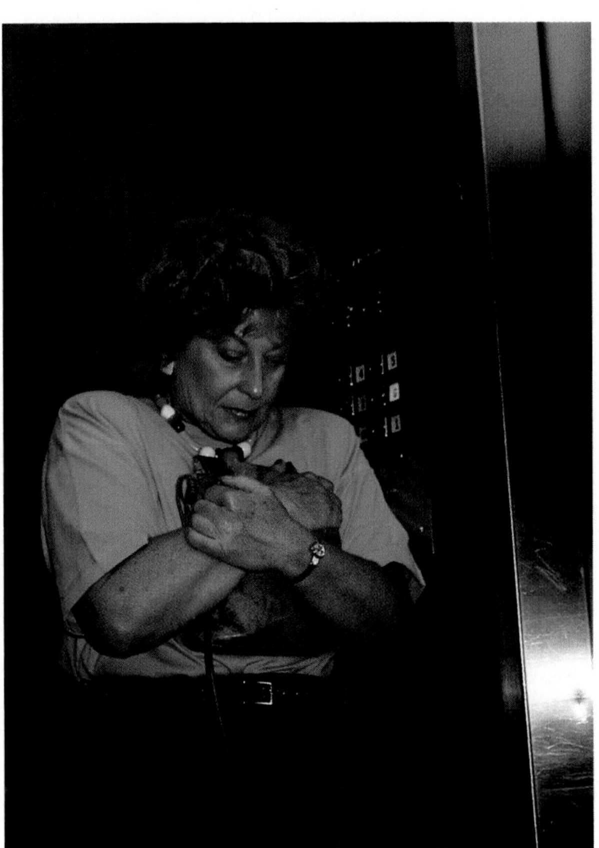

In the most frequent treatment for phobias, patients are exposed to what they fear most, here an enclosed space.

ploying it, except perhaps as a last resort when graduated exposure has not worked.

Behavior therapists who favor operant techniques ignore the fear assumed to underlie phobias and attend instead to the overt avoidance of phobic objects and to the approach behavior that must replace it. They treat approach to the feared situation like any other operant and shape it according to the principle of successive approximation. Real-life exposures to the phobic object are gradually achieved, and the client is rewarded for even minimal successes in moving closer to it.

Many behavior therapists attend both to fear and to avoidance, using techniques like desensitization to reduce fear and operant shaping to encourage approach. Lazarus, Davison, and Polefka (1965) first proposed this two-pronged strategy. At the initial stages of treatment, when fear and avoidance are both very great, the therapist concentrates on reducing the fear through relaxation training and graded exposures to the phobic situation. As therapy progresses, however, fear becomes less of an issue and avoidance more. A phobic individual has often over time settled into an existence in which other people cater to his or her incapacities and thus in a way reinforce the person for having a phobia. As the person's anxieties diminish, he or she is able to approach what used to be terrifying; this overt behavior should be positively reinforced—and avoidance discouraged—by relatives and friends as well as by the therapist.

Especially for agoraphobics, the spouse, who will usually be the husband, should be involved in treatment. Clinical reports suggest that, by being overly solicitous and supportive—perhaps out of his own understandable concern for his wife's plight, perhaps to satisfy some inner need of his own to be dominant—he may have unwittingly conspired to perpetuate his wife's agoraphobia (Brehony & Geller, 1981). Indeed, Milton and Hafner (1979) found that as the wife improves, an already distressed marital relationship can worsen.

This phenomenon is one of several lying at the core of the family therapy movement, described in detail in Chapter 20 (page 601). It should be mentioned, however, that this family systems view of agoraphobia has not gone unchallenged. Bland and Hallam (1981) argue that data do *not* support the contention that improvement in the wife's agoraphobia worsens the marital relationship. Rather, they suggest, "dissatisfied spouses remained dissatisfied; satisfied spouses tended to become more satisfied as the patient's phobia improved" (p. 338). Indeed, Barlow's clinical research program has found that successful real-life exposure treatment in which husbands are involved leads to *improved* marital satisfaction (Craske et al., 1992; Himadi et al., 1986). Perhaps the very process of involving the husband in his wife's therapy contributes to an improvement of marital problems per se, unrelated to the agoraphobia.

Agoraphobics, indeed, may present a unique set of problems for therapists in planning effective treatment strategies. The clinical literature notes in particular the "fear of fear" that most agoraphobics complain about. Theirs seems to be a "portable phobia" (Brehony & Geller, 1981). They are greatly concerned about becoming the slightest bit nervous, for fear that their nervousness will escalate into a panic attack in which they may lose control and suffer possible harm and social embarrassment (see the discussion of panic disorder later in this chapter).

Cognitive Approaches

Cognitive treatments for phobias have been viewed with skepticism because of a central defining characteristic. As stated in DSM-IV, the phobic fear is recognized by the individual as excessive or unreasonable. Thus if an otherwise well-functioning person is intensely afraid of something that, intellectually, he or she acknowledges to be relatively harmless, of what use can it be to alter the person's thoughts about it? One proposal comes from Ellis (1962). He suggests that a phobia is maintained by irrational beliefs such as "If something seems dangerous or fearsome, you must be terribly occupied with and upset about it" or "It is easier to avoid than to face certain life difficulties." The client is taught to dispute the irrational belief whenever encountering the phobic object or situation. But even Ellis, with his strong cognitive bias, uses behavioral approaches as well, by encouraging clients to approach and confront what they fear (Heimberg, Dodge, & Becker, 1987). His intellectual debates with clients may very well help goad them into real-life exposures, which will extinguish the fear. Indeed, there is no evidence that eliminating irrational beliefs alone, without exposures to the fearsome situations, reduces phobic avoidance (Turner et al., 1992; Williams & Rappoport, 1983).

All these various therapies for phobias have a recurrent theme, namely, the need for the phobic to desist from customary avoidance of the phobic object or situation and to begin facing what has been deemed too fearsome, too terrifying. To be sure, analysts consider the fear to reside in the buried past and therefore delay direct confrontation, but eventually they, too, encourage it (e.g., Zane, 1984). Even Freud stated: "One can hardly ever master a phobia if one waits until the patient lets the analysis influence him to give it up. One succeeds only when one can induce them to go about alone and to struggle with their anxiety while they make the attempt" (Freud, 1919, p. 400). Thus all these therapies reflect a time-honored bit of folk wisdom, one that tells us that we must face up to what we fear. As an ancient Chinese proverb puts it, "Go straight to the heart of danger, for there you will find safety."

Biological Approaches

Drugs that reduce anxiety are referred to as sedatives, tranquilizers, or **anxiolytics** (the suffix *-lytic* comes from the Greek word meaning to loosen or dissolve). Barbiturates were the first major category of drugs used to treat anxiety disorders, but because of undesirable side effects and their addictive properties, they were supplanted in the 1950s by two other classes of drugs—propanediols (e.g., Miltown) and benzodiazepines (e.g., Valium and Ativan). The latter are widely used today and are of demonstrated benefit; however, while the risk of lethal overdose is not as great as with barbiturates, they are addicting and produce a severe withdrawal syndrome (Schweizer et al., 1991). As with opiates, babies born of tranquilizer-dependent mothers are themselves dependent and suffer withdrawal. Some studies also suggest that antidepressants, such as imipramine, are useful in treating agoraphobia (Johnston et al., 1988; Zitrin, Klein, & Woerner, 1980), especially when dysphoria (depressed mood) is part of the clinical picture (Marks, 1983). However, in a study by Telch et al. (1985) comparing imipramine with exposure with imipramine and instructions *not* to enter fearsome situations, only the drug group that included exposure showed improvement.

The problem in treating phobias and other anxiety disorders with drugs is that the drugs may be difficult to discontinue. All too often people calmed down by anxiolytics find themselves still fearful when weaned from the drugs (Marks, 1981a); consequently, they tend to become dependent on them for long periods of time. In fact, in their efforts to reduce their anxiety, many phobics and other anxious people use anxiolytics or alcohol on their own. The use and abuse of drugs and alcohol are not uncommon among anxiety-ridden people.

Panic Disorder

In **panic disorder** there is a sudden and often inexplicable attack of a host of jarring symptoms—labored breathing, heart palpitations, chest pain, feelings of choking and smothering; dizziness, sweating, and trembling; and intense apprehension, terror, and feelings of impending doom. **Depersonalization** and **derealization**, feelings of being outside one's body and of the world's not being real, and fears of losing control, of going crazy, or even of dying may beset and overwhelm the patient. Panic attacks occur frequently, perhaps once weekly or more often; usually last minutes, rarely hours; and are sometimes linked to specific situations, such as driving a car. When associated with situational triggers, they are referred to as cued panic attacks. They can also occur in what seem to be benign situations, such as relaxation, and sleep, and in unexpected situations; in these cases they are referred to as uncued attacks. Recurrent uncued attacks are required for the diagnosis of panic disorder; the exclusive presence of cued attacks most likely reflects the presence of a phobia.

The rate of panic disorder is about 0.7 percent for men and slightly over 1 percent for women (Myers et al., 1984). It typically begins in early adulthood, and its onset is associated with stressful life experiences (Pollard, Pollard, & Corn, 1989).

In DSM-IV, panic disorder is diagnosed as either with or without agoraphobia, the former being much more common. Patients with panic disorder typically avoid the situations in which a panic attack could be dangerous or embarrassing. If the avoidance becomes widespread, panic with agoraphobia is the result.

As mentioned earlier, agoraphobia is sometimes seen as a result of a history of panic attacks, and it is indeed true that in clinical samples there is a high degree of overlap between the two. However, in a longitudinal study of a large sample from the general population, Eaton and Keyl (1990) found that only 21 percent of new cases of agoraphobia reported a prior history of panic attacks. Thus, the relationship between agoraphobia and panic seems more complex than was first thought. Some cases of agoraphobia may reflect avoidance of the situations that elicit panic, but others may actually be more like simple phobias (e.g., of tunnels or bridges).

Why does agoraphobia occur only in some patients with panic disorder? Several possibilities have some empirical support (Clum & Knowles, 1991). First, the cognitions of panic disorder patients who develop agoraphobia are more catastrophic than those of patients who do not develop agoraphobia. Believing that the symptoms of an attack mean that death is imminent could be a potent motivator of avoidance. Furthermore, patients who develop agoraphobia have fewer coping strategies to deal with the attack. Finally, gender differences seem to play a role. The rates of pure panic disorder (without agoraphobic symptoms) are about equal in men and women, but for panic disorder with agoraphobia, women outnumber men by about 4 to 1. It may be that this overrepresentation of women is linked to stereotypical sex roles that make it more acceptable for women to be housebound (recall Focus Box 6.2).

Over 80 percent of patients diagnosed as having one of the other anxiety disorders also experience panic attacks, although not with the frequency that justifies a diagnosis of panic disorder (Barlow et al., 1985). Coexistence of panic disorder and major depression is also common (Breier et al., 1986), as is comorbidity between panic and generalized anxiety disorder (Sanderson et al., 1990), alcoholism, personality disorders, and suicide (Johnson, Weissman, & Klerman, 1990). Comorbidity is associated with poor outcomes (Noyes et al., 1990).

Etiology of Panic Disorder

Panic disorder does run in families (Crowe et al., 1987) and has greater concordance in identical twin pairs than in fraternal twins (Torgersen, 1983). Further, evidence suggests a physiological cause for a proportion of diagnosed cases. Specifically, a cardiac malfunction, mitral valve prolapse (MVP) syndrome, can produce symptoms very similar to those of a panic attack. It has been hypothesized that some individuals with MVP syndrome become alarmed at their sensations of heart palpitations and thereby contribute to their escalation. They consider the palpitations a heart attack (Kantor, Zitrin, & Zeldis, 1980). Indeed, this physical problem is very frequent in patients diagnosed as having panic disorder (Crowe et al., 1980).

Another line of biological inquiry has focused on a number of experimental manipulations that can induce panic attacks. One approach proposes that panic attacks are linked to hyperventilation or overbreathing (Ley, 1987). Hyperventilation may activate the autonomic nervous system, thus leading to the familiar somatic aspects of a panic episode. Lactate (a product of muscular exertion) can also produce panic, and its level may become elevated in patients with panic disorder because of chronic hyperventilation. Based on the finding that breathing air containing higher than usual amounts of CO_2 can generate a panic attack, oversensitive CO_2 receptors have also been proposed as a mechanism that could stimulate hyperventilation (Gorman et al., 1988).

The data indicating that various biological challenges (e.g., carbon dioxide, hyperventilation) can induce panic also show that they do so only in those who have already been diagnosed with the disorder. This could be taken to mean that these stimuli activate some kind of biological abnormality or diathesis in patients with the disorder. However, the physiological responses of people with panic disorder to these biological challenges are very similar to those of people without the disorder. Only the self-reported levels of fear induced by the challenge differentiate the two groups (Margraf, Ehlers, & Roth, 1986). Therefore, the results may indicate that it is the psychological reaction to the challenge that is central.

The principal psychological theory of panic disorder (and its associated agoraphobia) is the fear of fear hypothesis (e.g., Goldstein & Chambless, 1978). The theory suggests that agoraphobia is not a fear of public places per se but a fear of having a panic attack in public. One idea about why panic disorder patients fear their own fear so acutely is that they misinterpret physiological sensations (Clark, 1986). They ruminate about serious illnesses, both physical and mental (Hibbert, 1984). In this overconcern they may amplify slight physical sensations into signs of impending disaster, which could then spiral into full-blown panic (Holt & Anderson, 1989). For example, a skipped heartbeat may be taken to mean that a heart attack is imminent. Patients with panic disorder also report high levels of anxiety in response to false physiological feedback indicating that their heart is beating quickly (Ehlers et al., 1988).

The concept of control is also relevant to panic. Patients with the disorder have an extreme fear of losing control, which would happen if they had an attack in public. The importance of control to the disorder is also clearly demonstrated in a study by Sanderson, Rapee, and Barlow (1989), extending earlier analogue work by Geer, Davison, and Gatchel (1970) on perceived control. Patients with panic disorder breathed carbon dioxide and were told that when a light turned on they could turn a dial to reduce the concentration of CO_2. For half the subjects the light was on continuously, whereas for the remainder it never came on. Turning the dial actually had no effect on CO_2 levels, so the study was of the effects of *perceived* control on reactions to the challenge. Eighty percent of the group with no control had a panic attack, compared with only 20 percent of the group who thought they could control CO_2 levels. Note that in addition to clearly demonstrating the importance of perceived control in panic disorder, the data show that it is not the biological challenge per se that elicits panic; rather, a person's psychological reaction is crucial.

Therapies for Panic Disorder

Both antidepressants and anxiolytics, such as the benzodiazepines, have shown some success as biological treatments. The evidence for the effectiveness of aprazolam, a benzodiazepine derivative, is particularly compelling as it has been obtained in a large-scale, multinational study (Ballenger et al., 1988).

In just the past several years, psychological treatment has been derived from the aforementioned hypotheses about the nature of panic disorder—that some mitral valve prolapse patients may become unduly alarmed by noticing irregular heartbeats, and that some people may attribute other sensations as well, such as hyperventilation, to an impending panic attack. The observation that treating agoraphobia with exposure did not always reduce panic attacks (Michelson, Mavissakalian, & Marchione, 1985) has also been taken into account. These factors have led to some innovative psychological therapies (e.g., Beck, 1988). Barlow and his associates (e.g., Barlow, 1988; Barlow & Cerny, 1988; Barlow, Craske, & Klosko, 1989; Klosko, et al., 1990) have developed a detailed and well-validated therapy that has three principal components: relaxation training; a combination of Ellis- and Beck-type cognitive-behavioral interventions; and, the most novel part, exposure to the internal cues that trigger panic. This third component has the client practice in the consulting room behaviors that can elicit feelings associated with panic. For example, a person whose panic attacks begin with hyperventilation is asked to breathe fast for three minutes; someone who gets dizzy might be requested to spin in a chair for several minutes. When sensations such as dizziness, dry mouth, lightheadedness, increased heart rate, and other signs of panic begin to be felt, the client (1) experiences them under safe conditions and (2) applies previously learned cognitive and relaxation coping tactics (which can include breathing from the diaphragm rather than hyperventilating). With practice and encouragement/persuasion from the therapist, the client learns to reinterpret internal sensations from signals of loss of control and panic to cues that are intrinsically harmless and can be controlled with certain skills. The intentional creation of these signs by the client coupled with success in coping with them reduces their unpredictability and their meaning for the client. Two-year follow-ups have shown that therapeutic gains from this cognitive and exposure therapy have been maintained and are superior to the use of aprazolam (Craske, Brown, & Barlow, 1992).

Generalized Anxiety Disorder

The patient, a twenty-four-year-old mechanic, had been referred for psychotherapy by his physician, whom he had consulted because of dizziness and difficulties in falling asleep. He was quite visibly distressed during the entire initial interview, gulping before he spoke, sweating, and continually fidgeting in his chair. His repeated requests for water to slake a seemingly unquenchable thirst were another indication of his extreme nervousness. Although he first related his physical concerns, a more general picture of pervasive anxiety soon emerged. He reported that he nearly always felt tense. He seemed to worry about anything and everything. He was apprehensive of disasters that could befall him as he worked and interacted with other people. He reported a long history of difficulties in interpersonal relationships, which had led to his being fired from several jobs. As he put it, "I really like people and try to get along with them, but it seems like I fly off the handle too easily. Little things they do upset me too much. I just can't cope unless everything is going exactly right."

The individual with **generalized anxiety disorder (GAD)** is persistently anxious. Chronic, uncontrollable worry about all manner of things is the hallmark of GAD; for example, the individual may experience chronic terror concerning a possible accident befalling a child. So pervasive is this distress that it is sometimes referred to as free-floating anxiety. Somatic complaints—sweating, flushing, pounding heart, upset stomach, diarrhea, frequent urination, cold, clammy hands, dry mouth, a lump in the throat, shortness of breath—are frequent and reflect hyperactivity of the autonomic nervous system. Pulse and respiration rates, too, may be high. The person may also report disturbances of the skeletal musculature: muscle tension and aches, especially of the neck and shoulders; eyelid and other twitches; trembling, tiring easily, and an inability to relax. He or she is easily startled, fidgety, restless, and sighs often. As for the state of mind, the person is generally apprehensive, often imagining and worrying about impending disasters, such as losing control, having a heart attack, or dying. Impatience, irritability, angry outbursts, insomnia, and distractibility are also common, for the person is always on edge.

Although generalized anxiety disorder is not commonly seen at mental health centers, its incidence is fairly high, occurring in about 4 percent of the general population (Rapee, 1991). It typically begins in the mid-teens, though many GAD sufferers report having had the problem all their lives (Barlow et al., 1986). Stressful life events appear to play some role in its onset (Blazer, Hughes, & George, 1987). It is somewhat more common in women than in men, and it has a high level of comorbidity with social phobia and obsessive-compulsive disorder (Barlow, 1986).

Etiology of Generalized Anxiety Disorder

Psychoanalytic View

Psychoanalytic theory regards the source of generalized anxiety as an unconscious conflict between the ego and id impulses. The impulses, usually sexual or aggressive in nature, are struggling for expression, but the ego cannot allow their expression because it unconsciously fears that punishment will follow. Since the source of the anxiety is unconscious, the person experiences apprehension and distress without knowing why. The true source of anxiety, namely, previously punished id impulses that are striving for expression, is ever present. In a sense there is no way to evade anxiety; if the person escapes the id, he is no longer alive. Anxiety is felt nearly all the time. The phobic may be regarded as more fortunate since, according to psychoanalytic theory, his or her anxiety is displaced onto a specific object or situation, which can then be avoided. The person with generalized anxiety disorder has not developed this type of defense and thus is constantly anxious.

Learning View

In attempting to account for generalized anxiety, learning theorists (e.g., Wolpe, 1958) examine the environmental elicitors of the anxiety. For example, a person anxious most of his or her waking hours might well be fearful of social contacts. If that individual spends a good deal of time with other people, it may be more useful to regard the anxiety as tied to these circumstances rather than to any internal factors. This behavioral model of generalized anxiety, then, is identical to one of the learning views of phobias. The anxiety is regarded as having been classically conditioned to external stimuli, although the range of conditioned stimuli is considerably broader.

Cognitive-Behavioral View

The focus of cognitive and behavioral views of generalized anxiety disorder mesh so closely that we will discuss them in tandem. Learning theory sees people as confronted with painful stimuli over which they have no control, which results in anxiety; cognitive theory emphasizes the perception of not being in control as a central characteristic of all views of anxiety (Mandler, 1966). As such, a cognitive-behavioral model of generalized anxiety focuses on control and helplessness.

In a classic experiment Mowrer and Viek (1948) trained rats to obtain food. Then they were all shocked at the feeding place. One group was able to terminate the shock by performing a certain behavior. Each member of the second group was yoked to, that is, paired with, a member of the first group, so that the amount and duration of shocks received by the pair were identical. But the members of the second group were unable to terminate the shock. The group of rats who had control over shock exhibited less fear than did those animals who were yoked helplessly to a partner.

Similar findings have emerged in studies of humans (e.g. Haggard 1943). In all experimental work with human beings, stressful events over which the subjects could exert some control were less anxiety-provoking than those over which no control could be exercised. Some research (e.g., Geer, Davison, & Gatchel, 1970) also suggests that in certain circumstances the control need only be perceived by the subject and not actually be real. Linking these findings to GAD, Barlow (1988) has shown that these patients indeed perceive threatening events to be out of their control. Furthermore, immunization against the anxiety-inducing effects of lack of control is possible. Exposure to controllable (escapable) shocks reduces the effects of subsequent exposure to inescapable shocks (Williams & Maier, 1977).

Some of the positive effects of having control may be mediated by the increased predictability of noxious events associated with the ability to control their cessation (see Mineka, 1992). Predictability is also relevant to the onset of noxious events. For example, animals prefer a signaled (and therefore predictable) shock to one that is not signaled (Seligman & Binik, 1977). In this case the absence of the signal can serve as a safety signal, indicating that no shock is forthcoming and there is no need to worry. Unsignaled and therefore unpredictable aversive stimuli may thus yield chronic vigilance and fear, or what in humans we would call worry (Borkovec & Inz, 1990).

In addition to the feeling that they cannot control stressors they encounter, a number of other cognitive processes may be linked to patients with GAD. The content of cognitions of such patients involves themes of danger. Benign events are misperceived as involving threats, and cognitions focus on anticipated future disasters (Beck et al., 1987; Ingram & Kendall, 1987; Kendall & Ingram, 1989). The attention of patients with GAD is easily drawn to stimuli suggesting possible physical harm or the possibility of social misfortune, such as criticism, embarrassment, or rejection (MacLeod et al., 1986). Furthermore, they are more likely to interpret ambiguous stimuli as threatening and to rate ominous events as more likely to occur to them (Butler & Matthews, 1983).

Genetic Studies

Genetic researchers have also examined generalized anxiety disorder. One study (Slater & Shields, 1969) compared seventeen pairs of identical twins and twenty-eight fraternal pairs; one twin of each pair had been diagnosed as having anxiety neurosis. Of the identical co-twins, 49 percent were also diagnosed as having anxiety neurosis. In contrast, only 4 percent of the fraternal co-twins were so diagnosed. Torgersen (1983), however, found the same concordance for generalized anxiety disorder in identical and fraternal twin pairs. Thus, at this time, the data are equivocal.

Neurobiology of Anxiety and Panic

In considering neurobiological factors relevant to generalized anxiety disorder, we will consider panic disorder again, because theorists in this area make an important distinction between the physiology of panic anxiety and what they often term anticipatory anxiety, which is viewed as similar to the anxiety of GAD (e.g., Gray, 1982).

Panic anxiety is viewed by many as being linked to the noradrenergic system (that is, neurons that use norepinephrine as a neurotransmitter) and particularly to the locus coeruleus, a nucleus in the pons. The locus coeruleus is the major noradrenergic nucleus and has projections to many other brain areas—cortex, limbic system, and brain stem. Redmond (1977) discovered that electrical stimulation of the locus coeruleus caused monkeys to respond with what appeared to be a panic attack, thus suggesting that naturally occurring panic might be based on noradrenergic overactivation. Subsequent research has indeed shown that drugs that stimulate the locus coeruleus (e.g., yohimbine) can elicit panic attacks whereas drugs that reduce activity in the locus coeruleus (e.g., clonidine) have anxiolytic properties (e.g., Charney et al., 1984; Siever & Uhde, 1984). Although all evidence does not support the theory (e.g., other measures of noradrenergic activation have failed to discriminate patients with panic disorder from controls; Woods et al., 1987), interest in it remains active.

The most prevalent neurobiological model for generalized anxiety comes from knowledge concerning the operation of the benzodiazepines, a group of drugs that are effective in treating anxiety. A receptor in the brain has been discovered that is linked to an inhibitory neurotransmitter called gamma-aminobutyric acid (GABA) (see page 33). It is believed that when there is neural excitation stimulated by anxiety, the benzodiazepines reduce anxiety by enhancing release of GABA. Similarly, drugs that block or inhibit the GABA system lead to increases in anxiety (Insell, 1986). As with most new theories, much remains to be learned, but the approach seems destined to enhance our understanding of anxiety.

Therapies for Generalized Anxiety Disorder

As might be expected from their view of generalized anxiety disorder, that it stems from repressed conflicts, most psychoanalysts work to help patients confront the true sources of their conflicts. Treatment is much the same as that for phobias.

Behavioral clinicians approach generalized anxiety in various ways. If they can construe the anxiety as a set of responses to identifiable situations, the free-floating anxiety can be reformulated into one or more phobias or cued anxieties. For example, through situational assessment (see page 93) a behavior therapist may determine that the generally anxious client seems more specifically afraid of critizing others and of being criticized by them. The anxiety appears free-floating only because the client spends so many hours with other human beings. Systematic desensitization becomes a possible treatment. However, difficulties in assessing specific causes of the anxiety suffered by such patients as well as by those with panic disorder have led behavioral clinicians to prescribe more generalized treatment, such as intensive relaxation training, in the hopes that its anxiety-inhibiting potential will help reduce the patient's overall tension level (Barlow et al., 1984; Borkovec & Mathews, 1988).

If a feeling of helplessness seems to underlie the pervasive anxiety, the therapist will help the client acquire whatever skills might engender a sense of competence, the vital self-efficacy that Bandura (1977) notes. The skills, including assertiveness, may be taught by verbal instructions, modeling, or operant shaping—and very likely some judicious combination of the three (Goldfried & Davison, 1976). Because chronic worrying is central to GAD, it is not surprising that cognitive techniques have been employed in its treatment. Perhaps a person worries needlessly because he or she interprets ambiguous stimuli as threats or overestimates the likelihood that a negative event will occur (Butler & Matthews, 1983). Helping GAD sufferers reappraise things may therefore help, and preliminary evidence suggests that it does (Durhman & Turvey, 1987).

Anxiolytics, such as those mentioned for the treatment of phobias, are probably the most widespread treatment for generalized anxiety disorder. A psychoactive drug is viewed by medical practitioners as especially appropriate for a disorder defined by its pervasiveness, for the simple reason that once it takes effect, it will continue to work for several hours in whatever situations clients encounter. Unfortunately, many tranquilizing drugs have undesirable side effects, ranging from drowsiness and depression to physical addiction and damage to certain bodily organs. In addition, when a patient withdraws from the drug, the gains achieved in treatment are usually lost (Barlow, 1988), perhaps because the person (rightfully) attributes the improvement to an external agent, the medication, rather than to internal changes and his or her own coping efforts (Davison & Valins, 1969); and thus the person continues to believe that the anxiety and the worrisome possibilities remain uncontrollable.

Obsessive-Compulsive Disorder

Bernice was forty-six when she entered treatment. This was the fourth time she had been in outpatient therapy, and she had previously been hospitalized twice. Her obsessive-compulsive disorder had begun twelve years ago, shortly after the death of her father. Since then it had waxed and waned and currently was as severe as it had ever been.

Bernice was obsessed with a fear of contamination, a fear she vaguely linked to her father's death from pneumonia. Although she reported that she was afraid of nearly everything, because germs could be anywhere, she was particularly upset by touching wood, "scratchy objects," mail, canned goods, and "silver flecks." By silver flecks Bernice meant silver embossing on a greeting card, eyeglass frames, shiny appliances, and silverware. She was unable to state why these particular objects were particular sources of possible contamination.

To try to reduce her discomfort, Bernice engaged in a variety of compulsive rituals that took up almost all her waking hours. In the morning she spent three to four hours in the bathroom, washing and rewashing herself. Between each bath she would have to scrape away the outside layer of her bar of soap so that it would be totally free of germs. Mealtimes also lasted for hours, as Bernice performed her rituals—eating three bites of food at a time, chewing each mouthful three hundred times. These were meant "magically" to decontaminate her food. Even Bernice's husband was sometimes involved in these mealtime ceremonies, and he would shake a teakettle and frozen vegetables over her head to remove the germs. Bernice's rituals and fear of contamination had reduced her life to doing almost nothing else. She would not leave the house, do housework, or even talk on the telephone.

Obsessive-compulsive disorder (OCD) is an anxiety disorder in which the mind is flooded with persistent and uncontrollable thoughts or the individual is compelled to repeat certain acts again and again, causing significant distress and interference with everyday functioning. Obsessive-compulsive disorder affects between 1 and 3 percent of the population (Myers et al., 1984). It usually begins in early adulthood, often following some stressful event such as pregnancy, childbirth, family conflict, and difficulties at work (Kringlen, 1970). Early onset is more common among men and is associated with checking compulsions; later onset is more frequent among women and is linked with cleaning compulsions (Noshirvani et al., 1991). During an episode of depression, patients occasionally develop obsessive-compulsive disorder, and significant depression is often found in obsessive-compulsive patients (Rachman & Hodgson, 1980). Obsessive-compulsive disorder shows comorbidity with other anxiety disorders as well, particularly panic and phobias (Austin et al., 1990), and with various personality disorders (Baer et al., 1990; Mavissikalian, Hammen, & Jones, 1990).

Obsessions are intrusive and recurring thoughts, impulses, and images that come unbidden to the mind and appear irrational and uncontrollable to the individual experiencing them. Whereas many of us may have similar fleeting experiences, the obsessive individual has them with such force and frequency that they interfere with normal functioning. Obsessions may also take the form of extreme doubting, procrastination, and indecision. The patient may be unable to come to a conclusion and cease reconsidering an issue (Salzman & Thaler, 1981).

A **compulsion** is a repetitive behavior that the person feels driven to perform in order to reduce distress or prevent some calamity from occurring. The activity is not realistically connected with its apparent purpose or is clearly excessive. Lady Macbeth washed her hands continually after the murder of Duncan. Often an individual who continually repeats some action fears dire consequences if the act is not performed. The sheer frequency with which an act is repeated may be staggering. Frequently reported compulsions have to do with cleanliness and orderliness, sometimes achieved only by elaborate ceremonies that take hours and even most of the day; with avoiding particular objects, such as staying away from anything brown; with repetitive "magical" protective practices, such as counting, saying particular numbers, touching a talisman or a particular part of the body; and with checking, going back seven or eight times to make certain that

This famous scene from Macbeth illustrates a compulsion involving handwashing.

already performed acts were actually carried out—lights, gas jets, or faucets turned off; windows fastened; doors locked. Sometimes compulsions take the form of performing an act, such as eating, extremely slowly.

In many cases, the line between obsessions and compulsions is not always sharp. Rather than being tormenting or anxiety-provoking, some obsessive thinking seems to function like compulsive behaviors, as when a person compulsively counts silently to herself as a way to control anxiety. These might be termed *cognitive compulsions* (White & Cole, 1990).

The content of obsessions and compulsions has been investigated by Akhter and his colleagues (1975). After interviews with eighty-two obsessive-compulsive patients, they identified five distinguishable forms of obsession and two of compulsion.

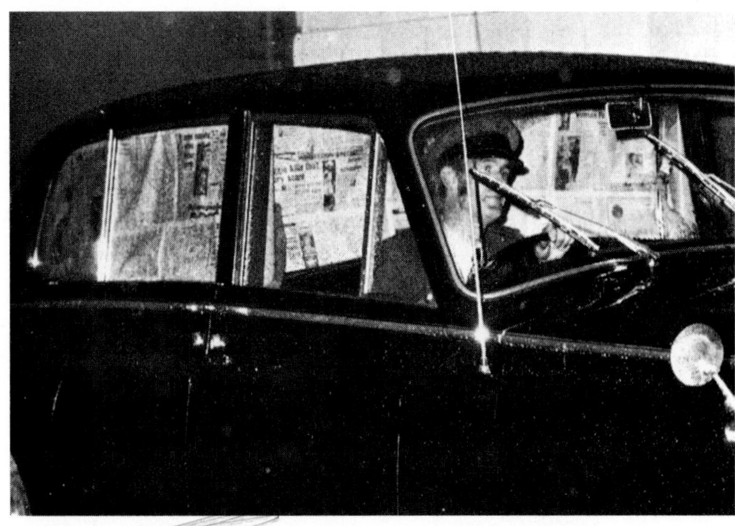

Howard Hughes, the famous industrialist, suffered from an obsessive fear of contamination. Here, on a trip to London, Hughes had the windows of his Rolls-Royce lined with newspaper to protect himself from unclean air.

Obsessions

1. **Obsessive Doubts.** Persistent thoughts that a completed task had not been adequately accomplished were found in 75 percent of the patients. "Each time he left his room a twenty-eight-year-old student began asking himself, 'Did I lock the door? Am I sure?' in spite of a clear and accurate remembrance of having done so" (p. 343).
2. **Obsessive Thinking.** Seemingly endless chains of thoughts, usually focusing on future events, were reported by 34 percent of those interviewed. A pregnant woman tormented herself with these thoughts: "If my baby is a boy he might aspire to a career that would necessitate his going away from me, but he might want to return to me and what would I do then, because if I . . ." (p. 343).
3. **Obsessive Impulses.** Seventeen percent of the patients had powerful urges to perform certain actions, ranging from rather trivial whims to grave and assaultive acts. "A forty-one-year-old lawyer was obsessed by what he understood to be the 'nonsensical notion' of drinking from his inkpot but also the serious urge to strangle an apparently beloved only son" (p. 343).
4. **Obsessive Fears.** Twenty-six percent of the patients were anxious about losing control and doing something that would be socially embarrassing. "A thirty-two-year-old teacher was afraid that in the classroom he would refer to his unsatisfactory sexual relations with his wife, although he had no wish to do so" (p. 344).
5. **Obsessive Images.** Persisting images of some recently seen or imagined event plagued 7 percent of the sample. A patient " 'saw' her baby being flushed away in the toilet whenever she entered the bathroom" (p. 344). Reprinted by permission of the Royal College of Psychiatrists.

Compulsions

1. **Yielding Compulsions.** Compulsive urges seemingly forced actions on 61 percent of the patients. "A twenty-nine-year-old clerk had [a notion] that he had an important document in one of his pockets. He knew that this was not true, but found himself impelled to check his pocket, again and again" (p. 344).
2. **Controlling Compulsions.** Diverting actions apparently allowed 6 percent of the patients to control a compulsive urge without giving in to it. "A sixteen-year-old-boy with incestuous impulses controlled the anxiety these aroused by repeatedly and loudly counting to ten" (p. 344).

Additional information on the content of compulsions is provided by Rachman and Hodgson's (1980) analysis of the responses of obsessive-compulsive patients to a questionnaire. The two major compulsions centered on cleaning and checking. In addition, many patients complained of what Rachman and Hodgson call primary obsessional slowness. Dressing, personal hygiene, folding clothes, and the like can occupy so much of the patients' days that they are unable to meet other obligations.

We hear people described as compulsive gamblers, compulsive eaters, and compulsive drinkers.

But even though such individuals may report an irresistible urge to gamble, eat, and drink, such behavior is not clinically regarded as a compulsion because it is often engaged in with pleasure and is not ego-alien. A true compulsion is often viewed by the person as somehow foreign to his or her personality. Stern and Cobb (1978), for example, found that 78 percent of a sample of compulsive individuals viewed their rituals as "rather silly or absurd."

A frequent consequence of obsessive-compulsive disorder is the negative effect it can have on the individual's relations with other people, especially with members of the family. People saddled with the irresistible need to wash their hands every ten minutes, or touch every doorknob they pass, or count every tile in a bathroom floor are likely to cause concern and even resentment in spouses, children, friends, or co-workers. And the antagonistic feelings experienced by these significant others are likely to be tinged with guilt, for at some level they understand that the person cannot really help doing these senseless things. Finally, the undesirable effects on others can, in turn, be expected to have additional consequences, engendering feelings of depression and generalized anxiety in the obsessive-compulsive person and setting the stage for even further deterioration of personal relationships. For such reasons family therapists (Hafner, 1982; Hafner et al., 1981) have suggested that obsessive-compulsive disorder is sometimes embedded in marital distress and actually substitutes for overt marital conflict. This speculative hypothesis cautions therapists to consider couples treatment as well as therapies that focus on the individual.

Etiology of Obsessive-Compulsive Disorder

Psychoanalyic Theory of Obsessive-Compulsive Disorder

In psychoanalytic theory obsessions and compulsions are viewed as similar, resulting from instinctual forces, sexual or aggressive, that are not under control because of overly harsh toilet training. The person is thus fixated at the anal stage. The symptoms observed represent the outcome of the struggle between the id and the defense mechanisms; sometimes the id predominates, sometimes the defense mechanisms. For example, when obsessive thoughts of killing intrude, the forces of the id are dominant. More often, however, the observed symptoms reflect the partially successful operation of one of the defense mechanisms. For example, an individual fixated at the anal stage may, by reaction formation, resist the urge to soil and become compulsively neat, clean, and orderly.

Alfred Adler (1931), an early colleague who broke with Freud because he did not agree with Freud's libido theory, viewed obsessive-compulsive disorders within the framework of his theory that pathology results when children are kept from developing a sense of competence by their doting or excessively dominating parents. Saddled with an inferiority complex, people may unconsciously adopt compulsive rituals in order to carve out a domain in which they exert control and can feel proficient. Adler proposed that the compulsive act allows a person mastery of *something*, even if only the positioning of writing implements on a desk.

Behavioral Theories of Obsessive-Compulsive Disorder

Behavioral accounts of obsessions and compulsions (Meyer and Chesser, 1970) consider the disorder to be learned behaviors reinforced by their consequences. One set of consequences is the reduction of fear. For example, compulsive hand washing is viewed as an operant escape-response that reduces an obsessional preoccupation with contamination by dirt or germs. Similarly, compulsive checking may reduce anxiety about whatever disaster the patient would anticipate were the checking ritual not completed. Anxiety as measured by self-report (Hodgson & Rachman, 1972) and psychophysiological responses (Carr, 1971) can indeed be reduced by such compulsive behavior. Research has also shown, however, that not all compulsive acts reduce anxiety to the same degree. Rachman and Hodgson (1980) reported that patients with a cleaning compulsion were more often able to lessen their anxiety than patients with a checking compulsion. Furthermore, the reduction of anxiety cannot account for obsessions. Indeed, the obsessions of obsessive-compulsive patients usually make them anxious (Rabavilas & Boulougouris, 1974), much as do the somewhat similar intrusive thoughts of normal subjects about stressful stimuli, such as a scary movie (Horowitz, 1975).

How, then, might we account for obsessive thoughts? First, Rachman and deSilva (1978) showed that most people occasionally experience unwanted ideas that are similar in content to obsessions. Among normal individuals, however, these cognitions are tolerated or dismissed. But for the obsessive individual, the thoughts may be particularly salient and elicit great concern. The obsessive person may then begin to try to actively suppress these troubling thoughts, with unfortunate consequences.

Wegner et al. (1987; in press) studied what happens when people are asked to suppress a thought. Two groups of college students were asked either to think about a white bear or not to think about one. One group thought about the white bear and then was told not to; the other group did the reverse. Thoughts were measured by having subjects voice their thoughts and also by having them ring a bell every time they thought about a white bear. Two findings are of particular note. First, attempts to inhibit were not fully successful. Second, the students who first inhibited thoughts of a white bear had more subsequent thoughts about it once the inhibition condition was over. Trying to inhibit a thought may therefore have the paradoxical effect of inducing preoccupation with it. Furthermore, attempts to suppress unpleasant thoughts are typically associated with intense emotional states, resulting in a strong link between the suppressed thought and the emotion. After many attempts at suppression, a strong emotion may lead to the return of the thought, accompanied by an increase in negative mood (Wenzlaff, Wegner, & Klein, 1991). The result would be an increase in anxiety.

Cognitive Views of Obsessive-Compulsive Disorder

In a related but more cognitive view, Carr (1974) proposes that obsessive-compulsive individuals, when in a situation that has a potentially undesirable or harmful outcome, overestimate the likelihood that the harmful outcome will occur. In other words, the obsessive-compulsive person has an "If anything can go wrong, it will" view of life. This cognitive set, according to Carr, necessitates avoiding the sources of threat and thus increases the likelihood of obsessive-compulsive behavior.

A study by Sher, Frost, and Otto (1983) used cognitive tasks to test the idea that college students who scored high on a measure of compulsive checking suffered from a memory deficit for actions performed—Did I turn off the stove?—and for distinguishing between reality and imagination—Maybe I just *imagined* I turned off the stove. In both instances the person would be inclined to reduce uncertainty by checking whether in fact the stove were turned off. The results supported the first hypothesis, that compulsive checkers had poorer recall of prior actions; the second hypothesis was not unequivocally supported. A replication study, using psychiatric patients as subjects, again showed that high scorers on a measure of compulsive checking were poor at remembering their own recent activities (Sher et al., 1989). These studies are significant in that they construe at least one kind of compulsivity as a problem in a certain kind of memory and test this hypothesis via procedures that come from basic experimental research in cognition. This kind of experimentation has been employed for some years in schizophrenia research but is only recently being followed in empirical work with other psychological disorders.

Biological Factors in Obsessive-Compulsive Disorder

Encephalitis, head injuries, and brain tumors have all been associated with the development of obsessive-compulsive disorder (Jenike, 1986). Neurochemically, interest has focused on serotonin. Clomipramine and fluoxetine, tricyclic antidepressants that block the reuptake of serotonin, have proved to be useful therapies for OCD (e.g., Pigott et al., 1990). Furthermore, patients with high pretest levels of serotonin or its major metabolite improve most when treated with a serotonin reuptake blocker, and the extent to which these drugs reduce levels of serotonin correlates with their clinical effectiveness (see Lesch et al., 1991, for a review of this evidence).

Similarly, research with drugs that can stimulate the serotonin receptor indicates that they can exacerbate the symptoms of OCD (Bastani, Nash, & Meltzer, 1990; Hollander et al., 1992; Zohar et al., 1988). Carey and Gottesman (1981) reported evidence consistent with a genetic contribution to OCD as do more recent studies. McKeon and Murray (1987) found high rates of anxiety disorders among the first-degree relatives of patients with OCD, and Lenane et al. (1990) found that 30 percent of the first-degree relatives in their study also had OCD. Although it is premature to conclude that biological factors are known to predispose people to OCD, we can expect the search for a biological diathesis to intensify in the coming years.

Therapies for Obsessive-Compulsive Disorder

Obsessive-compulsive disorder is overall one of the most difficult psychological problems to treat. Psychoanalytic treatment for obsessions and compulsions resembles that for phobias and generalized anxiety, namely, lifting repression and allowing the patient to confront what he or she is truly afraid of—that a particular impulse will be gratified. The intrusive thoughts and irresistible behavior are not appropriate targets for therapeutic change, serving as they do to protect the ego from the repressed conflict.

Psychoanalytic procedures have not been effective in treating obsessive-compulsive disorder. This shortcoming has prompted some analytic workers to take a more action-oriented, behavioral approach to these disorders and to regard the role of analytic understanding more as a way to increase compliance with behavioral procedures (Jenike, 1990). Salzman (1980), for example, warns that free association merely feeds into the patient's obsessionalism; hence he suggests that the analyst be more directive in guiding the discussion. He hypothesizes that the indecision one sees in most obsessive-compulsive patients derives from a need for guaranteed correctness before any action can be taken (Salzman, 1985). Patients therefore must learn to tolerate the uncertainty and anxiety that all people feel as they confront the reality that nothing is certain or absolutely controllable in life.[3] He suggests as well that the analyst encourage the patient to abandon the ego defense of acting compulsively. The ultimate focus of the treatment, however, remains on insight into unconscious determinants.

The most widely used and generally accepted behavioral approach to compulsive rituals entails exposure with response prevention (Rachman & Hodgson, 1980). This approach involves having the person expose himself or herself to situations that elicit the compulsive act—such as touching a dirty dish—and then refraining from performing the accustomed ritual—hand washing. The assumption is that the ritual reduces anxiety that is aroused by some environmental stimulus or event, such as dust on a chair, and that preventing the person from performing the ritual will expose him or her to the anxiety-provoking stimuli, thereby allowing the anxiety to extinguish. Controlled research (e.g., Foa et al., 1985) suggests that this is an effective treatment.

Although in the short term such curtailment is very arduous and unpleasant for clients, the extreme discomfort is believed worth enduring to alleviate these disabling problems. Clearly, however, conditions must be such that the client can be persuaded to go along with the treatment. Indeed, refusal to enter treatment and dropping out are generally recognized problems for all kinds of interventions for OCD (Jenike, 1990). For one thing, OCD patients tend to procrastinate, to fear changes, and to be overly concerned about others controlling them—characteristics that can be expected to create special problems for avowedly manipulative approaches like behavior therapy.

Sometimes control over obsessive-compulsive rituals is possible only in a hospital. Victor Meyer (1966), a renowned behavioral expert in the treatment of compulsions, pioneered the development of a controlled environment at Middlesex Hospital in London. There staff members were specially trained to restrict the patient's opportunities for engaging in ritualistic acts. Generalization of the treatment to the home required the involvement of family members. Suffice it to say that preparing them for this work was no mean task, requiring skills and care beyond whatever specific behavioral technique was being employed.

The monoamine oxidase inhibitors and the tricyclics, drugs that are more commonly used in treating depression (see Chapter 9), are sometimes given to obsessive-compulsive patients. Both classes of drugs have yielded beneficial results (Jenike, 1986). The largest study conducted to date (Clomipramine Collaborative Study Group, 1991) compared clomipramine to a placebo in a double-blind design and found clear evidence of effectiveness. On the other hand, in a study assessing the role of imipramine in enhancing improvement brought about by response prevention with depressed OCD patients, Foa et al. (in press) failed to find an effect from this antidepressant drug on OCD symptoms, although it did alleviate depression. Patients who received the response prevention treatment but not imipramine improved on depression as much as those who also received the drug. This finding suggests that depression in OCD patients may be secondary to, or caused by, the OCD symptoms themselves. In another study, the benefits of clomipramine on OCD were found to be short-lived: withdrawal from this drug led to a much higher relapse rate than that found with response prevention (Pato et al., 1988).

A recently published study (Baxter et al., 1992) comparing fluoxetine (Prozac) and response prevention found that improvement in OCD by *both* treatments was associated with the same changes in brain function, namely reduced metabolic activity in the caudate nucleus, overactivity of which has

---

[3]The hypothesized need of the obsessive-compulsive person not to err suggests that a rational-emotive approach might also be useful: the person may harbor an irrational belief that he or she must never make a mistake. In a rare clinical trial applying rational-emotive therapy to OCD, Emmelkamp, Visser, and Hoekstra (1988) found that Ellis's therapy achieved results comparable to those of an *in vivo* response prevention therapy and was superior to the more strictly behavioral therapy in reducing depressed mood.

been linked to OCD. Furthermore, only those patients who improved clinically showed this change in brain activity as measured by PET scans (p. 78). Such findings suggest that markedly different therapies may work for similar reasons, being different ways of affecting the same factors in the brain. We should note that a design problem with the Baxter et al. study was that patients were not randomly assigned to the treatment groups; rather, each patient selected either the drug or the response prevention treatment. While this flaw does not, in our view, invalidate the findings, another problem makes the comparisons of the two treatments not quite equivalent: during the posttreatment PET scan, the drug subjects were still on their medication, whereas the behavior therapy patients were not and could not be, in any meaningful sense, in treatment, that is, undergoing active response prevention for the rituals.

The desperation of mental health workers, surpassed only by that of the sufferers, explains the occasional use of psychosurgery in treating obsessions and compulsions. The procedure in current use is called cingulatomy; it involves destroying two to three centimeters of white matter in the cingulum, an area near the corpus callosum. While some clinical improvement has been reported (Jenike et al., 1991; Mitchell-Heggs et al., 1976; Tippin & Henn, 1982), this intervention is rightfully viewed as a treatment of very last resort, given the permanence of psychosurgery and the poorly understood ways in which it works.

All in all, regardless of treatment modality, OCD patients are seldom cured. While the improvement that many achieve in a variety of interventions can be significant, obsessive-compulsive tendencies usually persist to some degree, albeit under greater control and with less obtrusiveness into the conduct of their lives (White & Cole, 1990).

Posttraumatic Stress Disorder

A twenty-seven-year-old singer was referred by a friend for evaluation. Eight months before, her boyfriend had been stabbed to death during a mugging from which she escaped unharmed. After a period of mourning she appeared to return to her usual self. She helped the police in their investigation and was generally considered an ideal witness.

Nevertheless, shortly after the recent arrest of a man accused of the murder, the patient began to have recurrent nightmares and vivid memories of the night of the crime. In the dreams she frequently saw blood and imagined herself being pursued by ominous, cloaked figures. During the day, especially when walking somewhere alone, she often drifted off in daydreams, so that she forgot where she was going. Her friends noted that she began to startle easily and seemed to be preoccupied. She left her change or groceries at the store, or when waited on could not remember what she had come to buy. She began to sleep restlessly, and her work suffered because of poor concentration. She gradually withdrew from her friends and began to avoid work. She felt considerable guilt about her boyfriend's murder, although exactly why was not clear. (Spitzer et al., 1981, p. 17)

Posttraumatic Stress Disorder (PTSD) was introduced as a diagnosis in DSM-III and reflects an extreme response to a severe stressor including increased anxiety, avoidance of stimuli associated with the trauma, and a numbing of emotional responses. Although there had been prior awareness that the stresses of combat could produce powerful and adverse effects on soldiers, the aftermath of the Vietnam War (see Focus Box 6.4) spurred the acceptance of the new diagnosis. Like other disorders in the DSM, PTSD is defined by a cluster of symptoms. But unlike other psychological disorders, it also includes its presumed etiology, namely, a traumatic event which the person has directly experienced or witnessed that involved actual or threatened death, or serious injury, or a threat to physical integrity. In previous editions of the DSM, the traumatic event was defined as being "outside the range of human experience." This definition of the traumatic event was too restrictive as it would have ruled out the diagnosis of PTSD following occurrences such as an automobile accident.

There is a difference between posttraumatic stress disorder and **acute stress disorder**, a new diagnosis in DSM-IV. Nearly everyone who encounters a trauma experiences stress, sometimes to a very considerable degree. This is normal. Most people recover from an acute stress disorder after a few days or weeks and go on to lead lives that are not marked by PTSD.

FOCUS

6.4 • Posttraumatic Stress Disorder and the Vietnam War

During war, military personnel must contend with devastating stress, and some of them break down. The American Civil War was the first one in which the psychological disintegration suffered under the rigors of battle was acknowledged as a clinical entity. William Hammond, Surgeon General of the Union Army, considered it to be "nostalgia," meaning a severe melancholia brought on by protracted absence from home (Bourne, 1970). In World War I, the first global conflict, the term used was *shell shock*, reflecting the somatogenic belief that the soldier's brain suffered chronic concussions through the sudden and severe atmospheric pressure changes from nearby explosions.

In World War II and the Korean War the great weariness of soldiers, their sleeplessness, startle at the slightest sounds, inability to speak, terror, and either stupor or agitated excitement were called exhaustion and then combat fatigue (Figley, 1978a), putting the blame clearly on the stressful circumstances of battle.

What was unusual about the psychological breakdowns during and in the aftermath of the Vietnam War? As Figley (1978b) noted, this war was believed at first to have caused far fewer psychological casualties than did World War I or II—1.5 percent in Vietnam versus 10 percent in World War II—perhaps because battle duty was more intermittent and limited in time.

After veterans had been home for a few months or years however, signs of great distress began to appear. In 1984, Congress commissioned The National Vietnam Veterans Readjustment Study (NVVRS), the first comprehensive investigation designed to determine the social and psychological consequences of a country's involvement in a war. The NVVRS found a much higher percentage of PTSD sufferers than originally thought—15.2 percent of the 3.14 million men who served in Vietnam have PTSD today (Keane et al., 1992). Rates are higher among African-Americans and Hispanics than among non-Hispanic whites, a finding attributable to the fact that these minorities saw more combat. Women also served in Vietnam, albeit not in direct combat situations; for them PTSD was found in close to 9 percent. All of these rates are much higher than for comparable groups of American adults who did not serve in Vietnam.

The listing of posttraumatic stress disorder in DSM-III in 1980 eventually made it easier for Vietnam veterans to obtain help within the Veterans Administration system. They were acknowledged to have a recognized mental disorder. Their treatment centered on the combat stress itself and not on any emotional weakness presumed to have existed prior to the war, or on the veterans' own efforts to deal with their stress, such as abusing drugs.

Several factors other than the abbreviated and time-limited periods of combat differentiated the Vietnam War from others in recent history. It was extremely unpopular and controversial, and it was a war that this country did not win in spite of the infusion of billions of dollars, fatalities exceeding 58,000, and many more seriously wounded and permanently maimed. Military personnel, after their one-year tour of duty, returned home alone and quickly by jet. There were no battalions of soldiers arriving stateside together at war's end, no parades, no homecomings, indeed, none of the grateful hoopla that all of us have seen in newsreels taken of the end of World War II and more recently, the Persian Gulf War. To make matters worse, the soldiers were subjected to criticism and sometimes abuse from those who regarded them as murderers for their participation in what many in the United States had come gradually to regard as an immoral war. Here is one example from many cited by Figley and Leventman (1980).

> Walking across the Boston Commons his first day home, his service uniform and gear fully apparent, he was greeted by peace demonstrators with shouts of "Killer! How many babies did you burn over there?" Returning home, his brother offered, "You asshole! Why did you go to Vietnam anyway?" Seeking solace and companionship that night in the American Legion Hall, he was confronted with "Hey buddy! How come you guys lost the war over there?" (p. xxv)

Existential philosophy teaches us that people must find meaning and purpose in their lives. Sheer survival is important, but men and women suffer distress and depression if they cannot develop some sense of self-worth in what they do. It is terrible enough for soldiers to see a friend torn up by shrapnel or to plunge a bayonet into the throat of a person designated as the enemy. How much worse are these experiences if soldiers know that back home people are protesting the morality of their being in the war in the first place? Many American soldiers in Vietnam began to harbor their own doubts about the value and legitimacy of their being there.

Haley (1978), a social worker with extensive experience treating Vietnam veterans, provides a chilling and poignant account of how the particular nature of the war affected one soldier years afterward.

> Because of the guerrilla nature of the Vietnam war, the "enemy" could be anyone, including women and children. Thus, some stress responses are activated by closeness to women and the responsibility of marriage, a wife's pregnancy and the birth of a child. Veterans who have fought and killed women and children during combat often find it impossible to make a smooth transition to the roles of husband, protector and father. One veteran had warned his close friend, the squad medic, not to go near a crying baby lying in a village road until they had checked the area. In his haste to help the child, the medic raced forward and "was blown to bits" along with the child, who had been booby-trapped. The veteran came into treatment three years later, after a period of good adjustment, because he was made fearful and anxious by his eight-month-old daughter's crying. He had been unable to pick her up or hold her since her birth despite his conscious wish to "be a good father." (p. 263)

Why were there delays, sometimes years, before some of the combat-related PTSD symptoms began to show up in many returning Vietnam veterans? We would suggest that some of the stressors eliciting the symptoms did not occur until *after* the return home. The combat stressors themselves may have sensitized soldiers to react with great stress to the often hostile reception that awaited them after discharge. This lack of welcome (at best) may have robbed them of the healing effects that a warm and appreciative populace and family provided veterans who returned from our more popular, or at least more widely accepted, wars. Veterans of World War II, for example, may have also been predisposed to develop PTSD upon returning home but may have been protected from it by the strong social support that awaited them.

This hypothesis is consistent with the developing literature on secondary trauma, said to occur "when the survivor of a traumatic event subsequently is held responsible for the event or is seen in some vague, ill-defined, collusive relationship with agents of the primary traumatic event. . . . Examples could include the rape victim who 'brought it on herself . . . dressing, behaving seductively . . .' or the Vietnam veteran who 'deserved his misfortune . . . should feel guilty . . . shouldn't have been there in the first place.' " (Foy et al., 1987). Indirect but intriguing support for this idea can be found in research that shows the healing effects of social support in reducing the negative aftereffects of stress (e.g., Cohen & Wills, 1985); PTSD sufferers may find themselves rejected by others because of the very nature of their symptoms—suspiciousness, depression, apathy, low tolerance for intimacy.

This perspective implies that PTSD is virtually inevitable, with most people being spared its worst effects because of social support and acceptance once the actual crisis is past. Rather than focusing on why some people develop PTSD after a stressor, one might consider why most do not. When we discuss the aftermath of rape (page 351), we will see that rape crisis intervention is actually based on this posttrauma perspective: professional opinion holds that it is normal for a sexually abused individual to be traumatized and that therefore it is important to have in place readily available support systems to prevent the stressor from causing the development of PTSD. We see this also when crisis intervention professionals go to scenes of horror or destruction, for example, an unprovoked shooting spree at a school or other public place, immediately after the event and before any one individual seeks out mental health assistance.

Troops returning home from the Gulf War were welcomed with parades instead of the hostility that greeted Vietnam veterans. The unpopularity of the Vietnam War may well have contributed to the high frequency of PTSD.

The inclusion in the DSM of severe stress as a significant causal factor of PTSD represents no small change in overall point of view, for it constitutes a formal recognition that, regardless of their history, many people may be adversely affected by overwhelming catastrophic stress and that their reactions should be distinguished from other disorders. The cause of PTSD is primarily the event, not the person. Even well-adjusted people can develop PTSD (Foy et al., 1984). Instead of implicitly concluding that the person would be all right were he or she made of sterner stuff, the importance of the traumatizing circumstances is now formally acknowledged (Haley, 1978). Yet, the inclusion of this diagnostic criterion is not without controversy. Many people, for example, encounter traumatic life events but do not develop PTSD. Thus, the event itself cannot be the sole cause of PTSD.

The symptoms for PTSD are grouped into three major categories. The diagnosis requires that symptoms in each category last longer than one month.

1. **Reexperiencing the traumatic event.** The event is frequently recalled and nightmares about it are common. Intense emotional upset is produced by stimuli that symbolize the event (e.g., thunder reminding a veteran of the battlefield) or on anniversaries of some specific experience. In a laboratory confirmation of this disturbing symptom, McNally et al. (1990) administered the Stroop test to Vietnam veterans with and without PTSD. In this test, the subject sees a set of words printed in different colors and must name the color of each word as rapidly as possible and not simply say the word. Interference, measured as a slowing of response time, occurs because of the content of some words. In this study, words from several different categories—neutral (e.g., input), positive (e.g., love), obsessive-compulsive disorder (e.g., germs), and PTSD (e.g., bodybags)—were used. Veterans with PTSD were slower than non-PTSD veterans only on the PTSD words. The same effect has been documented for rape victims by Foa et al. (1991).

   The importance of reexperiencing cannot be underestimated, for it is the likely source of the

Witnessing the death of others, as happened to these people who saw the Challenger disaster, is among the types of stress related to Post Traumatic Stress Disorder.

Visiting the Vietnam War Memorial is an emotional experience for veterans.

other categories of symptoms. In fact, some theories of PTSD make this the central feature (e.g., Horowitz, 1986; Foa, Zinbarg, & Rothbaum, in press) by attributing the disorder to an inability to successfully integrate the traumatic event into an existing schema (the person's general beliefs about the world).

2. **Avoidance of stimuli associated with the event or numbing of responsiveness.** The person tries to avoid thinking about the trauma or encountering stimuli that will bring it to mind; there may actually be amnesia for the event. Numbing refers to decreased interest in others, a sense of estrangement, and inability to feel positive. Notice that the symptoms here seem almost contradictory to those in 1. In PTSD there is fluctuation: the person goes back and forth between reexperiencing and numbing.
3. **Symptoms of increased arousal.** Included here are difficulties falling or staying asleep, difficulty concentrating, hypervigilance, and exaggerated startle response. Laboratory studies have confirmed these clinical symptoms by documenting the heightened physiological reactivity of PTSD patients to combat imagery (e.g., Pitman et al., 1990).

Other problems are often associated with PTSD: anxiety, depression, anger, guilt, substance abuse (self-medication to ease the distress), marital problems, and occupational impairment (Keane, Gerardi, Quinn, & Litz, 1992). Suicidal thoughts and plans are also common, as are incidents of explosive violence and stress-related psychophysiological problems, such as low back pain, headaches, and gastrointestinal disorders (Hobfoll et al., 1991).

The DSM alerts us to the fact that children can suffer from PTSD but may manifest it differently from adults. Sleep disorders with nightmares about monsters are common, as are behavioral changes, for example, a previously outgoing youngster becoming quiet and withdrawn or a previously quiet youngster becoming loud and aggressive. Some traumatized children begin to think that they will not become adults. In addition, some children may lose already acquired developmental skills such as speech or toilet habits. Most importantly, young children have much more difficulty talking about their upset than do adults; this is especially important to remember in cases of possible physical or sexual abuse.

PTSD has a prevalence rate of about 1 percent in the general U.S. population (Helzer, Robins, & McEvoy, 1987). This represents about 2.4 million people. The rate rises to 3.5 percent among civilians who have been exposed to a physical attack and Vietnam veterans and to 20 percent among those wounded in Vietnam. An even higher percentage of PTSD was found in Rothbaum et al.'s (in press) longitudinal study of rape victims. The women were assessed weekly for twelve weeks following the rape. At the first assessment, 94 percent met the criteria for PTSD[4]; at the end of the study, the rate of PTSD had dropped to 47 percent. In a large-scale population study in Detroit, Breslau et al. (1991) found that 39 percent of adults had experienced a traumatic event. Of those who had experienced a trauma, 24 percent developed PTSD.

PTSD shows high rates of comorbidity: the long list of comorbid diagnoses includes alcoholism and suicide (Davidson et al., 1990) and dysthymia (Helzer, Robins, & McEvoy, 1987), in addition to conditions mentioned in the next section. Notably, these other diagnoses typically precede the onset of PTSD so they appear to potentiate the effects of traumatic events.

Etiology of Posttraumatic Stress Disorder

There are a number of risk factors for PTSD. In the Breslau study (1991), predictors of PTSD given exposure to a traumatic event were being female, early separation from parents, family history of a disorder, and a preexisting disorder (panic disorder, OCD, depression). The likelihood of PTSD increases with the severity of the traumatic event; for example, the greater the exposure to combat the greater the risk. With a high degree of combat exposure, the rates of PTSD are the same in veterans with or without family members with other disorders. But among those with a family history of disorder, even low combat exposure produces a high rate of PTSD (Foy et al., 1987).

Other research has also begun to examine person variables that distinguish between those who do and do not develop PTSD following combat. For example, in a study of Israeli veterans of the 1982 war with Lebanon, development of PTSD was associated with a depressive attributional style (see page 235) and a tendency to cope by focusing on their emotions (e.g., "I wish I could change how I feel.") rather than on the problems themselves (Mikhliner & Solomon, 1988; Solomon et al., 1988).

Both psychological and biological theories have been proposed to account for PTSD. Learning the-

[4]Technically, these women could not be diagnosed as having PTSD because the DSM specifies that the symptoms must last for at least one month.

orists assume that the disorder arises from a classical conditioning of fear (Fairbank & Brown, 1987; Keane, Zimering, & Caddell, 1985). In the case of rape, for example, the woman may come to fear walking in a certain neighborhood (the CS) that had previously caused her no second thoughts, because of having been assaulted there (the UCS). Based on this classically conditioned fear, avoidances are built up, and they are negatively reinforced by the reduction of fear that comes from not being in the presence of the CS. In a sense, PTSD is an example of the two-factor theory of avoidance learning proposed years ago by Mowrer (1947; p. 47). There is a developing body of evidence in support of this view (Foy et al., 1990) and for related cognitive-behavioral theories that emphasize the loss of control and predictability felt by PTSD sufferers (Chemtob et al., 1988; Foa & Kozak, 1986).

A psychodynamic theory proposed by Horowitz (1986, 1990) posits that the traumatic event is repeated constantly in the person's conscious mind but becomes so painful that it is either consciously suppressed (by distraction, for example) or repressed. The person is believed to engage in a kind of internal struggle to integrate the trauma into his or her existing beliefs about himself or herself and the world to make some sense out of it.

A biological theory of PTSD holds that the trauma damages the noradrenergic system, raising levels of norepinephrine and thereby making the person startle and express emotion more readily than normal (Krystal et al.,1989; Van der Kolk et al., 1985). Evidence consistent with this view is the finding of Kosten et al. (1987) that levels of norepinephrine were higher in PTSD hospital patients than among those diagnosed as having schizophrenic or mood disorders.

These theories do not fare well in accounting for why only some people develop PTSD in the aftermath of trauma. As mentioned earlier, some hints are now beginning to emerge concerning personal characteristics that render a person more vulnerable; these include a preexisting disorder, a family history of disorder, early separation from parents, and specific styles of coping with stress.

Therapies for Posttraumatic Stress Disorder

The treatment of combat-related stress has for some time been guided by the three principles of immediacy, proximity, and expectancy (Lifton, 1976). When signs of stress, such as sleeplessness, are detected in military personnel, they are removed immediately to a quiet area as near as possible to their fighting unit and comrades. There they are encouraged to talk things out and to rest and are made aware that a quick return to the unit is expected. Those severely affected are given more intensive therapy.

As stated earlier, during World War II combat-exhausted soldiers were hypnotized. They were also treated by narcosynthesis (Grinker & Spiegel, 1945), a procedure that might be considered a drug-assisted catharsis à la Breuer. A soldier was sedated with an intravenous injection of sodium Pentothal, enough to cause extreme drowsiness. The therapist then stated in a matter-of-fact voice that the soldier was on the battlefield, in the front lines, and, if necessary and possible, mentioned circumstances of the particular battle. The patient would usually begin recalling sometimes frightening events that had perhaps been forgotten, often with intense emotion. Many times the actual trauma was relived and even acted out by the patient. As the patient gradually returned to the waking state, the therapist would continue to encourage discussion of the terrifying events, in the hope that the patient would realize that they were in the past and no longer a threat. In this fashion a synthesis, or coming together, of the past horror with the patient's present life was sought (Cameron & Magaret, 1951).

The Veterans Administration, which had served veterans of World War II as well as those of the Korean War, was not prepared at first to address the psychological plight of Vietnam veterans. First of all, many had left the service with bad paper, that is, with less than honorable discharges. Some of the offenses for which a soldier could receive undesirable discharges included "character and behavior disorders," "alcoholism," and "drug addiction" (Kidder, 1978). It seems likely that some of these veterans were suffering from the trauma of combat. Not until 1979—six years after the truce was signed with North Vietnam—was upgrading of dishonorable discharges effected through the assistance of the American Civil Liberties Union (Beck, 1979).

But in 1971, earlier than these governmental efforts that have helped bring more Vietnam veterans within the purview of the Veterans Administration hospital system, the psychiatrist Robert Jay Lifton was approached by antiwar veterans from the New York–New Haven area to work with them in forming "rap groups." Initiated by the veterans themselves, these groups had a twofold purpose: a therapeutic one of healing themselves and a political one of forcing the American public to begin to understand the human costs of the war (Lifton, 1976). The rap groups spread outward from New York City until, in 1979, Congress approved a $25 million package establishing Operation Outreach, a net-

Rap groups, like the one shown here, played an important role in treating PTSD among Vietnam veterans.

work of ninety-one storefront counseling centers for psychologically distressed Vietnam veterans. In 1981 funding was extended for three additional years.

The rap groups focused on the residual guilt and rage felt by the veterans: guilt over what their status as soldiers had called on them to do in fighting a guerrilla war in which enemy and ally were often indistinguishable from one another; and rage at being placed in the predicament of risking their lives in a cause to which their country was not fully committed. Discussion extended as well to present-life concerns, such as relationships with women and feelings about masculinity, in particular, the macho view of physical violence. Antidepressant medication was also used, but with equivocal results (Lerer et al., 1987).

The treatment of PTSD should also, argued Stanton and Figley (1978), encompass the complexities of the veteran's family life. Does he feel guilt over infidelities, or rage at his wife's extramarital involvements while he was away? Is he having trouble with the increased independence of his wife, which she developed out of necessity in his absence and may be reluctant to give up on his return, especially in this era of raised feminist consciousness?

Group therapy is discussed in some detail in Chapter 20 (page 594). For now it suffices to say that in the rap groups—and in the more conventional group therapy sessions in the 172 Veterans Administration hospitals across the country—at least two factors have probably helped veterans. For perhaps the first time they could partake of the company of returned comrades-in-arms and feel the mutual support of others who had shared their war experiences. They were also able finally to begin confronting, in often emotional discussions, the combat events whose traumatic effects had been suppressed and therefore not examined. As people have known for many, many years, in order for individuals to come to terms with fearsome happenings, to loose themselves from the hold that events can have over them, they must, in effect, return to the events and expose themselves fully.

There is very little in the way of actual research on the kinds of approaches just described. But controlled research on the treatment of PTSD has accelerated in recent years as more attention has been focused on the aftermath of traumas such as natural disasters, rape, child abuse, and especially combat. Recent work in cognitive behavior therapy provides some findings based on studies that employed careful assessment, details of treatment, and appropriate control groups. (Interventions for the PTSD aftermath of child abuse and rape are described in Chapter 12.)

As reviewed by Rothbaum and Foa (in press), one general strategy that has been followed is to expose the patient to what he or she fears. We have already encountered exposure techniques in the behavioral treatment of other anxiety disorders, and this theme is present as well in nonbehavioral approaches to PTSD described above. The basic principle is that fears are best reduced or eliminated by having the person confront, in some fashion, whatever he or she most ardently wishes to avoid. In the case of

Social support plays a critical role in the treatment of PTSD.

PTSD, we almost always know what triggered the problem in the first place, as part of the very diagnosis of PTSD, so the decision is a tactical one, that is, how to expose the frightened patient to what is fearsome. Many techniques have been employed. In one well-designed study from the National Center for Post Traumatic Stress Disorder at the Boston Veterans Administration Medical Center, Terence Keane and his associates compared a no-treatment control group with an imaginal flooding condition that had patients visualize fearsome trauma-related scenes for extended periods of time. They found significantly greater reductions in depression, anxiety, reexperiencing of the trauma, startle reactions, and irritability in PTSD Vietnam veterans from the imaginal procedure (Keane et al., 1989). Case studies such as those of Fairbank, DeGood, and Jenkins (1981) and Muse (1986) demonstrate the clinical efficacy of systematic desensitization with victims of car accidents. Conducting such exposure therapy is difficult, however, for both patient and therapist, for it requires detailed review of the traumatizing events. As recently pointed out by Keane et al. (1992), patients may become temporarily worse in the initial stages of therapy, and therapists themselves may become upset by hearing of the horrifying events that their patients experienced.

Another cognitive-behavioral approach conceptualizes PTSD more generally as an extreme stress reaction and therefore amenable to the kind of multifaceted approach to stress management described in Chapter 8 (p. 220), entailing relaxation, rational-emotive therapy, and training in problem-solving. Among the problems addressed within this broader framework is the anger that many PTSD sufferers have, especially those who have seen combat. Assertion training and couples therapy are often called for in helping patients deal with their anger more appropriately (Keane et al., 1992).

Horowitz's (1988, 1990) psychodynamic approach has much in common with the aforementioned treatment, for he encourages patients to discuss the trauma and otherwise expose themselves to the events that led to the PTSD. But Horowitz emphasizes the manner in which the trauma interacts with a patient's pretrauma personality, and the treatment he proposes has much in common with other psychoanalytic approaches, including discussions of defenses and analysis of transference reactions by the patient. This complex therapy awaits empirical verification.

Finally, a range of psychoactive drugs have been used with PTSD patients, including antidepressants and tranquilizers. Some modest successes have been reported for the former (Davidson et al., 1990; Frank et al., 1987; Rosen & Bohon, 1990).

Whatever the specific mode of intervention, PTSD experts agree that social support is critical. Sometimes finding ways to lend support to others can help the giver as well as the receiver (Hobfoll et al., 1991). Belonging to a religious group, having family, friends, or fellow traumatized individuals listen nonjudgmentally to one's fears and recollections of the trauma—these and other ways of knowing that one belongs and that others wish to try to help ease the pain may even, as suggested in Focus Box 6.4, spell the difference between posttraumatic stress and posttraumatic stress disorder.

SUMMARY

People with anxiety-disorders feel an overwhelming apprehension that seems unwarranted. DSM-IV lists six principal diagnoses: phobic disorders, panic disorder, generalized anxiety disorder, obsessive-compulsive disorder, posttraumatic stress disorder, and acute stress disorder.

Phobias are intense, unreasonable fears that disrupt the life of an otherwise normal person. They are relatively common. Agoraphobia is fear of being outside one's home; social phobia is fear of social situations in which one may be scrutinized by other people. Other specific phobias are fears of animals, closed-in spaces, and heights. The psychoanalytic view of phobias is that they are a defense against repressed conflicts. Behavioral theorists have several ideas of how phobias are acquired—through classical conditioning, the pairing of an innocuous object or situation with an innately painful event; through operant conditioning, whereby a person is rewarded for avoidance; through modeling, imitating the fear and avoidance of others; and through cognition, by making a catastrophe of a social mishap that could be construed in a less threatening fashion. But not all people who have such experiences develop a phobia. Perhaps a genetically transmitted physiological diathesis, lability of the autonomic nervous system, predisposes certain people to acquire phobias.

A patient suffering from panic disorder has sudden inexplicable and periodic attacks of intense anxiety. Panic attacks sometimes precede the onset of agoraphobia. Some people who have panic attacks also suffer from mitral valve prolapse syndrome. They may regard their heart palpitations as evidence of anxiety and escalate them into full-blown panics. A number of laboratory manipulations (e.g., hyperventilation) can induce panic attacks in those with the disorder. Panic disorder patients, in general, ruminate about serious illnesses, both physical and mental; they may magnify slight physical sensations until they are overwhelmed.

In generalized anxiety disorder, sometimes called free-floating anxiety, the individual's life is beset with virtually constant tension, apprehension, and worry. Psychoanalytic theory regards the source as an unconscious conflict between the ego and id impulses. Behavioral theorists assume that, with adequate assessment, this pervasive anxiety can be pinned down to a finite set of anxiety-provoking circumstances, thereby likening it to a group of phobias. A sense of helplessness can also cause people to be anxious in a wide range of situations. Biological approaches focus on the therapeutic effects of the benzodiazepines and their relevance to the neurotransmitter GABA.

People with obsessive-compulsive problems have intrusive, ego-alien thoughts and feel pressured to engage in stereotyped rituals lest they be overcome by frightening levels of anxiety. This disorder can become quite disabling, interfering not only with the life of the unfortunate person who experiences the difficulties but also with the lives of those close to that person. Psychoanalytic theory posits strong id impulses that are under faulty and inadequate ego control. In behavioral accounts, compulsions are considered learned avoidance responses.

There are many therapies for anxiety disorders. Psychoanalytic treatment tries to lift repression so that childhood conflicts can be resolved; direct alleviation of the manifest problems is discouraged. In contrast, behavior therapists employ a range of procedures, such as systematic desensitization and modeling, designed to reduce the fear and avoidance. Preventing compulsives from performing their rituals is a useful although initially arduous technique. Rational-emotive therapy attempts to substitute more realistic self-statements for irrational beliefs.

Perhaps the most widely employed treatments are anxiolytic drugs dispensed by medical practitioners. Drugs, however, are subject to abuse, and their long-term use may have untoward and still inadequately understood side effects. Weaning a person from reliance on a chemical that reduces anxiety is also a problem.

Posttraumatic stress disorder is sometimes the fate of those who have experienced a traumatic event that would evoke extreme distress in most individuals. Treatment is by intense remembrances of the traumatic events. If we are to understand the veterans of Vietnam who suffer from this disorder and how best to render complete their return to and reintegration into society, we must grapple with the moral and political aspects of this conflict. The particular horrors and unpopularity of the war seem to lie at the core of the veteran's problems in adjusting to civilian life.

KEY TERMS

anxiety
neuroses
anxiety disorders
comorbidity
phobia
specific phobias
agoraphobia
social phobia
retrospective reports
vicarious conditioning
preparedness
autonomic lability
flooding
anxiolytics
panic disorder
depersonalization
derealization
generalized anxiety disorder (GAD)
obsessive-compulsive disorder (OCD)
obsessions
compulsion
posttraumatic stress disorder (PTSD)
acute stress disorder

c h a p t e r s e v e n

Somatoform and Dissociative Disorders

A twenty-seven-year-old male was brought to a hospital emergency room after being picked up by the police for lying down in the middle of a busy intersection. He said that he wanted to die and was very depressed. He had no memory of any events prior to being picked up by the police. He didn't know his name nor anything about his life history.

Several neurological tests were administered and revealed no abnormality. After six days in the hospital, hypnosis was begun. Over the first three hypnotic sessions, details of the patient's past life emerged but not his name nor the events that led up to his hospitalization. During the fourth and fifth sessions, the remaining details came forth. The man had just come to town, looking for work. Two men noticed his toolbox, approached him, and asked if he wanted a job. All three then left in a pickup truck, and, after smoking some marijuana, the patient was forced, at gunpoint, to have sex with the other men. (Kasniak et al., 1988)

Somatoform and dissociative disorders, our focus for this chapter, are related to anxiety disorders, which we discussed in the previous chapter. As we said, in earlier versions of DSM all these disorders were subsumed under the heading of neuroses because anxiety was considered to be the predominant underlying factor in each case. But starting with DSM-III, classification came to be based on observable behavior, not presumed etiology. In the anxiety disorders, signs of anxiety are obvious, but they are not necessarily observable in the somatoform and dissociative disorders. In **somatoform disorders,** the individual complains of bodily symptoms that suggest a physical defect or dysfunction—some rather dramatic in nature—but for which no physiological basis can be found. In **dissociative disorders,** the individual experiences disruptions of consciousness, memory, and identity, as illustrated in the opening case. The onset of both classes of disorder is typically related to some stressful experience and its associated anxiety. The DSM-IV categories for somatoform and dissociative disorders are listed in Table 7.1. We will examine each of these categories in this chapter, focusing in more depth on those disorders about which more is known. As before, we will look at symptoms, etiology, and therapies throughout the discussion.

Table 7.1 • Somatoform and Dissociative Disorders

Somatoform Disorders
Conversion disorder
Somatization disorder (Briquet's syndrome)
Pain disorder
Body dysmorphic disorder
Hypochondriasis
Dissociative Disorders
Dissociative amnesia
Dissociative fugue
Multiple personality (Dissociative identity disorder)
Depersonalization disorder

Somatoform Disorders

The physical symptoms of somatoform disorders, which have no known physiological explanation and are not under voluntary control, are assumed to be linked to psychological factors, presumably anxiety; they are assumed, therefore, to be psychologically caused. In this section, we look at two of the somatoform disorders in depth: conversion disorder and somatization disorder.

DSM-IV also includes three other categories of somatoform disorders, about which little information is available. Of these, **pain disorder** is diagnosed when the person experiences pain that causes significant distress and impairment and that cannot be accounted for by organic pathology, even after extensive investigation. The pain may have a temporal relation to some conflict or stress, or it may allow the individual to avoid some unpleasant activity and to secure attention and sympathy not otherwise available. Accurate diagnosis is difficult because the subjective experience of pain is always a psychologically influenced phenomenon; that is, pain is not just a sensory experience in the same way that vision and hearing are. Therefore, deciding when a pain becomes a somatoform pain is likely to be difficult.

With **body dysmorphic disorder,** a person is preoccupied with an imagined or exaggerated defect in appearance, for example, facial wrinkles, excess facial hair, or the shape or size of the nose. These concerns are distressing and lead to frequent consultations with plastic surgeons. Here again, though, subjective factors and matters of taste play a role.

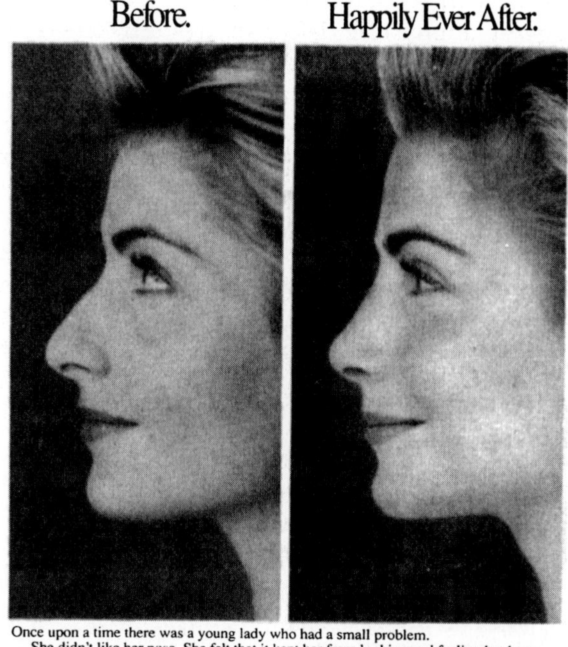

This ad illustrates the type of concern of someone with body dysmorphic disorder.

When, for example, does one's vanity become a body dysmorphic disorder? In a survey of college students, Fitts et al. (1989) found that 70 percent of the students indicated at least some dissatisfaction with their appearance, with a higher figure for women than for men. Determining when these frequent perceived defects become psychological disorders is difficult indeed. Social and cultural factors surely play a role.

Hypochondriasis is a somatoform disorder in which individuals are preoccupied with fears of having a serious disease. They overreact to ordinary physical sensations and minor abnormalities—such as irregular heartbeat, sweating, occasional coughing, a sore spot, stomachache—as evidence for this belief and cannot be medically persuaded otherwise. Hypochondriasis is not very well differentiated from somatization disorder.

Let us turn now to an in-depth discussion of conversion disorder and somatization disorder.

Conversion Disorder

In **conversion disorder,** the classic symptoms suggest an illness related to neurological damage of some sort, in spite of the fact that the bodily organs and nervous system are found to be fine. Individuals may experience partial or complete paralysis of arms or legs; seizures and coordination disturbances; a sensation of prickling, tingling, or creeping on the skin; insensitivity to pain; or the loss or impairment of sensations, called **anesthesias** (see Figure 7.1)—although they are physiologically normal people. Vision may be seriously impaired: the person may become partially or completely blind or have tunnel vision, in which the visual field is constricted as it would be if the observer were peering through a tunnel. *Aphonia,* loss of the voice and all but whispered speech; *anosmia,* loss or impairment of the sense of smell; and false pregnancy are other conversion disorders.

Conversion symptoms by their very nature suggest that they are linked to psychological factors. They usually appear suddenly in stressful situations, allowing the individual to avoid some activity or responsibility or to get badly wanted attention. The term *conversion* originally derived from Freud, who thought that the energy of a repressed instinct was diverted into sensory-motor channels and blocked functioning. Thus anxiety and psychological conflict were believed to be *converted* into physical symptoms. Some of the people suffering conversion disorders may in fact seem complacent, even serene, and not particularly eager to part with their symptoms. Nor do they connect them with whatever stressful situation they may be in.

Hysteria, the term originally used to describe what are now known as conversion disorders, has a long history dating back to the earliest writings on abnormal behavior. Hippocrates considered it an affliction limited solely to women and brought on by the wandering of the uterus through the body. The Greek word *hystera* means "womb." Presumably the wandering uterus symbolized the longing of the body for the production of a child. Freud considered the specific nature of the hysterical symptom to relate either to the repressed instinctual urge itself or to the attempt to suppress the urge, representing it in disguised form. A hysterical convulsion, for example, might be the symbolic expression of a forbidden sexual wish, and a hysterical paralysis the manifestation of self-punishment for a hidden aggressive urge. Conversion symptoms usually develop in adolescence or early adulthood. An episode may end abruptly, but sooner or later the disorder is likely to return, either in its original form or with

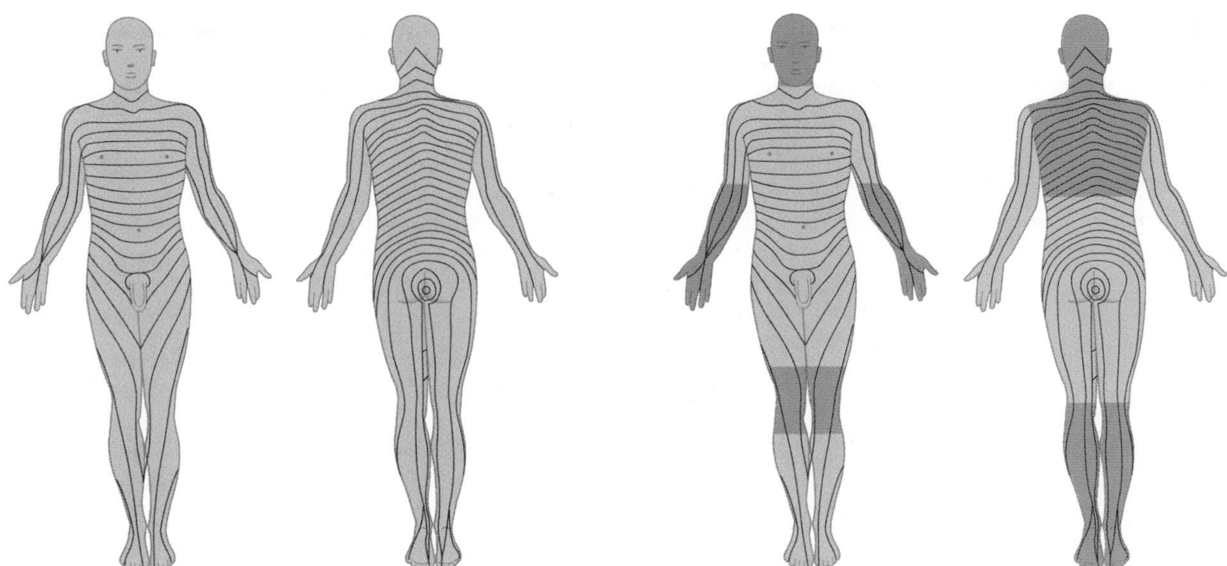

Figure 7.1 Hysterical anesthesias can be distinguished from neurological dysfunctions. On the left are shown the patterns of neural innervation. On the right are superimposed typical areas of anesthesias in hysterical patients. The hysterical anesthesias do not make anatomical sense. (Adapted from an original painting by Frank H. Netter, M.D. From *The CIBA Collection of Medical Illustrations*, copyright © by CIBA Pharmaceutical Company, Division of CIBA-GEIGY Corporation.)

a symptom of a different nature and site. More women than men are diagnosed as having conversion disorders (Viederman, 1986). At one clinic, for example, forty-four of the fifty individuals diagnosed with conversion disorder were women (Folks, Ford, & Regan, 1984). During both world wars, however, a large number of males developed conversionlike difficulties in combat (Ziegler, Imboden, & Meyer, 1960). This lends even more credibility to the point mentioned above that conversion symptoms typically help the individual avoid or escape some activity, in this case, combat.

Diagnostically, it is important to distinguish a conversion paralysis or sensory dysfunction from similar problems that have a true neurological basis. Sometimes this is an easy task, as when the paralysis does not make anatomical sense. A classic example is *glove anesthesia,* a rare syndrome in which the individual experiences little or no sensation in the part of the hand that would be covered by a glove (see Figure 7.1) For years this was the textbook illustration of anatomical nonsense because the nerves here run continuously from the hand up the arm. Yet even in this case, it now appears misdiagnosis can occur. A newly recognized disease, *carpal tunnel syndrome,* can produce symptoms like those of glove anesthesia. Nerves in the wrist run through a tunnel formed by the wrist bones and membranes; the tunnel can become swollen and may pinch the nerves, leading to tingling, numbness, and pain in the hand.

Since the majority of paralyses, analgesias, and sensory failures do have organic causes, true neurological problems may sometimes be misdiagnosed as conversion disorders. Slater and Glithero (1965) investigated this disturbing possibility in a follow-up of patients who nine years earlier had been diagnosed as suffering from conversion symptoms. They found that an alarming number, in fact 60 percent, of these individuals had either died in

Leon Fleischer, world famous pianist, lost use of his right hand due to carpal tunnel syndrome. He played lefthanded pieces for years and tried a comeback in 1983.

the meantime or developed symptoms of physical disease! A high proportion had diseases of the central nervous system. Similarly, Whitlock (1967) compared the incidence of organic disorders in patients earlier diagnosed as having depressive reactions, anxiety reactions, or both. Organic disorders were found in 62.5 percent of the patients earlier diagnosed as having conversion disorders and in only 5.3 percent of the other groups. The most common organic problem was head injury, generally found to have occurred about six months before the onset of the conversion symptoms. Other common organic problems were stroke, encephalitis, and brain tumors. Watson and Buranen (1979) and Fishbain and Goldberg (1991) found that many patients whose symptoms had been considered conversion disorders actually had physical disorders.

These are impressive data, and they suggest that conversion disorder may often be misdiagnosed when, in fact, the individual has a physical disorder. We have already learned that the assessment of organic problems is still far from perfect. Therefore, it is not always possible to distinguish between psychologically and organically produced symptoms. The damage that can result from inappropriate diagnoses is sobering to contemplate.

Another diagnostic problem with conversion disorder is distinguishing it from **malingering,** DSM-IV category in which the individual fakes an incapacity in order to avoid a responsibility. Malingering is diagnosed when the conversionlike symptoms are under voluntary control, which is not thought to be the case in true conversion disorders.

In trying to discriminate conversion reactions from malingering, clinicians may attempt to decide whether the symptoms have been consciously or unconsciously adopted. This means of resolving the issue is at best a dubious one, for it is difficult, if not impossible, to know with any degree of certainty whether behavior is consciously or unconsciously motivated. One aspect of behavior that can sometimes help distinguish the two disorders is known as **la belle indifférence,** which is characterized by a relative lack of concern or a blasé attitude toward the symptoms that is out of keeping with their severity and supposedly long-term consequences. Patients with conversion disorder sometimes demonstrate this behavior; they also appear willing and eager to talk endlessly and dramatically about their symptoms, but often without the concern one might expect. In contrast, malingerers are likely to be more guarded and cautious, perhaps because they consider interviews a challenge or threat to the success of the lie.

But this distinction is not foolproof, for only about one-third of people with conversion disorders show la belle indifférence (Stephens & Kamp, 1962). Further, a stoic attitude sometimes is found among patients with verified medical diseases.

Finally, we need to distinguish conversion disorders and malingering from yet another DSM category. **Factitious disorders** involve conversionlike symptoms that are under voluntary control, just as is the case with malingering. In malingering, however, the symptoms are obviously linked to a recognizable goal, the altering of the individual's circumstances. An example would be a claim of physical illness to avoid standing trial. In a factitious disorder the motivation for adopting the physical or psychological symptoms is much less clear. Apparently the individual for some unknown reason wants to assume the role of "patient."

Somatization Disorder

In 1859 the French physician Pierre Briquet described a syndrome that first bore his name, Briquet's syndrome, and now in DSM-IV is referred to as somatization disorder. Recurrent, multiple somatic complaints for which medical attention is sought but which have no apparent physical cause are the basis for this disorder. Common complaints include headaches; fatigue; allergies; abdominal, back, and chest pains; genitourinary symptoms; gastrointestinal symptoms; symptoms suggesting a neurological disorder; and heart palpitations. Table 7.2 gives a picture of the pervasiveness of health problems reported by people with somatization disorder. In fact, somatization disorder and conversion disorder share many of the same symptoms, and it is not uncommon for both diagnoses to be applicable to the same patient (e.g., Ford et al., 1984). Visits to physicians, sometimes to a number of them simultaneously, are frequent, as is the use of medication. Hospitalization and even surgery are common (Guze, 1967). Menstrual difficulties and sexual indifference are frequent (Swartz et al., 1986). Patients typically present their complaints in a histrionic, exaggerated fashion or as part of a long and complicated medical history. Many believe that they have been ailing all of their lives. The lifetime prevalence of somatization disorder is estimated at 0.1 percent (Robins et al., 1984), and the disorder is more frequent among women than men (Viederman, 1986). Comorbidity is high as well with anxiety disorders, mood disorders, and substance abuse. (Golding, Smith, & Kasher, 1991). In an epidemiological study conducted in Los Angeles, Escobar et al. (1987) found somatization more common among

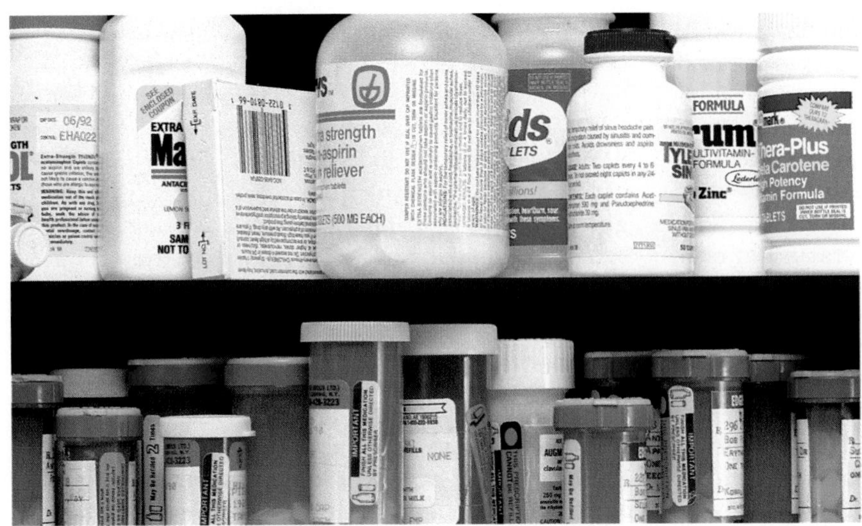

The medicine chest of a patient with a somatization disorder includes many drugs used to treat their numerous medical complaints.

Mexican-American women than among non-Hispanic white women. This difference may reflect the greater intensity of the stressors (e.g., financial strain, social isolation) these Mexican-American women face.

Somatization disorder typically begins in late adolescence (Kroll, Chamberlain & Halpern, 1979; Cloninger et al., 1986). Anxiety and depression are frequently reported, as are a host of behavioral and interpersonal problems, such as truancy, poor work

Table 7.2 • Somatization Disorder Symptoms and Their Frequency as Reported by a Sample of Patients

Symptom	*Percent Reporting*	*Symptom*	*Percent Reporting*	*Symptom*	*Percent Reporting*
Dyspnea (labored breathing)	72	Anorexia	60	Joint pain	84
Palpitation	60	Nausea	80	Extremity pain	84
Chest pain	72	Vomiting	32	Burning pains in rectum, vagina, mouth	28
Dizziness	84	Abdominal pain	80	Other bodily pain	36
Headache	80	Abdominal bloating	68	Depressed feelings	64
Anxiety attacks	64	Food intolerances	48	Phobias	48
Fatigue	84	Diarrhea	20	Vomiting all nine months of pregnancy	20
Blindness	20	Constipation	64	Nervous	92
Paralysis	12	Dysuria (painful urination)	44	Had to quit working because felt bad	44
Anesthesia	32	Urinary retention	8	Trouble doing anything because felt bad	72
Aphonia (loss of voice above a whisper)	44	Dysmenorrhea (painful menstruation, premarital only)	4	Cried a lot	70
Lump in throat	28	Dysmenorrhea (prepregnancy only)	8	Felt life was hopeless	28
Fits or convulsions	20	Dysmenorrhea (other)	48	Always sickly (most of life)	40
Faints	56	Menstrual irregularity	48	Thought of dying	48
Unconsciousness	16	Excessive menstrual bleeding	48	Wanted to die	36
Amnesia	8	Sexual indifference	44	Thought of suicide	28
Visual blurring	64	Frigidity (absence of orgasm)	24	Attempted suicide	12
Visual hallucination	12	Dyspareunia (painful sexual intercourse)	52		
Deafness	4	Back pain	88		
Olfactory hallucination	16				
Weakness	84				
Weight loss	28				
Sudden fluctuations in weight	16				

Source: After Perley & Guze, 1962.

records, and marital difficulties. Somatization disorders also seem to run in families; they are found in about 20 percent of the first-degree relatives of index cases, that is, individuals diagnosed as having somatization disorders (Arkonac & Guze, 1963). The following case illustrates one woman's complaints.

Alice was referred to the psychological clinic by her physician, Joyce Williams. Dr. Williams had been Alice's physician for about six months and in that time period had seen her twenty-three times. Alice had dwelt on a number of rather vague complaints—general aches and pains, bouts of nausea, tiredness, irregular menstruation, and dizziness. But various tests—complete blood workups, X rays, spinal tap, and so on—had not revealed any pathology.

Upon meeting her therapist, Alice immediately let him know that she was a somewhat reluctant client: "I'm here only because I trust Dr. Williams and she urged me to come. I'm physically sick and don't see how a psychologist is going to help." But when Alice was asked to describe the history of her physical problems, she quickly warmed to the task. According to Alice, she had always been sick. As a child she had had episodes of high fever, frequent respiratory infections, convulsions, and her first two operations, an appendectomy and a tonsillectomy. As she continued her somewhat loosely organized chronological account of her medical history, Alice's descriptions of her problems became more and more colorful (and probably exaggerated as well): "Yes, when I was in my early twenties I had some problems with vomiting. For weeks at a time I'd vomit up everything I ate. I'd even vomit up liquids, even water. Just the sight of food would make me vomit. The smell of food cooking was absolutely unbearable. I must have been vomiting every ten minutes." During her twenties Alice had gone from one physician to another. She saw several gynecologists for her menstrual irregularity and dyspareunia (pain during intercourse) and had undergone dilatation and curettage (scraping the lining of the uterus). She had been referred to neurologists for her headaches, dizziness, and fainting spells, and they had performed EEGs, spinal taps, and even a CAT scan. Other physicians had ordered X rays to look for the possible causes of her abdominal pain and EKGs for her chest pains. Both rectal and gallbladder surgery had also been performed.

When the interview finally shifted away from Alice's medical history, it became apparent that she was a highly anxious person in many situations, particularly those in which she thought she might be evaluated by other people. Indeed, some of her physical complaints could be regarded as consequences of anxiety. Furthermore, her marriage was quite shaky, and she and her husband were considering divorce. Their marital problems seemed to be linked to sexual difficulties stemming from Alice's dyspareunia and her general indifference toward sex. (Reprinted by permission of the New England Journal of Medicine.)

Etiology of Somatoform Disorders

Much of the theorizing in the area of somatoform disorders has been directed solely toward understanding hysteria, as originally conceptualized by Freud. This focus has by default encouraged the assumption that both conversion disorder and somatization disorder have similar etiological roots. Although this assumption is unsupported, it has dominated investigation into causality and thus left it with a distinctly psychoanalytic flavor. In this section, we will first examine those psychoanalytic views, but we will look, too, at what behavioral, cognitive, and biological theorists have to offer.

Psychoanalytic Theory

Conversion disorder occupies a central place in psychoanalytic theory, for in the course of treating such cases Freud developed many of the major concepts of psychoanalysis. Conversion disorders offered him a clear opportunity to explore the concept of the unconscious. Consider for a moment how you might try to make sense of a patient's report that she awakened one morning with a paralyzed left arm. Your first reaction might be to give her a series of neurological tests to assess possible biological causes of the paralysis. Let us assume that these tests are negative: no evidence of neurological disorder is present. You are now faced with choosing whether to believe or to doubt the patient's communication. On the one hand, she might be lying; she may know that her arm is not paralyzed but has decided to fake paralysis to achieve some end. This would be an example of malingering. But what if you believe the patient? Now you are almost forced to consider that unconscious processes are operating. On a conscious level the patient is telling the truth; she believes and reports that her arm is paralyzed. Only on a level that is not conscious does she know that her arm is actually normal.

In their *Studies in Hysteria* (1895) Breuer and Freud proposed that a conversion disorder is caused by an experience that created great emotional arousal. The affect, however, was not expressed, and the memory of the event was cut off from conscious experience. They proposed two explanations for why the affect associated with the experience was not expressed. The experience may have been so distressing that the person could not allow it to enter consciousness and therefore repressed it. Or the experience may have occurred while the person was in an abnormal psychological state, such as semihypnosis. In both situations, Breuer and Freud proposed, the specific conversion symptoms are causally related to the traumatic event that preceded them.

Anna O. (see p. 22), for example, while watching at the bedside of her seriously ill father, had dropped off into a waking dream with her right arm over the back of her chair. She saw a black snake emerge from the wall and come toward her sick father to bite him. She tried to ward it away, but her right arm had gone to sleep. When she looked at her hand, her fingers turned into little snakes with death's heads. The next day a bent branch recalled her hallucination of the snake, and at once her right arm became rigidly extended. After that, her arm responded in the same way whenever some object revived her hallucination. Later, when Anna O. fell into her absences and took to her own bed, the contracture of her right arm became chronic and extended to paralysis and anesthesia of her right side.

In his later writings Freud formulated a theory of conversion disorder in which sexual impulses became primary. Specifically, he hypothesized that conversion disorders are rooted in an early, unresolved Electra complex. The young female child becomes incestuously attached to her father, but these early impulses are repressed, producing both a preoccupation with sex and, at the same time, an avoidance of it. At a later period of her life, sexual excitement or some happenstance reawakens these repressed impulses, and they are transformed or converted into physical symptoms that represent in distorted form the repressed libidinal urges or the repressing forces. Thus the primary gain from conversion disorder is the avoidance of previously repressed id impulses. Freud allowed, however, that there could also be a secondary gain from the symptoms. That is, they might allow the patient to avoid or escape from some currently unpleasant life situation or to obtain attention from others.

A contemporary psychodynamic interpretation of one form of conversion disorder, hysterical blindness, has been offered by Sackeim, Nordlie, and Gur (1979). The starting point of their analysis is experimental studies of hysterically blind people whose behavior on visual tests shows that they are being influenced by the stimuli, even though they explicitly deny seeing them.

Two of the studies they reviewed involved cases of teen-aged women. The first case was described by Theodor and Mandelcorn (1973). The patient, a sixteen-year-old, had experienced a sudden loss of peripheral vision, reporting that her visual field had become tubular and constricted. Although a number of neurological tests had proved negative, the authors wanted to be even more certain that they were not dealing with a neurological problem. So they arranged a special visual test in which a bright, oval target was presented either in the center or in the periphery of the patient's visual field. On each trial there was a time interval, bounded by the sounding of a buzzer. Either a target was illuminated during the intervals or not, and the young woman's task was to report whether a target was present or not.

When the target was presented in the center of the visual field, the patient always correctly identified it. This had been expected since she had not reported any loss of central vision. What happened when the oval was presented peripherally? The patient could be expected to be correct 50 percent of the time by chance alone; the authors reasoned that this would be the outcome if she were truly blind in peripheral vision. For the peripheral showings of the target, however, the young woman was correct only 30 percent of the time. She had performed significantly more poorly than would a person who was indeed blind! The clinicians reasoned that she must have been in some sense aware of the illuminated stimulus, and that she wanted, either consciously or unconsciously, to preserve her blindness by performing poorly on the test.

Sackeim et al. also reviewed a seemingly contradictory case done by Grosz and Zimmerman (1970), in which a hysterically blind adolescent girl showed almost perfect visual performance. Fifteen-year-old Celia's initial symptom was a sudden loss of sight in both eyes, followed thereafter by severe blurring of vision. Celia claimed not to be able to read small or large print. She had set high standards for herself and did very well at school. Her busy parents, continually rushing off on their own many activities, professed concern about their four children's education but often left Celia responsible for the three younger children. When Celia's vision blurred so severely, her parents became obliged to read her studies to her. Even so, testing revealed that Celia could readily identify objects of various sizes and shapes and count fingers at a distance of fifteen feet. When three triangles were projected on three display windows of a console, two of the triangles inverted, one of them upright, in 599 trials out of 600 she pressed the switch under the upright triangle, the correct response, which then turned off a buzzer for 5 seconds.

We will return to Celia later in this chapter. For now, it is important to note that Sackeim et al. propose a two-stage defensive reaction to account for these conflicting findings. They argue that, at first, perceptual representations of visual stimuli are blocked from awareness, and on this basis people report themselves blind. Second, information is still extracted from the perceptual representations. If subjects feel that they must deny being privy to this information, they do more poorly than they would do by chance on perceptual tasks. If subjects do not need to deny to themselves having such information, they perform the task well but still maintain that they are blind. Whether hysterically blind people unconsciously need to deny receiving perceptual information is viewed as being dependent on personality factors and motivation.

Are the people who claim that they are blind and yet on another level respond to visual stimuli being truthful? Sackeim and his colleagues report that some patients with lesions in the visual cortex, rather than damage to the eye, say that they are blind and yet perform well on visual tasks. They have vision, but they do not *know* that they can see. So it is possible for people to claim truthfully that they cannot see and at the same time give evidence that they can. On a more general level, a dissociation between awareness and behavior has been reported in many perceptual and cognitive studies (see Focus Box 7.1). In a laboratory setting Sackeim and his colleagues tested their assumption that motivation has a bearing on whether an individual will dissociate behavior from awareness. They hypnotized two susceptible subjects, gave each a suggestion of total blindness, and then tested them on a visual discrimination task[1]. One was given instructions designed to motivate her to maintain her blindness. She was expected to deny her perceptions and perform more poorly than chance on the visual task. The other subject was not so explicitly urged to maintain her blindness and was expected to do better than chance on the task. A third subject was asked to simulate the behavior of someone who had been hypnotized and given a suggestion of total blindness.

The results agreed with the predictions. The subject highly motivated to maintain blindness indeed performed more poorly than chance, and the less motivated subject performed perfectly, even though still reporting that she was blind. The simulator performed, for the most part, at a chance level. In a postexperimental interview she stated that she had deliberately tried to simulate chance performance. Bryant and McConkey (1989) give further support to the Sackeim et al. findings. Over a large number of sessions, they tested a man with hysterical blindness, giving different instructions in some sessions. In the usual condition where visual feedback was present, the patient was correct 66 percent of the time. But when told that he had to do better, his percentage correct went up to 88 percent.

In sum, as Sackeim and his colleagues proposed, verbal reports and behavior can apparently be unconsciously separated from one another. Hysterically blind persons are able to say that they cannot see and yet at the same time be influenced by visual stimuli. The way in which they show signs of being able to see may depend on how much they need to be considered blind.

Behavioral Theory

A behavioral account of the development of conversion disorders was proposed by Ullmann and Krasner (1975). They view conversion disorders as similar to malingering in that the person adopts the symptom to gain some end. In their opinion the person with a conversion disorder attempts to behave according to his or her own conception of how a person with a disease affecting the motor or sensory abilities would act. This theory raises two questions. Are people capable of such behavior? Under what conditions might such behavior be most likely to occur?

Considerable evidence indicates the answer to the first question is yes: people can adopt patterns of behavior that match many of the classic conversion symptoms. For example, paralyses, analgesias, and blindness, as we have seen, can be induced in people under hypnosis. Similarly, chemically inert drugs, called placebos, have reduced the pain of patients who had been considered truly ill.

As a partial answer to the second question. Ullmann and Krasner specify two conditions that increase the likelihood that motor and sensory disabilities will be imitated. First, the individual must have some experience with the role to be adopted.

[1]Hypnotic susceptibility refers to whether someone will be a "good" hypnotic subject, that is, will be able to experience the suggestions of the hypnotist. It is most often assessed with the Stanford Hypnotic Susceptibility Scale (Weizenhoffer & Hilgard, 1959), in which subjects are asked to undertake a number of tasks. For example, the hypnotist may suggest that the subject's hand is so heavy that it cannot be raised and then ask the subject to try to raise it. The good hypnotic subject will not raise his or her arm or will have great difficulty doing so.

FOCUS 7.1 • Cognitive Factors: Awareness, the Unconscious, and Behavior

The first experimental psychologists working in the last two decades of the nineteenth century realized very soon that we are unaware of much that goes on in our minds as we perceive and encode stimuli from our environment. Much of the working of the mind proceeds out of our awareness. Consider an example. In studying selective attention, researchers often use a dichotic-listening task in which separate tapes are played to each ear; subjects are asked to attend to only one of them. Subjects usually report later on that they know little about the sounds that came into the unattended ear. *But these unattended stimuli can affect behavior.* For example, Wilson (1975) had people listen to a human voice played into one ear while tone sequences were played in the unattended ear. Subjects reported having heard no tones. Furthermore, in a memory task in which they listened to tone sequences played earlier and others that had not been played, the subjects were unable to distinguish between the two types. Despite this demonstration that the subjects did not recognize tone stimuli played previously, another measure revealed a startling result. When subjects in Wilson's study were asked to rate how much they liked a series of tone sequences, the ones that had been presented earlier to the unattended ear were preferred to novel sequences. Some aspects of the tone sequences played during the dichotic-listening task must have been absorbed, even though subjects said that they had not heard them and demonstrated that they did not recognize them.

It is known that familiarity affects judgments of tone stimuli similar to those Wilson used. Familiar sequences are liked better than novel ones. A similar phenomenon has been observed with vision (Kunst-Wilson & Zajonc, 1980). Subjects

A subject participates in a dichotic listening experiment. Although he attends to information presented to only one ear, the information reaching the unattended ear can affect behavior.

He or she may have had similar physical problems or may have observed them in others. Second, the enactment of a role must be rewarded. An individual will assume a disability only if it can be expected either to reduce stress or to reap other positive consequences.

Although this behavioral interpretation might seem to make sense, the literature does not support were presented with different shapes for one millisecond (one-thousandth of a second). Their ability to recognize later the shapes that they had seen was essentially nil. But when they rated how much they liked the shapes, they preferred the ones that they had "seen" to new ones that were presented.

A series of studies reported by Nisbett and Wilson (1977) also indicates that awareness, as measured by verbal report, is not always a very accurate indication of the effect stimuli have on behavior. In one of their studies, Nisbett and Wilson first had subjects memorize a list of word pairs. For some subjects the pairs of words were specially constructed so that they would be likely to have an effect on subjects' performance in the second part of the study. For example, one of the word pairs these subjects first memorized was "ocean–moon." This pair was expected to make them more likely to respond "Tide" when they were later asked to name a detergent. The results agreed with expectation: subjects who had memorized the special word pairs gave double the number of expected associations as subjects who had not memorized them. Right after the second part of the test, subjects were asked why they had given their particular responses. Even though they could still recall the word pairs, subjects almost never mentioned them as bringing their responses to mind. Instead they gave reasons such as "My mother uses Tide" or "Tide is the most popular detergent."

The studies just described provide laboratory evidence for the operation of unconscious processes. But do they generalize to more naturalistic dependent variables? A study by Bornstein, Leone, and Galley (1987) indicates that the answer is yes. They investigated whether subliminal exposure to a person's face would influence subsequent interactions with that person. Subjects participated with two confederates of the experimenter in a task in which they had to read ten poems and as a group decide on the gender of the author of each poem. By prior arrangement the two confederates disagreed on seven of the ten, putting the subject in the role of tie breaker. Prior to judging the poems, half of the subjects viewed, for four milliseconds, five presentations of a slide of one of the confederates. The other half saw a slide of the second confederate. (Pilot data had already shown that exposures like these could not be discriminated from blank flashes of light.) This manipulation, based on the earlier work of Wilson and Kunst-Wilson and Zajonc, was expected to increase liking for the confederate whose photograph had been viewed and hence change behavior toward that confederate. The major dependent measure was which confederate subjects chose to agree with concerning their judgments of the gender of the authors of the poems. Consistent with the hypothesis of the study, subjects agreed with the confederate whose slide they had seen 68 percent of the time, a statistically significant effect.

These experiments, which are but a small sampling of current research making a similar point, are closely related to the psychoanalytic concept of the unconscious. Contemporary investigators, many of whom would identify themselves as cognitive psychologists, have begun to corroborate Freud's view that some human behavior is determined by unconscious processes. Like many others (e.g., Kihlstrom, Barnhardt, & Tataryn, 1992), we are persuaded that unconscious processes are important. But the unconscious processes are understood in a different way. Freud postulated the existence of "the unconscious," a repository of instinctual energy and repressed conflicts and impulses. Contemporary researchers reject the energy reservoir and repression, holding more simply that we are not aware of everything going on around us and of some of our cognitive processes.* At the same time, these stimuli and processes of which we are unaware can affect behavior powerfully. This recent research suggests that understanding the causes of human behavior will be a difficult task. It will not be sufficient merely to ask someone, "Why did you do that?"

*In a sense, the distinction resides in whether *unconscious* is a noun, as Freud used it, or an adjective, as contemporary researchers employ the term. As an adjective, *unconscious* can encourage further exploration into the factors that render something unavailable to awareness.

it completely because there is clearly some question as to whether the patient is aware of the behavior—that is, whether this behavior is conscious or unconscious. Grosz and Zimmerman's patient Celia, for example, did not act in accord with Ullmann and Krasner's theory. The very intelligent Celia performed perfectly in the visual discrimination task while still claiming severely blurred vision. Such a pattern of behavior seems a rather clumsy enactment of a role. If you wanted to convince someone that you could not see, would you always correctly identify the upright triangle? Again, Celia's actions seem more consistent with the theorizing offered by Sackeim and his co-workers. On the level of conscious awareness, Celia probably saw only blurred images, as she claimed. But during the test the triangles were distinguished on an unconscious level, and she could pick out the upright one, wherever it appeared. It is interesting to note that Celia's visual problems gained her crucial attention and help from her parents, which is in the nature of conversion disorders as well as of malingering. Three years after the onset of her visual difficulties, Celia suddenly and dramatically recovered clear sight while on a summer trip with her parents across the country. Earlier in the summer, Celia had graduated from high school with grades well above average. The need to receive reinforcement for poor vision had perhaps passed, and her eyesight returned.

Another behavioral view of somatoform disorders, at least of somatization disorder, holds that the various aches and pains, discomforts, and dysfunctions are unrealistic anxiety manifesting itself in particular bodily systems. Perhaps the extreme tension of an individual localizes in stomach muscles, and he or she feels nauseous and even vomits. Once normal functioning is disrupted, the maladaptive pattern may strengthen because of the attention it receives or the excuses it provides. In a related vein, reports of physical symptoms have been seen as a strategy used to explain poor performance in evaluative situations. Attributing poor performance to illness is psychologically less threatening than attributing it to some personal failing (Smith, Snyder, & Perkins, 1983).

Sociocultural Theory

Sociocultural theories are based on the supposed decrease in conversion disorders over the last century. Although Charcot and Freud seemed to have had an abundance of female patients with this sort of difficulty, contemporary clinicians rarely see anyone with such problems. A number of hypotheses have been proposed to explain this apparent decrease. For example, those with a psychoanalytic bent point out that in the second half of the nineteenth century, when the incidence of conversion reactions was apparently high in France and Austria, sexual attitudes were quite repressive and may have contributed to the increased prevalence of the disorder. The decline of the conversion reaction, then, is attributed to a general relaxing of sexual mores and also to the greater psychological and medical sophistication of twentieth-century culture, which is more tolerant of anxiety than it is of dysfunctions that do not make physiological sense.

A study by Proctor (1958) provides evidence for the theory. The prevalence of conversion reaction was found to be particularly high (13 percent) among children who were patients at the University of North Carolina Medical School Psychiatric Clinic. In interpreting this very high prevalence, the author noted that most of the children came from rural areas where the socioeconomic status of the inhabitants was low and little education was provided for them. Moreover, the religious background of these people was generally strong and fundamentalist. The mid-twentieth-century conditions in this area of North Carolina may have approximated in some respects those prevailing in nineteenth-century France and Austria. Similarly, in the Folks et al. (1984) study of fifty cases, diagnoses of conversion disorder were more common among rural residents and those of lower socioeconomic status. Further evidence supporting this sociocultural view comes from studies showing that the diagnosis of hysteria has declined in industrialized societies (e.g., England: Hare, 1969) but has remained more common in undeveloped countries (e.g., Libya: Pu et al., 1986). These data, while consistent, are difficult to interpret. They could mean that increasing sophistication about medical diseases leads to decreased prevalence of conversion disorder. Alternatively, diagnostic practices may vary from country to country, producing the different rates. A cross-national study conducted by diagnosticians trained to follow the same procedures is clearly needed.

Biological Factors

Genetic factors have been proposed in the development of conversion disorders, but the research does not bear this proposal out. Slater (1961), for example, investigated concordance rates in twelve identical and twelve fraternal pairs of twins. Probands of each pair had been diagnosed as having the disorder, but none of the co-twins in either of the two groups manifested a conversion reaction. More recently, Torgerson (1986) reported the results of a twin study of somatoform disorders that included ten cases of conversion disorder, twelve of somatization disorder, and seven of pain disorder. No co-twin had the same diagnosis as his or her proband! Even the overall concordance for somatoform disorder was no higher in the identical twins than in the fraternal twins. Genetic factors, then, from the studies done so far, seem to be of no importance.

More promise seems to lie on the biological side. A hint of a neurophysiological explanation of why emotions connected with conversion disorders remain unavailable to conscious awareness comes from studies showing that conversion symptoms are more likely to occur on the left side of the body than on the right side (Galin, Diamond, & Braff, 1977; Ford & Folks, 1985; Stern, 1977). In most instances these left-side body functions are controlled by the right hemisphere of the brain. The majority of conversion symptoms, then, may be related to the functioning of the right hemisphere. Research on patients who have had the hemispheres of their brains surgically disconnected to prevent the spread of epileptic seizures has shown that the right hemisphere can separately generate emotions, and indeed it is suspected of generating more of them, particularly unpleasant ones, than does the left hemisphere. Conversion symptoms could in this way be neurophysiologically linked to emotional arousal. Furthermore, this same research indicates that the right hemisphere depends on the neural passageways of the corpus callosum for connection with the left hemisphere's verbal capacity to describe and explain emotions and thereby to gain awareness of them. In conversion disorders it may be that the left hemisphere somehow blocks impulses carrying painful emotional content from the right hemisphere. Thus individuals with a conversion disorder make no connection between it and their troubling circumstances or their emotional needs. This is an intriguing bit of speculation.

Therapies for Somatoform Disorders

Not surprisingly, people with somatic complaints as well as those with conversion disorders and pain disorder go far more often to physicians than to psychiatrists and nonmedical clinicians such as psychologists, for they define their problems in physical terms. They are not open to psychological explanations of their predicaments and therefore resent referrals to "shrinks." Many such people try the patience of their physicians, who often find themselves prescribing one drug or medical treatment after another in hopes of remedying the somatic complaint.

The talking cure that psychoanalysis developed into was based on the assumption that a massive repression had forced psychic energy to be transformed or converted into puzzling anesthesias or paralyses. The catharsis as the patient faced up to the infantile origins of the repression was assumed to help, and even today free association and other efforts to lift repression are commonly used to treat somatoform disorders. Psychoanalysis and psychoanalytically oriented psychotherapy have not been demonstrated to be particularly useful with conversion disorders, however, except perhaps to reduce the patient's concern about the disabling problems (Ochitil, 1982).

Behavioral clinicians consider the high levels of anxiety associated with somatization disorder to be linked to certain situations. Alice, the woman described earlier, revealed that she was extremely anxious about her shaky marriage and about situations in which other people might judge her. Techniques such as systematic desensitization or any of the cognitive therapies could address her fears, the reduction of which would help lessen somatic complaints. But it is likely that more treatment would be needed, for a person who has been "sick" for a period of time has grown accustomed to weakness and dependency, to avoiding everyday challenges rather than facing them as an adult. Chances are that people who live with Alice have adjusted to her infirmity and are even unwittingly reinforcing her for her avoidance of normal adult responsibilities. Family therapy would be called for to help Alice and the members of her family change the web of relationships in order to support her movements toward greater autonomy. Assertion training and social-skills training—for example, coaching Alice in effective ways to approach and talk to people, to keep eye contact, give compliments, accept criticism, make requests—could be useful in helping a patient acquire, or reacquire, means of relating to others and meeting needs that do not begin with the premise "I am a poor, weak, sick person."

In general, then, it seems advisable to shift the focus from what the patient *cannot* do because of illness to teaching the patient how to deal with stress, encouraging greater activity, and enhancing a sense of control—despite the physical limitations or discomfort the patient is experiencing. For patients with pain disorder, pain management therapy, such as that described in Chapter 19 (page 575) can also be useful (Seligman, 1990).

In vivo exposure was used in the treatment of two patients with psychogenic nausea. The individuals were encouraged to expose themselves to the situations that were making them nauseous, much as a phobic person would confront a particular fear. The authors concluded that the favorable outcomes were due to extinction of the anxiety underlying the nausea (Lesage & Lamoontagne, 1985).

Behavior therapists have applied to somatoform disorders a wide range of techniques intended to make it worthwhile for the patient to give up the symptoms. A case reported by Liebson (1967) is an

Assertion training is sometimes used as a way of reducing anxiety in patients with somatoform disorders.

example. A man had relinquished his job because of pain and weakness in the legs and attacks of giddiness. Liebson helped the patient return to full-time work by persuading his family to refrain from reinforcing him for his idleness and by arranging for the man to receive a pay increase if he succeeded in getting himself to work. A reinforcement approach, then, attempts to provide the patient with greater incentives to get better than to remain incapacitated. Another important consideration with any such operant tactic, as noted by Walen, Hauserman, and Lavin (1977), is that the therapist take measures to ensure that the patient not lose face when parting with the disorder. The therapist should appreciate the possibility that the patient may feel humiliated at becoming better through treatment that does not deal with the medical (physical) problem. An excellent, though curious illustration is provided by Macleod and Hemsley (1985).

A forty-nine-year-old man had developed aphonia, the inability to speak above a whisper, following an injection to his neck. Although physical examinations were all negative, the patient maintained that his speech difficulty was caused by the injection. Macleod and Hemsley decided not to challenge the patient's attribution and instead to accept it, telling the man that a series of exercises would be necessary to strengthen the damaged muscles. Treatment consisted of having the patient repeat nursery rhymes into a microphone attached to a polygraph that provided constant monitoring and feedback about volume. During each treatment session the patient was required to increase his speech level. Initially, volume increased steadily, but it soon reached a plateau. One day, however, the patient stopped for a beer before his therapy session and on this day his speech returned to normal.

Through a series of unfortunate incidents, however, the treatment gains were not maintained. The patient attributed his cure, in part, to the beer, and his wife decided that this was a newsworthy event and informed the local newspaper. The story was then picked up by the national press and television, and the manufacturer of the beer he had drunk even began an advertising campaign with him as the focus. The resulting humiliation was too much, and the aphonia returned as well as depressive symptoms that required hospitalization.

Because somatoform disorders are rarer than other problems people take to mental health professionals, no significant body of research exists on the relative efficacy of different treatments. Case reports and clinical speculation are, for now, the only sources of information on how to help people with these puzzling disruptions in bodily functions.

Dissociative Disorders

In this section we examine four dissociative disorders—dissociative amnesia, dissociative fugue, multiple personality disorder (dissociative identity disorder), and depersonalization disorder, all of which are characterized by changes in a person's sense of identity, memory, or consciousness. Individuals with these disorders may be unable to recall important personal events or may temporarily forget their identity or even assume a new identity. They may even wander far from their usual surroundings. High quality data concerning the prevalence of the dissociative disorders are not available.

Perhaps the best study to date found prevalences of 7.0 percent, 2.4 percent, and 0.2 percent for amnesia, depersonalization, and fugue, respectively (Ross, 1991). We will describe this study more fully when considering multiple personality disorder.

In our examination of the four major dissociative disorders, we'll look first at symptoms and then at theories of etiology and therapies.

Dissociative Amnesia

The person with **dissociative amnesia** is suddenly unable to recall important personal information, usually after some stressful episode, as was the situation in the chapter-opening case. The holes in memory are too extensive to be explained by ordinary forgetfulness.

Most often the memory loss is for all events during a limited period of time following some traumatic experience, such as witnessing the death of a loved one. More rarely the amnesia is for only selected events during a circumscribed period of distress; is continuous from a traumatic event to the present; or is total, covering the person's entire life. During the period of amnesia, the person's behavior is otherwise unremarkable, except that the memory loss may bring some disorientation and purposeless wandering. With total amnesia the patient does not recognize relatives and friends, but retains the ability to talk, read, and reason and perhaps retains talents and previously acquired knowledge of the world and how to function in it. The amnesic episode may last several hours or as long as several years. It usually disappears as suddenly as it came on, with complete recovery and only a small chance of recurrence.

Memory loss is also common in many organic brain disorders as well as in substance abuse. But amnesia and memory loss caused by a brain disease or substance abuse can be fairly easily distinguished. In degenerative brain disorders memory fails slowly over time and is not linked to life stress. Memory loss following a brain injury caused by some trauma (e.g., an automobile accident) or substance abuse can be easily linked to the trauma or the substance being abused.

Dissociative Fugue

If a person not only becomes totally amnesic but suddenly moves away from home and work and assumes a new identity, the diagnosis of **dissociative fugue** is made. Sometimes the assumption of the new identity can be quite elaborate, with the person taking on a new name, new home, new job, and even a new set of personality characteristics. He or she may succeed in establishing a fairly complex social life, all without questioning the inability to remember the past. More often, however, the new life does not crystallize to this extent and the fugue is of briefer duration. It consists for the most part of limited, but apparently purposeful, travel, during which social contacts are minimal or absent. Fugues typically occur after a person has experienced some severe stress, such as marital quarrels, personal rejections, war service, or a natural disaster. Recovery, although varying in the time it takes, is usually complete; the individual does not recollect what took place during the flight from his or her usual haunts.

In *Spellbound* Gregory Peck played a man with amnesia. Dissociative amnesia is typically triggered by a stressful event.

Multiple Personality Disorder

Consider what it would be like to have a multiple personality, as did Chris Sizemore, the woman with the famous three faces of Eve (see page 113). People tell you about things you have done that seem out of character, events of which you have no memory. You have been waking up each morning with the remains of a cup of tea by your bedside—and you do not like tea. How can you explain these happenings? If you were to seek treatment, might you not worry whether the psychiatrist or psychologist will believe you? Perhaps the clinician will think you psychotic.

We all have days when we are not quite ourselves. This is assumed to be quite normal and is not what is meant by multiple personality. According to DSM-IV, a proper diagnosis of **multiple personality disorder (MPD)** requires that a person have at least two separate ego states, or alters, different modes of being and feeling and acting that exist independently of each other, coming forth and being in control at different times. Gaps in memory are also common and are produced because at least one alter has no contact with the other; that is, alter A has no memory for what alter B is like, or even any knowledge of having an alternate state of being. The existence of different alters must furthermore be chronic (long-lasting) and severe (causing considerable disruption in one's life); it cannot be a temporary change resulting from the ingestion of a drug, for example.

Each alter is fully integrated and complex with its own behavior patterns, memories, and relationships: each determines the nature and acts of the individual when it is in command. Usually the personalities are quite different, even opposites of one another. Indeed, they may have different handedness, wear glasses with different prescriptions, and have allergies to different substances. The original and subordinate alters are all aware of lost periods of time, and the voices of the others may sometimes echo into their consciousness, even though they do not know to whom these voices belong. When an individual has more than two alters, each of these may to some extent be aware of the others. In fact, they may talk to each other and be constant companions.

Multiple personality disorder usually begins in early childhood, but it is rarely diagnosed until adolescence. It is more chronic and serious than other dissociative disorders, and recovery may be less complete. It is much more common in women than in men. The presence of other diagnoses—in particular, depression, borderline personality disorder, and somatization disorder—is frequent (Ross et al., 1990). In addition, MPD is commonly accompanied by headaches, substance abuse, phobias, suicidal ideas, and self-abusive behavior.

Cases of multiple personality are frequently mislabeled in the popular press as schizophrenic reactions. This diagnostic category, discussed in greater detail in Chapter 14, derives part of its name from the Greek root *schizo*, which means "splitting away from," hence the confusion. A split in the personality, wherein two or more fairly separate and coherent systems of being exist alternatively in the same person, is different from the split between cognition and affect that is said to produce the schizophrenic's behavior.

The very existence of multiple personality disorder has been the subject of much dispute (see Focus Box 7.2). Although it is formally recognized in that it is included in the official diagnostic manual, its existence violates a firmly held belief that each body is inhabited by only one person. The earliest mention of MPD occurred in the nineteenth century. In a review of the literature, Sutcliffe and Jones (1962) were able to identify a total of 77 cases, most of which were reported in the period between 1890 and 1920. After that period reports of MPD declined until the 1970s, when they increased markedly.

What caused this apparent decline and subsequent reemergence? We cannot be sure if diagnostic practice changed or whether clinicians have always seen a similar number of cases but chose to report them only when interest in MPD seemed high. One possibility is that the decline in diagnoses of MPD was due to the increasing popularity of the concept of schizophrenia. As we noted, cases of MPD may have been mistakenly diagnosed as schizophrenia (Rosenbaum, 1980). This diagnostic confusion may have declined over the past decades as schizophrenia has been more precisely defined (see Chapter 14). Another factor of possible relevance to the increase in MPD diagnoses was the publication of *Sybil*, which presented a dramatic case of MPD with sixteen personalities. This case attracted a great deal of attention and it is notable that in the post-*Sybil* era the number of alters in each case has risen dramatically (from two or three in past years to over ten at this point). Finally, changes in diagnostic criteria may have played a role. DSM-IIIR did not require that the alters be amnesic for one another. This raised the possibility that the diagnosis of MPD could be applied to people with high levels of variability in their behavior, as occurs in some of the personality disorders (Kihlstrom & Tataryn, 1991). As we have already mentioned, DSM-IV restored the memory dysfunction component of the diagnosis, but it is too early to know what effect this will have on prevalence.

To obtain data on the prevalence of MPD, Ross (1991) studied a sample of 454 adults in Winnipeg, Canada. Unfortunately, the sample was not representative of the population and the study had other flaws, such as the failure to have independent interviewers confirm diagnoses. Nonetheless, these are the most extensive data available on the prevalence of MPD, which was found to be 1.3 percent. Although this figure may not seem high, it is actually incredibly high compared with the typical clinical lore. For example, at the time of publication of *The Three Faces Of Eve,* occurrence of MPD was estimated to be one in a million. Clearly, more methodologically sophisticated studies need to be done, but it is fair to say that the prevalence of MPD is certainly higher than was thought several years ago.

The case of Eve White was at one time the most carefully documented report of multiple personality in the clinical literature. But many other cases have been described. One such account appeared in 1976 in the *Journal of Abnormal Psychology.* "The Three Faces of Evelyn" is a detailed history by Robert F. Jeans, the psychiatrist who treated the woman. Notice that the therapeutic outcome was an *integration,* or *fusion,* of several of the patient's personalities, not the elimination of all but one of them. Most contemporary workers regard the alters as having an important function and as important aspects of the whole person, hence the significance of trying to fuse them into a single personality (Ross, 1989).

Jeans provides the following background on his patient. He was consulted in December 1965 by a Gina Rinaldi, referred to him by her friends. Gina, single and thirty-one years old, lived with another single woman and was at the time working successfully as a writer at a large educational publishing firm. She was considered an efficient, businesslike, and productive person, but her friends had observed that she was becoming forgetful and sometimes acted out of character. The youngest of nine siblings, Gina reported that she had been sleepwalking since her early teens; her present roommate had told her that she would sometimes scream in her sleep.

Gina described her mother, then aged seventy-four, as the most domineering woman she had ever known. She reported that as a child she had been quite a fearful and obedient daughter. At age twenty-six Gina got braces for her teeth, and at age twenty-eight she had had an "affair," her first, with a former Jesuit priest, although it was apparently not sexual in nature. Then she became involved with "T.C.," a married man who assured her he would get a divorce and marry her. She indicated that she had been faithful to him since the start of their relationship. Partly on the basis of Jeans' analysis of one of Gina's dreams, the psychiatrist concluded that she was quite uncomfortable about being a woman, particularly when a close, sexual relationship with a man might be expected of her. But T.C. did not come through with his promised divorce, stopped seeing Gina regularly, and generally fell out of her favor.

After several sessions with Gina, Jeans began to notice a second personality emerging. "Mary Sunshine," as she came to be called by Jeans and Gina, was quite different from Gina. She seemed to be more childlike, more traditionally feminine, ebullient, and seductive. Gina felt that she herself walked like a coal miner, but Mary certainly did not. Some quite concrete incidents indicated Mary's existence. Sometimes Gina found in the sink cups that had had hot chocolate in them—neither Gina nor her roommate liked this beverage. There were large withdrawals from Gina's bank account that she could not remember making. One evening while watching television, Gina realized that she was crying and remarked to herself that it was stupid to feel sad about the particular program she was viewing. She even discovered herself ordering a sewing machine on the telephone, although she disliked sewing; some weeks later she showed up for her therapy session wearing a new dress that Mary had sewn. At work, Gina reported, people were finding her more pleasant to be with, and her colleagues took to consulting her on how to encourage people to work better with one another. All these phenomena were entirely alien to Gina. Jeans and Gina came to realize that sometimes Gina was transformed into Mary.

Then one day T.C. showed up again. Gina was filled with scorn and derision for him, yet she heard herself greeting him warmly with the words "Gee, I missed you so much! It's good to see you!" (Apparently the psychoanalytically oriented therapy was softening the hitherto impermeable boundaries between the separate ego states of Gina and Mary.) Gina was also surprised to hear T.C. reply on this occasion, "All you ever wanted was to please me. You've done nothing but cater to my every whim, nothing but make me happy." Mary must have been active in the earlier relationship that Gina had had with this man.

Now more and more often Jeans witnessed Gina turning into Mary right before his eyes in the consulting room. T.C. accompanied Gina to a session during which her posture and demeanor became more relaxed, her tone of voice warmer. When T.C. explained that he really cared for her,

Gina, or rather Mary, said warmly, "Of course, T., I know you do."

At another session Mary was upset and, as Jeans put it, chewed off Gina's fingernails. Then the two of them started having conversations with each other in front of Jeans.

A year after the start of therapy, an apparent synthesis of Gina and Mary began to emerge. At first it seemed that Gina had taken over entirely, but then Jeans noticed that Gina was not as serious as before, particularly about "getting the job done," that is, working extremely hard on the therapy. Jeans, probably believing that Mary wanted to converse with him, encouraged Gina to have a conversation with Mary. The following is what was said by the patient:

> "I was lying in bed trying to go to sleep. Someone started to cry about T.C. I was sure that it was Mary. I started to talk to her. The person told me that she didn't have a name. Later she said that Mary called her Evelyn. . . . I was suspicious at first that it was Mary pretending to be Evelyn. I changed my mind, however, because the person I talked to had too much sense to be Mary. She said that she realized that T.C. was unreliable but she still loved him and was very lonely. She agreed that it would be best to find a reliable man. She told me that she comes out once a day for a very short time to get used to the world. She promised that she will come out to see you [Jeans] sometime when she is stronger. (Jeans, 1976, pp. 254–255)

Throughout January Evelyn appeared more and more often, and Jeans felt that the patient was improving rapidly. Within a few months the patient seemed to be Evelyn all the time, and this woman soon married a physician. Now, years later, she has had no recurrences of the other personalities.

Depersonalization Disorder

Depersonalization order, in which the person's perception or experience of the self is disconcertingly and disruptively altered, is also included in DSM-IV as a dissociative disorder. Its inclusion is controversial, however, because depersonalization disorder involves no disturbance of memory, which is typical of the other dissociative disorders. In a depersonalization episode individuals rather suddenly lose the sense of self. Their limbs may seem drastically changed in size, or they may have the impression that they are outside their bodies, viewing themselves from a distance. Sometimes they feel mechanical, as though they and others, too, are robots, or they move as though in a dream, in a world that has lost its reality. Similar, but much more intense, episodes sometimes occur in schizophrenia (see Chapter 14). The schizophrenic's experience, however, does not have the "as if" quality that the person in depersonalization reports; in contrast, the schizophrenic's estrangement from the self is real and complete.

Etiology of Dissociative Disorders

According to psychoanalytic theory, all dissociative disorders are viewed as instances of a massive repression, usually relating to the unacceptable infantile sexual wishes of the oedipal stage. In adulthood these oedipal yearnings increase in strength until they are finally expressed, often as an impulsive sexual act. The ordinary form of repression is obviously no longer sufficient; the whole event must be obliterated from consciousness. The person succeeds in this by splitting off an entire part of the personality from awareness (Buss, 1966) or by acquiring a new identity for the dissociated portion of the self.

Learning theorists have generally construed dissociated phenomena as avoidance responses that serve to protect the individual from highly stressful

Severe trauma in childhood is regarded as a major cause of dissociative disorders.

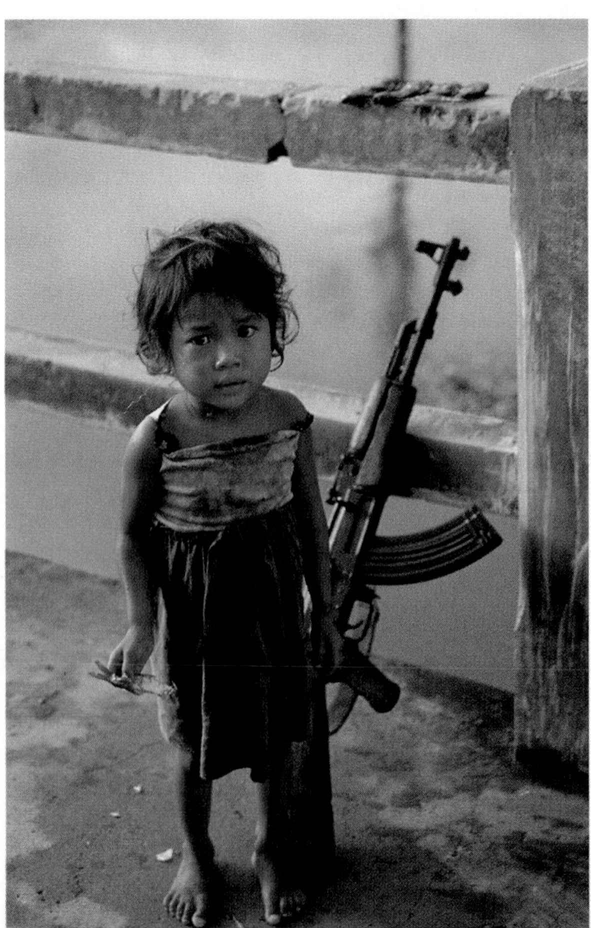

events. Although it does not employ the concept of repression nor emphasize the overriding importance of infantile sexual conflicts, the behavioral view of dissociative disorders is somewhat similar to psychoanalytic speculations about them.

Bliss (1980) believes that multiple personality is established in childhood by self-hypnosis as a way of coping with extremely disturbing events. Two pieces of evidence support Bliss's theory. First, available data indicate that multiple personalities are high in hypnotizability. Bliss (1983), for example, found that multiples scored much higher than controls on the Stanford Scales of Hypnotic Susceptibility. Second, cases of multiple personality report severe childhood traumas. For example, the results from a survey of therapists who work with multiple personalities indicated that 80 percent of their clients had suffered physical abuse in childhood and almost 70 percent had been subjected to incest (Putnam et al., 1983). Other estimates of physical and sexual abuse in childhood are even higher (Klutt, 1984; Ross et al., 1990).

In fact, much has been written in the past ten to fifteen years about the role of child abuse, sexual and otherwise, in dissociative disorders, especially MPD. Ross (1989), among others, believes that the decline in the reported incidence of MPD is linked to Freud's disavowal of his seduction theory (that some children, especially females, suffered abuse from their parents and other figures). He puts it very provocatively this way:

> After the repudiation of the seduction theory by Freud [in the early 1900s], an amnesia set in among psychologists and psychiatrists. Freud's evidence and argument about the traumatic origins of dissociation were lost. This occurred so suddenly that it cannot be attributed to passive scholarly forgetting. In fact the field developed a dissociative disorder, an active dismissal and forgetting of the role of sexual abuse and other childhood trauma in the formation of MPD. A feminist might comment that this was a convenient intellectual maneuver for the abusive patriarchy (Ross, 1989, p. 44).

This is an intriguing argument, one that has far-reaching social as well as scientific implications. We are reminded here that cultural contexts are important factors in the study of this disorder, as they are with any disorder. While we recognize child abuse today as a significant factor in MPD, in other times and in other cultures, it was not acceptable to do so. As we mentioned earlier in this text, Freud was under considerable social pressure to drop his seduction theory. Is this a situation in which societal pressures undermined real understanding? It would appear to be so.

Therapies for Dissociative Disorders

Dissociative disorders suggest, perhaps better than any other disorders, the plausibility of Freud's concept of repression. In three—amnesia, fugue, and multiple personality—people behave in ways that very assuredly indicate they have forgotten earlier parts of their lives. And since these people may at the same time be unaware even of having forgotten something, the hypothesis that they have repressed massive portions of their lives is a compelling one.

Consequently, for dissociative disorders, psychoanalytic treatment is perhaps more widespread as a choice of treatment than for other psychological problems. The goal of lifting repressions is the order of the day, pursued via the use of basic psychoanalytic techniques.

Combs and Ludwig (1982) suggested that some patients with rapid-onset amnesia can regain lost memories if the therapist patiently encourages them to tell their life stories as completely as possible, without skipping over difficult-to-remember parts. This recounting of their lives can be combined with a modified free-association technique focusing on remembered events that took place just before the hole in memory. Thus, if the patient seems to be jumping forward in time, the therapist encourages free association to the event just preceding the memory gap. The therapist should all along suggest strongly that memory will be regained and should not imply that the patient is deliberately lying or malingering. In some cases, Combs and Ludwig proposed, all that is necessary is the "tincture of time," a period during which the patient is separated from stressful surroundings and given quietness, general support, and encouragement.

Hypnosis is still used as a treatment for dissociative disorders by trying to restore memory for the traumatic event that led to the dissociation.

FOCUS 7.2. • Is Multiple Personality Disorder Real?

Questions have always been raised about whether MPD is a true disorder rather than a conscious effort to avoid punishment or to achieve gains not otherwise available. Is MPD little more than malingering? This question gained prominence during a trial in the early 1980s of a serial murderer in California who came to be known as the Hillside Strangler. Indeed, the differing views of several expert witnesses in the highly publicized trial were the subject of three articles in the *International Journal of Clinical and Experimental Hypnosis* (Allison, 1984; Orne, Dinges, & Orne, 1984; Watkins, 1984).

At around the time of the trial, a research team (Spanos, Weekes, & Bertrand, 1985) highly skeptical of the reality of MPD conducted an ingenious experiment that added a new perspective to the testimony of Kenneth Bianchi, the man accused of committing these murders. Their study supports the possibility that a person may adopt another personality just to avoid punishment. The experimental manipulations were derived from an actual interview with Bianchi, while he was supposedly under hypnosis during a pretrial meeting with a mental health professional to determine his legal responsibility for his crimes. The interviewer (I) asked for a second personality to come forward.

I: I've talked a bit to Ken but I think that perhaps there might be another part of Ken that I haven't talked to. And I would like to communicate with that other part. And I would like that other part to come to talk with me. . . . And when you're here, lift the left hand off the chair to signal to me that you are here. Would you please come. Part, so I can talk to you? . . . Part, would you come and lift Ken's hand to indicate to me that you are here? . . . Would you talk to me, Part, by saying "I'm here"? (Schwarz, 1981, pp. 142–143)

Bianchi (B) answered yes to the last question, and then he and the interviewer had the following conversation.

Ken Bianchi, the Hillside Strangler, attempted an insanity defense for his serial killings but the court decided that he had merely tried to fake a multiple personality.

I: Part, are you the same as Ken or are you different in any way. . . .
B: I'm not him.
I: You're not him. Who are you? Do you have a name?
B: I'm not Ken.
I: You're not him? Okay. Who are you? Tell me about yourself. Do you have a name I can call you by?
B: Steve. You can call me Steve. (pp. 139–140)

As we discussed in Chapter 1, psychoanalysis had its beginnings in hypnosis, with Mesmer's work in the late eighteenth century and Charcot's work in the nineteenth century. Both men believed that they could eliminate hypnotized patients' various hysterical symptoms by rather direct suggestion. Then Breuer and Freud encouraged patients to talk, while hypnotized, about their problems and especially about the earlier origins of them. Though Freud eventually abandoned the practice in favor of techniques such as free association, the use of hypnotism did not stop. Through the years practitioners have continued to hypnotize patients suffering from dissociative disorders, supposing that something spe-

While speaking as Steve, Bianchi stated that he hated Ken because Ken was nice, and that he, Steve, with the help of his cousin, had murdered a number of women. Bianchi's plea in the case became not guilty by reason of insanity; he claimed that he suffered from multiple personality.

In the Spanos study undergraduate subjects were told that they would play the role of an accused murderer and that, despite much evidence of guilt, a plea of not guilty had been entered. They were also told that they were to participate in a simulated psychiatric interview that might involve hypnosis. Then the subjects were taken to another room and introduced to the "psychiatrist," actually an experimental assistant. After a number of standard questions, the interview diverged for subjects assigned to one of three experimental conditions. Subjects in the *Bianchi condition* were given a rudimentary hypnotic induction and were then instructed to let a second personality come forward, just as Bianchi's interviewer had done. Subjects in the *Hidden Part condition* were also hypnotized and given information suggesting that they may have walled off parts of themselves. These instructions, however, were less explicit than those for the first condition. Subjects in a final condition were not hypnotized and were given even less explicit information about the possible existence of a hidden part.

After the experimental manipulations, the possible existence of a second personality was probed directly by the "psychiatrist." In addition, subjects were asked questions about the facts of the murders. Finally, in a second session, subjects who had acknowledged the presence of another personality were asked to take two personality tests twice—once each for their two personalities.

Eighty-one percent of subjects in the Bianchi condition adopted a new name, and many of these admitted guilt for the murders. Even the personality test scores of the two personalities differed considerably. Clearly, when the situation demands, people can adopt a second personality. Spanos et al. suggest that some people who present as multiple personalities may have a rich fantasy life and considerable practice imagining that they are other people, especially when they find themselves in a situation in which, like Bianchi, there are inducements and cues to behave as though a previous bad act had been committed by another personality. We should remember, however, that this demonstration illustrates only that such role-playing is possible and in no way demonstrates that all cases of multiple personality have such origins.

The Spanos study does, however, give us pause. Some professionals still consider multiple personality to be nothing more than role-playing. Others consider it a real, though rare, disorder. How can this dispute be resolved? The main method has been to compare cases of multiple personality with people asked to role-play or who are tested while hypnotized or deeply relaxed. The key comparisons are those of the main personality with the alters, and the reality of multiple personality is taken to be reflected by greater differences across the personalities for the clinical cases than for the role players. Physiological measures are frequently used as dependent variables because they are regarded as less subject to conscious control. Using this type of research strategy, Putnam, Zahn, and Post (1990) found greater differences in autonomic nervous system activity across personalities for the cases of multiple personality than for controls, and Miller (1989) found more differences in visual functioning. Do these data unequivocally indicate that multiple personality is more than mere role-playing? Not necessarily. They are interesting, but we must remember that the role players in these studies are considerably less practiced than the clinical cases in enacting their different personalities. Perhaps with greater practice the differences would lessen.

Returning to the actual trial, Bianchi was found guilty. His insanity plea did not hold up because evidence indicated that his role enactment differed in important ways from how true multiple personalities and deeply hypnotized subjects act (Orne, Dinges, & Orne, 1984).

cial about the hypnotic state would permit the person access to hidden portions of the personality—to lost identity or to a set of events precipitating or flowing from a trauma.

Some physicians have used sodium Amytal, truth serum, to induce a hypnoticlike state, again assuming that painful repressed memories will be brought forth and remove the need for the dissociative disorder. A number of dramatic case studies in the clinical literature suggest that both hypnosis and barbiturates like sodium Amytal can be helpful, but little of certainty can be said about their actual effectiveness because almost nothing approximating controlled research has been done (see Focus Box

7.3. • The Selective Nature of Publishing Case Studies

To illustrate the problem inherent to case studies, we offer this personal observation. While working in a mental hospital some years ago, one of the authors encountered on the ward a man suffering from partial amnesia. He did not recognize members of his family when they came to visit him but could still recall most other events in his life. Many efforts were made to restore his memory, ranging from hypnotic suggestions to drug therapy. Both sodium Amytal and Methedrine, a powerful stimulant, were administered, Methedrine intravenously. It was hoped that Methedrine would energize his nervous system and dislodge the blocks to memory, much as a drain cleaner is used to open a clogged drain. In all these attempts the patient was cooperative and even eager for a positive outcome, but none of them worked. The unsuccessful treatment was never written up for publication. There is a strong editorial bias against publishing reports of failed clinical treatments, as indeed there is against publishing inconclusive results of experiments. This, a general problem for psychology and psychiatry, is a special detriment when, as for dissociative disorders, there is little in the way of controlled research.

7.3). When Dysken (1979) compared the effects on amnesic patients of sodium amobarbital and normal saline acting as a placebo, he failed to find significant differences in the amount of new information remembered.

Despite differences in theoretical orientation, there seems to be widespread agreement on several principles of treatment of MPD (Bowers et al., 1971; Caddy, 1985; Kluft, 1985; Ross, 1989):

1. The goal is integration of the several personalities.
2. Each alter has to be helped to understand that he or she is part of one person.
3. The therapist should use the alters' names only for convenience, not as a way to confirm the existence of separate, autonomous personalities who do not share overall responsibility for the actions of the whole person.
4. All alters should be treated with fairness and empathy.
5. The therapist should encourage empathy and cooperation among personalities.
6. Gentleness and supportiveness are called for as consideration for the childhood trauma that probably gave rise to the splits.

The general goal of any approach to MPD can be seen as trying to convince the person that forgetting or splitting into different personalities is no longer necessary to deal with traumata, those in the past that triggered the original dissociation as well as those in the present and yet to be confronted in the future. In addition, on the assumption that MPD and the other dissociative disorders are in some measure an escape response to high levels of stress, teaching the patient to cope better with challenge can also enhance treatment. Because of the rarity of MPD and because it has often been misdiagnosed, there are no controlled outcome studies. Nearly all the well-reported outcome data come from the clinical observations of one highly experienced therapist, Richard Kluft (e. g., 1984a). Over a ten-year period, he had contact with 171 cases, of which he personally treated 117 and monitored the treatment of 6 others. Of these, 83, or 68 percent, achieved integration of their alters that was stable for at least three months (33 have remained stable for almost two and a half years). The greater the number of personalities, the longer the treatment took (Putnam et al., 1986), but in general, therapy took almost two years and upwards of 500 hours per patient. Ross (1989) concluded that therapies following the above-mentioned principles can be effective for most MPD patients, albeit at very high cost.

Additional information from Kluft (1984b), who has diagnosed some cases of MPD in children, suggests that early treatment of MPD may be more rapid and more successful than later treatment. That is, the longer the disorder persists, the more resistant it may be to therapy. If this turns out to be true, and if improved diagnosis can identify MPD at an earlier stage, it may be possible to prevent many cases of MPD in adults.

SUMMARY

In somatoform disorders there are physical symptoms for which no biological basis can be found. The sensory and motor dysfunctions of conversion disorders, one of the two principal types of somatoform disorders, suggest neurological impairments, but ones that do not always make anatomical sense; the symptoms do, however, seem to serve some psychological purpose. In somatization disorder, multiple physical complaints, not adequately explained by physical disorder or injury, eventuate in frequent visits to physicians, hospitalization, and even unnecessary surgery.

Theory concerning the etiology of these disorders is speculative and focuses primarily on conversion disorders. Psychoanalytic theory proposes that in conversion disorders repressed impulses are converted into physical symptoms. Behavioral theories focus on the more or less conscious and deliberate adoption of the symptoms as a means of obtaining a desired goal. In therapies for somatoform disorder, analysts try to help the client face up to the repressed impulses, and behavioral treatments attempt to reduce anxiety and reinforce behavior that will allow relinquishment of the symptoms.

Dissociative disorders are disruptions of consciousness, memory, and identity. An inability to recall important personal information, usually after some traumatic experience, is diagnosed as dissociative amnesia. In dissociative fugue the person moves away, assumes a new identity, and is amnesic for his or her previous life. In depersonalization disorder the person's perception of the self is altered; he or she may experience being outside the body or changes in the size of body parts. The person with multiple personality disorder has two or more distinct and fully developed personalities, each with unique memories, behavior patterns, and relationships. Psychoanalytic theory regards dissociative disorders as instances of massive repression of some undesirable event or aspect of the self, and in MPD the role of abuse in childhood is emerging as important. Behavioral theories similarly consider dissociative reactions to be escape-responses motivated by high levels of anxiety. Both analytic and behavioral clinicians focus their treatment efforts on the anxiety associated with the forgotten memories, since it is viewed as etiologically significant.

KEY TERMS

somatoform disorders
dissociative disorders
pain disorder
body dysmorphic disorder
hypochondriasis
conversion disorder
anesthesias
hysteria
malingering
la belle indifférence
factitious disorders
somatization disorder
dissociative amnesia
dissociative fugue
multiple personality disorder (MPD)
depersonalization disorder

c h a p t e r e i g h t

Psychophysiological Disorders

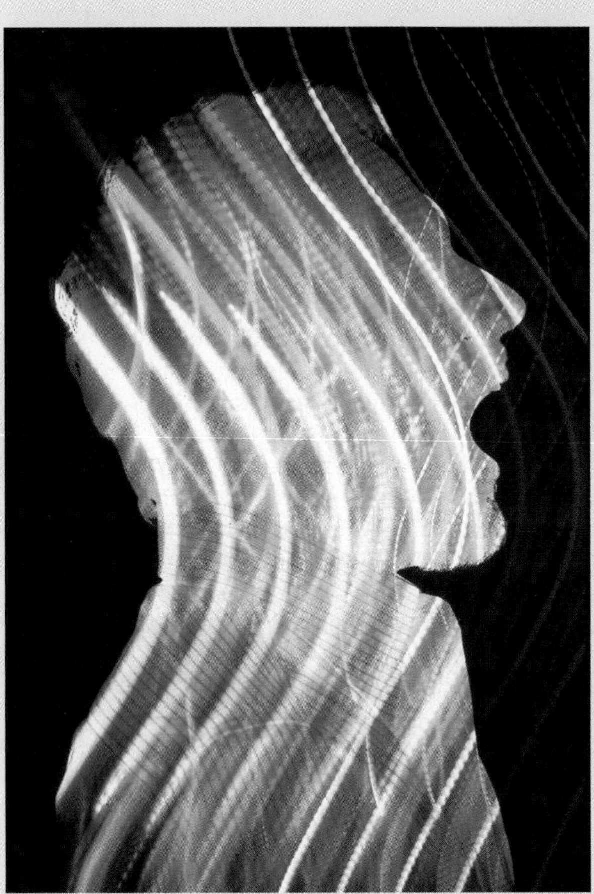

> A Brazilian Indian condemned and sentenced by a so-called medicine man is helpless against his own emotional response to this pronouncement—and dies within hours. In Africa a young Negro knowingly eats the inviolably banned wild hen. On discovery of his "crime" he trembles, is overcome by fear and dies in twenty-four hours. In New Zealand a Maori woman eats fruit that she only later learns comes from a taboo place. Her chief has been profaned. By noon the next day she is dead. (Basedow, 1925, cited in Richter, 1957, p. 191)

The opening quotation describes a case of voodoo death, a seemingly supernatural phenomenon whereby a curse from a medicine man dooms his victims to extreme physical suffering and death. To explain such events, Cannon (1942) proposed that vital bodily organs are irreparably harmed if the autonomic nervous system is maintained in a highly aroused state through prolonged psychological stress and there is no opportunity to take effective action to relieve the stress. Inasmuch as the arousal of the autonomic nervous system is also regarded as one of the bodily indications of emotion, it is not surprising that psychopathologists have been concerned with physical diseases involving this system in the belief that psychological factors may be implicated. In the expression of emotion, the bodily changes of autonomic arousal are viewed as transient; in psychophysiological disorders the usually reversible autonomic and hormonal responses to stress can cause irreversible tissue damage.

Psychophysiological disorders, such as asthma, ulcers, hypertension, headache, and gastritis, are characterized by genuine physical symptoms that are caused or can be worsened by emotional factors. The present term, psychophysiological disorders, is now preferred to one that is perhaps better known, psychosomatic disorders. **Psychosomatic** connotes quite well the principal feature of these disorders, that the psyche or mind is having an untoward effect on the soma or body. The structure of both these terms, in fact, implies that mind and body are separate and independent, although they may at times influence each other. This concept is known as **dualism,** and is a deeply ingrained paradigm of human thought (see Focus Box 8.1). Yet the hope was that these terms would foster a monistic rather than dualistic view of the human being since all diseases are both mental and physical. Instead of speaking of the emotions as causing bodily dysfunctions, we could instead, as Graham (1967) noted, regard the psyche and soma as one and the same. Psychological and physical explanations of disease are then simply alternative ways of describing the same events.

At the outset two important points must be firmly established. First, a psychophysiological disorder is a real disease involving damage to the body. The fact that such disorders are viewed as being caused by emotional factors does not make the affliction imaginary. People can just as readily die from psychologically produced high blood pressure or ulcers as from similar diseases produced by infection or physical injury. Second, psychophysiological disorders should be distinguished from conversion disorders, which were discussed in Chapter 7. Conversion disorders do not involve actual organic damage to the body and are generally considered to affect function of the voluntary musculature. In contrast, in psychophysiological disorders, bodily tissues *are* damaged (see Table 8.1).

Psychophysiological symptoms and disorders are quite common in industrialized societies, although they are apparently rare among nonindustrialized groups, such as Australian aborigines and Native Americans. Schwab, Fennell, and Warheit (1974), for example, interviewed a randomly selected sample of close to 1700 Americans (Table 8.2). Over 40 percent of the respondents reported having had headaches during the previous year, and 50 percent reported a range of gastrointestinal symptoms. Actual disorders such as hypertension, however, were not as common as the less serious symptoms the respondents were questioned about.

Psychophysiological disorders as such do not appear in DSM-IV as they did in some earlier versions of the DSM. DSM-IV requires a diagnostic judgment to indicate the presence of **psychological factors affecting a medical condition**. Notably, the diagnosis is coded in the broad section comprising "other conditions that may be a focus of clinical attention." The implication is that this is not to be considered a form of mental disorder. Nonetheless, we consider it in some detail because of its historical link to the field of psychopathology. The new approach to diagnosis is also broader in scope. Formerly, psychophysiological disorders were generally thought to be mediated by the autonomic nervous system and to include only a subset of all possible diseases (the classic psychosomatic diseases such as ulcers, head-

Table 8.1 • Comparing Psychophysiological and Conversion Disorders

Type of Disorder	*Organic Bodily Damage*	*Bodily Function Affected*
Conversion	No	Voluntary
Psychophysiological	Yes	Involuntary

8.1 • Descartes and the Mind–Body Problem

One of the most influential statements about the mind–body problem is found in the writings of the brilliant French philosopher of the seventeenth century, René Descartes (1596–1650). A deeply religious Catholic, he assumed that human beings differed from other animals by virtue of having a soul and thus being partly divine. But like the other animals, human beings had a body as well. Although the body was said to work on mechanical principles—Descartes was fascinated by the mechanical models of the body's workings that were prevalent at the time—these mechanics were seen to be under the control of the soul, or mind. But how could the body, operating like a machine, be affected by the soul, which is spiritual and nonphysical? How could two such basically different substances, in fact, touch each other? If the mind was to affect the body, there must be some point of *contact.* The pineal gland, located in the midbrain, was postulated by Descartes as the locus of this critical interaction, the point at which the mind could direct the mechanics of the body. By dualizing human beings in this way, with this vital connection between the mind and the body, Descartes felt that he could retain his religious view of people as being partly divine and yet an integral part of the rest of the animal world.

aches, asthma, and hypertension). The new diagnosis, in contrast, is applicable to any disease. The reason for this change is that it is now thought that any disease can be influenced by psychological factors, such as stress.

What is the evidence for the view that all illness is, in part, stress-related? For years it had been known that various physical diseases could be produced in laboratory animals who were exposed to severe stressors. Usually the diseases studied in this fashion were the classic psychophysiological disorders, such as ulcers and hypertension. But now a broader range of diseases appears to be stress-related. Sklar and Anisman (1979), for example, first induced tumors in mice with a transplant of cancerous tissue and then studied the impact of stress on growth of the tumors. In animals exposed to electric shock, the tumors grew more rapidly, and the animals died earlier.

The fields of **behavioral medicine** and **health psychology** are based on the many demonstrations of the pervasive role of psychological factors in health. Since the 1970s, these new areas have dealt with the role of psychological factors in all facets of health and illness. Beyond studying the etiological role that stress can play in illness, workers in these fields study psychological treatments (e.g., biofeedback for migraine headaches), the maintenance and promotion of healthful behaviors, (e.g., dietary change to reduce cholesterol intake and thus lessen the risk of heart attack), and the health care system itself (e.g., how to better deliver services to underserved populations) (Schwartz & Weiss, 1977; G. Stone, 1982). Many examples of behavioral medicine are discussed throughout this chapter as well as in Chapter 19 (page 574).

The DSM diagnosis of psychological factors affecting a medical condition is broader also because it includes the possibility that the psychological or behavioral factor can influence the course or treatment of the disorder, not just its onset. For example, a person with hypertension may continue to drink alcohol even though he or she knows that alcohol increases blood pressure. Or, a patient may fail to take prescribed medication regularly. The psychological or behavioral factors themselves include personality traits (e.g., the Type A personality), coping styles (e.g., expressing anger as opposed to holding it in), lifestyle factors (e.g., exercising regularly), as well as sociocultural factors (e.g., ethnic differences in the amount of stress to which people are exposed).

Stress and Health

In this chapter we will first examine general findings on the relationship between stress and health as well as theories about how stress can produce illness. We will then turn to an in-depth examination of two disorders—cardiovascular disease and asthma. In the final sections we consider psychological interventions.

Table 8.2 • Percentages of People[a] Reporting Psychophysiological Symptoms and Conditions for the Previous Year

Symptoms and Conditions	*Yes—Regularly, %*	*Yes—Occasionally, %*	*No, %*
Symptoms			
Headaches	8.7	38.0	53.4
Indigestion	6.4	27.5	66.1
Constipation	6.9	19.6	73.5
Nervous stomach	5.2	17.5	77.3
Stomachaches	3.7	18.8	77.5
Diarrhea	0.9	14.4	84.8
Conditions			
Hypertension	6.2	8.0	85.8
Asthma	1.9	2.9	95.2
Ulcers	0.9	1.4	97.6
Colitis	0.4	0.9	98.7

Source: From Schwab, Fennell, and Warheit, 1974.
[a]$N = 1647$.

The Concept of Stress

In 1936, Hans Selye, a physician, introduced the **general adaptation syndrome (GAS)**, a model used to describe the biological reaction to sustained and unrelenting physical stress. There are three phases of the model (see Figure 8.1). During the first phase, the alarm reaction, the autonomic nervous system is activated by the stress. If the stress is too powerful, gastrointestinal ulcers form, the adrenal glands become enlarged, and there is atrophy (wasting away) of the thymus. During the second phase, resistance, the organism adapts to the stress through available coping mechanisms. If the stressor persists or the organism is unable to respond effectively, the third phase, a stage of exhaustion, follows, and the organism dies or suffers irreversible damage (Selye, 1950).

Eventually, Selye's concept of stress found its way into the psychological literature, but with substantial changes in its definition. Some researchers followed Selye's lead and continued to consider stress a response to environmental conditions, defined on the basis of such diverse criteria as emotional upset, deterioration of performance, or physiological changes, such as increased skin conductance or increases in the levels of certain hormones. For other researchers, however, stress became a stimulus and was identified with a long list of environmental conditions—electric shock, boredom, uncontrollable stimuli, catastrophic life events, daily hassles, and sleep deprivation (Appley & Trumball, 1967). We prefer to use the term **stressor** to refer to events that can cause **stress,** the organism's biological and behavioral response to the stressor.

Figure 8.1 Selye's General Adaptation Syndrome.

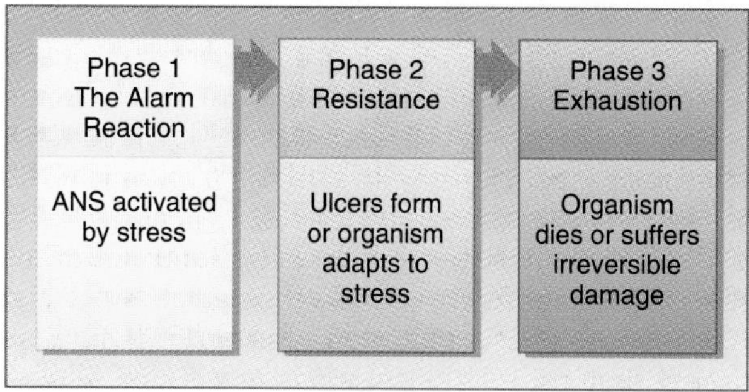

Richard Lazarus (1966) has been an important figure in the study of psychological stress and has elaborated it in several ways. For Lazarus, stress cannot be objectively defined. Rather, he suggests that the way we perceive or appraise the environment determines when stress is present. More specifically, stress is experienced when a situation is appraised as exceeding the person's adaptive resources. This is an important notion, for it allows us to account for individual differences in how people respond to the same event. Taking a final examination may create stress for some people and merely present a challenge for others.

Also relevant to individual differences in response to stressful situations is the concept of coping. Even among those who appraise a situation as stressful, the effects of the stress may vary depending on how an individual copes with the event. Lazarus and his colleagues have identified two broad dimensions of coping (Lazarus & Folkman, 1984).

Problem-focused coping includes taking direct action to solve the problem or seeking information that will be relevant to the solution. An example would be developing a study schedule to pace assignments over a semester and thereby reduce end-of-semester pressure. Emotion-focused coping subsumes efforts to reduce the negative emotional reactions to stress, for example, by distracting oneself from the problem, relaxing, or seeking comfort from others. It is important to mention that effective coping varies with the situation; distraction may be an effective way of dealing with the emotional upset produced by impending surgery but would be a poor way to handle the upset that could be produced by the discovery of a lump on the breast (Lazarus & Folkman, 1984).

Efforts to Measure Stress

Research on the effects of stress on human health has sought to measure the amount of life stress a person has experienced and then correlate this with illness. A number of instruments have been developed to measure life stress. We will examine two in some depth, the Social Readjustment Rating Scale and the Assessment of Daily Experience.

The Social Readjustment Rating Scale

Holmes and Rahe (1967) gave a list of life events to a large group of subjects and asked them to rate each item according to its "intensity and [the] length of time necessary to accommodate . . . *regardless of the desirability of the event.*" Marriage was arbitrarily assigned a stress value of 500; all other items were then evaluated using this reference point. For example, an event twice as stressful as marriage would be assigned a value of 1000, and an event one-fifth as stressful as marriage would be assigned a value of 100. The average ratings assigned to the events by the respondents in Holmes and Rahe's study are shown in Table 8.3.

Out of this study came the Social Readjustment Rating Scale (SRRS). The respondent simply checks off the life events that have been experienced during the time period in question. Ratings that indicate differential stressfulness of events are then totaled for all the events actually experienced to produce a Life Change Unit (LCU) score, a weighted sum of events. The LCU score has been related to a number of different illnesses, for example, to heart attacks (Rahe & Lind, 1971), fractures (Tollefson, 1972), onset of leukemia (Wold, 1968), and colds and fevers (Holmes & Holmes, 1970).

Table 8.3 • Social Readjustment Rating Scale

Rank	*Life Event*	*Mean Value*
1	Death of spouse	100
2	Divorce	73
3	Marital separation	65
4	Jail term	63
5	Death of close family member	63
6	Personal injury or illness	53
7	Marriage	50[a]
8	Fired from work	47
9	Marital reconciliation	45
10	Retirement	45
11	Change in health of family member	44
12	Pregnancy	40
13	Sex difficulties	39
14	New family member	39
15	Business readjustment	39
16	Change in financial state	38
17	Death of close friend	37
18	Change to different line of work	36
19	Change in number of arguments with spouse	35
20	Mortgage over $10,000	31
21	Foreclosure of mortgage or loan	30
22	Change in responsibilities at work	29
23	Child leaving home	29
24	Trouble with in-laws	29
25	Outstanding personal achievement	28
26	Spouse begins or stops work	26
27	Begin or end school	26
28	Change in living conditions	25
29	Revision of personal habits	24
30	Trouble with boss	23
31	Change in work hours or conditions	20
32	Change in residence	20
33	Change in schools	20
34	Change in recreation	19
35	Change in church activities	19
36	Change in social activities	18
37	Mortgage or loan less than $10,000	17
38	Change in sleeping habits	16
39	Change in number of family get-togethers	15
40	Change in eating habits	15
41	Vacation	13
42	Christmas	12
43	Minor violations of the law	11

Source: From Holmes and Rahe, 1967.
[a]Marriage was arbitrarily assigned a stress value of 500; no event was found to be any more than twice as stressful. Here the values are reduced proportionally and range up to 100.

We have, then, some promising information on the relationship between psychological stress and physical illness. But caution is in order before we assert that the relationship is a causal one. Illness,

Experiencing major life events such as marriage or starting school statistically increases risk for illness. Research on the effects of these major stressors assesses them with The Social Readjustment Rating Scale.

for example, could cause a high life change score, as when chronic absenteeism brings dismissal from a job. And the reports of stressful events in such studies could also be contaminated by knowledge of subsequently occurring illnesses. That is, someone who has experienced many illnesses may search hard for recent stressors to explain them. Furthermore, many of the studies have used a retrospective method; participants were asked to recall both the illnesses and the stressful life events that they had experienced over the previous two years. As mentioned again later (see page 274), retrospective reports are subject to considerable distortion and forgetting. Furthermore, self-reports of illness may not yield a true reflection of disease. For example, someone under stress may focus on minor physiological sensations and thereby increase reports of symptoms.

The SRRS can also be criticized for *assuming* a particular definition of stress, namely, that any change is stressful, whether it is a change usually regarded as negative, such as being fired from a job, or positive, such as marrying. The available evidence is, in fact, contradictory, but it would seem to indicate that the undesirable aspects of events are as important as the fact that they change lives (Redfield & Stone, 1979). Another problem is that items on the SRRS were not selected to sample systematically all major stressors. As you peruse Table 8.3, you can probably think of stressful events that you have experienced but that are not on the list. No doubt there are also cultural and ethnic differences in the kinds of potential stressors to which people are exposed, as discussed in Focus Box 8.2.

The Assessment of Daily Experience

Consideration of problems with the SRRS led Stone and Neale (1982) to develop a new assessment instrument, the Assessment of Daily Experience (ADE), designed to allow individuals to record and rate their daily experiences in prospective investigations. They chose a day as the unit of analysis because they felt that a thorough characterization of this period was possible without major retrospective-recall bias. With this period as the unit of analysis, the specific life events to be rated must include more mundane happenings than are found in previous life-event inventories. Yet the inventory does not exclude major events that have been retrospectively reported in other instruments; they can still be recorded, probably with greater reliability. Furthermore, there is theoretical and clinical support for the idea that minor daily events (hassles) are re-

FOCUS 8.2 • Stress Among African-Americans

For many years it has been recognized that the health, both physical and psychological, of African-Americans is worse than that of whites (Ozer, 1986; USDHS, 1984). Our later discussion of AIDS points up alarming statistics for the spread of the disease among African-Americans (p. 381), and we shall soon see that hypertension is generally higher than among whites. No doubt much of the problem has to do with the more impoverished conditions in which many African-Americans live (Brenner, 1973; Myers, 1982). But in addition to the direct negative effects that poverty has on people—from poor diet, high levels of physical violence, and deficient medical care—there are many psychological stressors that must be considered in understanding this situation. In a recent review and theoretical article, Anderson (1991) discussed the particular stressors confronted by African-Americans and some of the coping strategies employed in efforts to deal with them. He paid special attention to what he calls acculturative stress, emotional challenges posed by discrepancies between the values, beliefs, norms, and behaviors of African-Americans and those of the majority white community in which they reside, often as outcasts and strangers.

Following R. S. Lazarus's (1984) model, Anderson distinguished among three general categories of stressors.

Level I Stressors (chronic) Included here are stressors like racism, overcrowding, poor living conditions, and noise. It has been found, for example, that children who live near airports have severe academic problems and are very distractible (Cohen et al., 1980). Economic hardship is also known to be a major source of stress (Ross & Huber, 1985), associated with higher rates of mental hospitalization (Kessler & Neighbors, 1986). But, as Anderson cautioned, not all African-Americans living in deprived circumstances cope poorly.

Many would argue that the focus should be on changing potentially stressful environmental conditions rather than on determining how people can cope with them. We agree with the need to change these conditions, and we will look at many of the ethical issues involved with how we think about and can address chronic, Level 1 stressors in Chapters 20 and 21. Here, however, our focus is on the very real stressors that African-Americans face; these stressors will not be eliminated overnight, and the need to develop effective coping strategies to deal with them is paramount.

Level II Stressors (major life events) These are the kinds of stressors tapped by the Holmes and Rahe (1967) scale (Table 8.3). Research indicates that socioeconomic problems are a major stressor for African-Americans (e.g., McAdoo, 1982), but, as just noted, many find ways to cope with such stressors.

Level III Stressors (daily events, hassles) To paraphrase Woody Allen, 90 percent of life is just showing up. It turns out that the seemingly minor annoyances that people confront on a daily basis—what can be termed *hassles*—are a significant source of stress for people. Traffic delays, grouchy bosses, constant interruptions, unwanted phone calls—such daily stressors mount up and take their toll.

Anderson (1991) attached special significance to acculturative stress. As with other minority groups, there are pressures on African-Americans to become assimilated while at the same time there are obstacles to their being truly accepted by the majority community. Acculturative stress can be present at all levels of stress, but perhaps mostly on the level of daily hassles, when

lated to illness. These events may be subjectively important to individuals for reasons not addressed by the researcher. How events are appraised may be linked to past experience with similar events (e.g., many failures with it), to more general personality characteristics (an anxious individual faced with a public-speaking engagement), or to the cultural–religious background of the individual (divorce for a strict Catholic). Furthermore, there is now direct evidence that these minor events are related to illness (Jandorf et al., 1986).

The objective was to construct a checklist of daily events that would characterize an individual's experience. These events would then be rated on sev-

Table 8.4 • Sample Items from Acculturative Stress Measure *

Listed below are a number of statements concerning personal feelings for attitudes that you might have. Please indicate the most appropriate answer to each question on your answer sheet, using the following:

(A) Disagree (B) Somewhat Disagree (C) Somewhat Agree (D) Agree (E) Strongly Agree

1. I get especially nervous going into a room full of people if I am going to be the only one of my racial group.	A	B	C	D	E
2. I get nervous when several people from a different racial group approach me.	A	B	C	D	E
3. People from other racial groups seem to talk and act strangely and often don't know how to behave properly toward me.	A	B	C	D	E
4. It is difficult to really trust someone from a different racial background.	A	B	C	D	E
5. In this school I am often treated more like a member of my race than as an individual.	A	B	C	D	E
6. Many students at school put people down just because they're from racial groups other than their own.	A	B	C	D	E

decisions have to be made that can violate a person's sense of African-American identity. Self-esteem can suffer, and with that, stress can increase. Table 8.4 has several items from a self-report measure that Anderson developed with Williams. They found that African-American students' scores on this scale correlated with Spielberger's (1972) trait-anxiety scale (Williams & Anderson, in press).

How can African-Americans cope with such stressors? Anderson (1991) reported that, compared with whites, African-Americans use prayer more often as a way to control their emotional reactions to noxious situations (Neighbors et al., 1983). Self-esteem can be enhanced by developing a positive racial identity that can counteract prevailing negative stereotypes; the "Black is beautiful" slogan from the 1960s was designed to foster pride in African-Americans who had come to equate whiteness with superiority (a belief evidenced still in the use of hair-straightening agents as well as skin-tone lighteners among some African-Americans). Social supports may be particularly important among African-Americans, for whom membership in church and other social organizations is more prevalent on average than it is among whites (Raymond, Rhoads, & Raymond, 1980). Family ties are also instrumental as stress-reducing social supports (Wilson, 1984).

Much of the foregoing applies to stress among other minority groups as well, for example, Asian-Americans, Latinos, and Native Americans. As a group, Jews have made it in the American culture at large, but probably not without some emotional cost to their cultural and religious identity. Is America a melting pot or a garden salad? The former metaphor implies that minority groups—all of them immigrants except for Native Americans—lose their distinctiveness as they blend with the general culture. The salad imagery connotes the retention of one's uniqueness even as one becomes a part of the whole. There has always been prejudice in the United States, as indeed in all parts of the world. Psychological research is beginning to shed some light on the emotional costs that minority groups must pay as they negotiate their way in a society whose values and practices may threaten their sense of identity and self-esteem. The dilemmas faced by African-Americans provide difficult choices, both for minorities and for those in positions of power and influence.

eral dimensions to assess respondents' psychological reactions to them. Because the instrument was to be used on a daily basis over substantial time periods, it was important that the recording task itself not be excessively onerous. Devising a relatively small but representative set of event categories, rather than a lengthy checklist of specific events, was the solution to this problem. The first step in developing the scale was to obtain a sample of daily activities. A group of twenty-six couples from the local community recorded their experiences in a diary for fourteen days. These events were then independently reviewed and a list of categories was created and arranged in outline form.

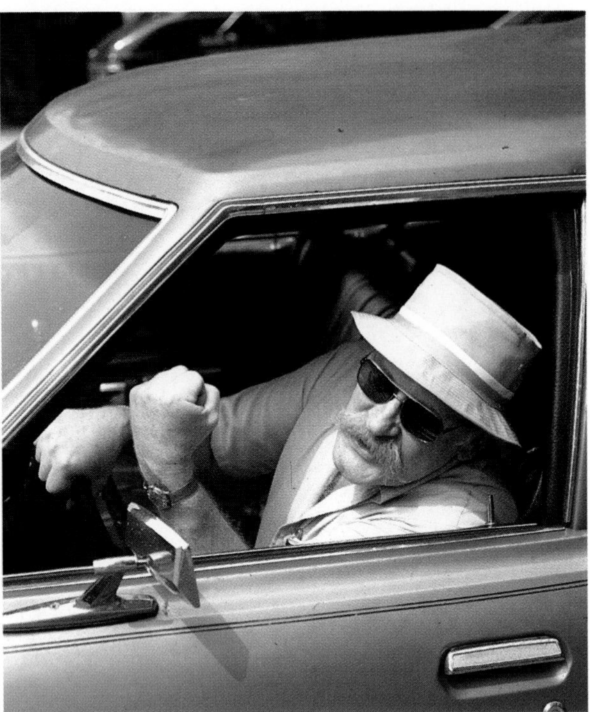

Daily hassles like being stuck in traffic can be emotionally upsetting and also increase risk for illness.

A sample page from the booklet is presented in Figure 8.2.

The procedure is as follows. Husbands (Targets) and wives (Observers) first work through the ADE independently, recording the husband's experiences of the day. They then reconvene and go through the event categories together to produce a master list of the husband's experiences that day. With this procedure the husband must confirm events he recorded but were not observed by his wife, she can remind him of some experiences, and the couple can discuss and agree upon how experiences are to be classified on the ADE.

With an assessment of daily experiences in hand, Stone, Reed, and Neale (1987) began a study of the relationship between life experience and health. Daily symptoms and health-related behaviors were collected using a modified version of the Daily Health Record from the Health in Detroit Study (Verbrugge, 1979). The section on symptoms asks if a subject had any symptoms or discomforts during the day; if so, they are recorded in an open-ended format along with any health-related behavior changes and treatments sought or administered.

Seventy-nine subjects provided at least twelve weeks of continuous, daily data. The goal was to examine the relationship between undesirable and desirable events and the onset of episodes of respiratory illness. Respiratory illness was selected as the criterion variable for two reasons. First, in a community sample, respiratory illness occurs with sufficient frequency to allow it to be analyzed as a distinct category. Second, respiratory infection maximizes the opportunity to detect lagged effects of events on the onset of symptoms. Lagged effects offer the clearest evidence that events are having an effect on symptoms. With rhinovirus infection (a principal cause of the common cold), for example, there is a two- to five-day lag between encountering the virus and peak symptom onset. Therefore, it would be possible for stress to increase risk of illness but with symptoms not being apparent for two to five days. In contrast, with other illnesses such as headaches, same-day effects are more probable and render causal interpretation of effects more difficult.

After examining each subject's data, thirty were identified as having episodes of infectious illness.

WORK RELATED ACTIVITIES

Concerning Boss, Supervisor, Upper Management, etc.

- ➤ Praised for a job well done □ ○ ○ △ 01
- ➤ Criticism for job performance, lateness, etc. □ ○ ○ △ 02

Concerning Co-workers, Employees, Supervisees, and/or Clients

- ➤ Positive emotional interactions and/or happenings with co-workers, employees, supervisees, and/or clients (work related events which were fulfilling, etc.) □ ○ ○ △ 03
- ➤ Negative emotional interactions and/or happenings with co-workers, employees, supervisees, and/or clients (work related events which were frustrating, irritating, etc.) □ ○ ○ △ 04
- ➤ Firing or disciplining (by Target) □ ○ ○ △ 05
- ➤ Socializing with staff, co-workers, employees, supervisees, and/or clients □ ○ ○ △ 06

General Happenings Concerning Target at Work

- ➤ Promotion, raise □ ○ ○ △ 07
- ➤ Fired, quit, resigned □ ○ ○ △ 08
- ➤ Some change in job (different from the above, i.e., new assignment, new boss, etc.) □ ○ ○ △ 09
- ➤ Under a lot of pressure at work (impending deadlines, heavy workload, etc.) □ ○ ○ △ 10

Figure 8.2 Sample page from Stone and Neale's (1982) Assessment of Daily Experience scale. Respondents indicate whether an event occurred by circling the arrows to the left of the list of events. If an event has occurred, it is then rated on the dimensions of desirability, change, meaningfulness, and control using the enclosed spaces to the right.

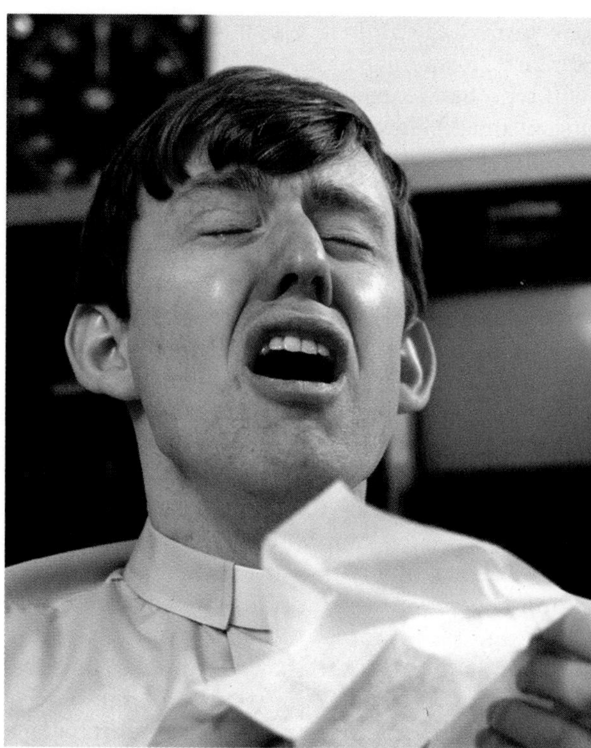

Stone and his colleagues have found that changes in the frequency of daily life events precede the onset of episodes of respiratory infection. The mechanism may be a stress-induced lowering of secretory IgA.

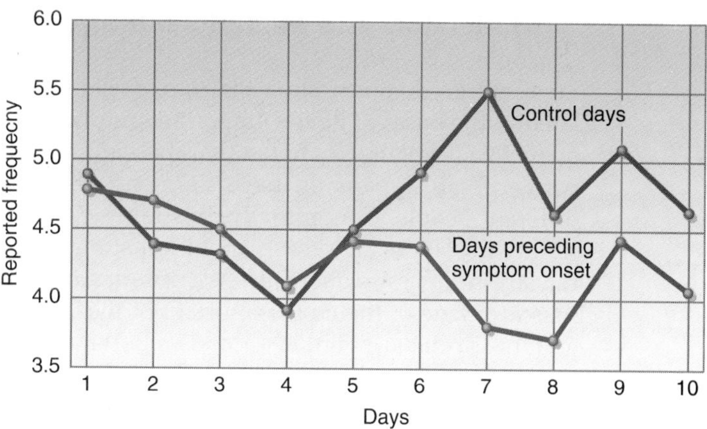

Figure 8.3 Number of desirable events for the ten days preceding an episode of respiratory infection. After Stone, Reed, and Neale (1987).

Next, the daily frequency of undesirable and desirable events that occurred from one to ten days before the start of an episode was examined. For each subject a set of control days, without an episode, was also selected with the restriction that the control days matched the others for day of the week. This was done to control for the higher frequency of desirable and lower frequency of undesirable events that are typically reported on weekends; since subjects serve as their own controls, any weekend effects would be the same for days preceding episodes and for control days. The means of desirable events for the days preceding episode starts is shown in Figure 8.3; parallel data for undesirable events are shown in Figure 8.4. It was expected that several days before the onset of the illness episode there would be an increase in undesirable events and a decrease in desirable events relative to control days. The results indeed showed that for desirable events there were significant decreases three and four days prior to episode onset. For undesirable events, there were significant increases at four and five days before the episode onset.

These results, which have subsequently been replicated (Evans & Edgerton, 1990), are the first to show a relationship between life events and health, with both variables measured in a daily, prospective design. Most sources of confounding in prior life-events studies have therefore been avoided in this study, and we can now come much closer to asserting that life events play a causal role in increasing vulnerability to episodes of infectious illness. One of the strongest and most interesting aspects of the pattern of events preceding symptom episodes is that there is a peak in undesirable events and a trough in desirable ones several days prior to onset, yet the two days just before onset have average rates of desirable and undesirable events. Speculation that the results are caused by some bias, such as individuals feeling poorly prior to flagrant symptom onset and thus influencing perception of events, is unlikely, as most potential biases would produce a change in the frequency of events on days just prior to the onset of symptoms.

Figure 8.4 Number of undesirable events in the ten days preceding an episode of respiratory infection. After Stone, Reed, and Neale (1987).

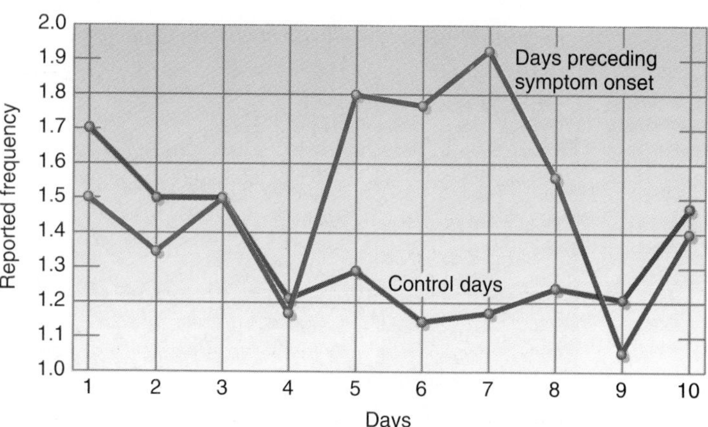

Moderators and Mediators of Stress

Even with a demonstration that life events are related to the onset of illness, important questions remain. We have already noted that the same life experience can apparently have different effects in different people. Conceptually, this raises the possibility that there are other variables that moderate the stress–illness relationship. We will describe research on one of the most important of these moderators—social support. A second important question concerns the mechanism, usually biological, by which stress exerts its effects. Through what process are the effects of psychological stress mediated? We will discuss one example of such a biological mediator—changes in the immune system.

Social Support

Cohen and Wills (1985) distinguished two major aspects of social support—structural and functional. **Structural social support** refers to a person's network of social relationships, for example, marital status and number of friends. **Functional social support** is concerned more with the *quality* of a person's relationships. For example, does a person believe he or she has friends to call on in a time of need?

Structural support is a well-established predictor of mortality. For example, Schoenbach et al. (1986) found that total mortality in an elderly population was related to lower levels of structural support. Similarly, Ruberman et al. (1984) found that among men who had experienced a myocardial infarction (heart attack), lower levels of structural support were related to subsequent death. The role of functional support in predicting death, however, is currently unclear (Cohen, 1988).

Both forms of social support have been related to disease onset. For example, Seeman and Syme (1987) found that higher levels of functional support were related to lower rates of atherosclerosis (clogging of the arteries) and to the ability of women to adjust to chronic rheumatoid arthritis (Goodenow, Reisine, & Grady, 1990). Structural support has been related to various aspects of cardiovascular disease (Reed et al., 1983).

How does social support exert its beneficial effects? One possibility is that higher levels of social support increase the occurrence of positive health behaviors, for example, eating a healthy diet, not smoking, and moderating alcohol intake. Such relationships were found in a study of the elderly (Blazer, 1982b). Alternatively, social support (or lack of it) could have a direct effect on biological processes. For example, low levels of social support are related to an increase in negative emotions (Kessler & McLeod, 1985; see also our earlier discussion of PTSD on page 157), which in turn could affect some hormone levels and the immune system (Kielcolt-Glaser et al., 1984).

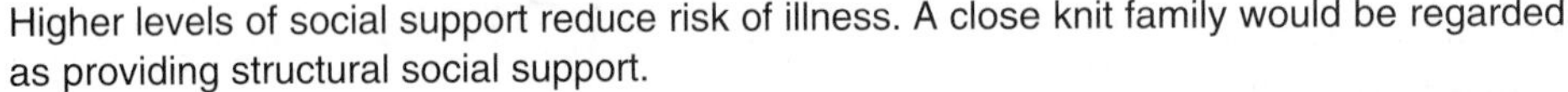

Higher levels of social support reduce risk of illness. A close knit family would be regarded as providing structural social support.

Biological Mediation

A host of biological changes occur during encounters with stressors that could mediate the role of stress on illness, for example, increases in heart rate and blood pressure or increases in secretions of hormones. Recent research also suggests that stress affects the immune system, which is an important consideration in infectious diseases, cancer, and allergies (Zakowski, Hall, & Baum, 1992). Depression and bereavement have also been shown to compromise immune function (Schleifer et al., 1983; Linn, Linn, & Jensen, 1984). As suggested by Zakowski et al., a sense of loss may underlie immunological changes, for similar effects have been found in divorced people (Kielcolt-Glaser et al., 1987; Kielcolt-Glaser et al., 1988) and those who have lost their jobs (Arnetz et al., 1987). Other kinds of stress also hamper the functioning of the immune system, for example, examination anxiety (Workman & La Via, 1987; Kielcolt-Glaser & Glaser, 1987), chronic illness (Levy, Herberman, Lippman, & d'Angelo, 1987) and even laboratory-induced stress (Zakowski, McAllister, Deal, & Baum, in press). Whether such immune system decrements lead to more negative clinical outcomes, such as early death from cancer, is yet to be determined, but researchers assume that it is a question well worth posing (Zakowski et al., 1992). To illustrate, we will discuss one aspect of the immune system—secretory immunity—in some detail and return to Stone and Neale's research described earlier.

The secretory component of the immune system exists in the fluids that bathe the mucosal surfaces of the body (i.e., tears; saliva; gastrointestinal, vaginal, nasal, and bronchial secretions) and at those surfaces at the ports of entry for invading bacteria and viruses. A substance found in these secretions, called Immunoglobulin A, or IgA, contains antibodies that are viewed as the body's first line of defense against invading viruses and bacteria. They prevent the virus or bacterium from binding to mucosal tissues.

A study by Stone et al. (1987) showed that changes in the number of antibodies in IgA were linked to changes in mood. Throughout an eight-week study period a group of dental students came to the laboratory three times a week to have their saliva collected and a brief psychological assessment conducted. When the students experienced relatively high levels of negative mood, there were fewer antibodies present than on days with low levels of negative mood. Similarly, antibody level was higher on days with higher levels of positive mood.

Prior research (e.g., Stone & Neale, 1984) had shown that daily events affect mood. It is therefore quite possible that daily events affect the fluctuations in mood, which in turn suppress synthesis of the secretory IgA antibodies. The process could operate as follows. An increase in undesirable life events coupled with a decrease in desirable life events produces increased negative mood, which in turn depresses antibody levels in secretory IgA. If, during this period a person is exposed to a virus, he or she will be at increased risk for the virus to infect the body. The overt symptoms of respiratory illness begin several days following infection.

Further information on the relationship between psychological and biological factors in the common cold is provided by the work of Cohen, Tyrrell, and Smith (1991), conducted at the Common Cold Unit in England. In this study volunteers took nasal drops containing a mild cold virus and also completed a battery of measures concerning recent stress. The advantage of this method is that exposure to the virus is an experimental variable, under the investigators' control. Increases in stress were clearly linked to the rate of infection. At the lowest level of recent stress about 71 percent of subjects became infected, while at the highest level the figure was over 90 percent. These findings illustrate well the complex interplay between psychological and biological variables in the etiology of psychophysiological disorders.

Theories of the Stress–Illness Link

In considering the etiology of psychophysiological disorders, we are confronted with three questions. (1) Why does stress produce illness in only some people who are exposed to it? (2) Why does stress sometimes cause an illness and not a psychological disorder? (3) Given that stress produces a psychophysiological disorder, what determines which one of the many disorders it will be? Answers to these questions have been sought by both biologically and psychologically oriented theorists.

Before reviewing some theories in this domain it is important to note that careful consideration needs to be given to the dependent variable in studies of stress and health. Much of the research in the field has attempted to link stress to self-reports of illness. The problem here is that self-reports may not be an accurate reflection of physical illness. For example, Watson and Pennebaker (1989), after an extensive review of the literature, concluded that an apparent association between negative emotional states and health actually was only a relationship between negative emotions and illness *reporting*. Perhaps high levels of stress increase vigilance about bodily changes and create a tendency to overreact to these sensations. The result would be an increase in self-reports of illness but not an actual change in health. It is possible that stress leads to health changes that are not due directly to biological or psychological variables but are due to changes in health behavior. That is, high stress may result in increased smoking, disrupted sleep, increased alcohol consumption, and altered diet (the opposite of what we saw with social support). These behavioral changes may then increase risk for illness. In this case the stress–illness association would be real, but mediated indirectly through changes in health behaviors.

Biological Theories

Biological approaches attribute particular psychophysiological disorders to specific weaknesses or overactivity of an individual's organ systems in responding to stress. Psychological theories account for specificity by positing particular emotional states or personality traits for particular disorders.

Somatic-Weakness Theory

Genetic factors, earlier illnesses, diet, and the like may disrupt a particular organ system, which may then become weak and vulnerable to stress. According to the **somatic-weakness theory**, the connection between stress and a particular psychophysiological disorder is the weakness in a specific bodily organ. Like a tire that blows out at its weakest or thinnest portion, in the human body a congenitally weak respiratory system might predispose the individual to asthma or a weak digestive system to ulcers.

Specific-Reaction Theory

Some investigators argue that there are differences, probably genetically determined, in the ways in which individuals respond to stress. People have been found to have their own particular patterns of autonomic response to stress. The heart rate of one individual may increase, whereas another person may react with increased respiration rate but no change in frequency of heartbeats (Lacey, 1967). According to **specific-reaction theory**, individuals respond to stress in their own idiosyncratic way, and the body system that is the most responsive may be a likely candidate for the locus of a subsequent psychophysiological disorder. For example, someone reacting to stress with elevated blood pressure may be more susceptible to essential hypertension. Later in this chapter, when we consider particular psychophysiological disorders, evidence in support of both somatic-weakness and specific-reaction theories will be presented.

Psychological Theories

Psychological theories try to account for the development of various disorders by considering factors such as unconscious emotional states, personality traits, cognitive appraisals, and specific styles of coping with stress.

Psychoanalytic Theories

Franz Alexander (1950) has perhaps had the greatest impact of the psychoanalytic theorists who have studied psychophysiological reactions. In his view the various psychophysiological disorders are products of unconscious emotional states specific to each disorder. For example,

> It would appear that the crucial factor in the pathogenesis of ulcer is the frustration of the dependent, help-seeking and love-demanding desires. When these desires cannot find gratification in human relationships, a chronic emotional stimulus is created which has a specific effect on the functions of the stomach. (p. 103)

Alexander assumed that ulcer patients have repressed their longing for parental love in childhood and that this repressed impulse causes the overactivity of the autonomic nervous system and of the stomach, leading to ulcers. Physiologically, the stomach is continuously preparing to receive food, which the person has symbolically equated with parental love.

Undischarged hostile impulses are viewed as creating the chronic emotional state responsible for essential hypertension.

> The damming up of his hostile impulses will continue and will consequently increase in intensity. This will induce the development of stronger defensive measures in order to keep pent-up aggressions in check. . . . Because of the marked degree of their inhibitions, these patients are less effective in their occupational activities and for that reason tend to fail in competition with others . . . envy is stimulated and . . . hostile feelings toward more successful, less inhibited competitors are further intensified. (p. 150)

Alexander formulated this unexpressed-anger or **anger-in theory** on the basis of his observations of patients undergoing psychoanalysis. His hypothesis continues to be pursued in present-day studies of the psychological factors in essential hypertension (see page 202).

Cognitive and Behavioral Factors

We perceive more than just physical threats (Simeons, 1961); we experience regrets about the past and worries about the future. All of these perceptions stimulate sympathetic system activity. But resentment and regret and worry cannot be fought or escaped as readily as external threats, nor do they easily pass. They may keep the sympathetic system aroused and the body in a continual state of emergency, sometimes for far longer than it can bear. Under these circumstances, moreover, the necessary balancing of sympathetic and parasympathetic actions is made that much more difficult and can go awry. Thus the distressed thoughts that evolution has made possible bring about bodily changes that persist longer than they were meant to and that contribute to an imbalance between sympathetic and parasympathetic activity. Our higher mental capacities, it is theorized, subject our bodies to physical storms that they are not built to withstand.

In our general discussion of stress we saw that the appraisal of a potential stressor is central to how it affects someone. Therefore people who continually appraise life experiences as exceeding their resources would be expected to be chronically stressed and at risk for the development of a psychophysiological disorder. Similarly, how people cope with stress could well be relevant. We will describe some findings on this point later and see that how people cope with anger is related to hypertension. Personality traits are also implicated in several disorders, notably cardiovascular disease. People with a Type A personality behave in ways that appear to be related to the development of heart problems. Finally, gender is an important variable in health as there are clear differences in the frequency with which men and women experience some health problems (see Focus Box 8.3).

Our general overview of theories concerning the etiology of psychophysiological disorders is complete. We turn now to a detailed review of two disorders that have attracted much attention from researchers—cardiovascular disorders and asthma.

Cardiovascular Disorders

Cardiovascular disorders are medical problems involving the heart and blood circulation system. Although the rate of death from cardiovascular disease has been decreasing since 1964, it still remains a problem of great magnitude: it accounts for almost half the deaths in the United States each year (Foreyt, 1990); affects over 300 people for every 10,000 (U.S. Census, 1990); and its treatment and research consume over 100 billion dollars a year (Weiss, 1986). In this section, we will focus on two forms of cardiovascular disease, hypertension and coronary heart disease. Coronary heart disease is of major significance because, of the cardiovascular diseases, it is the single greatest cause of death. It is generally agreed that many of the deaths from cardiovascular diseases are premature and can be prevented by dealing with one or more of the known risk factors (Price, 1982).

Essential Hypertension

Without question, one of the most serious psychophysiological disorders is hypertension, commonly called high blood pressure. This disease disposes people to atherosclerosis (clogging of the arteries), heart attacks, and strokes, and it can also cause death through kidney failure. In fact, no more than 10 percent of all cases in the United States are attributable to an identifiable physical cause. Hypertension without an evident organic cause is called **essential** (or sometimes primary) **hypertension**. Recent estimates are that varying degrees of hypertension are found in 15 to 33 percent of the adult population of the United States; it is twice as frequent in African-Americans as in whites. As many as 10 percent of American college students have hypertension, most of them unaware of their illness. Unless people have their blood pressure checked, they may go for years without knowing that they are hypertensive. The disease, then, is known as the silent killer.

Blood pressure is measured by two numbers; one represents *systolic pressure* and the other represents *diastolic pressure.* The systolic measure is the amount of arterial pressure when the ventricles contract and the heart is pumping; the diastolic measure is the degree of arterial pressure when the ventricles relax and the heart is resting. A normal blood pressure in

8.3 • Gender and Health

At every age from birth to eighty-five and older, more men die than women. Individual causes of death vary greatly between the sexes. A twofold or greater difference is found in automobile accidents, homicides, cirrhosis, heart disease, lung disease, lung cancer, and suicide. In spite of their reduced mortality, women have higher rates of morbidity (generalized poor health or several secific diseases). For example, women have higher rates of diabetes, anemia, gastrointestinal problems, and rheumatoid arthritis; they report more visits to physicians, use more prescription drugs, and account for two-thirds of all surgical procedures performed in the United States. In recent years, though, women's mortality advantage has been decreasing; for example, the death rate from cardiovascular disease has declined among men in the last thirty years but stayed about the same in women.

The statistics just mentioned were compiled by Rodin and Ickovics (1990) from several sources. They go on to note that, despite these data and the fact that several medical problems are unique to women (e.g., hysterectomy, breast cancer), most health research has focused on men. Clearly, they argue, there is an urgent need for more research on women's health.

What are some of the possible reasons for the differences in mortality and morbidity rates in women, and why is mortality increasing? As we have come to expect, tentative answers have been proposed by those in both the psychological and biological camps.

From a biological vantage point it might be proposed that women have some mechanism that protects them from life-threatening diseases. For example, the female hormone, estrogen, may offer protection from cardiovascular disease. Several lines of evidence support this idea. First, postmenopausal women and those who have had their ovaries removed (in both cases lowering estrogen) have higher rates of cardiovascular disease than do premenopausal women. Furthermore, hormone replacement therapy lowers the rate of mortality from cardiovascular disease, perhaps maintaining elevated levels of high-density lipoprotein (HDL), the so-called good cholesterol (Matthews et al., 1989).

Turning to a psychological proposal, we may note that women are less likely than men to be Type A personalities and are also less hostile than men (Waldron, 1976; Weidner & Collins, in

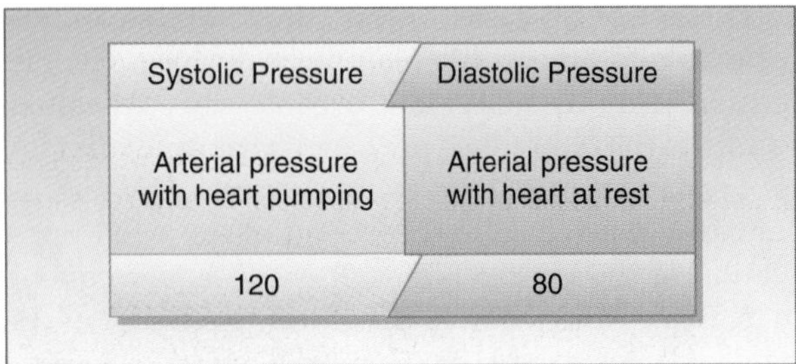

Figure 8.5 Normal young adult blood pressure.

a young adult would be 120 (systolic) over 80 (diastolic) (Figure 8.5).

Essential hypertension is currently viewed as a heterogeneous condition brought on by many possible disturbances in the various systems of the body that are responsible for regulating blood pressure. Blood pressure may be elevated by increased cardiac output, the amount of blood leaving the left ventricle of the heart per minute; by increased resistance to the passage of blood through the arteries, that is, by vasoconstriction; and by an increase in the body's volume of fluids. The combination of physiological mechanisms that contribute to regulation of blood pressure is extremely complex. The sympathetic nervous system, hormones, and salt and water metabolism, as well as central nervous system mechanisms, are all involved (Weiner, 1977). Many of these controlling physiological mechanisms can be affected by psychological stress.

Stress, Anger-In, and Blood Pressure Increase

Various stressful conditions have been examined to determine their role in the etiology of essential hypertension. Stressful interviews, natural disasters, anger, and anxiety have been found to produce short-term elevations in blood pressure (e.g., Innes, Millar, & Valentine, 1959). Kasl & Cobb (1970) examined the effects of the loss of employment. They studied a group of workers beginning two months before their jobs were terminated and for two years subsequent to the loss of employment. A control press). Eisler and Blalock (1991) hypothesize that the Type A pattern, discussed more fully below, is part and parcel of a rigid commitment to the traditional masculine gender role, which emphasizes achievement, mastery, competitiveness, not asking for help or emotional support, excessive need for control, and the tendency to become angry and to express it when frustrated. They link these attributes to the tendencies for men to be more prone to coronary problems and other stress-related health risks, such as hypertension (Harrison, Chin, & Ficarrotto, 1989). We describe elsewhere the role that both biological and psychological variables play in cardiovascular disease, but for now we simply state that it is significant and could well be relevant to the lower levels of mortality of women.

Why is the gap between mortality rates in men and women decreasing? In the early twentieth century most deaths were due to epidemics and infection, but now most deaths result from diseases that are affected by lifestyle. One possibility, then, is that lifestyle differences between men and women account for the sex difference in mortality and that these lifestyle differences are decreasing. Men smoke more than women and consume more alcohol. These differences are likely contributors to men's higher mortality from cardiovascular disease and lung cancer. It is also true that in recent years women have begun to smoke and drink more and that these changes have been paralleled by increases in lung cancer and the failure of the mortality rate for cardiovascular disease to decrease among them (Rodin & Ickovics, 1990). Perhaps some of the characteristics associated with Type A will come to be found more among women as they continue to work alongside men in occupations and professions previously closed to them.

There are several possible explanations for the difference in morbidity of men and women. First, because women live longer than men, they may be more likely to experience several diseases that are associated with aging. Second, women may be more attentive to their health than men and thus more likely to visit physicians and be diagnosed. Finally, women may cope with stress in a way that increases their risk for some illnesses (Weidner & Collins, in press).

In the case of many disorders, the gathering of scientific data on how best to minimize their risk has likely been compromised by the tendency to exclude women subjects from studies. As Rodin and Ickovics concluded, women have been understudied in health research. Future studies need to include equal samples of men and women and also to focus on the special health concerns of women.

group, consisting of men in similar occupations who did not lose their jobs, was examined for the same twenty-six month period. Each participant in the study was visited at home several times by a nurse during six separate periods so that blood pressure could be measured. For the control subjects there were no overall changes in blood pressure. In the men who lost their jobs, however, elevated blood pressure was found with anticipation of job loss, after termination of employment, and during the initial probationary period of a new job. Those who had great difficulty finding stable employment suffered the longest periods of high blood pressure. In general, chronic psychological stress such as this is widely accepted as an important factor in essential hypertension (Fredrikson & Mathews, 1990).

In another group of studies (Hokanson & Burgess, 1962; Hokanson, Burgess & Cohen, 1963; Hokanson, Willers, & Koropsak, 1968; Stone & Hokanson, 1969), based in part on psychoanalytic theory, Hokanson and his colleagues attempted to determine whether blood pressure elevation is associated with the inhibition of aggression. Subjects were given a task but were angered almost immediately

Because high blood pressure is typically not noticeable to the sufferer, regular check-ups are recommended, especially for those at higher than average risk.

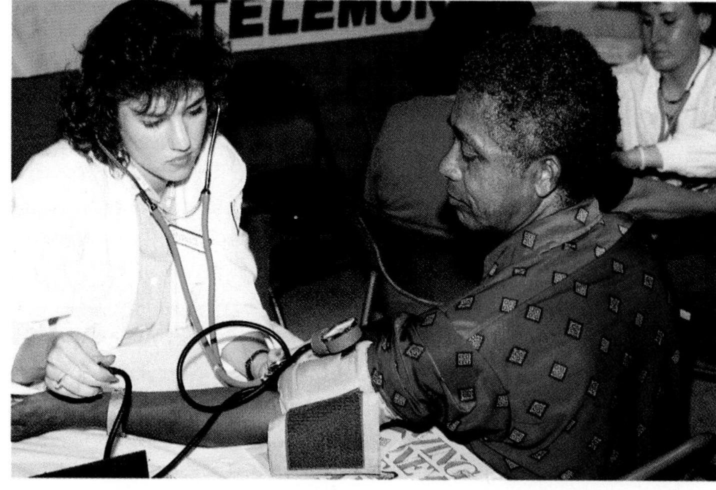

Harburg's research shows that among African-Americans, blood pressure is especially high among those living in a poor area of the city with high crime rates.

by the interruptions of a supposed fellow subject, actually a confederate of the experimenter. Later on, half the subjects were given the opportunity to retaliate against their harrasser. The results of this classic series of investigations indicate not only that harassment caused blood pressure to rise but that, for men, aggressing against a source of frustration then helps blood pressure to decrease.

A study by Harburg and others (1973) extended Hokanson's ideas to the natural environment and to the high incidence of hypertension among African-Americans. Harburg and his colleagues chose two areas of Detroit in which to conduct their investigation. In one area, the high-stress location, the crime rate was substantial; population density, mortality rates, and frequency of marital breakups were all high; and the socioeconomic status of residents was generally low. Conditions in the low-stress area were more favorable.

In each area groups of married African-American and white men were selected for study. During a visit to the participants' homes, blood pressure readings were taken, the respondents were interviewed, and a specially designed test was administered. The test presented hypothetical situations and asked the participants how they would respond. An example follows.

> Now imagine that you were searching to find another place to live in, and finally found one for sale or rent which you liked, but the owner told you he would not sell or rent to you because of your religion, national origin or race. How would you feel about that? The response categories . . . were as follows: (1) I'd get angry or mad and show it, (2) I'd get annoyed and show it, (3) I'd get annoyed, but would keep it in, (4) I'd get angry or mad but would keep it in, (5) I wouldn't feel angry or annoyed. (p. 280)

Participants were also asked how they would feel if they had become angry and showed it. The dimension assessed here was guilt, and the possible responses ranged from very guilty to no feelings of guilt at all.

Blood pressure was higher among the African-Americans than among the whites; and African-Americans living in the high-stress areas had higher blood pressure than those living in the middle-class neighborhoods. Thus previous statistics revealing racial differences in blood pressure were substantiated, but with the important qualification that environmental stress is also a major factor. When responses on the test were related to blood pressure, the following pattern emerged: for all subjects except African-Americans in the middle-class neighborhood, holding anger in and feeling guilt were related to higher blood pressure levels.

Harburg's findings, a reanalysis of them (Gentry et al., 1981, 1982), and a replication by Dimsdale et al. (1986) have pointed out the role of anger-in in the development and maintenance of high blood pressure. Other studies, however, do not find that anger-in predicts high blood pressure and have even found the reverse—that expressing anger predicts it. For example, Harburg et al. (1991) administered measures of anger-in and anger-out to a large sample of African-Americans and white men. Only anger-out predicted high blood pressure. In discussing their findings, Harburg et al. note that the immediate response to an anger-inducing situation may not be the key to understanding the relationship between anger and high blood pressure. More critical, they argue, is whether people later resolve the problem that aroused the anger or whether they remain angry and resentful. The latter circumstance may be most strongly related to hypertension. Harburg's findings are consistent with a recent intervention study by Davison and associates (1991, see page 218).

We should not conclude that anger is the only variable that increases blood pressure. As an illustration we can consider a series of studies involving what is termed active, effortful coping. In their research, Obrist and his colleagues (e.g., 1978) used a reaction time task in which subjects were told they would receive an electric shock if they did not respond quickly enough. Good performance led to a monetary bonus. The reaction time task yielded significant increases in both heart rate and systolic blood pressure.

The mechanism inducing long-term essential hypertension would necessarily involve some structural changes in the organism. For ethical reasons no experimental work has been done with human beings to determine whether short-term increases in blood pressure will develop into prolonged hypertension, but some research has been done on animals.

In general, true hypertension has proved elusive in the laboratory. In many studies using electric shock as a stressor, blood pressure increased during the period when the animal was stressed but returned to normal when the stressor was removed. Somewhat more successful in producing long-term blood pressure elevations are studies that have used more naturalistic stressors, such as competing with other animals for food (Peters, 1977). But the overall picture indicates that some predisposing factor or factors are required if stress, such as the activation of the autonomic nervous system by anger, is to bring on essential hypertension.

Predisposing Factors

In research with animals, several powerful diatheses have been identified—rearing in social isolation (Henry, Ely & Stephens, 1972), a high level of emotionality (Farris, Yeakel, & Medoff, 1945), and sensitivity to salt (Friedman & Dahl, 1975). In the salt study, the researchers worked with two strains of rats who had been bred to be either sensitive or insensitive to the impact of their diet. The sensitive rats developed hypertension and died on a high-salt diet. These salt-sensitive rats were also likely to show sustained blood pressure elevations when placed in an experimentally created conflict situation.

In the past decade there has been a great deal of interest in cardiovascular reactivity as a biological predisposition to hypertension (and coronary heart disease as well; see page 209). The general research strategy is to assess cardiovascular reactivity to a laboratory stressor (e.g., threat of electric shock) among people who are not currently hypertensive and then to follow up the participants some years later to determine whether the reactivity measure (usually the amount of change from a baseline condition to the stressor) predicts blood pressure. Two important points must be demonstrated to ensure the success of this approach. First, reactivity must be reliable if it is going to have predictive power. Indications are that it is (e.g., Kasprowicz et al., 1990). Second, the laboratory measure of reactivity must actually relate to what the cardiovascular system does during a person's day-to-day activities. (This is no trivial point because of what is called "white coat hypertension." A person's blood pressure may be high at the clinic or laboratory but normal elsewhere.) Though the literature on this issue is somewhat conflicting (see Manuck et al., 1990) studies that have compared laboratory reactivity with reactivity to stressors in the natural environment have shown some relationship.

What are the results of the studies that have tried to predict hypertension from reactivity? Again, there is some variability but those from a recent and well-conducted study are positive (Light et al., 1992). Cardiovascular measures were taken while subjects were threatened with shock if their responses were slow. A follow-up ten to fifteen years later included both office-based measures of cardiovascular functioning and a day of ambulatory monitoring (for the entire day subjects wore a device that obtained several measures of both heart rate and blood pressure every hour). Each of the cardiovascular reactivity measures taken earlier (heart rate and systolic and diastolic blood pressure) predicted blood pressure, with heart rate reactivity the strongest predictor. Importantly, these reactivity measures predicted subsequent blood pressure over and above the contribution of standard clinical predictors such as family history of hypertension.

This focus on reactivity as a predisposing factor in hypertension has led researchers to wonder whether increased cardiac reactivity might be related to the increased risk for the disease found in African-Americans. Although the topic is being actively pursued, results to date are contradictory (Anderson et al., 1990; Johnson, Nazaro, & Gilbert, 1991).

Further support for the importance of reactivity comes from high-risk research comparing individuals with and without a positive history for hypertension (e.g., Hastrup et al., 1982). As anticipated, people with a positive family history showed greater blood pressure reactivity to stress. Coupled with other research showing the heritability of blood pressure reactivity (Matthews & Rakaczky, 1987) and the heritability of hypertension, blood pressure reactivity becomes a good candidate for a genetically transmitted diathesis. There is little doubt that essential hypertension is caused by an interplay between a diathesis and a stressor.

Coronary Heart Disease

Coronary heart disease (CHD) takes two principal forms, angina pectoris and myocardial infarction or heart attack.

A Characterization of the Disease

The symptoms of **angina pectoris** are periodic chest pains, usually located behind the sternum and frequently radiating into the left shoulder and arm. The major cause of these severe attacks of pain is an insufficient supply of oxygen to the heart, which, in turn, is traced to coronary atherosclerosis, a narrowing or plugging of the coronary arteries by deposits of fatty material. Angina is generally precipitated by physical or emotional exertion and is commonly relieved by rest or medication. Serious physical damage to heart muscle rarely results from an angina attack, for blood flow is reduced but not cut off.

Myocardial infarction is a much more serious disorder and is the leading cause of death in the United States today. Like angina pectoris, myocardial infarction is caused by an insufficient supply of oxygen to the heart. The oxygen insufficiency, more extreme than in angina pectoris, results from coronary artery disease, a general curtailment of the heart's blood supply through atherosclerosis, or from coronary occlusion, a sudden obstruction of a large coronary artery by deposits or a blood clot. In both instances parts of the heart muscle die. In addition to increased severity and possibility of death, myocardial infarction differs from angina in that it is not necessarily precipitated by exertion and the pain is longer and more severe (Friedberg, 1966).

The American Heart Association lists seven factors related to increased risk for CHD: age, sex (males are at a greater risk), cigarette smoking, elevated blood pressure, elevated serum cholesterol, an increase in the size of the left ventricle of the heart as revealed by electrocardiogram, and diabetes (Insull, 1973). The risk for heart disease generally increases with the number and severity of these factors.

Still, Jenkins (1976) concluded that these traditional risk factors leave at least half the etiology of coronary heart disease unexplained. Indeed, less attention was paid earlier to contributing causes such as overweight, poor exercise habits, consumption of fatty foods, and smoking than now, and yet in earlier decades the incidence of CHD and related cardiovascular diseases was much less. Also, in the Midwest, where people's diets are highest in saturated fats and where smoking rates are especially high, the incidence of coronary heart disease is low compared with that in more industrialized parts of the United States. And anyone who has visited Paris is aware of the intemperate smoking and the fat-rich diets of the French population—yet CHD is relatively low there. *Why?*

Type A Behavior Pattern

The search for other causes of coronary heart disease has begun to focus on psychological factors such as stress and personality. Such considerations actually go back many years. In 1910 the Canadian physician Sir William Osler (1849–1919) described the typical angina patient as "vigorous in mind and body, and the keen and ambitious man, the indicator of whose engines is always set at full speed ahead" (Chesney, Eagleston, & Rosenman, 1980, p. 256). Further evidence indicates a relationship between CHD and such stressors as an overload of work, chronic conflict, and other life stressors (Jenkins, 1971, 1976; Rahe & Lind, 1971). The most promising evidence linking CHD to psychological variables, however, comes from investigations pioneered by two cardiologists, Meyer Friedman and Ray Rosenman (Friedman, 1969; Rosenman et al., 1975). In 1958 they identified a coronary-prone behavior pattern, called **Type A behavior pattern**.

The Type A individual has an intense and competitive drive for achievement and advancement; an exaggerated sense of the urgency of passing time, of the need to hurry; and considerable aggressiveness and hostility toward others. Type A persons are overcommitted to their work, often attempt to carry on two activities at once, and believe that to get something done well, they must do it themselves. They cannot abide waiting in lines and they play every game to win; even when their opponents are children they are impatient and hostile. Fast-thinking, fast-talking, and abrupt in gesture, they often jiggle their knees, tap their fingers, and blink rapidly. Too busy to notice their surroundings or to be interested in things of beauty, they tabulate success in life in numbers of articles written, projects under way, and material goods acquired. Some theorize that the ongoing struggle to achieve in a visible, tangible fashion is driven by an underlying sense of insecurity and low self-esteem (Price, 1982; Williams et al., 1992).

A second type of behavior pattern is called Type B. The Type B individual is less driven and relatively free of such pressures.

Assessment of Type A Type A and Type B individuals have been reliably identified by means of the Structured Interview (Rosenman et al., 1964), in which questions are asked about the intensity of ambitions, competitiveness, the urgency of deadlines, and hostility.

> **Interviewer:** When you are in your automobile, and there is a car in your lane going *far too slowly* for you, what do you do about it? Would you *mutter* and *complain* to yourself? Honk your horn? Flash your lights? Would anyone riding with you know that you were *annoyed?*
>
> **Interviewer:** If you make a date with someone for, oh, two o'clock in the afternoon, would you *be there* on *time?* Always? Never? If you are kept waiting, do you *resent* it? Would you *say* anything about it? Why or why not?

Seldom taking more than fifteen minutes, the interviewer asks the questions in a manner that is abrupt and fast-paced, rather than warm and empathic. Although the interview is highly structured, its protocol requires the interviewer to push the respondent with challenging, probing follow-up questions delivered in a pressured fashion. For example, if the respondent says that he or she played games with a child to win when the child was six, the interviewer might well ponder aloud, almost in disbelief, "Even with a six-year old?" The interviewer also interrupts the subject now and then in the middle of an answer in order to keep things moving and to try to elicit hostility. The originators of this novel assessment device believe that only by nudging and goading the interviewees can reliable discriminations be made between Type A and Type B individuals.

At the end of the interview, the interviewer makes a judgment as to whether the person is Type A or B, but the more critical assessment is made later on when highly skilled raters listen to or view tapes of the interview and attend very closely to two sets of information: the content of what the person says and how he or she said it. Indeed, the tenor of the responses is deemed more important. For example, question 13 is delivered in a hesitant, halting manner, almost as though the interviewer has lost his or her place or wandered off in thought to something else.

> **Interviewer:** Most people who work have to get up fairly early in the morning. In your particular case, uh-what-time-uh-do-you-uh, ordinarily uh-uh-uh-get up?

By the time the interviewer begins to uh-uh, it is obvious what the rest of the question is going to be. Note is taken whether the subject provides the answer before the question is completed, and whether he or she does so in an impatient, even hostile way, as if to say, "Hell, let's get on with this damned interview!" Answers to other questions also allow the raters to determine the subject's hostility, impatience, and sense of time urgency. Rosenman, in fact, believes that the interviewer should be a Type A person.

There are several other techniques for detecting a Type A personality (see Chesney, Eagleston, & Rosenman, 1980; Matthews, 1982). A self-report inventory of Type A behavior, the Jenkins Activity Survey (Jenkins, Rosenman, & Zyzanski, 1974), has been used extensively in the literature. It is now clear, however, that it does not relate well to the Structured Interview. Some of the inconsistencies in the Type A literature are likely the result of using different assessment devices (Matthews, 1982).

The Structured Interview is better than the Jenkins Activity Survey (JAS) at picking up hostility, which is increasingly being viewed as "the bad actor" (Weinstein et al., 1986) in contributing to coronary heart disease. In contrast, the JAS is better at detecting the person's job involvement, competitive striving, and fast pace of living (Matthews, 1982).

Evidence supporting the predictive validity of the Type A pattern comes from the classic Western Collaborative Group Study (WCGS) (Rosenman et al., 1975). In a double-blind prospective investigation, 3524 men aged thirty-nine to fifty-nine were to be followed over a period of eight and a half years. Some 3154 men completed their participation in the study. Individuals who had been identified as Type A by the Structured Interview were more than twice as likely to develop CHD than were Type B men. In addition, Type A men with CHD were more than five times as likely to have a second myocardial infarction than were other individuals with CHD. Traditional risk factors—parental history of heart at-

8.4 • Is Type A Really a Useful Construct?

> Like a shooting star that becomes brighter as it rises in the heavens and then falls to the earth extinguished, behavioral medicine's first cardiovascular risk factor, the Type A behavior pattern (TABP), seems to have finally burned itself out. (Foreyt, 1990, p. 158)

Clearly, serious doubts have arisen about the predictive validity of the Type A construct. In January 1988, *The New England Journal of Medicine* published an article by Ragland and Brand (1988) that reported on an analysis of men from the original Western Collaborative Group Study (WCGS) who had had one coronary event. They expected the data to indicate that subjects who had died from a subsequent coronary attack were more likely to have been Type A than Type B. They found the opposite to be true! Although Type A subjects were at higher risk for CHD within the eight and a half years of the study, *after* an initial coronary event they died less often from CHD than did Type B subjects. Perhaps Type A subjects reacted to their first coronary event in a more adaptive fashion, for example, by altering some of their health habits in a more conscientious and effective manner. Or maybe Type A is a risk factor only in younger populations (under age fifty, for example) or in those not suffering from irreversible artery damage (Taylor, Ironson, & Burnett, 1990). Among other things, this startling and unexpected finding casts serious doubt on the advisability of secondary prevention of CHD via reduction of Type A characteristics.

So controversial did the editors of the *Journal* consider the report that they invited a leading cardiovascular researcher, Dimsdale (1988), to write an introduction to place these negative findings in perspective. He did so by reviewing much of the literature we have just covered, but with attention to some unsuccessful attempts to replicate the original WCGS findings. His conclusions were several: (1) he lamented the fact that ideological fervor in opposing camps has apparently discouraged attempts to replicate or reconcile conflicting data; (2) he pointed to the heterogeneous nature of Type A and to the fact that different indexes of it correlate imperfectly (a conclusion Matthews, 1982, had come to earlier); and (3) he suggested that one of the components of Type A, hostility, might be worthy of special attention, a conclusion we came to in the fourth edition of this textbook (Davison & Neale, 1986).

Does this mean that Type A is dead as an organizing framework for research into coronary artery and heart disease? We think not. At a minimum, the heuristic function of the concept endures. It is through the attention to personality factors like Type A that behavioral scientists and physicians have examined closely the psychological variables in medical illnesses such as coronary artery disease and coronary heart disease,

tacks; high blood levels of cholesterol, triglycerides, and lipids; diabetes; elevated blood pressure; cigarette smoking; lack of education; and lack of exercise—were also found to be related to CHD, but even when these factors were controlled for, Type A individuals were still twice as likely to develop CHD.

These findings are sometimes misinterpreted as meaning that Type A individuals are highly likely to develop CHD. The WCGS did not show this, nor did its report intend such an implication. What the findings do reveal is *relative* risk: 7 percent of the initially well subjects had developed coronary disease at the eight-and-a-half-year point; of this small percentage two-thirds were Type A and one-third Type B. Since twice as many subjects who developed CHD were rated as Type A than as Type B, the risk was twice as high for the Type A subjects as for the Type B subjects (Chesney, Eagleston, & Rosenman, 1980). The overwhelming majority of Type A individuals do *not* develop CHD; rather, Type A personality is *one* of the significant risk factors in CHD. By the same token, many Type B's *do* develop CHD.

By the late 1970s enough evidence had accumulated to lead a distinguished group of researchers to conclude that Type A was a major independent risk factor in CHD, at least for men (Review Panel, 1981). Further research identified and studied Type A women (Waldron, 1978; Thoresen & Graff-Low, 1991) and attempted to identify subsets of Type A behavior that may be related to specific manifestations of coronary disease (Jenkins, Zyzanski, & Rosenman, 1978). Evidence collected by this second line of investigation suggested that "future angina" individuals may be more in a hurry, irritable, and

and it may seem ironic that it took two *physicians,* Rosenman and Friedman, to argue the case for psychological variables.

In fact, not all experts agree that the Type A construct is no longer useful. Bringing to mind W. C. Fields's comment that the reports of his death were greatly exaggerated, Thoresen and Powell (1992) recently analyzed conceptual as well as empirical issues in Type A theory and research and concluded that there is much potentially important work to be done with the construct, provided more careful attention is paid to its interactional, cognitive, and cultural aspects.

Even though Friedman and Rosenman originally conceived of Type A in terms of a person's interaction with the environment—a tendency to behave in hostile, competitive, and time-urgent ways *when confronted by challenge*—Thoresen and Powell point out that most research has taken an overly simplistic approach, neglecting the kinds of complex reciprocal interactions that are part of everyday life. For example, a Type A person, sensitive to threats to self-esteem, may react with hostility to implied criticism from others, which may then offend others and help create the very kind of social environment the person is uncomfortable in (Smith & Anderson, 1986). This general conceptualization resembles Wachtel's "cyclical psychodynamics" (page 105) and Bandura's "reciprocal causality," both ideas that sensitize us to the constant back-and-forth nature of human existence. Most research so far in Type A has not taken into account this interactional complexity.

There is also a need, argue Thoresen and Powell, to consider more carefully the cognitive components of Type A (cf. Glass, 1977; Matthews, 1982; Price, 1982; Strube, 1987; Weinstein et al., 1985; Williams et al., 1991), as well as the cultural context (viz., competitiveness and striving for achievement are common goals in a capitalistic society but probably not in a more communal one). More research on women and ethnic minorities is especially needed.

The fact of the matter is that there is a large body of evidence suggesting that something like Type A exists and that it bears some relationship to negative outcomes (e.g., early coronary death). Future research and theorizing will have to be much more complex in order to get to the core of the concept. There are skeptics, but there are also researchers who continue to believe that there is still something in the Type A mine that is worth digging for, but with more sophisticated and subtle tools.

For these reasons it is important to understand the course of theory and research on Type A, even if future findings encourage workers to drop the construct in favor of something less heterogeneous, like hostility. Indeed, twenty years from now it is likely that workers will criticize hostility as too global a construct and will focus on a narrower aspect of it.

competitive than "future myocardial infarction" individuals.

More recent studies have not, however, unequivocally supported the predictive utility of Type A behavior. For example, in the Multiple Risk Factor Intervention Trial (Shekelle et al., 1983), Type A failed to predict either mortality or myocardial infarction in subjects with multiple risk factors, although a reanalysis of the data scoring for potential for hostility from the Structured Interview did predict CHD incidence (Dembroski et al., 1989). Other studies have not found a relationship between Type A and angiographically determined coronary artery disease (Williams, 1987).

There are several reasons for these conflicting results. First, some of the negative findings have come from studies that did not use the Structured Interview to assess Type A; as we have already noted, such assessments probably do not adequately measure Type A. Second, the predictive power of Type A may be limited. For example, Williams et al. (1986) found that Type A predicted coronary artery disease only among people under the age of fifty. In fact, Type B individuals over age fifty had more severe disease! Thus, when studying a population with a broad age range, unless the data are analyzed separately according to age, it is unlikely that a Type A–CHD relationship will be established. Finally, it is possible that an overall Type A score is not the best measure of coronary-prone behavior (See Focus Box 8.4).

Mechanisms of Type A and CHD How does a set of psychological characteristics mediate a *physiological* disease of the heart? Type A individuals generally have higher heart rate reactivity to stressful

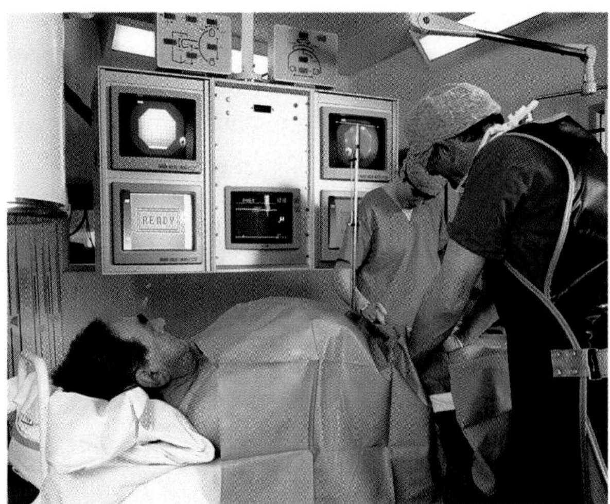

An angiogram is an X-ray based technique for detecting coronary artery disease. A catheter is inserted into a vein in the groin and maneuvered toward the heart. A dye is then released which reveals any blocked arteries.

laboratory situations than Type B individuals (see Manuck & Krantz, 1986, for a review). Excessive changes in heart rate and the consequent alterations in the force with which blood is pumped through the arteries could injure arteries. Heart rate reactivity has been related to CHD in several research contexts. Manuck, Kaplan, and Clarkson (1983) and Manuck et al. (1989) studied monkeys who were on a special diet designed to promote atherosclerosis. On the basis of a laboratory stress test the animals were divided into high versus low heart rate reactors. Subsequently, the high heart rate reactors developed twice as much atherosclerosis as the low reactors. In a study of humans, heart rate reactivity predicted the development of CHD in a twenty-three-year follow-up study (Keys et al., 1971). Alternatively, the release of catecholamines or corticosteroids in stressful situations could damage the arteries or increase the extent to which platelets aggregate, thus increasing the likelihood of blockage in the arteries (Herd, 1986).

On a psychological level, we can ask what there is about Type A personalities that puts them at risk. One answer to this question has been sought by investigating how Type A individuals cope with stress. When compared with Type B's, Type A people are more vigilant and active, which may lead to physical and mental exhaustion (Weidner & Collins, in press).

Another way of addressing this question is to examine individual items from the Structured Interview to see which ones are the best predictors of CHD. In the analysis of the interview data from the WCGS done by Matthews and her colleagues (1977), only seven of the whole set of items discriminated between Type A individuals who developed CHD and those who did not. Three of these items were related to self-reports of impatience and hostility, one was self-reported competitivenes, and the remainder were aspects of voice style, such as explosiveness. In further analysis of these data, hostility has emerged as the major predictor of CHD (Hecker et al., 1988). Hostility is also related to greater blood pressure reactivity to stress (Weidner et al., 1989) and to higher levels of cholesterol (Weidner et al., 1987).

Other findings (e.g., Almada, 1991; Williams et al., 1986) also suggest that cynicism is a major factor within the Type A complex. The amount of coronary artery blockage and coronary death were especially high in Type A subjects who had earlier endorsed MMPI items reflecting a cynical or hostile attitude. Similar findings were reported earlier by Barefoot, Dahlstrom, and Williams (1983). Following up medical students who were healthy when they took the MMPI twenty-five years earlier, they found a higher rate of CHD and death in those whose answers had indicated cynicism toward others. These MMPI-based findings have not always been replicated (e.g., Colligan & Offord, 1988; Hearn, 1989; McCraine et al., 1986). On the other hand, other findings concerning cynicism suggest a possible role for it in CHD. It is higher among men than women and among African-Americans than whites (Barefoot et al., 1991); it is also related to avoidance of seeking social supports, high levels of suppressed anger, greater consumption of alcohol, and being overweight (Houston & Vavak, 1991).

What is not yet clear is the best way to conceptualize these results. Is hostility the critical component? Or is it the cynical attitude that is assessed with the MMPI items? Further research will be needed to explore this issue.

Asthma

In **asthma** the air passages and bronchioles are narrowed, causing breathing to be extremely labored (particularly exhalation) and wheezy. This condition reflects a state of dominance of the parasympathetic division of the autonomic nervous system (see page 82). In addition, there is an inflammation of lung tissue mediated by the immune system, resulting in an increase in mucus secretion and edema (accumulation of fluid in the tissues) (Moran, 1991).

Somewhere between 2 and 5 percent of the population is estimated to have asthma. A third of asthma sufferers are children, and about two-thirds of these youngsters are boys (Graham et al., 1967; Purcell & Weiss, 1970). Williams and McNicol (1969) studied 30,000 seven-year-old Australian children. They found a high correlation between the age of onset of the symptoms and the length of time the disorder lasted. If onset occurred prior to age one, 80 percent were still wheezing five years later. With ages of onset from three to four, 40 percent were still wheezing five years later, and with an onset age of five or six, only 20 percent were still wheezing five years later. Thus the earlier the disorder begins, the longer it is likely to last.

A Characterization of the Disease

Asthma attacks occur intermittently and with variable severity; the frequency of some patients' attacks may increase seasonally when certain pollens are present. The airways are not continuously blocked; rather the respiratory system returns to normal or near normal either spontaneously or after treatment, thus allowing asthma to be differentiated from chronic respiratory problems such as emphysema (Creer, 1982). The major structures of the respiratory system are shown in Figure 8.6.

Most often, asthmatic attacks begin suddenly. The asthmatic individual has a sense of tightness in the chest, wheezes, coughs, and expectorates sputum. Subjective reactions can include panic-fear, irritability, and fatigue (Kinsman et al., 1974). A severe attack is a very frightening experience indeed. The asthma sufferer has immense difficulty getting air into and out of the lungs and feels as though he or she is suffocating; the raspy, harsh noise of the gasping, wheezing, and coughing compounds the terror. The sufferer may become exhausted by the exertion and fall asleep as soon as breathing is more normal.

Asthma attacks are often treated by using a nebulizer to spray a fine mist of a bronchodilator into the bronchial tubes.

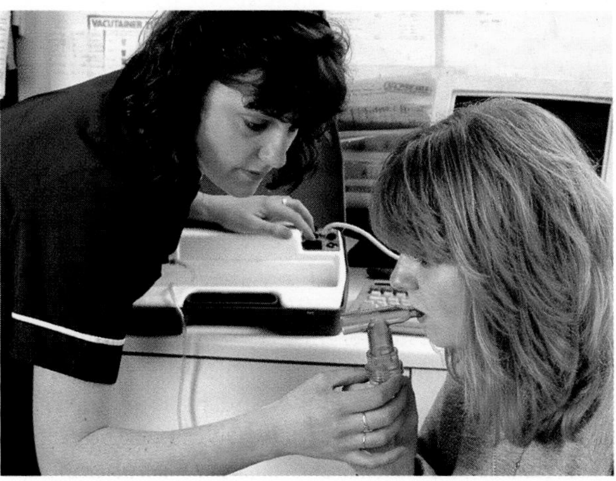

The asthma sufferer takes a longer time than normal to exhale, and whistling sounds, referred to as rales, can be detected throughout the chest. Symptoms may last an hour or less or may continue for several hours or sometimes even days. Between attacks no abnormal signs may be detected when the individual is breathing normally, but forced, heavy expiration often allows the rales to be heard through a stethoscope.

One patient, described in the following case history, had his first attack at age nine. His condition worsened until he was age thirteen, after which he was symptom-free for ten years. From that time on, however, his condition deteriorated to an unusual degree, and the patient eventually died of respiratory complications—an outcome that, fortunately, is rare. Notice that this patient appears to have more problems than just his asthma.

Abundant data from this patient's life suggest the importance of emotional factors in precipitating exacerbations of his asthma. He gives a graphic description of developing wheezing and shortness of breath upon separation from his mother. Once, while away on a trip with either her or his grandmother (it is not clear which), in a strange hotel, separated from his companion by a wall, he suffered through the night, having the feeling that his wheezes might be loud enough to be heard and bring her in to rescue him.

He described clearly the relationship of his symptoms to odors. His response to the scent of flowers may have had an allergic basis. That seems less likely in the case of the scent of "lovely ladies," which he stated also gave him asthma. So did certain "bad" smells, of asparagus and cigar smoke. . . . He had many conflicts around weeping, frequently described being dissolved in tears, but always with the implication that he never really was exhausting the reservoir of sobbing. . . .

At the time of his brother's marriage, the patient was jealous; he managed to forget to mail the 150 invitations to the ceremony that had been entrusted to him. In the church he was almost more prominent than the bride, walking down the aisle just before the ceremony, gasping for breath, and wearing a fur coat, although the month was July. (Knapp, 1969, p. 135)

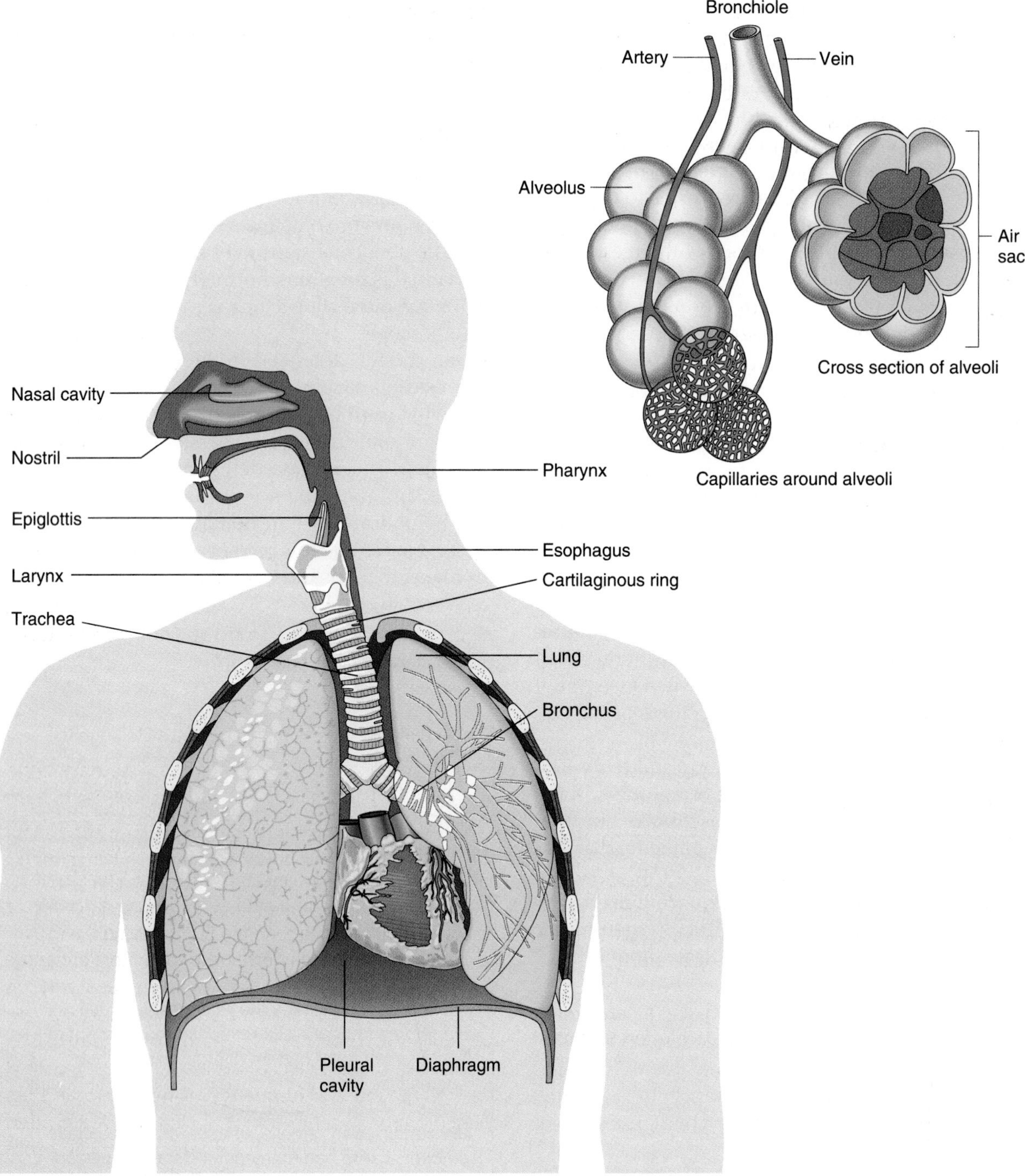

Figure 8.6 Major structures of the respiratory system—trachea, lungs, bronchi, bronchioles, and alveoli—and the ancillary organs.

The Etiology of Asthma

Much of the debate concerning the importance of psychological factors in the development of asthma relates to whether or not emotionality is always implicated. To investigate the etiology of asthma, Rees (1964) divided the various possible causes into three categories, allergic, infective, and psychological. (A related factor, not mentioned by Rees, is the effect of irritants, such as smoke and air pollution.) The cells in the respiratory tract may be especially sensitive to one or more substances or allergens, such as pollen, molds, fur, and dust, bringing on asthma. Respiratory infections, most often acute bronchitis, can also make the respiratory system vulnerable to asthma. Anxiety, tension produced by frustration, anger, depression, and anticipated pleasurable excitement are all examples of psychological factors that may, through induced emotionality, disturb the functioning of the respiratory system and thus cause asthma.

Rees studied 388 asthmatic children admitted consecutively to the asthmatic outpatient clinic of St. David's Hospital in Cardiff, Wales. The part played by allergic factors was assessed through the subjects' case histories and by conducting skin and inhalation reaction tests with suspected allergens. Patients were also exposed to suspected allergens and inert substances without knowing which was which. The importance of infective factors was determined through the case histories and X rays, by examining sputum, and by searching for pus or other evidence of infection in the nose, sinuses, and chest. The potential importance of psychological factors was assessed through the case histories and by direct behavioral observations. The principal results of Rees's study demonstrate the importance of conceptualizing asthma as a disease with multiple causes. As can be seen from Table 8.5, psychological factors were considered a dominant cause in only 37 percent of the cases, and in 30 percent of the cases psychological variables were regarded as totally unimportant—a conclusion at odds with the popular notion that asthma is always psychosomatic.

Rees's data showed also that the different causes of asthma varied in importance depending on the age of the individual. For those asthmatic individuals younger than five years of age, the infective factors predominated. From ages six to sixteen the infective factors still predominated, but psychological variables increased in importance. In the range from ages sixteen to sixty-five, psychological factors decreased in importance until about the thirty-fifth year, thereafter becoming more consequential again.

Table 8.5 • Relative Importance of Allergic, Infective, and Psychological Factors in the Etiology of Asthma

	Relative Importance, %		
Factors	*Dominant*	*Subsidiary*	*Unimportant*
Allergic	23	13	64
Infective	38	30	32
Psychological	37	33	30

Source: From Rees, 1964.

Psychological Factors Producing Asthma

Rees's studies have demonstrated that some, but by no means all, cases of asthma have psychological factors as a primary cause. Yet even when asthma is originally induced by an infection or allergy, psychological stress can precipitate attacks. Kleeman (1967) interviewed twenty-six patients over an eighteen-month period. According to the reports of these patients, 69 percent of their attacks began with an emotional disturbance.

In a more intensive study, Hyland (1990) had a group of asthmatics complete mood ratings and monitor their level of peak expiratory flow twice daily for fifteen days. (Peak expiratory flow is measured by blowing as hard as you can into a device that measures the force of the exhalation.) Agreeing with Rees's data that psychological factors are relevant for about one-third of asthmatics, three of ten participants showed a strong relationship between mood and peak expiratory flow.

The Role of the Family

Several researchers have considered parent–child interactions important in the etiology of asthma. In one investigation Mrazek et al. (1991) began with 150 pregnant women who had asthma. Because asthma has a genetic component, the investigators intended to study the at-risk offspring and assess parental characteristics as well. The parents were interviewed three weeks after the birth to determine their attitudes toward the infant, their sensitivity to the infant, their strategy for sharing parenting duties, and the presence of any emotional disturbance. The children were closely monitored over the next two years, and the frequency of asthma was then related to the parental characteristics noted earlier. Among the families who were rated as having problems, 25 percent of the children developed asthma as compared with only 8 percent of the children from the other families.

Not all research, however, finds that parent–child relationships figure in asthma. Earlier, Gauthier and his co-workers (1977, 1978) studied young asthmatic children and their mothers through a battery of questionnaires and interviews and by making observations in the home. Most of the children and their mothers were well-adjusted. The children's levels of development were normal for their age, and they were independent and successful at coping with their surroundings. Similarly, Eiser, Town, and Tripp (1991) found that parents of asthmatic children did not differ from controls in disciplinary practices.

The research we have reviewed is thus not completely consistent regarding the role played by the home life of asthmatics in their illness. Furthermore, even if we allow that family relations are consequential in asthma, we cannot always tell whether the various familial variables are causal agents or maintaining agents. Although certain emotional factors in the home may be important in eliciting early asthmatic attacks in some children, in others the illness may originally develop for nonfamilial reasons, and then the children's parents may unwittingly reward various symptoms of the syndrome. For example, parents may cater to asthmatic children and treat them specially because of the asthma. Current recommendations for the treatment of asthmatic children supply indirect support for this thesis. Doctors prescribe no special treatment and no overprotection. Instead, asthmatic children are urged to lead as normal a life as possible, even to the extent of participating in athletic events. An attempt is made, then, to keep the children from considering their sickness the dominating factor in their lives. This attitude is well illustrated in the following interaction presented by Kluger (1969, p. 361).

Patient: I can't go to school today because my asthma is worse.
Doctor: I know, but since it's not contagious why can't you be in school?
Patient (irritated): Because I'm having trouble breathing!
Doctor: I can see that, but you'll have trouble breathing whether you go to school or not. Remaining in bed won't help your breathing.
Patient (disgustedly): Boy, they don't even let you be sick in this hospital!

Personality and Asthma

It has often been suggested that particular constellations of personality traits are linked to asthma. Several investigators have found that asthmatic individuals have many neurotic symptoms such as dependency (Herbert, 1965), meekness, sensitivity, anxiety, meticulousness, perfectionism, and obsessions (Rees, 1964). But most of this work consisted of comparing asthmatics with a normal control population. Neuhaus (1958) compared the personality test scores of asthmatic children with those of both a group of normal children and a group of children with cardiac conditions. As in other studies, the asthmatics were found to be more neurotic than those who were normal. But, and this is the important point, *the cardiac children were like the asthmatics, more neurotic than normal children.* Thus the increased neuroticism of asthmatic children may reflect only reactions to a chronic illness; neuroticism scores on personality tests are higher the longer the patient has been sick (Kelly & Zeller, 1969).

Physiological Predisposition

Now that the importance of various stressors in eliciting asthmatic attacks has been documented, we must attempt to account for the fact that not all individuals exposed to such stressors develop asthma. Rees (1964) found that 86 percent of the asthmatics examined had had a respiratory infection before asthma developed. Only 30 percent of his control subjects had been so afflicted. This study can be regarded as evidence that inheriting a weak organ, establishing a reaction pattern, or both may figure in the etiology of asthma. Individuals whose asthma is primarily allergic may have an inherited hypersensitivity of the respiratory mucosa, which then overresponds to usually harmless substances such as dust or pollen. There is evidence that the incidence of asthma has a familial pattern consistent with genetic transmission of a diathesis (Konig & Godfrey, 1973). Finally, there is some indication that asthmatics have a less than normally responsive sympathetic nervous system (Miklich et al., 1973; Mathe & Knapp, 1971). Activation of the sympathetic nervous system is already known to reduce the intensity of an asthmatic attack.

In conclusion, a diathesis–stress explanation once again seems to fit the data on a psychophysiological disorder. Once the respiratory system is predisposed to asthma, any number of psychological stressors can interact with the diathesis to produce the disease.

Therapies for Psychophysiological Disorders

Since psychophysiological disorders are true physical dysfunctions, sound psychotherapeutic practice calls for close consultation with a physician. Whether high blood pressure is biologically caused or, as in essential hypertension, linked to psychological stress, a number of medications can reduce the constriction of the arteries. Asthma attacks can be alleviated by medications, taken either by inhalation or injection, that dilate the bronchial tubes; one of the most effective agents for controlling asthma is epinephrine. The help that drugs provide in ameliorating the damage and discomfort in the particular body systems cannot be underestimated. Mental health and medical professionals recognize, however, that most drug interventions treat only the symptoms; they do not deal with the fact that the person is reacting emotionally to psychological stress. Although the evidence suggests that the predisposition for a particular organ breakdown is inherited or at least somatically based, nonetheless, the importance of how a person responds psychologically indicates that psychotherapeutic interventions are appropriate.

Therapists of various persuasions agree in the most general terms that reducing anxiety or anger is the best way to alleviate the suffering from psychophysiological disorders. The particular disorder, whether it is essential hypertension, coronary heart disease, or an asthma attack, is considered a consequence of anxiety and/or anger or is linked with these emotions in some way. Psychoanalytically oriented workers employ techniques such as free association and dream analysis, as they do with other anxiety sufferers, in their efforts to help the egos of their patients confront the supposed infantile origins of their fears. Ego analysts, however, like Franz Alexander, consider specific emotional states to underlie the several disorders and try to strengthen present functioning. Thus they would encourage patients with essential hypertension, viewed as laboring under a burden of undischarged anger, to assert themselves and thereby siphon off the anger.

Behavior and cognitive therapists employ their usual range of procedures for reducing anxiety and anger—systematic desensitization, rational-emotive therapy, and assertion training—depending on the source of tension. If the person does not know how to act in a particular situation, behavior rehearsal and shaping may help him or her acquire necessary skills.

Psychophysiological disorders are of special interest to those in the field of behavioral medicine. Treatments are devised to lessen habits known to contribute to illness. For example, one important area of research is in helping people stop smoking cigarettes, which has been linked to a host of medical problems. These therapists also work on methods to help people lose weight (Marston & Marston, 1980). Carrying around extra pounds, especially as people grow older, can contribute to coronary heart disease and hypertension. One way to help asthma patients is to teach them how to recognize better when they are having an attack. Many patients do not recognize their own symptoms and do not respond appropriately. But they can become more attuned to the symptoms and thereby better able to follow a treatment regimen (Creer, Renna, & Chai, 1982).

In recent years behavioral researchers have been exploring the clinical uses of **biofeedback** as a means of improving somatic functioning. Biofeedback provides people with prompt and exact information, otherwise unavailable, on heart rate, blood pressure, brain waves, skin temperature, and other bodily functions. The particular internal physiological process is detected and amplified by a sensitive electronic recording device. The person knows instantaneously, through an auditory or visual signal, the rate of the process, whether it is too high or too low or just right. Numerous studies have shown that most people, if given the task, for example, of raising their heart rates or lowering their blood pressure, can do so with the help of biofeedback (Elmore & Tursky, 1978; Shapiro, Tursky, & Schwartz, 1970). What is not yet clear is whether, through biofeedback, they can achieve results that are clinically significant. Biofeedback will be evaluated in greater depth in Chapter 19. Focus Box 8.5 presents an example of promising clinical research.

Biofeedback is often used in the treatment of psychophysiological disorders. It can provide accurate information on physiological processes that hopefully will allow the patient to gain better control of them.

FOCUS

8.5 • Migraine Headache and Biofeedback

When I am in a migraine aura (for some people the aura lasts fifteen minutes, for others several hours), I will drive through red lights, lose the house keys, spill whatever I am holding, lose the ability to focus my eyes or frame coherent sentences, and generally give the appearance of being on drugs, or drunk. The actual headache, when it comes, brings with it chills, sweating, nausea, a debility that seems to stretch the very limits of endurance. That no one dies of migraine seems to someone deep into an attack, an ambiguous blessing. (From Joan Didion, *The White Album*, pp. 170–171. Reprinted by permission of Wallace Literary Agency, Inc. Copyright © 1968, 79 by Joan Didion.

Migraine headaches are extremely debilitating headaches caused by sustained dilation of the extracranial arteries, the temporal artery in particular. An estimated 10 percent of the general population is afflicted with migraine headaches. Some people have these attacks as often as every few days, others only a few times in their lives. The headache pain itself is usually on one side, almost as though the head were divided in two by an impermeable wall. It has been said that only those actually afflicted with this most common of psychophysiological disorders can know how extreme is the suffering associated with migraine.

A distinction is usually made between classic migraine and common migraine. In classic migraine (as described in the passage above) the person has *prodromal symptoms*, that is, symptoms experienced before the onset of the headache itself. They take the form of tension, wakefulness, declining energy and drive, and sometimes visual disturbances that are seen first as a shimmering haze, then as zigzag lines. Almost universally, the headache in both types is initially a pulsing pain on one side of the head, coinciding with each heartbeat as the blood is pumped through the expanded extracranial arteries. The pain is caused by these dilated arteries triggering pain-sensitive nerve fibers in the scalp. As the headache progresses, the pain becomes steadier. The arteries thicken and rigidify, making stimulation of the extracranial nerve fibers constant rather than pulsing (Elmore, 1979). Recent evidence indicates that the scalp arteries of migraine victims are more sensitive to autonomic nervous stimulation than are those of normal people. Other evidence points to a general instability in vasomotor control, which appears to be the inherited diathesis that predisposes some people to reacting to stress with this debilitating disorder.

For many years there has been a controversy about the causes of the extracranial vascular dilation. As we have already noted, in classic migraine, visual disturbances are among the precursors to the headache itself. According to some researchers, these disturbances are caused by intense constriction, or narrowing, of the internal carotid artery and its branches, the cranial arteries that supply blood to the brain and the visual system. Somehow, the theorizing goes, this initial constriction of the internal cranial arteries produces the subsequent dilation of the external arteries, which is the immediate cause of the migraine headache itself.

There are two competing schools of thought regarding the best way to treat migraine: one concentrates on the intracranial vasoconstriction during the prodromal stage, and the other on the extracranial vasodilation of the headache phase. The first tries to dilate internal arteries by reducing sympathetic activity, the second to constrict external arteries by increasing sympathetic activity. Sympathetic activity can be reduced through such psychological techniques as deep-muscle relaxation training (Jacobson, 1929); autogenic training, a method promoting relaxation through suggestions of heaviness and warmth (Luthe & Schultz, 1969); and a westernized version of transcendental meditation (Benson, 1975). Of particular importance for our present discussion are studies that employ biofeedback to increase hand temperature as a means of shifting blood supply to the periphery and away from the brain. Clinical reports of research conducted originally at the Menninger Clinic in Topeka, Kansas (Sargent, Green, & Walters, 1972, 1973) claimed marked improvement in a number of migraine patients who were taught to warm their hands through biofeedback training and then to initiate hand warming on their own at the slightest warning that a headache was coming on. Unfortunately, these studies were flawed by serious methodological problems. Nothing indicated that patients actually learned to warm their hands, and the judgments of improvement were unsystematic and impressionistic (Elmore, 1979). The Menninger reports, however, did stimulate a series of more rigorous clinical studies, some of which showed that *cooling* of the hands produced equally significant reductions in migraine (e.g., Gauthier, Bois, Allaire, & Drollet, 1981). Some researchers have concluded that it is the reduction in general sympathetic autonomic arousal that is the operative factor and that this can be brought about by a variety of techniques, including hypnosis and muscle relaxation (Blanchard et al., 1978).

The second treatment for migraine focuses on increasing sympathetic activity in order to halt extracranial artery dilation. Through biofeedback the individual is trained to constrict the arteries at the site of the actual migraine headache. Other researchers have demonstrated that patients find relief from migraine by learning to lower extracranial artery pulse via biofeedback (e.g., Friar & Beatty, 1976).

From an examination of the migraine treatment literature. Elmore and Tursky (1981) concluded that a study was needed to compare the two competing approaches to treatment. They also wanted to demonstrate by careful physiological measurement that whatever response was asserted to have been acquired via biofeedback was in fact acquired, and to determine whether therapy gains were maintained by following up patients for a period of time after their training.

Elmore and Tursky divided a sample of twenty-three adults suffering from migraine into two groups: one received eight sessions of biofeedback training to raise hand temperature, and the other eight sessions of biofeedback training to lower temporal pulse. Both groups had a ninth session without feedback to test whether members could perform the learned response on their own. To achieve the respective goals of their groups, raising hand temperature or lowering temporal pulse, subjects were to generate images of warmth or coolness, or to adopt any technique, other than tensing the muscles, that seemed to work for them. They were also encouraged to practice these strategies every day for about fifteen minutes and at the slightest warning that a headache was about to begin. For a month before and following treatment all subjects recorded the occurrence and intensity of headaches in a specially designed pain and discomfort diary. If the people lowering temporal pulse did better than the hand-warming people, it could be concluded that migraine should be treated by increasing sympathetic nervous system activity. To relieve migraine headaches people need merely constrict the extracranial arteries. Superiority of hand warming, in contrast, would indicate that vasodilation is necessary earlier on in order to prevent the intracranial vasoconstriction believed by the Menninger group to trigger the later extracranial vasodilation.

Physiological measurements taken during the biofeedback training showed that members of each group did in fact learn the skill they were being taught. Moreover, the subjects lowering temporal pulse showed a pattern of general sympathetic nervous system activation and the hand-warming group showed deactivation of this system, demonstrating that the respective training procedures had the intended effects on the autonomic nervous system. Finally, the all-important treatment results: the people lowering temporal pulse achieved significantly more improvement during the one-month posttreatment evaluation than did the hand-warming subjects. Specifically, they reported fewer than half the headaches suffered before treatment, ingested significantly less headache medication, and tended to rate as less painful whatever headaches they had. In contrast, members of the hand-warming group rated their posttreatment headaches as significantly more painful and somewhat longer lasting than those suffered before treatment.

The results, then, pose a serious challenge to the view that migraine is caused by sympathetic overarousal and that, generally speaking, people with this disorder should try to reduce their sympathetic nervous activity through relaxation training or tension-reducing drugs. Rather, treatment should be aimed more directly at constriction of the extracranial arteries. Nonetheless, other findings continue to lend support to the original Menninger idea about the benefits of biofeedback-induced hand warming to reduce vasoconstriction (Blanchard et al., 1982). In sum, consensus on appropriate therapy for migraines still requires further research.

Treating Hypertension

Because some antihypertensive drugs have undesirable side effects, such as drowsiness, lightheadedness, and erectile difficulties for men, and because medical research has suggested for some time that long-term use of certain drugs for mild hypertension may have harmful effects (Medical Research Council, 1981), many investigations have been undertaken on nonpharmacological treatments for borderline essential hypertension. Efforts have been directed at weight reduction, restriction of salt intake, aerobic exercise, and reduction in alcohol consumption. Each of these medical goals involves obvious behavioral change components, and success in achieving these goals has been mixed (Foreyt, 1990).

Another psychological approach has been to teach hypertensive individuals to lower sympathetic nervous system arousal, primarily via training in muscle relaxation, occasionally supplemented by biofeedback (Benson, Beary, & Carl, 1974; Blanchard et al., 1986). Results here have also been mixed (Kaufmann et al., 1988), and it is unclear how enduring the effects of relaxation treatment are (Patel et al., 1985). The success of this approach probably depends ultimately on whether the person maintains the acquired skill to relax, and that in turn depends on whether the person remains motivated to practice that skill.

DeQuattro and Davison (Lee et al., 1987) found that intensive relaxation, conducted in weekly sessions over two months and using at-home practice with audiotaped instructions, significantly reduced blood pressure in borderline hypertensive people (7 mm Hg systolic and 10 mm Hg diastolic), more so than did a control condition that included state-of-the-art medical advice and instructions concerning diet, weight loss, and other known risk factors. (It should be noted that the relaxation group also received the same medical information given to the control subjects.) Furthermore, these effects were stronger among those hypertensive subjects previously assessed to have high sympathetic arousal than among those with lower arousal levels. This result supports the hypothesis of Esler et al. (1977) that there is a subset of hypertensive individuals with relatively high resting levels of sympathetic arousal who may be especially well suited for sympathetic-dampening therapies such as relaxation.

This finding is one of the few in the psychotherapy or behavioral medicine literature that suggests a fit between a type of problem and a type of intervention. For example, hypertensive individuals with low levels of sympathetic nervous system arousal may benefit more from a cognitive therapy approach—their hypertension may be sustained by the thoughts they carry in their heads more than by what their sympathetic nervous system is doing. (Of course, the logical alternative exists that sympathetic arousal itself might be in part sustained by negative cognitive patterns and that cognitive interventions are one way to reduce this arousal and hence the consequent hypertension.)

Evidence suggesting the importance of cognitive change as well as the role of anger was reported by Davison, Williams et al. (1991) from the same data set as that used by Lee et al. These borderline hypertensive patients also achieved significant reductions in anger as expressed in their articulated thoughts. Interestingly, the reduction in angry thinking was positively correlated with decreased blood pressure: the less angry their articulated thoughts became, the lower their blood pressure became, a finding that is consistent with research linking anger with hypertension.

For several years the National Heart, Lung, and Blood Institute sponsored a large-scale multicenter study of different nonpharmacological ways of *preventing* hypertension in healthy women and men whose diastolic blood pressure was between 80 and 89 mm Hg, a range generally referred to as high normal (The Trials of Hypertension Prevention Collaborative Research Group, 1992). Without some kind of intervention, many such people gradually move into the borderline range (90 to 105 diastolic blood pressure), at which point treatment is strongly recommended. If ways could be found of reducing the number of people who develop borderline hypertension, there would be great savings in costs and in health over the long haul. The principal methods compared were weight reduction, cutback in sodium intake, stress management, and a usual care control group. The stress management condition is described briefly as "teaching four methods of relaxation (slow breathing, progressive muscle relaxation, mental imagery, and stretching), plus techniques to manage stress perceptions, reactions, and situations" (p. 1215). We will have more to say about the stress management condition in a moment.

Outcomes were evaluated at the end of the six-month treatment period as well as at follow-ups of twelve and eighteen months. Two basic kinds of outcome data were collected. The ultimate focus, of course, was on blood pressure. But also important was whether the behavioral changes aimed at via the three active groups were achieved. Specifically, did the weight reduction people lose weight? did the low sodium group reduce salt intake? and did the stress management group reduce their stress?

Looking at the latter results first, the sodium- and weight-reduction groups did achieve their goals of reducing salt usage and weight. But the stress management condition did not achieve its goals. First, as measured by a frequently used hassles questionnaire, this group got *worse* over time, reporting significantly more hassles at the eighteen-month follow-up than when treatment began. Furthermore, whereas the sodium- and weight-reduction groups improved on a psychological scale of general well-being, the stress management group did not. These results were mirrored in blood pressure improvements, that is, significant blood pressure drops were observed in the sodium- and weight-reduction groups but not in the stress management group.

The authors of this study concluded that people who are not yet hypertensive might be able to avoid entering the borderline range by losing weight and decreasing salt intake. They also dismissed, without good reason in our opinion, the role that stress management might have in preventing hypertension. In fact, nothing can be concluded about the latter because there is a serious flaw in the study. To determine what effect reducing stress might have on preventing the development of hypertension, one must first measurably reduce stress. In this study, that was not done. For what may be a variety of factors—including weak design or implementation of the stress management condition; poor compliance by patients to the complex cognitive and behavioral instructions; insensitive measures of outcome—the stress management techniques used by these researchers did not reduce stress. As we will see, stress can be reduced through effective stress management techniques. Because the study just discussed did not demonstrate stress reduction, it cannot provide valid information on the possible effectiveness of stress management techniques in preventing hypertension.

Changing Type A Behavior

Researchers in behavioral medicine also address the challenge of altering the driven, overcompetitive patterns of the Type A individual, who has been shown to be at higher risk for heart disease. Within the past fifteen years or so, about twenty studies have been conducted on how to lessen or change Type A behavior (Nunes, Frank & Kornfeld, 1987). Because most of them have provided a narrow treatment of short duration, for example, a few sessions of relaxation training, it is not surprising that their results have been modest (Price, 1982). A significant exception is the Recurrent Coronary Prevention Project (Friedman et al., 1982), funded by the National Heart, Lung, and Blood Institute.

The overall purpose of this project was to see whether the Type A behavior of men who had suffered a heart attack could be changed in the direction of Type B and whether fewer of these patients than those given only cardiological counseling would then have a second heart attack. The treatment expected to improve subjects the most attempted to alter their Type A behavior as well as the environmental, cognitive, and physiological factors believed to contribute to their personalities. Thus subjects practiced talking more slowly and listening to others more closely instead of interrupting them and were also encouraged to reduce excessive activities and demands and to relax more. They watched less television (an environmental switch), and they attempted to alter their silent, internal self-talk by believing that events are not necessarily direct challenges to them and by considering that Type A behavior may not be essential to success, which is a cognitive (actually philosophical) change. They also complied with their physicians' drug and diet prescriptions to improve their physiological states.

Results were encouraging: Type A behavior can be measurably changed. Moreover, after three years of treatment, for men who had received Type A counseling the risk of a second heart attack was 7.2 percent annually, compared with 13.2 percent for Type A men who received only cardiological counseling (Friedman & Ulmer, 1984; Friedman et al., 1984; Powell et al., 1984; Thoresen et al., 1985). Interestingly, there are indications that reductions in hostility may have been particularly important, consistent with its increasing importance in Type A research and in psychophysiological disorders generally (Haaga, 1987b).

There are, however, many obstacles to reducing Type A patterns in our culture. Price (1982) enumerates two. First, in an industrialized and competitive society such as ours, Type A behavior pays off, at least in the short run, in increased productivity and achievement, even though personal happiness may be sacrificed. Second, being a Type A person is in many ways a cultural norm in the United States and in other countries as well. Often it takes a heart attack to force a Type A person even to consider giving up the aggressive, individualistic struggle to gain as many material rewards as possible in the shortest amount of time and instead to treasure leisure time and to value people, including the self, for their intrinsic worth rather than for their achievements and status.

Some work by Matthews (e.g., 1978) assessed

8.6 • Coping with Cancer

There is a growing body of evidence that various psychosocial interventions can help people cope with cancer (Focus Box 15.4 describes such work with children). Groups conducted along cognitive-behavioral lines (Stolbach et al., 1988; Telch & Telch, 1986) demonstrate positive effects in alleviating anxiety and depression as well as fostering a fighting spirit, a nonpassive attitude that some research suggests may even enhance the capacity to survive cancer (Greer, Morris, & Pettigale, 1979).

A particularly noteworthy research program at Stanford University School of Medicine under the direction of psychiatrist David Spiegel confirms the utility of psychosocial interventions in improving the quality of life and even in extending the survival time of patients with terminal cancer. Supportive weekly group therapy—where patients offered understanding and comfort to each other, encouraged each other to live life as fully as possible in the face of death, openly discussed death and dying, and learned self-hypnosis techniques to control pain—reduced fatigue, anxiety, and depression in metastatic breast cancer patients (Spiegel, Bloom, & Yalom, 1981). Even more impressive are ten-year follow-up findings by the Spiegel group that this one-year supportive group intervention actually prolonged survival time; indeed, compared with control group patients, the group therapy patients lived twice as long (Spiegel et al., 1989; Spiegel, 1990).*

Speculating about these survival findings—which were not expected and were not a discussion topic for the group therapy—Spiegel and his associates suggested that perhaps the therapy helped patients better comply with medical treat-

*When surprising, even startling, findings are published in professional journals, the editor sometimes includes an accompanying comment. This was done with the Spiegel et al. (1989) report. Mindful that the results might be regarded as quite unorthodox, the editor took pains to comment favorably on the methodology and statistical analyses and to suggest that readers adopt an open-minded attitude toward the report, indicating that "the measures described by Spiegel et al. are at least life-enhancing, in stark contrast to the life impoverishment suffered by many terminally ill patients subjected to the vile diets, costly placebos, and exhausting introspections recommended by the more lunatic fringe among alternative practitioners. Other groups should pursue this intellectually honest approach to the psychosocial management of cancer" (Editorial, *The Lancet*, October 14, 1989).

Type A behavior in children and the ways in which young people learn the values and behavior of the Type A personality. She found, for example, that mothers of Type A boys continually up the ante for reinforcement. Ever-higher goals are set for the same degree of reward from the mother. The mass media and most of our schools exhort children to "Be number one," "Don't make mistakes," "Don't waste time," "Increase your production," "Upward and onward." It seems likely that developmental psychologists will find more and more evidence that Type A behavior is taught to youngsters from early childhood on and may therefore be extremely difficult to change.

Thus shifting from Type A behavior in an effort to prevent or at least reduce the incidence of coronary heart disease challenges the very essence of our advanced and advancing society. A perhaps unintended consequence of the burgeoning literature and research on the Type A personality may well be a searing examination of some of the most basic values on which modern Western civilization is built. Surely, however, psychology can advocate that different values be presented in schools and in the mass media. And the Recurrent Coronary Prevention Project, in which patients were encouraged to place less emphasis on achievement and rushing and more on pausing to smell the flowers, enjoying the moment, living life in the slow rather than in the fast lane, indicates that through their own efforts individuals can alter their Type A personalities and in the process make themselves happier as well as healthier. Of course these philosophical speculations will have to be revised if hostility, rather than excessive achievement and time-urgency, turns out to be the culprit in the contribution of Type A behavior to risk for cardiac disease.

Stress Management

In recent years the field of stress management, a set of varying techniques for reducing stress, has developed as part of the increased emphasis on stress and health that we discussed earlier. (We saw an ineffectual application of stress management in the ment or that it improved their appetite and diet by enhancing their mood. Ability to control pain might also have helped them be more physically active. And, consistent with research reviewed earlier on how stress affects the immune system, the therapy might have improved immune function by controlling stress, with social support a key factor (House, Landis, & Umberson, 1988; Levy et al., 1990).

Behavioral medicine research has also addressed preventive issues in cancer (in addition to the cigarette smoking research described in Chapter 11). A hurdle that must be overcome if women are to perform breast self-examination (BSE) is that examination significantly raises the probability of an aversive consequence, that is, finding a lump. Of course, logically, it is better to take this risk than not, but the fact is that the fear of learning something unpleasant is a major deterrent to doing the exam (Mahoney, 1977). In an effort to develop ways to help women do the BSE regularly, Meyerowitz and Chaiken (1987) compared a pamphlet that contained persuasive arguments to conduct BSE while emphasizing the negative consequences of not performing BSE with one emphasizing the positive consequences of performing BSE. Both pamphlets contained factual information about breast cancer and instructions about how to do BSE. Meyerowitz and Chaiken provided these examples. Words in parentheses were included in the positive condition, those in brackets in the negative:

> By [not] doing BSE now, you (can)[will not] learn what your normal healthy breasts feel like so that you will be (better)[ill] prepared to notice any small, abnormal changes that might occur as you get older.
>
> Research shows that women who do [not do] BSE have (an increased)[a decreased] chance of finding a tumor in the early, more treatable stage of the disease. (p. 504)

Compared with those receiving the positively framed information, the college-aged subjects in the negative group were no more likely right after reading the pamphlet to hold positive attitudes toward doing BSE *but*, four months later, were more likely to have engaged in such examination. This effect might be due to the fact that noncompliance with the very sensible advice to conduct BSE is maintained by an ignorance is bliss attitude; by making the possible negative consequences of not doing BSE more salient, doing the exam becomes more acceptable. This finding is particularly important because most pamphlets for women doing BSE stress the positive rather than the negative.

hypertension prevention project described on page 218.) In industry, in government, in universities, in the military, and among people generally, we read of individuals participating in workshops on **stress management**, even when they do not have diagnosable problems. Moreover, the increasing recognition of the role of stress in a variety of medical illnesses, including diseases affected by immune system dysfunction, has added impetus to stress management as a strategy for reducing stress-related deficits in the functioning of the immune system (Zakowski, Hall, & Baum, 1992; see also our discussion on page 384 on HIV infection).

There are several approaches under the rubric of stress management, and more than one are typically followed in any given instance (Davison & Thompson, 1988; Lehrer & Woolfolk, 1993).

Individual Approaches

Arousal Reduction In arousal reduction the person is trained in muscle relaxation, sometimes assisted by biofeedback. Although the evidence is uncertain for the need to use the complex instrumentation required for proper biofeedback of minute levels of muscle tension or certain patterns of electroencephalographic activity, there is confirmation that teaching people to relax deeply and to apply these skills to real-life stressors can be helpful in lowering their stress levels. There is also some preliminary evidence that immune function can be improved by relaxation training (Jasnoski & Kugler, 1987; Kiecolt-Glaser et al., 1985), although enduring benefits are doubtful unless relaxation is practiced regularly over the long haul (Davison & Thompson, 1988; Goldfried & Davison, 1976; Zakowski et al., 1992).

Cognitive Restructuring Included under cognitive restructuring is the work of Ellis (1962) and Beck (1976), already briefly described in Chapters 2 (page 51) and 6 (page 144) and described more fully in Chapters 9 (page 244) and 19 (page 565). The focus here is on altering people's belief systems and improving the clarity of their logical interpretations of experience on the assumption that our intellectual capacities can affect how we feel and behave. This includes what can simply be called the provision of information to reduce uncertainty and enhance people's sense of control, a theme from Chapter 6. Promising findings have been reported for various stress-related problems, including genital herpes lesions (McLarnon & Kaloupek, 1988). In a general sense, cognitive approaches can be seen as focusing on the appraisal processes that Lazarus researched for many years as a principal factor in how people react to environmental stressors (e.g., Lazarus, 1966; Folkman & Lazarus, 1984).

Behavioral Skills Training Because it is natural to feel overwhelmed if one lacks the skills to execute a challenging task, stress management often includes instruction and practice in necessary skills as well as in general issues such as time management and effective prioritizing. As an example of the complex interplay among behavior, emotion, and cognition, social-skills training can enhance a person's sense of self-efficacy (Bandura, 1986) by improving control over environmental stressors (Rodin, 1986).

Environmental Change Approaches

What can be regarded as an environmental approach draws on research mentioned earlier in this chapter (page 198) on the positive role that social support has on health. If, in fact, social support helps keep people healthy or helps them cope with illnesses, then it is reasonable to assume that enhancing such support can contribute to better functioning (see Focus Box 8.6 for a closer look at the role of social support with cancer patients).

The work of *community psychologists* is also relevant. Whereas the individual strategies described aim at helping the individual deal with a particular environment, one can also take the position that sometimes the environment is the problem and that change is best directed at altering it. (As we will see in Chapter 20, this approach highlights the political and ethical dimensions of any behavior-change enterprise.) For example, a work environment could be redesigned with partitions to provide some privacy, rather than requiring clerical workers to sit together in a large open area.

Our review of several therapeutic approaches to dealing with psychophysiological disorders—many of which can be subsumed under the rubric of behavioral medicine—illustrates the complex relationships between the soma and the psyche, the body and the mind. We come full circle to how we began this chapter, namely, an appreciation of the inseparability of bodily and mental processes and how these two ways of viewing the human organism can pose as many problems for people as they offer means of relieving suffering and promoting well-being.

SUMMARY

Psychophysiological disorders are physical diseases produced, in part, by psychological factors, primarily stress. Such disorders usually affect organs innervated by the autonomic nervous system, such as those of the respiratory, cardiovascular, gastrointestinal, and endocrine systems. Research has questioned how psychological stress produces a particular psychophysiological disorder. Some workers have proposed that the answer lies in the specifics of the stressor or psychological characteristics of the person. Theories and some evidence link inhibition of aggression to hypertension, and the Type A personality to heart attacks. Other theories propose that stress must interact with a biological diathesis: for hypertension, a tendency to respond to stress with increases in blood pressure; for heart attacks, a sympathetic nervous system that releases too much norepinephrine; and for asthma, a respiratory system that overresponds to an allergen or has been weakened by prior infection. Although we have spoken of psychological stress affecting the body, it must be remembered that the *mind* and the *body* are best viewed as two different ways of talking about the same organism.

Psychophysiological disorders no longer appear in the DSM. Instead, the diagnostician can make a diagnosis of psychological factors affecting a medical condition and then note the condition on axis III. This change reflects the growing realization that life stress is relevant to all disease, not just those that were previously considered psychophysiological disorders. For example, research shows that life stress is related to episodes of respiratory infection. Important issues in current work on life stress and health include moderators of the relationship (e.g., social support) and specifying the physiological mechanisms (e.g., the immune system) through which stress can exert its effects.

Because psychophysiological disorders represent true physical dysfunctions, medications are usually called for. The general aim of psychotherapies for these disorders is to reduce anxiety or anger. Behavioral medicine, a relatively new field of specialization in behavior therapy, tries to find psychological interventions that can improve the patient's physiological state. It has developed ways of helping people relax, smoke less, eat fewer fatty foods, and, using biofeedback, gain control over various autonomic functions, such as heart rate and blood pressure. One study has developed methods by which Type A victims of heart attacks can abandon their angry, driving ways.

The emergent field of stress management helps people without diagnosable problems avail themselves of techniques that allow them cope with the inevitable stress of everyday life and thereby ameliorate the toll that stress can take on the body.

KEY TERMS

psychophysiological disorders
psychosomatic disorders
dualism
psychological factors affecting a medical condition
behavioral medicine
health psychology
general adaptation syndrome (GAS)
stressor
stress
structural social support
functional social support
somatic-weakness theory
specific-reaction theory
anger-in theory
cardiovascular disorder
essential hypertension
coronary heart disease (CHD)
angina pectoris
myocardial infarction
Type A behavior pattern
asthma
biofeedback
migraine headaches
stress management

c h a p t e r n i n e

Mood Disorders

Mrs. M. was a thirty-eight-year-old factory worker who had been deeply depressed for about two months when she came to see a psychologist. The mother of four children, she had returned to work three years ago when the worsening economy made it impossible for her family to get by on just her husband's earnings. But seven months earlier she was laid off, and the family's financial situation deteriorated. Ever-present worries about money led to an increase in arguments with her spouse, not only about their finances but also about the children. She began to have difficulty sleeping and lost her appetite, resulting in weight loss. She had little energy and lost interest in activities that normally had been enjoyable to her. Even though she sat for hours in front of the television, she couldn't get interested in any of the shows that were previously her favorites, and she didn't even pay attention most of the time. Household chores became impossible, and her husband began to complain about this, leading to further arguments. Finally, realizing that something serious had happened to his wife, the husband cajoled her into making a first appointment with a psychologist.

Rod Steiger has suffered from episodes of depression and as a result has taken an active role in trying to gain increased public attention for this serious disorder.

Melancholia, a term derived from the Greek words *melan*, meaning "black," and *choler*, meaning bile, and *mania*, derived from the Greek word *mainesthai*, "to be mad," were two of the three types of mental disorder recognized by Hippocrates in the fourth century B.C. By the second century A.D. the physician Aretaeus of Cappadocia had suggested a relationship between melancholia and the apparently opposite emotional state of mania. In the late nineteenth century, as we have seen, the famous German psychiatrist Emil Kraepelin listed two major types of psychoses. One, schizophrenia, will be discussed in Chapter 14. The other, manic-depressive illness, is one of the principal **mood disorders**—disorders in which there are disabling disturbances in emotion—discussed in this chapter.

General Characteristics of Depression and Mania

Depression is an emotional state marked by great sadness and apprehension, feelings of worthlessness and guilt, withdrawal from others, loss of sleep, appetite, and sexual desire, or loss of interest and pleasure in usual activities. Just as most of us experience occasional anxiety, so, too, we will probably have more than an ample amount of sadness during the course of our lives, although perhaps not to a degree or with a frequency that warrants the diagnosis of depression. Often depression is associated with other psychological problems and with medical conditions. The man who has trouble maintaining his erection during intercourse can become depressed about his sex life. The woman who has had a hysterectomy may suffer depression over what she believes to be a loss of her femininity. Agoraphobics may become despondent because of their inability to venture out of their homes. Alcoholics may be depressed by their inability to control their drinking and by the social and employment problems that their drinking has provoked. In these and many other instances depression is best viewed as secondary to another condition. Our discussion of depression in this chapter focuses on people for whom this mood disorder is the *primary* problem.

The following eloquent account is from a person suffering from profound depression. Clearly, anxiety also plays a part in deepening the despair.

> I was seized with an unspeakable physical weariness. There was a tired feeling in the muscles unlike anything I had ever experienced. A peculiar sensation appeared to travel up my spine to my brain. I had an indescribable nervous feeling. My nerves seemed like live wires charged with electricity. My nights were sleepless. I lay with dry, staring eyes gazing into space. I had a fear that some terrible calamity was about to happen. I grew afraid to be left alone. The most trivial duty became a formidable task. Finally mental and physical exercises became impossible; the tired muscles refused to respond, my "thinking apparatus" refused to work, ambition was gone. My general feeling might be summed up in the familiar saying "What's the use?" I had tried so hard to make something of myself, but the struggle seemed useless. Life seemed utterly futile. (Reid, 1910, pp. 612–613)

Paying attention is an exhausting effort for the depressed. They cannot take in what they read and what other people say to them. Conversation is also a chore, for many prefer to sit alone and remain silent. They speak slowly, after long pauses, using few words and a low, monotonous voice. Others are agitated and cannot sit still. They pace, wring their hands, sighing and moaning all the while or complaining. When depressed individuals are confronted with a problem, no ideas for its solution occur to them. Every moment has a great heaviness, and their heads fill and reverberate with self-recriminations. Depressed people may also neglect personal hygiene and appearance and make numerous hypochondriacal complaints of aches and pains that apparently have no physical basis. Utterly dejected and completely without hope and initiative, they may be apprehensive, anxious, and despondent much of the time.

There is some variation in the symptoms and signs of depression across the life span. As we discuss in Chapters 15 and 17, depression in children sometimes results in their being overly active and aggressive; in adolescents, it is sometimes manifested by negativism, antisocial behavior, and a feeling of being misunderstood; and in older adults, depression is often characterized by distractibility and memory loss. Furthermore, an individual seldom shows all the aspects of depression: the diagnosis is typically made if at least a few signs are evident, particularly a *mood* of profound sadness that is out of proportion to the person's life situation and a loss of interest and pleasure in previously enjoyable activities. Fortunately, most depression, although recurrent, tends to dissipate with time. But an average untreated episode may stretch on for six to eight months or even longer. When depression becomes chronic, the patient does not always snap back to an earlier level of functioning between bouts.

Mania is an emotional state of intense but unfounded elation evidenced in hyperactivity, talkativeness, flight of ideas, distractibility, impractical grandiose plans, and spurts of purposeless activity. Some people who suffer from episodic periods of depression also at times suddenly become manic. Although there are clinical reports of individuals who experience mania but not depression, such a condition is apparently quite rare.

The manic stream of remarks is loud and incessant, full of puns, jokes, plays on words, rhyming, and interjections about nearby objects and happenings that have attracted the speaker's attention. This speech is very difficult to interrupt and reveals the manic's so-called flight of ideas. Although small bits of talk are coherent, the individual shifts rapidly from topic to topic. The manic need for activity may cause the individual to be annoyingly sociable and intrusive, constantly and sometimes purposelessly busy, and, unfortunately, oblivious to the obvious pitfalls of his or her endeavors. Any attempt to curb this momentum can bring quick anger and even rage. Mania usually comes on suddenly, over the period of a day or two. Untreated episodes may last from a few days to several months.

The following description of a case of mania comes from our files. The irritability that is often part of this state was not found in this patient.

Mr. W., a thirty-two-year-old postal worker, had been married for eight years. He and his wife lived comfortably and happily in a middle-class neighborhood with their two children. In retrospect there appeared to be no warning for what was to happen. On February the twelfth Mr. W. let his wife know that he was bursting with energy and ideas, that his job as a mail carrier was unfulfilling, and that he was just wasting his talent. That night he slept little, spending most of the time at a desk, writing furiously. The next morning he left for work at the usual time but returned home at eleven A.M., his car filled to overflowing with aquariums and other equipment for tropical fish. He had quit his job and than withdrawn all the money from the family's savings account. The money had been spent on tropical fish equipment. Mr. W. reported that the previous night he had worked out a way to modify existing equipment so that fish "won't die anymore. We'll be millionaires." After unloading the paraphernalia, Mr. W. set off to canvass the neighborhood for possible buyers, going door-to-door and talking to anyone who would listen.

The following bit of conversation from the period after Mr. W. entered treatment indicates his incorrigible optimism and provocativeness.

Therapist: Well, you seem pretty happy today.
Client: Happy! Happy! You certainly are a master of understatement, you rogue! (Shouting, literally jumping out of his seat.) Why I'm ecstatic. I'm leaving for the West Coast today, on my daughter's bicycle. Only 3100 miles. That's nothing, you know. I could probably walk, but I want to get there by next week. And along the way I plan to contact a lot of people about investing in my fish equipment. I'll get to know more people that way—you know, Doc, "know" in the biblical sense (leering at the therapist seductively). Oh, God, how good it feels. It's almost like a nonstop orgasm.

Formal Diagnostic Listings

Two major mood disorders are listed in DSM-IV, major depression and bipolar disorder. The symptoms of **major depression**, sometimes also referred to as **unipolar depression**, are profoundly sad mood and disturbances of appetite, weight, sleep, and activity level (becoming either lethargic or agitated).

There is general agreement on the most common signs and symptoms of depression. The formal DSM-IV diagnosis of a major depressive episode requires the presence of five of these symptoms for at least two weeks. Either depressed mood or loss of interest and pleasure must be one of the five symptoms.

1. Sad, depressed mood.
2. Loss of interest and pleasure in usual activities.
3. Difficulties in sleeping (insomnia); not falling asleep initially, not returning to sleep after awakening in the middle of the night, and early morning awakenings; or, in some patients, a desire to sleep a great deal of the time.
4. Shift in activity level, becoming either lethargic (psychomotor retardation) or agitated.
5. Poor appetite and weight loss, or increased appetite and weight gain.
6. Loss of energy, great fatigue.
7. Negative self-concept; self-reproach and self-blame; feelings of worthlessness and guilt.
8. Complaints or evidence of difficulty in concentrating, such as slowed thinking and indecisiveness.
9. Recurrent thoughts of death or suicide.

Major depression is one of the most widespread of the disorders considered in this book, with a lifetime prevalence rate of between 4 and 5 percent (Weissman et al., 1988). The average age of onset is between forty and fifty, and it is more common in women than in men. It is also more frequent among members of the lower socioeconomic classes (Hirschfeld & Cross, 1982). Major depression tends to be a recurrent disorder.

The critical symptoms of **bipolar disorder** are the elated or irritable mood, talkativeness, and hyperactivity of mania, as well as episodes of depression. These symptoms must be severe enough to cause serious impairment in social or occupational functioning or to require hospitalization. Of the criteria that follow, a formal diagnosis of a manic episode requires the presence of elevated or irritable mood plus three additional symptoms (four if the mood is irritable).

1. Increase in activity level—at work, socially, or sexually.
2. Unusual talkativeness, rapid speech.
3. Flight of ideas or subjective impression that thoughts are racing.
4. Less than the usual amount of sleep needed.

Patty Duke has experienced episodes of both mania and depression and therefore would be regarded as having bipolar disorder.

5. Inflated self-esteem; belief that one has special talents, powers, and abilities.
6. Distractibility; attention easily diverted.
7. Excessive involvement in activities that are likely to have undesirable consequences, such as reckless spending.

Bipolar disorder occurs less often than major depression, with a prevalence rate of about 1 percent of the population (Myers et al., 1984). The average age of onset is thirty, and it occurs equally often in men and women. Like major depression, bipolar disorder tends to recur; over 50 percent of cases have four or more episodes. Notably, some clinicians do not regard euphoria as a core symptom of mania and report that irritable mood and even depressive features are more common (e.g., Goodwin & Jamison, 1990). Interestingly, people who suffer only manic episodes are diagnosed as having bipolar disorder, because they are similar to those with episodes of both mania and depression on many other variables (e.g., family history, response to treatment).

Validity of the Unipolar–Bipolar Disorder Distinction

Only a few decades ago, distinctions were not typically made among the various mood disorders. Since then it has become clear that an important distinction can be drawn between bipolar and unipolar disorders (see Table 9.1). The disorders differ on many variables in addition to the presence or absence of manic episodes. For example, when people with bipolar disorder are depressed, they typically sleep more than usual and are lethargic, whereas people with unipolar depression have insomnia and are agitated. Also, as already mentioned, the age of onset of unipolar depression is usually later than that of bipolar disorder. More relatives of individuals with bipolar disorder have mood disorders than do relatives of those with unipolar depression. Lithium carbonate (see page 248) is more therapeutic for bipolar patients who are depressed than it is for patients with unipolar depression. All these differences bolster the validity of the bipolar–unipolar distinction (Depue & Monroe, 1978).

Although much of the evidence favors thinking about bipolar and unipolar disorders as distinct, the case is still not airtight. The fly in the ointment comes from research on genetic factors in the two disorders. Relatives of people with unipolar depression are at increased risk for unipolar disorder, whereas relatives of people with bipolar disorder are at increased risk for both unipolar and bipolar disorder, with a higher risk for unipolar disorder. These data can foster the argument that unipolar and bipolar disorder are not distinct entities but rather represent different levels of severity of the same disorder, with bipolar disorder the more severe variant (Faraone, Kremen, & Tsuang, 1990). Nonetheless, since most of the literature on the causes of mood disorders treats the two as distinct, we will discuss bipolar and unipolar disorders separately.

Heterogeneity within the Categories

A problem remaining in the classification of mood disorders is their great heterogeneity. Some bipolar patients suffer the full range of symptoms of both mania and depression almost simultaneously or alternating rapidly every few days. Other patients have only the symptoms of either mania or depression during a clinical episode. So-called bipolar II patients have episodes of major depression accompanied by **hypomania**, a change in behavior and mood that is not as extreme as mania.

Depressed patients are diagnosed as psychotic if

Table 9.1 • Differences between Unipolar and Bipolar Depression

Variable	*Unipolar*	*Bipolar*
Motor activity	Typically agitated	Typically retarded when depressed
Sleep	Difficulty sleeping	Sleeps more than usual when depressed
Age of onset	Late thirties to early forties	Thirty
Family history	First-degree relatives at high risk for unipolar depression	First-degree relatives at high risk for both unipolar and bipolar depression
Gender	Much more frequent among women	About equal in each gender
Biological treatment	Some response to lithium but better to tricyclics	Best response to lithium

Source: After Depue and Monroe, 1978.

they are subject to delusions and hallucinations. The presence of delusions appears to be a useful distinction among unipolar depressives (Nelson & Bowers, 1978; Glassman & Roose, 1981; Johnson, Horvath, & Weissman, 1991): depressed patients with delusions do not generally respond well to the usual drug therapies for depression, but they do respond favorably to these drugs when they are combined with the drugs commonly used to treat other psychotic disorders, such as schizophrenia.

According to DSM-IV, some episodes of depression may fit a melancholic subtype. They find no pleasure in any activity and are unable to feel better even temporarily when something good happens. Their depressed mood is worse in the morning. They awaken about two hours too early, lose appetite and weight, and are either lethargic or extremely agitated. Furthermore, they had no personality disturbance prior to their first episode of depression and respond well to biological therapies. The validity of the distinction between depressions with or without melancholia has not been well established (Zimmerman et al., 1986), although a recent study did find a relationship between it and poor outcome (Duggan et al., 1991).

Finally, DSM-IV states that both bipolar and unipolar disorders can be subdiagnosed as *seasonal* if there is a regular relationship between an episode and a particular time of the year. Most research on the concept of seasonal mood disorder has been done on patients who experienced depression in the winter and mania in the spring or summer (e.g., Rosenthal et al., 1986); the most prevalent explanation is that the mood disorders were linked to changes in the length of daylight hours. Indeed, therapy for these winter depressions involves exposing the patients to bright, white light (Rosenthal et al., 1985; Blehar & Rosenthal, 1989).

Seasonal depression is one of the subtypes of major depressive disorder. This woman is demonstrating light therapy which is an effective treatment for patients whose seasonal depression occurs during the winter.

Chronic Mood Disorders

DSM-IV lists two long-lasting, or chronic, disorders in which mood disturbances are predominant. Although the symptoms of individuals with either of these disorders must have been evident for at least two years, they are not severe enough to warrant a diagnosis of major depressive or manic episode. In **cyclothymic disorder**, the person has frequent periods of depressed mood and hypomania. These periods may be mixed with, may alternate with, or may be separated by periods of normal mood lasting as long as two months. People with cyclothymic disorder have paired sets of symptoms in their periods of depression and hypomania. During depression they feel inadequate: during hypomania their self-esteem is inflated. They withdraw from people, then seek them out in an uninhibited fashion. They sleep too much and then too little. Depressed cyclothymic patients have trouble concentrating and their productivity decreases; but during hypomania their thinking becomes sharp and creative and their productivity increases. Patients with cyclothymia may also experience full-blown episodes of mania and depression.

The person with **dysthymic disorder** is chronically depressed. Besides feeling blue and losing pleasure in usual activities and pastimes, the person has several other signs of depression, such as insomnia or sleeping too much; feeling inadequate, ineffective, and drained of energy; pessimism; inability to concentrate and to think clearly; and avoiding the company of others. Data collected by Klein and his associates (1988) have validated dysthymia as a form of depression and shown that it appears to be a particularly severe form of this disorder. Many dysthymics are both chronically depressed and have episodes of major depression as well.

Psychological Theories of Mood Disorders

Depression has been studied from several perspectives. We will discuss psychoanalytic views, which emphasize the unconscious conflicts associated with grief and loss; cognitive theories, which focus on the depressed person's self-defeating thought processes; interpersonal factors, which emphasize how depressed people interact with others; and biological theories, which concentrate on what the central nervous system is doing at the neurochemical level.

Psychoanalytic Theory of Depression

In his celebrated paper "Mourning and Melancholia," Freud (1917) wrote of the potential for depression being created early in childhood. He theorized that during the oral period a child's needs may be insufficiently or oversufficiently gratified, causing the person to remain in this stage and dependent on the instinctual gratifications particular to it. With this arrest in psychosexual maturation, this fixation at the oral stage, the person may develop a tendency to be excessively dependent on other people for the maintenance of self-esteem.

From this happenstance of childhood, how can the adult come to suffer from depression? The reasoning is complex. Freud hypothesized that after the loss of a loved one, the mourner first *introjects*, or incorporates, the lost person; he or she identifies with the lost one, perhaps in a fruitless attempt to undo the loss. Because, as Freud asserted, we unconsciously harbor negative feelings toward those we love, the mourner now becomes the object of his or her own hate and anger. In addition, the mourner also resents being deserted and feels guilt for real or imagined sins against the deceased. The period of introjection is followed by the period of *mourning work*, when the mourner recalls memories of the lost one and thereby separates himself or herself from the person who has died and loosens the bonds imposed by introjection.

The grief work can go astray in overly dependent individuals and develop into an ongoing process of self-abuse, self-blame, and depression. Such individuals do not loosen their emotional bonds with the person who has died; rather they continue to castigate themselves for the faults and shortcomings perceived in the loved one who has been introjected. The mourner's anger toward the lost one continues to be directed inward. This theorizing is the basis for the widespread psychodynamic view of depression as anger turned against oneself.

One further point must be made. Many people can become depressed and remain so without having recently suffered the loss of a loved one. In this case, psychoanalysts invoke the concept of symbolic loss in order to keep the theoretical formulation intact. For example, a person may unconsciously interpret a rejection as a total withdrawal of love.

Some research has been generated by psychoanalytic points of view, either Freud's or those of others not discussed here. The little information available does not support the theory. Dreams and projective tests should theoretically be means of expressing unconscious needs and fears. Beck and Ward (1961) analyzed the dreams of depressed people and found themes of loss and failure, not of anger and hostility. An examination of responses to projective tests established that depressives identify with the victim, not the aggressor. Other data also contradict psychoanalytic views. If depression comes from anger turned inward, we would expect depressed people to express little hostility toward others. This was not found to be the case; depressed individuals often express intense anger and hostility toward people close to them (Weissman, Klerman, & Paykel, 1971).

Although Freud cloaked his clinical impressions in theoretical terms that have been rejected by many contemporary writers, we must appreciate that some of his basic suppositions have a continuing influence. For instance, irrational self-statements such as "It is a dire necessity that I be universally loved and approved of," to which Ellis attributes much human suffering, might be devastating for Freud's oral personality in the deepening depression following the loss of a loved one. Similarly, a large body of evidence indicates that depression is precipitated by stressful life events, and these often involve losses, for example, a divorce or job separation (e.g., Brown & Harris, 1978).

Because cognitive theories of depression are those pursued most actively today in controlled studies, we now discuss two of them—Beck's schema theory and the helplessness/hopelessness theory—in some detail.

Cognitive Theories of Depression

Discussions of the feeling of helplessness in Chapter 6 and of Ellis's concept of irrational beliefs in Chapter 2 and elsewhere indicate that cognitive processes play a decisive role in emotional behavior. In some theories of depression, as in some concerning anxiety, thoughts and beliefs are regarded as major factors in causing or influencing the emotional state. In a way, Freud was a cognitive theorist, too, for he viewed depression as resulting from a person's belief that loss is a withdrawal of affection.

Beck's Theory

Levels of Cognition An important contemporary theory that regards thought processes as causative factors in depression is that of Aaron Beck (1967; 1985; 1987). His central thesis is that depressed individuals feel as they do because their thinking is biased toward negative interpretations. Figure 9.1 illustrates the interactions among three levels of cognitive activity believed by Beck to underlie depression.

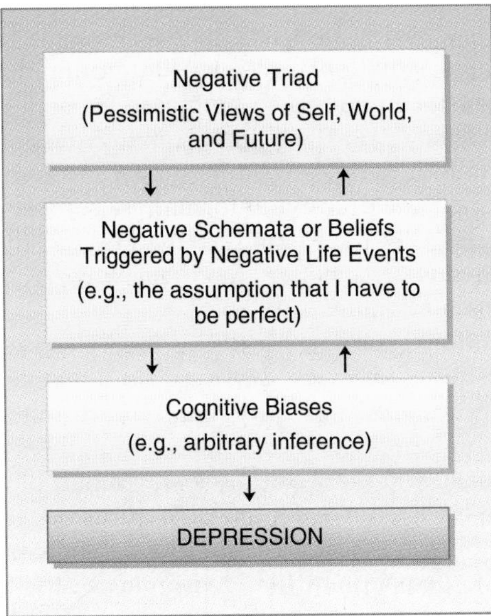

Figure 9.1 Beck's theory of depression, showing the interrelationships among different kinds of cognitions.

According to Beck, in childhood and adolescence, depressed individuals acquired a negative schema through loss of a parent, an unrelenting succession of tragedies, the social rejection of peers, the criticisms of teachers, or the depressive attitude of a parent. All of us have schemata of many kinds; by these perceptual sets, these miniparadigms, we order our lives. The negative schemata or beliefs acquired by depressed persons are activated whenever they encounter new situations that resemble in some way, perhaps only remotely, the conditions in which the schemata were learned. Moreover, the negative schemata of depressives fuel, and are fueled by, certain cognitive biases, which lead these sufferers to misperceive reality. Thus an ineptness schema can make depressives expect to fail most of the time; a self-blame schema burdens them with responsibility for all misfortunes; and a negative self-evaluation schema constantly reminds them of their worthlessness. The negative schemata, together with cognitive biases or distortions, maintain what Beck called the **negative triad**: negative views of the self, the world, and the future. The following is a list of the principal cognitive biases of the depressive individual.

1. **Arbitrary Inference.** A conclusion drawn in the absence of sufficient evidence or of any evidence at all. For example, a man concludes that he is worthless because it is raining the day that he is hosting an outdoor party.

According to Beck's theory, someone who is likely to develop depression will magnify or overgeneralize a negative experience like scoring poorly on the SAT.

2. **Selective Abstraction.** A conclusion drawn on the basis of but one of many elements in a situation. A worker feels worthless when a product fails to function, even though she is only one of many people who contributed to its production.
3. **Overgeneralization.** An overall sweeping conclusion drawn on the basis of a single, perhaps trivial, event. A student regards his poor performance in a single class on one particular day as final proof of his worthlessness and stupidity.
4. **Magnification and Minimization.** Exaggerations in evaluating performance. A man, believing that he has completely ruined his car (magnification) when he sees that there is a slight scratch on the rear fender, regards himself as good for nothing; or a woman still believes herself worthless (minimization) in spite of a succession of praiseworthy achievements.

These distortions could of course be used within a schema of positive self-evaluation by people who bias what they see so as to *enhance* their view of self. For example, a person can selectively abstract from the success of a project undertaken with many others the conclusion that he or she has great ability and was primarily responsible for the good outcome. The depressed person, however, by these errors in thinking, confirms the self-deprecatory schema and feels unworthy and responsible for calamities.

It is important to appreciate the thrust of Beck's position. Whereas many theorists see people as victims of their passions, creatures whose intellectual capacities can exert little if any control over feelings—this is Freud's basic position—in Beck's theory the cause–effect relationship operates in the opposite direction. Our emotional reactions are considered primarily a function of how we construe our world, and indeed the interpretations of depressives are found not to mesh very well with the way in which most people view the world. Beck sees depressives as the victims of their own illogical self-judgments.

Evaluation At least two points need to be demonstrated when evaluating Beck's theory. First, depressed patients, in contrast to nondepressed individuals, must actually judge themselves in the biased ways enumerated by Beck. This point was initially confirmed by Beck's clinical observations, which suggested that depressed patients do, in fact, manifest at least some of these biases (Beck, 1967).

Further support for this general proposition comes from a number of sources. Questionnaires have been developed to assess depressives' cognitive biases in reacting to stories about college students in problematic situations (Krantz & Hammen, 1979) and to allow subjects to report negative automatic thoughts (Hollon & Kendall, 1980). In general, depressives' responses to these questionnaires agree with expectations based on Beck's theory (e.g., Dobson & Shaw, 1986). Also, biased thinking as measured by the Automatic Thoughts Questionnaire decreases significantly after treatment to alleviate depression (Simons, Garfield, & Murphy, 1984). Furthermore, as indicated in Chapter 4, a study employing the Articulated Thoughts During Simulated Situations procedure found the thinking of depressive patients to be biased as Beck postulates (White et al., 1992). In perceiving and recalling information, depressives also have negative schemata, for they perceive information in more negative terms (Roth & Rehm, 1980) and recall their incorrect answers better than their correct ones (Nelson & Craighead, 1977).

Additional support for Beck's theory comes from many studies showing that depressed people think more negatively and, in general, more hopelessly than nondepressed individuals about themselves, the future, and the world. The world part of Beck's depressive triad, we should note, turns out to refer to the person's judgment that he or she can cope with the demands of the environment. It is highly personal—I cannot possibly cope with all these demands and responsibilities—rather than being a concern for global events that do not implicate the self directly, for example, "The world has been going south since the American League adopted the designated hitter rule" (Haaga et al., 1991, p. 218).

However, another body of research does not support the assertion that cognition is invariably distorted among depressives. For example, expectancy of success is actually quite accurate in depressives, whereas normal people overestimate the likelihood of success (Lobitz & Post, 1979). Similarly, in another study depressives were monitored while they engaged in a discussion with nondepressed students (Dykman et al., 1991). Ambiguous feedback was provided to the depressives about their performance, and the researchers attempted to predict how the depressed students would interpret the feedback from both a measure of negative schema and objective ratings of social competence. The depressed subjects' poor social performance and their negative schema were both significant predictors of their negative interpretations. Thus, although depressives are consistently pessimistic, they are not always cognitively distorted (Layne, 1986). An important task for future research will be to understand the conditions under which depressives distort reality and when they seem to perceive it more clearly than do normal people. Another challenge is to understand why a depressed person is saddened by sometimes accurate judgments whereas a nondepressed individual is not.

Some authors prefer the term *bias* to *distortion* (e.g., Haaga, Dyck, & Ernst, 1991). Drawing on related work by Coyne and Gotlib (1983), Alloy and Abramson (1988) defined *bias* as "a tendency to make judgments in a systematic and consistent manner across specific times and situations (e.g., a tendency to draw negative conclusions about oneself . . .)" (p. 227), contrasting it with *distortion*, a "judgment or conclusion that disagrees or is inconsistent with some commonly accepted measure of objective reality" (p. 226). In this light, it seems clear that Beck's theory describes biases in depressive cognition (e.g., accurately perceiving a negative event but then magnifying its importance and implications) rather than distorted perceptions. Indeed, in many important instances, such as one's hopes for the future, there seems to be no acceptable measure of objective reality with which to compare one's thoughts and thereby identify some of them as distortions.

Another challenge for researchers is to demonstrate that the cognitive bias of depressives does not follow upon an emotional disturbance, that it does in fact *cause* the depressed mood. Many studies in experimental psychology have in a general way shown that a person's mood can be influenced by how he or she construes events. But manipulating affect has also been shown to change thinking (e.g., Isen et al., 1978). No study that we know of directly demonstrates that the various emotional and physical aspects of depression are truly secondary to, or a function of, the negative schemata and biases that Beck believes operate in this disorder. Beck and others have found that depression and certain kinds of thinking are *correlated*, but a specific causal relationship cannot be determined from such data; depression could cause negative thoughts, or negative thoughts could cause depression.

Indeed, one longitudinal study of the relationship between cognition and depression found that negative thinking did not precede depression (Lewinsohn et al., 1981). A large sample of community residents completed a battery of tests measuring cognition and depression and were followed up eight months later. Of particular interest were the results of the earlier tests assessing the thinking of people who later became depressed.

> Prior to becoming depressed, [future depressives] did not subscribe to irrational beliefs, they did not have lower expectancies for positive outcomes or higher expectancies for negative outcomes . . . nor did they perceive themselves as having less control over the events in their lives. (p. 218)

In our view the relationship in all likelihood works both ways; depression can probably make thinking negative, and negative thinking can probably cause and can certainly worsen depression.

It is important to note that there is some confusion and disagreement in the literature about whether Beck assigns causal properties to cognition in depression, either as etiological or as maintaining factors. Certainly his influential writings on *therapy* emphasize the importance of altering self-statements and (sometimes unspoken) beliefs or schemata as *the* central way to alleviate depression, as we discuss later in this chapter and again in Chapter 19. But, especially in his more recent writings (Beck, 1987), Beck regards cognitions as a very important aspect of depression but not necessarily a cause of the disorder. The complexities of these interesting ambiguities and subtleties are discussed in a recent analysis by Haaga, Dyck, and Ernst (1991).

Despite these irresolutions, an important advantage of Beck's theory is that it is testable and has encouraged considerable research on depression. One of the areas now being pursued is how different schemata might interact with particular life stressors and lead to the onset of depression. For example, one person may regard the adequacy of social relationships as the most important aspect of well-being, whereas for another, occupational achievement might be central. For the socially oriented person, life stress related to interpersonal themes (e.g., divorce or breaking up a relationship) would have great impact; whereas for the achievement-oriented individual, a failure to meet some goal would do so. Evidence collected by Hammen and her colleagues (1985; 1989) supports the general usefulness of such a conceptualization. The relationship between life orientation and stressful events is especially pronounced for achievement events among those who are achievement oriented (Segal et al., 1992). Furthermore, the different personality styles of depressives are associated with different symptom patterns (Robins et al., 1989) and therefore may be related to the symptom heterogeneity problem discussed earlier. And as discussed later in this chapter (see page 244), Beck's work has encouraged therapists to focus directly on depressed patients' thinking in order to change and alleviate their feelings.

Helplessness/Hopelessness

In this section we will discuss in detail the evolution of an influential theory of depression. Actually, we will be describing three theories, the original helplessness theory, its subsequent, more cognitive, attributional version, and, finally, its transformation into the hopelessness theory (see Figure 9.2 for a summary of the three).

Learned Helplessness The basic premise of the **learned helplessness theory** is that an individual's passivity and sense of being unable to act and control his or her own life is acquired through unpleasant experiences and traumas that the individual tried unsuccessfully to control; this, then, brings on depression. Initially, this theory was a mediational learning theory formulated to explain the behavior of dogs who received inescapable electric shocks. Soon after receiving the first shocks, the dogs stopped running around in a distressed manner; they seemed to give up and passively accept the painful stimulation. In a subsequent part of the experiment the shocks could be avoided but the dogs did not acquire the avoidance response as efficiently and effectively as did the control animals. Most of them, in fact, lay down in a corner and whined. On the basis of these observations Seligman (1974) proposed that animals can acquire what might be called a sense of helplessness when confronted with uncontrollable aversive stimulation. This helplessness later tends seriously and deleteriously to affect their performance in stressful situations that *can* be controlled. They appear to lose the ability and motivation to learn to respond in an effective way to painful stimulation.

On the basis of this and other work on the effects of uncontrollable stress, Seligman felt that learned helplessness in animals could provide a model for at least certain forms of human depression. He noted similarities between the manifestations of helplessness observed in animal laboratory studies and at least some of the symptoms of depression. Like many depressed people, the animals appeared passive in the face of stress, failing to initiate action that might allow them to cope. They developed anorexia, having difficulty eating or retaining what they ate, and lost weight. Further, one of the neurotransmitter chemicals, norepinephrine, was depleted in Seligman's animals (see page 241). As we will see, drugs that increase levels of norepinephrine have been shown to alleviate depression in human beings. Although effectiveness of treatment does not, as we have indicated, prove etiology, the fact that depression is reduced by a drug that increases the level of norepinephrine is consistent with the finding that learned helplessness in animals is associated with lower levels of the chemical.

Experiments with human beings have yielded results similar to those of experiments done with animals. People who are subjected to inescapable noise, or inescapable shock, or who are confronted with unsolvable problems, fail later to escape noise and shock and solve simple problems (e.g., Hiroto & Seligman, 1975; Roth & Kubal, 1975). Moreover, the performance of tasks by college students who rate as depressed on the Beck Depression Inventory is similar to that of nondepressed students who have earlier been subjected to these same helplessness-inducing experiences (Miller, Seligman, & Kurlander, 1975; Klein & Seligman, 1976).

Attribution and Learned Helplessness By 1978, however, several inadequacies of the theory and unexplained aspects of depression had become apparent, and a revised version of the learned helplessness model was proposed by Abramson, Seligman, and Teasdale. Some studies with humans, for example, had indicated that helplessness inductions actually led to subsequent facilitation of performance (e.g., see Wortman & Brehm, 1975). In addition, many depressed people hold themselves responsible for their failures. If they regard themselves as helpless, how can they blame themselves? The essence of the revised theory lies in the concept of **attribution**—the explanation a person has for his or her behavior (Weiner et al., 1971), and in this way it blends cognitive and learning elements. Given a situation in which the individual has experienced failure, he or she will try to attribute the failure to some cause. In Table 9.2 the Abramson, Seligman,

Table 9.2 • Attributional Schema of Depression: Why I Failed My GRE Math Exam

	Internal (Personal)		***External (Environmental)***	
Degree	*Stable*	*Unstable*	*Stable*	*Unstable*
Global	I lack intelligence.	I am exhausted.	These tests are all unfair.	It's an unlucky day, Friday the thirteenth.
Specific	I lack mathematical ability.	I am fed up with math.	The math tests are unfair.	My math test was numbered "13."

and Teasdale formulation is applied to indicate the ways in which a college student might attribute failure on the mathematics portion of the GRE. Three questions are asked. Are the reasons for failure believed to be internal (personal) or external (environmentally caused)? Is the problem believed to be stable or unstable? How global or specific is the inability to succeed perceived to be?

The attributional revision of the helplessness theory postulates that the way in which a person explains failure will determine its subsequent effects. Global attributions should increase the generality of the effects of failure. Attributions to stable factors will make them long-term. Attributing the failure to internal characteristics is more likely to diminish self-esteem, particularly if the personal fault is also global and persistent.

People become depressed, the theory suggests, when they attribute negative life events to stable and global causes. Whether self-esteem collapses, too, depends on whether they blame the bad outcome on their own inadequacies. The depression-prone individual is also thought to show a "depressive attributional style," a tendency to attribute bad outcomes to personal, global, stable faults of character. When persons with this style (a diathesis) have unhappy, adverse experiences (stressors), they become depressed, and their self-esteem is shattered (Peterson & Seligman, 1984; see Focus Box 9.1).

Some research gives direct support to the reformulated theory. Seligman and his colleagues (1979) devised the Attributional-Style Questionnaire and, as the theory predicted, found that depressed college students did indeed more often attribute failure to personal, global, and persistent inadequacies than did nondepressed students.

Metalsky, Halberstadt, and Abramson (1987) linked attributional style to depressed mood. They conducted a study with college students taking a course in introductory psychology. Early in the semester the students completed the Attributional-Style Questionnaire and a questionnaire pertaining to their grade aspirations. A checklist was used to collect mood information on two occasions before the midterm exam, right after receipt of the exam grades, and again two days later.

According to the attributional helplessness theory, a tendency to attribute negative events to global and persistent inadequacies, as determined by the Attributional-Style Questionnaire, should predict more depressed mood in those students who received a poor grade. A poor grade was defined as a failure to match aspirations; this score was weighted by the importance attached to this negative event by the subjects.

The results differed depending on which of the postexam mood assessments was examined. The outcome of the exam was the major determinant of students' initial mood changes. Those who did poorly became more depressed. However, two days

Figure 9.2 The three helplessness theories of depression.

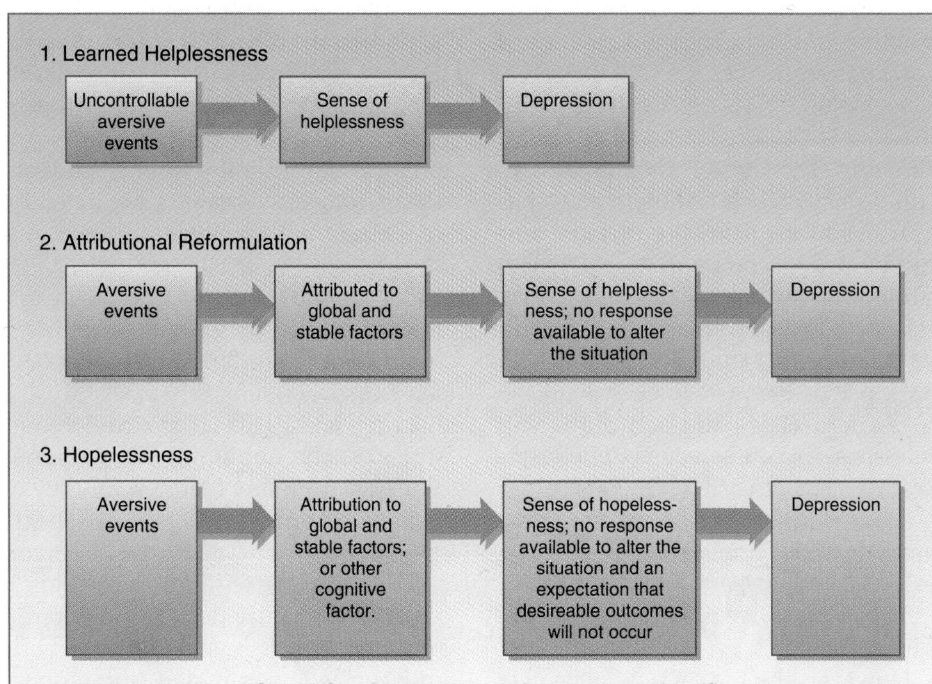

9.1 • Depression in Women: A Consequence of Learned Helplessness and Style of Coping?

Depression occurs more often in women than in men. Research involving both patients in treatment and surveys of community residents consistently yields a 2:1 female:male ratio (Nolen-Hoeksema, 1987). Understanding the cause of this gender difference may yield some further clues to the etiology of depression.

Radloff (1975) speculates that the higher levels of depression among women are best explained as a consequence of learned helplessness. The feminist literature would agree (e.g., Bernard, 1973; Chesler, 1972), for it blames the greater incidence of mental problems among women on their lack of personal and political power. Feminists take the position that more women than men become depressed because their social roles do not encourage them to feel competent. What women do does not seem to count compared with the greater power that men have in society. In fact, it may be that little girls are *trained* to be helpless (Broverman, Broverman, & Clarkson, 1970). Consistent with these speculations are data showing that girls' behavior is less likely than boys' to elicit consequences from both parents (Maccoby & Jacklin, 1974) and teachers (Dweck et al., 1978). Furthermore, girls are more likely to attribute success to luck or the favors of others (unstable) and failures to global and stable factors (Dweck, 1975).

In her research on factors influencing the duration of depressive episodes, Nolen-Hoeksema (1987; 1990) proposed an equally plausible account of these gender differences, referring to characteristic differences in the way men and women cope with stress. When responding to depression, men typically engage in activities that will distract them from their mood, for example, engaging in some physical activity or watching

later, the unstable, specific students had recovered but the stable, global students were still mildly depressed. Following a suggestion by Weiner (1986), Metalsky et al. proposed that a negative event elicits an immediate emotional response that occurs before any attributions are even made. Subsequently, causal interpretations are sought and a pattern of global, stable attributions makes the initial depressive response last longer.

Hopelessness Theory The latest version of the theory (Abramson, Metalsky, & Alloy, 1989) has moved even further away from the original formulation. Some forms of depression (hopelessness depressions) are now regarded as caused by a state of hopelessness, an expectation that desirable outcomes will not occur or that undesirable ones will occur and that the person has no responses available to change this situation. (The latter part of the definition of hopelessness, of course, refers to helplessness, the central concept of earlier versions of the theory.) As in the attributional reformulation, negative life events (stressors) are seen as interacting with diatheses to yield a hopelessness state. One diathesis is the attributional style pattern already described, attributing negative events to stable and global factors. However, the theory now considers the possibility that there are other diatheses—a tendency to infer that negative life events will have severe negative consequences and a tendency to draw negative inferences about the self. Metalsky and his colleagues (1993) have conducted the first test of the hopelessness theory in a study similar to his earlier one. Two new features were the direct measurement of hopelessness and another potential diathesis—low self-esteem. As in the earlier study, attributing poor grades to global and stable factors led to more persistent depressed mood. Furthermore, this pattern was found only among students whose self-esteem was low and was mediated by an increase in feelings of hopelessness, thus supporting the theory.

One advantage of the hopelessness theory is that it can deal directly with comorbidity of depression and anxiety disorders. In Chapter 6, we noted that panic disorder, agoraphobia, obsessive-compulsive disorder, and PTSD all occurred frequently with depression. Accounting for this pattern poses a major challenge for many theories, for they deal only with a single diagnosis. Alloy et al., (1990) pointed out several important features of comorbidity. First, cases of anxiety without depression are relatively common, but pure depression is rare. Second, longitudinal studies reveal that anxiety diagnoses typically precede depression (e.g., Rohde, Lewinsohn, & Seeley, 1991). On the basis of a good deal of prior television. Women, on the other hand, are less active, tend to ruminate about their situation, and blame themselves for being depressed (e.g., Kleinke et al., 1982). This ruminative reaction is then seen as amplifying the state of depression and negative mood, perhaps by interfering with attempts to solve problems.

Many studies support this hypothesis (Nolen-Hoeksema, 1991). People who report a tendency to ruminate over problems are less likely to engage in efforts at problem-solving (Carver, Scheier, & Weintraub, 1989; Nolen-Hoeksema & Morrow, 1991b), and this tendency to ruminate over problems rather than solve them is associated with longer periods of depression (Morrow & Nolen-Hoeksema, 1990; Nolen-Hoeksema & Morrow, 1991a). Moreover, women tend to ruminate more than men when depressed and to have longer periods of depressed mood, presumably as a result of their ruminative style (Nolen-Hoeksema, Morrow, & Frederickson, 1991, cited in Nolen-Hoeksema, 1991). This "response style" view of depression is concerned with the ways people cope with a depressed mood once it is evident, rather than with the reasons people become depressed in the first place.

How does it come about that women have more of a ruminative response style to stress and sadness than do men? Nolen-Hoeksema seeks answers in sex-role learning that begins during childhood. It is part of the masculine stereotype to be active and coping rather than reflecting on one's feelings and the reasons for them. Men learn to be less emotionally tuned in than women. By the same token this sex-linked learning may teach women that they are by nature more emotional and that therefore depressive episodes are natural and unavoidable.

The implications for treatment are clear according to this view. Depressed women—and men, to be sure—should be encouraged to increase their coping and pleasure-producing activity rather than dwell on their moods and search for causes of depression. Problem-solving skills should also be nurtured. In a preventive vein, Nolen-Hoeksema suggests that parents and other caretakers encourage girls to adopt active behavior in response to negative moods.

evidence (e.g., Mandler, 1972; Bowlby, 1980), Alloy and her colleagues proposed that an expectation of helplessness creates anxiety. When the expectation of helplessness becomes certain, a syndrome with elements of both depression and anxiety ensues. Finally, if the perceived probability of the occurrence of negative events becomes certain, hopelessness develops.

Issues in the Helplessness and Hopelessness Theories

Although the theories are promising, some problems do need to be addressed in future work.

1. Which type of depression is being modeled? In his original paper Seligman attempted to document the similarity between learned helplessness and reactive depression, depression thought to be brought on by stressful life events. But Depue and Monroe (1978) demonstrated that learned helplessness resembles the symptoms of a bipolar patient in a depressive episode more than it does those of any form of unipolar depression. Yet neither Seligman's dogs nor human beings in helplessness studies have exhibited both mania and depression. Seligman's (1978) solution to this problem was to bypass the traditional classification schemes and regard learned helplessness as a model for "helplessness depression." Similarly, Abramson et al. (1989) now talk about a hopelessness depression. Only future research will tell whether these solutions are more than circular statements.

2. Can college student populations provide good analogues? Although some research on learned helplessness has been done with clinical populations (e.g., Abramson et al., 1978), many studies have examined college students who are selected on the basis of scores on the Beck Depression Inventory. However, this inventory was not designed to *diagnose* depression, only to allow an assessment of severity in a clinically diagnosed group. Indeed, accumulating evidence indicates that selecting subjects solely on the basis of elevated BDI scores does not yield a group of people who can serve as a good analogue for those with clinical depression. Hammen (1980), for example, found that high scorers, with a mean of 18.37, were down to an average of only 10.87 when retested two to three weeks later.

3. Are the findings specific to depression? This issue is raised by the results of a learned helplessness study conducted by Lavelle, Metalsky, and Coyne (1979) with subjects classified as having high or low test anxiety. The subjects with high test anxiety performed a task poorly after going through a laboratory situation inducing helplessness. Thus the learned helplessness phenomenon may not be specific to depression. The newer hopelessness theory may fare better in distinguishing between anxiety and depression.

4. Are attributions relevant? At issue here is the underlying assumption that people actively attempt to explain their own behavior to themselves and that the attributions they make have subsequent effects on their behavior. Some research indicates that making attributions is not a universal process (Hanusa & Schulz, 1977). Indeed, in a series of experiments discussed in Chapter 7, Nisbett and Wilson (1977) showed that people are frequently unaware of the causes of their behavior.[1]

Even if we allow that attributions are relevant and powerful determinants of behavior, we should note that many findings supporting the learned helplessness theory have been gathered by giving individuals the Attributional-Style Questionnaire or by determining how they explain laboratory-induced successes or failures. When depressives were asked about the five most stressful events of their lives, however, their attributions did not differ from those given by normal subjects (Hammen & Cochran, 1981).

5. Some research has refuted some aspects of the theory. In a series of studies, Alloy and Abramson (1979) examined one of its central points, that depressed people perceive themselves as having little control over their lives. Subjects were placed in various experimental situations manipulated by the experimenter to give predetermined percentages of contingency between their responses and an outcome. After subjects had experienced some actual level of control, they were asked how much control they *believed* they had had. Contrary to the theory, depressed students did not underestimate their degree of control. Using a classic experimental situation to induce helplessness in subjects, Ford and Neale (1985) similarly found that the students did not underestimate their control on the subsequent task.

One key assumption of all versions of helplessness/hopelessness theory is that the depressive attributional style is a persistent part of the makeup of depressed people. Using a battery of measures, including the Attributional-Style Questionnaire, Hamilton and Abramson (1983) carefully tested diagnosed depressives on two occasions, first while they were in the midst of an episode of depression, and again just before they were discharged from the hospital. Results from the first assessment revealed the expected depressive pattern on the questionnaire. But the information gathered just before the patients were discharged indicated that the pattern was no longer present. Similar results were found by Dohr, Rush, and Bernstein (1989).

With all its problems, helplessness/hopelessness theory has clearly stimulated a great deal of research and further theorizing about depression. It seems destined to continue to do so for many years to come.

Interpersonal Theory of Depression

In this section we discuss behavioral aspects of depression that generally involve relationships between the depressed person and others. Some of the data we present may be relevant to the etiology of depression and some to its course.

In Chapter 8 we discussed the role of social support in health. The concept has also been applied to research on depression. Depressives have spare social networks and regard them as less supportive. This reduced social support lessens the individual's ability to handle negative life events (Billings, Cronkite, & Moos, 1983).

Is it simply fate that confronts the depressive with an inadequate level of social support? Perhaps, but it is also possible that the depressed person plays a role. Maybe depressed people are low in social skills

Depressed people often have sparse social support networks and may even elicit negative reactions from others. Both these factors can contribute to the onset and maintenance of depression.

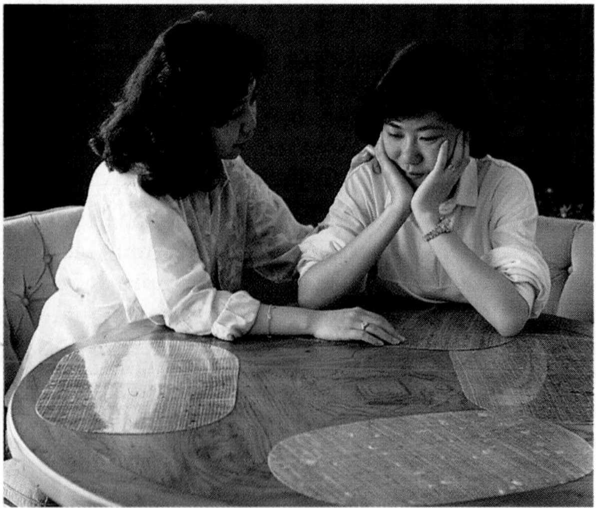

[1]The attribution literature makes the basic assumption that people care what the causes of their behavior are. This central idea is the brainchild of psychologists whose business it is to explain behavior. It may be that psychologists have projected their own need to explain behavior onto other people! Laypeople may simply not reflect on why they act and feel as they do to the same extent that psychologists do.

(Lewinsohn, 1974). A number of studies have indeed demonstrated such deficits across a variety of measures—interpersonal problem-solving (Gotlib & Asarnow, 1979), speech patterns, and maintenance of eye contact (Gotlib & Robinson, 1982; Gotlib, 1982). Similarly, in a longitudinal study of unipolar depressives, Hammen (1991) confirmed that they experience much stress (particularly of an interpersonal nature) and that their own behavior contributes to the high levels of stress that they experience. As an example, Hammen describes the stressors one woman with unipolar depression experienced in a one-year period:

> [She] had a car accident in which her knee was injured, failed a civil service exam that would have opened job opportunities, moved out of her home after conflict with her husband, had a serious argument with her daughter who remained with the father, divorced the husband, and got into a fight with her ex-husband over her new boyfriend. (p. 559)

As suggested by Coyne (1976), depressed people may elicit negative reactions from others. This possibility has been studied in a variety of ways, ranging from telephone conversations with depressed patients, listening to audiotapes of depressed patients, and even in face-to-face interactions. These data show that depressives have an aversive interpersonal style that elicits rejection from others. For example, Hokanson and his colleagues (1989) found that the roommates of depressed college students rated social contacts with them as being low in enjoyment and reported high levels of aggression toward them. Similarly, Joiner, Alfano, and Metalsky (1992) found that mildly depressed college students were likely to be rejected by their roommates. Not surprisingly given these findings, depression and marital discord frequently co-occur and the interactions of depressed people and their spouses are characterized by hostility (Kowalik & Gotlib, 1987). Indeed, Hooley and Teasdale (1989) have shown that the critical comments of spouses of depressed people are a significant predictor of recurrence of depression. The relationship between depression and marital discord is explored in Chapter 20.

Do any of these interpersonal characteristics of depressed people precede the onset of depression? Some research using the high-risk method (see page 119) suggests that the answer is yes. For example, the behavior of elementary-school-aged children of depressed parents is rated negatively by both teachers and peers (Weintraub, Liebert, & Neale, 1975; Weintraub, Prinz, & Neale, 1978). In sum, interpersonal behavior appears to play a major role in depression.

Theories of Bipolar Disorder

Bipolar disorder has been neglected by both psychological theorists and researchers, probably because only between 5 to 10 percent of depressed patients also have bouts of mania. In general, theories of the depressive phase of bipolar disorder are similar to theories of unipolar depression. The manic phase of the disorder is seen as a defense against a debilitating psychological state. The specific negative state that is being avoided varies from theory to theory. One of our own cases illustrates why many theorists have concluded that the manic state serves a protective function.

A forty-two-year-old man was currently in his third manic episode. During each he had had the classic pattern of manic symptoms, and much of his manic behavior centered on a grandiose delusion that he was the world's greatest businessman. "Did you know that I've already bought twenty companies today?" he stated at the beginning of a therapy session. "Not even Getty or Rockefeller have anything on me." From sessions between episodes, it was apparent that success in business was indeed a central concern to the patient. But he was far from successful. His parents had lent him money to start several companies, but each had gone bankrupt. He was obsessed with matching the business successes of his wealthy father, but as the years passed his opportunities to do so were slipping away. It seemed, therefore, that his manic grandiosity was protecting him from a confrontation with his lack of business success—a realization that would likely have plunged him into a deep depression.

Clinical experience with manics as well as studies of their personalities when they are in remission indicate that they appear relatively well adjusted between episodes. But if mania is a defense, it must be a defense against something, suggesting that the apparently good adjustment of manics between episodes may not be an accurate reflection of their true state. In an attempt to bypass what may be defensive responding, Winters and Neale (1985) used a specially developed test to examine the notion that manics, even when between episodes, have low self-esteem.

Manics, unipolar depressives, and normal subjects were given two tests, a self-esteem inventory and a pragmatic inference test. The second was meant to be a subtle measure of the manics' expected low self-esteem. In the pragmatic inference test subjects first read a paragraph describing a series of events, some of which had a positive outcome, the others a negative one. Subjects were then given a test that appeared to measure their recall of each story. Some items actually assessed recall of facts, but others forced the subject to go beyond the information and draw an inference. For example, one story concerned a man who was currently out of work. The reason for his unemployment was not stated directly, but the story was constructed to allow either of two inferences to be drawn. The subject could infer that the man was unemployed through no fault of his own but because the economy was poor. Or the subject could infer that the man's poor work record kept him unemployed. People with low self-esteem were expected to make the second inference.

The results agreed exactly with expectation. On the paper-and-pencil measure of self-esteem, both the manics and normal subjects scored higher than the depressives. But on the pragmatic inference test the manics performed like the depressives; both groups drew the second inferences and revealed their low self-esteem. Thus the self-esteem of manics may be very low. Generally, however, they successfully defend against their feelings of inadequacy.

Biological Theories of Mood Disorders

Since biological processes are known to have considerable effects on moods, it is not surprising that investigators have sought biological causes for depression and mania. Moreover, disturbed biological processes must of course be part of the causal chain if a predisposition for a mood disorder can be genetically transmitted. Evidence indicating that a mood disorder is, in part, inherited would then provide some support for the view that the disorder has a biological basis. We will look here at some of the research to date in the areas of genetics, neurochemistry, and the neuroendocrine system.

The Genetic Data

Research on genetic factors in unipolar depression and bipolar disorder has used the family, twin, and adoptee methods. Estimates of the frequency of mood disorders in first-degree relatives of bipolar patients range from about 10 to 20 percent (Perris, 1969; Brodie & Leff, 1971; Hays, 1976). Risk among the relatives increases with early onset of the disorder among the probands. These figures are higher than those for the general population. Curiously, among the first-degree relatives of bipolar probands, there are more cases of unipolar depression than of bipolar disorder. For example, James and Chapman (1975), in a thorough study conducted in New Zealand, found the morbidity risk estimates for the first-degree relatives of bipolar patients to be 6.4 percent for bipolar disorder and 13.2 percent for unipolar depression. Allen (1976) reviewed concordance data for bipolar disorder in twins. Overall, the concordance rate for bipolar disorder in identical twins was 72 percent and in fraternal twins only 14 percent. The evidence thus supports the notion that bipolar disorder has a heritable component.

The information available on unipolar depression indicates that genetic factors, although important, are not as decisive as they are in bipolar disorder. In fact, although the relatives of unipolar probands are at increased risk for unipolar depression, their risk is less than that among relatives of bipolar probands (Andreasen et al., 1987). Relatives of unipolar probands are also not at especially high risk for bipolar disorder. Early onset of depression and comorbidity with an anxiety disorder or alcoholism confer greater risk on the relatives (Weissman et al., 1988). Studies of unipolar depression in twins usually report monozygotic concordances of about 40 percent and dizygotic concordances of about 11 percent (Allen, 1976).

The family and twin studies together suggest that both *bipolar disorder* and *unipolar depression have heritable components*. This conclusion is further supported by several small-scale studies that have used the adoption method. Mendlewicz and Rainer (1977) found more mood disorders in the biological parents than in the adoptive parents of bipolar adoptees. Also, Cadoret (1978a) found more mood disorders in adopted children whose biological parents had a mood disorder. Finally, Wender et al. (1986) found that the biological relatives of adopted probands were eight times more likely than controls to have a mood disorder.

A recent development in genetic research on mood disorders is the use of what is called **linkage analysis**. The technique involves studying the occurrence of mood disorder over several generations in a family and simultaneously assessing some other characteristic—a genetic marker—for which the genetics are fully understood (e.g., red-green color blindness is known to result from mutations on the

X chromosome). When the genes for mood disorder and the genetic marker are linked, that is, when they are sufficiently close together on a chromosome, the family pedigree tends to show that the two traits being examined are inherited together. In a widely reported linkage study of the Old Order Amish, Egeland and her colleagues (1987) found evidence favoring the hypothesis that bipolar disorder results from a dominant gene on the eleventh chromosome. Unfortunately, the Egeland study as well as other apparently successful linkage studies have all failed to be replicated (e.g., Berrittini et al., 1990).

Neurochemistry and Mood Disorders

Numerous attempts have been made to link mood disorders to various neurotransmitters. The research here is still very much at the cutting edge, and as we will see, the need to change the focus of research can come at any time. We will describe an endeavor involving norepinephrine and another involving serotonin. The theory involving norepinephrine posits that a low level of norepinephrine leads to depression and a high level to mania. The serotonin theory suggests that a low level of serotonin, which frequently serves to modulate neural activity in other neurochemical systems, allows wild fluctuations in the activity of other neurotransmitters, thereby producing both mania and depression.

The actions of drugs provided the clues on which both theories are based. In the 1950s two particular groups of drugs, tricyclics and monoamine oxidase inhibitors, were found effective in relieving depression. **Tricyclic drugs** are a group of antidepressant medications so-named because their molecular structure is characterized by three fused rings; they interfere with the reuptake of norepinephrine and serotonin by a neuron after it has fired. **Monoamine oxidase inhibitors** are a group of antidepressant drugs that keep the enzyme monoamine oxidase from deactivating neurotransmitters. Both these types of drugs increase the levels of both serotonin and norepinephrine in the brains of animals. This information only suggested that depression is caused by low levels of these substances, but it encouraged further exploration.

Another piece of evidence favoring both theories was provided by reserpine, a drug sometimes used in the treatment of hypertension. Reserpine was isolated in the 1950s by a research team working in Switzerland. It is an alkaloid of the root of *Rauwolfia serpentina*, a shrub that grows in India. Hindu physicians have for centuries administered powdered rauwolfia as a treatment for mental illness. Reserpine was one of the compounds that initiated the modern era of psychopharmacology and revolutionized the care and treatment of mental patients. This drug and chlorpromazine were given to schizophrenics to calm their agitation. Reserpine did indeed relax and sedate them but was soon contraindicated since depression was a serious side effect in about 15 percent of the patients taking it (e.g., Lemieux, Davignon, & Genest, 1965). Reserpine was discovered to reduce levels of both serotonin and norepinephrine by impairing the process by which these substances are stored within the synaptic vesicles, allowing them instead to become degraded by monoamine oxidase.

So far we have examined indirect evidence for each theory. Two other approaches have been used. The first measures metabolites of these neurotransmitters, the by-products of the breakdown of serotonin and norepinephrine as they are found in urine, blood serum, and the cerebrospinal fluid. The problem with such measurements is that they are not direct reflections of *brain* levels of either serotonin or norepinephrine, since serotonin is involved in other bodily processes and norepinephrine also acts in the peripheral nervous system.

A second strategy is to choose drugs other than the antidepressants and reserpine that are known either to increase or to decrease the brain levels of serotonin and norepinephrine. A drug raising the level of a neurotransmitter should alleviate depression; one reducing it should deepen depression or induce it in normal subjects. This strategy also has its problems, however. Most drugs have multiple effects, making it difficult to choose one that accomplishes a specific purpose without complicating side effects.

These problems notwithstanding, what can be said of the validity of these theories that implicate low levels of norepinephrine or serotonin in depression and high levels of norepinephrine in mania? First, a series of studies conducted by Bunney and Murphy and their colleagues at the National Institute of Mental Health monitored closely the urinary levels of norepinephrine itself in a group of bipolar patients as they cycled through stages of depression, mania, and normalcy. Urinary levels of norepinephrine decreased as patients became depressed (Bunney et al., 1970) and increased during mania (Bunney, Goodwin, & Murphy, 1972). However, such changes could result from increases in activity level (increased motor activity in mania could increase norepinephrine activity). Nonetheless, there is evidence that stimulating a norepinephrine increase can precipitate a manic episode in a bipolar patient (Silberman et al., 1981). Turning to metabolites of norepinephrine, the evidence is mixed again. 3-Methoxy-4-hydroxyphenyl glycol (MHPG) is considered norepinephrine's principal metabolite. According to the theory, low levels of norepinephrine should be reflected in low levels of MHPG. Although depressed bipolar patients have generally been shown to have low levels of urinary MHPG, the amount of MHPG in the urine of unipolar patients does not differ from that of controls (e.g., Muscettola et al., 1984). However, MHPG levels are higher in bipolar manics than in depressed bipolar patients and higher also in manics than in normal people (Goodwin & Jamison, 1990).

Studies of serotonin examine 5-hydroxyindoleacetic acid (5-HIAA), a major metabolite of serotonin that is present in cerebrospinal fluid and can be measured to determine the level of the transmitter in the brain and spinal cord. A fairly consistent body of data indicates that 5-HIAA levels are low in the cerebrospinal fluid of depressives (see McNeal & Cimbolic, 1986, for a review). Studies also show that ingestion of L-tryptophan, which acts as a serotonin precursor, relieves depression, especially when used in combination with other drugs (Coppen et al., 1972; Mendels et al., 1975). Furthermore, a drug that suppresses serotonin synthesis reduces the therapeutic effect of drugs that usually lessen depression (Shopsin, Friedman, & Gershon, 1976). Finally, Delgado et al. (1988) reduced tryptophan in remitted depressives with a special diet and found that 67 percent experienced a return of their symptoms. When their normal diet was resumed, a gradual remission followed.

We have indicated that effective antidepressants increase levels of norepinephrine and serotonin and that knowledge of this formed a keystone of the norepinephrine and serotonin theories of depression. However, it now appears that the explanation of why these drugs work is not as straightforward as it seemed at first: the therapeutic effects of tricyclics and monoamine oxidase inhibitors do *not* depend solely on an increase in levels of neurotransmitters. The earlier findings were correct: tricyclics and monoamine oxidase inhibitors do indeed increase levels of norepinephrine and serotonin *when they are first taken*. But after several days the levels of neurotransmitters return to what they were earlier. This information is crucial because it does not fit with data on how much time must pass before antidepressants become effective. Both tricyclics and monoamine oxidase inhibitors take from seven to fourteen days to relieve depression! By that time, the neurotransmitter level has already returned to its previous level. It would seem, then, that a simple increase in norepinephrine or serotonin is not a sufficient explanation for why the drugs alleviate depression (Heninger, Charney, & Menkes, 1983).

Another key finding that has prompted a move away from the original theories of a simple increase in serotonin and norepinephrine levels comes from studies of new antidepressants. For example, mianserin and zimeldine seem to be effective antidepressants (Cole, 1986), and neither of these drugs simply increases the amount of norepinephrine or serotonin.

What is the impact of these new findings on the old theories? Researchers are now examining whether tricyclics and monoamine oxidase inhibitors act against depression by altering postsynaptic receptors. At this time, results are contradictory and difficult to interpret. Antidepressants seem to decrease the sensitivity of β-adrenergic receptors yet increase the sensitivity of serotonin receptors (McNeal & Cimbolic, 1986). This attention to receptors means that new methodologies must be developed to study receptor sensitivity in human beings. Most of our current knowledge of the functioning of receptors comes from animal studies. As yet, the methods used in human studies are indirect. The next few years of research will undoubtedly see further refinements so that receptor functions can be more thoroughly explored.

The Neuroendocrine System

Many studies also suggest a role for the neuroendocrine system in depression. The limbic area of the brain is closely linked to emotion and also has effects on the hypothalamus. The hypothalamus, in turn, controls various endocrine glands and thus the levels of hormones they secrete. Hormones secreted by the hypothalamus also affect the pituitary gland and the hormones it produces. Because of its relevance to the so-called vegetative symptoms of depression, such as disturbances in appetite and sleep, the hypothalamic–pituitary–adrenal cortical axis is thought to be overactive in depression.

Various findings support this proposition. Levels of cortisol (an adrenocortical hormone) are high in depressives; this finding even led to the development of a biological test for depression—the dexamethasone suppression test (DST). Dexamethasone suppresses cortisol secretion. When given dexamethasone during an overnight test, some depressives, especially those with melancholia, did not experience cortisol suppression (Carroll, 1982; Poland et al., 1987). The interpretation is that the failure of dexamethasone to suppress cortisol reflects overactivity in the hypothalamic–pituitary–adrenal cortical axis of depressive subjects. The failure to show suppression normalizes when the depressive episode ends, indicating that it might be a nonspecific response to stress. Another finding linking high levels of cortisol to depression is found in a disease called Cushing's syndrome. Abnormal growths on the adrenal cortex lead to oversecretion of cortisol and an ensuing depression. The oversecretion in depression may also be linked to the neurotransmitter theories just discussed. High levels of cortisol may lower the density of serotonin receptors (Roy et al., 1987) and impair the function of noradrenergic receptors (Price et al., 1986). Finally, the hypothalamic–pituitary–thyroid axis is of possible relevance to bipolar disorder. Disorders of thyroid function are often seen in bipolar patients, and thyroid hormones can induce mania in these patients (Goodwin & Jamison, 1990).

All these data lend some support to theories that mood disorders have biological causes. Does this mean that psychological theories are irrelevant or useless? Not in the least. To assert that behavioral disorders have a basis in biological processes is to state the obvious. No psychogenic theorist would deny that behavior is mediated by some kinds of bodily changes. The question, rather, is how psychological and biological factors interact. We have already grappled with this philosophical issue in Chapter 8. It may well be, for example, that alteration of norepinephrine receptors does cause certain kinds of depression, but that an earlier link in the causal chain is the sense of hopelessness or paralysis of will that psychological theorists have proposed as the disabler.

Therapy for Mood Disorders

Most episodes of depression lift after a few months,[2] although the time may seem immeasurably longer to the depressed individual and to those close to him or her. That most depressions are self-limiting is fortunate. However, mental health workers have not forsaken depressives. Depression is too widespread and too incapacitating, both to the sufferer and to those around him or her, not to treat the disorder. Furthermore, bouts of depression tend to recur (Keller et al., 1982). Current therapies are both psychological and biological. Singly or in combination, they turn out to be quite effective.

Psychological Therapies

Because depression is considered to be derived from a repressed sense of loss and from anger unconsciously turned inward, psychoanalytic treatment tries to help the patient achieve insight into the repressed conflict and often encourages outward release of the hostility supposedly directed inward. In the most general terms, the goal of psychoanalytic therapy is to uncover latent motivations for the patient's depression. A person may, for example, blame himself or herself for the death of a loved one, but repress this belief because of the pain it causes. The therapist must first guide the patient to confront the fact that he or she holds this belief, and can then help the patient realize that the guilt is unfounded. The recovery of memories of stressful circumstances of the patient's childhood, at which time feelings of inadequacy and loss may have developed, should also bring relief.

Research on the effectiveness of dynamic psychotherapy in alleviating depression is sparse (Craighead, Evans, & Robins, 1992; Klerman, 1988) and characterized by mixed results, in part owing to the high degree of variability among approaches that come under the rubric of psychodynamic or psychoanalytic psychotherapy. For example, early studies of psychoanalytic therapy combined with tricyclic drugs did not lift mood any more than did the drugs by themselves (Daneman, 1961; Covi et al., 1974). However, recent findings from a large-scale study (Elkin et al., 1989) suggest that a form of psychodynamic therapy that concentrates on present-day interactions between the depressed person and the social environment—Klerman and Weissman's interpersonal therapy (Klerman et al., 1984)—is quite effective for alleviating unipolar depression as well as for maintaining treatment gains (Frank et al., 1990). The core of the therapy is to help the depressed patient examine the ways in which his or her current interpersonal behavior might interfere with obtaining pleasure from relationships. For example, the patient might be taught how to improve communication with others to better meet his or her needs and to have more satisfying social interactions and support. Additional information on

[2]Depression can be more than a serious inconvenience. It can be life-threatening, for the risk of suicide is especially great in depressed individuals. The last section of this chapter is devoted to suicide.

interpersonal therapy is provided in the detailed discussion of the Elkin (1989) study in Chapter 19.

In keeping with their cognitive theory of depression, that the profound sadness and shattered self-esteem of depressed individuals are caused by errors in their thinking, Aaron Beck and his associates devised a cognitive therapy aimed at altering maladaptive thought patterns. The therapist tries to persuade the depressed person to change his or her opinions of events and of the self. When a client states that he or she is worthless because "Nothing goes right. Everything I try to do ends in a disaster," the therapist offers examples contrary to this overgeneralization, such as abilities that the client is either overlooking or discounting. The therapist also instructs the patient to monitor private monologues with himself or herself and to identify all patterns of thought that contribute to depression. The therapist then teaches the patient to think through negative prevailing beliefs to understand how they prevent making more realistic and positive assumptions and interpreting adversity more accurately.

Although developed independently of Ellis's rational-emotive method, Beck's analyses are similar to it in some ways. For example, Beck suggests that depressed people are likely to consider themselves totally inept and incompetent if they make a mistake. This schema can be considered an extension of one of Ellis's irrational beliefs, that the individual must be competent in all things in order to be a worthwhile person.

Beck also includes behavioral components in his treatment of depression. Especially when patients are severely depressed, Beck encourages them to *do* things, such as getting out of bed in the morning or going for a walk, and discourages them from doing other things, such as attempting suicide. Beck gives his patients activity assignments that will provide them with successful experiences and allow them to think well of themselves. But the overall emphasis is on cognitive restructuring, on persuading the person to think differently. If a change in overt behavior will help in achieving that goal, fine. Behavioral change by itself, however, without altering the errors in logic that Beck asserts depressed people commit, cannot be expected to alleviate depression in any significant way.

Over the past two decades considerable research has been conducted on Beck's therapy, beginning with a widely cited study by Rush et al. (1977), which indicated that cognitive therapy was more successful than the tricyclic imipramine (Tofranil) in alleviating unipolar depression. The unusually low improvement rate found for the drug in this clinical trial suggests that these patients might have been poorly suited for pharmacotherapy—and that therefore this was not a fair comparison. Nonetheless, the efficacy of Beck's therapy in this study and in a twelve-month follow-up (Kovacs et al., 1981) encouraged many other researchers to conduct additional evaluations, which have confirmed its efficacy (e.g., Hollon, DeRubeis, Tuason, Weimer, Evans, & Garvey, 1989; Seligman et al., 1988; Simons, Murphy, Levine, & Wetzel, 1985; Teasdale, Fennell, Hibbert, & Amies, 1984), including data showing that Beck's therapy has a prophylactic effect in preventing subsequent bouts of depression (Blackburn, Eunson, & Bishop, 1986; Evans et al., 1993; Hollon, DeRubeis, & Seligman, 1993). This growing body of research prompted Beck to conclude in a clinical vein that "it would seem desirable that if a patient is placed on drugs, to offer him cognitive therapy in addition. However, if he is receiving cognitive therapy [already], it is not clear that adding drugs would be indicated except for the more severely depressed patients in a hospital outpatient clinic" (Beck, 1986a, p. 3).

In Chapter 19 (page 568) we review in detail the large, multisite study comparing cognitive therapy with psychodynamic interpersonal therapy and imipramine drug therapy; we'll see that although cognitive therapy fares well, it does not appear superior to imipramine or psychodynamic therapy.

Since a key feature of depression is a lack of satisfying experiences with other people, behavioral treatments have also focused on helping the patient improve social interactions. Although there are cognitive components in these approaches—for example, encouraging the depressed patient not to evaluate his or her performance too harshly—evidence supports the effectiveness of a focus on enhancing overt social behaviors by such techniques as assertion and social-skills training (Hersen, Bellack, Himmelhoch, & Thase, 1984; Lewinsohn, 1974; Teri & Lewinsohn, 1986). Also, as described in our discussion of couples therapy (page 601), improvement in the kinds of interpersonal conflicts found in a distressed marriage or other intimate relationship also alleviates depression (O'Leary & Beach, 1990; Jacobson, Holzworth-Monroe, & Schmaling, 1989).

Clearly, determining the best therapy for each individual can be a challenge. A woman who is disheartened because of the way she is treated by men might be better advised by a feminist therapist, who will encourage her to resist continued subjugation by an overbearing spouse or boss, than by an equally well-intentioned cognitive therapist, who might try to teach her that the treatment she receives from husband or supervisor is not all that bad.

A preliminary effort to match type of patient to

type of treatment was reported by McKnight, et al. (1984). Adult women diagnosed as having a mood disorder were assigned to either rational-emotive therapy or social-skills training and then switched to the other treatment in an alternating treatments design. Significant and enduring (one-year follow-up) treatment effects, which did not differ from each other, were found on a variety of measures for both therapies. What is particularly interesting in this study is that, prior to treatment, a subset of three subjects had been identified as having special difficulties with irrational thinking and the other three with social skills deficits. A close analysis of session-by-session progress showed that the irrational group benefited more from RET than from social-skills training, with the reverse holding true for the socially deficient patients. The implication is clear: depression can be caused by a variety of factors, and optimal treatment should be chosen on the basis of efforts to match those factors with the nature of a given therapy (Haaga & Davison, 1989).

Other efforts to match certain kinds of depressed people with certain kinds of treatment have had mixed, though somewhat promising, results. Rosenbaum (1980), for example, developed the Self Control Schedule for measuring what he called learned resourcefulness. This self-report scale taps four dimensions of self-control: the use of self-instructions to cope with problems; the use of problem-solving strategies; the ability to delay gratification; and a belief in one's ability to control events. Investigators reasoned that a depressed person who is high on these abilities will do better with a cognitive therapy (which seems to capitalize on these skills) than with drug therapy, and, conversely, that patients low on the Self Control Schedule will do better with pharmacotherapy. Two studies lend support to the first proposition (Simons et al., 1985; Rehm, Kaslow, & Rabin, 1987), but others do not (e.g., Hoberman, Lewinsohn, & Tilson, 1988). It may be that having lots of learned resourcefulness is good no matter what the therapy. Psychoanalysts have for some time asserted that people with high levels of ego strength do better in analytic therapy. It may be that, regardless of one's therapy, it is preferable to have coping skills and a faith in one's ability to solve problems and to change than not to have such characteristics.

Finally, as with all forms of therapy for a wide range of human problems, the therapist must confront the moral and political implications of his or her work, and we shall turn to some of these issues in the last section of this chapter. Should I help the client alter his or her life situation, or should I help the client adjust? Indeed, the very fact that a person is depressed may indicate that he or she is ready for a change in social and personal relations with others (see Focus Box 9-2).

Biological Therapies

There are a variety of biological therapies for depression and mania. We will discuss the two most common, electroconvulsive shock and various drugs.

Electroconvulsive Therapy

Perhaps the most dramatic, and controversial, treatment for depression is **electroconvulsive therapy** (ECT). ECT was originated by two Italian physicians, Cerletti and Bini, in the early twentieth century. Cerletti had been interested in epilepsy and was seeking a means by which its seizures could be experimentally induced. The solution became apparent to him during a visit to a slaughterhouse, where he saw animals rendered unconscious by electric shocks administered to the head. Shortly thereafter he found that by applying electric shocks to the sides of the human head, he could produce full epileptic seizures. Not long thereafter, in 1938 in Rome, he used the technique on a schizophrenic patient.

Electroconvulsive therapy (ECT) is an effective treatment for depression. Using unilateral shock, anesthetics, and muscle relaxants has reduced its undesirable side-effects.

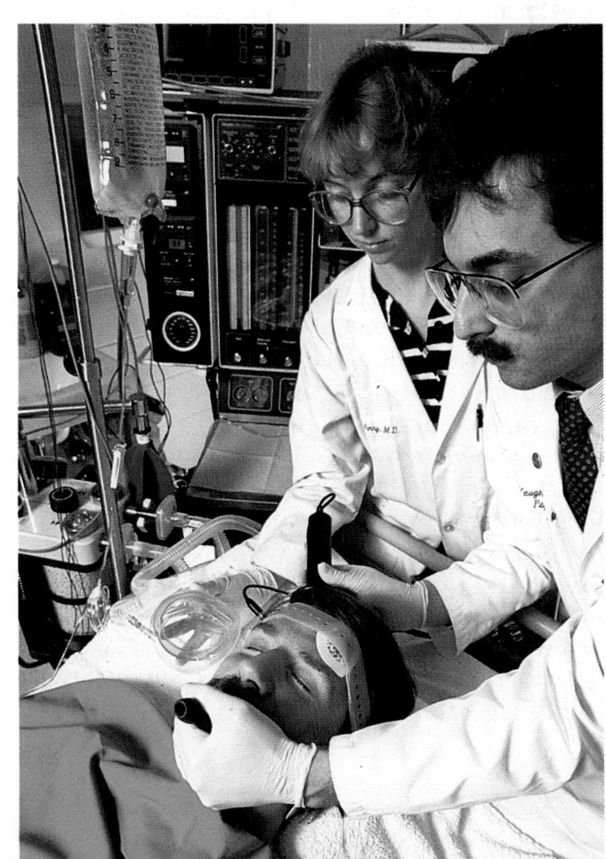

9.2 • An Existential Theory of Depression and Its Treatment

In 1959 a remarkable book, *From Death Camp to Existentialism*, was published by Viktor Frankl, an Austrian psychiatrist who during World War II had spent three horrible years in Nazi concentration camps. His wife, brother, and parents, imprisoned with him, all lost their lives. Revised since its initial appearance and retitled *Man's Search for Meaning* (1963), Frankl's book vividly describes the humiliation, suffering, and terror experienced by camp prisoners. Frankl goes on to tell how he and others managed to survive psychologically in the brutalizing conditions of the death camps.

Frankl concluded that he was sustained emotionally by having succeeded somehow in finding meaning in his suffering and relating it to his spiritual life. The spirit gives the individual freedom to transcend circumstances, and freedom makes the individual responsible for his or her life. Frankl believes that psychopathology, particularly depression, ensues when a person has no purpose in living. Out of his concentration camp experiences he developed a psychotherapeutic approach called **logotherapy**, after the Greek word *logos*, "meaning."

The task of logotherapy is to restore meaning to the client's life. This is accomplished first by accepting in an empathic way the subjective experience of the client's suffering, rather than conveying the message that suffering is sick and wrong and should therefore not be regarded as normal. The logotherapist then helps the client make some sense out of his or her suffering by placing it within a larger context, a philosophy of life in which the individual assumes responsibility for his or her existence and for pursuing the values inherent in life. As Nietzsche said, "He who has a why to live for can bear with almost any how."

It may be useful to relate Frankl's views on depression and its treatment to learned helplessness. Certainly the concentration camp induced helplessness and hopelessness, an utter disbelief that an individual could exert any control over his or her life. Profound depression was commonplace. Logotherapy might be an effective way to reverse the helplessness depressed people experience in contemporary society, under less horrific and brutal conditions. By accepting responsibility for their lives and by seeking some meaning even in trying circumstances, they may achieve a sense of control and competence indispensable for forging an acceptable existence.

In the decades that followed, ECT was administered to both schizophrenic and psychotically depressed patients, usually in hospital settings. For the most part its use nowadays is restricted to profoundly depressed individuals. ECT entails the deliberate induction of a seizure and momentary unconsciousness by passing a current of between 70 and 130 volts through the patient's brain. Electrodes were formerly placed on each side of the forehead, which allowed the current to pass through both hemispheres (**bilateral ECT**). Today, **unilateral ECT**, in which the current passes through the nondominant cerebral hemisphere only (e.g., Abrams, Swartz, & Vedak, 1991), is more commonly used. In the past the patient was usually awake until the current triggered the seizure, and the electric shock often created frightening contortions of the body, sometimes even causing bone fractures. Now the patient is given a short-acting anesthetic, then an injection of a strong muscle relaxant before the current is applied. The convulsive spasms of the body muscles are barely perceptible to onlookers, and the patient awakens a few minutes later, remembering nothing about the treatment.

Inducing a seizure still remains a drastic procedure, however. Why should anyone in his or her right but depressed mind agree to undergo such radical therapy, or how could a parent or a spouse consent to such treatment if the patient is judged legally incapable of giving consent? The answer is simple. Although we don't know why, ECT may be the optimal treatment for severe depression (Klerman, 1988). Most professionals, though, acknowledge the risks involved—confusion and memory loss that can be prolonged. However, unilateral ECT to the nondominant hemisphere now erases fewer memories than did bilateral ECT, and no detectable changes in brain structure result (Coffey et al., 1991). Clinicians typically resort to ECT only after less drastic treatments have been tried and found wanting. In considering *any* treatment that has negative side effects, the person making the decision must be aware of the consequences of not providing any treatment at all. Given that suicide is a real possibility among depressed people, and given a moral stance that values the preservation of life, the use of ECT, at least after other treatments have failed, is regarded by many as defensible and responsible.

Drug Therapy

Drugs are the most commonly used treatments for mood disorders. They do not work for all people, however, and side effects are sometimes serious (see Table 9.3). Determination of proper dosages can also be tricky.

The two major categories of antidepressant drugs are the tricyclics, such as imipramine (Tofranil) and amitriptyline (Elavil), and the monoamine oxidase (MAO) inhibitors, such as Parnate. Since the MAO inhibitors have by far the more serious side effects, the tricyclics are more widely used. These medications have been established as effective in a number of double-blind studies (Davidson et al., 1988; Morris & Beck, 1974) in addition to studies already mentioned. Both types of drugs are believed to ameliorate depression by facilitating neural transmission.

In recent years a number of new antidepressants have been introduced, the so-called second generation antidepressants. Although effective, many offer little or no therapeutic advantage over their older counterparts. The exceptions to this general rule are buproprion and fluoxetine. Buproprion appears to have a special role in the treatment of bipolar disorder, as it effectively reduces psychomotor retardation and is less likely than other antidepressants to induce a manic episode (Goodwin & Jamison, 1990). Fluoxetine (trade name Prozac) has achieved considerable notoriety. Hailed as a breakthrough drug, it even appeared on the cover of *Newsweek* (March 26, 1990). However, a number of anecdotal reports of serious side effects (especially a severe preoccupation with suicide and other violent acts) propelled the drug into the media and even the talk-show circuit. Although controlled research does not indicate that fluoxetine is likely to produce severe side effects, the controversy is by no means settled.

Although the various antidepressants hasten a patient's recovery from an episode of depression, relapse is still common after the drugs are withdrawn. Continuing to take imipramine after remission is of value in preventing recurrence—provided that maintenance doses are as high as the effective treatment doses (instead of lower, as is usually the case) and that the patient was involved during the drug therapy in a psychosocial treatment, such as Klerman and Weissman's interpersonal therapy (Frank et al., 1990). Indeed, antidepressant medication can be and often is used in combination with some kind of psychotherapy. If, for example, a person's depression is (partly) caused by lack of personal satisfaction because of problems or deficits in social skills, it is probably essential that the drug treatment be supplemented by psychosocial attention to those behavioral deficits (Klerman, 1988, 1990; Weissman et al., 1974).

Even if a chemical agent managers to alleviate a bout of depression only temporarily, that benefit in itself should not be underestimated, given the potential for suicide in depression and given the extreme anguish and suffering borne by the individual and usually by his or her family as well. Moreover, the judicious use of a drug may make unnecessary an avenue of intervention and control that many regard as very much a last resort, namely, being placed in a mental hospital.

People with the mood swings of bipolar disorder are often helped by carefully monitored dosages of lithium, an element, taken in a salt form, **lithium**

Table 9.3 • Drugs for Treating Mood Disorders

Category	*Generic Name*	*Trade Name*	*Side Effects*
Tricyclic Antidepressants	Imipramine Amitriptyline	Tofranil Elavil	Heart attack, stroke, hypotension, blurred vision, anxiety, tiredness, dry mouth, constipation, gastric disorders, erectile failure, weight gain
MAO Inhibitors	Tranylcyronize	Parnate	Possibly fatal hypertension, dry mouth, dizziness, nausea, headaches
Second Generation Antidepressants	Fluoxetine	Prozac	Nervousness, fatigue, gastrointestinal complaints, dizziness, headaches, insomnia
	Buproprion	Wellbutin	Agitation, dry mouth, insomnia, headache, constipation, tremor, seizures, weight loss
Lithium	Lithium	Lithium	Tremors, gastric distress, lack of coordination, dizziness, cardiac arrhythmia, blurred vision, fatigue

carbonate. The fact that lithium carbonate cannot be patented like other drugs discouraged pharmaceutical companies for years from marketing it; only minimal profits are to be made. Because the effects of lithium occur gradually, therapy typically begins with both lithium and a neuroleptic such as Haldol, which has an immediate calming effect. While a number of hypotheses are being pursued concerning how lithium works, none has good support at this time (e.g., Manji et al., 1991). Lithium is effective for bipolar patients when they are depressed as well as when they are manic and is much more effective than for unipolar patients (Baron et al., 1975)—another bit of evidence that these two mood disorders are basically different from each other.

Because of possibly serious, even fatal, side effects, lithium has to be prescribed and used very carefully. Furthermore, although it has great value in the elimination of a manic episode, discontinuation of lithium actually increases a person's risk for recurrence (Suppes et al., 1991). Thus, it is recommended that lithium be used continually. Finally, mention should be made of carbamazapine, originally used as an anticonvulsant; its use is on the upswing with manic patients and it has achieved good results (Small et al., 1991).

Suicide

In classical Rome, in the period just preceding the Christian era, the quality of life was viewed as far more important than how long one lived. "Living is not good, but living well. The wise man, therefore, lives as well as he should, not as long as he can. . . . He will always think of life in terms of quality not quantity" wrote the first-century Roman Stoic philosopher Seneca (as cited in Shneidman, 1973, p. 384). Then in its first centuries, Christianity was a persecuted religion; many early Christians committed suicide in acts of martyrdom (Heyd & Bloch, 1981). Western thought changed radically in the fourth century, when Saint Augustine proclaimed suicide a crime because it violated the Sixth Commandment, thou shalt not kill. Saint Thomas Aquinas elaborated on this view in the thirteenth century, declaring suicide to be a mortal sin because it usurped God's power over life and death. So, although neither the Old Testament nor the New explicitly forbids suicide, the Western world came to regard it as a crime and a sin (Shneidman, 1973). The irony is that the Christian injunctions against suicide, deriving from a profound respect for life, contributed to persecution of those who attempted to take their own lives. Indeed, as late as 1823 anyone in London who committed suicide was buried with a stake pounded through the heart, and not until 1961 did suicide cease to be a criminal offense in Great Britain. But what penalty can be imposed on someone who has committed suicide! Some states do categorize suicide attempts as misdemeanors, but these offenses are seldom prosecuted. On the other hand, there are laws in most states that make it a crime to encourage or advise suicide (Shneidman, 1987).

Suicide is discussed in this chapter because many depressives have suicidal thoughts and sometimes make genuine attempts to take their own lives. Moreover, it is generally believed that more than half of those who try to kill themselves are depressed and despondent at the time of the act. A significant number of people who are not depressed, however, make suicidal attempts, some with success. Other disorders are also associated with suicide (Linehan & Shearin, 1988). The suicide rate for male alcoholics is 75 times greater than that for the general population of men (Kessel & Grossman, 1961), and up to 13 percent of schizophrenics commit suicide (Roy, 1982). Our focus here is on issues and factors in suicide that transcend specific diagnoses.

Facts about Suicide

No single theory is likely to take into account all the available information about suicide. The diversity of known facts may help us appreciate how complex and multifaceted self-intentioned death is (Fremouw, et al., 1990; Hendin, 1982; Holinger, 1987; National Center for Health Statistics, 1988; Wright, 1992). For contrast to the facts listed below, see Focus Box 9.3 for myths about suicide.

1. Every twenty minutes someone in the United States kills himself or herself, and this rate—over 30,000 a year—is probably a gross underestimate. The suicide rate in the United States is about 12.8 per 100,000. It rises in old age; between the ages of seventy-five and eighty-four, the rate reaches 25.2 per 100,000.
2. Although no official data are available it is estimated that between 240,000 and 600,000 people attempt suicide each year. This means that for every actual suicide in the United States, between eight and twenty people have made

an attempt. Another way to look at these estimates is that at least five million living Americans have attempted to kill themselves.

3. About half of those who commit suicide have made at least one previous attempt, but two-thirds of attempters never make another attempt. Some differences between attempters and completers are shown in Table 9.4.
4. Almost four times as many men kill themselves as women, although the ratio may be approaching three times as many men as women, for women are becoming a higher risk group.
5. Three times as many women as men attempt to kill themselves but do not die.
6. Being divorced or widowed greatly increases suicide risk and may be a risk factor that becomes more influential with age. The importance of marital status may also be an aspect of the role of lack of social support in suicidal risk.
7. Suicide is found in both the very old and the very young—even in those older than ninety years and younger than ten years.
8. Suicide is found at all social and economic levels but is especially frequent among psychiatrists, physicians, lawyers, and psychologists.
9. No other kind of death leaves in friends and relatives such long-lasting feelings of distress, shame, guilt, puzzlement, and general disturbance. Indeed, these survivors are themselves victims, having an especially high mortality rate in the year following the suicide of their loved one.
10. Guns are by far the most common means of suicide in the United States. Men usually choose to shoot or hang themselves; women are more likely to use sleeping pills, which may account for their lower rate of completed suicide.
11. Suicide ranks eighth as a cause of death among adults in general; it ranks third after accidents and homicides among those aged fifteen to twenty-four. It is estimated that each year upwards of 10,000 American college students attempt to kill themselves and that as many as 20 percent consider suicide at least once during their college years.

Suicide involving violent death, such as jumping off a building, is more common among men than women.

Table 9.4 • Comparison of Suicide Attempters and Completers

Characteristic	*Attempters*	*Completers*
Gender	Majority female	Majority male
Age	Predominantly young	Risk increases with age
Method	Low lethality (pills, cutting)	More violent (gun, jumping)
Circumstances	Intervention likely	Precautions against discovery
Common diagnoses	Dysthymic disorder Borderline personality disorder	Major mood disorder Alcoholism Schizophrenia
Dominant affect	Depression with anger	Depression with hopelessness
Motivation	Change in situation Cry for help	Death
Hospital course	Quick recovery from dysphoria	
Attitude toward attempt	Relief to have survived Promises not to repeat	

Source: Adapted from Fremouw et al., 1990, p. 24. Reprinted by permission of Simon and Schuster International.

FOCUS 9.3 • Some Myths about Suicide

There are many prevalent misconceptions about suicide (Fremouw, Perczel, & Ellis, 1990; Pokorny, 1968; Shneidman, 1973).

1. **People who discuss suicide will not commit the act.** The fact is that up to three-quarters of those who take their lives have communicated beforehand, perhaps as a cry for help, perhaps to taunt.
2. **Suicide is committed without warning.** The falseness of this belief is readily indicated by the preceding statement. The person usually gives many warnings, such as saying that the world would be better off without him or her or making unexpected and inexplicable gifts to others, often of his or her most valued possessions.
3. **Only people of a certain class commit suicide.** Suicide is neither the curse of the poor nor the disease of the rich. People in all classes commit suicide.
4. **Membership in a particular religious group is a good predictor that a person will not consider suicide.** It is mistakenly thought that the strong Catholic prohibition against suicide makes the risk that Catholics will take their lives much lower. This is not supported by the evidence, perhaps because an individual's formal religious identification is not always an accurate index of true beliefs.
5. **The motives for suicide are easily established.** The truth is that we do not fully understand why people commit suicide. For example, the fact that a severe reverse in finances precedes a suicide does not mean that the reversal adequately explains the suicide.
6. **All who commit suicide are depressed.** This fallacy may account for the fact that signs of impending suicide are overlooked because the person does not act despondently. Many of the people who take their lives are *not* depressed. In fact, some people appear calm and at peace with themselves.
7. **A person with a terminal physical illness is unlikely to commit suicide.** A person's awareness of impending death does not preclude suicide. Perhaps the wish to end their own suffering or that of their loved ones impels many to choose the time of their death.

12. The rates for suicide among white and Native American youths are more than twice those for African-American youths, although in the inner cities, the rates among young African-American men are twice as high as those among young white men (similar to the higher incidence of violence and homicide among young urban African-Americans). The highest rates of suicide in the United States are for white males over 50.
13. The rates of suicide for adolescents and children in the United States are increasing dramatically. As many as 3,000 young people between the ages of fifteen and nineteen are believed to kill themselves each year, and attempts are made by children as young as six. But the rates are far below those of adults.
14. Hungary has the highest rate of suicide in the world. Czechoslovakia, Finland, Sweden, Japan, and Austria also have high incidences. The countries with the lowest rates are Greece, Ireland, and Italy.
15. Suicide rates go up during depression years, remain stable during years of prosperity, and decrease during war years.

Perspectives on Suicide

In imagining a suicide, we usually think of a person deliberately performing a dramatic act explicitly chosen to end life almost immediately—the woman on the ledge of the tall building, the man with the gun next to his temple, the child with the bottle of mother's sleeping pills. But suicidologists also regard people as suicidal when they act in self-destructive ways that can cause serious injury or death after a prolonged period of time, such as a diabetic who neglects insulin and a dietary regimen

8. **To commit suicide is insane.** Although most suicidal persons are very unhappy, most do appear to be completely rational and in touch with reality.
9. **A tendency to commit suicide is inherited.** Since suicides often run in families, the assumption is made that the tendency to think in terms of self-annihilation is inherited. There is no evidence for this.
10. **Suicide is influenced by seasons, latitude, weather fronts, barometric pressure, humidity, precipitation, cloudiness, wind speed, temperature, and days of the week.** There are no good data to substantiate any of these myths.
11. **Suicide is influenced by cosmic factors such as sunspots and phases of the moon.** No evidence confirms this.
12. **Improvement in emotional state means lessened risk of suicide.** The fact is that people often commit the act after their spirits begin to rise and their energy level improves; this appears to be especially true of depressed patients.
13. **Suicide is a lonely event.** Although the debate whether to commit suicide is waged within the individual's head, deep immersion in a frustrating, hurtful relationship with another person—a spouse, a child, a lover, a colleague—may be a principal cause.
14. **Suicidal people clearly want to die.** Most people who commit suicide appear to be ambivalent about their own deaths. Others are suffering from depression or alcoholism, which, if alleviated, reduces the suicidal desire. For many people the suicidal crisis passes, and they are grateful for having been prevented from self-destruction.
15. **Thinking about suicide is rare.** Estimates from various studies suggest that, among nonclinical populations, suicidal ideation runs from 40 percent to as high as 80 percent; that is, these percentages of people have thought about committing suicide at least once in their lives.
16. **Asking a person, especially a depressed one, about suicide will push him or her over the edge and cause a suicidal act that would not otherwise have occurred.** One of the first things clinicians learn in their training is to inquire about suicide in a deeply troubled patient; to ask about it can give permission to talk about what the person might harbor as a terrible, shameful secret, which could lead to further isolation and depression.
17. **People who attempt suicide by a low-lethal means are not serious about killing themselves.** This confuses lethality with intent. Some people, for example, are not well-informed about pill dosages or human anatomy. What turns out to have been an attempt unlikely to have led to death may nonetheless have been engaged in by someone who really wanted to self-destruct.

or an alcoholic who will not seek help, despite awareness of the damage being done to his or her body. Sometimes termed *subintentioned death,* these apparent suicides complicate still further the task of understanding and gathering statistics on suicide (Shneidman, 1973).

Perspectives on suicide can be found in many domains (Shneidman, 1987). Ordinary people have left letters and diaries that can be studied for insights into the phenomenology of people who commit suicide. Novelists, for example, Herman Melville and Leo Tolstoy, have provided insights on suicide, as have writers who have killed themselves, such as Virginia Woolf and Sylvia Plath. In his book *Immortality,* the Czech novelist Milan Kundera probes the reasons a person decides on a given day to commit suicide. The events immediately preceding the act can be trivial—but not to a person whose self-confidence is already weak and sense of hopelessness overwhelming:

> The longing for self-destruction slowly grew until one day she was no longer capable of resisting it. I am guessing that the wrongs done to her were probably quite minor: people didn't respond to her greeting; nobody smiled at her; she was waiting in line at the post office and some fat woman elbowed her way past; she had a job as a saleswoman in a department store and the manager accused her of not treating the customers with respect. Thousands of times she felt like protesting and shouting, but she never found the courage, because she had a weak voice that faltered in moments of excitement. She was weaker than anyone else and was continually being insulted. When evil strikes a man, he shifts it onto others. That's called conflict, quarrel, or revenge. But a weak man doesn't have the strength to shift the evil that strikes him; his own weakness insults and humiliates him, and he is totally defenseless in the face of it. He has no other choice but to destroy his weakness

along with his own self. And so the girl's dream of her own death was born. (Kundera, 1991, p. 253)

Many philosophers have also written searchingly on the topic, such as Descartes, Voltaire, and Kant, and, especially existentialists, such as Heidegger and Camus, who grapple with the inherent meaninglessness of life and the individual's need and responsibility to forge some meaning out of what appears to be a dark existence.

While acknowledging that perhaps 90 percent of suicides could be given a DSM diagnosis, Shneidman (1987) reminds us that the overwhelming majority of schizophrenics and those with mood disorders do *not* commit suicide and that the *perturbation* of mind that he posits as a key feature of a suicide is not a mental illness.

It appears that media reports of suicide may spark an increase in suicides. This disturbing possibility was discussed by Bandura (1986), who reviewed research by Phillips (1974, 1977, 1985) showing that (1) suicides rose by 12 percent in the month following Marilyn Monroe's death; (2) publicized accounts of self-inflicted deaths of people other than the famous also are followed by significant increases in suicide (suggesting that it is publicity rather than the fame of the suicide that is important); (3) publicized accounts of murder-suicides are followed by increases in fatal auto and plane crashes where the driver and others are killed; and, finally, (4) media reports of natural deaths of famous people are not followed by increases in suicide, suggesting that it is not grief per se that is the influential factor.

Mintz (1968) summarized the numerous motivations for suicide mentioned in the literature: aggression turned inward; retaliation by inducing guilt in others; efforts to force love from others; efforts to make amends for perceived past wrongs; efforts to rid oneself of unacceptable feelings, such as sexual attraction to members of one's own sex; the desire for reincarnation; the desire to rejoin a dead loved one; and the desire or need to escape from stress, deformity, pain, or emotional vacuum. Many contemporary mental health workers regard suicide in general as an individual's attempt at problem-solving, conducted under considerable stress and marked by consideration of a very narrow range of alternatives, of which self-annihilation appears the most viable (Linehan & Shearin, 1988).

A recent theory about suicide, based on current work in social and personality psychology, holds that some suicides arise from a strong desire to escape from aversive self-awareness, that is, from the painful awareness of shortcomings and lack of success attributed to oneself (Baumeister, 1990). This awareness is assumed to produce severe emotional suffering. Having unrealistically high expectations—and therefore being likely to fall short when one shouldn't (cf. Beck and Ellis)—plays a central role in this perspective on suicide. Of particular importance is a discrepancy between high expectations for intimacy and a reality that falls short, for example, suicidality in someone whose expectations for intimacy are dashed by denial of affection by their loved one (Stephens, 1985). The person considers emotional life so negative as to be intolerable. Oblivion through death can appear more tolerable than a continuation of the painful awareness of one's deficiencies. There is considerable research in support of this hypothesis (Baumeister, 1990). We turn now to several other perspectives on suicide, each of which attempts to shed light on this disturbing aspect of humankind.

Freud's Psychoanalytic Theories of Suicide

Freud proposed two major hypotheses to account for suicide. One, an extension of his theory of depression, basically views suicide as murder. When a person loses someone whom he or she has ambivalently loved and hated, and introjects that person, aggression is directed inward. If these feelings are strong enough, the person will commit suicide. The second theory postulates that the death instinct, Thanatos, can turn inward and make a person take his or her life.

Freud's views on suicide are subject to many of the criticisms raised earlier in this text about psychoanalytic theorizing. Moreover, a careful analysis of suicide notes by Tuckman, Kleiner, and Lavell (1959) found that only a minority of the notes expressed hostility. In fact, about half expressed gratitude and affection for others.

Durkheim's Sociological Theory of Suicide

Durkheim (1897), after analyzing the records of suicide for various countries and during different historical periods, viewed self-annihilation as a sociological phenomenon and distinguished three different kinds. **Egoistic suicide** is committed when a person has too few ties to society and community. These people feel alienated from others, cut off from the social supports that are important to keep them functioning adaptively as social beings. **Altruistic suicides**, in contrast, are viewed by Durkheim as responses to societal demands. Some people who commit suicide feel very much a part of a group and sacrifice themselves for what they take to be the good of society. The self-immolations of Buddhist monks and nuns to protest the fighting during the Vietnam War would fit into this category. Some altruistic suicides, such as the hara-kiri of the Japanese, are literally required as the only honorable recourse in the circumstances. Finally, **anomic suicide** may be triggered by a sudden change in a person's relation to society. A successful executive who suffers severe financial reverses may experience anomie, a sense of disorientation, because what he or she believed to be a normal way of living is no longer possible. Anomie can pervade a society in disequilibrium, making suicide more likely.

As with all sociological theorizing, Durkheim's hypotheses have trouble accounting for the differences among individuals in a given society in their reactions to the same demands and conditions. Not all those who unexpectedly lose their money commit suicide. It appears that Durkheim was aware of this problem, for he suggested that individual temperament would interact with any of the social pressures that he found causative.

Shneidman's Approach to Suicide

Shneidman's psychological approach to suicide (1987) is summarized in Table 9.5, which contains the ten most frequent characteristics of suicide, not all of them found in each and every case.

This view regards suicide as (almost always) a conscious effort to seek a solution to a problem that is causing intense suffering. To the sufferer, this solution ends consciousness and unendurable pain—what Melville in *Moby Dick* termed an "insufferable anguish". All hope and sense of constructive action are gone. Still—and this is of central importance in prevention—most suicides are ambivalent. "The prototypical suicidal state is one in which an individual cuts his or her throat, cries for help at the same time, and is genuine in both of these acts. . . . Individuals would be happy not to do it, if they didn't have to" (Shneidman, 1987, p. 170). Cognitively there is a narrowing of the perceived range of options; when not in a highly perturbed suicidal state, the person is capable of seeing more choices in dealing with stress. People planning suicide usually communicate their intention, sometimes as a cry for help, sometimes as a withdrawal from others, a search for inviolacy. Common behaviors include giving away treasured possessions and putting one's financial affairs in order.

Table 9.5 • The Ten Commandments of Suicide

I. The common purpose of suicide is to seek a solution.
II. The common goal of suicide is the cessation of consciousness.
III. The common stimulus in suicide is intolerable psychological pain.
IV. The common stressor in suicide is frustrated psychological needs.
V. The common emotion in suicide is hopelessness–helplessness.
VI. The common cognitive state in suicide is ambivalence.
VII. The common perceptual state in suicide is constriction.
VIII. The common action in suicide is egression.
IX. The common interpersonal act in suicide is communication of intention.
X. The common consistency in suicide is with lifelong coping patterns.

Source: From Shneidman, 1987, p. 167.

Neurochemistry and Suicide

Earlier we described data relevant to the serotonin theory of depression. Research has also established a link between serotonin, suicide, and impulsivity. Low levels of serotonin's major metabolite, 5-HIAA, have been found in suicide victims in several diagnostic categories—depression, schizophrenia, and various personality disorders (see Brown & Goodwin, 1986). Furthermore, postmortem studies of the brains of people who committed suicide have revealed increased numbers of serotonin receptors (presumably a response to a decreased level of serotonin itself). The link between 5-HIAA levels and suicide is especially compelling in the case of violent and impulsive suicide. Finally, 5-HIAA levels are correlated with questionnaire measures of both aggression and impulsivity (Brown & Goodwin, 1986).

Prediction of Suicide from Psychological Tests

Psychologists have attempted to predict suicide on the basis of scores on psychological tests. It would of course be of immense theoretical and practical advantage to be able to predict from test results who might consider the act. Many investigators have studied the personality characteristics of those who have attempted suicide. An unavoidable difficulty with this kind of research stems from the fact that the personality tests can seldom be given to num-

Jo Roman, in her early sixties and suffering from breast cancer that was not yet critical, methodically planned her death for fifteen months. She was determined to spare herself and her dear ones the pain and great emotional strain of a terminal illness. While she could still "function to my satisfaction," she bid her husband, daughter, and a close friend goodnight and farewell, swallowed thirty-five sleeping pills and a glass of champagne, and went quietly to bed.

bers of people who may *later* kill themselves. Furthermore, in addition to the problem of obtaining data before a suicide attempt has been made, it is impossible to collect information, other than biographical accounts from relatives and a few other sources, after the deed has been done. Much of the literature, then, consists of reports of psychological tests given to people *after* they have made an aborted attempt at suicide. Clearly, the information obtained from such tests will reflect the fact that those tested have recently tried and failed to kill themselves. Their state of mind is likely to be quite different from what it was before the attempt. For example, many who have tried unsuccessfully to take their lives feel extremely guilty and embarrassed. It is impossible to know exactly how test scores and interview behavior are affected by such postattempt factors.

Although these problems may have affected test results, several studies have found significant correlations between suicide intent and hopelessness. Especially noteworthy are Aaron Beck's findings, based on prospective data, that hopelessness is a strong predictor of suicide (Beck et al., 1985; Beck, 1986b; Beck et al., 1990), more so than is depression (Beck, Kovacs, & Weissman, 1975). The expectation that at some point in the future things will be no better than they are right now seems to be more instrumental than depression per se in propelling a person to take his or her life. Beck and his group also developed the Suicidal Intent Scale (Beck, Schuyler, & Herman, 1974) and the Scale for Suicide Ideation (Beck, Kovacs, & Weissman, 1979), both of which show promise in helping us understand and predict those at high risk for serious suicide attempts.

A self-report inventory still under development is Marsha Linehan's Reasons for Living (RFL) Inventory (Linehan, Goodstein, Nielsen, & Chiles, 1983; Linehan, 1985b). Clusters of items tap things that are important to the individual, such as responsiblity to family and concerns about children. The approach taken here is different from, and possibly more useful than, scales that focus only on negativism and pessimism, because knowing what there is in a person's life that *prevents* him or her from committing suicide has both assessment and intervention value. This instrument can discriminate between suicidal and nonsuicidal individuals and can also help the clinician by guiding intervention to reasons that the person has for not wanting to die.

Another avenue of research has focused on the cognitive characteristics of people who attempt suicide. It has been suggested that suicidal individuals are more rigid in their approach to problems (e.g., Neuringer, 1964) and less flexible in their thinking (Levenson, 1972). Constricted thinking could account for their apparent inability to seek solutions to life problems other than taking their own lives (Linehan *et al.*, 1987). In general, research confirms the hypothesis that people who attempt suicide are more rigid than control subjects, lending support to the clinical observation that they seem almost myopically incapable of thinking of alternative solutions to problems and might therefore tend to settle on suicide as the only way out.

The foregoing research adopts a trait approach to understanding and predicting behavior (cf. Chapter 4, page 193)—if we know how much of a given characteristic a person has, we are supposed to be able to predict pretty well how he or she will behave in the future. But as we also saw in Chapter 4, behavior is influenced a great deal by the environment, and this includes stressful events that themselves can be very difficult to predict. We cannot know, for example, whether a given individual is going to lose employment, suffer the loss of a loved one, or have a serious accident. In addition, it is very hard to predict with accuracy a very infrequent event, like suicide. Even with a highly reliable test, many suicides would be missed (false negatives) and many people would be designated future suicides who will not turn out to be (false positives). For these reasons the prediction of suicide is inexact and likely to remain so (Fremouw et al., 1990).

Suicide Prevention

Shneidman's (1985, 1987) general approach to suicide prevention is threefold: try to reduce the intense psychological pain and suffering; lift the blinders, that is, expand the constricted view by helping the individual see options other than the extremes of continued suffering or nothingness; and encourage the person to pull back even a little from the self-destructive act. He gives the example of a wealthy college student who was single, pregnant—and suicidal with a clearly formed plan. The only solution she could think of besides suicide was never to have become pregnant, even to be virginal again.

> I took out a sheet of paper and began to widen her blinders. I said something like, "Now, let's see: You could have an abortion here locally." She responded, "I couldn't do that." I continued, "You could go away and have an abortion," "I couldn't do that." "You could bring the baby to term and keep the baby." "I couldn't do that." "You could have the baby and adopt it out." Further options were similarly dismissed. When I said, "You can always commit suicide, but there is obviously no need to do that today," there was no response. "Now," I said, "let's look at this list and rank them in order of your preference, keeping in mind that none of them is optimal." (Shneidman, 1987, p. 171)

Shneidman reports that just drawing up the list had a calming effect. Her lethality—her drive to kill herself very soon—receded, and she was able to rank the list even though she found something wrong with each item. *But* an important goal had been achieved: she had been pulled back from the brink and was in a frame of mind to consider courses of action other than dying or being a virgin again. "We were then simply 'haggling' about life, a perfectly viable solution" (p. 171).

Suicide prevention centers usually provide round-the-clock consultation to persons who are suicidal. Workers are typically nonprofessional volunteers under professional supervision; they rely heavily on demographic factors (Shneidman, Farberow, & Litman, 1970). Workers receiving phone calls from people in suicidal crises have before them a checklist to guide their questioning of each caller, for they must immediately assess how great the risk of suicide may be. For example, a caller would be regarded as a lethal risk if he is male, middle-aged, divorced, and living alone and has a history of previous suicide attempts. And usually the more detailed and concrete the suicide plan, the higher the risk. More information on suicide prevention centers is provided in Chapter 20 (page 611).

Community mental health centers often provide a 24-hour-a-day hotline for those people who are considering suicide.

A widespread investigative procedure used to understand suicide is the **psychological autopsy**, pioneered at the Los Angeles Suicide Prevention Center (Shneidman, Faberow, & Litman, 1970). In this procedure workers analyze information obtained from crisis phone calls, from interviews with relatives and friends of those who are thinking about suicide or who are believed to have committed the act, and sometimes from notes left behind by those who have died. The purpose is to determine the actual mode of death and, if judged intentional, the reasons for it.

Of particular interest is a study of notes left by people who subsequently committed suicide

(Shneidman & Farberow, 1970). In the Los Angeles area at the time of this study about 15 percent of suicides left notes; the contents of these notes were analyzed by judges trained to rate them on the presence or absence of instructions and specific themes, such as self-blame, discomfort, death as relief, and the like. Having determined that such ratings could indeed be made reliably by independent judges, Shneidman and Farberow compared these actual suicide notes with simulated notes prepared for them by individuals who were *not* oriented toward killing themselves but who were matched to the suicides on such demographic variables as age, sex, and social class. These control subjects had been instructed to write *as if* they were about to commit suicide. The genuine notes contained a greater number of instructions, such as suggestions about raising the children and explicit orders about how to dispose of the body; there was also evidence of significantly more anguish and hostility in the genuine notes. Other research shows a higher degree of concreteness and specificity in suicide notes than in simulated ones (Ogilvie et al., 1983), reflecting tunnel vision (Shneidman, 1981). Lacking in real suicide notes is the kind of general and philosophical content that characterizes those written by simulators, for example, "Be sure to pay the electric bill" would more likely appear in a real suicide note than "Be good to others" (Baumeister, 1990).

Clinical and Ethical Issues in Dealing with Suicide

Although it is not true, as stated at the beginning of this section, that people are invariably depressed when they commit suicide or attempt to do so, suicide must always be considered a danger when working with those who are profoundly depressed. The despair and utter hopelessness of their existence may make them see suicide as the only solution, the only exit. In fact, sometimes the sole reason a depressed individual does *not* attempt suicide is that he or she cannot summon the energy to formulate and implement a suicide plan. In working with a seriously depressed individual, the clinician must be especially careful as the patient emerges from the low point of depression, because at this time the sadness and hopelessness may still be strong enough to make self-annihilation appear the only option and the person is beginning to have enough energy to do something about it. Because many who commit suicide are depressed, treatment of this condition is at the same time an intervention that clinicians hope will reduce the risk of suicide.

Professional organizations such as the American Psychiatric Association, the National Association of Social Workers, and the American Psychological Association all charge their members to protect people from harming themselves even if doing so requires breaking the confidentiality of the therapist–patient relationship; in Chapter 21 we discuss some legal obligations to protect others from the potentially harmful acts of patients (page 638). The suicide of a therapist's patient is frequently grounds for malpractice lawsuits, and therapists tend to lose such suits if the patient's agents can prove that there was negligence in making adequate assessments and taking reasonable precautions according to generally accepted standards of care for suicide prevention (Fremouw, Perczel, & Ellis, 1990).

But it is not always easy to agree about what reasonable care is, especially when the patient is not hospitalized and therefore not under surveillance and potential restraint. Ultimately clinicians have to work out their own ethic regarding a person's right to end his or her life. What steps is the professional willing to take to prevent a suicide? Confinement in a straitjacket on the back ward of a hospital? Or, as is more common today, sedation administered against the patient's wishes and strong enough that the person is virtually incapable of taking any action at all? And for how long will extraordinary measures be taken? The clinician realizes, of course, that most suicidal crises pass; the suicidal person is likely to be grateful afterward for being prevented from committing suicide when it seemed the only course. But to what extremes is the professional prepared to go in the interim to prevent a suicide at-

Jack Kervorkian, a Michigan physician, has assisted several patients in taking their own lives. The controversy stimulated by his actions has focused attention on the moral issues surrounding suicide.

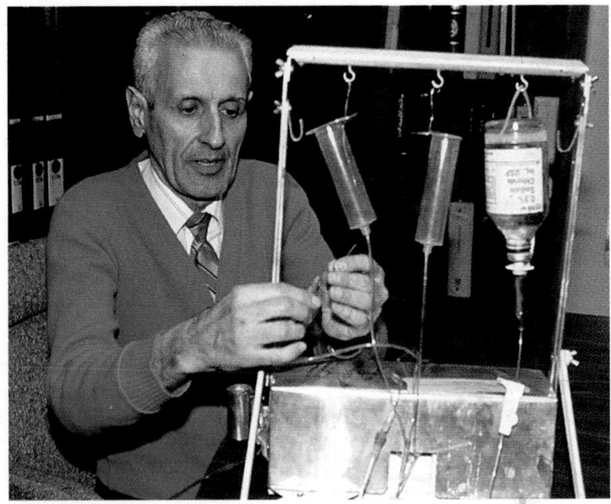

tempt? In Focus Box 9.4 we discuss some controversial views on this ethical dilemma.

On the other hand, can a professional ever properly *help* a person commit suicide? In a case similar to Jo Roman's (see photo on page 254), a fifty-four-year-old Oregon woman arranged for a Michigan physician to help her commit suicide. She pressed a button on a machine to inject a drug that induced unconsciousness and a lethal dose of potassium chloride that stopped her heart (Egan, 1990). Death was painless. This case was unusual not only because of the active assistance of a physician, but because the woman committed suicide while still in good health. What precipitated her decision was a diagnosis of probable Alzheimer's disease, an irreversible disease that destroys brain cells over a period of eight to fifteen years and leads during that time to gradual deterioration of memory as well as loss of the ability to perform functions such as toileting and other aspects of basic self-care.

The deceased's husband explained that he agreed with his wife's decision because she found intolerable the prospect of slowly but inevitably losing her ability to lead the kind of very active, interesting, and productive life she had enjoyed—from mountain climbing to playing and teaching music, from being a proud mother and grandmother to speaking and reading French. Objections were raised by some medical experts that her decision may have been too hasty—she was only fifty-four years old and was showing only slight signs of memory loss and impaired ability to play the piano. Indeed, she could still beat her son at tennis and could carry on normal conversations (Angier, 1990). The year she lived following the diagnosis was apparently as full and vital as her preceding years. It is very difficult to make a firm diagnosis of Alzheimer's disease, especially at the early stage at which this woman took her own life. One must be very careful, experts stated, to rule out other, reversible causes of the kinds of symp-

Table 9.6 • Guidelines for Treating Suicidal Clients

General Procedures

1. Talk about suicide openly and matter-of-factly.
2. Avoid pejorative explanations of suicidal behavior or motives.
3. Present a problem-solving theory of suicidal behavior, and maintain the stance that suicide is a maladaptive and/or ineffective solution.
4. Involve significant others, including other therapists.
5. Schedule sessions frequently enough, and maintain session discipline such that at least some therapy time is devoted to long-term treatment goals.
6. Stay aware of the multitude of variables impinging on patients, and avoid omnipotent taking or accepting of responsibility for patient's suicidal behaviors.
7. Maintain professional consultation with a colleague.
8. Maintain occasional contact with persons who reject therapy.

Precrisis Planning Procedures

9. Anticipate and plan for crisis situations.
10. Continually assess the risk of suicide and parasuicide.
11. Be accessible.
12. Use local emergency/crisis/suicide services.
13. Give the patient a crisis card: telephone numbers of therapist, police, emergency, hospital, significant others.
14. Keep telephone numbers and addresses of patients and their significant others with you.
15. Make a short-term antisuicide contract, and keep it up to date.
16. Contact the patient's physician regarding the risks of overprescribing medications.

Therapeutic Maintenance Procedures

17. Do not force the patient to resort to suicidal talk or ideation in order to get your attention.
18. Express your caring openly; provide noncontingent warmth and attention.
19. Clarify and reinforce nonsuicidal responses to problems.
20. Identify to the patient likely therapist responses to the patient's suicidal behaviors (e.g., if the patient dies, the therapist will be sad, but will continue on with life).
21. Ensure that the patient has realistic expectations about the responses of others to future suicidal behaviors.

Note: H. Glazer and J. Clarkin (eds.), *Depression: Behavioral and directive interpretation strategies* (pp. 229–294), by M. Linehan, 1981, New York: Garland, Copyright 1981 by Garland.

FOCUS 9.4 • An Argument against Coercive Suicide Prevention

In a bold and controversial article on coercive suicide prevention, Thomas Szasz (1986) argues that it is both impractical and immoral to prevent a person from committing suicide. It is impractical because we cannot really force people to live if they are intent on committing suicide unless—and this is where morality becomes an issue—we are prepared not only to commit them but to enslave them via heavy psychotropic medication or even physical restraints. Szasz asserts further that mental health professionals, in their understandable desire to help their patients, open themselves up to legal liability because, by taking it upon themselves to try to prevent suicide, they assume responsibility for something for which they cannot be responsible. In effect, they are promising more than they can deliver.

Arguing further from a moral position, Szasz asserts that health professionals *should* not assume such responsibility—even if it were practical to do so—because people, including those seriously disturbed, should be accorded freedom to make choices. He allows one exception for what he calls impulsive suicide, when people are temporarily agitated, perhaps truly deranged, and need to be protected for a short while from their uncontrollable impulses. He draws an analogy with patients coming out of general anesthesia, when it is common medical practice to strap them down lest their flailing about involuntarily lead to unintended and preventable harm. But there are limits here as well, including, in our own view, how we can know when we are dealing with an impulsive act rather than an act that the person has been thinking about and planning for a period of time.

Szasz is not against advising a person not to commit suicide or otherwise treating problems, like depression, which might have a good deal to do with self-destructive thinking. It is forcible prevention that he rails against. Indeed, he believes that if professionals exclude coercive suicide prevention from their intervention options, they will be able to be more empathic with their patients and perhaps more helpful. He also suggests a psychiatric will, according to which a patient, when not feeling suicidal, agrees ahead of time about how to be treated if, later on, he or she wishes to commit suicide. If the patient opts for coercive prevention in this will, then it would be all right. This strategy brings to mind the instructions Ulysses gave to his sailors before they were to pass by the coast of the Sirens, sea nymphs whose song compelled hapless mariners to commit suicide by throwing themselves into the sea:

> He filled the ears of his people with wax, and suffered them to bind him with cords firmly to the mast. As they approached the Sirens' island, the sea was calm, and over the waters came the notes of music so ravishing and attractive that Ulysses struggled to get loose, and by cries and signs to his people begged to be released; but they, obedient to his previous orders, sprang forward and bound him still faster. They held on their course, and the music grew fainter till it ceased to be

toms she was exhibiting. Still, the family was as comfortable as could be expected with the woman's decision.

After her death, a considerable outcry was raised in the press and in medical and legal circles about the propriety and legality of the physician helping her commit suicide. Indeed, was it really suicide? Initially the doctor was absolved of allegations of murder or professional misconduct, for there was no law in Michigan against assisting in someone else's suicide. He was, however, placed under a permanent court injunction not to help anyone else commit suicide, and his medical license in Michigan was revoked. In February 1992, he was indicted for murder after having assisted in two more suicides, one of a woman in debilitating pain and the other of a woman suffering from a degenerative nerve disease. Neither woman was terminally ill (Harrison, 1992). In July 1992, a judge dismissed the murder indictment for the same reason the earlier indictment was dropped, saying that, "For those patients, whether terminal or not, who have unmanageable pain, physician-assisted suicide remains an alternative" (*Los Angeles Times*, July 22, 1992, p. A11). Perhaps reflecting his own personal bias against such suicides, the judge went on to say that such suicides could be kept to a minimum if both physicians and the public were more aware of the benefits of hospices, facilities for the terminally ill that provide appropriate counseling to patients and their families and also administer suitably high doses of painkillers.[3] Despite the enactment of a law heard, when with joy Ulysses gave his companions the signal to unseal their ears, and they relieved him from his bonds. (*Bulfinch's Mythology*, 1979, p. 243).

Like the other arguments Szasz has made over the years involving freedom and responsibility (see Chapter 21, page 628, for a discussion of his seminal writings on mental illness and legal responsibility for crimes), his analysis is radical but worthy of serious consideration. In our view, the principal omission in his thesis is that many, if not most, people who somehow weather suicidal crises, including those forcibly prevented from killing themselves, are grateful afterwards for another chance at life. It may be the case, therefore, that if we were to follow Szasz's urgings, we would miss opportunities to save savable lives. Szasz's rejoinder, however, might be that one of the strongest predictors of a suicide attempt is a prior attempt. In other words, many people tend to try more than once to kill themselves, and we shall therefore be repeatedly challenged to decide how drastically we are prepared to limit freedom (and sometimes degrade the person by restraints of one kind or another) in the hopes of forestalling what may be inevitable. There are no easy answers here, but it is important to raise the questions.

Ulyſses & his Companions after his return from the Shades, escaping the Sirens, & paſsing between the Rocks Scylla & Charybdis.

The song of the Sirens was resisted by Ulysses, who was lashed to the mast of his ship to prevent his suicide. According to Szasz's views, this would be an acceptable instance of voluntary, coercive suicide prevention.

in Michigan prohibiting assisted suicide, this physician has continued to help terminally ill people take their own lives.

These cases are unusual, though they are likely to become less so as people concentrate more on the quality of life and the right to privacy, which may well include the right to take one's own life. For the most part, mental health workers try to prevent suicide, and in that context, as mentioned earlier, they should not hesitate to inquire directly whether a client has thought of suicide. It is also important to adopt a phenomenological stance, to view the suicidal person's situation as he or she sees it, rather than convey in any way that the patient is a fool or is crazy to have settled on suicide as a solution to his or her woes. This empathy for suicidal people is sometimes referred to as tuning in by those who work in suicide prevention centers. In addition, the clinician treating a suicidal person must be prepared to devote more energy and time than usual even for psychotic patients. Late-night phone calls and visits

[3]Decisions not to resuscitate terminally ill patients are made every day in hospitals. One informal estimate is that more than half the deaths in hospitals follow a decision to limit or withhold the kinds of life-sustaining equipment currently available. Many people do not consider this practice euthanasia or suicide, which is ending life. "It is, rather, a desire to end dying, to pass gently into the night without tubes running down the nose and a ventilator insistently inflating lungs that have grown weary from the insult" (*Newsweek*, 1991, p. 44). Major legal, religious, and ethical issues whirl around decisions about ending dying among the terminally ill. Is this physician-assisted suicide?

to the patient's home may be frequent. Finally, the therapist should realize that he or she is likely to become a singularly important figure in the suicidal person's life—and be prepared both for the extreme dependency of the patient and for the hostility and resentment that sometimes greet efforts to help. Table 9.6 contains general guidelines for dealing with suicidal patients.

SUMMARY

DSM-IV lists two principal mood disorders. In major or unipolar depression a person experiences profound sadness as well as a number of related problems, such as sleep and appetite disturbances and loss of energy and self-esteem. In bipolar disorder a person has episodes either of mania alone or of both mania and depression. With mania mood is elevated or irritable and the person becomes extremely active, talkative, and distractible. DSM-IV also lists two chronic mood disorders, cyclothymia and dysthymia. Both must last for two years. In cyclothymia the person has frequent periods of depressed mood and hypomania; in dysthymia the person is chronically depressed.

Psychological theories of depression have been couched in psychoanalytic, cognitive, and interpersonal terms. Psychoanalytic formulations stress unconscious identification with a loved one whose desertion of the individual has resulted in anger turned inward. Beck's cognitive theory ascribes causal significance to negative and illogical self-judgment. According to helplessness/hopelessness theory, early experiences in inescapable, hurtful situations instill a sense of hopelessness that can evolve into depression. These individuals are likely to attribute failures to their own general and persistent inadequacies and faults. Interpersonal theory focuses on deficits in depressed people and the negative responses they elicit from others. These same theories are applied to the depressive phase of bipolar disorder. The manic phase is considered a defense against a debilitating psychological state such as low self-esteem.

Biological theories suggest an inherited predisposition for mood disorders, particularly for bipolar disorder, and linkage analyses may provide information about the chromosome on which the gene is located. Early neurochemical theories related the phenomena of depression and mania to abnormally depleted amounts of the neurotransmitters that pass on neural impulses in particular nerve tracts of the brain. Recent research focuses on the postsynaptic receptor rather than simply the amount of various transmitters. Overreaction of the hypothalamic–pituitary–adrenal axis is also found among depressives.

There are several psychological and somatic therapies for mood disorders and especially for depression. Psychoanalytic treatment tries to give the patient insight into childhood loss and inadequacy and later self-blame. The aim of Beck's cognitive therapy is to uncover negative and illogical patterns of thinking and teach more realistic ways of viewing events, the self, and adversity. Frankl's existential therapy encourages depressed people to make spiritual sense of their suffering, to feel free and responsible for their lives, and to find meaning and purpose in existence.

A range of biological treatments is also available; often used in conjunction with psychological treatment, they can be very effective. Electroconvulsive shock and several antidepressant drugs have proved their worth in lifting depression. It has become possible for patients to avoid the excesses of manic and depressive periods through careful administration of lithium carbonate.

Finally, an exploration of suicide reveals that self-annihilative tendencies are not restricted to those who are depressed. A review of the facts and myths about suicide indicates that any single theory is unlikely to account for its great diversity, but that the information already gathered can be applied to prevent it.

Most large communities have suicide prevention centers, and most therapists at one time or another have to deal with patients in suicidal crisis. Clinical evidence suggests that suicidal persons need to have their fears and concerns understood but not judged, and that workers must gradually and patiently point out to them that alternatives to self-destruction are there to be explored.

KEY TERMS

mood disorders
depression
mania
major (unipolar) depression
bipolar disorder
hypomania
cyclothymic disorder
dysthymic disorder
negative triad
learned helplessness theory
attribution
linkage analysis
tricyclic drugs
monoamine oxidase inhibitors
lithium carbonate
logotherapy
electroconvulsive therapy (ECT)
bilateral ECT
unilateral ECT
egoistic suicide
altruistic suicides
anomic suicide
suicide prevention centers
psychological autopsy

c h a p t e r t e n

Personality Disorders

Mary was twenty-six years old at the time of her first admission to a psychiatric hospital. She had been in outpatient treatment with a psychologist for several months when her persistent thoughts of suicide and preoccupation with inflicting pain on herself (by cutting or burning) led her therapist to conclude that she could no longer be managed as an outpatient.

Mary's first experience with some form of psychological therapy occurred as an adolescent. Her grades had declined sharply in the eleventh grade, and her parents suspected she was using drugs. She began to miss curfews and even failed to make it home on a few occasions. She was also frequently truant. Family therapy was undertaken, and it seemed to go well at first. Mary was enthusiastic about her therapist and even wanted extra, private sessions with him. During the family sessions, her parents' fears were confirmed as Mary revealed an extensive history of drug use, including "everything I can get my hands on." She had been very promiscuous and had prostituted herself several times to get drug money. Her relations with her peers were changeable, to say the least. The pattern was a continual parade of new friends who were first thought to be the greatest ever, but who soon disappointed her in some way and were cast aside, often in a very unpleasant way. Except for the one person with whom she was currently enamored, she had no other friends and reported that she stayed away from others for fear that they would harm her in some way. She claimed to be totally uninterested in school and bored with everything but the altered states that drugs produced in her.

After several weeks of therapy Mary's parents noticed that her relationship with the therapist had cooled appreciably. In fact, the sessions were marked by angry and abusive outbursts on the part of Mary toward the therapist. Several weeks later she refused to attend any more sessions. In a subsequent conversation with the therapist, Mary's father learned that Mary had behaved very seductively toward the therapist during their private sessions and her changed attitude toward him coincided with the rejection of her advances, even though the therapist had tried to mix firmness with warmth and empathy. Mary managed to graduate from high school and enrolled in a local community college, but the old patterns returned. Poor grades, cutting classes, continuing drug use, and lack of interest in her studies finally led her to quit in the middle of the first semester of her second year.

After leaving school, Mary held a series of clerical jobs. Most of them didn't last long as some dispute with her co-workers typically led to her dismissal. Her relationships with co-workers paralleled her relationships with her peers in high school. On starting a new job, she would find someone she really liked a lot, but something would come between them and the relationship would end very angrily. She was frequently suspicious of her co-workers and reported that she often heard them talking about her, plotting how to prevent her from getting ahead on her job. She was quick to find hidden meanings in their behavior, as when she interpreted being the last person asked to sign a birthday card to mean that she was the least liked person in the office. She indicated that she "received vibrations" from others and could tell when they really didn't like her even in the absence of any direct evidence.

Mary's behavior was characteristic of many of the criteria of several personality disorders. Her frequent mood swings, including periods of depression and extreme irritability, led her to seek therapy several times. But after initial enthusiasm, her relationship with her therapist always deteriorated and led to premature termination. The therapist she had been seeing just before her hospitalization had been her sixth.

Personality disorders are a heterogeneous group of disorders regarded as long-standing, inflexible, and maladaptive traits that impair social and occupational functioning but not contact with reality. Some, but not all, can cause emotional distress. Previously called character disorders, personality disorders derive from a trait approach to personality (see page 104).

As will be apparent, many of the descriptions of personality disorders may seem to fit some members of our own families and some of our acquaintances, not to mention ourselves! This seems a good point to remind readers about the medical student syndrome, that is, the tendency to see oneself or one's family and friends in descriptions of the disorder being studied. With personality disorders we come closest to describing characteristics that we all possess. Therefore, it is especially important to be aware that an actual disorder is defined by the extremes of several personality traits. Each of us develops over the years some apparently persistent means of dealing with life's challenges, a certain style of relating to other people. One person is overly dependent; another challenging and aggressive; yet another is very shy and avoids social contact; and another is concerned more with appearance and bolstering his or her precious ego than with relating honestly and on a deep level with others. These individuals would not be diagnosed as having personality disorders unless the patterns of behavior were long-standing, pervasive, and dysfunctional.

With that in mind, we will look first at the problems of classifying personality disorders, then at the personality disorders themselves, at some of the theory and research on their etiology, and, finally, at therapies associated with them.

The Problems of Classifying Personality Disorders

In the DSM, personality disorders are to be indicated on axis II, which means that their presence or absence is to be considered whenever a diagnosis is made. They were placed on a separate axis to ensure that diagnosticians would pay greater attention to their possible presence. Sometimes, a diagnostic interview will point directly to the presence of a personality disorder, but often someone who has come to a clinic has an axis I disorder (such as panic disorder) that, quite naturally, is a primary focus of attention. Placing the personality disorders on axis II is meant to guide the clinician to consider whether a personality disorder is also present.

Over the years, personality disorders have had little diagnostic reliability, in spite of attempts to improve the clarity of their definitions. In the field trials of DSM-III, for example, although personality disorders were diagnosed in over 50 percent of the patients, the reliabilities of some of the individual personality disorders were totally inadequate (American Psychiatric Association, 1980). These low reliabilities, however, may have been caused by the lack of a good assessment device in the DSM-III field trials. More recent work with structured interviews specially designed for assessing personality disorders indicates that good reliabilities can be achieved (Loranger et al., 1987; Widiger et al., 1988).

Problems remain with this diagnostic category, however. It is often difficult to diagnose someone with a single, specific personality disorder because many disordered people exhibit a wide range of traits that make several diagnoses applicable. In fact, Mary, described in the case opening this chapter, met the diagnostic criteria for two personality disorders (borderline and paranoid) and almost met the criteria for a third (schizotypal).

Widiger, Frances, and Trull (1987) found that 55 percent of patients with borderline personality disorder also met the diagnostic criteria for schizotypal personality disorder; 47 percent met the criteria for antisocial personality disorder; and 57 percent for histrionic personality disorder. Such data are particularly discouraging when we try to interpret the results of research comparing patients who have a specific personality disorder with some control group. If, for example, we find that people with borderline disorder differ from normal people, have we learned anything specific to borderline personality disorder or do the findings relate to personality disorders in general or perhaps even to another diagnosis? Because the changes in diagnostic criteria in DSM-IV are relatively minor, it is unlikely that the overlap problem has been solved.

In Chapter 3 we noted that the diagnostic changes occurring from DSM-III to DSM-IIIR may have happened too quickly and without adequate empirical justification. The changes in the personality disorders category illustrate this problem. One of the goals of DSM-IIIR was to reduce the use of the atypical and other diagnoses, terms that are applied to individuals who do not meet the criteria for any specific personality disorder. Therefore, many of the changes were designed to allow expanded coverage by the specific diagnoses. In comparing DSM-III and DSM-IIIR diagnoses, Morey (1988) indeed found that the frequency of atypical or mixed diagnoses declined in DSM-IIIR. However, this apparently desirable change brought with it some costs, such as the sometimes dramatic changes in the frequency of certain diagnoses. Table 10.1 illustrates how diagnoses of the same patients by DSM-III and DSM-IIIR led to some striking differences (note especially the

Table 10.1 • Relationship of DSM-III and DSM-IIIR Personality Disorder Diagnoses

Personality Disorder	*Patients with Diagnosis, %*	
	DSM-III	*DSM-IIIR*
Borderline	32.0	33.3
Narcissistic	6.2	22.0
Histrionic	21.6	21.6
Antisocial	5.8	6.2
Avoidant	11.3	27.1
Dependent	14.1	22.3
Compulsive	8.9	7.9
Passive-aggressive	8.2	12.4
Paranoid	7.2	22.0
Schizoid	1.4	11.0
Schizotypal	17.2	9.3
Atypical, mixed	29.2	22.3

Source: From Morey, 1988.

frequencies for narcissistic, avoidant, dependent, paranoid, schizoid, and schizotypal). This kind of change is problematic because a dramatic change in diagnostic criteria means that the emerging research literature on patients diagnosed according to DSM-III may not be applicable to patients diagnosed according to DSM-IIIR or DSM-IV. A second difficulty created by the revised criteria is that they actually increased overlap among the categories. Morey found that, whereas only four DSM-III diagnoses overlapped other diagnoses by 50 percent, the corresponding figure for DSM-IIIR was eight. Of course one has to wonder about the validity of diagnoses that seem to be changing so quickly.

These data suggest that the categorical diagnostic system of DSM-IIIR may not be ideal for classifying personality disorders. The personality traits that constitute the data for classification form a continuum; that is, most of the relevant characteristics are present in varying degrees in most people. The diagnostic categories are in fact defined by the extremes; personality disorders represent extreme or rigid normal human tendencies or traits. This suggests that a dimensional approach to classification (see Chapter 3, page 68) may be more appropriate. Indeed, a dimensional system was considered for inclusion in both DSM-IIIR and DSM-IV but consensus could not be reached on which dimensions to include (Widiger et al., 1988). A promising effort in the direction of dimensional classification was reported by Widiger, Trull et al. (1987). A large sample of patients was assessed on all the symptoms relevant to a diagnosis of personality disorder. The correlations among the symptoms were then analyzed to see if a smaller number of dimensions could explain the relationships. Three dimensions were found to do so:

1. Social involvement: positive and friendly versus not involved with other people.
2. Assertion/dominance versus passive submission.
3. Anxious rumination versus behavioral acting out.

Using a dimensional approach to classification, each patient would be assessed, described, and scored on each dimension. For example, a person diagnosed as an avoidant personality would score below average on the first and second dimensions and above average on the third.

To sum up, a move is clearly on to at least formulate and try out a dimensional approach. However, the research on personality disorders conducted so far is based on the older categories, and we turn now to our examination of that work.

Specific Personality Disorders

For most of the personality disorders, research data are few; but in recent years interest and research has grown, and our discussion will reflect that. For one personality disorder in particular—antisocial personality—the diagnosis is reliable and the research is plentiful; we will thus focus in-depth on antisocial personality disorder after an overview of the other personality disorders.

Personality disorders are grouped into three clusters in DSM-IV. Individuals in Cluster A (paranoid, schizoid, and schizotypal) seem odd or eccentric; those in Cluster B (antisocial, borderline, histrionic, and narcissistic) seem dramatic, emotional, or erratic; and those in Cluster C (avoidant, dependent, and obsessive-compulsive) appear anxious or fearful.

Paranoid Personality Disorder

The **paranoid personality** is suspicious of people. He or she expects to be mistreated or exploited by others and thus becomes secretive and is continually on the lookout for possible signs of trickery and abuse. Such individuals are reluctant to confide in others and tend to blame others even when they themselves are at fault. They are extremely jealous and may unjustifiably question the fidelity of their spouse or lover.

Paranoid personalities are also preoccupied with unjustified doubts about the loyalty or trustworthiness of others. They may read hidden messages into events, for example, believing that a neighbor's dog deliberately barks in the early morning to disturb them. This diagnosis overlaps most strongly with borderline and avoidant personality disorders (Morey, 1988). Paranoid personality is more common among the first-degree relatives of patients with delusional disorder and schizophrenia, suggesting a genetic relationship among them (Kendler, Masterson, & Davis, 1985).

Schizoid Personality Disorder

The **schizoid personality** does not desire or enjoy social relationships and usually has few close friends. He or she appears dull and aloof and without warm, tender feelings for other people. These patients rarely report strong emotions, are not interested in sex, and experience few pleasurable activities. Indifferent to praise, criticism, and the sentiments of others, individuals with this disorder are loners and pursue solitary interests.

As we have indicated, the frequency of the schizoid diagnosis increased markedly from DSM-III to DSM-IIIR. Many patients formerly diagnosed as schizotypal are now diagnosed as schizoid. With regard to overlap with other personality disorder diagnoses, the percentages are highest for avoidant (53 percent) and paranoid (47 percent).

Schizotypal Personality Disorder

The modern concept of schizotypal personality disorder grew out of Danish studies of the adopted children of schizophrenics (Kety et al., 1968). While some of these children developed full-blown schizophrenia as adults, an even larger number developed what seemed to be an attenuated form of schizophrenia. The diagnostic criteria for schizotypal personality disorder were devised by Spitzer, Endicott, and Gibbon (1979) to describe these individuals. The Spitzer et al. criteria were incorporated by DSM-III and were then narrowed somewhat in DSM-IIIR and DSM-IV.

The **schizotypal personality** usually has the interpersonal difficulties of the schizoid personality and excessive social anxiety that does not diminish with familiarity. But there are a number of other, more eccentric symptoms as well, although they are not severe enough to warrant a diagnosis of schizophrenia (see Chapter 14). Schizotypal personalities may have *odd beliefs* or *magical thinking*—superstitiousness, beliefs that they are clairvoyant and telepathic—and recurrent *illusions*—they may sense the presence of a force or a person not actually there. Speech may also contain words used in unusual and unclear fashion. Behavior and appearance may also be eccentric (e.g., talking to oneself or wearing dirty and disheveled clothing); ideas of reference (the belief that events have a particular and unusual meaning for the person), suspiciousness, and paranoid ideation are common. Affect appears to be constricted and flat. In a study of the relative importance of these symptoms for diagnosis, Widiger, Frances, and Trull (1987) found that paranoid ideation, ideas of reference, and illusions were most telling.

The prevalence of schizotypal personality disorder is estimated at about 3 percent, and it is slightly more frequent in men than women (Zimmerman & Coryel, 1989). Furthermore, the relatives of people with schizotypal personality disorder are themselves at increased risk for the disorder (Siever et al., 1990). Patients with the disorder are also similar to schizophrenics on some biological measures (e.g., levels of monoamine oxidase, Baron et al., 1984). Schizotypal personality disorder and schizophrenia may be related to each other through genetic transmission of a predisposition. More first-degree relatives of schizophrenics are given the diagnosis than are relatives of individuals in control groups; the disorder may thus be a mild form of schizophrenia (Spitzer, Endicott, & Gibbon, 1979).

The biggest problem facing this diagnosis is its continuing overlap with other personality disorder diagnoses. Morey (1988), for example, found that 33 percent of DSM-IIIR diagnosed schizotypal personalities met the diagnostic criteria for borderline personality disorder, 33 percent for narcissistic personality disorder, 59 percent for avoidant personality disorder, 59 percent for paranoid personality disorder, and 44 percent for schizoid personality disorder. Clearly, these are unsatisfactory figures if we want to consider schizotypal personality disorder as a discrete diagnostic entity. This lack of distinctiveness also occurs in other domains. Squires-Wheeler et al. (1988), for example, found no differences in the rate of schizotypal personality disorder between the children of schizophrenics and those of parents with mood disorders.

Borderline Personality Disorder

The **borderline personality** reveals instability in relationships, mood, and self-image. For example, attitudes and feelings toward other people may vary considerably and inexplicably over short periods of time. Emotions are also erratic and can shift abruptly, particularly to anger. Borderline personalities are argumentative, irritable, and sarcastic. Their unpredictable and impulsive behavior, such as gambling, spending, sex, and eating sprees, is potentially self-damaging. These individuals have not developed a clear and coherent sense of self and remain uncertain about their values, loyalties, and choice of career. They cannot bear to be alone and have fears of abandonment. They tend to have a series of intense one-on-one relationships that are usually stormy and transient, alternating between idealization and devaluation. Subject to chronic feelings of depression and emptiness, they may make manipulative attempts at suicide. Paranoid ideation and dissociative symptoms may appear during periods of high stress. Of all these varied

The character portrayed by Glenn Close in the film *Fatal Attraction* had many characteristics of the borderline personality.

symptoms, unstable and intense interpersonal relationships appear as a critical feature (Modestin, 1987).[1]

Clinicians and researchers have used the term *borderline personality* for some time, but they have given it many meanings. Originally, the term implied that the patient was on the borderline between neurosis and schizophrenia; the DSM concept of borderline personality no longer has this connotation.

The current conceptualization of borderline personality derives from several sources. After reviewing the available literature and interview studies of borderline personalities, Gunderson, Kolb, and Austin (1981) devised an interview for collecting information necessary for the diagnosis. They also proposed a set of specific diagnostic criteria similar to those that ultimately appeared in DSM-III. The DSM-III criteria for borderline personality were established through a study done by Spitzer, Endicott, and Gibbon (1979). They identified schizotypal personality disorder as a cluster of traits related to schizophrenia; they also identified another syndrome not related to schizophrenia through a predisposition, and this became DSM-III's borderline personality disorder. DSM-IV maintains these distinctions.

Much controversy still surrounds the diagnosis of borderline personality disorder. It has become apparent that borderline personalities make up a very heterogeneous group. For example, Pope and his coworkers (1983) found that about half their sample of borderline personalities also had either major depression or bipolar disorder. These people responded well to the usual somatic treatments for these mood disorders. In addition, their first-degree relatives had a higher incidence of mood disorders than that of the general population. Pope and his colleagues found, too, that most of their borderline personalities could also be diagnosed as having another personality disorder—histrionic, narcissistic, or antisocial. A great deal of overlapping symptomatology has even been reported between DSM-III diagnosed borderline and schizotypal personality disorders (Serban, Conte, & Plutchik, 1987). With DSM-IIIR and DSM-IV criteria this picture may have changed, as Morey (1988) reported less overlap between schizotypal and borderline personality disorders but more overlap between borderline and histrionic, narcissistic, dependent, avoidant, and paranoid personality disorders.

Borderline personality disorder has a prevalence of almost 2 percent and is more common in women than in men (Swartz et al., 1990). High frequencies of childhood physical and sexual abuse are reported by borderline personalities (Ogata et al., 1990). The disorder begins in adolescence (McGlashan, 1983). Furthermore, it runs in families, with high rates in first-degree relatives of index cases (Baron et al., 1985; Loranger, Oldham, & Tulis, 1983).

Borderline personalities are very likely to have an axis I mood disorder (Manos, Vasilopoulou, & Sotorou, 1988), and even their relatives are more likely than average to have mood disorders (Zanarini et al., 1988). Therapeutic outcomes are generally poor (McGlashan, 1983), and there is a high rate of completed suicide (Paris, 1990). Lithium has been of some value in treating the impulsive aspects of the disorder (Links et al., 1990).

Because of the widespread interest in borderline personality disorder, we quote here from a colorful account written by Jonathan Kellerman, a clinical psychologist turned successful mystery writer:

> The borderline patient is a therapist's nightmare . . . because borderlines never really get better. The best you can do is help them coast, without getting sucked into their pathology. . . .

[1]Patients with both borderline and schizotypal personality disorders would probably have been diagnosed as schizophrenic using DSM-II criteria. Designating the behavior of these people as the criteria for these two personality disorders is one way that DSM-IIIR has narrowed the schizophrenia diagnosis (see Chapter 14).

They're the chronically depressed, the determinedly addictive, the compulsively divorced, living from one emotional disaster to the next. Bed hoppers, stomach pumpers, freeway jumpers, and sad-eyed bench-sitters with arms stitched up like footballs and psychic wounds that can never be sutured. Their egos are as fragile as spun sugar, their psyches irretrievably fragmented, like a jigsaw puzzle with crucial pieces missing. They play roles with alacrity, excel at being anyone but themselves, crave intimacy but repel it when they find it. Some of them gravitate toward stage or screen; others do their acting in more subtle ways. . . .

Borderlines go from therapist to therapist, hoping to find a magic bullet for the crushing feelings of emptiness. They turn to chemical bullets, gobble tranquilizers and antidepressants, alcohol and cocaine. Embrace gurus and heaven-hucksters, any charismatic creep promising a quick fix of the pain. And they end up taking temporary vacations in psychiatric wards and prison cells, emerge looking good, raising everyone's hopes. Until the next letdown, real or imagined, the next excursion into self damage.

What they don't do is change. (Kellerman, 1989, pp. 113–114)

Narcissistic personality disorder draws its name from Narcissus of Greek mythology. He fell in love with his own reflection, was consumed by his own desire, and was then transformed into a flower.

Histrionic Personality Disorder

The diagnosis **histrionic personality**, formerly called hysterical personality, is applied to people who are overly dramatic and attention seeking. These individuals, while displaying emotion extravagantly, are noted as actually being shallow of emotion. They are self-centered, overly concerned with physical attractiveness, and uncomfortable when not the center of attention. They can be inappropriately sexually provocative and seductive and are easily influenced by others.

The diagnosis is more common among women in hospital samples (Reich 1987), but this appears to be the result of sampling bias, as the rates for men and women were equal (2.1 percent) in a community survey (Nestadt et al., 1990). The frequency of the disorder is higher among separated and divorced people, and it is associated with high rates of depression and poor physical health (Nestadt et al., 1990). The major overlap is with borderline personality disorder.

Narcissistic Personality Disorder

People with a **narcissistic personality** have a grandiose view of their own uniqueness and abilities; they are preoccupied with fantasies of great success. To say that they are self-centered is almost an understatement. They require almost constant attention and excessive admiration and believe they can only be understood by special or high status people. Their interpersonal relationships are disturbed by their lack of empathy; feelings of envy; arrogance; taking advantage of others; and feelings of entitlement, expecting others to do special, not-to-be-reciprocated favors for them. Most of these characteristics, with the exception of lack of empathy and extreme reactions to criticism, have been validated as aspects of narcissistic personality disorder in empirical studies (Ronningston & Gunderson, 1990).

The diagnosis of narcissistic personality disorder was formally introduced in DSM-III. It is rooted in modern psychoanalytic writings. Kernberg (1970) described the grandiosity and egocentric behavior of narcissists as a defense against the rage that they feel toward their parents, whom they perceive as cold and indifferent. Kohut (1966) proposed that the narcissistic personality develops as a way of coping with perceived shortcomings in the self that rankle, because parents do not provide support and empathy. The child who receives such help learns to deal with his or her shortcomings more adaptively. Although these etiological speculations have not been empirically tested, the descriptions of narcissism by these psychoanalytic writers has a major impact on the DSM diagnosis (see Focus Box 10.1). From DSM-III to DSM-IIIR the frequency of the diagnosis has increased markedly, and it overlaps greatly with borderline personality disorder (Morey, 1988).

Avoidant Personality Disorder

Avoidant personality applies to people who are keenly sensitive to the possibility of criticism, rejection, or disapproval and are therefore reluctant to enter into relationships unless they are sure they will be liked. In social situations they are afraid of saying something foolish or of being embarrassed by blushing or other signs of anxiety. They believe they are incompetent and inferior to others and typically exaggerate the risks, dangers, or difficulties in doing something outside their usual routine. There is considerable overlap between the features of avoidant personality disorder and those of dependent personality disorder (Trull, Widiger, & Frances, 1987) and of borderline personality disorder (Morey, 1988).

Dependent Personality Disorder

The **dependent personality** lacks self-confidence and self-reliance. Such individuals passively allow their spouses or partners to assume responsibility for deciding where they should live, what jobs they should hold, with whom they should be friendly. They agree with others even when they know they are wrong, and they have difficulty initiating any activities on their own. They feel uncomfortable when alone and are often preoccupied with fears of being left to take care of themselves. They are unable to make demands on others, and they subordinate their own needs to ensure that they do not break up the protective relationships they have established. When close relationships end, they urgently seek another relationship to replace the old one.

The DSM-IV diagnosis of dependent personality disorder contains two types of symptoms: those describing dependent behavior and those describing what can be referred to as attachment problems (Livesley, Schroeder, & Jackson, 1990). Attachment is a process that has been studied by developmental psychologists and is regarded as important for personality development. The basic idea is that the young infant becomes attached to an adult and uses the adult as a secure base from which to explore and pursue other goals. Separation from the adult leads to anger and distress. As development proceeds, the child becomes less dependent on the attachment figure for security. It is possible that the abnormal attachment behaviors seen in dependent personalities reflect a failure in the usual developmental process.

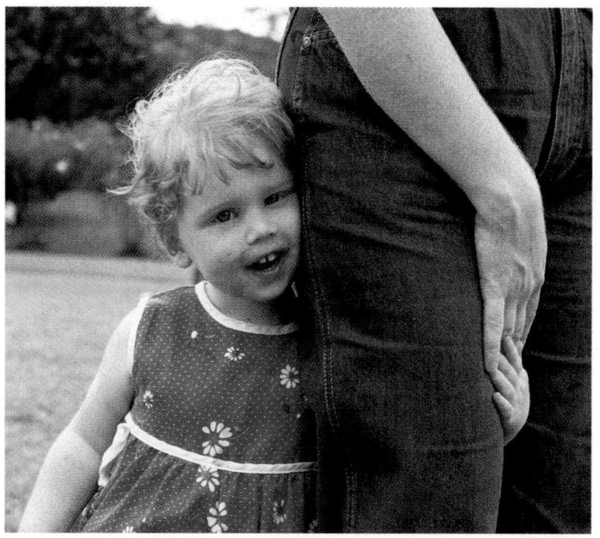

According to attachment theory, the young child uses an adult as a secure base from which to explore the world.

Although early studies using unstructured assessments found that dependent personality disorder was more frequent among women, later results from structured interviews have not confirmed this finding (Reich, 1987). However, there may be some differences between men and women who have the disorder. Reich (1990) found that relatives of men with dependent personality disorder showed a high rate of depression, whereas relatives of women with the disorder had a high rate of panic disorder. Dependent personality overlaps strongly with borderline and avoidant personality disorders (Morey, 1988) and is linked to several axis I diagnoses as well as poor physical health.

Obsessive-Compulsive Personality Disorder

The **obsessive-compulsive personality** is a perfectionist, preoccupied with details, rules, schedules, and the like. These people are work- rather than

FOCUS 10.1 • Kohut and the Narcissistic Personality

In recent years many psychoanalytically oriented clinicians have regarded as the prevalent disorder of our time the narcissistic personality, a person whose remarkable sense of self-importance, complete self-absorption, and fantasies of limitless success mask a very fragile self-esteem. Constantly seeking attention and adulation, narcissistic personalities are, underneath, extremely sensitive to criticism and deeply fearful of failure. Sometimes they seek out others whom they can idealize, because they are disappointed in themselves, but they generally do not allow anyone to be genuinely close to them. Their personal relationships are few and shallow: when people inevitably fall short of their unrealistic expectations, they become angry and rejecting. The inner lives of narcissists are similarly impoverished because, despite their self-aggrandizement, they actually think very little of themselves and are without resources.

At the center of this contemporary interest in narcissism is Heinz Kohut, whose two books *The Analysis of the Self* (1971) and *The Restoration of the Self* (1977) have established a variant of psychoanalysis known as self-psychology. His basic idea is that parents must respond to their children with respect, warmth, and empathy if the children are to acquire a normal sense of self-worth. But parents may further their own needs rather than being empathic with their children.

> A little girl comes home from school, eager to tell her mother about some great successes. But this mother, instead of listening with pride, deflects the conversation from the child to herself [and] begins to talk about her own successes which overshadow those of her little daughter. (Kohut & Wolf, 1978, p. 418)

Children neglected in this way have trouble accepting their own shortcomings. They may develop into narcissistic personalities, striving to bolster their sense of self through unending quests for love and approval from others.

---

pleasure-oriented and have inordinate difficulty making decisions and allocating time. Their interpersonal relationships are often poor because they demand that everything be done their way. They are generally serious, formal, and inflexible, especially regarding moral issues. They are unable to discard worn-out and useless objects, even if they have no sentimental value, and are likely to hoard money. This dysfunctional attention to work and productivity is found more often in men than in women. Notice that obsessive-compulsive personality disorder is quite different from obsessive-compulsive disorder and does not include the obsessions and compulsions that define the latter. Although the use of the two similar terms suggests that the two disorders should be related, it is not clear that they are.[2]

General Comments

The reader has no doubt noticed that descriptions of some of the personality disorders are similar to those of diagnostic categories discussed elsewhere. Generally speaking, a person judged to have, for example, a paranoid personality disorder is less disturbed than a person with paranoid schizophrenia or a delusional disorder (see page 397). People given one of these three diagnoses, however, all have in common a tendency to be overly suspicious, guarded, and thin-skinned. But it can be very difficult to distinguish personality disorders from others that bear a resemblance, underlining once again their problematic status as a separate group of psychological disturbances.

Another matter for debate in diagnosing personality disorders is the possible role of sex bias. Borderline personality disorder is more often diagnosed in women than in men, and, similarly, antisocial personality disorder (to be discussed next) is more often diagnosed in men than in women (Morey & Ochoa, 1989). Making a clear case for diagnostic bias, however, presents some thorny problems. For example, Widiger and Spitzer (1991) point out that it may be that the characteristics of borderline personality are, for sociocultural reasons,

[2]DSM-IIIR proposed diagnostic criteria for two new personality disorders that were not formal diagnoses but "categories in need of further study." The most controversial of these was self-defeating personality disorder. Another proposed personality disorder was sadistic personality disorder. These two diagnoses have been dropped entirely by DSM-IV. Passive-aggressive personality disorder, which was previously a formal diagnosis, has now been demoted to become a category in need of further study.

normally found more often among women than among men, and the opposite may be true for antisocial personality disorder. Society may shape women and men in these different directions. The diagnoses may not themselves be biased, rather they may be telling us something about our society that itself might merit attention.

Antisocial Personality Disorder (Psychopathy)

In current usage the terms *antisocial personality disorder* and *psychopathy* (and sometimes *sociopathy* as well) are often used interchangeably, although we will soon see that there are important differences between the two. Antisocial behavior is an important aspect of both terms, though, and the history of attempts to apply diagnoses to such antisocial behavior is interesting.

At the very beginning of the nineteenth century, Philippe Pinel conceived of *manie sans délire*. Pinel chose this term to indicate that the patient he described was violently insane (*manie*) but did not show other symptoms (*sans délire*) common among the insane. In 1835 James Prichard, an English psychiatrist, described the disorder "moral insanity" in an attempt to account for behavior so far outside the usual ethical and legal codes that it seemed a form of lunacy. The man whose nature prompted Prichard's term was an easily angered aristocrat who had whipped a horse, kicked a dog to death, and thrown a peasant woman into a well.

The current DSM-IV concept of antisocial personality disorder involves two major components. The first refers to the presence of a conduct disorder before the age of fifteen (see Chapter 15). Criteria include truancy, running away from home, frequent lying, theft, arson, and deliberate destruction of property. The second part of the DSM-IV definition refers to the continuation of this pattern of antisocial behavior in adulthood. The adult **antisocial personality** shows irresponsible and antisocial behavior by not working consistently, breaking laws, being irritable and physically aggressive, defaulting on debts, and being reckless. He or she is impulsive and fails to plan ahead. In addition, he or she shows no regard for truth nor remorse for misdeeds.

It is estimated that about 4 percent of adult American men and 1 percent of women are antisocial personalities (Robins et al., 1984). Pimps, confidence artists, murderers, and drug dealers are by no means the only antisocial personalities. Business executives, professors, politicians, physicians, plumbers, salespeople, carpenters, and bartenders have their share of antisocial personalities as well.

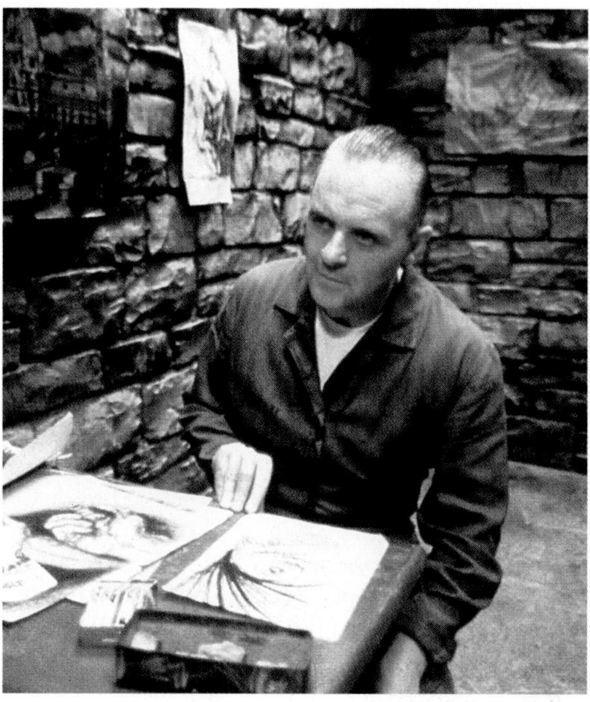

The character played by Anthony Hopkins in *The Silence of the Lambs* displayed many of the characteristics of the psychopath, especially his total lack of regard for the rights of others.

The concept of **psychopathy** is closely linked to the writings of Hervey Cleckley and his classic book, *The Mask of Sanity* (1976). On the basis of his vast clinical experience, he formulated a set of criteria by which to recognize the disorder. Unlike the DSM criteria for antisocial personality disorder, Cleckley's criteria for psychopathy refer less to antisocial behavior per se and more to the psychopath's psychology. For example, one of the key characteristics of the psychopath is poverty of emotions, both positive and negative. Psychopaths have no sense of shame and even their seemingly positive feelings for others are merely an act. The psychopath is superficially charming, and manipulates others for personal gain. The lack of negative emotions may make it impossible for psychopaths to learn from their mistakes, and the lack of positive emotions leads them to behave irresponsibly toward others. Another key point is that Cleckley describes the antisocial behavior of the psychopath as inadequately motivated; it is not due, for example, to a need for something like money but is performed impulsively, as much for thrills as anything else.

Currently, most researchers identify psychopaths using a checklist developed by Hare and his associates (Hare et al., 1990). The checklist identifies two major clusters of psychopathic behaviors. The first describes a selfish, remorseless individual who exploits others. The second characterizes an antisocial life-style. Among axis I diagnoses, psychopathy is often diagnosed as well when there is abuse of alcohol and other drugs (Smith & Newman, 1990). In an interesting study with cultural implications, Kosson, Smith, and Newman (1990) examined the validity of the psychopathy construct among African-American prison inmates. Although these researchers found some differences between African-Americans and whites, they also found many similarities in the pattern of scores on Hare's checklist and in passive avoidance learning (an important area of research in psychopathy described in detail later in this chapter).

We have, then, two related but not identical diagnoses—antisocial personality disorder and psychopathy. Hare, Hart, and Harpur (1991) have criticized the antisocial personality diagnosis because it requires accurate reports of events that took place many years ago by people who are habitual liars. In addition, it is important that the diagnostic concept here not be synonymous with criminality. But 75 to 80 percent of convicted felons meet the criteria for antisocial personality disorder. In contrast, the corresponding figure for psychopaths is 15 to 25 percent (Hart & Hare, 1989). Therefore, the concept of psychopathy seems to have some distinct advantages. As we review the research in this area, it will be important to keep in mind that it has been conducted on individuals diagnosed in different ways—some as antisocial personalities and some as psychopaths. Integrating these findings may therefore be somewhat difficult.

Before considering current research on psychopathy, we will examine an excerpt from a case history that illustrates the classic characteristics of the psychopath but is unusual in that the person described was neither a criminal nor in psychiatric treatment at the time the data for the case study were collected. This is an important point, for the majority of psychopaths who are the subjects of research studies have broken the law and been caught for doing so. Only rarely do we have the opportunity to examine in detail the behavior of an individual who fits the diagnostic definition yet has managed not to break the law.

The Case of Dan

This case history was compiled by a psychologist, Elton McNeil (1967), a personal friend of Dan's.

Dan was a wealthy actor and disc jockey who lived in an expensive house in an exclusive suburb and generally played his role as a personality to the hilt. One evening, when he and McNeil were out for dinner, Dan made a great fuss over the condition of the shrimp de Johnge he had ordered. McNeil thought that Dan deliberately contrived the whole scene for the effect it might produce, and he said to his companion,

> "I have a sneaking suspicion this whole scene came about just because you weren't really hungry." Dan laughed loudly in agreement and said, "What the hell, they'll be on their toes next time." "Was that the only reason for this display?" . . . "No," he replied, "I wanted to show you how gutless the rest of the world is. If you shove a little they all jump. Next time I come in, they'll be all over me to make sure everything is exactly as I want it. That's the only way they can tell the difference between class and plain ordinary. When I travel I go first class."
>
> "Yes, . . . but how do you feel about you as a person—as a fellow human being?"
>
> "Who cares?" he laughed. "If they were on top they would do the same to me. The more you walk on them, the more they like it. It's like royalty in the old days. It makes them nervous if everyone is equal to everyone else. Watch. When we leave I'll put my arm around that waitress, ask her if she still loves me, pat her on the fanny, and she'll be ready to roll over any time I wiggle my little finger." (p. 85)

Another incident occurred when a friend of Dan's committed suicide. Most of the other friends whom Dan and McNeil had in common were concerned and called McNeil to see whether he could provide any information about why the man had taken his life. Dan did not. Later, when McNeil mentioned the suicide to Dan, all he could say was, "That's the way the ball bounces." In his public behavior, however, Dan's attitude toward the incident appeared quite different. He was the one who collected money and presented it personally to the widow. In keeping with his character, however, Dan remarked that the widow had a sexy body that really interested him.

These two incidents convey the flavor of Dan's behavior. McNeil had witnessed a long succession of similar events, which led him to conclude that

> [The incidents] painted a grisly picture of lifelong abuse of people for Dan's amusement and profit. He was adept at office politics and told me casually of an unbelievable set of deceptive

> ways to deal with the opposition. Character assassination, rumor mongering, modest blackmail, seduction, and barefaced lying were the least of his talents. He was a jackal in the entertainment jungle, a jackal who feasted on the bodies of those he had slaughtered professionally. (p. 91)

In his conversations with Dan, McNeil was also able to inquire into Dan's life history. One early and potentially important event was related by Dan.

> I can remember the first time in my life when I began to suspect I was a little different from most people. When I was in high school my best friend got leukemia and died and I went to his funeral. Everybody else was crying and feeling sorry for themselves and as they were praying to get him into heaven I suddenly realized that I wasn't feeling anything at all. He was a nice guy but what the hell. That night I thought about it some more and found that I wouldn't miss my mother and father if they died and that I wasn't too nuts about my brothers and sisters for that matter. I figured there wasn't anybody I really cared for but, then, I didn't need any of them anyway so I rolled over and went to sleep. (p. 87)

The moral depravity described long ago by Pinel and Prichard clearly marks Dan's behavior. A person may be otherwise quite rational and show no loss of contact with reality and yet behave in a habitually and exceedingly unethical manner. This final excerpt illustrated Dan's complete lack of feeling for others, a characteristic that will later be seen to have considerable relevance in explaining the behavior of the psychopath.

Research and Theory on the Etiology of Psychopathy

We now turn to research and theory on the etiology of psychopathy. We will first examine two areas of biological interest—genetics and central nervous system activity—and then the psychological factors of the family and avoidance learning. A final section on underarousal and impulsivity ties several of the individual research domains together.

We should emphasize again that most research has been conducted on psychopaths who have already been convicted as criminals. Individuals such as Dan have rarely been studied in research settings. We must therefore keep in mind that the available literature may not allow generalization about the behavior of psychopaths who elude arrest.

Genetic Correlates of Psychopathic Behavior

Adoptee studies suggest that heredity may play a role in both criminality and psychopathy. With the help of the extensive social records kept in Denmark, Hutchings and Mednick (1974) and Mednick, Gabrielli, and Hutchings (1984) examined rates of criminality in the adoptive and biological relatives of adoptees who had acquired criminal records. Schulsinger (1972) performed a similar study with psychopathy as the misconduct of interest. Both studies of criminality found it at a higher rate in the biological relatives of criminals than in the adoptive relatives. Schulsinger found more psychopathy in the biological relatives of psychopaths. Studies done in the United States of adopted children whose biological parents were antisocial personalities also point to a genetic diathesis (e.g., Cadoret, 1978).

More complicated studies have examined both the criminality and the alcoholism of adoptees (Bohman et al., 1982; Cloninger et al., 1982). A large sample of adopted individuals were classified according to whether they had criminal records, a history of alcoholism, both, or neither. Criminals who were also alcoholic repeatedly committed violent offenses; risk for criminality in these individuals was linked to their own alcoholism but not to any criminal behavior of their biological parents. Nonalcoholic criminals tended to commit petty crimes, such as property offenses; their risk for criminality was associated with their biological parents' history of committing similar crimes as well as with instability in their placements before they were finally adopted. Thus these data suggest that some forms of criminal behavior may have a genetic component.

Central Nervous System Activity and Psychopathy

Many early studies examined brain-wave activity in psychopaths and various groups of control subjects. Fluctuations in voltage are recorded by an electroencephalograph and amplified so they can be viewed. The electrical activity of the brain changes depending on the state of the person (e.g., asleep or highly aroused). Ellingson (1954) reviewed these studies and reported that in thirteen out of fourteen, investigating a total of about 1500 psychopaths, between 31 and 58 percent of the psychopaths showed some form of electroencephalogram (EEG) abnormality. The most frequent form of abnormality was slow-wave activity, which is typical of infants and young children but not of normal adults. The slow waves were widespread throughout the brain.

Later findings reviewed by Syndulko (1978) generally agree with the earlier ones. Most studies report rather high frequencies of EEG abnormalities in psychopaths and the presence of slow waves and positive spikes in particular. These spikes occur in the temporal area of the brain and consist of bursts of activity with frequencies of 6 to 8 and 14 to 16 cycles per second (cps). Not all psychopaths show EEG abnormalities, however, and it is unclear whether those who do differ in any other way from those who do not. Furthermore, the brain waves of psychopaths are not abnormally slow in all experimental contexts. Hare and Jutai (1985), for example, found the usual high levels of slow-wave activity when psychopaths were resting, but later, when they played an exciting video game, their brain waves were the same as those of normal subjects.

Specific interpretations of the psychopath's EEG abnormalities remain highly speculative at this time. Hare (1970), for example, interprets the high frequency of slow-wave activity as indicating a dysfunction in inhibitory mechanisms, which, in turn, lessens the psychopath's ability to learn to forestall actions that are likely to get him or her into trouble. Although this interpretation is consistent with studies of the negligible effects of past punishment on psychopaths, it certainly is not the only one possible.

The Role of the Family

Since much psychopathic behavior violates social norms, it is not surprising that many investigators have focused on the primary agent of socialization, the family, in their search for the explanation of such behavior. McCord and McCord (1964) concluded, on the basis of a classic review of the literature, that lack of affection and severe parental rejection were the primary causes of psychopathic behavior. Several other studies have related psychopathic behavior to parents' inconsistencies in disciplining their children and in teaching them responsibility toward others (Bennet, 1960). Furthermore, the fathers of psychopaths are likely to be antisocial in their behavior.

But such data on early rearing must be interpreted with extreme caution. They were gathered by means of **restrospective reports**, individual recollections of past events. We have already seen (see page 193) that information obtained in this way is of questionable value. When people are asked to recollect the early events in the life of someone who is now known to be a psychopath, their knowledge of adult status may affect what they remember or report about childhood events. Deviant incidents are more likely to be recalled, whereas more typical or normal incidents that do not match with the person's current behavior may be overlooked. And as far as retrospective reporting by psychopaths themselves is concerned, it seems as imprudent to believe what they say about their past as it is to believe anything else they say.

One way of avoiding the problems of retrospective data is to follow up in adulthood a large group of individuals who as children were seen at child guidance clinics. In one such study very detailed records had been kept on the children, including the type of problem that had brought them to the clinic and considerable information relating to the family (Robins, 1966). Ninety percent of an initial sample of 584 cases were located thirty years after their referral to the clinic.[3] In addition to the clinic cases, 100 control subjects who had lived in the same geographic area served by the clinic but who had not been referred to it were also interviewed in adulthood.

By interviewing the now-adult people chosen for both the experimental and control samples, the investigators were able to diagnose and describe any maladjustments of these individuals. Then, adult problems were related back to the characteristics that these people had had as children to find out which of them predicted psychopathic behavior in adulthood. Robins's summary brings to mind the category of conduct disorder, introduced in the discussion of antisocial behavior in juveniles in Chapter 15:

> If one wishes to choose the most likely candidate for a later diagnosis of [psychopathy] from among children appearing in a child guidance clinic, the best choice appears to be a boy referred for theft or aggression who has shown a diversity of antisocial behavior in many episodes, at least one of which could be grounds for Juvenile Court appearance, and whose antisocial behavior involves him with strangers and organizations as well as with teachers and parents. . . . more than half of the boys appearing at the clinic [with these characteristics were later] diagnosed sociopathic personality. Such boys had a history of truancy, theft, staying out late, and refusing to obey parents. They lied gratuitously, and showed little guilt over their behavior. They were generally irresponsible about being where they were supposed to be or taking care of money. (p. 157)

In addition to these characteristics, aspects of family life mentioned earlier were again found to be

[3]It should be appreciated that tracking down this large a percentage of individuals thirty years after their contact with the clinic is an incredible feat.

consequential. Both inconsistent discipline and no discipline at all predicted psychopathic behavior in adulthood, as did antisocial behavior of the father.

In sum, the research we have reviewed emphasizes the importance of child-rearing practices. The fathers of psychopaths appear to provide a model for antisocial behavior. We must caution, however, that poor training in socialization has been implicated in the etiology of a number of clinical syndromes, including delinquent, neurotic, and even psychotic behavior (Wiggins, 1968), and that many individuals who come from what appear to be similarly disturbed social backgrounds do not become psychopaths or develop any other behavior disorders. This point is important: adults may have no problems whatsoever in spite of the inconsistent and otherwise undesirable manner of their upbringing. Thus, although family experience is probably significant in the development of psychopathic behavior, it is not the sole factor.

Avoidance Learning, Punishment, and Psychopathy

As previously noted, in defining the psychopathic syndrome, Cleckley pointed out the inability of these persons to profit from experience: they do not try to avoid the negative consequences of social misbehavior. Cleckley also remarked that they are not neurotic and are seldom anxious. From these clinical observations, Lykken (1957) deduced that psychopaths may have few inhibitions about committing antisocial acts because they experience so little anxiety. He performed several tests to determine whether psychopaths do indeed have low levels of anxiety. One of these tests involved avoidance learning. Because some of the discussion that follows is complicated and detailed, let us state at the outset the conclusion that the research seems to be heading toward, namely, it is not so much that psychopaths suffer from a general deficit in the ability to learn as that only certain punishments have meaning for them.

In the Lykken (1957) study, a group of male psychopaths, judged according to Cleckley's criteria, were selected from a penitentiary population. Their performance on an avoidance learning task was compared with that of nonpsychopathic penitentiary inmates and college students. It was, of course, critical to test only avoidance and not learning mediated by other possible rewards. For example, if a subject perceives that the task is to learn to avoid pain, he or she may be motivated not only by the desire to avoid the pain but also by a desire to demonstrate his or her cleverness to the investigator. To ensure that no other motives would come into play, Lykken made the avoidance learning task seem *incidental*, an apparently secondary aspect of the whole test. He used the following apparatus. On a panel in front of the subject there were four red lights in a horizontal array, four green lights below each of the red ones, and a lever below each column, as illustrated in Figure 10.1. The subject's task was to learn a sequence of twenty correct lever presses, but for each he first had to determine by trial and error which of the four alternatives was correct. The correct lever turned on a green light. Two of the remaining three incorrect levers turned on red lights, indicating an error. The third incorrect lever delivered an electric shock to the subject. The location of the correct lever was of course not always the same. The subject was told simply to figure out and to learn the series of twenty correct lever presses. He was not informed that avoiding shock was desirable or possible, only that shock was randomly administered as a stimulant to make him do well.

In terms of the overall number of errors made in learning the sequence, there were no significant differences among any of the groups in Lykken's study. The college students, however, made fewer errors that resulted in shock. The psychopaths made the most shocked errors. From these results, Lykken concluded that psychopaths operate under lower levels of anxiety than do normal individuals.

Figure 10.1 Lykken (1957) devised this apparatus for his study of avoidance learning in psychopaths. For the first lever press assume that lever 3 is correct, that is, that pressing it lights the green bulb; that levers 1 and 4 are incorrect, lighting red bulbs; and that pressing lever 2 lights a red bulb and gives the subject a shock. For the second lever press the meaning of the levers may change entirely; for example, lever 2 may be correct, levers 3 and 4 incorrect, and lever 1 may give the shock. The subjects had to learn a sequence of twenty correct lever presses.

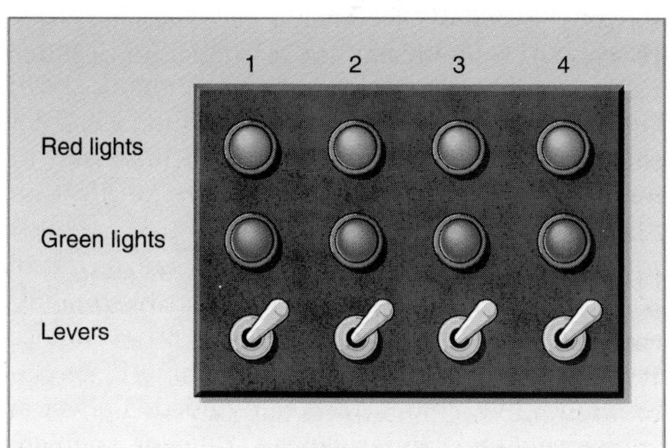

Lykken's pioneering work was subsequently followed up by Schachter and Latané (1964). These investigators reasoned that if psychopaths fail to learn to avoid unpleasant stimuli because they have little anxiety, a procedure that increases their anxiety should help them learn to shun punishment. Inasmuch as anxiety is viewed as being related to activity of the sympathetic nervous system, they injected Adrenalin, an agent whose effects mimic sympathetic activity, into the subjects to increase anxiety.

Psychopathic and nonpsychopathic prisoners from a penitentiary were studied with the task and apparatus devised by Lykken. The subjects were led to believe that the effects of a hormone on learning were being investigated. Testing took place on two consecutive days. Half received a placebo injection on the first day of testing and half an injection of Adrenalin. On the second day of testing, the injections received by the subjects were reversed.

The results of Schachter and Latané's experiment were important in several ways. First, the overall number of errors provided confirmation for Lykken's results: no difference was found between the psychopathic and nonpsychopathic prisoners in the total number of errors committed in learning the sequence, whether they had been injected with Adrenalin or the placebo. Second, the nonpsychopathic prisoners injected with the placebo markedly reduced their proportion of shocked errors after a number of trials, but the psychopaths injected with the placebo showed no such improvement. In this part of the study, the difference between the performances of the two groups of prisoners was greater than that revealed in Lykken's experiment and considerably larger than the amount necessary for statistical significance. Third, and most important, when injected with Adrenalin, the psychopaths showed a great reduction in the number of shocked errors, but the nonpsychopathic prisoners were adversely affected by the Adrenalin and did not learn to avoid the shock in their state of high arousal (Figure 10.2). Thus the hypothesis of the anxiety-free and underaroused psychopath received considerable support from the work of Schachter and Latané.

An avoidance learning study by Schmauk (1970) qualifies the findings of Lykken and of Schachter and Latané. He showed that a particular kind of punishment, losing money, can have an effect on psychopaths. He tested three groups: psychopathic prisoners, nonpsychopathic prisoners, and a control group consisting of farm workers and hospital attendants. As in the previous studies, an avoidance learning task was devised, but this time three different aversive stimuli could be avoided: a physical punishment—electric shock; a tangible punishment—losing a quarter from an initial pile of forty; and a social punishment—the experimenter's saying "wrong" to the subject. There were again no differences among the groups in the total number of errors made before the task was mastered. The major finding of this study (Figure 10.3) was that the psychopath's avoidance performance varied with the nature of punishment. When the punishments confronting them were physical and social, the members of the control group were vastly superior to the psychopaths in learning to avoid punishment. But the psychopaths outdid the controls in learning to avoid the tangible punishment of losing a quarter. The nonpsychopathic prisoners did better than the psychopaths in learning to avoid physical punishment but less well in avoiding social punishment.

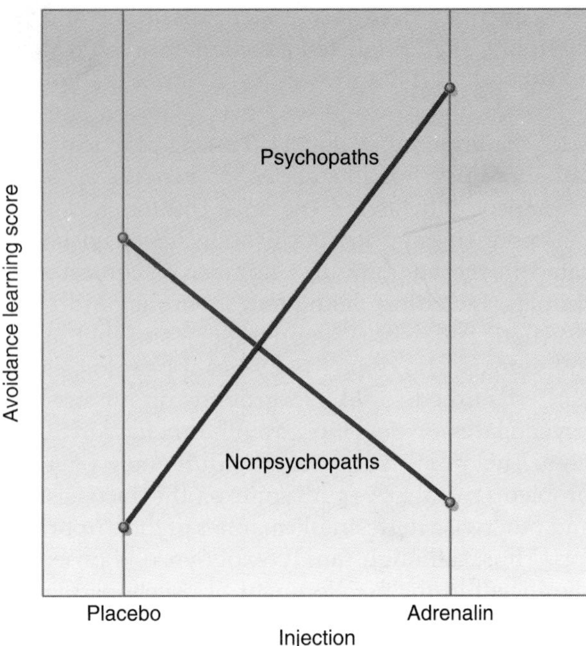

Figure 10.2 Results of Schachter and Latané's study (1964) of the effects of Adrenalin on avoidance learning in psychopathic and nonpsychopathic prisoners. Higher scores reflect better avoidance learning; increasing arousal through Adrenalin helped the psychopaths learn to avoid shock by activating their otherwise underaroused autonomic nervous systems.

It appears then that psychopaths *can* learn to avoid punishment. The differences found between psychopaths and nonpsychopaths in previous investigations may reflect not a general deficit in avoidance learning ability but rather the fact that some punishments have no meaning for the psychopath. Evidently, psychopaths will learn to avoid punishment that is relevant to their system of val-

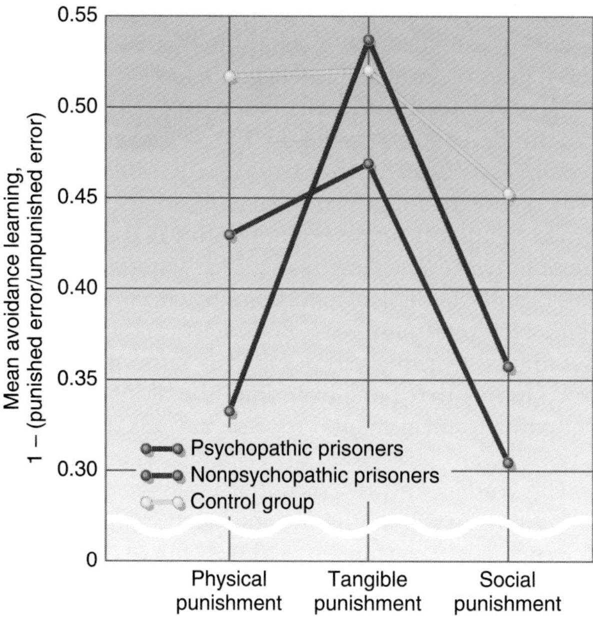

Figure 10.3 Mean avoidance learning scores plotted for three subject groups confronted by three different punishments: physical, tangible, and social. The psychopaths readily learned to avoid punishment when it cost them money. After Schmauk (1970).

ues, and money may very well be particularly motivating to them.

An alternative explanation of these results has been suggested by Newman and Kosson (1986). They pointed out that Schmauk's tangible punishment condition differed from shock avoidance in several respects. Most important to Newman and Kosson was the fact that in the tangible punishment condition the punishment was salient. Subjects saw the stack of quarters in front of them and could keep their winnings. In contrast, in the shock avoidance condition subjects were not even told that the shock could be avoided.

On the basis of this reasoning, Newman and Kosson hypothesized that salience of the punishment was the critical variable and tested their hypothesis by studying psychopaths and controls on two versions of a discrimination learning task. In one condition subjects were rewarded when they responded correctly and punished when they made an error. In the second condition subjects were not rewarded for a correct response; they were only punished for errors. The punishment should be more salient in the second condition because it is the only consequence to which a subject had to attend.

Comparison of the number of punished errors in each condition supported the hypothesis. Psychopaths did not differ from controls in the punishment-only condition, but in the reward and punishment condition they showed their usual performance deficit, making more punished errors than did controls. Getting the psychopath's attention may be what's needed for a punishment to be effective. Indeed, in situations where both rewards and punishments are present, psychopaths focus on the rewards rather than balancing their attention between both the rewards and punishments (Raine et al., 1990).

Gorenstein (1991) noted that although the avoidance learning theory of psychopathy is promising, it is also incomplete. It assumes, for example, that fear of punishment (going to prison) is what motivates us all to refrain from criminal activity. Lacking this fear, the psychopath commits frequent crimes. But it is likely that the reasons people don't commit crimes are much more complex. Most people are socialized into a value system that teaches them standards and moral values that they use to make decisions about acceptable conduct. Fear of punishment may play little role in the decisions most of us make about what's right and wrong. Furthermore, the avoidance learning model fails to account for other important aspects of psychopathy, such as gratuitous lying, insensitivity to others, and failure to follow a life plan.

Underarousal and Impulsivity

Psychopaths have often been described as not responding emotionally when confronted by both familiar and new situations that most people would find either stressful or unpleasant. Cleckley (1976) wrote about this aspect of their behavior.

> Regularly, we find in [the psychopath] extraordinary poise rather than jitteriness or worry, a smooth sense of physical well-being instead of uneasy preoccupations with bodily functions. Even under concrete circumstances that would for the ordinary person cause embarrassment, confusion, acute insecurity, or visible agitation, his relative serenity is likely to be noteworthy. (p. 340)

This description is remarkably consistent with the Schachter and Latané finding that psychopaths do not ordinarily avoid electric shock but that they do so when their autonomic arousal is increased by injections of Adrenalin. Because of the assumed central role of the autonomic nervous system in states of emotion, several investigators have examined psychopaths both for their resting levels of autonomic activity and for their patterns of autonomic reactivity to various classes of stimuli.

Most studies indicate that in resting situations

psychopaths have lower than normal levels of skin conductance. Furthermore, their skin conductance is less reactive when they are confronted with intense or aversive stimuli or when they anticipate an aversive stimulus (Harpur & Hare, 1990). A different picture emerges, however, when heart rate is examined. The heart rate of psychopaths is like that of normal people under resting conditions, and their heart rate reactivity to neutral stimuli is also unremarkable. But in situations in which psychopaths anticipate a stressful stimulus, their hearts beat faster than those of normal people anticipating stress.

These physiological reactions indicate that the psychopath cannot be regarded as simply underaroused, for measurements of skin conductance and heart rate are inconsistent. Basing his theorizing in part on Lacey's work (1967), Hare (1978) focused on the *pattern* of psychophysiological responses of psychopaths. Faster heartbeats are viewed as a concomitant of gating out or reducing sensory input and thus lowering cortical arousal. Thus the increased heart rate of psychopaths who are anticipating an aversive stimulus would indicate that they are tuning it out. Their skin conductance is then less reactive to an aversive stimulus because they have been able effectively to ignore it. That is, with skin conductance considered an index of anxiety, that of psychopaths does not increase to any extent after expected aversive stimulation because they have already dealt with it by screening it out. This interpretation of the physiological reactions of psychopaths is plausible and consistent with the studies reviewed earlier on avoidance learning; it has also been directly confirmed in subsequent research (Ogloff & Wong, 1990). Further research by Hare and his associates has confirmed that in both their behavior and their biological response (Jutai & Hare, 1983) psychopaths are particularly adept at ignoring stimuli and focusing their attention on what interests them (Forth & Hare, 1989).

An important addition to our current thinking about the causes of psychopathy might be the inclusion of something that would stimulate or push for antisocial behavior. In this vein Gorenstein and Newman (1980) proposed that a key element of psychopathy is heightened impulsivity and the inability to sustain goal-directed activity. They noted detailed similarities between aspects of psychopathy and the behavior of animals that have been lesioned in a neural system including the septum, hippocampus, and prefrontal cortex. For example, these animals show deficits in passive avoidance learning and impulsive responding to immediate rewards.

In a recent paper, Gorenstein (1991) elaborated on the earlier work in proposing that a lack of cognitive mediating processes may be the key feature of the lesioned animals and of psychopathy. By a lack of mediating cognitions Gorenstein means that, in the person's mind, the representations of events that are not immediately present in the environment are weak. The result is that behavior is often not directed toward long-term goals and instead is governed to an inordinate extent by stimuli that are immediately present. The theory adds what may be an important element of psychopathy; it is consistent with Newman and Kosson's interpretation of the avoidance learning data, and it is supported by a few studies that have examined the ability of psychopaths to form mental representations of events.

The studies and theories that we have reviewed show that psychopaths do not react as most of us do. In particular, they have almost no anxiety, so it can have little deterrent effect. Moreover, because psychopaths are in greater control of their negative emotional reactions, they actually seek arousal. And, because psychopaths are deficient in planning and in inhibition, they behave impulsively. These

Some of the psychopath's antisocial behavior seems to be motivated by thrill seeking, but in a more pervasive and intense way than simply engaging in bungee-jumping.

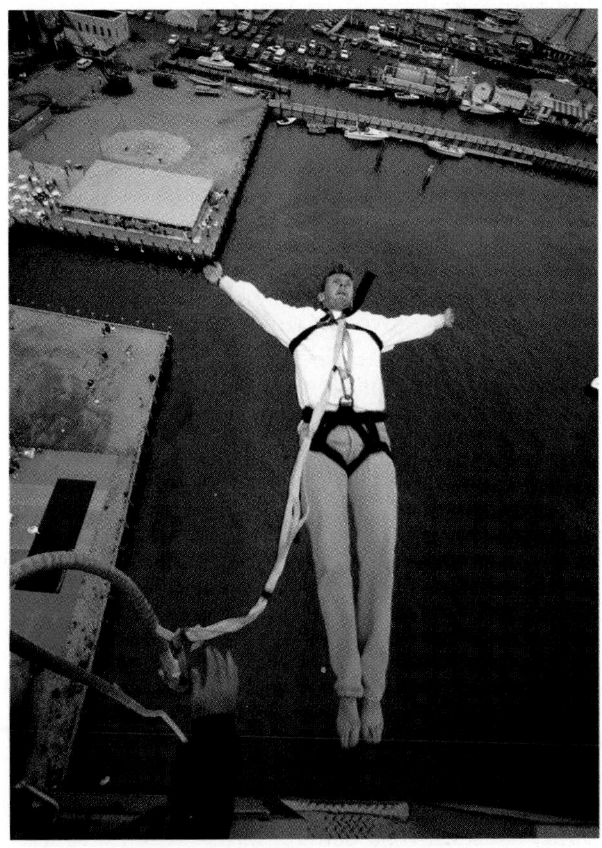

are possible reasons for the psychopath's misconduct without regret and thrill seeking without regard for society's rules.

Therapies for Personality Disorders

There is as little research-based information on treating personality disorders as there is information on how they develop. There is, though, a lively and burgeoning clinical case literature on therapies for many of the personality disorders. Though the ideas outlined here are for the most part based on the clinical experiences of a small number of mental health professionals and not on studies that contain suitable controls, these therapeutic guidelines are all that is available on treating personality disorders. As we review the clinical literature, it is also important to bear in mind that, for the most part, a therapist working with such patients is also concerned with axis I disorders. For example, an antisocial personality is likely to have substance abuse problems; an avoidant personality, social anxiety problems; an obsessive-compulsive personality, depression. In fact, it is typical that the axis I problem is what led the person to seek treatment.

Behavior and cognitive therapists, in keeping with their attention to situations rather than to traits, have had little to say until recently about specific treatments for the personality disorders designated by the DSM. Rather, they analyze the problems that, taken together, reflect a personality disorder. For example, a person diagnosed as having a paranoid personality will be very sensitive to criticism. This sensitivity may be treated by systematic desensitization or rational-emotive therapy (see Chapter 2, page 51). The person's argumentativeness and hostility when disagreeing with other people will push them away from him or her and provoke counterattacks from them. The behavior therapist may help the individual learn more adaptive ways of disagreeing with other people. Social-skills training in a support group might be considered a way to encourage avoidant personalities to be more bold in initiating contacts with other people. This technique, perhaps combined with rational-emotive therapy, may help them cope when their efforts to reach out do not succeed, as is bound to happen (Turkat & Maisto, 1985).

In a recent discussion of cognitive therapy for personality disorders, Beck and his associates (1990) apply the same kind of analysis as that found promising in the treatment of depression (cf. Chapter 9, p. 244 and Chapter 19, page 565). Beck analyzes each disorder in terms of logical errors and dysfunctional schemata. For example, cognitive therapy with an obsessive-compulsive personality entails first of all persuading the patient to accept the essence of the cognitive model, that feelings and behaviors are primarily a function of thoughts. Errors in logic are then explored, such as when the patient concludes that he or she cannot do anything right because of failing in one particular endeavor (an example of overgeneralization). The therapist also looks for dysfunctional assumptions or schemata that might underlie the person's thoughts and feelings, for example, believing that it is critical that every decision be a correct one (something adherents of Ellis's approach would also do). As one reads the clinical details in Beck's approach to personality disorders, what becomes clear is that it represents a sophisticated combination of a variety of behavioral and cognitive-behavioral techniques, all designed to address the particular, long-standing, and pervasive difficulties presented by patients. His approach to borderline personality disorder and antisocial personality disorder is described in the sections that follow.

Therapy for the Borderline Personality

A number of drugs have been tried in the pharmacotherapy of borderline personality disorder, most notably antidepressants and neuroleptics. However, most of the available data come from uncontrolled clinical trials (Gunderson, 1986). The exception is a double-blind, placebo-controlled study showing moderate effectiveness for neuroleptics (Soloff et al., 1986).

Object Relations Psychotherapy

Object relations theory, a branch of psychoanalytic theory, deals with the nature and development of mental representations of the self and others (the object relations). It includes not only the representations themselves but also the fantasies and emotions attached to these representations and how these variables mediate interpersonal functioning. Object relations theorists stress the impact of deprivation and abuse during childhood and draw on research such as that on attachment reviewed earlier. This theory has been particularly important in the field of personality disorders. The two leading contemporary object relations theorists are Heinz Kohut, whose views on narcissism were discussed earlier, and Otto Kernberg, who has written extensively about the borderline personality.

Kernberg (1985) operates from the basic assumption that borderline personalities have weak egos and therefore inordinate difficulty tolerating the regression (probing of childhood conflicts) that occurs in psychoanalytic treatment. The weak ego fears being flooded by primitive primary process thinking. Kernberg's modified analytic treatment has the overall goal of strengthening the patient's weak ego. Therapy involves analysis of a principal defense of the borderline person, namely, splitting, or dichotomizing into all good or all bad and not integrating positive and negative aspects of a person into a whole. Splitting is regarded as due to an inability to form complex object representations that do not fit a simple good–bad dichotomy. It causes extreme difficulty in regulating emotions because the person sees the world in black-and-white terms. Somehow this defense protects the borderline personality's weak ego from intolerable anxiety.

The borderline patient must also be helped to reality test (though it is not clear in what way this is different from the overall psychoanalytic goal of helping patients discriminate between irrational childhood-based fears and adult reality). Kernberg's approach is more directive than that of most analysts: he gives the patient concrete suggestions for behaving more adaptively and will hospitalize a patient whose behavior becomes dangerous to either the self or others. His opinion that such patients are inappropriate for classical psychoanalysis is consistent with a long-term study conducted at the world-famous analytically oriented Menninger Clinic (Stone, 1987).

Dialectical Behavior Therapy

An approach that combines client-centered empathy with behavioral problem-solving is suggested by Marsha Linehan (1987). What she calls **dialectical behavior therapy** (DBT) centers on the therapist's full acceptance of borderline personalities with all their contradictions and acting out, empathically validating their (distorted) beliefs with a matter-of-fact attitude toward their suicidal and other dysfunctional behavior. The behavioral aspect of the treatment involves helping patients learn to solve problems, that is, to acquire more effective and socially acceptable ways of handling their daily living problems and controlling their emotions. Work is also done on improving their interpersonal skills and in controlling their anxieties. After many months of intensive treatment, limits are set on their behavior, consistent with what Kernberg advocates.

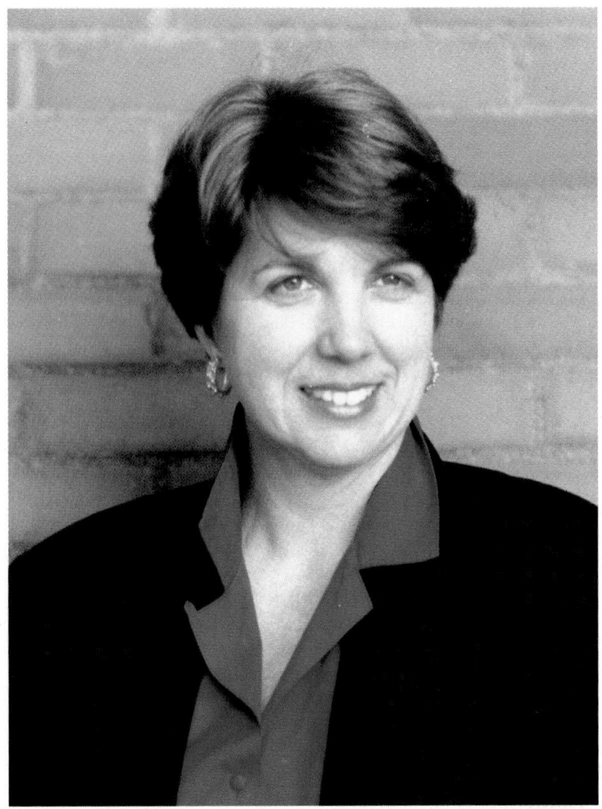

Marsha Linehan, created dialectical behavior therapy, which combines cognitive behavior therapy with Zen and Rogerian notions of acceptance.

Linehan and her associates have recently published the results of the first randomized, controlled study of a psychological intervention of borderline personality disorder (Linehan et al., 1991). Patients were randomly assigned either to dialectical behavior therapy or to treatment-as-usual, meaning any therapy available in the community (Seattle, Washington). At the end of one year of treatment and again six and twelve months later, patients in the two groups were compared on a variety of measures (Linehan, Heard, & Armstrong, 1992). The findings immediately after treatment revealed highly significant superiority of DBT on the following measures: intentional self-injurious behavior including suicide attempts, fewer dropouts from treatment, and fewer inpatient hospital days. At the follow-ups, superiority was maintained and, additionally, DBT patients had better work histories, reported less anger, and were judged as overall better adjusted than the comparison therapy patients. As a result of this study together with a new book and manual on dialectical behavior therapy (Linehan, in press-a, in press-b), increasing interest can be expected in this approach to borderline personality disorder (Focus Box 10.2).

10.2 • Acceptance in Linehan's Dialectical Behavior Therapy

Marsha Linehan's (1987; in press-a, in press-b) notion of acceptance within the framework of her dialectical behavior therapy is subtle, hence some elaboration is warranted. In a Zenlike way, Linehan argues that a therapist working with a borderline personality has to adopt what to the Western mind is an inconsistent posture: be clear with the patient about limits and work for change while at the same time accepting the person as client-centered therapists would, including the real possibility that no changes are going to occur. Linehan's reasoning is that the borderline personality is so exquisitely sensitive to rejection and criticism as well as so emotionally unstable that even gentle encouragement to behave or think differently leads to high levels of emotional arousal and subsequent misinterpretation of suggestions as a serious rebuke. The therapist who a moment earlier was revered is now vilified and spurned. Thus, while observing limits—"I would be very sad if you killed yourself so I hope very much that you won't"—the therapist must convey to the borderline patient that he or she is fully accepted even while threatening suicide and making everyone else's life miserable, including the therapist's! (Recall Kellerman's vivid description of this syndrome, page 267.)

This complete acceptance of the patient does not mean that the therapist *approves* of everything the patient is doing, only that the therapist accepts the situation for what it is. Indeed, argues Linehan, the therapist must truly accept the patient as he or she is; acceptance should not be in the service of change, an indirect way of encouraging the patient to behave differently. Such an instrumental use of acceptance, which Linehan rejects, reminds us of paradoxical therapy, an interesting approach discussed in detail in Chapter 19 (page 580). Briefly, paradoxical therapists foster change by instructing the patient either not to change or to increase the severity of the symptom they would like to eliminate. Although it might sometimes help a patient change if the therapist construes acceptance as one way to encourage change, Linehan's concept of acceptance is different, for it is not a means to an end. "Acceptance can transform but if you accept in order to transform, it is not acceptance. It is like loving. Love seeks no reward but when given freely comes back a hundredfold. He who loses his life finds it. He who accepts, changes" (Linehan, personal communication, November 16, 1992).

Thus, full and thoroughgoing acceptance does not, in Linehan's view, preclude change. Indeed, she proposes that it is the refusal to accept that prevents change. She puts it this way when talking to her patients: "If you hate the color purple, move into a house that is painted purple, and then refuse to accept that the house is indeed painted purple, it is unlikely that you will rush out and buy paint to repaint it. The person who immediately accepts that the house is painted purple—without excess ado or distortion or denial or outrage at the fact of the color or one's own preference—will probably get it repainted the quickest" (Linehan, personal communication, September 18, 1992). Linehan's ideas on acceptance bear some similarity to those of Hayes's Acceptance Commitment Therapy (Hayes, 1987) and have also been adapted recently by two cognitive-behavioral marital researchers, Jacobson and Christenson (in press; Jacobson, 1992), whose ideas are presented in Chapter 20 (page 606).

Cognitive Therapy

Recommendations from Beck et al. (1990) are consistent with Kernberg and Linehan in emphasizing the difficulties in establishing trust with borderline personalities: their tendencies to test the reliability of the therapist with threats and other demands, their low tolerance for intimacy and yet exquisite sensitivity to rejection, and the presentation in each session of constantly emergent crises that make it very hard to focus on a limited number of themes and goals. Beck even borrows a basic tenet of object relations, cautioning about *transference reactions* by the borderline patient. An example he provides is a patient who was convinced that people in authority were manipulative and controlling, a residue of her past dealings with her parents. Suggestions for specific behavioral changes from the therapist were met with anger and resistance because these efforts reminded the patient of sensitizing experiences from childhood. The therapist dealt with these transference reactions by taking care again and again to point out clearly and patiently what the reasons for the various suggestions were and what they were not.

Beck et al. theorize that borderline personalities operate with one or more of the following three negative schematas: that the world is dangerous and malevolent; that they themselves are vulnerable and powerless; and that they are unacceptable to others. The very specific and goal-oriented nature of Beck's cognitive therapy makes it a challenge to adapt it to the tumultuous, conflicted, and confusing picture commonly found in borderline patients. It is a daunting task (as indeed it is for *any* therapist). A general guideline is for the therapist to be more flexible than he or she would be with other kinds of patients, adapting techniques and foci to the idiosyncracies of the patient. For example, in collecting automatic thoughts (cf. page 232) from the patient, the therapist is advised to solicit the patient's suggestions for doing so rather than use a standard thought-listing procedure commonly found in the clinical and research literature on cognitive therapy. The kind of directiveness and certainty that can be reassuring to a depressed patient by imposing such structure can be threatening and anger-provoking to a borderline patient, yet it is also important to work toward particular goals in order to implement Beck's basic principles.

A central feature of borderline personality disorder is, as noted earlier, splitting, or dichotomous thinking. As we have seen in Beck's approach to depression, such all-or-none thinking is a familiar therapeutic target for the cognitive therapist. The general strategy is to (gently) show the borderline patient that he or she is, in fact, thinking in a dichotomous fashion and then to persuade the patient that it would be in his or her best interest to experiment with looking at the world in terms of shades of gray rather than black and white. As thinking becomes less dichotomous, the rapid and extreme emotional fluctuations typical of borderline personalities also tend to moderate. Exactly how this cognitive change is effected is exceedingly subtle and difficult, and beyond the scope of this book, but suffice it to say that such cognitive shifts are not achieved easily or quickly. Indeed, Beck et al. caution that, whereas many depressed patients can be helped by cognitive therapy in fewer than twenty sessions, borderline personalities may need up to two years of weekly sessions.

Therapy for Psychopathy

As for the treatment of antisocial personality disorder, there is unusual—and unfortunate—agreement among therapists of varying theoretical persuasions: psychopathy is virtually impossible to treat (Cleckley, 1976; McCord & McCord, 1964).

It may be that people with the classic symptoms listed by Cleckley are, by their very natures, incapable of benefiting from any form of psychotherapy. The most likely reason is that they are unable to form any sort of trusting, honest relationship with a therapist. People who lie almost without knowing it, who care little for the feelings of others and understand their own even less, who appear not to realize that what they are doing is morally wrong, who lack any motivation to obey society's laws and mores, and who, living only for the present, have no concern for the future are all in all extremely poor candidates for therapy. In fact, one clinician experienced in working with psychopaths has suggested three general principles.

> First, the therapist must be continually vigilant with regard to manipulation on the part of the patient. Second, he must assume, until proven otherwise, that information given him by the patient contains distortions and fabrications. Third, he must recognize that a working alliance develops, if ever, exceedingly late in any therapeutic relationship with a psychopath. (Lion, 1978, p. 286)

To be sure, many valiant attempts have been made to establish tenable connections with psychopaths, but both the published literature and informal communications among mental health professionals support the conclusion that true psychopathy cannot be reached through psychological efforts. Similar negative conclusions are to be drawn as well about somatic methods—electroconvulsive shock, drugs such as Dilantin, stimulants, and sedatives, and psychosurgery.[4] There is, however, some evidence that large doses of antianxiety agents can reduce hostility in psychopaths (Kellner, 1982), and there is some very tentative evidence that psychopaths who had attention-deficit disorder (see Chapter 15, page 428) as children might benefit from the drug Ritalin, which has had some positive effects with hyperactive youngsters (Stringer & Josef, 1983).

Beck and associates (1990) proposed that antisocial personality disorder be conceptualized in terms of particular kinds of thoughts and assumptions.

[4]An ethical problem can arise from the notion that psychopaths have a poor prognosis. If a prisoner is considered a psychopath, those in charge of decisions about parole and release are naturally concerned about whether he or she has really reformed. Good behavior in prison may merely reflect the prisoner's manipulativeness and ability to con people. The person designated a psychopath may thus be at a serious disadvantage in obtaining just treatment from the judicial system.

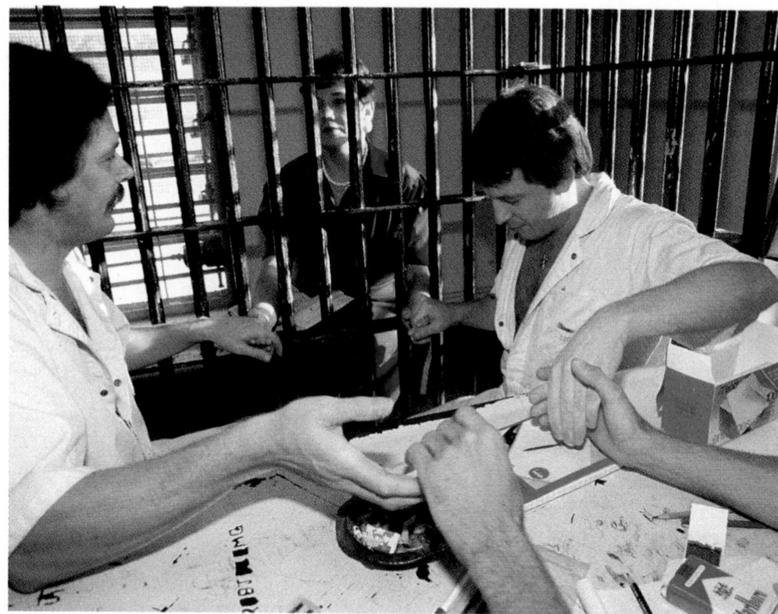

Although therapy is sometimes offered to prison inmates, its results have not been very encouraging.

> [They have] self-serving beliefs that emphasize immediate, personal satisfactions and minimize future consequences. The underlying belief that they are always right makes it unlikely that they will question their actions. . . . Instead of evaluating the potential helpfulness of [guidance and counseling from others, such] patients tend to dismiss input from others as irrelevant to their purposes. . . . Antisocial patients' lack of concern for future outcomes might be placed on the opposite end of a continuum from obsessive-compulsive patients' excessive striving toward perfectionistic future goals. (Beck et al., 1990, p. 154)

Specific beliefs are said to include justification (merely wanting something justifies any actions to attain it), personal infallibility (believing that one always makes good choices), the impotence of others (what others think doesn't matter), and low-impact consequences (negative outcomes will happen, and if they do, it will not matter). The general goal of cognitive therapy is to challenge such beliefs and try to bring the patient's ideas and behaviors in line with those of a lawful society where people respect the rights and sensibilities of others and in which their behavior is responsive to social controls. Efforts are made to demonstrate to the patient that his or her goals can be more readily achieved by altering behavior so that it is less impulsive, more empathic, and in general more conforming to societal standards. Considering the feelings of others might be more advantageous to them than continuing to ignore them. It remains to be seen whether this cognitive-behavioral conceptualization will generate interventions any more successful than others that have been tried in vain.

Since many psychopaths spend time in prison for committing crimes, the discouraging results of imprisonment as rehabilitation are traced at least in part to the inability to modify psychopathic behavior. As criminologists have stated repeatedly, our prison system seems to operate more as a school for crime than it does as a place where criminals, and psychopaths, can be rehabilitated.

An interesting argument in favor of incarceration is that psychopaths often settle down in middle age and thereafter (Craft, 1969). Whether through biological changes, eventual insight into their self-defeating natures, or simply becoming worn out and unable to continue in their finagling ways, many psychopaths grow less disruptive as they approach age forty. Prison, therefore, protects society from the antisocial behavior of active psychopaths, with release considered more plausible when the prisoner enters a stage of life in which the excesses of the disorder are less in evidence.

SUMMARY

The category of personality disorders is extremely broad and heterogeneous. Personality disorders are grouped into three clusters in DSM-IV. Individuals in the first cluster are odd and eccentric; those in the next, dramatic and emotional; and those in the last, anxious and fearful. There is little information on many of the personality disorders. Because many of the diagnoses overlap considerably, it is not uncommon for a single person to meet criteria for several of the personality disorder diagnoses. This high rate of comorbidity, coupled with the fact that personality traits are continuous variables, has led to proposals to develop a dimensional model of classification for these disorders.

The one personality disorder about which more is known is psychopathy; its dominant pattern is repeated antisocial behavior without regret or shame. Psychopaths are thought to be unable to learn from experience, to have no sense of responsibility, and to establish no genuine emotional relationships with other people. Research on their families indicates that psychopaths have fathers who themselves are antisocial and that discipline during upbringing was either absent or inconsistent. Genetic studies, particularly those using the adoptee method, suggest that a predisposition to psychopathy is inherited. The core problem of the psychopath may be that impending punishment creates no inhibitions about committing antisocial acts. A good deal of overlapping evidence supports this view: (1) psychopaths have abnormal amounts of slow-wave EEG activity, which may reflect a failure of the usual inhibitory processes; (2) psychopaths are slow at learning to avoid shock, a deficit that can be reduced by heightening their level of autonomic arousal; and (3) psychopaths, according to their electrodermal responses, show little anxiety but, as indicated by their faster heart rates, seem better able than normal people to tune out aversive stimuli.

Little is known about effective therapy for the various personality disorders for several reasons. The poor reliability of the diagnoses and the tendency to use the category as a grab bag make it difficult to evaluate reports of therapy. Some promising evidence is emerging, however, for the utility of dialectical behavior therapy for borderline personality disorder. Therapy for the psychopath holds little promise for a successful outcome. In addition to the pervasiveness and apparent intractability of the uncaring and manipulative life-style, the antisocial personality is by nature a poor candidate for therapy. People who habitually lie and lack insight into their own or others' feelings—and have no inclination to examine emotions—will not readily establish a trusting and open working relationship with a therapist.

KEY TERMS

personality disorders
paranoid personality
schizoid personality
schizotypal personality
borderline personality
histrionic personality
narcissistic personality
avoidant personality
dependent personality
obsessive-compulsive personality
antisocial personality
psychopathy
retrospective reports
dialectical behavior therapy

c h a p t e r   e l e v e n

Substance Related Disorders

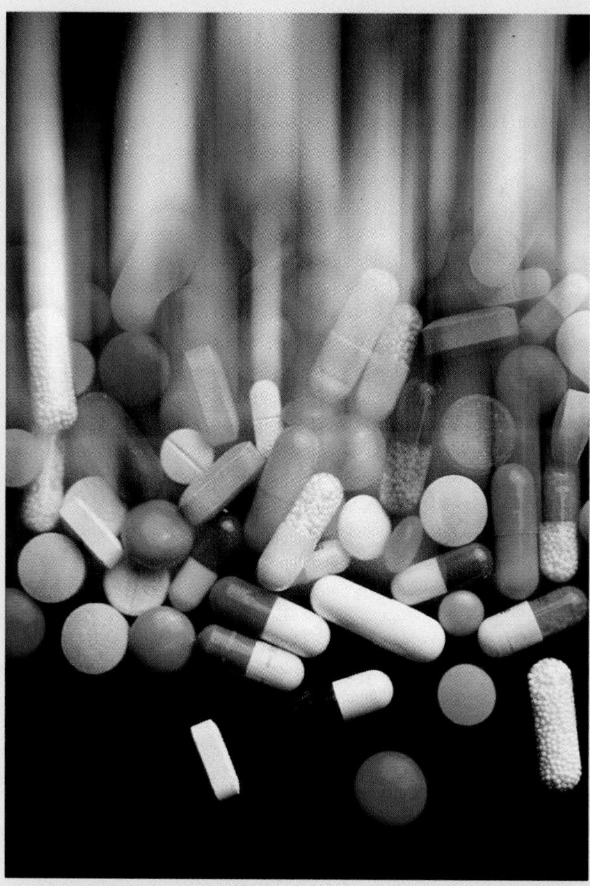

Alice was fifty-four years old when her family finally persuaded her to check into an alcohol rehabilitation clinic. She had taken a bad fall down her bedroom steps while drunk and it may have been this event that finally got her to admit that something was wrong. Her drinking had been out of control for several years. She began each day with a drink, resulting in total intoxication by the afternoon. She seldom had any memory for events after noon of any day.

Since early adulthood she had drunk regularly, but rarely during the day, and never to the point of drunkenness. The sudden death of her husband in an automobile accident two years earlier had triggered a quick increase in her drinking, and within six months she had slipped into a pattern of severe alcohol abuse. She had little desire to go out of her house and had cut back on social activities with family and friends. Repeated efforts by her family to get her to curtail her intake of alcohol had only led to angry confrontations.

From prehistoric times humankind has used various substances in the hope of reducing physical pain or altering states of consciousness. Almost all peoples have discovered some intoxicant that affects the central nervous system, relieving physical and mental anguish or producing euphoria. Whatever the aftermath of taking such substances into the body, their initial effects are usually pleasing.

The United States is a drug culture. We use drugs on awakening (coffee or tea), throughout the day (cigarettes, certain soft drinks), as a way to relax (alcohol) and to reduce pain (aspirin). The widespread availability and frequent use of various drugs sets the stage for the potential abuse of drugs, the topic of this chapter. The most recent data on the frequency of use of several drugs, both legal and illegal, are presented in Table 11.1. These figures do not represent the frequency of abuse (figures for abuse will be presented in the discussion of individual drugs), but simply provide an indication of how pervasive drug use is in this country.

Many, perhaps even most (Wilkinson et al., 1987), of those who abuse drugs use more than one at any given time. This multiple usage, called **polysubstance abuse,** poses a serious health problem because the effects of some drugs when taken together are synergistic, that is, the effects of each interact to produce an especially strong reaction. For example, mixing barbiturates with alcohol is a common means of suicide, intentional or accidental. Alcohol is believed to have contributed to deaths from heroin, for evidence indicates that alcohol can dramatically reduce the amount of narcotic that makes a dose lethal. The pathological use of substances that affect the central nervous system falls into two categories: substance abuse, and substance dependence. Together these constitute the major DSM-IV category substance related disorders.

It is important to define here a number of terms that are key to this discussion. In **substance abuse** a person uses a drug to such an extent that he or she is often intoxicated throughout the day and fails in important obligations and in attempts to abstain, but there is no physiological dependence. **Substance dependence,** also called **addiction,** is more severe abuse of a drug accompanied by a physiological dependence on it, made evident by tolerance and withdrawal symptoms. **Tolerance** is a physiological process whereby greater and greater amounts of an addictive drug are required to produce the same effect. **Withdrawal symptoms** are negative physiological and psychological reactions experienced when a person suddenly stops taking an addictive drug; cramps, restlessness, and even death are examples.

DSM-IV delineates the criteria for substance *dependence* as the presence of at least three of the following:

1. Tolerance develops, indicated by (a) larger doses of the substance are needed to produce the desired effect; (b) the effects of the drug become markedly less if the usual amount is taken; or (c) the person can appear to function normally after taking an amount that would impair a casual user.

Table 11.1 • Use of Various Drugs in One Month

Substance	*U.S. Population Reporting Use, %*
Alcohol	50.9
Cigarettes	27.0
Marijuana	4.8
Smokeless tobacco	3.4
Psychotherapeutics[a]	1.5
Cocaine	0.9
Inhalants	0.6
Hallucinogens	0.3
Crack	0.2
PCP	0.2

Source: From NIDA, 1991.
[a]Includes tranquilizers, sedatives, stimulants, and analgesics.

2. Withdrawal symptoms develop when the person stops taking the substance or reduces the amount. The person may also use the substance to relieve or avoid withdrawal symptoms.
3. The person uses more of the substance or uses it for a longer time than intended.
4. The person recognizes excessive use of the substance; may have tried to reduce it but has been unable to do so.
5. Much of the person's time is spent in efforts to obtain the substance or recover from its effects.
6. Substance use continues despite psychological or physical problems caused or made worse by the drug (e.g., smoking despite knowledge that it increases the risk for cancer and cardiovascular disease).
7. Many activities (work, recreation, socializing) are given up or reduced in frequency because of the use of the substance.

For the diagnosis of substance abuse the person must have one of the following problems due to recurrent use of the drug:

1. Failure to fulfill major obligations, for example absences from work or neglect of children.
2. Exposure to physical dangers such as operating machinery or driving while intoxicated.
3. Legal problems such as arrests for disorderly conduct or traffic violations.
4. Persistent social or interpersonal problems such as arguments with spouse.

The DSM-IV section on substance use disorders considers only the *behavior* associated with the regular use of substances that interfere with everyday life. If a person who is addicted to a drug is denied it and therefore experiences withdrawal, that person would be diagnosed as having a substance dependence and, in addition, would receive a diagnosis of substance withdrawal. An example is alcohol withdrawal delirium, commonly known as the DTs (see page 292). We must also remember that drugs can cause dementia and the symptoms of other Axis I disorders.

With this background, we turn now to an overview of the major substance-related disorders, including alcoholism, nicotine and cigarette smoking, marijuana, sedatives and stimulants, and the hallucinogens. We will then look at etiological factors suspected in substance abuse and dependence and conclude with an examination of the therapies available for alcoholism, drug abuse, and cigarette smoking.

Alcoholism

Written reports of the use of wine, beer, and other alcoholic beverages date back to 3000 B.C., but not until about 800 B.C. was the distillation process applied to fermented beverages, making possible the preparation of the highly potent liquors that are available today. Alcohol consumption has risen in the United States and in most other countries (Hasin et al., 1990). In 1940, for example, 30 percent of the U.S. population were drinkers and 2 percent problem drinkers. By 1970, 68 percent of the population drank and 9 percent were problem drinkers (Caddy, 1983). As of 1985, 86 percent of the U.S. population reported having consumed alcohol, and about 12 percent reported using it twenty or more days each month (NIDA, 1988). Alcohol use is especially frequent among college-aged adults, and concern about this use has led some colleges to establish alcohol-free residences or even to ban the drug from campus.

Polysubstance abuse involves the use of multiple drugs. Alcohol and nicotine are a frequent combination, although most people who smoke and drink in social situations do not become substance abusers.

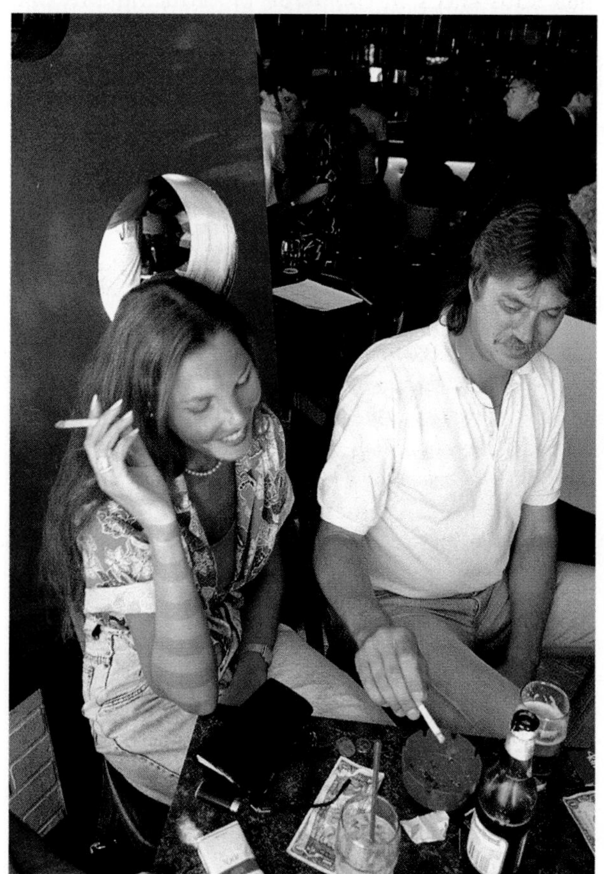

In the large U.S. epidemiological study described on page 115, lifetime prevalence rates for alcoholism defined by DSM-III criteria were over 20 percent for men and just under 5 percent for women (Robins et al., 1984). Robins et al. (1988) reported only small differences in drinking patterns among different ethnic groups (whites, African-Americans, and Hispanics). They also reported comorbidity of alcohol abuse with antisocial personality disorder, mania, other drug use, schizophrenia, and panic disorder. Fortunately, it appears that the use of alcohol has begun to decline in recent years.

Although most people who have a drinking problem do not seek professional help, alcoholics do constitute a large proportion of new admissions to mental and general hospitals. The suicide rate of alcoholics, especially of female alcoholics, is much higher than that of the general population. Alcohol is a contributing cause in one-third of all suicides. Moreover, some estimate that alcohol is implicated in at least 25,000 highway deaths each year, about half the total number. Alcohol may be a factor as well in airplane crashes, industrial accidents, and mishaps in the home. Alcohol also presents law-enforcement problems; about one-third of all arrests in the United States are for public drunkenness. Homicide is an alcohol-related crime—it is believed that over half of all murders are committed under its influence—and so, too, are parental child abuse, spouse abuse, and sexual offenses (Brecher, 1972; National Institute on Alcohol Abuse and Alcoholism, 1983).

The overall cost of problem drinking in the United States—from absenteeism to damaged health—was estimated in 1983 at more than 116 billion dollars (National Council on Alcoholism, 1986). Up to 40 percent of patients in general hospitals are thought to be under treatment for alcohol-related disorders. Alcoholics use health services four times more than do nonalcoholics, and their medical expenses are twice as high as those of nondrinkers (*The Harvard Medical School Mental Health Letter,* 1987). The human costs, in terms of broken lives and losses to society, are incalculable (Jaffe, 1985).

Alcohol is implicated in vehicular accidents. The driver of this New York subway train, which derailed, killing 5 and injuring over 100, was intoxicated.

As in the more general diagnoses of substance abuse and dependence, DSM-IV distinguishes between *alcohol dependence* and *alcohol abuse.* Important components of alcohol dependence include tolerance or withdrawal reactions, such as morning shakes and malaise, which can be relieved only by taking a drink. Persons who begin drinking early in life develop the first withdrawal symptoms in their thirties or forties. The pattern of drinking indicates that it is out of control. Individuals need to drink daily and are unable to stop or cut down despite repeated efforts to abstain completely or to restrict drinking to certain periods of the day. They may go on occasional binges, remaining intoxicated for two, three, or more days. Sometimes they consume a fifth of alcohol at a time. They may suffer blackouts for the events that took place during a bout of intoxication; their craving may be so overpowering that they are forced to ingest alcohol in a nonbeverage form such as hair tonic. Such drinking, of course, causes social and occupational difficulties, quarrels with family or friends, sometimes violence when intoxicated, frequent absences from work or loss of job, and arrest for intoxication or traffic accidents. Polysubstance abuse often involves alcohol, and DSM-IV indicates that nicotine dependence is especially common in association with heavy drinking, as any visit to a cocktail lounge will confirm (though we do not mean to imply that all those in cocktail lounges are alcoholics).

Short-term Effects of Alcohol

After being swallowed, alcohol does not undergo any of the process of digestion. A small part of the alcohol ingested passes immediately into the bloodstream through the stomach walls, but most of it goes into the small intestines and from there is absorbed into the blood. It is then broken down, primarily in the liver, which can metabolize about one ounce of 100 proof (that is, 50 percent alcohol) whiskey per hour. Quantities in excess of this amount remain in the bloodstream. Whereas absorption of alcohol can be very rapid, removal is always slow.

Many of the effects of alcohol vary directly with the level of concentration of the drug in the bloodstream, which in turn depends on the amount ingested in a particular period of time, the presence or absence of food in the stomach to retain the alcohol and reduce its absorption rate, the size of the individual's body, and the efficiency of the liver.

Because drinking alcoholic beverages is accepted in most societies, alcohol is rarely regarded as a drug, especially by those who drink. But it is indeed a drug and acts as a depressant on the central nervous system. The initial effect of alcohol is stimulating. Tensions and inhibitions are reduced, and the drinker may experience an expansive feeling of sociability and well-being. Some people, though, become suspicious and even violent. Larger amounts of alcohol interfere with complex thought processes; motor coordination, balance, speech, and vision are impaired. At this stage of intoxication, some individuals become depressed and withdrawn. Alcohol is capable of blunting pain and, in larger doses, of inducing sedation and sleep. Before modern techniques of anesthesia were discovered, liquor was often administered to patients about to undergo surgery.

There are many beliefs about the effects of alcohol: it is thought to reduce anxiety, increase sociability, relax inhibitions, and the like. But it appears that some of the short-term effects of ingesting small amounts of alcohol are as strongly related to the drinker's expectations about the effects of the drug as they are to its chemical action on the body. For example, alcohol is commonly thought to stimulate aggression and increase sexual responsiveness. Research has shown, however, that these reactions may not be caused by alcohol itself but by the drinker's beliefs about alcohol's effects. In experiments demonstrating these points, subjects are told that they are consuming a quantity of alcohol but, in fact, are given an alcohol-free beverage with its taste disguised. They subsequently become more aggressive (Lang et al., 1975) and report increased sexual arousal (Wilson & Lawson, 1976). Subjects who actually drink alcohol also report increased sexual arousal, even though alcohol makes them less aroused physiologically (Farkas & Wilson, 1976). Once again, cognitions have a demonstrably powerful effect on behavior.

Long-term Effects of Prolonged Alcohol Abuse

The possible long-term effects of prolonged drinking are vividly illustrated in the following case history.

At the time of his first admission to a state hospital at the age of twenty-four, the patient, an unmarried and unemployed laborer, already had a long history of antisocial behavior, promiscuity and addiction to alcohol and other drugs. . . . There had been eight brief admissions to private sanatoria for alcoholics, a number of arrests for public intoxication and drunken driving, and two jail terms for assault.

The patient had been born into a wealthy and respected family in a small town. The patient's father, a successful and popular businessman, drank excessively and his death at the age of fifty-seven was partly due to alcoholism. The mother also drank to excess. The parents exercised little control over the patient as a child, and he was cared for by nursemaids. His father taught him to pour drinks for guests of the family when he was very young and he reported that he began to drain the glasses at parties in his home before he was six; by the time he was twelve he drank almost a pint of liquor every weekend and by seventeen was drinking up to three bottles every day. His father provided him with money to buy liquor and shielded him from punishment for drunken driving and other consequences of his drinking.

The patient was expelled from high school his freshman year for striking a teacher. He then attended a private school until the eleventh grade, when he changed the date on his birth certificate and joined the Army paratroops. After discharge, he was unemployed for six months; he drank heavily and needed repeated care at a sanatorium. When a job was obtained for him he quit within a month. On his third arrest for drunken driving he was jailed. His father bailed him out with the warning that no more money would be forthcoming. The patient left town and worked as an unskilled laborer—he had never acquired any useful skills—but returned home when his father died. During the next few years he was jailed for intoxication, for blackening his mother's eyes when he found a male friend visiting her, and for violating probation by getting drunk. He assaulted and badly hurt a prison guard in an escape attempt and was sentenced to two additional years in prison. When released, he began to use a variety of stimulant, sedative and narcotic drugs as well as alcohol. (Rosen, Fox & Gregory, 1972, p. 312)

Course of the Disorder

For some time the life histories of male alcoholics were thought to have a common progression. On the basis of an extensive survey of 2000 such men, Jellinek (1952) described the male alcoholic as passing through four stages on the way to addiction. In the *prealcoholic* phase the individual drinks socially and on occasion drinks rather heavily to relieve tension and forget about his problems. In the second, *prodromal*, stage drinking may become furtive and may also be marked by blackouts. The drinker remains conscious, talks coherently, and carries on other activities without appearing to be greatly intoxicated, but later has no recall of the occasion. Alcohol begins to be used more as a drug and less as a beverage.

Jellinek terms the third phase *crucial*, choosing this adjective because he sees the alcoholic in this stage as in severe danger of losing everything that he values. He has already lost control of his drinking. Once he takes a single drink, he continues to consume alcohol until he is too sick or in too much of a stupor to drink anymore. The individual's social adjustment also begins to deteriorate. He starts to drink during the day, and his drinking becomes evident to employers, family, and friends. The alcoholic neglects his diet, has his first bender—a several-day period of excessive drinking—and may experience hallucinations and delirium when he stops drinking. At this stage the individual still has the ability to abstain. He can give up alcohol for several weeks or even months at a time, but if he has just one drink the whole pattern begins again.

The skid row alcoholic provides a good example of Jellinek's chronic stage of alcoholism.

In the final, *chronic*, stage drinking is continual and benders are frequent. The individual lives only to drink. His bodily systems have become so accustomed to alcohol that its absence triggers withdrawal reactions. If liquor is not available, he consumes any liquid he can find that contains alcohol—shaving lotion, hair tonic, various medicinal preparations, whatever. He suffers from malnutrition and other physiological changes. He neglects his personal appearance and, having lost his self-esteem, feels little remorse about any aspect of his behavior. Finally, he ceases to care at all about family and home, about friends, occupation, and social status.

Jellinek's description has been widely cited, but the available evidence is not always corroborative. One study found that blackouts do *not* occur in conjunction with modest drinking and that many alcoholics have never experienced a blackout (Goodwin, Crane, & Guze, 1969). Other data question the commonly accepted notion that a single drink stimulates an irresistible impulse to continue drinking (Marlatt, Demming, & Reid, 1973). Alcoholics primed with an initial drink, one they believed to be nonalcoholic, later consumed no more alcohol than did social drinkers. Finally, there is much less consistency in the progression from problem drinking to alcoholism than Jellinek implied. Progression also seems to vary depending on the comorbidity of alcoholism with other disorders and on the age at which the individual begins drinking. If antisocial personality disorder or depression is present, remission is less likely. Comorbidity with other disorders is more frequent if alcoholism begins at an early age (Roy et al., 1991). In a four-year follow-up of problem drinkers, Clark and Cahalan (1976) also found much variability in outcome. Contrary to the widespread belief that a person who is once an abuser of alcohol is always an abuser, data show considerable fluctuations in many drinkers, from heavy drinking for periods of time to abstinence or lighter drinking at others. Furthermore, patterns of maladaptive use of alcohol are more variable than Jellinek implied. For example, heavy use of the drug may be restricted to weekends or long periods of abstinence may be interspersed with binges of continual drinking for several weeks (Robins et al., 1988).

A growing body of evidence also indicates that Jellinek's account does not apply to female alcoholics. Alcoholism usually begins at a later age in women than in men and very often after an inordinately stressful experience, such as the death of a husband or a serious family crisis. For women the time interval between the onset of problem drinking and alcoholism is briefer. Alcoholic women tend more than men to be steady drinkers and to drink alone; they are also less likely to engage in binge drinking (Hill, 1980; Wolin, 1980).

Biological Effects

In addition to psychological deterioration, severe biological damage is a serious consequence of chronic drinking. Almost every tissue and organ of the body is affected by prolonged consumption of alcohol. The malnutrition suffered may be severe. Because alcohol provides calories—a pint of 80 proof spirits supplies about half a day's caloric requirements—alcoholics often reduce their intake of food. But the calories provided by alcohol are empty; they do not supply the nutrients essential for health. Alcohol also contributes directly to malnutrition by impairing the digestion of food and absorbtion of vitamins. In older chronic alcoholics, a deficiency of B-complex vitamins can cause *amnestic syndrome,* a severe loss of memory for both recent and long-past events. These memory gaps are often filled in by reporting imaginary events (confabulation) that are highly improbable.

A drastic reduction in the intake of protein contributes to the development of cirrhosis of the liver, a disease in which some liver cells become engorged with fat and protein, impeding their function, and some cells die, triggering an inflammatory process. When scar tissue develops, blood flow is obstructed. Cirrhosis ranks ninth among causes of death in the United States (USDHHS, 1990), and for many years deaths from alcohol-related cirrhosis have remained constant at approximately five per 100,000 of the population (Malin et al., 1982). The disease is more common in female alcoholics than in male. Alcohol per se also disturbs liver functions and damages liver cells. Other common physiological changes include damage to the endocrine glands and pancreas, heart failure, hypertension, and capillary hemorrhages, which are responsible for the swelling and redness in the face, and especially of the nose, of chronic alcoholics. Prolonged use of alcohol appears to damage brain cells, especially those in the frontal lobes, causing cortical atrophy and other changes in structure (Parsons, 1975). Alcohol also reduces the effectiveness of the immune system, resulting in increased susceptibility to infection.

Heavy alcohol consumption during pregnancy can retard the growth of the fetus and infant and can cause cranial, facial, and limb anomalies as well as mental retardation, a condition known as **fetal alcohol syndrome**. Even moderate drinking can produce less severe but undesirable effects on the fetus, leading the National Institute on Alcohol Abuse and Alcoholism to counsel total abstention during pregnancy as the safest course (*Alcohol, Drug Abuse and Mental Health Administration News,* May 2, 1980). Indeed, in 1989 a law was enacted requiring the inclusion of warnings about birth defects on packaging for all alcoholic beverages (NIAA, 1990).

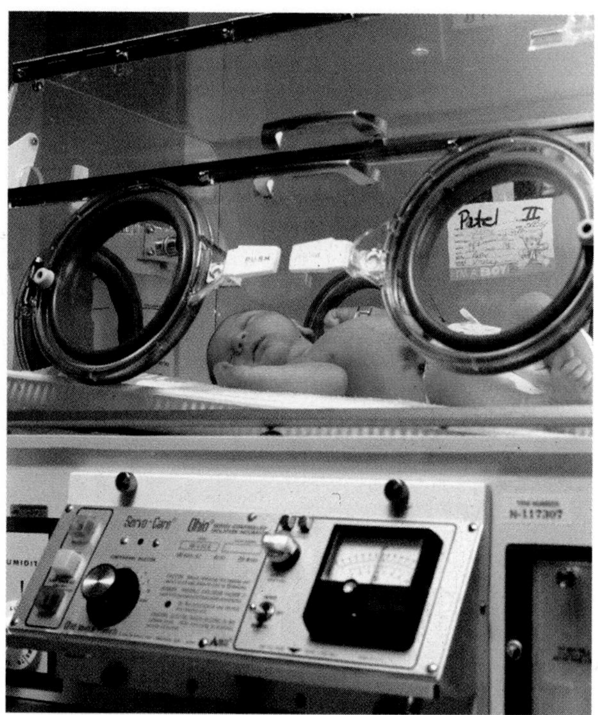

Heavy drinking during pregnancy can lead to premature birth as well as physical and mental abnormalities in the fetus. This condition is called fetal alcohol syndrome.

Although it is appropriate and accurate to concentrate on the deleterious effects of alcohol, tantalizing evidence suggests positive health benefits for some people: light drinking, especially of wine, is related to decreased risk for coronary heart disease in both men and women (Stampfer et al., 1988). This may be a direct physiological effect, or it may be associated with a less driven life-style and decreased levels of hostility (page 210). This situation is implicated in the so-called French paradox—the fact that, despite diets rich in saturated fats, the French may be offsetting their cholesterol levels by consuming low to moderate amounts of red wine. (Of course, the French life-style includes eating more fresh foods and getting more daily exercise, for example, walking instead of driving to work, than does the American life-style). Nevertheless,

An etching displaying the vivid portrayal of a delirium tremens scene in a play.

promoting alcohol in the American diet may set the stage for a dangerous flirtation with potential alcohol abuse.

The effects of the abrupt withdrawal of alcohol from an alcoholic may be rather dramatic, because the body has become accustomed to the drug. Subjectively, the patient is often anxious, depressed, weak, restless, and unable to sleep. Tremors of the muscles, especially of the small musculatures of the fingers, face, eyelids, lips, and tongue, may be marked, and there is an elevation of pulse, blood pressure, and temperature. In relatively rare cases an alcoholic who has been drinking for a number of years may also suffer from **delirium tremens** (DTs) when the level of alcohol in the blood drops suddenly. The person becomes delirious as well as tremulous and suffers from hallucinations that are primarily visual, but may be tactile as well. Unpleasant and very active creatures—snakes, cockroaches, spiders, and the like—may appear to be crawling up the wall or all over the alcoholic's body, or they may fill the room. Feverish, disoriented, and terrified, the alcoholic may claw frantically at his or her skin to get rid of the vermin or may cower in the corner to escape an advancing army of fantastic animals.

The delirium and physiological paroxysms caused by withdrawal of alcohol indicate that the drug is addictive. Increased tolerance is also evident. Mello and Mendelson (1970) found that some alcoholics could drink a quart of bourbon a day without showing signs of drunkenness. Moreover, levels of alcohol in the blood of these people were unexpectedly low after what would usually be viewed as excessive drinking.

Although changes in the liver enzymes that metabolize alcohol can account to some extent for tolerance, most researchers now believe that the central nervous system is implicated. Alcohol can, for example, increase the fluidity of nerve cell membranes and by this process alter electrical conduction in the brain (National Institute on Alcohol Abuse and Alcoholism, 1983). Other processes being studied in relation to the biology of tolerance include levels of serotonin, catecholamine metabolism, and alterations in neurotransmitter receptors (Meyer, 1988). None has good support at this time.

In short, *the psychological, biological, and social consequences of prolonged consumption of alcohol are extremely serious.* Because the alcoholic's own functioning is so severely disrupted, the people with whom he or she interacts are also deeply affected and hurt by this conduct. Society, too, suffers, for the alcoholic is unlikely to be able to hold a job. As mentioned earlier, the accumulated costs—money spent on liquor, time lost in work efficiency, damage of traffic accidents, expense of physicians and psychologists—run to well over 100 billion dollars each year. The human tragedy, much more devastating, is virtually incalculable.

Nicotine and Cigarette Smoking

The history of tobacco smoking bears much similarity to the use of other addictive drugs (Brecher, 1972). Its popularity spread through the world from Columbus's commerce with Native Americans. It did not take long for sailors and merchants to imitate the Native Americans' smoking of rolled leaves of tobacco, and to experience, as they did, the increasing craving for it. When not smoked, tobacco was chewed or ground into small pieces and inhaled as snuff.

Nicotine is the principal alkaloid of tobacco and its addicting agent. Some idea of the addictive qualities of tobacco can be appreciated by considering how much people would sacrifice to maintain their supplies. In sixteenth-century England, for example, tobacco was exchanged for silver ounce for ounce. Poor people squandered their meager resources for their several daily pipefuls. Even the public tortures and executions engineered as punishment by the Sultan Murad IV of Turkey during the seventeenth century could not dissuade those of his subjects who were addicted to the weed.

Prevalence of Smoking

The threat to health posed by smoking has been documented convincingly by the surgeon general of the United States in a series of reports since 1964. Among the medical problems associated with, and almost certainly caused or exacerbated by, long-term cigarette smoking are lung cancer, emphysema, cancer of the larynx and of the esophagus, and a number of cardiovascular diseases. The most probable harmful components in the smoke from burning tobacco are nicotine, carbon monoxide, and tar; the latter consists primarily of certain hydrocarbons, many of which are known carcinogens (Jaffe, 1985).

The twentieth surgeon general's report, published in 1989 (U.S. Department of Health and Human Services, 1989), and a report from the Centers for Disease Control (Cimons, 1992), drew several conclusions from twenty-five years' experience in focused federal government efforts to discourage cigarette smoking:

1. The prevalence of habitual smoking among American adults decreased from a little over 40 percent in 1965 to about 25 percent in 1990, a hefty 25 percent decrease; almost half of all living adults who ever smoked quit. The rate of quitting since 1987 was more than double that between 1965 and 1985.
2. Prevalence remains higher among Native Americans, African-Americans, blue-collar workers, and less-educated individuals than in the general population, though some of the sharpest declines have occurred among African-American men since 1965.
3. Prevalence is lowest among college graduates and people over the age of seventy-five.
4. Prevalence has declined much less among women than among men.
5. People begin to smoke primarily in childhood and adolescence; the age at which smoking begins, especially among young women, is decreasing (see also Focus Box 11.1).
6. Cigarette smoking is responsible in some way for one of every six deaths in the United States, killing about 1000 people each day. It remains the single most preventable cause of premature death. The risks are significantly less for cigar and pipe smokers, because they seldom inhale the smoke into their lungs, but cancers of the mouth and lips are enhanced by such consumption.

Health risks decline dramatically over a period of five to ten years following cessation, to levels only slightly above those of nonsmokers, although the destruction of lung tissue is not reversible (Jaffe, 1985). As with alcohol, the socioeconomic cost is considerable: smokers compile each year over 80 million extra days of lost work and 145 million extra days of disability. Health costs associated with cigarettes in the United States run more than 30 billion dollars annually.

Of concern is that smoking by youths between the ages of twelve and seventeen has only declined to 40 percent, and the use of smokeless tobacco has increased in recent years (Chassin et al., 1985). The attraction of smoking for young people is worrisome, because smoking is extremely difficult to give up once the habit and the addiction have been established. Researchers surmise that the widely publicized health dangers of smoking may be making an impact. Through peer pressure and social support not to smoke, the macho image of the male smoker and the supersophisticated image of the female smoker seem to be losing their appeal. But young people emulate their familial elders as well as their peers. If both parents and an older sibling smoke, a youngster is four times more likely to do so than if none of the other family members smokes.

FOCUS 11.1 • Selling "Loosies" to Minors

In most jurisdictions it is unlawful to sell cigarettes to minors, but such laws are seldom enforced. Even more disturbing to those who believe that prevention of smoking in young people is of paramount importance, there is a lively business in many parts of the country in the sale of single cigarettes, which is also unlawful in some cities and states.

A recent article in the *Los Angeles Times* (Levin & Kaplan, 1992) reported widespread sales of "loosies" to minors for as much as 20 cents each (the equivalent of $4.00 a pack, to be compared with the prevailing price of $2.45 a pack). Most buyers of loosies are from the lower socioeconomic classes, and many are in their early teens. Health officials regard such sales as equivalent to free doses of other addicting drugs that pushers offer to would-be addicts. Laws against sales to minors are seldom enforced because police are more concerned with violent crime and most people in California, including some public officials, are not even aware of the 1991 law against selling single cigarettes. While tobacco critics contend that cigarette manufacturers at least tacitly support the sale of singles, representatives of the industry say that they oppose it, because in the future people who began smoking in this way might claim that they were not exposed to the health warnings required on cigarette packs. Ironically, recent increases in taxes on cigarettes, designed in part to discourage smoking, may actually be fostering the sale of loosies.

Another factor in recruiting young people to cigarettes is the availability and promotion of low-nicotine cigarettes. Adolescent women especially find such cigarettes easier to get used to, and, therefore, they may be more likely to experiment with cigarette smoking because these cigarettes are available (Silverstein, Feld, & Kozlowski, 1980).

Consequences of Smoking

Most people who smoke acknowledge that it is hazardous to their health, and yet they continue to engage in what might be viewed as suicidal behavior. Perhaps one of the most tortured addicts was Sigmund Freud, who continued smoking up to twenty cigars a day in the full knowledge that they were seriously taxing his heart and causing cancerous growths in his mouth. When his jaw was later almost entirely removed and replaced by an awkward artificial one, Freud suffered great difficulty swallowing and endured excruciating pain. But he was still unable to bear the anguish of abstaining from smoking. Although many heavy smokers do succeed in stopping, Freud's tragic case was certainly not the exception.

As we have known for many years (Bennett, 1980), the health hazards are not restricted to those who smoke. The smoke coming from the burning end of a cigarette, so-called secondhand smoke, contains higher concentrations of ammonia, carbon monoxide, nicotine, and tar than does the smoke actually inhaled by the smoker. Nonsmokers can suffer lung damage, possibly permanent, from extended exposure to cigarette smoke. At the very least, many nonsmokers greatly dislike the smell of smoke from burning tobacco, and some have allergic reactions to it. Also, babies of women who smoke during pregnancy are more likely to be born prematurely and to have lower birth weights and birth defects.

In recent years various local governments have passed ordinances regulating cigarette smoking in

Smoking is now banned in many public places, including elevators. Some smokers, however, ignore the ban and regard it as an infringement on their rights.

public places and work settings. Smoking is banned in many supermarkets, buses, hospitals, government buildings, and on all domestic U.S. airline flights. Restaurants must often post signs indicating whether they have an area for nonsmokers, and, especially on the West Coast, some restaurants are banning smoking altogether. Workplaces with more than fifty employees must either ban smoking on the premises or restrict it to designated areas. One of the most talked-about bans is in a well-known indoor sports arena, where not only smoking but also smoking advertisements are forbidden. Many nonsmokers express enthusiastic approval of such measures, but pressure from smokers and from the tobacco industry sometimes defeats efforts to enact laws. Some smokers object virulently to what they view as undue infringement on their rights.

Marijuana

Marijuana consists of the dried and crushed leaves and flowering tops of the hemp plant, *Cannabis sativa*. It is most often smoked, but it may be chewed, prepared as a tea, or eaten in baked goods. **Hashish**, much stronger than marijuana, is produced by removing and drying the resin exudate of the tops of high-quality cannabis plants. Both marijuana and hashish have been known for thousands of years, and their poor reputation among the general public dates back many centuries. For example, the English word *assassin* comes from the Arabic word *hashishāshīn*, referring to those addicted to hashish, which was the name given an order of Muslims who took hashish and murdered Christians at the time of the Crusades. In early U.S. history the plant was extensively cultivated not for smoking but for its fibers, which were used in the manufacture of cloth and rope. By the nineteenth century the medicinal properties of cannabis resin were noted, and it was a recommended treatment for rheumatism, gout, depression, cholera, and neuralgia, as well as being smoked for pleasure. Until 1920 marijuana was little seen in the United States, but with the passage of the Eighteenth Amendment prohibiting the sale of alcohol, members of the lower classes began to smoke marijuana brought across the border from Mexico. Unfavorable reports in the press attributing crimes to marijuana use led to the enactment of a federal law against the sale of the drug in 1937. It is today illegal in most countries, many of which are bound by a United Nations treaty prohibiting its sale (Goodwin & Guze, 1984).[1]

Early recreational use of hashish occurred in a fashionable apartment in New York City. An 1876 issue of the *Illustrated Police News* carried this picture with the title "Secret Dissipation of New York Belles: Interior of a Hasheesh Hell on Fifth Avenue."

Prevalence of Marijuana Use

Periodically the National Institute of Drug Abuse (NIDA), a federal agency charged to investigate drug use in this country, publishes the results of surveys taken of youths, ages twelve to seventeen; young adults, eighteen to twenty-five; and people over twenty-six years old. The participants are questioned about current drug use, past use, frequency of use, range of drugs used, and so forth. In general, trends over the past twenty years suggest that the use of marijuana peaked in 1979 and is now showing a decline. For example, the following percentages of those between the ages of twelve and seventeen reported having used marijuana at least once: 14 percent in 1972, 31 percent in 1979, 24 percent in 1985, and 13 percent in 1991 (*Marijuana Research Findings: 1980; National Survey on Drug Abuse*, 1979; *National Survey on Drug Abuse*, 1982, 1991; Kozel & Adams, 1986). Among adults aged eighteen to twenty-five, the figures were 48 percent in 1972, 53 percent in 1974, 68 percent in 1979, 61 percent in 1985, and 50 percent in 1991.

An interesting relationship is found between use among high school seniors and their perceptions of the harmfulness of marijuana. Use peaked in 1978, when almost 11 percent of seniors reported use daily; at that time only 12 percent of seniors believed there was risk associated with occasional use

[1]As will be seen, the marijuana story is full of ironies. One is that marijuana is a lucrative cash crop in agriculture-rich California.

and 35 percent believed there was risk with regular use. Compare this with 1985, when daily use had plummeted to 5 percent; 25 percent of high school seniors believed marijuana was harmful if used occasionally, and 70 percent believed it was harmful if used on a regular basis (Kozel & Adams, 1986).

Effects of Marijuana

A great deal of research has been conducted on marijuana. Like most other drugs it is apparently not without its risks. Science has generally found that the more we learn about a drug, the less benign it turns out to be. Marijuana is no exception (see Focus Box 11.2).

Psychological Effects of Marijuana

The intoxicating effects of marijuana, as of most drugs, depend in part on potency and size of the dose. Smokers of marijuana find it makes them feel relaxed and sociable. Large doses have been reported to bring rapid shifts in emotion, to dull attention, fragment thoughts, and impair memory. Extremely heavy doses have sometimes been found to induce hallucinations and other effects similar to those of LSD, including extreme panic, sometimes arising from the belief that the frightening experience will never end. Dosage can be difficult to regulate because the behavioral effects can lag behind actual inhalation by more than half an hour; many users have in this way gotten themselves much higher than they had intended. People who have had psychological problems before using any psychoactive drug are generally believed to be at highest risk for negative reactions to it.

The major active chemical in marijuana has been isolated and named delta-9-tetrahydrocannabinol (THC). Since 1974 the marijuana available in the United States has been very potent, as much as ten times stronger than that sold earlier.[2] Thus in the early 1970s the most widely available domestic cannabis contained about 0.4 percent THC; samples studied in 1979, in contrast, averaged more than 4 percent THC, and in the early 1980s, as much as 6 percent. Hash oil, a concentrated liquid marijuana extract, has been found to be as much as 28 percent THC. The picture is complicated, however, by the fact that cannabis contains more than 400 compounds in addition to THC. Many of these compounds are believed to exert psychological effects either by themselves or in conjunction with one another and with THC.

Let us examine the psychological effects of marijuana more closely. An abundance of scientific evidence indicates that marijuana interferes with a wide range of cognitive functions. And since cannabis available in recent years is stronger, actual short-term effects on people's minds are probably greater than they were found to be in the laboratory studies conducted for the most part in the late 1960s. A number of tests—digit-symbol substitution (substituting symbols for numbers), reaction time tests, repeating series of digits forward and backward, arithmetic calculations, reading comprehension and speech tests—all revealed intellectual impairment *(Marijuana Research Findings: 1980).* Of special significance are loss of short-term memory and state-dependent learning—the inability, when sober or straight, to recall material learned when high. Given both the numbers of high school students who use marijuana regularly and the strength of cannabis today, it would seem that significant numbers of students may be seriously hindering their learning.

Several studies have demonstrated that being high on marijuana diminishes complex psychomotor skills necessary for driving. Highway fatality and driver arrest figures indicate that marijuana plays a role in a significant proportion of accidents and arrests. Marijuana has similarly been found to impair manipulation of flight simulators. Some performance decrements measurable after smoking one or two joints containing 2 percent THC can persist for up to eight hours after a person believes he or she is no longer high, creating the very real danger that people will attempt to drive or to fly when they are not functioning adequately.

Does long-term use of marijuana affect intellectual functioning in any consistent way? Studies requiring memory and problem-solving conducted in Egypt and India in the late 1970s indicated some deterioration in users compared with nonusers (Soueif, 1976; Wig & Varma, 1977). It is impossible to know, however, whether these differences existed before heavy drug use and whether they might have been associated with poor diet. American college students do not show these deficits, so it would be premature to conclude that chronic use of the drug brings intellectual deterioration.

Survey findings suggest, however, that heavy use of marijuana during teenage years may well contribute to psychological problems in adulthood. Kandel et al. (1986) interviewed 1004 adults in their mid-twenties who had been part of a 1971 New York public high school survey of drug use. They

[2]The potency of the leaves is thought to vary with the region in which the hemp plant is cultivated. The leaves of plants grown in hot, relatively dry climates contain larger amounts of THC.

FOCUS 11.2 • The Stepping-Stone Theory—From Marijuana to Hard Drugs

A concern that has been prevalent for some time is expressed in the so-called stepping-stone theory of marijuana use. According to this view, marijuana is dangerous not only in itself but as a first step that can lead young people to become addicted to hard drugs like heroin. In the late 1960s, when information on the harmfulness of marijuana was scant, the issue was basically a political and generational one. People in their teens and college years believed that the older generation, lacking scientific data to discourage marijuana use, had concocted the stepping-stone theory, which itself lacked empirical support, to justify harsh legal penalties for the use and sale of marijuana. Since there was little doubt that the hard drugs were very harmful, marijuana was said to be so too, because it was a first step to a career of abusing these drugs.

Studies done in the late 1970s and early 1980s established several specific dangers from using marijuana, as described in the text (Jones, 1983). The scientific question remains whether marijuana is, in fact, a stepping-stone to more serious substance abuse. The question may not be a difficult one to answer. It is clear that most people who have used marijuana do *not* go on to use drugs like heroin and cocaine. So, if by stepping-stone we mean that there is an inevitability of escalating to a more serious drug, the case is definitely not made. However, we do know that many—but far from all—who abuse heroin and cocaine began their drug experimentation with marijuana. Indeed, cigarette smokers are more likely to use marijuana than nonsmokers, and, at least in the United States, users of marijuana are more likely than nonusers to experiment later with heroin and cocaine (Kandel, 1984). Furthermore, the single best predictor of cocaine use in adulthood is heavy use of marijuana during adolesence (Kozel & Adams, 1986; Kandel, Murphy, & Karus, 1985). Perhaps there is a third variable that can link all such drugs, including the legal drug alcohol. There is growing evidence that users of even legal drugs are at higher risk for using illegal drugs. It is likely that the use of an illegal (or legal) substance puts one in the company of like-minded others.

Indeed, it should come as no surprise that the use of legal drugs is sometimes related to the use of illegal drugs, for our laws lack consistency in designating certain drugs as legal and others as illegal—the psychological and medical dangers of alcohol and tobacco use are no less severe than the risks associated with the use of heroin and marijuana. Social supports develop that even encourage the use of drugs to escape from stressors and from the tedium of many people's lives.

Thus, better than a stepping-stone theory might be a network theory, for *network* implies a complex set of relationships, with cause and effect virtually impossible to isolate but in which some degree of association among many variables is acknowledged. Marijuana is part of the picture, but only one of many contributing factors to involvement in harmful substance use.

found indications of deleterious effects of heavy marijuana use, including higher rates of separation or divorce, more delinquency, increased tendencies to consult mental health professionals, and less stable employment patterns among women. The authors caution, however, that the specific effects of a single drug such as marijuana are very difficult to disentangle from the effects of other drugs that marijuana smokers sometimes use, especially alcohol and cocaine.

Somatic Effects of Marijuana

In the short term, marijuana makes the eyes bloodshot and itchy, dries the mouth and throat, increases appetite, and may raise blood pressure somewhat. There is no evidence that smoking marijuana has untoward effects on the normal heart. The drug apparently poses a danger to people with already abnormal heart function, however, for it elevates heart rate, sometimes dramatically. As a NIDA report suggests, this fact may be of particular concern as present smokers grow older. The relatively healthy thirty-year-old marijuana users of today are the fifty-year-olds of tomorrow, with a statistically greater chance of having a cardiovascular system impaired for other reasons, such as atherosclerosis. If they are still using the drug then, their hearts will be more vulnerable to its effects. In addition, it is possible that long-term use of marijuana, like the chronic use of tobacco, may be harmful in ways that cannot be predicted from the short-term effects studied so far (Jones, 1980).

Long-term use of marijuana may seriously impair lung structure and function. Even though marijuana users smoke far fewer cigarettes than do persons using tobacco, most inhale marijuana smoke more deeply and retain it in their lungs for much longer periods of time. Since marijuana has some of the same carcinogens found in tobacco cigarettes, harmful effects may be greater than would be expected were only the absolute number of cigarettes or pipefuls considered. What are these unfavorable pulmonary effects? First, a research team at the University of California at Los Angeles found that the amount of air a person can expel following a deep breath, called vital capacity, is reduced as much from smoking one marijuana cigarette a day as from smoking sixteen conventional cigarettes a day (Tashkin, Clavarese & Simmons, 1978). Second, since marijuana cigarettes are generally homemade, they are not filtered as are most tobacco cigarettes; the smoke contains significantly higher levels of tar, which, like the tar from conventional cigarettes, has been found to cause cancer when applied to the skin of laboratory animals. Moreover, marijuana smoke contains 70 percent more benzopyrene, another known cancer-causing agent, and 50 percent more carcinogenic polyaromatic hydrocarbons than does the smoke from regular cigarettes (Cohen, 1981). The risk of lung cancer from regular, prolonged use of marijuana cannot be overlooked.

Evidence indicates that marijuana may be harmful to reproduction. Two studies of chonic male users found lower sperm counts and less motility of the spermatozoa, suggesting that fertility might be decreased, especially in men who are already marginally fertile (Hembree, Nahas, & Huang, 1979; Issidorides, 1979).

A study with female street users yielded consistent findings, namely, frequent failure to ovulate normally and shortened fertility periods. Moreover, researchers have discovered that marijuana constituents can cross the placental barrier[3] in rats and thus may affect fetal development (Vardaris et al., 1976). Experiments with female rhesus monkeys, using THC levels comparable to fairly heavy marijuana use by human beings, found abnormally frequent loss of the fetus in those who became pregnant (Sassenrath, Chapman & Goo, 1979). All these studies have their share of methodological problems, but the outcomes for animals and human beings do raise the possibility that moderate and heavy use of marijuana interferes with reproduction. People interested in bearing children need to exercise caution and prudence with *any* drug and should avoid the use of all but strictly necessary and medically supervised drugs if they believe that they might be pregnant.

Is marijuana addictive? It indeed may be, contrary to widespread earlier belief that it is not. The development of tolerance began to be suspected when American service personnel returned from Vietnam accustomed to concentrations of THC that would be toxic to domestic users. Controlled observations have confirmed that habitual use of marijuana does produce tolerance (Nowlan & Cohen, 1977; Compton, Dewey, & Martin, 1990). Whether long-term users suffer physical withdrawal when accustomed amounts of marijuana are not available is less clear. When subjects abstain after a period of heavier-than-normal smoking in the laboratory, appetite is lost and other withdrawal symptoms, such as irritability, nausea, and diarrhea develop (Jones, 1977; Jones & Benowitz, 1976; Jones, 1983). Withdrawal was also found in a study in which users selected their own number of joints, smoked in their usual manner, and then stopped (Mendelson, Rossi, & Meyer, 1974). If people do develop a physical dependency on marijuana, it is far less serious than what we know to be the case with nicotine, cocaine, and alcohol.

The question whether marijuana is physically addicting is complicated by reverse tolerance. Experienced smokers need only a few hits or puffs to become high from a marijuana cigarette that a less experienced user puffs many times in order to reach a similar state of intoxication. Reverse tolerance is directly opposite to tolerance for an addicting drug like heroin. The substance THC, after being rapidly metabolized, is stored in the body's fatty tissue and then released very slowly, over as long a period as a month, which may explain people's reverse tolerance for it.

Ours is known to be a drug-taking culture. At any one time many individuals have circulating in their bloodstreams one or more chemicals that have been swallowed, injected, sniffed, or smoked. How drugs *interact* with one another, the combination of marijuana and alcohol in particular, is of concern.

Evidence from studies of both animals and human beings indicates that simultaneous use of al-

[3]The placenta is the porous membrane forming the sac in which a fetus develops. In studying whether a chemical in a pregnant woman's body might affect the fetus, scientists try to determine whether it can penetrate the placenta or whether the placenta filters it out. If the agent can get through this barrier, there is presumptive—suggestive but not definite—evidence that the fetus is affected.

cohol and marijuana more seriously impairs perception, cognition, and motor activity than does use of either drug alone. The synergistic effect also extends to physiological processes; for example, heart rate is faster and eyes become more bloodshot. Marijuana can enhance the effects of other drugs, such as barbiturates and amphetamines. Although this interactive force of THC is complex and inadequately understood, people should be aware of it and govern themselves accordingly (Siemens, 1980).

Therapeutic Effects of Marijuana

In a seeming irony, therapeutic uses of marijuana came to light during the same period that negative effects of regular and heavy usage of the drug were indicated. In the 1970s a number of double-blind studies (e.g., Salan, Zinberg, & Frei, 1975) showed that THC and related drugs can reduce for some cancer patients the nausea and loss of appetite that accompany chemotherapy. Marijuana often appears to reduce nausea when other antinausea agents fail, and THC is available for oral administration in hundreds of hospitals today under special arrangement with the U.S. government (Jaffe, 1985; Poster et al., 1981).[4] It is also a treatment for the discomfort of AIDS and for glaucoma, a disease in which outflow of fluid from the eyeball is obstructed. A 1971 study by Hepler and Frank shows that smoking marijuana reduces intraocular pressure in normal subjects. Later studies showed that oral ingestion of delta-9-THC, especially when combined with conventional treatment of the eye disease, reduces intraocular pressure in glaucoma sufferers (Hepler, Frank & Petrus, 1976).

However controversy exists over the therapeutic use of marijuana. Klein (1992) describes an AIDS sufferer in California who derives relief from smoking the drug—it stimulates his appetite, helps him relax, eases his nausea, and helps him sleep. Instead of wasting away, his weight is still normal, despite a very low T-cell count. He had been accepted into a federal program that supplied marijuana to about two dozen terminal patients, but in March 1992 the program was canceled and new applications were denied. The reason: marijuana is bad for one's health. THC is still available in pill form but many sick patients cannot take it without vomiting. These pills also do not seem to be as helpful to AIDS patients and to others who benefited from smoking the drug, for example, paralyzed people, people with glaucoma, and people with multiple sclerosis. Those not in the terminal stages of AIDS are often in severe pain, suffer muscle spasms, or are going blind. Smoking marijuana helps them. Court and federal agencies have been inconsistent. In the meantime, many such patients violate the law by smoking the drug.

[4]Phenothiazines, used in the treatment of schizophrenia, havebeen used with some success to reduce the subjective effects of marijuana that can be troubling to patients undergoing chemotherapy. Also used is Nabilone, a synthetic compound that produces fewer of marijuana's psychological effects (Weintraub & Standish, 1983).

Sedatives and Stimulants

Addiction to drugs was disapproved of but tolerated in the United States until 1914, when the Harrison Narcotics Act made the unauthorized use of various drugs illegal and those addicted to them criminals. The drugs we will discuss, not all of which are illegal, may be divided into two general categories: Sedatives and stimulants.

Sedatives

The major **sedatives**, called downers, slow the activities of the body and reduce its responsiveness. In this group of drugs are the organic narcotics—opium and its derivatives morphine, heroin, and codeine—and the synthetic barbiturates, such as seconal.

Narcotics

Narcotics represent a group of addictive sedatives that in moderate doses relieve pain and induce sleep. Foremost of the narcotics is **opium,** originally the principal drug of illegal international traffic and known to the people of the Sumerian civilization dating as far back as 7000 B.C. They gave the poppy that supplied this narcotic the name by which it is still known, meaning "the plant of joy." Opium is a mixture of about eighteen alkaloids, but until 1806 people had no knowledge of these substances to which so many natural drugs owe their potency.

In that year the alkaloid **morphine**, named after Morpheus, the Greek god of dreams, was separated out from raw opium. This bitter-tasting powder proved to be a powerful sedative and pain reliever. Before its addictive properties were noted, it was

Opium is typically smoked in special pipes. These harem women appear in a photograph taken around 1870.

commonly used in patent medicines. In the middle of the nineteenth century, when the hypodermic needle was introduced in the United States, morphine began to be injected directly into the veins to relieve pain. Many soldiers wounded in battle and those suffering from dysentery during the Civil War were treated with morphine and returned home addicted to the drug.

Concerned about administering a drug that could disturb the later lives of patients, scientists began studying morphine. In 1874 they found that morphine could be converted into another powerful pain-relieving drug, which they named **heroin**. It was used initially as a cure for morphine addiction and was substituted for morphine in cough syrups and other patent medicines. So many maladies were treated with heroin that it came to be known as G.O.M., or "God's own medicine" (Brecher, 1972). Heroin however, proved to be even more addictive and more potent than morphine, acting more quickly and with greater intensity. In 1909, President Theodore Roosevelt called for an international investigation of opium and the opiates.

Heroin was synthesized from opium in 1874 and soon was being added to a variety of medicines that could be purchased without prescription. The ad shown here is for a teething remedy containing heroin. It probably worked.

Opium and its derivatives morphine and heroin produce euphoria, drowsiness, reverie, and sometimes a lack of coordination. Heroin has an additional initial effect, the rush, a feeling of warm, suffusing ecstasy immediately following an intravenous injection. The addict sheds worries and fears and has great self-confidence for four to six hours, but then experiences letdown, bordering on stupor. Because these drugs are central nervous system depressants, they relieve pain. All three are clearly addicting in the physiological sense, for users show both increased tolerance of the drugs and withdrawal symptoms when they are unable to obtain another dose.

Reactions to not having a dose of heroin may begin within eight hours of the last injection, at least after high tolerance has built up. During the next few hours the individual typically has muscle pain, sneezes, sweats, becomes tearful, and yawns a great deal; the symptoms resemble influenza. Within thirty-six hours the withdrawal symptoms become more severe. There may be uncontrollable muscle twitching, cramps, chills alternating with excessive flushing and sweating, and a rise in heart rate and blood pressure. The addict is unable to sleep, vomits, and has diarrhea. These symptoms typically persist for about seventy-two hours and then diminish gradually over a five- to ten-day period.

In spite of enormous difficulties in gathering data, the considered opinion is that there are more than a million heroin addicts in the United States. Most of these began using heroin in the 1960s and have continued to use it (Kozel & Adams, 1985). Among young adults aged eighteen to twenty-five, the frequency of heroin addiction has declined steadily from 4.6 percent in 1972 to 1.2 percent in 1982 and 0.6 percent in 1990 (*HHS News,* 1990). However, heroin use is increasing in the upper socioeconomic classes. For many years dependence has been many times higher among physicians and nurses than in any other group with a comparable educational background. This problem is believed to arise from a combination of the relative availability of opiates in medical settings and the stresses under which people often work in such environments (Jaffe, 1985).

Even more serious than the physical effects are the social consequences of narcotic addiction. The drug and obtaining it become the center of the abuser's existence, governing all activities and social relationships. Since narcotics are illegal, addicts must deal with the underworld to maintain their habits. The high cost of the drugs—addicts must often spend upwards of 200 dollars per day for their narcotics—means that they must either have great wealth or acquire money through illegal activities, such as prostitution or selling drugs themselves. Thus, the correlation between addiction and criminal activities is rather high, undoubtedly contributing to the popular notion that drug addiction per se causes crime. In recent years, a problem associated with intravenous drug use is exposure, due to the sharing of needles, to the human immunodeficiency virus (HIV) and AIDS (see page 383).

Barbiturates and Other Sedatives

Barbiturates were synthesized as aids for sleeping and relaxation. The first was produced in 1903, and since then hundreds of derivatives of barbituric acid have been made. When properly prescribed and used, barbiturates can be safe and effective. Two types are usually distinguished—long-acting barbiturates for prolonged sedation, and short-acting barbiturates for prompt sedation and sleep. The short-acting drugs are usually viewed as addicting. Initially, the drugs were considered highly desirable and were prescribed very frequently. In the 1940s, however, a campaign was mounted against them because they were discovered to be addicting, and physicians prescribed barbiturates less frequently. Today in the United States they are manufactured in vast quantities, enough, it is estimated, to supply each man, woman, and child with fifty pills per year. Many are shipped legally to Mexico and then brought back into the country and trafficked illegally. The majority of polysubstance abusers choose a barbiturate or other sedative as one of their drugs.

Barbiturates (pentobarbital, secobarbital, and amobarbital) relax the muscles and in small doses produce a mildly euphoric state.[5] With excessive doses, however, speech becomes slurred and gait unsteady. Impairment of judgment, concentration, and ability to work may be extreme. The user loses emotional control and may become irritable and combative before falling into a deep sleep. Very large doses can be fatal because the diaphragm muscles relax to such an extent that the individual suffocates. As we indicated in Chapter 9, barbiturates are frequently chosen as a means of suicide. But many users accidently kill themselves by drinking alcohol, which potentiates, or magnifies the depressant effects of barbiturates. With prolonged excessive use the brain can become damaged and personality deteriorates.

Increased tolerance follows prolonged use of the barbiturates, and the withdrawal reactions after abrupt termination are particularly severe and long lasting and can even cause sudden death. The delirium, convulsions, and other symptoms resemble those following abrupt withdrawal of alcohol.

Three types of abusers can be distinguished. The first group fits the stereotype of the illicit drug abuser: adolescents and young adults, usually male and often antisocial, who use the drugs to alter their moods and consciousness, sometimes mixing them with other drugs. The second group consists of middle-aged, middle-class individuals who begin their use of sedatives under a physician's orders, to alleviate sleeplessness and anxiety, and then come to use larger and larger doses until they are addicted. These people rely less on street purchases because they are generally able to obtain refills of their drug prescriptions whenever they wish, sometimes changing physicians so as not to raise suspicion. The third group comprises health professionals, physicians and nurses who have easy access to these drugs and often use them to self-medicate for anxiety-related problems (Shader, Caine, & Meyer, 1975; Liskow, 1982).

Stimulants

The second group, the **stimulants** or uppers, such as cocaine, act on the brain and the sympathetic nervous system to increase alertness and motor activity. The amphetamines, such as benzedrine, are synthetic stimulants; cocaine is a natural stimulant extracted from the coca leaf.

Amphetamines

In seeking a treatment for asthma, the Chinese-American pharmacologist Chen studied ancient Chinese descriptions of drugs. He found a desert shrub called mahuang commended again and again as an effective remedy. After systematic effort Chen was able to isolate an alkaloid from this plant be-

[5]Methaqualone, a sedative sold under the trade names Quaalude and Sopor, is similar in effect to barbiturates and has become a popular street drug. Besides being addictive, it has other dangers—internal bleeding, coma, and even death from overdose.

longing to the genus *Ephedra*, and ephedrine did indeed prove highly successful in treating asthma. But relying on the shrub for the drug was not viewed as efficient, and so a search began for a synthetic substitute. **Amphetamines** were the result of this search (Snyder, 1974).

The first amphetamine, Benzedrine, was synthesized in 1927. Almost as soon as it became commercially available in the early 1930s as an inhalant to relieve stuffy noses, the public discovered its stimulating effects. Physicians thereafter prescribed it and the other amphetamines soon synthesized to control mild depression and appetite. During World War II soldiers on both sides were supplied with the drugs to ward off fatigue; today amphetamines are sometimes used to treat hyperactive children (see page 432).

Amphetamines, such as Benzedrine, Dexedrine, and Methedrine, produce effects similar to those of norepinephrine in the sympathetic nervous system. They are taken orally or intravenously and can be addicting. Wakefulness is heightened, intestinal functions are inhibited, and appetite is reduced—hence their use in dieting. The heart rate quickens and blood vessels in the skin and mucous membranes constrict. The individual becomes alert, euphoric, and more outgoing and is possessed with seemingly boundless energy and self-confidence. Larger doses can make a person nervous, agitated, and confused, subjecting him or her to palpitations, headaches, dizziness, and sleeplessness. Sometimes the high-level user becomes so suspicious and hostile that he or she can be dangerous to others. Large doses taken over a period of time induce a state quite similar to paranoid schizophrenia, including its delusions. This state can persist beyond the time that the drug is present in the body. Frequent ingestion of large amounts of amphetamines is also believed to cause brain damage.

Tolerance develops rapidly so that mouthfuls of pills are required to produce the stimulating effect. As tolerance increases, the user may stop taking pills and inject Methedrine, the strongest of the amphetamines, directly into the veins. The so-called speed freaks give themselves repeated injections of the drug and maintain intense and euphoric activity for a few days, without eating or sleeping (a run), after which they are exhausted and depressed and sleep, or crash, for several days. Then the cycle starts again. After several repetitions of this pattern, the physical and social functioning of the individual deteriorate considerably. Behavior is erratic and hostile, and the speed freak may become a danger to self and to others. Fortunately, the use of stimulants has been declining regularly over the past several years (NIDA, 1991), although the abuse of a smokable form of methamphetamine (ice) has increased, particularly in Hawaii (Focus Box 11.3 discusses a more prevalent and less risky stimulant—caffeine).

Cocaine

The Spanish conquistadors introduced coca leaves to Europe. The Indians of the Andean uplands, to which the coca shrubs are native, chew the leaves, but the Europeans chose to brew them instead in beverages. The alkaloid **cocaine** was extracted from the leaves of the coca plant in 1844 and has been used since then as a local anesthetic. In 1884, while still a young neurologist, Sigmund Freud began using cocaine to combat his depression. Convinced of its wondrous effects, he prescribed it to a friend with a painful disease and published one of the first papers on the drug, "Song of Praise," which was an enthusiastic endorsement of the exhilarating effects he had experienced. Freud subsequently lost his enthusiasm for cocaine after nursing a physician friend to whom he had recommended the drug through a night-long psychotic state brought on by it. Perhaps the most famous fictional cocaine addict is Sherlock Holmes.

One of the early products using coca leaves in its manufacture was Coca-Cola, concocted by an Atlanta druggist in 1886. For the next twenty years Coke was the real thing, but in 1906 the Pure Food and Drugs Act was passed and the manufacturer switched to coca leaves from which the cocaine had been removed.

In addition to its pain-reducing effects, cocaine acts rapidly on the cortex of the brain, heightening sensory awareness and inducing a thirty-minute state of euphoria. Sexual desire is accentuated, and feelings of self-confidence, well-being, and indefatigability suffuse the user's consciousness. An overdose may bring on chills, nausea, and insomnia, as well as a paranoid breakdown and terrifying hallucinations of insects crawling beneath the skin. Chronic use often leads to changes in personality that include heightened irritability, impaired social relationships, paranoid thinking, and disturbances in eating and sleeping (*Scientific Perspectives on Cocaine Abuse*, 1987). As users take larger and larger doses of the purer forms of cocaine now available, they are more often rushed to emergency rooms and may die of an overdose, often from a myocardial infarction (heart attack) (Kozel, Crider, & Adams, 1982). Because of its strong vasoconstricting properties, cocaine may pose special dangers in pregnancy, for the blood supply to the developing fetus may be compromised.

FOCUS 11.3 • Our Tastiest Addiction—Caffeine

What may be the world's most popular drug is seldom viewed as a drug at all, and yet it has strong effects, produces tolerance in people, and even subjects habitual users to withdrawal (Hughes et al., 1991). Users and nonusers alike joke about it, and most readers of this book have probably had some this very day. We are, of course, referring to caffeine, a substance found in coffee, tea, cocoa, cola and other soft drinks, in some cold remedies, and in some diet pills.

Two cups of coffee, containing between 150 and 300 milligrams of caffeine, affect most people within half an hour. Metabolism, body temperature, and blood pressure all increase; urine production goes up, as most of us will attest; there may be hand tremors, appetite can diminish, and, most familiar of all, sleepiness is warded off. Panic disorder can be exacerbated by caffeine, not surprising in light of the heightened sympathetic nervous system arousal occasioned by the drug. Extremely large doses of caffeine can cause headache, diarrhea, nervousness, severe agitation, even convulsions and death. Such deaths, though, are virtually impossible unless the individual grossly overuses tablets containing caffeine, for the drug is excreted by the kidneys without any appreciable accumulation.

Although it has long been recognized that drinkers of very large amounts of caffeinated coffee daily can experience withdrawal symptoms when consumption ceases, a recently published study indicates that people who drink no more than two cups of regular coffee a day can suffer from clinically significant headaches, fatigue, and anxiety if caffeine is withdrawn from their daily diet (Silverman et al., 1992), and these symptoms can markedly interfere with social and occupational functioning. These findings are disturbing because over three-quarters of Americans consume a little more than two cups of caffeinated coffee a day (Roan, 1992). Although parents usually deny their children access to coffee and tea, often they do allow them to imbibe caffeine-laden cola drinks, hot chocolate, and cocoa, and to eat chocolate candy and coffee and chocolate ice cream. Thus our addiction to caffeine can begin to develop as early as six months of age, the form of it changing as we move from childhood to adulthood.

Cocaine can be sniffed (snorted), smoked in pipes or cigarettes, swallowed, or even injected into the veins like heroin; some heroin addicts in fact mix the two drugs in a combination known as speedball, which is taken orally. In the 1970s cocaine devotees in this country adopted a practice similar to that used in parts of South America for enhancing the effects of the drug. To separate, or free, the most potent component of cocaine, they heat cocaine with ether. When purified by this chemical process, the cocaine base—or freebase—is extremely powerful. Called white tornado, baseball, or snow toke, it is usually smoked in a water pipe or sprinkled on a normal or marijuana cigarette. It is rapidly absorbed into the lungs and carried to the brain in a few seconds and induces an intense two-minute high, followed by restlessness and discomfort. Some freebase smokers go on marathon binges lasting up to four days (Goodwin & Guze, 1984). The freebasing process is hazardous, however, because ether is flammable. Comedian Richard Pryor nearly died from the burns he suffered when the ether he was using ignited.

In the mid-1980s a new form of freebase, called crack, appeared on the streets. The presence of crack has brought about an increase in freebasing and in casualties. Because it is available in small, relatively inexpensive doses (ten dollars for about 100 milligrams versus the 100 dollars per gram that users formerly had to shell out to obtain cocaine), younger and less-affluent buyers have begun to experiment with the drug and to become addicted (Kozel & Adams, 1986). Many public health and police officials regard crack as the most dangerous and perhaps most addicting illicit drug that society has to cope with today.

Cocaine use soared in the 1970s and 1980s. The dramatic increase in use is evident in the following statistics. In 1974 it was estimated that 5.4 million Americans had tried cocaine at least once; in 1982 this figure had risen to 21.6 million. Users of the drug numbered 1.6 million in 1974; in 1982 they numbered 4.2 million (National Institute on Drug Abuse, 1983); and in 1985, 5.8 million (Kozel & Adams, 1986). Thus, use increased over 260 percent in 11 years! Since those alarming data were obtained, use of cocaine has dramatically decreased. The number of users declined to 2.9 million in 1988 and 1.6 million in 1990 (*HHS News*, 1990). The frequency of use of crack, however, has not followed suit. Figures for crack use in the past month have remained stable at about 0.3 percent for young (ages eighteen to thirty-four) whites and about triple that number for young African-Americans (NIDA, 1991).

The economics of cocaine provides staggering figures for money spent by heavy users. In 1985 people snorting cocaine once a day spent more than 1500 dollars a week for the drug. Others using it more often reported spending much more, being able to support their expensive habit because they themselves sold the drug or were independently wealthy (Siegel, 1982). In the early 1980s cocaine cost 2000 dollars an ounce, making it approximately five times more expensive than gold. It was a status symbol in the 1920s among Hollywood performers, and in the 1980s it reemerged with similar meaning for actors, rock stars, athletes, and others in the better-paid strata of our society. When the cost of cocaine decreased, people from all segments of society began using it.

Is cocaine addicting? Until recently it was believed not to be, but data gathered over the past decade indicate otherwise (*Scientific Perspectives on Cocaine Abuse*, 1987); ceasing cocaine use appears to cause a severe withdrawal syndrome. Descriptions of withdrawal from cocaine vary. Based on clinical observations of outpatients, Gawin and Kleber (1986) suggested the existence of three phases. In *crash*, craving is first intense and the person cannot sleep and is depressed and paranoid. Then fatigue sets in and a desire to sleep takes over. *Withdrawal* follows, with a period of near normalcy, but within a few days craving increases again. *Extinction* is the third phase and includes periodic episodes of controllable craving that can last for a long time. In contrast, Weddington et al. (1990) made direct observations of cocaine addicts as they withdrew in an inpatient setting and found a steady improvement in mood, craving, and sleep over the twenty-eight days of the study.

Current laboratory as well as field-based research indicates more and more that cocaine can take hold of people with as much tenacity as that demonstrated for years with the established addictive drugs. As with alcohol, developing fetuses are markedly and negatively affected in the womb by the mother's use of cocaine during pregnancy, and many babies are born addicted to the drug. The mass media are full of reports on the social, psychological, economic, and legal damage to which people will subject themselves in order to continue taking the drug.

LSD and Other Hallucinogens

In 1943, a Swiss chemist, Albert Hofmann, recorded a description of an illness he had seemingly contracted.

> Last Friday . . . I had to interrupt my laboratory work . . . I was seized with a feeling of great restlessness and mild dizziness. At home, I lay down and sank into a not unpleasant delirium, which was characterized by extremely exciting fantasies. In a semiconscious state with my eyes closed . . . fantastic visions of extraordinary realness and with an intense kaleidoscopic play of colors assaulted me. (Cited by Cashman, 1966, p. 31)

Earlier in the day Dr. Hofmann had manufactured a few milligrams of *d*-lysergic acid diethylamide, a drug that he had first synthesized in 1938. Reasoning that he might have unknowingly ingested some and that this was the cause of his unusual experience, he deliberately took a dose and confirmed his hypothesis.

After Hofmann's experiences with **LSD** in 1943, the drug was referred to as psychotomimetic because it was thought to produce effects similar to the symptoms of a psychosis. Then the term psychedelic, from the Greek words for "soul" and "to make manifest," was applied to emphasize the subjectively experienced expansions of consciousness reported by users of LSD. The term in current use is **hallucinogen**, a term that describes one of the main effects of such drugs, producing hallucinations. Two other hallucinogens are important to mention, mescaline and psilocybin. In 1896 **mescaline**, an alkaloid and the active ingredient of peyote, was isolated from small, disklike growths of the top of the peyote cactus. The drug has been used for centuries in the religious rites of Indian peoples living in the Southwest and northern Mexico. **Psilocybin** is a crystalline powder that Hofmann isolated from the mushroom *Psilocybe mexicana* in 1958. The early Aztec and Mexican cultures called the sacred mushrooms "god's flesh," and the Indians of Mexico still use them in their worship.

During the 1950s these drugs were given in research settings to study what were thought to be psychotic experiences. In 1960 Timothy Leary and Richard Alpert of Harvard University began an investigation of the effects of psilocybin on institutionalized prisoners. The early results, although subject to several confounds, were encouraging: released prisoners who had a psilocybin trip proved less likely to be rearrested. At the same time the investigators started taking trips themselves and soon had gathered around them a group of people interested in experimenting with psychedelic drugs. By 1962 their activities had attracted the attention of law-enforcement agencies. As the investigation continued, it became a scandal, culminating in Leary's and Alpert's departure from Harvard. The affair seemed to give tremendous impetus to the use of the hallucinogens, particularly since the manufacture of LSD and the extraction of mescaline and psilocybin were found to be relatively easy and inexpensive.

After leaving Harvard, Leary and Alpert founded the International Foundation for Internal Freedom, an organization that emphatically espoused the desirability of psychedelic trips. It can probably be said that the proselytizing efforts of Leary and Alpert shifted attention from the supposedly psychotic experiences induced by the drugs to their mind-expanding effects.[6]

The use of LSD and other hallucinogens peaked in the 1960s; by the 1980s and into the 1990s only 1 or 2 percent of people could be classified as regular users, and even these acid heads do not indulge more than once or twice every two weeks (*National Survey on Drug Abuse: Main Findings 1982*, 1983; *HHS News*, 1990). However, marijuana is used fairly frequently between trips. There is no evidence of withdrawal symptoms during abstinence and only equivocal evidence of tolerance (Jaffe, 1985).

A new hallucinogen joined the ranks of illegal drugs on an emergency basis on July 1, 1985. **Ecstasy**, which refers to two closely similar synthetic compounds. MDA (methelenedioxyamphetamine) and MDMA (methylenedioxymethamphetamine) is chemically similar to mescaline and the amphetamines and is the psychoactive agent in nutmeg. MDA was first synthesized in 1910, but it was not until the 1960s that its psychedelic properties came to the attention of the drug-using, consciousness-expanding generation of the sixties. Today it is popular on some college campuses. Users report that the drug enhances intimacy and insight, improves interpersonal relationships, elevates mood, and promotes aesthetic awareness. It can also cause muscle tension, rapid eye movements, nausea, faintness, chills or sweating, and anxiety, depression, and confusion. The Drug Enforcement Administration considers the use of Ecstasy and other so-called designer drugs to be unsafe and a serious threat to health. Indeed, a number of deaths have been reported from accidental overdose (Climko, Roehrich, Sweeney, & Al-Razi, 1987). (See Focus Box 11.4 on nitrous oxide.)

[6]Like many of the old timers in the psychedelic drug revolution, Alpert went on to espouse an Eastern meditation philosophy that urged people to forsake drugs and work instead on creating their own meaningful trips without the aid of chemical agents. Known as Baba Ram Dass, he has lectured and written eloquently about the possibility of cultivating expanded states of consciousness: those who would devote the necessary time and energy to meditation techniques will be open to such experiences, according to Ram Dass. Most recently, Ram Dass seems to have rediscovered his Jewish roots and is exploring the possibilities of integrating Judaism with the teachings of Eastern mystics.

In the 1960s Timothy Leary was one of the leading proponents of the use of hallucinogens to expand consciousness.

The Effects of Hallucinogens

The typical dose of LSD is extremely small, from about 100 to 350 micrograms, administered as a liquid absorbed in sugar cubes or as capsules or tablets; for psilocybin the usual dose is about 30,000 micrograms; and for mescaline the usual dose is between 350,000 and 500,000 micrograms. The effects of LSD and mescaline usually last about twelve hours and those of psilocybin about six hours. Although the chemical structure of LSD is well-known, how it produces its psychological effects is not.

The following description is of the general effects of LSD, but it is also appropriate for the other hallucinogens.

> Synesthesias, the overflow from one sensory modality to another, may occur. Colors are heard and

FOCUS 11.4 • Nitrous Oxide—Not a Laughing Matter*

Nitrous oxide is a colorless gas that has been available since the nineteenth century. Within seconds it induces lightheadedness and a state of euphoria in most people. For some, important insights seem to flood the mind. Clinical reports and some controlled research (e.g., Devine et al., 1974) confirm that this gaseous mixture raises pain thresholds, perhaps by an induction of positive feelings that dull sensations that would normally be experienced as noxious. Many people find otherwise mundane events and thoughts irresistibly funny, hence the nickname laughing gas.

Perhaps readers of this book have had nitrous oxide at a dentist's office, to facilitate relaxation and otherwise make a potentially uncomfortable and intimidating dental procedure more palatable (and to make it easier for the dentist to work on the patient). For dentists a major advantage of nitrous oxide over other analgesics and relaxants is that the person can return to the normal waking state within minutes of breathing enriched oxygen or normal air. An additional advantage is that patients can be taught to control how deep they go by taking a few breaths of regular air through the mouth (the gas is administered through a small mask that covers only the nose—otherwise the dentist could not work on the person's teeth). The health professional, of course, can easily make continuing adjustments based on experienced judgment of how intoxicated the patient is becoming.

Since it was first available, nitrous oxide has been used recreationally, though for many years it has been illegal in most states. As with the other mind-altering drugs we have examined here, illegality does not prevent its unsupervised use. Illicit use is not a priority for police, perhaps because there is no evidence that nitrous oxide is physically addicting. And because it is thus far legally available for refilling aerosol canisters and souping up race-car engines, its use is not (yet)

> sounds may be seen. Subjective time is also seriously altered, so that clock time seems to pass extremely slowly. The loss of boundaries [between one's sense of self and one's environment] and the fear of fragmentation create a need for a structuring or supporting environment; and in the sense that they create a need for experienced companions and an explanatory system, these drugs are "cultogenic." During the "trip," thoughts and memories can vividly emerge under self-guidance or unexpectedly, to the user's distress. Mood may be labile, shifting from depression to gaiety, from elation to fear. Tension and anxiety may mount and reach panic proportions. After about 4 to 5 hours, if a major panic episode does not occur, there may be a sense of detachment and the conviction that one is magically in control. . . . The user may be greatly impressed with the drug experience and feel a greater sensitivity for art, music, human feelings, and the harmony of the universe, . . . (Jaffe, 1985, p. 564)

The effects of the hallucinogens, like those of other kinds of drugs, depend on a number of psychological variables in addition to the dose itself. A subject's set, that is, attitudes, expectancies, and motivations about taking drugs, are widely held to be important determinants of reactions to hallucinogens. Important also is the setting in which the drug is experienced. Among the most prominent dangers of taking LSD is the bad trip: some aspect of experience after taking the drug creates anxiety, which escalates and can sometimes develop into a full-blown panic attack. Often the specific fear is of going crazy. These panics are usually short-lived and subside as the drug is metabolized. A minority of people, however, go into a psychotic state that can require hospitalization and extended treatment (see Focus Box 11.5).

Pahnke (1963) performed a remarkable and original piece of research. He attempted to maximize all the situational variables that might contribute to a religious or mystical experience. Subjects in his investigation were theological students who first attended a meeting at which they were told of the possibilities of having religious experiences after taking psilocybin. Twenty students were given psilocybin and twenty an active placebo by a double-blind procedure. Nicotinic acid was given as the placebo because it does produce some similar effects, such as a tingling sensation in the skin. After receiving the drug or the placebo, each subject participated in a two-and-a-half-hour-long religious service that included meditation, prayers, and the associated with crime as is the case with heroin and cocaine. It also does not directly provoke violent behavior like phencyclidine (PCP). But it does carry serious risk.

An important difference between the way in which dentists use nitrous oxide and the way in which it is used casually is that, in the dental office, the air mixture is seldom more than 80 percent nitrous oxide, the rest being oxygen. This mixture allows for the safe and effective use of the gas. Such was not the case for three men who were found dead in the closed cab of a pickup truck in the early morning hours of March 6, 1992. They had apparently been asphyxiated from the nitrous oxide in an eighty-pound industrial-sized canister that was lying across their laps. Evidence at the scene suggested that they had been filling balloons with the gas and, perhaps inadvertently, allowed the gas to escape freely into the sealed cab. With little air from the outside, the men had been breathing pure nitrous oxide and their own exhaled carbon dioxide—and very little oxygen. They were not the first victims. In 1988 four young adults had met a similar death in a dental storage room in Cedar City, Utah. And in Birmingham, Alabama, a party host was charged with manslaughter in 1990 for allegedly giving the gas to a teenager who died after inhaling it.

In recent years many underground parties in some large cities have featured the sale of balloons filled with nitrous oxide costing about five dollars each. Flyers promoting these parties proclaim such things as "Free Balloons for the Kiddies." T-shirt logos, like "Just Say NO," tout the gas, NO referring to nitrous oxide. Sometimes called hippie crack, nitrous oxide balloons are often supplemented with the use of Ecstasy and other designer drugs in a psychedelic atmosphere full of bright laser lights and loud dance music. The illegal use of nitrous oxide appears to be on the increase, and promoters of some of these rave parties make a great deal of money selling both nitrous oxide and Ecstasy. Police fear that gangs and organized crime are moving into this arena as has happened with other illicit drugs.

*Some of the material here comes from two *Los Angeles Times* articles, Connelly (1992) and Romero (1992).

like. To heighten the significance of the occasion, Pahnke had chosen to conduct the experiment on Good Friday. After the service, each subject wrote a description of the experience and answered an extensive questionnaire. The mystical and transcendental experiences of those who took psilocybin were found to be significantly greater than the experiences of those who took the placebo.

One of the principal concerns about ingesting LSD is the possibility of a **flashback**, an unpredictable recurrence of psychedelic experiences after the physiological effects of the drug have worn off. Little is known about these flashback trips except that they cannot be predicted or controlled. The available evidence does not support the hypothesis that they are caused by drug-produced physical changes in the nervous system. For one thing, only 15 to 30 percent of users of hallucinogenic drugs are estimated ever to have flashbacks (e.g., Stanton & Bardoni, 1972). Moreover, there is no independent evidence of measurable neurological changes in these drug users. The flashback, which seems to have a force of its own and may come to haunt people weeks and months after they have taken the drug, is a very upsetting phenomenon for those who experience it.

The Etiology of Substance Abuse and Dependence

In trying to understand the causes of substance abuse and dependence disorders, researchers have generally distinguished the variables that lead someone to begin using the substance, to then use it heavily, and finally to abuse or become dependent on it. The general idea is that for abuse or dependence to occur, there must first be a period of heavy use. After prolonged heavy use the person becomes ensnared by the biological processes of tolerance and withdrawal.

Although there is certainly some truth to this model, it is not likely to account for all cases. There are, for example, documented cases of heavy use of both tobacco and heroin that did not eventuate in addiction. Nevertheless, guided by this general model, most research has examined variables related to initial use and its subsequent escalation, and so we will examine sociocultural, psychological, and biological factors. As we discuss these variables it is important to keep in mind that they are likely to be differentially related to different substances.

FOCUS

11.5 • Not an Upper or a Downer but an Inside-Outer

In 1956 Parke Davis and Company, a large pharmaceutical firm, synthesized a new anesthetic. Although effective in large doses, it was found to cause agitation and disorientation as a patient regained consciousness. When administered in smaller doses, it induced a psychoticlike state. In 1965 this new drug, **phencyclidine (PCP)**, was taken off the market, and by 1978 its legal manufacture was discontinued in the United States.

PCP was first seen in illegal use in Los Angeles in 1965. It soon turned up in the Haight-Ashbury district of San Francisco under the name PeaCe Pill and was sold as a psychedelic, but it quickly gained a bad reputation because many users had negative reactions. In the late 1960s and early 1970s the drug spread to other parts of the country until, by 1979, it had turned up in most states. Its prevalence declined sharply in the 1980s.

On the street PCP is known by dozens of names, among them angel dust, elephant tranquilizer, cadillac, cozmos, Detroit Pink, embalming fluid, Killerweed, horse crystal, PeaCe Pill, wac, and zombie, and has been marketed falsely as LSD, psilocybin, cocaine, and other drugs. It is available in many forms and degrees of purity and in most colors. In granular form it contains between 50 and 100 percent phencyclidine. The most popular ways of taking PCP are in mint or parsley flavored joints and in commercial cigarettes that have been dipped in liquid PCP or had a string dipped in liquid PCP passed through them. But the drug can also be injected intravenously, swallowed, put in the eyes as drops, snorted like cocaine, and smoked in a pipe.

The effects of PCP depend largely on the dosage. The user generally has jerky eye movements (nystagmus) alternating with a blank stare, is unable to walk heel-to-toe in a straight line (gait ataxia), and has great rigidity of the muscles. Hallucinations and delusions are also experienced by some. All the sensory systems become overly sensitive so that users are extremely susceptible to any stimulation and are best left alone. When touched, they are likely to flail and become so agitated and combative that it takes several people to restrain them. Their incoherence and lack of

Genetics, for example, may play some role in alcoholism but be irrelevant to crack abuse.

Sociocultural Variables

Variables considered here range from the molar to the molecular and are relevant to promoting initial use of a substance and continued heavy use. Beginning at the molar level there is great cross-national variation in alcohol consumption. The data in Figure 11.1 are from a large-scale longitudinal study, and, besides the great differences in consumption, several other points can be gleaned from the figure. First, over the study period (1950–1980) alcohol consumption rose greatly in each country. Second, the differences in consumption decreased with the passage of time. Earlier research also found striking cross-national differences in alcohol consumption, some of them even greater than those shown in the figure. For example, in deLint's (1978) report the highest consumption rates were found in wine-drinking societies such as those of France, Spain, and Italy. Cultural attitudes and patterns of drink-

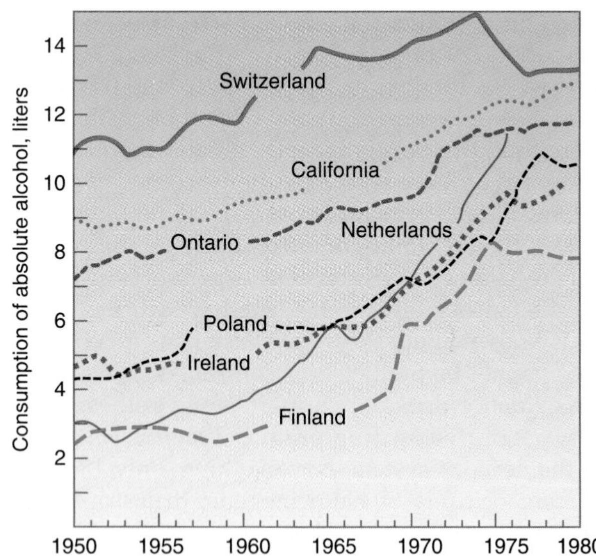

Figure 11.1 Total consumption of alcoholic beverages (in liters of absolute alcohol per head) of population aged 15 years and over in countries studied in ISACE, from 1950–1980. After Mäkelä et al., 1981.

communicativeness do not allow them to be talked down from their high. Very high dosages—actually, as little as a single gram—usually result in a deep and prolonged coma, seizures, apnea or periods of no breathing, sustained high blood pressure, and sometimes even death from heart and lung failure or from ruptured blood vessels in the brain. No medication to reverse the effects of PCP has yet been found. People seldom remember afterward what happened while they were on the drug.

Phencyclidine is not an upper or a downer, nor is it a psychedelic. Some workers refer to it as an inside-outer, a term that to some extent conveys the bizarre and extreme nature of its effects.

How long do the effects of PCP last? The way in which it is ingested and the dosage seem to play a role. Onset is usually between one and five minutes after smoking a treated cigarette; effects peak after about half an hour and then do not dissipate for up to two days. Since PCP remains in the body for several days, it can accumulate if ingested repeatedly. Chronic users who have taken the drug several times a week for six months experience cognitive distortions and disorientation for several months afterward, even for as long as two years after use has ceased. In addition, personality often changes, there can be memory loss, and the user may experience severe anxiety, depression, and aggressive urges (Aniline & Pitts, 1982). The addictiveness and other consequences are difficult to determine because most PCP users take other drugs as well, such as alcohol.

More than 100 deaths from ingesting PCP were reported in Los Angeles County in 1978 alone. These fatalities were caused in a number of ways. One man who was swimming drowned because he lost his spatial orientation; others died because of severe respiratory depression or an uncontrollable increase in body temperature.

Those who use PCP frequently are apparently very young, averaging fifteen years of age. Abusers tend to be arrested more often for substance-related offenses than those taking the other drugs discussed in this chapter, and they tend as well to have overdosed on more occasions. The PCP user, then, seems to be more socially deviant, perhaps more often psychopathic, than abusers of other illicit substances.

In light of how terrifying and dangerous the drug is, it is not surprising that its popularity declined in the 1980s. More surprising perhaps is that it is enjoying a resurgence in the 1990s.

Alcoholism is higher in countries in which alcohol use is heavy, such as vinicultural societies. Note that everyone is drinking wine in this French bar.

ing thus influence the likelihood of drinking heavily and therefore of abusing alcohol.

Turning to studies within the population of a single country (the United States), there is also considerable variation in the use of substances. For example, Fillmore and Caetano (1980) found unusually high levels of alcoholism among sailors, railroad workers, and people in the drink trade—restaurant owners, bartenders, waiters, and liquor dealers. In all these occupations heavy drinking is normative, that is, almost expected as part of the job, and alcohol is readily available.

Similarly, tobacco use among high school students is highest in an identifiable subgroup: those with poor grades, behavior problems, and a taste for heavy metal music (Sussman et al., 1990), as well as those with little adult supervision after school (Richardson et al., 1989). Peer influence is important in the decision of adolescents to smoke, but those who have a high sense of self-efficacy (Bandura, 1986) to resist social pressure—e.g., "I can imagine refusing to use tobacco with students my age and still have them like me" (Stacy et al., 1992, p. 166)—are influenced less by their peers. Finally, heroin and crack abuse is most common in ghettos, and marijuana and hallucinogen use was linked to social activism and other characteristics of the late 1960s. In all these cases, members of a subcultural group are likely to be exposed to multiple exemplars of drug use, peer pressure to conform, and substances that are readily available.

The use of particular substances is often linked to subgroups of a culture or even to particular periods of time. For example, marijuana and hallucinogen use was prevalent for the Woodstock generation.

Another variable to be considered in this context is the media. We are bombarded with TV commercials in which beer is associated with athletic-looking males, bikini–clad women, and good times. The message is clear: alcohol promotes fun. As another example we can consider the Marlboro Man, a clear attempt to present smoking as a macho activity.[7]

More recent, and particularly pernicious, is the Old Joe Camel campaign for Camel cigarettes. With the number of smokers declining, the tobacco industry's profitability depends on recruiting new smokers to replace those who are quitting. The obvious target—elementary and high school students. Camel launched its campaign in 1988 with the Joe Camel character modeled after James Bond or the character played by Don Johnson in "Miami Vice." Prior to the campaign (1976–1988) Camels were the preferred brand of less than 0.5 percent of seventh through twelfth graders. By 1991 Camel's share of this *illegal* market had increased to 33 percent (Di Franza et al., 1991)! In March 1992, the surgeon general as well as the American Medical Association (AMA) asked R. J. Reynolds, the manufacturer of Camel cigarettes, to drop Old Joe Camel from its ads for these very reasons. Billboard companies and print media were also requested to stop running the ads. The response from R. J. Reynolds? "We have no reason to believe that this campaign is causing anyone to begin smoking. If we thought it was causing young people to smoke, we'd pull it" (spokesperson for the company, quoted in Horovitz, 1992). And from the media: "With all due respect to the surgeon general's opinion, we are very committed to free speech in all of its various forms" (spokesperson for Time Inc. Magazines, quoted in Horovitz, 1992). The surgeon general herself exercised the right of free speech when, on June 21, 1992, she joined leaders of the AMA as well as schoolchildren in a march through downtown Chicago to protest ads featuring Joe Camel, whom they called a merchant of death (*Los Angeles Times*, June 21, 1992, p. A4).

Psychological Variables

We examine next two classes of psychological variables. The first class comprises the effects of alcohol on mood. The second includes the personality traits that may make it more likely for some people to drink heavily.

[7]The actor who portrayed the Marlboro Man in the mid 1970s was diagnosed with lung cancer in 1991.

Mood Alteration

Many studies suggest that a principal reason for using drugs is to alter mood. Drug use is therefore reinforcing, either by enhancing positive mood states or diminishing negative ones. Drugs like alcohol, marijuana, sedatives, nicotine, and caffeine are thought to reduce anxiety and distress and to be relaxing, while stimulants and narcotics promote positive feelings.[8] Most of the research in this area has focused on the tension-reducing properties of alcohol. Early animal experiments (Conger, 1950) showed that alcohol reduces avoidance responding, which is usually regarded as mediated by anxiety. Some later experiments with humans (e.g., Sher & Levenson, 1982) indicate that alcohol can reduce tension in people who are not yet alcoholic, but there are also conflicting findings (e.g., Thyer & Curtis, 1984).

Some investigators who have examined the reasons for these inconsistent results focus on the situation in which alcohol is consumed. Steele and Josephs (1988; 1990) have proposed that alcohol produces its tension-reducing effect by altering cognition and perception. Specifically, they theorize that alcohol impairs cognitive processing and narrows attention to the most immediately available cues, resulting in what the authors term *alcohol myopia*; the intoxicated person has less cognitive capacity to distribute between ongoing activity and worry. If a distracting activity is available, attention will be diverted to it rather than focusing on worrisome thoughts, with a resultant decrease in anxiety. However, in some situations alcohol could increase tension, for example, when no distractors are present and an intoxicated person therefore focuses all his or her limited processing capacity on unpleasant thoughts. In this case, the discouraged person can become even more depressed while drinking alone.

In an experiment designed to test this theory, Steele and Josephs (1988) led subjects to believe that they would have to give a speech on the topic "What I dislike most about my body and personal appearance." Half the subjects were given alcohol (gin and tonic; 1 ml ethanol/kg of body weight); the other half thought they were getting alcohol but got just tonic (disguised so the deception would not be obvious). A fifteen-minute waiting period followed consumption of the beverages. During the waiting period, half the subjects in each group were given a distracting task of making aesthetic judgments of art slides, while the other half sat quietly.

The dependent variable was anxiety, which had been assessed several times by a self-report measure. Some of the data are shown in Table 11.2. As can be seen, anxiety ratings remained virtually unchanged among the no alcohol subjects from the beginning of the waiting period to the halfway point and, as predicted by the theory, anxiety decreased in subjects who were given alcohol and were distracted by the slides. The cognitive and perceptual effects of the alcohol altered the subjects so that their focus was on the art slides and not on the upcoming self-deprecating speech. Also as predicted, anxiety increased in subjects who received alcohol and were

Table 11.2 • Results of the Steele and Josephs (1988) Experiment Showing Differential Effects of Alcohol on Anxiety[a]

	Amount of Anxiety during Wait Period, %	
Group	*Beginning*	*Halfway Through*
No alcohol/slides	54.6	56.4
No alcohol/no slides	56.5	55.5
Alcohol/slides	63.5	53.0
Alcohol/no slides	57.4	66.8

[a]The larger the percentage the higher the anxiety.

The tension reduction theory argues that people become heavy drinkers because of alcohol's stress reducing properties. The stock market crash of 1987 apparently drove many financiers to the nearest bar. Although some came to read and some to talk, others undoubtedly had an extra drink or two.

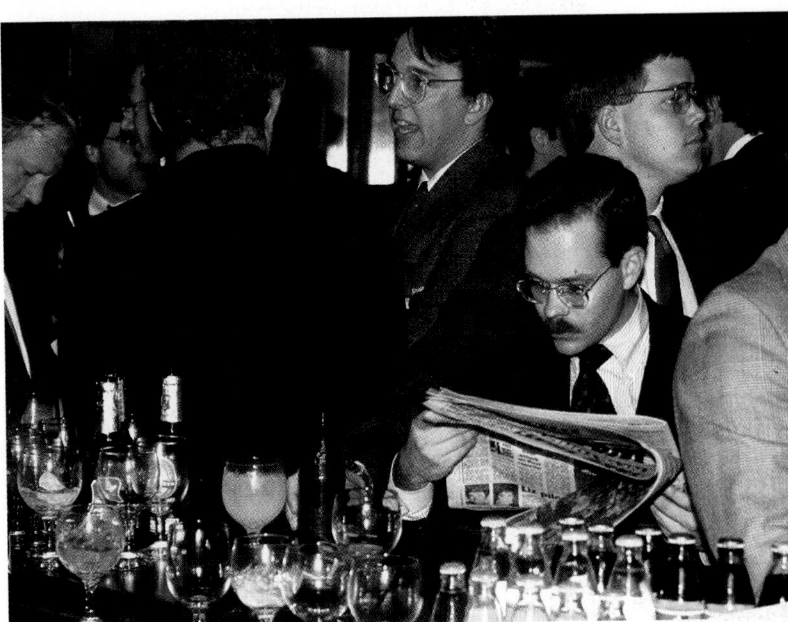

[8]It might seem strange that drugs that increase physiological arousal are reported to be relaxing, but the literature suggests that the link between physiology and phenomenological states is far from one-to-one.

not distracted. Apparently, these people focused excessively on the upcoming stress and became even more anxious as time passed.

Another situational variable related to the tension-reducing effects of alcohol is whether alcohol consumption precedes or follows stress. The notion most people have about alcohol and tension reduction is that an increase in tension (for example, from a bad day at the office) leads to increased consumption to reduce the effects of the earlier stressor. Empirical support for this idea comes from studies showing that increases in life stress precede relapses in reformed alcoholics (e.g., Brown et al., 1990). Notably, however, experimental research on the tension-reducing properties of alcohol has typically reversed the order of the two variables, having subjects drink and then encounter a stressor. Sayette and Wilson (1991) compared alcohol's effects in both orders (stress–alcohol vs. alcohol–stress) and found tension reduction only in the alcohol–stress sequence. Based on these results, alcohol may not be a potent tension reducer in many life situations when it is consumed after stress.

What, then, can we conclude about the tension-reduction theory? Returning to a concept introduced earlier in this chapter (page 289), it may be that people use alcohol after stress not because it reduces distress directly but because they *expect* it will reduce their tension. In support of this idea, studies of college undergraduates (Rather et al., 1992) and children of alcoholic parents (Sher et al., 1991) demonstrate that positive expectancies about alcohol's effects predict use of the drug. That is, people who expect alcohol to reduce stress and anxiety are those likely to be frequent users. Indeed, Stacy, Newcomb, and Bentler (1991) have shown that positive expectancies about a drug's effects predict drug use in general.

Personality and Drug Use

Neither the sociocultural nor mood alteration theories can completely account for individual differences in drug use. That is, not all members of a particular culture or subculture are heavy users nor does everyone who experiences stress increase drug usage. Personality variables attempt to explain why certain people seem to need these effects. An association has often been noted between criminality, drug abuse, and antisocial personality disorder. In this context drug abuse may be considered part of the thrill-seeking behavior of the psychopath discussed in Chapter 10. We might also expect narcotics to be used by anxious individuals in order to reduce their distress.

Drug addicts have been found to be deviant on various personality questionnaire measures. But we must question whether these personality characteristics antedated the addiction and caused it. For example, we might find that drug addicts tend to be more suspicious than nonusers. To conclude that suspiciousness contributes to the use of drugs would not be justified, for it might well be the addict's *reaction* to illegal status as a drug user.

A number of studies, however, have employed a longitudinal design, which is more appropriate for studying the relationship between personality and drug use. Several personality characteristics of drug users have emerged from this work. The first is hyperactivity in childhood. For example, in a prospective study spanning over ten years, Hechtman, Weiss, and Perlman (1984) found that hyperactivity was an important predictor of later alcohol abuse. Another trait is antisocial behavior (Jones, 1968). Notably, hyperactivity and antisocial behavior are themselves highly correlated, and there are some indications that antisocial behavior has the greater ability to predict adult outcomes. Indeed, antisocial personality, linked to similar patterns in biological parental background, is predictive of drug abuse problems generally (Cadoret et al., 1986).

Finally, in a longitudinal study spanning the years from preschool to age eighteen, Shadler and Block (1990) investigated personality characteristics that predict frequent marijuana use. Compared with those who only experimented with the drug, heavy users were described in the following way at age seven: not getting along well with others, unconcerned with moral issues (e.g., fairness), showing physical symptoms of stress, indecisive, not trustworthy or dependable, unable to admit to negative feelings, and lacking confidence and self-esteem. At age eleven the following differences emerged: very emotionally labile, inattentive and unable to concentrate, lacking involvement in activities, stubborn, and deviant from their peers.

Biological Variables

Most of the research on biological factors in substance abuse has addressed the possibility that a genetically transmitted alteration in some biological process serves as a predisposition for alcoholism. We will focus on these data.

Among animals a preference for alcohol or indifference to it varies with the species. By using selective mating within a species, animals that greatly prefer alcohol to other beverages can be bred (Segovia-Riquelme, Varela, & Mardones, 1971). There is also evidence that alcoholism in human beings runs in families. A number of studies indicate that relatives and children of alcoholics have higher than expected rates of alcoholism (e.g., Shu et al., 1991). Studies indicating greater concordance for alcoholism (e.g., McGue, Pickens, & Suikis, 1992) and caffeine, nicotine, and opiate use (Look & Gurling, 1988) in identical twins than in fraternal twins also point toward a possible role of heredity. Although these findings are consistent with the genetic transmission of a predisposition, these individuals might also have become substance users through exposure to their parents' drug-related behavior.

One major study, however, examined alcoholism in the adopted male offspring of alcoholics, thus allowing the role of heredity to be more precisely specified (Goodwin et al., 1973). From an initial pool of 5483 male babies who were adopted in Copenhagen between 1924 and 1947, 174 subjects were chosen. Subjects were divided into three groups.

1. **N = 67.** One and sometimes both biological parents of each subject (proband) in the experimental group had been hospitalized for alcoholism. The probands had been adopted within six weeks of birth by nonrelatives and had had no subsequent contact with biological relatives.
2. **N = 70.** Each subject in this control group was matched for age and time of adoption with a subject in group 1. None of the biological parents of these control subjects had a record of psychiatric hospitalization.
3. **N = 37.** The subjects in this control group were matched for age and time of adoption with subjects in group 1. At least one biological parent of each of these control subjects had been hospitalized for a psychiatric condition other than alcoholism or schizophrenia.

When this original sample was followed up, 133 subjects were located and interviewed. (Those who could not be located or who refused to be questioned were proportionately distributed across groups.) The subjects, who had a mean age of thirty at the time of the follow-up, were interviewed by a psychiatrist blind to their group assignment. Questions covered their drinking practices, psychopathology, and demographic variables. Since the subjects in the two control groups did not differ on any of the classificatory variables except having or not having a parent with a record of psychiatric hospitalization, they were combined into one comparison group for purposes of analysis. Problems that significantly discriminated between the two groups are given in Table 11.3.

Table 11.3 • Alcohol-Related Problems of Offspring of Alcoholics, Adopted and Raised by Others, Compared with Those of Controls

Problems	*Probands, % (N = 55)*	*Controls, % (N = 78)*
Nondrinking		
Ever divorced	27	9
Any psychiatric treatment	40	24
Psychiatric hospitalization	15	3
Drinking		
Hallucinations (as withdrawal symptoms)	6	0
Loss of control	35	17
Repeated morning drinking	29	11
Treated for drinking	9	1
Alcoholic diagnosis	18	5

Source: From Goodwin et al., 1973.

As shown, the two groups are easily distinguishable on the basis of alcohol-related measures. Thus the results suggest that in men a predisposition toward alcoholism can be inherited. That a predisposition to alcoholism may be found only in men is also shown in the McGue et al. (1992) twin study. For the males the concordance rate for MZ pairs was 76 percent and for the DZs, 54 percent. The corresponding figures for the female MZs and DZs were 39 percent and 41 percent.

Large-scale adoptee research conducted in Sweden has also raised the possibility that there are subtypes of alcoholism with different genetic bases (Cloninger et al., 1981). The investigators divided their sample of biological parents into two groups according to their pattern of alcohol abuse. One group of biological parents had an adult onset of alcoholism, no history of criminal behavior, and were believed to be episodic alcoholics (bingers). The second group of parents had both an early onset of drinking problems and a history of antisocial behavior. They were viewed as the continual alcoholics.

For the first adoptee subtype, both genes and environment seemed necessary to produce disorder. An alcoholic parent and exposure to a pattern of heavy drinking in the adoptive home predicted alcoholism in these subjects. In contrast, only a genetic effect was evident in the children whose biological parents continually used alcohol, but their risk of alcoholism was increased markedly. This effect held only for male adoptees. Similarly, the McGue (1992) twin study showed that genetic factors were much more important in the case of early onset alcoholism. On a more molecular level, researchers have also been pursuing the specific gene or genes that might confer increased vulnerability to their carriers. Interest has focused on a gene for a receptor for the neurotransmitter dopamine (the D2 gene). Results to date are promising (Uhl, Perscio, & Smith, 1992).

In speculating on what might be inherited as a diathesis for alcoholism, Goodwin (1979) proposed the ability to tolerate alcohol. To become an alcoholic, a person first has to be able to drink a lot, in other words, be able to tolerate large quantities of alcohol. Some ethnic groups, notably Asians, may have a low rate of alcoholism because of their physiological intolerance, which is caused by a deficiency in an enzyme that metabolizes alcohol. Indeed, about three-quarters of Asians experience unpleasant effects from small quantities of alcohol. Noxious effects of the drug may then protect a person from alcoholism.

Goodwin's hypothesis focuses on short-term effects, possibly on how alcohol is metabolized or on how the central nervous system responds to alcohol. Animal research indicates that genetic components are at work in both these processes (Schuckit, 1983). Corroborating this notion are recent findings from research using the high-risk method. Typically, studies have compared young, nonalcoholic adults with a first-degree alcoholic relative to similar individuals without a positive family history for the disorder. Although there have been inconsistencies in published results, two findings have been replicated by Schuckit and Gold (1988) in one of the best studies yet reported. Of a number of variables examined, two were the strongest discriminators between groups:

1. Sons of alcoholics self-reported less intoxication than controls after a dose of alcohol.
2. Sons of alcoholics showed a smaller hormonal response (cortisol and prolactin) to the alcohol.

The smaller response of the sons of alcoholics may at first seem puzzling but it may well fit with the notion that you have to drink a lot to become an alcoholic. A small response to alcohol may set the stage for heavier than normal drinking. However, as persuasive as the case is for a heritable predisposition to becoming alcoholic, it must be emphasized that the vast majority of children of alcoholics do *not* become alcoholics themselves.

Therapy for Alcoholism

The havoc created by alcoholism, both for the drinkers and for their families, friends, employers, and communities, makes this problem a serious public health issue in this country. Again, no dollar figure can be put on the human tragedy that is a direct result of this most prevalent form of drug abuse. Industry spends large sums of money in support of various alcohol rehabilitation programs for employees, in the knowledge that for every dollar spent in this way, many more dollars will be returned in improved functioning of workers. Television and radio carry public service messages about the dangers of alcoholism in attempts to discourage people from beginning to drink excessively and encourage those already affected to own up to their problem and seek help. Calling excessive drinking a disease is believed preferable to holding persons responsible for their drinking; presumably this lessens guilt and allows them to mobilize their resources to seek help and combat their alcoholism.

The treatment of alcoholics is very difficult, not only because of the addictive nature of the drug but also because many other psychological problems are likely to be present, for example, depression, anxiety, and severe disruptions in the person's social and occupational functioning. Risk of suicide is also very high (Galanter & Castenada, 1985). Although some of these problems may have preceded, indeed, contributed to, the abuse of alcohol, by the time an alcoholic is treated it is seldom possible to know what is cause and what is effect. What *is* certain is that the person's life is usually a shambles, and any treatment worth attempting has to address more than the excessive drinking per se. There are both biological and psychological interventions for alcoholism. Regardless of the kind of intervention, the first step is to admit the problem and decide to do something about it.

Traditional Hospital Treatment

Public and private hospitals worldwide have for many years provided retreats for alcoholics, sanctums where individuals can dry out and avail themselves of a variety of individual and group therapies. The withdrawal from alcohol—**detoxification**—can be difficult, both physically and psychologically, and usually takes about one month. Tranquilizers are sometimes given to ease the anxiety and general discomfort of withdrawal. However, because many alcoholics misuse tranquilizers, some clinics try gradual tapering off without tranquilizers rather than a sudden cutoff of alcohol. Alcoholics also need carbohydrate solutions, B vitamins, and perhaps anticonvulsants.

Holder et al. (1991) pointed out that the number of for-profit hospitals treating alcoholism increased almost fourfold from 1978 to 1984, fueled by the fact that such treatment is covered in large measure by both private insurance companies and the federal government. Inpatient alcoholism treatment is a big and profitable business! Miller and Hester (1986b) indicated that the cost of all treatment modalities is at least 10 billion dollars a year, most of it for inpatient care. Because inpatient treatment is much more expensive than outpatient treatment, its cost-effectiveness should be questioned. From the available data, Miller and Hester found that the higher costs of inpatient treatment are not matched by higher degrees of effectiveness. For one thing, detoxification can be safely managed on an outpatient basis for most people, and, in general, the therapeutic results of hospital treatment are not superior to those of outpatient treatment.

Antabuse

Among the treatments available for alcoholics is disulfiram, or **Antabuse,** a drug that discourages drinking by causing violent vomiting if alcohol is ingested. Introduced in Europe in 1948, Antabuse is the only available drug that has specific relevance for the treatment of alcoholism (Moss, 1990). As one can imagine, adherence to an Antabuse regimen can be a problem. Indeed, *if* an alcoholic is able or willing to take the drug every morning as prescribed, the chances are good that drinking will lessen because of the negative consequences of imbibing (Sisson & Azrin, 1989). However, in a large multicenter study with placebo controls, Antabuse was not shown to have any specific benefit (Fuller et al., 1986; Fuller, 1988). There can also be serious side effects (Moss, 1990).

Alcoholics Anonymous

The largest and most widely known self-help group in the world is Alcoholics Anonymous (AA), founded in 1935 by two recovered alcoholics. It currently has 30,000 chapters and membership numbering more than a million people in the United

Alcoholics Anonymous is the largest self-help group in the world. At their regular meetings, newcomers rise to announce their addiction and receive advice and support from others.

States and ninety-one other countries throughout the world. An AA chapter runs regular and frequent meetings at which newcomers rise to announce that they are alcoholics and older, sober members give testimonials, relating the stories of their alcoholism and indicating how their lives are better now. The group provides emotional support, understanding, and close counseling for the alcoholic as well as a social life to relieve isolation. Members are urged to call upon one another around-the-clock when they need companionship and encouragement not to relapse into drink.

The belief is instilled in each AA member that alcoholism is a disease one is never cured of, that continuing vigilance is necessary to resist taking even a single drink lest uncontrollable drinking begin all over again. The basic tenet of AA was vividly articulated in the classic film *Lost Weekend,* for which Ray Milland won an Oscar for best actor. In a scene in which he is confronted with his denial of the seriousness of his drinking problem, his brother remonstrates, "Don't you ever learn that with you it's like stepping off a roof and expecting to fall just one floor?"

The important religious and spiritual aspect of AA is evident in the twelve steps of AA shown in Table 11.4. Two related self-help groups are of more recent origin. The relatives of alcoholics meet in Al-Anon Family Groups for mutual support in dealing with their alcoholic family members. Alateen is for the children of alcoholics, who also require support and understanding.

Table 11.4 • Twelve Suggested Steps of Alcoholics Anonymous

1. We admitted we were powerless over alcohol—that our lives had become unmanageable.
2. Came to believe that a power greater than ourselves could restore us to sanity.
3. Made a decision to turn our will and our lives over to the care of God *as we understood Him.*
4. Made a searching and fearless moral inventory of ourselves.
5. Admitted to God, to ourselves, and to another human being the exact nature of our wrongs.
6. Were entirely ready to have God remove all these defects of character.
7. Humbly asked Him to remove our shortcomings.
8. Made a list of all persons we had harmed, and became willing to make amends to them all.
9. Made direct amends to such people wherever possible, except when to do so would injure them or others.
10. Continued to take personal inventory and, when we were wrong, promptly admitted it.
11. Sought through prayer and meditation to improve our conscious contact with God *as we understood Him*, praying only for knowledge of His will for us and the power to carry that out.
12. Having had a spiritual awakening as the result of these steps, we tried to carry this message to alcoholics and to practice these principles in all our affairs.

Note: The Twelve Steps and Twelve Traditions. Copyright © 1952, by Alcoholics Anonymous World Services, Inc. Reprinted with permission of Alcoholics Anonymous World Services, Inc.

Unfortunately, the claims made by AA about the effectiveness of its treatment have rarely been subjected to scientific scrutiny. Findings from uncontrolled studies must be viewed with caution: AA has high drop-out rates, and the dropouts are not factored into the results (Edwards et al., 1967). In addition, there is a lack of long-term follow-up of AA clients. Results from the best controlled study to date are mixed (Walsh et al., 1991).

Alcohol-abusing workers at a General Electric manufacturing plant were randomly assigned to one of three treatments: three weeks of hospitalization followed by AA; AA alone; or a choice of treatment. Of the seventy-one people in the choice group, twenty-seven elected hospitalization, thirty-three AA, and six no treatment. At a two-year follow-up of the entire group, 23 percent of the hospitalization group had required rehospitalization for alcoholism, compared with 63 percent of the AA group and 38 percent of the choice group. On the other hand, it is important to note that those who *chose* AA did well in the study; it is when alcoholics were randomly *assigned* to AA that they did not fare at all well. Many people who choose AA and stay with it for more than three months—a select group, to be sure—remain abstinent for at least a few years (Emerick, Lassen, & Edwards, 1977). The needs of such people seem to be met by the fellowship, support, and religious overtones of AA. For them it becomes a way of life. As with other forms of intervention, it remains to be determined for whom this particular mode is best suited.

Insight Therapy

It is noteworthy that insight-oriented psychotherapists see the need for active and directive intervention when it comes to treating alcoholics and other substance abusers, even on an outpatient basis. "The concept of therapist and patient enclosed in an inviolable envelope must be modified; immediate circumstances that may expose the patient to drug use must take precedence over issues of long-term understanding and insight (Galanter & Cataneda, 1990, p. 467)." Unlike traditional insight-oriented treatment—but similar to the approach used with suicidal patients—the therapist should be available between sessions to provide support and understanding as the patient wrestles with the challenge of living without alcohol. If the patient has a social support system, such as a spouse or companion or other relative, that person is involved as well in treatment as part of a network to discourage drinking. Also recommended is the use of Antabuse as well as attendance at AA meetings, and the patient's network is often necessary to ensure compliance with these assignments, for example, by having a spouse watch the patient take the Antabuse each morning. With these rather behavioral aspects in place, an insight therapist can proceed with the usual exploration of conflicts and, if psychodynamic in orientation, uncovering unconscious motivation for the drinking problem (Galanter & Castaneda, 1990).

The use of a network of people in this kind of treatment differs in an important way from the involvement of significant others in family therapy (page 600, Chapter 20): the focus is on the alcoholic or drug abuser as the one with the problem. Stress from close relationships might be part of the picture, but the alcoholic is considered the patient. "The therapist's relationship to the network is like that of a team leader rather than that of a family therapist. The network is established to implement a straightforward task: that of aiding the therapist to sustain the patient's abstinence" (Galanter & Cataneda,

1990, p. 472). However, there is a similarity as well: the members of the network have to be carefully chosen, and their effectiveness as helpers in the therapy depends a good deal on their relationship with the patient. The therapist has to be sensitive to possible conflicts between the patient and a network member, and in this way relationship issues such as those dealt with in family and couples therapy may arise.

Aversion Therapy

Behavioral researchers have been studying the treatment of alcoholism for many years. In fact, one of the earliest articles on behavior therapy concerned aversive "conditioning" of alcoholism (Kantorovich, 1930). With these procedures a problem drinker is shocked or made nauseous while looking at, reaching for, or beginning to drink alcohol. The aversive stimulus may also be vividly imagined in a procedure called **covert sensitization** (Cautela, 1966). Using a hierarchy of scenes designed to extinguish the desire to drink, the alcoholic is instructed to imagine being made violently and disgustingly sick by his or her drinking.

Originally used by themselves, aversion therapies are best implemented (if at all) in the context of broadly based programs that attend to the patient's particular life circumstances, for example, marital conflict, social fears, and other factors often associated with problem drinking (Tucker, Vuchinich, & Downey, 1992).

Contingency Management

An operant approach to treating alcoholism was originated by Nathan Azrin, one of behavior therapy's pioneers. Working with severe alcoholics, Azrin and his associates arranged for people significant in the patients' social environments—or hospital staff in the case of institutionalized substance abusers—to monitor them and reinforce such behaviors as taking Antabuse regularly and engaging in behaviors inconsistent with drinking. In addition, Azrin set up job clubs to help the patients develop or enhance employment-seeking skills and social networks for recreational activities that did not include alcohol. Assertiveness training for refusing drinks was also provided. This community reinforcement approach has generated promising results (Azrin, 1976; Hunt & Azrin, 1973; Azrin, Sisson, Meyers, & Godley, 1982; Keane, Foy, Nunn, & Rychtarik, 1984).

Nathan Azrin was one of the originators of the token economy and later extended this work to a community reinforcement approach to alcoholism.

Building on this work is a strategy sometimes termed *behavioral self-control training* (Tucker et al., 1992), which emphasizes patient control and includes one or more of the following: (1) stimulus control, whereby patients narrow the situations in which they allow themselves to drink, for example, with others on a special occasion; (2) modification of the topography of drinking, for example, having only mixed drinks and taking small sips rather than gulps; and (3) reinforcing abstinence or controlled drinking, for example, allowing themselves a nonalcoholic treat if they resist the urge to drink.

In our view a central issue not formally addressed by advocates of behavioral self-control training is getting the person to abide by restrictions and conditions that, if implemented, will in fact reduce or eliminate drinking (see page 582 on the limits of self-control in a behavioral paradigm). In other words, the challenge seems not so much to discover the means necessary to control drinking as it is to get the alcoholic to employ these tools without constant external supervision and control. There is evidence for the general effectiveness of this approach (Hester & Miller, 1989), some of it in the context of controlled drinking programs, to which we turn now.

Controlled Drinking

Until recently it was generally agreed that alcoholics had to abstain completely if they were to be cured,[9] for they were said to have no control over their imbibing once they had taken that first drink. Although this continues to be the abiding belief of Alcoholics Anonymous, the research mentioned earlier called this assumption into question: drinkers' *beliefs* about themselves and alcohol may be as important as the physiological addiction to the drug itself. Indeed, considering the difficulty in our society of avoiding alcohol altogether, it may even be *preferable* to teach the problem drinker to imbibe with moderation. A drinker's self-esteem will certainly benefit from being able to control a problem and from feeling in charge of his or her life.

Controlled drinking refers to a pattern of alcohol consumption that is moderate and avoids the extremes of total abstinence and inebriation. During early controlled drinking programs, outpatients were allowed to drink to a moderate level of intoxication and blood alcohol. They were then informed if the level of blood alcohol rose above a certain percent (Lovibond & Caddy, 1970). Thereafter when they drank, they were supposedly able to keep the blood level of alcohol low.

Findings of one well-known treatment program suggest that at least some alcoholics can learn to control their drinking and improve other aspects of their lives as well (Sobell & Sobell, 1976, 1978). Alcoholics attempting to control their drinking were given shocks when they chose straight liquor rather than mixed drinks, gulped their drinks down too fast, or took large swallows rather than sips. They were also given problem-solving and assertiveness training, watched videotapes of themselves inebriated, and identifed the situations precipitating their drinking so that they could settle on a less self-destructive course of action. Their improvement was greater than that of alcoholics who tried for total abstinence and who were given shocks for any drinking at all.

In contemporary controlled drinking treatment programs, patients are taught other ways of responding to situations that might lead to excessive drinking. Learning to resist social pressures to drink: assertiveness, relaxation, and stress management training, sometimes including biofeedback and meditation; and exercise and better diets all help bolster them. They are also taught that a lapse will not inevitably precipitate a total relapse and should be regarded as a learning experience (Marlatt & Gordon 1985). Sources of stress in their work, family, and relationships are examined. To be able to control their drinking, they must become active and responsible in anticipating and resisting situations that might tempt excesses (Marlatt, 1983, Sobell et al., 1990).

The trend toward controlled drinking, however, has not gone unchallenged. An attack against the early work of the Sobells was launched by Pendery, Maltzman, and West (1982), who argued that some of the patients believed to have been drinking moderately had in fact reverted to uncontrolled and self-destructive drinking. Groups like AA also object to moderation in drinking as a sensible treatment goal.

A Rand Corporation study (Armor, Polich, and Stambul, 1976, 1978) offered a way to resolve the controversy by suggesting that abstinence is a better goal for older, more addicted drinkers, while moderation is viable for younger, less dependent drinkers. Findings published in the late 1980s of well-controlled studies that had at least a twelve-month follow-up indicated that controlled drinking is often a viable outcome even when the original goal was abstinence. Success at controlled drinking is especially associated with younger age and lighter drinking, as suggested by the Rand study (see reviews by Miller & Hester, 1986a, and by Sobell, Toneato, & Sobell, 1990, of studies other than their own). The patient's ability to choose his or her own goals may also improve outcome (Sanchez-Craig & Wilkinson, 1987).

The abstinence versus controlled drinking issue is controversial, for it pits influential forces, such as AA, who uphold abstinence as the *only* proper goal for problem drinkers, against more recent workers, such as the Sobells and those adopting their general approach, who have shown that moderation can work for many alcoholics, even those with serious drinking problems. If the therapeutic means of achieving the goal of moderate drinking are available—and research strongly suggests that they are—then controlled drinking may be a more realistic goal even for an addicted alcoholic. As of this writing, controlled drinking is much more widely accepted in Canada and Europe than it is in the United States.

Clinical Considerations

A general problem with attempts to treat alcoholism has been the therapist's often unstated assumption

[9]It is widely believed that alcoholics are in fact never really cured, rather, that they can be in remission and must constantly fight the temptation to drink to excess.

that all people who drink to excess do so for the same reasons. Thus an analyst may assume that problem drinkers are trying to escape from intolerable feelings of dependency. A humanistic theorist may hold that the excessive drinker escapes into the haze of alcohol because he or she lacks courage to face problems and deal with them in an open, direct fashion (see Chapter 18). A behavior therapist favoring aversive treatment believes that reducing the attraction alcohol or its taste has for drinkers will help them abstain. As we might expect, excessive drinking is a complex human problem, and it may be too simple to assume that all people drink for the same reason (Lazarus, 1965). A more sophisticated and comprehensive clinical assessment considers the place that drinking occupies in the person's life (Tucker et al., 1992). A woman in a desperately unhappy marriage, with meaningless time on her hands now that her children are in school and no longer need her constant attention, may seek the numbing effects of alcohol just to help the time pass and to avoid facing her life dilemmas. Making the taste of alcohol unpleasant for this patient by pairing it with shock or an emetic seems neither sensible nor adequate. The therapist should concentrate on the marital and family problems and try to reduce the psychological pain that permeates her existence. She will also need help in tolerating the withdrawal symptoms that come with reduced consumption. Without alcohol as a reliable anesthetic, she will need to mobilize other resources to confront her hitherto avoided problems. Social-skills training may help her to do so.

In addition, alcoholism is sometimes associated with other mental disorders, in particular mood disorders and psychopathy (Goodwin, 1982). The clinician must conduct a broad-spectrum assessment of the patient's problem, for if heavy drinking stems from the desperation of deep depression, a regimen of Antabuse or any other treatment focused only on alcohol is unlikely to be of lasting value.

Concerted research attention has yet to be focused on treating polysubstance abuse (Sobell et al., 1990). It is known, for example, that up to 95 percent of problem drinkers also smoke cigarettes regularly, and are probably addicted, therefore, to both alcohol and nicotine (Istvan & Matarrazo, 1984). Should a therapist try to wean an alcoholic from both alcohol and cigarettes simultaneously or sequentially (Kozlowski et al., 1989)? Should no attempt at all be made to discourage the use of both drugs, on the assumption that the patient somehow needs to be reliant on at least one of them? Or should, in fact, both dependencies be treated, on the assumption that cigarettes have become so closely associated with drinking that an alcoholic trying to remain dry will be drawn to drinking if he or she smokes? These are important and unanswered questions.

Even with the many treatment programs to help alcoholics live without their drug, it has been estimated that no more than 10 percent of alcoholics are ever in professional treatment and upwards of 40 percent cure themselves. How does such spontaneous recovery take place? Among the apparent factors are new marriage, new job, religious or spiritual experience or conversion, near-fatal auto accident while driving drunk, or being shaken by a serious illness. What is not clear is why some people can stop drinking after a serious crisis while others react by seeking the solace of the bottle (Valliant, 1983).

It seems unlikely that a single event, even a dramatic one, can bring about the kind of profound changes necessary to wean a person from an addiction. It is more likely that successful abstinence, whether from treatment or not, relies on a confluence of many life events and forces that can support the recovering alcoholic's efforts to lead a life without substance abuse. Whatever combination of factors helps alcoholics become abstinent or controlled drinkers, what seems important is *social support* for their efforts, from family, friends, work, or self-help groups such as AA (McCrady, 1985).

Therapy for the Use of Illicit Drugs

Some of what we have just reviewed for the treatment of alcoholism is relevant also to the treatment of those addicted to illegal drugs. We focus here on issues and data that have special relevance for those who abuse illicit drugs.

Central to the treatment of those who use illegal drugs is detoxification, withdrawal from the drug itself. Heroin withdrawal reactions range from relatively mild bouts of anxiety, nausea, and restlessness for several days, to more severe and frightening bouts of delirium and apparent madness, depending primarily on the purity of the heroin that the individual has been using. Someone high on amphetamines can be brought down by appropriate dosages of one of the phenothiazines, a class of drugs more commonly used to treat schizophrenics (see page 414), although it is important to remember that the speed freak may also have been using other drugs in conjunction with amphetamines. Withdrawal reactions from barbiturates, as already noted, are especially severe, even life-threatening; they begin about twenty-four hours after the last dose and reach their maximum two or three days later. They usually abate by the end of the first week, but they may last a month if doses have been large. Withdrawal from these drugs is best done gradually, not cold turkey,[10] and should take place under close medical supervision (Honigfeld & Howard, 1978).

Detoxification is but the first way in which therapists try to help an addict or drug abuser, and perhaps ironically it is the easiest part of the rehabilitation process. Finding a way to enable the drug user to function without drugs is an arduous task that promises more disappointment and sadness than success for both helper and client. Nonetheless, a great number of efforts are made, many of them financed heavily by federal and state governments.

Biological Treatments

Two widely used drug therapy programs for heroin addiction are the administration of **heroin substitutes**, narcotics that can replace the body's craving for heroin, and of **heroin antagonists**, drugs that prevent the user from experiencing the heroin high. The first category includes **methadone** and methadyl acetate, both synthetic narcotics. Originally developed by Dole and Nyswander (1966), these agents are designed to take the place of heroin. Since they are themselves narcotics, successful treatment merely converts the heroin addict into a methadone addict. This conversion occurs because methadone is **cross-dependent** with heroin; that is, by acting on the same central nervous-system receptors, it becomes a substitute for the original dependency. Abrupt discontinuation of methadone results in its own pattern of withdrawal reactions, which are not as severe as those of heroin, hence its potential therapeutic properties for weaning the addict altogether from drug dependence (Jaffe, 1985). The addict must come to a clinic and swallow the drug in the presence of a staff member, once a day for methadone and three times a week for methadyl acetate. Indeed, many methadone users manage to hold jobs, commit no crimes, and stay away from other illicit drugs (Cooper et al., 1983), but many others do not. Some abuse alcohol.

[10]This expression comes from the goose bumps that commonly appear during abrupt withdrawal from opiates: the skin of the person resembles that of a plucked turkey (Jaffe, 1985).

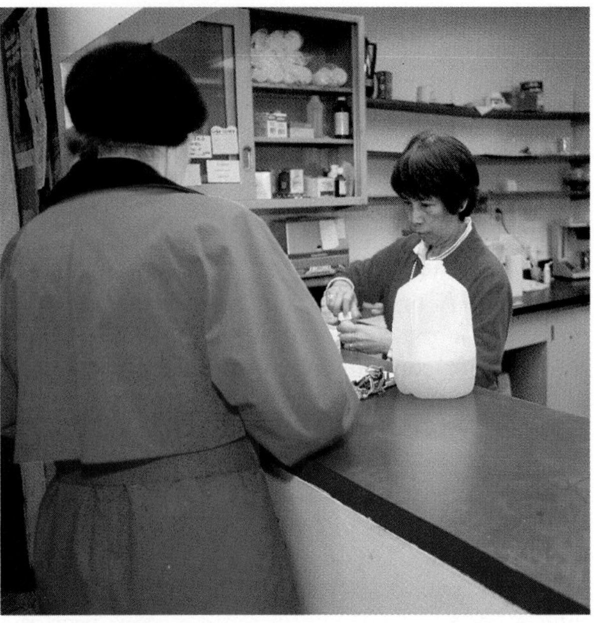

Methadone is a synthetic narcotic substitute. Former heroin addicts come to clinics each day and swallow their dose.

Clearly, preexisting behavioral patterns and life circumstances play a role in how a given individual will react to methadone treatment. Moreover, since methadone does not give the addict a euphoric high, many will return to heroin if it becomes available to them. In addition, when methadone is injected, rather than taken orally as it is supposed to be, its effects on some addicts are similar to those of heroin (Honigfeld & Howard, 1978). In this era of AIDS and the transmission of the human immunodeficiency virus through shared needles (page 383), the fact that methadone *can* be swallowed is a big advantage. Not surprisingly, an illegal market in methadone has developed, which would seem to be defeating the purpose of its use. Finally, a great number of people drop out from methadone programs, in part because of side effects, such as insomnia, constipation, excessive sweating, and diminished sexual function.

Cyclazocine and naloxone are heroin antagonists. After being gradually weaned from heroin, addicts receive increasing dosages of one of these drugs, which prevents them from experiencing any high should they later take heroin. The drugs have great affinity for the receptors that heroin usually binds to. Their molecules occupy the receptors, without stimulating them, and heroin molecules have no place to go. The antagonist, then, changes the whole nature of heroin; it simply will not produce the euphoric effect that the addict seeks. As with methadone, however, addicts must make frequent and regular visits to a clinic, which requires motivation and responsibility on their part. In addition, addicts do not lose the actual craving for heroin for some time. Thus patient compliance is very poor with opiate antagonists (Ginzburg, 1986).

The societal need to address opiate dependence has been accentuated in recent years by the AIDS epidemic. So serious is the problem that proposals have been made to provide addicts with free sterile needles without attempting to influence them to stay off the drug.

As mentioned earlier, cocaine is now viewed as a physically addicting drug. One consequence of this is a search for drugs that will ease the symptoms of withdrawal and perhaps also attack the physical basis of the addiction. While some favorable results were reported with the antidepressants imipramine (Tennant & Ranson, 1982) and desipramine (Gawin et al., 1989), the findings from two more recent and better controlled studies were decidedly less positive. In two similarly conducted double-blind experiments, use of desipramine by cocaine abusers did not lead to differential use of cocaine as compared to a placebo at the end of 8 weeks (Kosten et al., 1992) and was significantly *worse* than that of placebo subjects at three- and six-month follow-up after a 12 week treatment period (Arndt et al., 1992). Focus Box 11.6 discusses the utility of **clonidine**, an antihypertensive medication, in easing withdrawal in a variety of addicting drugs including cocaine. Bromocriptine shows some promise in reducing craving, perhaps by reversing the depletion of dopamine that is believed to underlie cocaine's addicting properties (Dackis & Gold, 1986; Moss, 1990).

Psychological Treatments

Drug abuse cannot be dealt with solely by some form of chemotherapy, and it has been suggested that pharmacological treatment should be resorted to only if psychosocial efforts have failed (Peachey, 1986). People turn to drugs for many reasons, and even though in most instances drug-use is controlled primarily by a physical addiction, the entire pattern of their existence is bound to be influenced by the drug and must therefore command the attention of whoever would hope to remove the drug from their lives. The difficulty of maintaining abstinence is attributable in a major way to environmental stimuli that can influence the recovering addict. The presence of needles, neighborhoods, and others with whom a person used to take drugs can readily become secondary reinforcers, thereby eliciting a craving for the substance (Wikler, 1980). Alcoholics and cigarette smokers have similar experiences.

Drug abuse is treated in the consulting rooms of psychiatrists, psychologists, and other mental health workers. The several kinds of psychotherapy are applied to drug use disorders as they are to the other human maladjustments. Little can be said, however, about the relative efficacy of psychoanalytic and humanistic therapies in helping people break their dependence on drugs (Liskow, 1982). What little evidence there is for behavioral approaches indicates some reduction in drug use when contingency management (operant) procedures are in effect but poor maintenance during follow-up periods. Somewhat better results are emerging with cognitive-behavioral approaches (Sobell et al., 1990).

Self-help residential homes or communes, with which most readers are familiar, are the most widespread psychological approach to dealing with heroin addiction and other drug abuse. Modeled after Synanon, a therapeutic community of former drug addicts founded by Charles Dederich in Santa Monica, California, in 1958, these residences are designed to restructure radically the addict's outlook on life so that illicit drugs no longer have a place. Daytop Village, Phoenix House, Odyssey House, and other drug rehabilitation homes share the following features.

1. A total environment in which drugs are not available and continuing support is offered to ease the transition from regular drug use to a drug-free existence.
2. The presence of often charismatic role models, former addicts who appear to be meeting life's challenges without drugs.
3. Direct, often brutal confrontation in group therapy, in which addicts are goaded into accepting

Many contemporary drug rehabilitation centers, like Daytop Village shown here, are modeled after Synanon. A confrontational style of group therapy is one of the components of treatment.

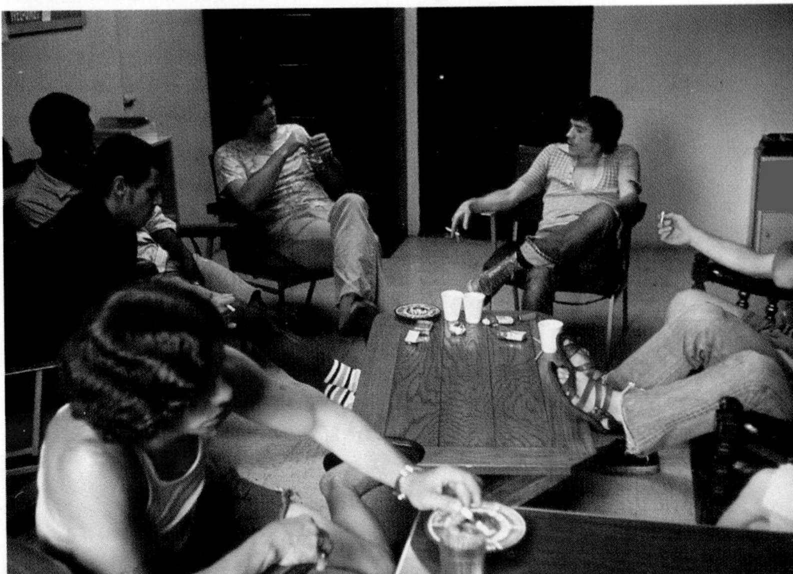

FOCUS 11.6 • Clonidine and Drug Withdrawal

A promising development in the treatment of substance dependence is the use of clonidine, an antihypertensive drug that appears to ease the withdrawal symptoms from alcohol, opiates, cocaine, and nicotine. An early report by Bjorkqvist (1975) with alcoholics was followed by a brief account on opiates by Gold, Redmond, and Kleber in 1978, who gave clonidine to five former morphine addicts who had become addicted to methadone. The clonidine alleviated the withdrawal symptoms from methadone abstention and also helped actually wean them from the methadone. These results were subsequently replicated (e.g., Charney, Heninger, & Kleber, 1986; Gold, Pottash, Sweeney, & Kleber, 1980; Washton & Resnick, 1980) and confirmed by controlled studies (Wilkins, Jenkins, & Steiner, 1983; Baumgartner & Rowen, 1987), though some users have found that the effects of clonidine are not quite so good as those of morphine itself (Jasinski, Johnson, & Kocher, 1985).

Why did workers try this drug at all? Previous research by Gold et al. (1978) with monkeys had shown that stimulating the locus coeruleus, a nucleus in the brain that produces most of the norepinephrine, mimicked the effects of withdrawal from morphine. It is known that both morphine and clonidine also reduce noradrenergic activity. Since morphine reduces withdrawal from itself (obviously), the investigators reasoned that perhaps clonidine could, too, without the negative addicting effects of morphine.

responsibility for their problems and for their drug habits, and are urged to take charge of their lives.

4. A setting in which addicts are respected as human beings rather than stigmatized as failures or criminals.
5. Separation of addicts from previous social contacts, on the assumption that these relationships have been instrumental in fostering the addictive life-style.

There are several obstacles to evaluating the efficacy of residential drug treatment programs. First, since entrance is voluntary, only a small minority of dependent users enter such settings (Jaffe, 1985). Furthermore, because the drop-out rate is high, those who remain cannot be regarded as representative of the population of people addicted to illicit drugs. Their motivation to go straight is probably much higher than average: therefore any improvement they might make will in part reflect their uncommon desire to rid themselves of their habit, rather than the specific qualities of the treatment program. Moreover, the role of mental health professionals is either nonexistent or marginal because of an explicit antagonism toward shrinks and social workers. Further, adequately designed research on the outcomes of these programs has not been undertaken. Such self-regulating residential communities, however, may help a large number of those who stay in them for a year or so (Jaffe, 1985).

Prevention

It is generally acknowledged that by far the best way to deal with drug abuse is to *prevent* it in the first place. In recent years we have seen well-known sports and entertainment figures urge audiences not to experiment with illicit drugs, especially cocaine. The message in the 1960s and the 1970s was often that certain drugs—especially the psychedelics—would help people realize their potential or at least provide an escape from the humdrum and the stressful. The message in the 1990s, however, is that mind-altering drugs interfere with psychological functioning and the achievement of one's personal best and that, above all, these drugs are harmful to the body and can even cause unexpected death. "Just say no" has replaced "Turn on, tune in, drop out." Also better appreciated are the relationships among drug usage patterns. As mentioned earlier, it now appears that marijuana may be one factor in subsequent more serious drug abuse, a hypothesis that in the 1960s was ridiculed by young people for whom marijuana was as much a form of political and social protest as a mind-altering excursion.

Adequate prevention requires more knowledge of the developmental paths to drug use. For example, are youngsters from particular family and socioeconomic backgrounds at risk for initiation into the use of a drug that, once taken, quickly fosters dependency? Does the early use of tobacco predis-

According to Glassman et al. (1988), the fact that clonidine has been found to reduce withdrawal discomfort among opiate, alcohol, and nicotine addicts and the fact that clonidine is known to reduce noradrenergic activity in the brain lend support to the physiological hypothesis that high levels of noradrenergic activity in the locus coeruleus underlie withdrawal from addicting drugs. Future research will have to examine these effects more closely, especially their interactions with psychosocial interventions that have to be included once the acute withdrawal period is past. The hope is that by combining the interventions, the former addict will be less likely to resume his or her reliance on harmful drugs to escape from life stress.

Indeed, emergent data and theorizing about the biological substrates of positive and negative reinforcement suggest that treatment for addicting drugs must attend not only to easing the pain of withdrawal, as clonidine does, but also to the positive reinforcing effects of the drug (Wise, 1987). These two effects seem to be subserved by different parts of the brain, consistent with the well-known clinical observation that a detoxified addict—one who has gotten past withdrawal—can still have a positive craving for the particular drug based on memories of its initially positive reinforcing effects. Arguing from animal and biological research, Wise proposes that treatment programs must attend to the pleasures that can be achieved with use of a drug and not only to detoxification. Nondrug substitutes for the positive rewards of drugs such as cocaine and heroin have to be found.

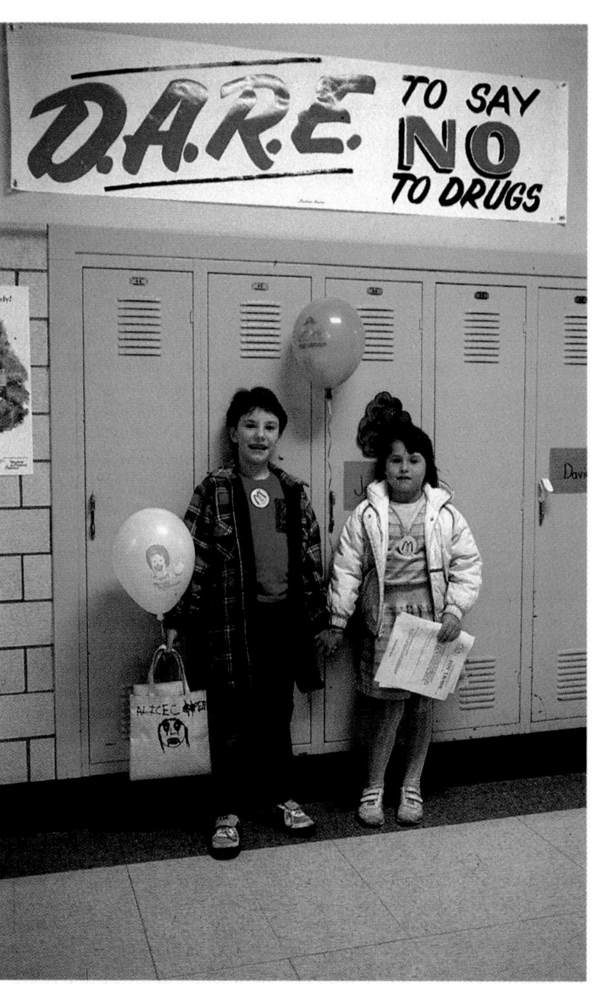

pose to the snorting of cocaine or the smoking of marijuana? Are young people who have low self-esteem or who show conduct disorder problems at risk for drug abuse? Such information will not only help clinical researchers target subgroups toward whom preventive efforts can be most fruitfully directed but can also shed light on the whys and hows of people's initiation into and continuation of substance abuse and dependence.

Treatment and Prevention of Cigarette Smoking

Of the more than forty million smokers who have quit since 1964, it is believed that 90 percent did so without professional help (National Cancer Institute, 1977; U. S. Department of Health and Human Services, 1982, 1989). Each year more than 30 percent of cigarette smokers try to quit with minimal outside assistance, but fewer than 10 percent succeed even in the short run (Fiore et al., 1990). Research is under way on smokers' use of self-help

In the 1980s and 1990s, several programs have appeared that try to prevent substance abuse. They are typically directed at elementary school children and provide information on the harmful effects of drugs.

methods outside the framework of formal smoking-cessation programs (Orleans et al., 1991).

Some smokers attend smoking clinics or consult with professionals for specialized smoking reduction programs. The American Cancer Society, the American Lung Association, and the Church of the Seventh Day Adventists have been especially active in offering programs to help people stop smoking. And, as mentioned earlier, more and more nonsmokers object to people smoking in restaurants, trains, airplanes, and public buildings. The social context, then, provides more incentive and support to stop smoking than existed in 1964, when the surgeon general first warned of the serious health hazards associated with cigarette smoking. Indeed, it is estimated that 2.1 million smoking related deaths will be postponed or avoided between 1986 and the year 2000 owing to the publicity from the surgeon general's reports and associated programs to discourage the habit (Foreyt, 1990). Even so, it is estimated that not more than half of those who go through smoking cessation programs succeed in abstaining by the time the program is over; and only about one-third of those who have succeeded in the short term actually remain away from cigarettes after a year (Hunt & Bespalec, 1974; Schwartz, 1987).

Psychological Treatments

Many efforts have been made within behavioral and cognitive-behavioral frameworks to reduce or eliminate cigarette smoking. Although short-term results are often very encouraging—some programs (e.g., Etringer, Gregory, & Lando, 1984) report as many as 95 percent of smokers abstinent by the end of treatment—longer term results are more modest. Regardless of how well things look when an intervention ends, the overwhelming majority of smokers return to their drug dependence within a year. This evidence does not deny the fact that a substantial minority of smokers can be helped; as with other efforts to change behavior, though, the task is not an easy one.

Many techniques have been tried. The idea behind all of them is to make smoking unpleasant, even nauseating. For a while in the 1970s, there was considerable interest in *rapid-smoking treatment*, in which a smoker sits in a poorly ventilated room and puffs much faster than normal, perhaps as often as every six seconds (e.g., Lando, 1977). Newer variations include *rapid puffing* (rapid smoking without inhaling), *focused smoking* (in which the person smokes for a long period of time but at a normal rate), and *smoke holding* (retaining smoke in the mouth for several minutes but without inhaling). Although such treatments reduce smoking and foster abstinence more than no-treatment control conditions, they usually do not differ from each other or from other credible interventions and, as noted, show high rates of relapse at follow-ups of several months to a year (Schwartz, 1987; Sobell et al., 1990).

Cognitively oriented investigators have tried to encourage more control in the smoker with treatments that have people develop and utilize various coping skills, such as relaxation and positive self-talk, when confronted with tempting situations, for example, following a meal or sitting down to read a book. Results here are not very promising (Schwartz, 1987).

Behavioral treatments have thus far focused on the overt act of smoking. Given the addictive nature of the smoking habit, the disappointing results are not surprising. Until more is known of how to eliminate the addiction or at least how ex-smokers might learn to tolerate withdrawal symptoms for long periods of time, it is unrealistic to expect great advances in treatment.

Probably the most widespread intervention is advice or direction from a physician to stop smoking. Each year millions of smokers are told by their doctors to stop smoking—because of hypertension, heart disease, lung disease, diabetes, or on general grounds of preserving or improving health. At the same time it is doubtful that this medical advice does much good (Mothersill, McDowell, & Rosser, 1988)! Although there is some evidence that a physician's advice can get some people to stop smoking, at least for a while, especially when this advice is combined with chewing nicotine gum (Russell, Merriman, Stapleton, & Taylor, 1983), much more needs to be learned about the nature of the advice, the manner in which it is given, its timing, and other factors that must surely play a role in whether an addicted individual is prepared and able to alter his or her behavior primarily on a physician's say-so.

As in the other addictions, one smoker may also have trouble quitting for psychological reasons, and they may be quite different from the reasons that keep another smoker puffing away. When two such smokers are exposed to the same treatment package, it is unlikely to help both. Unfortunately, in their zeal to make an impact on the smoking problem, workers have for many years put smokers in standardized programs. Since people probably have trouble quitting for many different reasons, there will have to be diverse methods to help them.

Biological Treatments

We examine next two biological treatments aimed at satisfying the smoker's need for nicotine without the deleterious effects of smoking, nicotine gum, and nicotine patches.

Nicotine Gum

Each of the thousands of hits that a smoker takes each day during the consumption of a pack or two of cigarettes delivers nicotine to the brain in seven seconds. Available in the United States since 1984 by doctor's prescription, gum containing nicotine may help smokers endure the nicotine withdrawal that accompanies any effort to stop smoking. The nicotine in gum is absorbed much more slowly and steadily. The rationale is that providing the addicting drug by gum will help unlink the act of smoking from the nicotine hit. At the same time cessation of smoking is disconnected from the nicotine fit, or withdrawal. The long-term goal, of course, is for the former smoker to be able to cut back on the use of the gum as well, eventually eliminating reliance on nicotine altogether.

There is evidence, however, that ex-smokers can become dependent on this gum. Moreover, in doses that deliver an amount of nicotine equivalent to smoking one cigarette an hour, the occurrence of cardiovascular changes, such as increased blood pressure, can be dangerous to people with cardiovascular diseases. Even so, some experts believe that even prolonged continued use of the gum is healthier than obtaining nicotine by smoking, because at least the poisons in the smoke are avoided. Some well-controlled double-blind studies suggest that nicotine gum is useful in a limited way (Jarvis et al., 1982; Jarvik et al., 1983), especially among heavier smokers (Jarvik & Schneider, 1984).

However, nicotine gum does not duplicate the effects of an inhaled cigarette. It does not produce the peak in plasma nicotine produced by an average cigarette, nor does it raise nicotine blood levels as high (Russell, Feyerabend, & Cole, 1976). These differences probably account for the limited (though significant) benefits of the gum in reducing withdrawal once a smoker abstains. Smokers prefer to get their nicotine from a cigarette! On the other hand, these differences are an integral part of the process of weaning the nicotine addict from the drug.

Research indicates that clinic support is important. This entails monitoring the use of the gum for the first week, daily encouragement, and discussion of coping skills. The gum must be chewed slowly as well as intermittently and then discarded after about twenty minutes: enough pieces must be chewed to provide relief from withdrawal, as many as fifteen pieces a day, and this regimen may last for several months, with a gradual tapering; and it should be kept on hand for emergencies (Schneider, 1987). Data do point clearly to the gum's usefulness in reducing withdrawal symptoms in the first few crucial days of abstinence (Schneider & Jarvik, 1984), but something other than replacement of cigarette nicotine is clearly necessary to keep people from later smoking.

The best results are found when the gum is combined with a behaviorally oriented treatment (Hall et al., 1985; Killen, Maccoby, & Taylor, 1984; Killen et al., 1990). When nicotine gum was prescribed as part of a physician's *unsolicited* advice to stop smoking, it had no measurable effect (Crofton et al., 1983; Hughes et al, 1989).

Nicotine Patches

In December 1991 we began to see the active marketing of nicotine patches, a transdermal nicotine delivery system that slowly and steadily releases the drug into the bloodstream and thence to the brain through a polyethylene patch taped to the arm. An advantage of this method over nicotine gum is that the person need only apply a patch each day and not remove it, which ought to make compliance easier. A program of treatment usually lasts ten to twelve weeks, with smaller and smaller patches used as treatment progresses. A caution is that a person who continues smoking while wearing the patch risks increasing the amount of nicotine in the body to dangerous levels.

Preliminary evidence suggests that the nicotine patch is superior to the use of a placebo patch in terms of abstinence as well as subjective craving (Abelin, Buehler, et al., 1989; Abelin, Ehrsam, et al., 1989; Mueller et al., 1990). However, as with nicotine gum, the patch is not a panacea; abstinence rates are still under 40 percent even right after the termination of treatment, and at nine-month follow-ups, drug–placebo differences disappear. The manufacturers themselves state that the patch is to be used only as part of a psychological smoking-cessation program and then for not more than three months at a time. The manufacturers offer psychological support via free 800 telephone numbers.

Like nicotine gum, the patch is probably helpful for some smokers in temporarily easing the discomfort from smoking cessation or tapering off; but, as is the case for most other drugs that have behavioral effects, the person's commitment, will, and use of behavior-change procedures are necessary for breaking one of the most stubborn of addictions.

Relapse Prevention

Since most smokers relapse within a year of stopping, regardless of the means used to stop, attention needs to be given to helping ex-smokers maintain their gains. This challenge is proving difficult. Data (and common sense) tell us that ex-smokers who do not have a smoker in the home do better at follow-up than those who do (McIntyre-Kingsolver, Lichtenstein, & Mermelstein, 1986). So-called booster or maintenance sessions help, but in a very real sense they represent a continuation of treatment; when they stop, relapse is the rule (Brandon, Zelman, & Baker, 1987). What is to be appreciated, however, is that, at least in the United States, there is considerably more social support for not smoking than there was just ten years ago. Perhaps as time goes on, societal sanctions against smoking will help those who have succeeded in quitting to remain abstinent.

Another approach to the relapse problem is to study the cognitions of ex-smokers (Baer & Lichtenstein, 1988). Using the articulated thoughts paradigm (Davison et al., 1983; see page 98), Haaga (1989) found that recent ex-smokers who tended to think of smoking without prompting relapsed more readily three months later. He found also that the presence of effective cognitive coping tactics in thoughts articulated during simulated situations previously linked with smoking (feeling bad, experiencing social pressure to smoke, and drinking alcohol) was associated with better maintenance of abstinence. In another analysis of the articulated thoughts data, he discovered that subjects with moderate levels of self-efficacy (SE, the belief that they could abstain; Bandura, 1977) for returning to abstinence after a lapse were more likely to be abstinent months later than those with high or low levels of self-efficacy in their articulated thoughts (Haaga & Stewart, 1992). Using a questionnaire measure of self-efficacy, he found that self-efficacy in their most difficult challenge situation—their Achilles' heel—was a good predictor of abstinence a year later (Haaga, 1990). What these and related studies indicate is that the prediction of maintenance or relapse in smoking cessation is enhanced by measuring the cognitions of ex-smokers. Such information may help therapists design programs that will improve the ability of a person to remain a nonsmoker.

Smoking Prevention Programs

In light of the difficulties in stopping smoking once the habit and addiction are established, *prevention* of smoking, developing ways of discouraging young people even from experimenting with tobacco, has become a top priority among health researchers, with encouragement from the surgeon general. What measures hold promise for persuading young people to resist smoking? Although many now apparently do fear disastrous consequences later in life and resist cigarettes, both young and old smokers seem able to discount the possibility that they are at higher risk of coronary heart disease or lung cancer—the "It won't happen to me" syndrome. Indeed, although heavy smokers are eleven times as likely as nonsmokers to develop lung cancer, large numbers of heavy smokers live longer and healthier lives than do nonsmokers. In addition, it is the nature of young people to have a limited time perspective. Teenagers would seem to be more concerned with next Saturday evening's festivities or Friday's math exam than with their life situation at age sixty.

Recent years have seen scores of school-based programs aimed at preventing the onset of tobacco use by young people. A review of 143 such programs indicates marked success in delaying the onset of smoking (Tobler, 1986). Several components are found in such efforts (Hansen et al., 1988):

1. **Peer Pressure Resistance Training.** Instruction is given about the nature of peer pressure and ways to say no. Evans and his co-workers (1981), for example, developed films that portray teenagers resisting appeals from friends to try smoking. The idea is to teach assertive ways to refuse invitations to smoke, not an easy matter for young people, for whom peer approval and acceptance are acutely important. Schinke and Gilchrist (1985) taught resistance strategies to sixth-graders and found less smoking two years later than among a control group who received only attention and information about the harmful effects of smoking. Interestingly, refusal-skills training is much more effective for girls than for boys (Graham et al., 1990).
2. **Correction of Normative Expectations.** Since many young people believe that cigarette smoking is more prevalent (and by implication, more okay) than it actually is, some programs provide factual information about true prevalence rates. Establishing conservative norms—that it is *not* okay to smoke cigarettes (or drink alcohol or use marijuana)—appears to be a powerful tool in discouraging adolescents from indulg-

ing, and is perhaps significantly more effective than resistance training (Hansen & Graham, 1991).

3. **Inoculation against Mass Media Messages.** Some programs try to counter the positive images of smokers put forth in the media, for example, the Joe Camel ads mentioned earlier. For several years there have been no cigarette ads on television or radio, and print ads have to contain explicit warnings about the dangers of smoking.
4. **Information about Parental and Other Adult Influences.** Since it is known that parental smoking is strongly correlated with (and most probably contributes to) smoking by their children, some programs point out this fact and argue that this aspect of one's parents' behavior does not have to be imitated.
5. **Peer Leadership.** Most programs involve peers of recognized status to enhance the impact of the nonsmoking messages being conveyed.
6. **Affective Education, Self-Image Enhancement.** A number of programs focus on the idea that intrapsychic factors, such as poor self-image and inability to cope with stress, underlie the onset of smoking in young people. A careful comparison of this approach with a program that emphasized social-pressure resistance training combined with most of points 1 through 5 found that it was far less effective in preventing the use of tobacco as well as alcohol and marijuana (Hansen et al., 1988). In fact, there were indications that the affective education program actually *increased* drug use over a period of three years, perhaps by unintentionally suggesting drug experimentation to deal with life stress.
7. **Other Components.** Additional features of preventive programs include information about the harmful effects of smoking (a common element in adult smoking-cessation programs) and efforts to produce a public commitment not to smoke, for example, making a commitment on videotape.

An interesting perspective on discouraging children and preadolescents from smoking can be found in the controversy about bubble gum and candy made to resemble cigarettes. Some of today's fake cigarettes even emit puffs of sugar powder, simulating smoke. More recently available is shredded bubble gum packaged in pouches, like chewing tobacco. Should these products be available for sale to children?

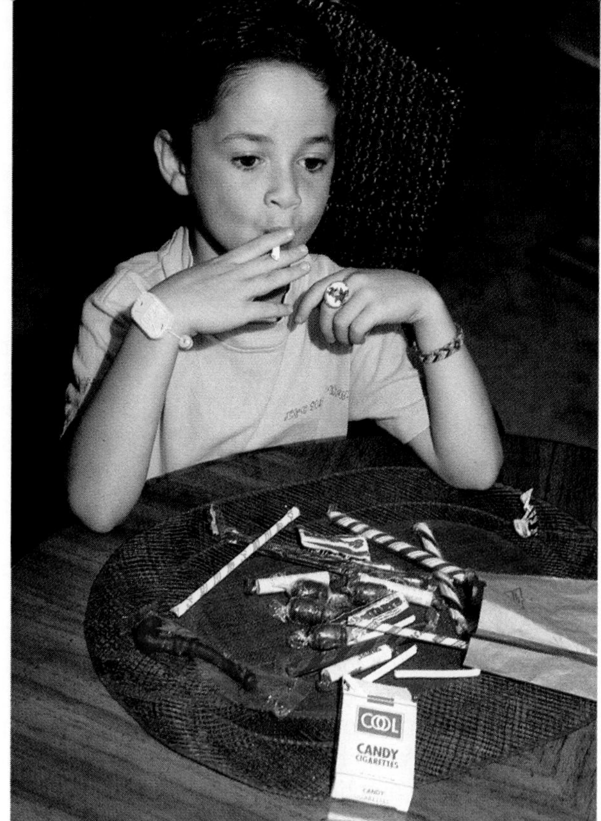

A controversy surrounds the sale of candy cigarettes. Some groups believe that the candies promote the later use of real tobacco products. The other side counters with the claim that any legislation would be an infringement on a harmless pleasure.

Many national health organizations, such as the American Cancer Society and the American Lung Association, support legislation to ban sales to children. Such a ban would almost certainly discourage manufacture of these products, for it is doubtful that sales would be strong enough to warrant their continued manufacture if their primary market, children, were removed.[11] Such efforts are all part of campaigns to prevent young people from starting an addiction that we have seen is very hard to break, but advocates of these children's playthings argue against Big Brotherism and a law that would deprive children of harmless enjoyment and access to materials that, they assert, might even discourage tobacco use. (It is unclear to us, however, how this would come about—do advocates imply that children who use these candy or gum products will continue to use them as adults instead of smoking real cigarettes?) Besides, supporters of the candy and gum "tobacco" products say, "the substances they are designed to emulate are themselves not illegal." Good data are less available than passionately held opinions (Hurst, 1992).

[11]A surreal scenario occurs to us. In much the same way that minors sometimes arrange for someone with the proper ID card to purchase alcohol for them, consider the possibility of fifth-graders asking their older siblings to buy them a package of bubble gum cigarettes!

SUMMARY

Using substances to alter mood and consciousness is virtually a human characteristic, and so also is the tendency to abuse them. DSM-IV distinguishes between substance dependence and substance abuse. Dependence refers to excessive use of the substance and serious impairments due to its use. Some workers equate it with physical addiction, especially when tolerance and withdrawal are present. Substance abuse is a less severe version of dependence.

Alcohol has a variety of short-term and long-term effects on human beings, and many are tragic in nature, ranging from poor judgment and motor coordination and their dire consequences for the alcoholic and society, to addiction, which makes an ordinary, productive life impossible and is extremely difficult to overcome. As with other addicting drugs, people come to rely on alcohol less for how good it makes them feel than for an escape from feeling bad.

Less prevalent but more notorious, perhaps because of their illegality, are the narcotic heroin and the barbiturates, such as Seconal, which are sedatives, and the amphetamines and cocaine, which are stimulants; all are addicting, most of all cocaine. Heroin has been of special concern in recent years because stronger varieties have become available. Barbiturates have for some time been implicated in both intentional and accidental suicides; they are especially lethal when alcohol is taken at the same time. Cocaine use has risen dramatically in recent years. Its extremely high cost and elaborate attendant paraphernalia made it a rather trendy drug in some circles, but now it costs somewhat less and is used by all segments of society.

Nicotine, especially when taken into the body via the inhaled smoke from a cigarette, has worked its addictive power on humankind for centuries and, in spite of somberly phrased warnings from public health officials, continues in widespread use. Of special concern is the smoking of school-aged youngsters and teenagers. Each year the government and private individuals spend millions of dollars to dissuade people from beginning the habit or to help those already addicted to stop smoking; and each year millions of dollars are spent by the government and private individuals promoting the cultivation and sale of tobacco products. Neither the psychological-medical nor the economic-political issues have easy solutions.

Marijuana is smoked by a large number of young Americans, although its use declined in the 1980s. Arguments for deregulation of marijuana have stressed its supposed safety in comparison with the known harm caused by the habitual use of alcohol, which is a legal and integral part of our culture. But currently available evidence indicates that marijuana when used regularly is not benign. Varieties of marijuana significantly stronger than those of the early 1970s are now available. Furthermore, there is evidence that constituents in marijuana may adversely affect fertility, fetal development, heart function in people who already have coronary problems, and pulmonary function. It also appears to be addicting. Ironically, at the same time that the possible dangers of this drug began to be uncovered, marijuana was found to ease the nausea of cancer patients undergoing chemotherapy and to reduce the excessive intraocular pressure of glaucoma sufferers.

Phencyclidine, known as PCP or angel dust, is a relative newcomer on the drug abuse scene. Though it is used by very few, there is a legal and public health concern about it, for people on PCP are unpredictable and often violent and have such seriously impaired judgment that they can inadvertently kill themselves.

The hallucinogens, LSD, mescaline, and psilocybin, are taken to alter or expand consciousness. Their use reflects humankind's desires not only to escape from unpleasant realities but to explore inner space as well.

We examined a number of factors related to the etiology of substance abuse and dependence. Sociocultural variables such as attitudes toward the substance, peer pressure, and how the substance is portrayed by the media are all related to how frequently a substance is used. On a psychological level, many substances are used to alter mood (for example, reducing tension) and people with certain personality traits are especially likely to use drugs. Finally, a genetic diathesis appears to play a role in the use of some substances, particularly alcohol.

Therapies to discourage use of many of these drugs are often confrontational in nature. Residential and outpatient programs confront alcoholics and other drug addicts with the immorality or stupidity of their behavior and encourage in them a resolve to alter the mode of their lives, leaving no room for chemical crutches. Behavioral clinicians, until fairly recently, employed primarily aversive techniques with abusers of alcohol and tobacco, but they now include procedures designed to reduce anxiety and enhance social skills. Anxiety and the lack of such skills may be underlying reasons that people turn to drugs as a means of coping with life.

KEY TERMS

polysubstance abuse
substance abuse
substance dependence
addiction
tolerance
withdrawal symptoms
fetal alcohol syndrome
delirium tremens (DTs)
nicotine
marijuana
hashish
sedatives
stimulants
narcotics
opium
morphine
heroin
barbiturates
amphetamines
cocaine
LSD
hallucinogen
mescaline
psilocybin
Ecstasy
nitrous oxide
phencyclidine (PCP)
flashback
detoxification
Antabuse
covert sensitization
controlled drinking
heroin substitutes
heroin antagonists
methadone
cross-dependent
clonidine

c h a p t e r   t w e l v e

Sexual Disorders: Gender Identity Disorders and the Paraphilias

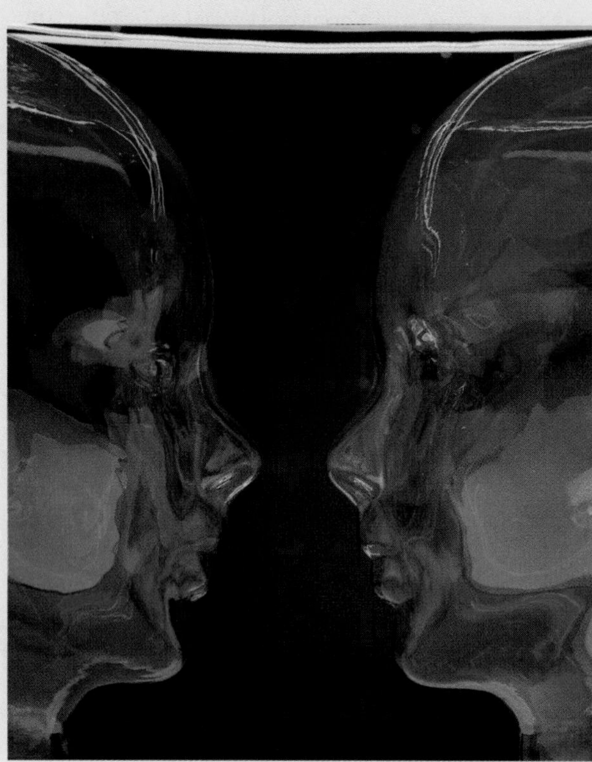

William V. is a twenty-eight-year-old computer programmer who currently lives alone. He grew up in a rural area within a conservative family with strong religious values. He has two younger brothers and an older sister. William began to masturbate at age fifteen; his first masturbatory experience took place while he watched his sister urinate in an outdoor toilet. Despite considerable feelings of guilt, he continued to masturbate two or three times a week while having voyeuristic fantasies. At the age of twenty he left home to spend two years in the navy.

On a summer evening at about 11:30 P.M., William was arrested for climbing a ladder and peeping into the bedroom of a suburban home. Just before this incident he had been drinking heavily at a cocktail lounge featuring a topless dancer. When he had left the lounge at 11:15 P.M. he had intended to return to his home. Feeling lonely and depressed, however, he had begun to drive slowly through a nearby suburban neighborhood, where he noticed a lighted upstairs window. With little premeditation, he had parked his car, erected a ladder he found lying near the house, and climbed up to peep. The householders, who were alerted by the sounds, called the police, and William was arrested. Although this was his first arrest, William had committed similar acts on two previous occasions.

The police referred William's case for immediate and mandatory psychological counseling. William described a lonely and insecure life . . . to his therapist—six months before the arrest, he had been rejected in a long-term relationship, and he had not recovered from this emotional rejection. As an unassertive and timid individual, he had responded by withdrawing from social relationships, and increasing his use of alcohol. His voyeuristic fantasies, which were present to begin with, became progressively more urgent as William's self-esteem deteriorated. His arrest had come as a great personal shock, although he recognized that his behavior was both irrational and self-destructive. (Rosen & Rosen, 1981, pp. 452–453). Reprinted by permission of McGraw-Hill Book Company.

Of all the aspects of human suffering that command the attention of psychopathologists and clinicians, few touch the lives of more people than problems involving sex. Often the problem is exacerbated by bad counsel and misinformation—such as the belief held not so long ago that masturbation should be avoided at all costs because it was immoral and might weaken the mind. This chapter and the next consider the full range of human sexual thoughts, feelings, and actions that are generally regarded as abnormal and dysfunctional and are listed in DSM-IV as **sexual and gender identity disorders** (Table 12.1).

Our study of these disorders is divided into two chapters: the present chapter examines theory and research in gender identity disorders and paraphilias, with some critical discussion of homosexuality, which, though it is no longer considered a sexual disorder in the DSM, has such a history of controversy regarding its status that it warrants some consideration here. Included also in the present chapter are incest and rape. Incest is a subcategory of pedophilia, and while rape does not appear as a separate listing in DSM-IV, it merits examination in an abnormal psychology textbook. The next chapter addresses sexual dysfunctions, disruptions in normal sexual functioning found in many people who are in otherwise reasonably sound psychological health.

Table 12.1 • Sexual and Gender Identity Disorders

A. Gender Identity Disorders
B. Paraphilias
   1. Fetishism
   2. Transvestic fetishism
   3. Pedophilia
   4. Exhibitionism
   5. Voyeurism
   6. Sexual masochism
   7. Sexual sadism
   8. Frotteurism
   9. Paraphilias not otherwise specified (e.g., coprophilia, necrophilia)
C. Sexual Dysfunctions
   1. Sexual desire disorders
      a. Hypoactive sexual desire disorder
      b. Sexual aversion disorder
   2. Sexual arousal disorders
      a. Female sexual arousal disorder
      b. Male erectile disorder
   3. Orgasm disorders
      a. Female orgasm disorder (inhibited female orgasm)
      b. Male orgasm disorder (inhibited male orgasm)
      c. Premature ejaculation
   4. Sexual pain disorders
      a. Dyspareunia
      b. Vaginismus

Source: From DSM-IV.

Gender Identity Disorders

"Are you a boy or a girl?" "Are you a man or a woman?" For virtually all people—even those with serious mental disorders such as schizophrenia—the answer to such questions is immediate and obvious. Also unequivocal is the fact that others will agree with the answer given. Our sense of ourselves as male or female, or what is called **gender identity**, is so deeply ingrained from earliest childhood that, no matter the stress suffered at one time or another, the vast majority of people are certain beyond a doubt of their gender.

Some people, however, men more often than women, feel deep within themselves from early childhood that they are of the opposite sex. The evidence of their anatomy—normal genitals and the usual secondary sex characteristics, such as beard growth for men and developed breasts for women—does not persuade them that they are what others see them to be. A male transsexual can look at himself in a mirror, see a biological man, and yet announce to himself that he is a woman. Furthermore, he will often try to convince the medical profession to bring his body in line with his gender identity; many transsexuals undergo genital surgery and hormone treatment to make their bodies assume as much as possible the anatomy of the opposite sex.

We will look first at gender identity disorder in adults, which is evident in transsexualism, then at gender identity disorder as it is first evidenced in childhood.

Transsexualism

A **transsexual** is an adult who experiences persistent discomfort with his or her sex or gender role and identifies strongly with the opposite sex to the point of believing that he or she really is the opposite sex. Such an individual often tries to pass as a member of the opposite sex and frequently desires sex-reassignment surgery. Excluded from this category are schizophrenics who on very rare occasions claim to be of the other sex, as well as hermaphrodites, individuals who have both male and female reproductive organs.

Transsexuals generally suffer from anxiety and depression, not surprising in light of their psychological predicament. A male transsexual's interest in men will be interpreted by him as a conventional heterosexual preference, given that he considers

A transsexual or person with gender identity disorder experiences great discomfort with their gender and often has sex-reassignment surgery to become as much as possible like someone of the opposite sex. The transsexual shown here was running for mayor of a town in California.

himself really a woman. Predictably, transsexuals often arouse the disapproval of others when they choose to cross-dress in clothing of the other sex. Indeed, for a man to dress as a woman is illegal in many states. Many male-to-female transsexuals who are preparing for sex-reassignment surgery carry letters from their physicians or therapists to inform police authorities that their cross-dressing is an important early aspect of treatment. Cross-dressing is less of a problem for female-to-male transsexuals because contemporary fashions allow women to wear clothing very similar to that worn by men. The prevalence rates for transsexualism are slight, one in 30,000 for males and one in 100,000 in females.

The long-standing and apparently unchangeable nature of the transsexual's incongruous gender identity has led researchers to speculate that transsexuals are hormonally different from those with normal gender identity. Perhaps a woman who believes that she is a man has an excess of androgens, such as testosterone and androsterone, hormones known to promote the development and maintenance of male secondary sex characteristics. In a review of several such investigations, Gladue (1987) found few if any differences in hormone levels among adult male transsexuals, male heterosexuals, and male homosexuals. In another survey, Meyer–

Bahlburg (1979) found the results to be equivocal: some female transsexuals have elevated levels of male hormones, but most of them do not. Differences, when they are found, are difficult to interpret. Many transsexuals use sex hormones in an effort to alter their bodies in the direction of the sex to which they believe they belong. Even though a researcher may study only transsexuals who have not taken such exogenous hormones for a few months, relatively little is known at present about the long-term effects of earlier hormonal treatment. In any event, the available data do not clearly support an explanation of transsexualism in terms of hormones. Even less conclusive is the research on possible chromosomal abnormalities, and efforts to find differences in brain structure between transsexuals and control subjects have likewise been negative (Emory et al., 1991).

Gender Identity Disorder of Childhood

We know that most transsexuals who have been studied by sex researchers report a history of profound opposite-sexed styles in childhood—femininity in boys and masculinity in girls (Green, 1969; Tsoi, 1990). An examination of **gender identity disorder of childhood** might therefore provide clues to the etiology of transsexualism. The children given this diagnosis are profoundly feminine boys and profoundly masculine girls, youngsters whose behavior, likes, and dislikes do not fit our culture's ideas of what is appropriate for the two sexes. Thus a boy may not like rough-and-tumble play, may prefer the company of little girls, dress up in women's clothing, and insist that he will grow up to be a girl. He may even claim that his penis and testes are disgusting. Many gender-disordered children harbor the belief that as they grow, their genitalia will somehow change into those of the opposite sex, a belief that can be construed as a child's version of the adult transsexual's wish for sex-reassignment surgery. The onset of the disorder is before the age of six.

The very categorization of boys and girls as having their own masculine and feminine ways is so heavily laden with value judgments and stereotyping that considering opposite behavioral patterns abnormal may seem unjustified. But some evidence suggests that these patterns can come from a physical disturbance. Human and other primate offspring of mothers who have taken sex hormones during pregnancy may frequently behave like members of the opposite sex *and* have anatomical abnormalities. For example, girls whose mothers took synthetic progestins to prevent uterine bleeding during pregnancy were found to be tomboyish during their preschool years (Ehrhardt & Money, 1967). Progestins are considered precursors of androgens, the male sex hormones. Other young tomboys also had genitalia with male characteristics (though this is quite rare), which suggests a link between the progestins taken by their mothers and male physical features (Green, 1976). Young boys whose mothers ingested female hormones when they were pregnant were found to be less athletic as young children and to engage less in rough-and-tumble play than their male peers (Yalom, Green, & Fisk, 1973). Although such children were not necessarily abnormal in their gender identity, the mother's ingestion of prenatal sex hormones did give them higher than usual levels of cross-gender interests and behavior.

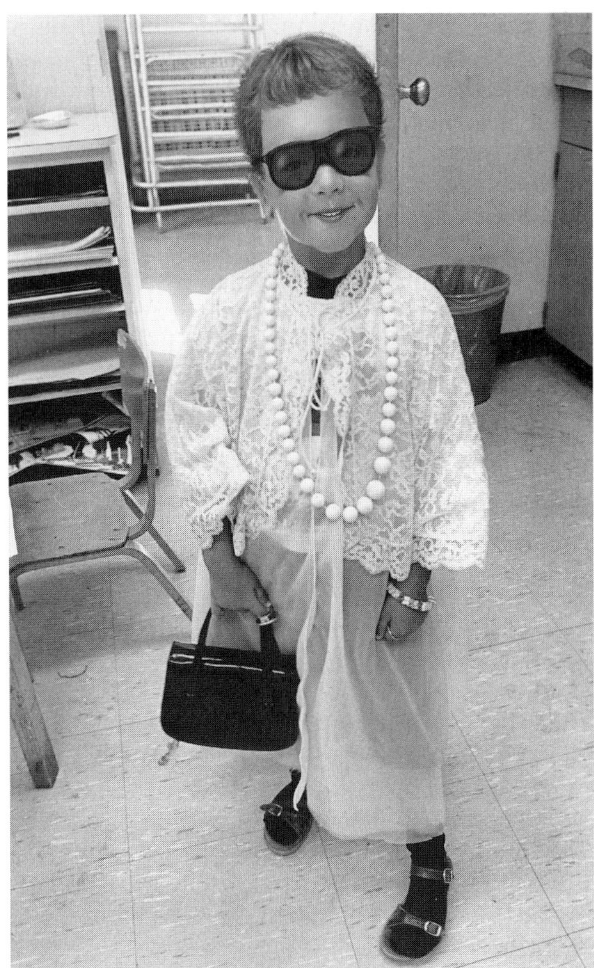

Most transsexuals trace their gender identity disturbance to childhood and report dressing in gender-inappropriate clothes.

The cross-gender behavior that many, perhaps most, young children engage in now and then may, in some homes, receive too much attention and reinforcement from parents and other relatives. Interviews with the parents of children who have become atypical frequently reveal that they did not discourage, and in many instances clearly encouraged, cross-dressing behavior. This is especially true for feminine boys. Many mothers, aunts, and grandmothers found it cute when the boys dressed in mommy's old dresses and high-heeled shoes, and very often they instructed the youngsters on how to apply makeup. Family albums often contain photographs of the young boys attired in women's clothing. Such reactions on the part of the family to an atypical child probably contribute in a major way to the conflict between his or her anatomical sex and the acquired gender identity (Green, 1974). Indeed, Richard Green's noteworthy prospective, longitudinal study of feminine boys and tomboys[1] revealed that, compared with a control group of nontomboys, tomboys were more likely to choose their fathers as a favored parent (and presumably to regard their fathers rather than their mothers as a role model); they were also more likely to have mothers who themselves were tomboys as children and who were more accepting of their daughters' masculine behavior. The possible modeling and operant shaping of more masculine behavior within the family may be supplemented by the positive reinforcement these girls might experience from their male peer groups as a result of their tomboyish behavior (Williams, Goodman, & Green, 1985).

Research with infants and very young children whose genitals have both male and female characteristics indicates that surgery to correct this problem needs to be performed by the age of three, the time by which a child has achieved a sense of gender identity that is very difficult to change later on (Money, Hampson, & Hampson, 1955). Indeed, the gender assigned several of these children was later found to conflict with at least one anatomic sex criterion, such as the indication of sex by their chromosomes. Such children over the age of three kept the gender to which they had been assigned. The web of evidence points to the criticalness of how a very young child, under three years of age, is treated by the adults around him or her. Dressing a child as a boy, giving him (or her!) a male name, and encouraging him or her to engage in traditional masculine activities are major influences on the development of a male gender identity. In contradiction to widespread belief, anatomy is not always destiny.

These findings, however, should *not* be interpreted to mean that encouraging gentleness in a little boy or assertiveness, even aggressiveness, in a little girl will probably lead to a gender identity disorder. Indeed, *most gender identity disordered children do not become transsexual in adulthood, even without professional intervention* (Zucker et al., 1984), although many demonstrate a homosexual orientation (Coates & Person, 1985; Green, 1985).

Investigators working in this field are very much aware of the culture-relative aspects of masculinity and femininity and of the difference between enjoying activities more typical of the opposite sex and actually believing that one *is* of the opposite sex. We do know that the vast majority of little boys engage in varying amounts of feminine play and little girls in varying amounts of masculine play with no identity conflicts whatsoever (Green, 1976). This is not to say that feminine boys are not subject to considerable stress. Our society has a low tolerance for boys who act like girls. In contrast, girls can be tomboys and still conform to acceptable standards of behavior for girls (Williams, Goodman, & Green, 1985). In any case, gender identity disorder of childhood and the adult disorder of transsexualism are extremely rare, far less prevalent than could be expected from the numbers of little boys who play with dolls and of little girls who engage in contact sports.

Indeed, Sandra Bem (1984) takes the radical view that we need not consider any behavior or interest as gender-related except those that concern anatomy or reproduction. She argues that children should enjoy the freedom to behave in both conventional and nontraditional ways without risking punishment from parents or peers. A little boy who shows tenderness to a doll and a little girl who does not should not be made to worry and doubt themselves. Taking the argument a step further, would transsexuality itself disappear if sex-role stereotyping ceased to exist? Then a man would regard his traditionally feminine traits and interests as a normal *masculine* variation, rather than as a pathognomonic sign of being a woman trapped in a man's body (see Raymond, 1979). He would need to be more accepting of any sexual attraction to members of his own sex, however, an attraction that transsexuals regard as heterosexual.

[1]What is a tomboy? This study defined a tomboy as a girl who was regarded as one by her parents and had the following characteristics: "(1) a peer group which was at least half male; (2) a preference for traditionally masculine attire such as a baseball jacket and cap; (3) a low interest in dress-up dolls (e.g., Barbie); (4) a preference for male roles when engaging in make-believe games; (5) a stronger interest in sports than most same-age girls; and (6) a more than rarely expressed desire to be a boy" (Williams et al., 1985, p. 722). The data described here were collected on Long Island, New York, during the mid-1970s.

Therapies for Gender Identity Disorders

We turn now to the interventions available to help people with gender identity disorders. They are of two main types: one attempts to alter the body to suit the person's psychology; the other is designed to alter the psychology to match the body.

Sex-Reassignment Surgery

Innovations in surgical procedures, coupled with advances in hormonal treatments and a sociocultural atmosphere that permits their implementation, have allowed many transsexuals to pursue their wish to become in some respects a member of the opposite sex. **Sex-reassignment surgery** is an operation in which the existing genitalia of a transsexual are removed and a substitute for the genitals of the opposite sex is constructed. It is important to remember, however, that such surgery does *not* biologically transform a man or woman into the opposite sex.

For male-to-female reassigment surgery, the male genitalia are almost entirely removed, with some of the tissue retained to form an artificial vagina. At least a year before the operation, appropriate female hormones are given to develop the breasts, soften the skin, and change the body in other ways; hormones have to be taken indefinitely after the surgery (Green & Money, 1969). Most male-to-female transsexuals have to undergo extensive and costly electrolysis to remove beard and body hair and receive training to raise the pitch of their voice; the female hormones prescribed do not make hair distribution and the voice less masculine. Some male-to-female transsexuals also have plastic surgery on their chin, nose, and Adam's apple to rid them of masculine largeness. At the same time the transsexual begins to live as a female member of society in order to experience as fully as possible what it is like. The genital surgery itself is usually not done until a one- or two-year trial period has been completed. Conventional heterosexual intercourse is possible for male-to-female transsexuals, although pregnancy is out of the question since only the external genitalia are altered.

For female-to-male reassignment surgery, the process is more arduous. The penis that can be constructed is small and not capable of normal erection; artificial supports are therefore needed for conventional sexual intercourse. An operation now available extends the urethra into the newly constructed

James Morris (in a 1960 picture), after sex-change surgery, became Jan Morris (in a 1974 photograph).

penis to allow the person the social comfort of being able to use public urinals. Less cosmetic follow-up is needed than for male-to-female transsexuals because the male hormones prescribed drastically alter fat distribution and stimulate the growth of beard and body hair. The relatively greater ease of the female-to-male change may come in part from our society's lesser focus on the physical attributes of men. A small, soft-spoken man may be more acceptable to society than a large, hulking woman.

The ratio of male transsexuals to female transsexuals seeking help ranges from a high of eight to one to a low of one to one. In the first comprehensive book on female-to-male transsexuals, Lothstein (1983) reported that each year more and more women apply for sex-reassignment surgery.

The first sex-reassignment operation took place in Europe in 1930, but the surgery that attracted worldwide attention was performed on an ex-soldier, Christine (originally George) Jorgensen, in Copenhagen in 1952. Some years later Jan (originally James) Morris, a well-known journalist, published *Conundrum* (1974), a sensitive and highly personal account of her life as a man and her subsequent alteration to a woman.

Over the years, controversy has existed over the benefits of sex-reassignment surgery. One of the first outcome studies (Meyer & Reter, 1979) found no advantage to the individual "in terms of social rehabilitation" (p. 1015). The findings of this study led to the termination of the Johns Hopkins University School of Medicine sex-reassignment program, the largest such program in the United States. However, other studies criticized the Meyer–Reter findings. Abramovitz's (1986) careful review of twenty years of research indicated an overall improvement in social adaptation rate resulting from sex-reassignment surgery, with female-to-male transsexuals showing somewhat greater success than male-to-female.

However, caution is warranted in drawing conclusions because of glaring inadequacies in research design in most of the studies. These include such problems as subjects appearing in more than one report; subjects who committed suicide not being counted as no-improvement because they were not available at follow-up; and inadequate information provided on the exact nature of hormonal and surgical modification. As for the Meyer–Reter (1979) study, Abramovitz (1986) pointed out that the markedly shorter follow-up period for the unoperated controls worked against finding better results for the surgical group of transsexuals (the longer follow-up period for the surgery patients may well have allowed more problems to come to light over time). He concluded that "an observer [of reactions to the Meyer–Reter report] may well suspect that this incident warrants a chapter in the social psychology of medicine" (p. 187).

A more recent review by Green and Fleming (1990) of reasonably controlled outcome studies published between 1979 and 1989 with at least a one-year follow-up drew more favorable conclusions: of 130 female-to-male surgeries, about 97 percent could be judged satisfactory; and of 220 male-to-female surgeries, 87 percent were satisfactory. Preoperative factors that seemed to predict favorable postsurgery adjustment were (1) reasonable emotional stability, (2) successful adaptation in the new role for at least one year, (3) adequate understanding of the actual limitations and consequences of the surgery, and (4) psychotherapy in the context of an established gender identity program (see Figure 12.1). The authors caution, however, that ratings of satisfactory meant only that the patients reported they did not regret having had the surgery. And perhaps such patient reports constitute an overly generous criterion for favorable outcome, especially reports that follow the investment of considerable time, money, and energy for an outcome that is, for the most part, irreversible. Green and Fleming also properly point out that many more people have sex-reassignment surgery than are reported on in published studies.

It may be that the best surgery and overall best care are to be found in settings that collect data and publish their findings. In our view, it is more likely than not that the highly favorable outcomes reviewed here overestimate the success of such surgery. On the other hand, Green (personal communication, February 20, 1992) points out that an opposite bias might be operating, to wit, transsex-

Figure 12.1 Factors that contribute to good outcomes in Sex-Reassignment Surgery.

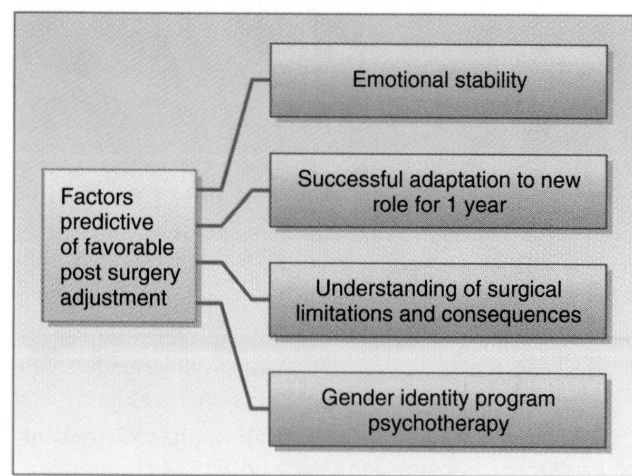

uals who are the most satisfied with their surgery tend to drift away, losing contact with the people who performed the surgery. It tends to be patients who are troubled or dissatisfied with the outcomes of treatment who keep in touch with medical–psychological teams and complain to them.

In the face of these controversies, sex-reassignment programs continue in many medical–psychological settings; it is estimated that each year in the United States upwards of 1000 transsexuals are surgically altered to the opposite sex. And yet, the long-term effectiveness, or even wisdom, of sex-reassignment surgery is still difficult to evaluate (Lothstein, 1980). Given that people who go to great lengths to have this surgery performed claim that their future happiness depends on the change, should this surgery be evaluated in terms of how happy such people are afterward? If so, it can probably be said that most transsexuals who have crossed over anatomically are better off, although some are not. But as people make their way through life, many events bring them a greater or lesser amount of fulfillment or even ease. If a surgically altered transsexual becomes dismally unhappy, is the venture to be indicted as antitherapeutic? Transsexuals who undergo these procedures often cut their ties to former friends and family members and to aspects of their previous lives—"Was it *I* who played tailback on the football team?" Considerable stress is the lot of those who choose to divorce themselves from the past, for the past contributes to our sense of ourselves as people, as much as do the present and the future. A transsexual who has surgery, then, confronts challenges few others have occasion to face; adjustment to the new life should perhaps be evaluated more leniently.

All experienced therapists, whatever their theoretical persuasion, are wary of a client who says, "If only . . ." The variations are legion: "If only I were not so fat. . . ." "If only I were not so nervous. . . ." "If only I had not left school before graduation. . . ." Following each "if only" clause is some statement indicating that life would be far better, even wonderful . . . if only. Most of the time the hopes expressed are an illusion. Things are seldom so simple. The transsexual, understandably focusing on the discrepancy between gender identity and biological makeup, blames present dissatisfactions on the horrible trick nature has played. But he or she usually finds that sex reassignment falls short of solving life's problems. It may handle this one set of them, but it usually leaves untouched other difficulties to which all human beings are subject, such as conflicts at work, with intimates, and even within oneself.

Alterations of Gender Identity

Are sex-reassignment operations indeed the only option? They used to be considered the only viable treatment for gender identity disorders because psychological attempts to shift gender identity had consistently failed. Gender identity was assumed too deep-seated to alter. Some successful procedures for altering gender identity through behavior therapy have been reported, however.

One treatment (Rekers & Lovaas, 1974) was of a five-year-old boy who, since age two, had been cross-dressing and showing the other familiar signs of gender identity disorder. Concurring with the therapist's judgment that conforming to societal standards of masculinity would benefit the boy in both the short and long runs, the child's parents began, as instructed, to compliment and otherwise support him whenever he played with traditionally male toys, rather than those commonly preferred by girls, and whenever he engaged in other traditionally male activities. Feminine mannerisms were discouraged. After only six months of intensive treatment, the boy was typically masculine, and he was still so at a two-year follow-up. Although it might be objected that encouraging play with guns while discouraging play with dolls only reinforces cultural stereotypes (Winkler, 1977), this child may have been spared considerable psychological hardship by bringing his gender identity into conformity with his biological makeup. We reiterate that most children with gender identity disorders do not become transsexuals, even without special treatment. Not knowing whether this particular child would grow out of it, the parents and the therapists decided to intervene.

An even more dramatic reversal of gender identity was reported by Barlow, Reynolds, and Agras (1973). In their behavioral treatment of a seventeen-year-old male transsexual, gender role was broken down into concrete components, such as mannerisms, interpersonal behavior, and fantasies, and the client was given training to change each component. He was initially made aware of the effeminate manner in which he stood, sat, walked, and talked. Then, through modeling, rehearsal, and video feedback and through voice retraining, he was taught to do these things in ways judged masculine by the culture. Almost immediately the staring and ridicule of his peers lessened, and he returned to high school part-time. The young man's social skills improved as he was taught to make eye contact and conversation and to express his positive feelings through appropriate smiles and other means.

He still felt himself to be a female, however, and

had fantasies and urges to have intercourse with men. Therapy then focused on his fantasy life. During training sessions a female therapist encouraged him to imagine himself in sexual situations with attractive women; she also embellished his fantasies by describing foreplay in explicit detail. He was instructed to generate such fantasies when encountering women as he went about his daily activities. After thirty-four training sessions over a period of two months, the client's desire to change sex dropped dramatically, and fantasies about men decreased in number as those about women increased. He was now beginning to think of himself as a man, and the attraction he still occasionally felt toward men took place without gender role reversal, that is, the attraction was that felt by one man toward another.

Even with these changes, however, physiological measures of sexual arousal with the penile plethysmograph, a device for measuring the circumference of the penis (shown in Figure 12.2), more definitely revealed that he was still attracted to men and not women, so therapeutic effort was now devoted to increasing the arousal felt toward women and decreasing that felt toward men. Slides of women were paired with slides of men, the idea being to classically condition sexual arousal to women by associating them with the arousal felt toward slides of men. This procedure, followed by aversion therapy sessions to reduce the attractiveness of slides of men, promoted the desired change to a heterosexual pattern of arousal.

Interestingly, during this period the young man's manner of standing, sitting, and walking became even more traditionally masculine. He also felt much better about himself and had returned to high school on a full-time basis. Five months after the end of treatment, the young man reported for the first time masturbating to orgasm while imagining himself with a woman. A one-year follow-up found him going steady with a woman and engaging in light petting. He no longer thought of himself as a woman. Five years later the man's gender identity continued to be masculine and his sexual orientation heterosexual. In their follow-up report on this seventeen-year-old transsexual, Barlow, Abel, and Blanchard (1979) described two additional cases treated in the same way. These two men, in their mid-twenties, were on the route to sex-reassignment surgery but then had second thoughts. The behavioral retraining succeeded again in altering gender identity but not their attraction to men; that is, their sexual orientation remained homosexual.

The work of Barlow and his colleagues represents the first carefully documented change of gender identity in adult transsexuals. As such it demonstrates that cross-sex identity is amenable to change. The clinicians themselves acknowledge that their clients might have been different from other transsexuals because they did consent at the outset to participate in a therapy program aimed at changing gender identity. Most transsexuals refuse such treatment as inappropriate; for them sex-reassignment surgery is the only legitimate goal. There are significant ethical issues inherent in the alteration of gender identity, as well as in the sex-reassignment surgery discussed earlier. Some of these dilemmas are

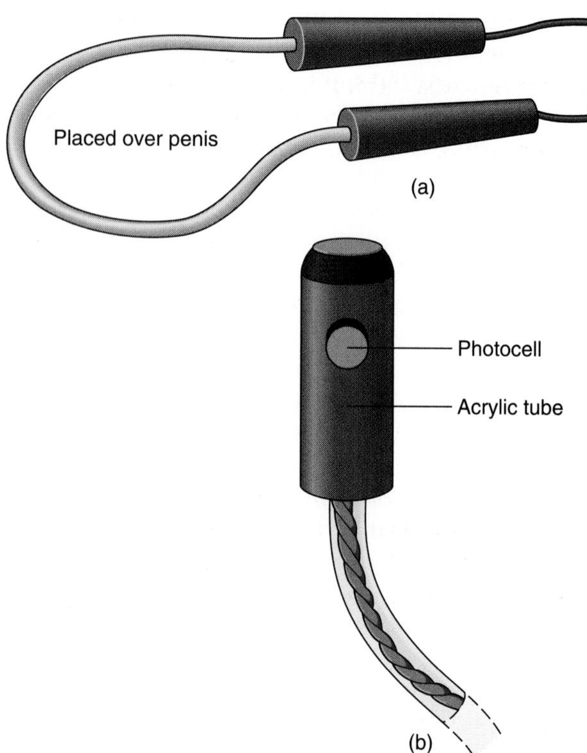

Figure 12.2 Behavioral researchers use two genital devices for measuring sexual arousal in men and in women; both provide rather specific measurements of sexual excitement (e.g., Adams et al., 1992; Barlow et al., 1970; Geer, Morokoff, & Greenwood, 1974; Heiman et al., 1991). Both are sensitive indicators of vasocongestion of the genitalia, that is, the flooding of the veins with blood, a key physiological process in sexual arousal. (a) For men, the penile plethysmograph measures changes in the circumference of the penis by means of a strain gauge, consisting of a very thin rubber tube filled with mercury. As the penis is engorged with blood, the tube stretches, changing its electrical resistance, which can then be measured by a suitably configured polygraph. (b) Sexual arousal in women can be measured by a vaginal plethysmograph, such as the device invented by Sintchak and Geer (1975). Shaped like a menstrual tampon, this apparatus can be inserted into the vagina to provide direct measurement of the increased blood flow characteristic of female sexual arousal.

examined later in the context of sexual reorientation change for homosexuality (page 359). Suffice it to say for now that ethical judgments are *always* present when therapists help clients to change their ways of being and behaving.

The Paraphilias

In DSM-IV the **paraphilias** represent a group of disorders in which sexual attraction is to unusual objects, and sexual activities are unusual in nature; in brief, there is a deviation (*para*) in what the person is attracted to (*-philia*). This attraction has to be intense and last at least six months. The diagnosis is made only if the person has acted on these urges or experiences significant distress from them. It is important to note that people can have the same fantasies and urges that a paraphiliac has (like exhibiting the genitals to an unsuspecting stranger) but not be diagnosed if the fantasies are not recurrent and intense and if he or she has never acted on the urges *or is not markedly distressed by them.*

Paraphilias are often multiple rather than single and can also be an aspect of other mental disorders, such as schizophrenia or one of the personality disorders. Prevalence statistics indicate that paraphiliacs, of whatever sexual orientation, are almost always men; only in masochism does one find appreciable numbers of women, but even here they are outnumbered by a ratio of twenty to one. Finally, the fact that some paraphiliacs seek nonconsenting partners indicates that there are often legal consequences to the disorders.

Fetishism

Fetishism involves a reliance on an inanimate object for sexual arousal. The fetishist, almost always a male, has recurrent and intense sexual urges toward nonliving objects, called fetishes, like a woman's shoes; and the fetish is strongly preferred or even necessary for sexual arousal to occur.

Beautiful shoes, sheer stockings, gloves, toilet articles, fur garments, and especially underpants are common sources of arousal for fetishists. An unusual fetishistic attraction was reported by King (1990), who described a twenty-six-year-old man who was aroused by other people sneezing. Some can carry on their fetishism by themselves in secret by fondling, kissing, smelling, or merely gazing at the adored object as they masturbate. Others need their partner to don the fetish as a stimulant for intercourse. Fetishists sometimes become primarily interested in making a collection of the desired objects, and they may commit burlgary week after week to add to their hoard.

Subjectively, the attraction felt by the fetishist toward the object is involuntary and irresistible. The degree of the erotic focalization distinguishes fetishisms from the ordinary attraction that high heels and sheer stockings may hold for heterosexual men. The disorder usually begins by adolescence, although the fetish may have acquired special significance even earlier, during childhood.

Psychoanalytic theorists generally consider fetishisms and other paraphilias to serve some sort of defensive function, warding off castration anxiety about normal sexual contacts. Learning theorists usually invoke some kind of classical conditioning in the person's social-sexual history. For example, a young man may, early in his sexual experiences, masturbate to pictures of women dressed in black leather. Indeed, one experiment (Rachman, 1966) lends some mild support to learning propositions. Male subjects were repeatedly shown slides of nude and alluring females interspersed with slides of women's boots. The subjects were eventually aroused by the boots alone. The fetishistic attraction induced, however, was weak and transient.

In Chapter 6 (page 138) we discussed the possibility that people are prepared to learn to become phobic to certain objects. It is also possible that human beings are prepared to learn to be sexually stimulated by certain classes of stimuli. If mere association with sexual stimulation were all there is to acquiring a fetishism through classical conditioning, one would expect objects such as ceilings and pillows to be high on the list of fetishes (Baron & Byrne, 1977). Clearly they are not, and at this point it would be premature to conclude that fetishisms are established solely through classical conditioning.

Transvestic Fetishism

When a man is sexually aroused by dressing in women's clothing while still regarding himself as a man, the term **transvestic fetishism**, or transvestism, is applied to this behavior. A transvestite may also enjoy appearing socially as a woman; some female impersonators become performers in nightclubs, catering to the delight that many sexually conventional people take in skilled cross-dressing. Unless the cross-dressing is associated with sexual arousal, however, these impersonators are not con-

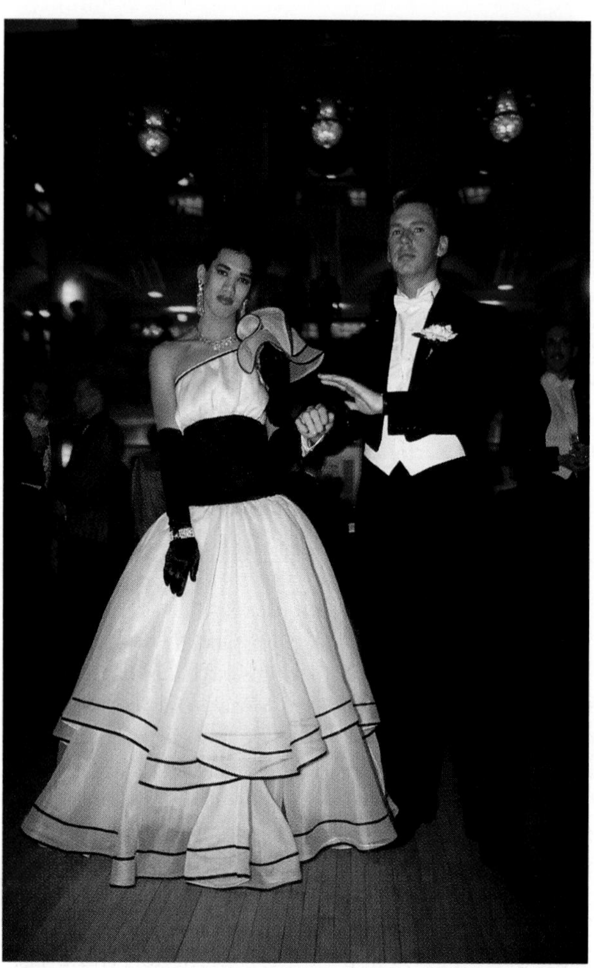

Transvestic fetishism or transvestism is diagnosed when the person produces sexual arousal by dressing in opposite sex clothing. This transvestite is attending a fund raiser for AIDS at the Waldorf Astoria in New York.

sidered transvestic. Transvestism should not be confused with homosexuality; transvestites are heterosexual, and only a few homosexuals ever on occasion go in drag. As mentioned earlier, it is illegal in many jurisdictions to appear cross-dressed in public.

Transvestites, who are always males, by and large cross-dress episodically rather than on a regular basis. They tend to be otherwise masculine in appearance, demeanor, and sexual preference. Most are married. Cross-dressing usually takes place in private and in secret and is known to few members of the family. The urge to cross-dress may become more frequent over time but only rarely develops to a change in gender identity, that is, to the man's believing that he is actually a female. On the other hand, some transvestites do report *feeling* like a woman when they are cross-dressing. Transvestism usually begins with partial cross-dressing in childhood and adolescence.

Case histories of transvestites often refer to childhood incidents in which the little boy was praised and fussed over for looking cute when wearing female attire. Paradoxically, some male transvestites recall "petticoat punishment" from their childhood—being punished through the humiliation of being forced to wear girls' clothing (American Psychiatric Association, 1987, p. 289). Learning accounts assume the disorder results from the conditioning effects of repeatedly masturbating when cross-dressing, similar to the supposed classical conditioning connection between arousal and the object adopted as a fetish. Some clinicians believe transvestism represents for a beleaguered male a refuge from the responsibilities he sees himself bearing solely by virtue of being male in our society. Female clothing, then, is believed to have meaning for transvestites that is more complex and encompassing than sheer sexual arousal; trying to explain transvestism solely in sexual terms may therefore be an oversimplification. Perhaps changing gender roles will alter the meaning that female clothes have for such men.

Incest

The taboo against **incest**, sexual relations between close relatives for whom marriage is forbidden, seems virtually universal in human societies (Ford & Beach, 1951). A notable exception was the marriages of Egyptian pharaohs to their sisters or other females of their immediate families. In Egypt it was believed that the royal blood should not be contaminated by that of outsiders. Some anthropologists consider the prohibition against incest to have served the important function of forcing more widely spread social ties and consequently greater social harmony than would have been likely had family members chosen their mates only from among their own. The incest taboo makes sense according to present-day scientific knowledge. The offspring from a father–daughter or a brother–sister union has a greater probability of inheriting a pair of recessive genes, one from each parent. For the most part, recessive genes have negative biological effects, such as serious birth defects. The incest taboo, then, has adaptive evolutionary significance (Geer, Heiman, & Leitenberg, 1984). Incest is listed in DSM-IV as a subtype of pedophilia.

Incest, which includes all forms of sexual contact, seems most common between brother and sister. The next most common form, which is considered more pathological, is between father and daughter. In a well-known study on sex offenders, Gebhard and his associates (1965) found that most fathers who had relations with physically mature daughters tended to be very devout, moralistic, and fundamentalistic in their religious beliefs.[2] There is also evidence that the structure of families in which incest occurs is unusually patriarchal and traditional, especially with respect to the subservient position of women relative to men (Alexander & Lupfer, 1987). There is in addition parental neglect of and emotional distance from the children (Madonna, VanScoyk, & Jones, 1991). Furthermore, it is believed that incest is more prevalent when the mother is absent or disabled (Finkelhor, 1979); this may happen because mothers otherwise usually protect their daughters from intrafamilial sexual abuse.

Fathers who commit incest may be sexually frustrated in their marriage yet feel constrained, for religious reasons, from seeking gratification through masturbation, prostitutes, or extramarital affairs. (This in no way implies that it is necessarily the wife's fault for not sexually satisfying her husband.) For such men it is apparently preferable to keep sexual contact within the family (Frude, 1982), though one wonders how molesting one's own child can be more acceptable than having sex with an adult other than one's wife. However, recent evidence suggests that it is not sexual dissatisfaction so much as it is lack of a satisfying emotional relationship with his wife that is associated with incest by the father (Lang et al., 1990). Other factors that put a child at risk for being subjected to this type of incest are having a stepfather, having a mother who did not graduate from high school, having a poor relationship with the mother, and having fewer than two close friends in childhood (Finkelhor, 1984).

Incest is now acknowledged to occur much more often than had earlier been assumed. A study of 796 college students found that an astounding 19 percent of the women and 8.6 percent of the men had been sexually victimized as children. Of the victimized women, 28 percent had had incestuous relations, of the men, 23 percent (Finkelhor, 1979). More recent survey data confirm these findings (Siegel et al., 1987). When states pass more effective legislation on reporting incidents of incest, confirmed cases increase 50 to 500 percent.

Explanations of incest run the gamut from sexual deprivation to the Freudian notion that human beings have basic human desires for such relationships. Some older explanations tended to blame the victim (Ryan, 1971); Bender and Blau (1937) described a number of children who had been involved in incestuous relationships as having "unusually attractive and charming personalities" (p. 511) and, because of their seductiveness, as not being totally innocent parties. In addition to being morally repugnant, this hypothesis is refuted by the information available (Meiselman, 1978).

Pedophilia

Pedophiles (*pedos*, Greek for child) are adults, usually men as far as police records indicate, who derive sexual gratification through physical and often sexual contact with prepubertal children unrelated to them. DSM-IV requires that the offender be at least 16 years old and at least 5 years older than the child. The pedophile can be either heterosexual or homosexual. Violence is seldom a part of the molestation, although some pedophiles frighten the child by, for example, killing a pet and threatening further harm if the youngster tells his or her parents. Sometimes the pedophile is content to stroke the child's hair, but he may also manipulate the child's genitalia, encourage the child to manipulate his, and, less often, attempt intromission. The molestations may be repeated over a period of weeks, months, or years if they are not discovered by other adults or if the child does not protest. A minority of pedophiles, who might also be classified as sexual sadists or antisocial (psychopathic) personalities, inflict serious bodily harm on the object of their passion. Groth et al. (1982) regard such individuals, whether psychopathic or not, as child rapists and fundamentally different from pedophiles by virtue of their wish to hurt the child physically at least as much as to obtain sexual gratification.

Two major distinctions are drawn between incest and pedophilia. First, by definition, incest is between members of the same family. Second, and more importantly, most incest victims tend to be older than the object of a pedophile's desires. It is more often the case that a father becomes interested in his daughter when she begins to mature physically, whereas the pedophile is interested in the youngster precisely because he or she is sexually immature. Data from penile plethysmography studies confirm that men who molest children un-

[2]The association that some have reported between strong religious beliefs and the disorders of incest and pedophilia should not be taken to mean that being religious, even rigidly so, predisposes one to these sexual disorders. It may be that some people, overcome by the intensity of their attraction to their own or others' children, seek solace and forgiveness in religion. In any event, the data are correlational and hence are open to different interpretations.

related to them are sexually aroused from photographs of nude children, whereas men who molest children within their families show greater penile arousal from adult heterosexual cues (Marshall, Barabee, & Christophe, 1986). In defining pedophilia, state laws vary on a prescribed upper age limit for those considered children.

Pedophiles are often rigidly religious and moralistic. As with most of the aberrant sexual behavior that has been described, there is a strong subjective attraction that draws the pedophile to the child. According to Gebhard and his colleagues (1965), pedophiles generally know the children they molest; they are neighbors or friends of the family. Clinical observations suggest that pedophiles are low in social maturity, self-esteem, impulse control, and social skills (Finkelhor & Araji, 1986), views that have been confirmed in recent research (Kalichman, 1991; Overholser & Beck, 1986). Most older heterosexual pedophiles are or have been married at some time in their lives.

As with incest, it is not known with any degree of precision how widespread nonfamilial child molestation is; since most instances occur between the child and someone known to him or her and to the family, many more cases are assumed to go unreported to authorities than come to their attention. Indeed, in 1984 several day-care centers across the country were alleged to be the sites of ongoing child molestation by the owners and staff, heightening public awareness of, and outrage at, the extent of the problem. The general estimate is that from 10 to 15 percent of children and young adolescents are subjected to at least one incident of molestation by an adult (Mrazek, 1984).

Common among psychoanalytic hypotheses are nonsexual bases for child molestation, such as an idealization of childhood, the need for mastery, debilitating anxiety about adult sexual relationships, and a sense of having failed socially and professionaly in the adult world (Lanyon, 1986).[3] The widespread belief that pedophilia is caused by having been sexually abused in childhood (American Psychiatric Association, 1987) actually has very little support from research data (Hindman, 1988; Freund, Watson, & Dickey, 1990). Child abuse, whether incestuous or not, often does have deleterious consequences (Kendall-Tackett et al., 1993), but these consequences are probably not specific to the creation of yet another cohort of molesters. For more detailed discussion of the effects of both pedophilia and incest, see Focus Box 12.1.

Voyeurism (Peeping)

Now and then a man may by chance happen to observe a nude woman without her knowing he is watching her. If his sex life is primarily conventional, his act is voyeuristic, but he would not generally be considered a voyeur. **Voyeurism** is a marked preference for obtaining sexual gratification by watching others in a state of undress or having sexual relations. The looking, often called peeping, is what helps the individual become sexually aroused and is sometimes essential for arousal. The voyeur's orgasm is achieved by masturbation, either while watching or later, remembering what he saw. Sometimes the voyeur fantasizes about having sexual contact with the observed person, but it remains a fantasy; in voyeurism, there is seldom contact between the observer and the observed.

A true voyeur, almost always a man, does not find it particularly exciting to watch a woman who is undressing for his special benefit. The element of risk seems important, for the voyeur is excited by the anticipation of how the woman would react if she knew he was watching. Some voyeurs derive special pleasure from secretly observing couples having sexual relations. As with all categories of behavior that are against the law, frequencies of occurrence are difficult to assess, since the majority of *all* illegal activities go unnoticed by the police.

From what we know, voyeurs tend to be young, single, submissive, and fearful of more direct sexual encounters with others (Katchadourian & Lunde, 1972; McCary, 1973). Their peeping serves as a substitute gratification and possibly gives them a sense of power over those watched. They do not seem to be otherwise disturbed, however. That voyeurs have an impoverished social life and engage in surreptitious peeping instead of making conventional sexual and social contacts with women suggests another way to understand their preference for spying on unaware women. If the woman were aware of the man's actions and continued nonetheless to allow herself to be watched, the man might well conclude that she had some personal interest in him. This possibility would be very threatening to the voyeur and, because of his fear, less sexually arousing. Perhaps, then, it is not the risk of being discovered that arouses the voyeur. Rather, undiscovered peeping, because it protects the heterosexual voyeur from a possible relationship with a woman, is the

[3]It is interesting to note that psychoanalytic views of sexual problems often implicate nonsexual factors such as those just mentioned, whereas analytic theorizing about nonsexual disorders usually implicates sexual urges.

least frightening way for him to have contact with her.

After all restrictions against the sale of pornographic materials to adults had been lifted in Denmark, one of the few observed effects of this liberalization was a significant reduction in peeping, at least as reported to the police (Kutchinsky, 1970). It may be that the increased availability of completely frank pictorial and written material, typically used in masturbation, satisfies the needs that earlier made voyeurs of some men without other outlets.

"When I said you were allowed one phone call, I did not mean *another* obscene one."

(Drawing by Charles Addams, © 1974, The New Yorker Magazine, Inc.)

Exhibitionism

Exhibitionism is a recurrent, marked preference for obtaining sexual gratification by exposing one's genitals to an unwilling stranger. As with voyeurism, there is seldom an attempt to have actual contact with the stranger. Sexual arousal comes from fantasizing that one is exposing himself or from actually doing so, and the exhibitionist masturbates either while fantasizing or even during the actual exposure. In most cases there is a desire to shock or embarrass the observer.

Voyeurism and exhibitionism together account for close to a majority of all sexual offenses that come to the attention of the police. Again, the frequency of exhibitionism is much greater among men, who are often arrested for what is legally termed *indecent exposure.*

The urge to expose seems overwhelming and virtually uncontrollable to the exhibitionist, or flasher, and is apparently triggered by anxiety and restlessness as well as by sexual arousal. One exhibitionist persisted in his practices even after suffering a spinal cord injury that left him without sensation or movement from the waist down (DeFazio et al., 1987). Because of the compulsive nature of the urge, the exposures may be repeated rather frequently and even in the same place and at the same time of day. Apparently exhibitionists are so strongly driven that, at the time of the act, they are usually oblivious to the social and legal consequences of what they are doing (Stevenson & Jones, 1972). In the desperation and tension of the moment, they may suffer headaches and palpitations and have a sense of unreality. Afterward they flee in trembling and remorse (Bond & Hutchison, 1960). Only rarely do exhibitionists seek physical contact with their unwilling observers; even less often is there danger of a more violent sexual offense, such as rape. (Rooth, 1973). Generally exhibitionists are immature in their approaches to the opposite sex and have difficulty in interpersonal relationships. Over half of all exhibitionists are married, but their sexual relationships with their spouses are not satisfactory (Mohr, Turner, & Jerry, 1964).

The penile plethysmograph was used in a study of male exhibitionists in an effort to determine whether they are sexually aroused by stimuli that do not arouse nonexhibitionists (Fedora, Reddon, & Yeudall, 1986). Compared with normal subjects and with sex offenders who had committed violent assaults, the exhibitionists showed significantly greater arousal to slides of fully clothed women in nonsexual situations, such as riding on an escalator or sitting in a park, while showing *similar* levels of sexual interest to erotic and sexually explicit slides. These results are consistent with the hypothesis that exhibitionists misread cues in the courtship phase of sexual contact, in the sense that they construe certain situations to be sexual that are judged to be nonerotic by nonexhibitionists. In this same study, measures indicated that exhibitionists were *less* aroused than either control group by slides that depicted violence. This would seem to undermine the widespread concern that exhibitionists might be physically threatening.

The search to determine how exhibitionism develops has turned up very little. One of many psychodynamic theories views the problem as stemming from a repressed fear of castration and the male exhibitionist's need to reassure himself that he is still a man. Such speculations are unsupported

FOCUS 12.1 • Child Sexual Abuse—Effects on the Victim and Modes of Intervention

Both pedophilia and incest are forms of **child sexual abuse**. They should be distinguished from nonsexual child abuse. Both can have very negative consequences, and sometimes they co-occur. Nonsexual child abuse includes such things as neglecting the child's physical and mental welfare, for example, punishing the child unfairly; belittling the child; intentionally withholding suitable shelter, food, and medical care; and striking or otherwise inflicting physical pain and injury. Both are reportable offenses, but parents often engage in nonsexual abuse of their children when no sexual abuse is involved.

Child sexual abuse generally refers to such physical contact as penetration of the child's vagina or anus with the perpetrator's penis, finger, or other object; fellatio, cunnilingus, or analingus; and fondling or caressing. Also included are exhibitionism and child pornography, which may not involve actual sexual activity between an adult and a child (Wolfe, 1990). Most child sexual abuse victims are female.

There is a growing body of evidence attesting to the long-term adverse effects of incest and pedophilia (Felitti, 1991). In a questionnaire study of well-functioning college women, Jackson et al. (1990) found that those who had suffered incest as children had more severe problems than control subjects in dating relationships, in general social adjustment, in sexual satisfaction, in self-esteem, and with depression. Subjects' recollections of their home life also suggested that certain aspects might have contributed to some of the later psychological problems. For example, the high frequency of domination by the father in incestuous homes might have contributed to a sense of helplessness that, apart from the sexual abuse, could have made these women more vulnerable to depression (cf. page 236). Other research implicates incest in subsequent prostitution, sexual promiscuity, substance abuse, anxiety disorders, and sexual dysfunctions (Burnam et al., 1988). We have already indicated that sexual abuse in childhood is implicated in multiple personality disorder (page 183) and in borderline personality disorder (page 267; Saunders, 1991). One study found that a long-term effect of child sexual abuse is an increased vulnerability to subsequent sexual assault. "The actual occurrence of abuse, regardless of perpetrator, appeared to [play a role] . . . in instilling an expectation of victimization" (Alexander & Lupfer, 1987, p. 244). Although it is important to emphasize that this interpretation is not equivalent to a degrading "she asked for it," it does point to the possibility that victims of sexual abuse are adversely affected in their adult years by not having learned to deal assertively with unwanted sexual advances.

In recent years many communities have developed programs to reduce the incidence of child sexual abuse. The programs are reminiscent of the caveats that most of us (even those old enough to be the parents of most readers of this book) recall: "Don't talk to strangers" and "Don't take candy from strangers." Few of us had the image of this dangerous stranger as being other than a man, and the data bear this out, for very few child sexual abusers are women. But few of us were told that a molester was usually *not* a stranger, that it could be an uncle, a father, a brother, a teacher, a coach, a neighbor, or even a cleric. These are very difficult things to discuss with a child, difficult also to confront for ourselves. But the child molester is often a male adult whom the child knows and probably also trusts. The betrayal of this trust makes the crime even more abhorrent than if there were no prior relationship between perpetrator and victim.

An important goal of any prevention program—in a later chapter we discuss prevention as a key aspect of what is called community psychology (page 608)—is to reduce the incidence, prevalence, and severity of a particular problem. As one might expect, prevention efforts have focused on

by any data; nor have they contributed to the development of effective therapies. An intriguing learning hypothesis emphasizes the reinforcing aspects of masturbation. McGuire, Carlisle, and Young (1965) reported on the development of exhibitionism in two young men who were surprised during urination by an attractive woman. When the embarrassment had passed and they were in private, the thought of being discovered in this way aroused them and they masturbated while fantasizing the earlier experience. After repeated masturbating to such fantasies, they began to exhibit. The elementary schools. While content varies from program to program, common elements include teaching children how to recognize inappropriate adult behavior, to resist inducements, to leave the situation quickly, and report the incident to an appropriate adult (Wolfe, 1990). Children are taught to say no in a firm, assertive way when an adult talks to or touches them in a way that makes them feel uncomfortable. Instructors use such things as comic books, films, and descriptions of risky situations to try to teach about the nature of sexual abuse and how children can protect themselves. Evaluations of school programs tend to support the notion that they increase awareness of sexual abuse among children, but less is known about whether the children are able to translate what they have learned into *overt behavior* and whether such changes reduce the problem (Wolfe, 1990). At the very least, programs seem to legitimize discussion of the problem at home (Wurtele & Miller-Perrin, 1987) and might therefore achieve one important goal, namely, to increase the *reporting* of the crime by encouraging and empowering children to tell their parents or guardians that an adult has made a sexual overture to them.

Efforts are necessary to encourage parents to raise the issue with their children, something that many adults are quite uncomfortable about doing. Physicians as well need to be sensitized to signs of sexual abuse, both physical and psychological. Indeed, in many states, licensed health professionals and teachers are *required* to report sexual abuse (as well as nonsexual child abuse) when they become aware of it; in California, licensed psychologists also need to take a day-long course in the subject to ensure that they are at least minimally knowledgeable about it and aware of their legal responsibilities to report sexual abuse to child protection agencies.

And yet, it is not a straightforward matter for a child or developing adolescent to report molestation. We tend to forget how helpless and dependent a youngster feels and how frightening it can be to tell Daddy that he or she has been fondled by a brother or grandfather. Probably even more threatening are advances from Daddy himself, for the child is likely to be torn by allegiance to and love for his or her father on the one hand and by fear and revulsion on the other, coupled with the knowledge that what is happening is wrong. And when, as sometimes is the case, the mother suspects what is happening to her child and yet (implicitly) allows it to continue, the victim's complaints to the mother can be met with lack of support, with disbelief, and even with hostility.

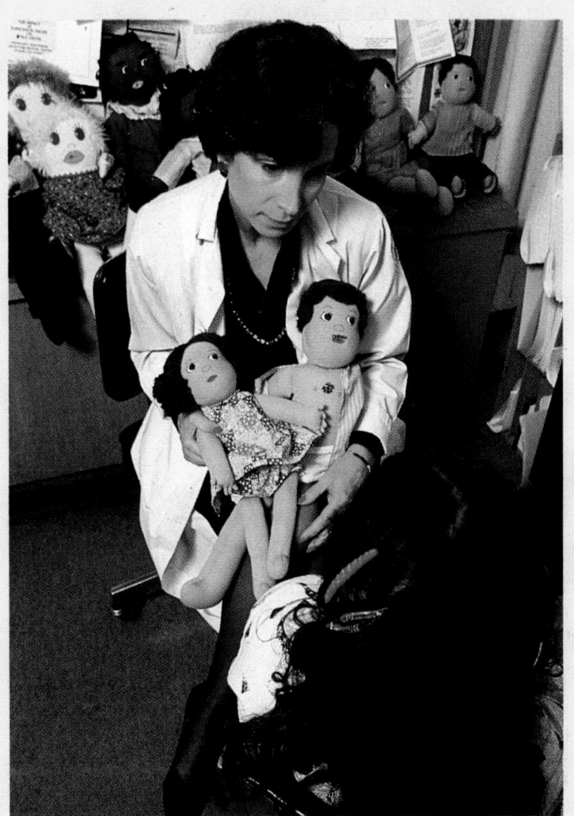

Great sensitivity is required when interviewing a child about the possibility of sexual abuse. Anatomically correct dolls are often used to facilitate the process.

Great skill is required in questioning a child about possible sexual abuse to ensure that the report is accurate, to avoid biasing the youngster

report suggests that repeated association of sexual arousal with images of being seen by a woman classically conditioned the men to become aroused through exhibiting. No controlled evidence, however, clearly supports this learning explanation of exhibitionism.

Sexual Sadism and Sexual Masochism

A marked preference for obtaining or increasing sexual gratification by inflicting pain or psychological suffering (e.g., humiliation) is the key characteristic of **sexual sadism**; a marked preference for one way or the other, and to minimize the stress that is inevitable in recounting a disturbing experience, especially if a decision is made to prosecute. Taking formal legal action is still relatively rare, but some jurisdictions use innovative procedures that can reduce the stress on the victim while still protecting the rights of the accused, such as videotaped testimony, closed-courtroom trials, closed-circuit televised testimony, and special assistants and coaching sessions to explain courtroom etiquette and what to expect (Wolfe, 1990). Having the child play with anatomically correct dolls can be useful in getting at the truth, but it should be but one part of an assessment, because many nonabused children will portray such dolls having sexual intercourse (Jampole & Weber, 1987). The professional consensus, though, is that very few cases of sexual abuse are fabricated by children. Still in all, it is little wonder that many, perhaps most, occurrences of child molestation within families go unreported and become a developing adult's terrible secret that can lower self-esteem, distort what could otherwise be positive relationships, and even contribute to serious mental disorders.

Parents go through their own crisis when they become aware that someone has been molesting their child. If incest is involved, it is a true family crisis; and if it is the father, then there is often conflict about what to do, for he is frequently the dominant figure in the family and is feared as well as loved. Shame and guilt abound within the home, and the family may well be struggling with other serious problems, such as alcoholism in one or both parents. Decisions have to be made about how to protect the youngster from further sexual abuse or vindictive threats or actions from a frightened, angry perpetrator. The incest victim's mother is in a particularly difficult situation, sometimes torn between her husband and her child, sometimes facing financial uncertainty should he leave the home or be arrested. It is impossible to know what percentage of incest cases are not reported to the police, but it is safe to say that it is sizable, perhaps the great majority (Finkelhor, 1983). More frequently reported to police and prosecuted in court are pedophilic offenses, when the perpetrator is a nonfamily member.

Parents also need help in knowing how to respond to the child's allegations. To freak out (an understandable reaction) will likely only make the child feel worse, yet the complaints must be taken seriously. It is important to remember that children construe things differently than do adults, and although molestation of any kind is serious, preschool-aged children may well not understand the exact nature of what has been done to them. Yet they must be protected and sometimes treated for physical injuries.

After the immediate crisis is past, many children may still need professional attention (Wolfe, 1990). Like adult victims of rape (page 351)—and in a very real sense molested children are often rape victims—posttraumatic stress disorder can be a consequence. Many interventions are similar to those used for PTSD in adults (page 160), the emphasis being on exposure to memories of the trauma through discussion in a safe and supportive therapeutic atmosphere (Johnson, 1987). Also important is learning that human sexuality is not dirty and can be a bolstering part of one's personality as one continues to mature (McCarthy, 1986). Inhibitions about body contact can be addressed in group therapy settings via structured, nonsexual hand-holding and back rubs (Wolfe, 1990). As with rape, an important focus is externalizing the blame for what happened, changing the victim's attribution of responsibility from an "I was bad" self-concept to "He/she was bad." Intervention varies with the subject's age—a fourteen-year-old does not need dolls to recount what was done, and a three-year-old child is not an appropriate candidate for group therapy. As yet, there is no controlled research on these various and complex interventions, but clinical reports are encouraging.

obtaining or increasing sexual gratification through subjection to pain or humiliation is the key characteristic of **sexual masochism**. Both these disorders are found in heterosexual and homosexual relationships, though it is estimated that upwards of 85 percent of people with these disorders are exclusively or predominantly heterosexual (Moser & Levitt, 1987). Unlike the situation with the other paraphilias, some sadists and masochists are women. The disorders seem to begin by early adulthood, and most sadists and masochists are relatively comfortable with their unconventional sexual practices (Spengler, 1977).

The majority of sadists establish relationships with masochists to derive mutual sexual gratification. Moser and Levitt (1987) estimate that millions of Americans engage in sexual practices that involve the infliction of pain or humiliation (though far fewer engage in such practices often or intensively enough to be diagnosed as sadists or masochists). The majority of sadists and masochists lead otherwise conventional lives, and there is some evidence that they are above average in income and educational status (Moser & Levitt, 1987; Spengler, 1977). The sadist may derive full orgasmic pleasure by inflicting pain on his or her partner, and the masochist may be completely gratified by being subjected to pain. For other partners the sadistic and masochistic practices are a prelude or aspect of sexual intercourse. A married couple seen for behavior therapy had practiced the following ritual, which they wanted to eliminate.

> As a prelude to sexual intercourse, the young man would draw blood by cutting a small incision on the palm of his wife's right hand. She would then stimulate his penis, using the blood of her right palm as a lubricant. Normal intercourse would then ensue, and the moment the wife felt her husband ejaculating, she was required to dig her nails deep into the small of his back or buttocks. (Lazarus & Davison, 1971, pp. 202–203)

Although a great many are switchable, that is, able to take both dominant and submissive roles, masochists outnumber sadists. For this reason bondage and discipline services may constitute a considerable portion of the business of a house of prostitution. The manifestations of sexual masochism are also varied. Examples include restraint (physical bondage), blindfolding (sensory bondage), spanking, whipping, electrical shocks, cutting, and humiliation (such as being urinated or defecated on, being forced to bark like a dog, or being subjected to verbal abuse). The term *infantilism* refers to a desire to be treated as a helpless infant and clothed in diapers. One particularly dangerous form of masochism, called hypoxyphilia, involves sexual arousal by oxygen deprivation. This can involve a noose, plastic bag, chest compression, or a chemical that produces a temporary decrease in brain oxygenation by peripheral vasodilation (American Psychiatric Association, 1987).

The sexual sadist obtains sexual gratification from inflicting pain or humiliation on another person, often a sexual masochist who is aroused by being dominated or humiliated.

Some sadists do murder and mutilate, and are among sex offenders who are imprisoned for torturing victims, mostly strangers, and deriving sexual satisfaction from this (Dietz, Hazelwood, & Warren, 1990). Fortunately, however, most of the time sadism and masochism are restricted to fantasies and are not then regarded as disorders, according to the DSM, unless the person is "markedly distressed by them." This is a constant theme in DSM-IV, that is, that it is okay to have very unconventional fantasies provided that one does not act on them or that one is not bothered by them. If, then, the social milieu supports creativity, at least in fantasies, we can expect more people not to be bothered by the stories they tell themselves and the pictures they generate in their minds while having sex. We may have, then, more sadistic and/or masochistic fantasies but less diagnosable sadism and masochism.

The shared activities of a sadist and a masochist are heavily scripted. Pain, humiliation and domination, or both take place as part of a story that the two agree to act out together. Themes of submission–domination appear to be as important as inflicting physical pain. The activities of the masochist and sadist assume for both parties a certain fictional *meaning* that heightens sexual arousal. The masochist, for example, may be a mischievous child who must be punished by a discipline-minded teacher; or a slave from ancient times, recently sold to a powerful sultan. Cognitive theorists, such as Gagnon and Simon (1973), hold that any explanation of sadomasochistic sexual patterns must take into account the fabrications that the partners weave into their actions.

How can it happen that a person, often quite normal in other respects, must inflict or experience suffering, directly or vicariously, in order to become sexually aroused? If it is assumed, as some psychoanalysts do, that pain provides sexual pleasure, the answer is readily available; unfortunately, this explanation really explains nothing. Another psychoanalytic theory, restricted to men, holds that the sadist has a castration complex and inflicts pain to assure himself of his power and masculinity. It may also be that in childhood or adolescence sadomasochistic elements were present while orgasms were experienced. Although it is plausible to suggest that classical conditioning may have occurred, there are as yet no data to support this theory. A related hypothesis suggests that the physiological arousal from inflicting and experiencing pain is not, in fact, dissimilar to sexual excitement. In the early stages of being sexualized, discriminations may be difficult to make, especially if the pain-inducing act also includes sexual elements. In this way the individual may learn to label pain-produced arousal as sexual. Interesting as it may be, this hypothesis is also purely speculative at this time.

Paraphilias Not Otherwise Specified

The paraphilias here are a miscellaneous group of unconventional activities, all with impressive and mysterious names, none of them well understood. Among them are the following.

Coprophilia. Obtaining sexual gratification from handling feces.

Frotteurism. Obtaining sexual gratification by rubbing against or fondling an unsuspecting, nonconsenting person. Intercourse is not involved. Note: In DSM-IV this diagnosis has its own separate listing, whereas the other paraphilias discussed in this section continue to be relegated to a catchall miscellaneous category.

Klismaphilia. Achieving sexual excitement by means of an enema administered by another person.

Necrophilia. Being sexually intimate with a corpse.

Telephone scatologia. Seeking sexual gratification by making obscene phone calls to unconsenting adults.

Zoophilia. Being sexually intimate with animals.

Therapies for the Paraphilias

A prevalent psychoanalytic view of the paraphilias is that they arise from a character disorder, an older term for personality disorder, and that they are therefore exceedingly difficult to treat with any reasonable expectation of success. This perspective is probably the one also held by the courts and by the lay public (Lanyon, 1986). Although psychoanalytic views have had an impact on views of causation, they have made few contributions to effective therapy for these disorders.

Behavior therapists have made relatively few assumptions about deep-seated personality defects among paraphiliacs and have instead concentrated on the particular pattern of unconventional sexuality and tried to develop therapeutic procedures for changing only this aspect of the individual's makeup.

In the earliest stages of behavior therapy, paraphilias were narrowly viewed as attractions to inappropriate objects and activities. Looking to experimental psychology for ways to reduce these attractions, workers fixed on aversion therapy. Thus a boot fetishist would be given shock or an emetic when looking at a boot, a transvestite when cross-dressing, a pedophile when gazing at a photograph of a nude child, and so on. Sometimes these negative treatments were supplemented by training in social skills and assertion, for many of these individuals relate poorly to others in ordinary social situations and even more poorly, if at all, through conventional sexual activity. There is some reason to believe that aversion therapy can have some beneficial effects on pedophilia, transvestism, exhibitionism, and fetishism (Marks & Gelder, 1967; Marks, Gelder, & Bancroft, 1970; Marshall & Barsbee, 1990), though it is very unlikely that such techniques work by conditioning. Although aversion therapy may not actually eliminate the attraction, it does in some cases provide the patient with a greater measure of control over the overt behavior itself (McConaghy, 1990).

Increasing conventional arousal seems to depend more on positive therapeutic approaches. **Orgasmic reorientation** is one such behavioral technique used to alter classes of stimuli to which people are sexually attracted (Brownell, Hayes, & Barlow, 1977). Paraphiliacs are confronted with a conventionally arousing stimulus while they are responding sexually for other, undesirable reasons. In the first clinical demonstration of this technique, Davison (1968a) instructed a young man troubled by sadistic fantasies to masturbate at home in the following manner.

> When assured of privacy in his dormitory room . . . he was first to obtain an erection by whatever means possible—undoubtedly with a sadistic fantasy, as he indicated. He was then to begin to masturbate while

> looking at a picture of a sexy, nude woman (the "target" sexual stimulus). . . . If he began losing his erection, he was to switch back to his sadistic fantasy until he could begin masturbating effectively again. Concentrating again on the . . . picture, he was to continue masturbating, using the fantasy only to regain the erection. As orgasm was approaching, he was at all costs to focus on the . . . picture. . . . (p. 84)

The client was able to follow these instructions and over a period of weeks began to find conventional pictures, ideas, and images sexually arousing. The therapist, however, had to complement the orgasmic procedure with some aversion therapy (Cautela, 1966) for the sadistic imaginings. The follow-up after a year and a half found the client capable of conventional arousal, although he apparently reverted to his sadistic fantasies every now and again. This dubious outcome has been reported for other instances of orgasmic reorientation, but behavior therapists continue to explore its possibilities, and some workers believe it to be the treatment of choice for increasing conventional sexual arousal in paraphiliacs (Abel, Mittelman, & Becker, 1985).

In Focus Box 12.1, we discussed child sexual abuse from the victim's perspective. Efforts to reduce its incidence, prevalence, and severity must also focus on the sex offender. One strategy is to teach an ethic that condemns exploitative sex (Cohen, 1986). Aversion therapy to reduce sexual arousal toward children has also been advocated (Wolfe, 1990; Ryan et al., 1987).

As mentioned at the beginning of this chapter, most paraphilias are illegal and some of them pose dangers to society. It is therefore to be expected that many child molesters and rapists (discussed in next section) are imprisoned or committed to mental hospitals (Chapter 21). How effective is treatment in these institutional settings? Success rates are difficult to determine, ranging from more than 90 percent to as low as 30 percent (Marshall et al., 1991). One reason that published data are hard to interpret is that some programs select the most problematic prisoners to treat whereas others treat those with the most promising prognoses, for example, first offenders. Also, treated offenders are seldom compared with matched no-treatment control groups, a serious (yet understandable) problem in light of the fact that some pedophiles do not commit another offense for up to twenty years following release, even if they received no treatment while incarcerated (Soothill & Gibbons, 1978). Some programs do not have follow-up sessions after release, while others do. Recidivism increases as the years go by, especially when two years have passed since termination of treatment (Marshall & Barabee, 1990). Some reviews (e.g., Furby, Weinrott, & Blackshaw, 1989) do not distinguish carefully among kinds of treatment, an omission that makes it understandable that success rates vary so much.

A variety of medical interventions have also been tried. Psychosurgery, usually lesioning parts of the hypothalamus in the midbrain, was attempted primarily by a group of surgeons in Germany with largely negative results, sometimes with serious unintended side effects, such as loss of intellect or even death (Muller, Roeder, & Orthner, 1973). One reason for these failures is probably the fact that too little was known about the role of the hypothalamus in complex human sexual behavior to justify such radical and irreversible interventions. Castration, or removal of the testes, was used a great deal in western Europe a generation ago, with apparently some efficacy in terms of reducing the incidence of paraphiliac behavior (e.g., Langeluddeke, 1963). However, as Marshall et al. (1991) point out, those operated on were a heterogeneous group, among whom were homosexuals involved in *noncoercive* sex with other adults. It is unclear how many were offenders whose crimes really harmed innocent others, that is, child molesters and rapists. The lack of clarity of outcome, coupled with major ethical concerns, has led to very infrequent use of castration these days.

Efforts to control illegal and socially disapproved paraphiliac behavior among sex offenders have also turned to the use of certain drugs. Treatment has employed Medroxyprogesterone acetate (MPA), a drug that is believed to reduce testosterone levels in men, reduce the frequency of erections and ejaculations, and thereby, presumably, inhibit unconventional sexual arousal and consequent disapproved behavior, but the results so far are inconclusive. Berlin and Meinecke (1981) found that after periods of MPA administration ranging from five to twenty years, seventeen of twenty sex offenders did not engage in paraphiliac behaviors; however, when the drug was discontinued, most reverted to their forbidden ways. It would appear that this sexual appetite suppressant may have to be taken indefinitely, a possibility that raises many ethical issues, including the sometimes serious side effects of long-term use, such as infertility and diabetes.

Conflicting findings have been reported also with the short-term use of MPA: Wincze, Bansal, and Malamud (1986) showed persistence of paraphiliac arousal and behavior even when testosterone levels were reduced (a finding also reported by Cooper, 1987b, and Gagne, 1981), whereas McConaghy, Blaszczynski, and Kidson (1988) found significant reductions in paraphiliac urges at a one-year follow-up. In reviewing these and many other studies of MPA, Marshall et al. (1991) concluded that the short-term administration of the drug might bring paraphiliac and rape behavior under enough control in some individuals to permit psychological intervention that might have a more enduring effect.

A sensible program of treatment must always consider the multifaceted nature of a particular disorder. An exhibitionist, for example, may experience a great deal of tension in connection with the urge to expose himself; it would therefore make sense to desensitize him to women who turn him on. After imagining them in a succession of street and other public scenes, until they no longer make him anxious, he may be more relaxed when he encounters these types of women in public places and so may not feel the urge to expose (Bond & Hutchison, 1960). Other paraphiliacs might be questioned about social situations and aspects of relating to women that cause them undue discomfort. They could be desensitized to these women in hopes of becoming generally less anxious. Social-skills training and sex education are often called for as well, to address deficits that are commonly found among paraphiliacs. The availability of an adult sexual partner also strengthens the potential for long-term improvement.

There is a call for a multifaceted approach in the treatment of incest, a problem that is increasingly viewed as involving an entire family—the victim, the spouse, and siblings as well. A **family systems approach** is advocated, whereby the entire family is involved in therapy sessions that are primarily insight oriented, aimed at helping all members understand why the father (in most instances) turns to a daughter for emotional support and sexual gratification. The best known program of this kind is the Child Sexual Abuse Treatment Program in Santa Clara County, California, which reports that over 90 percent of fathers can be returned to their families and that there is only a 1 percent recidivism rate (Giarretto, 1982). Considerable research is needed, however, to replicate these findings and to uncover why this complex (and expensive) treatment approach effects beneficial change (Lanyon, 1986).

In general, cognitive-behavioral approaches have become more sophisticated and broader in scope since the 1960s, when the paraphilias were dealt with almost exclusively in terms of sexual attraction to inappropriate environmental stimuli. In many instances, therapy is modeled on Masters and Johnson (1970; cf. page 378), the assumption being that some paraphilias develop or are maintained by unsatisfactory sexual relationships with consenting adults (Marshall & Barabee, 1990). Overall, both institution-based and outpatient programs that follow a cognitive-behavioral model with sex offenders often reduce recidividism more than what one would expect if no treatment at all had been attempted. These outcomes are much better for child molesters than for rapists. Although sex offenders generally evoke disgust and fear from people more than genuine interest, society often overlooks the fact that efforts to treat such people, even if only minimally effective, are not only cost-effective but stand the chance of protecting others when the person is ultimately released (Prentky & Burgess, 1990).

We have mentioned rape several times in our discussion of the paraphilias, especially pedophilia and incest. But forcible sexual contact occurs far more often between adults than between an adult and a child. We turn now to an examination of the important topic of rape.

Rape

Few other antisocial acts are viewed with more disgust and anger than **forcible rape**, sexual intercourse with an unwilling partner. A second category, **statutory rape**, refers to sexual intercourse between a male and a female minor, someone under the age of consent. The typical age of consent, as decided by state statutes, is eighteen years. It is assumed that a younger person should not be held responsible for her sexual activity, but it has been suggested in recent years that the age be lowered. A charge of statutory rape can be made even if it is proved that the girl entered into the situation knowingly and willingly. Thus statutory rape need not involve force, being simply a consummated intercourse with a female minor that was reported to the police. We focus here on forcible rape.

The Crime

In what is sometimes termed *sadistic rape*, the rapist inflicts serious physical harm on the victim's body, such as inserting foreign objects into the vagina or pulling and burning her breasts. Some rapists murder and mutiliate (Holmstrom & Burgess, 1980). Little wonder then that rape is considered as much an act of violence and aggression as a sexual act. In many jurisdictions the definition of rape includes not only vaginal penetration but oral and anal entry as well. Focusing on the victim's reactions—the helplessness, the fear, the humiliation—rather than on the specifics of the perpetrator's acts, Calhoun and Atkeson (1991) construe *any* act of sexual domination as rape. This expanded definition may be useful for purposes of helping victims but is different from legal definitions. In our discussion, we will distinguish whenever possible rape that involves penile penetration or oral sex from unwanted sexual activity that does not (even though the latter may be as traumatic to some women as the former). Also, although men can be victims of sexual assault—especially by other men in prison—our discussion focuses on women because rape is primarily an act of men against women.

As many as 25 percent of American women will be raped during their lifetimes (Kilpatrick & Best, 1990), and it is likely that more than 80 percent of sexual assaults are not reported. Expanding the purview to coerced sexual activity that stops short of rape, Koss (1985) determined that as many as 75 percent of female college students have been subjected to unwanted sexual activity.

The Victim, the Attack, and the Aftermath

A prevalent belief is that the victims of rape are always young and attractive. This is a myth. Although many victims do indeed fit this description, many others do not. Age and physical appearance are no barriers to some rapists; they might choose children as young as one year old and women in their eighties.

Rape victims are often traumatized by the experience, both physically and mentally (Calhoun, Atkeson, & Resick, 1982; Resick, Veronen, Calhoun, Kilpatrick, & Atkeson, 1986). In the minutes or seconds preceding rape, the woman begins to recognize her dangerous situation but can scarcely believe what is about to happen to her. During the moments of the attack, she is first and foremost in great fear for her life. The physical violation of her body and the ripping away of her freedom of choice are enraging. But the victim also feels her vulnerability in not being able to fight off her stronger attacker and usually finds her capacity for resistance seriously compromised by her terror. For weeks or months following the rape, many victims are extremely tense and deeply humiliated; they feel guilt that they were unable to fight harder and have angry thoughts of revenge. Many have nightmares about the rape.

In a study of women admitted to a large city hospital for emergency treatment immediately following rape, Burgess and Holmstrom (1974) found that half ultimately changed their place of residence or their telephone number. Such changes can seriously disrupt social relationships, lead to loss of time at work and even of employment, and contribute to depression because of a withdrawal from social supports (Calhoun & Atkeson, 1991).

A large number of these women had trouble in sexual relationships with their husbands or lovers. Masters and Johnson (1970), too, found among their dysfunctional couples a number of women who had developed negative attitudes toward sex with their husbands following rape. So certain are Calhoun and Atkeson (1991), two experienced clinical researchers on rape, that sexual problems are a frequent long-term consequence of untreated rape trauma that they urge clinicians always to suspect rape or sexual assault in women who have sexual dysfunctions. For some women, even though frequency of sex and of orgasms may not be diminished, satisfaction with sex can be reduced for years (Feldman-Summers, Gordon, & Mengler, 1979). Some victims of rape develop phobias about being outdoors or indoors or in the dark, depending on where the rape took place. They may also fear being alone or in crowds or having anyone behind them.

Without intervention, symptoms of anxiety and depression can persist in some women for years following an assault (Calhoun & Atkeson, 1991). Suicidal risk is also high for many victims (Cohen & Roth, 1987; Kilpatrick et al., 1985), as is substance abuse (Burnam et al., 1988), which is probably an attempt to self-medicate to reduce anxiety and general dysphoria. We have already seen (page 344) that multiple personality and borderline personality have been linked to sexual trauma in childhood. Moreover, consistent with research on the effects of stress on physical health, rape victims can suffer a variety of somatic problems and tend to increase their utilization of medical services (Phelps, Wallace, & Waigant, 1989).

Of course, the nature and duration of what some call rape trauma syndrome (Burgess & Holstrom, 1974) depend a great deal on what the victim's life is like both prior to and following the attack. Such variables as marital status, partner's reactions, social support, prior psychological health, experiences testifying in court, and crisis intervention or longer term therapy can all worsen or mitigate the emotional consequences of rape (Atkeson et al., 1982; Ruch & Leon, 1983). And yet results from research are inconclusive as to whether the emotional consequences of rape correlate with the violence of the assault, the setting, or the familiarity of the rapist, leading Calhoun and Atkeson (1991) to conclude that the aftermath is more a function of how the victim appraises the events than of the circumstances themselves. Again we see the apparent importance of how people *construe* events.

It is of interest that many jurisdictions allow the very existence of rape trauma syndrome in a victim to be admitted as evidence supporting an allegation of rape. It can also be used to explain behavior of the victim that might otherwise be taken to mean that there had been consent, for example, delays in reporting the crime, memory loss, and inconsistent statements by the victim (Block, 1990). For good reason DSM-IV mentions rape as one of the traumata that can give rise to posttraumatic stress disorder.

The Rapist

The vast majority of rapes are almost surely planned—it is inaccurate to say that rape is the spontaneous act of a man whose sexual impulses have gone out of control (Harrington & Sutton-Simon, 1977). The rapist may have a sadistic streak, but unlike the sadist, he often does not know the victim beforehand and attacks someone who is unwilling. Moreover, a sadist usually has an established, ongoing relationship with a masochist that involves voluntary mutual exchange of sexually pleasurable pain. In many cases, a pattern of repeated rape is part of a psychopathic life-style.

The incidence of sexual dysfunction during rape may be high. Interviews with 170 men convicted of sexual assault revealed that erectile failure as well as premature and retarded ejaculation during their criminal act had occurred for a third of these men, although almost none reported having these problems in his consenting sexual relations. Only one-fourth of the men gave no evidence of sexual dysfunction during rape (Groth & Burgess, 1977). Rapists often abuse alcohol, so the frequency of erectile failure might be due in part to the inhibitory effects of alcohol on sexual arousal (Wilson & Lawson, 1976). Also, the violence that is intrinsic to rape may arise from the *dis*inhibitory effects of alcohol on aggression (Barabee, Marshall, & Yates, 1983).

Sexism and the subjugation of women through rape were explored in depth by Susan Brownmiller (1975) in her best-selling book *Against Our Will*. Her thesis is that rape is "nothing more or less than a conscious process of intimidation by which all men keep all women in a state of fear" (p. 5). She garners evidence from history, both ancient and modern. In the Babylonian civilization (3000 B.C.), for example, a married woman was the property of her husband. If she was raped, both she and the rapist were bound and tossed into a river. The husband could choose to save her, or he could let her drown, just punishment for her adultery. The views of the ancient Hebrews were no more enlightened; a married woman who had been raped was commonly stoned to death along with her attacker. When an unbetrothed virgin was raped within the walls of the city, she was similarly stoned, for it was assumed that she could have prevented the attack simply by crying out.

Such penalties imposed by different societies on raped women, together with the fact that men with their generally superior strength can usually overpower women, buttress Brownmiller's argument that rape has served in the past and still serves to intimidate women. The Crusaders raped their way across Europe in the eleventh through thirteeth centuries on their holy pilgrimages to free Jerusalem from the Muslims; the Germans in World War I raped as they rampaged through Belgium; U.S. forces raped in Vietnam as they searched and destroyed; and Iraqi soldiers raped and brutalized women as they occupied Kuwait just a few years ago. Brownmiller contends that rape is actually *expected* in war. In her view, membership in the most exclusive males-only clubs in the world—the fighting forces of most nations—encourages a perverse sense of masculine superiority and creates a climate in which rape is acceptable.

Who is the rapist? Is he primarily the psychopath who seeks the thrill of dominating and humiliating a woman through intimidation and often brutal assault? Is he an ordinarily unassertive man with a fragile ego who, feeling inadequate after disappointment and rejection in work or love, takes out his frustrations on an unwilling stranger? Or is he the teenager, provoked by a seductive and apparently available young woman who, it turns out, was not as interested as he in sexual intimacy? Is he a man whose inhibitions against expressing anger have been dissolved by alcohol? The best answer is that the rapist is all these men, probably in a combination of several of these circumstances. What many rapists probably have in common is unusually high hostility toward women, arising from beliefs of having been betrayed, deceived, or demeaned by them (Duke & Durham, 1990). From a sociological perspective, the more a society accepts interpersonal violence as a way to handle conflict and solve problems, the higher the frequency of rape (Sanday, 1981).

If we rely on crime reports for information, men arrested for rape tend to be young—usually between fifteen and twenty-five years of age—poor, unskilled, and not well educated. They come from the lower classes, in which, sociologists assert, violence is more the norm than in the middle class. About half of them are married and living with their wives at the time of the crime. A fourth to a third of all rapes are carried out by two or more men. Given the knowledge that rape is seriously underreported, however, it would be a mistake to generalize about rapists from information gleaned from police files. Indeed, in some instances the rapist is the victim's husband. Russell (1982) estimates a 14 percent incidence rate among married women.

Bandura (1986) suggested that exposure to certain forms of pornography may dispose some men to act aggressively toward women in sexual situations. In a review of research on the topic, he concluded that, whereas pleasant erotica does not increase sexual aggressiveness, erotica that demeans women or entails violence toward and domination of them does (Malamuth, Feshbach, & Jaffe, 1977). Indeed, there is evidence that hard-core pornography—which typically derogates women—leads male viewers to become more lenient in their thinking about rape offenders (Linz, Donnerstein, & Penrod, 1988; Zillman & Bryant, 1984). Violent pornography that portrays women as initially resisting but then enjoying rape fosters the idea that women like to be sexually assaulted (Malamuth & Check, 1981). Moreover, one-third of a sample of college men admitted that they might rape if they could avoid arrest, and they tended to subscribe to the myth that women who are raped ask for it by the way they dress and act (Malamuth, 1981).

Even male students who regard rape as unacceptable are aroused by portrayals of rape if the woman is depicted as having an orgasm during the assault (Malamuth & Check, 1983). What comes to mind is what is regarded as one of the most memorable and romantic kisses portrayed on film, that of Clark Gable as Rhett Butler and Vivien Leigh as Scarlett O'Hara in the classic movie *Gone with the Wind.* At the foot of the stairs in an elegant Southern mansion, Gable grabs Leigh, embraces her forcefully, and kisses her. She initially resists but within a few seconds gives in to the passion of the moment and allows herself to be carried upstairs, thrown on the bed, and, as it used to be quaintly phrased, "taken." What kind of message is conveyed to men who would be masculine? What kind of message to women who would be feminine? And what kind of message to generations of film buffs about the nature of male–female sexual relationships? (See Focus Box 12.2 for a review of what we know today as date rape or acquaintance rape.)

Emerging from the study of rape, and of other patterns of unconventional sexual behavior, is the fact that sexuality can serve many purposes. Indeed, an act we label as sexual because it involves the genitalia may sometimes be better understood in nonsexual terms. The classic study of sex offenders (Gebhard et al., 1965) concluded that up to 33 percent of rapists carried out the act to express aggression rather than for sexual satisfaction. Rapists, in the opinion of many (e.g., Brownmiller, 1975; Gagnon, 1977), aggress against others for reasons only remotely related to sex per se. Recent research by Knight and Prentky (1990) suggests four motivations: opportunism (involving an unplanned, impulsive assault), pervasive anger (consisting of inflicting pain and injury), sex (reflecting an enduring sexual preoccupation), and vindictiveness (entailing actions designed to humiliate and degrade).

Many feminist groups object to the classification of rape as a *sexual* crime at all, for it can mask the basically assaultive and typically brutal nature of the act, and it creates an atmosphere in which the sexual motives of the *victim* are questioned. Although a person who is beaten and robbed (without being sexually abused) is hardly suspected of secretly wanting to be attacked, by cruel irony the victims of rape must often prove their moral purity to husbands, friends, police—even to themselves. What, after all, did *they* do that might have contributed to the incident, especially if the rapist is not a

This famous scene from *Gone with the Wind* illustrates one of the myths about rape—that despite initial resistance women like to be "taken".

FOCUS

12.2 • Acquaintance Rape

Rape between two people who know, who may even be dating, each other is called **acquaintance rape** or **date rape**. Such attacks may outnumber those between strangers by as much as three to one (Kilpatrick & Best, 1990). Given the still-prevalent tendency to question the complicity, even seductiveness, of the victim (who is almost always a woman), it is not surprising that date rapes are infrequently reported—indeed, they are the least reported type of rape (Warshaw, 1988), perhaps because victims tend even more than in assaults from strangers to blame themselves for what happened. Some assert that if a woman permits a man to embrace and kiss her, she has at least implicitly given him permission to have intercourse or to engage in other intimate sexual acts with her. This permission-giving viewpoint is vehemently rebutted by the contention that the weaker party in a sociosexual situation always has the right to say no, and that there is no justification in the claim that the man has been all stirred up by the woman's alleged seductiveness and can't help himself. The uncontrollable passion claim is especially weak when the rape involves force that results in bodily harm to the victim.

According to a survey conducted by *Ms Magazine*, only one-quarter of women who said that they had had sexual intercourse against their will said they had ever been raped (Warshaw, 1988). In a related vein, several studies by Malamuth and his colleagues (e.g., Malamuth, Haber, & Feshbach, 1980; Malamuth, 1981) found that about half of male college student respondents admitted that they would force sex with a woman if they believed they would not get caught. It's little surprise, then, that date rape is still poorly understood and infrequently reported.

Some theoreticians believe that rape is part and parcel of the cultural stereotypes of masculinity and femininity, whereby the male's role in sexual relationships is to be aggressive and the female's, passive yet seductive. The woman is expected to resist the man's advances; the man is expected to overcome her resistance. It may be that some acts of rape are committed through faulty communication between the man and the woman. The woman's "maybe" is interpreted as "yes" by the man, who proceeds on the assumption that the woman really wants to be intimate, only to be sorely disappointed and unable to accept her ultimate refusal (Gagnon, 1977; Margolin, 1990). This view of rape would of course apply only to instances in which the two people know each other, not to the large number of assaults that occur on streets and through forced entry into homes. Nor does this view account for the extreme brutality that is often part of the assault.

There may be a message here that can reduce date rape. In addition to being more assertive and demanding if they feel unwanted pressure being applied, women can learn to understand the different scripts that men and women often operate with and thereby become more mindful of the possibility that some of their messages can be received and interpreted by men in unintended ways. This is not to shift the responsibility to the woman, rather to provide her with some tools that can improve communication and lessen the chances that an acquaintance or date will construe her friendliness and affection as an invitation to go further. Certainly any preventive efforts directed at women have to be complemented by educational programs for men, who need to examine their attitudes and practices in dealing with women as possible sexual partners (rather than objects) and need to understand the different scripts as well.

complete stranger? But there are indications that the stigma of rape is being lessened by more enlightened views, coming in large measure from women's liberation groups and from books such as Brownmiller's (Focus Box 12.3).

Therapy for Rapists and Rape Victims

Unlike most of the disorders dealt with in this book, rape has the dubious distinction of presenting two different challenges to the mental health professional: treating the man who has committed the act and treating the woman who has been the victim.

A number of therapy programs have been developed to reduce the tendency of men to rape. In some prisons confrontational group therapy has been employed in efforts to encourage convicted rapists to take responsibility for their violence toward women and to explore more decent ways of handling their anger and relating to the opposite sex. But the effectiveness of these programs has not been adequately studied. Most rapists perpetrate their assaults many times in their lives, and prison terms have limited effect on reducing the future incidence of rape. Therapists who try to help men who rape have to consider a wide range of causes that might underlie the problem—loneliness, deficient social skills (Overholser & Beck, 1986), fear of dealing with women in conventional ways, hatred of women, inability or unwillingness to delay gratification, especially after excessive drinking, and exaggerated conceptions of masculinity that relegate women to an inferior status.

Biological interventions, such as surgical castration and the chemical lowering of testosterone rest on the assumption that rape is primarily a sexual act. It should be kept in mind, however, that erectile capacity is not necessary for rape; the violent behavior itself is not directly addressed by these drastic medical measures (Geer, Heiman, & Leitenberg, 1984). Further, there is the question of the effectiveness of castration as a therapy.

Considerable effort is expended in helping the victims of sexual assaults (e.g., Calhoun & Atkeson, 1991). A number of rape crisis centers and telephone hot lines have been established across the country, some of them associated with existing hospitals and clinics, others operating on their own. Staffed both by professionals and by female volunteers who may themselves have been rape victims, these centers offer support and advice within what is called a crisis intervention framework. The focus is on normalizing the victim's emotional reactions—"Everyone goes through this emotional turmoil after an assault"; encouraging her to talk about her feelings; helping her meet immediate needs, such as arranging for child care or improving the security arrangements in her home; in short, helping her solve problems and cope with the immediate aftermath of the traumatic event (Calhoun & Atkeson, 1991; Sorenson & Brown, 1990).

Withdrawal and inactivity are not to be encouraged in the victim. Reporting the rape to the police is encouraged: women from the crisis center can accompany the rape victim to the hospital and to the police station, where they help her with the legal procedures and with recounting the events of the attack. They may later arrange for examinations for pregnancy and venereal disease and for psychological counseling. The possibility of HIV infection also has to be addressed. The empathic companions from the crisis center help the victim get started in expressing her feelings about her ordeal, and they urge her to continue her venting with her own relatives and friends. If the attacker or attackers have been apprehended, the women from the center urge the victim to go through with the prosecution. They attend both her meetings with the district attorney and the trial itself.

As already indicated, rape victims, far more than the victims of other violent crimes, tend to examine their own role in provoking or allowing the attack; counseling, therefore, has to concentrate on allevi-

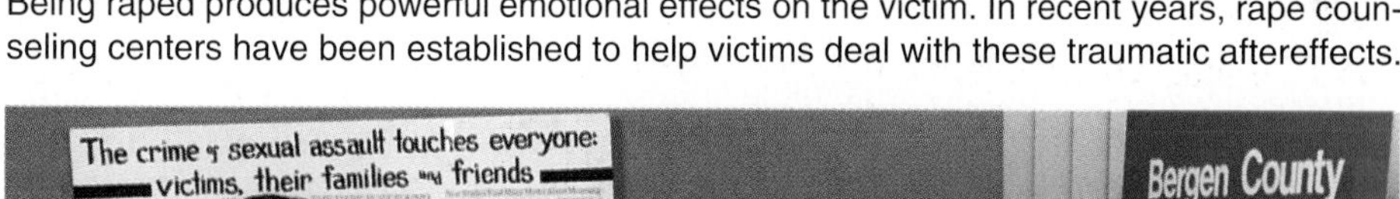
Being raped produces powerful emotional effects on the victim. In recent years, rape counseling centers have been established to help victims deal with these traumatic aftereffects.

FOCUS 12.3 • A Psychophysiological Analysis of Rape: Promise Unrealized?

Discussions of rape are based almost entirely on the work of historians, sociologists, political analysts, and journalists. Psychophysiologists also have been trying to bring something of the phenomenon into the laboratory. The work of Abel and his colleagues (1977) is a good example of this kind of research.

In their initial study these workers developed a methodology that relied on the penile plethysmograph to help them distinguish between rapists and nonrapists. Most of the rapists had long histories of forcible sexual assaults on women, and some on men as well. Control subjects had histories of other types of unconventional sexual behavior, such as exhibitionism, pedophilia, and homosexuality.

The independent variable in the experiment consisted of two kinds of erotic audiotapes. The story recorded on one tape was of mutually enjoyable intercourse with a suitable partner; the other audiotape was of a rape of that same partner. The enjoyable scene of intercourse portrayed the partner as willing, loving, and utterly involved with the subject. In the rape scene the victim resisted and was in physical as well as emotional pain. According to the plethysmograph, rapists were significantly more aroused by the rape tape than were the nonrapist subjects, the expected pattern. But, interestingly, the rapists were highly aroused by the mutually enjoyable intercourse tape as well! In fact, this tape aroused them no less than the rape scene. And the nonrapists, although much more aroused by the lovemaking than by the rape, nonetheless showed some mild arousal when listening to the rape story.

Abel then used the same method to investigate the rapist's response to aggression. Are rapists aroused by aggression if the incident does not conclude with sexual assault? How does arousal from aggression relate to arousal from rape? Some of the rapists already studied listened to three additional tapes. One of them depicted a man slapping, hitting, and holding a woman down against her will, but without ensuing intercourse. On the second the man had forcible intercourse with the same victim. The rapists also listened to a tape of nonviolent sexual intercourse with a willing partner. Results revealed that the aggression scene generated some sexual arousal, but only 40 percent of that generated by the rape scene and an even smaller percent than was generated by the tape of mutually satisfying nonaggressive intercourse.

Abel and his colleagues then compared the plethysmograph records of individual rapists with their case histories. Some case histories indicated a preference for conventional intercourse, with rape resorted to if the victim was unwilling. These men had relatively small erections to the aggression story, greater response to the rape, and the greatest response to the conventional intercourse. For other rapists, whose histories showed repeated, often sadistic assaults of women, erections to mutually enjoyable intercourse were minimal, but arousal was markedly increased when aggression was added, enough to equal rape. Moreover, high levels of arousal were elicited by the aggression-only tape. Hence the picture is not a simple one. Some men apparently resort to rape only when loving inter-

ating the woman's feelings of responsibility and guilt (Frazier, 1990).

When long-term counseling is available, attention is often paid to the woman's ongoing relationships, which may be disrupted or negatively affected by the rape. Friends and family, especially spouses and lovers, will also need attention to help them handle their own emotional turmoil so that they can provide the kind of nonjudgmental support that rape victims need. Although anxiety-reduction approaches vary, they share in common with the treatment of PTSD (Keane et al., 1989) that the victim must be exposed to the fearsome events of the attack so that the learned anxiety can be extinguished (Calhoun & Atkeson, 1991; Rothbaum & Foa, 1992). As with other kinds of anxieties, it is no easy task to encourage the person to reflect on her fears, because denial and avoidance are the usual coping methods used by rape victims—for the most part unsuccessfully. Depression can be addressed by helping the woman reevaluate her role in the rape—as previously mentioned, many victims tend to see them-

course is unavailable, whereas others seem to *require* violence with sex forced on an unwilling and frightened victim. These findings have been fairly well replicated with other samples of rapists and nonrapist controls (Barabee, Marshall, & Lanthier, 1979; Quinsey & Chaplin, 1984), and similar research has been done with child molesters (Abel, Becker, Murphy, & Flanagan, 1981) and other paraphiliacs (Abel, Blanchard, & Barlow, 1981).

The technology used in these studies has, however, been criticized on both technical and conceptual grounds. McConaghy (1990) has criticized the methodology of many of the studies and contends that the methods used to assess arousal are not valid. (Interestingly, for someone who has been involved himself in penile plethysmographic research, he makes a case for more reliance on self-reports.) Although his arguments have not gone unchallenged (McAnulty & Adams, 1992; and rebuttal by McConaghy, 1992), there is a legitimate question as to whether penile plethysmography really taps into the processes underlying aggressive sexual behavior such as rape (Blader & Marshall, 1989). The very use of this genital instrument to distinguish sex offenders from nonoffenders assumes that sexual arousal measurable by enlargement of the penis is an early and necessary stage in the production of sexually coercive behavior. Although this central assumption enjoys some support in the laboratory study of pedophiles (e.g., Freund, Watson, Dickey, & Rienzo, 1991; Marshall, Barbaree, & Christophe, 1986), it lacks clear support in studies of rapists, as we have just seen in the work of Abel and as can also be seen in reports from others (e.g., Barbaree, Baxter, & Marshall, 1989; Baxter et al., 1984; Langevin et al., 1985).

Consider also that in date rape, the male usually tries to obtain consent first, but, if thwarted, exerts force in the hope that the woman will change her mind or in the belief that she really wants intercourse and perhaps does not want to take responsibility for it. Since this kind of scenario is believed to characterize the *majority* of rapes (Williams, 1984), this constitutes a serious problem for the role of sexual arousal as a significant precursor to rape—for there is nothing deviant in the stimuli that elicit the *early* stages of sexual arousal. Rather, there must be factors in the rapist that have him respond with aggression to resistance from the woman. This characteristic is not detectable by an assessment of sexual arousal, psychophysiological or otherwise.

How does this sort of research relate to the discussions in the text? Consider, for example, Brownmiller's thesis that rape is man's way of intimidating, even denigrating, women. Her historical–political analysis might at first appear a world apart from the laboratory research of Abel. But this is not really the case. The question that Abel's kind of laboratory research does not address—and can probably *never* address—is *why.* Why are certain men sexually stimulated when pain is inflicted on an unwilling victim? What is there about the one-down relationship between a rapist and his victim that excites him? Brownmiller and others find the causes in the broad sweep of history and more particularly in the power relationship between men and women. Their independent variables, if you will, are male machismo, the deliberate degradation of women, and the desire to intimidate by aggression. Abel and other laboratory researchers examine men at the end of a long shaping process. The rapists they have studied are products of their social-learning history. To figure out *why* they aggress is the larger, more important question. The search should take investigators into the domain of sociologists, political scientists, and historians.

selves as (partly) responsible. A little-researched topic is the anger and rage that many victims have toward their assailant, feelings that they are often afraid of expressing or not well socialized to express (Calhoun & Atkeson, 1991).

Attitudes and support systems now encourage the victim to report rape and pursue the prosecution of the alleged rapist, but the legal situation is still problematic. Rape continues to be one of the most underreported of crimes. A national crime survey conducted by the U.S. Bureau of Justice estimates that not more than 53 percent of rapes committed between 1973 and 1987 were reported to the police; the actual figure is probably much lower. Interviews with half a million women indicated three reasons for reluctance to report rape: considering the rape a private matter, fearing reprisals from the rapist or his family or friends, and believing that the police would be inefficient, ineffective, or insensitive (Wright, 1991). Furthermore, estimates are that only a very small percentage of rapists are convicted of their crimes. Any familiarity of the victim with her assailant argues strongly against his ultimate conviction. The victim's role in her own assault continues to be examined. And even though many rapists rape hundreds of times, they are only occasionally imprisoned for an offense. Society must be attentive and active to ensure that the victim's rights are defended by the legal system.

A Comment on Homosexuality

Although homosexuality does not appear in DSM-IV as a clearly definable category, we believe that sufficient controversy remains about these patterns of emotion and behavior—among both lay people and health professionals—to warrant consideration of the topic. A historical overview will provide a perspective on some of the many issues surrounding the ways we view those whose sexual preferences include or are restricted to members of their own sex. (See Focus Box 12.4 for several other problems and issues on the topic.)

From the publication of DSM-II in 1968 until 1973, **homosexuality**, sexual desire or activity directed toward a member of one's own sex, was listed as one of the sexual deviations. In 1973, the Nomenclature Committee of the American Psychiatric Association, under pressure from many professionals and particularly from gay activist groups, recommended to the general membership the elimination of the category homosexuality and the substitution of *sexual orientation disturbance*. This new diagnosis was to be applied to gay men and women who are "disturbed by, in conflict with, or wish to change their sexual orientation." The members of the psychiatric association voted on the issue, in itself a comment on the conduct of science in the twentieth century. The change was approved, but not without vehement protests from a number of renowned psychiatrists who had for some time been identified with the traditional view that homosexuality reflects a fixation at an early stage of psychosexual development and is inherently abnormal.

The controversy continued among mental health professionals, but as DSM-III was being developed during the late 1970s, it became increasingly clear that the new nomenclature would maintain the tolerant stance toward homosexuality that had become evident in 1973. The DSM-III category **ego-dystonic homosexuality** referred to a person who is homosexually aroused, finds this arousal to be a persistent source of distress, and wishes to become heterosexual.

Ego-Dystonic Homosexuality in DSM-III

As for all categories of disorder, DSM-III contained for ego-dystonic homosexuality a discussion of predisposing factors.

In DSM-II, homosexuality was listed as one of several sexual deviations. In subsequent editions of the DSM, homosexuality was gradually dropped as a mental disorder, in part due to pressure from gay rights groups.

> Since homosexuality itself is not considered a mental disorder, the factors that predispose to homosexuality are not included in this section [or anywhere in DSM-III]. The factors that predispose to Ego-Dystonic Homosexuality are those negative societal attitudes toward homosexuality that have been internalized. In addition, features associated with heterosexuality, such as having children and [a] socially sanctioned family life, may be viewed as desirable and incompatible with a homosexual arousal pattern. (American Psychiatric Association, 1980, p. 282)

What did these statements mean? Consider the plight of the homosexual growing up in contemporary society.

> To suggest that a person comes voluntarily to change his sexual orientation is to ignore the powerful environmental stress, oppression if you will, that has been telling him for years that he should change. To grow up in a family where the word "homosexual" was whispered, to play in a playground and hear the words "faggot" and "queer," to go to church and hear of "sin" and then to college and hear of "illness," and finally to the counseling center that promises to "cure," is hardly [to live in] an environment of freedom and voluntary choice. The homosexual is expected to want to be changed and his application for treatment is implicity praised as the first step toward "normal" behavior. (Silverstein, 1972, p. 4)

DSM-III took the position that a homosexual was abnormal if he or she had been persuaded by this prejudiced society-at-large that his or her sexual orientation was inherently deviant. Yet DSM-III also asserted that homosexuality was not abnormal! Ego-dystonic homosexuality could also develop when a homosexual was frustrated or hurt by societal prejudices against his or her desire to establish a home with another person of the same sex.

DSM-IIIR, DSM-IV, and Homosexuality

When we commented on DSM-III's ego-dystonic homosexuality category in a previous edition of this textbook, we suggested that

> if DSM-III's explicit support of homosexuality is able to help win for the life-style greater acceptance than it has today, eventually there will be fewer social and legal sanctions against homosexual partners' setting up households and raising children, whether they be adopted or the offspring of earlier heterosexual liaisons of one or both of them. The homosexual will then be able to enjoy more of what is now the heterosexual "package." The DSM will have influenced itself out of this new category, ego-dystonic homosexuality. (Davison & Neale, 1986, p. 309)

This may well have happened, for DSM-IIIR and now DSM-IV contain no specific mention of homosexuality as a disorder in its own right. In the years following publication of DSM-III in 1980, very little use was made by mental health professionals of the ego-dystonic homosexuality diagnosis. Was it because homosexuals in therapy were no longer asking for sexual reorientation? Perhaps the greater tolerance of homosexuality—despite the AIDS crisis (page 381) and the erroneous allegation that it was a homosexual problem and maybe even God's punishment for their sins—helped gay people seek therapy for problems unrelated to their sexual orientation. Perhaps also some gay people, as gay activists had been urging for the previous twenty years, were no longer willing to tolerate the prejudice against their sexual orientation and were seeking assistance in resisting societal biases against them. It may also have been that clinicians had begun to focus more on problems like anxiety and depression in gay clients without seeing these problems as necessarily connected with a wish to become heterosexual. It is impossible to establish the exact reasons, but it is clear that by the time the American Psychiatric Association was ready in 1987 to publish DSM-IIIR, it had decided that even the watered-down diagnosis of ego-dystonic homosexuality should not be included. Instead, its catchall category of Sexual Disorder Not Otherwise Specified referred to "persistent and marked distress about one's sexual orientation" (p. 296); it appears also in DSM-IV.

It is noteworthy that this definition does not specify a particular sexual orientation. Thus, while the door is still open for a diagnosis of ego-dystonic homosexuality, the psychiatric nosology now appears to allow as well for ego-dystonic *hetero*sexuality. Our own expectation is that *neither* of these diagnoses is going to be made very often.

Future Research

The position that has evolved over the past fifteen to twenty years, that homosexuality per se is not a mental disorder, along with the position that to be considered disordered a person must be markedly distressed by his or her sexual orientation, has important implications for how social scientists might spend their time studying homosexuality. Rather than searching for why some people prefer members of their own gender as sexual mates and rather than investigating and applying methods for changing homosexuals' orientation in the direction of heterosexuality, clinicians and researchers might better focus on how people in general deal with their sexuality and on how to help those homosexually inclined to resist the pressures that are still applied by

FOCUS 12.4 • Some Problems in Logic and Theory in the Study of Homosexuality

Homophobia and Exclusive Homosexuality

Those who argue that heterosexuality is normal and homosexuality abnormal often make the statement that exclusive homosexuality is unknown in the animal kingdom when members of the opposite sex are available. It is also proposed that heterosexual contacts are maximized in all species so that adequate reproduction can take place. Moreover, it is apparently the case that in no human culture has exclusive homosexuality been encouraged for sizable numbers of people.

These arguments are cogent, but they overlook one essential characteristic of human sexuality, namely, that *bisexuality is more prevalent than exclusive homosexuality* (Kinsey, Pomeroy, & Martin, 1948). Churchill (1967) made the provocative suggestion that exclusive homosexuality may well be encouraged by antihomosexual societies such as our own. Because sexual contacts between members of the same sex are so severely condemned, some bisexuals may be forced into making a choice and *thereby* become committed to contacts with members of their own sex rather than continuing to find sexual relationships with members of both sexes meaningful. What some call *homophobia* (Weinberg, 1972) may actually help create exclusive homosexuality.

Gender Identity and Homosexual Preference

Psychoanalytic theory and to a degree behavioral theories as well hold male homosexuality to be a problem in gender identity: a man can become homosexual because he has not adopted his society's definition of manhood. Making love to a man rather than to a woman is assumed to be possible only for men who do not share a given society's conception of masculinity.

Other theorists and writers dispute whether homosexuals have an inappropriate gender identity. Churchill (1967), for example, referred to the comradeship and homosexual love that existed among many Greek warriors; Plato commented on the military advantages of homosexual relationships, for they seemed to foster great ferocity in battle on the part of men driven to protect their lovers. Is it reasonable to regard a brave soldier as lacking a masculine gender identity?

Moreover, only 2 percent of homosexuals were rated by their analysts as effeminate (Bieber et al., 1962); this finding of masculinity among male homosexuals was borne out in a study by Evans (1969), in which 95 percent of the homosexuals rated themselves as "moderately or strongly masculine." Indeed, in his renowned "Three Contributions to the Theory of Sex" (1905), Freud asserted, "In men, the most perfect psychic manliness may be united with homosexuality."

The vast majority of male homosexuals have a firm identification of themselves as masculine (Silverstein, 1972); the same holds true for lesbians, who usually consider themselves quite feminine (Martin & Lyon, 1972). To be sure, the stereotype of the limp-wristed, lisping fag probably contributes to the misconception, or at least overgeneralization, of male homosexuality as feminine behavior. And the stereotype of the butch or dyke who wears her hair clipped and dresses in tailored clothing similarly fosters the misconception that the lesbian is somehow less of a woman and more of a man. But we must bear in mind that

those directing them toward heterosexuality. Furthermore, as discussed in Focus Box 21.5 (page 656), mental health workers might direct their energies to the institutional, community psychology level and try to eliminate societal prejudices against homosexuality; homophobia continues to be quite prevalent among both lay and professional people (Forstein, 1988), and mental health professionals could be attempting more vigorously to reduce this widespread fear and abhorrence of homoeroticism. Fewer and fewer state laws legislate against homosexuality; as these legal proscriptions are eliminated, social biases may also slowly mollify. As a consequence of all these changes, the very societal conditions that underlie distress about one's sexual orientation may disappear and with them, as indicated above, the last vestige of homosexuality from the list of recognized mental disorders.

homosexuals grow up in the same cultures as everyone else! They learn that preferring a same-sexed partner implies being less of a man or less of a woman, and they may therefore come to adopt traits of the opposite gender. To explain homosexuality itself as simply an error in gender identity is probably wrong. "Gender roles are not a mold in which we pour our sexuality" (Gagnon, 1977, p. 242).

Differences and Pathogenics

For many years theories have been proposed, and data collected, on the origins of homosexuality. Psychoanalysts, learning theorists, and physiologically oriented workers have compared homosexuals with heterosexuals for differences in their psychological or physical makeup. Perhaps the most widely cited study is that carried out by Bieber and several of his colleagues (1962). Case records of 106 homosexual patients were compared with those of 100 heterosexual patients. These two groups were being seen by 77 New York psychoanalysts. Among the differences found was that the homosexual male patients more often had "close-binding intimate mothers" and emotionally detached, hostile fathers. Overlooking for present purposes a number of methodological flaws in the study—the most important being that all the 106 homosexuals were being analyzed and were not representative of homosexuals en masse, most of whom are not in therapy—we ask whether these differences demonstrate that homosexuality per se is pathological and that having such parents is pathogenic, that is, causes illness.

Bieber and his colleagues clearly believe so.

> [The close-binding intimate mother] exerted an unhealthy influence on her son through preferential treatment and seductiveness on the one hand and inhibiting, over-controlling attitudes on the other. In many instances, the son was the most significant individual in her life and the husband was usually replaced by the son as her love object. . . . We are led to believe that . . . maternal close-binding intimacy and paternal detachment-hostility is the "classic", pattern and most conducive to promoting homosexuality . . . in the son. (pp. 47, 144)

The implication of this study and of many others is that any differences found between homosexuals and heterosexuals constitute evidence that homosexuality is abnormal and that the difference itself is pathogenic. Is there anything wrong with this line of reasoning?

Let us take an analogous situation. Suppose we found that women who are now good golfers had as children attended public schools more often than did women who are poor golfers. Suppose also that their golfing ability is the only consistent difference between the two groups. Under what circumstances would we conclude that childhood experiences in private schools are pathogenic, causing pathology or illness? The answer is simple: going to a private school is pathogenic if its outcome, being a poor golfer, has already been judged pathological. If we do not make this a priori judgment, we cannot talk of a difference between two groups as indicative of pathology in one of the groups and we cannot regard the presumed cause a pathogenic one. The most we can say is that the two groups are *different* from each other.

This logic can be applied to Bieber's study.

> One cannot attach a pathogenic label to a pattern of child rearing unless one a priori labels the adult behavior pattern as pathological. . . . What is wrong with [a "close-binding intimate mother"] unless you happen to find her in the background of people whose current behavior you judge beforehand to be pathological? (Davison, 1976, p. 159).

SUMMARY

In this chapter we examined three categories of sexual disorders. The gender identity disorders—transsexualism and gender identity disorder of childhood—are deep and persistent convictions of individuals that their anatomic sexual makeup and psychological sense of self as a man, woman, boy, or girl are discrepant. Thus a man who is a transsexual is physically masculine but considers himself a woman and would like to live as such. Early child-rearing practices may have encouraged the young child to believe that he or she was of the opposite sex. These problems are of significant theoretical interest, for they illustrate the early plasticity of our beliefs about ourselves as males and females. For a time the only kind of help available to such individuals was sex-reassignment surgery, to bring their bodies into line in some degree with gender identity. Now, however, there is preliminary evidence that behavior therapy can alter specific aspects of the transsexual's behavior—mannerisms, tone of voice, sexual fantasies—and bring gender identity into line with anatomy.

In the paraphilias, unusual imagery and acts are persistent and necessary for sexual excitement or gratification; fetishism, transvestic fetishism, pedophilia, incest, and sexual sadism are examples of such problems. Rape, although it is not separately diagnosed in DSM-IV, is a pattern of behavior that results in considerable social and psychological trauma for the victim. The very inclusion of rape in a discussion of human sexuality is a matter of some controversy, for many workers regard rape as an act of aggression and violence rather than of sex. The most promising treatments for the paraphilias are behavior therapies, such as training in social skills to help the person have ordinary relations with members of the opposite sex. Treatment for rape victims involves social support and frank discussion of the traumatic event.

Like DSM-IIIR, DSM-IV does not contain any specific mention of homosexuality, thus continuing a process of liberalization that began in 1973, when DSM-II introduced a variation of the diagnosis that was to be applied only to those homosexuals disturbed by their sexual orientation. The current nomenclature alludes to those distressed by their sexual orientation without specifying whether that orientation is hetero- or homosexual.

KEY TERMS

sexual disorders
gender identity
transsexual
gender identity disorder of childhood
sex-reassignment surgery
paraphilias
fetishism
transvestic fetishism
incest
pedophiles
child sexual abuse
voyeurism
exhibitionism
sexual sadism
sexual masochism
orgasmic reorientation
family systems approach
forcible rape
statutory rape
acquaintance (date) rape
homosexuality
ego-dystonic homosexuality

c h a p t e r   t h i r t e e n

Sexual Dysfunctions

Robert S. was a highly intelligent and accomplished twenty-five-year-old graduate student in physics at a leading East Coast university who consulted us for what he called "sexual diffidence." He was engaged to a young woman whom he said he loved very much and with whom he felt compatible in every conceivable way except in bed. There, try as he might, and with apparent understanding from his fiancée, he found himself interested very little either in initiating sexual contact or responding to it when initiated by his fiancée. Both parties believed for the two years of their friendship and later engagement that academic pressures on the man lay at the root of the problem, but an early discussion with the therapist revealed that the client had had little interest in sex—either with men or women—for as far back as he could remember, and that his desire for sex did not increase when pressures from other obligations lessened. He asserted that he found his fiancée very attractive and appealing, but, as with other young women he had known, his feelings were not passionate.

He had masturbated very infrequently in adolescence and did not begin dating until late in college, though he had had many female acquaintances. His general approach to life, including sex, was quite analytical and intellectual, and he described his problems in a very dispassionate way with the therapist. In fact, he freely admitted that he would not have contacted a therapist at all were it not for the quietly stated wishes of his fiancée, who worried that his disinterest in sex would interfere with their future marital relationship.

After a few individual sessions, the therapist asked the young man to invite his fiancée to a therapy session, which the client readily agreed to do. During a conjoint session, the couple appeared to be very much in love and looking forward to a life together, though the woman expressed concern about her fiancé's lack of interest in her sexually. The following session was held just with the client, and the therapist outlined a tentative course of treatment, beginning with general discussions of sexual values and asking the client to masturbate once or twice before the next session, to get a clearer idea of what his sexual responsiveness might be to pictorial materials of his own choosing. The client said he would try to follow through, though he did not have a specific idea of what kinds of pictures he would find sexually arousing. Two days later he phoned the therapist to thank him for his efforts but to indicate that he did not want to continue therapy.

The preceding chapter described the unconventional patterns of sexual behavior of a small minority of the population. But many ordinary people are likely to have problems that interfere with conventional sexual enjoyment during the course of their lives. Our concern in this chapter is with **sexual dysfunctions**, the range of sexual problems that are usually considered to represent inhibitions in the normal sexual response cycle.

What is defined as normal and desirable in human sexual behavior varies with time and place. Contemporary views point to *inhibitions* of sexual expression as causes of abnormality. In contrast, during the nineteenth and early twentieth centuries the Western world regarded *excess* as the culprit. It is well to keep these varying temporal and cultural norms in mind as we continue our study of human sexual dysfunctions.

A psychological problem has consequences not only for the individual but also for those with whom he or she is involved. People who are unable to interact socially with others are inevitably cut off from many opportunities in life and, furthermore, often have low opinions of themselves. They can be a source of frustration and guilt for a spouse, a child, or a friend. This aspect of human emotional problems is especially important in our consideration of sexual dysfunctions, for they are usually evident in intimate personal relationships. A marriage is bound to suffer if one or both of the partners fear sex. And most of us, for better or for worse, base part of our self-concept on our sexuality. Do we please the people we love, do we gratify ourselves, or, more simply, are we able to enjoy the fulfillment and relaxation that can come from a pleasurable sexual experience? Sexual dysfunctions can be so severe that tenderness itself is lost, let alone the more intense satisfaction of sexual activity.

We will look first at the human sexual response cycle as it normally functions and then at sexual dysfunctions that can occur. We will then discuss etiologies and therapies of sexual dysfunctions and conclude with an examination of the very critical problem of AIDS.

Sexual Disorders and the Human Sexual Response Cycle

As indicated in Table 12.1 (page 331), DSM-IV divides sexual dysfunctions into four principal categories: sexual desire disorders, sexual arousal disorders, orgasm disorders, and sexual pain disorders. These disorders were called psychosexual dysfunctions in DSM-III; the *psycho* part of the term was dropped in DSM-IIIR and in the current edition in formal recognition of the accumulating evidence that biological factors play a role in many of these problems.

In the most general terms, sexual dysfunctions are defined as inhibitions of the normal sexual response cycle. The difficulty should be persistent and recurrent, a clinical judgment acknowledged in the DSM to entail a degree of subjectivity. New in DSM-IV is the requirement that the disturbance cause marked distress or interpersonal problems, a change that allows the person's *own* reactions to, say, having no interest in sex, play a role in whether he or she should be diagnosed. The diagnosis is not to be made if the disorder is believed to be due entirely to a medical illness (such as advanced diabetes, which can cause erectile problems in men) or if it is believed to be due to another axis I disorder (such as major depression).

Most conceptualizations of the sexual response cycle are a distillation of proposals by Havelock Ellis (1906, no relation to Albert Ellis), Masters and Johnson (1966), and Kaplan (1974). The work of Masters and Johnson almost thirty years ago signaled a revolution in the nature and intensity of research in and clinical attention to human sexuality. They extended the earlier interview-based breakthroughs of the Kinsey group (Kinsey et al., 1948,

At the turn of the century, Havelock Ellis (1859–1939) began writing about sexuality and is considered one of the major pioneers of the field.

Helen Singer Kaplan is the noted sex therapist who introduced the appetitive phase to the sexual response cycle.

The pioneering work of the sex therapists William H. Masters and Virginia Johnson helped launch a more candid and scientific appraisal of human sexuality.

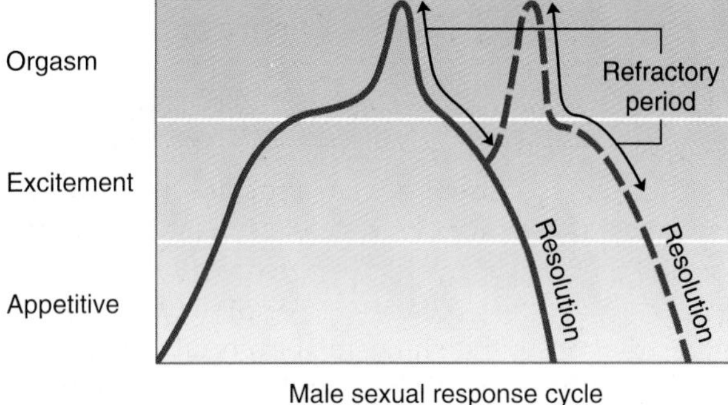

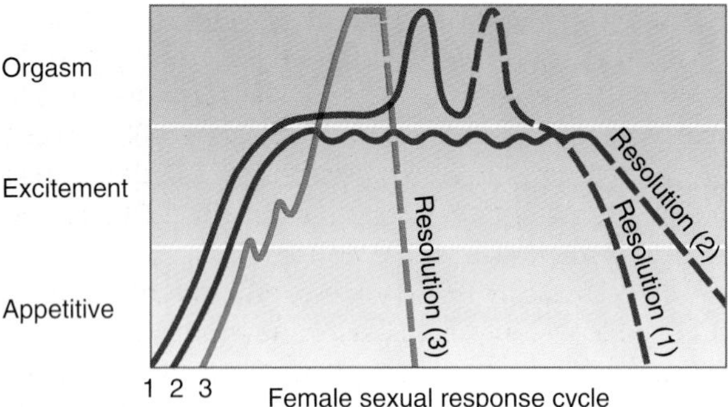

Figure 13.1 The stage of the human sexual response cycle.

1953) to make direct observations and physiological measurements of people masturbating and having sexual intercourse. Four phases in the human sexual response cycle are typically identified; they are considered quite similar in men and in women:

1. **Appetitive.** Introduced by Kaplan (1974), this stage refers to sexual interest or desire, often associated with sexually arousing fantasies.[1]
2. **Excitement.** Masters and Johnson's original first stage, a subjective experience of sexual pleasure associated with physiological changes brought about by increased blood flow to the genitalia and, in women, to the breasts. This **tumescence**—the flow of blood into tissues—shows up as erection of the penis in men and, in women, as enlargement of the breasts and changes in the vagina, for example, increased lubrication.
3. **Orgasm.** In this phase sexual pleasure peaks in ways that have fascinated poets and the rest of us ordinary people for thousands of years. In men, ejaculation feels inevitable and indeed almost always occurs (in rare instances some men can have an orgasm without ejaculating and vice versa). In women, the walls of the outer third of the vagina contract. In both sexes there is general muscle tension and involuntary pelvic thrusting.
4. **Resolution.** This last of Masters and Johnson's stages refers to the relaxation and sense of well-being that usually follow an orgasm. In men there is an associated refractory period, during which further erection and arousal are not possible (but for varying periods of time across individuals and even within the same person across occasions). Women, however, are often able to respond again with sexual excitement almost immediately, an ability that permits multiple orgasms.

It is important to note the constructive nature of this rendition of the human sexual response cycle. As we said, there have been different proposals over time; Havelock Ellis, for example, spoke only of tumescence and **detumescence** (the flow of blood out of tissue). The view just described is one of many conceivable inventions or conceptual schemes created by scientists as a way to organize and discuss a body of information (Gagnon, 1977; Kuhn, 1962). We are about to see how the DSM uses this scheme to describe sexual dysfunctions. It is also worth mentioning that sex researchers speak in terms of averages, which, after all, are by definition a mathematical way to summarize a range of scores or observations. So, a given individual's responses can differ noticeably from a group average and yet not be considered abnormal (Focus Box 13.1).

The Sexual Dysfunctions: Descriptions and Etiology

A particular disorder may be lifelong, or it may have been acquired after a period of normal functioning; it may be generalized, or it may occur only in particular situations or with certain partners; and it may be total or partial. Each disorder may show up either during sexual activity with another person or during masturbation. The prevalence of disturbances is believed to be so great that people should not assume that they need treatment because they sometimes experience one or more of these problems. In the diagnostic criteria for each sexual dysfunction, the phrase "persistent or recurrent" is

[1]Masters and Johnson omitted this stage because, we believe, they used well-functioning volunteers in their landmark laboratory work. The issue of desire or readiness to be sexual did not arise. This is a good example of how the nature of knowledge-gathering techniques—in this case the kinds of subjects studied—constrains the kinds of information obtained.

included to underscore the fact that a problem must be serious indeed before a diagnosis is made. Further, DSM-IV does not state whether the sexual partner is of the opposite sex or same sex, another sign of the growing liberalization of the attitude of the mental health professions toward homosexuality.

We will report prevalence rates for the dysfunctions, but their accuracy is sometimes difficult to determine because of several methodological problems (Spector & Carey, 1990). First, it is not easy to obtain a representative sample of the general population—those who respond to magazine surveys (e.g., Hite, 1976), for example, may be people who are themselves distressed or concerned—and reliance on clinical groups confounds help-seeking behavior with the actual extent of the particular dysfunction. Peple may also be reluctant to respond honestly to questions about sensitive material such as this. Furthermore, disagreement exists on how best to define some of the human sexual dysfunctions. Finally, it is worth noting that dysfunction does not necessarily mean dissatisfaction; in a survey of happily married heterosexual couples, for example, it was found that almost half the men reported erectile and ejaculatory problems and more than half the women, arousal or orgasmic problems—yet 80 percent of the couples regarded their marital and sexual relations to be positive and satisfying (Franks, Anderson, & Rubenstein, 1978).

In the following discussions of DSM-IV categories of sexual dysfunctions, we will touch on what is believed to cause these human problems, and then later in the chapter we will examine more general theories of etiology. It is important to bear in mind, however, that most of the generalizations about etiology are based on clinical reports of investigators such as Masters and Johnson (1970), Kaplan (1974), and other sex therapists. As with all clinical reports, information provided by clients and interpreted by therapists is subject to distortion and selective attention. Moreover, no studies compare groups of dysfunctional patients with appropriate control groups for the presence or absence of causative factors. For example, an unpleasant experience with a prostitute at age seventeen may seem to be a major cause of a thirty-year-old man's erectile problem, but countless other men have similar negative experiences *without* developing a sexual problem.

Any points made about etiology are therefore necessarily tentative. Although this caveat can be issued for any section of this book, it is particularly appropriate to bear in mind here, considering the likelihood that the lives of many readers will be touched in some way by what is being discussed.

Sexual Desire Disorders

DSM-IV distinguishes two kinds of sexual desire disorders: **hypoactive sexual desire disorder** refers to deficient or absent sexual fantasies and urges; **sexual aversion disorder** represents a more extreme form of the first, in which the person actively avoids nearly all genital contact with another. In making either diagnosis the clinician should take into consideration the patient's age, health, and life circumstances. About 20 percent of the general adult population has hypoactive sexual desire disorder, although accurate estimates are difficult to come by because of definitional problems. Among people seeking treatment for sexual dysfunctions, more than half complain of low desire; of these, 60 percent are men. In general, hypoactive sexual desire has increased in clinical samples from the 1970s to the 1980s (Spector & Carey, 1990).

Of all the DSM-IV diagnoses, what is colloquially referred to as low sex drive (as illustrated in the case that opened the chapter) seems the most problematic. How frequently *should* a person want sex? In practice, the reason a person even goes to a clinician in the first place and ends up with this diagnosis is probably that *someone else* is dissatisfied with that person's interest in sex *with him or her*. The hypoactive desire category appeared for the first time in DSM-III in 1980, under the title of inhibited sexual desire,[2] and may owe its existence to the high expectations people have about being sexual. It is striking that entire books, for example, Leiblum and Rosen (1988), have been written about a disorder that twenty years ago was hardly talked about in professional sexology circles.

We know little about the causes of either hypoactive sexual desire or sexual aversion disorder. Among those proposed by LoPiccolo and Friedman (1988) on the basis of clinical experience are religious orthodoxy, trying to have sex with a partner of the nonpreferred gender, fear of loss of control, fear of pregnancy, depression, side effects from medications, such as antihypertensives and tranquilizers, interpersonal tensions (as in marital or couples conflict), lack of attraction resulting from such factors as poor personal hygiene in the partner. Other possible causes include a past history of sexual trauma, such as rape or child sexual abuse (Stuart & Greer, 1984), and fears of contracting sexually transmitted diseases, such as AIDS (Katz, Gipson, Kearl, & Kris-

[2]It is interesting to note that the DSM-III term *inhibited* was deemed by those who produced DSM-IIIR as suggesting psychodynamic causality. For DSM-IIIR and DSM-IV, preference was given to the more descriptive term *hypoactive* (Lief, 1988).

13.1 • Some Sexual Myths Dispelled by Masters and Johnson

The impact of Masters and Johnson's work was considerable in contributing to our knowledge of the physiology of human sexuality. Perhaps more important, it helped make the scientific study of sex legitimate and acceptable. By knowing how the body functions to achieve maximum sexual response, Masters and Johnson were able to develop methods of treating sexual dysfunctions. Even before their 1966 book was published, the information obtained through research was being put to use in the treatment phase of their work (Masters & Johnson, 1970).

The artificial circumstances in which Masters and Johnson gathered their findings limit their generality somewhat, however. And we should be mindful that their physiological research can tell us little about the *psychological* components of human sexuality, particularly the romantic aspects of a relationship. Masters and Johnson were nonetheless able to provide firm data on certain controversial points and to dispel a few myths.

1. Although the **clitoris** (the small, heavily innervated erectile structure located above the vaginal opening) is very important in transmitting sexual stimulation in the female, it has been a mistake to advise continual stimulation during intercourse. During the excitement phase the clitoris retracts, making access to it extremely difficult and even painful for some women. In point of fact, it is very difficult to have intercourse without stimulating the clitoris *indirectly,* which is the type of stimulation that some women seem to prefer.
2. Masters and Johnson were able to document that orgasms in women obtained from stimulation of the clitoris, without entrance into the vagina, are as intense as and indeed physiologically indistinguishable from orgasms obtained by having an erect penis in the vagina.

Probably few pieces of misinformation have caused more consternation than Freud's insistence that the vaginal orgasm is superior to the clitoral orgasm. He asserted, and practitioners have echoed to hundreds of thousands of people for years since, that a woman who can have an orgasm only by stimulation of her clitoris is settling for second best; further, that failure to have an orgasm via stimulation of the vagina by the man's penis is a sign of psychosexual fixation and immaturity.

Even before the work of Masters and Johnson, some sexologists had been trying to disabuse people of this notion (e.g., A. Ellis, 1961), pointing out that the walls of the vaginal barrel are poorly supplied with sensory nerve endings, whereas the clitoris, like the glans of the penis, is amply supplied. The fact that orgasms achieved by masturbation

kovich, 1989). Stuart, Hammond, and Pett (1987) found that relationships in which hypoactive desire disorder is present are marked by distrust, anger, power struggles, and poor communication. In general, the importance that sex has in someone's life can vary tremendously. Unlike hunger and thirst, an appetite for sex need not be satisfied or even exist in order for the individual to survive and, it seems, to live happily.

Sexual Arousal Disorders

The two subcategories of arousal disorders are **female sexual arousal disorder** and **male erectile disorder**. The former used to be called frigidity, and the latter, impotence. These and the orgasm disorders assume that the person has adequate sexual stimulation. In other words, if the situation is simply that the person's partner does not do what the person *likes,* the diagnosis is not to be made; the problem in this case is likely to center on relationship issues that might have little or nothing to do with sex.

In the woman, there is inadequate vaginal lubrication for comfortable completion of intercourse. In the man there is failure to attain or maintain an erection through completion of the sexual activity. Prevalence rates for female sexual arousal disorder range from 11 percent (Levine & Yost, 1976) to as high as 48 percent (Frank, Anderson, & Rubenstein, 1978); the actual figure is probably closer to 11 percent (Spector & Carey, 1990). For male erectile disorder prevalence is estimated at between 3 percent and 9 and manual manipulation by the partner, both of which typically concentrate on the clitoris and surrounding areas, were found to create at least as much excitation as intercourse pretty much puts to rest the bugaboo about clitoral orgasms.

Many authorities now believe that all female orgasms are evoked by stimulation of the clitoris, whether the friction is applied directly or through coitus. The orgasm itself, however, is expressed by rhythmic contractions of vaginal muscles. This dichotomy may be the source of the myth of clitoral versus vaginal orgasms (Kaplan, 1974). Of course these findings in no way imply that the insertion of the penis and the movements of coitus are not extremely enjoyable to women.

3. Having simultaneous orgasms, a goal held up in numerous marriage manuals as indicating true love and compatibility, was not shown to be a mark of superior sexual achievement. In fact, it can often distract the partners from their own sexual pleasure. Some experts believe simultaneous orgasms are actually rare (Wincze & Carey, 1991).
4. Most women do not object to intercourse during menstruation. Recent laboratory evidence reported by Meuwissen and Over (1992) shows little variation in the ability to become sexually aroused across different phases of the menstrual cycle.
5. During the second trimester of pregnancy, women seem to desire intercourse at least as much as when not pregnant. Although there is some danger of spontaneous abortion in the early stages, particularly for women who have a history of spontaneous miscarriage, most women continue to desire sexual stimulation, sometimes until they go into labor. At any rate, little harm seems to come to the woman or to the fetus through intercourse, at least during the first six months of pregnancy.
6. Various myths about the male's penis were also dispelled, including the idea that the size of a man's penis is an index of his virility. The size of a man's erect penis was not found to be a factor in the enjoyment he can derive himself or impart to his sexual partner. For the most part, the vagina is a potential, not an actual, space; that is, it distends just enough to accommodate the penis. Hence a very large penis really does not create more friction for the man or the woman than a smaller one. Furthermore, penises that are small when flaccid may double in size when erect, whereas penises that are large in the limp state increase less proportionately. In other words, there does not seem to be as much variation in the size of the *erect* penis as had been assumed. We should add that some women have voiced disagreement with Masters and Johnson's conclusion about the merit of a large penis. No doubt psychological variables, as well as the purely physiological ones that Masters and Johnson have dealt with, play a part in determining how an individual woman reacts.

percent (e.g., Ard, 1977; Frank et al., 1978) and increases greatly in older adults (Kinsey et al., 1948). Arousal problems account for about half the complaints of men and women who seek help with sexual dysfunctions (Frank et al., 1976; Renshaw, 1988).

Besides the fears of performance and the spectator role discussed later as general causes of sexual dysfunctions, some specific causes are believed to underlie female arousal problems. A woman may not have learned adequately what she finds sexually arousing and may even lack knowledge about her own anatomy. Coupled with a shyness about communicating her needs, she may find the behavior of her partner unstimulating and even aversive.

Helen Singer Kaplan (1974) outlined a wide range of erectile problems for men. Some get an erection easily but lose it as they enter the woman's vagina. Others are flaccid when intercourse is imminent but maintain an erection easily during fellatio. Some men are erect when the partner dominates the situation, others when they themselves are in control. Some suffer complete erectile failure, being unable to maintain an erection under any circumstances. Others have problems only with people they care for deeply. Moreover, an obvious aspect of the problem is that it is, in fact, obvious. A woman can go through the motions of lovemaking, but sexual intercourse is usually stalemated if the man is not erect. A great deal is at stake if the penis becomes flaccid when it "should" be erect. For this reason, perhaps, an impotent male is sometimes and unfortunately regarded as less than a man.

Recent reviews (e.g., LoPiccolo, 1992a; Mohr & Beutler, 1990) suggest that as many as two-thirds of erectile problems have some organic basis, usually combined with psychological factors. In general, any disease or hormonal imbalance that can affect the nerve pathways or blood supply to the penis (Geer, Heiman, & Leitenberg, 1984) can contribute to erectile problems, for example certain drugs, such as Mellaril and some hypertensive medications, and illnesses, such as diabetes and chronic alcoholism. But it is probably a mistake to think in terms of *either–or*, for somatic and psychological factors usually interact to produce and maintain erectile difficulties.

There is no doubt about it: male erectile problems are complicated. Although an extended discussion is beyond the scope of this book, a few additional observations would seem in order. The fact that the state of a man's penis is obvious both to him and his partner is generally regarded as placing a unique set of pressures on him that are not the fate of a woman who suffers from sexual arousal disorder. But the woman's situation is not easy either. The very fact that she can have sexual relations without being aroused has no doubt contributed to neglect of the woman's needs and desires. Moreover, the man's self-esteem is not the only one threatened if he becomes flaccid; the partner too, whether it be a woman or another man, often has doubts about sexual adequacy—is she or he not sexy enough, not lovable enough, not creative or liberal enough? Replacement of the words *impotence* and *frigidity* by the phrase *sexual arousal disorder* can be considered an advance. Impotence implies that the man is not potent, or in control, or truly masculine, and negatively backs up the macho conception of masculinity that many people are challenging. Frigidity implies that the woman is emotionally cold, distant, unsympathetic, unfeeling. Both terms are derogatory and encourage as well a search for causes *within* the person, rather than focusing attention on the relationship, the domain contemporary investigators explore for answers and solutions.

Orgasm Disorders

Three kinds of orgasm disorders are described in DSM-IV, one found in women and two in men. **Female orgasm disorder (inhibited female orgasm)** refers to absence of orgasm after a period of normal sexual excitement. Stimulation can come from masturbation or from having sex with a partner.

The published prevalence rates for female orgasm disorder vary widely. The classic Kinsey study reported that 10 percent of all women said they had never experienced an orgasm (Kinsey et al., 1953); a quarter of a century later Levine and Yost (1976) found only 5 percent to be nonorgasmic over their lifetime. If low frequency of orgasm is included, however, the rates jump to 20 percent (Spector & Carey, 1990), and it seems that women from lower socioeconomic strata have higher prevalence rates for this disorder (Levine & Yost, 1976). Whatever the true prevalence rate, this problem is the one most frequently presented to practitioners (Kaplan, 1974).

Until recently a distinction was not generally made between problems a woman may have in becoming sexually aroused and those she may have in reaching an orgasm. Although as many as 10 percent of adult women have never experienced an orgasm (Anderson, 1983), far fewer are believed to remain unaroused during lovemaking. Kaplan (1974) argued that this distinction is an important one, for, "as a general rule, women who suffer from orgasmic dysfunction [female orgasm disorder] are responsive sexually. They may fall in love, experience erotic feelings, lubricate copiously, and also show genital swelling" (p. 343). In fact, she argued that failure to have orgasms should not be regarded as a disorder at all, rather as a normal variation of female sexuality.

Numerous reasons have been put forward to explain the problem. Perhaps many women, unlike men, have to *learn* to become orgasmic. That is, the capacity to have an orgasm may not be innate in females as it is in males. In men, ejaculation, which almost always is accompanied by orgasm, is necessary for reproduction. A woman may to some extent learn to have coital orgasms through earlier masturbation; survey findings indicate that women who masturbated little or not at all before they began to have intercourse were much more likely to be nonorgasmic than others (Kinsey et al., 1953; Hite, 1976; Hoon & Hoon, 1978). These are, of course, correlational data; some third factor may be responsible both for infrequent masturbation and for diminished ability to have orgasms. Lack of sexual knowledge also appears to play a role according to clinical data; many nonorgasmic women, as well as those who experience little excitement during sexual stimulation, are unaware of their own genital anatomy and therefore have trouble knowing what their needs are and communicating them to a partner. Chronic use of alcohol may be a somatic factor in orgasmic dysfunction in women (Wilsnak, 1984); the role of the female hormone estrogen is much less clear (Sherwin, Gelfand, & Brender, 1985).

Women have different thresholds for orgasm. Although some have orgasms quickly and without much clitoral stimulation, others seem to need intense and prolonged stimulation, whether during foreplay or intercourse. Because a man may conclude that he and his penis are inadequate if the female asks for manual stimulation of her clitoris during intercourse, the reaction of a woman's partner can contribute to the problem.

Another factor may be fear of losing control. The French have an expression for orgasm, *la petite mort*, "the little death." Some women fear that they will begin screaming uncontrollably, make fools of themselves, or faint. A related source of inhibition is a belief, perhaps poorly articulated, that to let go and allow the body to take over from the conscious, controlling mind is somehow unseemly. The state of a relationship is also not to be overlooked: although some women can enjoy making love to a person they are angry with, or even despise, most hold back under such circumstances. Certainly the nonsexual feelings each partner has for the other play a role.

Male orgasm disorder and premature ejaculation are the two orgasm disorders described for men in DSM-IV. Masters and Johnson (1970) used the somewhat pejorative term *ejaculatory incompetence* for the inability of the man to ejaculate within the vagina. The DSM-IV diagnosis **male orgasm disorder** (called **inhibited male orgasm** in DSM-IIIR) is applied to problems of ejaculating during intercourse, masturbation, manual or oral manipulation by a partner, and anal intercourse.

Difficulty in ejaculating is relatively rare. Causes that have been put forth include fear of impregnating a female partner, withholding love, expressing hostility, and, as with female orgasm problems, fear of letting go. In rare instances the problem may be traced to a physical source, such as taking certain tranquilizers (Munjack & Kanno, 1979).

Masters and Johnson (1970) spoke of **premature ejaculation** when a man was unable to inhibit his orgasm long enough for his partner to climax in 50 percent of their sexual encounters. Many people were concerned about couching the problem in terms of a *partner's* responsiveness. In DSM-IV these concerns were addressed by including the man's own desires and preferences as well as such factors as his age and the novelty of the sexual partner or situation. This may be an improvement, but in our view, it would be naive to overlook the extent to which a partner may influence a patient's judgment that ejaculation is occurring before he wishes it.

Premature ejaculation is probably the most prevalent sexual dysfunction among males, a problem for 30 percent of men at any given time (American Psychiatric Association, 1987). There is some laboratory-based evidence that men who have such problems ejaculate at lower levels of sexual arousal and that they have longer periods of abstinence from climactic sex than do men who are not premature ejaculators (Spiess, Geer, & O'Donohue, 1984). In general, premature ejaculation is associated with considerable anxiety. Sometimes the man ejaculates even before he penetrates the vagina, but more usually within a few seconds of intromission. Atlhough the human being is more than a relatively hairless ape, evolutionary theory informs us that rapid ejaculation has survival value, for any animal is particularly vulnerable to surprise attack when copulating. Hence the more quickly copulation can occur, the better. Kinsey, himself a biologist, suggested that ejaculating quickly should not be regarded as a problem in human beings. Such a view, however, considers only the reproductive function of intercourse, ignoring its recreational and interpersonal functions (Rosen & Rosen, 1981).

Indeed, concern about ejaculating too soon may be regarded as part and parcel of the undue emphasis placed on coitus as the ultimate in sexual behavior. The problem for couples who prize conventional sexual intercourse above all other sexual activities is that erection is slowly lost after an ejaculation, with many men finding continued stimulation unpleasant and sometimes painful. If lovemaking stops when the penis is no longer hard, ejaculation may indeed sometimes be premature. But if, as sex therapists advise, couples expand their repertoire of activities to include techniques not requiring an engorged penis, gratification of the partner is eminently possible *after* the man has climaxed. Indeed, when the focus is removed from penile–vaginal intercourse, a couple's anxieties about sex usually diminish sufficiently to permit greater ejaculatory control in the male and sexual intercourse of longer duration. It will be interesting to observe whether shifts in sexual norms and practices alter the concept of premature ejaculation.

Sexual Pain Disorders

Two pain disorders associated with sex are listed in the DSM, dyspareunia and vaginismus. **Dyspareunia** is diagnosed when there is persistent or recurrent pain before, during, or after sexual intercourse. In women the diagnosis should not be made when the pain is believed to be due to lack of vaginal lubrication (when presumably female sexual arousal disorder would be diagnosed); nor should it be made when it is judged to be a function of the second pain disorder, **vaginismus**, which is marked by involuntary spasms of the outer third of the vagina to such a degree that intercourse is not possible. Prevalence rates for dyspareunia in women range from 8 percent (Schover, 1981) to 23 percent (Hite, 1976); it is generally accepted that the disorder is far less often found in men, perhaps in as few as 1 percent (Bancroft, 1989). Estimates for vaginismus vary widely but are not based on good epidemiological data; the disorder is regarded as rare, far less prevalent than the other female sexual dysfunctions (Wincze & Carey, 1991).

Although dyspareunia should not, according to DSM-IV, be diagnosed if the pain is caused by a drug or a medical condition, the fact of the matter is that genital pain associated with intercourse is almost always caused by a medical problem, such as infections of the vagina or uterus or, in the male, infections of the glans of the penis. Vaginismus, though defined in sexual terms by DSM-IV, can occasionally be observed during pelvic examinations.

Since the spastic contractions of the muscles prevent intercourse, it is not surprising that one theory supposes that the woman wishes, perhaps unconsciously, to deny herself, her partner, or both the pleasures of sexual intimacy. As plausible as this idea may seem, no evidence supports it. Indeed, women with vaginismus can often have sexually satisfying lives through clitoral stimulation if the partner agrees. Clinical reports also suggest fear of pregnancy and negative attitudes about sex in general, the latter often traceable to rape or to having been molested in childhood (LoPiccolo & Stock, 1987). Masters and Johnson found that for a number of couples the man's inability to maintain an erection preceded the development of vaginismus in his wife; for some women, then, the sexual problems of their partners are so anxiety–provoking that a condition like vaginismus may develop.

General Theories of Sexual Dysfunctions

Having reviewed descriptions of the sexual dysfunctions and the causes believed to underlie each, we turn now to a consideration of general theoretical perspectives.

Prior to modern scientific theorizing, sexual dysfunctions were generally viewed as a result of moral degeneracy. As recently reviewed by LoPiccolo (1992a), excessive masturbation in childhood was widely believed to lead to sexual problems in adulthood. Von Krafft-Ebing (1902) and Havelock Ellis (1910) postulated that such early masturbation damaged the sexual organs and exhausted a finite reservoir of sexual energy, resulting in lessened abilities to function sexually in adulthood. Even in adulthood excessive sexual activity was thought to underlie such problems as erectile failure, and the general Victorian view was to restrain dangerous sexual appetite. To discourage handling of the genitals by children, metal mittens were promoted; and to distract adults from too much sex, outdoor exercise and a bland diet were recommended. In fact, Kellogg's Corn Flakes and graham crackers were developed as foods that would lessen sexual interest. They didn't.

Psychoanalytic views have assumed that sexual dysfunctions are symptoms of underlying repressed conflicts. The analyst considers the symbolic meaning of the symptom both to understand its etiology and to guide treatment. Since sexual dysfunctions bring discomfort and psychological pain to both the individual and to his or her partner, and since unimpaired sexuality is inherently pleasurable, the theme of repressed anger and aggression competing with the gratification of sexual needs pervades psychoanalytic writings. Thus a man who ejaculates so quickly that he frustrates his female partner may be expressing repressed hostility to women who remind him unconsciously of his mother. A woman with vaginismus may be expressing her repressed penis envy by threatening to castrate a man who would hope to enter her vagina. Many contemporary psychoanalysts now recognize the limits of their therapy in helping people with sexual dysfunctions and supplement it with more direct cognitive-behavioral techniques (LoPiccolo, 1977). The spirit of rapprochement has also affected cognitive-behavioral approaches to the treatment of sexual dysfunctions, as these therapists are coming to appreciate the role of psychodynamic themes in what used to be straightforward behavioral treatments (cf. page 586).

The most comprehensive account of the etiology of human sexual dysfunctions was offered by Masters and Johnson in their widely acclaimed book *Human Sexual Inadequacy* (1970). Let us first examine their suggestions and then consider modifications and extensions of their ideas that have been proposed more recently.

The Theoretical Model of Masters and Johnson

Masters and Johnson (1970) used a two-tier model of current and historical causes to conceptualize the

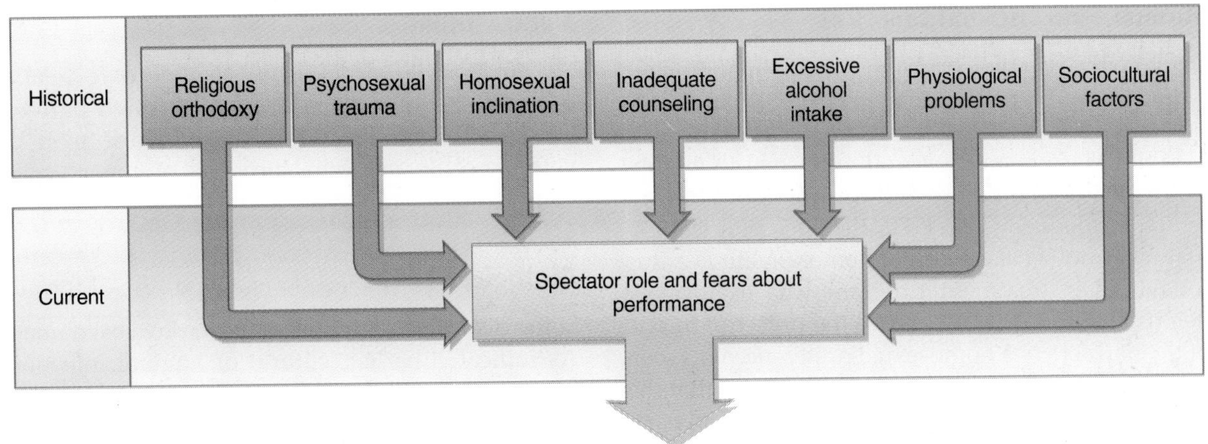

Figure 13.2 Historical and current causes of human sexual inadequacies, according to Masters and Johnson.

etiology of human sexual inadequacy (Figure 13.2). Current variables can be distilled down to two, **fears of performance** and the adoption of a **spectator role**. Both involve a pattern of behavior in which the individual's focus on and concern for sexual performance impedes his or her natural sexual responses. As they put it, "fear of inadequacy is the greatest known deterrent to effective sexual functioning, simply because it so completely distracts the fearful individual from his or her natural responsivity by blocking reception of sexual stimuli" (Masters & Johnson, 1970, pp. 12–13).

Viewed as the *current* or proximal reasons for sexual dysfunctions, performance fears and the spectator role were hypothesized to have any one of several *historical* antecedents, which we will review here.

Religious Orthodoxy

One or both partners may have negative attitudes toward sex because they have been brought up with strict religious beliefs that denigrate sexual enjoyment. For example, a woman with vaginismus who was interviewed by Masters and Johnson had been

> taught that almost any form of physical expression might be suspect of objectionable sexual connotations.... She was prohibited when bathing from looking at her own breasts either directly or from reflection in the mirror for fear that unhealthy sexual thoughts might be stimulated by visual examination of her own body. Discussion with a sibling of such subjects as menstruation, conception, contraception, or sexual functioning were taboo.... Mrs. A. entered marriage without a single word of advice, warning, or even good cheer from her family relative to marital sexual expression. The only direction offered by her religious advisor relative to sexual behavior was that coital connection was only to be endured if conception was desired. (p. 254)

Psychosexual Trauma

Some patients trace their fears of sexual contact to particularly frightening or degrading experiences during early sexual encounters. One young man had been assured by a prostitute that "He would never be able to get the job done for any woman—if he couldn't get it done here and now with a pro." One woman could date her vaginismus to a gang rape from which she suffered severe physical and psychological damage.

The Accused depicted a gang rape and its legal aftermath. A traumatic event like this is regarded by Masters and Johnson as a possible cause of sexual dysfunction.

Homosexual Inclinations

Men with erectile problems and nonorgasmic women may be unable to enjoy heterosexual relations because they have homosexual inclinations.

When Masters and Johnson published their clinical report on the nature and treatment of "human sexual inadequacy" in 1970, the sociopolitical climate was not as accepting of homosexuality as it is today. Their treatment program was exclusively heterosexual in its focus; hence the presence in one of the partners of a homosexual preference was seen as an etiological factor. The alternative view that the problem lay with a decision of the homosexual partner to try to maintain a heterosexual marriage was not explicitly considered.

Inadequate Counseling

Bad advice from professional workers may create or exacerbate sexual inadequacies. Some men were told by physicians that erectile problems are incurable, others that they are a natural part of the aging process. A few had been warned by clerics that their problem was God's punishment for sins.

Excessive Intake of Alcohol

An erectile problem sometimes begins with undue concern about a normal reduction in sexual responsiveness brought on by excessive drinking (see page 289). In the typical pattern suggested by Masters and Johnson, a man who works very hard may develop a habit of drinking a good deal. Large amounts of alcohol are known to interfere with erections, while at the same time, ironically, lowering inhibitions. Having drunk too much, the man may find later in bed that no erection develops. Instead of attributing his lack of sexual arousal to drinking, however, he begins to ruminate. Fear accumulates, and after a number of failures he may become unable to have an erection. The wife often attempts to be understanding and supportive of the husband. He, for any number of reasons, interprets this solicitude as further questioning of his masculinity. Or the wife, concerned that she may no longer be sexually attractive to her husband, pushes for sexual encounters and aggravates the situation. Soon she may refrain from any physical contact whatsoever, even affectionate hugs and kisses, for fear that the husband will interpret this as a demand for intercourse. The communication of the couple worsens, intensifying the man's anxiety and setting a pattern difficult to reverse without professional assistance.

Vaginismus

As yet another example of the intimate relation between the sexual reactions of the two partners, Masters and Johnson found that some men develop erectile problems because of the partner's vaginismus.

Biological Causes

Some disorders are attributable to physical damage. As indicated earlier, clitoral or vaginal infections, torn ligaments in the pelvic region, scar tissue at the vaginal opening from incisions made during childbirth (episiotomies), and—especially in postmenopausal women—insufficient lubrication of the vagina may make intercourse painful for women. Infection of the glans of the penis, which can develop when it is not kept clean, may cause dyspareunia in men. Some men with erectile problems are found to suffer from metabolic disturbances due to diabetes, and in others sexual arousal is dulled by the use of certain tranquilizers.[3]

Sociocultural Factors

Especially in female dysfunctions, cultural biases play a role. "Sociocultural influence more often than not places the woman in a position in which she must adapt, sublimate, inhibit, or even distort her natural capacity to function sexually in order to fulfill her genetically assigned role. Herein lies a major source of woman's sexual dysfunction" (Masters & Johnson, 1970, p. 218). The man has the blessing of society to develop sexual expressiveness, but the woman, at least until recently, had not had this freedom, and her needs have often been ignored. And of course compounding her difficulties is the fact that she does not require sexual arousal to function adequately as a partner during sexual intercourse.

According to laboratory studies reported in *Human Sexual Response,* women seem capable both of multiple orgasms and of more sustained, more frequent, and more physiologically intense sexual arousal than men, which makes the neglect of their sexuality particularly ironic.

One question suggested by the distinction drawn by Masters and Johnson between the historically rel-

[3]Spinal cord lesions, depending on how complete they are and where they are located, may cause paralysis and loss of sensation either in the legs (paraplegia) or in both arms and legs (quadraplegia). A person who cannot move his or her arms and legs is sometimes considered incapable of sexual excitement. This is not so. A review by Higgins (1978) documents erections and ejaculation in a number of paralyzed men.

evant factors and the spectator role factors and fear of performance is whether causes alleged to be of only historical importance might not be of more immediate concern to some people. Might not a woman's *current* religious beliefs inhibit her involvement in and enjoyment of sexual relations? Or consider the woman who was traumatized as a teenager by a gang rape. Might not the memory of that incident intrude itself upon her consciousness whenever she finds herself in an intimate situation? Masters and Johnson would reply that a religious belief or memory acts on the present by putting the person in a spectator role rather than as an uncritical participant, thus preserving the integrity of their theoretical model. Be that as it may, religious beliefs and sexual traumata might conceivably hinder a person's sexual behavior in a very direct and immediate way.

Other Contemporary Views

Masters and Johnson considered sexual dysfunctions as problems in and of themselves and not inevitably caused by deep-seated intrapsychic or nonsexual interpersonal difficulties. The couples whose treatment formed the basis of their second book, *Human Sexual Inadequacy* (1970), had marriages that, in spite of sexual problems, were marked by caring and closeness. But as the Masters and Johnson therapy techniques became widespread and were applied by others, sex therapists were seeing people whose relationships were seriously impaired. It is not difficult to imagine why a marriage or other relationship might deteriorate when the couple had not had intercourse for years. By the time a therapist is consulted, he or she is faced with the chicken-and-egg conundrum. It is impossible to know whether the hostility between the two people caused the sexual problem or vice versa. The working assumption of most therapists is that couples have both sexual and interpersonal problems. Clearly, it is unrealistic to expect a satisfying sexual encounter when, for example, the man is angry with the woman for spending more and more time outside the home, or when the woman resents the man's insensitive dealings with their children. Such negative thoughts and emotions can intrude themselves into the sexual situation and thereby inhibit whatever arousal and pleasure might otherwise be found.

As mentioned earlier, people may lack knowledge of sexual anatomy and functioning and more specifically be unaware of the likes and dislikes of a partner. Unfortunately, just caring for the partner may not be enough in establishing a mutually satisfying sexual relationship. In fact, Kaplan (1974) suggested that inhibiting anxiety can arise when one partner wants *too much* to please the other; this may, though, be a special case of performance anxiety. People who have sexual problems are often found to lack knowledge and skill in this area (LoPiccolo & Hogan, 1979). Or, the partner may lack knowledge or skill; the husbands of nonorgasmic women are often reported to be awkward lovers (Kaplan, 1974; LoPiccolo, 1977).

The assumption that sexual anxiety inhibits sexual arousal and performance has been challenged by data from psychophysiology laboratories that show that anxiety experimentally induced by certain films or by the threat of electric shock actually *increases* genital arousal as compared with no-anxiety conditions (Barlow, Sakheim, & Beck, 1983; Hoon, Wincze, & Hoon, 1977). This finding, however, holds only for fully functional subjects; those who have been identified as sexually dysfunctional become *less* aroused under shock-threat conditions (Beck et al., 1984). Perhaps there is something arousing for functional people when there is danger involved during sex, a theme many people can relate to from their earliest sexual experiences in parked cars and other similar situations. If so, anxiety may play less of a role in the etiology of some sexual dysfunctions than it does in the maintenance of them.

Another problem is poor communication between partners. For any number of reasons—embarrassment, distrust, dislike, resentment, depression, to name but a few—one lover may not inform the other of his or her preferences, likes, and dislikes. Then he or she often misinterprets the failure of the partner to anticipate or mind read as not really caring. Although sexual communication is frequently inadequate in distressed marriages and is therefore tended to in couples therapy (see page 601), it can also be poor in people who are otherwise compatible. Open discussions of sex by partners, among friends, in the media, and even in professional training programs are, after all, relatively recent phenomena.

Although concerns about contracting a venereal disease have probably long been a distractor and hence an inhibitor of having sexual pleasure with a partner, the spread of acquired immunodeficiency syndrome among sexually active individuals has no doubt become yet another reason for many of the sexual dysfunctions. We will discuss the critical topic of AIDS in detail at the end of this chapter.

Finally, as with many other psychological problems, it is not known why some people have in their backgrounds or in their present lives one or more

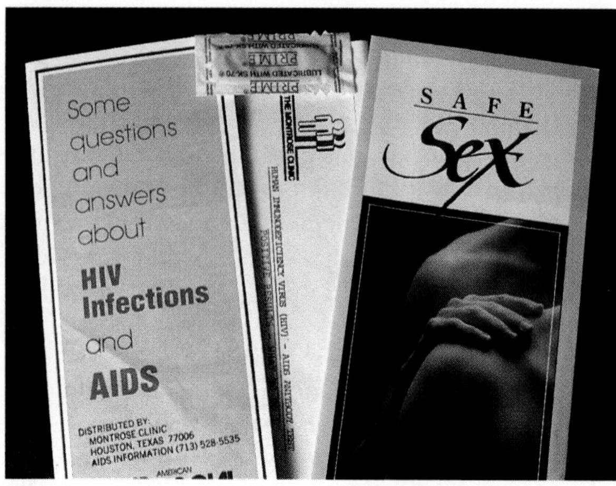

Sexual dysfunctions can arise due to fears about contracting a venereal disease or AIDS.

of the factors believed to be of etiological significance and yet do not have a sexual dysfunction. Why a person develops one sexual dysfunction rather than another is also a puzzle.

Therapies for Sexual Dysfunctions

Perhaps in no area of psychotherapy have behavioral and cognitive therapies been more notably successful than in treating sexual dysfunctions, as demonstrated by several adequately controlled outcome studies (e.g., D'Amicis et al., 1985; LoPiccolo et al., 1985) plus the overwhelming weight of clinical evidence. The overall success rates for the kind of direct cognitive-behavioral approaches described below, however, are far from perfect.

The pioneering work of Masters and Johnson (1970) in the treatment of sexual dysfunctions is described in Focus Box 13.2. Over the past twenty years therapists and researchers have elaborated on this early report and added to the armamentarium of clinicians who seek to improve the sexual lives of dysfunctional patients. Furthermore, there is a consensus (e.g., LoPiccolo, 1992-a; Wincze & Carey, 1991) that the patients being seen by sex therapists in the 1990s are more diverse in background and circumstances and are beset with more complicated and serious problems than were the traditional, comparatively well-adjusted, upper and upper-middle class couples reported on in 1970 by Masters and Johnson.

We will describe several approaches and procedures. A therapist may choose only one technique for a given case, but the complex and multifaceted nature of sexual dysfunctions usually demands several.

Sex Education

Because many dysfunctional people are ignorant of basic facts about human sexuality, most therapists devote time and effort to educating their clients in sexual anatomy and the physiological processes of intercourse. An unintentional but important effect of such instruction is to make legitimate the explicit discussion of sex, taking it out of the realm of unspoken taboo and mystery and reducing some of the anxiety and embarrassment surrounding this previously avoided topic.

Anxiety Reduction

Well before the publication of the Masters and Johnson therapy program, behavior therapists appreciated that their frightened clients needed gradual and systematic exposure to anxiety-provoking aspects of the sexual situation. Wolpe's systematic desensitization and in vivo desensitization (that is, desensitization by real-life encounters) have been employed with high degrees of success (Hogan, 1978; Andersen, 1983), especially when combined with skills training; people highly anxious about sex have often failed to learn to do a number of necessary and preliminary things. In vivo desensitization would appear to be the principal technique of the Masters and Johnson program, although additional components probably contribute to its overall effectiveness.

Directed Masturbation

Employed primarily for women who have seldom if ever had an orgasm, this technique involves persuading the patient of the propriety and normality of masturbation (for often such women have never masturbated), instructing her in female anatomy, encouraging stroking oneself in pleasurable ways, and finally exploring those masturbation methods that are most effective in bringing her to high levels of sexual arousal and to orgasm (LoPiccolo & Lobitz, 1972). An important covert message in directed masturbation is that it is okay to be sexual and okay to seek sexual gratification. This implicit theme is common to all the strategies and techniques described here and no doubt contributes a great deal to clinical improvement.

Those women who have partners are invited to include them in the various stages of the program. Sessions with the therapist can be supplemented by assigned reading, such as *Becoming Orgasmic*, a self-help book by Heiman and LoPiccolo (1988), and occasionally by specially designed videotapes that illustrate masturbation. In most instances nonorgasmic women learn to have orgasms while masturbating and while their partners manually or orally bring them to orgasm. However, this ability transfers to conventional penile–vaginal intercourse in fewer than half of the cases (LoPiccolo & Stock, 1986).

Skills and Communication Training

To improve sexual skills and communication, therapists assign written materials, show clients videotapes and films that demonstrate explicit sexual techniques, discuss techniques with them, and encourage them to express their likes and dislikes to their partners (e.g., McMullen & Rosen, 1979). These training procedures also expose the client to anxiety-laden material; this desensitizing aspect appears to be an additional benefit.

Procedures to Change Attitudes and Thoughts

In what are called **sensory-awareness procedures,** clients are encouraged to tune in to the pleasant sensations that accompany even incipient sexual arousal. The sensate-focus exercises described in Box 13.2, for example, are a way of opening the individual to truly sensual and sexual feelings. Rational-emotive therapy tries to substitute less self-demanding thoughts for "musturbation," the "I must" thoughts often causing problems for people with sexual dysfunctions.

Couples Therapy

As noted earlier, sexual dysfunctions are often embedded in a distressed marital or other close relationship. Troubled couples usually need special training in communications skills. Recent writings on sex therapy (e.g., LoPiccolo, 1992a) emphasize that a systems perspective is necessary, that is, the therapist must appreciate that a sexual problem is embedded in a complex network of factors and that it sometimes even "works for" the couple, as when a man's erectile problems relieve the woman of concerns she might have of satisfying his sexual desires. Couples therapy is discussed in more detail in Chapter 20.

Psychodynamic Techniques

A man may not at first admit that he cannot have an erection, in which case the therapist must listen for clues in what he says. A woman may be reluctant to initiate sexual encounters because, although she may not verbalize it to the therapist, she considers such assertiveness unseemly and inappropriate to her traditional female role. In such instances the general analytic view that clients are often unable to express clearly to their therapists what truly bothers them can help in proper assessment and planning for behavioral treatment. Kaplan (1974) articulated well the blend of psychodynamic therapy with direct behavioral treatment. No doubt elements of nonbehavioral therapy are to be found in the actual practices of sex therapists, even if they are usually not made explicit by these workers when they discuss their techniques in journals or with colleagues. Readers may wish to recall the earlier discussion of eclecticism in therapy (page 55) to remind themselves of the complexity of the therapeutic enterprise.

Medical and Physical Procedures

As more and more is discovered about organic factors in sexual dysfunctions, it becomes increasingly important for therapists to consider underlying somatic contributors and the possible utility of medical interventions (LoPiccolo, 1992b), especially if dyspareunia and complete erectile dysfunction are the disorders. Dyspareunia can be ameliorated in postmenopausal women by estrogen treatments, which can reduce the thinning of vaginal tissue and improve vaginal lubrication (Masters, Johnson, & Kolodny, 1988; Walling, Anderson, & Johnson, 1990). When depression is part of the clinical picture along with severely diminished sex drive, antidepressant drugs can be helpful. Tranquilizers are also used as an adjunct to anxiety reduction techniques, although the depressant effects of these drugs may be detrimental to sexual functioning. Most therapists use drugs only when psychological procedures are found wanting.

Also available are surgical procedures, such as

FOCUS 13.2 • Masters and Johnson's Therapy for Sexual Dysfunctions

In 1970 the publication of Masters and Johnson's *Human Sexual Inadequacy* generated an excitement in the mental health community that is seldom encountered. This book reported on a therapy program carried out with close to 800 sexually dysfunctional people. Each couple had traveled to St. Louis and spent two weeks attending the Reproductive Biology Research Foundation for intensive therapy by day and doing sexual homework in a motel at night. Away from home, they were free of domestic distractions and able to make their stay a sort of second honeymoon. Many of the Masters and Johnson techniques had been used by therapists for some time; and, although some methodological problems have been uncovered by close examination of their report (Zilbergeld & Evans, 1980), other therapists using their techniques have had the same high rates of success (Andersen, 1983). Masters and Johnson virtually created the sex therapy movement, and their work therefore deserves a detailed description.

The therapy attempts to reduce or eliminate fears of performance and to take the participants out of their maladaptive spectator role. It is hoped that these steps will enable the couple to enjoy sex freely and spontaneously.

Each day the couple meets with a dual-sex therapy team, the assumption being that men best understand men and women best understand women. For the first several days the experiences of all couples are the same, regardless of their specific problem. An important stipulation in these early days is that sexual activity between the two partners is expressly forbidden. A complete social and sexual history is obtained during the first two days, and physical examinations are conducted to determine whether there are organic factors present.

During the assessment interviews considerable attention is paid to the so-called **sexual value system**, the ideas of each partner about what is acceptable and needed in a sexual relationship. Sometimes this sexual value system must be changed for one or both partners before sexual functioning can improve. For example, if one partner regards sexuality as ugly and unacceptable, it is doubtful whether even the most powerful therapy can help that person and the partner enjoy sex.

On the third day the therapists begin to offer interpretations about why problems have arisen and why they are continuing. In all cases the emphasis is on the problems in the relationship, not on particular difficulties of either partner. A basic premise of the Masters and Johnson therapy is that "there is no such thing as an uninvolved partner in any marriage in which there is some form of sexual inadequacy" (1970, p. 2). Whatever the problem, the couple is encouraged to see it as their mutual responsibility. At this time the clients are introduced to the idea of the spectator role. They are told, for example, that a male with erectile problems usually worries about how well or poorly he is doing rather than participating freely. It is pointed out to the couple that this pattern of observing himself, although totally understandable in context, is blocking his natural responses and greatly interfering with sexual enjoyment.

At the end of the third day an all-important assignment is given to the couple, namely to engage in **sensate focus**. The couple is instructed to choose a time when they feel "a natural sense of warmth, unit compatibility . . . or even a shared sense of gamesmanship" (Masters & Johnson, 1970, p. 71). They are to undress and give each other pleasure by touching each other's bodies. The cotherapists appoint one marital partner to do the first "pleasuring," or "giving"; the partner who is "getting" is simply to enjoy being touched. The one being touched, however, is *not* required to feel a sexual response and, moreover, is responsible for immediately telling the partner if something becomes distracting or uncomfortable. Then the roles are switched. Attempts at intercourse are still forbidden. To Masters and Johnson this approach is a way of breaking up the frantic groping common among these couples. The sensate-focus assignment may promote contact where none has existed for years; if it does, it is a first step toward gradually reestablishing sexual intimacy.

Sensate focusing may uncover deep animosities that have hitherto remained hidden. Most of the time, however, partners begin to realize that encounters in bed can be intimate without necessarily being a prelude to sexual intercourse. On the second evening the partner being pleasured is instructed to give specific encouragement and direction by placing his or her hand on the hand of the giving partner in order to regulate pressure and rate of stroking. The touching of genitals and breasts is also now allowed. Still, however, there is no mention of an orgasm, and the prohibition on intercourse remains in effect. Diagrams are presented if the partners are ignorant of basic female and male anatomy, as they often are. After this second day of sensate focusing, treatment branches out according to the specific problem or problems of the couple. As an illustration, we will outline the therapy for female orgasm disorder.

After the sensate-focus exercises have made the couple more comfortable with each other in bed, the woman is encouraged to focus on maximizing her own sexual stimulation without trying to have an orgasm. As a result, her own sexual excitement usually builds. The therapists give her partner explicit instructions about generally effective means of manually stroking the female genital area, although ultimate decisions are made by the female partner, who is encouraged to make her wishes clear to the man, moment by moment. In the treatment of this dysfunction, as in the treatment of others, it is emphasized that at this stage having orgasms is not the focus of interaction between partners.

After the woman has begun to enjoy being pleasured by manual stimulation, the next step is to move the source of sensate pleasure from the man's hand on her body to his penis inside her vagina. She is told to place herself on top of the man and gently insert the penis; she is encouraged simply to tune in to her feelings. When she feels inclined, she can begin slowly to move her pelvis. She is encouraged to regard the penis as something for her to play with, something that will provide her with pleasure. The male can also begin to thrust slowly. At all times, however, the woman must be able to decide when and what should happen next.

When the couple is able to maintain this containment for minutes at a time, without the man thrusting forcefully toward orgasm, a major change has usually taken place in their sexual interactions: for perhaps the first time the woman has been allowed to feel and think sexually, and indeed selfishly, about her own pleasure. In their subsequent encounters most couples begin to have mutually satisfying intercourse.

Clinicians must be extremely sensitive in presenting these various treatment procedures to a couple whose problems may stretch back many years. Sometimes the couple discusses sex for the very first time at the Masters and Johnson clinic. The calm and open manner of the therapists puts the couple at ease, encouraging in them both a commitment to follow certain instructions and a more open attitude toward sex and the activities that people may engage in together when making love. Although behavioral prescriptions are specific, the therapists can never lose sight of the atmosphere that must be maintained in the consulting room and, it is hoped, transferred over to the privacy of the bedroom, where much of the *actual* therapy takes place. As in other forms of behavior therapy, there is a strong emphasis on technique, but interpersonal factors set the stage for behavior to change.

A caveat about sensate focus is in order. As LoPiccolo (1992a) points out, more and more people are aware of the belief that not getting an erection from sensate focus is at the same time expected and not expected! That is, although the instruction from the therapist is not to feel sexual, even the moderately knowledgeable man knows that, *at some point*, he is supposed to get an erection from this nonsexual situation (which, after all, is not really nonsexual at all, involving as it does two nude people who care for each other enough to be spending time and money to feel more sexual towards each other.) Thus, rather than reducing performance anxiety and the spectator role, sensate focus may create in some men meta-performance anxiety, taking the form of self-statements like, "OK, I don't have any pressure to get an erection and have intercourse. Right. So now ten minutes have passed, there's no pressure to perform, but I don't have an erection yet. When am I going to get an erection? And if I do, will I be able to maintain it long enough to insert it?" The sensate-focus stage of treatment, and indeed other aspects of Masters and Johnson's sex therapy, have elements of a very subtle approach to intervention, paradoxical therapy, something we discuss later in some detail (page 580).

In the 1970s and 1980s, sex clinics sprang up everywhere, based in general on the Masters and Johnson model, and many mental health professionals elaborated on their thinking (e.g., LoPiccolo & LoPiccolo, 1978; Gagnon, 1979; LoPiccolo, 1992a, 1992b) and incorporated direct sex therapy techniques into their practices. Researchers have investigated various aspects of the treatment package. One question is whether a dual-sex therapy team is really necessary for all couples; this does not seem to be the case (Fordney-Settlage, 1975; Husted, 1975). Another question concerns the effectiveness of daily intensive therapy compared with the more usual outpatient practice of once weekly sessions; data indicate no advantage to the intensive Masters and Johnson regimen (Heiman & LoPiccolo, 1983).

implanting a semirigid silicone rod in a chronically flaccid penis or removing the clitoral hood in the hopes of enhancing clitoral stimulation. These are radical steps, however. Such alterations for females seem unnecessary, since the clitoris can be gently rubbed either during or separately from intercourse. For males, implantations can allow for erection. However, long-term follow-ups of men who have had such implants indicate that poor sexual functioning continues in many cases (Tiefer, Pedersen, & Melman, 1988); if the psychological components of the problem are not addressed, men may continue to have sexual problems, only with a penis that is never flaccid (for one thing, sexual interest and arousal are now not necessary for intercourse, and this is usually not favorable for long-term adjustment). Vascular surgery involves correction of problems with blood inflow via arteries or outflow via veins in the penis. Results here are mixed at best (Melman & Rossman, 1989), but the possibility does exist for restoration of normal functioning because, unlike with implants, erection will occur only with desire and arousal (Wincze & Carey, 1991).

More recently, the drug yohimbine taken orally has been used with some success with male patients in whom biological factors are suspected (Sonda, Mazo, & Chancellor, 1990); it is believed to work by increasing blood flow into the penis and reducing outflow from it (Meyer, 1988). There is also some very mixed evidence that injection of the drug papaverine into the spongy portion of the penis improves erections in some men, though for many the continuing existence of interpersonal conflicts with their mates negates whatever improvement in erectile capacity is achieved. Dependency on the injections and serious side effects also seem to be significant problems with this mode of treatment (Turner et al., 1989).

In all instances of medical intervention, consideration of psychosocial factors remains important, for sexual dysfunctions are almost always embedded in a complex set of interpersonal and intrapsychic conflicts.

Treating Low Sexual Desire: An Integrative Approach

As noted earlier in this chapter, sexual desire disorders have only recently been isolated as problems in their own right. It is believed by many in the field that in the 1970s low sex drive arose as a concept among both professionals and laypersons because the era of sex therapy legitimized sexual activity in ways that encouraged people to apply pressure on partners who were much less interested in sex than they were. Also, as indicated by LoPiccolo and Friedman (1988), several well-designed follow-up studies of sex therapy (e.g., D'Amicis et al., 1985; LoPiccolo et al., 1985) revealed relapses among people who had apparently been treated successfully. Examination of these cases suggested that at least one of the partners was showing little if any interest in initiating sexual encounters at all.

We have already mentioned some of the reasons hypothesized as causing low sexual desire and aversion to sex (page 367). We now turn to some of the treatments designed to help people with these problems, relying heavily on the programmatic work of Joseph LoPiccolo (LoPiccolo, 1980; LoPiccolo & Friedman, 1988). His work in turn shows the influence of Helen Kaplan (1974), who made the early argument that sexual desire disorders require therapists to go beyond the largely behavioral techniques devised by Masters and Johnson (1970) for dealing with arousal and orgasm disorders. A consideration of how low sexual desire is treated by experienced sex therapists will provide a useful glimpse into the complexities of treatment and how ideas and techniques from different approaches are being blended these days by many psychotherapists who deal with sexual dysfunctions.

A first step entails *sensory awareness exercises* à la Masters and Johnson, but with the purpose of helping the low desire or sex-aversive partner become more aware of his or her actual feelings about sex. It turns out in clinical cases that the problem revolves much more often around an actual *aversion* (fear, anger, disgust, embarrassment) to sex rather than a lack of interest in it. The person, in other words, is more often negative than neutral, a very important finding, for it can suggest leads to work on later in the therapy. Useful in this initial stage of treatment are exercises from Gestalt therapy (see page 547), which help people become cognizant of feelings of which they have been unaware. For example, the therapist may ask the patient to imagine sexual activity and then encourage, even goad, the patient to verbalize his or her negative feelings about it, paying close attention to bodily cues and facial expressions that are subtle manifestations of the aversive feelings and attitudes.

The second stage, often undertaken in conjunction with the first, entails *insight* into the reasons for the negative feelings. For example, a sixty-year-old man may believe that this is "just the way I am," perhaps because of his age, whereas it may appear to the therapist that his hypoactive sexual desire is due (more) to his anger at his partner for things having nothing to do with sex per se. Changing the patient's attribution, something we saw as important in treating anxiety (page 146) and depression (page 244), can lay the foundation for positive therapeutic change. Useful here are Rogerian empathy statements that help the person become more aware of factors that might underlie the sexual problem.

The third phase of treatment is *cognitive restructuring*, which represents in part the application of Albert Ellis's rational-emotive therapy to low sexual desire. Specific self-statements, based on what was learned in the first two stages of therapy, are created for the patient to counteract ideas that are blocking sexual desire or making it aversive to have sexual feelings. For example, a coping self-statement like "Just because I feel sexy does not mean I am a bad person" could make sense for a person who learned that sexuality made him or her unworthy of respect and love. Of course, it is not easy for patients to accept these more constructive self-statements or beliefs. One of the continuing challenges to any cognitive-behavioral therapy is how people internalize new ideas that can help them function better. This and related problems are addressed in depth in Chapter 19.

The fourth and final treatment stage involves *behavioral interventions*. Here we find the various techniques pioneered by Masters and Johnson (1970) as well as others that are reviewed in this text. For example, a person with little experience in frankly sexual situations can be expected to need instruction and support in particular sexual techniques for pleasuring his or her partner. Encouragement, indeed, permission, to view erotic films and read erotic books can further legitimize sex and can also serve to prime the pump. As with more traditional Masters and Johnson therapy, the partner of the patient is best involved in the treatment, for he or she is an inextricable part of the problem and therefore a necessary part of the solution.

AIDS: A Challenge for the Behavioral Sciences

There is no greater public health threat today than **AIDS (acquired immunodeficiency syndrome)**. This invariably fatal illness has two unique, interrelated characteristics that make it appropriate for discussion in an abnormal psychology textbook: (1) it is not presently curable or preventable by medical means; and (2) it *is* preventable by psychological means. Indeed, for the present and foreseeable future, the only realm in which we *know* progress can be made is in changing people's attitudes and behavior, and in particular their sexual activities.

Scope of the Problem

First identified in 1981, AIDS has emerged as the most serious infectious epidemic of modern times. Indeed, it has been compared with the Black Plague of the Middle Ages. By mid-1992, 150,000 people in the United States had died from complications from the disease and between one and 1.5 million were HIV-positive (carrying the virus that causes AIDS; Sarngadharan et al., 1984). There were also 206,000 documented living cases of AIDS. The U.S. Centers for Disease Control estimate that by the end of 1993, as many as 170,000 more Americans will have died from AIDS; thus the total number of fatalities in the United States would be as high as 320,000. Another way to portray the spreading epidemic is to note that every thirteen minutes someone in the United States becomes infected with the human immunodeficiency virus (HIV).

Figures like these can be so numbing that it is instructive to put them in perspective. The Vietnam War, the morality and casualties of which have been constantly debated in this country, claimed about 58,000 lives in the ten years of American involvement (1964 to 1973). The analogous ten-year figure for AIDS is 150,000, or two and a half times higher. But since the worst fatality figures are yet to come, the magnitude of the loss of human life in the United States alone is going to be many times greater than U.S. deaths in Vietnam.

The prevalence of AIDS among African-Americans and Hispanics is more than double the percentages of these groups in the U.S. population—about 40 percent of U.S. AIDS cases are members of these minorities (Centers for Disease Control, 1989; Foreyt, 1990). The imbalance is even greater for women; most women with AIDS are intravenous (IV) drug users or have had sexual contact with IV drug users. In 162 countries reporting data to the World Health Organization, close to 350,000 cases have been isolated, but this figure is believed to be a gross underestimate because detection and reporting of cases lag in many countries (underreporting in Africa may be as high as 90 percent). Perhaps even more daunting are future estimates of the number of people in the world believed to be HIV-positive but not yet diagnosed as having AIDS (e.g., Earvin "Magic" Johnson, formerly of the Los Angeles Lakers basketball team): according to the World Health Organization, as of 1991 as many as 10 million people throughout the world were HIV-positive and about one-third of these will have developed AIDS by 1993 (Wright, 1991).

AIDS was first proclaimed in this country to be a disease of homosexuals. As of the late 1980s, almost three-quarters of AIDS patients were homosexual men, with intravenous drug users accounting for approximately 20 percent. Before blood screening began in 1985, many hemophiliacs received contaminated blood transfusions that ultimately resulted in their contracting AIDS. But AIDS never was a homosexual disease at all, and there are signs that the disease is increasing among heterosexuals, both men and women (Centers for Disease Control, 1989). Indeed, in Africa and parts of Latin America, AIDS is found primarily among heterosexuals, and throughout the world, infected women are giving birth to babies who are HIV-positive. Even in parts of the world in which AIDS is not yet a significant health problem, it is likely to become one.

Description of the Disease

Although the medical intricacies of AIDS are beyond the scope of this book, it is important to understand a few fundamentals. AIDS is a disease in which the body's immune system is severely compromised, putting the individual at high risk for opportunistic diseases, such as Kaposi's sarcoma, rare forms of lymph cancer, and a wide range of dangerous fungal, viral, and bacterial infections. Medical authorities suspect AIDS when an otherwise healthy person presents with an illness that he or she would not likely have with a properly functioning immune system. (People who have had an organ transplant, for example, are at risk for such opportunistic diseases because they are given drugs that suppress the immune system so that the body will not reject the new organ. In a sense, the AIDS patient is someone who presents similarly, without having taken the antirejection, immunosuppressant medication. The big difference, of course, is that the transplant patient is kept in an antiseptic intensive care hospital environment while his or her immune system is being *artificially*—and *temporarily*—compromised.) Strictly speaking, people do not die of AIDS as much as they die of fatal infectious diseases that AIDS makes them vulnerable to.

The HIV-infection may also attack the central nervous system directly (Nurnberg, Prudic, Fiori, & Freedman, 1984), sometimes leading to problems in memory and concentration many months before an AIDS-related illness appears. One study (Navia, Cho, Petito, & Price, 1986) found that of seventy AIDS patients autopsied at death, fewer than 10 percent had normal brains and most of them had exhibited what has come to be called AIDS dementia complex, a deterioration in memory, thought, judgment, and motor coordination that is believed to be caused directly by the AIDS virus prior to the suppression of the immune system that is the hallmark of AIDS. However, many studies fail to show this direct damaging effect of the HIV infection, leaving the question a complex and open one at the present time (Grant & Heaton, 1990).

If a person tests positive for HIV, the body has produced antibodies to the AIDS virus. AIDS is diagnosed when the virus has destroyed a large number of T-4 or helper T lymphocytes, cells that are at the core of the body's immune system, the system that fights off the many infections that humans are exposed to daily but resist rather routinely most of the time. All people who test HIV-positive develop AIDS, usually within eight years, but some first develop AIDS-related complex, ARC, which is less severe than AIDS and which develops into AIDS, usually within a year (Redfield, Wright, & Tramat, 1986).

Spread of the Disease

The AIDS crisis is exacerbated by the fact that many untested HIV-positive people feel healthy and are unaware of their illness. Though little talked about in the media, there is an illness called acute HIV syndrome, characterized by flulike symptoms such as fever, night sweats, and headaches, that occurs about a month after infection and lasts two to three weeks (Glasner & Kaslow, 1990; Ho et al., 1985). Because it affects only about half the people infected (Fox et al., 1987) and because of its nonspecific nature, it is generally overlooked as people go into a symptom-free incubation or latency period that can last for eight to ten years (Hessol et al., 1988).

HIV-positive individuals can infect others, in the ways described below, and contribute to what some have called a ticking time bomb in the health of the human race. Complicating efforts to control transmission of HIV is the fact that the most widely employed tests detect antibodies to infection, and these antibodies do not appear in most infected people until several months following infection (McCutchan, 1990). Thus even if a test is negative, a person recently exposed to an infected individual may have HIV.

Once diagnosed with AIDS, drugs such as AZT can bring about some improvement and perhaps even prolong life, but available data offer little encouragement that lives can be saved over the long haul (and "long" is seldom more than a few years).

Although millions are being spent on developing a vaccine against HIV, the focus is now squarely on behavioral science research and practice for prevention and control.

The core of the problem is risky sexual practices, not sexual orientation. HIV is present only in blood, semen, and vaginal secretions and can be transmitted only when infected liquids get into the bloodstream. AIDS cannot be caught through casual social contact or even by living with an AIDS or HIV-positive person, provided that reasonable care is taken to avoid contact with blood. Unprotected receptive anal intercourse (i.e., having a penis inserted into one's anus) is the riskiest of sexual practices (Kingsley et al., 1987). Considerably less risky but still chancy is vaginal intercourse without a condom, and probably also unprotected oral–genital contact and finger or hand insertion into the anus or vagina. The other category of risky behavior is found among *intravenous drug users who share unsterilized needles* and thus can introduce HIV-carrying blood into the bloodstream of another. The use of alcohol and drugs during sex increases the probability of risky sexual practices (Stall et al., 1986). Perhaps the most tragic victims are infants born to HIV-positive mothers, for the virus can cross the placental barrier and infect the developing fetus. The virus can also be transmitted through breast-feeding.

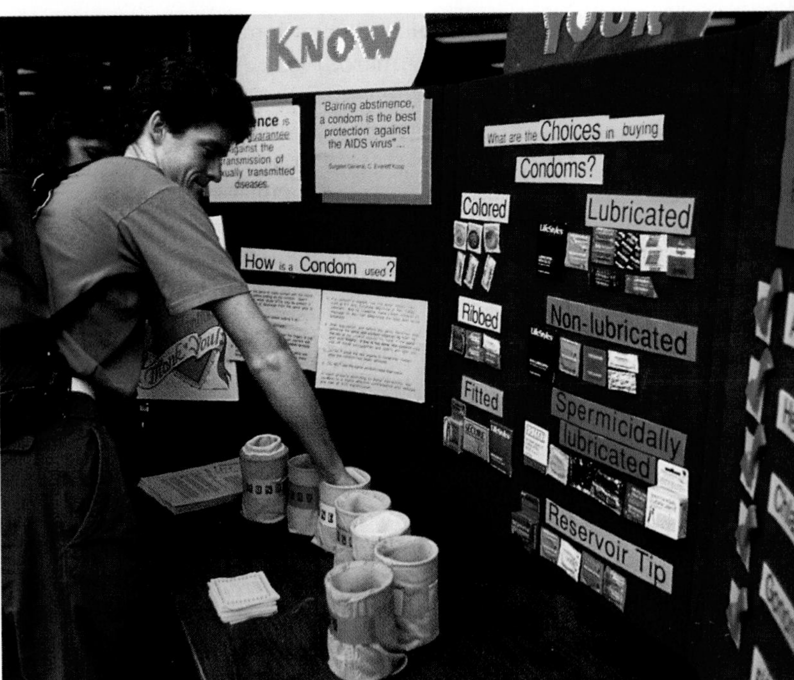

Risky sexual practices are a major factor in the spread of AIDS. Because condoms significantly reduce the risk of infection, efforts are underway to make people more aware of them and to increase their availability.

Prevention of the Disease

The primary focus in prevention of sexually transmitted AIDS is on changing sexual *practices*. Exposure can of course be eliminated by being in a monogamous relationship with a partner who tests negative for HIV. However, monogamous relationships are very rare among young people, and are not invariably found among married people or those in other committed relationships. Prevention is best directed at encouraging sexually active people to use condoms, which are about 90 percent effective in preventing HIV infection. Employing sophisticated probability modeling techniques, Reiss and Leik (1989) demonstrated that risk is far more significantly reduced by using condoms—even though they are less than 100 percent effective—than by reducing the number of partners with whom a person has sex. Of course, the safest strategy would be to use condoms in a monogamous relationship, a tack that is probably unrealistic and that is also contrary to the strictures of some religious groups (since condoms are a form of birth control). More prevalent in the public health arena, however, is advocacy of monogamous relationships, a recommendation that is based more on morality than on data.

People are also urged to explore the pleasures of low-risk sex, such as mutual masturbation and frottage (body rubbing without insertion of the penis into the vagina, mouth, or anus of the partner). Note that for the most part this advice holds for same- or opposite-sexed partners. Prevention for IV drug users includes the aforementioned measures, but should also include the use of new or sterilized needles. The best precaution would be getting off drugs altogether.

In cities where AIDS is less of a problem than it is in centers like New York and San Francisco, high-risk behavior is much more common. Perhaps there is a (mistaken) sense of personal invulnerability when there is not an epidemic in one's immediate vicinity (St. Lawrence, et al., 1988). This certainly seems to be the case, especially among young heterosexuals (both male and female) who continue to see the problem as mostly limited to gays and drug users and who perhaps wish to distance themselves from a disease that bears the social stigma of those whom it affects the most at the present time. There is, then, little evidence that high-risk behavior among heterosexuals has markedly changed, especially among African-Americans and Hispanics (Thomas, Gilliam, & Iwrey, 1989), whose attitudes toward the use of condoms are quite negative (Marin, 1989; Amaro, 1989). Adolescents in general see AIDS as a personal threat less than do people in their twenties and beyond (Strunin & Hingson, 1987). These facts pose a serious problem, because the most prudent judgment for people to make—regardless of sexual orientation—when they consider having sexual relations, particularly with a new partner, is that their partner could be HIV-positive.

But how can changes be brought about, especially (at least for heterosexuals) in a generation of sexually active people for whom the pill marked a welcome liberation from the need to use condoms? Also daunting is the challenge of changing the attitudes and practices of adults for whom the 1960s ushered in a period of sexual liberation, restrained to be sure by the danger of herpes and other venereal diseases but not by the certainty of dying. Kelly and St. Lawrence (1988a, 1988b) draw on social psychological and behavior therapy theory and research to suggest principles that can form the basis of effective interventions. Educational messages should (1) emphasize the risk of certain behaviors; (2) make clear the vulnerability of people who engage in such behaviors; (3) demonstrate how changes in behavior can reduce risk; and (4) persuade the person that the benefits of making behavioral changes outweigh any inconvenience and loss of satisfaction. The information needs to be presented so that people know exactly what they should be doing and why; and communication has to be frequent and conveyed in a supportive, optimistic (yet realistic) way by respected persons with whom the audience can identify. Also important are social support and encouragement, as we saw in Chapter 11 with cigarette smokers trying to kick the habit.

Interventions implementing these principles lead to reductions in unprotected anal intercourse and increased use of condoms in gay and bisexual men (Kelly et al., 1989; Kelly et al., 1990). Such efforts are having a positive impact in reducing the spread of HIV infection among gays. For example, in the San Francisco Men's Health Study, unprotected anal intercourse was reported by about 35 percent of gay men in 1985 but only by 2 to 4 percent by 1988 (Ekstrand & Coates, in press). Similarly sharp drops were found in Denver (Judson, Cohn, & Douglas, 1989) and in Long Beach, Chicago, and Seattle (O'Reilly et al., 1989).

Such cognitive-behavioral approaches to prevention might, we believe, benefit from some social psychological research inspired by Milton Rokeach's work on values (1973; Ball-Rokeach & Rokeach, 1984). Rokeach held that human behavior is controlled in important ways by values, for example, involvement in civil rights is associated with a person valuing equality more than freedom of choice. In a technique he called value self-confrontation, Rokeach and others have shown that if one confronts an individual with a discrepancy between the values held by those whom the person wishes to emulate and the values the person currently holds, one can influence the individual to change his or her behavior in an enduring fashion.

What might be the implications for AIDS prevention? It is possible—and remains to be researched—that people who are successful in changing from high- to low-risk sexual practices differ in their *values* from those who do not. For example, they may value wisdom more than short-term pleasure. If this is the case, then informing HIV-negative people of this fact may encourage them to change their own values (or maintain them if they match those of successful behavior changers) and thereby regard their sexuality in a way that promotes more healthful, less risky behavior in the interests of a long-term benefit. Research inspired by Rokeach (e.g., Schwarz & Inbar-Saban, 1988) would seem to be of particular importance to social scientists concerned with behavioral risk reduction in AIDS, because, to be meaningful, any behavioral changes brought about need to be enduring ones. Cognitive change aimed at a deep level, such as a change in values, is likely to be superior to a more superficial change.

Therapy for HIV-Positive and AIDS Patients

What can mental health professionals offer HIV-positive people and those afflicted with AIDS? Anxiety and depression are common, as is a sense of outrage that Nature has perpetrated such a sick joke on humankind.

In the chapter on psychophysiological disorders, we discussed a growing body of evidence that psychological stress can have a negative impact on the immune system (page 199). Alleviating such stress can have positive benefits (Kielcolt-Glaser et al., 1986). This kind of work is being applied to therapy for HIV-positive and AIDS patients because the infection results in a suppression of the immune system. For example, there is some promising evidence that, in the early stages of HIV infection, aerobic exercise can increase T-4 cell levels and reduce anxiety and depression (see Antoni et al., 1990, and Antoni et al., in press, for reviews). A possible mechanism for these preliminary gains may be an enhanced sense of control and well-being.

As with other stressful situations, patients with AIDS can benefit from the support they receive from joining a group.

For those with full-blown AIDS, therapy entails supporting the person in seeking available and acceptable experimental medical treatments and helping the person make contact with AIDS support groups in the area. Stress management approaches (page 220) can also be beneficial, though one cannot and should not deny the objective gravity of the situation. What also seems in our view to be emerging in the clinical literature is the appropriateness of an existential approach that encourages examination of the meaning of one's life and of one's impending death and the importance of achieving some manner of resolution, including making out a will, saying goodbye, in short, doing what has long been believed to be useful and meaningful as one confronts his or her mortality and obligations to those about to be left behind. No doubt a religious belief in an afterlife can bring comfort both to the patient and to his or her loved ones. Social support from family and friends and from other AIDS sufferers is also beneficial (Kelly, St. Lawrence, Hood, Smith, & Cook, 1988). Since many terminal AIDS patients have been estranged from their families because of their sexual orientation, drug use, or family members' fears of contagion, concerted efforts are needed to effect what can sometimes be remarkable and bolstering reconciliations (McCutchan, 1990).

The fact that most of those dying of AIDS are young and in what would have been their most productive years underscores the personal and social tragedy. Those who test HIV-positive but do not yet have AIDS or ARC are under stress as they face the knowledge that they will almost certainly contract AIDS. With such individuals Kelly and St. Lawrence advise encouragement of healthful practices such as exercise, decreased alcohol consumption, and good nutrition, all of which *may* have positive effects on the immune system. Indeed, since little is known about the biological and psychological factors that may determine when an HIV-positive individual will develop AIDS, there is much research to be done in hopes of buying time.

AIDS and Public Policy

Any discussion of AIDS prevention is fraught with moral, political, and public policy implications. In the early 1990s we are witnessing heated debate about how much information to convey to children and young adults in elementary and secondary school. Most young people in the United States have had intercourse by the time they enter high school (Hofferth & Hayes, 1987), and perhaps as few as 15 percent of sexually active teenagers use condoms (Nicholas et al., 1989). Should society distribute free condoms to junior high school children? Or should abstinence from sexual intercourse be advocated? At what age do we believe that people should become sexually active? If condoms are sold or distributed gratis in secondary schools, does this condone premarital teenage sex? Or does it represent a realistic and humane confrontation with the real world?

Should we distribute free clean needles to intravenous drug users, or does this, too, condone a pattern of behavior that can be regarded as harmful, both to the abuser and to society?

Should we require mandatory testing and of whom should we require it? Health care workers only? If so, are we prepared to protect those who test positive for the AIDS virus from job discrimination and quarantine? And if we do not offer legal protection, will that not undermine voluntary testing? And isn't that undesirable, given that such testing could reduce the spread of the virus and might also prolong life in infected individuals by enabling them to make choices for drugs, like AZT, which if begun in the early stages of infection can improve the quality and length of life (Weiss & Hardy, 1990)?

Also critical for society to face are the attitudes and practices of health care providers. Although the risks of contagion from treating HIV-infected or AIDS patients are known, very small, and eminently controllable, many workers are still reluctant to treat such patients. It is also the case that recruitment and training of physicians and other health care workers to care for AIDS patients are not keeping pace with the growing needs (Cotton, 1988; Weiss & Hardy, 1990), and the ultimate impact of this epidemic has not even yet been felt.

As the world is affected more and more by AIDS, we will all ultimately have to confront our values and our prejudices, our deepest fears and most urgent desires, as we negotiate a period of uncertainty and threat that few of us have ever had to face.

SUMMARY

Few emotional problems are of greater interest to people nowadays than the sexual dysfunctions, disruptions in the normal sexual response cycle that are often caused by inhibitions and that rob many people of sexual enjoyment. DSM-IV categorizes these disturbances in four groups: sexual desire disorders, sexual arousal disorders, orgasm disorders, and sexual pain disorders. Disorders can vary in severity, chronicity, and pervasiveness, occurring generally or only with certain partners and in particular situations. In no instance should a person believe that he or she has a sexual dysfunction unless the difficulty is persistent and recurrent; all of us quite normally experience sexual problems on an intermittent basis throughout our lives.

The particular sexual dysfunctions and their presumed causes were described. Although biological factors must be considered, especially for dyspareunia and complete erectile failure, the etiology of the disorders usually lies in a combination of unfavorable attitudes, difficult early experiences, fears of performance, assumption of a spectator role, and lack of specific knowledge and skills. Sex-role stereotypes may play a part in some dysfunctions: a man who has trouble maintaining his erection is often called impotent, the implication being that he is not much of a man; and a woman who does not have orgasms with regularity is often termed frigid, the implication being that she is generally cold and unresponsive. The problems of females in particular appear to be linked to cultural prejudices against their sexuality, ironic in light of laboratory data indicating that women are capable of more frequent sexual enjoyment than men.

Information on the causes of sexual dysfunctions derives almost entirely from uncontrolled case studies and must therefore be viewed with caution. The absence of solid data on etiology, however, has not deterred therapists from devising effective behavioral and cognitive interventions. Direct sex therapy, aimed at reversing old habits and teaching new skills, was propelled into public consciousness by the appearance of the Masters and Johnson book *Human Sexual Inadequacy* in 1970. Their method hinges on gradual, nonthreatening exposure to increasingly intimate sexual encounters and the sanctioning of sexuality by credible and sensitive therapists. Other means applied by sex therapists include education in sexual anatomy and physiology; anxiety reduction techniques; skills and communication training; procedures to change attitudes and thoughts; couples therapy when the sexual problem is embedded, as it often is, in a snarled relationship; psychodynamic techniques; and a variety of medical and other physical procedures. Controlled data are just beginning to appear, but there is good reason to be optimistic about the ultimate ability of the mental health professions to help many people achieve at least some relief from sexual problems.

Acquired Immunodeficiency Syndrome (AIDS) has created a health crisis. Behavioral scientists have attempted to help people reduce their chances of contracting AIDS by changing from risky to safer sexual practices.

KEY TERMS

sexual dysfunctions
tumescence
detumescence
hypoactive sexual desire disorder
sexual aversion disorder
clitoris
female sexual arousal disorder
male erectile disorder
female orgasm disorder
inhibited female orgasm
male orgasm disorder
inhibited male orgasm
premature ejaculation
dyspareunia
vaginismus
fears of performance
spectator role
sensory-awareness procedures
sexual value system
sensate focus
AIDS (acquired immunodeficiency syndrome)

chapter fourteen

Schizophrenia

All of a sudden things weren't going so well. I began to lose control of my life and, most of all, myself. I couldn't concentrate on my schoolwork, I couldn't sleep, and when I did sleep, I had dreams about dying. I was afraid to go to class, imagined that people were talking about me, and on top of that I heard voices. I called my mother in Pittsburgh and asked for her advice. She told me to move off campus into an apartment with my sister.

After I moved in with my sister, things got worse. I was afraid to go outside and when I looked out of the window, it seemed that everyone outside was yelling, "kill her, kill her." My sister forced me to go to school. I would go out of the house until I knew she had gone to work; then I would return home. Things continued to get worse. I imagined that I had a foul body odor and I sometimes took up to six showers a day. I recall going to the grocery store one day, and I imagined that the people in the store were saying "Get saved, Jesus is the answer." Things worsened—I couldn't remember a thing. I had a notebook full of reminders telling me what to do on that particular day. I couldn't remember my schoolwork, and I would study from 6:00 P.M. until 4:00 A.M. but never had the courage to go to class on the following day. I tried to tell my sister about it, but she didn't understand. She suggested that I see a psychiatrist, but I was afraid to go out of the house to see him.

One day I decided that I couldn't take this trauma anymore, so I took an overdose of thirty-five Darvon pills. At the same moment, a voice inside me said, "What did you do that for? Now you won't go to heaven." At that instant I realized that I really didn't want to die. I wanted to live, and I was afraid. I got on the phone and called the psychiatrist whom my sister had recommended. I told him that I had taken an overdose of Darvon and that I was afraid. He told me to take a taxi to the hospital. When I arrived at the hospital, I began vomiting, but I didn't pass out. Somehow I just couldn't accept the fact that I was really going to see a psychiatrist. I thought that psychiatrists were only for crazy people, and I definitely didn't think I was crazy yet. As a result, I did not admit myself right away. As a matter of fact I left the hospital and ended up meeting my sister on the way home. She told me to turn right back around because I was definitely going to be admitted. We then called my mother, and she said she would fly down on the following day. (O'Neil, 1984, pp. 109–110)

The young woman described in this case study was diagnosed as schizophrenic. Although the diagnosis of schizophrenia has existed now for about a century and the disorder has spawned more research than any other, we are far from understanding this serious mental disorder. **Schizophrenia** is a group of psychotic disorders characterized by major disturbances in thought, emotion, and behavior—disordered thinking in which ideas are not logically related; faulty perception and attention; bizarre disturbances in motor activity; and flat or inappropriate affect. It causes a patient to withdraw from people and reality, often into a fantasy life of delusions and hallucinations. It is important to remember that schizophrenia is not at all the same as multiple personality disorder, although the two are often confused in the media. In this chapter we will provide first detailed descriptions of the clinical features of schizophrenia, in all their dizzying diversity. Next we will consider the history of the concept, how it was first conceptualized and how it has changed over the years. Then we will examine research on the etiology of schizophrenia and therapies for the disorder.

Clinical Symptoms of Schizophrenia

The symptoms of schizophrenic patients involve disturbances in several major areas—thought, perception, and attention; motor behavior; affect or emotion; and life functioning. The range of problems of people diagnosed as schizophrenic is extensive, although patients who are so diagnosed typically have only *some* of them. The DSM determines for the diagnostician how many problems must be present, and in what degree, to justify the diagnosis. Unlike most diagnostic categories that we have considered, there is *no essential* symptom that must be present. Thus schizophrenic patients differ from one another more than do patients with other disorders. The heterogeneity of schizophrenia suggests that it would be appropriate to try to subdivide schizophrenics into types who manifest particular constellations of problems, and we will examine several recognized types later in this chapter. Here we will review the major symptoms of schizophrenia. These symptoms derive from the DSM criteria as well as from information collected in a large-scale investigation of schizophrenia, the International Pilot Study of Schizophrenia (IPSS), conducted by the World Health Organization (Sartorius, Shapiro, & Jablonsky, 1974). We will present the main symptoms of schizophrenia divided into two categories, positive and negative, and also describe some symptoms that do not fit into these two categories. Although we describe the symptoms in detail, it must be kept in mind that diagnostically the duration of the disorder is regarded as at least as important, if not more so, in distinguishing schizophrenia from the symptomatically similar schizophreniform disorder and brief psychotic disorder.

Positive Symptoms

Positive symptoms consist of excesses, such as hallucinations, delusions, and bizarre behavior.

Disorganized Speech

Disorganized speech, also known as formal **thought disorder**, refers to problems in the organization of ideas and in speaking so that a listener can understand.

> **Interviewer:** Have you been nervous or tense lately?
> **Schizophrenic:** No, I got a head of lettuce.
> **Interviewer:** You got a head of lettuce? I don't understand.
> **Schizophrenic:** Well, it's just a head of lettuce.
> **Interviewer:** Tell me about lettuce. What do you mean?
> **Schizophrenic:** Well, . . . lettuce is a transformation of a dead cougar that suffered a relapse on the lion's toe. And he swallowed the lion and something happened. The . . . see, the . . . Gloria and Tommy, they're two heads and they're not whales. But they escaped with herds of vomit, and things like that.
> **Interviewer:** Who are Tommy and Gloria?
> **Schizophrenic:** Uh, . . . there's Joe DiMaggio, Tommy Henrich, Bill Dickey, Phil Rizzuto, John Esclavera, Del Crandell, Ted Williams, Mickey Mantle, Roy Mantle, Ray Mantle, Bob Chance . . .
> **Interviewer:** Who are they? Who are those people?
> **Schizophrenic:** Dead people . . . they want to be fucked . . . by this outlaw.
> **Interviewer:** What does all that mean?
> **Schizophrenic:** Well, you see, I have to leave the hospital. I'm supposed to have an operation on my legs, you know. And it comes to me pretty sickly that I don't want to keep my legs. That's why I wish I could have an operation.
> **Interviewer:** You want to have your legs taken off?
> **Schizophrenic:** It's possible, you know.
> **Interviewer:** Why would you want to do that?
> **Schizophrenic:** I didn't have any legs to begin with. So I would imagine that if I was a fast runner, I'd be scared to be a wife, because I had a splinter inside of my head of lettuce. (Neale & Oltmanns, 1980, p. 103–104)

This excerpt illustrates the **incoherence** sometimes found in the conversation of schizophrenics: although the patient may make repeated references to central ideas or a theme, the images and fragments of thought are not connected. It is difficult to understand exactly what the patient is trying to tell the interviewer.

Speech may also be disordered by **loose associations** or **derailment**, in which case the patient may be more successful in communicating with a listener but has difficulty sticking to one topic. He or she seems to drift off on a train of associations evoked by an idea from the past. Schizophrenic patients have themselves provided descriptions of this state.

> My thoughts get all jumbled up. I start thinking or talking about something but I never get there. Instead, I wander off in the wrong direction and get caught up with all sorts of different things that may be connected with things I want to say but in a way I can't explain. People listening to me get more lost than I do. . . .
>
> My trouble is that I've got too many thoughts. You might think about something, let's say that ashtray and just think, oh! yes, that's for putting my cigarette in, but I would think of it and then I would think of a dozen different things connected with it at the same time. (McGhie & Chapman, 1961, p. 108)

Disturbances in speech were regarded at one time as the principal clinical symptom of schizophrenia and remain one of the criteria for the diagnosis. But evidence indicates that the speech of many schizophrenics is not disorganized. Furthermore, the presence of disorganized speech does not discriminate well between schizophrenics and other psychotic patients, such as some of those with mood disorders (Andreasen, 1979). For example, manic patients show as much loosening of associations as do schizophrenics.

Delusions

Deviance in the *content* of thought seems more central to schizophrenia than confusion in speech and in the form of thought. The thoughts of 97 percent of schizophrenics in the IPSS were found disordered in a very fundamental way, through lack of insight. When asked what they thought was wrong or why they had been hospitalized, schizophrenics seemed to have no appreciation of their condition and little realization that their behavior was unusual.

No doubt all of us, at one time or another, are concerned because we believe that others think badly of us. Perhaps much of the time this belief is well justified. Who, after all, can be universally loved? Fortunately, we either learn to live with this belief, or, if it is false, are readily able to dispel it.

Many schizophrenics, however, are subject to **delusions**, holding beliefs that the rest of society would generally disagree with or view as misinterpretations of reality.

Consider for a moment what life would be like if you were firmly convinced that numbers of people did not like you, indeed that they disliked you so much that they were plotting against you. Some of these persecutors have sophisticated listening devices that allow them to tune in on your most private conversations and gather evidence in a plot to discredit you. Not one of those around you, including your loved ones, is able to reassure you that these people are not spying on you. In fact, even your closest friends and confidants are gradually joining your tormentors and becoming members of the persecuting community. You are naturally quite anxious or angry about your situation, and you begin your own counteractions against the imagined persecutors. Any new room you enter must be carefully checked for listening devices. When you meet a person for the first time, you question him or her at great length to determine whether he or she is part of the plot against you.

Simple persecutory delusions were found in 65 percent of the IPSS sample. Schizophrenics' delusions may also take several other forms. Some of the most important of these were described by the German psychiatrist Kurt Schneider (1959). The following descriptions of these delusions are drawn from Mellor (1970).

1. **Somatic Passivity.** The patient is a passive, unwilling recipient of bodily sensations imposed by an external agency.

   A twenty-nine-year-old teacher described "X-rays entering the back of my neck, where the skin tingles and feels warm, they pass down the back in a hot tingling strip about six inches wide to the waist. There they disappear into the pelvis which feels numb and cold and solid like a block of ice. They stop me from getting an erection." (p. 16)

2. **Thought Insertion.** Thoughts, which are not the patient's own, have been placed in his or her mind by an external source.

   A twenty-nine-year-old housewife said "I look out of the window and I think the garden looks nice and the grass looks cool, but the thoughts of Eamonn Andrews come into my mind. There are no other thoughts there, only his. . . . He treats my mind like a screen and flashes his thoughts on it like you flash a picture." (p. 17)

3. **Thought Broadcast.** The patient's thoughts are transmitted, so that others know them.

   A twenty-one-year-old student [found that] "As I think, my thoughts leave my head on a type of mental ticker-tape. Everyone around has only to pass the tape through their mind and they know my thoughts." (p. 17)

4. **Thought Withdrawal.** The patient's thoughts are "stolen" from his or her mind by an external force, suddenly and unexpectedly.

   A twenty-two-year-old woman [described such an experience]. "I am thinking about my mother, and suddenly my thoughts are sucked out of my mind by a phrenological vacuum extractor, and there is nothing in my mind, it is empty. . . ." (pp. 16–17)

The next three delusions pertain to the patient's experiencing feelings and carrying out actions and impulses imposed on him or her by some external agent.

5. **Made Feelings.**

   A twenty-three-year-old female patient reported, "I cry, tears roll down my cheeks and I look unhappy, but inside I have a cold anger because they are using me in this way, and it is not me who is unhappy, but they are projecting unhappiness onto my brain. They project upon me laughter, for no reason, and you have no idea how terrible it is to laugh and look happy and know it is not you, but their emotions." (p. 17)

Kurt Schneider, a German psychiatrist, proposed that particular forms of hallucinations and delusions, which he calls first-rank symptoms, are central to defining schizophrenia.

6. **Made Volitional Acts.**

> A twenty-nine-year-old shorthand typist described her [simplest] actions as follows: "When I reach my hand for the comb it is my hand and arm which move, and my fingers pick up the pen, but I don't control them. . . . I sit there watching them move, and they are quite independent, what they do is nothing to do with me. . . . I am just a puppet who is manipulated by cosmic strings. When the strings are pulled my body moves and I cannot prevent it." (p. 17)

7. **Made Impulses.**

> A twenty-nine-year-old engineer [who had] emptied the contents of a urine bottle over the ward dinner trolley [tried to explain the incident]. "The sudden impulse came over me that I must do it. It was not my feeling, it came into me from the X-ray department, that was why I was sent there for implants yesterday. It was nothing to do with me, they wanted it done. So I picked up the bottle and poured it in. It seemed all I could do." (p. 18)

Although delusions are found among over 50% of schizophrenics, as with speech disorganization, they also are found among patients in other diagnostic categories, notably mania and delusional depression.

Hallucinations and Other Disorders of Perception

Schizophrenic patients frequently report that the world seems somehow different or even unreal (derealization) to them. Some mention changes in the way their bodies feel. Parts of their bodies may seem too large or too small, objects around them too close or too far away. Or there may be numbness or tingling and electrical or burning sensations. Patients may feel as though snakes are crawling inside the abdomen. Or the body may become so depersonalized that it feels as though it is a machine. Some patients become hypersensitive to sights, sounds, and smells. They may find it torment to be touched. Light may seem blinding, and noise becomes an agony. Others remark that their surroundings are not as they used to be, that everything appears flat and colorless. Some schizophrenics report difficulties in attending to what is happening around them.

> I can't concentrate on television because I can't watch the screen and listen to what is being said at the same time. I can't seem to take in two things like this at the same time especially when one of them means watching and the other means listening. On the other hand I seem to be always taking in too much at the one time, and then I can't handle it and can't make sense of it. (McGhie & Chapman, 1961, p. 106)

The most dramatic distortions of perception are called **hallucinations**, sensory experiences in the absence of any stimulation from the environment. They occur most often in the auditory modality and less often in the visual. Seventy-four percent of the IPSS sample reported having auditory hallucinations.

Some hallucinations are thought to be particularly important diagnostically because they occur more often in schizophrenics than in other psychotic patients. Schneider (1959) described these, and we again rely on Mellor (1970) for examples.

1. **Audible Thoughts.**

> A thirty-two-year-old housewife complained of a man's voice speaking in an intense whisper from a point about two feet above her head. The voice would repeat almost all the patient's goal-directing thinking—even the most banal thoughts. The patient would think, "I must put the kettle on" and after a pause of not more than one second the voice would say "I must put the kettle on." It would often say the opposite, "Don't put the kettle on." (p. 16)

2. **Voices Arguing.**

> A twenty-four-year-old male patient reported hearing voices coming from the nurse's office. One voice, deep in pitch and roughly spoken, repeatedly said "G.T. is a bloody paradox," and another higher in pitch said "He is that, he should be locked up." A female voice occasionally interrupted, saying "He is not, he is a lovely man." (p. 16)

3. **Voices Commenting.**

> A forty-one-year-old housewife heard a voice coming from a house across the road. The voice went on incessantly in a flat monotone describing everything she was doing with an admixture of critical comments. "She is peeling potatoes, got hold of the peeler, she does not want that potato, she is putting it back, because she thinks it has a knobble like a penis, she has a dirty mind, she is peeling potatoes, now she is washing them. . . ." (p. 16)

Negative Symptoms

Negative symptoms consist of behavioral deficits, such as avolition, alogia, anhedonia and flat affect.

Avolition

Avolition, or apathy, refers to a lack of energy and seeming absence of interest in what are usually routine activities. Patients may be inattentive to grooming and personal hygiene, with uncombed hair, dirty nails, unbrushed teeth, and disheveled clothes. They have difficulty persisting at work, school, or household chores and spend much of their time just sitting around doing nothing.

Alogia

Alogia can be considered a negative thought disorder and has several components. In poverty of speech, the amount of speech is greatly reduced. In poverty of content of speech, the amount of discourse is adequate but it conveys little information, tending to be vague and repetitive. Patients are typically very slow in responding to questions and sometimes don't respond at all. The following excerpt illustrates poverty of content of speech.

> **Interviewer:** O.K. Why is it, do you think, that people believe in God?
> **Patient:** Well, first of all because, He is the person that, is their personal savior. He walks with me and talks with me. And uh, the understanding that I have, a lot of peoples, they don't really know their personal self. Because they ain't, they all, just don't know their personal self. They don't know that He uh, seems to like me, a lot of them don't understand that He walks and talks with them. And uh, show 'em their way to go. I understand also that, every man and every lady, is not just pointed in the same direction. Some are pointed different. They go in their different ways. The way that Jesus Christ wanted 'em to go. Myself. I am pointed in the ways of uh, knowing right from wrong, and doing it, I can't do any more, or not less than that. (American Psychiatric Association, pp. 403–404)

Anhedonia

Anhedonia refers to an inability to experience pleasure. It manifests itself as a lack of interest in recreational activities, failure to develop close relationships with other people, and lack of interest in sex. Patients are aware of this symptom and report that what are usually considered pleasurable activities are not enjoyable for them.

Flat Affect

In patients with **flat affect** virtually no stimulus can elicit an emotional response. The patient may stare vacantly, the muscles of the face flaccid, the eyes lifeless. When spoken to, he or she answers in a flat and toneless voice. Flat affect was found in 66 percent of the IPSS schizophrenics.

It is important to be clear that the concept of flat affect refers only to the outward expression of emotion and not to the patient's inner experience, which may not be impoverished at all. In a study by Kring (1990), schizophrenics and normal subjects watched excerpts from films while their facial reactions and skin conductance were recorded. After each film clip subjects self-reported on the moods the films had elicited. As expected, schizophrenics were much less facially expressive than normal people, but they reported about the same amount of emotion and were even more physiologically aroused.

Other Symptoms

Several other symptoms of schizophrenia do not fit neatly into the positive–negative scheme we have presented. One of these is catatonia, in which schizophrenics may grimace or adopt strange facial expressions. They may gesture repeatedly, using peculiar and sometimes complex sequences of finger, hand, and arm movements—which often seem to be purposeful, odd as they may be. Some schizophrenics manifest an unusual increase in their overall level of activity, including much excitement, wild flailing of the limbs, and great expenditure of energy similar to that seen in mania. At the other end of the spectrum is **catatonic immobility**: unusual postures are adopted and maintained for very long periods of time. A patient may stand on one leg, with the other tucked up toward the buttocks, and remain in this position virtually all day. Catatonic patients may also have what is referred to as **waxy flexibility**: another person can move the patient's

A schizophrenic with catatonic immobility adopts unusual and seemingly uncomfortable postures for long periods of time.

limbs into strange positions that will then be maintained for long periods of time.

Some schizophrenic patients have **inappropriate affect**. The emotional responses of these individuals are out of context—the patient may laugh on hearing that his or her mother just died or become enraged when asked a simple question about how a new garment fits. These schizophrenics are likely to shift rapidly from one emotional state to another for no discernible reason. Although this symptom is quite rare, when it does appear it is of considerable diagnostic importance. Finally, many patients exhibit various forms of bizarre behavior. They may talk to themselves in public, hoard food, or collect garbage.

With the principal symptoms of schizophrenia described, we turn now to a review of the history of the concept. As we will see, our ideas of what schizophrenia is have changed over time.

Emil Kraepelin (1856–1926), the German psychiatrist, articulated descriptions of dementia praecox that have proved remarkably durable in the light of contemporary research.

History of the Concept

Kraepelin's and Bleuler's Early Descriptions

The concept of schizophrenia was initially formulated by two European psychiatrists, Emil Kraepelin and Eugen Bleuler. Kraepelin first presented his concept of **dementia praecox**, the early term for schizophrenia, in 1898. Two major groups of endogenous, or internally caused, psychoses were differentiated, manic-depressive illness and dementia praecox. Dementia praecox included several diagnostic concepts—dementia paranoides, catatonia, and hebephrenia—already singled out and regarded as distinct entities by clinicians in the previous few decades. Although these disorders are *symptomatically* diverse, Kraepelin believed that they shared a common core. His term, *dementia praecox*, reflected what he believed the common core to be—an early onset (praecox) and a progressive intellectual deterioration (dementia). It is important to note that the *dementia* in dementia praecox is not the same as the dementias we will discuss in Chapter 17 on aging. The latter are defined principally by severe memory impairments, whereas Kraepelin saw in schizophrenia what he termed a general "mental enfeeblement." Among the major symptoms that Kraepelin saw in such patients were hallucinations, delusions, negativism, attentional difficulties, stereotyped behavior, and emotional dysfunction. Thus Kraepelin focused on both the course and the symptoms in defining the disorder, although he often emphasized the former over the latter.

Eugen Bleuler (1857–1939), the Swiss psychiatrist, contributed to our conceptions of schizophrenia and coined the term.

Kraepelin did not move much beyond a narrow definition of schizophrenia and an emphasis on description. In the eighth edition of his textbook, for example, he grouped the symptoms of dementia praecox into thirty-six major categories, assigning hundreds of symptoms to each. He made little effort to interrelate these separate symptoms and stated only that they all reflected dementia and a loss of the usual unity in thinking, feeling, and acting. The view of the next major figure, Eugen Bleuler, however, represented both a specific attempt to define the core of the disorder and a move away from Kraepelin's emphasis on prognosis in the definition.

In describing schizophrenia, Bleuler broke with Kraepelin on two major points: he believed that the disorder in question did not necessarily have an early onset and that it did not inevitably progress toward dementia. Thus the label *dementia praecox* was no longer considered appropriate, and in 1908 Bleuler proposed his own term, *schizophrenia*, from the Greek words *schizein*, meaning "to split," and *phren*, meaning "mind," to capture what he viewed as the essential nature of the condition.

With age of onset and deteriorating course no longer seen as defining features of the disorder, Bleuler faced a conceptual problem. Recognizing that the symptoms of schizophrenia could vary widely among patients, he had to provide some justification for putting them into a single diagnostic category. Bleuler therefore tried to specify a common denominator or essential property that would link the various disturbances together. The metaphorical concept that he adopted for this purpose was the "breaking of associative threads." For Bleuler associative threads joined not only words but thoughts. Thus goal-directed, efficient thinking and communication were possible only when these hypothetical structures were intact. The notion that associative threads are disrupted in schizophrenics was then used to account for other problems. The attentional difficulties of schizophrenics, for example, were viewed by Bleuler as resulting from a loss of purposeful direction in thought, which in turn caused passive responding to objects and people in the immediate surroundings. In a similar vein, blocking, a seeming total loss of a train of thought, was considered a complete disruption of the associative threads for the subject under discussion.

Although Kraepelin recognized that a small percentage of patients who originally manifested symptoms of dementia praecox did not deteriorate, he preferred to limit this diagnostic category to patients who had a poor prognosis. Bleuler's work, in contrast, led to a broader concept of schizophrenia and a more pronounced theoretical emphasis. He placed patients with a good prognosis in his group of schizophrenias and in addition included as schizophrenic "many atypical melancholias and manias of other schools, especially hysterical melancholias and manias, most hallucinatory confusions, some 'nervous' people and compulsive and impulsive patients and many prison psychoses" (1923, p. 436).

The Broadened American Concept

Bleuler had a great influence on the American concept of schizophrenia. Over the first part of the twentieth century, its breadth was extended considerably. At the New York State Psychiatric Institute, for example, about 20 percent of the patients were diagnosed schizophrenic in the 1930s. The numbers increased through the 1940s and in 1952 peaked at a remarkable 80 percent. In contrast, the European concept of schizophrenia remained narrower. The percentage of patients diagnosed schizophrenic at Maudsley Hospital in London stayed relatively constant, at 20 percent, for a forty-year period (Kuriansky, Deming, & Gurland, 1974).

The reasons for the increase in the frequency of American diagnoses of schizophrenia are not difficult to find. Several prominent figures in the history of American psychiatry, following Bleuler's lead, expanded the concept of schizophrenia to an even greater extent.

Adolf Meyer (1866–1950), considered by many the dean of American psychiatry (e.g., Zilboorg & Henry, 1941), argued that diagnostic categories were often arbitrary and artificial (e.g., Meyer, 1917, 1926). His approach to schizophrenia was flexible and did not rely on either specific symptoms or progressive deterioration for a definition of the disorder.

The American conception of schizophrenia was also broadened by investigators who suggested additional schizophrenic subtypes. (Both Kraepelin and Bleuler had suggested that schizophrenia could be divided into specific types, but the subtypes discussed here went considerably beyond their proposals.) For example, in 1933 Kasanin described nine patients who had all been diagnosed with dementia praecox. The onset of the disorder had been sudden for all of them and their recovery relatively rapid. Noting that theirs could be said to be a combination of both schizophrenic and affective symptoms, Kasanin suggested the term *schizoaffective psychosis* to describe the disturbances of these patients. This diagnosis subsequently became part of the American concept of schizophrenia and was listed in DSM-I (1952) and DSM-II (1968).

The schizophrenia category was further expanded by Hoch and his colleagues, who argued that schizophrenia often masquerades as other disorders. They suggested the terms *pseudoneurotic schizophrenia* (Hoch & Polatin, 1949) and *pseudopsychopathic schizophrenia* (Hoch & Dunaif, 1955) to describe anxious, withdrawn persons with serious interpersonal problems who also have neurotic or psychopathic symptoms. Hoch argued that even though these patients often lack the more classic symptoms of schizophrenia, they reveal, on closer examination, the cognitive and emotional disorganization he considered the hallmark of the disorder. As a result of such opinions, many patients who would otherwise have been diagnosed as suffering from neuroses, mood disorders, and personality disorders were considered schizophrenic in the United States.

In the 1960s and 1970s the **process-reactive dimension** was another key means of maintaining the broad concept of schizophrenia in the United States. As soon as Bleuler had observed that the onset of schizophrenia was not always at a young age and that deterioration was not a certain course, clinicians began to observe other differences between those whose onset was later and who sometimes recovered and those whose onset was earlier and who usually deteriorated further. Some schizophrenics had been relatively deviant, apathetic individuals for many of their young years, suffering gradual but insidious depletion of thought, emotion, interests, and activity. Others, usually later in life, had a rather rapid onset of more severe symptoms. The term *process*, indicating some sort of basic physiological malfunction in the brain, was chosen for insidiously developing schizophrenia, and *reactive*, for what appeared suddenly after stress. For the last forty years in the United States the process-reactive dimension has been extensively studied. Earlier social and sexual adjustment, as measured, for example, by the Phillips Scale (1953), became a means of distinguishing schizophrenics and determining their chances for recovery. Those with a *good premorbid* adjustment were more likely to have only an episodic problem and to have a good prognosis. On the other hand process schizophrenia following an earlier poor adjustment of patients at school, work, and in their sexual and social lives, was equated with Kraepelin's original description of dementia praecox. The inclusion of reactive patients in the definition helped extend the American concept.

A prevailing interest in treatment also played a role in broadening the American concept of schizophrenia. Both Bleuler and Meyer had rejected the notion that deterioration was inevitable, thus allowing the possibility of intervention and the restitution of reason. Harry Stack Sullivan (1892–1949) shared this optimistic view and became the first major theorist to develop a systematic psychological treatment for schizophrenia. He emphasized the underlying emotional and cognitive factors motivating what he considered the schizophrenic's withdrawal from interpersonal relationships. Other behavior did not play an important role in Sullivan's definition of the disorder. Because he believed that personality could be observed only in interpersonal relations, he, in fact, maintained that there were *no* fundamental criteria for the disorder (Sullivan, 1929). This view is not held by many contemporary researchers.

The DSM-IV Diagnosis

Subsequent to the publication of DSM-III, the American concept of schizophrenia has moved considerably from the broad definition we have been discussing to a new definition that narrows the range of patients diagnosed schizophrenic in four ways. First, the diagnostic criteria are presented in explicit and considerable detail. Second, patients with symptoms of a mood disorder are specifically excluded. Many patients with a DSM-II diagnosis of schizophrenia actually had a mood disorder (Cooper et al., 1972). Schizophrenia, schizoaffective type, is now listed as *schizoaffective disorder* in a separate section as one of the Psychotic Disorders. Schizoaffective disorder consists of a mixture of the symptoms of schizophrenia and mood disorders.

Third, DSM-IV requires at least six months of disturbance for the diagnosis. The six-month period must include at least one month of the active phase, defined by the presence of at least two of the following: delusions, hallucinations, disorganized speech, grossly disorganized or catatonic behavior, and negative symptoms. The remaining time required can be either a prodromal (before the active phase) or residual (after the active phase) period. Problems during either the prodromal or residual phases include social withdrawal, impaired role functioning, blunted or inappropriate affect, lack of initiative, vague and circumstantial speech, impairment in hygiene and grooming, odd beliefs or magical thinking, and unusual perceptual experiences. Thus are eliminated patients who have a brief psychotic episode, often stress related, and then recover quickly. DSM-II's acute schizophrenic episode is now diagnosed as either *schizophreniform disorder* or *brief psychotic disorder*, which are also listed in the new section. The symptoms of schizophreniform disorder are the same as those of schizophrenia but last only from one to six months. Brief psychotic disorder lasts from one day to one month and is often brought on by extreme stress, such as bereavement. Fourth, what DSM-II regarded as mild forms of schizophrenia are now diagnosed as personality disorders—schizotypal and borderline—as we saw in Chapter 10 (page 267).

Earlier we mentioned that the heterogeneity of schizophrenic symptoms gave rise to proposals concerning the presence of subtypes of the disorder. Three types of schizophrenic disorders now included in DSM-IV—disorganized, catatonic, and paranoid—were initially proposed by Kraepelin many years ago. The present descriptions of Kraepelin's original types provide further information on what schizophrenia is like and on the great diversity of behavior that relates to the diagnosis.

Disorganized Schizophrenia

Kraepelin's hebephrenic form of schizophrenia is called **disorganized schizophrenia** by DSM-IV and is characterized by a number of rather diffuse and regressive symptoms. Hallucinations and delusions—sexual, hypochondriacal, religious, and persecutory—are profuse and poorly organized. The patient may be subject to bizarre ideas, often involving deterioration of the body. The patient speaks incoherently, stringing together similar-sounding words and even inventing new words. He or she may have flat affect or be constantly changeable, breaking into inexplicable fits of laughter and crying. All in all, the patient's behavior is very disorganized. He or she may tie a ribbon around a big toe or move incessantly, pointing at objects for no apparent reason. The patient frequently deteriorates to the point of incontinence, voiding anywhere and at any time, and completely neglects his or her appearance, never bathing, brushing teeth, or combing hair.

Catatonic Schizophrenia

The most obvious symptoms of **catatonic schizophrenia** are the motor disturbances discussed earlier. Such individuals typically alternate between catatonic immobility and wild excitement, but one or the other type of motor symptom may predominate. These patients are negativistic, resisting instructions and suggestions, and often echo (repeat back) the speech of others. The onset of catatonic reactions may be more sudden than other forms of schizophrenia, although the person has probably already shown some apathy and withdrawal from reality. The limbs of the immobile catatonic may become stiff and swollen; in spite of apparent obliviousness, he or she may later relate all that occurred during the stupor. In the excited state the catatonic may shout and talk continuously and incoherently, all the while pacing with great agitation. This form of schizophrenia is seldom seen today, perhaps because drug therapy works effectively on these bizarre motor processes. Alternatively, Boyle (1991) has argued that the apparent high prevalence of catatonia during the eary part of the century reflected misdiagnosis. Specifically, she details similarities between encephalitis lethargica (sleeping sickness) and catatonic schizophrenia and suggests that many cases of the former were misdiagnosed as the latter. This point was dramatized in the film *Awakenings*, based on the work of Oliver Sachs.

Paranoid Schizophrenia

A diagnosis of **paranoid schizophrenia** is assigned to a substantial number of incoming patients to mental hospitals. The key to this diagnosis is the presence of prominent delusions. Usually they are of persecution, but sometimes they may be **grandiose delusions**: individuals may have an exaggerated sense of their own importance, power, knowledge, or identity. Or they may be plagued by **delusional jealousy**, believing their sexual partner to be unfaithful. Vivid auditory hallucinations may also accompany the delusions. These patients often develop what are referred to as **ideas of reference**: they incorporate unimportant events within a delusional framework, reading personal significance into the trivial activities of others. They think that segments of overheard conversations apply to them, and the frequent appearance of a person on a street where they customarily walk means that they are being watched. What they see on television or read in magazines also somehow refers to them. Paranoid schizophrenics are agitated, argumentative, angry, and sometimes violent. But they remain emotionally responsive, although they may be somewhat stilted, formal, and intense with others. And they are more alert and verbal than other schizophrenics: their thought processes, although deluded, have not fragmented (see Focus Box 14.1).

Evaluation of the Subtypes

The subtypes described here still form the basis of current diagnostic systems, yet many have ques-

FOCUS 14.1 • Paranoid Delusions and Psychoanalytic Theory

According to DSM-IV, paranoid delusions are the most obvious symptoms of both paranoid schizophrenia and the **delusional (paranoid) disorders**. A person with a delusional disorder is troubled by persistent persecutory delusions or by delusional jealousy, the unfounded conviction that a spouse or lover is unfaithful. Other delusions that may occur are delusions of being followed, delusions of erotomania (believing that one is loved by some other person, usually a complete stranger with a higher social status), and somatic delusions (e.g., believing that some internal organ is malfunctioning). But unlike the paranoid schizophrenic, he or she has no thought disorder, no hallucinations, and his or her delusions are less bizarre (i.e., more plausible) than those of schizophrenics. The person speaks and reasons coherently and carries out daily responsibilities. A circumscribed delusional system is the one and fundamental loss of contact with reality. People with delusional disorder rarely seek treatment through their own volition, but when they become contentious and initiate litigation, others may bring them for care. Delusional disorder is quite uncommon and typically begins in later life. In family studies, it does not appear to be related to schizophrenia (e.g., Kendler, Masterson, & Davis, 1985).

Freud's theory, accepted even today by many analytic workers, is that paranoid delusions result from repressed homosexual impulses striving for expression. The anxiety stemming from their threatened expression is handled primarily by the defense mechanism of projection, attributing to others feelings that are unacceptable to one's own ego (Freud, 1915). The basic unconscious thought is "I, a man, love him" or "I, a woman, love her." Freud considered the common paranoid delusions of persecution and grandiosity to derive from distortions, and then projection, of this basic homosexual urge.

In **delusions of persecution** the homosexual thought "I, a man, love him," being unacceptable to the ego, is converted into the less threatening statement "I, a man, hate him." Since the emotion expressed by this premise is also less than satisfactory, it is further transformed by projection into "He hates me, so I am justified in hating him." The final formulation may be "I hate him because he persecutes me." Freud asserted that the persecutor is always a person of the same sex who is unconsciously a love object for the individual.

Delusions of grandiosity (megalomania) begin with a contradiction of the homosexual impulse. The sentence "I, a man, love him" is changed into "I do not love anyone." But since libido must be invested in or attached to something or someone, the psychic reality becomes "I love only myself."

One of Freud's lesser known cases of a patient with paranoid delusions is of special interest, for it seems initially to challenge Freud's basic tenet that the persecutor must be a person of the same sex. The kinds of inferences that constitute the argument of this case study are typical of those made by Freud in his attempts to understand his clinical data and to test his hypotheses.

Freud was consulted by a lawyer in Vienna who had been hired by a woman to sue a male business associate for making indecent allegations about her. She stated that the man had had photographs taken of them while they were making love and was now threatening to bring disgrace upon her. Because of the unusual nature of her allegation, the lawyer had persuaded her to see Freud so that he could offer an opinion.

The woman, about thirty years old, was an attractive single person who lived quietly with her mother, whom she supported. A handsome man in her firm had recently begun to court her. After much coaxing he had persuaded her to come to his apartment for an afternoon. They became intimate, at which point she was frightened by a clicking noise coming from the direction of a desk in front of the window. The lover told her that it was probably from a small clock on the desk. As she left the house that afternoon, she encountered two men, one of them carrying a small package. They appeared to whisper something to each other secretively as she passed. By the time she reached home that evening, she had put together the following story. The box was a camera, the men were photographers, and her lover was an untrustworthy person who had arranged for photographs to be taken of them while they were undressed. The following day she began to berate the lover for his untrustworthiness, and he tried equally hard to rid her mind of her unfounded suspicions. Freud read one of the letters that the man had written to the woman. It struck him that the lover was indeed sincere and honest in denying involvement in such a plot.

At this point Freud faced a dilemma common in scientific inquiry. What should the investigator do when confronted with an instance that negates his hypothesis? The persecutor of the young woman appeared to be a member of the opposite sex. Freud could, of course, have completely abandoned his theory that paranoid delusions originate in homosexual impulses. Instead, he looked more closely into the case to see whether there were subtle factors that would allow him, in the end, to preserve the integrity of his theory.

During the second meeting with Freud, the woman changed the story somewhat. She admitted that she had visited the man twice in his apartment, not once, and that only on the second occasion had she heard the suspicious noise. After the first and uneventful visit—as far as her paranoia was concerned—she had been disturbed by an incident that she had witnessed at the office. The next day she had seen her new lover speaking in low tones to an older woman who was in charge of the firm. The older person liked the younger woman a great deal, and the younger woman in turn found that her employer reminded her of her own mother. She was therefore very concerned about their conversation and became convinced that her suitor was telling the woman about their lovemaking the previous afternoon.

Then it occurred to her that her lover and her employer had been having a love affair for some time. At the first opportunity she berated her lover for telling their employer of their lovemaking. He naturally protested and after a while succeeded in undoing her suspicions. Then she made her second visit to his apartment and heard the reputed clicking.

Let us examine Freud's comments on this portion of the case history.

> These new details remove first of all any doubts as to the pathological nature of her suspicion. It is easy to see that the white haired elderly manageress is a mother-substitute, that in spite of his youth the lover had been put in the place of the father, and that the strength of the mother-complex has driven the patient to suspect a love-relationship between these ill-matched partners, however unlikely such a relation might be. Moreover, this fresh information resolves the apparent contradiction with the view maintained by psychoanalysis, that the development of a delusion of persecution is conditioned by an overpowerful homosexual bond. The original persecutor—the agency whose influence the patient wishes to escape—is here again not a man but a woman. The manageress knows about the girl's love-affairs, disapproves of them, and shows her disapproval by mysterious allusions. The woman's attachment to her own sex hinders her attempts to adopt a person of the other sex as a love object. (1915, p. 155)

To protect herself unconsciously from her own homosexual impulses, the young woman is presumed to have developed a paranoid delusion about the man and her employer. A crucial aspect of the case, according to Freud, was the click that the woman had heard and interpreted as the sound of a camera shutter. Freud assumed that this click was actually a sensation or beat in her clitoris. Her sexual arousal, then, provided the basis for her paranoid delusion of being photographed.

Freud allowed himself a great deal of unverified inference in this particular case. Because he wanted to hold to a homosexuality-based theory of paranoia, he inferred that the woman regarded her female superior as a substitute for her mother, that she had an undue homosexual attachment to her own mother and by generalization to this older woman, and that the click that she heard and construed in paranoid fashion was the sound of a camera shutter was really sexual excitement.*

*A more general problem with the psychoanalytic theory of paranoia is that many paranoids are *aware* of their homosexual interests. If so, they should have no need unconsciously to form defensive projections.

tioned their usefulness. Diagnosing types of schizophrenia is extremely difficult, which often means that diagnostic reliability is dramatically reduced. Furthermore, the types have little predictive validity: knowing that a patient has been diagnosed as having one or another form of schizophrenia provides little information that is helpful in treatment or in predicting the course of the problems. Finally, there is considerable overlap among types. For example, with all forms of schizophrenia patients may have delusions. Thus Kraepelin's system of subtyping has not proved to be an optimal way of trying to deal with the variability in schizophrenic behavior.

Supplemental types that have been included in DSM-IV are also flawed, as definitions of undifferentiated and residual schizophrenia indicate. The diagnosis of **undifferentiated schizophrenia** is for patients who meet the diagnostic criteria for schizophrenia but not for any of the subtypes we described previously. The diagnosis of **residual schizophrenia** is used when the patient no longer meets the full criteria for schizophrenia, though signs of the illness persist. Clearly, schizophrenia is a disorder with a wide range of possible symptoms. Indeed, Bleuler wrote of the "group of schizophrenias," implying that it is not one but a set of disorders, each perhaps with a different etiology.

Because of this symptomatic variability among schizophrenics, there is continuing interest in establishing subtypes of symptoms. As we have already indicated, the system currently attracting much interest distinguishes between positive and negative symptoms (Crow, 1980; Strauss, Carpenter, & Bartko, 1974), permitting distinctions among schizophrenic patients with positive symptoms, negative symptoms, and mixed symptoms. Andreasen and Olsen (1982), for example, evaluated fifty-two schizophrenic patients and found that sixteen could be regarded as having predominantly negative symptoms, eighteen, positive symptoms, and eighteen, mixed symptoms. Although these data indicate that it is possible to talk about types of schizophrenia, subsequent research indicates that most schizophrenics show a mixed symptom picture (e.g., Andreasen et al., 1990), so that there are actually very few patients who fit into the pure positive or negative types. Nonetheless, the distinction between positive and negative symptoms is increasingly being used in research on the etiology of schizophrenia, and we will give evidence relevant to the validity of this distinction in the discussion of the possible roles of genetics, dopamine, and brain pathology in the etiology of schizophrenia.

Research on the Etiology of Schizophrenia

We have considered how schizophrenics differ from normal people in the ways they think, speak, perceive, and imagine. We are now ready to ask what can explain the scattering and disconnections of their thoughts, their inappropriate emotions or lack of them, their misguided delusions and bewildering hallucinations. In contrast with other disorders considered in this book, broad theoretical perspectives, such as psychoanalysis, have not had much of an impact on research in schizophrenia. Therefore we provide only a brief overview of two theoretical positions in Focus Box 14.2. Specific areas of etiological research are examined in detail, however.

The Genetic Data

Suppose you want to find an individual who you know will one day be diagnosed as a schizophrenic and you cannot consider any behavior patterns or other symptoms. This problem, suggested by Paul Meehl (1962), has one solution with close to an even chance of picking a potential schizophrenic. *Find an individual who has a schizophrenic identical twin.* There now exists a convincing body of literature indicating that a predisposition for schizophrenia is transmitted genetically. The major methods employed in this research, as in other behavior genetics research projects, are family, twin, and adoption studies. It is important to note at the outset that most of the major genetic studies of schizophrenia were conducted before the publication of DSM-III. Fortunately, genetic investigators collected extensive descriptive data on their samples, allowing them to be rediagnosed using newer diagnostic criteria. Reanalyses using DSM-III criteria have substantiated the conclusions reached earlier (e.g., Kendler & Gruenberg, 1984).

Family Studies

Table 14.1 presents a summary, compiled by Gottesman, McGuffin, and Farmer (1987), of the risk for schizophrenia in various relatives of schizophrenic index cases. In evaluating the figures of this table, bear in mind that the risk for schizophrenia in the general population is a little less than one percent. Quite clearly, relatives of schizophrenics are at in-

Table 14.1 • Summary of Major European Family and Twin Studies of the Genetics of Schizophrenia

Relation to Proband	*Percentage Schizophrenic*
Spouse	1.00
Grandchildren	2.84
Nieces/nephews	2.65
Children	9.35
Siblings	7.30
DZ twins	12.08
MZ twins	44.30

Source: After Gottesman, McGuffin, & Farmer, 1987.

creased risk, and the risk increases as the genetic relationship between proband and relative becomes closer. Therefore the data gathered by the family method support the notion that a predisposition for schizophrenia can be transmitted genetically. And yet relatives of a schizophrenic proband share not only genes but also common experiences. A schizophrenic parent's behavior could be very disturbing to a developing child. The influence of the environment cannot be discounted as a rival explanation for the higher morbidity risks.

Twin Studies

Concordance rates for MZ and DZ twins also appear in Table 14.1. Concordance for identical twins (44.3) is clearly greater than that for fraternal twins (12.08), but it is less than 100 percent. This is important, for if genetic transmission were the whole story of schizophrenia and one twin was schizophrenic, the other twin would almost certainly have a similar fate because MZ twins are genetically identical.

Gottesman and Shields (1972) studied all twins treated at the Maudsley and Bethlem hospitals in London between the years 1948 and 1964. One of the problems of any twin study of schizophrenia is how to judge concordance. Recognizing the potential problems and biases involved in making psychiatric diagnoses, often of people who were not hospitalized, Gottesman and Shields devised a three-grade system of concordance. All probands were, of course, hospitalized schizophrenics. The co-twins with the first grade of concordance were also hospitalized and diagnosed schizophrenic. Co-twins with the second grade of concordance were hospitalized but not diagnosed as schizophrenic; those with the third grade were abnormal but not hospitalized. Concordance rates for the MZ and DZ twins in the sample, figured cumulatively for the three grades, are shown in Table 14.2. As the definition of concordance is broadened, its rate increases in both MZ and DZ pairs, but concordance of the MZs is always significantly higher than that of the DZs.

Gottesman and Shields also examined the relationship between severity of schizophrenia in the proband and the rate of concordance. Severity was defined in terms of the total length of hospitalization and the outcome, that is, whether the patient recovered enough to leave the hospital and then engage in gainful employment. When one of a pair of MZ twins was judged severely ill, concordance rates went up dramatically. For example, pairs of MZ twins were divided into two groups; in one group the probands had had less than two years of hospitalization and in the other more than two years of hospitalization. The concordance rate for the first group was 27 percent and for the second, 77 percent.

Questions have been raised about the interpretation of data collected on twins. Some have argued that the experience of being an identical twin may itself predispose toward schizophrenia. If schizophrenia is considered an identity problem, it might be argued that being a member of an identical pair of twins could be particularly stressful. But schizophrenia occurs about as frequently in single births as in twin births. If the hypothesis were correct, simply being a twin would have to increase the likelihood of becoming schizophrenic—which it does not (Rosenthal, 1970).

But the most critical problem of interpretation remains. Since the twins were reared together, a common deviant environment rather than common genetic factors could account for the concordance rates. A clever analysis, supporting a genetic interpretation of the high concordance rates found for identical twins, was performed by Fischer (1971). She reasoned that if these rates indeed reflected a genetic effect, the children of even the discordant,

Table 14.2 • Concordance in MZ and DZ Twins

Definition of Concordance	*Concordance, %* MZ	DZ
1. Hospitalized and diagnosed schizophrenic	42	9
2. Hospitalized but not schizophrenic, plus those with first-grade concordance	54	18
3. Not hospitalized but abnormal, plus those with first-grade and second-grade concordance.	79	45

Source: From Gottesman & Shields, 1972.

14.2 • Two Theoretical Positions on the Etiology of Schizophrenia

Psychoanalytic Theory

Because Freud dealt primarily with neuroses, he had relatively little to say about schizophrenia. He did occasionally speculate on its origins, though, using some of the psychoanalytic concepts that he applied to all disordered personalities. His basic notion was that schizophrenics have regressed to a state of primary narcissism, a phase early in the oral stage before the ego has differentiated from the id. There is thus no separate ego to engage in reality testing. By regressing to narcissism, schizophrenics have effectively lost contact with the world; they have withdrawn the libido from attachment to any objects external to themselves. Freud thought that the cause of the regression was an increase, during adulthood, in the intensity of id impulses, especially sexual ones. Contemporary psychoanalytic theorists give primacy to aggressive impulses. Whether the threats of the intense id impulses provoke schizophrenia or a neurosis depends on the strength of the ego. Neurotics, having developed a more stable ego, will not regress to the first psychosexual stage, as schizophrenics do, and consequently will not lose contact with reality.

Few data bear on the psychoanalytic position. The theory has generated intriguing and speculative analysis of case history material but little research. Studies showing that schizophrenics have cognitive deficits could be said to demonstrate that the egos of schizophrenics have been impaired. But even so, ego impairment need not be precipitated by an increase in id impulses, nor need it end in a regression to a childhood state. Finally, no one has presented evidence that ego impairments cause schizophrenia.

Labeling Theory

In a radical departure from the traditional conceptualization of schizophrenia, Scheff (1966) suggested that the disorder is a learned social role. This position, also known as **labeling theory**, is essentially unconcerned with etiology. Rather, Scheff argues that the crucial factor in schizophrenia is the act of assigning a diagnostic label to the individual. Presumably this label then influences the manner in which the person will continue to behave, based on the stereotypic notions of mental illness, and at the same time determines the reactions of other people to the individual's behavior. The social role, therefore, *is* the disorder, and it is determined by the labeling process. Without the diagnosis, Scheff argues, deviant behavior—or to use his term, residual rule breaking—would not become stabilized. It would presumably be both transient and relatively inconsequential.

By residual rules Scheff means the rules that are left over after all the formal and obvious ones, about stealing and violence and fairness, have been laid down. The examples are endless. "Do not stand still staring vacantly in the middle of a busy sidewalk." "Do not talk to the neon beer sign in the delicatessen window." "Do not spit on the piano." Scheff believes that one-time violations of residual rules are fairly common. However, normal people, through poor judgment or bad luck, may be caught violating a rule and be diagnosed as being mentally ill. Once judged so, they are very likely to accept this social role and will find it very difficult to rejoin the sane. They will be denied employment, and other people will know about their pasts. In the hospital they will receive attention and sympathy and be free of all responsibilities. So once there, they actually perceive them-

or nonschizophrenic, identical co-twins of schizophrenics should be at high risk for schizophrenia. These nonschizophrenic twins would presumably have the genotype for schizophrenia, even though it was not expressed behaviorally, and thus might pass along an increased risk for the disorder to their children. In agreement with this line of reasoning, the rate of schizophrenia and schizophreniclike psychoses in the children of nonschizophrenic co-twins of schizophrenic probands was 9.4 percent. The rate among the children of the schizophrenic probands themselves was only slightly and nonsignificantly higher, 12.3 percent. Both rates are substantially higher than those found in an unselected population.

Dworkin and his colleagues reevaluated the major twin studies according to the positive–negative symptom distinction discussed earlier (Dworkin & Lenzenweger, 1984; Dworkin et al., 1987). Ratings of positive and negative symptoms were compiled selves as mentally ill and settle into acting crazy as they are expected to do.

Scheff's theory has some intuitive appeal. Most people who have worked for any amount of time at a psychiatric facility have witnessed abuses of the diagnostic process. Patients are sometimes assigned labels that are poorly justified.

Scheff's theory has a number of serious problems, however, indicating that it is, at most, of secondary importance to our understanding of schizophrenia. First of all, Scheff refers to deviance as residual rule breaking, and as described it is indeed merely that. However, calling schizophrenia residual rule breaking trivializes a very serious disorder. Second, very little evidence indicates that unlabeled norm violations are indeed transient, as Scheff implies. Third, information regarding the detrimental effects of the social stigma associated with mental illness is inconclusive (Gove, 1970).

An important correlate of the labeling position is the notion of cultural relativism, according to which definitions of abnormality should be very different in cultures different from our own because of the wide variation in social norms and rules. As an example, proponents of labeling theory might argue that the visions of a shaman are the same as the hallucinations of a schizophrenic but that cultural differences allow a favorable response to shamans.

This and several other questions were addressed by Murphy (1976) in a report of her investigations of the Eskimo and Yoruba. Contrary to the labeling view, both cultures had a concept of being crazy that is quite similar to our definition of schizophrenia. The Eskimo call it *nuthkavihak*, and it includes talking to oneself, refusing to talk, delusional beliefs, and bizarre behavior. The Yoruba call the phenomenon *were* and include similar symptoms under this rubric. Notably, both cultures also have shamans but draw a clear distinction between their behavior and that of crazy people.

A final perspective on labeling theory is found in an anecdote related by colleagues of Paul Meehl, the famous schizophrenia theorist. Meehl

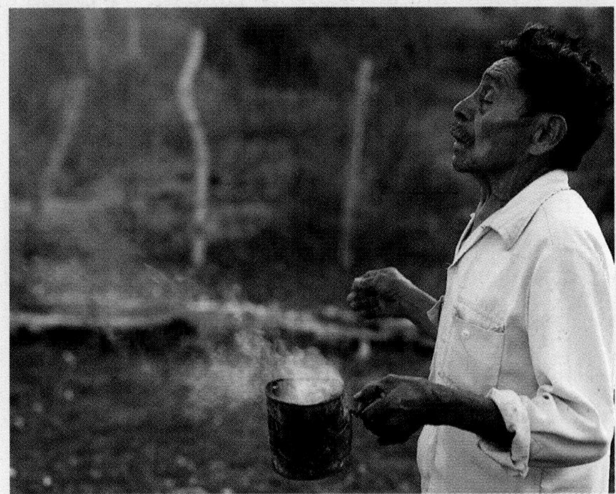

Some writers have held that the trances of shamans are the same as the hallucinations of schizophrenics. Murphy's research, however, finds that the behavior of shamans is clearly distinguished from psychopathology.

was giving a lecture on genetics and schizophrenia when someone in the audience interrupted him to point out that he thought that schizophrenics behaved in a crazy way because others had labeled them schizophrenic. Meehl had the following reaction:

> I just stood there and didn't know what to say. I was thinking of a patient I had seen on a ward who kept his finger up his ass "to keep his thoughts from running out," while with his other hand he tried to tear out his hair because it really "belonged to his father." And here was this man telling me that he was doing these things because someone had called him a schizophrenic. What could I say to him? (Kimble, Garmezy, & Zigler, 1980, p. 453)

In sum, neither the psychoanalytic nor the labeling position has much support. Freud's views of regression to the oral stage and labeling theory, which postulates that schizophrenia is role taking reinforced by the attitudes of diagnosticians and mental hospital staff, are both without substantiating evidence.

from published case histories of the twins and compared for probands of concordant and discordant pairs. No differences emerged for positive symptoms, but probands from concordant pairs were higher in negative symptoms than probands from discordant pairs. These data suggest that negative symptoms have a stronger genetic component than positive ones.

Adoptee Studies

The study of children of schizophrenic mothers reared from early infancy by adoptive parents has provided more conclusive information on the role of genes in schizophrenia by eliminating possible effects of a deviant environment. Heston (1966) was able to follow up forty-seven people who had been born to schizophrenic mothers while they were in a state mental hospital. The infants were separated from the mothers at birth and raised by either foster or adoptive parents. In addition, fifty control subjects were selected from the same foundling homes that had placed the children of schizophrenic mothers. The control group was matched to the schizophrenics by sex, where they were eventually placed, and for the length of time in a child-care institution; as one might expect, exact matching in each case was not always possible. All forty-seven subjects were born between 1915 and 1945.

The follow-up assessment, conducted in 1964, consisted of an interview, MMPI, IQ test, social class ratings, and the like. A dossier on each of these subjects was then rated independently by two psychiatrists, and a third evaluation was made by Heston. Ratings were made on a 0 to 100 scale of overall disability and, whenever possible, diagnoses were offered. Ratings of disability proved to be quite reliable, and when the number of diagnostic categories was reduced to four—schizophrenia, mental deficiency, psychopathy, and neurosis—diagnostic agreement was also acceptable.

The control subjects were rated as less disabled than were the children of schizophrenic mothers. Similarly, thirty-one of the forty-seven children of schizophrenic mothers (66 percent) were given a diagnosis, but only nine of fifty control subjects (18 percent) were. None of the control subjects was diagnosed schizophrenic, but 16.6 percent of the offspring of schizophrenic mothers were so diagnosed.[1] In addition to the greater likelihood of being diagnosed schizophrenic, the children of schizophrenic mothers were more likely to be diagnosed mentally defective, psychopathic, and neurotic (Table 14.3). They had been involved more frequently in criminal activity, had spent more time in penal institutions, and had more often been discharged from the armed services for psychiatric reasons. Heston's study clearly supports the importance of genetic factors in the development of schizophrenia. Children reared without contact with their so-called pathogenic mothers were still more likely to become schizophrenic than were the controls.

A study similar to Heston's was carried out in Denmark under Kety's direction (Kety et al., 1968, 1976). The starting point for the investigation was a culling of the records of all children who had been adopted at an early age between the years 1924 and 1947. All adoptees who had later been admitted to a psychiatric facility and diagnosed schizophrenic were selected as the index cases. From the remaining cases the investigators chose a control group who had no psychiatric history and who were matched to the index group on variables such as sex and age. Both the adoptive and the biological parents and the siblings and half-siblings of the two groups were then identified, and a search was made to determine who among them had a psychiatric history. As might be expected if genetic factors figure in schizophrenia, the biological relatives of the index cases were diagnosed schizophrenic more often than were members of the general population. The adoptive relatives were not.

[1]The 16.6 percent figure was *age-corrected*. By this process raw data are corrected to take into account the age of the subjects involved. If a subject in Heston's sample was only twenty-four years old at the time of the assessment, he or she might still have become schizophrenic at some point later in life. The age-correction procedure attempts to account for this possibility.

Evaluation of the Genetic Data

All the data collected so far indicate that genetic factors play an important role in the development of schizophrenia. Earlier twin and family studies deserved the criticism of environmentalists, who found that in-

Table 14.3 • Subjects Separated from Their Mothers in Early Infancy

Assessment	*Offspring of Schizophrenic Mothers*	*Control Offspring, Mothers Not Schizophrenic*
Number of subjects	47	50
Mean age at follow-up	35.8	36.3
Overall ratings of disability (low score indicates more pathology)	65.2	80.1
Number diagnosed schizophrenic	5	0
Number diagnosed mentally defective	4	0
Number diagnosed psychopathic	9	2
Number diagnosed neurotic	13	7

Source: From Heston, 1966.

vestigators had not acknowledged upbringing as a possible contributing factor. But later studies of children of schizophrenic mothers and fathers, who were reared in foster and adoptive homes, plus the follow-up of relatives of adopted schizophrenics, indicate the importance of genetic transmission, because the potential biasing influence of the environment had been virtually removed. As Seymour Kety, the highly regarded schizophrenia researcher, quipped, "if schizophrenia is a myth, it is a myth with a heavy genetic component" (1974).

We cannot conclude, however, that schizophrenia is a disorder completely determined by genetic transmission, for we must always keep in mind the distinction made between phenotype and genotype (see page 29). The diathesis–stress model, introduced in Chapter 2, seems appropriate for guiding theory and research into the etiology of schizophrenia. Genetic factors can only be predisposers for a behavioral disorder. Stress is required to render this predisposition an observable pathology. And yet the exact sources of stress are rather vague at this point. Low social class and certain patterns of family interaction are two areas we will discuss. There is also some evidence that, in the weeks preceding hospitalization, schizophrenics experience an increased number of stressful life events (Brown & Birley, 1968). But on the whole, additional research is needed on how particular environmental stressors trigger schizophrenia in an already predisposed person.

Biochemical Factors[2]

Speculation concerning possible biochemical causes of schizophrenia began almost as soon as the syndrome was identified. Kraepelin thought in terms of a chemical imbalance, as already indicated, for he believed that poisons secreted from the sex glands affected the brain to produce the symptoms. Carl Jung suggested the presence of "toxin X," a mystery chemical that he thought would eventually be identified. The demonstrated role of genetic factors in schizophrenia also suggests that biochemicals should be investigated, for it is through the body chemistry and biological processes that heredity may have an effect.

The extensive and continuing search for possible biochemical causes faces a key difficulty. If an aberrant biochemical is found in schizophrenics and not in control subjects, the difference in biochemical functioning may have been produced by a third variable rather than by the disorder. Most schizophrenic patients, for example, take psychoactive medication. Although the effects of such drugs on behavior diminish quite rapidly once they are discontinued, traces of them may remain in the bloodstream for very long periods of time, making it difficult to attribute a biochemical difference between schizophrenic and control subjects to schizophrenia per se. Prolonged drug therapy may also lead to changes in the very process of neural transmission. Institutionalized patients may also smoke more, drink more coffee, have a less nutritionally adequate diet than various control groups, and they may be relatively inactive. All these variables can conspire to produce biochemical differences between schizophrenic and control patients that confound attempts to seek deviant biochemicals in schizophrenics. Nonetheless, the search for biochemical causes of schizophrenia proceeds at a rapid rate. Improved technology now allows a much greater understanding of the relation between biochemistry and behavior. At present no biochemical theory has unequivocal support, but because of the great amount of effort that continues to be spent in the search for biochemical causes of schizophrenia, we shall review one of the best researched factors.

Dopamine Activity

The theory that schizophrenia is related to activity of the neurotransmitter dopamine is based principally on information concerning the mode of action of drugs that are effective in treating schizophrenia. If the biochemical activity of a therapeutically effective drug is understood, or at least hypothesized, the process responsible for the disorder may be guessed at too.[3] The phenothiazines (see page 414), in addition to alleviating some symptoms of schizophrenia, produce side effects resembling Parkinson's disease. Parkinsonism is known to be caused, in part, by low levels of dopamine in a particular nerve tract of the brain. It is therefore supposed that phenothiazines lower dopamine activity. Phenothiazine molecules are assumed, because of the struc-

[2]This section is necessarily technical, and for readers who have not studied biochemistry, it may be unusually difficult to follow. We want to provide the details, however, for those who have this background. For those who lack it, we hope at least to convey the logic and general trends in the research on biochemical factors.

[3]Although the therapeutic effects of a drug may provide a *clue* to the causes of the disorder it helps to alleviate, we must be mindful once again that treatment effects cannot logically prove the case for etiology or even for the current causes of the problem in question.

tural similarities to the dopamine molecule (Figure 14.1), to fit into and thereby block postsynaptic receptors in dopamine tracts. From this speculation about the action of the drugs that help schizophrenics, it is but a short inductive leap to view schizophrenia as resulting from excess activity in dopamine nerve tracts.

Further indirect support for the **dopamine activity theory** of schizophrenia comes from the literature on amphetamine psychosis. Amphetamines can produce a state that closely resembles paranoid schizophrenia, and they can exacerbate the symptomatology of a schizophrenic (Angrist, Lee, & Gershon, 1974). The amphetamines are thought to act either by directly releasing catecholamines into the synaptic cleft or by preventing their inactivation (Snyder et al., 1974). We can be relatively confident that the psychosis-inducing effects of amphetamines come from their impact on dopamine, rather than norepinephrine, for phenothiazines are antidotes to amphetamine psychosis.

The major metabolite of dopamine, homovanillic acid (HVA), has been examined, with the expectation that it would be present in greater amounts in schizophrenics. HVA can be measured in cerebrospinal fluid by treating patients with probenecid, a drug that prevents the transfer of homovanillic acid from cerebrospinal fluid to blood. But Bowers (1974) found that before drug treatment schizophrenics had lower levels of HVA than patients with mood disorders and that levels of HVA in schizophrenics increased when they were reassessed during treatment. HVA, when measured in blood plasma, however, does correlate with severity of illness and predicts response to phenothiazines (Davila et al., 1988).

The theory of excess dopamine transmission is not strongly refuted by the evidence collected in the studies of HVA. Dopaminergic overactivity has not, perhaps, been specified precisely enough. The predictions of increased levels of HVA assume that the dopamine-releasing neurons are overactive. But it may be that in schizophrenia dopamine *receptors* are overactive or oversensitive. In fact, the work on the phenothiazines' mode of action would suggest that the dopaminergic receptors are a more likely locus of disorder. Indeed, some postmortem studies of schizophrenics' brains as well as PET scans of schizophrenics have revealed that dopamine receptors may have either increased in number or been hyperactive (Lee & Seeman, 1977; Mackay et al., 1982; Wong et al., 1986). If increased activity of the dopaminergic receptors is the key to schizophrenia, the data concerning levels of HVA are not crucially relevant.

Other research on the excess dopamine activity theory has revealed that it may not be applicable to all schizophrenics. Some studies have now shown, for example, that amphetamines do not worsen the symptoms of all patients (e.g., Kornetsky, 1976), and one study has even reported that symptoms lessen after an amphetamine has been administered (Kammen et al., 1977). Furthermore, phenothiazines have been shown to benefit only a subgroup of patients. In both instances the divergent results are related to the positive–negative symptom distinction noted earlier. Amphetamines worsen positive symptoms and lessen negative ones. Phenothiazines lessen

Figure 14.1 Conformations of (a) chlorpromazine, a phenothiazine, and (b) dopamine and (c) their superimposition, determined by X-ray crystallographic analysis. Chlorpromazine blocks impulse transmission by dopamine by fitting into its receptor sites. Adapted from Horn and Snyder (1971).

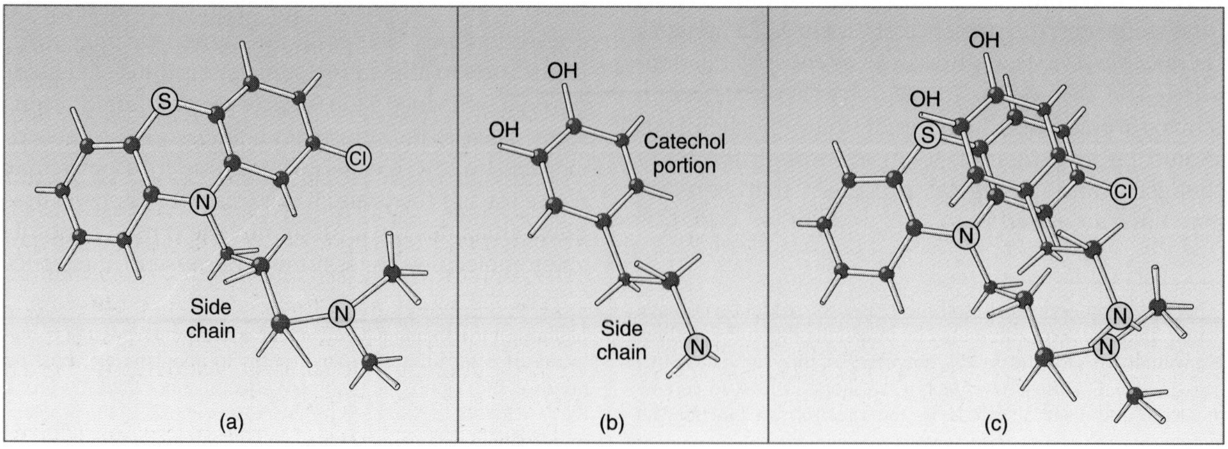

positive symptoms but their effect on negative symptoms is less clear; some studies show no benefit (e.g., Haracz, 1982) and others, a positive effect (e.g., vanKammen et al., 1987). The dopamine theory appears to apply mainly to the positive symptoms of schizophrenia.

More recent developments in the dopamine theory (e.g., Davis et al., 1991) have expanded its scope. The key change involves the recognition of differences among the neural pathways that use dopamine as a transmitter. The excess dopamine activity that is thought to be most relevant to schizophrenia is localized in the mesolimbic pathway (see Figure 14.3), and the therapeutic effects of phenothiazines on positive symptoms occur by blocking dopamine receptors there. The mesocortical dopamine pathway begins in the same brain region as the mesolimbic but projects to the prefrontal cortex. The prefrontal cortex also projects to limbic areas that are innervated by dopamine. These dopamine neurons in the prefrontal cortex may be underactive and thus fail to exert inhibitory control over the dopamine neurons in the limbic area. The underactivity of the dopamine neurons in the prefrontal cortex may also be the cause of the negative symptoms of schizophrenia. This proposal has the advantage of allowing the simultaneous presence of positive and negative symptoms in a schizophrenic patient. Furthermore, because phenothiazines do not have major effects on the dopamine neurons in the prefrontal cortex, we would expect them to be relatively ineffective as treatments for negative symptoms (and this is true). Finally, when we examine some of the research on structural abnormalities in schizophrenics' brains, we will see some close connections between these two domains.

Despite these favorable developments, the dopamine hypothesis cannot be regarded as having been proved, for it has difficulty accounting for some other effects. For example, phenothiazines gradually lessen positive schizophrenic symptoms over a period of several weeks, but the drugs rapidly block dopamine receptors, and after several weeks tolerance should develop (Davis, 1978). This disjunction between the behavioral and pharmacological effects of phenothiazines is difficult to understand within the context of the theory. It is also puzzling that phenothiazines have to reduce dopamine levels or receptor activity to *below normal*, producing parkinsonian side effects, if they are to be therapeutically effective. According to the theory, reducing dopamine levels or receptor activity to normal should be sufficient for a therapeutic effect, but apparently it is not. Thus, although the dopamine explanation remains the most actively researched biochemical position, it is not likely to be a complete theory of the biochemistry of schizophrenia.

Figure 14.2 Dopamine theory of schizophrenia.

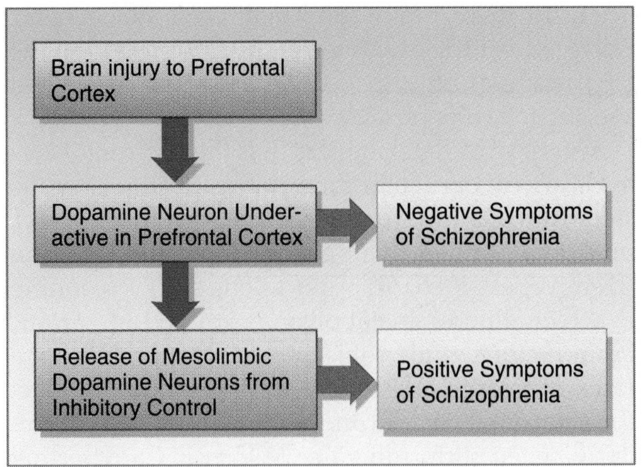

Evaluation of Biochemical Data

The history of research on whether biochemicals figure in schizophrenia has been one of discovery followed by failures to replicate. Many methodological problems plague this research, and many confounds, unrelated to whether or not a subject is schizophrenic, can produce biochemical differences. Thus we must maintain a cautious attitude toward the dopamine activity theory. Furthermore, studies on biochemicals can indicate only that a particular substance and its physiological processes are associated with schizophrenia. Dopamine activity might become changed *after* rather than *before* the onset of the disorder.

The Brain and Schizophrenia

The search for a brain abnormality that causes schizophrenia, like the search for a biochemical, began as early as the syndrome was identified. But the research did not prove promising, for studies when replicated did not yield the same findings. Interest gradually waned over the years. In the last two decades, however, spurred by a number of methodological advances, the field has reawakened and yielded some promising evidence (Seidman, 1983; Weinberger, Wagner, & Wyatt, 1983). A percentage of schizophrenics—the exact number cannot be specified—have been found to have observable brain pathology. The controversy is whether these abnormalities are localized in a small number of brain areas or are widespread.

Postmortem analysis of the brains of schizo-

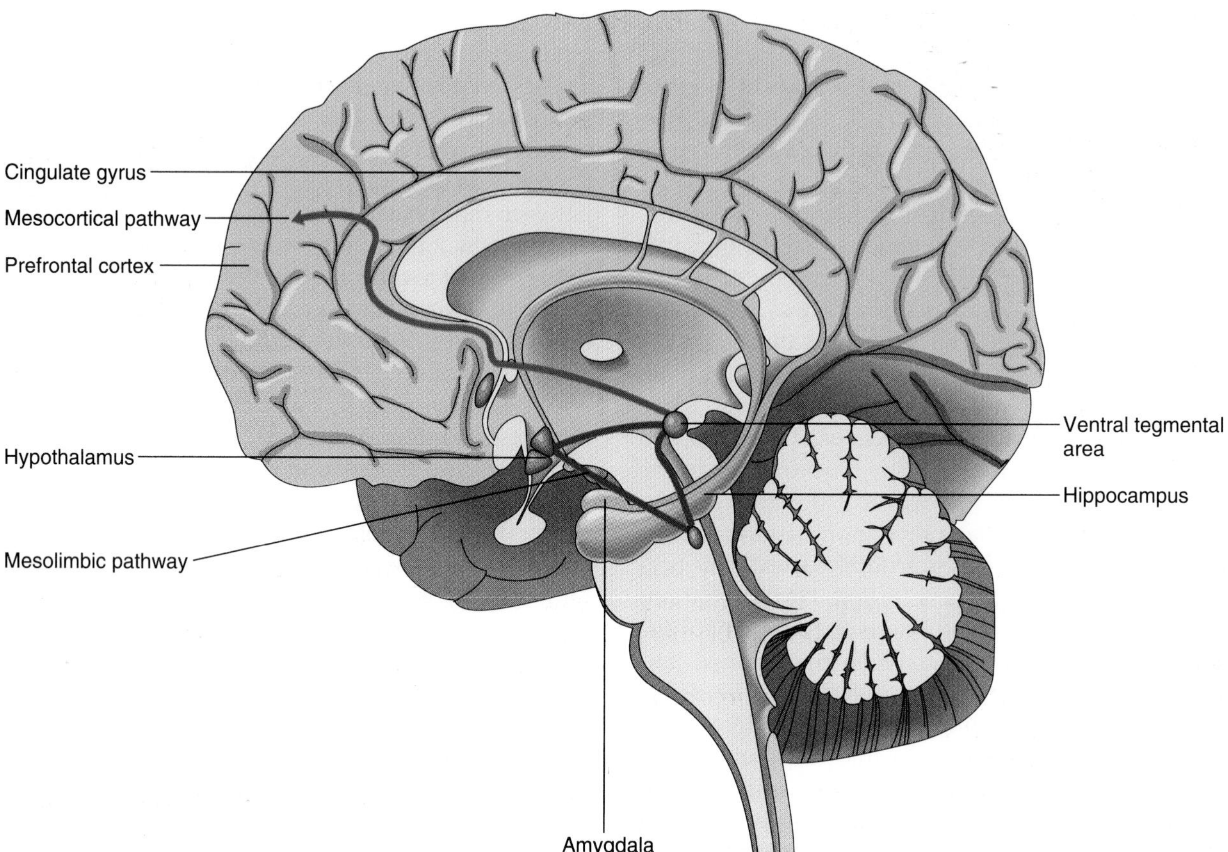

Figure 14.3 The brain and schizophrenia. The mesocortical pathway begins in the ventral tegmental area and projects to the prefrontal cortex. The mesolimbic pathway also begins in the ventral tegmental area but projects to the hypothalamus, amygdala, hippocampus, and nucleus accumbens.

phrenic patients is one source of this evidence. These studies consistently reveal abnormalities in schizophrenics' brains, although the specific problems reported vary from study to study (Weinberger et al., 1983). However, the most consistent findings indicate structural problems in limbic areas, the diencephalon, and the prefrontal cortex (Benes et al., 1992).

Even more impressive are the images obtained in CAT scan and MRI studies. Researchers were quick to apply these new tools to the living brains of schizophrenics. Thus far these images of living brain tissue, with a resolution of less than one millimeter, have most consistently revealed that some schizophrenics, especially males (Andreasen et al., 1990), have enlarged ventricles, suggesting deterioration or atrophy or brain tissue, particularly limbic areas.[4] Large ventricles are in turn correlated with impaired performance on neuropsychological tests, poor premorbid adjustment, and poor response to drug treatment (Andreasen et al., 1982; Weinberger et al., 1980). Further evidence concerning large ventricles comes from an MRI study of fifteen pairs of MZ twins who were discordant for schizophrenia (Suddath et al., 1990). For twelve of the fifteen pairs the schizophrenic twin could be identified by simple visual inspection of the scan. Because the twins were genetically identical, these data also suggest that the origin of these brain abnormalities is not genetic. Enlarged ventricles, however, are also found in the CAT scans of other psychotic patients and are not specific to schizophrenia (Rieder et al., 1983).

A variety of data suggest that the prefrontal cortex is also of particular importance. In studies of the sulci (the shallow furrows in the cerebral cortex), prefrontal rather than general atrophy is found (Doran et al., 1985). In applications of PET scanning in which glucose metabolism is studied in various brain regions while subjects perform psychological tests, schizophrenics show low metabolic rates in the prefrontal cortex (Buchsbaum et al., 1984). Similarly, when performing the Wisconsin Card Sorting

[4]This difference between male and female schizophrenics prompts us to mention that there are other gender effects here. For example, schizophrenic men are more likely to express negative symptoms and to have more of a deteriorating course than women (Goldstein et al., 1990; Haas et al., 1990).

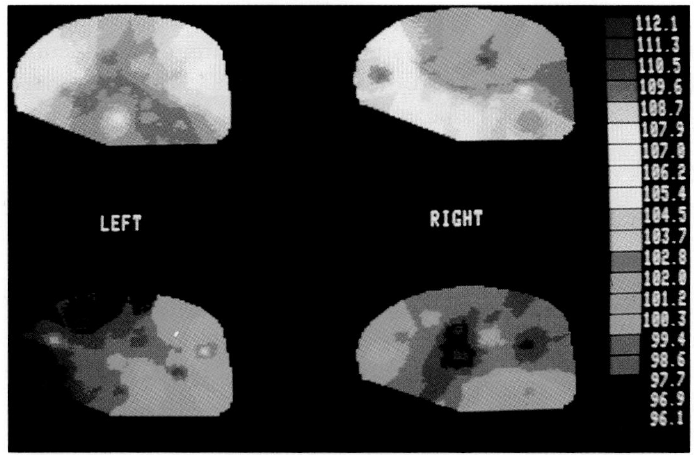

Differences in regional cerebral blood flow between schizophrenics (bottom) and normals (top) for each hemisphere. The values shown were scored as the percentage change in cerebral blood flow from a control task to the Wisconsin Card Sort, which was expected to activate prefrontal cortex. The normals showed greater prefrontal cortical activation as indexed by the "hotter" color of this brain region. Source: Weinberger, Berman, & Illowsky, 1988

Task (a measure of prefrontal function), schizophrenics do poorly and also fail to show activation in the prefrontal region as measured by the amount of blood flowing to this area (Weinberger, Berman, & Illowsky, 1988; Rubin et al., 1992). Note that the findings regarding the importance of the prefrontal area and limbic system parallel the work on dopamine already discussed.

A possible interpretation of these neurological abnormalities is that they result from infection by a virus that invades the brain and damages it. Some data suggest that the infection could occur during fetal development. Mednick and his colleagues (1988) addressed this possibility in a study performed in Helsinki. During a five-week period in 1957 Helsinki experienced an epidemic of influenza virus. Rates of schizophrenia were examined in adults who had been exposed during their mothers' pregnancies. Those exposed during the second trimester of pregnancy had much higher rates than those exposed in either of the other trimesters or in nonexposed controls. This is an intriguing finding, especially since cortical development is in a critical stage of growth during the second trimester. Corroborating evidence has been reported by Barr, Mednick, and Munk-Johnson (1990), who found that the highest rates of birth of future schizophrenics coincided with elevated rates of influenza in the sixth month of gestation.

If schizophrenics' brains are damaged early in development, why does the disorder begin in adolescence or early adulthood? Weinberger (1987) proposed one answer to this question. He hypothesized that the brain injury interacts with normal brain development and that the prefrontal cortex is a brain structure that matures late, typically in adolescence. Thus, an injury to this area may remain silent until the period of development when the prefrontal cortex begins to play a larger role in behavior. Notably, dopamine activity also peaks in adolescence, which may further set the stage for the onset of schizophrenic symptoms. Further work on the brain and schizophrenia is proceeding at a rapid rate and will no doubt lead to more insights about this disorder over the next years.

Psychological Stress and Schizophrenia

Thus far we have discussed several possible diatheses for schizophrenia. We now turn to the role of stressors. Data show that, like many of the disorders we have discussed, general life stress can precipitate a relapse of the condition (Ventura & Neuchterlein, 1989). But more specific stressors have also played an important role in schizophrenia research. We now consider two of them—social class and the family. Note that these are psychological stressors, to be contrasted with the biological stressor of exposure to a virus just discussed.

Social Class and Schizophrenia

Numerous studies have shown a relation between social class and the diagnosis of schizophrenia. We have known for many years that the highest rates of schizophrenia are found in central city areas inhabited by the lowest socioeconomic classes (e.g., Hollingshead & Redlich, 1958; Srole et al., 1962). The relationship between social class and schizophrenia does not show a continuous progression of higher rates of schizophrenia as the social class becomes lower. Rather, there is a decidedly sharp difference between the number of schizophrenics in the lowest social class and those in others. In the classic ten-year Hollingshead and Redlich study of social class and mental illness in New Haven, Connecticut, the rate of schizophrenia was found to be twice as high in the lowest social class as in the next to the lowest. The findings of Hollingshead and Redlich have been confirmed cross-culturally by similar community studies carried out in countries such as Denmark, Norway, and England (Kohn, 1968).[5]

The correlations between social class and schizophrenia are consistent, but they are still difficult to interpret in causal terms. Some people believe that being in a low social class may in itself cause schizophrenia. This is called the **sociogenic hypothesis**. The degrading treatment a person receives from others, the low level of education, and the unavailability of rewards and opportunity, taken together, may make membership in the lowest social class such a stressful experience that the individual develops schizophrenia.

Another explanation of the correlation between schizophrenia and low social class has also been suggested, the **social-selection theory**. During the course of their developing psychosis, schizophrenics may drift into the poverty-ridden areas of the city. The growing cognitive and motivational problems besetting these individuals may so impair their earning abilities that they cannot afford to live elsewhere. Or they may by choice move to areas where little social pressure will be brought to bear on them and where they can escape intense social relationships.

One way of resolving the conflict between these two differing theories is to study the social mobility of schizophrenics. Three studies (Schwartz, 1946; Lystad, 1957; Turner & Wagonfeld, 1967) found that schizophrenics are downwardly mobile in occupational status. But an equal number of studies have shown schizophrenics *not* to be downwardly mobile (Hollingshead & Redlich, 1958; Clausen & Kohn, 1959; Dunham, 1965). Kohn (1968) suggested another way of examining this question. Are the fathers of schizophrenics also from the lowest social class? If they are, this could be considered evidence in favor of the hypothesis that lower-class status is conducive to schizophrenia, for class would be shown to *precede* schizophrenia. If the fathers are from a higher social class, the social selection hypothesis would be the better explanation.

Goldberg and Morrison (1963) conducted such a study in England and Wales. They reported that the occupations of male schizophrenic patients were less remunerative and prestigious than those of their fathers. Turner and Wagonfeld (1967) conducted a similar study in the United States and found evidence for both the sociogenic and selection hypotheses. Fathers of schizophrenics were more frequently from the lowest social class, supporting the sociogenic hypothesis. But at the same time many of these schizophrenics were lower in occupational prestige than their fathers, supporting the selection hypothesis.

A recent study relevant to the two theories (Dohrenwend et al., 1992) employed a new methodology, simultaneously investigating both social class and ethnic background. The rates of schizophrenia were examined in Israeli Jews of European ethnic background as well as in more recent immigrants to Israel from North Africa and the Middle East. The latter group experiences considerable racial prejudice and discrimination. Applying the sociogenic hypothesis to this study led to the prediction that, because they experience high levels of stress at all levels of social class, the members of the disadvantaged ethnic group should have consistently higher rates of schizophrenia at all levels of social class. In contrast, the social-selection process should affect the two groups differently. Because of prejudice and discrimination, only the most healthy and able members of the disadvantaged ethnic group should be able to move upward in social class. Upward mobility should be easier and more frequent for the advantaged group, leaving more disabled members behind. The result should be that rates of schizophrenia are higher for the advantaged group. And in fact this is the pattern of results that emerged. Thus some, but not all, of the relationship between social class and schizophrenia can be accounted for by the selection hypothesis. Social class also appears to play a role as a stressor, but the exact way in which the stresses associated with it exert their effect remains unknown.

The Family and Schizophrenia

Many theorists have regarded family relationships, especially those between a mother and her son, as crucial in the development of schizophrenia. The view has been so prevalent that the term **schizophrenogenic mother** was coined for the supposedly cold and dominant, conflict-inducing parent who is said to produce schizophrenia in her offspring (Fromm-Reichmann, 1948). These mothers have also been characterized as rejecting, overprotective, self-sacrificing, impervious to the feelings of others, rigid and moralistic about sex, and fearful of intimacy.[6]

[5]There is perhaps one exception to this finding: the relationship may disappear in nonurban areas (Clausen & Kohn, 1959).

[6]It is noteworthy that most theories implicating family processes in the etiology of abnormal behavior focus almost exclusively on the mother. Sexism?

Another prominent early view is the **double-bind theory** proposed by Bateson and his colleagues (1956). These writers believed that an important factor in the development of schizophrenic thought disorder is the constant subjection of an individual to a so-called double-bind situation which includes the following elements.

1. The individual has an intense relationship with another, so intense that it is especially important to be able to understand communications from the other person accurately so that the individual can respond appropriately.
2. The other person expresses two messages when making a statement, one of which denies the other.
3. The individual cannot comment on the mutually contradictory messages and cannot withdraw from the situation or ignore the messages.

In their original paper Bateson and his colleagues gave the following example.

> A young man who had fairly well recovered from an acute schizophrenic episode was visited in the hospital by his mother. He was glad to see her and impulsively put his arm around her shoulders whereupon she stiffened. He withdrew his arm and she asked, "Don't you love me anymore?" He then blushed and she said, "Dear, you must not be so easily embarrassed and afraid of your feelings." The patient was able to stay with her only a few minutes more and following her departure he assaulted an aide. . . .
>
> Obviously, this result could have been avoided if the young man had been able to say, "Mother, it is obvious that you become uncomfortable when I put my arm around you, and you have difficulty accepting a gesture of affection from me." However, the schizophrenic patient doesn't have this possibility open to him. An intense dependency in training prevents him from commenting upon his mother's communicative behavior, though she comments on his and forces him to accept and to attempt to deal with the complicated sequence. . . .
>
> The impossible dilemma thus becomes: "If I am to keep my tie to my mother, I must not show her that I love her, but if I do not show her that I love her then I will lose her." (pp. 258–259)

Controlled studies evaluating these two theories have not yielded supporting data. Studies of families of schizophrenics have, however, revealed that they differ in some ways from normal families, for example, showing vague patterns of communication and high levels of conflict. But whether these family processes should be viewed as playing a causal role in the development of schizophrenia is questionable. It is equally plausible that the conflict and unclear communication are a response to having a young schizophrenic in the family. Indeed, some evidence favors this interpretation.

The faulty communications of parents may, however, play a role in the etiology of schizophrenia. Indeed, some findings suggest that they do. One of these studies is the University of California at Los Angeles Family Project (Goldstein & Rodnick, 1975). Adolescents with behavior problems were studied intensively along with their families. A five-year follow-up revealed that a number of the young people had developed schizophrenia or schizophrenia-related disorders. The investigators were then able to relate these disorders discovered at follow-up to any deviance in the communications of parents that had been evident five years earlier. Communication deviancies of parents were indeed found to be a predictor of the later onset of schizophrenia in their offspring, supporting its significance (Norton, 1982). It does not appear, however, that communication deviance is a *specific* etiological factor for schizophrenia, since parents of manics are equally high on this variable (Miklowitz, 1985).

Further evidence favoring some role for the family comes from a very substantial adoption study by Tienari and his colleagues (1987) underway in Finland. A large sample of adopted offspring of schizophrenic mothers is being studied along with a control group. As of 1987, 112 children of schizophrenics and 135 controls had been assessed. Unlike Heston's adoption study, extensive data were collected on various aspects of family life in the adoptive families. Data on the adjustment of the children were related to data collected on their adoptive families. The families were categorized into levels of maladjustment based on material from clinical interviews as well as psychological tests. The major data are shown in Table 14.4. As can be seen, more severe problems in adopted children of schizophrenics are clearly associated with more pathological environments. Also notable in this study was the fact that family environment was *not* related to

Table 14.4 • Adjustment of Adopted Children of Schizophrenic Parents Related to Maladjustment of Adoptive Families

Clinical Ratings of Children	Degree of Family Maladjustment: None to Mild	Moderate	Severe
Healthy or mild disturbance	39	9	3
Moderate	10	9	24
Severe	0	11	16

Source: From Tienari et al., 1987. Reprinted by permission.

psychopathology in the control adoptees. Both a genetic predisposition (diathesis) and a noxious environment (stress) are therefore necessary to increase risk for psychopathology.

A series of studies conducted in London indicate that the family can also have an important impact on the adjustment of patients *after* they leave the hospital. Brown and his colleagues (1966) conducted a nine-month follow-up study of a sample of schizophrenics who returned to live with their families after being discharged from the hospital. Interviews were conducted with parents or spouses before discharge and rated for the number of critical comments made about the patient and for expressions of hostility toward or emotional overinvolvement with him or her. On the basis of this variable, called **expressed emotion (EE)**, families were divided into those revealing a great deal, high-EE families, and those revealing little, low-EE families. At the end of the follow-up period, 10 percent of the patients returning to low-EE homes had relapsed. In marked contrast, 58 percent of the patients returning to high-EE homes had gone back to the hospital in the same period!

This research, which has since been replicated (Vaughn & Leff, 1976; Leff, 1976; MacMillan et al., 1981; Koenigsberg & Hadley, 1986), indicates that the environment to which patients are discharged has great bearing on whether or not they are rehospitalized. What is not yet clear, however, is exactly how to interpret the effects of EE. Is EE causal or do these attitudes reflect a reaction to the patients' behavior? For example, if the condition of a schizophrenic begins to deteriorate, family concern and involvement may be increased. The other side of this coin is that family criticism and efforts to control the schizophrenic may also increase. Indeed, bizarre or dangerous behavior by the schizophrenic can be seen to call for limit setting and other familial efforts that come under the rubric of expressed emotion (Kanter, Lamb, & Loeper, 1987). Finally, a focus on expressed emotion runs the risk of needlessly blaming the family for the patient's illness, provoking the kind of guilt and hurt that will be addressed in our discussion of infantile autism (Focus Box 16.6). The EE work, though, has laid the foundation for some promising research in intervention (page 416).

High-Risk Studies of Schizophrenia

How does schizophrenia develop? We know that the clinical symptoms begin in adolescence and early adulthood, somewhat earlier for men than for women. But what are these individuals like before their symptoms begin? An early method of answering this question was to construct developmental histories by examining the childhood records of those who had later become schizophrenics. This research did indeed show that those who became schizophrenic were different from their contemporaries even before any serious problems were noted in their behavior. Three decades ago, Albee and Lane and their colleagues repeatedly found preschizophrenics to have a lower IQ than members of various control groups, which usually consisted of siblings and neighborhood peers (Albee, Lane, & Reuter, 1964; Lane & Albee, 1965). Investigations of the social behavior of preschizophrenics yielded some interesting findings; for example, teachers described male schizophrenics as disagreeable in childhood and female schizophrenics as passive (Watt et al., 1970; Watt, 1974). Both males and females were described as delinquent and withdrawn (Berry, 1967).

The major limitation of this type of developmental research is that the data on which it relies were not originally collected with the intention of describing preschizophrenics or of predicting the development of schizophrenia from childhood behavior. More specific information is required if developmental histories are to be a source of new hypotheses.

The high-risk method, described in Chapter 5, can yield such information. The first such study of schizophrenia was begun in the 1960s by Sarnoff Mednick and Fini Schulsinger (Mednick & Schulsinger, 1968). They chose Denmark because the Danish registries of all people make it possible to keep track of them for long periods of time. Mednick and Schulsinger selected as their high-risk subjects 207 young people whose mothers were chronic schizophrenics and had had poor premorbid adjustment. It was decided that the mother should be the parent suffering the disorder because paternity is not always easy to determine and because schizophrenic women have more children than do schizophrenic men. Then, 104 low-risk subjects, individuals whose mothers were not schizophrenics, were matched to the high-risk subjects on variables such as sex, age, father's occupation, rural–urban residence, years of education, and institutional upbringing versus rearing by the family.

In 1972 the now-grown men and women of the high-risk sample and of the low-risk group were followed up through a number of measures, including a diagnostic battery. Fifteen of the high-risk subjects were diagnosed schizophrenic. None of the control men and women was so diagnosed. Looking back to the information collected on the subjects when they were children, the investigators found that sev-

Sarnoff Mednick is a psychologist at the University of Southern California who pioneered the use of the high-risk method for studying schizophrenia. He has also contributed to the hypothesis that a viral infection is implicated in this disorder.

eral circumstances predicted the later onset of schizophrenia. These data, granted that they come from a small study, seem to suggest that the etiology of schizophrenia may differ for positive and negative symptom patients. In the most recent analysis of the data, the schizophrenics were divided into groups with either predominantly positive or predominantly negative symptoms (Cannon, Mednick, & Farnas, 1990). Variables predicting schizophrenia were different for the two groups. Negative symptom schizophrenia was preceded by a history of pregnancy and birth complications and by a failure to show electrodermal responses to simple stimuli. Positive symptom schizophrenia was preceded by a history of family instability, such as separation from parents and placement in foster homes or institutions for periods of time.

In the wake of Mednick and Schulsinger's pioneering study a number of other high-risk investigations began. Some of them have also yielded information concerning the prediction of adult psychopathology. The New York High-Risk Study found that a composite measure of attentional dysfunction predicted behavioral disturbance at follow-up (Cornblatt & Erlenmeyer-Kimling, 1985). Furthermore, low IQ was a characteristic of the first high-risk children to be hospitalized (Erlenmeyer-Kimling & Cornblatt, 1987). In an Israeli study, poor neurobehavioral functioning (poor concentration, poor verbal ability, lack of motor control and coordination) predicted schizophrenialike outcomes, as did earlier interpersonal problems (Marcus et al., 1987). As subjects in other studies mature we will gain further glimpses of the development of this debilitating disorder.

Therapies for Schizophrenia

The puzzling, often frightening array of phenomena that plague schizophrenics makes one wonder how they can possibly be helped. The history of psychopathology, reviewed in Chapter 1, is in many respects a history of humankind's efforts, often brutal and unenlightened, to deal with schizophrenia. Although some of the insane people confined centuries ago in foul asylums may have suffered from problems as prosaic as food poisoning or syphilis (see pages 10 and 19), there seems little doubt that many, were they to be examined now, would carry a diagnosis of schizophrenia.

We described mental hospitals in Chapter 1 (page 20). For the most part clinical research indicates that traditional hospital care does little to effect meaningful, enduring changes in the majority of patients. The overwhelming body of evidence indicates rehospitalization rates of 40 to 50 percent after one year and upwards of 75 percent after two years (Anthony et al., 1986; Paul & Menditto, 1992). Similar studies specifically designed to follow only schizophrenics also show generally poor outcomes (Breier et al., 1991; Carone, Harrow, & Westermeyer, 1991). We turn now to a closer look at the treatment of schizophrenia, most, but not all, of which is hospital based.

Biological Treatments

Shock and Psychosurgery

The general warehousing of severely disturbed patients in mental hospitals earlier in this century, coupled with the shortage of professional staff, created a climate that allowed, perhaps even subtly encouraged, experimentation with radical biological interventions. In the early 1930s, inducing a coma with large dosages of insulin was introduced by Sakel (1938), who claimed that up to three-quarters of the schizophrenics he treated showed significant improvement. But later findings by others were less encouraging, and insulin coma therapy, which presented serious risks to health, including irreversible coma and death, was gradually abandoned.

In 1935 Moniz, a Portuguese psychiatrist, introduced the **prefrontal lobotomy**, a surgical procedure that destroys the tracts connecting the frontal lobes to lower centers of the patient's brain. His initial reports, like those of Sakel for insulin coma

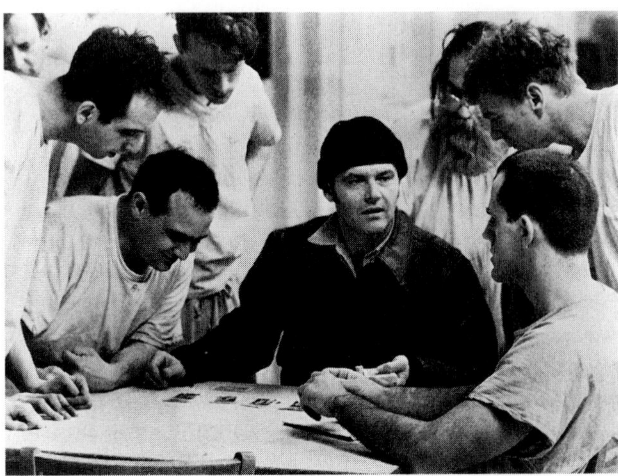

One Flew Over the Cuckoo's Nest provides a compelling illustration of the horrors of older mental hospitals and the treatments then in use.

therapy, claimed high rates of success (Moniz, 1936), and for twenty years thereafter thousands of mental patients underwent variations of psychosurgery, especially if their behavior was violent. Many of them did indeed quiet down and could even be discharged from hospitals. But during the 1950s this intervention, too, fell into disrepute for several reasons. Many patients suffered serious losses in their cognitive capacities—which is not surprising, given the destruction of parts of their brain believed responsible for thought—and became dull and listless, or even died. The principal reason for its abandonment, however, was the introduction of drugs that seemed to reduce the behavioral and emotional excesses of many patients.

Electroconvulsive therapy (ECT) has been used since its development in 1938 by Cerletti and Bini. Electrodes are placed on both temples, more recently on only one temple, and a current of between 70 and 130 volts is applied for a fraction of a second. A seizure is thereby induced, followed by a period of unconsciousness. In the treatment of schizophrenia, ECT has, like psychosurgery, proved to be basically ineffective and has given way to the several psychotropic medications, although it remains an effective treatment for profoundly depressed patients.

Drug Therapies

Without question the most important development in the treatment of the schizophrenia disorders was the advent in the 1950s of several drugs collectively referred to as antipsychotic medications. They are also called **neuroleptics** because, in addition to their beneficial effects, they have side effects similar to the behavioral manifestations of neurological diseases. One of the more frequently prescribed neuroleptic drugs, *phenothiazine,* was first produced by a German chemist in the late nineteenth century and used to treat parasitic worm infections of the digestive system of animals. However, it was not until the discovery of the antihistamines by Bovet in the 1940s that phenothiazines were given any attention; antihistamines have a phenothiazine nucleus! Reaching beyond their use to treat the common cold and asthma, the French surgeon Laborit pioneered the use of antihistamines to reduce surgical shock. He noticed that they made his patients somewhat sleepy and less fearful about the impending operation. Laborit's work encouraged the drug companies to reexamine antihistamines in light of their tranquilizing effects. Shortly thereafter a French chemist, Charpentier, prepared a new phenothiazine derivative and called it chlorpromazine. It proved very effective in calming schizophrenics. Phenothiazines are now believed to block dopamine receptors in the brain, which gives them their therapeutic properties.

Chlorpromazine (trade name Thorazine) was first used therapeutically in the United States in 1954 and rapidly became the preferred treatment for schizophrenics. By 1970 over 85 percent of all patients in state mental hospitals were receiving chlorpromazine or one of the other phenothiazines. In recent years two other neuroleptics have also been given to schizophrenics, the *butyrophenones* (e.g., haloperidol, Haldol) and the *thioxanthenes* (e.g., navane, Taractan). Both seem generally as effective as the phenothiazines. Each class of drug seems able to reduce positive schizophrenic symptoms but has less effect on the negative ones.

Although the phenothiazine regimen reduces the positive symptoms of schizophrenia, so that patients can be released from the hospital, it should not be viewed as a cure. Typically, patients are kept on so-called *maintenance doses* of the drug—that is just enough to continue the therapeutic effect. They take their medication and return to the hospital or clinic on occasion for adjustment of the dose level. But released patients who are maintained on phenothiazine medication may make only marginal adjustment to the community. As mentioned earlier, the phenothiazines keep the positive symptoms from returning but have little effect on negative symptoms, such as social incompetence. In addition, reinstitutionalization is frequent. Although the phenothiazines reduced long-term institutionalization significantly, they also made possible the revolving-door pattern of admission, discharge, and readmission.

Some progress has been made in at least slowing down the revolutions per minute of the door. We know that applying social-learning principles in aftercare homes is one way of helping deinstitutionalized patients remain in the community (Paul & Lentz, 1977) There is also some evidence that a maintenance program of drugs plus social skills training is effective at preventing relapse (Hogarty et al., 1974).

Finally, the potentially serious side effects of phenothiazines must be noted. Patients generally report that taking the drug is disagreeable, causing dryness of the mouth, blurred vision, grogginess, and constipation. Among the other common side effects are low blood pressure and jaundice. Perhaps this unpleasantness is one of the reasons maintenance programs have proved so difficult. It is a problem to get patients to take these drugs initially and to keep them on medication once they have left the hospital (Van Putten et al., 1981). Thus patients are now frequently treated with long-lasting neuroleptics (e.g., fluphenazine decanoate) that require an injection every few weeks.

Even more disturbing are the extrapyramidal side effects, that is, those that stem from dysfunctions of the nerve tracts that descend from the brain to spinal motor neurons. Extrapyramidal side effects resemble symptoms of neurological diseases. These side effects most closely resemble the symptoms of Parkinson's disease. People taking phenothiazines have pill-rolling tremors of the fingers, a shuffling gait, muscular rigidity, and drooling. Other side effects include dystonia, a disordered tonicity of tissues, and dyskinesia, an abnormal motion of voluntary and involuntary muscles. They cause arching of the back and a twisted posture of the neck and body. Akasthesia is an inability to remain still; people pace constantly, fidget, and make chewing movements and other movements of the lips, fingers, and legs. These perturbing symptoms can be treated by drugs used with patients who have Parkinson's disease. In a muscular disturbance of older patients, called tardive dyskinesia, the mouth muscles involuntarily make sucking, lip-smacking, and chin-wagging motions. This syndrome affects from 10 to 20 percent of patients treated with phenothiazines for a long period of time (Kane et al., 1986).

Because of these serious side effects some clinicians believe that it is unwise to take phenothiazines for extended periods of time. Current clinical practice calls for treating patients with the smallest possible doses of drugs. The routine use of maintenance doses is also regarded as risky, and many patients now take drug holidays—scheduled periods when they do not take any medication. Some relief from the symptoms of tardive dyskinesia is obtained from the administration of GABA agonists (Thaker et al., 1987).

Recent research indicates that a new drug, clozapine (Clozaril), can produce therapeutic gains in schizophrenics who do not respond positively to phenothiazines (Kane et al., 1988). Interestingly, clozapine does not appear to produce its therapeutic effect by blocking dopamine receptors and does not produce extrapyramidal side effects. Unfortunately, it can impair the functioning of the immune system, making patients vulnerable to infection, and it can produce seizures. In addition, clozapine is controversial because of its high cost, about seven thousand dollars per year of treatment. The cost is due not so much to the drug per se but to the fact that patients must be carefully monitored to check for adverse effects on the immune system.

In spite of the many difficulties, phenothiazines are an indispensible part of treatment for schizophrenics and will undoubtedly continue to be the primary treatment until something better is discovered. They are surely preferable to the straitjackets formerly used to restrain patients.

Psychological Treatments

Although Freud did not advocate psychoanalysis as a treatment for schizophrenia, others have proposed adaptations, and we will review some of them now. In addition, we will examine recent family and behavioral therapies for schizophrenics and will suggest at the end of this section that it is best to combine biological and psychological treatments in an integrated approach to these debilitating disorders.

Psychodynamic Therapy

Freud did little, either in his clinical practice or through his writings, to adapt psychoanalysis to the treatment of schizophrenics; he believed them to be incapable of establishing the close interpersonal relationship that is essential for analysis. It was Harry Stack Sullivan, the American psychiatrist, who pioneered the use of psychotherapy with schizophrenic hospital patients. Sullivan established a ward at the Sheppard and Enoch Pratt Hospital in Towson, Maryland, in 1923 and developed a psychoanalytic treatment reported to be markedly successful. He held that schizophrenia reflects a return to early childhood forms of communication. The fragile ego of the schizophrenic, unable to handle the extreme stress of interpersonal challenges, regresses. Therapy therefore requires the patient to learn adult forms of communication and achieve insight into the role that the past has played in current problems. Sullivan advised the very gradual, nonthreatening development of a trusting relationship. For example, he recommended that the therapist sit somewhat to the side of the patient in order not to force eye contact, which is deemed too frightening in the early stages of treatment. After many sessions, and with the establishment of greater trust and support, the analyst begins to encourage the patient to examine his or her interpersonal relationships.

A similar ego-analytic approach was proposed by Frieda Fromm-Reichmann (1889–1957), a German psychiatrist who emigrated to the United States and worked for a period of time with Sullivan at Chestnut Lodge, a private mental hospital in Rockville, Maryland. Fromm-Reichmann was sensitive to the symbolic and unconscious meaning of behavior, attributing the aloofness of schizophrenics to a wish to avoid the rebuffs suffered in childhood and thereafter judged inevitable. She treated them with great patience and optimism, making it clear that they need not take her into their world or give up their sickness until they were completely ready to do so. Along with Sullivan, Fromm-Reichmann (1952) helped establish psychoanalysis as a major treatment for schizophrenia.

The overall evaluation of analytically oriented psychotherapy with schizophrenics thus far justifies little enthusiasm for applying it with these severely disturbed people (Feinsilver & Gunderson, 1972). Results from a long-term follow-up of patients bearing a diagnosis of schizophrenia and discharged after treatment between 1963 and 1976 at the New York State Psychiatric Institute confirm the lack of success (Stone, 1986). These patients had received drugs in addition to what was described as analytically oriented therapy. An analysis of data from half the sample of more than 500 indicated that the patients were doing poorly. It may be, as Stone hypothesized, that gaining psychoanalytic insight into one's problems and illness may even worsen a schizophrenic patient's psychological condition (Focus Box 14.3). Earlier, great claims of success were made for the analyses done by Sullivan and Fromm-Reichmann, but a close consideration of the patients they saw indicates that many tended to be only mildly disturbed and might not even have been diagnosed schizophrenic by the strict DSM-IV criteria for the disorder.

Family Therapy and Expressed Emotion (EE)

Recent family therapy research has attempted to help schizophrenics discharged from a mental hospital remain at home. Since high levels of expressed emotion have been linked with relapse and reinstitutionalization, a family therapy team at the University of Southern California decided to try to lower, through cognitive and behavioral means, the emotional intensity of the households to which schizophrenics returned (Falloon et al., 1982, 1985).

Family therapy sessions took place in the patients' homes, with family and patient participating together. The importance of the patient's taking his or her medication regularly was stressed. The family was also instructed in ways to express both positive and negative feelings in a constructive, empathic manner and to defuse tense, personal conflicts through collaborative problem-solving. The patient's symptoms were explained to the family, and ways of coping with them and of reducing emotional turmoil in the home were suggested. It was made clear to patient and family alike that schizophrenia is primarily a biochemical illness, but that proper medication and the kind of psychosocial treatment they were receiving can reduce stress on the patient and prevent relapses and deterioration. Treatment extended over the first nine months after the patient returned home, when the danger of relapse is especially great.

This family treament, aimed at calming the home life of the family, was compared with an individual therapy in which the patient was seen alone at a clinic, with supportive discussions centering on problems in daily living and on developing a social network. Family members of patients in this control group were seldom seen, and when they were, it was not in conjoint home sessions with the patients. These control patients received the typical, individual, supportive management in widespread use in aftercare programs for schizophrenics.

Ongoing assessments were made of the patient's symptomatology, with special attention given to signs of relapse, such as delusions of control and hallucinations. Family members were also evaluated for their problem-solving skills and for the emotions they expressed toward the patient. All patients, including the controls, were maintained on antipsychotic medication, primarily Thorazine (chlorpromazine), which was monitored and adjusted throughout the project by a psychiatrist unaware of which patients were receiving family therapy and which individual therapy.

In all, thirty-six patients were treated over a two-year period, eighteen in the family therapy group and eighteen in the individual therapy control group. Those receiving family therapy fared much better. Only one person in this group had a major clinical relapse, compared with eight in the control

FOCUS 14.3 • Some Negative Effects of Therapies with Schizophrenics

A discussion of therapy with schizophrenics must include mention of iatrogenic (caused by the method of treatment) negative effects. In a review of such negative effects, Drake and Sederer (1986) note the following cautions:

1. Intensive, intrusive, especially psychoanalytic treatments can be more than some schizophrenics can handle, especially when close therapeutic relationships are encouraged. Many patients subjected to such treatments need longer hospitalizations, become symptomatically worse, and are more likely to leave treatment. It is believed that the problem is emotional overstimulation (see page 412 for the data on harmful effects of expressed emotion in families), especially when regression is encouraged (as is frequently the case in analytically oriented therapies). Therapies that appear to be more effective are those that focus on practical issues, such as finding a job or behaving in nondisruptive ways, and that permit the therapist to give straightforward advice and be a sounding board for reality testing.*
2. Milieu therapy (see page 559) can be harmful if, as above, the environment is overly stimulating, for example, when there are lively group discussions that encourage affective exploration of self and others, or otherwise emotionally provocative discussions. Furthermore, milieu therapies that encourage democratic decision making and antihierarchical power can be confusing and negative for many schizophrenic patients. Although this latter generalization is inconsistent with data such as those reported by Paul and Lentz (1977), as well as other proponents of milieu therapy, the cautionary note is useful as a check on unbridled professional enthusiasm for assuming that seriously mentally ill patients (at least when they are actively psychotic) have the same needs and capacity for power sharing as do normal individuals. There are probably also differences along milieu therapies, and those that are only moderately stimulating may be best suited to schizophrenics.
3. As in milieu therapy, excessive uncovering and self-disclosure during group therapy is not as helpful as groups that foster reality testing and teach social skills. A review of forty-three studies of group therapy with hospitalized schizophrenics suggests that although there may be some benefit from both psychodynamic insight-oriented and behaviorally oriented approaches, there is some indication that the former carries a risk of negative effects (Kanas, 1986).
4. The noted negative side effects of neuroleptics (see page 415) and other pharmacotherapies that are used with schizophrenics present serious iatrogenic problems. In addition to physical sequelae such as tardive dyskinesia, patients can develop psychotic explanations for drug-produced effects, such as concluding that the FBI is interfering with their thinking via malevolent radio waves.

*It is sometimes said that this kind of intervention is not *therapy* at all, rather *just* advice-giving and such. The issue depends of course on one's definition of therapy, a question considered in Chapter 18.

group. Further, of the schizophrenic episodes occurring in the control group, two-thirds were considered major, whereas only one-third in the family therapy group were so categorized. Finally, hospital readmission rates were consistently different: half (nine) of the eighteen control patients were returned to the hospital, whereas only 2 of the eighteen family therapy patients had to return.

In interpreting their results, the investigators were properly mindful of the possibility that the patients in family therapy may have improved more than the controls because they took their medications more faithfully; indeed, family therapy subjects did comply better with their medication regimens. On the other hand, results from other studies show that drugs alone do not prevent deterioration in such patients. The conclusion is that this kind of EE-lowering family therapy was of major importance in the patients' improvement.

Falloon's findings have been replicated and extended by a larger scale study by Hogarty et al. (1986), who also found that patients could be taught social skills, like handling conflict better and abstaining from behavior that might elicit high EE reactions in their families. After one year, this patient-focused social-skills treatment achieved low relapse results just as good as those of the Falloon family therapy. Furthermore, *no* patient whose family EE diminished had to return to the hospital—including a handful of patients in the control group, which received only maintenance medication and nonspecific support from a nurse practitioner. Conversely, among households that remained high on EE, relapse rates were similar regardless of treatment conditions. In a treatment group that combined family therapy with patient-focused social-skills training, there were no relapses whatsoever after a year.

After two years of treatment, however, the pattern of results changed. Relapse rates no longer differed among groups (Hogarty et al., 1991). It is also important to bear in mind when interpreting the Hogarty study as well as all others that the actual real-life adjustment of the nonrelapsing patients remained marginal. Prevention or delay of rehospitalization are very worthwhile goals, but these patients do not, as a rule, become fully functioning members of society; they continue to require care and treatment.

Behavior Therapy

Social-skills training as a means of reducing expressed emotion is generally viewed as a form of behavioral therapy. In addition, operant conditioning techniques, another means of behavior therapy, have been employed in mental hospitals; this work is discussed in greater detail in Chapter 19. For our present purposes we should note that hundreds of hospitalized patients, most of them carrying a diagnosis of schizophrenia, have lived in a token economy instituted to eliminate specific behavior, such as hoarding towels, to teach more socially appropriate responses, such as combing hair and arriving on time at dining halls, and to encourage activity, such as doing chores on the ward (Ayllon & Azrin, 1968). The study by Paul and Lentz (1977) demonstrated the potential of a carefully designed and meticulously implemented therapy program based on social-learning principles (see Chapter 19). Some seriously ill schizophrenics were released to shelter care or to independent living.

At the present time it is generally acknowledged among mental health professionals that therapy programs with a learning framework are the most effective psychological procedures for helping schizophrenics function better. But the changes brought about by behavior therapy are seldom so thoroughgoing that we can speak of curing people with this group of mental illnesses. Behavioral interventions do, however, reverse somewhat the effects of institutionalization, fostering social skills such as assertiveness in people who have been reinforced by hospital staff for passiveness and compliance.

General Trends in Treatment

A general trend seems to be emerging in attitudes toward and treatment of schizophrenia. Only a generation ago many if not most mental health professionals and lay people believed the primary culprit to be the psychological environment, and most especially the family—because the seeds for schizophrenia were seen as having been sown in early childhood. The thinking now is that a biological, and probably a genetic, factor predisposes a person to become schizophrenic. The twin and high-risk studies reviewed earlier in this chapter provide strong supporting evidence for this view. More careful research is needed on the *kind of stressor* that can trigger a schizophrenic break in a predisposed individual. In our view, the most promising contemporary approaches to treatment, discussed below, make good use of this increased understanding.

1. Information about current scientific knowledge is conveyed to both family and patient. They are given realistic information about schizophrenia as a disability that can be controlled but that is probably lifelong. As with many other chronic disabilities, medication is necessary to maintain control and allow the patient to perform daily activities. But what is *not* necessary, and what is even counterproductive is the guilt of family members, especially parents, believing that something in the patient's upbringing has caused the problem. Considerable effort is devoted in many treatment programs to dispel this sense of culpability while encouraging a focus on the biological diathesis and the associated need for medication.

2. Efforts are made to reduce the stress experienced by the patient on discharge. This is done both by reducing hostility, overinvolvement or intrusiveness, and criticality of the family—what has been termed *expressed emotion* (EE)—and by providing medication that is believed to have a quieting effect, perhaps by helping the patient think more clearly about the world. The means employed to reduce stress include teaching family members to reduce their EE, teaching the patient how to interact with the family so as to reduce EE in the home, and in general trying to improve the patient's social skills so that he or she can function more normally outside the hospital and probably reduce the EE encountered both inside and outside the home.

3. Networking among affected families is also being encouraged (Greenberg et al., 1988) to reduce the isolation and stigma associated with having a family member who is schizophrenic. Support groups and even formal organizations are increasingly available to help families cope with the stress associated with having a member who is schizophrenic.

Concluding Remarks on the Integration of Biological and Psychological Interventions

The justified enthusiasm for drugs that reduce hallucinations and delusions and even sometimes improve the clarity of thought runs a risk of ignoring psychological components that are necessary for effective and humane intervention. Biological and psychological approaches need to be integrated for many reasons.

1. We know that long-term use of phenothiazines and other neuroleptics can have seriously negative side effects, such as tardive dyskinesia. Some patients complain of affective blunting and interference with thinking, reminiscent of the "fog machine" that Ken Kesey talked about being turned on in the hospital ward in his classic novel *One Flew Over the Cuckoo's Nest*. Although there are hopes that newly developed drugs will avoid some of these drawbacks, the general history of medication cautions us to remain mindful of the iatrogenic problems of many pharmaceuticals.

2. As already noted, neuroleptics have only modest effects on negative symptoms, such as social withdrawal and behavioral deficits. Many schizophrenics need to learn or relearn ways of interacting with their world, of dealing with the emotional challenges that all people face as they negotiate life. A wonder drug that alleviates symptoms still leaves untouched the basic tendency of the predisposed individual to react abnormally in later stressful situations.

3. Another consideration, sometimes lost when only group averages are examined, is that many patients do not improve from the available antipsychotic drugs. Much more needs to be learned about *individual differences*, and although some of these variations no doubt exist in the biological realm, some experts hold that psychological factors, including the phenomenological realm of the patient, will prove to be important (Carpenter, 1986).

4. The family therapy work with high EE has alerted us to the interplay between the biological and the psychological. At the very least, even a highly effective drug cannot have its effects on a patient who does not take it. Although medication can be forced on a person in a hospital setting, and new technologies may make it possible to administer a drug to an uncooperative patient—for example, with a slow release device implanted under the skin—issues of civil rights and respect for human dignity are not to be overlooked. An empathic, supportive, and trusting relationship with the patient is always necessary and important.

Regrettably, professional turf battles threaten to interfere with the integration of biological and psychological therapies. In the late 1980s and early 1990s some medical practitioners have blocked psychologists from obtaining hospital privileges. Some psychological practitioners have taken antagonistic stances against drug therapies and neuropsychological discoveries on grounds that seem to be less than purely scientific. These interdisciplinary squabbles are not new, but they seldom contribute to advances in knowledge or improvements in patient care. We would do well to recall some of the past extreme positions taken by in-groups believing themselves to be the recipients of Truth, only to find years later that these positions taken with utmost certainty and not a little bigotry to the out-group were discredited and seen to be ridiculous at best and harmful at worst. Well before all the answers are in, logic and experience dictate that comprehensive treatment should be both biological and psychological.

SUMMARY

The symptoms of schizophrenia are typically divided into positive and negative types. Positive symptoms refer to behavioral excesses, such as delusions, hallucinations, and disorganized speech. Negative symptoms refer to behavioral deficits, such as flat affect, avolition, alogia, and anhedonia. Schizophrenics also show deterioration in functioning in occupational and social roles. The diagnosis requires that these symptoms be present for at least a month and also requires that there be a prodromal or residual phase of at least five months wherein some symptoms persist but at a lower level of severity. Schizophenia is typically divided into subtypes, such as paranoid, catatonic, and disorganized. These subtypes are based on the prominence of particular symptoms (e.g., delusions in the paranoid subtype) and reflect the fact that the behavior of people diagnosed schizophrenic varies considerably from case to case.

Historically, the concept of schizophrenia arose from the pioneering efforts of Kraepelin and Bleuler. Kraepelin's work fostered a descriptive approach and a narrow definition, whereas Bleuler's theoretical emphasis led to a very broad diagnostic category. Bleuler had a great influence on the American concept of schizophrenia. His influence, together with the American interest in treatment and the addition of several poorly defined types of schizophrenia, served to make the American concept excessively inclusive. By the middle of the twentieth century the differences in the way schizophrenia was diagnosed in America and Europe were vast. Subsequent to the publication of DSM-III, the American concept of schizophrenia has become narrower and more similar to the European view.

Research has tried to determine the etiological role of specific biological variables, such as genetic and biochemical factors and brain pathology as well as that of stressors, such as low social class and the family. The data on genetic transmission are impressive. The adoptee studies, which are relatively free from most criticisms that can be leveled at family or twin studies, show a strong relation between having a schizophrenic parent and the likelihood of developing the disorder. Perhaps the genetic predisposition has biochemical correlates, although research in this area permits only tentative conclusions. At this point it appears that increased sensitivity of dopamine receptors in the limbic area of the brain is related to the positive symptoms of schizophrenia. The negative symptoms may be due to dopamine underactivity in the prefrontal cortex. The brains of schizophrenics, especially those with negative symptoms, have enlarged ventricles, prefrontal atrophies, and a reduced metabolism in the frontal areas.

The diagnosis of schizophrenia is more frequently applied to members of the lowest social class. Available information indicates this is so in part because the stresses of lower-class existence are great and in part because the disorder keeps schizophrenics from achieving higher social status. Vague communications and conflicts are evident in the family life of schizophrenics and probably contribute to their disorder. The level of expressed emotion (EE) in families has been shown to be an important determinant of relapse.

Much of the information we have reviewed is consistent with a diathesis–stress view of schizophrenia. Investigators have turned to the high-risk method, studying children who are particularly vulnerable to schizophrenia by virtue of having a schizophrenic parent. Mednick and Schulsinger found that circumstances predicting maladjustment in adulthood differ depending on whether positive or negative symptoms are most prominent.

There are both biological and psychological therapies for schizophrenia. Insulin and electroshock treatments and even surgery were in vogue earlier in the century, but none is employed to any extent now, primarily because of the availability of neuroleptic drugs, in particular the phenothiazines. In numerous studies these medications have been found to have a major and beneficial impact on the disordered lives of schizophrenic patients. They have also been very much a factor in the deinstitutionalization of hospital patients. But drugs alone are unlikely to be the answer, for schizophrenics need to be taught or retaught ways of dealing with the challenges of everyday life, and perhaps as well of resolving the intrapsychic problems believed by some therapists to underlie their symptoms.

Psychoanalytic theory assumes that schizophrenia represents a retreat from the pain of childhood rejection and mistreatment; the relationship gradually and patiently established by the analyst offers the patient a safe haven in which to explore repressed traumas. Good evidence for the efficacy of analytic treatments is not plentiful, although case studies of dramatic cures are many in both the professional and popular literature. Family therapy, aimed at reducing high levels of expressed emotion, has been shown to be valuable in preventing relapse. More recently, behavioral treatments have helped patients discharged from mental hospitals meet the inevitable stresses of family and community living, and, when discharge is not possible, lead more ordered and constructive lives within an institution. The most effective treatments for schizophrenia are likely to involve both biological and psychological components.

KEY TERMS

schizophrenia
positive symptoms
disorganized speech (thought disorder)
incoherence
loose associations (derailment)
delusions
hallucinations
negative symptoms
avolition
alogia
anhedonia
flat affect
catatonic immobility
waxy flexibility
inappropriate affect
dementia praecox
process-reactive dimension [of schizophrenia]
disorganized schizophrenia
catatonic schizophrenia
paranoid schizophrenia
grandiose delusions
delusional jealousy
ideas of reference
delusional (paranoid) disorders
delusions of persecution
delusions of grandiosity
undifferentiated schizophrenia
residual schizophrenia
labeling theory
dopamine activity theory
sociogenic hypothesis
social-selection theory
schizophrenogeic mother
double-bind theory
expressed emotion (EE)
prefrontal lobotomy
neuroleptics

PART THREE

Life-Span Developmental Disorders

chapter fifteen

Emotional and Behavioral Disorders of Childhood and Adolescence

Mr. and Mrs. Berg had taken Robert to doctors and clinics repeatedly. One Sunday night they even took him to the emergency room of the city hospital after they found him panic-stricken, writhing in bed with pain. A nice-looking, curly haired, underweight eight-year-old, Robert, now in second grade, had always been very much afraid of school. Recently, his fears were becoming tinged with a morbid depression that had begun to alarm his parents. . . .

Without fail, Sunday through Thursday evenings found the boy eating little at dinner, staring morosely at his plate, picking idly at his food, and wondering whether it was really worth eating, since he would probably be vomiting it all up one to two hours later. His skinny little body was beset with a host of twitches and rituals that simply became more pronounced if someone commented on them. Robert felt as ill equipped to resist them as he felt helpless to control the anxiety that mounted as the evening wore on.

Bedtime offered little solace. Robert found it necessary to observe whether he would fall asleep before 9 P.M.; when that did not happen before 9:30 P.M., and on later into the evening, he would sometimes break into tears that brought his mother into bed with him. In a fruitless effort to distract his worrying mind and ease him into sleep, she told Robert fanciful stories and promised him rewards if he would manage to go to school the following day without the usual somatic complaints and pitiful entreaties that he be allowed to stay home "just for today."

But it was the morning that really threw the household into total chaos. Rising by 6:00 A.M., Robert would pace the floor of the small apartment, causing the boards to creak and usually waking up his older brother. By 7:00 A.M. everyone was awake. While preparations for the day occupied everyone else, Robert spent the time groaning in a corner of the kitchen, rubbing his stomach, and occasionally dashing into the bathroom to throw up in the toilet. His mother would plead, cajole, insist that he at least drink a glass of milk for breakfast, but Robert would generally refuse, whining that it would only make him vomit more. . . .

He had no way to express adequately to another human being, even to this mother, how terrified school made him. It was not just the separation from home that frightened him—although, to be sure, he did not ever stray far from his neighborhood or even spend much time at friends' houses. There was something particular about *school.* Yes, his present teacher in second grade was not an especially warm person, but she was always nice to Robert, both out of pity and out of appreciation for how good a student he was. The building itself seemed to him as cheery and attractive as a haunted house, and the authoritarian atmosphere did little to make the boy feel better. It is not an exaggeration to say that Robert's sorrowful walk to school in the morning resembled that of a convicted murderer as he was led from his death cell to the room being readied for him with cyanide gas. (Oltmanns, Neale, & Davison, 1991, pp. 275–276)

Few events in an adult's life are more emotionally draining than being close to a child who is hurt, physically or psychologically. Until now we have discussed psychological problems that affect a significant proportion of the adult population. As upsetting as it may be to have a friend or relative who suffers from depression, or from unpredictable bouts of anxiety, or from the myriad of thought and emotional disruptions of schizophrenia, it is much more disturbing to see such problems in a child. Children are judged to have few emotional resources with which to cope with problems. The extreme dependency of troubled children on their parents and guardians adds to the sense of responsibility that these people feel, and to their guilt, whether justified or not.

Most psychodynamic, behavioral, cognitive, and even biological theories consider childhood experience and development critically important to adult mental health. In addition, most theories regard children as more malleable than adults and thus more amenable to treatment. We might therefore expect the disorders of children to have been the focus of voluminous research into etiology, prevention, and therapy. Until recently, however, they have been given considerably less attention than adult problems. The recently published *National Plan for Research on Child and Adolescent Mental Disorders* (National Advisory Mental Health Council, 1990) is likely to have an impact on the future funding and direction of research in child psychopathology. Recommending an increase in NIMH funding for research on child and adolescent mental disorders from 92 million dollars in 1990 to 283 million dollars in 1995, the council has pushed Congress to put research dollars behind its hope to "hasten the day when no child or adolescent need be too hard to handle, too sad to survive, too strange and angry to live among us, too ill to laugh, play and love" (p. xiv).

Disorders associated with the course of adult development and aging have received even less attention than those of childhood. The disorders of these two periods, childhood and aging, can be treated together as a new research and clinical endeavor, the study of the problems of life-span development. In this chapter we discuss emotional and behavioral disorders of childhood and adolescence. Chapter 16 covers disorders in which the acquisition of cognitive, language, motor, or social skills is disturbed. These disorders include learning disabilities and the most severe of developmental disorders, mental retardation and pervasive developmental disorders (especially autism), which are usually chronic and often persist into adulthood. Chapter 17 discusses the psychological disorders of older adults.

Classification

The classification of childhood disorders has changed radically over the last thirty years. Consistent with the scant research efforts then expended on the problems of childhood, DSM-I and DSM-II treated them primarily as downward extensions of adult disorders. Children were often given diagnoses that had originally been created for adults. The ineffectiveness of this system is indicated by the fact that most children seen by mental health professionals received a diagnosis of adjustment reaction, a very broad one indeed, or no diagnosis at all (Achenbach, 1982). Following scrutiny of this classification system by the Group for Advancement of Psychiatry (GAP, 1966), a developmentally oriented diagnostic system tailored specifically to childhood disorders was incorporated into DSM-III and expanded in DSM-IIIR and now DSM-IV.

Revisions of the diagnostic manual reflect the growing influence of the field of developmental psychopathology, which studies disorders of childhood within the context of knowledge about normal life-span development. Understanding normal developmental changes allows us to identify behaviors that are appropriate at one stage but are considered disturbed at another. For example, although defiant behavior is quite common at age two or three, the persistence of such behavior at ages five or six is considered much more problematic. Maturational differences in children also affect the manner in which symptoms are expressed and make many childhood disorders both distinct from adult psychopathology and more difficult to classify. Although we agree that childhood problems should not be viewed merely as downward extensions of adult problems, it is also possible to diagnose children as having disorders such as major depression or posttraumatic stress disorder if they meet the adult criteria.

Before proceeding further, it is important to note that childhood disorders differ from adult disorders in a very central way. Whereas most adults identify *themselves* as having a problem, most children are so identified *by others.* The difference between "I have a problem" and "You have a problem" is great. When adults are referred for treatment, we can be reasonably sure that they have problems for which they desire help. When a child is referred for treatment, on the other hand, all we really know is that someone perceives this child as disordered. Why does the person see this child as needing treatment? Is this boy really unmanageable or does he just remind his mother of her divorced husband? Is this girl really distractible or is she merely bored by school? The evidence indicates that although the child's actual behavior plays a major role in how adults perceive him or her, many other factors also enter into the perception (Ross, 1981).

In our survey of childhood and adolescent disorders, we make only partial use of DSM-IV. More useful in our view is a consideration based on a review of the studies of disordered children that found consistent evidence for two broad clusters of childhood symptoms. Children with symptoms from one cluster are called **undercontrolled,** or externalizers, and are said to show behavior excesses. Children who have symptoms from the other cluster are said to be **overcontrolled,** to be internalizers, or to have behavior deficits and emotional inhibitions (Achenbach & Edelbrock, 1978). A distinction between these clusters lies in whether the child's way of reacting creates a problem for others or primarily affects the self. These two clusters are prevalent across cultures of many different countries, including England (Collins, Maxwell, & Cameron, 1962), Japan (Hayashi, Toyama, & Quay, 1976), Greece, Finland, and Iran (Quay & Parskeuopoulos, 1972). Consistent also across cultures is that undercontrol problems are found more often among boys, overcontrol, among girls (Weisz et al., 1987). Focus Box 15.1 discusses the possible role of culture in the varying degrees of prevalence of undercontrolled and overcontrolled behavior problems in children. These two groupings are discussed first, followed by a discussion of the eating disorders anorexia nervosa and bulimia nervosa.

FOCUS

15.1 • Culture and Childhood Problems

The values and mores of a culture play a role in whether a certain pattern of child behavior develops or is considered a problem. In a study comparing clinic referrals in Thailand and the United States, Weisz et al. (1987) found that problems of overcontrol (for example, fearfulness) were reported more often for Thai than for American youngsters, whereas problems of undercontrol (for example, fighting) were reported more often for American than for Thai children. The authors attribute these differences to Thailand's widely practiced Buddhism, which disapproves of and discourages aggression and is revealed in child-rearing practices that reflect parental intolerance of undercontrolled behavior such as disrespect and aggression. The additional finding that, within Thailand, problems of overcontrol were reported at clinics more often for adolescents than for children is, they suggest, due to the fact that Buddhist strictures are especially strong in the teen years, when young men may serve as novices in the temples.

The underlying assumption of this study is that because undercontrol is actively discouraged, Thai children, virtually by default, are more likely than American children to develop problems of overcontrol. A complementary reason is that the Buddhist culture fosters such patterns of inhibition. It could be, though, that adults in Thailand have a lower tolerance for problems of undercontrol. If this were the case, however, the study would have shown more clinic referrals for such problems and would have reflected adult bias toward referring youngsters with undercontrolled behaviors for treatment. The fact that this did not happen is taken as evidence against this "adult distress threshold" notion and in support of the supposition that the different clinic referrals reflect actual prevalence of problems.

We wonder about the main findings, however. If the Buddhist culture encourages inhibition of feelings and other so-called problems of overcontrol, why would not such behavior patterns be seen as desirable and praiseworthy by both adults and children? If so, why would a youngster who is inhibited, submissive, and even fearful of others be regarded as abnormal enough to be referred by his or her parents to a clinic? Weisz et al.'s response to such an argument is that it is just such a cultural pattern—one that discourages outward displays of emotionality—that may foster psychological problems of excessive inhibition (Boesch, 1977; Sangsingkeo, 1969). We find this interesting in that it implies that there is a certain amount of emotional expressiveness that is normal for a child or adolescent, regardless of what the culture sanctions. Suppress emotional expression, as in Buddhist Thailand, and children may become abnormally inhibited and show problems of overcontrol that lead to their being referred relatively frequently for treatment.

Disorders of Undercontrolled Behavior

The undercontrolled child lacks or has insufficient control over behavior that is expected in a given setting and is appropriate to the child's age. Because of such failings, the undercontrolled child is frequently an annoyance to both adults and peers. Two general categories of undercontrolled behavior are frequently differentiated, attention-deficit hyperactivity disorder and conduct problems.

Problems of undercontrol are defined by the type, form, and frequency of the behavior. The high frequency of much problem behavior in the general population of children, such as fidgeting in class, makes it questionable, however, whether isolated incidents should be considered abnormal. Other behavior, such as assaulting a teacher, is considered abnormal by most people.

Attention-Deficit Hyperactivity Disorder

Everybody probably knows at least one child considered to be hyperactive, and this child is most likely to be a school-age boy. These youngsters often behave impulsively or act before thinking, a pattern that may lead both to social friction and to academic failure. They have difficulty focusing on a single activity and often shift erratically from one task to another without finishing those projects they begin. Many of these children tend not to maintain the behaviors expected of them for more than a few minutes—whether this involves sustained attention to a task or a game, patient waiting for a desired event, or modulation of spontaneous verbal and motor behaviors. They seem to have remarkably high energy levels, approaching activities with striking and sometimes formidable intensity.

A hyperactive child's mother might report that he has difficulty remembering not to trail his dirty hand along the clean wall as he runs from the front door to the kitchen. His peers may find that he spontaneously changes the rules while playing Monopoly or soccer. His teacher notes that he asks what he is supposed to do immediately after detailed instructions were presented to the entire class. He may make warbling noises or other strange sounds that inadvertently disturb anyone nearby. He may seem to have more than his share of accidents—knocking over the tower his classmates are erecting, spilling his cranberry juice on the linen tablecloth, or tripping over the television cord while retrieving the family cat—and thereby disconnecting the set in the middle of the SuperBowl game.

A hyperactive child is all too frequently "in trouble"—with his peers, his teachers, his family, his community. His social faux pas do not seem to stem from negativism or maliciousness. In fact, he is often quite surprised when his behaviors elicit anger and rejection from others. Nor does he seem to have any basic deficits or disabilities—either in intellectual or in interpersonal spheres. He seems *almost* normal in every way, but yet he has inordinate and pervasive difficulties getting along in the everyday world. This is the puzzle of hyperactivity—a puzzle that continues to perplex and intrigue child health and education specialists. (Whalen, 1983, pp. 151–152)

As the foregoing description suggests, the term *hyperactive* is familiar to most people, especially to parents and teachers. Other diagnoses that have in the past been used to describe inattentive and impulsive youngsters include minimal brain dysfunction, which clearly suggested that subtle brain damage caused the behavioral problems, and hyperkinesis, from the Greek word *hyper,* meaning "over," and *kinesis,* meaning "motion." DSM-IIIR renamed these terms **attention-deficit hyperactivity disorder (ADHD).** The focus was shifted to the difficulty the child has in concentrating on the task at hand for an appropriate period of time and on the child's involvement in non-goal-directed overactivity. These inattentive children seem to have particular difficulty controlling their activity in situations that call for sitting still, such as at school or at mealtimes. When required to be quiet, they appear unable to stop moving or talking. They are often described as being on the go or "running like a motor." They are also disorganized, erratic, tactless, obstinate, and bossy. Their activities and movements seem haphazard. They quickly wear out their shoes and clothing, smash their toys, and soon exhaust their family, teachers, and friends.

As Whalen (1983) cautioned,it is important not to apply the ADHD diagnosis to youngsters who are rambunctious, overactive, or a bit distractible, for in the early school years children are often so. ADHD is best reserved for truly extreme and persistent cases. Those who worry that DSM diagnoses may stigmatize children unnecessarily (e.g., Garmezy, 1977) remind us that words like rambunctious may really mean no more than that the child is more lively and more difficult to control than a parent or teacher would like.

Because the symptoms described in DSM-IIIR represented such a heterogeneous group of behaviors, some researchers advocated returning to an earlier subgrouping of the ADHD diagnosis, separating those children with both attention deficits *and* hyperactivity from those with attention-deficit disorder (ADD) alone. This is what DSM-IV proposes. Research indicates that ADHD children (with attentional problems *and* hyperactivity) are more likely to develop conduct problems and oppositional behavior, to be placed in special classes for behavior-disordered children, and to have peer difficulties (Barkley, DuPaul, & McMurray, 1990). ADD children (with attentional problems but normal activity levels), on the other hand, appear to have more problems with focused attention or speed of information processing (Barkley, Grodzinsky, & DuPaul, 1990). These studies, along with preliminary evidence suggesting different neuroanatomical loci for different types of attentional problems (Mirsky, 1987; Posner, 1988), suggest that it may be best to think of these as two separate disorders (Barkley, 1990). Most of the theory and research, however, does not yet make this distinction.

Not surprisingly, the inattention and impulsiveness of ADHD children are often associated with academic difficulties. About 20 to 25 percent of children with ADHD have been found to have a learning disability (see page 455) in math, reading, or spelling (Barkley, DuPaul, & McMurray, 1990), and many more ADHD children are placed in special educational programs because of their difficulty in adjusting to a typical classroom environment. Still, it is clear that ADHD and learning disabilities are two separate disorders, despite some overlap between the two.

A more difficult distinction to make is that between ADHD and conduct disorder. Since an overlap of 30 to 90 percent between the two categories has been found (Hinshaw, 1987), some researchers have asserted that the two types of undercontrolled behavior are actually the same disorder (Quay, 1979). On the other hand, validational studies have revealed differences between the two; hyperactivity is associated more with off-task behavior in school, cognitive and achievement deficits, and a better long-term prognosis, whereas children with conduct problems and aggression are more likely to have antisocial parents, family hostility, low socioeconomic status, and a much higher risk for delinquency and substance abuse in adolescence (Hinshaw, 1987; Loney, Langhorne, & Paternite, 1978). The comorbidity of both disorders, which is frequent in clinic-referred children, apparently combines the worst features of both, as these children are the most likely to be rejected by their peers and have the poorest long-term prognosis. In concluding a careful review of the literature comparing the two disorders, Hinshaw (1987) recommended continuing to view hyperactivity and conduct disorder as separate but related disorders. Unfortunately, much of the research on hyperactive children confounds ADHD with conduct problems and aggressiveness, making the findings about hyperactivity less clear.

Indeed, the prevalence of ADHD has been difficult to establish because of varied definitions of the disorder over time and in different countries. Estimates vary from 1 to 20 percent (DuPaul, 1991; Ross & Ross, 1982, Szatmari et al., 1989) with a consensus that about 3 to 5 percent of children currently have ADHD (American Psychiatric Association, 1987). The disorder is certainly more common in boys than in girls, although exact figures depend on whether the sample studied is taken from clinic referrals (boys are more likely to be referred because of a higher likelihood of aggressive behavior in addition to their ADHD symptoms) or from the general population. Very few studies of girls with ADHD have been conducted, but few differences between girls and boys with ADHD have been found thus far (Breen, 1989; Horn, Wagner, & Ialongo, 1989; McGee, Williams, & Silva, 1987).

Although many preschoolers are considered quite inattentive and overactive by their parents and teachers, the majority of these youngsters are going through a normal developmental stage that will not become a persistent pattern of ADHD (Campbell, 1990). On the other hand, most children who *do* go on to develop ADHD began to exhibit excessive activity and temperamental behavior quite early in life. Their insatiable curiosity and vigorous play make child proofing a necessity to avoid such tragedies as accidental poisoning and tumbling down stairs and out windows. Although the preschool years are stressful for parents coping with ADHD, the problems are most salient when the children enter school and are suddenly expected to comply with demands that they sit in their seats for periods of time, complete assignments independently, and negotiate with peers on the playground.

Many hyperactive children have inordinate difficulties getting along with peers and establishing friendships (Whalen & Henker, 1985), probably because their behavior is annoying to others. Although these children are usually friendly and talkative, they often miss subtle social cues, misinterpret peers' intentions, and make unintentional social mistakes. (Such cognitive misattributions are found as well in some conduct-disordered children, as we shall see shortly.) ADHD children are often knowledgeable about correct social actions in hypothetical situations but do not translate this knowledge into appropriate behavior in real-life social interactions. This ineptitude, often combined with impulsive aggressiveness, leads hyperactive children to be rejected by their peers, even in new social groups (Whalen & Henker, 1985).

At one time it was thought that hyperactivity simply went away by adolescence. However, this belief has been challenged by several longitudinal studies completed during the 1980s (Barkley, Fischer, Edelbrock, & Smallish, 1990; Gittelman, Mannuzza, Shenker, & Bonagura, 1985; Weiss & Hechtman, 1986). In one study, over 70 percent of children with ADHD were found to meet criteria for the disorder in adolescence (Barkley et al., 1990); Table 15.1 provides a catalogue of behaviors that are found more often among ADHD adolescents than among normals. In addition to these fidgety, distractible, impulsive behaviors, adolescents with ADHD are far more likely to drop out of high school. In adulthood, although most are employed and financially independent, they generally reach a lower level of socioeconomic status than would be expected and change jobs more frequently. Although most adults with a history of ADHD continue to exhibit some symptoms of the disorder, most also learn to adapt to these symptoms, perhaps by finding a niche for themselves in the working world.

Biological Theories of ADHD

The search for causes of ADHD is complicated by the heterogeneity of children given this diagnosis; any factor found to be associated with the syndrome is perhaps linked with only some of those carrying the diagnosis.

A predisposition toward ADHD is probably inherited. In a study of 238 twin pairs, for example,

Table 15.1. • Prevalence of Symptoms in ADHD and Normal Adolescents

Symptom	*ADHD, %*	*Normal, %*
Fidgets	73.2	10.6
Difficulty remaining seated	60.2	3.0
Easily distracted	82.1	15.2
Difficulty waiting turn	48.0	4.5
Blurts out answers	65.0	10.6
Difficulty following instructions	83.7	12.1
Difficulty sustaining attention	79.7	16.7
Shifts from one uncompleted task to another	77.2	16.7
Difficulty playing quietly	39.8	7.6
Talks excessively	43.9	6.1
Interrupts others	65.9	10.6
Doesn't seem to listen	80.5	15.2
Loses things needed for tasks	62.6	12.1
Engages in physically dangerous activities	37.4	3.0

Source: Adapted from Barkley et al., 1990.

Goodman and Stevenson (1989) found concordance for clinically diagnosed hyperactivity in 51 percent of identical twins and 33 percent of fraternal twins. But what is it that ADHD children inherit? Preliminary studies of brain *functioning* (as opposed to anatomical structures) suggest that neurological differences between ADHD and normal children, specifically involving the frontal-limbic system, may be the biological basis for the disorder. Zametkin and his colleagues (1990) used PET scans of the brain to demonstrate that adults with childhood-onset ADHD have reduced cerebral glucose metabolism; that is, their brains are less active than the brains of normal adults during an auditory-attention task. The difference was most striking in those regions of the brain involved in self-regulation of motor functions and attentional systems. Evidence of the poorer performance of ADHD children on neuropsychological tests of frontal lobe functioning (such as inhibiting behavioral responses) provides further support for the theory that a basic deficit in this part of the brain may be related to the symptoms of the disorder (Chelune, Ferguson, Koon, & Dickey, 1986; Heilman, Voeller, & Nadeau, in press).

Popular theories of ADHD over the years have involved the role of environmental toxins in the development of hyperactivity. A biochemical theory of hyperactivity put forth by Feingold (1973) enjoyed much attention in the popular press for many years. He proposed that food additives upset the central nervous systems of hyperactive children, and he prescribed a diet free of them. It is unlikely, though, that more than a small percentage of cases of hyperactivity are caused by sensitivity to food additives. Well-controlled studies of the Feingold diet have found that very few children respond positively to it (Goyette & Conners, 1977). Similarly, the popular view that refined sugar can cause ADHD (Smith, 1975) has not been supported by careful research (Gross, 1984; Wolraich et al., 1985). Although some evidence suggests that lead poisoning may be associated to a small degree with symptoms of hyperactivity and attentional problems (Thompson et al., 1989), most children with ADHD do not show elevated levels of lead in the blood. Thus, environmental toxins have not proved a productive avenue in the search for the cause of most cases of attention-deficit disorder.

Using the PET scan, Zametkin has found that the brains of hyperactive adults have decreased rates of glucose metabolism compared to controls. Left: control. Right: Hyperactive adult. White, red, and orange indicate high levels of glucose metabolism.

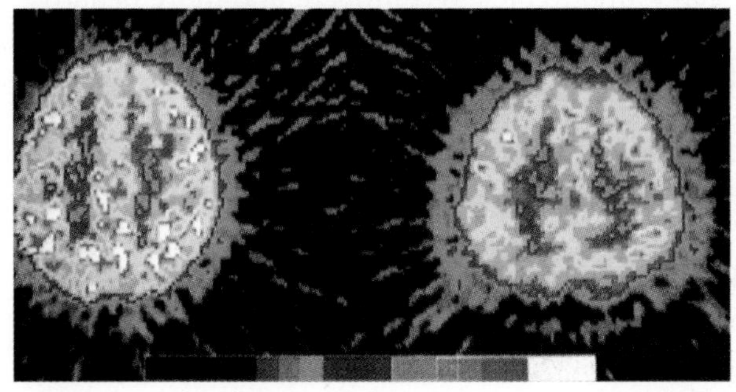

The success of psychostimulant medication in treating hyperactive children was once considered evidence in support of a biological theory of hyperactivity. Amphetamines, as discussed in Chapter 11, heighten the adult's sense of energy. Yet they have the effect of increasing attention and decreasing activity level in hyperactive children. This apparently paradoxical effect was taken as evidence for abnormal biological processes in hyperactive children. Such an interpretation is no longer viable, for some evidence demonstrates that normal children also respond to amphetamines with increased attention and decreased activity (Rapoport et al., 1978). The once presumed paradoxical effect has proved to be the normal response of children to psychostimulants. This is another case of the logical fallacy of concluding etiology from the effectiveness of treatment.

Psychological Theories of ADHD

Bettelheim (1973) proposed a diathesis–stress theory, suggesting that hyperactivity develops when a predisposition to the disorder is coupled with unfortunate rearing by parents. A child with a disposition toward overactivity and moodiness is stressed further by a mother who easily becomes impatient and resentful. The child is unable to cope with the mother's demands for obedience, the mother becomes more and more negative and disapproving, and the mother–child relationship ends up a battleground. With a disruptive and disobedient pattern already established, the demands of school cannot be handled, and the behavior of the child is often in conflict with the rules of the classroom.

Learning might figure in hyperactivity as well. First, hyperactivity could be reinforced by the attention it elicits. Second, as Ross and Ross (1982) suggested, hyperactivity may be modeled on the behavior of parents and siblings.

The parent–child relationship is, of course, bidirectional. While parents of hyperactive children give them more commands and have negative interactions with them, hyperactive children have also been found to be less compliant and more negative in their interactions with their parents (Barkley, Karlsson, & Pollard, 1985; Tallmadge & Barkley, 1983). As indicated in the section on treatment, stimulant medication has been shown to reduce hyperactivity and increase compliance in ADHD children. Significantly, when such medication is used, the parents' commands and negative behavior also decrease (see Barkley, 1990).

Treatment of ADHD

We have already mentioned the two biological treatments used for hyperactivity. Stimulant drugs, especially methylphenidate or Ritalin, have been prescribed since the early 1960s (Sprague & Gadow, 1976). One estimate is that during the school year 1 to 2 percent of American children are given Ritalin or one of the amphetamines in an effort to control their hyperactivity (Safer & Krager, 1983). Recently, prescription of these medications has continued into adolescence for many youngsters in light of the accumulating evidence that the symptoms of ADHD often do not disappear with the passage of time.

A number of controlled studies comparing stimulants with placebos in double-blind designs indicate dramatic short-term improvements in concentration, goal-directed activity, classroom behavior, fine motor activity, and reduced aggressive behavior and impulsivity in many ADHD children (Weiss, 1983). One ingenious study even demonstrated that Ritalin helped children playing softball to assume the ready position in the outfield and keep track of the status of the game. Children given placebos, in contrast, frequently threw or kicked their gloves while the pitch was in progress (Pelham, McBurnett, et al., 1990). However, research indicates that such drugs may not improve academic achievement over the long haul (Weiss, 1983), or improve batting and throwing skills, for that matter!

The other biological intervention is the so-called Feingold diet, promulgated by Feingold's 1975 book, *Why Your Child Is Hyperactive,* and by numerous parent associations throughout the country. These associations publish complete diets comprising foods that do not contain artificial flavors and colorings, preservatives, and natural salicylates, among other things. We have already said that few hyperactive children are helped by the Feingold diet.

Despite the absence of a comprehensive theory, treatments of ADHD children based on learning principles have demonstrated at least short-term success in improving both social and academic behavior. In these treatments the behavior of the children is monitored both at home and in school, and they are reinforced for doing the appropriate thing, such as remaining in their seats and working on assignments. Point systems and star charts are frequently a part of these programs; the youngsters earn points and the younger children earn stars for behaving in certain ways. They can then, of course, spend their earnings for rewards. It is of special interest that the focus of these operant programs is on improving academic work, completing household tasks, or learning specific social skills, rather than on reducing signs of hyperactivity, such as running around and jiggling (O'Leary et al., 1976). The therapists devising these interventions conceptualize hyperactivity as a deficit in certain skills rather than as an excess of disruptive behavior. Although hyperactive children have proved very responsive to these programs, the optimal treatment for the disorder may require the use of both stimulants and behavior therapy (Barkley, 1990; Gittelman et al., 1980).

Conduct Disorders

The term **conduct disorders** encompasses a wide variety of undercontrolled behavior and does not have a single definition. Aggression, lying, destructiveness, vandalism, theft, and truancy are actions usually covered by the general, and rather vague, category conduct disorders. The connecting thread in this array of behaviors is the violation of societal norms and the basic rights of others. The patterns and severity of the acts go beyond the mischief and pranks common among children and adolescents.

Perhaps more than any other childhood disorder, conduct problems are defined by the impact of the child's behavior on people and surroundings. Schools, parents, and peers usually decide what undercontrolled behavior is unacceptable conduct. Preadolescents and adolescents are often identified as conduct problems by legal authorities. In this case the child might be considered a juvenile delinquent. *Juvenile delinquency* is a legal, not a psychological, term, referring to acts committed by a young person, usually under eighteen years of age, that are either generally illegal, such as assault or robbery, or illegal only for people of a certain age, such as truancy. It is not surprising, then, that many youngsters who are diagnosed as conduct-disordered run afoul of the law and are judged to be juvenile delinquents by our system of juvenile justice. A young person with a conduct disorder, however, might well evade legal detection.

Clearly, moral judgments are inherent in our conception of the disorder, for the very term *conduct* carries with it the connotation of good or bad. Moreover, since much of the behavior considered a conduct problem has a high base rate in the general population, a certain level of aggression or disobedience should probably be deemed normal. For example, a survey of sixth-grade students in a middle-class suburb revealed that 26 percent had committed minor shoplifting, 22 percent had defaced property, and 45 percent had fought with another student (Richards, Berk, & Forster, 1979).

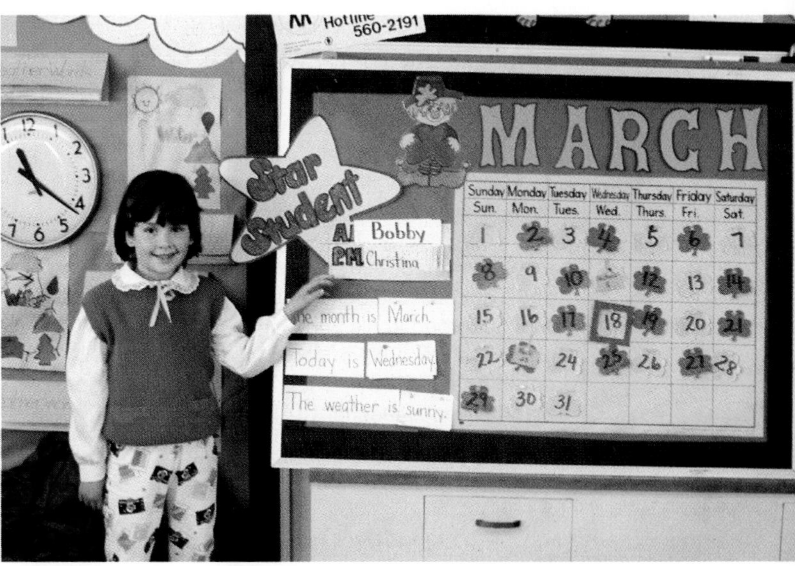

Successful treatment of attention deficit/hyperactivity disorder often involves the use of point systems or star charts to reward children for completing assignments, being attentive, and remaining in seats.

An excerpt from the case history of Tom serves to illustrate the difficulty of defining conduct disorders in terms of behavior alone.

Conduct disorders are identified by the frequent occurrence of antisocial behaviors such as aggression, theft, vandalism, and truancy.

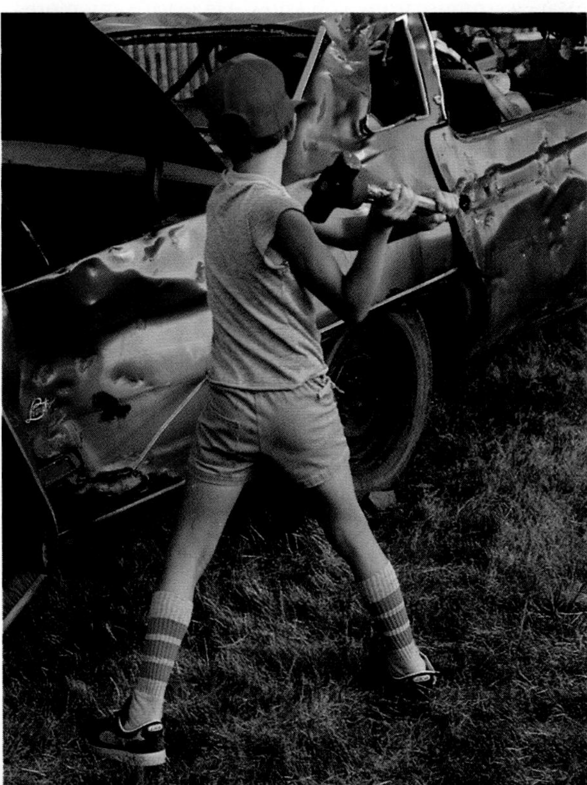

He entered the church, now, with a swarm of clean and noisy boys and girls, proceeded to his seat and started a quarrel with the first boy who came handy. The teacher, a grave, elderly man, interfered; then turned his back a moment and Tom pulled a boy's hair in the next bench, and was absorbed in his book when the boy turned around; stuck a pin in another boy, presently, in order to hear him say "Ouch!" and got a new reprimand from his teacher.

Based on this sample of Tom's behavior, are we to conclude that he has a conduct disorder? Certainly he is aggressive and disobedient, two of the more frequent indications. And the impact of Tom's behavior on his companions and the Sunday school session is a disruptive one, as we can be sure both Tom's Sunday school teacher and his classmates would report. The excerpt, however, was taken from *The Adventures of Tom Sawyer,* by Mark Twain (1876, p. 494). Tom Sawyer a conduct problem? No! For over one hundred years Tom has been considered the prototypical all-American boy. Something about Tom, perhaps his cleverness and his affection for Becky, keeps us from thinking of him as a boy with conduct problems. Although he was devilish, even Aunt Polly acknowledged that Tom was not *really* a ruffian.

> "But as I was saying," said Aunt Polly, "he warn't bad, so to say—only mischievous. Only, just giddy, and harum-scarum, you know. He warn't any more responsible than a colt. He never meant any harm, and he was the best-hearted boy that ever was." (p. 503)

The factors that cause the actions of one child to be considered a conduct problem and the same actions of another to be accepted as normal are intriguing. Unfortunately, they are largely unspecified in the psychological literature. Fertile ground for speculation is provided by the contrast between Tom Sawyer and Huck Finn, who *would* likely be diagnosed as having a conduct disorder. "Huckleberry was cordially hated and dreaded by all the mothers of the town, because he was idle, and lawless, and vulgar and bad" (p. 464). The fact that Huck had no proper family may have been one factor swaying the opinions of the townspeople.

We do not wish to overstate the labeling bias of society, however. Many qualities of the child's behavior itself must be considered in the diagnosis of conduct disorders. Perhaps the two most important criteria for deciding whether a given act is aggressive or problematic are the frequency with which it occurs and the intensity of the behavior (Herbert, 1978). Thus one fight in a year is not a problem, but one fight per week is. Similarly, whereas stealing a candy bar is a minor incident, stealing a car is a felony. These criteria of frequency and intensity do not fully solve the problem of defining conduct disorders, but they are important considerations.

Many children with conduct disorders display other problems as well. We have already discussed the high degree of overlap between conduct disorders and attention-deficit hyperactivity disorder. Substance abuse is another behavior commonly co-occurring with conduct problems. Investigators from the Pittsburgh Youth Study, a longitudinal study of conduct problems in boys, found a strong association between substance use and delinquent acts (Van Kammen, Loeber, & Stouthamer-Loeber, 1991). For example, among seventh-graders who reported having tried marijuana, more than 30 percent had attacked someone with a weapon and 43 percent admitted breaking and entering. Fewer than 5 percent of children who reported no substance use had committed these acts.

Because of the definitional difficulties, the prevalence of conduct disorders is almost impossible to estimate accurately. With little doubt, however, they are quite common. For example, a recent population-based study of over 2500 children in Ontario, Canada, found that 8 percent of boys and about 3 percent of girls aged four to sixteen met the DSM criteria for conduct disorder (Offord, Boyle, et al., 1987). Juvenile crime is a major problem, particularly the more violent crimes of robbery and aggravated assault. The rate of juvenile crime increased greatly in the 1960s and 1970s and then leveled off at this higher frequency.

The prognosis for children diagnosed as having conduct disorders is poor. Robins (1978) summarized several longitudinal studies examining antisocial behavior in a number of cohorts, from the 1920s to the 1970s, with follow-ups over as long as thirty years. She concluded that the vast majority of highly antisocial adults had also been highly antisocial as children. However, more than half the antisocial children did *not* go on to become antisocial adults. Thus, it appears that conduct problems in childhood are a necessary but not a sufficient condition for antisocial behavior in adulthood. Interestingly, a child's own behavior was a better predictor of later antisocial behavior than any family characteristics or social-status variables.

Although almost all the research in this area has

been conducted with males, a recent study followed for several years fifty-five hospitalized adolescent girls with conduct disorders (Zoccolillo & Rogers, 1991). As with boys, the majority of these subjects had a history of substance use and most also met diagnostic criteria for depression or an anxiety disorder. The outcome for these girls paralleled the poor prognosis found in male subjects: 88 percent of the sample had problems, including premature death (6 percent), dropping out of school (41 percent), encounters with the legal system (50 percent), running away (48 percent), pregnancy before age seventeen (32 percent), and suicide attempts (22 percent).

Aggressive behavior, in particular, has been found to be as stable as IQ, persisting from preschool and childhood into adulthood (Huesmann et al., 1984; Olweus, 1979; Quay, 1986). It is clear that conduct problems, like hyperactivity, are not simply outgrown.

Etiology of Conduct Disorders

Numerous theories have been offered for the etiology of conduct disorders. Data showing a high prevalence of antisocial personality disorder in both mothers and fathers of children with conduct disorders suggest familial transmission (Lahey et al., 1988). Since adoptive parents of conduct-disordered children have *not* been found to have antisocial problems or alcoholism (Jary & Stewart, 1985), the connection between parents' and childrens' conduct problems may be at least partly genetic. Furthermore, twin studies show consistently higher concordance rates for antisocial behavior in identical pairs than in fraternal pairs (Eysenck, 1975). The effects of upbringing are indicated by findings that families of these children frequently lack cohesiveness (Craig & Glick, 1963) and have experienced the stresses of marital discord and divorce (Rutter, 1971; Emery & O'Leary, 1979; see Focus Box 15.2).

An important part of normal child development is the growth of moral awareness, acquiring a sense of what is right and wrong and the ability, even desire, to abide by rules and norms. Most people refrain from hurting others, not only because it is illegal but because it would make them feel guilty to do otherwise. Research into the backgrounds of conduct-disordered youngsters has shown a pattern of family life lacking in factors believed to be central to the development of a strong moral sense. Affection between child and parents; making firm moral demands on the child; using sanctions in a consistent manner; punishing psychologically rather than physically to induce anxiety and guilt rather than anger; and reasoning and explaining things to the child all help in this development (Herbert, 1982; Hoffman, 1970; Wright, 1971).

Conduct-disordered children, like the psychopaths discussed in Chapter 10, seem to be deficient in this moral awareness, viewing antisocial acts as exciting and rewarding, indeed as central to their very self-concept (Ryall, 1974). Some psychodynamic theorists have explained conduct problems and delinquency as "disorder(s) in the functioning of the superego" (Kessler, 1966, p. 303).

Several other psychological theories have merit. Learning theories that look to both modeling and operant conditioning have received considerable attention as explanations of the development and maintenance of conduct problems. Bandura and Walters (1963) were among the first to point out the obvious, that children can learn aggressiveness from parents who behave in this way. Children may also imitate aggressive acts that are seen elsewhere, such as on television (Liebert, Neale, & Davidson, 1973). Since aggression is an effective, albeit unpleasant, means of achieving a goal, it is likely to be reinforced. Thus, once imitated, aggressive acts will probably be maintained.

Patterson (1986) offered a specific explanation of how conduct problems are rewarded in families. His *coercion hypothesis* is best demonstrated by an example from our clinical files.

Chris was an eight-year-old boy brought to the clinic by his mother, who described him as unmanageable. Whenever his mother refused to comply with Chris's requests, he became upset. At these times Chris would be stubborn, uncooperative, and verbally abusive. Occasionally he would throw a temper tantrum and lie down on the floor, kicking his feet and screaming. His mother usually ignored Chris's behavior for a few minutes, but she gave in to his demands when his tantrums became too difficult for her to bear. This sequence of agitation and giving in had become habitual, particularly when the mother was busy. When she felt rushed and perturbed, she gave in to Chris almost immediately.

The coercion hypothesis postulates that both Chris and his mother are rewarded in this sequence of events. Chris is rewarded by getting his own way, his mother by the cessation of Chris's obnoxious behavior. Through this mutual rewarding both Chris's

FOCUS 15.2 • The Role of Marital Discord in Conduct Disorders

The role that separation and divorce play in fostering conduct problems and delinquency has been an issue of debate. Rutter's (1971) classic study pointed to the association between marital discord and antisocial behavior in sons. Although this connection has been confirmed in later studies (e.g., O'Leary & Emery, 1984), explaining it has been more difficult.

Most researchers agree that it is marital discord, not separation or divorce itself, that is related to problem behavior in the children (e.g., Rutter, 1979). Emery (1982) discussed several theories proposed to explain how marital discord adversely affects children. The modeling hypothesis suggests that interparental conflict sets an example of using hostility and aggression as a way of handling problems; the parents' behaviors are imitated by the children (particularly boys), who are then seen as conduct disordered. Another theory suggests that parents who have marital problems are less consistent in their discipline techniques, leading to undercontrolled behavior in the children. A third possibility, proposed by Minuchin (1974), is that children develop problems as a way of distracting parents from their own conflict. Finally, it has been suggested that having a conduct-disordered child can create marital conflict.

An alternative to these hypotheses has been proposed by Frick and his colleagues in their study of the relationship between conduct problems in boys and maternal variables (Frick, Lahey, Hardagen, & Hynd, 1989). They suggest that a third variable, antisocial personality disorder in the parent, may explain both the marital discord and the child's conduct problems. Their data suggest that it may be that parents with antisocial personalities relate poorly to their spouses *and* pass on their inappropriate behavior to their sons (perhaps through genetic mechanisms and not directly through the effects of marital discord).

Each of these theories may prove useful in describing the mechanism that links marital turmoil with children's problems. They all seem to suggest that parents should minimize their children's involvement in marital conflict, for example, by not arguing about marital or discipline issues in front of the children.

Marital discord is associated with increased prevalence of conduct disorder but it is unclear how the relationship is mediated. Among the possibilities are that parents with marital problems are inconsistent in their disciplinary practices or that children imitate their parent's hostility and aggressiveness.

A good deal of evidence indicates that modeling is involved in increasing aggressiveness. Viewing televised violence is one way in which this can occur.

conduct problems and his mother's acquiescence are likely to be maintained. Therapy based on the coercion hypothesis would direct the mother not to give in to Chris while he is misbehaving and thereby extinguish his conduct problem. The coercion hypothesis seems a likely model, but it explains only how obstreperous behavior is *maintained,* not how it first *develops.*

In any discussion of conduct disorders and delinquency, the work of sociologists must be recognized. Social class and urban living in particular are related to the incidence of delinquency. High unemployment, poor educational facilities, disrupted family life, and a subculture that deems delinquency acceptable have all been found to be contributing factors (Gibbons, 1975). Any comprehensive theory of delinquency and conduct disorders needs to include these consistent sociological findings.

Treatment of Conduct Disorders

The management of conduct disorders poses a formidable challenge to contemporary society. Sociologists and politicians, as well as community psychologists, working on the assumption that poor economic conditions create most of the problem, argue for a fairer distribution of income and for job programs and other large-scale efforts to alleviate the material deprivation of the lower classes, among which, as previously noted, delinquency is often found. Although sociological considerations may play some role in planning treatments, we emphasize here psychological methods aimed more at the particular individuals and their families.

Some of the young people with conduct disorder are the psychopaths of tomorrow. Just as precious little in the way of effective psychological treatment has been found for psychopathy, so are there few ways to reach young people who commit violent and antisocial acts with little remorse or emotional involvement. These callous young individuals, most of them male, graduate from training schools and youth farms to lives of crime and dissoluteness, interrupted by extended periods of incarceration. Recidivism is the rule. One of society's most enduring problems is how to deal with people whose social consciences appear grossly underdeveloped.

Some of the most promising approaches to treating conduct disorders involve intervening with the parents or families of the antisocial child. Gerald Patterson and his colleagues have worked for almost three decades developing and testing a behavioral program of parent management training, in which parents are taught to modify their responses to their children so that prosocial rather than antisocial behavior is consistently rewarded. Parents are taught social-learning principles through readings and presentations and are taught to use techniques such as positive reinforcement when the child ex-

Some people with conduct disorders become adult psychopaths, in part due to the ineffectiveness of penal institutions in rehabilitating them. What does life hold for Amy Fisher once she has served her term in prison?

hibits positive behaviors and time-out and loss of privileges for aggressive or antisocial behavior. Sessions include practicing the techniques and a discussion of difficulties the parents may encounter when applying the methods to an antisocial child. Patterson's group has demonstrated the effectiveness of this program as evidenced both by parents' and teachers' reports of children's behavior and by direct observation of behavior at home and at school (Patterson, 1982). Parent management training has even been shown to improve the behavior of siblings and reduce depression in mothers involved in the program (Kazdin, 1985).

Although parent-focused intervention is often the treatment of choice for children with conduct disorders, in some situations direct intervention with the disturbed individual is more appropriate. Parent management training requires a great deal of time and effort from at least one parent and can be difficult to carry out in families with multiple social problems. In fact, research has demonstrated that parent-focused training is much less effective in families with low socioeconomic status or marital discord and when there is psychopathology in one or both parents (Kazdin, 1985).

Research by Dodge and Frame (1982) suggests a direction for cognitive therapy. They examined the cognitive processes associated with aggressive behavior and found a cognitive bias that might underlie such antisocial behavior. Their finding was that aggressive boys interpret ambiguous acts (such as being bumped in line) as hostile. This biased view may lead such boys to retaliate aggressively to actions that may not have been intended to be provocative. Their peers, remembering these aggressive acts, may tend to aggress more often against them, further angering the aggressive children. This cycle can lead to peer rejection and further aggression.

In a series of programmatic studies, Dodge (in press; Dodge & Coie, 1987) distinguished between reactive and proactive aggression in children. The reactively aggressive child is said to respond with aggression to perceived wrongs by others, as just described. In contrast, the proactively aggressive youngster is said to regard aggression as a means to an end, as a way to get what he wants from other people; the neighborhood bully is an example. Although some youngsters can show both kinds of aggression, this distinction may have important implications for intervention: in the case of proactive aggression, treatment would focus on the expected payoff for antisocial behavior, whereas for reactive aggression, attention would best be paid to how the child interprets the intentions of others, especially when those intentions are ambiguous.

Anger-control training is a promising method of teaching aggressive children self-control in anger-provoking situations. Hinshaw, Henker, and Whalen (1984) helped children learn to withstand verbal attacks without responding aggressively using distracting techniques such as humming a tune, saying calming things to themselves, or turning away. The children then practiced these self-control methods while a peer provoked and insulted them.

Another cognitive-behavioral approach to conduct-disordered children, based on the work of Kendall and Braswell (1985) and Spivack, Platt, and Shure (1976), is illustrated in a study by Kazdin et al. (1989). They taught antisocial children problem-solving skills as well as empathy, or taking the perspective of others, all in an effort to help them better handle interpersonal conflict and academic tasks. This multifaceted program also included role-playing and practicing newly learned cognitive and behavioral skills, as well as reinforcement—chips could be earned for later exchange for back-up reinforcers, and chips could be lost (response cost) for failure to carry out problem-solving. The results were encouraging in promoting prosocial behavior. Although conduct disorders remain very resistant to all sorts of interventions and although cognitive-behavioral treatments still fall short of curing conduct disorders, there is some promise in approaches that focus on deficient problem-solving skills, impulsivity, and anger control (Kendall et al., 1990; Salovey & Singer, 1991).

Most of the methods just described are preventive, focusing mainly on younger children who have not yet exhibited serious criminal or delinquent behavior. Once conduct-disordered children or adolescents have come into contact with the juvenile justice system, it becomes much more difficult to redirect them to a prosocial way of life. In fact, studies suggest that avoiding contact with the court system is essential to success in treating delinquents. Davidson et al. (1987) compared several types of treatments, all having the common element of pairing a college student with a juvenile delinquent for six to eight hours per week in the community. They found that the specific content of those meetings (behavioral contracting versus focusing on empathy, unconditional positive regard, and communication skills) was less important than the factor of removal from the justice system. Even a watered-down treatment involving minimal supervision by the college volunteers was superior to a more rigorous treatment where supervision was administered within the court building by a court caseworker (even though the juveniles had no contact with the court during treatment).

FOCUS 15.3 • Enuresis

It is well-known that infants have no bladder or bowel control. As they become older, the inevitable toilet training begins. Some children learn toileting at eighteen months, others at thirty months, and so on. When is it no longer normal to be unable to control the bladder? The answer, determined by cultural norms and statistics, is fairly arbitrary.

DSM-IV and other classification systems distinguish between those who wet during sleep, which is nocturnal enuresis, and those who wet while awake, which is diurnal enuresis. Daytime continence is established earlier. When a child falls behind in bladder control, it is usually for the nighttime hours. It is estimated that at age five, between 16 and 25 percent of children wet at night (this figure includes those who used to stay dry but have regressed). By age seven and one-half, 7 percent are still wetting, and by age ten, 5 percent remain nocturnal bed wetters (Pierce, 1980, 1985).

In the United States, the most commonly accepted cutoff for regarding nocturnal wetting as an actual problem is between three and four years of age (age five in DSM-IV), at which time the estimated incidence of bed-wetting is 10 to 15 percent of the age group (Baller, 1975). Primary enuretics, who represent two-thirds of all enuretics (Starfield, 1972), have wet the bed from infancy, whereas secondary enuretics were once able to remain dry at night but have apparently lost the capacity. Bed-wetting usually occurs about four hours after the onset of sleep, or after the last enuretic incident (Sorotzin, 1984).

One consistent finding about enuresis is that the likelihood of an enuretic having a first-degree relative who also wets is very high, approximately 75 percent (Bakwin, 1973), evidence for either biological or psychological theories of etiology.

Theories of Enuresis

As many as 10 percent of all cases of enuresis are caused by purely medical conditions. The most common of the known physical causes is urinary tract infection. Approximately one in twenty female and one in fifty male enuretics have such an infection. Treatment of the infection oftentimes does not stop the enuresis, however. Other infrequent but known physical causes are chronic renal or kidney disease, tumors, diabetes, and seizures (Kolvin, MacKeith, & Meadow, 1973). Because of the substantial incidence of physical causes of enuresis, most professionals refer enuretics to physicians before beginning psychological treatment.

Some psychoanalytic theorists have suggested that enuresis serves as a symbol for other conflicts. Enuresis has been hypothesized to be both symbolic masturbation and a disguised means of demonstrating spite toward parents (Mowrer, 1950). A related notion considers enuresis a symptom of a more general psychological disorder. Many investigators disagree, however, finding other personal problems to be a reaction to the embarrassment and guilt of wetting, rather than causes of enuresis. Children will, of course, lose self-esteem if their peers ostracize them and their parents become angry and rejecting. When bladder control is gained, most of the correlated problems are also likely to disappear (Baller, 1975; Moffatt, Kato, & Pless, 1987; Starfield, 1972).

Learning theorists propose that children wet when toilet training begins at too early an age, when training is lax and insufficient reinforcement is given for proper toileting, and more specifically when children do not learn to awaken as a conditioned response to a full bladder or to inhibit sufficiently relaxation of the sphincter muscle that controls urination (Mowrer & Mowrer, 1938; Young, 1965; Baller, 1975). Bladder control, the inhibition of a natural reflex until voluntary voiding can take place, is, after all, a skill of considerable complexity. Recent medical evidence involving activity of the pelvic floor muscles provides support for the idea that children who wet the bed are failing to spontaneously contract these muscles at night (Norgaard, 1989a, 1989b).

Some preliminary research suggests another biological theory to account for nocturnal enuresis: Danish researchers found that adolescents with enuresis had a night-time deficiency of antidiuretic hormone (ADH) (Rittig et al., 1989). In normal children, ADH concentrates in the urine more during sleep than during the waking hours.

Alternative theories, such as the idea that enuretic children have sleep and arousal problems or an abnormally small functional bladder capacity, have not been supported by research (Houts, 1991).

Treatment of Enuresis

Home remedies for bed-wetting have run the gamut from restricting fluids to making children sleep on golf balls or hang "the incriminating evidence," wet sheets, out the window (Houts, 1991); most have been ineffective. Similarly, waiting for the child to grow out of the problem has not been satisfactory. Only about 15 percent of enuretics between ages five and nineteen show spontaneous remission within a year (Forsythe & Redmond, 1974).

The two most widely used treatments prescribed by professionals involve either medication or urine alarm systems. The latter first came on the scene in 1938, when Mowrer and Mowrer introduced the bell and pad. (Recall from Chapters 2 and 6 that O. H. Mowrer was a leading re-

Figure 15.A The bell and pad apparatus for halting bed-wetting, devised by Orval Hobart and Willie Mae Mowrer.

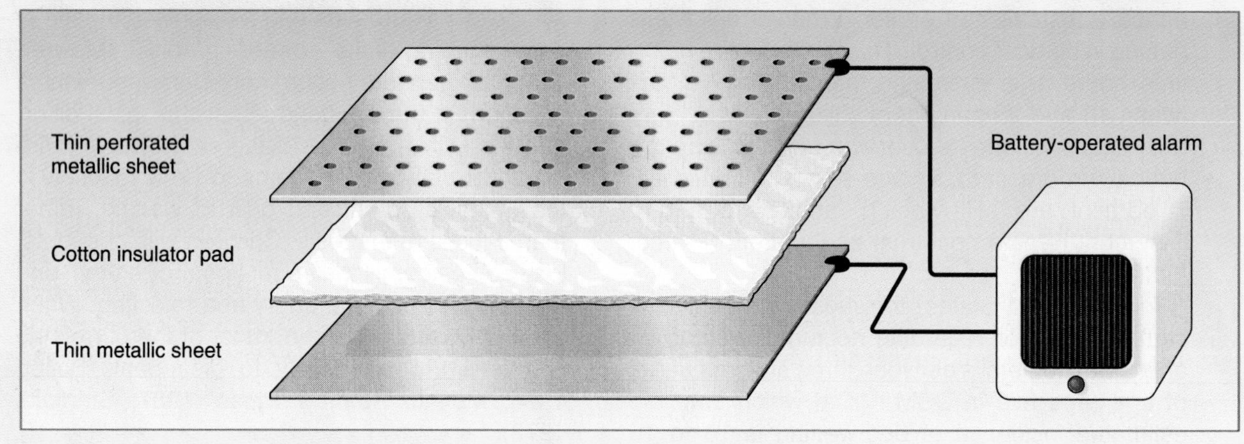

Disorders of Overcontrolled Behavior

Overcontrolled behavior, as indicated earlier, usually creates more problems for the individual child than for others, although we must not underestimate the toll taken on parents, family members in general, and teachers by the problems described in this section. Unlike undercontrolled children, whose behavior is judged negatively by others, children with problems of overcontrol frequently complain of bothersome fears and tenseness; of feelings of shyness, of being unhappy and unloved; and of being inferior to other children. Symptoms of overcontrolled behavior are similar to those of the adult problems of anxiety and depression. The three specific problems of overcontrol we will discuss are frequently found in the same child: childhood fears, social withdrawal, and depression (Quay, 1979). Some childhood fears are listed under **separation anxiety disorder** in the DSM-IV section on childhood disorders. School phobia is one of the manifestations of separation anxiety disorder. Other fears, like those found in social withdrawal, are to be diagnosed as a social phobia in the adult section of DSM-IV. Similarly, depression in children is diagnosed in much the same way as depression in adults is. Focus Box 15.3 discusses **enuresis**, a disorder in which, through faulty control of the bladder, the child repeatedly wets after an age at which continence is expected.

Childhood Fears

Most children have fears and worries that are part of the normal course of development. For example, Bell-Dolan, Last, and Strauss (1990) interviewed sixty-two children between the ages of five and eighteen who had no history of psychiatric disor-

searcher and theoretician whose work was important in laying the foundations for behavioral approaches to psychopathology and intervention.) Over the years the treatment has proved markedly successful in reducing or eliminating bed-wetting. Although relapses can be common, it is estimated that 77 percent of enuretic children will learn to stay dry through the night with the help of this remarkably simple device, which Houts (1991) termed "one of the most clear and lasting accomplishments of the behavior therapy movement" (p. 147).

The bell and a battery are wired to the pad, which is composed of two metallic foil sheets, the top one perforated, separated by a layer of absorbent cloth (Figure 15.A). The pad is inserted into a pillowcase and placed beneath the child at bedtime. When the first drops of urine, which act as an electrolyte, reach the cloth, the electric circuit is completed between the two foil sheets. The completed circuit sets off the bell, which awakens the child immediately or soon after beginning to wet. The child can then stop urination, turn off the device, and go to the bathroom.

Mowrer and Mowrer (1938) viewed the bell and pad as a classical conditioning procedure wherein an unconditioned stimulus, the bell, wakes the child, the unconditioned response. The bell is paired with the sensations of a full bladder so that these sensations eventually become a conditioned stimulus that produces the conditioned response of awakening before the bell sounds. Others have questioned the classical conditioning theory, suggesting instead that the bell, by waking the child, serves as a punisher and thus reduces the undesirable behavior of wetting. In actual practice the bell usually wakes the child's parents too; their reactions may serve as an additional incentive for the child to remain dry. Other methods that use an operant conditioning approach without the help of the urine alarm have not been nearly as successful (Houts, 1991).

Pharmacological treatment is another approach; about one-third of enuretics who seek professional help are prescribed medications, such as imipramine and, more recently, desmopressin, by their physicians. Such medications work by either changing the reactivity of the muscles involved in urinating (imipramine) or concentrating urine in the bladder (desmopressin). Although an immediate positive effect is usually seen, in the vast majority of cases children relapse as soon as the medication is stopped (see Houts, 1991). Treatments combining medication with the behavioral approach described earlier are only just beginning to be tested; preliminary research has been promising (Sukhai, Mol, & Harris, 1989).

ders or mental health treatment. One-third of the children expressed overconcern about their competence and an excessive need for reassurance, and about one-fifth reported fears of heights and public speaking, shrinking from contact with others, and somatic complaints. Although many symptoms of anxiety were present in these normal children, none met the criteria for a DSM disorder, and many did not exhibit any significant fears at a follow-up interview one year later. Thus, fears and anxieties appear to be a normal part of child development. Focus Box 15.4 explores further some of the problems of otherwise psychologically normal children who have serious medical illnesses.

In order for fears and worries to be classified as disorders, children must show impairment of their functioning; using this definition, it has been estimated that 6 to 8 percent of children and adolescents have an anxiety disorder, making these the most common disorders of childhood (Costello, 1989; Kashani & Orvaschel, 1988; McGee et al., 1990).

School Phobia

One childhood fear, **school phobia,** has attracted the most attention, for not only is it disabling to the child and disruptive to the household, but it also appears to be a true phobia, an extreme avoidance that does not usually just go away with the passage of time. Furthermore, it has serious academic and social consequences for the youngster and can be a very disabling childhood disorder. The case that opened this chapter illustrates many of the clinical features of school phobia.

The frequency of school phobia has been estimated at seventeen per 1000 children per year (Kennedy, 1965). Two types have been identified. In the most common, that associated with separation anxiety, children worry constantly that some harm will befall their parents or themselves when they are away from their parents; when home, they shadow one or both of their parents and often try to join them in bed.

FOCUS

15.4 • Behavioral Pediatrics

An earlier discussion of behavioral medicine (see page 215) enumerated several applications of psychological knowledge to the prevention and treatment of physical disease, for example, altering the Type A behavior pattern as a way of reducing the incidence of later coronary heart disease. Psychological attention has been paid to childhood and adolescent diseases as well.

Russo and Varni (1982) proposed a normal person–abnormal situation (NPAS) model as a way of conceptualizing **behavioral pediatrics**, a branch of behavioral medicine concerned with the psychological aspects of childhood medical problems. An acutely or chronically ill child is a young person who may have psychological problems because he or she has been placed, by illness, in a complex and stressful predicament. Many sick children suffer considerable pain and sometimes defacement and have to spend long periods of time in a hospital, away from parents, siblings, and the comforting surroundings of their homes and neighborhoods.

In general, behavioral pediatrics combines behavior therapy and pediatrics to manage disease in children. It concerns itself with parent–child, school–child, and medical team–child relations (Varni & Dietrich, 1981). Some specific examples will convey the scope and aims of this field (Kellerman & Varni, 1982).

In recent years, many forms of childhood cancer, such as acute lymphoblastic leukemia, have become treatable; some types can even be treated so effectively that they go into remission and the children are alive five years after the onset of cancer. With such improvement, however, come new problems of a psychological nature for both patients and families—learning to live with the disease and its treatment.

Concealing from a youngster the true nature of his or her illness and how life-threatening it is increases rather than decreases anxiety (e.g., Spinetta, 1980). Open communication with the child is advocated. Research advises maintaining the child in his or her regular school as much as possible (Katz, 1980). Because cancer and its treatment can bring physical difigurement, such as hair loss, the child should be taught to handle the teasing that often awaits any youngster who looks different; assertion training and learning to ignore the hurtful remarks can be helpful.

Pain accompanies both the diagnosis and treatment of childhood cancer. A child with leukemia must undergo frequent and regular bone marrow aspiration. The doctor inserts a long needle into the middle of the thigh bone and extracts some marrow. It hurts. And it is not the kind of pain to which the individual readily habituates (Katz, Kellerman, & Siegel, 1980). The experience takes a toll on the young patient and on the parents as well. Specialists in behavioral pediatrics have developed hypnotic imagery techniques

Behavioral pediatrics is a branch of behavioral medicine dealing with children's health problems. For example, a leukemia patient may be taught relaxation to cope with pain and given assertion training to deal with teasing about hair loss.

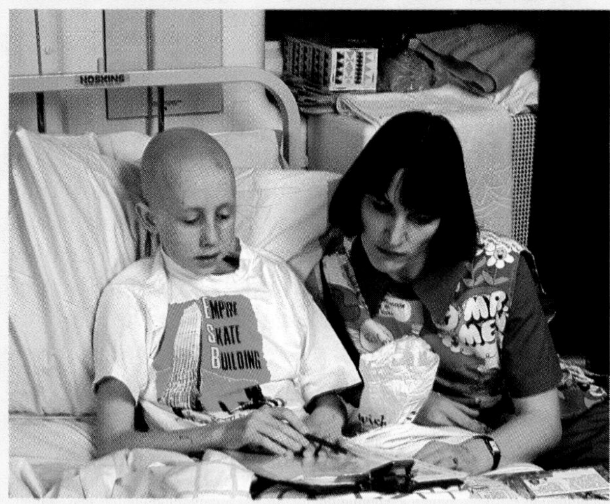

Since the beginning of school is often the first circumstance that requires lengthy and frequent separations of children from their parents, separation anxiety is frequently a principal cause of school phobia. One study found that 75 percent of children who have school refusal caused by separation anxiety have mothers who also refused school in childhood (Last & Strauss, 1990). It has been hypothesized that the child's refusal or extreme reluctance to go to school stems from some difficulty in the mother–child relationship. Perhaps the mother communicates her own separation anxieties and unwittingly reinforces the child's dependent and avoidant behavior.

The second major type of school refusal is that associated with a true phobia of school—either a that teach the child to relax, thereby reducing the trauma of this inevitable medical event. Other interventions have also proved useful for this painful procedure. Jay et al. (1987) compared Valium with a cognitive-behavioral package that included breathing exercises and distraction from the pain, and found that the psychological intervention was superior to the tranquilizer in reducing behavioral and self-report indexes of stress as well as pulse rate.

Children who develop anticipatory anxiety before undergoing other painful medical procedures have been helped by viewing films of a coping model (Jay et al., 1982). Systematic desensitization to situations associated with the pain, such as entering the hospital and sitting in the waiting room, can reduce the level of anxiety with which a patient comes to the medical procedure and, in turn, alleviate the pain. Reducing anxiety can be of more general importance. An extremely anxious child, for example, may avoid the medical procedure or may begin to lose weight. Weight loss decreases the chances of surviving cancer (Dewys et al., 1980).

Children and adolescents with other medical problems have also been helped by behavioral pediatrics. Chronic arthritic pain in the joints is a serious problem for hemophiliacs, people whose blood lacks a critical clotting factor. Varni (1981) successfully treated such pain by hypnotic imagery techniques, teaching his patients both to relax and to increase blood flow to the affected joint. A higher surface temperature about the joint diminishes the need for pain medications, many of which have the undesirable side effect of inhibiting platelet aggregation, thus worsening an already bad blood-clotting condition. Varni's recent work in pain management for children with rheumatoid arthritis also exemplifies the kind of research-based behavioral medicine that is having a positive impact on helping children and their families cope with serious medical illnesses (Varni & Bernstein, 1991; Walco, Varni, & Ilowite, 1992).

Obesity in children is highly predictive of obesity in adulthood, which is, as we know, a major risk factor for such diseases as hypertension, heart disease, and diabetes. Childhood obesity has also been associated with low social competence, behavior problems, and poor self-concept (Banis et al., 1988). Behavioral investigators have been working to help overweight youngsters alter their eating habits, exercise practices, and other aspects of their life-styles that appear to contribute to the caloric intake and how it is or is not burned off (Epstein, Masek, & Marshall, 1978). For example, obese children, like obese adults, eat faster, take bigger bites, and chew their food less than do age peers of normal weight (Drabman et al., 1979). When their parents are also involved in treatment, weight can be lost permanently (Aragone, Cassady, & Drabman, 1975).

Another topic in behavioral pediatrics is known as *therapeutic compliance*. How can we get people to do the things that are necessary to prevent or manage an illness (Varni & Wallander, 1984)? Juvenile diabetes serves as a good example of the challenge facing the youngsters and families affected. Urine must be tested several times a day to determine glucose (sugar) levels so that food intake and the amount of insulin can be adjusted. Indeed, diet itself poses a major challenge to youngsters. They must learn to resist candy and other sweets. Their meals need to be timed to coincide with the peak action of an insulin injection so that the insulin does not lower glucose levels abnormally. Activity and exercise must also become part of the regimen, for they exert their own natural, insulin-like effect of utilizing glucose in the cells (Hobbs, Beck, & Wansley, 1984). With no cure of diabetes in sight, diabetics need to accept both their condition and the required regulation of some of the most basic of human drives. The complex set of self-care skills that a young person needs in order to cope with this serious but treatable disease is now benefiting from clinical research in behavioral pediatrics (Epstein et al., 1981).

fear specifically related to school or a more general social phobia. These school phobics generally begin refusing to go to school later in life and have more severe and pervasive avoidance of school. Their fear is more likely to be related to specific aspects of the school environment, such as worries about academic failure or discomfort with peers. (See Chapter 6 for general discussion of phobias.)

Treatment of Childhood Fears

How are childhood fears overcome? As discussed earlier, many simply dissipate with time and maturation. Perhaps the most widespread means of helping children overcome fears, employed by millions of parents, is to expose them gradually to the feared object, often while acting simultaneously to

School phobia is most commonly associated with separation anxiety disorder, an intense fear of being away from parents or other attachment figures.

inhibit their anxiety. If a little girl fears strangers, a parent takes her by the hand and walks her slowly toward the new person. Mary Cover Jones (see page 555) was the first psychologist to explain this bit of folk wisdom as a counterconditioning procedure.

Indeed, contemporary therapists have by and large built on folk wisdom in helping children overcome fears. Exposure is generally agreed to be the most effective way of eliminating baseless fear and avoidance. Modeling has also proved effective, both in laboratory studies (e.g., Bandura, Grusec, & Menlove, 1967) and in countless clinical treatments; for example, another child, one the fearful child is likely to imitate, demonstrates fearless behavior. Offering rewards for moving closer to a feared object or situation can also be encouragement to a fearful child. Of course, both modeling and operant treatments involve exposure to what is feared. When the fear and avoidance of a school phobic child are very great and of long duration, they may require desensitization through direct, graduated exposure plus operant shaping.

In one of our cases, the therapist started with walks to school with nine-year-old Paul. Next, the boy, one step at a time on successive days, entered the school yard, then an empty classroom after school, attended the opening morning exercises and then left, sat at the desk, spent time in school, all with the therapist beside him, then with the therapist out of sight but still nearby. In the last steps, when anxiety seemed to have lessened, promises to play the guitar for Paul at night, comic books, and tokens that would eventually earn the boy a baseball glove were the enticements for attending school (Lazarus, Davison, & Polefka, 1965).

Finally, some new situations may be threatening not only for children but for adults as well, because the person lacks the knowledge and skills to deal with them. Thus a child's fear of the water may very well be based on a reasonable judgment that danger lurks there because he or she cannot swim. Parents and therapists must see to it that children have the opportunity to acquire knowledge and relevant skills.

Treatment outcome studies suggest that time-limited treatment of children's phobias can be very effective. For example, Hampe et al. (1973) treated sixty-seven phobic children for eight weeks, using either a behavioral or insight-oriented therapy. Sixty percent of the treated children were free of their phobia at the end of the eight-week period and did not experience a relapse or additional emotional problems during the two-year follow-up period. Eighty percent of the sample (those just mentioned plus others who sought further treatment elsewhere) were free of symptoms after two years, with only 7 percent continuing to experience a severe phobia. The authors concluded that although many childhood phobias go away on their own, treatment greatly hastens recovery. Another comparative study demonstrated the superiority of behavioral treatment over home tutoring and psychotherapy for school phobic children (Blagg & Yule, 1984). The average duration of treatment for the behavior therapy group was only two and a half weeks, and 83 percent were still attending school at the one-year follow-up. In contrast, the home tutoring and psychotherapy treatment took an average of seventy-two weeks, and *all* of these children relapsed within one year (Focus Box 15.5).

Social Withdrawal

Most classrooms have in attendance at least one or two children who are extremely quiet and shy. Often these same children will play only with family members or familiar peers, avoiding strangers both young and old. Their shyness may prevent them from acquiring skills and participating in a variety of activities that most of their age-mates enjoy, for they avoid playgrounds and games played by neighborhood children. Although some youngsters who are shy may simply be slow to warm up, withdrawn children never do, even after prolonged exposure to new people. Extremely shy children may refuse to speak at all in unfamiliar social circumstances; this is called **elective mutism.** In crowded rooms they cling and whisper to their parents, hide behind the furniture, and cower in corners. At home they ask their parents endless questions about situations that worry them. Withdrawn children usually have warm and satisfying relationships with family members and family friends, and they do show an eagerness for affection and acceptance. Because the point at which shyness or withdrawal becomes a problem varies, no statistics have been compiled on the frequency of this disorder.

Some children exhibit intense anxiety in specific social situations, showing social phobia similar to that of adults (see page 134). When such children were asked to keep daily diaries of anxiety-producing events, they reported experiencing anxiety three times more frequently than a normal control group, with concerns about such activities as reading aloud before a group, writing on the board, and performing in front of others. When faced with these events, they reported using negative coping strategies, such as crying, avoidance, and somatic complaints. In a behavioral task, the children were asked to read *Jack in the Beanstalk* aloud before a small audience of research assistants. The social phobic children showed dramatic increases in pulse rate during the task (Beidel, 1991).

Theories of the etiology of social withdrawal are not well worked out. It is often suggested that anxiety interferes with social interaction and thus causes the child to avoid social situations. Or withdrawn children may simply not have the social know-how that facilitates interaction with their agemates. The finding that isolated children make fewer attempts to make friends and are less imaginative in their play may indicate a deficiency in social skills. Finally, isolated children may have become so because they have in the past spent most of their time with adults; they do interact more freely with adults than with other children (Scarlett, 1980).

Treatment of Social Withdrawal

Treatment of social withdrawal is similar to the treatment of childhood fears. In one innovative study, youngsters were helped by viewing films in which other isolated children gradually engaged in and came to enjoy play with their peers (O'Connor, 1969). Another group of researchers paired undergraduate volunteers with socially isolated children on the playground during recess (Allen et al., 1976). The goal was to help start group games that would include the target child and give in vivo feedback to the child about which behavior promoted or inhibited positive interactions with other children. By the end of the six-month program, the volunteers were standing on the sidelines, observing the children playing with their peers.

Some shy children lack specific social skills needed for peer interaction. Skills such as asking questions (Ladd, 1981), giving compliments, and starting conversations with age-mates (Michelson, Sugai, Wood, & Kazdin, 1983) may be taught in small groups or pairs, with interactions videotaped so the child and coach can observe and modify the new behaviors.

Depression in Childhood and Adolescence

Considering our typical image of children as happy-go-lucky and carefree, it is distressing to observe that major depression and dysthymia occur in children and adolescents as well as in adults. DSM-IV includes mood disorders in children under the adult criteria, while allowing for age-specific features such as irritability instead of depressed mood.

Recent studies have found both similarities and differences in symptomatology in children and adults with major depression (Mitchell, McCauley, Burke, & Moss, 1988). Children and adolescents ages seven to seventeen resembled adults in depressed mood, anhedonia (loss of the ability to experience pleasure), fatigue, concentration problems, and suicidal ideation. Symptoms differing between children and adults were higher rates of suicide attempts and guilt among the children and adolescents, and more terminal insomnia (waking up early in the morning), loss of appetite and weight loss, and early morning depression among adults. Recent cognitive research with depressed children indicates that their outlooks (schemata) are more negative than those of nondepressed children and similar to those of depressed adults (Prieto, Cole, & Tageson, 1992). Such findings provide a possibly useful connection between childhood depression and Beck's theory and research on depressed adults.

As with adults, depression in children is recurrent. Longitudinal studies have demonstrated that both children and adolescents with major depression are likely to continue to exhibit significant depressive symptoms when assessed even four to eight years later (Garber et al., 1988; McGee & Williams, 1988).

Researchers have reported widely varying findings on the prevalence of childhood depression. Rutter, Tizard, and Whitmore (1970), using conservative criteria, conducted an extensive survey of children on the Isle of Wight; they found that fewer than 1 percent were depressed. In marked contrast, other studies (e.g., Weinberg et al., 1973) have reported much higher figures. Reasons for the contradictory findings lie in part in using a wide age range

FOCUS

15.5 • Play Therapy and Family Therapy: Two General Methods of Treating Childhood Problems

Many of the childhood disorders discussed in the present chapter, and even the more serious problems reviewed in the next, are treated by two general methods, **play therapy,** the use of play as a means of uncovering what is troubling a child and of establishing rapport, and **family therapy,** a form of group therapy in which members of a family are helped to relate better to one another.

Children are usually less verbal than adults, at least in the sense that is needed for psychoanalytic and client-centered therapy. Moreover, children are often more reluctant than older clients to voice their concerns and complaints directly and openly. Through the pioneering work of Melanie Klein (1932) and Anna Freud (1946b), play became an analytic vehicle for delving into a child's unconscious, taking the place of the free association and recounting of dreams that are important in analytic treatment of adults. It is assumed that in play therapy a child will express his or her feelings about problems, parents, teachers, and peers. A play therapy room is equipped with puppets, blocks, games, puzzles, drawing materials, paints, water, sand, clay, toy guns and soldiers, and a large inflated rubber clown to punch. These toys will, it is hoped, help draw out inner tensions and concerns. A dollhouse inhabited by parental and child dolls is a common fixture. The therapist may encourage a young male client to place the figures in "any room you wish," to position the dolls in a way "that makes you feel good." The child may assemble members of the family in the living room, except for the father, who is placed in the study. "What is Daddy doing?" the therapist will ask. "He's working. If he weren't such a meanie, he'd come out and play with the kids." The therapist will then, as he or she would for an adult, interpret for the boy the wish he seems reluctant to express openly.

In nondirective play therapy, such as that practiced by Virginia Axline (1964), the relationship between the therapist and child developed through play is used to provide a corrective emotional experience for the child. Rather than interpreting the child's symbolic expressions, the client-centered therapist responds to the child's words and actions in an empathic manner, demonstrating unconditional acceptance.

There has been little controlled research to evaluate the claims made for play therapy by its adherents. What evidence is available, however, does not find it to be notably effective (Barrett, Hampe, & Miller, 1978; Phillips, 1985). One area of promise is play therapy with cognitive-behavioral components. For example, short-term puppet play containing rehearsal and modeling has been demonstrated to help reduce anxiety in children about to undergo surgery (Cassell, 1965).

Whatever ultimate purposes may be served by play therapy, at the very least it is likely to help the adult therapist establish rapport with a youngster. An adult client might respond favorably to a

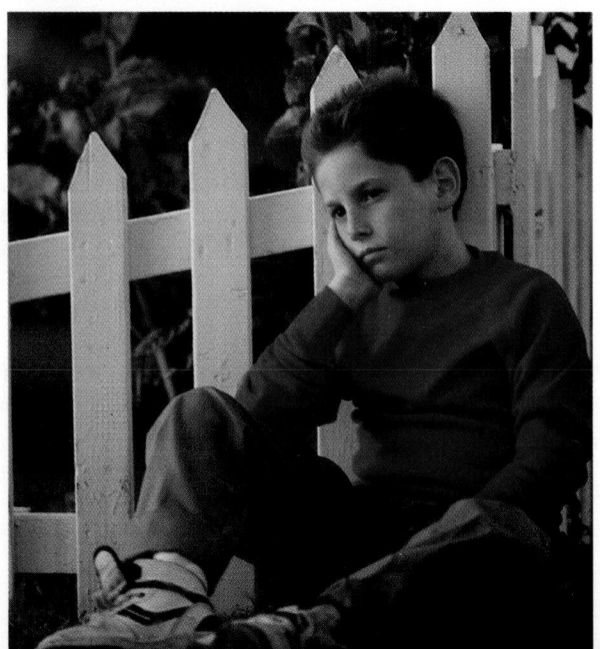

Although there has been some controversy about the existence of depression in children, recent data indicate that it does occur and that its symptoms are basically like those of adult depression.

of subjects as well as different sex ratios, varying patient samples (such as inpatient versus outpatient), and different diagnostic criteria (Cantwell, 1983).

Another problem complicating the diagnosis of depression in children are the high rates of comorbidity with other disorders. Several studies have estimated the overlap between depression and separation anxiety to be close to 50 percent (Kovacs et al., 1984; Puig-Antich & Rabinovich, 1986; Hershberg et al., 1982). Depression is also quite common

Because children are often less verbal than adults, play therapy was developed to help them better express their concerns as they play with a toy house and dolls representing their parents and siblings.

therapist who is empathic, kindly, and replete with professional degrees, but a young child is likely to be suspicious and regard "Dr. X" as an ally of his or her parents or teacher, with no real interest in the child. Therapists of varying persuasions, including cognitive and behavior therapists who would eschew the symbolic significance an analytic worker might see in the child's play, commonly use a playroom to establish a relationship with a young client and perhaps also to determine from what the child says and does with toys the youngster's perspective of the problem.

Because children usually live with their parents and siblings, and because their lives are so inextricably bound up with them, many therapists examine and attempt to alter patterns of interactions in families rather than see the troubled child or young adolescent alone. Family therapy (page 601), too, is practiced by therapists of all persuasions. Practitioners hold that the child's problem has been caused or is maintained by disturbed relationships within the family. For example, the father may have defaulted on his own responsibilities, forcing a male child to take a more adult role than he feels ready to assume. As we have pointed out many times, however, treatments that help alleviate a problem may in no way indicate its etiology. The fact that clarifying and altering disturbed family relationships relieves the disorders of children does not mean that the disturbed relationships themselves caused the problems in the first place. Many clinical reports and the intrinsic plausibility of family therapy suggest that future studies will back up claims of success made by enthusiasts.

in children with conduct disorders, and, conversely, many conduct-disordered children are also depressed (Chiles, Miller, & Cox, 1980; Puig-Antich, 1982). Indeed, comorbidity of a mood disorder with either a conduct or attention deficit disorder worsens the symptoms or behavioral problems of children on measures of social functioning in school and with peers, although this exacerbation does not show up on interview measures (Kelly, 1992).

Etiology of Depression

What causes a child to become depressed? Several theories of etiology have been suggested. As discussed in Chapter 9, evidence supports the role of a genetic factor in adult depression. Perhaps genetics are implicated in childhood depression as well. Studies of children have also focused on family relationships, hypothesizing that such factors play an important role in child psychopathology.

Puig-Antich and colleagues (Puig-Antich et al., 1985) interviewed mothers of three groups of children: depressed, normal, and a group with psychiatric diagnoses other than mood disorders. Several aspects of interpersonal functioning distinguished depressed children from the other groups: the mother–child relationship of depressed children was characterized by less communication, less warmth, more hostility, and less time spent in activities together; relationships between the fathers and the depressed children revealed more tension and hostility and less warmth; depressed children were less able to maintain a best friend and were more likely to be teased by their peers; and the sibling relationships of depressed children were especially difficult. Although these interpersonal problems were less pronounced after successful treatment with antidepressant medication (peer relationships, in particular, showed improvement), the previously depressed children still experienced interpersonal relationships that were significantly worse than those of normal children. The authors point out that it is not yet clear whether poor social bonds cause depression in children, whether depression produces persistent impairments in social relationships, or whether some third variable causes both depression and interpersonal difficulties.

Suicide is the third most common cause of death among young people in the United States, exceeded only by accidents and homicide. As with adults, it is conceivable that some of the deaths deemed accidental are actually suicides, a number of them subintentioned.[1] The finding that mothers are often completely unaware of their children's suicidal ideation and even of their attempts suggests the importance of parents talking openly with their children about suicidal thoughts (Velez & Cohen, 1988). Depression in young people heightens suicide risk, especially for those between the ages of fifteen and nineteen. But even at much younger ages children can become so despondent, so completely without hope of things becoming better, that they attempt to end their lives. However, as previously discussed (see page 248), suicide is not always linked to depression. Adolescents appear to commit suicide far less from depression than from personal conflicts and developmental crises, such as the breakup of a love affair (Achenbach, 1982; Cytryn & McKnew, 1979), arguments with parents, and problems at school (Hoberman & Garfinkel, 1988). Moreover, one study found that adolescents treated for a suicide attempt were three to six times more likely than controls to have had previous contact with the Department of Social Services because of child abuse or neglect charges (Deykin, Alpert, & McNamarra, 1985).

Treatment of Childhood Depression

Far less research has been done on therapy with depressed children and adolescents than with adults (Kaslow & Racusin, 1990). Nearly all the literature is composed of uncontrolled case reports, including some promising work with psychodynamic approaches (Boverman & French, 1979). Research with some measure of experimental control indicates that the use of antidepressant drugs has little support (Puig-Antich et al., 1987). Social-skills training shows promise in providing depressed youngsters the behavioral and verbal means to gain access to pleasant, reinforcing environments, like making friends and getting along with peers (Frame et al., 1982). Some comparative research on cognitive-behavioral interventions offers some limited evidence for its efficacy as compared with role-playing social skills (Stark et al., 1987). A case report by Braswell and Kendall (1988) illustrates a cognitive-behavioral therapy with a depressed fifteen-year-old girl.

When initially seen, Sharon was extremely dysphoric, experienced recurrent suicidal ideation, and displayed a number of vegetative signs of depression. A psychiatric consultation was obtained and she was placed on antidepressant medication. In individual therapy she was introduced to a cognitive-behavioral approach to depression, and she completed self-monitoring and mood ratings on a regular basis. She was able to understand how her mood was affected by her thoughts and behavior and was able to engage in behavioral planning to increase the occurrence of pleasure and mastery-oriented events. Sharon manifested extremely high standards for evaluating her performance in a number of areas, and it became clear that her parents also ascribed to these standards, so that family therapy sessions were held to encourage Sharon and her parents to reevaluate their standards.

Sharon had difficulty with the notion of changing her standards and noted that when she was not depressed she actually valued her pefectionism. At that point she resisted the therapy because she perceived it as trying to change something she valued in herself. With this in mind, we began to explore and identify those situations or domains in which her perfectionism worked for her and when and how it might work against her. She became increasingly comfortable with this perspective and decided she wanted to continue to set high standards regarding her performance in mathematical

[1]This loss of life is clearly tragic, but the fact that suicide is the third-ranked cause of death in young people should be placed in perspective. Young people and children are far less likely than adults to die from disease. Therefore their deaths are more likely to be from accidents and suicide. The *rates* of suicide in children and adolescents are actually quite low, nowhere near those of adults.

coursework (which was a clear area of strength), but she did not need to be so demanding of herself regarding art or physical education. (p. 194)

Eating Disorders

Anorexia Nervosa

Anorexia nervosa is a life-threatening disorder unaccounted for by any known physical disease. The term *anorexia* means severe loss of appetite, and *nervosa* indicates for emotional reasons. Interestingly, the word anorexia is a misnomer because many anorexics initially do not so much lose their appetites as fear gaining weight (Achenbach, 1982). They refuse to eat enough to maintain minimal weight, and have an intense fear of becoming obese. The self-starvation imposed by anorexics brings about physiological changes that are sometimes difficult to reverse; estimates vary, but approximately 5 percent die. Another 25 percent of anorexics continue in the unremitting course of their disorder at two-year follow-ups, and the remainder gain weight back as a result of treatment (Hsu, 1980).

An essential feature of anorexia is a distorted body image. Despite their protruding ribs and hipbones, their skull-like faces, their broomstick limbs, anorexics do not view themselves as being too thin. Rather, in frequent scrutiny of their figures in mirrors, they either continue to see themselves as too fat or feel that they have finally arrived at an attractive weight. Garner, Olmstead, and Polivy (1983) measured body dissatisfaction with a self-report questionnaire that contained items like "I think that my stomach is too big," "I like the shape of my buttocks," and "I think that my thighs are too large." In their study comparing normal men and women with anorexic and bulimic men and women, they found that normal women scored significantly higher in dissatisfaction than normal men but significantly lower than anorexics and bulimics. This is consistent with the fact that many more women than men suffer from eating disorders and that these problems are associated with, and perhaps caused by, uncommonly high levels of unhappiness with the shape of their bodies.

Indeed, a recent survey by Whitaker et al. (1990) found a prevalence rate of 0.3 percent for young women in grades nine through twelve and a virtual absence of anorexia in young men of the same age. Onset of the weight loss most commonly begins during early adolescence, shortly after the beginning of menstruation. Amenorrhea, failure to menstruate regularly, is a characteristic feature of anorexia nervosa, often starting before weight loss has become noticeable. Other physiological changes include dry, cracking skin, fine downy hair on the face and neck, brittle fingernails, yellowish discoloration of the skin, increased heart rate, constipation, reduced body temperature, and muscular weakness (Kaplan & Woodside, 1987). Anorexics may take laxatives and exercise extensively and frantically to lose weight. The manic energy expended in excessive physical activity is amazing, considering their emaciation.

Anorexia nervosa is defined by major weight loss and fear of becoming fat. Karen Carpenter, a popular singer, died from it.

Some anorexics are preoccupied with food, even when they are struggling not to ingest it. They become interested in its preparation, collecting cookbooks, trying new recipes, and planning and cooking elaborate meals of many courses and special dishes for others. Many anorexics do not admit to feeling any hunger, but others say they do feel hungry but force themselves not to eat. Anorexics in general deny having a problem that needs treatment. Often described as good girls, they are well-behaved, conscientious, quiet, and often perfectionists.

Etiology of Anorexia Nervosa

Theories of anorexia are varied and largely unsubstantiated. Some psychological explanations of the disorder have been based on Freud's notion that eating can be a substitute for sexual expression. Thus the anorexic's refusal to eat is thought to indicate fear of increasing sexual desires or perhaps of oral impregnation (Ross, 1977). Some view anorexia as a reflection of conflict between wanting to attain independence and selfhood within the family and a fear of growing up.

Learning theorists have suggested that anorexia may be a weight phobia (Crisp, 1967) or a striving to effect the image of of the beautiful slim woman so extensively modeled and emulated by our society (Bemis, 1978). In order to achieve the same figure as Barbie, the doll who represents the ideal body to many girls, the average American woman (who weighs 124 pounds) would have to increase her bust by twelve inches, reduce her waist by ten inches, and reach seven feet two inches in height (Moser, 1989)! Given such cultural standards of the ideal figure, it is not surprising that most American women are dissatisfied with their bodies (Harris, 1987). As shown in Figure 15.1, Fallon and Rozin (1985) found that women rate their ideal figure and the figure they think men find attractive as much thinner than they judge their own current figure. Men, in contrast, rate their current, ideal, and attractive figures as virtually the same.

Finally, a variety of biological explanations for anorexia have been offered. Abnormal functioning of the part of the hypothalamus known to control eating, sexual activity, and menstruation is perhaps the leading physiological theory; however, it is not yet known whether disturbance in hypothalamic functioning is a cause of anorexia, a result of the weight loss and caloric restriction, or a result of the emotional distress of the patient (Garfinkel & Garner, 1982).

Figure 15.1 Ratings by women (*top*) and men (*bottom*) of their own figures: ideal, attractive to the opposite sex, and current. Other attractive represents the figure rated by the opposite sex as most attractive. From "Use of the Danish Adoption Register for the Study of Obesity and Thinness" by A. Stunkard, T. Sorensen, and F. Schulsinger, in *The Genetics of Neurological and Psychiatric Disorders*, edited by S. Kety, 1980, p. 119. Copyright 1983 by Raven Press. Adapted by permission.

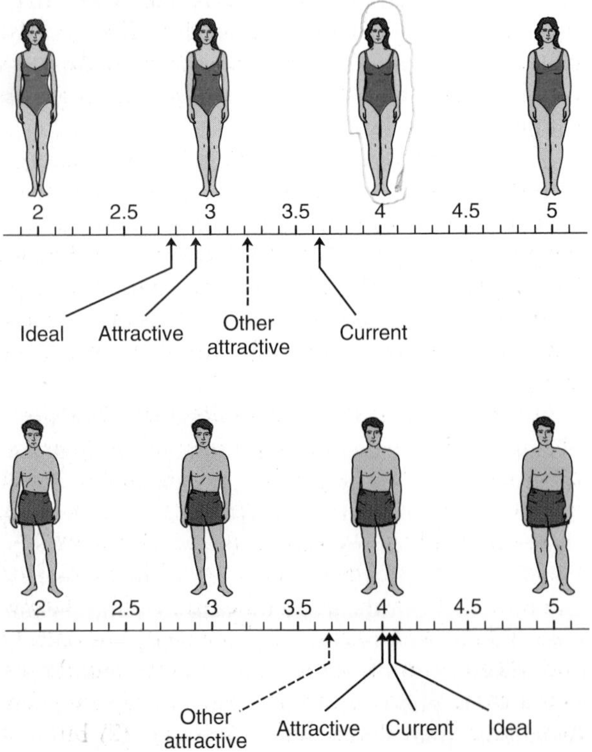

Treatment of Anorexia Nervosa

Therapy for anorexia is a two-tiered process. The immediate goal is to help the anorexic gain weight in order to avoid medical complications and the possibility of death. Hospitalization may be necessary to ensure that the patient ingests some food. The anorexic is often so weak and physiological functioning so disturbed that hospital treatment is imperative. Intravenous feeding provides necessary nourishment in life-threatening situations. Some success in producing immediate increases in body weight has been achieved by behavior therapy programs in which the hospitalized anorexic is isolated as much as possible and given mealtime company, then periods of access to a television set, radio, or stereo, walks with a student nurse, mail, and visitors as rewards for eating and gaining weight (Hsu, 1986). The second goal of treatment, long-term maintenance of gains in body weight, is not reliably achieved by medical, behavioral, or traditional psychodynamic interventions (Bemis, 1978).

One mode of treatment that may be able to produce long-term gains for anorexics is family therapy. Like most other treatments, family therapy has been insufficiently studied for its long-term effects. One report, however, suggests that as many as 86 percent of fifty anorexic daughters treated with their families were still functioning well when assessed at times ranging from three months to four years after treatment (Rosman, Minuchin, & Liebman, 1976). Salvador Minuchin and his colleagues, who represent but one of several schools of family therapy, have done considerable work on anorexia nervosa. The treatment they have developed is called the "family lunch session."

Before the specific treatment is described, a basic assumption in Minuchin's family treatment has to be made clear. He believes that sick family members, especially children, serve to deflect attention away from underlying conflict in family relationships. The illness is the family psychopathology become manifest, so to speak. In these families, members are both rigid and deeply enmeshed in one another's lives; they overprotect their children and do not acknowledge conflicts. Thus the sickness acts to reduce friction surrounding these basic family disturbances. By providing an alternative focus of attention, the illness lessens the tension among family members. Minuchin believes that troubled families therefore act in a way that keeps the sick family member in the patient role (Minuchin et al., 1975).

A review of studies on the family interactions of anorexia nervosa patients provides some support for Minuchin's theory. For example, families of anorexics were found to be more enmeshed, as evidenced by stronger coalitions between each parent and the anorexic child than between the parents as marital partners. Videotaped role-plays among anorexic families revealed a lack of conflict resolution, a focus on the daughter, and parents rarely talking directly to one another (Kog & Vandereycken, 1985).

To treat the disorder, Minuchin attempts to redefine it as interpersonal rather than individual and to bring the family conflict to the fore. Thus, it is theorized, the symptomatic family member is freed from having to maintain his or her problem, for it no longer deflects attention from the dysfunctional family.

Families of anorexics are seen by the therapist during mealtime, since the conflicts related to anorexia are believed to be most evident then. There are three major goals for these lunch sessions: (1) changing the patient role of the anorexic; (2) redefining the eating problem as an interpersonal one; and (3) preventing the parents from using their child's anorexia as a means of avoiding conflict. One strategy is to instruct each parent to try individually to force the child to eat. The other parent may leave the room. The individual efforts are expected to fail. But through this failure and the frustration of each, the mother and father may now work *together* to persuade the child to eat. Thus, rather than being a focus of conflict, the child's eating will produce cooperation and increase parental effectiveness in dealing with the child (Rosman, Minuchin, & Liebman, 1975). Given the only moderate successes of other treatments devised for anorexics, family therapy appears promising.

Bulimia Nervosa

For some time **bulimia nervosa** was regarded as an occasional accompaniment to anorexia, but it is recognized in DSM-IV as an eating disorder separate from anorexia nervosa. *Bulimia* is from the Greek words, *bous,* meaning ox, and *limos,* meaning "hunger." Often referred to as the binge–purge syndrome, it consists of episodes of gross overeating followed by induced vomiting or overdoses of laxatives to rid the body of the enormous amount of food just ingested. Unlike the anorexic, the bulimic does not necessarily have abnormally low weight, but patients with both disorders do share an abnormal concern with body size, having a morbid fear of becoming fat. Individuals in whom aspects of both disorders are found are sometimes referred to as *bulimarexics.*

The foods bulimics choose have a texture that allows them to be eaten rapidly. They gobble them down, with little chewing, in a short span of time, and then may go in search of more food. A typical binge might consist of three packages of cookies, a loaf of bread, ten pieces of fried chicken, two pounds of candy, and two gallons of milk. Bulimics are painfully aware that their uncontrollable eating pattern is abnormal. They often feel disgust, helplessness, and panic during a binge. The purge is a source of relief for most victims. In fact, Rosen and Leitenberg (1985) assert that bulimics purge to reduce the anxiety caused by a binge. Their vomiting serves as an escape-response that frees them from normal inhibitions against overeating. Thus, binges often become more extreme after the individual has discovered the use of purging to control the previous anxiety about overeating.

Estimates of the prevalence of bulimia nervosa vary depending on the type of measures used (questionnaires vs. interviews) and definitions of the binge and purge behaviors (Fairburn & Beglin, 1990). Probably about 1 to 2 percent of college women meet DSM criteria for the disorder; very few studies have been conducted other than on college campuses.

In her review of the bulimia literature, Schleiser-Stropp (1984) provided a portrait of the typical binge eater. She is likely to be a white woman in her mid-twenties who began overeating at about age eighteen and began purging, usually by vomiting, about a year later. She is typically within the normal weight range for her age and height, and her family history has an unusually high incidence of obesity and alcoholism. Several other points should be noted from Schlesier-Stropp's review: (1) very few men have been diagnosed as bulimic; (2) bulimia

15.6 • Depression and the Eating Disorders

It has long been noticed that both anorexics and bulimics are often depressed. In a sample of 105 hospitalized anorexics, Ecker and his colleagues (1982) found high levels of depression, especially in those with the most severe eating difficulties.

For some women, the onset of depression precedes symptoms of an eating disorder (Piran et al., 1985), and depressed and nondepressed anorexics may show biochemical differences (Biederman et al., 1984). Rather than trying to prove either that the depression is always the *result* of the eating disorder or that anorexia and bulimia are caused by mood disturbances, Swift and colleagues suggested a multidimensional model, where biological, psychological, familial, and sociocultural factors interact reciprocally (Swift, Andrews, & Barklage, 1986).

Let us assume that depression is indeed connected to anorexia and bulimia. Which is the cause and which the effect? If an anorexic loses 25 percent of body weight, the drop in body temperature and the starvation may cause biochemical changes that bring on depression. Similar harmful somatic changes can take place with bulimia. From a psychological point of view, the loss of control, guilt, and shame that accompany these eating disorders could easily eventuate in a clinical depression. On the other hand, depression could conceivably cause anorexia. Bruch (1980), a psychoanalytic theorist, suggests that a young woman may compensate for her depressed feelings by seeking to be thin and desirable; finding that as she loses weight her depression does not lift, she seeks to lose still more. Bruch (1981) also suggests that anorexia might be regarded as an adolescent female manifestation of depression. Looking to her appearance as both the cause and potential cure of her depression, the young woman loses more and more weight. The strong association between eating disorders and depression has led some researchers to view them as a variant of depression. A review of this literature by Hinz and Williamson (1987), however, suggests that depression and eating disorders should be viewed as two separate, but often cooccurring, disorders.

is a problem of adolescence and early adulthood, with very, very few cases beginning after age thirty; (3) overeating tends to precede purging by as much as three years; (4) the frequency of binge–purge cycles varies considerably, from once a day to once a week or so or as often as thirty times a week.

Bulimics also frequently suffer periods of depression (see Focus Box 15.6) and anxiety as well as guilt over their inability to control their binges. Their costly binge–purge behavior can take up so many of their hours that social activities are restricted and financial resources squandered. In a study of 275 bulimics, Mitchell et al. (1985) found that 70 percent experienced difficulties with intimate or interpersonal relationships, 53 percent reported family problems, and 50 percent had work impairment. Many bulimics are suicidal as well.

There are also physiological consequences, especially if the purging is done by vomiting. Sore throats, swollen salivary glands, and destruction of tooth enamel by the acidic vomitus have been reported in a significant number of bulimics: intestinal damage, nutritional deficiencies, and dehydration can also result. Menstrual irregularities, found frequently among female anorexics, are less severe among female bulimics (Ely, 1983; Schlesier-Stropp, 1984). Decreased levels of potassium and electrolyte abnormalities can be life-threatening; bulimics have been known to experience heart failure leading to sudden death (Kaplan & Woodside, 1987).

Treatment of Bulimia

When untreated, bulimia is unlikely to go away. Recent controlled research suggests the value of cognitive behavior therapy to alter maladaptive beliefs about body image and weight (Fairburn et al., 1986). A review by Garner, Fairburn, and Davis (1987) indicated that the median reduction in frequency of binging is 79 percent with such interventions, with improvement continuing after termination of therapy. Wilson et al. (1986) found that the benefits of cognitive behavior therapy were markedly enhanced by the addition of response prevention, that is, exposing the bulimic to forbidden foods and preventing him or her from vomiting after eating them. Some success has been achieved as well with antidepressant drugs (Hughes, Wells, Cunningham, & Ilstrup, 1986; Pope & Hudson, 1984).

SUMMARY

DSM-III greatly expanded the range of diagnoses applicable to children, and DSM-IV reflects the continued burgeoning of interest in childhood disorders.

Attention-deficit disorders and conduct problems are disorders of undercontrolled behavior. Genetic studies and evidence of altered neurological functioning point to a biological cause in attention-deficit disorders, many of which are associated with hyperactivity. The role of parents in influencing the course of the disorder is also supported by some data. Stimulant drugs and rewards for staying focused on a task help to calm such children. Conduct disorders include aggression, lying, theft, vandalism, and other acts that violate social norms. A genetic predisposition, marital discord of parents, inadequate teaching of moral awareness, modeling and direct reinforcement of deviant behavior, and living in city slums are considered etiological factors. Teaching parents to reinforce prosocial behavior and diverting delinquents from the court system have proved promising interventions.

School phobia, social withdrawal, and depression are disorders of overcontrolled behavior. School phobia, a fear and refusal to go to school, is usually treated by gradual exposure to the feared situation, sometimes coupled with rewards for attending school. Children who withdraw socially are assumed to do so because of anxiety and poor social skills. Depression is surprisingly common in both children and adolescents. Play therapy and family therapy are often applied to disorders of overcontrolled behavior. Behavioral pediatrics help children adjust to serious illness.

The final disorders discussed are two enormously irregular eating patterns that usually develop in adolescence. In anorexia nervosa the individual does not eat enough to maintain a healthy weight and, if not stopped, starves to death. It is much more common in adolescent women than in men. None of the several theories of anorexia—fear of becoming sexually mature, weight phobia, striving for the slim image so esteemed by our society, conflict between wanting selfhood within the family and a fear of growing up, and biological dysfunctions—has clear support. Treatment of the disorder is difficult, although family therapy appears promising. In bulimia, sometimes found in anorexics but also considered a separate disorder, the individual indulges in binges of eating and then induces vomiting or takes a laxative to rid the body of the food. Bulimics suffer serious health consequences from their vomiting and forced bowel movements, such as tooth decay and damage to the intestines. In both eating disorders, depression may play a role, not just as an understandable consequence but as a cause as well.

KEY TERMS

undercontrolled [behavior]
overcontrolled [behavior]
attention-deficit hyperactivity disorder (ADHD)
conduct disorders
separation anxiety disorder
enuresis
school phobia
behavioral pediatrics
elective mutism
play therapy
family therapy
anorexia nervosa
bulimia nervosa

c h a p t e r   s i x t e e n

Learning Disabilities, Mental Retardation, and Autistic Disorder

Recently, a dyslexic young man was enrolled in one of our undergraduate courses. The student's oral comments in class were exemplary, but his handwriting and spelling were sometimes indecipherable. After the instructor had noted these problems on the student's midterm examination, the undergraduate explained that he was dyslexic and that it took him longer to complete the weekly reading assignments and to write papers and exams. The instructor thus accorded him additional time for preparing written work. The student was obviously of superior intelligence and highly motivated to excel. Excel he did, earning an A in the seminar and upon graduation being admitted to a leading law school.

In the previous chapter we examined several emotional and behavioral disorders of childhood. This chapter focuses on developmental disorders: learning disabilities, mental retardation, and autistic disorder, which are characterized predominantly by a disturbance in the acquisition of cognitive, language, motor, or social skills. The course of these disorders tends to be chronic, usually persisting into adulthood. Learning disabilities signify inadequate development in a specific area of academic, language, speech, or motor skills, which is not due to mental retardation, autism, a demonstrable physical or neurological disorder,[1] or deficient educational opportunities. Children with these disorders are usually of average or above average intelligence, but have difficulty learning some specific skill (e.g., arithmetic or reading); thus their progress in school is impeded.

In contrast, mental retardation and autism interfere markedly with the entire developmental process, and many of the children affected are unlikely to become well-functioning adults. Not only are these disorders lifelong but, if severe, they disrupt all of a life. Mentally retarded and autistic children are similar in a number of respects. The majority of autistic children score significantly below average on intelligence tests, and many children with mental retardation make ritualistic hand movements, rock their bodies, and injure themselves, actions that are even more frequent in those with autism. Educational interventions can also be similar for children with the two disorders. Both autism and the moderate, severe, and profound forms of mental retardation become evident in infancy or in very early childhood. Retardation and autism are, however, different problems of development.

[1]Of course, physical bases for one or more learning disabilities may be uncovered by future research; see later discussion.

Learning Disabilities

DSM-IV does not use the term learning disabilities. We are using it to group together three disorders that appear in DSM-IV: learning disorders, communication disorders, and motor skills disorder. In each of these a child fails to develop to the degree expected by his or her intellectual level in a specific academic or language or motor skill area. Learning disabilities are usually identified and treated within the school system rather than through mental health clinics. The disorders are from two to four times more common in males than in females. Though learning-disabled individuals cope with their problems, it should come as no surprise that their academic and social development is affected, sometimes quite seriously.

DSM-IV divides Learning Disorders into three categories: reading disorder, mathematics disorder, and disorder of written expression. None of these diagnoses is appropriate if the disability can be accounted for by a sensory deficit like visual or auditory problems.

Learning Disorders

Children with **reading disorder,** better known as **dyslexia,** have significant difficulty with word recognition, reading comprehension, and, typically, with written spelling as well. When reading orally, they omit, add, or distort the pronunciation of words to an unusual extent for their age. In adulthood, problems with fluent oral reading, comprehension, and written spelling persist (Bruck, 1987). This disorder, present in 2 to 8 percent of school-age children, does not preclude great achievements. Like the college student described at the opening of this chapter, it is widely known that Nelson Rockefeller, former governor of New York and former vice president of the United States, suffered from dyslexia.

In **mathematics disorder,** the child may have difficulty with linguistic skills, such as coding written problems into mathematical symbols, perceptual skills, such as recognizing numerical symbols, attention skills, such as remembering to add in "carried" numbers, and mathematical skills, such as counting objects or following sequences of mathematical steps. Poor achievement in mathematics is at least as common as poor achievement in reading and spelling, and often the three overlap (Badian, 1983; Rourke & Finlayson, 1978).

Disorder of written expression describes an impairment in the ability to compose the written word (including spelling errors, grammatical or punctuation errors, or poor paragraph organization) that is serious enough to interfere significantly with academic achievement or daily activities requiring such writing skills. Few systematic data have yet been collected on the prevalence of this disorder.

Communication Disorders

In **receptive language disorder,** the child has trouble understanding spoken language. In **expressive language disorder,** the child has difficulty expressing himself or herself in speech. A child with the receptive form may be so deficient in comprehending what is being said that he or she appears to be deaf. A youngster with the expressive form of the disorder may seem eager to communicate but have inordinate difficulty finding the right words. By age four, the child speaks only in short phrases. Old words are forgotten when new ones are learned, and the use of grammatical structures is considerably below age level.

Unlike children who have trouble understanding or finding words, youngsters with **phonological disorder** both comprehend and are able to use a substantial vocabulary, but their words sound like baby talk. *Blue* comes out *bu,* and *rabbit* sounds like *wabbit.* They have not learned articulation of the later acquired speech sounds, such as *r, sh, th, f, z, l,* and *ch.* With speech therapy, complete recovery occurs in almost all cases, and milder cases may recover spontaneously by age eight.

A speech therapist works with a child with phonological disorder by having him practice the sounds he finds difficult.

Motor Skills Disorder

In **motor skills disorder,** also referred to as developmental coordination disorder, children show marked impairment in the development of motor coordination that is not explainable by mental retardation or a known physical disorder, such as cerebral palsy. The young child may have difficulty tying shoelaces and buttoning shirts and, when older, with model building, playing ball, and printing or handwriting. The diagnosis is made only if the impairment interferes significantly with academic achievement or with the activities of daily living.

Etiology of Learning Disabilities

Both biological and psychological factors are possible causes of the several learning disabilities. Answers are far from in. Twin studies several years ago confirmed the heritability of learning disabilities (Mathaney, Dolan, & Wilson, 1976), and more recent research has begun to pinpoint which specific learning problems are inherited and which may have psychological or other biological bases. Evidence reviewed by Pennington and Smith (1988) suggests that, whereas simple word reading and spelling skills are genetically influenced, reading comprehension seems not to be.

Some evidence suggests that neurological problems may be responsible for learning disabilities. Autopsies of the brains of eight individuals with childhood dyslexia revealed microscopic abnormalities in the location, number, and organization of neurons. The anomalies were predominantly localized in the left hemispheric language regions (Galaburda, 1989). The source of these developmental defects remains unknown.

In the past, psychological theories have focused on visual perceptual deficits as the basis for dyslexia. One popular hypothesis suggested that children with reading problems *perceive* letters in reverse order or mirror image, mistaking, for example, a *d* for a *b.* However, no relationship has been found between letter confusions at age five or six and subsequent reading ability (Calfee, Fisk, & Piontkowski, 1985), and one does not need to be able to *see* to have reading problems—blind people may have difficulty learning to read Braille (McGuiness, 1981). Recent research points to one or more problems in language processing that might underlie dyslexia. These include perception of speech and the analysis of the sounds of spoken language and their relation to printed words (Mann & Brady, 1988). A series of longitudinal studies suggests that some early language problems can predict later dyslexia: difficulties recognizing rhyme and alliteration at age four (Bradley & Bryant, 1985), problems in rapidly naming familiar objects at age five (Scarborough, 1990; Wolf, Bally, & Morris, 1986), and delays in learning syntactic rules at age two and a half (Scarborough, 1990).

McGuiness (1985) noted that any theory of learning disabilities must explain the clear sex difference in the disorders. It may be that structural or hormonal differences between male and female brains account for some of the difference in learning between the sexes. For example, damage to the left hemisphere causes more deficits in language in males than in females; females have a greater representation of language in the right hemisphere than do males (Kimura, 1983; Mateer, Polen, & Ojemann, 1982). This finding suggests that boys are more vulnerable to language and reading disabilities.

Another promising hypothesis concerns differences between boys and girls in sensorimotor integration (McGuiness, 1985). Boys are said to be involved in more gross motor activities as young children. Gross motor control skills become integrated primarily with sensory input to the *visual* system and the position of limbs in space, leading to efficiency in visuomotor integration (which males are better at than females). In contrast, it is hypothesized that girls are geared more toward fine motor control, which includes speech structures, that becomes integrated primarily with the *auditory* system, leading to girls' superior language skills.

Intervention with Learning Disabilities

One cannot underestimate the anxiety of parents whose otherwise normal child lags behind in reading or cannot speak effectively and normally for his or her age. Professional attempts to remedy learning disabilities have been subject to somatic, educational, and psychological fads—from the use of stimulants and tranquilizers to training the child in motor activities believed to have been inadequately mastered at a younger age in hopes of reorganizing neuronal connections in the brain.

Currently, several methods are being used to treat learning disabilities. Linguistic approaches, which are primarily used in cases of reading and writing difficulties, focus on instruction in listening, speaking, reading, and writing skills in a logical sequential and multisensory manner (Lyon & Moats, 1988). In young children, readiness skills, such as letter discrimination, phonetic analysis, and learning letter–sound correspondences, may need to be taught before explicit instruction in reading is attempted. Dyslexic individuals often can succeed in college with the aid of instructional supports, such as tape-recorded lectures, tutors, writing editors, and untimed tests (Bruck, 1987).

In recent years researchers have focused on the possibility that some learning-disabled children lack certain teachable skills rather than an ability to learn and plan (Braswell & Kendall, 1988). The implication of this assumption is important, for it suggests that one can help such children learn better if adaptive cognitive strategies can be provided. For example, Harris (1986) videotaped children putting together a puzzle of a superhero (Shazam) and observed their private speech during the task. Compared with normally achieving children, the self-talk of the learning-disabled youngsters was marked by irrelevant comments, such as word play ("a dogie, dogie, dogie"), descriptions of irrelevant stimuli ("that's a funny noise"), noisemaking ("criminy," "Pheweee"), and negative evaluations of their performance or the task ("This is a stupid puzzle"; "I can't do this"). In contrast, the control children were more likely to employ useful self-talk to guide themselves through the task. Explicitly teaching the children to use self-talk constructively helped both the controls and the learning-disabled children to persist at the task for longer periods.

For all children, but especially those with learning disabilities, a success-oriented approach is essential. Most learning-disabled children have probably experienced a great deal of frustration and failure that erode their motivation and confidence. Behavioral programs that reward small steps can be helpful in increasing the child's motivation, focusing attention on the learning task, and reducing behavioral problems caused by frustration.

Mental Retardation

Kevin is a twenty-three-year-old man who was diagnosed in childhood as having moderate to severe mental retardation. He has been in educational programs since he was six years of age. At present he feeds and dresses himself but needs help in selecting clothing to wear and must be "checked" to ensure that everything is appropriate before going out. He finds his way around his community without getting lost, but he cannot take buses alone. He can go on errands to the grocery store about two blocks from his home, but he takes a note for the storekeeper and does not know whether he has been given the correct change. He is reliable in helping with simple household chores, such as making beds, setting the table, running the vacuum cleaner, and helping with simple tasks in the kitchen. His scores on the Wechsler Adult Intelligence Scale are very much below normal. The psychologist reported that Kevin did not respond on some verbal tasks, which had to be marked "Fail"; she did not know, however, whether he could have responded correctly were his speech better. Kevin's speech is indeed barely understandable, with many articulation problems, but he does respond to directions and requests. He functions adequately in a sheltered workshop on simple tasks, such as stuffing bags, simple assembly, and attaching stickers in correct places. He understands that he is paid for work and talks about using the money he makes, but he must be supervised in selecting purchases. (Adapted from Grossman, 1983, pp. 213–214).

The Concept of Mental Retardation

In DSM-IV mental retardation is defined as significantly subaverage intellectual functioning along with deficits in adaptive behavior and occurring prior to age 18. We will examine these several criteria.

Intelligence Test Scores as a Criterion

The first component of the definition requires a judgment of intelligence. Scores on most IQ tests are standardized in such a way that 100 is the mean and 15 or 16 is the standard deviation (a measure of how scores are dispersed both above and below the average). This means that approximately two-thirds of the population receive scores between 85 and 115. Those with a score below 70 are two standard deviations below the mean of the population and are considered to have "significant subaverage general intellectual functioning." Approximately 2.5 percent of the population fall into this category.

The use of standardized IQ tests to assess mental retardation has been criticized because of the lack of normative data for children who are not from white middle-class backgrounds and for children with IQs below 70. More recently, IQ tests have been revised with these criticisms in mind. The third edition of the Wechsler Intelligence Scale for Children (1991), for example, used the 1988 census data to obtain a stratified sample of varied ethnicity, socioeconomic status, and region of the country. In addition, the test developers validated the scale on a number of special groups, including children with mental retardation, learning disabilities, hearing impairments, and attention-deficit hyperactivity disorder. See Focus Box 16.1 for a discussion of how intelligence in infants might be measured.

Adaptive Functioning as a Criterion

Adaptive functioning refers to childhood skills such as caring for the self; acquiring concepts of time and money; being able to use tools, to shop, and to travel by public transportation; and becoming socially responsive and self-directive. An adolescent is expected to be able to apply academic skills, reasoning, and judgment to daily living and to participate in group activities. The adult, of course, is expected to be self-supporting and to assume social responsibilities.

Several tests have been constructed to assess adaptive behavior; the best known are the American Association of Mental Deficiency Adaptive Behavior Scale (ABS) (Nihira et al., 1974) and the Vineland Adaptive Behavior Scales (Sparrow, Balla, & Cicchetti, 1984; Table 16.1).

Table 16.1 • Sample items from the Vineland Adaptive Behavior Scales

Age Level	*Adaptive Ability*
2 years	Says at least fifty recognizable words.
	Removes front-opening coat, sweater, or shirt without assistance.
5 years	Tells popular story, fairy tale, lengthy joke, or plot of television program.
	Ties shoelaces into a bow without assistance.
8 years	Keeps secrets or confidences for more than one day.
	Orders own meal in a restaurant.
11 years	Uses the telephone for all kinds of calls without assistance.
	Watches television or listens to radio for information about a particular area of interest.
16 years	Looks after own health.
	Responds to hints or indirect cues in conversation.

Source: From Sparrow, Balla, & Cicchetti, 1984.

16.1 • Measuring Infant Intelligence

For the past fifty years, psychologists have been searching for a way to predict later intelligence from the performance of infants. Most such attempts have involved measuring sensory and motor functioning, such as hand–eye coordination, response to sound, and social responsiveness during the first year of life (Brooks & Weinraub, 1976). Although these measures are useful for learning about normal development and cross-cultural differences in infancy, they have proved to be poor predictors of later intellectual functioning as well as ineffective measures of the efficacy of intervention or enrichment programs.

Fagan and Singer (1983) made strides in the development of a new type of measure that holds promise for tapping the intelligence of infants. Their work explored the *visual recognition memory* of infants, that is, the child's ability to recognize a familiar stimulus. Capitalizing on the infant's predilection to attend more to novel stimuli than to familiar objects, Fagan and Singer determined whether an infant recognized a previously presented object. They discovered that infants' ability to remember and recognize visual stimuli was far better at predicting intelligence measured at age seven than were the sensorimotor measures. In addition, groups of infants expected to differ in later intelligence (such as Down syndrome and premature babies versus normal infants) were found to differ in visual recognition memory.

In addition to contributing to our understanding of the nature of intelligence at different ages, Fagan and Singer's work may result in a test that can be used to screen infants suspected to be at risk for a slower rate of development, to determine the effects of early intervention programs, and to measure cognitive functioning in individuals for whom verbal tests are inappropriate, such as those who have a severe mental disability.

Although impairments in adaptive functioning have long been included in the definition of mental retardation, only recently have the tests been adequately standardized with firmly established norms. One problem with many assessments of adaptive behavior, however, is that they fail to consider the environment to which the person must adapt. A person who lives in a small rural community where everyone is acquainted may not need skills as complex as those needed by someone who lives in New York City. Youngsters who are quite competent working at farm chores, walking to school, and shopping at the local general store may, when transported to a city, be considered deficient in adaptive behavior if they are not able to ride the subway to school or buy groceries at a store where a foreign language is spoken. By the same token, city children may find themselves at a loss with some of the activities expected of youngsters living on a farm! An effective and valid assessment of adaptive behavior should therefore consider the interaction between the child and the surroundings in which he or she must function.

Another problem with assessing adaptive behavior is that the distinction between it and intelligence is sometimes blurred. Charlesworth (1976), an ethological psychologist who studies intelligence from an evolutionary perspective, believes that the ability to adapt to the environment is the hallmark of intelligence. According to this view, adaptive behavior scores are a more valid measure of intelligence than scores on IQ tests, which require more abstract thinking. Critics of the ethological perspective, however, point out that the cockroach has been best able to adapt to the environment, as evidenced by its length of time on earth, longer than that of any other creature. Not many people would be willing to claim that the cockroach is more intelligent than human beings.

Time of Onset as a Criterion

A final definitional criterion mandates that mental retardation be manifest before adulthood, that is, before age eighteen. This rules out classifying as mental retardation any deficits in intelligence and adaptive behavior from traumatic accidents or illnesses occurring later in life. For the majority of children with more severe impairments, diagnosis can usually be made during infancy, or sometimes, through amniocentesis (see page 468), even before the child is born. The majority of children considered mentally retarded, however, are not identified as such until they enter school. These children have no obvious physiological, neurological, or physical manifestations, and thus their problems become apparent only when they are not able to keep up with their peers in school. In fact, the increased prevalence of mild mental retardation in school-age children has led some researchers to consider it a school-specific phenomenon; once these mildly retarded children leave school and become absorbed into the community and work world, their mental retardation may become less evident once again.

Classification of Mental Retardation

Four levels of mental retardation are recognized by DSM-IV, each of them a specific subaverage range on the far left of the normal distribution curve of measured intelligence. As noted earlier, the IQ ranges given are not the sole basis of diagnosis, for deficiencies in adaptive behavior are also a criterion of mental retardation. Some persons falling in the mildly retarded range based on IQ may have no deficits in adaptive behavior and thus would not be considered mentally retarded. The American Association on Mental Deficiency suggests that the IQ criterion be applied only after deficits in adaptive behavior have been identified. The following is a summary of how individuals at each level of mental retardation are described by Robinson and Robinson (1976).

In addition to low intelligence, the diagnosis of mental retardation requires the presence of deficits in adaptive behavior, a set of skills including self-care.

Mild Mental Retardation (50–55 to 70 IQ) About 85 percent of all those who have IQs less than 70 are classified as having **mild mental retardation**. They are not always distinguishable from normal youngsters until they enter school. By their late teens they can usually learn academic skills at about a sixth-grade level. As adults they are likely to be able to maintain themselves in unskilled jobs or in sheltered workshops, although they may need help with social and financial problems. Further, they may marry and have children of their own. Only about one percent are ever institutionalized, usually in adolescence for behavior problems. Most of the mildly retarded show no signs of brain pathology and are members of families whose formal education, psychometric (or measured) intelligence, and socioeconomic levels are low.

Moderate Mental Retardation (35–40 to 50–55 IQ) About 10 percent of those with IQs less than 70 are classified as having **moderate mental retardation**. Brain damage and other pathologies are frequent. The moderately retarded may have physical defects and neurological dysfunctions that hinder fine motor skills, such as grasping and coloring within lines, and gross motor skills, such as running and climbing. During childhood these individuals are eligible for special classes that emphasize the development of self-care skills rather than academic achievement. The moderately retarded are unlikely to progress beyond the second-grade level in academic subjects and can manage this learning only in later childhood or as adults. They may, however, learn to travel alone in a familiar locality. Many are institutionalized. Although most can do useful work, few hold jobs except in sheltered workshops or in family businesses. Most live dependently within the family or in supervised group homes. Few have friends of their own, but they may be left alone without supervision for several hours at a time. Their retardation is likely to be identified in infancy or early childhood, for they have poor sensorimotor coordination and are slow to develop verbal and social skills. In contrast with mildly retarded children, moderate retardates and those more seriously retarded are found in all socioeconomic groups.

Severe Mental Retardation (20–25 to 35–40 IQ) Of those with IQs less than 70, about 3 to 4 percent come under the category of **severe mental retarda-**

tion. They commonly have congenital physical abnormalities and limited sensorimotor control. Genetic disorders and environmental insults, such as severe oxygen deprivation at birth, account for most of this degree of retardation. Most are institutionalized and require constant aid and supervision. For children in this group to be able to speak and take care of their own basic needs requires prolonged training; the self-care training that is provided in the special classes within the school system is usually inadequate except for the upper portion of this group. As adults the severely retarded may be friendly but can usually communicate only briefly on a very concrete level. They engage in very little independent activity and are often lethargic, for their severe brain damage leaves them relatively passive and the circumstances of their lives allow them little stimulation. They may be able to perform very simple work under close supervision.

Profound Mental Retardation (below 20–25 IQ) One to two percent of the retarded are classified as having **profound mental retardation**, requiring total supervision and often nursing care all their lives. Intensive training may improve motor development, self-care, and communication skills. Many have severe physical deformities as well as neurological damage and cannot get around on their own. The profoundly mentally retarded have a very high mortality rate during childhood.

Classification and Educability

Educational psychologists have developed an education classification system that parallels DSM-IV and aids in the instructional programming of those with mental retardation.

The labels *educable* and *trainable* are sometimes substituted for *mild* and *moderate* mental retardation, respectively. The present trend, however, is away from educational placement based on the student's degree of mental retardation and toward an individualized placement based on the person's strengths, weaknesses, and the amount of instruction needed. For example, in New York State a student who needs considerable one-on-one instruction because of deficient intellectual functioning may be placed in the same classroom with a child who needs intensive instruction because of emotional problems or physical disabilities. Thus students are identified by the classroom environment that they are judged to need. This approach can lessen the stigmatizing effects of being considered retarded and may also encourage a focus on what can be done to improve the student's learning rather than just settling on how to label the child.

Nature of Mental Retardation

Figure 16.1 presents a visual scheme to illustrate the nature and etiology of mental retardation. We will refer to this figure several times in the chapter.

Deficiencies in Adaptive Skills

As pictured in the outer ring of Figure 16.1, a retarded person is generally limited at least to some extent in six skills needed for daily living—communication, social skills, academic skills, sensorimotor skills, self-help skills, and vocational skills. A discussion of these adaptive skills provides a means of comparing degrees of mental retardation and the assistance that these children need.

Communication Although most children develop spontaneously the ability to speak and communicate, children with mental retardation may need help. Those with mild disabilities may require only minimal support to achieve effective communication, such as being assigned to a speech class. Children with more severe disabilities, however, may need years of intensive language training in order to express effectively their basic needs and feelings.

Figure 16.1 The nature and causes of mental retardation and the adaptive skills and general cognitive abilities that retarded people lack.

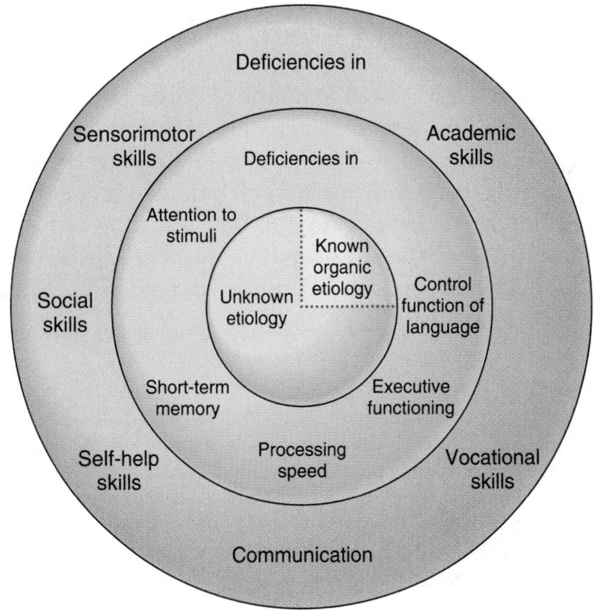

Social Skills It is not uncommon for children who are mildly retarded to have difficulty making and keeping friends. The more seriously retarded children show little awareness of social conventions. For example, many moderately and severely retarded youngsters seem overly friendly, wanting to be held and hugged by people whom they have just met. Children who are profoundly retarded may appear to be unaware of those who approach them.

Even children who are profoundly retarded, however, are capable of some social behavior. A child with multiple physical disabilities may be unable to talk or to reach out to someone but will smile at a favorite person. Lack of expressive social behavior does not mean that the person is not responding to social events. The individual may be experiencing more emotion than he or she is able to express.

Academic Skills Mastering reading, writing, and mathematics poses difficult problems for children with even mild mental disabilities. Still, many can learn enough arithmetic to shop effectively, to balance checkbooks, and to budget money. They may also competently read recipes, how-to-manuals, or just-for-fun books. Few teachers attempt to teach these skills, in their usual sense, to children with more severe disabilities. But many of these children have learned, with adequate instruction, functional academics, for example, reading signs and labels frequently found on their daily route or using a calculator at a store.

Sensorimotor Skills The degree of sensorimotor impairment is not consistently related to the degree of mental retardation. To be sure, many severely and profoundly retarded children have serious motor and sensory impairments. Children may also have physical disabilities but little or no mental impairment. Unfortunately, many children with physical disabilities, such as cerebral palsy[2] or hearing loss, may appear to be mentally retarded and subsequently be given an inappropriate educational curriculum. As clinicians become more aware of these problems and as assessment procedures become more sophisticated, fewer diagnostic errors are being made.

[2]Some people with cerebral palsy are very likely to be underestimated. Difficulties in walking and speaking, problems in using hands in a smooth, coordinated fashion, uncontrollable facial grimaces—these are frequently interpreted by others as signs of defective intelligence. Although the majority of those with cerebral palsy do have IQs below average, many achieve uncommonly high levels of distinction that require superior intellectual functioning.

Self-Help Skills Self-help skills are exercised in the routine activities of daily living—bathing, dressing, eating, using a telephone. Many children with mild and moderate retardation have all these skills. Children with profound retardation often require extensive, arduous training and supervision in order to perform these basic tasks. But many of these children also have physical disabilities; a movement that is simple for a nondisabled person may pose a real challenge for someone with a limited range of motion.

Vocational Skills One goal of education is to prepare children for a vocation. By the time most youngsters with mild mental retardation have finished school, they have acquired most of the skills needed to support themselves with a job in a competitive marketplace. In fact, although mild disabilities may be readily apparent in an academic setting, they may not be apparent in the world of work. Children with moderate mental retardation may also have acquired some work skills, and many gain employment, usually in simple jobs, structured and

Training in vocational skills is an important component of the education of the mentally retarded. Even children with moderate retardation can acquire work skills.

supervised, in sheltered workshops or family businesses.

Some retarded people do clerical, maintenance, and laundry work; packaging; electronic and other light assembly; metal cutting, drilling, and other machine work; farming, gardening, and carpentry. They also work in the domestic and food services. Some are taught to participate in the care and training of those more retarded than themselves and benefit greatly from the experience. Many retarded workers are very persistent, accurate, and punctual employees. The character of Benny on the television series "L. A. Law" portrays such achievements in a dramatic and compelling way.

Deficiencies in General Cognitive Abilities

The middle ring of Figure 16.1 consists of general cognitive abilities that people with mental retardation lack, at least to some extent. Researchers who specialize in mental retardation have studied two aspects of cognitive abilities that are hypothesized as responsible for the observed deficits in adaptive behavior. *Structural features,* for example, the frontal lobe, refer to fixed, unmodifiable components of the brain that affect cognitive and adaptive functioning. *Control processes,* in contrast, are those aspects of cognitive abilities that can presumably be improved through training (Atkinson & Shiffrin, 1969; Baumeister, 1984). Although researchers differ in their emphases on fixed versus modifiable aspects of cognitive functioning, most agree that both components are important to an understanding of mental retardation.

In this scene from "L. A. Law," Benny appears in court trying to regain the right to vote, which had been taken away from him just before election day.

Attention to Stimuli Zeaman and Hanley (1983) reviewed evidence indicating that persons with mental retardation attend to different dimensions of a stimulus than do people of normal intelligence. Discrimination learning tasks require subjects to select correctly between two objects on the basis of one or more specific dimensions, such as color, size, or shape. Researchers have found that younger children and retarded individuals attend more to color, whereas older children and normal adults pay more attention to form. In addition, mentally retarded individuals attend more readily to the position of the object than to its other dimensions. For example, a retarded person may use a response set, such as always selecting the choice on the left, or alternating left and right positions, and ignore dimensions of the problem such as color or shape that could guide him or her to a correct solution.

Does the preference of retarded individuals for the position of a stimulus indicate the presence of a control process or a structural feature? Evidence that retarded persons can be taught to attend to the relevant dimensions rather than to position suggests that control processes are functioning. On the other hand, several findings indicate that structural features are predominant: (1) prior to training, most retarded individuals show the preference for position; (2) despite countertraining in attention to the relevant dimensions of the problem, retarded individuals sometimes continue to attend to an irrelevant dimension, such as position; and (3) when training ends, subjects usually regress to their earlier preferences (Zeaman & Hanley, 1983).

Short-Term Memory Deficits The well-documented presence of short-term memory deficits in mentally retarded persons again raises the question of fixed versus modifiable deficiencies in cognitive functioning. Although the long-term memories of normal children and those with mild mental retardation have been found to be the same, retarded individuals have much poorer short-term memory.

A control process hypothesis to explain this deficit centers on a correctable failure to use rehearsal strategies in solving problems. Given a list of ten items, normal children will rehearse the items or find cues to help remember them. Some researchers (Butterfield & Belmont, 1975; Detterman, 1979) suggest that although retarded children do not use such rehearsal strategies on their own, they can be taught to do so, with a resulting improvement in their short-term memory abilities.

More recent evidence, however, points to a structural deficit in the memory capacity of mentally retarded children. To study short-term memory capacity separately from voluntary cognitive processes, such as rehearsal, Ellis, Deacon, and Wooldridge (1985) presented stimuli (letters or pictures) briefly, and prevented rehearsal by requiring both normal and mentally retarded children to attend immediately to a distracting stimulus. In this procedure, the superior rehearsal strategies of the normal subjects are inhibited, enabling the experimenter to examine short-term memory ability apart from the effects of rehearsal. The data demonstrated greater deficiencies in short-term memory in mentally retarded individuals than in normal individuals, suggesting a structural deficit in their memory capacity.

Processing Speed Further evidence for structural deficits in the functioning of mentally retarded individuals is found in research on the speed of processing information. An example of this type of experiment is the inspection time study, which attempts to measure processing speed while keeping cognitive strategies (control processes) to a minimum. Nettelbeck (1985) gave subjects a simple discrimination task, such as identifying the longer of two lines. The task (stimulus) is flashed briefly on a screen, followed by a mask (a different pattern) to halt processing. Inspection time is defined as the length of exposure to the initial stimulus that the subject requires to reach 100 percent accuracy. Mildly retarded subjects require about twice as much exposure time as nonretarded control subjects, suggesting a deficit in their processing speed, a presumed structural problem.

Executive Functioning Other researchers suggest that retarded children have general deficits in executive functioning (Butterfield & Belmont, 1977). The children fail to generalize strategies to other times and to other settings. Although the appropriate use of memory strategies is one aspect of executive functioning, it includes as well metacognitive activities, such as knowing how to plan, monitor progress, solve problems, and check outcomes for completeness and corrections. People with and without retardation may have strategic ability but not be able to apply it.

Control Function of Language Lev Semenovich Vygotsky (1896–1934), a Russian neuropsychologist, had an extensive theory of thought and speech that regarded them as stemming from separate roots but later coinciding. He also theorized that private speech branches off from social speech and assumes a control function. The control function of language is crucial to intelligent behavior and develops in three stages (Vygotsky, 1978). A child's behavior is first controlled or regulated by instructions from other people. Then the child imitates these instructions aloud, and they serve as a cue or guide to behavior. The process is completed when the child's formerly spoken words become internalized, when they become inner speech. This connection between language and action may fail to develop in retarded children, leading to deficits in self-regulation (Whitman, 1990).

Etiology of Mental Retardation

The innermost circle of Figure 16.1 (page 461), which we focus on in this section, represents the responsible causal agent of mental retardation. In only 25 percent of the mentally retarded population can this primary cause be specifically identified.

No Identifiable Etiology

In general, persons with severe or profound mental retardation have an identifiable organic brain defect, whereas persons with less severe mental retardation do not. Persons whose mental retardation is associated with identifiable organic impairments are found in much the same percentages throughout all socioeconomic, ethnic, and racial groups. In contrast, persons with mild or moderate mental retardation are overrepresented in the lower socioeconomic classes.

Two theories have been proposed to explain why some people with no identifiable brain defect do not function within the normal range of intelligence. One proposed by Yale psychologist Edmund Zigler (1967) is called the developmental theory. Zigler argued that a person with mild retardation for which no organic cause is indicated should not be viewed as having a structural deficit, but rather as "a perfectly normal expression of the population gene pool, of slower and more limited intellectual development than the individual of average intellect" (Zigler, 1967, p. 298). According to this model, the differences found between retarded persons and normal children with matched mental age are not due to a cognitive defect, but to motivational factors. Specifically, the social deprivation common in institutions for the retarded, the history of task failures, and the lesser importance of reinforcers such as being told one is correct lead retarded individuals to have lower motivation for performing cognitive tasks than normal children of the same mental age. Presumably, strengthening those motivational variables should improve the performance of mildly retarded children, although they still would not be expected to perform at normal levels because of their slower growth and lower peak of intellectual development.

Research reviewed by Weisz and colleagues has lent support, albeit inconsistent, to this developmental theory of mental retardation. Weisz and Yeates (1981) found that mentally retarded subjects with no organic cause for their retardation performed comparably to mental-age-matched controls on certain intellectual tasks, suggesting that retarded persons develop cognitively in the same way as normal persons, just more slowly. This finding supports Zigler's view. However, Weiss, Weisz, and Bromfield (1986) found that on information-processing tasks, retarded individuals performed significantly below their mental-age-matched controls. This latter finding suggests that there are indeed structural differences between mentally retarded and normal individuals, challenging the developmental theory.

The alternative view to Zigler's is that brain damage, too slight to be detected by currently available methods, causes mild retardation. Baumeister and MacLean (1979), for example, proposed that a trauma during the birth of infants, as well as other prenatal and perinatal conditions, damages the brain enough to cause mild retardation. But other factors, including the environment, may make the same degree of impairment manifest itself differently. The effects of the environment could explain the relatively few persons in the upper socioeconomic classes with mild retardation. Consider two persons with equal structural impairment, one from an upper socioeconomic level and one from a lower level. The first individual's slight deficit could be compensated for by the enriched background. The second individual's deficit might be exaggerated by impoverished circumstances. To show signs of retardation, a socially advantaged person must have more extensive damage, which is impervious to help from an enriched upbringing.

Although researchers have attempted to determine the nature of the proposed physical brain impairment, results have thus far been inconclusive (Baumeister & MacLean, 1979; Karrer, Nelson, & Galbraith, 1979). Some evidence suggests, however, that the synaptic connections in the brains of children with mental retardation are less complex and less differentiated than those of normal children (Huttenlocher, 1974; Purpura, 1976). Unfortunately, the minor physical defects responsible for mild to moderate retardation are readily observable only in postmortem studies. Their presence is also somewhat of a children-and-egg question. Does the environmental deprivation or the structural deficit occur first? For example, studies of animals raised in a deprived environment found their brains to be smaller in size (Krech, Rosenzweig, & Bennett, 1966).

Known Organic Etiology

The approximately 25 percent of people whose mental retardation has a known single organic cause inflates the incidence of retardation in the population over what would be statistically expected were no abnormal conditions present. These individuals create what is referred to as a bump at the bottom end of the normal curve (Figure 16.2). Genetic conditions, infectious diseases, accidents, prematurity, chemicals, and environmental hazards are six categories of organic impairment.

Genetic or Chromosomal Anomalies Four percent of all recognized pregnancies have chromosomal abnormalities. The majority of these pregnancies,

Figure 16.2 Normal curve showing the theoretical distribution of IQ scores. The bump on the left represents the actual frequency of severe and profound retardation with organic causes.

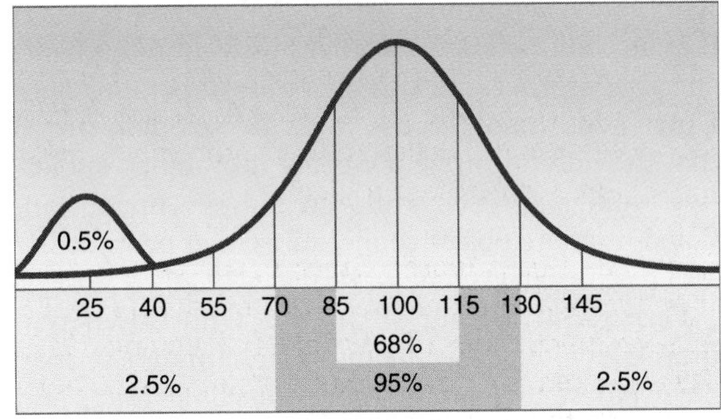

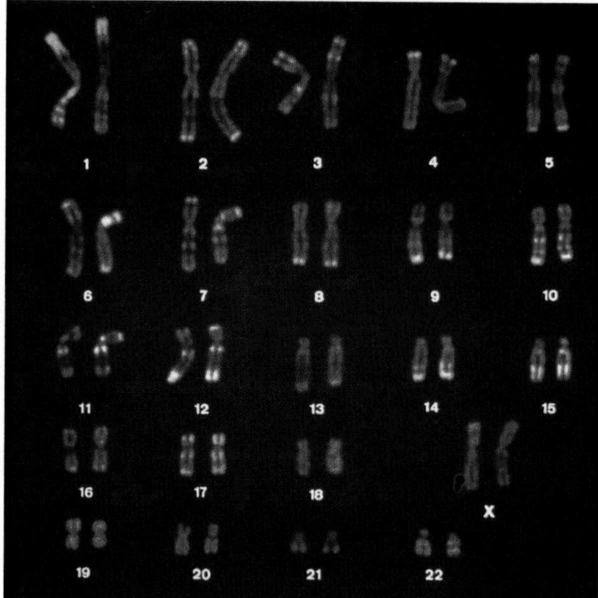

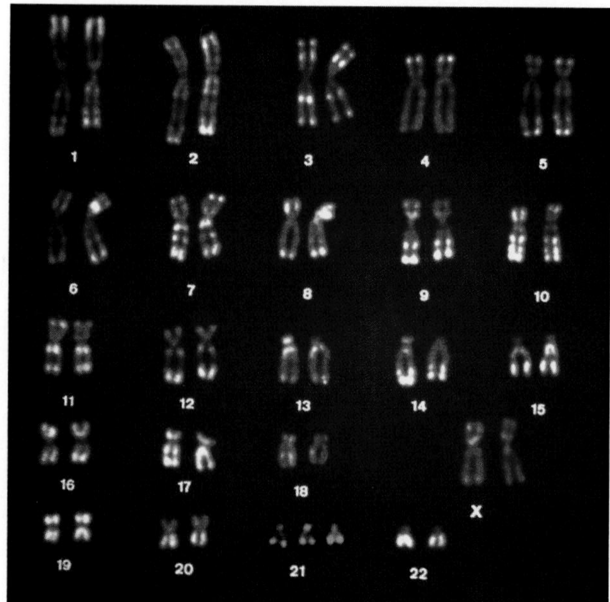

Left: The normal complement of chromosomes is 23 pairs. Right: In Down syndrome there is a trisomy of chromosome 21.

however, end in spontaneous abortions or miscarriages. Only about one-half of one percent of the babies who are born have a chromosomal abnormality (Smith, Bierman, & Robinson, 1978). A significant proportion of these infants die soon after birth. Of the babies that survive, the largest percent have **Down syndrome**, or **trisomy 21**.

The IQs of people with Down syndrome are in the mild to moderate range of mental retardation. In addition, they have many rather distinctive physical signs of the syndrome: short and stocky stature; oval, upward-slanting eyes; the epicanthic fold, a prolongation of the fold of the upper eyelid over the inner corner of the eye; sparse, fine, straight hair; a wide and flat nasal bridge; square-shaped ears; a large, furrowed tongue, protruding because the mouth is small and its roof low; short, broad hands with stubby fingers; a general loose-jointedness, particularly in the ankles; and a broad-based walk. Plastic surgeons have recently attenuated some of the more obvious facial distinctions of young people with Down syndrome. Although proponents assert that, in conjunction with other interventions, plastic surgery improves the quality of life of persons with Down syndrome (Strauss et al., 1989), others argue that the only improvements are in parents' subjective ratings of their children, ratings unsubstantiated by more objective measures of appearance or social acceptance (Katz & Kravetz, 1989).

Perhaps 40 percent of children with Down syndrome have heart problems; a small minority may have blockages of the upper intestinal tract; and about one in six dies during the first year. Mortality after age forty is high; at autopsy, brain tissue generally shows deterioration similar to that in Alzheimer's disease (page 494). Despite their mental retardation, most of these children can learn to read, write, and even do math.

Down syndrome is named after the British physician Langdon Down, who first described the clinical signs in 1866. In 1959 the French geneticist Jerome Lejeune and his colleagues identified its genetic basis. Human beings usually possess forty-six chromosomes, inheriting twenty-three from each parent by means of the germ cells. Individuals with Down syndrome almost always have forty-seven chromosomes instead of forty-six. During maturation of the egg, something goes wrong so that the two chromocomes of pair 21, the smallest ones, fail to separate. If this egg is fertilized, uniting with a sperm, there will be three of chromosome 21; thus the technical term *trisomy 21*. Down syndrome is found in approximately one out of 800 to 1200 live births.

All of a woman's eggs remain in a suspended state of division from the time that they were formed, when the woman was merely a fetus, until they begin to mature after puberty, usually one at a time. The longer this period, the greater the chance for damage to pairs of chromosomes that would prevent their eventual separation. For this reason the incidence of Down syndrome increases dramatically for mothers over the age of thirty-five; in 1973 women over thirty-five had little more than 13 percent of all pregnancies but bore more than one-half of the infants with trisomy 21.

Unlike women, after puberty men form new germ cells daily. Research, however, indicates that in as many as 25 percent of Down syndrome cases the father's sperm carries the extra chromosome (Magenis et al., 1977). Again, age at conception is implicated, in this instance advanced paternal age.

Researchers have identified certain individuals with malformations of the X chromosome (Harvey, Judge, & Wiener, 1977). Specifically, the X chromosome may actually break in two—hence the name **fragile X syndrome**. Physical symptoms associated with fragile X include facial features such as large, underdeveloped ears, a long, thin face and a broad nasal root, and enlarged testicles in males. More importantly, the majority of males and about one-third of females with fragile X are moderately mentally retarded, and many also show attention deficits and hyperactivity. Females who do not manifest outward symptoms can still be carriers and may pass the syndrome on to their children. Among those who are not retarded, many have learning disabilities and speech and language difficulties (Bergman et al., 1987). Fragile X is the second leading cause of mental retardation with a chromosomal basis, after Down syndrome (Dykens et al., 1988), and has recently been implicated as a cause of some cases of autism as well (Fisch et al., 1986).

Recessive-Gene Diseases When a pair of defective recessive genes misdirects the formation of an enzyme, metabolic processes are disturbed. The problem may affect development of the embryo in the uterus or become important only much later in life.

In **phenylketonuria (PKU)** the infant, born normal, soon suffers from a deficiency of liver enzyme, phenylalanine hydroxylase, which is needed to convert phenylalanine, an amino acid of protein food, to tyrosine. Phenylalanine and its derivative phenylpyruvic acid build up in the body fluids, eventually giving the urine a musty odor and ultimately causing irreversible brain damage. The unmetabolized amino acid interferes with the process of myelination, the sheathing of neuron axons. This sheathing is essential for the rapid transmittal of impulses and thus of information; the neurons of the frontal lobes are particularly affected. Little wonder that mental retardation is profound.

Although PKU is a rare disease, with an incidence of about one in 14,000 live births, it is estimated that one person in seventy is a carrier of the recessive gene. There is a blood test for prospective parents who have reason to suspect that they might be carriers. Fortunately too, after the PKU newborn has consumed milk for several days, an excess amount of unconverted phenylalanine can be detected in its blood. State laws require that the necessary test be given. If the test is positive, the parents are urged to provide the infant a diet low in phenylalanine.

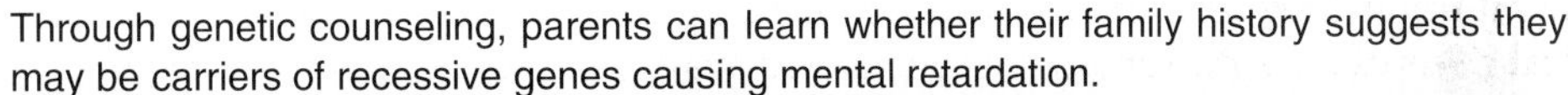

Through genetic counseling, parents can learn whether their family history suggests they may be carriers of recessive genes causing mental retardation.

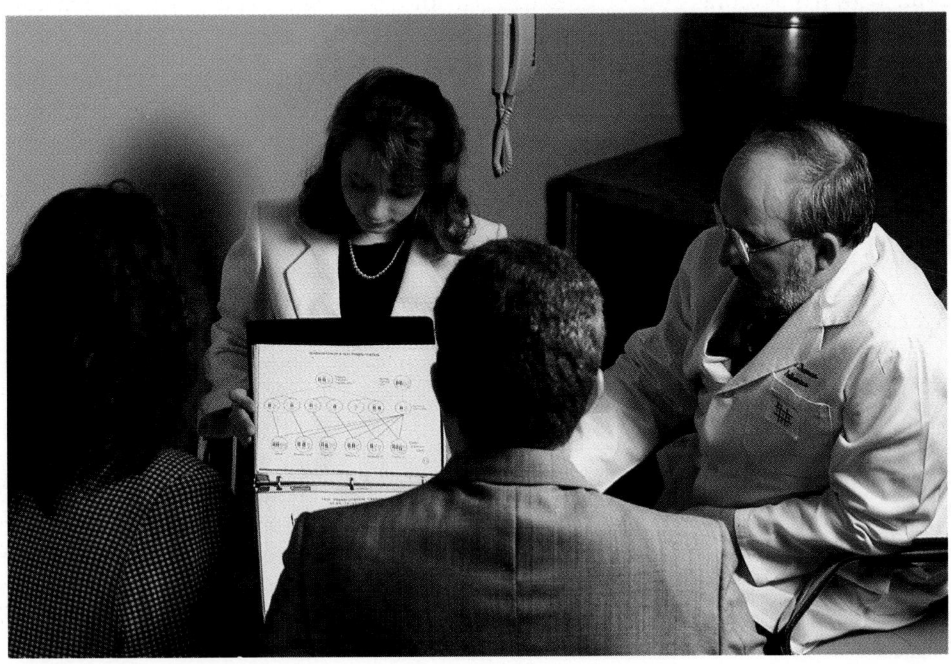

When the diet is restricted as early as the third month and until the age of six, when brain differentiation is relatively complete, cognitive development improves, sometimes to within the normal range (*Collaborative Study of Children Treated for Phenylketonuria*, 1975).

Several hundred other recessive-gene diseases have been identified, many of them causing mental retardation. Only a very small percentage of cases of mental retardation is accounted for by any *single* disease. Genetic counseling can help future parents find out whether their backgrounds suggest that they are at risk for carrying certain of these recessive genes.

Amniocentesis and chorionic villi biopsy can reveal the presence of some of these problems in the fetus. The amniotic fluid in which the fetus is immersed within the uterus contains cells and other substances from the fetus. A small amount of the fluid can be withdrawn by needle in the sixteenth week, a process called *amniocentesis.* The cells are cultured and later reveal whether there are three of chromosome 21. A new procedure, *chorionic villi biopsy*, can be performed even earlier, in the tenth week, which is an important advantage. The villi, tiny protrusions on the chorion, the outermost membrane surrounding the fetus, are sampled by suction or clipping and removed directly through the mother's cervix. Cells of this tissue are cultured and then analyzed.

If the fetus is found to have genetic abnormalities, the parents usually have the option of abortion. Supporters of selective abortion refer to the poor quality of life of a retarded individual as well as to the emotional costs to the parents and the monetary costs to society to provide care. Opponents of selective abortion claim that all life is sacred and that such fetuses have the right to life. It is not an easy issue.

Infectious Diseases While in utero, the fetus is at increased risk of mental retardation from maternal infectious diseases. The consequences of these diseases are more serious during the first trimester of pregnancy, when the fetus has no detectable immunological response. In addition, the first trimester is a critical period in the development of the brain. Cytomegalovirus, toxoplasmosis, rubella, herpes simplex, and syphilis are all maternal infections that may cause both physical deformities and mental retardation of the fetus. The mother may experience slight or even no symptoms from the infection, but the effects on the developing fetus can be devastating. Pregnant women who go to prenatal clinics are given a blood test for syphilis. Today women who contemplate having a child can take a blood test to determine whether they are immune to rubella (German measles); nearly 85 percent of American women are. A woman who is not should be vaccinated at least six months before becoming pregnant. If a fetus contracts rubella from its mother, it is likely to be born with brain lesions that cause mental retardation.

After birth, infectious diseases can also affect a child's developing brain. Encephalitis and meningococcal meningitis may cause irreversible brain damage and even death if contracted in infancy or early childhood. These infections in adulthood are usually far less serious, probably because the brain is largely developed by about the age of six. There are several forms of childhood meningitis, a disease in which the protective membranes of the brain are acutely inflamed and fever is very high. Even if the child survives and is not severely retarded, it is likely that onset of moderate or mild retardation will occur. Other disabling aftereffects are deafness, paralysis, and epilepsy.

Accidents In the United States accidents are the leading cause of severe disability and death in children over one year of age. Falls and automobile accidents are among the most common mishaps in early childhood and may cause varying degrees of head injury and mental retardation. The institution of laws mandating that children riding in automobiles wear seat belts may play a major role in reducing the incidence of mental retardation in young children.

Prematurity A baby is considered premature if delivered three or more weeks before term. Premature infants who survive have an increased risk of developing mental retardation. Although the relation between prematurity and mental retardation is quite high, it is difficult to substantiate prematurity per se as a causal factor. Many factors—poverty, teenage motherhood, inadequate nutrition, alcohol and drug abuse, and poor prenatal care—all figure in prematurity. Additionally, premature infants may develop other medical problems that place them at increased risk for mental retardation. Of course, many children born prematurely grow up quite normally.

There is some evidence that preterm infants may not get off to a good start in social development. Field and her colleagues (1979, 1980) compared the patterns of mothers' interactions with their preterm infants with those of mothers with full-term infants. Those between mothers and preterm infants had less synchrony, sensitivity, give-and-take, and turn taking. Field suggests that parents of preterm in-

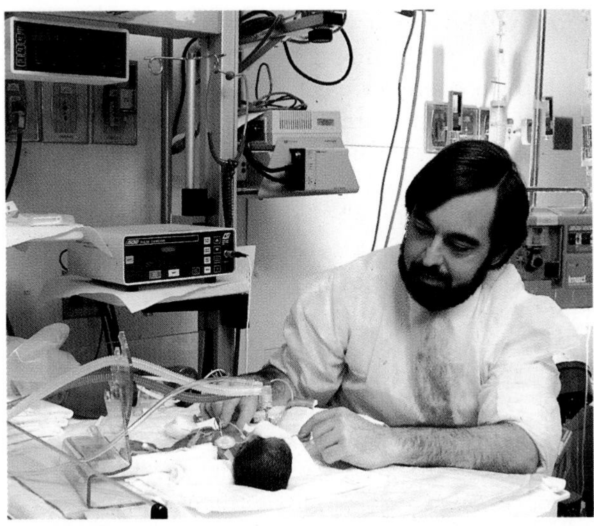

Related to factors such as poverty, poor prenatal care, and drug use during pregnancy, premature birth itself is a cause of mental retardation.

fants may be disappointed in their babies because they expect them to act their birth age, rather than their age since conception in the womb.

Noxious Chemical Substances In the early 1960s a presumably harmless drug called thalidomide was prescribed in England, Canada, West Germany, and Scandinavia for pregnant women experiencing morning sickness. Many of the babies born to these mothers had arms and legs resembling the buds that precede limb development in the human embryo. Although thalidomide was quickly taken off the market, for thousands of infants the damage was already done.

The havoc wreaked by thalidomide was extreme, but it can serve to underscore the point that the ingestion of any chemical substance by a pregnant woman may cause the development of the fetus to diverge in a serious way from its normal track. In chapter 11, we discussed two such substances, alcohol and cocaine.

Environmental Hazards Several environmental pollutants can cause poisoning and mental retardation. These include mercury, which may be transmitted through affected fish, and lead, which is found in lead-based paints, smog, and the exhaust from automobiles burning leaded gasoline. Lead poisoning can cause kidney and brain damage as well as anemia, mental retardation, seizures, and death. Lead-based paint is now prohibited, but it is still found in older homes where it may be flaking.

The increasing technology of our society creates environmental hazards. The intent of a medical treatment is to do good, but an unforeseen consequence may be mental retardation. One such medical procedure—the diphtheria–pertussis–tetanus (DPT) vaccine—carries such iatrogenic dangers, that is, problems induced inadvertently by the treatment. The DPT vaccine protects thousands of children from pertussis, a dangerous childhood disease more commonly known as whooping cough. The pertussis part of the vaccine, however, causes a high rate of adverse reactions in the children inoculated. These range from redness and swelling around the vaccinated area, to persistent crying or high-pitched screaming, to brain damage and sometimes even death. The DPT vaccine is estimated to be responsible for approximately fifty cases of severe mental retardation each year.

Although the potential side effects of the DPT vaccine were known in the early 1940s, the majority of the population remains unaware of the risks. A group of parents, Dissatisfied Parents Together, whose children have been adversely affected by the DPT vaccine, advocates federal legislation that would allow compensation for the families of DPT victims. The proposed legislation would also require doctors to give parents all the information available on the vaccine before it is administered and to report all adverse reactions. Such warnings are now issued in many states.

Although lead-based paint is now illegal, it can still be found in older homes. Eating chips of it can cause lead poisoning and mental retardation.

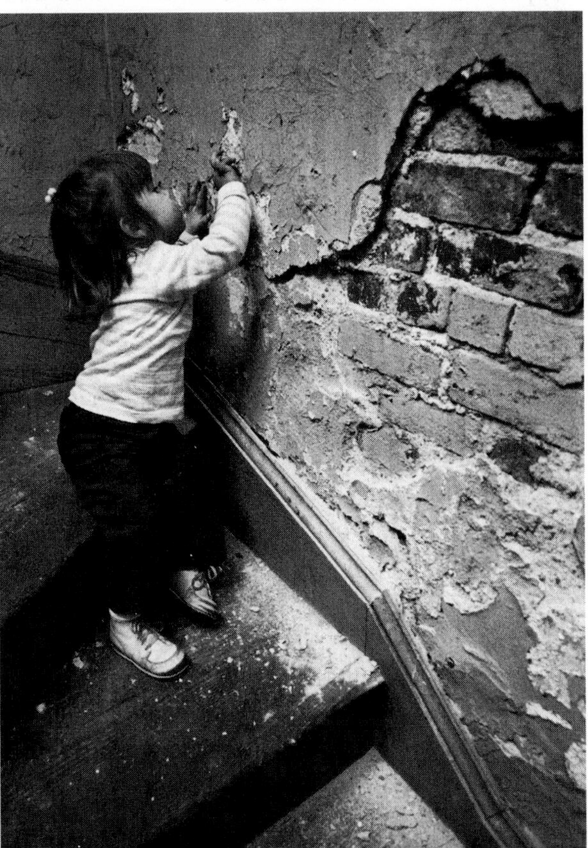

Prevention of Mental Retardation

Prevention depends, of course, on understanding the factors causing retardation. The known organic causes present a fairly straightforward challenge and opportunity, and many of them can now be counteracted, as already indicated. For the majority of cases in which etiology is not as obvious, prevention becomes considerably more problematic.

Eugenics Movement

Historically, eugenics[3] has been practiced in an effort to decrease the numbers of mentally retarded people. Eugenics advocates that breeding be selective to increase, from one generation to another, the proportion of persons with better than average hereditary endowments. Social Darwinism had contributed the belief that mental retardation was caused largely by heredity. In 1903 the American Breeders Association was formed to devise guidelines and set up policies to control which people should be allowed to conceive and bear children. Two remedies for mental retardation were advocated, segregation and sterilization.

Many large institutions were built so that retarded individuals could live apart from the rest of the population. Most were no more than warehouses for anyone unfortunate enough to do poorly on newly constructed intelligence tests (Blatt, 1966). The majority of residents were newly arrived immigrants, members of racial minorities, children with physical disabilities, and indigents. Recall the example of the bigoted attitudes held by one of the pioneers in standardized IQ testing in this country, presented in Chapter 4 (page 103).

Although forced segregation reduced the number of children born to couples with one partner of questionable intelligence, it did not stop couples within institutions from bearing children. In Indiana in 1907 the first mandatory sterilization law for women with mental retardation was passed. By 1930 twenty-eight states had these laws. Although their constitutionality was questioned, forced sterilization—especially for undereducated minority and immigrant groups—continued to be practiced in many institutions through the 1950s. In the 1960s safeguards were passed to protect the rights of mentally retarded individuals to marry and bear children.

Early in the twentieth century, large institutions were created so the mentally retarded could be segregated from the rest of society. Newly arriving immigrants were tested at Ellis Island to determine whether they should be institutionalized.

In contrast to the eugenics movement, current workers in the field promote the rights of mentally retarded adults to freedom of sexual expression. Abramson, Parker, and Weisberg (1988) reviewed evidence indicating that adults with mild mental retardation are sexually competent in terms of their physical development, desire for sexual relationships, and ability to maintain satisfying marriages. Therefore, they advocate sex education for mildly retarded adults to teach skills required for informed consent, sexual hygiene, and contraception. Again, the television character Benny from "L.A. Law" comes to mind. In one series of episodes he became romantically involved with a mentally retarded young woman and almost married her. In another group of episodes he became a foster parent of a nonretarded but delinquent boy whom authorities removed from his care when the youngster got into legal trouble.

Early Intervention

As the importance of environmental factors in the incidence of mental retardation became more

[3]Eugenics should be distinguished from genetic counseling, in which parents learn through a counselor that they are at risk for giving birth to a disabled infant, are advised about the odds and the care that would be necessary for the child, and are given other information that might help them reach a decision in a difficult predicament. In contrast, eugenics tries to create babies who will have certain qualities that it is believed will make them superior. During the Third Reich the Nazis wanted to increase the numbers of blond, blue-eyed Aryan children. Today there are sperm banks that store the frozen sperm of men of uncommon professional distinction such as scientists and writers, in the hope that, at some later time, a woman will apply to be impregnated by sperm judged genetically superior.

widely recognized, prevention efforts turned to early intervention for children at risk through the impoverished circumstances of their upbringing. Prevention of mild mental retardation depends on early identification and training of susceptible people. Researchers are working both to improve the procedures for identifying children at risk and to design the most effective preventive programs.

Certainly the best-known, large-scale effort to raise the achievement and intellectual level of disadvantaged children is Project Head Start. Its purpose is to prepare children socially and culturally to succeed in the regular school setting by giving them experiences that they are missing at home. The impetus for Head Start came during the 1960s, when national attention was directed to problems of hunger and civil rights. If the thousands of children from culturally disadvantaged families were to have the same educational opportunities as other children, the poverty cycle would have to be broken and the standard of living raised considerably.

The core of the Head Start program is community-based preschool education, focusing on the development of early cognitive and social skills. In addition, Head Start contracts with professionals in the community to provide children with health and dental services, including vaccinations, hearing and vision testing, medical treatment, and nutrition information (North, 1979). Mental health services are an important component of Head Start programs. Psychologists may help to identify children with psychological problems and consult with teachers and staff to help make the preschool environment sensitive to psychological issues, for example, by sharing knowledge of child development, consulting on an individual case, or helping staff address parents' concerns (Cohen, Solnit, & Wohlford, 1979). Social workers can serve as advocates for the child's family, linking families with needed social services and encouraging parents to get involved with their children's education (Lazar, 1979).

A comparison of Head Start children with other disadvantaged children who attended either a different preschool or no preschool was conducted by Lee, Brooks-Gunn, and Schnur (1988). The Head Start children improved significantly more than both control groups on social-cognitive ability and motor impulsivity; the relative improvement was especially strong for African-American children, particularly those with initial ability below average. Although the Head Start program succeeded in enhancing the functioning of the neediest children, the authors note that these children were still behind their peers in terms of absolute cognitive levels after one year in the program.

Treatment for Mental Retardation

Over the past two hundred years attitudes have swung like a pendulum from optimism and interest in educating the feeble-minded to bleak pessimism (Crissey, 1975). Edouard Seguin, a French physician and educator of the nineteenth century, was convinced that education was a universal right and that "idiots" were among the neediest. Considering mental retardation a weakness in the nervous system, he devised teaching methods to correct specific disabilities. After leaving Paris in 1848, he settled in Ohio and was instrumental in setting up special schools throughout the northeastern United States, one of them the Pennsylvania Training School for Idiots. (The reader will note how the connotative meanings of terms change. Nowadays health professionals would never use the word *idiot*, let alone include it in the name of an institution.) But disil-

Early intervention, as illustrated by Head Start programs, is a way of counteracting the impoverished environments of retarded children.

lusionment set in later in the century when the goals that had been confidently worked toward earlier were not attained. The children did not become normal, and the institutions grew and grew. Perhaps retarded individuals were just born that way and little could be done for them, except to maintain them and protect them from the intellectual demands of society. But in the past few decades of this century, there have again been serious and systematic attempts to educate retarded children to as full an extent as possible. Most retarded people can acquire the competence needed to function effectively in the community.

Deinstitutionalization

Since the 1960s the trend has been to provide retarded individuals with educational and community services rather than institutional care. Like the emptying of mental hospitals, this is called deinstitutionalization. According to the Developmentally Disabled Assistance and Bill of Rights Act, passed by Congress in 1975, retarded individuals have a right to appropriate treatment in the least restrictive residential setting. Ideally, moderately retarded people live in small- to medium-sized homelike residences that are integrated into the community. A transition period gradually prepares the individual for the move from the institution to the community home. Medical care is provided and trained, live-in supervisors and aides attend to the residents' special needs around the clock. Residents are encouraged to participate in the household routines to the best of their ability. Severely retarded children may live at home or in foster-care homes provided with educational and psychological services. Many mildly retarded persons who have jobs and are able to live independently have their own apartments. Others live together in semi-independent apartments of three to four retarded adults. The aid of a counselor is generally provided only in the evening.

Unfortunately, some large institutions have been closed down and the residents discharged without having a supervised community residence to which to go. At present, the majority who remain in institutions are severely and profoundly retarded people who have physical disabilities as well (Cunningham & Mueller, 1991).

Early Intervention

Whereas programs such as Head Start can help prevent mild mental retardation in disadvantaged children, other early intervention programs have been developed to improve the eventual level of functioning of more seriously retarded individuals (without actually preventing the retardation). A number of pilot projects with Down syndrome children have intervened during infancy and early childhood to attempt to improve the functioning of these children. These programs typically include systematic home- and treatment-center-based instruction in language skills, fine and gross motor skills, self-care, and social development. Specific behavioral objectives are defined, and, in an operant fashion, children are taught skills in small sequential steps (e.g., Clunies-Ross, 1979).

Studies of these programs indicate consistent improvements in fine motor skills, social acceptance, and self-help skills. Unfortunately, the programs appear to have little effect on gross motor skills and linguistic abilities, and long-term improvements in IQ and school performance have not been demonstrated. It is not yet clear whether the benefits of the programs are greater than what parents can provide in the home without special training (Gibson & Harris, 1988).

Public Laws 94-142 and 99-457

In 1975 the United States Congress passed Public Law 94-142, the Education for All Handicapped Children Act. Passage of this law represented substantial gains for the educational rights of children with disabilities and, in addition, secured their integration into the community. The law guarantees children between the ages of three and twenty-one a free, appropriate public education in the least restrictive environment. Such an environment is one that allows the disabled student to develop mentally, physically, and socially with the fewest barriers while providing necessary support. The goals for each child are set forth in an individual educational program (IEP) that is evaluated annually. To some, the least restrictive environment means that the children are educated at the same schools as normally achieving youngsters and are mainstreamed into some of their classrooms. Others would say that a segregated school provides the resources and intensive training required by disabled children.

Public Law 99-457, passed in 1986, extended the earlier statute by requiring that all public schools serve disabled preschoolers by 1991 or lose their federal funding. This law has led to interagency agreements between Head Start centers and public schools, resulting in more extensive services for young children not previously involved in the educational system.

These laws apply to all children with exceptional needs, including those with mental retardation, autism, and learning disabilities, as well as children with speech, hearing, or visual impairments, gifted and talented children,[4] and those with serious emotional disturbances that interfere with their school progress. Especially in the South, African-Americans are overrepresented among the educable mentally retarded and in special education classes conducted under these two laws. Since scores on standardized intelligence tests are central in deciding on such placement, there is some concern that African-Americans may be unfairly stigmatized and otherwise disadvantaged by being assigned to such classes, even though the classes are in public schools (Heller, Holtzman, & Messick, 1982). The reasons for the disproportionately large numbers of African-Americans in classes for the educable mentally retarded are complex; they include historical patterns of discrimination that can lead to poor economic conditions, disrupted home lives, malnutrition, poor-quality school instruction, and other disadvantages that contribute to low test scores and poor school performance. Personal biases of teachers and administrators may also play a role in whether a child is placed in a special class. These are weighty social issues that our heterogeneous society has been grappling with for well over a hundred years.

Overall, programs that are sensitive to the problems inherent in mainstreaming appear likely to yield positive results for students both with and without disabilities (Gottlieb, 1990; Zigler, Hodapp, & Edison, 1990). Normal children can learn early in life that there is tremendous diversity among human beings and that a child may be different in some very important ways and yet be worthy of respect and friendship. With support from parents and teachers, normal children may reach adulthood without the burden of prejudice of earlier generations. Such an eventuality would benefit both the normal child and the emotionally or cognitively disadvantaged age-mate.

Teaching Strategies

Therapies based on the writings of Freud and Rogers, which rely heavily on verbal ability, indeed verbal facility, have had limited applicability in treating retarded people. But verbal exchanges with retarded individuals are of course possible and necessary. Moderately and mildly retarded children can use advice from a counselor or other adult; they all need to be reassured about their abilities; and they can obtain encouragement and support from kind and trustworthy people (Robinson & Robinson, 1976).

Many therapists treat retarded children with behavioral methods, in particular, with **applied behavior analysis**[5] and cognitive behavior therapy. The former is most often used to teach severely and profoundly retarded children and those with autism the adaptive skills mentioned earlier: communication, self-help, and social and vocational skills. Children with mild and moderate mental retardation are given cognitive therapy to improve their general cognitive functioning. Other teaching approaches focus on nonvocal communication and computer-assisted instruction. Here are some examples.

Applied Behavior Analysis Children with severe and profound retardation usually need intensive instruction to be able to feed, toilet, and groom themselves. To teach a severely retarded child a particular routine, the therapist usually begins by analyzing and dividing the targeted behavior, such as eating, into smaller components: pick up spoon, scoop food from plate onto spoon, bring spoon to mouth, remove food with lips, chew and swallow food. Operant conditioning principles are then applied to teach the child these components of eating. For example, the child may be reinforced for successive approximations to picking up the spoon until he or she is able to do so.

Applied behavior analysis is used also to reduce inappropriate and self-injurious behavior. Children with severe and profound mental impairment who live in institutions are especially prone to stereotyped behaviors performed in isolation—repetitive, rhythmic, self-stimulatory motions, such as rocking back and forth, swaying, rolling the head—and to aggression against the self or toward other children and staff. These maladaptive movements and injurious actions can often be reduced by reinforcing substitute responses (see Focus Box 16.2).

The significance of learning self-care and of reducing stereotyped and injurious actions must not be underestimated. Toilet-trained children, for example, are more comfortable, are liked better by the

[4]It may seem odd that gifted and talented children are covered by this law, apparently designed for those with serious disabilities. Surely being uncommonly bright or talented in an area such as music or art is not a disability! True. But parents of such children know that the public schools sometimes do damage to gifted youngsters by not challenging them sufficiently and sometimes by discouraging, even disparaging, their abilities and interests. Such young people, then, also have special educational needs, but it is understandable that, when budgets are tight, resources are directed toward those who are retarded and otherwise intellectually or physically compromised.

[5]In the behavioral literature on mental retardation, this term is used more frequently than operant conditioning, but the two terms refer to the same kinds of assessments and interventions.

FOCUS

16.2 • Treatment of Self-Injurious and Stereotyped Behavior

Many mentally retarded and autistic individuals, particularly those with severe disabilities, engage in persistent, repetitive, stereotyped behavior. Some of these behaviors are self-injurious, such as head banging, face slapping, biting, pinching, and scratching, whereas others, such as rocking, twirling, mouthing, or wall patting, do not present a physical danger. Nevertheless, these maladaptive behaviors compete with more socially acceptable adaptive behaviors and interfere with attempts at education.

A fourteen-member task force organized by the Association for the Advancement of Behavior Therapy (AABT) explored the effectiveness of behavior therapy for treating self-injurious behavior (Favell et al., 1982). One effective combination involves giving positive reinforcement when the child is *not* engaging in the target behavior and using overcorrection (having the child practice alternative behaviors over and over) after each instance of self-injurious or stereotyped behavior. These procedures have been found to be effective for many children, but not for all.

A controversial alternative is punishment. Behavior therapists have used such aversive consequences as squirting lemon juice in the mouth or applying a mild shock (enough to be noxious, but not physically harmful) to the arm or leg immediately following each incident of self-injurious behavior. Of course, some therapists and lay people have understandably been concerned about the morality of aversive procedures, particularly in institutional settings with patients who may be unable to give informed consent. Heated debate followed the publication of a monograph by the Association of Persons with Severe Handicaps (TASH) that asserted that aversive procedures should never be used (Guess, Helmstetter, Turnbull, & Knowlton, 1986; see commentary by Mulick, 1990).

But research has demonstrated that punishment may be the most effective, indeed the only effective, method of reducing self-injurious behavior in intractable cases (Gorman-Smith & Matson, 1985). Proponents of the procedure assert that dangerous behaviors, for example, those that may cause serious head injury, justify the use of aversive procedures. The AABT task force concluded their report by advocating that punishment be reserved for situations in which more benign procedures have failed, in which the client is in imminent and extreme physical danger, or the self-injurious behavior is so intrusive as to prevent participation in rehabilitative and humanizing activities. In addition, they proposed guidelines for ensuring that the procedures are used with caution, including required training and supervision by qualified experts, review of treatment by a Human Rights Committee and a Peer Review Committee, informed guardian consent, and rigorous evaluation of the effects of the treatment in each individual case. Similar guidelines have more recently been adopted by the American Psychological Association's Division on Mental Retardation (APA, 1989). We will return to the ethics of aversion therapy in the final chapter of the book.

staff, and can leave the ward for other rooms and leave the building to play on the grounds. Mastering toilet training and learning to feed and dress themselves may even mean that severely retarded children can live at home. Most retarded people face discrimination from others, based in part on the violations of norms that they commit. Being able to act more normally will increase their chances of interacting meaningfully with others. Moreover, the self-esteem that comes from learning to take better care of oneself is extremely bolstering.

Cognitive Behavior Therapy As indicated earlier, retarded children fail to use strategies in solving problems, and when they do have strategies, they often do not apply them effectively. **Self-instructional training**, based on the Vygotsky work described earlier (page 464), teaches retarded children to guide their actions through speech. Meichenbaum and Goodman (1971) outlined a five-step procedure. First the instructor performs the task, speaking instructions aloud to himself or herself while the child watches and listens. Then the child listens and performs the task while the instructor says instructions to the child. The child repeats the task twice again, first giving himself or herself instructions aloud, then whispering them. Finally, the child is ready to perform the task while uttering instructions to himself or herself.

Self-instructions have been employed to teach

retarded children self-control and how to pay attention as well as master more academic tasks. Johnston and her colleagues (1980) found self-instruction effective for teaching metacognitive skills in helping mildly retarded children learn to add and subtract. The children ask themselves, "How do I begin?" and "What kind of math problem is this?" They are also given answers to these questions. For example, "It's an add problem. I can tell by the sign." To self-instruct in specific arithmetic techniques for carrying and borrowing, the children may learn to say, "I start with the top number in the one column. Since it has two numbers, I have to carry." A question designed to foster monitoring or checking skills might be, "Is the answer right? I need to check it." Finally, the children learn to reinforce themselves for correct answers. "I got it right. I'm doing very well."

Ross and Ross (1973) implemented an exemplary modeling program based on a finding by Milgram (1973) that retarded children do not use mediators to make associations as effectively as normal children do. They gave one group of children whose IQs ranged from 40 to 80 special game sessions in which they watched nonretarded children using sentences to link words together. Control retarded children continued in the usual curriculum of the school at which the study was being carried out. During the school year the special group of retarded children showed marked increases in their measured IQ, and eleven of the thirty were actually transferred from the special classes to regular ones; the control children did not show such improvement.

Cognitive behavior therapy has also been applied to improving the social skills of retarded individuals. Although focus on concrete behavioral skills is important, it is also clear that many mentally retarded individuals experience ridicule during adolescence and may develop negative attitudes about social interaction that prevent them from forming satisfying social relationships, even with adequate social skills. Lindsay (1986) used cognitive therapy methods to reduce anxiety and negative self-statements in mildly mentally retarded adults and found that negative attitudes toward socializing could be reduced.

Nonvocal Communications It is estimated that over 70 percent of mentally retarded individuals have some type of speech difficulty (Fristoe & Lloyd, 1979). Though some of these people can be taught to communicate through speech, behavior modification techniques for teaching speech have not been successful with many retarded and autistic individuals. These failures have led to a shift in emphasis from trying to teach articulation and language to other means of communication. Most promising have been efforts to teach severely retarded and autistic individuals to communicate through sign language and other nonvocal methods. Communication systems taught include the American Sign Language used by the deaf and communication boards with pictures or symbols that mute persons use to indicate wants or needs. Individuals who are unable to point can direct a beam of light mounted on the head to communicate. Some encouraging findings of studies on nonvocal communication suggest that not only can disabled individuals often learn to communicate more easily through nonvocal means than through speech, but people who have learned to sign often begin using speech spontaneously (Lloyd & Karlan, 1984).

Computer-Assisted Instruction Evidence suggests that computer-assisted instruction may be especially well suited to the education of mentally retarded individuals. The visual and auditory components of computers maintain the attention of often distractible students; the level of material presented can be individualized, ensuring success experiences; and the computer can meet the needs of mentally retarded individuals for numerous repetitions of material without becoming bored or impatient (as a human teacher might). Computer-assisted instruction programs are shown to be superior to traditional methods for teaching the mentally retarded spelling, money handling, number conservation, text reading, word recognition, handwriting, and visual discrimination (Conners, Caruso, & Detterman, 1986).

Autistic Disorder

Imagine that you are walking into a community group home for children with developmental disabilities. You are taking a class on mental retardation, and one of the requirements is to volunteer some time in this home. As several of the children rise to greet you, you become aware of some minor or major physical signs. One child has slanted eyes and a flat nose, characteristic of Down syndrome. Another makes spastic movements, which you recognize as signs of cerebral palsy. A third child may call to you from a wheelchair with grunting noises and communicate with a combination of hand gestures and pictures. So far the children are as you expected from your readings.

Finally, you notice a fourth child in the room. He is standing in front of the fish tank. As you approach him, you notice his graceful, deft movements, the dreamy, remote look in his eye, and you find him hauntingly attractive. You naturally assume that he is a visitor to the group home or a sibling of one of the residents. You start talking to him about the fish. Instead of acknowledging your comment, or even your presence, he begins rocking back and forth while continuing to smile, as if enjoying a private joke. When the group home director enters the room, your first question is about the boy at the fish tank. The director tells you that he is autistic.

Descriptive Characteristics

From the time it was first distinguished, **autistic disorder** has seemed to have a mystical aura. The syndrome was first identified in 1943 by a psychiatrist at Harvard, Leo Kanner, who noticed that eleven disturbed children behaved in ways that were not common in children with mental retardation or schizophrenia. He named the syndrome *early infantile autism,* because he observed that "there is from the start an *extreme autistic aloneness* that, whenever possible, disregards, ignores, shuts out anything that comes to the child from the outside" (Kanner, 1943). Kanner considered autistic aloneness the most fundamental symptom, but he also found that these eleven children had been unable from the beginning of life to relate to people in the ordinary way, were severely limited in language, and had a strong obsessive desire that everything about them remain exactly the same. Despite its early description by Kanner and others (e.g., Rimland, 1964), the disorder was not accepted into official diagnostic nomenclature until the publication of DSM-III in 1980.

In fact, there has been a good deal of confusion in the classification of serious disorders that begin in childhood. DSM-II used the diagnosis childhood schizophrenia for these conditions, implying that autism was simply an early-onset form of adult schizophrenia. But the available evidence indicates that childhood-onset schizophrenia and autism are separate disorders. The syndrome of schizophrenia described in Chapter 14 does occasionally have an onset in late childhood, but researchers now identify this childhood-onset schizophrenia as distinct from autism (Frith, 1989; Rutter & Schopler, 1987). Although the social withdrawal and inappropriate affect seen in autistic children may appear similar to the negative symptoms of schizophrenia, autistic children do not exhibit hallucinations and delusions and do not grow up to become schizophrenic (Wing & Attwood, 1987). Further, people with autism do not have a higher prevalence of schizophrenia in their families, as do children and adults with schizophrenia. Features associated with autism but not schizophrenia include a higher male–female ratio, onset in very early childhood, and co-occurrence of mental retardation and epileptic seizures.

In part to clarify the differentiation of autism from schizophrenia, DSM-III introduced (and DSM-IIIR retained) the term **pervasive developmental disorders**. This term emphasized that autism involves a serious abnormality in the developmental process itself and thus differs from the mental disorders originating in adulthood. In DSM-IV, autistic disorder is but one of several pervasive developmental disorders, the others being Rett's Disorder, Child Disintegrative Disorder, and Asperger's Disorder. Because these newly included categories have not been researched much, our focus here is on autism.

Autism begins in early childhood and indeed can be evident in the first weeks of life. It occurs relatively infrequently in the general population, in approximately three or four infants in 10,000. Studies indicate that about four times more boys than girls have autism. Autism is found in all socioeconomic classes and in all ethnic and racial groups.

Parents may attribute an autistic infant's behavior to several factors. They may believe that the baby will grow out of it and become more responsive as he or she matures. They may adapt to the infant, believing that the behavior is normal, just different from what they expected. Other parents may realize that something is very wrong but be unable to admit it to themselves. Sometimes they fear that the baby is deaf. Parents may first realize that something is seriously awry when the infant misses an important developmental marker. For example, the absence or peculiarity of speech development by age two often compels parents to determinedly pursue an accurate diagnosis.

Autism and Mental Retardation

Kanner believed that children with autism were probably of average intelligence. He based this conclusion on their good physical condition and on their skill at some tasks requiring rote memory or spatial ability. Empirical investigations indicate, however, that approximately 80 percent of autistic children score below 70 on standardized intelligence tests. Because of the significant number of autistic children who are also mentally retarded, it is sometimes difficult to differentiate the two disabilities.

But there *are* important differences. Although retarded children usually score consistently poorly on all parts of an intelligence test, the scores of autistic children may have a more differentiated pattern. In general, autistic children do worse on tasks requiring abstract thought, symbolism, or sequential logic, all of which may be associated with language. They usually obtain better scores on items requiring visual–spatial skills, such as matching designs in block design tests and putting together disassembled objects (DeMyer, 1975; Rutter, 1983). In addition, as described in Focus Box 16.3, they may have isolated skills reflecting great talent, such as multiplying two four-digit numbers rapidly in their heads. They may also have exceptional long-term memory, being able to recall the exact words of a song heard years earlier. In addition, sensorimotor development is the area of greatest relative strength among autistic children. Retarded children are much more delayed in areas of gross motor development, such as learning to walk. In contrast, autistic children, who may show severe and profound deficits in cognitive abilities, can be quite graceful and adept at swinging, climbing, or balancing.

Because of the social nature of autistic children's disability, standard scores on intelligence tests have been questioned. In fact, autistic children used to be referred to as untestable. Although testing an autistic child is difficult because such children generally will not sit still, follow directions, or attend to the task at hand, modifications of testing procedures have made it possible to evaluate autistic youngsters meaningfully. For example, concrete reinforcements, such as giving candy for paying attention to a task and not hand flapping, usually succeed in focusing the child's attention long enough to administer a test. In addition, care must be taken to choose tests that are appropriate for the child's developmental level and skills; administering a test requiring expressive verbal responses is clearly inadequate for determining the cognitive abilities of a nonverbal autistic child (Freeman & Ritvo, 1976).

Extreme Autistic Aloneness

The social deficits of autistic children also differentiate them from the mentally retarded. In a sense autistic children do not withdraw from society—they never joined it to begin with. Table 16.2 shows how such children have been described by their parents. Note that there is much variability in the autistic signs observed.

Normal infants may show signs of attachment, usually to their mothers, as early as three months of age. In autistic children this early attachment is virtually absent. They do not smile or reach out or look at their mothers when being fed. Infants may reject parents' affection by refusing to be held or cuddled, arching their backs when picked up to minimize the contact normal infants—and parents—love. Although normal infants often coo or cry or fret to attract parental attention, autistic children seldom initiate contact with the caregiver, except when hungry or wet. Indeed, such children are often de-

Table 16.2. • Parental Report of Social Relatedness in Autistic Children before Age 6

	Percentage of Responses				
Relatedness Measure	*Never*	*Rarely*	*Often*	*Very Often*	*Almost Always*
1. Ignored people	0	4	22	29	45
2. Emotionally distant	0	8	23	19	50
3. Avoided eye contact	2	4	20	16	58
4. No affection or interest when held	11	11	35	26	17
5. Going limp when held	30	33	17	17	2
6. Stiff/rigid when held	33	24	7	18	18
7. Ignored affection	6	30	34	11	19
8. Withdrew from affection	12	33	29	10	15
9. Cuddling when held	26	24	29	10	15
10. Accept/return affection	30	34	26	4	6
11. Looked through people	4	10	22	22	41
12. Seemed not to need mother	12	20	32	8	28
13. Responsive smile to mother	14	30	30	14	12
14. Unaware of mother's absence	17	25	25	14	19

Source: Adapted from "An Evaluation of DSM-III Criteria for Infantile Autism" by F. R. Volkmar, D. J. Cohen, and R. Paul, 1986, *Journal of the American Academy of Child Psychiatry, 25,* p. 193. Copyright 1986 by the American Academy of Child Psychiatry. Adapted by permission.

FOCUS 16.3 • The Idiot or Autistic Savant

A classic case reported by Scheerer, Rothman, and Goldstein (1945) set forth a syndrome called idiot savant, referring to a retarded person with superior functioning in one narrow area of intellectual activity. In recent years the term *autistic savant* has also been applied, the assumption being that these individuals are really autistic. The autism is believed to discourage the individuals from using their intact intellectual abilities for normal pursuits, instead channeling their abilities into internal mental games that occupy their time and focus their concentration. This might be seen as analogous on the mental level to self-stimulation and twirling on the psychomotor level, two other characteristics of autistic children.

In a wonderfully written book about people suffering from a wide range of neuropsychological disorders, the physician Oliver Sacks (1985) describes twins John and Michael, twenty-six years old at the time he met them. They had been hospitalized since age seven, diagnosed at various times as autistic, psychotic, or severely retarded. They had been on television many times because of their ability to say immediately on what day of the week a date far in the past or future had fallen or would fall.

> Their memory for digits is remarkable—and possibly unlimited. They will repeat a number of three digits, of thirty digits, of three hundred digits, with equal ease. . . . But when one comes to test their ability to calculate—the typical forte of arithmetical prodigies and "mental calculators"—they do astonishingly badly, as badly as their IQs of sixty might lead one to think. They cannot do simple addition or subtraction with any accuracy, and cannot even comprehend what multiplication or division means. . . .
>
> And yet, even in some of their performances, their "tricks," there is a quality that takes one aback. They can tell one the weather, and the events, of any day in their lives—any day from about their fourth year on. Their way of talking . . . is at once childlike, detailed, without emotion. Give them a date, and their eyes roll for a moment, and then fixate, and in a flat, monotonous voice they tell you of the weather, the bare political events they would have heard of, and the events of their own lives—this last often including the painful or poignant anguish of childhood, the contempt, the jeers, the mortifications they endured, but all delivered in an even and unvarying tone, without the least hint of any personal inflection or emotion. (p. 197–198)

When Sacks met them, they were in the hospital where they lived. The following scene is reminiscent of an incident in the movie *Rain Man*, starring Dustin Hoffman.

> A box of matches on their table fell, and discharged its contents on the floor: "111," they both cried simultaneously; and then, in a murmur, John said "37." Michael repeated this, John said it a third time and stopped. I counted the matches—it took me some time—and there were 111.
>
> "How could you count the matches so quickly?" I asked. "We didn't count," they said. "We *saw* the 111." . . .
>
> "And why did you murmur '37,' and repeat it three times?" I asked the twins. They said in unison, "37, 37, 37, 111." And this, if possible, I found even more puzzling. That they should *see* 111—111-ness"—in a flash was extraordinary. . . . But they had then gone on to "factor" the number 111—without having any method, without even "knowing" (in the ordinary way) what factors meant. . . .
>
> "How did you work that out?" I said, rather hotly. They indicated, as best they could, in poor, insufficient terms—but perhaps there are no words to correspond to such things—that they did not "work it out," but just "saw" it, in a flash. John made a gesture with two outstretched fingers and his thumb, which seemed to suggest that they had spontaneously *trisected* the number, or that it

scribed as good babies because they make few demands. Autisic infants are usually content to sit quietly in their playpens, completely self-absorbed, never noticing the comings, goings, and doings of other people. However, by age two or three many autistic children do form some emotional attachment to their parents or to other caregivers.

Impaired attachment to parents is not the only way in which the autisic child's social development is poor. The child rarely approaches others and may look through or past people or turn his or her back on them. When play is initiated by someone else, however, the autistic child may be compliant and engage in the selected activity for a period of time.

"came apart" of its own accord, into these three equal parts, by a sort of spontaneous, numerical "fission." They seemed surprised at my surprise—as if *I* were somehow blind; and John's gesture conveyed an extraordinary sense of immediate, *felt* reality. . . .

[Another time I saw the twins], they were seated in a corner together, with a mysterious, secret smile on their faces, a smile I had never seen before, enjoying the strange pleasure and peace they now seemed to have. I crept up quietly, so as not to disturb them. They seemed to be locked in a singular, purely numerical, converse. John would say a number—a six-figure number. Michael would catch the number, nod, smile, and seem to savour it. Then he, in turn, would say another six-figure number, and now it was John who received, and appreciated it richly. They looked, at first, like two connoisseurs wine-tasting, sharing rare tastes, rare appreciations. I sat still, unseen by them, mesmerized, bewildered.

What were they doing? What on earth was going on? I could make nothing of it. It was perhaps a sort of game, but it had a gravity and an intensity, a sort of serene and meditative and almost holy intensity, which I had never seen in any ordinary game before, and which I certainly had never seen before in the usually agitated and distracted twins. I contented myself with noting down the numbers they uttered—the numbers that manifestly gave them such delight, and which they "contemplated," savoured, shared, in communion.

Had the numbers any meaning, I wondered on the way home. . . . As soon as I got home I pulled out tables of powers, factors, logarithms and primes—mementos and relics of an odd, isolated period in my own childhood. . . . I already had a hunch—and now I confirmed it. *All the numbers, the six-figure numbers, which the twins had exchanged were primes*—i.e., numbers that could be evenly divided by no other whole number than itself or one. Had they somehow seen or possessed such a book as mine—or were they, in some unimaginable way, themselves "seeing" primes, in somewhat the same way they had "seen" 111-ness, or triple 37-ness? Certainly they could not be *calculating* them—they could calculate nothing.

I returned to the ward the next day, carrying the precious book of primes with me. I again found them closeted in their numerical communion, but this time, without saying anything, I quietly joined them. They were taken aback at first, but when I made no interruption, they resumed their "game" of six-figure primes. After a few minutes I decided to join in, and ventured a number, an eight-figure prime. They both turned towards me, then suddenly became still, with a look of intense concentration and perhaps wonder on their faces. There was a long pause—the longest I had ever known them to make, it must have lasted a half-minute or more—and then suddenly, simultaneously, they both broke into smiles.

They had, after some unimaginable internal process of testing, suddenly seen my own eight-digit number as a prime—and this was manifestly a great joy, a double joy, to them; first because I had introduced a delightful new plaything, a prime of an order they had never previously encountered; and, secondly, because it was evident that I had seen what they were doing, that I liked it, that I admired it, and that I could join in myself.

They drew apart slightly, making room for me, a new number playmate, a third in their world. Then John, who always took the lead, thought for a very long time—it must have been at least five minutes, though I dared not move, and scarcely breathed—and brought out a nine-figure number; and after a similar time his twin, Michael, responded with a similar one. And then I, in my turn, after a surreptitious look in my book, added my own rather dishonest contribution, a ten-figure prime I found in my book.

There was again, and for even longer, a wondering, still silence; and then John, after a prodigious internal contemplation, brought out a twelve-figure number. I had no way of checking this, and could not respond, because my own book . . . did not go beyond ten-figure primes. But Michael was up to it, though it took him five minutes—and an hour later the twins were swapping twenty-figure primes, at least I assume this was so, for I had no way of checking it. (pp. 199–203)

Physical play such as tickling and wrestling may actually appear to be enjoyable to the child. Observations of spontaneous play in an unstructured setting demonstrate that children with autism spend much less of their time engaged in symbolic play, such as making a doll drive to the store or pretending that a block is a car, than do either mentally retarded or normal children of comparable mental age (Sigman, Ungerer, Mundy, & Sherman, 1987).

Few autistic children may be said to have friends. Not only do they seldom initiate play with other children, but potential companions, like parents, usually receive little responsiveness from the autistic child. Autistic infants may avert their gaze if parents try to communicate with them, and they are described as engaging in less eye contact than their peers. The sheer amount of gazing may sometimes be relatively normal, but not the way in which it is used. Normal children gaze to gain someone's attention or to direct the other person's attention to an object. The autistic child generally does not do this (Mirenda, Donnellan, & Yoder, 1983).

Some autistic children appear not to recognize or distinguish one person from another. They do become preoccupied with and form strong attachments to keys, rocks, a wire mesh basket, light switches, a large blanket; to mechanical objects such as refrigerators and vacuum cleaners. If the object is something that they can carry, they walk around with it in their hands, thus preventing them from learning to do more useful things.

There are conflicting views of whether social withdrawal is a primary or secondary characteristic of autism. Kanner (1943) believed it was primary, and that other features were a result of this emotional withdrawal and failure to interact with the world. Fein and colleagues (Fein et al., 1986) present evidence in favor of viewing social withdrawal as the primary feature of autism, noting that even children with Down syndrome, severe retardation, brain damage, or environmental deprivation do not show the kinds of social aloofness present even in high-functioning autistic children. However, it is also possible that the core deficit is an inability to process certain kinds of sensory input, which leaves the child helpless to understand and respond to the world around him or her (Rimland, 1964).

Communication Problems

Even before the period when language is usually acquired, autistic children have deficits in communication. Babbling, a descriptive term for the utterances of infants before they actually begin to use words, is less frequent in infants with autism and conveys less information than does that of other infants (Ricks, 1973).

By two years of age, most normally developing children use words to represent objects in their surroundings and construct one- and two-word sentences to express more complex thoughts. About 50 percent of all autistic children never learn to speak at all (Rutter, 1966). Even when they do, many peculiarities are found, among them **echolalia**. The child echoes, usually with remarkable fidelity and in a high-pitched monotone, what he or she has heard another person say. The teacher may ask an autistic boy, "Do you want a cookie?" The child's response will be "Do you want a cookie?" This is immediate echolalia. In delayed echolalia the child may be in a room with the television on and with others conversing and appear to be completely uninterested. Several hours later or even the next day, the child may echo a word or phrase from the conversation or television program. Mute autistic children who later do acquire some functional speech through training usually first pass through a stage of echolalia.

In the past most educators and researchers believed that echolalia served no functional purpose. But Prizant (1983) and others have suggested that echolalia may actually be an attempt to communicate. The boy who was offered a cookie decides at a later time that he does want one. He will approach the teacher and ask, "Do you want a cookie?" Although the child may not know what each of the individual words means, he has certainly learned that the phrase is connected with getting a cookie.

Another abnormality common in the speech of autistic children is **pronoun reversal**. The children refer to themselves as "he," or "you," or by their own proper names. Pronoun reversal is closely linked to echolalia. Since autistic children often use echolalic speech, they will refer to themselves as they have heard others speak of them; pronouns are misapplied. For example:

Parent: What are you doing, Johnny?
Child: He's here.
Parent: Are you having a good time?
Child: He knows it.

If normal speech is developed, this pronoun reversal might be expected to disappear. It has been reported, however, to be highly resistant to change (Tramontana & Stimbert, 1970); some children have required very extensive training even after they have stopped parroting the phrases of other people.

Neologisms, made-up words or words used with other than their usual meaning, are another characteristic of the speech of autistic children. Neologisms may also be a consequence of echolalia. If a word or phrase heard earlier is repeated later by the autistic child, it may be inappropriate to the present situation. Autistic children may also change slightly the original words or phrase. These alterations may develop into made-up words. Of course, all children make up words in this fashion. Normal children, however, alter their idiosyncratic words as they listen to the speech of others and are corrected by those who care for them.

Children with autism are very literal in their use of words. If a father provided positive reinforcement by putting the child on his shoulders when he or she learned to say the word yes, then the child might say yes to mean that he or she wants to be lifted onto the father's shoulders. In the reverse, called metaphorical language, the child may say, "Do not drop the cat" to mean the more general no, because his or her mother had used these emphatic words when the child was about to drop the family kitten.

Communication deficiencies may leave a lasting mark of social retardation on the child. The link between social skills and language is made evident by the often spontaneous appearance of affectionate and dependent behavior in these children after they have been trained to speak (Churchill, 1969; Hewett, 1965). Even after they learn to speak, however, people with autism often lack verbal spontaneity and are sparse in their verbal expression and less than entirely appropriate in their use of language (Paul, 1987).

Compulsive and Ritualistic Acts

Autistic children become extremely upset over changes in daily routine and their surroundings. An offer of milk in a different drinking cup or a rearrangement of furniture may make them cry or bring on a temper tantrum. Even common greetings must not vary.

> Each morning she had to be greeted with the set phrase "Good morning, Lily, I am very, very glad to see you." If even one of the very's was omitted, or another added she would start to scream widly. (Diamond, Baldwin, & Diamond, 1963, p. 304)

An obsessional quality, similar to the preservation of sameness, pervades the behavior of autistic children in other ways. In their play they may continually line up toys or construct intricate patterns with household objects. They may become preoccupied with train schedules, subway routes, and number sequences. By adolescence, full-blown obsessions sometimes appear.

Autistic children are also given to stereotypical behavior, peculiar ritualistic hand movements, and other rhythmic movements, such as endless body rocking, hand flapping, and walking on tiptoe. They spin and twirl string, crayons, sticks, and plates, twiddle their fingers in front of their eyes, and stare at fans and spinning things. They may also become preoccupied with manipulating a mechanical object and be very upset when interrupted. Often toys are used in a compulsive and ritualistic manner rather than for their intended purpose.

Prognosis in Autistic Disorder

What happens to such severely disturbed children when they reach adulthood? Kanner (1973) reported on the adult status of nine of the eleven children

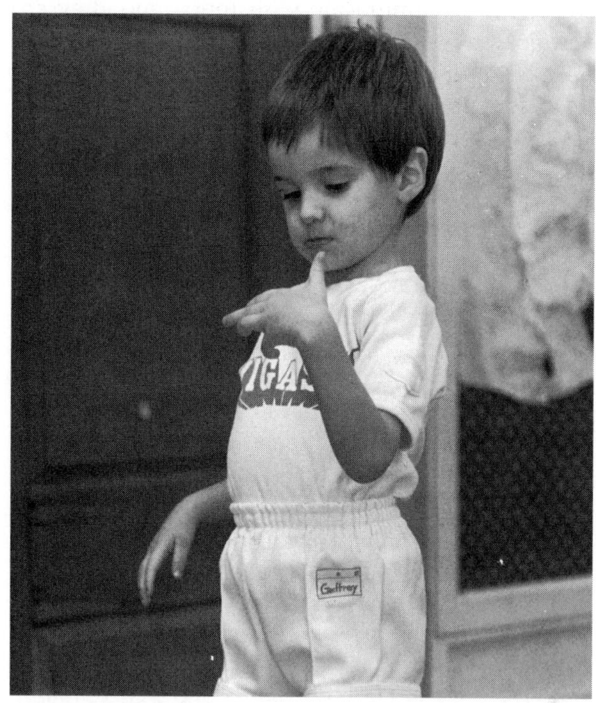

Autistic children frequently engage in stereotypical behaviors such as ritualistic hand movements which they stare at.

whom he had described in his original paper on autism. Two developed epileptic seizures; one of them died, and the other was in a state mental hospital. Four others had spent most of their lives in institutions. Of the remaining three, one had remained mute but was working on a farm and as an orderly in a nursing home. The last two made at least somewhat satisfactory recoveries. Although both still lived with their parents and had little social life, they became gainfully employed and developed some recreational interests.

Other follow-up studies corroborate the generally gloomy picture of adult autistics (e.g., Lotter, 1974; Rutter, 1967; Treffert, McAndrew, & Dreifuerst, 1973). From his review of all published studies, Lotter (1978) concluded that only 5 to 17 percent of autistic children had made a relatively good adjustment in adulthood, leading independent lives but with some residual problems, such as social awkwardness. Most of the others had limited lives, and about half were institutionalized (see Focus Box 16.4). Prior to the passage of Public Law 94-142 in 1975 (page 472), autistic children were often excluded from educational programs in the public schools. Thus most of the autistic children followed into adulthood have not had the benefit of intensive educational interventions or the kind of intensive behavioral program described below (p. 486). New follow-up studies are needed to determine whether the prognosis for autism will remain as universally

FOCUS

16.4. • A First-Person Account of an Adult Autistic Man

Excerpted below, with some punctuation and spelling corrections made by the professionals who published the account (Volkmar & Cohen, 1985), is a first-person report by a twenty-two-year-old man who had been treated for autism as a very young child at the Yale Child Study Center and who had returned to gain access to his records. In the course of many meetings with the staff, he decided to write an account of his experiences as an autistic child and now as a young adult. This depiction is unusual because autistic children seldom acquire enough cognitive and linguistic abilities to communicate in this way.

"Tony" had been described by his parents as, from the first weeks of life, avoiding human contact, never smiling responsively to others, and being preoccupied with his hands and with spinning objects. When examined at twenty-six months of age at the Yale center, he did not speak, exhibited bizarre and highly stereotyped behavior, and showed no interest in others. After treatment at the center, he was able to enter a special education program in a public school and was even able to attend a private high school until the tenth grade. His WAIS IQ at the time he wrote his autobiographical account was 94 Verbal, 92 Performance, and 93 Full Scale, which placed him just a little below the average and was described as "a testament to his intellectual abilities" (Volkmar & Cohen, 1985, p. 48). When he contacted the center, he was employed as an assembler in a local industry.

Tony's account of his life contains features that are often found in people with autistic disorder, such as his sense of social isolation, inability to empathize with others, unusual sensory experiences, and pervasive anxiety (and occasional abuse of alcohol in attempts to diminish it). Less typical of such individuals are the anger and aggressive tendencies he reports, and perhaps also his desire to be considered normal and his interest in the opposite sex. The reader should note that Tony succeeded in obtaining a driver's license and enlisting in the army.

AUTISM: "THE DISEASE OF ABOMINATION"

Tony W.

I was living in a world of daydreaming and Fear revolving aboud my self I had no care about Human feelings or other people. I was afraid of everything! I was terrified to go in the water swimming, (and of) loud noises; in the dark I had severe, repetitive Nightmares and occasionally hearing electronic noises with nightmares. I would wake up so terrified and disoriented I wasnt able to Find my way out of the room for a few miniuts. It felt

devastating as was the case before the training and education of people with autism were taken seriously by society.

Etiology of Autistic Disorder

Psychological Bases of Autism

Since Kanner first described autism, researchers have been seeking its cause. Some of the same reasons that led Kanner to consider autistic children to be average in intelligence, their normal appearance and apparently normal physiological functioning, led some to regard autism as environmentally caused.

One of the best known of the psychological theories was formulated by Bruno Bettelheim (1967). The basic supposition of his theory was that autism closely resembles the apathy and hopelessness found among inmates of German concentration camps during World War II. Bettelheim hypothesized that the young infant has rejecting parents and is able to perceive their negative feelings. The infant finds that his or her own actions have little impact on their unresponsiveness. The child comes to believe "that [his or her] own efforts have no power to influence the world, because of the earlier conviction that the world is insensitive to [his or her] reactions" (p. 46). Thus, the autistic child never really enters the world but builds the "empty fortress" of autism against pain and disappointment.

Some behavioral theorists, like those who are psychoanalytically oriented, have postulated that certain childhood learning experiences cause autism. Ferster (1961), in an extremely influential article, suggested that the inattention of the parents, especially of the mother, prevents establishment of the associations that make human beings reinforcers.

> like I was being draged to Hell. I was afraid of simple things such as going into the shower, getting my nails cliped, soap in my eyes. . . . I rember Yale Child Study Ctr. I ignored the doctors and did my own thing such as make something and played or idolize it not caring that anybody was in the room. I was also very hat(e)full and sneakey. I struggled and breathed hard because I wanted to kill the gunia pig; as soon as the examiner turned her back I killed it. I hated my mother becaus she try to stop me from being in my world and doing what I liked; so I stoped and as soon as she turn her back I went at it agen. I was very Rebellious and sneaky and distructive. I would plot to kill my mother and destroy the world. . . . I also (had) a very warp sence of humor and learn(ed) perveted thing(s) verry quickly. I used to lash out of controll and repeat sick, perverted Phrases as well as telling people violent, wild, untrue things to impress them. . . . I like machanical Battery Power toys or electronic toys. Regular toys such as toy trucks, cars that wernt battery powered didnt turn me on at all. I was terrified to learn to ride the bybycle. One thing I loved that not even the Fear could stop was Airplanes. I saw an air show the planes—f4s—were loud. I was allway(s) Impressed by Airplanes. I drew picutres and had severeal Airplane models. The Test came when we went to D.C. I was so Anxious and Hyper to go on the plane I drove my Parrents nut. The only peace they had is when I heard the turbines reving at the end of the runway. Then I knew we were taking off. Soon as the plane took off I was amazed. I started to yell y(a)h HO! I loved every minuit of it. I allways loved Hi tech thing(s)—Planes, Rockets. . . . I dont or didnt trust anybody but my self—that still (is) a problem today. And (I) was and still (am) verry insucure! I was very cold Harted too. I(t) was impossible for me to Give or Receive love from anybody. I often Repulse it by turning people off. Thats is still a problem today and relating to other people. . . . I woudl hear electronic Noises and have quick siezious (seizures) in bed and many other ph(y)sical problems. Often I have to be Force to get things done and (was) verry uncordinated. And was verry Nervious about everything. And Feared People and Social Activity Greatly. . . . I lived with my father and the(n) saw the so call(ed) normal, sick teenage world. I was 14. I set my will (to) be normal like everybody else. (I) look(ed) up to people in school and did what they did to be accepted and put (up) more of a show to hide the problems and be Normal. I forced(d) my self to Know all the top rock groups, smoke pot, and drink and (tried to) have a girl friend. This was the 9th grade and 10th. I constantly got in trouble in school and did som(e) real crazy things to be cool. Like everybody else I thought I was all normal. Most of it was a failure. More people hated me then ever. . . . I went into the army and got in lots of Fights with people. So I got dicarged (discharged). . . . I worked a few more Jobs and hung around w/some Crazy people I knew from school and got drunk a lot and did distructive things. Magnified Fears and Peronia on pot. I never got Fired from a job. My problems havn't changed at ALL from early childhood. I was Just able to Function. And it still (is) the same today—1983. (*Volkmar & Cohen, 1985, pp. 49–52*)

And because the parents have not become reinforcers, they cannot control the child's behavior, the result being autistic disorder.

Both Bettelheim and Ferster, as well as others, have stated that parents play the crucial role in the etiology of autism. Many investigators have therefore studied the characteristics of these parents; for a psychogenic theory of a childhood disorder to have any plausibility at all, something very unusual and damaging about the parents' treatment of their children would have to be demonstrated.

In his early papers, Kanner described the parents of autistic children as cold, insensitive, meticulous, introverted, distant, and highly intellectual (Kanner & Eisenberg, 1955). Singer and Wynne (1963) described several means by which these parents "disaffiliate" themselves from their children. Some are cynical about all interpersonal relations and are emotionally cold; others are passive and apathetic; and still others maintain an obsessive, intellectual distance from people.

Systematic investigations, however, have failed to confirm these clinical impressions. For example, Cox and his colleagues (1975) compared the parents of autistic children with those of children with receptive aphasia (a disorder in understanding speech); the two groups did *not* differ in warmth, emotional demonstrativeness, responsiveness, and sociability. This and other studies (e.g., Cantwell, Baker, & Rutter, 1978) provide overwhelming evidence that there is nothing remarkable about the parents of autistic children. In fact, such parents raise other perfectly normal and healthy siblings.

Even if we were to ignore these findings, the direction of a possible correlation between parental characteristics and autism is not easily determined. Any deviant behavior could be a reaction to the child's abnormality rather than the other way

FOCUS 16.5. • The Pernicious Nature of Psychogenic Theories

Readers of this book have no doubt noticed that the authors are often critical of some psychogenic theories, both psychoanalytic and learning. In addition to our aspirations to provide as scientifically accurate a textbook as possible, we are concerned about the impact that theories may have on people. Consider, for a moment, what your feelings might be if a psychiatrist or psychologist were to tell you that your unconscious hostility has caused your child to be mute at the age of six. Or how would you feel if you were told that your commitment to professional activities has brought about the autistic behavior patterns of your child? The fact is, of course, that the truth of these allegations has never been demonstrated, and considerable information even contradicts these views. But in the meantime a tremendous emotional burden is placed on parents who have, over the years, been told that they are at fault.

As Rimland (1964) suggested, considering autism psychogenic in origin is not only an incorrect hypothesis, but also a pernicious one.

around. Moreover, there is no evidence that any kind of emotional maltreatment, deprivation, or neglect can produce behavior that resembles the syndrome of autism (Ornitz, 1973; Wing, 1976) (see Focus Box 16.5). Indeed, the very early onset of autism and an accumulation of neurological and genetic evidence imply a biological basis for this puzzling disorder.

Biological Bases of Autism

Genetic Factors Genetic studies of autism are difficult to conduct because the disorder is so rare. Indeed, the family method presents special problems because autistic persons almost never marry. In cases where autistics have siblings, the rate of autism in their brothers and sisters is about 2 percent (Rutter, 1967). Although this is a small percentage, it represents a fiftyfold increase in risk compared with the morbidity risk in the general population.

Further evidence of the importance of genetic factors in autism is provided by a methodologically sound study conducted by Folstein and Rutter (1978). In ten pairs of fraternal twins, one of whom had autism, there was no concordance of the co-twins. But in eleven pairs of identical twins, one of whom had autism, the concordance rate was 36 percent; four of the co-twins had autism. Even stronger evidence for genetic transmission of autism comes from a study by Steffenberg et al. (1989), who found 91 percent concordance in MZ twins and zero percent in DZ twins.

In addition to examining concordance for autism, Folstein and Rutter also looked for cognitive disabilities, such as delayed speech, problems in saying words properly, and low IQ, in the co-twins. Concordance for cognitive impairment was 82 percent for the MZ pairs and 10 percent for the DZ pairs. Thus the identical twin of an autistic child is very likely to have difficulties of speech and intellect, but the fraternal twin of an autistic child is not. Autism is apparently linked genetically to a broader deficit in cognitive ability. Further support for this position comes from finding a higher incidence of a spectrum of learning disabilities in the families of autistic children (August, Stewart, & Tsai, 1981). Taken together, the evidence from family and twin studies supports a genetic basis for autistic disorder.

Neurological Factors Early EEG studies of autistic children indicated that many had abnormal brain wave patterns (e.g., Hutt et al., 1964). Other types of neurological examination also revealed signs of damage in many autistic children (e.g., Campbell et al., 1982; Gillberg & Svendsen, 1983). Further evidence supporting the possibility of neurological dysfunction includes a recent study using magnetic resonance scans of the brain, which found that portions of the cerebellum were underdeveloped in autistic children (Courchesne et al., 1988). This abnormality was present in fourteen of eighteen autistic subjects. The degree of neurological abnormality or central nervous system dysfunction seems to be related to the severity of the autistic symptoms. In adolescence 30 percent of those who had severe autistic symptoms as children begin having epileptic seizures. Furthermore, the prevalence of autism in children whose mothers had rubella during the prenatal period is approximately ten times higher than that in the general population of children. A syndrome similar to autism may follow in the aftermath of meningitis, encephalitis, and tuberous sclerosis, all of which may affect central nervous system functioning. These findings, plus the degree of mental retardation, would seem to link autism and brain damage.

Treatment of Autistic Disorder

Special Problems in Treating Autistic Children

Educational programs for autistic children usually try to relieve their symptoms and improve their communication, social skills, and adaptive behavior so that they can become more independent. Autistic children have several problems that make teaching them difficult, however. First, they do not adjust normally to changes in routines, and efforts to teach necessarily involve such changes. Second, their behavior problems and self-stimulatory movements may interfere with effective teaching. Although the similar behavior of children with other disabilities may intrude on the teacher's efforts, it does not do so with the same frequency and severity.

Third, it is particularly difficult to find reinforcers that motivate autistic children. Normal children like to explore and control their surroundings, but not children with autism. For reinforcers to be effective with autistic children, they must be explicit, concrete, or highly salient. A widely used method of increasing the range of reinforcers that autistic children respond to is to pair social reinforcement with primary reinforcers, such as food. A further problem that often interferes with the learning of autistic children is their overselectivity of attention. When the child's attention becomes focused on one particular aspect of a task or situation, other properties, including relevant ones, may not even be noticed.

An additional concern, one that educators and therapists of autistic children share with educators of retarded children, is the youngsters' inability to generalize learning. The overselective nature of autistic children's attention makes generalization especially difficult for them. For example, the child who has learned several words by watching the instructor's lip movements may not comprehend the same words spoken by another person with less pronounced lip movements. In other words, the child's response may be contingent on a nonessential aspect of the situation, which is usually not present if the context is changed. In spite of all these problems, educational programs for students with autism have achieved some positive results.

Primary reinforcers such as food are typically used in therapy with autistic children.

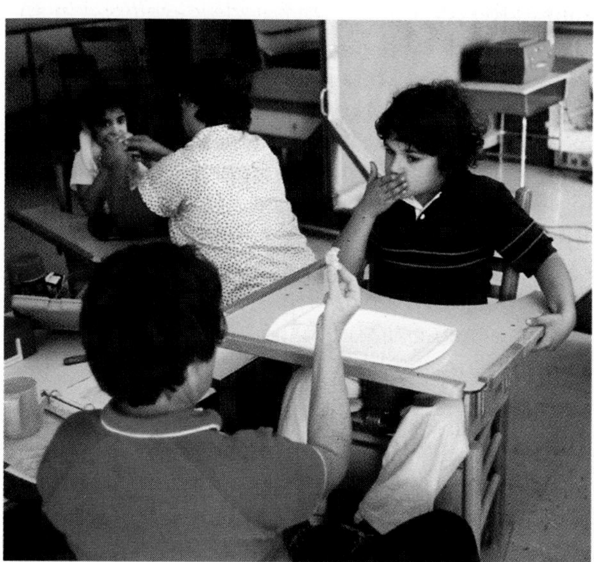

Behavioral Treatments

Mental health professionals agree that autistic children have been helped through modeling and operant conditioning. Behavior therapists have taught autistic children to talk (Hewett, 1965), modified their echolalic speech (Carr, Schreibman, & Lovaas, 1975), encouraged them to play with other children (Romanczyk et al., 1975), and helped them become more generally responsive to adults (Davison, 1964).

Clara Park (1987), mother of an autistic child grown up, writes of her discovery of an innovative behavioral program to teach her daughter essential social skills.

> There is a sense in which the most important thing Jessy every learned was to smile and say hello. How did she learn to do this? Certainly a cheerful household contributed. But it was by no means enough. . . . However we coaxed and encouraged, she did not in fact learn to greet another human being until she was 14 years old. She learned it not through imitation or osmosis, but through a behavior-modification program. . . . Jessy learned to say "Hello, Mrs. Jones" via an ordinary, score-keeping golf counter, available at any sporting goods store. "Hello" earned her one point; eye contact, another; the proper name, a third. "Hello, Mrs. Jones" . . . and people at school began to report their astonishment. Jessy was suddenly so much more friendly. Of course they were all smiles, greeted for the first time after Jessy had so long ignored them. Social reinforcement could hardly have been stronger or more naturally delivered. It was some time before they noticed the click-click-click of Jessy's counter.
>
> This was only one of the many behaviors which could gain or lose points. Jessy kept track of them all, with autistic literalness. Autistic people don't cheat. We had stumbled onto the system by accident: Jessy had seen the counter on a visiting child, been fascinated with an instrument that combined two of her strongest interests, clicks and numbers, and decided she wanted one of her own. Only slowly did we discover how to use it, to utilize her strengths—her exactitude and thoroughness, her grasp of num-

bers—to address her weaknesses. . . . We watched in amazement as Jessy . . . rapidly acquired a large repertoire of new behaviors and eliminated others we had assumed we must live with forever, spurred on by something no more concrete than a rising tally. (Years later, she was to watch with the same satisfaction the rising balance in her bank account.) (pp. 291–292)

Ivar Lovaas, a leading clinical researcher at the University of California at Los Angeles, describes an intensive operant program with very young (under four years) autistic children (Lovaas, 1987). Therapy encompassed all aspects of the children's lives for more than forty hours a week over more than two years. Parents were trained extensively so that treatment could continue during almost all the children's waking hours. Nineteen youngsters receiving this intensive treatment were compared with forty controls who received a similar treatment for less than ten hours per week. All children were rewarded for being less aggressive, more compliant, and more socially appropriate, including talking and playing with other children. The goal of the program was to mainstream the children, the assumption being that autistic children, as they improve, benefit more from being with normal peers than by remaining by themselves or with other seriously disturbed children.

The results were quite dramatic and encouraging for the intensive therapy group. Their measured IQs averaged 83 in first grade (after about two years in the intensive therapy) compared with about 55 for the controls; twelve of the nineteen reached the normal range, compared with only two (of forty) in the control group. Furthermore, nine of the nineteen intensives were promoted to second grade in a normal public school, whereas only one of the much larger control group achieved this level of normal functioning. Although critics have pointed out weaknesses in the study's methodology and outcome measures (Schopler, Short, & Mesibov, 1989), this ambitious program confirms the need for heavy involvement of both professionals and parents in dealing with the extreme challenge of autistic disorder.

Ivar Lovaas, a behavior therapist, is noted for his operant conditioning treatment of autistic children.

Autism, like mental retardation, places considerable stress on a family. Because autistic children have few or no physical disabilities and some isolated normal and even superior abilities, their parents may even hope that the diagnosis is erroneous. One way to ease the parents' burden is to instruct them about the nature of autistic disorder, especially the virtual certainty that it does not have a psychogenic cause. Relieved of the guilt associated with this pernicious belief, some parents will want to become involved in the education of their child. There is reason to expect that the education provided by parents is more beneficial to the child than clinic- or hospital-based treatment. In work similar to that of Lovaas, Koegel and his colleagues (1982) demonstrated that after only 25 to 30 hours of parent training, autistic children's improvements on standardized tests and behavioral measures were similar to those after over 200 hours of direct clinic treatment. Koegel concluded that parent training is superior in generalizing learning because parents are present in many different situations, and, when training their children, they may actually spend more time with them in recreational and leisure activities.

At the same time, it must be clearly stated that some autistic and other severely disturbed children can be adequately looked after only in a hospital or in a group home staffed by mental health professionals. Moreover, the circumstances of some families preclude the home care of a seriously disturbed child. The fact that effective treatments can be implemented by parents should not be transformed into a must-do for those who are already living their lives and taking care of other normal children under trying circumstances.

Psychodynamic Treatment

A very different treatment of autism was developed over many years by Bruno Bettelheim (1967, 1974) at the Orthogenic School of the University of Chicago. Bettelheim argued that a warm, loving atmosphere must be created to encourage the child to enter the world. Patience and what Rogerians would call unconditional positive regard were believed to be necessary for the child to begin to trust others and to take chances in establishing relationships. Bettelheim and his colleagues reported many instances of success, but the uncontrolled nature of their observations makes it difficult to know what the active ingredients might have been. Bettelheim's treatment may contain more direct instruction, systematic reinforcement, and extinction than comes through in the published reports. By the same token, of course, reports of behavior therapists usually underplay the rapport building that undoubtedly provides the context for their programs.

Drug Treatment

The most commonly used medication for treating autistic behaviors is haloperidol, an antipsychotic medication. However, many autistic children do not respond positively to this drug, consistent with the differentiation of autism from early-onset schizophrenia (page 476), and it also has potentially serious side effects (Campbell, 1987).

There is some evidence that autistic children have elevated blood levels of serotonin (Anderson & Hoshino, 1987). Researchers from eighteen to twenty medical centers under the leadership of Ritvo at the University of California at Los Angeles studied the effectiveness of fenfluramine, a drug known to lower serotonin levels in rats and monkeys. Results of early studies administering fenfluramine to autistic children were quite positive; not only were serotonin levels lowered, but IQs and behavior were significantly improved (Geller et al., 1982, 1984; Ritvo et al., 1983). However, although several reports replicated the initial findings (Ritvo et al., 1986), concerns have been raised about negative side effects (particularly excessive sedation, increased irritability, and transient weight loss). Furthermore, several investigators have failed to demonstrate improvements in cognitive or behavioral functioning (Campbell, 1987, 1988). Future research is needed to identify reasons for the discrepant findings in different laboratories and to clarify which autistic children, if any, are likely to benefit from the drug.

Other researchers have studied an opioid receptor antagonist, naltrexone, and found this drug to reduce self-injurious behavior in autistic children and to reduce hyperactivity, increase attention span, and reduce the severity of autistic behaviors (Campbell et al., 1989). The first double-blind, placebo-controlled study of naltrexone produced mixed results: although the children on naltrexone improved more than the placebo group in terms of global ratings by staff (who were blind to treatment condition), more specific behavioral ratings did not show significant differences in favor of the drug (Campbell et al., 1990). Clearly, more controlled studies are needed to determine whether naltrexone will prove to be a helpful medication for use with autistic children.

SUMMARY

Learning disorders are diagnosed when a child fails to develop to the degree expected by his or her intellectual level in a specific academic, language, or motor skill area. These disorders, which are two to four times more prevalent in males than in females, are usually identified and treated within the school system rather than through mental health clinics.

The diagnostic criteria for mental retardation are subaverage intellectual functioning and deficits in adaptive behavior, with onset before the age of eighteen. Four levels of retardation are designated, ranging from the profound, when IQ is less than 20, to mild, when IQ is 50 to 70. The more severe forms of mental retardation usually have a biological basis, such as the chromosomal trisomy that causes Down syndrome. Certain infectious diseases suffered by the pregnant mother, such as rubella and syphilis, or affecting the child directly, for example, encephalitis, can stunt cognitive and social development. So can malnutrition, severe falls, and automobile accidents that injure the brain. For the mild range of retardation, which is by far the most prevalent, no identifiable brain damage is evident. Environmental factors are considered the principal causes. Among the specific findings are that these people come from lower-class homes in which deprivation is great.

Researchers try to prevent mild retardation by giving children at risk through impoverished circumstances special preschool training and social opportunities. Many retarded children who would formerly have been institutionalized are now being educated in the public schools under the mainstreaming provisions of Public Law 94-142. In addition, using applied behavioral analysis, self-instructional training, and modeling, behavior therapists have been able to treat successfully many of the behavioral problems of retarded individuals as well as improve their intellectual functioning.

Autistic disorder, one of the pervasive developmental disorders, usually begins before the age of thirty months. The major symptoms are extreme autistic aloneness, a failure to relate to other people; communication problems, either a failure to learn any language or speech irregularities such as echolalia and pronoun reversal; and preservation of sameness, an obsessive desire that daily routines and surroundings be kept exactly the same. On the basis of early clinical reports, some psychologically biased theorists concluded that the alleged coldness and aloofness of parents and their rejection of their children bring on autism, but recent research gives no credence to such notions. Although no certain biological basis of autism has been found, a number of facts make such a cause plausible; its onset is very early; both family and twin studies give evidence of a genetic predisposition; neurological tests often reveal abnormalities; a syndrome similar to autism can develop after meningitis and encephalitis; and many autistic children have the low intelligence associated with brain dysfunctions.

The most promising treatments of autism have often used procedures that rely on modeling and operant conditioning. Although the prognosis for autistic children remains poor in general, Lovaas's recent work suggests that with intensive behavioral treatment, some of these children may be able to lead normal lives.

KEY TERMS

learning disorders
learning disabilities
reading disorder (dyslexia)
mathematics disorder
disorder of written expression
language disorders
receptive language disorder
expressive language disorder
phonological disorder
motor skills disorder
mild mental retardation
moderate mental retardation
severe mental retardation
profound mental retardation
Down syndrome (trisomy 21)
fragile X syndrome
phenylketonuria (PKU)
applied behavior analysis
self-instructional training
autistic disorder
pervasive developmental disorders
echolalia
pronoun reversal

c h a p t e r   s e v e n t e e n

Aging and Psychological Disorders

The patient is a fifty-six-year-old right-handed businessman who had entered the hospital for cervical disk surgery. Because of his busy schedule and his anxiety relating to surgery, he had canceled his admission on two previous occasions. The patient was a fairly heavy social drinker but not to the point of interfering in any way with his business performance. The surgery was uneventful and there were no immediate complications of the procedure. The patient was greatly relieved and seemed to be making a normal recovery until the third postoperative night. During that night he became quite restless and found it difficult to sleep. The next day he was visibly fatigued but otherwise normal. The following night his restlessness became more pronounced, and he became fearful and anxious. As the night progressed, he thought that he saw people hiding in his room, and shortly before dawn he reported to the nurse that he saw some strange little animals running over his bed and up the drapes. At the time of morning rounds, the patient was very anxious and frightened. He was lethargic, distractible, and quite incoherent when he tried to discuss the events of the night before. He knew who he was and where he was but did not know the date or when he had had his surgery. During that day his mental status fluctuated, but by nightfall he had become grossly disoriented and agitated. At this point, psychiatric consultation was obtained.

The consultant's diagnosis was acute postoperative confusional state [delirium]. The cause was probably due to a combination of factors: withdrawal from alcohol, fear of surgery, use of strong analgesics, stress of the operation, pain, and the sleepless nights in an unfamiliar room. The treatment consisted of a reduction in medications for pain, partial illumination of the room at night, and a family member in attendance at all times. These simple changes in conjunction with 50 mg of chlorpromazine (Thorazine) three times daily and 500 mg of chloral hydrate at bedtime reversed his confusional state within two days, and he was able to return home in a week with no residual evidence of abnormal behavior. To date there has been no recurrence of these problems. (Strub & Black, 1981, pp. 89–90).

The more fortunate readers of this book will grow old one day. When and as you do, physiological changes are inevitable, and there may be many emotional and mental changes as well. Are the aged at higher risk for mental disorders than the young? Are earlier emotional problems of anxiety and depression likely to become worse in old age? Do these emotional problems develop in people who did not have them when younger? Is it reasonable to expect a satisfying sex life in old age? Do societal attitudes play a role in how people feel about themselves as they grow old? Finally, are some therapies especially appropriate to our elders, and does society devote suitable monetary and intellectual resources to the development of effective ways of helping our older citizens? As life expectancy extends into the seventies and beyond, what is the professional community doing *now* to acquire knowledge and techniques that can make old age more meaningful than it has been for past generations, in the United States and in many other countries?

In contrast to the esteem in which they are held in most Asian countries, the elderly are generally not treated very well in the United States. The process of growing old, although inevitable for us all, is abhorred, even resented, by many. Perhaps the lack of regard for senior citizens stems for our own deep-seated fear of and misconceptions about growing old. The old person with serious infirmities is an unwelcome reminder that some of us may one day walk with a less steady gait, see less clearly, taste food less keenly, enjoy sex less frequently and with apparently less intensity, and fall victim to some of the many diseases and maladies that are the lot of most old people before they depart this world.

The psychological problems of aging may be especially severe for women. Even with the consciousness-raising of the past three decades, our society does not readily accept in women the wrinkles and sagging that become more and more prominent with advancing years. The cosmetics and plastic surgery establishments make billions of dollars each year exploiting the fear inculcated in women about looking their age. Although gray hair at the temples and even a bald head are often considered distinguished in a man, a great many women who have the financial means to buy a few more years of youthful appearance do so.

Elderly individuals from minority ethnic groups experience a double jeopardy: African-American and Mexican-American elders have considerably lower income and poorer health, as well as lower life satisfaction, than their white counterparts (Dowd & Bengston, 1978; Gerber, 1983). And societal biases against women contribute to what some consider triple jeopardy, with elderly minority women running the greatest risk of economic dependency and associated problems (Blau, Oser, & Stephens, 1979).

Older adults often suffer discrimination because of **ageism**, which can be defined as discrimination against any person, young or old, based on chronological age. In this chapter, our focus is on ageism as it relates to prejudicial attitudes and behavior toward older adults. Ageism can be seen when a professor in her sixties is considered too old to continue teaching at a university as well as when a person older than seventy-five is ignored in a social gathering on the assumption that he has nothing to contribute to the conversation. Like any prejudice, ageism ignores the *diversity* among people in favor of employing stereotypes (Gatz & Pearson, 1988).

A more subtle form of ageism is potentially as pernicious, for example, when we smile a special smile or shout a special hooray as a ninety-two-year-old man crosses the finish line at a sporting event. Gatz, Pearson, and Fuentes (1984) call this positive kind of ageism countermyth, a reaction to the negative myths just mentioned, which emphasize disadvantage and deterioration. Countermyths assert that there are no problems in growing old. As we shall see, the truth seems to lie somewhere in between.

Mental health professionals have until recently almost phobically ignored the behavioral and emotional problems of the elderly. There is misinformation, such as the belief that intellectual deterioration is prevalent and inevitable, that depression among old people is widespread and untreatable, that sex is a lost cause. Although those who provide mental health services are probably not extremely ageist (Gatz & Pearson, 1988), their attitudes and practices merit special attention because of the influence they have over policies that affect the lives of older adults. In the past decade research and training in gerontology have been introduced into the curricula of many schools and universities that prepare people for the health professions, although there is still a dearth of professionals primarily committed to serving the needs of older adults (Gatz & Sruyer, 1992).

This relative neglect of older adults is problematic, considering their growing numbers. In 1900 only 4 percent of the U.S. population was over age sixty-five. Due to such factors as better health care and the control of illnesses such as cancer and cardiovascular diseases, this figure rose to more than 12 percent by 1987. It is predicted that by the year 2040, the percentage will rise to between 21 and 25, a result of the baby boomers of the 1950s reaching age sixty-five and older (Guralnik, Yanagashita, & Schneider, 1988; U.S. Bureau of the Census, 1986). And the oldest-old, those above age eighty-five, are expected to grow to nearly 24 million by the year 2040. Thus is it important to examine what we know about the psychological and neuropsychological problems of older adults. We will first review some general concepts and issues critical to the study of aging. Then we will look at brain disorders of old age, after which we will examine psychological disorders—most of which we have already discussed—with a particular focus on how these disorders are manifest in old age. Finally, we will discuss general issues of treatment and care for the elderly.

Concepts and Methods in the Study of Older Adults

Diversity in Older Adults

In any discussion of the differences between the elderly and those not yet old, the elderly are usually defined as those over the age of sixty-five. The decision to use this age was set largely by social policies, not because age sixty-five is some critical point at which the physiological and psychological processes of aging suddenly begin. To have some rough demarcation points for better describing the diversity of the elderly, gerontologists usually divide those over age sixty-five into three groups: the young-old, those aged sixty-five to seventy-four; the old-old, those aged seventy-five to eighty-four; and the oldest-old, those over age eighty-five. The health of these groups differs in important ways. The word *diversity* is well applied to the older population. Not only are older people different from one another, but they are more different from one another than are individuals in any other age group! In essence, people tend to become less alike as they grow older.[1]

Age, Cohort, and Time-of-Measurement Effects

Chronological age is not as simple a variable in psychological research as we might expect, for being any age is associated with a host of other factors. For example, diet, medical care, and social habits all

[1]That all old people are alike is a prejudice held by many younger people. To know that a person is sixty-seven years old is, in itself, to know very little about him or her. And yet a moment's honest reflection may indicate to the reader that certain traits come to mind when we hear that a person is age sixty-seven. The many *differences* in people who are sixty-five and older will become increasingly evident in the course of reading this chapter.

Cohort effects refer to the fact that people of the same chronological age may differ considerably depending on when they were born.

change with time; we must be cautious when we attribute differences in age groups solely to the effects of aging, because other factors associated with age may be at work. Being age seventy in 1994 is different from having been seventy in 1964. In the field of aging, therefore, as in studies of earlier development, including childhood, a distinction is made among the contributions of what are called **age effects,** the consequences of being a given chronological age; **cohort effects,** the consequences of having been born in a given year and having grown up during a particular time period with its own unique pressures, problems, challenges, and opportunities; and **time-of-measurement effects,** a possible confound in research whereby events at a particular point in time can have a specific effect on a variable that is being studied over time (Schaie & Hertzog, 1982). The two major research designs used to assess developmental change, the cross-sectional and the longitudinal, clarify these terms.

In **cross-sectional studies** the investigator compares different age groups at the same moment in time on the variable of interest. Suppose that in 1985 I took a poll and found that many of my interviewees over seventy spoke with a European accent, whereas those in their thirties and forties did not. Could I conclude that as people grow older they develop European accents? Hardly! Cross-sectional studies do not examine the same people over time; they allow us to make statements only about age differences in a particular study or experiment, not about age changes over time.

In the hypothetical study just mentioned, many people in the older sample, or cohort, came to this country from abroad. In **longitudinal studies,** the researcher selects one cohort and then periodically retests it, using the same measure over a number of years. Thus it allows us to trace individual patterns of consistency or change over time and to analyze how behavior in early life relates to behavior in old age.

Conclusions drawn from longitudinal studies are restricted to the particular cohort chosen, however, for each cohort is unique. This limitation is a problem of longitudinal studies. For example, if a cohort is studied from 1940 to 1980 and its members are found to decline in sexual activity as they enter their sixties, we cannot conclude that the sexuality of those in a cohort studied from 1980 to 2020 will decline when they reach the same age. Improvements over time in health care and changes in other variables such as social mores might enhance the sexual activity of the younger cohort. Another problem with longitudinal studies is that subjects often drop out of them as the studies proceed, creating a source of bias commonly called **selective mortality.** The least able subjects are the most likely to drop from a study; the nonrepresentative people who remain are usually healthier than the general population. Thus, findings based on longitudinal studies may be too optimistic concerning the amount of decline in something like sexual activity over the life span.

Contrary to popular belief, longitudinal studies do not allow us to measure pure age changes. Time-of-measurement effects also have to be considered. For example, because of a coronary risk scare in 1980, many people in a cohort may have given up smoking cigarettes between the time of their first measurement in 1970 and their next measurement in 1985. At the next evaluation their physical health—which usually declines—may actually have *improved* because fewer have smoked since the 1980 scare, a time-of-measurement effect.

Diagnosing Psychopathology in Later Life

The DSM criteria are basically the same for older adults as they are for younger. The nature and manifestations of mental disorders are apparently assumed to be the same in adulthood and old age, even though little research supports this assumption (LaRue, Dessonville, & Jarvik, 1985). We often do not know what certain symptoms of older adults mean because we have few specifics about psychopathology in the elderly (Zarit, Eiler, & Hassinger, 1985). For example, somatic symptoms are generally more prevalent in late life, but these symptoms are also evident in depression in older adults. Are the somatic symptoms of a depressed older adult necessarily a part of depression? Or might they (also) reflect physical decline?

Range of Problems

We already know that mental health may be tied to the physical and social problems in a person's life. Although this can be true at any age, no other group of people have more of these problems than the aged. They have them all—physical decline and disabilities, sensory and neurological deficits, the cumulative effects of a lifetime of many unfortunate experiences and social stresses. However, it is important also to remember that in addition to a lifetime of exposure to losses and to other stressors, both expected and unexpected, older adults may have many positive life experiences, coping mechanisms, and wisdom on which to draw. Moreover, we are just beginning to investigate how some cultural and ethnic factors mitigate the negative effects of aging. Older adults who belong to groups that provide meaningful, strong roles for the elderly seem to have an easier time adjusting to growing old than do those who are not allowed such input into the family or society (Amoss & Harrell, 1981; Keith, 1982).

Old Age and Brain Disorders

Although the majority of older people do not have organic brain disorders, these problems account for more admissions and hospital inpatient days than any other condition of geriatric adults (Christie, 1982). Two principal types of brain disorders are distinguished, dementia and delirium; we will examine both.

Dementia

Clinical Description

Dementia is what laypeople call senility; it is a gradual deterioration of intellectual abilities to the point that social and occupational functioning are impaired. Difficulty in remembering things, especially recent events, is the most prominent symptom of dementia. People may leave tasks unfinished because they forget to return to them after an interruption. A person who had started to fill a teapot at the sink leaves the water running. A parent may be unable to remember the name of a daughter or son and later not even recall that he or she has children. Hygiene may be poor and appearance slovenly because the person forgets to bathe or how to dress adequately. Dementia patients also get lost, even in familiar surroundings.

Judgment may become faulty, and the person may have difficulty in comprehending personal situations and making plans or decisions. The demented also lose their standards and control of their impulses; they may use coarse language, tell inappropriate jokes, shoplift, and make sexual advances to strangers. The ability to deal with abstract ideas also declines, and disturbances in the emotions are common, including both flatness of affect and sporadic emotional outbursts. The course of dementia may be progressive, static, or remitting, depending on the cause. Eventually, many with progressive dementia become withdrawn and apathetic. In the terminal phase of the illness, the personality loses its sparkle and integrity. Relatives and friends say that the person is just not himself or herself anymore. Social involvement with others keeps narrowing. In the end, the person is oblivious to his or her surroundings.

The prevalence of definite cases of dementia in the aged has been estimated at approximately 2 to 5 percent when noninstitutionalized adults are considered, and another 2 to 3 percent are added from the institutionalized aged (Folstein et al., 1991; Gurland & Cross, 1982). Only a small proportion of persons under age sixty suffer from dementia, but approximately 30 percent of individuals over the age of eighty do (Gurland & Cross, 1982; Heston & White, 1991; Jarvik, Ruth, & Matsuyama, 1980; LaRue, Dessonville, & Jarvik, 1985). **Cerebrovascular diseases,** illnesses that disrupt blood supply to the brain, represent a major cause of dementia (see Focus Box 17.1).

Causes of Dementia

Dementias are usually divided into two categories, primary and secondary. Primary dementia is produced directly by brain impairment, as in the case of cerebrovascular disease. The secondary dementias are caused by diseases that do not attack the brain directly.

Primary Dementia Alzheimer's disease accounts for 50 percent of dementia in the elderly. It is usually referred to as dementia of the Alzheimer's type (DAT) because a definitive diagnosis can be made only by microscopic examination of the brain tissue after death. When the person is alive, a diagnosis of Alzheimer's is made by exclusion, that is, by ruling out other possible causes of the person's cognitive and behavioral symptoms. Much research is being done, though, to develop tests that can more reliably identify living people with the disease (Matsuyama & Jarvik, 1989).

In **Alzheimer's disease** the brain tissue irreversibly deteriorates, with death usually occurring ten or twelve years after the onset of symptoms. About 100,000 Americans die each year from the disease. The disorder is somewhat more prevalent among women than among men. The disease was first described by the German neurologist Alois Alzheimer in 1860. It commences with difficulties in concentration and memory for newly learned material; the individual appears absentminded and irritable, shortcomings that soon begin to interfere with daily living. The person blames others for personal failings and has delusions of being persecuted. Memory continues to deteriorate, with the individual becoming increasingly disoriented and agitated.

The primary physiological change in the brain, evident at autopsy, is a general atrophy of the cerebral cortex as neurons are lost, particularly axons and dendrites rather than the cell bodies themselves (Kowall & Beal, 1988). The fissures widen and the ridges become narrower and flatter. The ventricles also become enlarged. Moreover, senile plaques—small round areas consisting of the remnants of the lost neurons, and amyloid, a waxy substance deposited when protein synthesis is disturbed—are scattered throughout the cortex; tangled abnormal protein filaments, neurofibrillary tangles, accumulate within the cell bodies of neurons. These plaques and tangles are present throughout the cerebral cortex and the hippocampus. The cerebellum, spinal cord, and sensory areas of the cortex are less affected, which is why Alzheimer's patients do not appear to have anything physically wrong with them until late in the disease process. In addition to being able to walk around normally, overlearned habits, like making small talk, remain intact for some time so that, in short encounters, strangers may not notice that there is anything amiss.

Although neural pathways using different transmitters (e.g., serotonin, norepinephrine) deteriorate (Lawlor et al., 1989; Wester et al., 1988), those using acetylcholine are of particular importance. There is evidence that anticholinergic drugs can produce in normal subjects memory impairments similar to

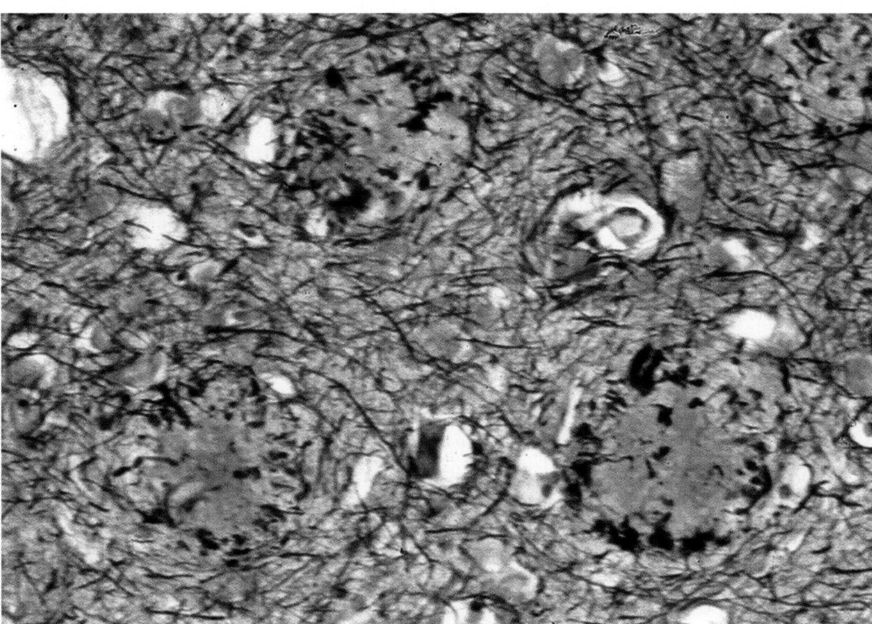

In this photograph of brain tissue from a patient with Alzheimer's Disease, the waxy amyloid shows up as areas of dark pink.

those found in Alzheimer's patients. The number of acetylcholine terminals are reduced in the brains of DAT patients (Strong et al., 1991), and levels of the major metabolite of acetylcholine are low in Alzheimer's patients and are related to the extent of the patient's mental deterioration (Wester et al., 1988).

The risk for Alzheimer's is increased in first-degree relatives of afflicted individuals (Mohs et al., 1987), and among some families the pattern of inheritance suggests the operation of a single dominant gene. Furthermore, the gene controlling the protein responsible for the formation of plaques has been shown to be on the long arm of chromosome 21, and a recent linkage study has demonstrated an association between this gene and the expression of the disease (Tanzi et al., 1987). Although another linkage study did not confirm these results (Schellenberg et al., 1988), it involved patients of a much younger age. Therefore, early and late onset of Alzheimer's may have different etiologies (Nyth et al., 1991; Small et al., 1989) and only a subset of cases of DAT may be genetically linked to chromosome 21.

Aluminum may also play a role in some Alzheimer's type dementias. Animal research shows that aluminum can induce lesions such as those found in DAT and is found in excess quantity in the brains of DAT patients (Heston & White, 1991). Finally, the immune system may also be involved. The amyloid found in the brains of patients with DAT is also present in other diseases in which the immune system plays a significant role. Furthermore, some researchers have reported finding a novel antigen in the brains of DAT patients that could be attacking the brain (Bisette et al., 1991). We are, though, far from understanding the causes of Alzheimer's.

A number of infectious diseases can also produce irreversible primary dementia. *Encephalitis,* a generic term for any inflammation of brain tissue, is caused by viruses that enter the brain either from other parts of the body (e.g., the sinuses or ears) or from the bites of mosquitoes or ticks. *Meningitis,* an inflammation of the membranes covering the outer brain, is usually caused by a bacterial infection. The organism (*Treponema pallidum*) that produces the venereal disease syphilis can also invade the brain and cause dementia. Finally, several rare viral illnesses can be causes (Creutzfeld-Jacob disease, kuru, and Gerstmann-Straussler syndrome).

Neurological diseases, such as *Huntington's chorea,* can also produce dementia. Huntington's is caused by a single dominant gene located on chromosome 4 and is diagnosed principally by the presence of writhing (choreiform) movements. Similarly, *Parkinson's disease,* marked by muscle tremors, muscular rigidity, and akinesia (an inability to initiate movement) can lead to dementia. Finally, in *normal pressure hydrocephalus* an impairment in the circulation of the cerebrospinal fluid leads to an accumulation in the brain's ventricles (water on the brain). Pressure builds and creates dementia as well as difficulty standing and walking. The condition is reversible with surgery to restore normal circulation of cerebrospinal fluid.

17.1 • Cerebrovascular Diseases—Stroke and Its Aftermath

The blood vessels supplying the brain are subject to several types of malfunction. In atherosclerosis, deposits of fatty material narrow the lumen, or inner passageway, of the arteries of the body. When those in the brain are affected, some areas may not receive enough blood and hence insufficient oxygen and glucose. If the shortage is prolonged, the brain tissue, which is particularly dependent on receiving adequate supplies, softens, degenerates, and is even destroyed. The effects of cerebral atherosclerosis vary widely, depending on what area of the brain has clogged arteries and whether it is also supplied by nonaffected blood vessels. About three million Americans are presently incapacitated in some way by cerebral atherosclerosis.

In **cerebral thrombosis** a blood clot forms at a site narrowed by atherosclerosis and blocks circulation. Carbon dioxide builds up and damages the neural tissues. The loss of consciousness and control is referred to as apoplexy or **stroke.** The patient may suffer paralysis or decreased sensation on one side of the body or on an arm or leg, lose other motor and sensory functions, or die. The impairments of the patients who survive may disappear spontaneously, or they may be lessened through therapy and determined effort. Usually there is some residual damage. When only a small vessel is suddenly blocked, the patient suffers transient confusion and unsteadiness. A succession of these small strokes brings cumulative damage, however.

In **cerebral hemorrhage** a blood vessel ruptures because of a weakness in its wall, damaging the brain tissue on which the blood spills. Cerebral hemorrhages are frequently associated with hypertension. The psychological disturbance produced depends on the size of the vessel that has ruptured and on the extent and the location of the damage. Often the person suffering a cerebral hemorrhage is overtaken suddenly and rapidly loses consciousness. When a large vessel ruptures, the person suffers a major stroke. All functions of the brain are generally disturbed—speech, memory, reasoning, orientation, and balance. The person usually lapses into a coma, sometimes with convulsions, and may die within two to fourteen days. If the person survives, he or she will probably have some paralysis and difficulties with speech and memory, although in some cases appropriate rehabilitation restores nearly normal functioning.

A frequent impairment is **aphasia,** a disturbance of the ability to use words. The cause of this damage may be a clot in the middle cerebral artery supplying the parietotemporal region, usually of the dominant cerebral hemisphere. A right-handed person depends on the parietotemporal region in the left hemisphere for language skills; a left-handed person may depend on this region in the right hemisphere or in the left.

The following case illustrates the human impact of a stroke and efforts that can be made to restore some semblance of normalcy.

At age sixty-eight, Mr. H., a retired small businessman, was active in community affairs and with his hobby of woodworking. He had high blood pressure that was well controlled on medication and had had diabetes for several years, which was controlled with insulin. Mr. H. was accustomed to being independent and in charge of things, and this was acceptable to his wife of forty-five years. Mr. H. believed that any reduction of his independent status would be a sign of weakness. He was generally even tempered but would become angry when he was hindered from completing a task he had set out to do. . . .

Mrs. H. was active with her church group and had frequent visitors. She was in good health but had only moderate physical strength. She prepared well-balanced meals for both of them, including the special diet required for Mr. H. because of his diabetes and high blood pressure. They had two children, both of whom were married and living out of state, but who visited at holiday times.

One morning Mrs. H. entered her husband's workshop and found him sitting on a chair and unable to speak. The right side of his face drooped and he was unable to move his right arm or leg. He did not seem to see her when she approached him from his right but could see her when she moved to his left side. He made a few attempts to speak but was unsuccessful. Mrs. H. called their physician, who arranged for ambulance transportation to the

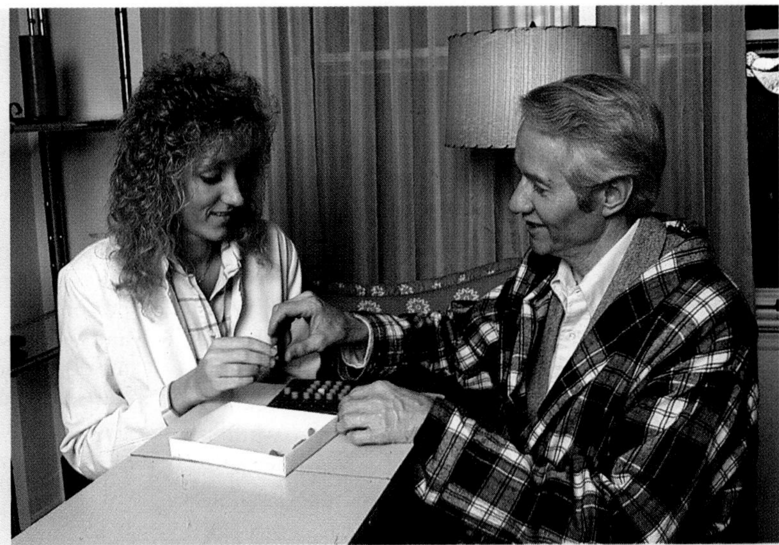

In recovering from a stroke, patients need therapy to help them regain lost skills such as fine motor control.

hospital. Detailed examination and testing revealed that Mr. H. had sustained a stroke due to the occlusion [the complete blockage] of an artery supplying the left side of his brain. After receiving acute care including that necessary to prevent complications and reaching a stabilized condition, Mr. H. was transferred to a comprehensive medical rehabilitation center. . . .

Mrs. H. found that she would be part of the rehabilitation process, that the staff would work closely with her, and that she would receive training necessary to help in her husband's care when he returned home. She would also receive counseling to aid her in coping skills and help her adapt to this change in their life situation. . . . As Mr. H. progressed in the program, they taught him how to inject his insulin with his left hand and taught his wife how to draw up the proper amount in the syringe.

Mr. H. began to regain some communication ability, and his function was carefully evaluated by the speech pathologist, who aided him in improving general communication abilities. She informed Mrs. H. and the rehabilitation team members about how best to communicate with Mr. H. Speech therapy was also used to improve the volume and clarity of his speech.

As communication abilities improved, a psychologist evaluated Mr. H.'s mental status and cognitive skills and helped him to adapt to the frustrations of his disability and his feelings of [not] being in control. The psychologist also helped Mr. H. direct his anger in a more productive manner rather than diffusely taking out frustrations on the staff or on his wife. . . .

The physical therapist gradually helped Mr. H. improve his bed mobility and transfers, and eventually he progressed to the point where he was ambulating, first with a broad-based four-pointed cane and maximum assistance, and ultimately with a straight cane with his wife standing by. The occupational therapist worked on teaching Mr. H. to use his nondominant hand while he was also working to improve function in the weak right hand. He was taught to feed himself, to dress himself, and to perform the basic activities of daily living. He was also given exercises and training that would [allow him to pursue] his woodworking hobby, at least to a limited degree.

The recreational therapist helped Mr. H. to reach some self-fulfillment during his leisure time. His leisure activities were geared to those he had previously enjoyed, adapted to his disability. Transportation and financial status were discussed with Mrs. H. and also with her husband, and appropriate community agency referrals were made. An occupational therapist went out to the house to evaluate the existence of architectural barriers and to make recommendations for safety.

During this course of events, the rehabilitation team met weekly to discuss the problems that Mr. H. was experiencing, to compare ideas on solving these problems, and to plan the treatment approach for the forthcoming week. After about a month of this treatment Mr. H was able to return home with his wife at a semi-independent level, with plans to return for outpatient treatment in order further to increase his strength, mobility, self-care, and communication skills. (Zarit, 1980, pp. 179–180)

Secondary Dementias Secondary dementias can arise from a number of diseases or conditions. Depression, particularly one that includes psychomotor retardation (Heston & White, 1991), is a significant cause. When the depression lifts, the dementia lifts also. Other causes of secondary dementia include hormonal imbalances, drugs (including alcohol), and atherosclerosis (see Focus Box 17.1). In the latter case, *multi-infarct dementias* develop gradually and have a variable course (brain tissue can partially recover from the damage caused by a series of small strokes). The specific symptoms of multi-infarct dementia depend on whether the infarcts affect the cerebral cortex or subcortical areas. Various infections (e.g., pneumonia, infections of the urinary system) can also produce dementia. HIV infection and AIDS cause irreversible dementia, but this kind of brain damage is currently a problem of younger people.

Treatment of Dementia

If the dementia has a reversible cause, appropriate medical treatment should begin immediately, for example, correcting a hormonal imbalance. To date no clinically significant treatment has been found for Alzheimer's disease, although investigations are numerous. It is a degenerative disease, resulting in continued deterioration of the patient.

Because of the death of brain cells that secrete acetylcholine in DAT, various studies have attempted to increase the levels of this neurotransmitter. Research using choline (a precursor of the enzyme that catalyzes the reaction producing acetylcholine) and physostigmine (a drug that prevents the breakdown of acetylcholine) have been disappointing. Tetrahydroaminoacridine (THA), which also prevents the breakdown of acetylcholine, has yielded positive effects on short-term memory, but it is not known if any longer term benefits will be produced (Heston & White, 1991). In March 1993, the Food and Drug Administration approved the marketing of the drug, also known as tacrine, in recognition of the lack of promising alternatives to the treatment of this fatal disease. Long-term strategies focus on slowing the progression of the disease. Growth factors and other drugs that prevent alterations in cell metabolism offer hope of actually preventing neural degeneration (Whitehouse, 1991), underscoring ongoing efforts to develop tests for early detection of Alzheimer's. Management of other symptoms of DAT includes many of the drugs previously discussed, for example, phenothiazines for paranoia, diazepine for anxiety, and sedatives for sleep difficulties.

Turning to psychosocial interventions, Zarit (1980) succinctly summarized those that make sense.

> The treatment of persons with [progressive] senile dementia is basically supportive both of affected individuals and of their social networks. . . . Treatment involves minimizing the disruption caused by the disorder. Goals for treatment include: maintaining the person in a community setting; allowing affected persons the opportunity of discussing their illness and its consequences; giving information to family members and other concerned persons about the nature of this disorder; supporting family members so that they can continue to provide assistance to the affected person; and using behavioral and problem-solving methods to deal with specific issues that arise as the result of the brain disorder. (p. 356)

For every individual with a severely disabling dementia living in an institution, there are two living in the community (Gurland & Cross, 1982), usually supported by a spouse, daughter, or other family member. The burden of caring for the elderly with dementia usually falls on family members. Thus treatment should concern not only the individual, but the family as well. As discussed later (p. 520) family caregivers and friends, faced with taxing demands on their time, energies, and emotions, can become depressed. One form of support is accurate information on the nature of the patient's problems. For example, because people with Alzheimer's have great difficulty placing new information into memory, they can engage in a reasonable conversation but forget a few minutes later what has been discussed. A caregiver may become impatient unless he or she understands that this impairment is to be expected because of the underlying brain damage. Making increased demands on the patient, perhaps in the belief that he or she is expressing hostility in a passive–aggressive manner, is likely to be aggravating for the person making the demands and for other family members and is not likely to help the elderly person's recollections. Homespun memory drills are also ill-advised, for there are no known techniques for improving the memories of persons with this disease.

Families can be taught, however, how to help their relatives cope with lost functions. Substituting recognition for recall in daily situations may help patients and families better manage their lives. Families can be taught to ask questions embedding the answer. It is much easier to respond to "Was the person you just spoke to on the phone Harry or Tom?" than to "Who just called?" Labels on drawers, appliances, and rooms help orient a person. If the individual has lost the ability to read, pictures

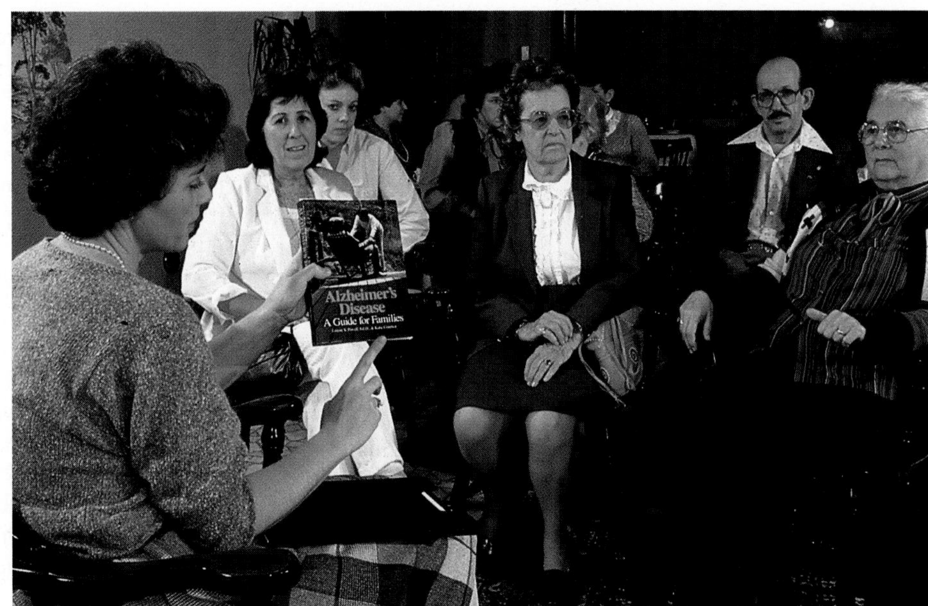

The task of caring for demented patients often falls on their families, who themselves need support and information on how to cope.

can be used instead of verbal labels. Prominent calendars, clocks, and strategic notes can also help, as can an automatic dialer on a telephone.

Caregivers should also be informed that patients do not always appreciate their limitations and may attempt to engage in activities beyond their abilities, sometimes in a dangerous manner. Although it is not advisable to coddle patients, it is important to set limits in light of their obliviousness to their own problems and impairments. Sometimes the caregiver's reactions to the patient's problems require attention. In one case, the daughter-in-law of a woman was offended by the woman's color combinations in clothing and wished to take over responsibility for coordinating her wardrobe, even though the patient was capable of dressing herself in an adequate, although not spiffy, fashion. The caregiver was urged not to impose her standards and taste on the patient, and to understand that her ability to dress herself and to take responsibility for her clothes was more important than adherence to conventional appearance (Zarit, 1980).

The counselor must bear in mind that some of the tensions between caregiver and patient may well have their roots in aspects of the relationship that predate the onset of the dementia. There is a tendency to consider the most obvious facet of a situation, here the impairments of a sick person, as the cause of all difficulties. Counseling directed to longstanding problems may be called for.

The paranoid delusions sometimes found in dementia can be disruptive. As with paranoia generally, the beliefs should not be challenged directly. It is better to try to work around them, concentrating on aspects of the person's behavior that are more intact. The delusions in dementia diminish with time, as memory worsens with the progressive cerebral deterioration; the prognosis for this aspect of the illness is, in a sad sort of way, good.

Counseling the impaired person is difficult and, with the more severely deteriorated, of apparently little long-term benefit because of their cognitive losses. But some patients seem to enjoy and be reassured by occasional conversations with professionals and with others not directly involved in their lives. It would appear important not to discount entirely their ability to participate in their caregiver's discussions of ways to cope with the problems they face. Their inherent cognitive limitations must be appreciated, however; Zarit (1980) even suggested that no efforts be made to get patients to admit to their problems, for their denial may be the most effective coping mechanism available.

The cognitive limitations of senile persons should always be treated with gentleness. Others should not consider them nonbeings, talking about their disabilities in their presence, making fun of their occasional antics and forgetfulness, discounting their paranoid suspicions about others. Older people, even those with no organic disorder, are often infantilized or ignored by their juniors, a sign of disrespect that demeans not only the elderly person but the person showing the discourtesy.

Perhaps the most heartrending decision is

Providing memory aids is one way of combating the severe memory loss of dementia.

whether and when to institutionalize the impaired person. At some point the nursing needs may become so onerous and the mental state of the person so deteriorated that placement in a nursing home is the only realistic option, for the benefit not only of the person but of the family. The conflicts encountered in making this decision are not to be underestimated. The counselor can be a source of information about nearby facilities as well as a source of support for making and implementing the decision (Zarit, 1980).

Delirium

Clinical Description

The term **delirium** is derived from the Latin words *de,* meaning "from" or "out of," and *lira,* meaning "furrow" or "track." The term thus implies being off track or deviating from the individual's usual state (Wells & Duncan, 1980). Although delirium is one of the most frequent organic mental disorders in older adults, it has been neglected in research and is, like dementia, often misdiagnosed. Progress in diagnosis has been impeded largely by terminological chaos. The literature reveals thirty or more synonyms signifying delirium (Liston, 1982); acute confusional state and acute brain syndrome are the two most common. The case that opened this chapter is illustrative.

People of any age are subject to delirium, but it is more common in children and older adults. Investigators have reported that 10 to 15 percent of older general-surgery patients become delirious after their operations (Miller, 1981). A review of the literature on delirium concluded that between one-third and one-half of all the hospitalized elderly are likely to be delirious at some point during their stay (Lipowski, 1983). Although the rates vary widely, even the lowest figures indicate that delirium is a serious health problem for older adults. Indeed, the mortality rate for delirium is extremely high; approximately 40 percent of the patients die, either from the underlying condition or from exhaustion (Rabins & Folstein, 1982). In fact, when fatality rates for dementia and delirium are compared over a one-year period, the rates are higher for delirium than for dementia, 37.5 compared with 16 percent.

Delirium is typically described as a "clouded state of consciousness." The patient, sometimes rather suddenly, has great trouble concentrating and focusing attention and cannot maintain a coherent and directed stream of thought. In the early stages of delirium, the person is frequently restless, particularly at night. The sleep–waking cycle becomes disturbed so that the person is drowsy during the day and awake, restless, and agitated during the night. The individual is generally worse during sleepless nights and in the dark. Vivid dreams and nightmares are common.

Delirious patients may be impossible to engage in conversation because of their wandering attention and fragmented thinking. Words are slurred, or they have difficulty finding them, and handwriting and spelling may become impaired. In severe delirium, speech is sparse or pressured and incoherent. Bewildered and confused, delirious individuals may become disoriented for time, place, and sometimes for person. But very often they are so inattentive that they cannot be questioned about orientation. In the course of a twenty-four-hour period, however, they do have lucid intervals and become alert and coherent. These fluctuations help to distinguish delirium from other syndromes, especially dementia.

Perceptual disturbances are common; individuals mistake the unfamiliar for the familiar. For example, they state that they are in a hotel instead of a hospital, and see the attending nurse as a room clerk. Moreover, they may see objects as too small, too big, misshapen, or duplicated. Although illusions and hallucinations are common, particularly visual and mixed visual–auditory ones, they are not always present in delirium. Paranoid delusions have been noted in 40 to 70 percent of the delirious aged. These delusions tend to be poorly worked out, fleeting, changeable, and tied to the surroundings.

Accompanying their disordered thoughts and perceptions are swings in activity and mood. Delirious people can be erratic, ripping their clothes one moment and sitting lethargically the next. They are in great emotional turmoil and may shift rapidly from one emotion to another—depression, anxiety, and fright, anger, euphoria, and irritability. Fever, flushed face, dilated pupils, rapid tremors, rapid heartbeat, elevated blood pressure, and incontinence of urine and feces are also common. If the delirium proceeds, the person will completely lose touch with reality and may become stuporous (Lipowski, 1980, 1983; Strub & Black, 1981).

The accurate diagnosis of delirium and its differentiation from conditions that resemble it are obviously critical to the welfare of older persons. Recognition and differentiation, however, presuppose knowledge of the distinguishing clinical symptoms. An elderly woman, for example, was found in a filthy apartment with no food. Initially believed by a poorly informed physician to be demented, she was simply given routine custodial care in a nursing home. Fortunately, a professional knowledgeable about delirium learned that she had become depressed over the loss of a loved one and had neglected her diet. Once this was recognized, appropriate attention was given to her nutritional deficiencies, and her condition improved to the point that she was discharged back to her own home after one month (Zarit, 1980).

This case is not atypical. Cameron et al. (1987) assessed 133 consecutive admissions to an acute medical ward. They found fifteen cases of delirium, but only one of these had been detected by the admitting physician. Older adults are often mistaken for senile and therefore beyond hope. A decision for long-term institutional care is all too often viewed as the only sound one, in spite of the fact that the person may have a reversible condition. The older adult who has cognitive impairment must be examined thoroughly for all possible reversible causes of the disorder, such as drug intoxications, infections, fever, malnutrition, and head trauma, and then treated accordingly.

Causes of Delirium

The causes of delirium in the aged can be grouped into several general classes: drug intoxications, metabolic and nutritional imbalances, infections or fevers, neurological disorders, and the stress of a change in the person's surroundings (Habot & Libow, 1980; Lipowski, 1980). It may also occur following major surgery (hip surgery is especially common; Gustafson et al., 1988), during psychoactive substance withdrawal, and following head trauma or seizures. Common physical illnesses causing delirium in this age group include congestive heart failure, pneumonia, urinary tract infection, cancer, uremia, malnutrition, dehydration, and cerebrovascular accidents or strokes. Probably the single most frequent cause of delirium in the aged is intoxication with prescription drugs (Besdine, 1980; Lipowski, 1983). In most cases, however, the delirium has more than one cause (Sloane, 1980).

Although delirium usually develops swiftly, within a matter of hours or days, the exact mode of onset depends on the underlying cause. Delirium resulting from a toxic reaction or concussion has an abrupt onset; when infection or metabolic disturbance underlies delirium, the onset of symptoms is gradual, over an extended period of time.

Why are the elderly especially vulnerable to delirium? Many explanations have been offered: the physical declines of aging, the increased general susceptibility to chronic diseases, the many medications prescribed for older patients, and vulnerability to stress. One other factor, brain damage, increases the risk of delirium. The elderly with dementing disorders appear to be the most susceptible of all. A retrospective review of 100 hospital admissions of people of all ages who had a diagnosis of delirium revealed that 44 percent of them had a delirium superimposed on another organic brain condition (Purdie, Honigman, & Rosen, 1981).

Treatment of Delirium

As already indicated, complete recovery from delirium is possible if the syndrome is correctly identified and the underlying cause promptly and effectively treated. Generally, the condition takes one to four weeks to clear, although it takes longer in the elderly than in the young. If the underlying causative condition is not treated, however, the brain can be permanently damaged and the patient may die.

One often neglected aspect of the management of delirium is educating the family of a senile parent to recognize the symptoms of delirium and its reversible nature. They may interpret the onset of delirium as a new stage of a progressive dementing condition. For example, a patient with Alzheimer's disease may run a high fever from an internal infection and begin to hallucinate and otherwise act bizarrely. These new symptoms, superimposed on the intellectual deterioration to which members of the family have become accustomed, may alarm them into concluding that the patient is losing ground fast and irreversibly. They may be rushed into a premature decision to institutionalize him or her. Proper diagnosis and treatment, however, can usually return the person to the earlier state, which, although problematic, could be coped with in the home.

Old Age and Psychological Disorders

An earlier discussion pointed out that transsexuals tend to attribute whatever personal unhappiness they experience to the discrepancy between their anatomy and their gender identity (page 337). A similar process operates with older adults, at least as they are viewed by others. The most obvious characteristic of a seventy-five-year-old man is that he is old. If he is cranky, it is because he is old. If he is depressed, it is because he is old. Even when he is happy, it is assumed to be because of his age. Moreover, the old-age explanation is generally a somatic one, even if this is not made explicit. Some ill-defined physical deterioration is assumed to underlie not only the physical problems of old people but all their psychological problems as well.

Although a psychological disorder at any age may have at least a partial physical explanation, this explanation can be problematic with older adults because it locates the cause of their problems within them and can blind us to other factors that may have much to do with whatever mental or emotional distress they are suffering. The fact is that most psychopathology found in the aged has *not* been directly linked to the physiological processes of aging. Whether the person brings maladaptive personality traits and inadequate coping skills into old age plays a role, as do health, genetic predisposition, and life stressors.

With these considerations in mind, we will first look at how common mental disorders are in late life and then survey a number of them, paying specific attention to how they manifest themselves in the elderly.

Overall Prevalence of Mental Disorders in Late Life

Is age itself a contributing factor to emotional and mental malfunction? Do more old people than young people have mental disorders? Whether mental disorders become more prevalent with age is not clear, partly because of the methodological and conceptual difficulties that we have already discussed. Comprehensive and systematic research on the incidence and prevalence of various psychiatric disorders in late adulthood is just beginning (LaRue, Dessonville, & Jarvik, 1985; Stenmark & Dunn, 1982). The already mentioned extensive cross-sectional study conducted by the National Institute of Mental Health yielded valuable data on mental disorders in all age groups, including the elderly.

Current prevalence rates indicated that persons over age sixty-five had the lowest overall rates of all age groups when the disorders were grouped together. Indeed, schizophrenia and substance abuse are extremely rare in people in the upper age ranges. The primary problem of old age was found to be *cognitive impairment.* In the NIMH study, rates for mild cognitive impairment were about 14 percent for elderly males and females, and for severe cognitive impairment rates were 5.5 percent for men and 4.7 percent for women (Myers et al., 1984). These rates tell us only the overall prevalence of cognitive impairment in the aged, not whether the causes were reversible or irreversible. As we have seen, this is an important issue.

What of lifetime prevalence? We would expect that because older adults have lived through a longer risk period in which disorders could develop, they would have the highest overall lifetime rates. Again, however, the lifetime rates of those aged sixty-five and older were the lowest.

What can explain these findings? Disordered older people might have been absent from the community samples through mortality or institutionalization. Older adults may also have attributed their symptoms to physical illness or may have forgotten past episodes (Robins et al., 1984). Moreover, as we have said before, we do not really know whether we can measure disorders the same way in the old as we do in younger people. Some disorders, such as schizophrenia, were said to have a maximum age for onset; DSM-III held that individuals do not become schizophrenic after age forty-five. Finally, perhaps there has been a true historical increase in psychiatric disorders in the last few generations, as compared with our current generation of older adults. Today's younger and middle-aged adults may have significantly higher rates of mental disorders than did their parents and grandparents (Robins et al., 1984).

All in all, the majority of persons sixty-five years of age and older are free from serious psychopathology, but 10 to 20 percent do have psychological problems, either cognitive or mental, severe enough to warrant professional attention (Birren & Sloane, 1980; Gurland, 1991; Gurland & Cross, 1982; LaRue, Dessonville, & Jarvik, 1985).

Depression

According to NIMH and other data, mood disorders are less common in older adults than in younger adults (Eaton et al., 1989; Myers et al., 1984; Regier et al., 1988), but they are estimated to account for nearly half the admissions of older adults to acute psychiatric care (Gurland & Cross, 1982; Redick & Taube, 1980). Unipolar depressions are much more common in the elderly than are bipolar depressions (Post, 1978; Regier et al., 1988). In fact, the onset of bipolar disorder after the age of sixty-five is believed to be rare (Jamison, 1979); Regier et al. found almost no person aged sixty-five or older who met diagnostic criteria for mania. For this reason the following discussion addresses unipolar depression in older adults.

Women have more periods of depression than men for most of their lives, except possibly when they reach old-old age. More than 30 percent of older individuals who have chronic health problems or are confined in hospitals are depressed (Blazer, 1982). Moreover, as mentioned earlier, people with a dementing disorder, such as Alzheimer's, may also be depressed; 20 percent of those with dementia are estimated to have a superimposed depression (Reifler, Larson, & Hanley, 1982).

Sometimes the term *secondary depression* is applied when the depression is believed to accompany or result from any of the many physical illnesses to which older adults are subject. It is the prevalence of these kinds of depressions that give rise to estimates that depression is generally more common among older than among younger adults (Cohen, 1990; Kermis, 1986).

Depression in Older versus Younger Adults

Is depression in older adults the same as or different from that in younger adults? Blazer (1982) stated that worry, feelings of uselessness, sadness, pessimism, fatigue, inability to sleep, and volitional difficulties are common symptoms of depression in the elderly. These symptoms are of course similar to those of depression in other age groups. When Blazer (1982) and Small et al. (1986) compared the symptoms of depression in the aged with those of younger depressed adults, however, some interesting differences emerged. Feelings of guilt were found less often in the depressed elderly, whereas somatic complaints were more common. Other differences noted by Musetti et al. (1989) are that older depressed patients show greater motor retardation, more weight loss, more of a general physical decline, less hostility, and less suicidal ideation. This latter difference—to the extent that suicide is associated with depression in some people—contrasts with our knowledge that actual suicide attempts and successes increase in older men (see page 250). Finally, memory complaints—not necessarily actual memory problems—are more common in older than in younger depressed individuals (Kahn et al., 1975; O'Connor et al., 1990).

Depression versus Dementia

As noted earlier, a number of case histories and research studies document that symptoms of elderly individuals, seemingly of dementia, remit spontaneously or improve with treatment for depression (Folstein & McHugh, 1978; Kiloh, 1961; McAllister & Price, 1982; Plotkin, Mintz, & Jarvik, 1985; Post, 1975). On the other hand, cases of depression are often misdiagnosed as a dementing disorder. This is an important issue in differential diagnosis because depression is generally reversible whereas dementia is not.

Depressed patients may complain more of forgetfulness than do patients with dementia, a distinction that may be clinically useful (Kahn et al., 1975; Raskin & Rae, 1981). Those with dementia may forget that they forget! In testing, depressed patients tend to underestimate their abilities and to be preoccupied with negative feedback (Miller, 1975; Weingartner & Silberman, 1982). Depressed older adults, although they complain more than nondepressed controls about memory problems, do not in fact perform less well than do controls on laboratory memory tests (O'Connor et al., 1990; O'Hara et al., 1986), and their performance on memory tests is above average or superior even if they complain about memory deficits (Williams et al., 1987). This discrepancy between memory complaints and actual memory deficits among depressed people is found as well among younger subjects (page 232) and probably reflects self-deprecating evaluations in the clinical syndrome of depression.

The depressed also tend to have more errors of omission: they may not answer a question because it is just too much effort for them or because they expect to make mistakes. Those with dementia, on the other hand, tend to make random or confabulatory errors (Whitehead, 1973). Finally, as noted earlier, patients can suffer from both dementia and depression: an Alzheimer's patient can become depressed over his or her growing physical and cognitive limitations (Reifler et al., 1982; Teri & Reifler, 1987).

Correlates of Depression in the Aged

As might be expected, many aged in poor physical health are depressed. In a survey of 900 elderly people living in the community, Blazer & Williams (1980) found that 44 percent of people with depressive symptoms were medically ill. Moreover, older men who have their first onset of depression in late life are likely to have undergone surgery before psychiatric admission, to have unusually high rates of chronic illness, and to have suffered from more medical conditions than have other persons (Roth & Kay, 1956). Many physicians who care for elderly medical patients are insensitive to the likelihood of depression coexisting with physical illnesses and more often than not fail to diagnose and therefore to treat the psychological condition (Rapp et al., 1988; Rapp, Parisi, & Walsh, 1988). This oversight can worsen not only the depression but the medical problem itself.

Physical illness and depression are linked for reasons other than the disheartening aspects of an illness. Medications prescribed to treat a chronic condition can aggravate a depression that already exists, cause a depression to start, or produce symptoms that resemble the disorder but are not in fact a true depression (Klerman, 1983). The drugs that are the most likely to do this are antihypertensive medications. Other possibilities include hormones, corticosteroids, and antiparkinsonian medications. Longitudinal and retrospective studies have pointed out that, on the other side of the coin, individuals who are originally depressed may be predisposed to develop physical illness (Vaillant, 1979; Wigdor & Morris, 1977).

As we grow older, we almost inevitably experience a number of life events that could cause depression. Various studies have documented higher rates of illness and death among the widowed (Clayton, 1973; Parkes & Brown, 1972), and bereavement has been hypothesized to be a common precipitating factor for depressions that hospitalize elderly patients (Turner & Sternberg, 1978). And yet longitudinal studies have found relatively low rates of depression in the bereaved, and it has been concluded that the symptoms of depression in bereft individuals are generally less severe and fewer than those in individuals institutionalized for depression (Bornstein et al., 1973; Clayton et al., 1972; Gallagher et al., 1982). Few older people, then, appear to develop a disabling depressive illness following an expected loss of a loved one.

Although retirement has also been assumed to have negative consequences for the person, research does not generally support this assumption (Atchley, 1980; George, 1980). Any ill effects of retirement may have to do with the poor health and low incomes of the retirees.

Each older person brings to late life a developmental history that makes his or her reactions to common problems unique. Their coping skills and personality determine how effectively they will respond to new life events (Butler & Lewis, 1982). We should not assume that depression rather than adaptation is the common reaction to losses and stress in late life.

Treatment of Depression

Although clinical lore commonly holds that depressions in the elderly last longer and are more resistant to treatment, these claims are not substantiated (Small & Jarvik, 1982). Indeed, there is considerable evidence that depressed older adults can be helped by psychological interventions. Gallagher and Thompson (1982, 1983) compared cognitive, behavioral, and brief psychodynamic psychotherapies for older depressed individuals. All three were found equally effective, and in a subsequent study (Thompson, Gallagher, & Breckenridge, 1987), 70 percent of the patients were judged either completely cured or markedly improved. This compares very favorably with psychotherapy in younger depressed age groups. Another notable finding is that untreated control patients did not improve, suggesting that older adults are less likely than younger to recover unless they are treated.

The use of antidepressant drugs with older adults is complicated by side effects, such as postural hypotension; some patients treated with tricyclic antidepressants become dizzy and fall. There is also risk to the cardiovascular system, with the danger of a heart attack. Moreover, older people are at high risk for toxic reactions to medications generally. Since the efficacy of antidepressants with older adults is in question (Beutler et al., 1987; Gerson, Plotkin, & Jarvik, 1988), nonpharmacological approaches to depression in the elderly are particularly important (Bressler, 1987). Interestingly, electroconvulsive therapy (page 245) is back in favor among many geriatric psychiatrists (Hay, 1991).

Delusional (Paranoid) Disorders

A sixty-six-year-old married woman reluctantly agreed to a clinical evaluation. She [had] a six-week history of bizarre delusions and hallucinations of her husband spraying the house with a fluid that smelled like "burned food." She complained that he sprayed the substance everywhere around the house, including draperies and furniture, although she had never seen him do it. She could smell the substance almost constantly, and it affected her head, chest, and rectum. She also complained that someone in the neighborhood had been throwing bricks and rocks at her house. In addition, she suspected her husband of having affairs with other women, whose footprints she claimed to have seen near home. . . .

. . . Interviews revealed a sullen woman who was extremely hostile toward her husband. She focused on the delusion that he was spraying an unusual substance in an attempt to upset her; other issues in the relationship seemed secondary. She looked very sad at times and would occasionally wipe away a tear; but her predominant affect was extreme hostility and consternation about her husband's alleged behavior (Varner & Gaitz, 1982, p. 108).

In addition to the distress experienced by the patient, paranoia may have a disturbing and immediate impact on others, often bringing angry reactions and contributing to a decision to institutionalize the older adult (Berger & Zarit, 1978). Assessments of 800 older patients at the Texas Research Institute of Mental Science for a period of five years revealed a 2 percent prevalence for outpatients and a 4.6 percent prevalence for inpatients (Varner & Gaitz, 1982). Paranoid symptomatology is held to be a general complaint of many elderly psychiatric patients (Pfeiffer, 1977). One study of geriatric inpatients found that 32 percent of them had paranoid symptoms associated with some other form of mental illness (Whanger, 1973).

Clinicians report an interesting and striking difference between the paranoid delusions of older people and those of younger individuals. The suspicions of older adults are more down-to-earth, concerned with persons in their immediate surroundings—such as neighbors, sons and daughters, people in stores, and the like. In contrast, the persecutors of younger paranoids are often located far away, in the CIA or the FBI or even outer space. Younger paranoids are given to more grandiosity than older ones (Post, 1987). Moreover, older patients are more likely to be women who are in good health, except for problems with vision and, as we will see, hearing.

Causes of Paranoia

Paranoia in the elderly may be the continuation of a disorder that began earlier in life. It may also accompany organic brain conditions, such as delirium and dementia. In fact, paranoia may serve a function for the demented, filling in the gaps caused by memory loss. Instead of admitting, "I can't remember where I left my keys," they think, "Someone must have come in and taken my keys" (Zarit, 1980). Paranoid ideation has also been linked to sensory losses, in particular loss of hearing. Older people with severe paranoid disorders tend to have long-standing hearing loss in both ears, which makes them socially deaf (Post, 1980). An older person who is deaf may believe that other people are whispering about him or her, so that he or she cannot hear what is being said. The person's paranoid reactions may be an attempt to fill in the blanks caused by sensory loss (Pfeiffer, 1977; see Focus Box 17.2). By explaining bewildering events, delusions are in a sense adaptive and understandable. Often the earlier social adjustment of paranoid patients has been poor; the onset of their symptoms may follow a period in which they have become increasingly isolated. And isolation itself limits a person's opportunities to check his or her suspicions about the world, making it easier for delusions to take hold. The individual builds a pseudocommunity rather than social relations based on good communication and mutual trust (Cameron, 1959).

Older people are especially vulnerable to all kinds of abuse from others. They may be talked about behind their backs, or even to their faces, as though they were not present, and taken advantage of by others in many ways. There is thus a danger that a complaint of persecution from an older person will be quickly dismissed as just a sign of late-life paranoia. An older client of one of the authors complained bitterly about being followed by a detective hired by her evil husband. Inquiry revealed that the husband was worried that she was having an affair and had indeed hired someone to follow her! It should always be determined whether suspicions have any bases in reality before they are attributed to paranoia.

Treatment of Paranoia

The treatment of paranoia in older adults is much the same as in younger adults. Although controlled data are lacking, clinicians suggest that a patient, supportive approach is best; the therapist should provide empathic understanding of the person's concerns. Directly challenging the paranoid delusion or attempting to reason the person out of his or her beliefs is seldom effective. Rather, recognition of the distress caused by the paranoia is more likely to promote a therapeutic relationship with the person. When the patient trusts and feels safe with the therapist, the delusions can gradually be questioned. Therapists should be mindful, however, that

FOCUS 17.2 • Partial Deafness, Growing Old, and Paranoia

A relationship between hearing problems in old age and the development of paranoid thinking was noted many years ago by Emil Kraepelin and has been verified since by careful laboratory studies (Cooper et al., 1974). The connection appears to be specific to paranoia, for the relationship between difficulties in hearing and depression in older individuals is not as great. Since hearing losses appear to predate the onset of paranoid delusions, this may be a cause–effect relationship of some importance.

Stanford psychologist Philip Zimbardo and his associates conducted an ingenious experiment to study the relation of poor hearing to paranoia. They reasoned that loss of hearing acuity might set the stage for the development of paranoia if the person does not acknowledge, or is unaware of, the hearing problem (Zimbardo, Andersen, & Kabat, 1981). If I have trouble hearing people around me, which makes them seem to be whispering, I may conclude that they are whispering *about me*, and that what they say is unfavorable. I will think this way, however, only if I am unaware of my hearing problem. If I know that I am partially deaf, I will appreciate that I do not hear them well because of my deafness and will not think that they are whispering. A hard-of-hearing grandfather may eventually challenge the light-voiced, gesturing grandchildren he believes are whispering about him; and they will deny that they are. A tense cycle of allegations, denials, and further accusations will isolate the increasingly hostile and suspicious grandfather from the company of his grandchildren.

Unrecognized hearing loss may lead some elderly people to conclude that others are whispering about them and therefore to the development of delusions.

The experiment done by Zimbardo and his group examined the initial stage of this hypothesized development of paranoia. College students, previously determined to be easily hypnotized and capable of responding to a posthypnotic suggestion of partial deafness, participated in what they believed to be a study of the effects of various hypnotic procedures on creative problem-solving. Each of the subjects sat in a room with two others who were actually confederates of the experimenter. The trio were provided a task to perform either cooperatively or by themselves; they were to make up a story concerning a TAT picture. The picture was shown on the screen, and projected first was the word FOCUS. The confederates, as planned, began to joke with each other as they made decisions about the story, inviting the subject to join them in the cooperative venture. After the story was completed, the subject was left alone to fill out the questionnaires, among them MMPI measures of paranoia and an adjective checklist to assess mood.

As described so far, there is nothing particularly interesting about the experiment. The actual manipulations took place earlier, *before* the TAT picture was presented. Each subject had been hypnotized and given one of the three following posthypnotic suggestions.

1. **Induced partial deafness without awareness.** Members of the first group were told that when they saw the word FOCUS projected on a screen in the next room, they

by the time the patient sees a health professional, many others—family, friends, the police—have probably tried, to no avail, to reason the person out of his or her delusional beliefs.

If the person has a hearing or visual problem, a hearing aid or corrective lenses may alleviate some of the symptoms. If the individual is socially isolated, efforts can be made to increase his or her activities and contacts. Regular supportive therapy may help the patient in reestablishing relations with would have trouble hearing noises and whatever other people might be saying, that the others would seem to be whispering, and that they would be concerned about not being able to hear. They were also instructed that they would not be aware of this suggestion until an experimenter removed the amnesia by touching their shoulder.

2. **Induced partial deafness with awareness.** Subjects in the second group, the control group, were given the same partial-deafness suggestion, but they were instructed to remember that their hearing difficulty was by posthypnotic suggestion.
3. **Posthypnotic-suggestion control.** Subjects in the third group, controls for the effects of posthypnotic suggestion, were instructed to react to the word FOCUS by experiencing an itchiness in the left earlobe, with amnesia for this suggestion until touched on the left shoulder by the experimenter.

After being given their posthypnotic suggestions, all subjects were awakened from the hypnotic state and ushered into the next room, where the experiment proceeded with the TAT picture, as described. It can now be appreciated that participants who had deafness without awareness might perceive the joking of the confederates as directed toward them, for they would have trouble hearing what was being said and would be unlikely to attribute this difficulty to any hearing problem of their own. Subjects who had deafness with awareness would have the same problem hearing the joking, but they would know that they had a temporary decrement in hearing through hypnotic suggestion. The other control subjects would have no hearing problems, just itchy earlobes. At the completion of the study, all subjects were carefully informed about the purposes of the study, and steps were taken to ensure that the posthypnotic suggestions of partial deafness and itchy earlobes had been lifted.

The results were fascinating. The experience of being partially deaf without awareness showed up significantly on cognitive, emotional, and behavioral measures. Compared with members of the two control groups, these subjects scored more paranoid on the MMPI scales and described themselves as more irritated, agitated, and hostile. The two confederates who were in the same room with these subjects rated them as more hostile than the controls. (The confederates were not aware of which group a given subject was in.) When the confederates invited each subject to work with them in concocting the TAT story, only one of six experimental subjects accepted the overture, although most of the control subjects agreed. At the end of the study, just before the debriefing, all subjects were asked whether they would like to participate in a future experiment with the same partners; none of the deafness-without-awareness subjects responded affirmatively, but most of the controls did.

The overall reaction of subjects who had trouble hearing and had no ready explanation for it, other than that others were whispering, was suspicion, hostility, agitation, and unwillingness to affiliate with these people. This pattern is similar to what Zimbardo hypothesized to be the earliest stage of the development of some paranoid delusions. The creation of this "analogue incipient paranoia" in the laboratory by inducing deafness without awareness of the deafness is consistent with the view that when people's hearing becomes poor in old age, they are susceptible to paranoia *if*, for whatever reasons, they do not acknowledge their deafness.

In subsequent research, Zimbardo strengthened these findings by inducing physiological arousal via hypnotic suggestion and then suggesting amnesia for the true source of the arousal. Unexplained arousal was experienced as significantly more distressing than arousal that could be attributed to the hypnosis (Zimbardo, LaBerge, & Butler, in press). Other studies indicate that if people look to the actions of others to understand the reasons for their unexplained arousal, they become more paranoid than people whose search for the causes of the arousal is guided into other domains, for example, something in the physical environment (P. Zimbardo, personal communication, September 29, 1992).

family members and friends. Attention should be provided for appropriate behavior. Even if these straightforward measures do not relieve paranoia, they may be beneficial in other areas of the person's life.

Studies of therapy outcomes indicate that delusions in the elderly can be treated successfully with phenothiazines (Post, 1980). Unfortunately, paranoid individuals are generally suspicious of the motives of those who give them drugs. Toxicity from medications must also be considered, given the particular sensitivity of older people to drugs. Institutionalization, best considered as a last resort, may do little good. In practice, the decision depends more on how tolerant the person's social environment is than on how severe and disruptive are the paranoid beliefs.

Schizophrenia

Does schizophrenia ever appear for the first time in old age? Debate on this question has raged for years—even Kraepelin had doubts that it was always appropriate to use the adjective *praecox*, meaning early onset, to describe schizophrenia.

When schizophrenia does make an appearance for the first time in older adults, it is often called **paraphrenia** (Roth, 1955). Symptoms are reported to be quite similar to those of earlier onset schizophrenia, with paranoid symptoms perhaps more often present. The patients tend to be unmarried, live in isolation, have few surviving relatives, have hearing losses and a family history of schizophrenia, and belong to the lower socioeconomic classes (Harris & Jeste, 1988; Post, 1987). In the United States the term *paraphrenia*, like paranoia, has been inconsistently used (Berger & Zarit, 1978; Bridge & Wyatt, 1980). Some researchers believe that the older patients diagnosed by Roth as having paraphrenia actually had a mood disorder (Cooper, Garside, & Kay, 1976; Cooper & Porter, 1976; Kay et al., 1976), for in many with prominent symptoms, cognition and overall functioning were preserved. And in a study of patients who appeared to have become schizophrenic for the first time after age sixty-five, roughly two-thirds were actually suffering from dementia or from a mood disorder (Leuchter, 1985).

What happens to schizophrenic symptomatology as people become older? Some researchers claim that schizophrenia sometimes burns out (Bridge, Cannon, & Wyatt, 1978)—that positive symptoms (see Chapter 14, page 390) become somewhat muted; hallucinations and delusions decrease in intensity and frequency; and the capacity for social interactions improves. But, as Lawton (1972) cautioned, these findings are based primarily on hospitalized patients who were taking drugs.

Substance Related Disorders

Alcohol Abuse and Dependence

Alcoholism is generally believed to be less prevalent in the elderly than in younger cohorts. It is estimated that between 2 and 10 percent of the elderly are alcoholic or abuse alcohol. Prevalence estimates vary, however, because studies employ different definitions of the older age group (Whittington, 1984). In a more recent study examining NIMH Epidemiological Catchment Area data of one-month prevalence rates (Regier et al., 1988), only 0.9 percent of community-dwelling adults aged sixty-five and over were found to be abusing alcohol. This rate was much lower than for younger adults. More men than women had alcohol problems.

Many problem drinkers do not survive to old age. The peak years for death from cirrhosis are between fifty-five and sixty-four years of age. Older people may also develop physiological intolerance for alcohol, counteracting its positive effects on mood (Gurland & Cross, 1982).

It is believed that older alcoholics fall into two groups, the two-thirds or more who began drinking in early or middle adulthood and who continued their pattern into late life, and the small percentage who took to drink after age fifty (Rosin & Glatt, 1971). Alcoholics who started late either had intermittent drinking problems in the past and now abuse alcohol regularly in late life or had no history of alcohol problems until their late years (Zimberg, 1987). The late-starting abuser is more likely to be separated or divorced, to live alone, and to have serious health difficulties (Schuckit & Moore, 1979). Age-related circumstances, such as retirement, may have provoked some of them to drink (Rosin & Glatt, 1971).

However, not all researchers support this distinction; Borgatta, Montgomery, and Borgatta (1982), for example, argued that there is no firm evidence for late-onset alcoholism. One conclusion that *can* be drawn from research is that alcoholism is not a self-limiting problem: if a person is a problem drinker in the younger years, chances are that he or she will remain so later in life (if the person lives that long).

As people age, their tolerance for alcohol is reduced, for they metabolize it more slowly. Thus the drug may cause greater changes in their brain chemistry than in that of the young and may more readily bring on toxic effects, such as delirium. A number of neuropsychological studies have shown that cognitive deficits associated with alcohol abuse are likely to be more pronounced in the aged alcoholic than in younger individuals with comparable drinking histories (Brandt et al., 1983). Although some intellectual functioning is recovered with abstinence, residual effects may remain long after the older person has stopped drinking.

Unfortunately, clinicians may be less likely to look for alcoholism in older people and instead attribute symptoms such as poor motor coordination and impaired memory to an organic problem or to late-life depression. If alcohol abuse goes unrecognized, treatment of the patient will be severely compromised.

Illegal Drug Abuse

The current older population abuses illegal drugs infrequently compared with other age groups. In the previously cited NIMH survey (Regier et al., 1988), none of those aged sixty-five and older, and only 0.1 percent of those between forty-five and sixty-four years of age, had a drug abuse or dependency disorder, compared with much higher rates for younger age groups. Studies of the few older narcotics abusers indicate that they began their habit early in life and reduced their drug intake as they grew older (Ball & Chambers, 1970). Many experts believe, however, that the abuse of illegal drugs is higher than these formal estimates indicate and that as younger cohorts age, there will be explosive growth in the prevalence of drug abuse in the elderly (Whittington, 1984). Early beliefs that addicts mature out of their drug abuse (Winick, 1962) are unfounded (Schuckit & Moore, 1979).

Medication Misuse

The misuse of prescription and over-the-counter medicines is a much greater problem in the aged population than drug or alcohol abuse (LaRue, Dessonville, & Jarvik, 1985). Since all phases of drug intake are altered in the elderly—absorption, distribution, metabolism, and excretion—they are more likely, as noted, to react adversely to medications in even normal doses and to experience more side effects to a wider range of drugs. Community surveys of the elderly show that they have a higher overall rate of legal drug intake than any other group (Warheit, Arey, & Swanson, 1976); although they constituted only 11.3 percent of the population, they consumed 25 percent of all prescribed medications at that time.

Abuse of prescription or legal drugs can be deliberate or inadvertent. Some may seek drugs to abuse, obtaining medications from a number of sources. Others may not take medications as they are prescribed, perhaps through misunderstanding, ignorance, or limited financial resources. One study showed that more than half of a group of aged patients could not afford to take their medications as prescribed (Brand, Smith, & Brand, 1977). A careful interview study of 141 well-functioning middle-class elderly people living in their own homes found that almost half reported having misused prescription or over-the-counter drugs at least once over a period of six months (Folkman, Bernstein, & Lazarus, 1987). The chance for misuse is believed to increase the greater the number of medications and the more complex the instructions. Dependence on medications can develop, particularly in anxious, depressed, and hypochondriacal older adults (LaRue, Dessonville, & Jarvik, 1985). One side effect of medications, confusion or even delirium, may be misdiagnosed as dementia, and the side effect of lethargy may be mistaken for depression.

Medication misuse is a serious problem among the aged and can cause delirium.

Individuals of any age need to understand why they are taking a drug, what it is called, when and how often they should take it, and under what conditions, for example, after meals, on an empty stomach, and so on. Their comprehension of the instructions should be tested. An older woman who had been given an antibiotics prescription that cautioned against taking it before or after meals came to the attention of one of the authors. She believed that this warning meant she could not eat at all while taking the medication! Since visual acuity declines with age and susceptibility to glare increases, printing instructions in small type on a shiny label—a common practice of drug companies—is bad. A chart on which the forgetful person can check off when he or she has taken medication, taped in a prominent place, serves as a useful reminder.

Hypochondriasis

Older adults complain of a multitude of physical problems, among them sore feet and backs, poor digestion, constipation, labored breathing, and cold extremities. All are to be taken seriously by responsible health professionals. But some of the elderly only believe themselves to be ill and complain unendingly about aches and pains for which there are no plausible physical causes. Indeed, it has been widely believed that hypochondriasis is especially common in the elderly.

Data, however, suggest that the prevalence of hypochondriasis is *not* greater in old age than at any other age (Siegler & Costa, 1985). In fact, the elderly as a whole tend to *under*report somatic symptoms rather than overreport them and often fail to seek help for serious illnesses (Besdine, 1980), perhaps out of concern for health care costs or out of a belief—probably veridical—that aches and pains are an inevitable part of aging and may not reflect a medical problem per se.

Longitudinal survey data indicate that health concerns do not increase with age but rather remain fairly stable over the life span; since actual health *problems* do increase with age without accompanying increases in *concerns* about health, such data support the idea that people do not become more hypochondriacal as they get older (Costa et al., 1987). Rather, as Siegler and Costa (1985) stated, older persons who have many physical complaints have long-standing personality traits that predict such complaining. Their excessive somatic complaints appear to be associated with neuroticism or poor adjustment, which are *not* associated with age. In addition, the NIMH study (Regier et al., 1988) found only 0.1 percent of those aged sixty-five years or older to have somatization disorder, which is the same rate as in younger age groups.

Treatment of Hypochondriasis

No controlled studies of the treatment of hypochondriasis in older adults have been done. Clinicians generally agree, however, that reassuring the person that he or she is really healthy is generally useless, for these people are not swayed by negative laboratory tests or authoritative pronouncements from official sources. Some tentative evidence suggests that ignoring the somatic complaints and concentrating instead on more positive aspects of existence can be helpful (Goldstein & Birnbom, 1976). "I know that you're feeling bad and that your feet really hurt, but let's take a walk in Palisades Park anyway." Diverting activities may allow these individuals at least to function in the face of their perceived medical ills and perhaps obtain some positive satisfaction from life.

Insomnia

Insomnia is a frequent complaint among the elderly. One national survey found serious sleep disturbances in 25 percent of respondents aged sixty-five to seventy-nine, as compared with 14 percent in the eighteen to thirty-four age group; another 20 percent have less serious but still problematic insomnia (Mellinger, Balter, & Uhlenhuth, 1985).

The most common problems are awakening often at night, frequent early-morning awakenings, difficulty falling asleep, and daytime fatigue (Miles & Dement, 1980). These complaints have been found to parallel the physiological changes that occur normally in the sleep patterns of older adults (Bootzin, Engle-Friedman, & Hazelwood, 1983). For example, the total time that the elderly devote to sleep appears to be somewhat less than or the same as that of younger age groups. But sleep is more often spontaneously interrupted as people grow older. Thus older people generally sleep less in relation to the total time they spend in bed. In addition, the elderly spend less absolute time in a phase known as rapid eye movement (REM) sleep; and stage 4 sleep, the deepest, is virtually absent. In general, elderly men appear to have more disturbances of their sleep than do women, a difference found to a lesser extent in young adults (Dement, Laughton, & Carskadon, 1981).

Causes of Insomnia

Besides the changes in sleep associated with aging, various illnesses, medications, caffeine, stress, anxiety, depression, lack of activity, and poor sleep habits may make insomniacs of older adults. Depressed mood—even in the absence of a full-blown mood disorder—has been shown to be related to sleep disturbances in older adults, especially early-morning awakening (Rodin, McAvay, & Timko, 1988). Pain, particularly that of arthritis, is a principal disrupter of their sleep (Prinz & Raskin, 1978). Sleep apnea, a respiratory disorder in which breathing ceases for a period of ten seconds or more repeatedly through the night, increases with age (Bliwise et al., 1984). Whatever the cause of insomnia at any age, it is worsened by self-defeating actions such as ruminating over it and counting the number of hours slept and those spent waiting to fall asleep. Sleeping problems can also be worsened by medications that are taken to deal with them, as noted below.

Treatment of Insomnia

Over-the-counter medications and prescription drugs are taken by many older insomniacs. The little bottle of sleeping pills is a familiar companion to the many medications that sit on the night table. The elderly are major consumers of sleep aids, yet these rapidly lose their effectiveness and with continuous use, may even make sleep light and fragmented. REM rebound sleep, an increase in REM sleep after prolonged reliance on drugs, is fitful (Bootzin et al., 1983). In fact, medications can bring about what is called a drug-dependent insomnia. These so-called aids can also give people drug hangovers and increase respiratory difficulties, which in the elderly is a great hazard, given the increased prevalence of sleep apnea. Side effects of tranquilizers like the benzodiazepines (e.g., Valium) include problems in learning new information—anterograde amnesia—and serious difficulties in thinking clearly the following day (Ghoneim & Mewaldt, 1990; Schatzberg, 1991).

Indeed, there is now considerable evidence that sleep medication is not the appropriate treatment for the chronic insomniac of any age, but particularly not for the elderly insomniac. Still, sleep medications are prescribed for most nursing home residents, and in many instances they are administered daily even without evidence of a sleep disturbance (Cohen et al., 1983).

Nonpharmacological treatment of sleep disorders in the elderly has not been researched much, perhaps because workers have assumed that the normal age-related changes in sleep patterns noted earlier preclude effective intervention (Bootzin & Engle-Friedman, 1987). Nonetheless, improvement is possible. Explaining the nature of sleep and the changes that take place as a normal part of the aging process can reduce the worry that older persons have about their sleep patterns, concern that itself can interfere with sleep. The therapist should also reassure patients that going without sleep is not a calamity; it will not cause irreversible brain damage or insanity, as some people fear. Some individuals are given relaxation training to help them fall asleep and instructions to help them develop good sleep habits—rising at the same time every day; avoiding activities at bedtime that are inconsistent with falling asleep, such as watching television and reading; lying down only when sleepy, and, if unable to go to sleep, getting up and going into another room. All these tactics can loosen the grip of insomnia in adults of all ages (Bootzin et al., 1983, Morin & Azrin, 1988).

Suicide

Several factors put people in general at especially high risk for suicide: serious physical illness, feelings of hopelessness, social isolation, loss of loved ones, dire financial circumstances, and depression (see Chapter 9). Because these problems are widespread among the elderly, we should not be surprised to learn that suicide rates for people over age sixty-five are high, perhaps three times greater than the rate for younger individuals (Manton, Blazer, & Woodbury, 1987; Osgood, 1984; Pfeiffer, 1977).

An examination of cross-sectional data indicates that the suicide rate for males rises from youth and increases in a linear fashion with age (Atchley, 1982). Older white men are more likely to commit suicide than any other group; the peak ages for taking their lives are from eighty to eighty-four. The rate for white women peaks before they reach the age of fifty and declines steadily thereafter. Thus rates of suicide in white men increase sharply during old age, and rates for white women decline somewhat. Throughout the life span men have higher suicide rates than women, but the difference is most notable in the old-old. Marked increases have also been noted recently among nonwhite men (Manton, Blazer, & Woodbury, 1987). What all of this means is that, as more and more people survive longer, the number of suicides in the over sixty-five age group could double over the next forty years (Blazer, Bachar, & Manton, 1986).

Older persons communicate their intentions to commit suicide less often than do the young and make fewer attempts. When they do make an attempt, however, they are more often successful in killing themselves. Suicide attempts by people younger than thirty-five fail more often than they succeed, but those of people over age fifty are more likely to be lethal. Once people are past age sixty-five, their attempts rarely fail (Butler & Lewis, 1982). Furthermore, the statistics given are probably underestimates; older adults have many opportunities to give up on themselves by neglecting their diet or medications, thus killing themselves in a more passive fashion. Moreover, Butler and Lewis (1982) argued that the suicide of older adults may more often be a rational or philosophical decision than that of younger people. Consider, for example, the elderly person who faces the intractable pain of a terminal illness and knows that with each passing day the cost of medical care is using up more and more of the money that might otherwise be left to his or her family. Recall also our earlier discussions of how some older people with Alzheimer's and other debilitating diseases have arranged to take their own lives (page 257).

Intervention to prevent the suicide of an older person is similar to that discussed earlier. In general, the therapist tries to persuade the person to regard his or her problems in less desperate terms. Mental health professionals, who are usually younger and healthier, may unwittingly try less hard to prevent an older person's suicide attempt. But even an older person, once the crisis has passed, is usually grateful to have another chance at life.

Sexuality and Aging

Bias against the expression of sexuality in old age and disbelief in the capacity for sex among older people have abounded in our culture. Men and women alike have been expected to lose interest in and capacity for sex once they reach their senior years. Some believe that old people are unable to enjoy anything more passionate than an affectionate hug and a kiss on the cheek. An older male who shows sexual interest in much younger women is called a dirty old man. And, after the strong sexual value placed on them when younger, older women are no longer considered especially sexual (Steuer, 1982). Furthermore, their capacity for sexual arousal is confused with their postmenopausal inability to procreate.

Contrary to the stereotypes, many older people maintain an active interest in sex. Studies indicate that the frequency of sexual activity among those in their 70s is as high as among middle-aged people.

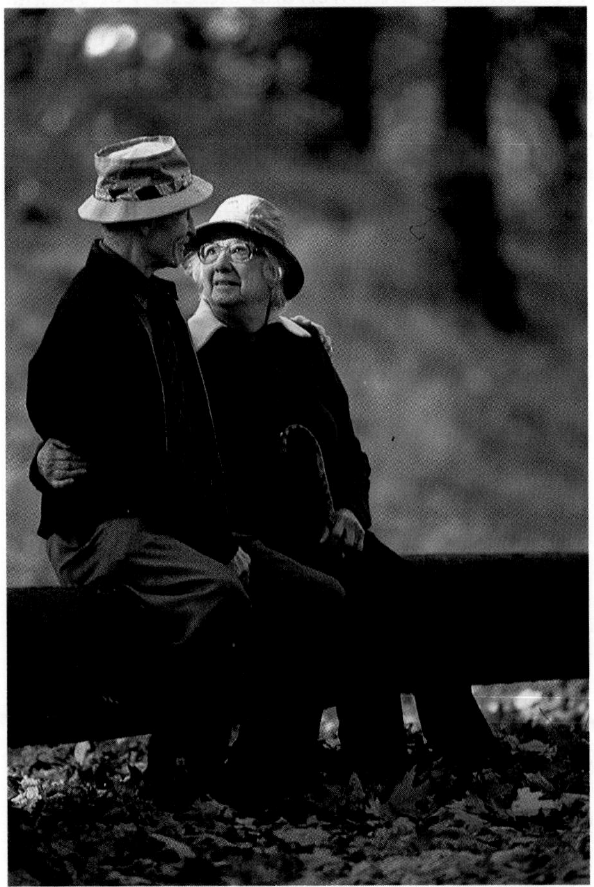

The facts are that most older people have considerable sexual interest and capacity. This holds true even for many healthy eighty- to one-hundred-year-old individuals, the preferred activities being caressing and masturbation, with some occasions of sexual intercourse as well (Bretschneider & McCoy, 1988). As we review the data, it will be important to bear in mind that sexual interest and activity vary greatly in younger adults; disinterest or infrequent sex on the part of an older person should not be blithely taken as evidence that older people are inherently asexual. The sixty-eight-year-old man who has no sex life may well have had little if any interest at age twenty-eight. Whether the person is twenty-eight or sixty-eight, one of the best predictors of continued sexual activity is past sexual enjoyment and frequency (Solnick & Corby, 1983).

Early studies of the frequencies of sexual activity, such as the famous Kinsey reports (Kinsey, Pomeroy, & Martin, 1948; Kinsey et al., 1953) and the Duke Longitudinal Studies (George & Weiler, 1980; Pfeiffer, Verwoerdt, & Wang, 1968, 1969), noted a decline in heterosexual intercourse, masturbation, and homosexual intercourse beginning around age thirty and continuing across the life span. The belief that sex necessarily becomes less important to people in their middle years and in old age was not substantiated by later research, however. The second Duke study (George & Weiler, 1980), which covered the years 1968 through 1974, indicated no decline in the sexual activity of people between ages forty-six and seventy-one and, in fact, indicated that 15 percent of older persons increased their sexual activity as they aged. Other studies show that about half those between the ages of sixty and seventy-one still have regular and frequent intercourse (Comfort, 1980; Turner & Adams, 1988). A recent study of cognitively unimpaired men living in nursing homes confirms high levels of sexual interest and, when partners were available, sexual intercourse and other forms of sexual activity (Mulligan & Palguta, 1991).

These facts can be interpreted in several ways. Clearly older people can be sexually active; even the earlier surveys indicated that. But it is noteworthy that the second Duke study did not reveal the decline of the first. The older people surveyed in the second study may have had less negative stereotyping to contend with and they may have been healthier, both of which would be cohort effects. They may also have been more willing to discuss their sexual interests and activities with researchers because the cultural atmosphere had become more supportive, a time-of-measurement effect. Historical factors and sexual attitudes in society at large may affect sexuality among older adults. In one study seventy- and eighty-year-olds reported rates of intercourse similar to those that Kinsey found in forty-year-olds in the 1940s and 1950s (Starr & Weiner, 1981). Perhaps sexual activity in the elderly will continue to rise as today's young grow older.

A largely invisible group of older adults are homosexuals. It has been suggested that between 5 and 10 percent of older adults are lesbian or gay, consonant with estimates for the general population (Lipman, 1984). Although, as we have seen recently, there is a measure of greater acceptance of homosexuality as an alternative life-style rather than as a mental illness, it seems likely that the current cohort of older homosexuals is less open about their sexual orientation than are younger people and thus suffer from isolation and self-stigmatization (Kimmel, 1979). And although many older homosexuals are in close-couple committed relationships, they face discrimination that older heterosexual couples do not: Social Security benefits do not go to the surviving partner; one partner may not be consulted on medical decisions affecting the other; and support networks are more limited for older gays and lesbians who do not have children.

Physiological Changes in Sexual Response with Aging

Among the volunteer subjects studied by Masters and Johnson (1966) were a number of older adults. We know a great deal about sexuality in older adults both from their physiological research and from later work by Comfort (1984), O'Donohue (1987), and Weg (1983). What is true of both sexes is that there are wide individual differences in sexual capacity and behavior among older adults, as indeed is the case for other areas in the lives of seniors. The following differences have been found between older and younger adults.

Men Older men take longer to have an erection, even when they are being stimulated in a way they like. They can maintain an erection longer before ejaculating than younger men, however, and the feeling that ejaculation is inevitable may disappear. It is not known whether physiological changes or control learned over the years explains this. During the orgasm phase, contractions are less intense and fewer in number, and less seminal fluid is expelled under less pressure. Once orgasm has occurred, erection is lost more rapidly in older men, and the capacity for another erection cannot be regained as quickly as in younger men. In fact, the refractory period begins to lengthen in men in their twenties (Rosen & Hall, 1984).

Older men are capable of the same pattern of sexual activity as younger men, the major difference being that things take longer to happen, and when they do, there is less urgency. The way men and their partners view normal, age-related physiological changes may contribute to sexual dysfunction, however. If, for example, a man or his partner reacts with alarm to a slow buildup of sexual arousal, the stage is set for performance fears, a principal reason for sexual dysfunction. Unfortunately, changes that occur with aging are often misinterpreted as evidence that older men are becoming impotent (LoPiccolo, 1991). An important point to remember is that an older man does not lose his capacity for erection and ejaculation unless physical or emotional illness interferes (Kaiser et al., 1988).

Women A number of age-related differences have been found in older women, but again none of them justifies the conclusion that older women are incapable of a satisfactory sex life (Morokoff, 1988). In fact, like younger women, they are capable of at least as much sexual activity as are men. There are even reports of women becoming orgasmic for the first time in their lives at age eighty. Like men, older women need more time to become sexually aroused. Vaginal lubrication is slower and reduced because estrogen levels are lower, and there may be vaginal itching and burning. Steroid replacement can reduce many of these symptoms and also help protect against osteoporosis, a disease causing brittleness of the bones. There are risks, however, such as developing endometrial (uterine) cancer. Vaginal contractions during orgasm are fewer in number compared with those of younger women. Spastic contractions of the vagina and uterus, rather than the rhythmic ones of orgasm in younger women, can cause discomfort and even pain in the lower abdomen and legs. Estrogen deficiency, which can be corrected, can change skin sensitivity such that caressing the breast and having a penis inside the vagina may not feel as pleasurable as it did when the woman was younger (Morokoff, 1988). Like older men, older women return more quickly to a less aroused state. There is some evidence that these physical changes are not as extensive in women who have been sexually stimulated on a regular basis once or twice a week throughout their sexual lives.

Age-Related Problems Physical illness can interfere with sex in older people as it can in younger people. Because the elderly suffer from many chronic ailments, however, the potential for interference from illness and medications is greater

(Mulligan et al., 1988). This is particularly true for men; any disease that disrupts male hormone balance, the nerve pathways to the pelvic area, or blood supply to the penis can prevent erection. Diabetes is one such disease, and it affects men and women similarly in terms of nerve damage and reduction of blood supply to the genitalia. But older women seem to complain less than do older men about its negative effects on their sexuality. As LoPiccolo (1991) pointed out, it may be that the current cohorts of older women, raised at a time when female sexuality was downplayed and even denigrated, suffer as much from diabetes-related reduction in vaginal lubrication as men do from erectile difficulties, but they do not tell their partners and physicians and may use a lubricant to reduce vaginal pain during intercourse.

Tranquilizers and antihypertensive drugs can also bring about sexual dysfunctioning, as can fatigue and excessive drinking and eating (Moss & Procci, 1982). Older adults are sometimes challenged as well by having to adjust to disease-related bodily changes, such as alterations in the genitalia from treatment of urological cancer (Anderson & Wolf, 1986).

Fears of resuming sexual activities after a heart attack or coronary bypass surgery have inhibited older adults and their lovers, but for most of them the fears are exaggerated (Friedman, 1978). Regrettably, physicians often fail to provide accurate information to such patients; for example, heart rate is frequently higher during such activities as climbing stairs than it is during intercourse. The situation for patients with congestive heart failure, in which the heart is unable to maintain an adequate circulation of blood in the tissues of the body or to pump out venous blood returned by the venous circulation, does create for some a risk in intercourse, but less strenuous sexual activity is usually not a problem (Kaiser et al., 1988).

Although women experience fewer physical problems than men, they are subject to all the myths about aging women's sexuality (Gatz, Pearson, & Fuentes, 1984). In addition, a heterosexual woman's sexual activity typically centers on having a partner and on whether or not he is well (Caven, 1973). Thus sexual activity of older women is less than that of older men, perhaps because they lack a partner or because, if they are married, their husbands tend to be older and to have significant health problems. Women live longer than men, thus losing their spouses more often than men lose theirs; and divorced or widowed men tend to remarry women younger than themselves, sometimes considerably so. Indeed, elderly widowers have a remarriage rate seven times that of elderly widows (U.S. Bureau of the Census, 1986).

Treatment of Sexual Dysfunction

Making the facts of sexuality in old age available to the general public and to the professionals who look after their medical and mental health needs is likely to benefit many older people. As with younger adults, a degree of permission giving is useful, especially in the light of widespread societal stereotypes of the asexuality of seniors. Physicians in particular have been guilty of telling older patients to forget about sex or of not raising the issue when discussing patients' adjustment, perhaps because of their own discomfort, lack of knowledge, or ageism (LoPiccolo, 1991). Clinicians need to bear in mind that the current cohort of people over age sixty-five was socialized into sexuality at a time when the open discussion of sex was in no way as prevalent as it has been for the past thirty years. Nursing homes are often intolerant of sexuality among their residents; a married couple residing in the same nursing home may not be allowed to share a room (Comfort, 1984); the situation for homosexuals is even worse. The authors have also witnessed nurses in geriatric wards caution residents against stimulating themselves in public but without allowing for privacy.

Some older people prefer not to be sexually active, but for older adults who are experiencing and are troubled by sexual dysfunctions, indications are that they are good candidates for the type of sex therapy devised by Masters and Johnson (Berman & Lief, 1976), with particular attention to providing the kind of information we have just reviewed about normal age-related changes in sexual functioning. A caveat is that most of today's older adults acquired their attitudes toward sex at a time when, for example, genital foreplay was not emphasized, indeed, was often discouraged. Clinicians have to be very tactful, therefore, about asking an older woman to fondle her male lover's penis in order to provide the tactile stimulation older men often need to become erect (LoPiccolo, 1991).

With older adults greater attention must be paid to physical condition than is usual with younger adults, including creative and open discussion of sexual techniques and positions that take into consideration physical limitations from illnesses such as arthritis (Zeiss, Zeiss, & Dornbrand, 1988).

This focus on sexuality per se should not blind us to the links between sexual satisfaction and nonsexual aspects of a relationship between adults especially if the people are married or in an otherwise committed relationship. As with younger adults, nonsexual distress in a couple can be both a cause and an effect of sexual problems. The situation can be particularly complex with older partners, who must deal with transitions arising from retirement and illness. Many couples who have been together for decades encounter distress in their relationship for the first time in their senior years. One particularly daunting challenge arises when one of the partners is cast in the role as caregiver for the other, especially when the ill spouse has a deteriorative disorder, such as Alzheimer's disease. Communication and problem-solving training of the kind discussed in Chapter 20 may be of value (page 604; Smyer et al., 1990).

General Issues in Treatment and Care

In spite of improvements in recent years, older adults still do not receive their just share of mental health services (Gatz, Karel, & Wolkenstein, 1991). One survey found that fewer than one percent of psychological practitioners nationwide devote more than half their time to seeing older adults (Turner & Turner, 1987); a more recent study covering Los Angeles County in California found just under 5 percent specializing in serving the mental health needs of older adults (Gatz et al., 1991). Although they constitute about 12 percent of the U.S. population, older adults represent only 6 percent of those served by community mental health centers and only 2 percent of those seen by private therapists (Burns & Taub, 1990; Flemming et al., 1986; MacDonald, 1987; Roybal, 1988). This underservice is especially serious for minority and rural elderly.

Why this apparent underservice to the mental health needs of older adults? Some feel that those who are currently elderly are reluctant to define their problems in psychological terms and that this lack of psychological mindedness keeps them out of therapy (Lawton, 1979). Research suggests, however, that older adults are really not more reluctant to seek treatment (Knight, 1983; Zarit, 1980), nor are they more likely than members of other age groups to drop out of treatment (Knight, 1983).

The way in which services are provided may fail the elderly. Older adults often come to mental health centers through referrals. Yet research has shown that older people are less likely than younger adults to be referred (Ginsburg & Goldstein, 1974; Kucharski, White, & Schratz, 1979). Indeed, one recent study found that general practitioners usually fail to detect depression in older patients (Bowers et al., 1990). This may be due in part to inadequate geriatric training for medical professionals. The reimbursement system may pose some problems as well, for it is biased toward inpatient care and pays less for outpatient therapy, especially for mental health services (Gatz & Pearson, 1988). Moreover, Medicare does not cover supportive care for persons with Alzheimer's disease.

Various studies have shown that clinicians do not expect to treat the elderly with as much success as the young (Dye, 1978; Ford & Sbordonne, 1980; Settin, 1982). In one study older patients were rated by therapists as having more severe psychopathology, less motivation for treatment, a poorer prognosis, and less insight than younger patients (Karasu, Stein, & Charles, 1979). Yet, in fact, research does not suggest that psychotherapy of the elderly is less successful (Garfield, 1978; Knight, 1989; Knight, Kelly, & Gatz, 1992). If the elderly are viewed as having limited possibilities for improvement, they may not be treated. But a therapist may also lack the knowledge necessary to give good treatment to older people, which would keep them from improving.

Provision of Services

Admissions of older adults to state and county mental hospitals and to psychiatric wards of city hospitals have substantially decreased in the past few years. Most older people needing mental health treatment now live in nursing homes or receive community-based care.

Nursing Homes

The evidence indicates that nursing homes are now the major locus for institutional care for the elderly with severe chronic illnesses and mental disorders (Gatz & Smyer, 1992; Kramer, 1977). Given projected future increases, it does not appear that enough people are being trained to provide mental health services within these nursing homes.[2] This is a matter of concern, particularly since only 30 percent of the nation's 15,000 nursing homes offer

[2]Especially in large urban centers, nursing homes often have nonprofessional staff who do not speak English and who take care of residents who speak only English. A related problem is the non-English-speaking resident who is dependent for care on staff who do not speak his or her language.

counseling as a routine service, and between 43 and 94 percent of patients have diagnosed emotional disorders (National Center for Health Statistics, 1989; Rovner et al, 1986). Worse still, recent nursing home reforms aim to exclude from such settings older adults with mental disorders, a step that is likely to place further strains on state and private psychiatric hospitals as well as on general hospitals with psychiatric units (Gatz & Smyer, 1992). It is unlikely that care in these settings will be any better.

Twenty years ago the news media were filled with exposés and lawsuits concerning ineptitude and brutality in some nursing homes. Violations of building codes, neglect, overmedication, intimidation, excessive billing, and other unethical and illegal practices made people wary about the honesty of nursing home operators and occasioned considerable anxiety among families and old people themselves about whether the nursing home is the best place to spend final months or years.

These concerns were vividly expressed in a federal government report from the Health Care Financing Administration (Rosenblatt & Spiegel, 1988). Among the negative findings about the nation's nursing homes were the following:

17 percent failed to give residents adequate privacy during treatments and for the care of personal needs

43 percent did not ensure that food was properly refrigerated and served under sanitary conditions

30 percent did not provide consistent daily hygiene care

18 percent failed to provide adequate care to residents with catheters

22 percent did not provide rehabilitation services to prevent residents from losing the ability to walk or move about freely

29 percent failed to administer drugs according to physician's instructions

15 percent failed to keep electrical and mechanical equipment in safe operating condition

25 percent failed to follow proper isolation procedures to reduce the spread of infection

These problems are all the more serious given the frail state of most nursing home residents. Although objections to the report were raised by various nursing home organizations (especially in California, where the figures were considerably worse than the national averages), the report drives home the point that many major problems are still with us. More alarming still are the conditions of so-called board-and-care homes, institutional settings, usually in houses and seldom licensed, that are frequently crawling with cockroaches, totally lacking in professional supervision, and preying on the fears that some seniors have of being entirely without shelter. Oversight of these residential settings seems thus far to have fallen through the cracks of federal and state governments.

There may be subtle complications in placing someone in a nursing home, perhaps even in the absence of the more flagrant violations noted here. A dramatic study by Blenker (1967) highlights the problem. Elderly people who came to a family service center were *randomly* assigned to one of three treatments, intensive, intermediate, and minimal. Intensive treatment involved the services of a nurse and a social worker, and intermediate somewhat less professional attention. Minimal treatment consisted of information and referral to community-based services. We might expect intensive treatment to be the most effective, but quite the opposite was the case. After half a year the death rate of members of the intensive-care group was four times that of people in the minimal-care group! The intermediate-care group was better off than the intensive-care group; the death rate of its members was "only" twice that of the minimal-care group. What happened? It turned out that the major factor was being placed in an institution such as a nursing home. A person was much more likely to be institutionalized if a nurse and social worker were intensively involved in planning his or her care, and that is where excessive death rates were found. Since people had been assigned randomly to the three treatments, it is unlikely that the death rates were related to differences existing before treatment began.

What is there about nursing homes that contributes to such decline? First, relocation to a new setting is in itself stressful and is believed to play a role in increased mortality (Aldrich & Mendkoff, 1963; Schulz & Brenner, 1977). Once in the nursing home, the extent and nature of care discourage rehabilitation and even maintenance of whatever self-care skills and autonomous activities the resident may be capable of. For example, a resident able to feed himself or herself, but slowly and with occasional spills, will be assisted at mealtime and even fed like a child to shorten the time devoted to serving meals as well as to decrease the chances of messes on the floor and stains on the patient's clothing. The resident no longer thinks of himself or herself as someone able to eat without help, which is likely to lead to still more loss of function and lowered morale. Muscles weaken and deteriorate through disuse (DeVries, 1975). Relatives of the resident, anxious to know that they have made the right decision and

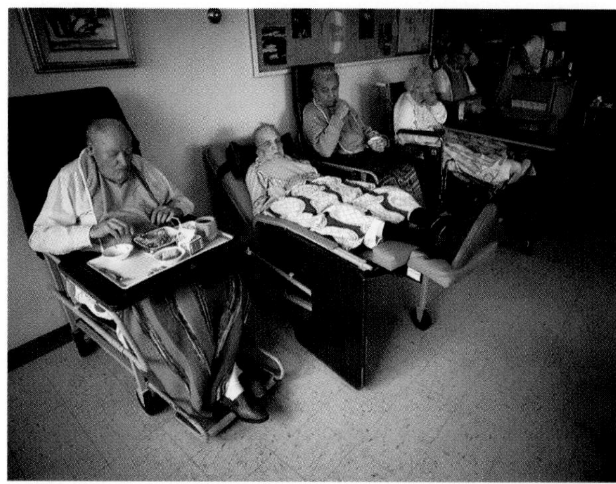

Nursing homes play a major role in the institutional care of the aged, providing for people with a variety of physical and psychological needs. They have often been severely criticized for the poor care they provide. While conditions and care can differ widely across different homes, advances in knowledge about the processes of aging have aided many homes in better meeting the needs of all their residents.

that their parent is being well cared for, are pleased by the tidiness and orderliness that are the result of excessive staff involvement in all details of living.

Custodial care may be excessive, but treatments to improve a patient's mental condition do not have priority. We know that depression is found in some older people, especially those in nursing homes. The type of psychoactive drug prescribed, however, is more likely to be a tranquilizer than an antidepressant; a less agitated, relatively inactive patient is easier to handle. Psychological interventions are virtually unheard of, for the staff either is untrained in their implementation or operates under the widely held assumption that such therapy is inappropriate for an old person (Zarit, 1980).

In sum, all the problems of institutionalization are in bold and exaggerated relief in nursing homes. Independence is inadvertently, but with sad consequences, discouraged, and both physical and mental deteriorations, because they are expected, are obtained (see Focus Box 17.3).

The prevalent myth is that families dump their older relatives into institutions at the first sign of frailty. The data indicate, however, that families usually explore all their alternatives and exhaust their own resources before they institutionalize an older relative. Thus the decision to institutionalize comes as a last resort, not as a first choice. Institutionalization is also believed to have a negative impact on family relations. One study, however, found that for a large number of families, moving the parent to a nursing home strengthened family ties and brought a renewed closeness between the parent and the child who was the primary care giver. The care provided by the home alleviated the strain and pressure caused by the multiple physical or mental problems of the parent. In only about 10 percent of the families were relations worsened by the move (Smith & Bengston, 1979).

Community-Based Care

Since 95 percent of the elderly at any given time reside in the community, what in general can be said about community-based care for them? Traditional individual, family, and marital counseling, pet therapy,[3] and peer counseling have all been shown effective to some degree in relieving depression, anxiety, and loneliness; most of these therapies are described elsewhere. The frail elderly have an urgent need for help with their daily living arrangements. Services that are not geared to the needs of an ethnically and racially diverse community, such as those of most metropolitan areas, may create a reluctance on the part of minorities to use those services. We discuss here some general principles that can foster the development of effective and comprehensive community care (Zarit, 1980).

Comprehensive Community-based Services Sound community care should provide a continuum of aid,

[3]Pet therapy builds on age-old observations that people who have pets to care for benefit from the companionship of their animals. The dependence of a domesticated animal on a human being can help the person physically and emotionally, by keeping him or her active and feeling useful. A pet's acceptance of us is usually more nearly unconditional than that given by people. Sheer physical contact with an animal is also beneficial. We do not argue that older adults, or anyone else, are better off taking care of household pets than having human companions. But the repsonsibility and pleasure of taking care of a cat, dog, or bird does enhance simple daily living, fosters healthful thoughts and actions (Brickel, 1984), and improves the morale of those living alone (Goldmeier, 1988).

FOCUS 17.3 • Loss of Control and Mindlessness in Nursing Homes

Ellen Langer and Judith Rodin have advanced an argument relating lack of control over life circumstances to the deterioration in both physical and mental health often found in some of the elderly. Since we know that a perceived or actual lack of control leads to deterioration in adaptive behavior, at least some of what we regard as senility—the inactivity of elderly people and their poor adjustment to changing circumstances—may be caused by loss of control rather than by progressive brain disease (Langer, 1981). Indeed, diminution in a sense of self-efficacy and control appears to have especially negative effects in the elderly (Rodin, 1986).

Langer points out that our society actually *teaches* the elderly—and sometimes the nonelderly as well!—that older adults are incompetent, or at least far less competent than they were before they became old. In our eagerness to help them, we seem to protect old people from having to make decisions that they might, in fact, be able to make. In our concern to protect them from physical harm, we arrange environments that require little effort to control. And, of course, we set ages for compulsory retirement, overlooking the large individual differences of old people. These practices, especially in a society that values competence and activity, do much to destroy an elderly person's belief that he or she is still effective, that indeed life is worthwhile.

Langer and Rodin (1976b) argue that the crucial problem in nursing homes is loss of opportunity to exercise control and personal responsibility. In one study patients were assigned a particular fifteen-minute period during which the nurse would be on call specifically for them, thus increasing each individual's control over his or her own caretaking. The health of these patients improved more than that of the control group, and they were more sociable (Rodin, 1980).

In another study Langer and Rodin (1976a) told one group of residents that they would be given a variety of decisions to make, instead of the staff's making decisions for them; they were also given plants to take care of. A control group was told how eager the staff was to take care of them; the plants they were given would be looked after by the staff. Although initially matched on variables such as health, these two groups of elderly residents differed three weeks later on several measures of alertness, happiness, and general well-being. Members of the group given enhanced responsibility—and presumably a sense of greater control—tested superior on these measures. Even more impressive was the finding eighteen months later that only half as many of the experimental group as of the control group had died, seven of forty-seven, compared with

ranging from information to services that allow the frail elderly to remain in their homes. Some communities are organized to provide telephone reassurance, daily phone calls to old persons living alone to check that they are all right; home services, such as Meals on Wheels, which bring a hot meal each day to the old person's door, visits from volunteers who cook meals and do household chores, shopping help from young people, light repair work by volunteers; a community center for older people, which may also serve a hot lunch and provide help with state and federal forms; sheltered housing, apartments in which several old people may live together semi-independently; home visits by health professionals and social workers, who can assess the actual needs of old people and treat them; and regular social visits from community neighbors. A range of available services allows a true match with the needs of the older person. Otherwise he or she will have too much or not enough help. There is some research indicating that such community psychology projects can enhance the quality of life of elderly people and reduce their dependency on institutional care (e.g., Knight, 1983; Nocks et al., 1986). However, current incentives encourage more expensive inpatient care or not seeking mental health services at all (Gatz & Smyer, 1992).

It is estimated that over two million adults in the United States are involved in looking after frail dependent elders in the home, from those with physical disabilities, such as broken hips, to those whose minds are compromised by a dementing illness such as Alzheimer's disease (Stone et al., 1987). More than three-quarters of these caregivers are women (spouses or daughters), and about half also work outside the home. Although part-time outside thirteen of forty-four. Moreover, the group given responsibilities continued to show better psychological and physical health (Rodin & Langer, 1977). In a subsequent study, Rodin (1983) found that nursing home residents who were taught coping skills manifested lower stress in self-reports, on physiological measures, and on physicians' judgments of health. Rodin's presumption is that the skills training enhanced both their perceived and actual control over problems commonly arising in nursing homes. Other research generally shows that people who feel in greater control actually do more things that enhance their health, such as complying with medical regimens, losing weight, and engaging in other self-care behaviors (Rodin, 1986).

Increased control is not positive under all circumstances and for all individuals, however, as Rodin concluded after a review of work in diverse areas on control (Rodin, 1986). With increased control comes more responsibility, and some people may convert this into self-blame when such an internal attribution is not warranted, for example, in the case of a dementing illness caused by factors beyond the patient's control. And if one's actual environment is not supportive of increased efforts to exert control and assume responsibility, people are likely to feel worse. With this caveat in mind, Rodin concludes that health professionals as well as family members should look for ways to enhance control in older adults, including those in institutional settings, such as nursing homes.

Not only may our treatment of old people engender in them a sense of lost control, but their repetitious, unchallenging environments—especially the surroundings of those who are hospital patients or live in nursing homes—may encourage a mode of cognitive functioning that Langer termed *mindlessness.* Mindlessness is a kind of automatic information processing studied by cognitive psychologists, a mode of thinking that is adaptive when people are in situations that recur frequently, for example, remembering a familiar sequence such as tying one's shoes. In fact, attending to such overlearned activities—making the information processing conscious, not mindless—can actually *interfere* with performance! But when a situation is novel and requires our attention, we want to operate *mindfully.*

What are the clinical implications of too much mindlessness, this mode of mental functioning that entails little cognitive effort? The elderly may be afforded too few opportunities to be thoughtful and to maintain an alert state of mind. Because of the restricted mobility of nursing home residents and hospital patients and because little is demanded of them, their experiences tend to be repetitious and boring. The Langer and Rodin nursing home research may well demonstrate that conscious *thinking* per se as well as perceived control are essential in maintaining emotional and physical well-being. Lack of control and mindlessness are probably related, for what is there really to think about when people believe that they have lost control over the events in their lives?

Among community-based services are day care centers where the aged participate in various activities such as exercise classes.

help, for example, from paid home aides, is often available, the pressures on these people—and on their own families—are enormous.[4]

Members of families who care for older relatives need information on how to handle problem situations and on how to keep the older relative as independent as possible. They also need support and encouragement, opportunities to vent their feelings of guilt and resentment. Some may need permission to take time off, or to feel that they will be able to should the pressure become too great.

Especially stressful is caring for a person with Alzheimer's disease (Anthony-Bergstone, Zarit & Gatz, 1988; Gwynther & George, 1986; Zarit, Todd, & Zarit, 1986). Two recent studies (Dura, Stukenberg, & Kielcolt-Glaser, 1991; Schulz & Williamson, 1991) documented unusually high levels of clinical depression and anxiety in adult children and spouses caring for their demented parents or spouses as compared with non-caregiver controls. Other studies found more physical illness (Haley et al., 1987; Potashnik & Pruchno, 1988) and decreased immune functioning (Kielcolt-Glaser et al., 1991) among caregivers. In many instances the disorders seem to be attributable to the stresses of caregiving; prior to these challenges, the families of caregivers usually did not experience psychological difficulties (Gatz, Bengston, & Blum, 1990). Factors that increase depression and anxiety among caregivers include the severity of the patient's problem behaviors, perceived availability of social support, and concerns about financial resources to handle expenses during the long, debilitating, and often expensive illness.

Other researchers have begun to examine cognitive factors in how caregivers handle the challenge (e.g., Gatz, Bengston, & Blum, 1990; Knight & Davison, 1993; Pearlin et al., 1990; Zarit, 1989). It may be, for example, that less distressed caregivers adopt a fatalistic attitude to the patient's behavior—"There's nothing I can do to change the situation, so let me just resign myself to it"—rather than a more active coping approach, which is more suitable to dealing with challenges that are amenable to modification (Fiore, Becker, & Coppel, 1983; Folkman & Lazarus, 1985). In a recent study by Knight, Lutzky, and Olshevski (1992), efforts to help distressed caregivers solve problems and accept responsibility actually *increased* their stress as measured by cardiovascular reactivity. Knight et al. speculate that problem-solving training may, in fact reinforce the view that the caregiver is responsible for the patient's problem behaviors.[5]

Coordination of Services Mere availability of services is not enough. They must be coordinated, and regrettably they are not in most localities. All too often an older person and his or her family are shuffled from one agency to another, getting lost in Kafkaesque bureaucracies. In fact, even professionals who have experience with the system often have difficulties working through it to get needed services for their clients! Moreover, frustrating rules can interfere with the very goals for which programs were instituted. In California, for example, Medicare does not always pay for rehabilitation services, such as physical therapy after a broken hip has healed. As a consequence, many older people do not regain the function that they might have and may suffer additional physical and emotional deterioration, exacerbations that require more expensive services.

Assuming the elderly can obtain and pay for medical care, how good is it? The answer seems to be, not very. The chronic health problems of old people are not appealing to physicians because they seldom diminish. In fact, many maladies of old people—such as hearing loss, visual impairments, loss of mobility, aches and pains, especially in the feet (Pearson & Gatz, 1982), and a steadily declining cardiovascular system—are unlikely to get better and must somehow be adjusted to. The elderly come to rely heavily on their relationships with health care providers, but these providers may become impatient with them because, as Zarit (1980) suggested, the illnesses of older people violate a "law" that the medical profession lives by, for these maladies are often incurable. Furthermore, older people do not always take medication as instructed, and even when they do, adverse drug reactions are not uncommon (Leach & Roy, 1986). Relations with family members who must look after them are likely

[4]Although the emphasis here is on the help provided by the caregiver to the disabled family member, Gatz et al. (1990) remind us that it is not a one-way street, for the recipient of care often contributes to the household, for example, through financial assistance, help with some household chores, and the less tangible gifts that older adults can give to younger generations. A sense of satisfaction and enhanced self-efficacy can also be rewards to caregivers.

[5]This brings to mind our observations in the previous chapter (page 484) on the pernicious nature of psychogenic theories of psychopathology. Those who are entrusted with the care of children as well as demented older adults are often subtly encouraged to accept responsibility and hence blame for the predicament of their charges. We do not wish to advocate inaction and neglect, rather only to place a caregiver's responsibilities in proper perspective.

to suffer. The ailing elderly are sometimes torn both by feelings of guilt for needing so much from others and by anger against these younger people whom they have spent so many of their good years looking after and sacrificing for. The sons and daughters also have feelings of guilt and anger (Zarit, 1980).

Issues Specific to Therapy with Older Adults

As mentioned throughout this chapter, discussing a group of people who share only chronological age runs the risk of overlooking important differences in their backgrounds, developmental histories, and personalities (Smyer, Zarit, & Qualls, 1990). Although adults over age sixty-five do have in common physical and psychological characteristics that make them different from younger adults, they are nonetheless *individuals*, each of whom has lived a long time and experienced unique joys and sorrows. In spite of this uniqueness, there are a few general issues important to consider in the conduct of therapy with older people. They can be divided into issues of content and issues of process (Zarit, 1980).

Content

The incidence of brain disorders does increase with age, but other mental health problems of older adults are not that different from those experienced earlier in life. Although the clinician should appreciate how physical incapacities and medications may intensify psychological problems, consistency and continuity from earlier decades of the older person's life should be noted too.

The clinician must also bear in mind that the emotional distress of older adults may be a realistic reaction to problems in living. Medical illnesses can create irreversible difficulties in walking, seeing, and hearing. Finances may be a problem, particularly for the older woman who lives alone. To suggest that all psychological distress is pathological rather than an understandable response to real-life problems is unfair and inaccurate.

In a thoughtful analysis of psychotherapy for seniors, Steuer (1982) pointed out that older women suffer doubly as psychotherapy patients: not only ageist but also sexist attitudes can negatively influence the direction of psychotherapy. For example, stress in an older couple can increase when the husband retires. A common therapeutic goal is for the woman to accommodate to the husband's loss of status and to learn to spend more time with him each day. But, Steuer pointed out, less often does the woman get to retire from her long-standing role as homemaker. Nor are therapists, who are almost always closer in age to an older patient's children than to the patient herself, always understanding of the loss experienced by many mothers when their grown children blame them for being too controlling and otherwise responsible for their own problems as adults. (As mentioned elsewhere in this book, mom bashing is prevalent in the lore of the mental health professions.)

The older person's worries about impending death are another realistic source of stress. Much psychological turmoil about dying can be reduced by encouraging the client to attend to such concrete details as ensuring that estate and will are in order and that funeral or cremation plans are explicit and satisfactory. If clients deplore and dread the artificial life-support treatments sometimes applied in cases of terminal illness, the therapist should suggest that they consider a living will to provide direction to those who will be responsible for them. Family members are wisely included in discussions, for their own concerns about death often influence their dealings with the old person.

Older clients may also be counseled to examine their lives from a philosophical or a religious perspective. Leo Tolstoy was but one of many people who become increasingly religious as they grow old. Philosophical and religious perspectives can help the client transcend the limitations aging imposes on human existence. When the person is finally dying, discussions of the meaning of the individual's life can facilitate self-disclosure and enhance his or her sense of well-being and personal growth (see the discussion of life review that follows). The loved ones, who will experience the inevitable loss, will also benefit from such discussions.

Process

Many clinicians have asked whether older adults require entirely different treatments from younger adults, or whether they can benefit from the same treatments. Behavior therapy made the early assumption that no substantive changes from techniques found useful for younger populations were necessary in working with older adults (Cautela, 1966, 1969). We have already indicated that traditional individual, family, and marital therapies are effective with the elderly (Gatz et al., 1985). Some clinicians make adaptations and focus on here-and-now problems. They hold that therapy with the elderly needs to be more active and directive, providing information, taking the initiative in seeking out agencies for necessary services, and helping the client and his or her family through the maze of federal and local laws and offices that are in place to help the elderly.

In a recent historical overview of psychotherapy with older adults, Knight, Kelly, and Gatz (1992) discuss life review, proposed by Butler (1963) as a psychotherapeutic approach uniquely suitable for older adults. It reflects the influence of Erik Erikson's (1950, 1968) life-span developmental theory, which postulated stages of conflict and growth extending well into the senior years (page 40). Life review basically facilitates what appears to be a natural tendency of older adults to reflect on their lives and to try to make sense of what has happened to them. In Eriksonian terms, it helps the person address the conflict between ego integrity and despair. Methods include having the patient bring in old photographs, travel to a childhood home, and write an autobiography. As one might imagine, people can feel worse as well as better from this kind of therapy; it takes considerable skill on the part of the therapist to guide the patient to a positive view of life and to the coming end of existence.

Psychoanalytically oriented therapy for older adults has been studied in recent years, especially the shorter term therapy that concentrates more on strengthening ego functions than on exploring childhood repressions through analysis of the transference (Kahana, 1987; pages 43 and 534). A previously mentioned effort by Gallagher and Thompson (1982, 1983; Thompson et al., 1987, p. 494) showed equivalent improvement in depressed older patients from cognitive, behavioral, and brief psychodynamic therapies, lending support to the efficacy of present-oriented dynamic intervention. Other research also provides promising preliminary results (Smyer et al., 1990).

Dependency on therapists and caregivers is, however, a problem. Baltes (1988) observed that older adults, whether institutionalized or living at home with caregivers, received much more social reinforcement (attention, praise) for dependent behaviors than for instances of independent functioning. These kinds of data are part of the growing specialization of behavioral gerontology (Nemeroff & Karoly, 1991), where careful behavioral analysis of and operant intervention into the lives of the elderly are helping seniors to enhance their self-esteem by controlling their toileting better (Whitehead, Burgio, & Engel, 1985), increasing self-care and mobility (Burgio et al., 1986), and improving their telephone conversational skills as a way to enhance social contacts (Praderas & MacDonald, 1986). Other behavioral and cognitive-behavioral approaches also show promise (e.g., Beutler et al., 1987). Moreover, caregivers benefit from learning the principles of operant conditioning and how to apply them to the challenges they face in dealing with the sometimes exasperating behavior of their demented parents at home (Pinkston & Linsk, 1984). Groups conducted within various theoretical orientations also seem to help older adults, especially by providing social contacts and support and by normalizing some of their experiences as they grow older (Lieberman & Videka-Sherman, 1986).

An aspect of psychotherapy, regardless of theoretical orientation, that is highlighted by working with elders is reminiscent of the analytic concept of countertransference. Therapists, usually many years younger than these patients, can be troubled by the patients' problems, for these difficulties can touch on sensitive personal areas of their own, such as unresolved conflicts with their own parents, worries about their own aging process, and a reluctance to deal with issues of death and dying. As Knight et al. (1992) speculated, "the perception that therapy is different with older adults is now thought to be due more to the emotional impact on the therapists of working with the elderly than to actual differences in technique, process, or likelihood of success. . . . [Working with older adults] will challenge therapists intellectually and emotionally to reach a maturity beyond their years (pp. 540, 546)."

SUMMARY

Until recently the psychological problems of older people have been neglected by mental health professionals. As the proportion of people who live beyond age sixty-five continues to grow, it will become ever more important to learn about the disorders suffered by some older people and the most effective means of preventing or ameliorating them. Although physical deterioration is an obvious aspect of growing old, it appears that most of the emotional distress to which old people are prone is psychologically produced.

Serious brain disorders affect a very small minority of older people, fewer than 10 percent. Two principal disorders have been distinguished, dementia and delirium. In dementia the person's intellectual functioning declines; memory, abstract thinking, and judgment deteriorate. If the dementia is progressive, as most are, the individual seems another person altogether and is in the end oblivious to his or her surroundings. A variety of diseases can cause this deterioration; the most important is an Alzheimer's-type disease, in which cortical cells waste away. In delirium there is sudden clouding of consciousness and other problems in thinking, feeling, and behaving—fragmented and undirected thought, incoherent speech, inability to sustain attention, hallucinations, illusions, disorientation, lethargy or hyperactivity, and mood swings. The condition is reversible, provided that the underlying cause is self-limiting or adequately treated. Brain cells malfunction but are not necessarily destroyed. Causes include overmedication, infection of brain tissue, high fevers, malnutrition, dehydration, endocrine disorders, head trauma, and cerebrovascular problems.

The treatments of these two disorders are quite different from each other. If delirium is suspected, there should be a search for the cause so that the pathogenic situation can be rectified. Dementia, on the other hand, usually cannot be treated, but the person and the family affected by the disease can be counseled on how to make the remaining time tolerable and even rewarding. If adequate support is given to caregivers, many dementia patients can be looked after at home. There usually comes a time, however, when the burden of care impels most families to place the person in a nursing home or hospital.

Older people suffer from the entire spectrum of psychological disorders, in many instances brought with them from their earlier years. The newer cognitive behavior therapies are being applied to depression of the elderly, and results so far are encouraging.

Although not as widespread as depression, paranoia is a problem for older people and for those who have a relationship with them. In contrast to the persecutors of young paranoids (distant agencies such as the FBI and aliens from outer space), those of older individuals live closer to home (the neighbor who opens the person's mail, the ungrateful child who is conniving to steal his or her elderly parent's money, the physician who prescribes drugs that pollute the mind). Paranoia is sometimes brought on by brain damage in dementia, but more often it is apparently caused by psychological factors. Paranoia may be a reaction to hearing difficulties. If I cannot hear what they are saying—especially if I do not acknowledge my hearing problem—perhaps it is because they are whispering nasty things about me. Isolation as well can be a factor; when a person has little social intercourse, and indeed many old people have too little, it is difficult to verify impressions and suspicions, setting the stage for the development of delusions. Other psychological disorders experienced in old age include schizophrenia; substance abuse, in particular the misuse of medication; hypochondriasis; and insomnia.

White males as they enter old age are at increasing risk of suicide. More of the suicide attempts of old people result in death than do those of younger people. Mental health professionals, most of them younger than age sixty-five, may assume that the old and debilitated have nothing to live for. This attitude may reflect their own fear of growing old.

Considerable mythology has surrounded sexuality and aging, the principal assumption being that at the age of sixty-five sex becomes improper, unsatisfying, and even impossible. Evidence indicates otherwise. Barring serious physical disability, older people, even those well into their eighties, are capable of deriving enjoyment from sexual intercourse and other kinds of lovemaking. There are differences as people age; it takes longer to become aroused and the orgasm is less intense. Dissemination of accurate information about sexual capacity in old age would probably prevent much unnecessary sexual dysfunction and disinterest.

Nursing homes and other extended-care facilities often do little to encourage residents to maintain or enhance whatever skills and capacities they still have; both physical and mental deterioration are the rule. Today care is provided in the community whenever possible. There should be comprehensive services, such as Meals on Wheels, regular home visits by health professionals, and support for caregivers. Such services should be coordinated so that people do not have to confront a bureaucratic maze. And intervention should be minimal so that older people remain as independent as their circumstances permit.

Many older people can benefit from psychotherapy, but several issues specific to treating the older adult should be kept in mind. The emotional distress of the elderly is sometimes realistic in content. They have often suffered irreplaceable losses and face real medical and financial problems; it is unwise always to attribute their complaints to a psychopathological condition. Death is a more immediate issue as well. As for the process of therapy, clinicians should sometimes be active and directive, providing information and seeking out the agencies that give the social services needed by their clients. Therapy should also foster a sense of control, self-efficacy, and hope and should help the older person elucidate a sense of meaning as the end of life is approached.

KEY TERMS

ageism
age effects
cohort effects
time-of-measurement effects
cross-sectional studies
longitudinal studies
selective mortality
dementia
cerebrovascular disease
Alzheimer's disease
cerebral thrombosis
stroke
cerebral hemorrhage
aphasia
delirium
paraphrenia

PART FOUR

Intervention and Legal and Ethical Issues

c h a p t e r   e i g h t e e n

Insight Therapies

In ordinary conversation, you usually try to keep a connecting thread running through your remarks, excluding any intrusive ideas or side issues so as not to wander too far from the point, and rightly so. But in this case you must talk differently. As you talk various thoughts will occur to you which you like to ignore because of certain criticisms and objections. You will be tempted to think, "That is irrelevant or unimportant or nonsensical," and to avoid saying it. Do not give in to such criticism. Report such thoughts in spite of your wish not to do so. Later, the reason for this injunction, the only one you have to follow, will become clear. Report whatever goes through your mind. Pretend that you are a traveler, describing to someone beside you the changing views which you see outside the train window. (Ford & Urban, 1963, p. 168)

What is Psychotherapy?

Throughout our account of the various psychopathologies, we have considered the ways in which therapists attempt to prevent, lessen, and even eliminate mental and emotional suffering. Our descriptions in Chapter 2 of the several paradigms of treatment—biological, psychoanalytic, learning, and cognitive—laid the groundwork for a variety of ways in which to approach the task. In Chapters 6 through 17, we learned that some forms of intervention are more appropriate than others for particular problems. For example, because of advances in our understanding of biological processes, new parents now have means to halt or at least reduce certain forms of genetically transmitted mental retardation. And through better understanding of the process of learning, retarded children now acquire more cognitive, social, and self-care skills than was earlier thought possible. As we have seen, psychoanalytic theory helps therapists treat dissociative disorders, for it alerts them to the possibility that an amnesic patient, for example, cannot remember because the pain of certain past events forced them to be massively repressed. Instructions to free-associate, an important technique in psychoanalysis, opened this chapter. Humanistic and existential therapies help clients explore the depth and causes of their psychological pain and encourage them to take action, make choices, and assume responsibility for bettering their lives.

It is time now to take a closer, more intensive look at therapy, to consider issues of general importance, to explore controversies, and to make comparisons. What we have studied so far of psychopathology and treatment should enable us to do so with some sophistication and perspective.

Shorn of its theoretical complexities, any **psychotherapy** is a social interaction in which a trained professional tries to help another person, the client or patient, behave and feel differently. The therapist follows procedures that are, to a greater or lesser extent, prescribed by a certain theory or school of thought. The basic assumption, indeed article of faith, is that particular kinds of verbal and nonverbal exchanges in a trusting relationship can achieve goals such as reducing anxiety and eliminating self-defeating or dangerous behavior.

Basic as this explanation may seem, there is little general agreement about what really constitutes psychotherapy. A person's next-door neighbor might utter the same words of comfort as a clinical psychologist, but should we regard this as psychotherapy? In what way is psychotherapy different from such nonprofessional reassurance? Is the distinction made on the straightforward basis of whether the dispenser of reassurance has a particular academic degree or license? Does it relate to whether the giver of information has a theory that dictates or at least guides what he or she says? Does it depend on how sound the basic assumptions of the theory are? These are difficult questions, and, as in other areas of abnormal psychology, there is less than complete agreement among professionals.

It is important to note at the outset that the people who seek or are sent for *professional* help have probably tried nonprofessional avenues to feeling better and have failed to obtain relief. Before most individuals go to a therapist, they have confided in friends or in a spouse, perhaps spoken to the family doctor, consulted with a member of the clergy, and maybe tried several of the vast number of self-help books and programs that are so popular now. For most people in psychological distress, one or more of these options provide enough relief, and they seek no further help (Bergin, 1971). But for others these attempts fall short, and individuals are left feeling helpless, often hopeless. These are the people who go to mental health clinics, university counseling centers, and the private offices of independent practitioners.

Theories and therapies are great in number. There are scores, perhaps hundreds, each with its enthu-

18.1 • The Placebo Effect

Any study of the effects of psychotherapy—whether insight or action oriented—should include a consideration of the **placebo effect**. This term refers to an improvement in physical or psychological condition that is attributable to a patient's expectations of help rather than to any specific active ingredient in a treatment. Frank (1973) related placebo effects to faith healing in prescientific or nonscientific societies. For centuries, suffering human beings have derived benefit from making pilgrimages to sanctified places and from ingesting sometimes foul-smelling concoctions.

Many people dismiss placebo reactions as not real or as second-best. After all, if a person has a tension headache, what possible benefit can he or she hope to get from a pill that is totally devoid of chemical action or direct physiological effect? The fact is, however, that such benefits can sometimes be significant and even long lasting. For example, Frank (1973) furnished extensive evidence attesting to improvement in a variety of physical and mental problems after ingestion of placebo sugar pills and from exposure to other ministrations that, in themselves, could not possibly account for this relief.

It is not a simple matter, however, to extend the findings of research on chemical placebos directly to research on psychological placebos. In psychotherapy, the mere expectation of being helped can be an active ingredient! If the theory adopted by the therapist holds that positive expectancy of improvement is an active ingredient, then improvement arising from the expectancy would, by definition, *not* be considered a placebo effect. Indeed, Lambert, Shapiro, and Bergin (1986) argued that "placebo factors" should be replaced with the concept "common factors" in the study of the effects of psychotherapy. They reiterated Rosenthal and Frank's (1956) early caveat that a placebo as something therapeutically inert can be understood only from the standpoint of a particular *theory* of change, and they defined common factors as "those dimensions of the treatment setting . . . that are not specific to a particular technique. Those factors that are common to most therapies (such as expectation for improvement, persuasion, warmth and attention, understanding, encouragement, etc.) should not be viewed as theoretically *inert* nor as *trivial;* they are central to psychological treatments and play an active role in patient improvement" (p. 163). Indeed, patients in so-called placebo control groups, as Lambert et al. (1986) pointed out, generally improve more than patients in no-treatment groups—though often not as much as patients in treatment groups. The issue of common factors is important in the movement toward psychotherapy integration, a topic we examine closely near the end of Chapter 19, after we have had the opportunity to review the principal insight and action therapies.

The place of placebo control groups in psychotherapy research is an often-debated and complex topic, the intricacies of which are beyond the scope of this book. We should note, though, that a study that compares a particular therapy to no treatment at all and finds that therapy brings more improvement does tell us something important, namely, that being treated is better than receiving no treatment. But a given therapy usually tries to create improvement in a particular way, by removing the person's defenses, by easing the individual's way to self-actualization, by enhancing responsible choices, by counterconditioning fears, and so forth. To determine whether these *processes* are at work and are effective, a study needs, at the very least, a control group of patients who are instilled with expectancies of help, who believe that something worthwhile and beneficial is being done for them. *All* therapies derive at least some of their power from the faith that people have in the healer and from their profound desire to get better.

siastic supporters. We present in this and the following two chapters a close look at the more prominent theories of intervention and the research supporting them. Our intent is to provide enough detail about the major approaches to allow a grasp of the basic issues and an overall perspective on the therapeutic enterprise. We hope, too, that this will provide the reader with the means to evaluate critically new therapies that arise, or at the very least to know the questions to ask in order to evaluate them effectively.

Our principal concern in this chapter and the next

Troubled people may talk about their problems with friends or seek professional therapy. Therapy is typically sought by those for whom the advice and support of friends have not provided relief.

is individual therapy, that is, therapy conducted by a clinician with one patient or client. Nearly everything said in these two chapters is relevant also for therapy in groups, a subject dealt with more completely as one of three principal topics in Chapter 20.

London (1964; 1986) categorized psychotherapies as *insight* or *action* (behavioral) therapies. Behavior therapy is discussed in Chapter 19. **Insight therapy,** discussed in depth in this chapter, assumes that behavior, emotions, and thoughts become disordered because people do not adequately understand what motivates them, especially when their needs and drives conflict. Insight therapy tries to help people discover the true reasons for behaving, feeling, and thinking as they do. The premise is that greater awareness of motivations will yield greater control over and subsequent improvement in thought, emotion, and behavior.

It is important to note here that *insight* is not exclusive to the so-called insight therapies. Clearly the action therapies bring insight to the individual as well, and the newer cognitive therapies, also discussed in Chapter 19, can be seen as a blend of insight and behavioral therapies. It is a matter of emphasis, a matter of focus. In the behavioral therapies, the focus is on changing behavior; insight is often a peripheral benefit. In the insight therapies, the focus is less on changing people directly than on enhancing their understanding of their motives, fears, and conflicts. To facilitate such insights, therapists of different theoretical persuasions have employed a variety of techniques, ranging from the free association of psychoanalysis to the reflection of feelings practiced in client-centered therapy (see Focus Box 18.1 for an important issue in evaluating the effects of psychotherapy).

Psychoanalytic Therapies

Psychoanalysis and its many offshoots are an important force in psychiatry and clinical psychology. In this section we summarize and evaluate the important elements of classical (Freudian) psychoanalysis, ego-analysis, and interpersonal therapies.

Basic Techniques and Concepts in Psychoanalysis

At the heart of classical **psychoanalysis** is the therapeutic attempt to remove repressions that have prevented the ego from helping the individual grow into a responsible, healthy adult. Psychopathology, it is assumed, develops when people remain unaware of their true motivations and fears. They can be restored to healthy functioning only by becoming conscious of what has been repressed. When people can understand *what* is motivating their actions, they have a greater number of choices. Where id is, let there ego be, to paraphrase a maxim of psychoanalysis. The ego—being the primarily conscious, deliberating, choosing portion of the personality—can better guide the individual in rational, realistic directions if repressions are at a minimum.

Wachtel's (1977) woolly mammoth (see page 42) is an apt metaphor for the unresolved, buried conflicts from which psychoanalytic theory assumes psychological problems arise. The proper focus of therapy, then, is not on the presenting problem, such as fears of being rejected, but on unconscious conflicts existing in the psyche from childhood. Only by lifting the repression can the person confront the underlying problem and reevaluate it in the context of his or her adult life.

Free Association

Psychoanalysts use a number of techniques to help the patient recover repressed conflicts. Perhaps the best known and most important is **free association:** the patient, reclining on a couch, is encouraged to give free rein to thoughts and feelings and to verbalize whatever comes to mind. The quotation opening this chapter presents the kind of instruction that might be given to a patient. The assumption is that, with enough practice, free association will facilitate the uncovering of unconscious material. The adjective *free* does not mean uncaused, only free from conscious censorship and control. "As an avowed determinist, Freud believed that unconscious mechanisms governed by psychological laws produced the flow of free associations. Free associations are thus not truly free" (Morse, 1982, p. 215). Indeed, it is the assumption that they are *not* free that makes this technique important in psychoanalysis.

In therapy, the patient must follow the fundamental rule of reporting thoughts and feelings as accurately as possible, without screening out the elements that might seem unimportant or shameful. Freud assumed that thoughts and memories occurred in associative chains and that recent ones reported first would ultimately trace back to earlier crucial ones. In order to get to these earlier events, however, the therapist has to be very careful not to guide or direct the patient's thinking and usually sits behind the patient to minimize such influence.

Resistance

Blocks to free association do arise, however, virtually thrusting themselves across the thoughts supposedly given free rein. Patients may suddenly change the subject or be unable to remember how a long-ago event ended. They try any tactic to interrupt the session, remaining silent, getting up from the couch, looking out the window, making jokes and personal remarks to the analyst. Patients may even come late or "forget" sessions altogether. Such obstacles to free association—**resistances**—were noted by Freud and contributed to the development of the concept of repression. He asserted that interference with free association can be traced to unconscious control over sensitive areas; it is precisely these areas that psychoanalytic therapists want to probe. Indeed, in some respects resistances provide the analyst with the most critical information about the patient.

Analysis of Dreams

Akin to free association is **dream analysis,** a classic analytic technique in which the therapist guides the patient in remembering and later analyzing his or her dreams. Freud assumed that during sleep the ego defenses are lowered, allowing repressed material to come forth, usually in disguised form. Concerns of the patient are often expressed in symbols (**latent content**) to help protect the conscious ego from the true significance of dream material. The **manifest content** of dreams—what is immediately apparent—may be regarded as a sort of compromise between repression of true meaning and a full expression of unconscious material. The cutting down of a tall tree (manifest content) might symbolize the patient's anger toward his or her father (latent content). The content of dreams, then, is distorted by unconscious defensive structures, which, never completely abandoned, even in sleep, continue their fight to protect the ego from repressed impulses.

Interpretation and Denial

As presumably unconscious material begins to appear, another technique comes into play, **interpretation.** According to Freud, this stage helps the person finally face the emotionally loaded conflict that was previously repressed. At the right time the analyst begins to point out the patient's defenses and the underlying meaning of his or her dreams, feelings, thoughts, and actions. The analyst must be careful not to offer this interpretation too soon, for the patient may totally reject it and leave treatment. To be effective, the analyst's interpretations should reflect insights that the patient is on the verge of making; the patient can then regard these insights as their own, rather than viewing them as coming from the analyst. Presumably an interpretation that a patient attributes to himself or herself will be more readily accepted and thereby have a stronger therapeutic effect.

Interpretation is the analyst's principal weapon against the continued use of defense mechanisms. The analyst may point out how certain verbalizations of the patient relate to repressed unconscious material, or suggest what the manifest content of dreams *truly* means. If the interpretation is timed correctly, the patient starts to examine the repressed impulse in the light of present-day reality. In other words, the patient begins to realize that he or she no longer has to fear the awareness of the impulse.

Feeling safe under the undemanding conditions arranged by the analyst, the patient should uncover more and more repressed material. The analyst's interpretations are held to be particularly helpful in establishing the meaning of the resistances that disturb the patient's free association. The analyst may, for example, point out how the patient tends to avoid a particular topic, and it is common for the patient to deny the interpretation. Interestingly, this denial is sometimes interpreted as a sign that the analyst's interpretation is correct rather than incorrect. In the slow process of working through the disturbing conflicts, of confronting them again and again, the patient gradually faces up to the validity of the analyst's interpretations, often with great emotion.

Determining when a patient's **denial** of an interpretation means that it is correct is, in our opinion, one of the thorniest problems in psychoanalysis. When, in truth, is it appropriate to consider that a no is really a yes? It would seem a scenario ripe for mistakes. But the analyst, like any clinician, does not judge in a vacuum. He or she formulates hypotheses over time about the patient, noticing how one problem area relates to others. The analyst searches for clues in a slowly developing picture, and every statement, every gesture of the patient, is viewed within this scheme. A patient's no is considered a yes only in the *context* of other ideas already formed by the analyst. And the analyst bases that judgment, in part, on how vigorously the patient denies an interpretation, generally regarding as defensive a denial expressed in an excessive manner. As Queen Gertrude in Shakespeare's *Hamlet* commented, "The lady doth protest too much, methinks" (act III, scene 2).

Transference

The core of psychoanalytic therapy is the **transference neurosis**. Freud noted that his patients sometimes acted toward him in an emotion-charged and unrealistic way. For example, a patient much older than Freud would behave in a childish manner during a therapy session. Although these reactions were often positive and loving, many times they were quite negative and hostile. Since these feelings seemed out of character with the ongoing therapy relationship, Freud assumed that they were relics of attitudes *transferred* to him from those held in the past toward important people in the patient's history, primarily parents. That is, Freud felt that patients responded to him *as though* he were one of the important people in their past. Freud used this transference of attitudes, which he came to consider an inevitable aspect of psychoanalysis, as a means of explaining to patients the childhood origin of many of their concerns and fears. This revelation and explanation tended also to help lift repressions and allow the confrontation of buried impulses. In psychoanalysis, transference is regarded as essential to a complete cure. Indeed, it is precisely when analysts notice transference developing that they take hope that the important repressed conflict from childhood is getting closer to the surface.

Analysts encourage the development of transference by intentionally remaining shadowy figures, generally sitting behind the patient while the patient free-associates and serving as relatively blank screens on which important persons in the repressed conflicts can be projected. They take pains to reveal as little as possible of their own personal lives. Analysts are also caring persons, which may remind the patient of attributes, real or hoped for, in his or her parents. Because the therapy setting is so different from the childhood situation, analysts can readily point out to patients the irrational nature of their fears and concerns (see Focus Box 18.2).

Countertransference

Related to transference is **countertransference**, the feelings of the analyst toward the patient. The analyst must be careful not to allow his or her own emotional vulnerabilities to affect the relationship with the patient. The analyst's own needs and fears must be recognized for what they are: the analyst should have enough understanding of his or her own motivations to be able to see the client clearly, without distortion. The problem is well articulated in the following discussion of therapy with depressed people, during which countertransference is a continuing challenge to a therapist.

> Depressed patients bring their hopelessness and despair into therapy, and the therapist may be affected. If the depression improves slowly, or not at all, the therapist may feel guilty, angry, and/or helpless. After seeing several severely depressed patients in a day, the therapist may feel quite drained and eventually may become unwilling to work in the future with similar patients. Suicidal patients can evoke particularly difficult countertransferences. . . .
>
> One safeguard against such difficulties is the therapist's continuing awareness of these feelings and their relation to his or her own psychodynamics. A suffering patient may mobilize the therapist's fantasy of being able to heal and earn gratitude, deftly and single-handedly; or may stir up the therapist's anger at the existence of suffering. An abiding awareness of these reactions will help the therapist

18.2 • Excerpt from a Psychoanalytic Session—An Illustration of Transference

Patient: (a fifty-year-old male business executive): I really don't feel like talking today.

Analyst: (Remains silent for several minutes, then) Perhaps you'd like to talk about why you don't feel like talking.

Patient: There you go again, making demands on me, insisting I do what I just don't feel up to doing. (Pause) Do I always have to talk here, when I don't feel like it? (Voice becomes angry and petulant) Can't you just get off my back? You don't really give a damn how I feel, do you?

Analyst: I wonder why you feel I don't care.

Patient: Because you're always pressuring me to do what I feel I can't do.

Comments

This excerpt must be viewed in context. The patient had been in therapy for about a year, complaining of depression and anxiety. Although extremely successful in the eyes of his family and associates, he himself felt weak and incompetent. Through many sessions of free association and dream analysis, the analyst had begun to suspect that the patient's feelings of failure stemmed from his childhood experiences with an extremely punitive and critical father, a man even more successful than the client, and a person who seemed never to be satisfied with his son's efforts. The exchange quoted was later interpreted by the analyst as an expression of resentment by the patient of his *father's* pressures on him and had little to do with the analyst himself. The patient's tone of voice (petulant), as well as his overreaction to the analyst's gentle suggestion that he talk about his feelings of not wanting to talk, indicated that the patient was angry not at his analyst but at his father. The expression of such feelings to the analyst, that is, transferring them from the father to the analyst, was regarded as significant by the therapist and was used in subsequent sessions in helping the patient to reevaluate his childhood fears of expressing aggression toward his father.

> maintain the patience and satisfaction with small gains that are necessary for conducting psychotherapy with severely depressed patients. At the same time, the therapist must avoid overstepping his/her role and trying to do all the work for an apparently weak patient. (Jacobson & McKinney, 1982, p. 215)

Thus a training analysis (*Lehranalyse*, wherein the trainee is psychoanalyzed by a senior analyst) is a formal part of the education of an analyst. Although many therapists of different theoretical persuasions consider it useful to have been in therapy themselves, it is *required* in analytic training institutes. It is essential that analysts reduce to a minimum the frequency and intensity of countertransference toward their clients.

Detachment

The analyst must *not* become actively involved in helping the patient deal with everyday problems. He or she carefully avoids any intervention, such as a direct suggestion about how to behave in a troublesome situation. Short-term relief might deflect the patient's efforts to uncover the repressed conflicts. Freud was emphatic on this point, writing in 1918 that the analyst must take care not to make the patient's life so comfortable that he or she is no longer motivated to delve into the unconscious. He put it this way in his criticism of nonanalytic helpers.

> Their one aim is to make everything as pleasant as possible for the patient, so that he may feel well there and be glad to take refuge there again from the trials of life. In so doing, they make no attempt to give him more strength for facing life and more capacity for carrying out his actual tasks in it. In analytic treatment, all such spoiling must be avoided. As far as his relations with the physician are concerned, the patient must be left with unfulfilled wishes in abundance. It is expedient to deny him precisely those satisfactions which he desires most intensely and expresses most importunately. (Freud, 1955, p. 164)

The detachment of the analyst has often been ridiculed or misinterpreted, which does an injustice both to analytic theory and to the people who apply it. When a person is in pain and is needy, the initial impulse is, figuratively, to take the sufferer into one's arms and comfort him or her, providing reassurance that all will be well, that the patient will be taken care of. But the analyst views it from a different perspective: a patient in therapy has likely had others try to provide solace; if sympathy and support were going to help, they probably would already have done so. The analyst must work hard to resist showing concern through expressions of support and with concrete advice. Moreover, acting in a directive fashion will interfere with transference, for the therapist necessarily becomes less of a blank screen if he or she expresses opinions, voices objections, and gives advice and direction. The distance kept by the analyst from the patient is intended to help the patient. This strategem is consistent with analytic theory and is rather rigidly applied by the more orthodox psychoanalysts.

Concluding Comment

Classical psychoanalysis is directly opposite in thrust to cognitive and behavior therapy. Practitioners of the latter are unconcerned with factors presumed by analysts to be buried in the unconscious and they concentrate precisely on what analysts ignore, namely, helping patients change their attitudes, feelings, and overt behavior in concrete, current life situations. What the analyst, and to a large degree the ego analyst, terms *supportive therapy*, the cognitive behavior therapist regards as the essence of therapy. By the same token, what the behavior therapist sees as unnecessary and even detrimental to the client—digging into the repressed past and withholding advice on how to make specific changes in the here and now—is judged by the analyst to be essential to complete psychotherapeutic treatment.

Contemporary Analytic Therapies

Current analytic therapies include ego analysis, brief psychodynamic therapy, and interpersonal psychodynamic therapy.

Ego Analysis

After Freud's death some important modifications in psychoanalytic theory came from a group generally referred to as ego analysts. Their views are sometimes described as psychodynamic rather than psychoanalytic. The major figures in this loosely formed movement include Karen Horney (1942), Anna Freud (1946), Erik Erikson (1950), David Rapaport (1951), and Heinz Hartmann (1958). Although Freud by no means ignored the interactions of the organism with the environment, his view was essentially a push model, one in which people are driven by intrapsychic urges. Those who subscribe to **ego analysis** place greater emphasis on a person's ability to control the environment and to select the time and the means for satisfying certain instinctual drives. Their basic contention is that the individual is as much ego as id. They also focus on current living conditions to a greater extent than did Freud, although they still sometimes advocate delving deeply into the historical causes of an individual's behavior.

Important for the ego analysts is a set of ego functions that are primarily conscious, capable of controlling both id instincts and the external environment, and that, more significantly, do not depend on the id for their energy. Ego analysts assume that these functions and capabilities are present at birth and then develop through experience. Underemphasized by Freud, ego functions have energies and gratifications of their own, usually separate from the reduction of id impulses. And whereas society was, for Freud, essentially a negative inhibition against the unfettered gratification of libidinal impulses, the ego analysts hold that an individual's social interactions can provide their own special kind of gratification.

Brief Psychodynamic Therapy

Although many lay people assume that patients usually spend many months, even years, in psychodynamic psychotherapy, most therapies last fewer than ten sessions (Garfield, 1978). Among many reasons for the short duration of therapy is that fewer people today are interested in the personality overhaul that was the goal of classical analytic treatment. Another factor both in shortening treatment and in encouraging analytically oriented workers to adapt analytic ideas to time-limited psychotherapy, called **brief therapy**, is, no doubt, the growing reluctance of insurance companies to cover more than, say, twenty-five psychotherapy sessions in a given calendar year, with other limits set as well on the amount of reimbursement provided. The emergence of cognitive and behavioral therapies over the past twenty or thirty years has also played a role; these approaches focus on discrete problems and eschew long-term therapy, as explained in greater detail in the next chapter. Combined with the growing acceptability of psychotherapy in the population at large, the stage has been set for a stronger focus on time-limited psychodynamic therapy.

Another strand in the history of brief psychodynamic therapy can be found in the challenges faced by mental health professionals to respond to psychological emergencies (Koss & Shiang, in press). Shell shock emergencies in World War II led to Grinker and Spiegel's (1944) classic short-term analytic treatment of what is now called posttraumatic stress disorder (page 155). A related contribution came from Eric Lindemann's (1944) crisis intervention with the victims of the famous Coconut Grove nightclub fire in 1943.

Interestingly, Freud's original conception was that psychoanalysis should be relatively short-term; the analyst should focus on specific problems, make it clear to the patient that therapy would not exceed a certain number of sessions, and structure sessions in a directive fashion. Thus Freud envisioned a more active psychoanalysis than what eventually developed. The early pioneers in brief therapy were the psychoanalysts Ferenczi (1920) and Alexander and French (1946).

Brief therapies share several common elements (Koss & Shiang, in press):

1. Assessment tends to be rapid and early.
2. It is made clear right away to the patient that therapy will be limited and that improvement is expected within a small number of sessions, ranging from six to twenty-five.
3. Goals are concrete and focused on the amelioration of the patient's worst symptoms, on helping the patient understand what is going on in his or her life, and on enabling the patient to cope better in the future.
4. Interpretations are directed more toward present life circumstances and patient behavior than on the historical significance of feelings.
5. Development of a transference neurosis is not encouraged. Some positive transference to the therapist, however, is fostered in an effort to encourage the patient to follow the therapist's suggestions and advice.
6. There is a general understanding that psychotherapy does not cure, but that it can help troubled individuals learn to deal better with life's inevitable stressors.

Interpersonal Psychodynamic Therapy

A variant of brief ego-analytic therapy is a group of psychodynamic therapies, often referred to as **interpersonal therapy**, that emphasize the interactions between a patient and his or her social environment. A pioneer in the development of this approach was the American psychiatrist Harry Stack Sullivan. Sometimes called a neo-Freudian, Sullivan held that the basic difficulty of patients is misperceptions of reality (parataxic distortions) stemming from disorganization in the interpersonal relations of childhood, primarily those between child and parents. This is traditionally Freudian.

Harry Stack Sullivan modified the traditional psychoanalytic concept of transference and instead proposed that the therapist was a participant observer.

Sullivan departed from Freud, however, in his conception of the analyst as a "participant observer" in the therapy process. In contrast with the classical or even ego-analytical view of the therapist as a blank screen for the transference neurosis, Sullivan argued that the therapist, like the scientist, is inevitably a part of the process he or she is studying. An analyst does not see patients without at the same time affecting them.

In a searching critique of transference, Wachtel (1977) placed even greater emphasis on the interpersonal nature of therapy. Opposing the orthodox psychoanalytic view that a shadowy therapist enables transference to develop, Wachtel hypothesized that such unvarying behavior on the part of the therapist frustrates the client, who may be seeking some indication of how the therapist feels about what he or she is doing and saying. The sometimes childish reactions assumed to be part of the transference neurosis Wachtel regarded, in part, as the normal reactions of an adult who is thwarted! The troubled client sees the analyst as a professional person who remains distant and noncommittal in the face of his or her increasing expression of emotion. Thus, rather than being exclusively an unfolding of the client's personality, transference may actually be in some measure his or her extreme frustration with minimal feedback. Moreover, because the analyst restricts his or her own behavior so severely in the consulting room and intentionally limits the setting to which the client is exposed, he or she can sample only a limited range of the client's behavior, attitudes, and feelings. Wachtel's blend of psychoanalytic and behavioral viewpoints will be explored when we describe recent developments toward a rapprochement between these major paradigms (page 586).

A contemporary example of a psychodynamic interpersonal therapy was proposed by Klerman and Weissman (Klerman et al., 1984). Their Interpersonal Therapy (IPT) was mentioned earlier (page 244) as an effective treatment of depression and will be discussed again in the next chapter when we examine a major study comparing their therapy with Beck's cognitive therapy and with imipramine, a widely used antidepressant medication (page 247). IPT concentrates a good deal on current interpersonal difficulties and on discussing with the patient—even teaching the patient directly—better ways of relating to others. The kind of major personality change sought by classical psychoanalysis is not a goal of IPT. The clinical literature cautions against brief therapy for several kinds of patients, including those who are extremely anxious, passive-dependent, self-destructive, or psychotic (Wolberg, 1965).

There can be confusion about what is considered brief psychotherapy. Our own reading suggests that the term almost always refers to the ego-analytic and interpersonal approaches described here. A defining characteristic seems to be that psychoanalytic ideas and practices are adapted for short-term use. But sometimes the term has been applied to therapies based on other paradigms, for example, Wolpe's desensitization and related techniques, Ellis's rational-emotive therapy, and Beck's cognitive therapy; the common characteristic here is the typically short-term nature of these interventions (Koss & Shiang, in press). In our view, the latter categorization is not useful, for it would include *any* intervention that happens to involve a patient in fewer than two dozen sessions, such as electroconvulsive therapy, many drug therapies, and even psychosurgery. Our discussion, therefore, assumes the more substantive definition of brief therapy as equivalent to some variation of psychoanalysis that is designed for short-term application.

Evaluation of Analytic Therapies

In clinical circles there are few issues more controversial than the question of whether classical psychoanalysis and related therapies work. Some clinicians are uneasy with the classical psychoanalytic concepts themselves, especially those that seem wedded to a notion of *an* unconscious.

Paradigmatic differences bear on any evaluation of the effectiveness of psychoanalysis, in all its various forms. It is very difficult to study scientifically. What, for example, are the criteria for improvement? A principal one is the lifting of repressions, making the unconscious conscious. But how is that to be demonstrated? How do we determine whether a repression has been lifted? Attempts to assess outcome have sometimes relied on projective tests, such as the Rorschach, which, in turn, rely on the concept of the unconscious. For those who reject the very concept of an unconscious, data from projective tests are not very convincing.

The central concept of insight has also been questioned. Rather than accept insight as the recognition by the client of some important, externally valid, historical connection or relationship, several writers (e.g., Bandura, 1969; London, 1964) have proposed that the development of insight is better understood as a *social conversion process*, whereby the patient comes to accept the belief system of his or her therapist. Marmor (1962) suggested that insight means different things depending on the school of therapy; a patient treated by a proponent of any one of the various schools develops insights along the lines of its particular theoretical predilections. Freudians tend to elicit insights regarding oedipal dilemmas, Sullivanians insights regarding interpersonal relationships, and so forth.

Should we be concerned whether an insight into the past is a true one? If an insight is in fact part of a social conversion process, do we need to concern ourselves with the truth of it? When we examine cognitive behavior therapy in the next chapter, especially Ellis's rational-emotive therapy, we encounter this question again. Therapists who encourage clients to look at things differently—as do all the therapists discussed in this chapter and the cognitive behavior therapists of the next—believe that an insight may help the client change an outlook, whether or not the insight is true. Because of the immense complexity of human lives, it is impossible to know with any degree of certainty whether an event really happened and, if it did, whether it caused the current problem.

The issue has other ramifications. In our discussion of ethics in therapy in Chapter 21, we review suggestions that psychotherapy is inherently, ultimately, a moral enterprise. That is, therapists, sometimes unwittingly, convey to clients messages about how they *ought* to live their lives. They assume a "secular priest" role (London, 1964, 1986). In this framework the usefulness of a given insight would depend on whether it helps the client lead a life more consonant with a particular set of shoulds and oughts.

With all these cautions in mind, let us consider the efforts researchers have made to evaluate the efficacy of classical psychoanalytic, ego-analytic, and interpersonal therapies. Although there is often some overlap, the psychotherapy research literature often distinguishes between outcome studies and process studies. **Outcome studies** ask whether therapy works. **Process studies** focus on what happens *during* therapy that can be related to the outcome. For example, does transference have to occur for beneficial change to take place?

Research on Classical Psychoanalysis

The following generalizations about Freudian psychoanalysis were made by Luborsky and Spence (1978), who relied on outcome research conducted with some measure of controlled observation.

1. Patients with severe psychopathology (e.g., schizophrenia) do not do as well as those with anxiety disorders. This is understandable in view of Freud's admitted emphasis on neurosis rather than psychosis and in view of the heavy reliance psychoanalysis places on rationality and verbal abilities.
2. The more education a patient has, the better he or she does in analysis, probably because of the heavy emphasis on verbal interaction.
3. There is conflicting evidence as to whether the outcome of psychoanalysis is any better than what would be achieved through the mere passage of time or by engaging other professional help, such as a family doctor (Bergin, 1971). This is *not* to say that psychoanalysis does no good, only that clear evidence is as yet lacking. Given the great diversity in the characteristics of both patients and therapists and in the severity of patients' problems, the question is probably too complex to yield a single, scientifically acceptable answer.

Research on Ego-Analytic, Brief, and Interpersonal Therapies

A widely cited study by Sloane and his colleagues (1975) at the Temple University Outpatient Clinic had three behavior therapists and three psychoanalysts of an ego-analytic bent—all of them highly experienced and recognized leaders in their respective fields—treat a total of ninety adult patients for a period of four months. Most of the participants in this study can best be described as neurotic; they were the individuals typically seen in outpatient clinics or in private consulting rooms. For the most part they were troubled by anxiety and disturbed relationships. After being matched on age and sex, as well as severity of problems, they were randomly assigned to behavior therapy or to short-term analytic therapy. In addition to the ninety people treated, some who had gone through the same comprehensive assessment were assigned to a wait-list control group. They were promised therapy later but were asked to wait while others were in treatment. The purpose of this control group was to judge the effects on patients of having taken steps to enter therapy.

Sloane and his colleagues drew up for their therapists a list of defining characteristics of the analytic and behavior therapy that they intended to compare (Table 18.1) and instructed the therapists to adhere to these criteria as closely as possible. Audiotape recordings of the fifth session of each treatment were analyzed to determine whether these rules were being followed. The judgment was made that they were.

Outcome measures, taken immediately after treatment and at an eight-month follow-up, included personality tests, such as the MMPI, ratings of how much symptoms had improved, structured interviews to determine how well the clients were doing in their work and social adjustment, and a global rating of improvement. In addition to the psychiatrist or psychologist who had conducted the therapy, the client, a clinician who had not been involved in treatment and did not know which treatment each participant had received, and a close friend or relative joined in the judgments.

Depending on how we look at the data—and there are many ways given the complexity of the study and the several measures taken—the findings favor behavior therapy, analytic therapy, or even no treatment at all! Immediately after termination of therapy, independent clinicians rated 80 percent of the clients in each treatment group improved or cured and 48 percent of the wait-list control group improved or recovered. *But*, at the eight-month follow-up, the superiority of the two treated groups over the wait-list control group had vanished, for the subjects in the control group had improved markedly. The people waiting for treatment had received a fair amount of attention, because in addition to the initial and later assessments, they were called regularly and given encouragement and support.

We can view negatively the fact that the wait-list control group caught up with the two therapy

Table 18.1 • Characteristics of Behavior Therapy and Analytically Oriented Psychotherapy in the Temple University Study

Defining Characteristic	*Ego-Analysis*	*Behavior Therapy*
Specific advice	Given infrequently	Given frequently
Transference interpretation	May be given	Avoided
Interpretation of resistance	Used	Not used
Dreams	Interest in reported dreams; may be used in treatment	Polite lack of interest; not used in treatment
Level of anxiety	Maintain some anxiety as long as it does not disrupt behavior	Diminished when possible except in implosive therapy
Training in relaxation	Only an indirect consequence of sitting, and perhaps the example of the therapist	Directly undertaken
Desensitization	Only an indirect consequence of talking in comfortable circumstances with uncritical therapist	Directly undertaken
Practical retraining	Not emphasized	Directly undertaken
Training appropriately assertive action	Only indirectly encouraged in everyday life; assertive or aggressive speech that would be inappropriate in everyday life permitted in therapeutic session	Directly undertaken and encouraged in everyday life
Symptoms	Report of symptoms discouraged; may interpret symbolically	Interest in the report of symptoms; may explain biologically
Childhood memories	Usually further memories looked for	Usually history-taking only
Aversion, e.g., electric shock	Not used	May be used
Observers of treatment session	Not usually permitted	May be permitted
Deliberate attempts to stop behavior, such as thoughts, that makes the patient anxious	Rarely directly attempted	May be used
Role training	Not used	May be used
Repetition of motor habits	Not used	May be used

Source: From Sloane et al., 1975.

groups at the eight-month follow-up. But the same finding can be regarded as positive. The therapy, whether insight or behavioral, *speeded up* the rate of improvement, thus lessening overall the suffering of the clients and those close to them. In this way both types of therapy were helpful and could be judged superior to the attention given the wait-list group.

Many other studies have examined the effectiveness of brief psychodynamic therapy (Beutler & Grago, 1991), and a general conclusion reached by Koss and Butcher (1986) is that it is no less effective than time-unlimited psychoanalysis, perhaps because both patient and therapist work harder and focus on more specific and manageable goals than a personality overhaul. In their review of individual psychotherapy research, Goldfried, Greenberg, and Marmar (1990) concluded that brief dynamic therapy is effective in treating stress and bereavement (Marmar & Horowitz, 1988), late-life depression (Thompson, Gallagher, & Breckenridge, 1987), and mood and personality disorders (Marziali, 1984). Other literature reviews have concluded that brief psychodynamic therapy is useful with job-related distress and a variety of anxiety disorders (Koss & Shiang, in press), including posttraumatic stress disorder (Horowitz, 1988). Furthermore, the NIMH Treatment of Depression Collaborative Research Program, described in detail in the next chapter, provides additional evidence that Interpersonal Psychotherapy is effective in treating depression, confirming some earlier research by Weissman, Klerman, and associates (DiMascio et al., 1979). However, according to Beutler, a noted psychotherapy researcher, it is too soon to conclude that brief therapy is specifically effective with certain kinds of patients, for the very concept of brief therapy covers so many different variations—300, he estimates!—as to render general conclusions risky indeed (Beutler, 1991).

Process research in brief therapy has improved in just the past fifteen years, with more careful delineation of therapeutic procedures, the use of manuals, and more operational measurement of concepts such as the working alliance developed between therapist and patient (e.g., the Vanderbilt Therapeutic Alliance Scale of Hartley and Strupp, 1983; and the Therapeutic Bond Scales of Saunders, Howard, and Orlinsky, 1989). Therapeutic or working alliance refers to rapport and trust and to a sense that the therapist and the patient are working together to achieve mutually agreed upon goals. A study by Kolden (1991), for example, found that the better this bond, the more favorable the outcome after an average of twenty-five sessions. Luborsky et al.'s (1990) and Howard et al.'s (1991) review of other such studies confirm that the stronger the therapeutic relationship, or alliance, the better the outcome (Luborsky et al., 1988). Interestingly, Luborsky et al. were unable to point to research supporting the central doctrine of "where id was there shall ego be" (Freud, 1933/1964), that is, that therapeutic progress is brought about by the patient coming to understand better what has hitherto been unconscious.

A positive factor in working with ethnic minorities is the cultural sensitivity of the therapist (Gim, Atkinson, & Kim, 1991), something we encountered earlier in the discussion of Lopez's work on therapist biases in assessing the needs of minority patients (page 104). Preparing patients, especially those from less sophisticated strata of society, via films that provide information on what to expect from psychotherapy seems to improve therapeutic outcome as well (Warren & Rice, 1972). Also associated with improvement is patient openness, the degree to which the patient is unguarded about discussing his or her problems, fears, and aspirations (Orlinsky & Howard, 1986).

All of these process variables may well be related to a factor that has for some time been known to be correlated with positive outcome, namely, patient involvement in the therapy (Gomes-Schwartz, 1978). The evidence from these process studies should not, however, be taken to indicate a particular direction of causality. Although, for example, patient involvement is positively correlated with outcome, it may itself be a consequence of outcome rather than a cause of it. A patient who feels improvement—for reasons that may have nothing to do with how much energy he or she invests in the therapy—may, *as a consequence of beginning to feel better*, become more interested in treatment. Subsequently, this increased involvement may indeed contribute to some of the therapeutic improvement later on. Our own hunch is that there is a complex interplay and bidirectionality in most process research. (Focus Box 18.3 discusses a statistical strategy for comparing the relative effectiveness of different therapies.)

Humanistic and Existential Therapies

Sometimes called experiential therapies, **humanistic** and **existential therapies**, like psychoanalytic therapies, are insight-focused, based on the assumption that disordered behavior can best be treated by increasing the individual's awareness of motivations and needs. But there are useful contrasts between psychoanalysis and its offshoots on the one hand and humanistic and existential approaches on the other. The psychoanalytic paradigm assumes that human nature, the id, is something in need of restraint, that effective socialization requires the ego to mediate between the environment and the basically antisocial, at best, asocial, impulses stemming from biological urges. (As we have seen, though, ego-analytic theorizing deemphasized these features of classical Freudian thought and introduced concepts that bring contemporary psychoanalytic thinking closer to humanistic and existential approaches.) Humanistic and existential therapies also place greater emphasis on the person's freedom of choice. Free will is regarded as our most important characteristic. Free will is, however, a double-edged sword, for it not only offers fulfillment and pleasure but also threatens acute pain and suffering. It is an innately provided gift that *must* be used and that requires special courage to use. Not all of us can meet this challenge: those who cannot are regarded as candidates for client-oriented, existential, and Gestalt therapies.

Carl Rogers's Client-Centered Therapy

Carl Rogers was an American psychologist whose theorizing about psychotherapy grew slowly out of years of intensive clinical experience. After teaching at the university level in the 1940s and 1950s, he helped organize the Center for Studies of the Person in La Jolla, California. Rogers made several basic

18.3 • Meta-analysis and the Effects of Psychotherapy

A development in psychotherapy research that has attracted enormous attention in recent years is meta-analysis. Devised by Smith, Glass, and Miller (1980), it can be summarized as:

> a quantitative method for averaging . . . the standardized results of a large number of different studies. The unit of analysis is the effect size (ES), a quantitative index of the size of the effect of therapy . . . [arrived at] by subtracting the mean of the control group from the mean of the treatment group and dividing that difference by the standard deviation of the control group . . . The larger the ES, the greater the effect of therapy.

The basis of comparison need not be therapy A versus therapy B, rather, one can compare on dimensions such as type of subjects and settings in which therapy was administered. The independent variables, in other words, can be any factors considered influential in the outcome of an intervention. The great advantage of meta-analysis is that it provides a common metric across studies conducted in diverse settings by different investigators at different times (Kazdin, 1986).

In their original and oft-cited report, Smith et al. (1980) meta-analyzed 475 psychotherapy outcome studies involving more than 25,000 subjects and 1700 effect sizes and came to two conclusions that have attracted considerable attention and created controversy. First, they concluded that a wide range of therapies produce larger effect sizes than no treatment. Specifically, treated patients were found to be better off than almost 80 percent of untreated patients. Second, Smith et al. contended that effect sizes across diverse modes of intervention do not differ from each other.

The psychotherapy research literature has been full of references to and use of meta-analysis in efforts to sort through scores of studies and to try to bring a sense of order and fairness to the task of making comparative statements on the merits of contrasting kinds of therapy. Indeed, a standard handbook of psychotherapy and behavior change (Garfield & Bergin, 1986) relied heavily on literature reviews utilizing this technique. As part of a growing trend toward eclecticism in psychotherapy, reviewers of the literature have relied increasingly on meta-analysis as an evaluative and comparative tool. In this spirit, Lambert et al. (1986) drew several conclusions about psychotherapy *in general*, that is, without explicit consideration of *differences among* theoretical orientations. Although in our view this tactic runs the risk of comparing the proverbial apples and oranges, their conclusions are nonetheless useful in our broad-gauged study of this field.

1. Lambert et al. (1986) went beyond the findings of Smith et al. (1980) as well as others and found that many psychotherapeutic interventions were more effective than a number of so-called attention-placebo control groups. They concluded that psychotherapists are more than "placebologists" (p. 163). By the same token, what Lambert et al. call "common factors" (see page 589), rather than placebo factors, namely, warmth, trust, and encouragement, do themselves effect significant and even lasting improvement in a broad range of anxiety and mood disorders.
2. They found that the positive effects of psychotherapy tend to be maintained for many months following termination. Lambert et al. (1986) based this sanguine conclusion on a meta-analysis of sixty-seven outcome studies by Nicholson and Berman (1983), mostly behavioral in nature, with patients other than those diagnosed as psychotic, brain-disordered, antisocial personality, or addictive-disordered. Posttreatment status correlated well with follow-up status and, in general, group differences at follow-up were similar to those immediately following termination of therapy. This finding is obviously important to the client and to the individual therapist (who hopes that patients will continue to do well once they stop coming for regular sessions); it is important as well to psychotherapy researchers, who often have to undertake expensive and arduous follow-up measures to convince their colleagues that the effects of a given treatment are enduring. And yet Lambert et al. (1986) remind us that some disorders probably need to be followed up more than others, for example, depression, which is known to be recurrent.
3. There is considerable variability in therapy effects. Although treatment group X may, on average, show significant improvement, there are often patients in that group who get worse. This deterioration effect is discussed in greater detail in Focus Box 20.1
4. Recent meta-analytic studies comparing insight therapy with the cognitive and behav-

ioral interventions reviewed in the next chapter show a slight but consistent advantage to the latter, although there is criticism by proponents of insight therapy that behavioral and cognitive therapies focus on milder disorders.*

However, meta-analysis has been criticized by a number of psychotherapy researchers for the following reasons.

1. The behavioral researchers Wilson and Rachman (Rachman & Wilson, 1980; Wilson & Rachman, 1983) alleged that many behavior therapy studies, in particular those employing single-subject designs (see page 123), were omitted in the Smith et al. (1980) review. The claim is that the exclusion of these studies weakened the case for behavior therapy.
2. A more general problem is the quality control of studies that are included in a meta-analysis. Therapy studies differ in their internal and external validity *as judged by particular researchers*. By giving equal weight to all studies, the meta-analyses of Smith et al. created a situation in which a poorly controlled outcome study received as much attention as a well-controlled one. When Smith et al. attempted to address this problem by comparing effect sizes of good versus poor studies and found no differences, they were further criticized for the criteria they employed in separating the good from the not-so-good (Rachman & Wilson, 1980)! They were criticized also for using the results of this closer scrutiny to conclude that good and bad studies can be lumped together, the criticism being that "if poor-quality research agrees with good research, include it. . . . If poor research disagrees, disregard it" (Mintz, 1983, p. 74). O'Leary and Wilson (1987) considered other critiques as well and concluded that the ultimate problem is that *someone* has to make a judgment of good versus poor quality in psychotherapy research and that *others* can find fault with that judgment.

   This would appear to be an insoluble problem, one that has existed for years in reviews of therapy outcome research. There are times when a scholar has no choice but to make his or her own judgment about the validity of a piece of research and to decide whether or not to ignore it. Perhaps Mintz (1983) was correct in saying that the move toward meta-analysis in this field has at least sensitized us to the subjectivity that is inherent in passing judgment on research and has also encouraged greater explicitness in the criteria used to accept or to reject the findings of a given outcome study. Moreover, meta-analysis has uncovered deficiencies in some published research, for example, inadequate reporting of means and standard deviations and the collection of outcome data by persons who were aware of the treatment condition to which subjects were assigned (Shapiro & Shapiro, 1983). A long-term beneficial effect of meta-analysis may, then, be an improvement in research practices and a tightening of publication standards (Kazdin, 1986).
3. The overwhelming majority of outcome studies employ more than one measure. In their original work, Smith et al. (1980) computed effect sizes separately for each measure in each study; this led to greater weight being given to studies with larger numbers of outcome measures. Efforts to correct this inequity (e.g., Landman & Dawes, 1980; Prioleau, Murdock, & Brody, 1983) included combining separate measures to come up with a single effect size estimate for each study. At first blush this seems a good and fair solution, but as O'Leary and Wilson (1987) pointed out, it obscures the different information that disparate measures can provide and also overlooks the fact that different measures may change at different rates from a given intervention. They pointed out, for example, that rapid weight reduction programs can lead to quick weight loss *but* to an increase in depression (Stunkard & Rush, 1974). If one statistically combines these two measures into a single one, a finding of no significant effect emerges, thus concealing a clinically important outcome.
4. Insight-oriented therapists claim that there is a bias against them because most of the therapy outcome research has been done by cognitive and behavioral therapists (Lambert et al., 1986). This is troublesome because Smith et al. (1980) found larger effect sizes for those techniques to which the investigator had a prior allegiance.

A continuing challenge, in our view, is the seemingly inescapable role of the investigator's own paradigm in judging the merits of another's meta-analysis.

---

*As one might expect, charges of bias go back and forth between proponents of diverse approaches. Dispassionate, paradigm-free interpretations of data are no less difficult to come by in therapy research than in psychopathology.

Carl Rogers, a humanistic therapist, proposed that the key ingredient in therapy is the attitude and style of the therapist rather than specific techniques.

assumptions about human nature and the means by which we can try to understand it (Ford & Urban, 1963; Rogers, 1951, 1961).

1. People can be understood only from the vantage point of their own perceptions and feelings, that is, from their phenomenological world. To understand individuals, then, we must look at the way they experience events rather than at the events themselves, for each person's phenomenological world is the major determinant of behavior and makes that person unique.
2. Healthy people are aware of their behavior. In this sense Rogers's system is similar to psychoanalysis and ego analysis, for it emphasizes the desirability of being aware of motives.
3. Healthy people are innately good and effective: they become ineffective and disturbed only when faulty learning intervenes.
4. Healthy people are purposive and goal-directed: they do not respond passively to the influence of their environment or to their inner drives. They are self-directive. In this assumption Rogers is closer to ego analysts than to orthodox Freudian psychoanalysis.
5. Therapists should not attempt to manipulate events for the individual; rather they should create conditions that will facilitate independent decision making by the client. When people are not concerned with the evaluations, demands, and preferences of others, their lives are guided by an innate tendency for *self-actualization.*

Therapeutic Intervention

Assuming that a mature and well-adjusted person makes judgments based on what is intrinsically satisfying and actualizing, Rogers avoided imposing goals on the client during therapy. According to him, the client is to take the lead and direct the course of the conversation and of the session. The therapist's job is to create conditions so that during their hour together the client can return once again to his or her basic nature and judge which course of life is intrinsically gratifying. Because of his very positive view of people, Rogers assumed that their decisions would not only make them happy with themselves but also turn them into good, civilized people. Of course, the road to these good decisions is not an easy one.

According to Rogers and other humanistic and existential therapists, people must take responsibility for themselves, even when they are troubled. It is often difficult for a therapist to refrain from giving advice, from taking charge of a client's life, especially when the client appears incapable of making his or her own decisions. But these workers hold steadfastly to the rule that an individual's innate capacity for growth and self-direction will assert itself provided that the therapeutic atmosphere is warm, attentive, and receptive. Indeed, it is believed that if the therapist steps in, the process of growth and self-actualization will only be thwarted. Whatever short-term relief might come from the therapist's intervening will sacrifice long-term growth. The therapist must not become yet another person whose wishes the client strives to satisfy.

Rogers's thinking evolved from a clear specification of techniques (Rogers, 1942) to an emphasis on the attitude and emotional style of the therapist and a deemphasis of specific procedures (Rogers, 1951). The therapist should have three core qualities: genuineness, unconditional positive regard, and empathic understanding.

Genuineness, sometimes called congruence, encompasses spontaneity, openness, and authenticity. The therapist has no phoniness and no professional facade, disclosing his feelings and thoughts informally and candidly to the client. In a sense the therapist, through honest self-disclosure, provides a model for what the client can become by being in touch with feelings and able to express them and to accept responsibility for doing so. The therapist has the courage to present himself or herself to others as he or she really is.

The second attribute of the successful therapist, according to Rogers, is being able to extend **unconditional positive regard**. Other people set what Rogers called "conditions of worth"—I will love you if. . . . The client-centered therapist prizes clients as they are and conveys unpossessive warmth for them, even if he or she does not approve of their behavior. People have value merely for being people, and the therapist must care deeply for and respect a client, for the simple reason that he or she is another human being, engaged in the struggle of growing and being alive.

The third quality, **accurate empathic understanding,** is the ability to see the world through the eyes of clients from moment to moment, to understand the feelings of clients both from their own phenomenological vantage point, which is known to them, and from perspectives of which they may be only dimly aware.

Empathy

Let us examine empathy more closely. Empathy is the therapist's acceptance, recognition, and clarification of the client's feelings. It is one of the few techniques of Rogerian therapy. Within the context of a warm therapeutic relationship, the therapist encourages the client to talk about his or her most deeply felt concerns and attempts to restate the emotional aspects, not just the content of what the client says. This reflection of feelings to the client is meant to remove gradually the emotional conflicts that are blocking self-actualization. Because feelings are mirrored without judgment or disapproval, the client can look at them, clarify them, and acknowledge and accept them. Feared thoughts and emotions that were previously too threatening to enter awareness can become part of the self-concept. If therapeutic conditions allowing self-acceptance are established, clients begin to talk in a more honest and emotional way about themselves. Rogers assumed that such talk in itself is primarily responsible for changing behavior.

The therapist, it should be noted, is not being truly nondirective, a term often applied to Rogers, for he or she selectively attends to evaluative statements and feelings expressed by the client. The therapist believes that these are the matters the client should be helped to examine.

Rogers's application of empathy is sometimes mistakenly assumed to be an easy, straightforward matter, but it is not. In fact, it requires much subtlety and constitutes strong medicine indeed. The therapist does not always restrict himself or herself to merely finding words for the emotional aspects of what the client says but, in what one writer called **advanced accurate empathy** (Egan, 1975), he or she goes beyond to what he or she believes *lies behind* the client's observable behavior and most obvious thoughts and feelings (see Focus Box 18.4). The therapist makes an inference about what is troubling the client and interprets what the client has said in a way that seems different from the client's actual statements. In a sense, advanced empathy represents theory building on the part of the therapist: after considering over a number of sessions what the client has been saying and how he or she has been saying it, the therapist generates a hypothesis about what may be the true source of distress and yet remains hidden from the client.[1] The following is an example.

> **Client:** I don't know what's going on. I study hard, but I just don't get good marks. I think I study as hard as anyone else, but all of my efforts seem to go down the drain. I don't know what else I can do.
> **Counselor A:** You feel frustrated because even when you try hard you fail [primary empathy].
> **Counselor B:** It's depressing to put in as much effort as those who pass and still fail. It gets you down and maybe even makes you feel a little sorry for yourself [advanced emphathy]. (Egan, 1975, p. 135)

In **primary empathy** the therapist tries to restate to clients their thoughts, feelings, and experiences *from their own point of view.* The work here is at the phenomenological level: the therapist views the client's world from the client's perspective and then communicates to the client that this frame of reference is understood and appreciated. In advanced empathy the therapist generates a view that takes the client's world into account but conceptualizes things, it is hoped, in a more constructive way. The therapist presents to the client a way of considering himself or herself that may be quite different from the client's accustomed perspective.

To understand this important distinction, we must bear in mind that therapists operating within the client-centered framework assume that the client views things in an unproductive way, as evidenced by the psychological distress that has brought the client into therapy. At the primary empathic level the therapist accepts this view, understands it, and communicates to the client that it is appreciated. But at the advanced or interpretive level the therapist offers something new, a perspective that he or she hopes is better and more productive and implies new modes of action. Advanced empathizing builds on the information provided over a number of sessions in which the therapist concentrated on making primary-level empathic statements.

The client-centered therapist, operating within a phenomenological philosophy, *must* have as the goal the movement of a client from his or her present phenomenological world to another one; hence the importance of the advanced empathy stage. Since people's emotions and actions are determined

---

[1]Whether an advanced empathy statement by the therapist should even be regarded as *accurate* is another interesting question. These interpretations by client-centered therapists can never be known for sure to be true. Rather, like scientific theories and insights into the past, they may be more or less *useful.*

FOCUS

18.4 • Excerpt from a Client-Centered Therapy Session

Client: (an eighteen-year-old female college student): My parents really bug me. First it was Arthur they didn't like, now it's Peter. I'm just fed up with all their meddling.

Therapist: You really are angry at your folks.

Client: Well, how do you expect me to feel? Here I am with a 3.5 GPA, and providing all sorts of other goodies, and they claim the right to pass on how appropriate my boyfriend is. (Begins to sob.)

Therapist: It strikes me that you're not just angry with them. (Pause) Maybe you're worried about disappointing them.

Client: (Crying even more) I've tried all my life to please them. Sure their approval is important to me. They're really pleased when I get A's, but why do they have to pass judgment on my social life as well?

Comments

Although the emotion expressed initially was one of anger, the therapist believed that the client was really fearful of criticism from her parents. She therefore made an advanced empathic statement in an effort to explore with the client what was only implied but not expressed. Previous sessions had suggested that the client worked hard academically primarily to please her parents and to avoid their censure. She had always been able to win their approval by getting good grades, but more recently the critical eye of her mother and father were directed at the young men she was dating. The client was beginning to realize that she had to arrange her social life to please her parents. Her fear of disapproval from her parents became the focus in therapy after the therapist had helped her see beyond her anger.

by how they construe themselves and their surroundings, by their phenomenology, those who are dysfunctional or otherwise dissatisfied with their present mode of living are in need of a *new* phenomenology. From the very outset, then, client-centered therapy—and all other phenomenological therapies—concentrated on clients' adopting frameworks different from what they had upon beginning treatment. Merely to reflect back to clients their current phenomenology cannot in itself bring therapeutic change. A new phenomenology must be acquired.

Evaluation

Largely because of Rogers's own insistence that the outcome and process of therapy be carefully scrutinized and empirically validated, numerous studies have attempted to evaluate client-centered therapy. Indeed, Rogers can be credited with originating the whole field of psychotherapy research. He and his students deserve the distinction for removing the mystique and excessive privacy of the consulting room; for example, they pioneered the tape recording of therapy sessions for subsequent analysis by researchers.

Research on Rogerian therapy has focused principally on relating outcome to the personal qualities of therapists and has yielded inconsistent results, suggesting that the widely held assumption that positive outcome is strongly related to the therapist's empathy, genuineness, and warmth may not be the case (Beutler, Crago, & Arizmendi, 1986; Lambert et al., 1986). It is probably useful to continue emphasizing such qualities in the training of young clinicians, however, for they would seem to help create for the client an atmosphere of trust and safety within which to reveal the deep inner workings of the self. But it is not justifiable, from a research perspective, to assert that these qualities, by themselves, are sufficient to help clients change.

In keeping with Rogers's phenomenological approach, self-reports by clients have been the usual measures of the effectiveness of therapy. Research on Rogerian therapy has until recently paid little attention to how patients actually *behave* following therapy. Rogers's basic data were the individual's own phenomenological evaluation of and reaction to the self and events in his or her world; the overt behavior, believed to follow from these perceptions, has not generally been the focus of study by client-centered therapy researchers.

Rogers's emphasis on subjective experience raises epistemological problems, for the therapist must be able to make accurate and incisive inferences about what the client is feeling or thinking. Validity is a real issue here. Although the method seems to rely entirely on what the client says, Rogers asserted that clients can be unaware of their true feelings; indeed, this lack of awareness brings most of them into therapy in the first place. As with psychoanalysis, we must ask how a therapist is to make an inference about internal processes of which a client is seemingly unaware and then by what procedures the usefulness or validity of that inference is to be evaluated.

The early use of only self-descriptive measures of outcome from client-centered therapy has given way to more direct and theoretically neutral measures that tap into the patient's daily functioning in life, such as the adequate performance of social roles. An associated trend is the use of multiple methods of assessing therapeutic change (Beutler, 1983; Lambert et al., 1986) as investigators have come increasingly to appreciate the complex nature of behavior and the need to assess it along many dimensions. For example, physiological measures can be supplemented with self-reports from the patients as well as with reports from significant others (e.g., spouses). Valuable and differing kinds of information are available from looking at change in a multidimensional fashion. We saw examples of this in the Sloane et al. (1975) study and earlier in Gordon Paul's (1966) classic study of anxiety in public speaking (page 95).

Rogers may also be criticized for assuming that self-actualization is the principal human motivation. He inferred the self-actualization motive from his observation that people seek out situations offering fulfillment. But then the self-actualization tendency is proposed as an *explanation* of the search for these situations. Circular reasoning again!

Another point to consider is how faulty ideas are learned from the evaluation of others. Why does the master motive not always dominate the individual's learning? If the person is indeed always self-actualizing, under what circumstances does faulty learning take place, and what motives and needs are satisfied by such faulty learning?

Finally, Rogers assumed both that the psychologically healthy person makes choices to satisfy self-actualizing tendencies and that people are by their very natures good. But some social philosophers have taken a less optimistic view of human nature. Thomas Hobbes, for example, stated that life is "nasty, brutish, and short." How do we explain a person who behaves in a brutish fashion and yet asserts that this behavior is intrinsically gratifying and, indeed, self-actualizing?

It may be that the problem of extreme unreasonableness was not adequately addressed by Rogers because he and his colleagues concentrated on people who were only mildly disturbed. As a way to help unhappy but not severely disturbed people understand themselves better (and *perhaps* even to help them behave differently), client-centered therapy may very well be appropriate and effective. This humanistic approach remains popular in the encounter group movement (see page 596). Rogerian therapy may not, however, be appropriate for a severe psychological disorder, as Rogers himself warned.

Existential Therapy

Together with the humanistic perspective, the existential approach constituted in the 1950s what Abraham Maslow (1968) termed a "third force" in psychology (psychoanalysis and behaviorism being the other two forces). Humanism and existentialism have much in common, but the humanistic work of Americans like Rogers can be contrasted with the more European existential approach that derives from the writings of such philosophers as Sartre, Kierkegaard, and Heidegger, and such psychiatrists as Binswanger and Boss of Switzerland and Viktor Frankl of Austria, whose logotherapy and views on depression were discussed earlier (page 246). In an influential book on existential psychotherapy, Stanford University psychiatrist Irvin Yalom portrayed the differences between these approaches.

> The existential tradition in Europe has always emphasized human limitations and the tragic dimensions of existence. Perhaps it has done so because Europeans have had a greater familiarity with geographic and ethnic confinement, with war, death, and uncertain existence. The United States (and the humanistic psychology it spawned) bathed in a Zeitgeist of expansiveness, optimism, limitless horizons, and pragmatism. Accordingly, the imported form of existential thought has been systematically altered [as American humanistic psychology has absorbed some of European existentialism]. . . . The European focus is on limits, on facing and taking into oneself the anxiety of uncertainty and non-being. The humanistic psychologists, on the other hand, speak less of limits and contingency than of development of potential, less of acceptance than of awareness, less of anxiety than of peak experiences and oceanic oneness, less of life meaning than of self-realization [and self-actualization], less of apartness and basic aloneness than of I-thou and encounter. (Yalom, 1980, p. 19)

The existential point of view, like humanism, emphasizes personal growth. There are, though, some important distinctions. Humanism, exemplified by Rogers's views, stresses the goodness of human nature. If unfettered by groundless fears and societal restrictions, human beings will develop normally, even exceptionally, much as a flower will sprout from a seed if only given enough light, air, and wa-

Humanistic therapist Abraham Maslow made Carl Jung's self-actualization a central factor in his psychology.

ter. Existentialism is gloomier, having a strain of darkness within it. Although it embraces free will and responsibility, existentialism stresses the anxiety that is inevitable in making important choices, the existential choices on which existence depends, such as staying or not staying with a spouse, with a job, or even with this world. Hamlet's famous soliloquy beginning "To be, or not to be—that is the question" (act III, scene 1) is a classic existential statement. To be truly alive is to confront the anxiety that comes with existential choices. Existential anxiety comes from several sources (Tillich, 1952).

1. We are all aware that one day we shall die; when we honestly confront this inescapable reality, we face up to existential anxiety.
2. We are also aware of our helplessness against chance circumstances that can forever change our lives, such as a crippling automobile accident.
3. We are aware that we must ultimately make decisions, act, and live with the consequences.
4. We must ourselves create the meaning of our lives; the ultimate responsibility for endowing our world and our lives with substance and purpose rests with each of us.
5. We know that we are ultimately alone.

To avoid choices, to pretend that they do not have to be made, may protect people from anxiety, but it also deprives them of living a life with meaning and is at the core of psychopathology. Thus, whereas the humanistic message is upbeat, almost ecstatic, the existential is tinged with sadness and anxiety, but not despair, unless the exercise of free will and assumption of responsibility that accompanies it are avoided.

The Goals of Therapy

"So oftentimes it happens that we live our lives in chains, and we never even know we have the key."
(Jack Tempchin and Robb Strandlund, "Already Gone" 1973, 1975)

According to existentialism, a person is the sum of the choices he or she makes. Difficulties in making choices can be understood only by exploring experience. A goal of the existential therapist is to offer support and empathy through the adoption of the individual's phenomenological frame of reference; the therapist then helps the individual explore his or her behavior, feelings, relationships, and what life means. The therapist encourages the client to confront and clarify past and present choices. Present choices, however, are considered the most important.

Another goal of the existential therapist is to help the individual relate *authentically* to others, a tenet borrowed and greatly elaborated by the encounter group movement. People are assumed to define their identity and existence in terms of their personal relationships; a person is threatened with nonbeing—or alienation—if isolated from others. Even though the person may be effective in dealing with people and the world, he or she can become anxious if deprived of open and frank relationships. Hence, although the existential view is a highly subjective one, it strongly emphasizes *relating to others* in an open, honest, spontaneous, and loving manner. At the same time each of us is ultimately and basically *alone*. Although existentialism asserts that we must relate authentically to others, the paradox of life is that we are inherently separate from others, that we came into the world alone and must create our own existence in the world alone.

The existential therapist strives to make the therapeutic relationship an authentic encounter between two human beings so that the patient has some practice in relating to another individual in a straightforward fashion.[2] The therapist, through honesty and self-disclosure, helps the client learn authenticity. This can take the form of the therapist's openly expressing strong disapproval of what the client is doing—but without rejecting the client as a worthwhile human being.

The ultimate goal of existential therapy is to make the patient more aware of his or her own potential for choice and growth. In the existential view people create their existence anew at each moment. The potential for disorder as well as for growth is ever present. Individuals must be encouraged to accept

[2]It is interesting to note that this approach, which places so much emphasis on a person's perceptions, understanding, feelings, and other internal processes, is in a way very behavioristic. The person must at some point during therapy begin to behave differently, both toward the therapist and toward the outside world, in order to change his or her own existential condition.

Rollo May, an American psychotherapist, one of the central figures in existential therapy.

the responsibility for their own existence and to realize that, within certain limits, they can redefine themselves at any moment and behave and feel differently within their own social environment. But this freedom to choose and the responsibility that comes with it are not easy for humankind to accept and work with. Many people are afraid of this freedom, and as they begin to make choices, they realize that fulfillment is a *process*, that they must constantly choose and accept responsibility if they are to be truly human and fulfill their potential. Their prospects then are not cheery; with greater awareness of their freedom to choose comes more existential anxiety. One of the goals of therapy is to bolster their resolve and ability to cope with this inescapable anxiety and to continue growing.

The existential writers, however, are very vague about what therapeutic techniques will help the client grow. Indeed, a reliance on technique may be seen as an objectifying process, that is, a process in which the therapist acts upon the client as though he or she were a thing to be manipulated (Prochaska, 1984). As such, the existential approach is best understood as a general *attitude* taken by certain therapists toward human nature rather than a set of therapeutic techniques.

Evaluation

Existential therapy lacks the definable, concrete operations on which scientific research can be conducted. Indeed, no research has been done, although existential therapists have published numerous case reports relating successes with a variety of clinical problems.

Moreover, existential therapists tend to see contemporary science as dehumanizing and hence to be avoided. They believe that applying science to individuals denies their unique humanness.

Clearly, many of the criticisms of client-centered therapy apply as well to existential treatment. Since by definition a person's subjective experience is unique, how can the therapist know that he or she is truly understanding a patient's world as it appears to the patient? Yet attention to subjective impressions is not necessarily unproductive. Paying heed to our freedom to choose and ability to change at any time may be an important means of improving behavior. Indeed, the message implicit in existentialism, that our existence is constantly being reaffirmed and that we are not prisoners of our past mistakes and misfortunes, might well be incorporated into *any* therapy.

Gestalt Therapy

A therapy that has both humanistic and existential elements, **Gestalt therapy** derives from the work of Frederich S. (Fritz) Perls. After receiving a medical degree in Germany in 1921, Perls became a psychoanalyst. But he was rejected by European analysts because he challenged some of the basic precepts of psychoanalytaic theory, particularly the important place accorded to the libido and its various transformations in the development of neurosis (Perls, 1947). He emigrated to the Netherlands in 1933, shortly after Hitler came to power, because he was opposed to totalitarianism, and to South Africa in 1934, as the country's first teaching analyst. There he developed the basis of Gestalt therapy. He took up residence in the United States in 1946 and eventually settled at Esalen, a center for humanistic-existential therapy in Big Sur, California. Here his ideas and techniques of therapy underwent impressive growth, especially as applied in groups (Perls, Hefferline, & Goodman, 1951; Perls, 1970). In fact, during his lifetime, Perls had a near cultlike following (see Focus Box 18.5).

Basic Concepts of Gestalt Therapy

Like Rogers, Perls held that people have an innate goodness and that this basic nature should be allowed to express itself. Psychological problems originate in frustrations and denials of this inborn

FOCUS

18.5 • A Glimpse of Fritz Perls

As Joe got on the elevator, he hardly noticed the short, gray-bearded man standing against the wall. Then recognition hit him. "Uh, Dr. Perls, I'm, uh, honored to meet you. I've read your work, and it's such—such an honor to meet—to be in your presence. . . ." Joe's stammering speech trailed away with no effect. The old man did not move.

The elevator slowed and Joe, realizing that an opportunity was slipping away, heard himself say, hopelessly, "I'm really nervous." Perls turned and smiled at him. As the doors opened, he took Joe's arm and said. "Now let us talk." (Gaines, 1974)

Frederich (Fritz) Perls (1893–1970) was the colorful founder of Gestalt therapy.

virtue. Gestalt therapists, along with other humanistic therapists, emphasize the creative and expressive aspects of people, rather than the negative and distorted features on which psychoanalysts often seem to concentrate.

A central goal of Gestalt therapy is to help patients understand and accept their needs, desires, and fears, to enhance their awareness of how they block themselves from reaching their goals and satisfying their needs. A basic assumption is that all of us bring our needs and wants to any situation. We do not merely perceive situations "as they are"; instead we engage our social environment by projecting our needs, or fears, or desires onto what is "out there." Thus if I am talking to a stranger, I do not merely react to the person as that person exists: I react to the stranger in the context of my needs. Sometimes there is unfinished business with a significant person from one's past, which can affect how we deal with someone in the present.

Perls and his followers have concentrated on the here and now and on the individual as an actor, as a being who is responsible for his or her own behavior and who is capable of playing a central role in bringing about beneficial changes.

Gestalt therapy draws from Gestalt psychology, a branch of psychology concerned primarily with perception. Their closest similarity may be in their attention to *wholes*. Perls wanted to make individuals *whole* by increasing their awareness of unacknowledged feelings and having them reclaim the parts of the personality that had been denied or disowned.

Gestalt Therapy Techniques

Gestalt therapists focus on what a client is doing in the consulting room here and now, without delving into the past, for the most important event in the client's life is what is happening at this moment. In Gestalt therapy all that exists is the now. If the past is bothersome, it is brought into the present. Questions of why are discouraged, because searching after causes in the past is considered an attempt to escape responsibility for making choices in the present, a familiar existential theme. Clients are exhorted, cajoled, sometimes even coerced into awareness of what is happening now. Awareness is an immediate and direct thinking and sensing. Individuals must know what is going on about them, what they think and fantasize, want and feel, what they are doing at the moment, and they must also sense posture, facial expressions, muscular tensions, and gestures, the words they use, the sound of their voice. Perls believed that awareness is curative. People have only to be moved away from their ideas about themselves to an awareness of what they are feeling and doing at this exact moment.

Gestalt therapy is noted for its emphasis on techniques, in contrast to their paucity in the humanistic and existential therapies discussed so far. We should caution, however, that at its core, Gestalt therapy is not merely a collection of techniques, rather it is a set of *attitudes* about the nature of humankind, a philosophy that values creativity and openness to experience. The Gestalt therapist aims to help the patient be as creative and open as the therapist is, to encounter the world on an immediate, nonjudgmental, nonreflective basis. The means to this end are the many techniques for which this approach is well-known, and some of them have even been taken over and adapted by therapists of other theoretical persuasions. We describe here a small sample of current Gestalt practices.

Gestalt therapists use the empty-chair technique to help clients confront their feelings more directly.

1. **"I-Language."** To help patients bear responsibility for their present and future lives, the therapist instructs them to change "it" language into "I language."

   Therapist: What do you hear in your voice?
   Patient: My voice sounds like it is crying.
   Therapist: Can you take responsibility for that by saying, I am crying? (Levitsky & Perls, 1970, p. 142)

   This simple change in language, besides encouraging the patient to assume responsibility for feelings and behavior, reduces the sense of being alienated from aspects of his or her very being. It helps the patient see the self as active rather than passive, as an open and searching person rather than as someone whose behavior is determined entirely by external events.
2. **The Empty Chair.** In the empty-chair technique, a client projects and then talks to the projection of a feeling, or of a person, object, or situation. For example, if a patient is crying, the Gestalt therapist might ask the patient to regard the tears as being in an empty chair opposite him or her and to speak *to* the tears. This tactic often seems to help people confront their feelings. Indeed, to ask a person to talk *about* his or her tears is assumed to encourage the person to establish an even greater distance from his or her feelings—something Gestalt therapists assert interferes with psychological well-being.
3. **Projection of Feelings.** Gestalt therapists working with groups sometimes have people pair off, close their eyes, and imagine the face of an individual to whom they have a strong emotional attachment. They are encouraged to concentrate on the feelings they have about that person. Then all open their eyes and look at their partner. After a few moments they are instructed to close their eyes again and think now of something neutral, such as an arithmetic problem. They then open their eyes again and look a second time at their partner. Finally, they are asked whether there was an important difference in the way they felt about their partner in the two situations. This exercise is designed to exaggerate what is assumed to be inevitable in all our social interactions, namely, the intrusion of our feelings into whatever is happening at any particular moment.
4. **Reversal.** Another technique is to have the person behave opposite to the way he or she feels. Someone who is excessively timid might be asked during the therapy session to behave like an outgoing person. Perls assumed that the opposite side of the coin actually lies within the being of the person and that acting out feelings not usually expressed allows the person to become aware of a part of the self that had been submerged.
5. **Attending to Nonverbal Cues.** All therapists pay attention to nonverbal and paralinguistic cues given by the client. Nonverbal cues are body movements, facial expressions, gestures, and the like; paralinguistic cues are the tone of voice, the rapidity with which words are spoken, and other audible components of speech beyond its content. People can negate with their hands or their eyes what they are saying with the larynx. Perls placed special emphasis on these nonlinguistic signals, closely observing them to determine what clients might really be

feeling. "What we say is mostly lies or bullshit. But the voice is there, the gesture, the posture, the facial expression, the psychosomatic language" (Perls, 1969, p. 54).

6. **The Use of Metaphor.** During the therapy session Gestalt therapists often create unusual scenarios to externalize, to make more vivid and understandable, a problem they believe a client is having. In one session that we observed, a husband and wife sat together on a sofa, bickering about the woman's mother. The husband seemed very angry with his mother-in-law, and the therapist surmised that she was getting in the way of his relationship with his wife. The therapist wanted to demonstrate to the couple how frustrating this must be for both of them, and he also wished to goad both of them to do something about it. Without warning, he rose from his chair and wedged himself between the couple. Not a word was said. The husband looked puzzled, then hurt, and gradually became angry at the therapist. He asked him to move so that he could sit next to his wife again. The therapist shook his head. When the husband repeated his request, the therapist removed his jacket and placed it over the wife's head so that the husband could not even see her. A long silence followed, during which the husband grew more and more agitated. The wife meanwhile was sitting quietly, covered by the therapist's coat. Suddenly the husband stood up, walked past the therapist, and angrily removed the coat; then he pushed the therapist off the sofa. The therapist exploded in good-natured laughter. "I wondered how long it would take you to do something!" he roared.

   This staged scene drove several points home in a way that mere words might not have. The husband—having been trained already by the therapist to get in better touch with his feelings and to express them without fear or embarrassment—reported tearfully that he had felt cut off from his wife by the therapist, in much the same way that he felt alienated from her by her mother. The mother was intruding, and he was not doing anything about it. He did not trust himself to assert his needs and to take action to satisfy them. The fact that he was able to remove the coat and the therapist as well made him wonder whether he might not behave similarly toward his mother-in-law. As he spoke, his wife began to sob; she confided to her husband that all along she had been wanting him to take charge of the problem with her mother. So far so good. But then the therapist turned to the woman and asked her why she had not removed the coat herself! The husband grinned as the therapist gently chided the wife for being unduly passive about her marital problems. By the end of the session, the clients, although emotionally drained, felt in better contact with each other and expressed resolve to work together actively to alter their relationship with her mother.

7. **Dream Work.** The interpretation of dreams is another important part of Gestalt therapy. In contrast to psychoanalytic approaches, the Gestalt therapist does not consider the dream a rich source of symbolism relating to unconscious processes; rather,

> Every image in the dream, whether human, animal, vegetable, or mineral, is taken to represent an alienated portion of the self. By reexperiencing and retelling the dream over and over again in the present tense, from the standpoint of each image, the patient can begin to reclaim these alienated fragments, and accept them, live with them and express them more appropriately. (Enright, 1970, p. 121)

   For example, a woman in Gestalt therapy dreamed of walking down a crooked path among tall, straight trees. The therapist asked her to *become* one of the trees, and this made her feel serene and more deeply rooted. She then expressed her desire for such security. When she was asked to become the crooked path, tears welled as she confronted the deviousness of the way in which she lived. Once again the Gestalt therapist helped the client externalize feelings customarily avoided, so that she could become aware of them, acknowledge them as her own, and then perhaps decide to change them.

   Consistent with their phenomenological approach, Gestalt therapists encourage clients to recount, with emotion, the meaning that the dream has for them at that very moment. Even though the therapist may have a hypothesis about what a particular dream means to the client, the therapist takes care not to impose that meaning on the dreamer, for it is the dreamer's dream. The only significance it has for the dreamer is the meaning it holds as it is discussed in the session. In this sense Gestalt therapy does not have a theory of dreams; rather it is concerned with dream *work*, the analysis of dreams by the client with support from the therapist. Since only the phenomenal world has importance for each client, his or her immediate experience is the one thing worth focusing on.

Evaluation

The clinical literature suggests that Gestalt therapists spend much or most of their time urging clients to be more expressive, spontaneous, and responsive to their own needs. Perls described this activity as making the person more attentive to emerging gestalts. Therapy also attempts to make the person whole by encouraging a reclamation of parts of the personality until now denied. The psychotherapy is therefore aligned with the experimental findings of Gestalt psychology. It is open to question, however, whether Perls's description is the most accurate or parsimonious way of talking about the techniques, and, more importantly, whether such concepts assist in the effective training of good therapists.

Gestalt therapy does forcefully convey the existential message that a person is not a prisoner of the past, that he or she can at any time make the existential choice to be different, and that the therapist will not tolerate stagnation. No doubt this optimistic view helps many people change. If the person does not know how to behave differently, however, considerable damage can be done to an already miserable individual. For example, if a socially inhibited patient never learned *how* to talk assertively to others, it would do little good only to have the person become more aware of this nonassertiveness and to encourage him or her to become more expressive. Lacking social skills, the person would probably behave awkwardly and ineffectually with others and could end up feeling even worse about himself or herself than before.

Perls's emphasis on responsibility is not to be confused with commitment or obligation to others. Even as a therapist Perls did not present himself as a person who assumed responsibility for others, and he did not urge this on his patients either. The individual has the responsibility to take care of himself or herself, to meet his or her *own* needs as they arise. This apparent egocentrism may be troubling for people with a social conscience and for those who have in the past made commitments to others. Indeed, Perls believed that such commitments should never be made (Prochaska, 1984).

According to humanists like Perls and Rogers, people are, by their very nature, good, purposive, and resourceful. If they are, it would be reasonable to trust this intrinsic good nature and to encourage direct expression of needs. But are people always good? Sometimes clients—especially those who are psychologically troubled—feel they must do something that, in the judgment of the professional, is not in their own best interest. Suppose that a client feels the need to murder someone or to engage in other behavior that, to outside observers, is surely undesirable. What is the therapist's responsibility? At what point does the therapist intervene and impose his or her judgment? When patients threaten to act in destructive ways, few therapists stand by and do nothing. In fact, as seen in the discussion of the Tarasoff ruling in Chapter 21, therapists now have no choice *but* to take action in such circumstances, even against the wishes of the patient. But beyond this legal constraint, we believe that Gestalt therapists do *not* abdicate all decisions to their clients and that they *do* exert considerable influence on them, if only by virtue of the models they themselves provide. We have already indicated that Perls was a very charismatic figure. It is likely that most people adopt the values of their therapist, regardless of theoretical orientation (Pentony, 1966; Rosenthal, 1955), and it seems preferable to us to admit this social influence so that it can be dealt with, rather than to deny that such influence exists and perhaps allow for even greater tyranny of therapists over patients. This issue is also discussed at length in Chapter 21.

A few studies have attempted to examine aspects of Gestalt therapy, in particular the empty-chair technique. Conoley and his colleagues (1983) found, in an analogue study with college undergraduates, that self-rated anger was reduced after a twenty-minute empty-chair exercise. Greenberg and Rice (1981) reported that the technique increases awareness and emotional expression, and Clarke and Greenberg (1986) found it superior to problem-solving in helping people make decisions. Data from our own lab lend support to the empty-chair technique as a more powerful method than a conventional interview for uncovering affect (Davison & Binkoff, unpublished).

All therapies are subject to abuse; Gestalt is no exception. Indeed, it may present special problems. It is not difficult, even for trainees with a minimum of experience, to induce clients to express their feelings. Some Gestalt techniques may in themselves be so powerful in opening people up that clients can be harmed unintentionally. The forcefulness of Perls's personality and his confrontational style have led some therapists to mimic him without the thoughtfulness, skill, and caring he appeared to possess in unusual abundance. The responsible Gestalt therapist is a professional who keeps the client's interests at the forefront, and who understands that the expression of strong emotion for its own sake is seldom enough to ease an individual's suffering. The nature of Gestalt therapy and the fact that a cult has grown up around the memory of Fritz Perls are reasons that practicing Gestalt therapists should strive for an extra measure of caution and humility.

SUMMARY

Insight therapies share the basic assumption that behavior is disordered because the person is not aware of what motivates his or her actions. Psychoanalysis emphasizes factors from the past, whereas most humanistic and existential approaches, such as those of Rogers and Perls, emphasize the current determinants of behavior. A concern with present-day factors in the patient's life is also found in many contemporary variants of classical psychoanalysis, like ego analysis and psychodynamic interpersonal therapy.

Consistent with Freud's second theory of neurosis, classical psychoanalysis tries to uncover childhood repressions so that infantile fears of libidinal expression can be examined by the adult ego in the light of present-day realities. Ego analysis puts more emphasis on the need and ability of the patient to achieve greater control over the environment and over instinctual gratification. Much ego analysis now takes the form of brief, time-limited therapy, in which expectations are set for fewer than two dozen sessions. There is a focus on concrete goals and learning ways to cope with life's inevitable stressors, forsaking the goal of psychoanalysis for a personality overhaul through analysis of the transference neurosis.

Rogers trusted the basic goodness of the drive to self-actualize, and he proposed the creation of nonjudgmental conditions in therapy. Through empathy and unconditional positive regard for their clients, Rogerian therapists help them view themselves more accurately and trust their own instincts for self-actualization. Existential therapists, influenced primarily by European existential philosophy, similarly regard people as having the innate ability to realize their potential; they also have the freedom to decide at any given moment to become different. Both Rogerians and existentialists assume that the only reality is the one experienced by the individual; thus the therapist must try to view the world from the client's phenomenological frame of reference, rather than from his or her own.

The Gestalt therapy of Perls is usually regarded as humanistic, yet it is different in important ways from the therapies of Rogers and the existentialists. Perls stressed living in the now, and the many techniques he and his followers have introduced are designed to help clients experience their current needs and feel comfortable about satisfying them as they emerge.

A growing body of research supports the efficacy of some of the insight therapies, and some of it is process oriented, that is, examining the factors responsible for improvement. The working alliance between therapist and patient, for example, is emerging as an important variable. Psychotherapy research, though, is exceedingly complex and difficult, and scientifically based conclusions are not as available as strongly held unsubstantiated beliefs about how to help people change. The next two chapters continue our study of therapeutic intervention, and some of the same problems in evaluating outcome and process will be encountered again.

KEY TERMS

psychotherapy
placebo effect
insight therapy
psychoanalysis
free association
resistance
dream analysis
latent content
manifest content
interpretation
denial
transference neurosis
countertransference
ego analysis
brief therapy
interpersonal therapy
outcome studies
process studies
humanistic and existential therapies
client-centered therapy
genuineness
unconditional positive regard
accurate empathic understanding
advanced accurate empathy
primary empathy
Gestalt therapy

c h a p t e r   n i n e t e e n

Cognitive and Behavior Therapies

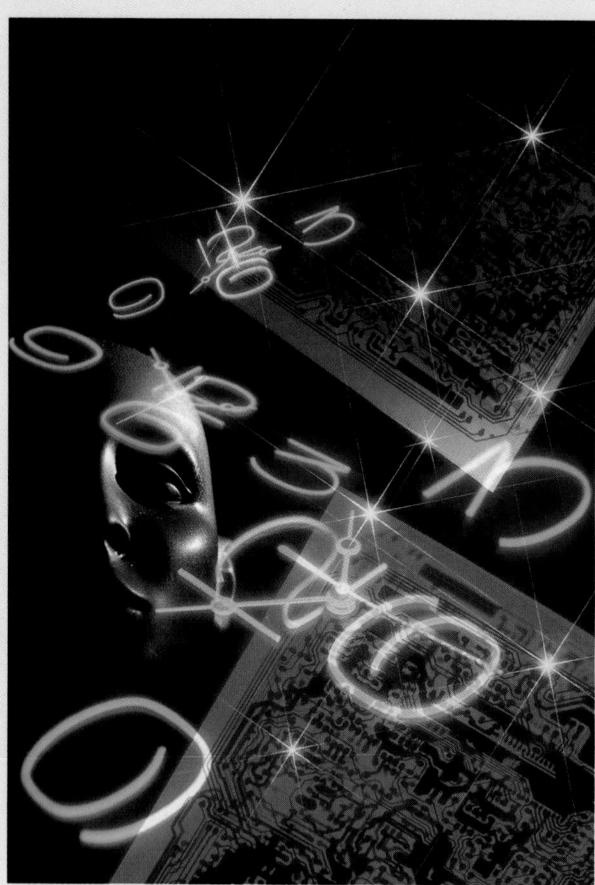

A middle-aged construction worker sought help for his depression. He was having trouble getting out of bed in the morning and viewed his job and life in general with dread and foreboding. Careful assessment by the clinician revealed that the man was inordinately concerned whether the men working under him liked and approved of him. His depression had set in after he had been promoted to foreman, a position that required him to issue orders and monitor and criticize the activities of other workers. His men would occasionally object to his instructions and comments, and the client found their resentful stares and sullen silences very upsetting. He agreed with the therapist that he was unduly anxious when criticized or rejected. The reduction in job-related anxiety that followed treatment by systematic desensitization succeeded in lifting his depression (Goldfried & Davison, 1976).

Over the past four decades a new way of treating psychopathology has been developed. Called **behavior therapy**, it was initially restricted to the application of procedures based on classical and operant conditioning to alter clinical problems. Although there is considerable ferment over how to define the field itself (e.g., Fishman, Rotgers, & Franks, 1988; Mahoney, 1993), today behavior therapy is characterized more by its epistemological stance—its search for rigorous standards of proof—than by allegiance to any particular set of concepts (Davison & Goldfried, 1973). In brief, behavior therapy is an attempt to change abnormal behavior, thoughts, and feelings by applying in a clinical context the methods used and the discoveries made by experimental psychologists in their study of both normal and abnormal behavior. Sometimes the term *behavior modification* is used interchangeably with behavior therapy; therapists who use operant conditioning as a means of treatment often prefer this term.

That the most effective clinical procedures will be developed through science is an *assumption*. There is nothing inherent in the scientific method that guarantees victories for those studying human behavior by its principles. Because we have reached the moon and beyond by playing the science game does not mean that the same set of rules should be applied to human behavior. The existentialists, who emphasize free will, assume that the nature of humankind cannot be meaningfully probed by following the rules favored by the authors of this textbook. Although we are placing our bets on the scientific work described in this chapter, it nonetheless remains an article of faith that behavior therapy will prove the best means of treating disordered behavior, cognition, and affect.

Just when behavior therapy first began to be developed is difficult to date. Some social scientist did not wake up one morning and proclaim that from this day forward people with psychological problems should be treated with techniques suggested by experimental findings. Rather, over a number of years, people in the clinical field began to formulate a new set of assumptions about dealing with the problems that they encountered. Although there are areas of overlap, we have found it helpful to distinguish four theoretical approaches applied in behavior therapy—counterconditioning, operant conditioning, modeling, and cognitive therapy. After reviewing these, we discuss behavioral medicine, a new specialization that blends behavioral and biomedical knowledge to enhance physical health and lessen physical illness. Then we consider how gains made in therapy can be generalized to real life and effectively maintained. We go on to examine some important problems and issues as they pertain to cognitive and behavior therapies. Finally, we consider the growing interest in eclecticism and theoretical integration in psychotherapy, examining both the advantages and some of the pitfalls in any such effort.

Counterconditioning

In counterconditioning, illustrated in Figure 2.5 (page 48), a response (R_1) to given stimulus (S) is eliminated by eliciting different behavior (R_2) in the presence of that stimulus. For example, if an individual is afraid (R_1) of enclosed spaces (S), the therapist attempts to help the person have a calm reaction (R_2) when he or she is in such situations. Experimental evidence suggests that unrealistic fears can be eliminated in this way. An early and now famous clinical demonstration of counterconditioning was reported by Mary Cover Jones (1924). She successfully eliminated a little boy's fear of rabbits by feeding him in the presence of a rabbit. The animal was at first kept several feet away and then gradually moved closed on successive occasions. In this fashion the fear (R_1) produced by the rabbit (S) was crowded out by the stronger positive feelings associated with eating (R_2).

We will examine here systematic desensitization and aversion therapy, two behavioral techniques assumed to be effective because of counterconditioning.

Systematic Desensitization

Joseph Wolpe (1958) employed with fearful adults techniques similar to those used by Jones three decades earlier. He found that many of his clients could be encouraged to expose themselves gradually to the situation or object they feared if they were at the same time engaging in behavior that inhibited anxiety. Rather than have his patients eat, however, Wolpe taught these adults deep muscle relaxation. His training procedures were adapted from earlier work by Edmond Jacobson (1929), who had shown that strong emotional states, such as anxiety, could be markedly inhibited if a person were in a state of deep relaxation.

Many of the fears felt by Wolpe's patients were so abstract—for example, fear of criticism and fear of failure—that it was impractical to confront them with real-life situations that would evoke these fears. Wolpe reasoned that he might have fearful patients *imagine* what they feared. Thus he formulated a new technique that he called **systematic desensitization**, in which a deeply relaxed person is asked to imagine a graded series of anxiety-provoking situations; the relaxation tends to inhibit any anxiety that might otherwise be elicited by the imagined scenes. If relaxation does give way to anxiety, the client signals to the therapist by raising an index finger, stops imagining the situation, rests, reestablishes relaxation, and then reimagines the situation. If anxiety drives out relaxation again, the client goes back to an earlier situation and later tries to handle the more difficult one. Over successive sessions a client is usually able to tolerate increasingly more difficult scenes as he or she climbs the hierarchy in imagination. As documented by Wolpe as well as by many other clinicians, the ability to tolerate stressful imagery is generally followed by a reduction of anxiety in related real-life situations. The case study on page 48 illustrates the application of this technique.

Joseph Wolpe, one of the pioneers in behavior therapy, is known particularly for systematic desensitization, a widely applied behavioral technique.

Between therapy sessions clients are usually instructed to place themselves in progressively more frightening real-life situations. These homework assignments help move their adjustment from imagination to reality. As noted in Chapter 6 (page 142), exposure to feared real-life situations has long been known to be an important means of reducing unwarranted anxieties.

Clinicians have treated a great variety of anxiety-related problems by systematic desensitization. The technique appears deceptively simple. However, as with any therapy for people in emotional distress, its proper application is a complicated affair. First, the clinician must determine, by means of a comprehensive behavioral assessment, that the situations the client is reacting anxiously to do not warrant such fearful reactions. If a person is anxious because he or she lacks the skills to deal with a given set of circumstances, desensitization would not be appropriate; for example, to be anxious about piloting an airplane is logical when you don't know how to operate the aircraft! Desensitization, then, is an appropriate treatment if a client seems to be inhibited by anxiety from behaving in customary and known ways. Sometimes the technique can be used when the client does not appear openly anxious, as in the case that opened this chapter.

As with all the techniques described here, very rarely is only one procedure used exclusively. A person fearful of social interactions might well be given training in conversational and other social skills in addition to desensitization. In the most general sense, the treatments chosen and their applicability depend largely on the therapist's ingenuity in discovering the source of the anxiety underlying a client's problems.

Researchers became interested in studying desensitization because clinical reports indicated that the technique is effective. Scores of controlled studies have lent credence to the prior clinical claims beginning with the earliest experiments in the 1960s (e.g., Davison, 1968b; Lang & Lazovik, 1963; Paul, 1966).

Like researchers in the insight therapies, behavioral researchers are interested not only in whether a given technique works—the outcome question—but also in why—the process question. Wolpe suggests that counterconditioning underlies the efficacy of desensitization; a state or response antagonistic to anxiety is substituted for anxiety as the person is exposed gradually to stronger and stronger doses of what he or she is afraid of. Many experiments (e.g., Davison, 1968b) confirm that there may be a specific learning process underlying the technique and that, indeed, it may be counterconditioning. But a number of other explanations are possible. Some workers attach importance to exposure to what the person fears per se; relaxation is then considered merely a useful way to encourage a frightened individual to confront what he or she fears (Wilson & Davison, 1971).

Aversion Therapy

Aversion therapy is a procedure that pairs negative stimuli with stimuli that are considered inappropriately attractive, with the intent of making the latter less appealing.[1] The literature on classical aversive conditioning of animals (i.e., pairing a neutral or positive stimulus with an unpleasant unconditioned stimulus, such as shock; see Focus Box 6.3, page 138) led therapists to believe that negative reactions could be conditioned in human beings, and they formulated treatment programs along these lines. The method is similar to desensitization but has the opposite goal, since the new response of anxiety, or an aversion reaction, is to be substituted for a positive response. Among the problems treated with aversion therapy are excessive drinking, smoking, transvestism, exhibitionism, and overeating. For example, an excessive drinker who wishes to be discouraged from drinking is asked to taste, see, or smell alcohol and is then made uncomfortable while doing so. In addition to employing painful but not harmful shock to the hands as the unconditioned stimulus, some therapists have adopted use of emetics, drugs that make the client nauseous when presented with the undesirable stimulus.

Recent research in chemical aversion with alcoholism and nicotine dependence lends some support to the proposition that nausea paired with the taste of alcohol or with inhaling a cigarette can produce stable conditioned aversions and subsequent abstinence from alcohol or tobacco (e.g., Baker & Brandon, 1988; Cannon et al., 1986). These and similar findings, however, have been criticized by Wilson (1987), among others. Debate continues to be lively.

Aversion therapy has been controversial also for ethical reasons. A great outcry was raised about inflicting pain and discomfort on people, even when they asked for it. Perhaps the greatest ethical concern was voiced by gay liberation organizations. They believed that homosexuals who requested painful treatment to help them shift sexual preference were actually seeking to punish themselves for behavior that a prejudiced society had convinced them was dirty. These groups accused behavior therapists of impeding the acceptance of homosexuality as a legitimate life-style when they acceded to such requests (Silverstein, 1972). We explore this issue later (Focus Box 21.5).

Behavior therapists who choose aversive procedures seldom use them alone. In addition, more positive techniques are instituted to teach new behavior to replace responses that have been eliminated. Even if the effects of aversion therapy are ephemeral, or short-lived, the temporary reduction in undesirable behavior can create some space, which can be taken up by responses judged by the person or the culture to be more appropriate. When aversion therapy is employed, it is generally chosen as a last resort.

[1]Some commentators (e.g., Sandler, 1986) consider aversion therapy a form of punishment and place it under the general rubric of operant conditioning. Our preference is otherwise, though we accept the widely held assumption in learning theory that all classical conditioning procedures have operant elements and that all operant conditioning procedures have Pavlovian features. The issue appears to be whether, as in classical conditioning, the therapist or experimenter attempts to pair a *stimulus* with an aversive event, regardless of what the person is doing; or whether, as in operant conditioning, the effort is made to pair a *response* with an aversive event. In practice there is more overlap than the conceptual scheme implies.

Operant Conditioning

In the 1950s a number of investigators suggested that therapists should try to shape overt behavior in humans through rewards and punishments (Skinner, 1953). In the belief that they could through operant conditioning exercise some control over the complex, puzzling, often frenetic behavior of hos-

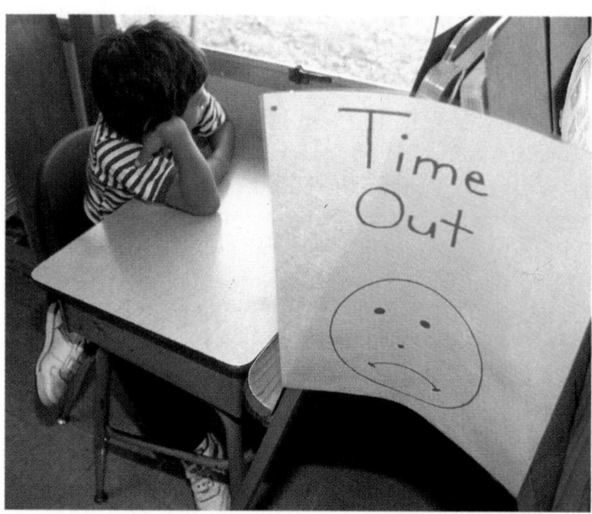

Time-out is an operant procedure wherein the consequence for misbehavior is removal to an environment with no positive reinforcers.

pitalized patients, many experimentally minded psychologists set about the task of bringing practical order into the chaos of institutions for the severely disturbed.

In addition to the familiar use of praise, tokens, and food as positive reinforcers, and of verbal or physical punishment as negative reinforcers, operant workers developed other reinforcers. The *Premack principle* (Premack, 1959) holds that in a given situation a more probable behavior can serve as a reinforcer for a less probable behavior. For example, if you know that John would rather watch a football game than do the laundry, you can make the former contingent on the latter: allowing John to watch football can function as a positive reinforcer for washing the clothes. Most of us have applied this principle to our own behavior many times, resolving not to reward ourselves with going to a movie unless we first complete a task that holds less appeal for us.

Another operant tool is *time-out*, which refers to removing a person from an environment in which he or she can earn positive reinforcers. For example, rather than just ignoring undesirable behavior—the typical extinction method—one banishes the person for a stated period of time to a dreary room where positive reinforcers are unavailable. Finally, *overcorrection* is a punisher that requires the person not only to restore an environment he or she has sullied but also to improve upon its original condition (e.g., Azrin, Sneed, & Foxx, 1973). Thus, if a destructive child tears the sheets off the bed instead of making it, the therapist requires the child to make not only that bed but others as well. Generally speaking, operant treatments work best with clients whose intellectual capacities are limited and in situations in which considerable control can be exercised by the therapist. We will look first at the token economy and then at operant procedures with children.

The Token Economy

An early example of work within the operant tradition is the **token economy**, a procedure in which tokens (such as poker chips or stickers) are given for desired behavior; the tokens can later be exchanged for desirable items and activities. On the basis of research that Staats and Staats (1963) conducted with children, Ayllon and Azrin (1968) set aside an entire ward of a mental hospital for a series of experiments in which rewards were provided for activities such as making beds and combing hair and were not given when behavior was withdrawn or bizarre. The forty-five female patients, who averaged sixteen years of hospitalization, were systematically rewarded for their ward work and self-care by receiving plastic tokens that could later be exchanged for special privileges, such as listening to records, going to the movies, renting a private room, or enjoying extra visits to the canteen. The entire life of each patient was as far as possible controlled by this regime.

The rules of the token economy—the medium of exchange; the chores and self-care rewarded and by what number of tokens; the items and privileges that can be purchased and for how many tokens—

Shown here is a token economy conducted by the Social-Learning Program at Fulton State Hospital, Fulton, Missouri. The patient is receiving a token and verbal praise from the staff member for actively participating in an academic class.

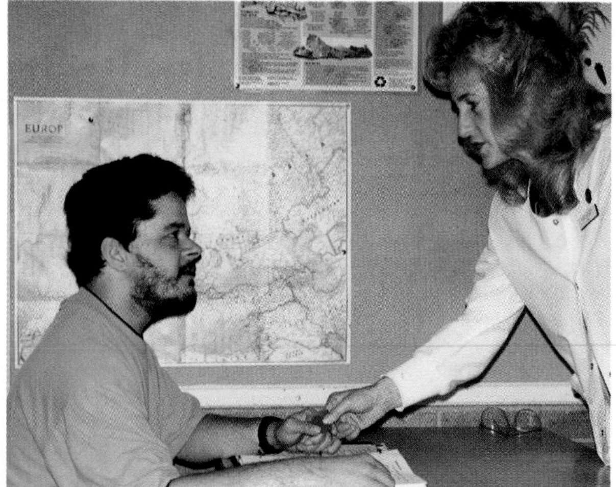

are carefully established and usually posted. These regimes have demonstrated how even markedly regressed adult hospital patients can be significantly affected by systematic manipulation of reinforcement contingencies, that is, rewarding some behavior to increase its frequency or ignoring other behavior to reduce its frequency. To show that a stimulus following behavior actually reinforces it, an experiment has to demonstrate not only that behavior increases when followed by a positive event, but also that behavior declines when nothing positive happens as a consequence. In Chapter 5 the ABAB design was presented as a method for studying the effect of contingencies. Ayllon, Aztin, and others demonstrated in this way the effect of contingencies on the behavior of their ward patients. Figure 19.1 indicates that conduct such as brushing teeth and making beds markedly decreased when rewards were withdrawn but became more frequent again when rewards were reinstated.

Since the publication of these early studies of the token economy, many similar programs have been instituted throughout the country. The most impressive was reported by Gordon Paul and Robert Lentz (1977) and has already been cited (page 418). The long-term, regressed, and chronic schizophrenic patients in their program are the most severely debilitated institutionalized adults ever studied systematically. Some of these patients screamed for long periods, some were mute; many were incontinent, a few assaultive. Most of them no longer used silverware, and some buried their faces in their food. The patients were matched for age, sex, socioeconomic background, symptoms, and length of hospitalization and then assigned to one of three wards—social learning (behavioral), milieu therapy, and routine hospital management. Each ward had twenty-eight residents. The two treatment wards shared ambitious objectives: to teach self-care, housekeeping, communication, and vocational skills; to reduce symptomatic behavior; and to release patients to the community.

Figure 19.1 When receiving tokens, patients on a ward spent more time grooming themselves and doing chores than when they were given no reward. Adapted from Ayllon and Azrin (1965).

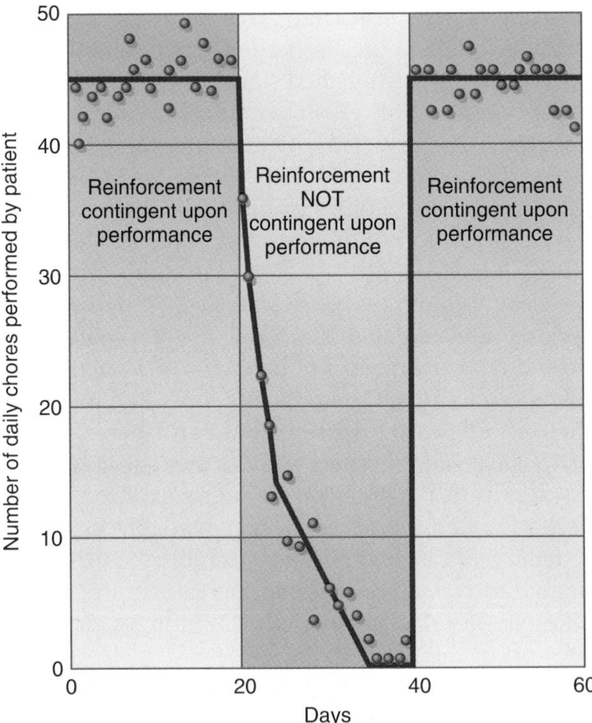

1. **Social-Learning Ward.** Located in a new mental health center, the social-learning ward was operated on a token economy embracing all aspects of the residents' lives. Their appearance had to pass muster each morning, in eleven specific ways, in order to earn a token. Well-made beds, good behavior at mealtime, classroom participation, and socializing during free periods were other means of earning tokens. Residents learned through modeling, shaping, prompting, and instructions. They were also taught to communicate better with one another and participated in problem-solving groups. Tokens were a necessity, for they purchased meals as well as small luxuries. In addition to living by the rules of the token economy, individuals received behavioral treatments tailored to their needs. Residents were kept busy 85 percent of their waking hours learning to behave better.
2. **Milieu Therapy Ward.** Another ward of the center operated on the principles of Jones's (1953) therapeutic community, an approach reminiscent of Pinel's moral treatment of the late eighteenth century (page 14). These residents, too, were kept busy 85 percent of their waking hours. Both individually and as a group, they were expected to act responsibly and to participate in decisions about how the ward was to function. In general, they were treated more as normal individuals than as incompetent mental patients. Staff members impressed on the residents their positive expectations and praised them for doing well. When they behaved symptomatically, staff members stayed with them, making clear the expectation that they would soon behave more appropriately.

3. **Routine Hospital Management.** These patients continued their accustomed hospital existence in an older state institution, receiving custodial care and heavy antipsychotic medication. Except for the 5 percent of their waking hours occupied by occasional activity, and recreational, occupational, and individual and group therapies, these people were on their own.

Before the program began, the staffs of the two treatment wards were carefully trained to adhere to detailed instructions in therapy manuals; regular observations confirmed that they were implementing the principles of a social-learning or a milieu therapy program. Over the four and a half years of hospitalization and the one and a half years of follow-up, the patients were carefully evaluated at regular six-month intervals by structured interviews and by meticulous, direct, behavioral observations.

The results? Both the social-learning and the milieu therapy reduced positive and negative symptoms, with the social-learning ward achieving better results than the milieu ward on a number of measures. The residents also acquired self-care, housekeeping, social, and vocational skills. The behavior of members of these two groups within the institution was superior to that of the residents of the hospital ward. By the end of treatment, more of them had been discharged. In fact, over 10 percent of the social-learning patients left the center for independent living; 7 percent of the milieu patients achieved this goal; and none of the hospital treatment patients did.

An interesting finding emerged on medication usage. Not surprisingly, about 90 percent of the patients in all three groups were receiving neuroleptics at the outset of the study. Over time, use among the routine hospital management group increased to 100 percent while in the other two groups the percentage of patients on drugs dropped dramatically, to 18 percent in the milieu group and 11 percent in the social-learning ward. In addition, many more patients from all three groups were discharged to community placements, such as boarding homes and halfway houses, where there was supervision but also considerably less restraint than patients had been experiencing for an average of seventeen years. Members of the social-learning group did significantly better at remaining in these community residences than did patients in the other two groups.

Considering how poorly these patients had been functioning before this treatment project, these results are remarkable. And the fact that the social-learning program was superior to the milieu program is also significant, for milieu treatment is used in many, perhaps most, mental hospitals. As implemented by Paul's team of clinicians, it provided patients with more attention than was given those on the social-learning ward. This greater amount of attention would appear to control well for the placebo effect of the social-learning therapy.

These results, though, should not be accepted as confirming the usefulness of token economies per se, for the social-learning therapy contained elements that went beyond operant conditioning of overt motor behavior. Staff provided information to residents and attempted verbally to clarify misconceptions. Indeed, Paul (personal communication, 1981) relegated the token economy to a secondary, although not trivial, role. He saw it as a useful device for getting the attention of severely regressed patients in the initial stages of treatment. The token economy created the opportunity for his patients to acquire new information, or, in Paul's informal phrase, to "get good things into their heads."

Paul and Lentz never claimed that any one of these patients was cured. Although they were able to live outside the hospital, most continued to manifest many signs of mental disorder, and few of them had gainful employment or participated in the social activities that most people take for granted. (The aftercare aspects of the Paul and Lentz project are discussed in detail in Chapter 20 page 615.) The outcome, though, is not to be underestimated: chronic mental patients, those typically shut away on back wards and forgotten by society, can be resocialized and taught self-care. They can learn to behave normally enough to be discharged from mental institutions. Reports published since the Paul and Lentz study support the effectiveness of social-learning programs (see review by Paul & Menditto, 1992).

Yet the success of the Paul–Lentz work has had little impact on the care of hospitalized mental patients. In 1983, Boudewyns, Fry, and Nightingale (1986) surveyed all 152 Veterans Administration Medical Centers. A phenomenal 100 percent response rate revealed that only twenty centers reported having any sort of behavior modification or token economy. Of these twenty, only half modeled their efforts on the work of Paul and Lentz. Thus, of 46,360 schizophrenics with an average stay of 98 days, only 1.01 percent were being exposed to the best-validated therapy program available for them. Fifteen years later, Paul and Menditto (1992) were unable to report much of an increase in the use of token economies, in spite of even more evidence in support of their effectiveness.

Why is this model for treatment not more widely used? Speculation includes staff resistance (it requires a way of interacting with patients and of keeping records that is new and perhaps objectionable to mental health staff), problems finding effective reinforcers for chronic patients, high cost, and concerns for patient rights. Paul and Menditto (1992) blame political factors such as negative biases in the psychiatric and medical establishments, bureaucratic inertia in the face of new approaches, and the conservative federal administrations of the 1980s that reduced funding for research in the behavioral and social sciences. But they sense a backlash developing in the 1990s as legislators, taxpayers, and insurance companies demand better evidence that what is being paid for actually works as well as can be expected.

Operant Work with Children

Some of the best operant conditioning behavior therapy has been done with children, perhaps because much of their behavior is subject to the control of others. Children, after all, tend more than adults to be under continual supervision. At school their behavior is scrutinized by teachers, and when they come home, parents frequently oversee their play and other social activities. In most instances the behavior therapist works with the parents and teachers in an effort to change the ways in which they reward and punish the children for whom they have responsibility. It is assumed that altering the reinforcement practices of the adults in a child's life will ultimately change the child's behavior.

The range of childhood problems dealt with through operant conditioning is broad, including bed-wetting, thumb sucking, nail biting, aggression, tantrums, hyperactivity, disruptive classroom behavior, poor school performance, language deficiency, extreme social withdrawal, and asthmatic attacks (Nemeroff & Karoly, 1991). Self-mutilation has also been effectively treated with punishment procedures, sometimes involving the response-contingent application of painful electric shock to the hands or feet (see page 474). Such extreme measures are, of course, used only when less drastic interventions are ineffective and when the problem behaviors are health- or life-threatening (Sandler, 1991). Even gender identity appears susceptible to operant procedures (see page 337). In general, rates of improvement for these kinds of problems are superior to those reported for traditional forms of therapy (Franks et al., 1990).

Before applying this therapy, one must first determine that the problem behavior is an operant, that is, under the control of a contingent reinforcer. A child who is crying because of physical pain, for example, should be attended to. Encouraging results have also been achieved by applying operant techniques to therapy with retarded and autistic children. As indicated in Chapter 16, many operant conditioners have challenged assumptions about the limited trainability of such children, much to the benefit of the children and their families.

Modeling

Modeling is the third theoretical approach employed by behavior therapists. The importance of modeling and imitation in behavior is self-evident, for children as well as adults are able to acquire complex responses and eliminate emotional inhibitions merely by watching how others handle themselves. We look first at the variety of problems that can be treated by modeling and then at the role of cognition in modeling.

Problems Treated by Modeling

The effectiveness of modeling in clinical work was shown in an early study by Bandura, Blanchard, and Ritter (1969) in which they were attempting to help people overcome snake phobias. The researchers had fearful adults view both live and filmed confrontations of people and snakes. In these engagements the models gradually moved closer to the animals. The fears of the patients were decidedly reduced. The pioneering work of Ivar Lovaas mentioned in Chapter 16 has from its inception employed modeling to teach complex skills, such as speech, to autistic children (Lovaas et al., 1966). Sex therapy researchers have found that inhibited adults can become more comfortable with their sexuality if shown tastefully designed explicit films of people touching themselves, masturbating, and having intercourse (McMullen & Rosen, 1979; Nemetz, Craig, & Reith, 1978). Other films or slide presentations have significantly reduced children's fears of dogs (Hill, Liebert, & Mott, 1968), of hospitalization (Roberts et al., 1981), of surgery (Melamed & Siegel, 1975), and of dental work (Melamed et al., 1975). Modeling films for reducing children's fears of medical treatments are considered one of the new behavioral medicine or health psychology procedures (see page 443).

Some of the clinical work of Arnold Lazarus, one of the earliest behavior therapists, is also regarded as modeling treatment. As indicated in Chapter 2 (page 49), in *behavior rehearsal* Lazarus (1971) demonstrates for a client a better way to handle a difficult interpersonal problem. The client observes the therapist's exemplary performance and then attempts to imitate it during the therapy session. By continual practice and observation, the client can frequently acquire entire repertoires of more effective and more satisfying behavior. Videotape equipment can be creatively used to facilitate such modeling and imitation.

In their review of cognitive-behavioral interventions with children, Braswell and Kendall (1988) indicate that nearly all such efforts entail a model, usually an adult, providing exemplars of desired performance. For example, in an early report, Meichenbaum (1971) found that having a model verbalize his or her thoughts while solving a problem—"Let's see, if I can't get anywhere, I'll try another way altogether"—led to greater improvement than when the model merely solved the problem without thinking aloud. Kendall and Braswell (1985) also encourage child behavior therapists to use naturally occurring events as modeling opportunities, for example, thinking out loud while trying to find a suitable room for the therapy session or figuring out when to schedule the next meeting. Children learn a great deal from observing others, both adults and peers; this work indicates that patterns of thought can be acquired as readily as overt behavior (Kendall, 1990).

Behavior therapy programs for hospitalized patients also make use of modeling. Bellack, Hersen, and Turner (1976) contrived social situations for three chronic schizophrenic patients and then observed whether they behaved appropriately. For instance, a patient was told to pretend that he had just returned home from a weekend trip to find that his lawn had been mowed. As he gets out of the car, his next-door neighbor approaches him and says that he has cut the patient's grass because he was already cutting his own. The patient must then respond to the situation. As expected, patients were initially not very good at making a socially appropriate response, which in this instance might have been some sort of thank-you. Training followed: the therapist encouraged the patient to respond, commenting helpfully on his efforts. If necessary, the therapist also modeled appropriate behavior so that the patient could observe and then try to imitate it. This combination of role-playing, modeling, and positive reinforcement effected significant improvement in all three patients. There was even generalization to social situations that had not been worked on during the training. This study and others like it (e.g., Wallace et al., 1985) indicate that many severely disturbed patients can be taught new social behavior that may help them function better both inside *and outside* the hospital.

The Role of Cognition

It is still unclear, however, *how* the observation of a model is translated into changes in overt behavior. In their original writings on modeling, Bandura and Walters (1963) asserted that an observer could, somehow, learn new behavior by watching others. Given the emphasis that much of experimental psychology places on learning through doing, this attention to learning *without* doing was important. But it left out the processes that could be operating. A moment's reflection on the typical modeling experiment suggests the direction theory and research have taken in recent years. The observer, a child, sits in a chair and watches a film of another child making a number of movements, such as hitting a large inflated plastic doll in a highly stereotyped manner, and hears the child in the film uttering peculiar sounds. An hour later the youngster is given the opportunity to imitate what was earlier seen and heard. The child is able to do so, as common sense and folk wisdom would predict. How can we understand what happened? Since the observer did not *do* anything of interest in any motoric way while watching the film, except perhaps fidget in the chair, it would not be fruitful to look at overt behavior for a clue. Obviously, the child's cognitive processes were engaged, including the ability to remember later on what had happened.

Bandura (1986) has written extensively on the cognitive factors involved in modeling, which he defines as a process by which a person rather efficiently acquires rules for the generation of behavior. This interest has led Bandura to formulate a social cognitive theory of behavior, in which the person's symbolic, cognitive processes play a key role. For example, Bandura, Jeffrey, and Bachica (1974), drawing on experimental cognitive research, showed that having a code by which to summarize information helps a person retain it better. In addition, they found that the use of such a code helped observers pattern their actions on what they had seen modeled. Other theories about memory storage and retrieval may shed light on how people acquire new and complex patterns of behavior "simply" by watching others. The word *simply* is placed in quotation marks because, in fact, the process is not simple at all. The literature on modeling, which at first offered straightforward, commonsensical, social-learning explanations, now regards modeling interventions as a type of cognitive behavior therapy, to which we now turn.

Cognitive Behavior Therapy

In the therapies discussed thus far, the emphasis has been on the direct manipulation of overt behavior and occasionally of covert behavior. Relatively little attention has been paid to direct alteration of the thinking and reasoning processes of the client. Perhaps it was in reaction to insight therapy that behavior therapists initially discounted the importance of cognition, regarding any appeal to thinking as a return to the "mentalism" that John Watson had vigorously objected to in the early part of the twentieth century.

If behavior therapy is to be taken seriously as applied experimental psychology, however, it should incorporate theory and research on cognitive processes. Indeed, for a number of years behavior therapists have paid attention to private events—to thoughts, perceptions, judgments, self-statements, and even tacit (unconscious) assumptions—and have studied and manipulated these processes in their attempts to understand and modify overt and covert disturbed behavior (Mahoney, 1974). The cognitive-restructuring treatment of the man with pressure points described in Chapter 2 (page 51) is one early example. **Cognitive restructuring** is a general term for changing a pattern of thought that is presumed to be causing a disturbed emotion or behavior. It is implemented in several ways by cognitive behavior therapists.[2]

Ellis's Rational-Emotive Therapy

The principal thesis of Ellis's **rational-emotive therapy (RET)** is that sustained emotional reactions are caused by internal sentences that people repeat to themselves, and these self-statements reflect sometimes unspoken assumptions—irrational beliefs—about what is necessary to lead a meaningful life. The aim of therapy is to eliminate self-defeating beliefs through a rational examination of them. As indicated earlier, anxious persons may create their own problems by making unrealistic demands on themselves or others, such as "I must win the love of everyone." Or a depressed person may say several times a day, "What a worthless jerk I am." Ellis proposes that people interpret what is happening around them, that sometimes these interpretations can cause emotional turmoil, and that a therapist's attention should be focused on these beliefs rather than on historical causes or, indeed, overt behavior (Ellis, 1957, 1962, 1984).

Ellis lists a number of irrational beliefs that people can harbor. One very common notion is that people must be thoroughly competent in everything they do. Ellis suggests that many people actually believe this untenable assumption and evaluate every event within this context. Thus if a person makes an error, it becomes a catastrophe because it violates the deeply held conviction that he or she must be perfect. It sometimes comes as a shock to clients to realize that they actually believe such strictures and as a consequence run their lives so that it becomes virtually impossible to live comfortably or productively.

Clinical Implementation

After becoming familiar with the client's problems, the therapist presents the basic theory of rational-emotive therapy so that the client can understand and accept it.[3] The following transcript is from a session with a young man who had inordinate fears about speaking in front of groups. The therapist guides the client to view his inferiority complex in terms of the unreasonable things he may be telling himself. The therapist's thoughts during the interview are indicated in italics.

Client: My primary difficulty is that I become very uptight when I have to speak in front of a group of people. I guess it's just my own inferiority complex.
Therapist: [*I don't want to get sidetracked at this point by talking about that conceptualization of his problem. I'll*

[2]There is a terminological issue here. As mentioned in Chapter 9 and discussed further in this chapter, Aaron Beck's therapy is called cognitive therapy; the word *behavior* is not included. Ellis's rational-emotive therapy is regarded as one of the "cognitive behavior therapies." As will become clear, both approaches have an important place for overt behavior while emphasizing the cognitive component of therapy. We will follow general practice by regarding both Beck's cognitive therapy (CT) and Ellis's RET as cognitive behavior therapies. More generally, we find that people today use "cognitive therapy" and "cognitive behavior therapy" interchangeably.

[3]We said in Chapter 18 that the usefulness of an empathy statement or insight into the past does not depend on whether it is true. Nor does the usefulness of rational-emotive therapy. Ellis's views may be only partially correct, or even entirely wrong, and yet it may be helpful for a client to act as though they are true.

just try to finesse it and make a smooth transition to something else.] I don't know if I would call it an inferiority complex but I do believe that people can, in a sense, bring on their own upset and anxiety in certain kinds of situations. When you're in a particular situation, your anxiety is often not the result of the situation itself, but rather the way in which you *interpret* the situation—what you tell yourself about the situation. For example, look at this pen. Does this pen make you nervous?
Client: No.
Therapist: Why not?
Client: It's just an object. It's just a pen.
Therapist: It can't hurt you?
Client: No. . . .
Therapist: It's really not the object that creates emotional upset in people, but rather what you think about the object [*Hopefully, this Socratic-like dialogue will eventually bring him to the conclusion that self-statements can mediate emotional arousal.*] Now this holds true for . . . situations where emotional upset is caused by what a person tells himself about the situation. Take, for example, two people who are about to attend the same social gathering. Both of them may know exactly the same number of people at the party, but one person can be optimistic and relaxed about the situation, whereas the other one can be worried about how he will appear, and consequently be very anxious. [*I'll try to get him to verbalize the basic assumption that attitude or perception is most important here.*] So, when these two people walk into the place where the party is given, are their emotional reactions at all associated with the physical arrangements at the party?
Client: No, obviously not.
Therapist: What determines their reactions, then?
Client: They obviously have different attitudes toward the party.
Therapist: Exactly, and their attitudes—the ways in which they approach the situation—greatly influence their emotional reactions. (Goldfried & Davison, 1976, pp. 163–165)

Having persuaded the client that his or her emotional problems will benefit from rational examination, the therapist proceeds to teach the person to substitute for irrational self-statements an internal dialogue meant to ease the emotional turmoil. At the present time therapists who implement Ellis's ideas differ greatly on how they persuade clients to change their self-talk. Some rational-emotive therapists, like Ellis himself, argue with clients, cajoling and teasing them, sometimes in very blunt language. Others, believing that social influence should be more subtle and that individuals should participate more in changing themselves, encourage clients to discuss their own irrational thinking and then gently lead them to discover more rational ways of regarding the world (Goldfried & Davison, 1976).

The rational-emotive therapist believes that a person's reluctance to interact with others at a party is due to anxiety caused by overconcern with the possible reactions of others.

Once a client verbalizes a different belief or self-statement during a therapy session, it must be made part of everyday thinking. In recent years, Ellis and his followers have paid particular attention to homework assignments designed to provide opportunities for the client to experiment with the new self-talk and to experience the positive consequences of viewing life in less catastrophic ways. Indeed, Ellis emphasizes the importance of getting the patient to *behave* differently, both to test out new beliefs and to learn to cope with life's disappointments.

Evaluation of Rational-Emotive Therapy

While the outcome research on RET is not without its problems (Haaga & Davison, 1993), several conclusions can be offered (Haaga & Davison, 1989):

1. RET reduces self-reports of general anxiety, speech anxiety, and test anxiety.
2. In social anxiety RET effects improvements in both self-report and behavior though it may be inferior to systematic desensitization.
3. RET is inferior to exposure-based treatments for agoraphobia, but it remains to be studied whether combining the two approaches leads to better maintenance of exposure-produced gains.
4. Preliminary evidence suggests that RET may be useful in treating excessive anger, depression, and antisocial behavior.
5. RET has utility only as part of more comprehensive behavioral programs for sexual dysfunction.
6. As described in Chapter 8, RET shows promise in reducing the Type A behavior pattern but, as with other psychological interventions, has not

yet shown its utility in preventing coronary heart disease (Haaga, 1987).

7. There is some preliminary evidence that RET may be useful in a preventive fashion for untroubled people, that is, to help emotionally healthy people cope better with everyday stress.
8. Rational-emotive education, whereby teachers explain to children in classrooms the principles of RET and how they can be applied to their everyday lives, has been used in the spirit of primary prevention (page 608) in hopes of forestalling full-blown emotional problems later in life. Evidence suggests that it can improve self-concept (Cangelosi, Gressard, & Mines, 1980) and reduce test anxiety (Knaus & Bokor, 1975).
9. There is only some tentative evidence (e.g., Smith, 1983) that RET achieves its effects through a reduction in the irrationality of thought. Not to be underestimated in importance is the support RET gives patients to confront what they fear and to take risks with new, more adaptive behavior.

As with most other clinical procedures, the relevance of RET to a given problem is dependent in part on how the clinician *conceptualizes* the patient's predicament. Thus, if one is trying to help an overweight person lose pounds, one might conceptualize eating as a way of reducing anxiety; in turn, the anxiety might be viewed as due to social distress that is itself caused by extreme fear of rejection arising from an irrational need to please everyone and never make a mistake. The RET therapist would direct his or her efforts to the irrational beliefs about pleasing others and being perfect, the rationale being that this will alleviate the patient's distress and ultimately the overeating. This kind of analysis into underlying causes is discussed at the end of this chapter.

Defining Irrationality and the Issue of Ethics in RET

Like other therapists, Ellis preaches an ethical system, and this becomes clear when one tries to define irrational or rational thinking. If we say simply that irrational thinking is what creates psychological distress, the definition is unsatisfyingly circular. If one then proposes that we regard as irrational any thought that is not objective and rigorous, then we would have to conclude that much of the thinking of *nondistressed* people is irrational, for considerable research indicates that the stories people tell themselves in order to live (Didion, 1979) frequently have illusory elements (e.g., Geer et al., 1970; Taylor & Brown, 1988). Indeed, it is possible that, in order to achieve something unique or outstanding, one sometimes *has* to harbor beliefs that might be seen by those not committed to a cause as unrealistic. Albert Bandura put it this way:

> Visionaries and unshakable optimists, whose misbeliefs foster hope and sustain their efforts in endeavors beset with immense obstacles, do not flock to psychotherapists. . . . Similarly, the efforts of social reformers rest on illusions about the amount of social change their collective actions will accomplish. Although their fondest hopes are likely to be unrealized during their lifetime, nevertheless their concerted efforts achieve some progress and strengthen the perceived efficacy of others to carry on the struggle. For those leading impoverished, oppressed lives, realism can breed despair. . . . Clearly the relationship between illusion and psychological functioning is a complex one. (Bandura, 1986, p. 516)

In our view, one cannot construct a definition of irrational thinking on empirical or scientific grounds at all. Ultimately, RET therapists—*and their clients*—decide that it would be more useful or appropriate to think about the world in certain ways. This decision is based on what one believes is functional or ethical, not necessarily on what is strictly objective or rational.

Beck's Cognitive Therapy[4]

As noted earlier, (see page 231), Beck holds that numerous disorders, particularly depression, are caused by negative beliefs that individuals have about themselves, the world, and the future. These dysfunctional beliefs, or negative schemata, are maintained by one or more biases or errors in logic, such as arbitrary inference or selective abstraction. The overall goal of Beck's **cognitive therapy (CT)** is to provide the client with experiences, both in and outside the consulting room, that will alter the negative schemata in a favorable way. Thus a client who, through an ineptness schema, bemoans his or her witlessness for burning a roast, is encouraged to view the failure as regrettable but not to overgeneralize (one of the cognitive biases) and conclude, through a hopelessness schema, that he or she can do no good on future occasions. The therapist tries to break into the vicious cycle of a negative schema fueling an illogicality, which in turn fuels the negative schema.

Clinical Implementation

Attempts to change negative thinking are made at both the behavioral and the cognitive levels. One

[4]Some of this section is based on Haaga and Davison (1991).

behavioral technique, useful for clients who are convinced that they are depressed all the time and who become still more deeply depressed because of this belief, is to have them record their moods at regular intervals during the day. If it turns out that these reports show some variability, as indeed often happens even with very depressed people, this information can serve to challenge their general belief that life is always miserable. This change in thinking can then serve as the basis for a change in behavior, such as getting out of bed in the morning, doing a few chores, or even going to work.

Similarly, depressed clients often do very little because tasks seem insurmountable and they believe they can accomplish nothing. To test this belief or schema of insurmountableness, the therapist breaks down a particular task into small steps and encourages the client to focus on just one step at a time. If this tactic is skillfully handled—and a good therapeutic relationship is obviously important—the client finds that he or she can, in fact, accomplish *something.* These accomplishments are then discussed with the therapist as inconsistent with the notion that tasks are beyond the client's efforts. As the client's view of the self begins to change, tasks of greater difficulty appear less forbidding, and success can build upon success, with still further beneficial changes in the client's beliefs about the self and his or her world.

Collaborative empiricism is inherent to Beck's therapy. Therapist and client work as co-investigators to uncover and examine any maladaptive interpretations of the world that may be aggravating the client's depression and general life condition. They try to uncover both automatic thoughts and dysfunctional assumptions. Automatic thoughts are the things we tell or picture to ourselves as we go about our daily business, the running dialogue we have with ourselves as we drive to school, listen to a friend, or watch others crossing the street. Clients usually need practice in taking note of such thoughts and images, especially the ones that are associated with depressed mood. For example, a parent hears a child say that he or she failed a test at school and thinks, "What a lousy parent I am." Thereafter the parent feels blue. The therapist helps the client monitor such thoughts, and together they examine their validity. Why should your child's problems at school mean that you are a bad parent? What else affects your youngster and determines whether he or she does well at school? In this fashion the therapist teaches the client to check his or her thoughts against the available information and to entertain hypotheses that might attribute the child's failure on the test to factors other than having a bad parent.

This phase of identifying and modifying automatic thoughts is followed by a more subtle phase, the identification of underlying dysfunctional assumptions, schemata, or beliefs. These can be likened to a leitmotiv in music, a dominant, recurring theme. The parent may come to realize that he or she has taken on responsibility for the happiness and welfare of the entire family, including how good a student the child is. The therapist can examine with the client the implications of the worst possible case, that the evidence does indeed indicate that he or she is not an omnipotent parent. Is this something to be clinically depressed about? To be sure, concern and desire to do something about the child's problems are understandable, but these reactions can energize a person to new action, not plunge him or her into despair.

How can the therapist help the individual alter his or her dysfunctional assumptions? In addition to verbal persuasion, the therapist may encourage the client to behave in a way inconsistent with them. For example, a person who believes that he or she must please everyone at the office can decline the next unreasonable request made and see whether, as he or she has been assuming, the sky will fall. If the situation has been properly analyzed ahead of time by client and therapist, clearly a necessary step, the client can experience what happens when he or she acts against this absolutist belief.

Beck's therapy, like others that alter thinking, is *difficult!* Clients would probably not be depressed if they were readily convinced by mastery experiences that they are worthwhile individuals. Our brief account is only an outline; the implementation is invariably less systematic, less unidirectional, and certainly more arduous than the description implies.

Evaluation of Cognitive Therapy

The effectiveness of Beck's approach is under intensive study. A number of experiments with depressed patients lent early support to it (Rush et al., 1977; Shaw, 1977; Wilson, Goldin, & Charbonneau-Powis, 1983). Moreover, CT may have a preventive effect relative to drug treatment, a consideration of major importance in light of the oft-observed tendency for depressive episodes to recur (Blackburn, Eunson, & Bishop, 1986). Perhaps cognitive therapy patients acquire some useful cognitive behavior skills that they are able to use following termination of therapy. And, as seen in Chapter 17, because older patients can be extremely sensitive to medications and can also suffer from medical problems that contraindicate prescribing psychoactive drugs, nonpharmacological interventions are especially appropriate.

A meta-analysis of outcome studies of diverse therapies concluded that Beck's therapy achieves greater short-term improvement than wait-list controls, drug therapies, noncognitive-behavioral treatments, and a heterogeneous group of other psychotherapies (Dobson, 1989). Such research laid the foundations for the widely publicized comparative outcome study sponsored by the National Institute of Mental Health (Elkin et al., 1985), a study that did *not* find CT superior to a drug therapy and a particular kind of psychotherapy but nonetheless supported the utility of Beck's approach to the treatment of depression (see Focus Box 19.1).

Yet to be demonstrated is that when cognitive therapy works, it does so because it helps patients change their cognitions. As Hollon and Beck (1986) pointed out, predictable changes in cognitions do occur in cognitive therapy—*but* they are found as well in successful treatment of depression by drugs (e.g., Rush et al., 1982). Cognitive change may be the *consequence* of change produced by other means. Or, at least with depression (the disorder in which cognitive therapy has been researched), cognitive change may be the mediator of therapeutic improvement brought about by *any* therapy, whether Beck's cognitive therapy, psychoanalysis, or drugs.

The Therapies of Beck and Ellis—Some Comparisons

The views and techniques of Ellis and Beck are widely used by therapists today. With the inevitable changes that inventive clinicians make as they apply the work of others, and with the evolution in the thinking of the theorists themselves, the differences between the two therapies can sometimes be difficult to discern. They do contrast, however, in interesting ways (Haaga & Davison, 1991, 1992).

To the parent who became depressed upon learning that his or her child had failed a test at school, Ellis would say immediately, in essence, "So what if you are an inadequate parent? It is irrational to be depressed about that." Beck, in contrast, would first examine the evidence for the conclusion. His is a more empirical approach. "What evidence is there for thinking that you are an inadequate parent?" If proof is lacking, this discovery in itself will be therapeutic. Ellis regards his own type of solution as more thoroughgoing. *Even if* the person is wanting as a parent, the world will not end, for a person does not have to be competent in everything he or she does. Beck will also eventually question with the client whether one has to be competent in everything to feel good about oneself, but maybe not until the evidence that they accumulate suggests that the person is an inadequate parent.

The therapist adopting Beck's approach certainly has preconceptions about negative schemata and especially about the forms that maladaptive, illogical or biased thinking takes, such as overgeneralization. But working with a depressed individual is a collaborative, *inductive* procedure by which client and therapist attempt to discover the *particular* dysfunctional assumptions underlying the client's negative thoughts. Rational-emotive therapists, by contrast, are *deductive*. They are confident that a distressed person subscribes to one or more of a predetermined list of irrational beliefs.

Beck's therapy and standard rational-emotive practices differ in style on this inductive–deductive basis. Beck suggests that the therapist avoid being overly didactic, but Ellis often uses minilectures and didactic speeches. Beck proposes calling negative thoughts "unproductive ideas" to promote rapport with clients. He does not favor adjectives such as irrational or nutty, which might be heard—with supportive humor, it must be pointed out—from Ellis. Finally, Beck recommends that the therapist begin by acknowledging the client's frame of reference and asking for an elaboration of it. Having had a chance to present his or her case and feel understood, the client may be more willing to go through the collaborative process of undermining beliefs. Ellis, on the other hand, supposes that quite forceful interventions are necessary to disrupt a well-learned maladaptive pattern of thinking; he will therefore directly confront the client's irrational beliefs, sometimes within minutes in the first session.

Both approaches have one thing in common, and this factor makes Beck and Ellis soul mates of the experiential (humanistic and existential) therapies reviewed in Chapter 18: they convey the message that people can change their psychological predicaments by thinking differently. They emphasize that the way people construe themselves and their world is a major determinant of the kind of person they will be—and people have *choice* in how they will construe things. They assert also that people can, sometimes with great effort, choose to behave differently. However, unlike behavior therapists who are not cognitive—but like the humanists and existentialists—Beck and Ellis believe that new behavior is important for the evidence it can provide about how one looks at oneself and the world. Thus, the focus remains on the cognitive dimension of humankind and on the abiding belief that people's minds are difficult to enslave and that our thinking can provide the key to positive psychological change.

19.1. • NIMH Treatment of Depression Collaborative Research Program

In 1977 the National Institute of Mental Health undertook a large, complex, and expensive three-site study of Beck's cognitive therapy, comparing it with brief psychodynamic psychotherapy and pharmacotherapy (Elkin et al., 1985). Called the Treatment of Depression Collaborative Research Program (TDCRP), this is the first multisite coordinated study initiated by NIMH in the field of psychotherapy (the NIMH has fruitfully conducted such research in pharmacology).

Selection of Therapies

Three criteria were employed in selecting a psychotherapy to be compared with Beck's: it had to have been developed for treating depression; it had to be explicit and standardized enough to allow for instructing other therapists (preferably using a manual); and it had to have empirically shown some efficacy with depressed patients. It was also preferable that there be little overlap with Beck's cognitive therapy.

The NIMH team selected Gerald Klerman's Interpersonal Psychotherapy, which, as we saw in Chapter 18, is a psychodynamic, Sullivanian, insight-oriented approach that focuses on current problems and interpersonal relationships and has demonstrated effectiveness for depression (Klerman et al., 1984; Weissman et al., 1979). It is, however, not as much intrapsychic as it is interpersonal; it emphasizes better understanding of the interpersonal problems assumed to give rise to depression and aims at improving relationships with others. As such, the focus is on better communication with others, reality-testing, developing more effective social skills, and meeting present social-role requirements. Actual techniques include somewhat nondirective discussion of interpersonal problems, exploration of and encouragement to express unacknowledged negative feelings, improvement of both verbal and nonverbal communications, and problem-solving.*

A pharmacological therapy, imipramine (Tofranil), a well-tested tricyclic drug widely regarded as a standard therapy for depression, was used as a reference against which to evaluate the two psychotherapies. Dosages were adjusted according to predetermined guidelines that were flexible enough to allow for some clinical judgment of the psychiatrist in the context of clinical management, that is, in a warm, supportive atmosphere (Fawcett et al., 1987). Indeed, Elkin et al. (1985) regarded this almost as a drug-plus-supportive therapy condition, *supportive* referring to the nature of the doctor–patient relationship, not to the application of any explicit psychotherapeutic techniques.

A fourth and final condition was a placebo–clinical management group, against which to judge the efficacy of imipramine. It was also conceived of as a partial control for the two psychotherapies because of the presence of strong support and encouragement. In a double-blind design like that used in the imipramine condition, patients in this group received a placebo that they believed might be an effective antidepressant medication; they were also given direct advice when considered necessary. As placebo conditions go, this was a very strong one, that is, it included much more psychological support and even intervention than do most placebo control groups in both the psychotherapy and pharmacotherapy literatures. It should be noted that clinical management—support and advice—was common to both this and the imipramine group.

All treatments lasted sixteen weeks, with slight differences in numbers of sessions, depending on the treatment manuals. For example, cognitive therapy patients received twelve sessions during the first eight weeks, followed by weekly sessions during the second half of the study. These twenty sessions exceeded the sixteen for interpersonal therapy, which, however, could number as many as twenty at the therapist's discretion. Throughout all therapies, patients were closely monitored and all professional safeguards were employed to minimize risk, for example, excluding imminently

*Technique differences have been noted between the therapies of Beck and Klerman (DeRubeis et al., 1982), and in the present study CT and IPT therapists adhered well to the procedures required of their respective therapies (Hill, O'Grady, & Elkin, 1992). Nonetheless, in our eyes there is considerable overlap, for both emphasize improving accuracy in perception as well as efficacy in social behavior. The reader may want to consider this when the results of this milestone study are described.

suicidal patients and, in general, maintaining close and regular contact during the study. These considerations were particularly important in the placebo condition.

Selection and Training of Therapists

An important feature of this study was the care and thoroughness of therapist selection and training at each of the treatment sites. This phase took almost two years, beginning with careful screening of recruits for general clinical competence and some experience in one of the three modalities under study. Altogether twenty-eight therapists were selected—ten each for interpersonal therapy and drug therapy and eight for cognitive therapy.

Clearly this was not a random selection of therapists, for they had to seek participation, be accepted after rigorous screening, and agree to adhere to an established treatment protocol, as well as have each of their therapy sessions videotaped for concurrent as well as subsequent scrutiny to ensure adherence to the respective therapy protocol. Training took months and was very rigorous, involving 119 patients. This selection and training phase itself constituted an achievement in psychotherapy research and has already been reported on by those involved in instruction and supervision (Rounsaville, Chevron, & Weissman, 1984; Shaw, 1984; Waskow, 1984). This lengthy procedure was taken to ensure the integrity of the independent variable, the therapy each subject received; these training and supervision efforts were in fact successful (Hill et al., 1992). Only recently have psychotherapy outcome studies devoted suitable attention to the training and monitoring of therapist-experimenters to ensure that the independent variables are, in fact, being manipulated in the study. Subjects began to be treated in May 1982.

Selection of Patient Subjects

The overall design of the study called for 240 patients, 60 in each of the four conditions. They had to meet the criteria for major depressive disorder but could not be imminently suicidal or have medical contraindications for the use of imipramine (in case they were assigned to the drug condition). All were outpatients, nonbipolar and nonpsychotic. Many other pieces of information were gathered on the patients so that they could later be related to treatment outcome (e.g., is melancholia a negative factor in cognitive therapy? do minority patients drop out of therapy more often than others?). Seventy percent of the sample were female (which corresponds well to the 2:1 ratio of women to men with this disorder), and patients were on average moderately to severely depressed for an outpatient sample. Of those who began treatment, 162, or 68 percent, completed at least fifteen weeks and twelve sessions; although more patients in the placebo condition dropped out of treatment, their number was not statistically greater than those in the other three, active treatment groups.

Types of Assessments

A wide range and large number of assessments were made at pre- and posttreatment, as well as three times during treatment and again at six-, twelve-, and eighteen-month follow-ups. Measures included some that might shed light on processes of change. For example, do interpersonal therapy patients learn to relate better to others during therapy, and, if so, is this improvement correlated with clinical outcome? Do cognitive therapy patients manifest less cognitive distortion during the later sessions than at the beginning of treatment, and, if so, is this shift associated with better clinical outcome? Assessment instruments included those that tap the perspectives of the patient, the therapist, an independent clinical evaluator blind to treatment condition, and, whenever possible, a significant other from the patient's life, for example, a spouse. Three domains of change were assessed: depressive symptomatology, overall symptomatology and life functioning, and functioning related to particular treatment approaches (e.g., the Dysfunctional Attitudes Scale of Weissman and Beck [1978], to assess cognitive change).

Results

Analyses of the data suggest variations among research sites, between those who completed treatment and the total sample (including dropouts), and among assessments with different perspectives (e.g., patient versus clinical evaluator judgments). Some of the complex findings thus far published can be summarized as follows (Elkin et al., 1986; Elkin et al., 1989; Imber et al., 1990; Shea et al., 1990; Shea et al., 1992).

1. At termination and without distinguishing subjects according to severity of depression, there were no significant differences in reduction of depression or improvement in overall functioning between cognitive therapy (CT) and interpersonal therapy (IPT) or between either of them and imipramine plus clinical management. In general, then, the three active treatments achieved significant *and equivalent* degrees of success. The placebo plus clinical management subjects also showed significant improvement. Imipramine was faster than the other treatments in reducing depressive symptoms. By the end of sixteen weeks, however, the two psychotherapies had caught up with the drug.
2. On some measures the less severely depressed placebo subjects were doing as well at termination as were the less depressed people in the three active treatment conditions.
3. Severely depressed patients did not fare as well in the placebo condition as did those in the three active treatments.
4. There was little evidence that particular treatments effected change in expected domains, such as IPT patients showing more improvements in social functioning than imipramine or CT patients.
5. For IPT and pharmacotherapy, but not for CT, patients diagnosed with personality disorders were more likely to have residual depressive symptoms after therapy than those without these axis II diagnoses.
6. Follow-up study eighteen months after the end of treatment found that the different treatment conditions did *not* differ significantly, and of those patients across the four conditions who had markedly improved immediately at the end of treatment, only between twenty and thirty percent remained nondepressed.

Much remains to be learned about effecting even short-term improvement in depressed patients; and even less is known about how to maintain over the long haul any benefits that are evident right after treatment ends. Certainly there is little in the many findings from this milestone study of comparative outcome that can gladden the hearts of proponents of any of the interventions.

Social Problem Solving

Some psychological distress can be regarded as a reaction to problems for which people believe they have no solution. I am late with a term paper and am upset about it. Shall I approach the professor, or is it better to deal at least initially with the teaching assistant? Should I request an Incomplete, or will it look bad on my transcript, which is going to be sent out soon to the graduate programs I am applying to? But isn't an Incomplete better than a C? Students caught in such a predicament can be helped by knowing how to solve a problem in the most effective, efficient manner.

Therapists have devised what is called **social problem solving (SPS)** (D'Zurilla & Goldfried, 1971; Goldfried & D'Zurilla, 1969; Kanfer & Busenmeyer, 1982). Training clients in SPS consists of a number of steps. They are first taught to regard their distress as a reaction to unsolved problems and even to regard problems as challenges or opportunities rather than as threats (D'Zurilla, 1986). They are then taught to identify what the problems might be; to brainstorm—to generate as many alternative solutions as possible without evaluating their feasibility or possible effectiveness; to assess the likely consequences of each solution; and to implement a decision and evaluate its effectiveness for achieving their particular goals.

Some clinical research finds SPS training useful. For example, depressed older adults in a nursing home alleviated more of their depression after such training than did patients given a more behaviorally based treatment (Hussian & Lawrence, 1981). Similarly good outcomes were achieved by Nezu (1986), who found greater reductions in depression among subjects who received the entire SPS package compared with a control condition whose group discussions about problems did not contain systematic procedures for solving them and evaluating the effectiveness of the solutions. In another study, school-age children acquired problem-solving skills that generalized to situations different from those dealt with in the SPS training (Weissberg et al.,

1981), and other work (e.g., Elias & Clabby, 1989) applied the approach to entire elementary school curricula. SPS training has also been found useful for enhancing social skills in psychiatric patients (Bedell, Archer, & Marlow, 1980) and for treating alcohol abuse (Chaney, O'Leary, & Marlatt, 1978). In the best of all possible worlds, clients learn a general attitude and set of skills that they can apply to a wide range of future situations, thereby enhancing their general well-being.

Metacognition, that is, what people know about knowing (Meichenbaum & Asarnow, 1979), is also applied in solving social problems. If I come to a new city, I am likely to get lost without a map. But once I obtain a street map, granted that I have earlier learned the general skill of map reading, I am well able to find my way around. At the metacognitive level I know that to locate streets and areas in a new city, I should get a city map and then read it.

Another example of metacognition is how we react to a problem that we find difficult to solve. We call it an interesting challenge; tell ourselves to go slowly; think of as many solutions as possible, without committing ourselves to any particular one; and carefully and without rushing test each of our alternatives.

The SPS approach might be criticized because it conveys the message that people *should* always strive to take effective action against any frustration or problem in order to gain control over it (e.g., Goldfried, 1980). To view one's world as full of challenges to be overcome might encourage the development of a Type A personality. D'Zurilla (1986, 1990) recently expanded the social problem-solving perspective to include "emotion-focused solutions," adapted from Richard Lazarus's (Lazarus & Folkman, 1984) classic work on cognition and stress. According to this view, if a situation is judged unchangeable or uncontrollable, a sensible approach to solving the problem is to change one's emotional reaction to it (by relaxing, for example) and thereby to adapt to the difficult environmental situation.

Multimodal Therapy

Multimodal therapy is a cognitive-behavioral approach proposed by Rutgers University psychologist Arnold Lazarus (1973, 1989), who broke with Wolpe in the late 1960s out of dissatisfaction with what he viewed as undue constraints that the behavioral paradigm placed on assessment and on the design of maximally effective psychotherapeutic interventions. Lazarus's basic premise is that people are a composite of seven dimensions, according to the acronym BASIC IB: Behavior, Affective processes, Sensations, Images, Cognitions, Interpersonal relationships, and Biological functions. Effective therapy, according to Lazarus, must designate problems in all or in some subset of these areas, decide the order in which problems should be treated, and then apply to each problem area the techniques that are best suited to it.

If, for example, a patient's duress seems to be triggered by aberrant thought processes, attention should focus on the C, for cognition, and procedures suggested by clinical and experimental research to be well-suited to altering how people think about things should be applied. But the first B, behavior, might itself be problematic and, although set in motion by an aberrant thought, might require specific attention in and of itself, for example, when a person has learned to act in ways that are not reinforced by his or her present environment.

For each patient, Lazarus draws up a Modality Profile, which helps him and the patient to see the areas that merit attention. In a sense, this scheme is similar to (and preceded by several years) the multiaxial system of the DSM, in that it is designed to draw attention to domains that are worthy of attention, basically *forcing* the clinician to focus on particular categories or areas. But the BASIC IB approach goes further in that Lazarus attempts to outline for each of the seven areas a range of procedures that can be effective.

So far Lazarus's approach fits easily into a general cognitive-behavioral framework. But he goes on to argue that the decision to use a given technique should be guided not by theoretical approach or school affiliation, rather by an open-minded consideration of the data. Given what we believe we know about how to change cognitions, for example, what techniques might be used to change the maladaptive beliefs of this particular client? If a technique from Gestalt therapy could be useful, then use it, he suggests. In this sense, Lazarus was one of the early principal figures in the psychotherapy integration movement, although he works at the technique level rather than, like Wachtel, attempting to integrate at a conceptual or theoretical level (see the last section of this chapter for a lively debate between Lazarus and Messer on Lazarus's borrowing of techniques from other approaches). Lazarus (1989, pp. 219–222) has reviewed research over the past twenty years in support both of the reliability of assessment within the BASIC IB framework and of the general effectiveness of the approach for helping people with a wide array of problems (Focus Box 19.2).

19.2 • Assertion Training

"Children should be seen and not heard." "Keep a stiff upper lip." "He's the strong silent type." Our society does not generally value the open expression of beliefs and feelings, and yet people seem to pay an emotional price for concealing their thoughts and suppressing their feelings. Peoples' wants and needs may not be met if they shy away from stating them clearly. As we have seen, poor communication between sexual partners is one of the major factors contributing to an unsatisfying sexual relationship. Therapists of all persuasions spend a good deal of time encouraging clients to discover what their desires and needs are and then to take responsibility for meeting them. If they have trouble expressing their feelings and wishes to others, assertion training, conducted individually or in groups (see page 598) may be able to help them.

Andrew Salter, in his book *Conditioned Reflex Therapy* (1949), was the first behavior therapist to set assertiveness as a positive goal for clients. Using Pavlovian, classical conditioning terms, Salter said that much human psychological suffering is caused by an excess of cortical inhibition; therefore greater excitation is warranted. He encouraged socially inhibited people to express their feelings to others in an open, spontaneous way. They should do so verbally, telling people when they are happy or sad, angry or resolute, and nonverbally, with smiles and frowns, what Salter called facial talk. They should also contradict people they disagree with, and with appropriate feeling; use the pronoun *I* as often as possible; express agreement with those who praise them; and improvise, that is, respond intuitively in the moment without ruminating. In helping clients to assert themselves, behavior therapists, whether they acknowledge it or not, are doing therapeutic work with goals similar to those of humanistic therapists, who also regard expression of positive and negative feelings as a necessary component of effective living.

How are we to define assertion? Might it not be inconsiderate to put ourselves forward and express our beliefs and feelings to others? What if we hurt someone else's feelings in doing so? Much effort has gone into articulating the differences between assertive behavior and aggressive behavior. A useful distinction was drawn by Lange and Jakubowski (1976); they consider assertion

> expressing thoughts, feelings, and beliefs in direct, honest, and appropriate ways which respect the rights of other people. In contrast, aggression involves self-expression which is characterized by violating others' rights and demeaning others in an attempt to achieve one's own objectives. (pp. 38–39)

People may be unassertive for any number of reasons. The specific therapy procedures chosen depend on the reasons believed to be causing the individual 's unassertiveness. Assertion training, then, is actually a set of different techniques, having in common the goal of enhancing assertiveness, or what Lazarus (1971) calls "emotional freedom." Goldfried and Davison (1976) suggested several factors that can underlie unassertiveness, one or more of which may be found in an unassertive individual.

1. The client may not know what to say. Some unassertive people lack information on what to say in situations that call for expressiveness. The therapist should supply this information.

Some Reflections on Cognitive Behavior Therapy

As we have indicated, behavior therapy initially aligned itself with the study of classical and operant conditioning, the assumption being that principles and procedures derived from conditioning experiments could be applied to lessen psychological suffering. This orientation came from behaviorists, such as Watson and Skinner, who had become dissatisfied with the work done on the contents of the mind and consciousness in Wundt's and Titchener's laboratories and with their use of introspection in these studies. What developed into cognitive behavior therapy (or cognitive therapy) may appear to be a radical and novel departure, given the earlier focus of behavior therapists on classical and operant

2. Clients may not know how to behave assertively. They may not assume the tone and volume of voice, the fluency of speech, the facial expression and eye contact, and the body posture necessary for assertiveness. Modeling and role-playing can help these people acquire the signals of firmness and directness.

3. Clients may fear that something terrible will happen if they assert themselves. Systematic desensitization may reduce this anticipatory anxiety. In others assertiveness seems to be blocked by negative self-statements, such as "If I assert myself and am rejected, that would be a catastrophe" (Schwartz & Gottman, 1976). These clients may profit from rational-emotive therapy.

4. The client may not feel that it is proper or right to be assertive. The value systems of some people preclude or discourage assertiveness. For example, some of the problems of a Catholic nun undergoing therapy seemed to relate to her unassertiveness, but through discussion it became clear that she would violate some of her vows were she more expressive and outspoken. By mutual agreement assertion training was not undertaken; instead, therapy focused on helping her work within her chosen profession in ways that were more personally satisfying and yet not more assertive.

Assertion training may begin with conversations in which the therapist tries to get the client to distinguish between assertiveness and aggression. For people who are submissive, even making a reasonable request or refusing a presumptuous one may make them feel that they are being hostile. Then therapists usually give clients sample situations that will leave them feeling put upon if they are unable to handle them. The situations usually require that they stand up for their rights, their time, and their energies.

> You have been studying very hard for weeks, taking no time off at all for relaxation. But now a new film, which will play for only a few days, interests you and you have decided to take a few hours and go late this evening to see it. On the way to an afternoon class, your very good friend tells you that she has free tickets to a concert this evening and asks you to go with her. How do you say no?

Behavior rehearsal is a useful technique in assertion training. The therapist discusses and models appropriate assertiveness and then has the client role-play situations. Improvement is rewarded by praise from the therapist or from other members of an assertion training group. Graded homework assignments, such as asking the mechanic to explain the latest bill for repairs, then telling a relative that his or her constant criticisms are resented, are given as soon as the client has acquired some degree of assertiveness through session work.

Assertion training raises several ethical issues. To encourage assertiveness in people who, like the nun mentioned earlier, believe that self-denial is a greater good than self-expression would violate the client's value system and could generate an unfavorable ripple effect in other areas of the person's life. Drawing a distinction between assertion and aggression is also an ethical issue. Behavior considered assertive by one person may be seen by another as aggressive. If we adopt the distinction made by Lange and Jakubowski, that assertion respects the rights of others whereas aggression does not, we still have to make a judgment about what the rights of others are. Thus assertion training touches on moral aspects of social living, namely, the definition of other people's rights and the proper means of standing up for one's own.

conditioning. But in a historical sense it actually represents a return to the cognitive foci of the earliest period of experimental psychology, and many experimental psychologists have continued through the years to do research into cognition—into the mental processes of perceiving, recognizing, conceiving, judging, and reasoning, of problem-solving, imagining, and other symbolizing activities.

Ellis and Beck try directly to change cognitive processes in order to relieve psychological distress. From the beginning, however, behavior therapists have relied heavily on the human being's capacity to symbolize, to process information, to represent the world in words and images. Wolpe's systematic desensitization is a clear example. This technique, believed by Wolpe to rest on conditioning principles, is inherently a cognitive procedure, for the client *imagines* what is fearful. Indeed, the most exciting overt behavioral event during a regimen of desensitization is the client's occasional signaling of anxiety by raising an index finger! If anything important is happening, it is surely going on under the skin, and some of this activity is surely cognitive.

As behavior therapy goes cognitive, however, it is important to bear in mind that many contemporary researchers continue to believe that behavioral *procedures* are more powerful than strictly verbal ones in affecting cognitive *processes* (Bandura, 1977). That is, they favor behavioral techniques while maintaining that it is important to alter a person's beliefs in order to effect an enduring change in behavior and emotion. Bandura suggests, in fact, that all therapeutic procedures, to the extent that they are effective, work their improvement by giving the person a sense of mastery, of self-efficacy. At the same time he finds that the most effective way to gain a sense of self-efficacy, if one is lacking, is by changing behavior. Whether or not we believe self-efficacy to be as important as Bandura does, a distinction can be made between processes that underlie improvement and *procedures* that set these processes in motion.

Cognitive behavior therapists continue to be behavioral in their use of performance-based procedures and in their commitment to behavioral change, but they are cognitive in the sense that they believe that cognitive change (e.g., enhanced self-efficacy) is an important mechanism that accounts for the effectiveness of at least some behavioral procedures. Indeed, cognition and behavior continually and reciprocally influence each other—new behavior can alter thinking, and that new mode of thinking can in turn facilitate the new behavior. In addition, the environment influences both thought and action and is influenced by them. The model, termed **triadic reciprocality** by Bandura (1986), highlights the close interrelatedness of thinking, behaving, and the environment.

But, as Salovey and Singer (1991) recently pointed out, Bandura's triadic reciprocality underemphasizes the concept of emotion. People have many cognitions that are affect-laden—sometimes referred to as "hot cognitions"—and these tend to relate to the self (Cantor et al., 1986), to one's dreams and fantasies, fondest hopes and direst fears, what Singer (1984) called the private personality. "The therapist must be alert to emotions that color the maladaptive cognitions that are traditionally the focus of treatment. Even though feelings often also arise as a consequence of cognition, it may still be possible to alter maladaptive cognitions by first assessing and then intervening at the level of feelings" (Salovey & Singer, 1991, p. 366). Both clinical observations (Greenberg & Safran, 1984) and experimental findings (e.g., Snyder & White, 1982) point to the importance of emotion in personality and should be included more systematically in cognitive-behavioral conceptions of disorder and treatment.

All cognitive behavior therapists heed the mental processes of their clients in another way. They pay attention to the world as it is perceived by the client. It is not what impinges on us from the outside that controls our behavior, the assumption that has guided behavioral psychology for decades. Rather our feelings and behavior are determined by how we view the world. The Greek philosopher Epictetus stated in the first century: "Men are disturbed not by things, but by the view they take of them." Thus cognitive behavior therapy is being brought closer to the humanistic and existential therapies reviewed in Chapter 18. A central thesis of experiential therapists, like Rogers and Perls, is that clients must be understood from their own frame of rerference, from their phenomenological world, for it is this experience of the world that controls life and behavior.

From the philosophical point of view, such assumptions on the part of those who would understand people and try to help them are profoundly important. Experimentally minded clinicians and researchers are intrigued by how much the new field of cognitive behavior therapy has in common with the experientialists and their attention to the phenomenological world of their clients. To be sure, the *techniques* used by cognitive behavior therapists are usually quite different from those of the followers of Rogers and Perls. But as students of psychotherapy and of human nature, these surface differences should not blind us to the links between the two approaches. Further discussion of integration among diverse therapeutic modalities is found at the end of this chapter.

Behavioral Medicine

Behavioral medicine is "the interdisciplinary field concerned with the development of behavioral and biomedical science, knowledge, and techniques relevant to the understanding of health and illness, and the application of this knowledge and these techniques to prevention, diagnosis, treatment, and rehabilitation" (Society of Behavioral Medicine, 1989, p. 1). What is noteworthy about this definition—and what clearly reflects the nature of the field—is that the approach is *interdisciplinary*, drawing on the knowledge and skills of a variety of researchers and practitioners, including psychologists, psychiatrists, nonpsychiatric physicians, nurses, and social workers, who bring to the analysis and treatment of health-related behaviors their own particular perspective and expertise and often collaborate with one another on such diseases as essential hypertension and coronary heart disease (Chapter 8), the problems of seriously ill children (Chapter 15), substance abuse (Chapter 11), and AIDS (Chapter 13). Indeed, the 1980s and 1990s have seen increasing recognition by the federal government that illnesses hitherto regarded as strictly medical have important psychological components and that a key to addressing the medical health crisis in the United States and elsewhere lies in altering people's thoughts and behaviors relevant to maintaining health and treating illness (Department of Health and Human Services, 1990).

Behavioral medicine is not restricted to a set of techniques or particular principles of changing behavior. Rather, workers in this field employ a wide variety of procedures—from contingency management through operant conditioning, to desensitization through counterconditioning, and a variety of cognitive-behavioral approaches—all of which have in common the goal of altering bad living habits, distressed psychological states, and aberrant physiological processes in order to have a beneficial impact on a person's physical condition. A sampling of three important areas of behavioral medicine—the management of pain, chronic diseases and lifestyle, and biofeedback—will convey an even better sense of the scope of this emerging multidisciplinary field of research and treatment.

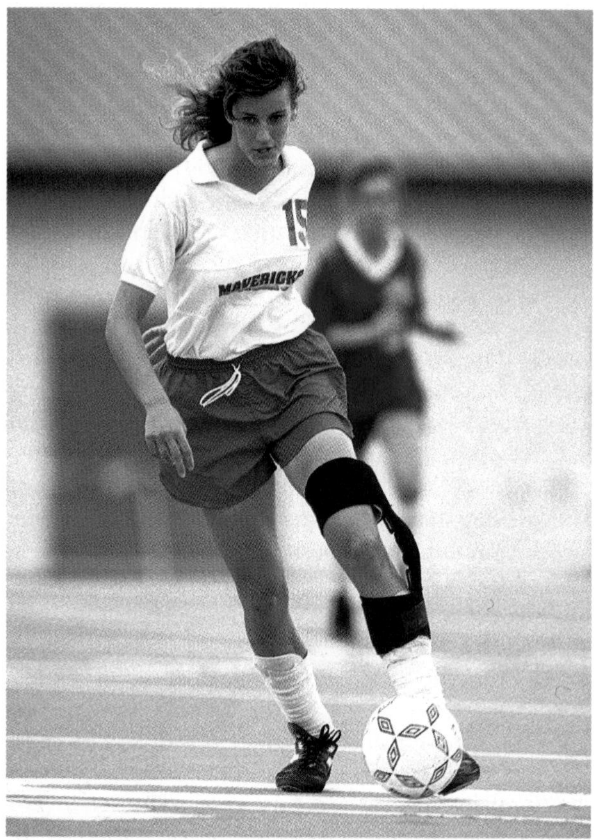

The ability to continue playing soccer despite a painful injury is an example of how distraction reduces the experience of pain. Distraction is used systematically in pain-management programs.

The Management of Pain[5]

Like anxiety, pain can be adaptive. People with congenital inability to feel pain are at an extreme disadvantage, indeed, are at serious risk for injury. Imagine how dangerous it would be if you could not feel pain from contact with a hot stove or a sharp knife. Our concern here is with pain that is *mal*adaptive, pain that is out of proportion to the situation and unduly restricts a person's capacity for meaningful and productive living.

We know enough about pain to appreciate the fact that there is no one-to-one relationship between a stimulus that is capable of triggering the experience of pain, referred to as nociceptive stimulation, and the actual sensation of pain. Soldiers in combat, for example, can be wounded by a bullet and yet be so involved in their efforts to survive and inflict harm on the enemy that they do not feel any pain until later. This well-known fact tells us something important about pain even as it hints at ways of controlling it: if one is *distracted* from a nociceptive stimulus, one may not experience pain or at least not as much of it as when one attends to the stimulation (Turk, Meichenbaum, & Genest, 1983). The importance of distraction in controlling pain, both acute and chronic, is consistent with research in experimental cognitive psychology; each person has only a limited supply of attentional resources such that attention to one channel of input blocks the processing of input in other channels (Kahneman, 1973). This human limitation can thus be seen as a positive benefit when it comes to the experience of pain. In addition to distraction, other factors that reduce pain are lowered anxiety, feelings of optimism and control (Geer et al., 1970), and a sense that what one is engaged in has meaning and purpose (Gatchel et al., 1989; Gendlin, 1962).

[5]This section on pain is based on Davison and Darke (1991).

Acute Pain

Psychologists have contributed to our understanding of both acute and chronic pain. Acute pain is linked to nociception. Chronic pain can evolve from acute pain and refers to pain that is experienced after the time for healing has passed, when there is little reason to assume that nociception is still present.

The importance of a sense of personal control in dealing with acute pain is readily seen in situations where the patient is allowed to administer his or her own painkillers (with a preset upper limit). Compared with the more common hospital situation, where a patient has to ask a nurse for pain medication, it has been found that patients who control the administration of the medication experience greater relief from pain and even use less analgesic medication (White, 1986). It is significant that this patient-controlled analgesia reduces pain even though it requires the person to focus on it, something that goes against the well-documented benefits of distraction. Apparently the positive effects of control outweigh the negative consequences of focusing on the pain.

Of course, relying on a nurse to administer pain medication also causes the patient to focus on the pain, perhaps even more so than when the patient administers the drug. With nurse-administered analgesia, the patient learns to wait until the pain is substantial before requesting medication; then, after making the request, the patient usually waits until the nurse has time to fulfill it. This system obviously does not enhance distraction from the pain!

Patients allowed to administer their own pain killers use less medication and experience more relief from pain.

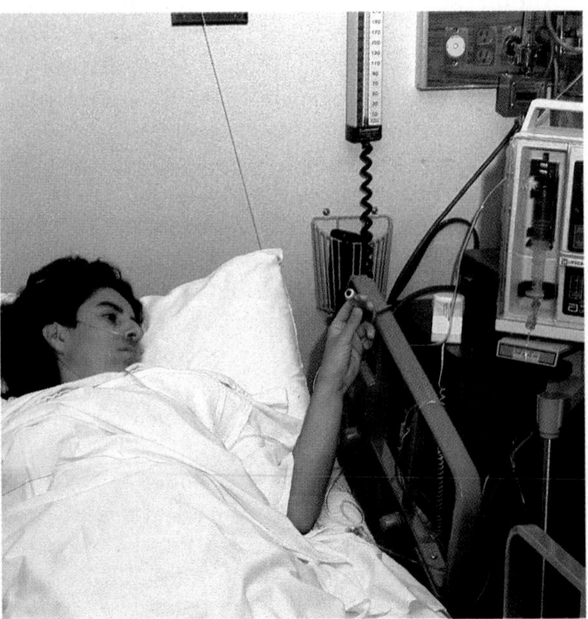

Chronic Pain

Chronic pain is the lot of millions of Americans (Bonica, 1981), accounting for millions of dollars of lost work time and incalculable personal and familial suffering. Traditional medical treatments seldom help with this kind of pain. To understand chronic pain, it is useful to distinguish between pain per se, that is, the perception of nociceptive stimulation (as we have just seen in acute pain) and *suffering* and *pain behaviors*. Suffering refers to the emotional response to nociception and can be present even in the absence of pain, as when a loved one leaves a person. Pain behaviors—chronic pain—refer to observable behaviors associated with either pain or with suffering; examples include moaning, clenching teeth, irritability, and avoidance of activity (Turk, Wack, & Kerns, 1985). The treatment of chronic pain, therefore, focuses on suffering and pain behaviors rather than on whether the person is actually experiencing pain. The emphasis is on toughing it out, working through the pain rather than allowing oneself to be incapacitated by it. If handled properly, the result is often increased activity and function that can sometimes even reduce the actual experience of pain.

A well-researched example of chronic pain is back pain caused by severe muscle spasms. Initially, the person is unable to engage in activity any more vigorous than getting in and out of bed. In the acute phase this is sensible behavior. As the spasms ease, and if no other damage has occurred, such as to the disks between the vertebrae, the patient should begin moving more normally, stretching, and eventually attempting exercises to strengthen the very muscles that went into spasm. Fordyce and his colleagues (Fordyce et al., 1986) showed the superiority of a behavioral over a traditional medical program for management of back pain. In the traditional program patients exercised and otherwise moved about only until they felt pain, whereas the behavioral management program encouraged them to exercise at a predetermined intensity for a predetermined period of time, even if they experienced pain. Low back pain patients have also been given relaxation training and encouraged to relabel their pain as numbness or tickling (Rybstein-Blinchik, 1979), a cognitive-restructuring procedure. Obviously care must be taken not to push patients beyond activities their bodies are actually ready for. The implicit message seems to be that traditional medical practice has underestimated what chronic pain patients are capable of (Keefe & Gil, 1986). Indeed, a frequent outcome is that increased activity improves muscle tone, which can itself reduce nociception over time and even reduce the likelihood of future recurrences of muscle spasms.

Chronic Diseases and Life-style

Behavioral medicine is concerned not only with alleviation of illness and pain but with their prevention; when it has this purpose, it is often called **health psychology**. At the beginning of this century, the leading causes of death were infectious diseases, such as influenza and tuberculosis. In the 1980s, with these illnesses largely under medical control, Americans succumbed most often to heart diseases, cancer, cerebrovascular diseases, such as stroke, and accidents. For each of these diseases the behavior of people over their lifetime—their life-style—is implicated. We have already seen in Chapter 8 that, along with Type A personality, a diet high in cholesterol, lack of exercise, and smoking contribute to heart disease.

Physicians have for years been dispensing sound advice about diet, exercise, and smoking, usually with little effect on life-style. Getting people to do what is in the best interest of their health is a challenge! Merely telling a sedentary accountant to exercise for at least fifteen minutes three times a week at 70 percent of maximum heart rate will probably not rouse him or her to adhere to such a schedule.

In one study (Epstein et al., 1980) female college students agreed that they would run one to two miles a day for five weeks and made a five-dollar deposit, which was returned to them a dollar at a time as they complied. These young women ran more consistently than those in a control group who had no contingency. A number of similar programs for encouraging regular exercise have also been reported. Of particular interest was the posting of a cartoon at the base of a public stairway and escalator (Brownwell, Stunkard, & Albaum, 1980). It portrayed a glum, unhealthy-looking heart taking the escalator, next to a robust, happy heart bounding up a flight of stairs; the caption read, "Your heart needs exercise . . . here's your chance." Simple and inexpensive, the cartoon effected a dramatic change in people passing that way: three times as many used the stairs as had been observed earlier. Stairs are of course far more available than aerobics exercise sessions, and climbing them is easier than instituting a jogging regimen. Regular stair use is known to be a very healthful cardiovascular exercise for people throughout their lives.

Many industries and corporations now maintain their own health and fitness programs, screening their employees for such illnesses as hypertension and providing facilities and incentives for taking regular exercise, even during work hours. More than magnanimity is operating here; such programs often reduce absenteeism and improve health generally, making them cost-effective for the company.

Biofeedback

A visit to the commercial exhibit area of any psychological or psychiatric convention will reveal a plentiful display of complex biofeedback apparatus, touted as an efficient, even miraculous, means of helping people control one or another bodily-mental state. Basically, by using sensitive instrumentation, **biofeedback** gives a person prompt and exact information, otherwise unavailable, on muscle

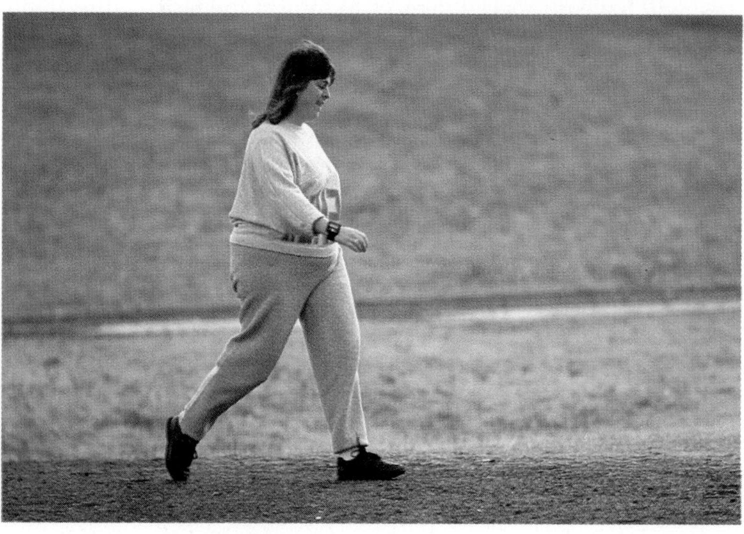

Exercise is an important aspect of life-style that is related to health. The application of contingencies can yield life-style changes.

activity, brain waves, skin temperature, heart rate, blood pressure, and other bodily functions. It is assumed that a person can achieve greater voluntary control over these phenomena—most of which were once considered to be under involuntary control and completely unresponsive to will—if he or she knows immediately, through an auditory or visual signal, whether a somatic activity is increasing or decreasing. Because anxiety has generally been viewed as a state involving the autonomic (involuntary) nervous system, and because psychophysiological disorders afflict organs innervated by this system, it is obvious why researchers and clinicians became intrigued with biofeedback. Indeed, biofeedback was for a time virtually synonymous with behavioral medicine.

In a series of studies at Harvard Medical School, Shapiro, Tursky, and Schwartz (1970; Schwartz, 1973) demonstrated that human volunteers could achieve significant short-term changes in blood pressure and in heart rate. They found that some subjects could even be trained to increase their heart rate while decreasing blood pressure. Achievement of this fine-grained control lent impetus to biofeedback work with human beings and awakened hope that certain clinical disorders might be alleviated in this new way.

In the move from analogue to the more challenging world of the clinic, at least three vital questions must be asked. First, can persons whose systems are *malfunctioning* achieve the same biofeedback control over bodily events that normal subjects can acquire? Second, if actual patients can achieve some degree of control, will it be enough to make a significant difference in their problems? And third, can the control achieved by patients hooked up to and receiving immediate feedback from a remarkable apparatus be carried over to real-life situations in which they will have no special devices to inform them of the state of the bodily functions that they have learned to control?

Research with patients suffering from essential hypertension has been somewhat encouraging, but results have not been certain enough to establish biofeedback as a standard treatment for the problem (Shapiro & Surwit, 1979). Moreover, some (Blanchard et al., 1979) believe that relaxation training, which is often given along with biofeedback, does more to reduce blood pressure than the biofeedback itself, a conclusion drawn in reviews by Emmelkamp (1986), O'Leary and Wilson (1987), and Reed, Katkin, and Goldband (1986).

The control of migraine headache by biofeedback was reviewed in Chapter 8 (page 216). Tension headaches, believed to be caused by excessive and persistent tension in the frontalis muscles of the forehead and in the muscles of the neck, have also been handled within this framework, the standard treatment entailing feedback of tension in the frontalis muscles. Although such biofeedback has indeed been shown to be effective (e.g., Birbaumer, 1977), some studies suggest that cognitive factors may play a role. For example, Holroyd et al. (1984) found that *believing* that one was reducing frontalis tension via biofeedback was associated with reductions in tension headaches, whether or not such reductions were actually being achieved. Enhanced feelings of self-efficacy and internal control appear to have inherent stress-reducing properties, a theme encountered in Chapter 6 when we discussed control and anxiety. It is possible that biofeedback strengthens the sense of control, thereby reducing general anxiety levels and ultimately tension headaches. Other studies (e.g., Blanchard et al., 1982; Cox, Freundlich, & Meyer, 1975) suggest that relaxation per se is the critical variable, similar to the beliefs about treating essential hypertension.

Attempts have also been made to alleviate other medical problems with biofeedback, with mixed success. Increasing finger temperature, which dilates the blood vessels in the hands, has been found somewhat useful in helping people with Raynaud's disease, in which blood flow to the extremities is reduced by spasms of small peripheral arteries (Surwit, 1982). But since relaxation is also typically employed along with biofeedback (a common practice in many kinds of biofeedback studies), it is far from clear whether the biofeedback itself was critical (Reed, Katkin, & Goldband, 1986). Biofeedback has also been used to increase and enhance muscular control in such neuromuscular disorders as cerebral palsy and poststroke paralysis (Basmajian, 1977). If a neuromuscular dysfunction is caused in part by the faintness of the signs of muscle movement in damaged tissue, then amplifying these proprioceptive signals by biofeedback might make the patient aware of them and possibly allow control (Runck, 1980).

For the most part, there is only limited evidence that biofeedback has any specific effects other than distraction, relaxation, and instilling a beneficial sense of control. In addition, clinicians must remain mindful of the complexities of human problems. A person with high blood pressure, for example, might have to alter a tense, driven life-style before he or she can significantly reduce blood pressure through biofeedback. It is unwise, and a sign of naive clinical practice, to assume that one technique focused on a specific malfunction or problem will invariably cure the patient.

Generalization and Maintenance of Treatment Effects

As we have indicated, generalizing to real life and maintaining whatever gains have been achieved in therapy is a problem common to all treatments. Insight therapists assume that therapeutic effects are made more general through restructuring of the personality. Looking a good deal to the environment for factors that affect people, behavior therapists wonder how therapeutic changes can be made to persist once clients return to their everyday situations, which are often assumed to have been a factor in creating their problems in the first place! This challenge has been addressed in several ways.

Intermittent Reinforcement

Because laboratory findings indicate that intermittent reinforcement—rewarding a response only a portion of the times it appears—makes new behavior more enduring, many operant programs take care to move away from continuous schedules of reinforcement once desired behavior is occurring with satisfactory regularity. For example, if a teacher has succeeded in helping a disruptive child spend more time sitting down by praising the child generously for each arithmetic problem finished while seated, the teacher will gradually reward the child for every other success, and ultimately only infrequently.

Another strategy is to move from artificial reinforcers to those that occur naturally in the social environment. A token program might be maintained only long enough to encourage certain desired behavior, after which the person is weaned to natural reinforcers, such as praise from peers.

Environmental Modification

Another strategy for bringing about generalization takes the therapist into the province of community psychology, which will be discussed in the next chapter. Behavior therapists manipulate surroundings, or attempt to do so, to support changes brought about in treatment. For example, Lovaas and his colleagues (1973) found that the gains painstakingly achieved in therapy for autistic children were sustained only when their parents continued to reinforce their good behavior.

Eliminating Secondary Gain

Most behavior therapists assign their clients homework tasks to do between sessions. For example, clients may be asked to listen to audiotapes containing relaxation-training instructions. They sometimes fail to follow through in a consistent fashion, however, complaining of not having enough quiet time at home to listen to the tapes, or saying that they forgot about the assignment. Many patients are so resistant to doing on their own what they consciously and rationally agree is in their best interests that therapists often invoke as an explanation the psychoanalytic concept of secondary gain, that the patient derives benefit from his or her problem. For complex and poorly understood reasons people sometimes act as though they unconsciously wish to keep their symptoms. Therapists, whatever their persuasion, may have to examine the client's interpersonal relationships for clues to why a person suffering directly from a problem seems to prefer to hold on to it (Focus Box 19.3).

Relapse Prevention

Marlatt (1985) proposed the "abstinence violation effect" as a focus of concern in relapse prevention. His research on alcoholism sensitized him to the generally negative effects of a slip, as when a former drinker, after a successful period of abstinence, imbibes to a stupor after taking a single drink. Marlatt suggested that the ways the person reacts both cognitively and behaviorally to the slip determines whether he or she will overcome the setback and stay on the wagon or relapse and resume drinking to excess. The consequences of the slip are hypothesized to be worse if the person attributes it to internal, stable, and global factors believed to be uncontrollable—in much the same way that Abramson, Seligman, and Teasdale (1978) theorized about helplessness and depression (see page 234). An example would be a belief that the lapse was caused by an uncontrollable disease process that overwhelms the person once a single drink is taken. In contrast, relapse is assumed to be less likely if the individual attributes the slip to causes that are external, unstable, specific, and controllable, such as an unexpectedly stressful life event. In essence, the client is encouraged to distinguish between a lapse and relapse. Cognitive behavior therapists attempt to minimize the abstinence violation effect by encouraging attributions to external, unstable, and specific factors *and* by teaching strategies for coping with life stressors.

FOCUS

19.3 • You're Changed If You Do and Changed If You Don't

Have you ever tried to persuade a friend to do something by asking him or her not to do it? Intuition tells us that this sneaky ploy might be effective when a person is spiteful or doesn't like to be controlled by others. The thinking of such an individual might be as follows: "So, he wants me to continue arriving late, huh? I'll show him—I'll start arriving *early*!"

Over the past twenty-five years, since the publication of *Pragmatics of Human Communication*, a book by Watzlawick, Beavin, and Jackson (1967) on complex communication and interaction, a small but committed number of psychotherapists have been drawn to what have come to be called paradoxical interventions. These attempts to effect change have in common a request or prescription by the therapist for the client to continue the problem or to increase its severity or frequency. Thus, if a client cannot go to sleep, he or she is asked to *remain awake.* If a client cannot stop thinking of a disturbing event, he or she is asked to think of it *more often.* If a client becomes anxious for no apparent reason, the client is asked to *make himself or herself anxious.* Clinical reports from enthusiasts of the approach suggest that at least some clients benefit from such counterintuitive efforts (e.g., Frankl, 1967; Seltzer, 1986; Shoham-Salomon & Rosenthal, 1987), but only recently have paradoxical interventions been studied experimentally (e.g., Asher & Turner, 1979).

An example is the program of research of Shoham-Salomon and her co-workers at the University of Arizona. They postulate two mechanisms that could account for the beneficial changes reported clinically for some clients: reactance and increase in self-efficacy. Reactance refers to a motivational state aroused when people perceive that their range of freedom is being limited; they then make efforts to restore their freedom (Brehm & Brehm, 1981). Thus, a reactant client, when asked by the therapist to become more anxious, will see this symptom prescription as an infringement of freedom and will protect himself or herself from this perceived threat by becoming *less* anxious. The second mechanism proposed by Shoham-Salomon, this one underlying the response of *non*reactant patients to a paradoxical directive, is Bandura's (1986) concept of self-efficacy, the sense that one is capable of performing a desired behavior. In the context of psychotherapy this would entail gaining control over one's problem. Bandura's research suggests that self-efficacy is enhanced when people have successful experiences. Thus, if a nonreactant client given a paradoxical directive does in fact follow it, for example, increases his or her anxiety, the short-term outcome for this patient is not symptom reduction, as with the reactant client, but cognitive change, namely, a belief that he or she is not helpless and can in fact exert some control over the previously uncontrollable problem (even if the control leads to something that is opposite to what the person really wants). The implication is promising: if patients can make themselves worse, then maybe they can make themselves better.

Thus, both kinds of clients are expected to change in positive ways from paradoxical treatment, but for different reasons and at different times. The reactant client is expected to change rather quickly because he or she is defying the therapist's directive. In contrast, the nonreactant client is expected not to change behaviorally right away; instead the groundwork is laid for later behavioral change via an increase in self-efficacy. This type of person will not improve in the short term, but will construe his or her symptomatic behavior as more controllable and may improve later on.

These predictions were confirmed in two studies of college students suffering from procrastination, as reported in an article by Shoham-Salomon, Avner, and Neeman (1989), part of the title of which appears as the title of this focus box. First, they divided their subjects into reactant and nonreactant groups, using procedures that detected spitefulness in tone of voice. Then the experimenters had the subjects undergo one of two

Self-Reinforcement

Generalization can also be enhanced by assigning the client a more active role, as done by Drabman, Spitalnik, and O'Leary (1973). In a three-month after-school program for disruptive young boys, the teacher rewarded nondisruptive classroom behavior and appropriate reading behavior. Later the boys were allowed to self-rate their behavior according to the teacher's criteria and reward their treatments, each conducted for two weekly sessions. In the *paradoxical intervention*, the therapist explained to the subjects that they needed to understand their procrastination problem better and become more aware of it. To this end, they were to observe the problem carefully by trying to procrastinate deliberately. Subjects were instructed to gather all their study materials on their desks but not to study for half an hour, to resist any impulse to study, and to concentrate on procrastinating, for example, by ruminating about the problem as they usually did when procrastination occurred normally. *Studying at these times was not permitted.* If they succeeded in this unusual observation task for six days, then on the seventh day they could either study or not study, as they wished and whenever they wished. At the second therapy session, subjects discussed this assignment. Those who were able to do it were congratulated and reminded that their not studying had allowed them to better understand their problem and therefore to begin to deal with it. If a subject reported having studied *more*, he or she was not praised; in fact, the change was regarded with skepticism by the therapist as probably only temporary. And if subjects did not schedule procrastination time, the therapist exhorted them to try it again in the coming week.* Above all, subjects were not encouraged to procrastinate less or study more.

The contrasting intervention was one of *self-control.* Procrastination was described to the subjects as a learned habit; the subjects needed to develop new behaviors incompatible with procrastination. They were directed to select a place in which they could study more effectively and to try to study as much as possible there, the idea being that these new stimulus conditions would become associated with improved study habits. Any reported successes were praised by the therapist.

Results showed that study time as well as self-efficacy were improved via both treatments, but the really interesting results concern interactions between reactance and treatment modality. Higher reactance was correlated with improvement in study habits (less procrastination) in the paradoxical but not the self-control group, as expected. Thus, subjects who were motivated to restore freedom that they saw as being threatened engaged in behavior that went against the instructions of the therapist—told to study less, they studied more. This contrariness was not found among reactant subjects in the self-control condition. As for self-efficacy, increases were correlated with better studying in the self-control condition, consistent with many findings that show a link between behavioral improvement and self-efficacy (Bandura, 1986); *but* this link was not found in the paradoxical treatment group, where increases in self-efficacy were associated with *lack of behavioral change*, as predicted. The findings from this mixed-design study (reactance was a correlational variable embedded in an experimental design, cf, page 124) were replicated in a second experiment.

Further research with more clinically disturbed subjects and with long follow-ups needs to be conducted, and Shoham-Salomon and her colleagues are engaged in such efforts. But these two analogue experiments provide strong empirical support for the idea that, for some people, telling them *not* to change their problematic behaviors may be more effective than, as is usually done, encouraging them to work directly on behavioral changes.

A number of important issues are raised by the success of paradoxical interventions. Do some treatments or therapists arouse more reactance in patients than others? Is reactance fairly stable and traitlike in people (Beutler, 1979), or is it more situational in nature, aroused by particular social influence efforts (Brehm & Brehm, 1981)? Are changes brought about by paradoxical maneuvers as stable as those effected by less indirect procedures? Does trust in the therapist suffer if the patient comes to realize that the therapist is saying one thing but intending another? Can the problems that all therapies have with compliance be addressed more effectively by studying therapeutic paradoxes?

*An interesting problem arises in paradoxical therapy when a reactant patient defies the therapist's directive to exacerbate a problem behavior. One might label this "meta-defiance." If one is not careful, one can get caught in an infinite regress!

own good conduct. That is, the pupils were taught that they could earn special privileges not only by behaving well when the teacher dispensed rewards but through honest evaluation of their own good behavior. The findings for the first part of the study were similar to those of many other studies: problem behavior decreased and academic behavior improved when the teacher judged them and dispensed the tokens. This improvement then generalized to periods of each class during which the

FOCUS 19.4 • Self-Control—Outside a Behavioral Paradigm?

Operant research and theory seem to assume that the human being is a relatively passive recipient of stimulation from the environment. Given this apparent dependence on the external world, how can we account for behavior that appears to be autonomous, willed, and often contrary to what might be expected in a particular situation? How, for example, do we account for the fact that a person on a diet refrains from eating a luscious piece of chocolate cake even when hungry?

Psychoanalytic writers, including ego analysts, handle the issue by positing within the person some kind of internal agent. Thus many ego analysts assert that the ego can operate on its own power, making deliberate decisions for the entire psychic system—including decisions that go against the wishes of the id. Behaviorists, especially Skinner (1953), have objected to this explanation, regarding it as simply a relabeling of the phenomenon.

Perhaps the most widely accepted behavioral view of self-control is Skinner's: an individual engages in self-control when he or she arranges the environment so that only certain controlling stimuli are present. A person wishing to lose weight rids the house of fattening foods and avoids passing restaurants when hungry. Behavior remains a function of the surroundings, but they are controlled by the individual.

A related behavioral conception of self-control is reflected in Bandura's (1969) explanation of aversive conditioning. Rather than being passively conditioned to feel distaste for stimuli that have been paired with shock, a person learns a skill of aversive self-stimulation that he or she deliberately applies in real life. According to this view, a person resists a temptation by *deliberately* recalling the earlier aversive experience of being shocked or nauseated during therapy. Here, then, the individual is said to create symbolic stimuli that, in turn, control behavior.

A familiar means of exercising self-control, also discussed in the behavior therapy literature, is setting standards for oneself and denying oneself reinforcement unless they are met (Bandura & Perloff, 1967). One example is a tactic often employed by the authors of this book: I will not leave this desk for a snack until I have finished writing this page. When a person sets goals, makes a contract with himself or herself about achieving them before enjoying a reward, and then keeps to the contract without obvious external constraints, that person can be said to have exercised self-control.

Self-control can be applied with *any* therapy technique. The only stipulation is that the client implement the procedure on his or her own, after receiving instructions from the therapist. For example, a client who was being desensitized decided on his own to imagine some of the hierarchy scenes while relaxing in a warm tub. A sophisticated and intelligent man, he felt that he understood the rationale of desensitization well enough and had enough control over the processes of his imagination to meet the procedural requirements of the technique. Consequently, after achieving what he felt to be a state of deep relaxation in the bathtub, he closed his eyes and carried out the scene presentation and scene termination as he had learned to do from the behavior therapist. Later, when he was with the therapist, they were able to skip the items to which he had desensitized himself in the tub and proceed more rapidly through the anxiety hierarchy.

Implicit in all concepts of self-control are three criteria: (1) there are *few external controls* that could explain the behavior; (2) control of self is difficult enough that the person has to *put forth*

child *himself judged* how well he was doing and *reinforced himself* accordingly; in other words, improved performance was extended to periods of time when the pupils were not under direct external control (see Focus Box 19.4).

Attribution to Self

Attribution, a subject usually studied by social psychologists, may offer insight on how to maintain treatment gains once therapy is over. How people explain to themselves why they are behaving or have behaved in a particular way presumably helps determine their subsequent actions. Might not a person who has been in therapy and attributes improvement in behavior to an external cause, such as the therapist, lose ground once what that person considers the external justification for change is gone?

In an analogue study on attribution and maintaining a change in behavior (Davison & Valins, 1969), college undergraduates were shocked on their fingertips to determine how much they could bear. Then they took a "fast-acting vitamin com-

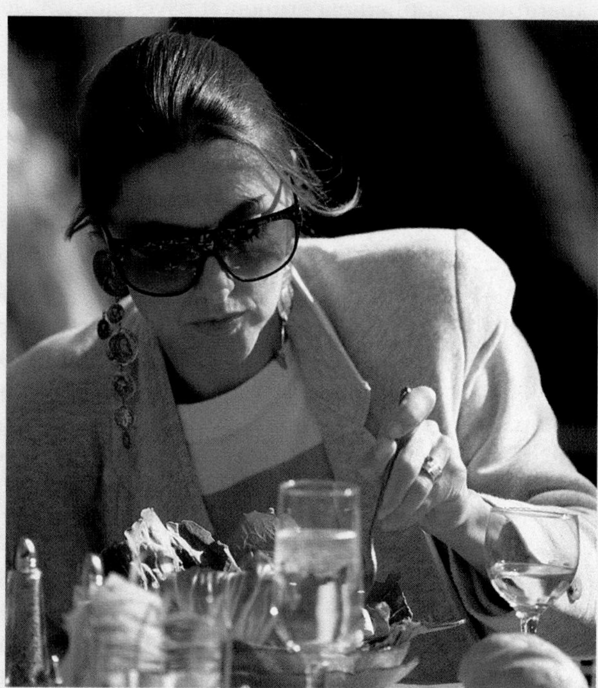

Self-control, as illustrated by dieting, is difficult to explain within a behavioral paradigm.

some effort; and (3) the behavior in question is engaged in with *conscious deliberation and choice.* The individual actively decides to exercise self-control either by performing some action or by keeping himself or herself from doing something, such as overeating. The person does not do it automatically, and is not forced by someone else to take action.

Let us take the example of a male jogger. If an army sergeant is goading the jogger along, the first criterion is not met and the running is not an instance of self-control, even though considerable effort is probably required to maintain it.

If the jogger finds it pleasurable to run, so enjoyable that he would rather do so than engage in other activities, the running cannot be considered an instance of self-control. Self-control is to be seen only in the *earliest* stages of jogging, when the man may indeed be exerting great effort. He groans as he dons his Nikes, looks at his watch after only a few minutes of running to see how long this torture has been going on, and collapses in relief after half a mile, glad that the ordeal is over.

The third criterion, acting with conscious deliberation and choice, distinguishes self-control from actions people perform in a mindless way. It is probably a good thing that much of our everyday behavior is mindless, for imagine how fatiguing (and boring!) it would be to mull over and make specific decisions to do such things as tie our shoelaces. But these very acts would be categorized as instances of self-control if, on a given occasion, we have to decide whether to engage in them. Eating would require self-control if we were on a strict diet and had agreed, with our partner, or doctor, or self, to reduce caloric intake.

In our opinion, the concept of self-control places a strain on the behavioristic paradigm, for people are described as acting independently, putting forth effort, deliberating and choosing. Each of these verbs supposes the person to be an *initiator* of action, as the place where control *begins.* Ardent behaviorists, though, will counter by asserting with Skinner that our view of the person as an initiator only indicates our ignorance of the external forces that ultimately control behavior. Thus the person who denies himself an extra dessert is not really controlling the self; rather this self-denial is controlled by some subtle reward unappreciated by the observer or by a distant reinforcer, such as being able later on to wear clothes of a smaller size. The flaw in this line of reasoning is that it is purely *post hoc* and irrefutable. We can *always* assert that, down the road, there will arrive the reinforcer that sustains the behavior. Such an explanation should be as unsatisfactory to the behaviorist as the psychoanalyst's *post hoc* invocation of an unconscious defense mechanism to account for an action.

pound'' (actually an inert placebo) and were told that they would be able to endure greater amounts of shock. And indeed they were, at least in their own minds. The experimenters had surreptitiously lowered the voltage levels to create this belief. Half the subjects were then told that the capsule ingested was only a placebo, the others that its effects would soon wear off. Those who believed that they had taken a placebo attributed to themselves the greater ability to withstand discomfort and endured higher levels of shock on the third test. Those who believed that they had been given a real drug that was no longer effective were in the third round able to endure only lesser amounts of shock, mirroring findings with most psychoactive drugs.

In an experiment with a similar design, conducted with people who were having trouble falling asleep, Davison, Tsujimoto, and Glaros (1973) obtained comparable results, indicating that real problems may be treated by helping patients attribute improvements to themselves. Individuals attempting to reduce smoking (Chambliss & Murray, 1979; Colletti & Kopel, 1979) and lose weight (Jeffrey, 1974) have similarly benefited from attributing gains to their own efforts and changes in attitudes rather than to external forces. In a series of nonbehavior therapy outcome studies from the Johns Hopkins Psychotherapy Research Unit, patients who attributed their gains to a drug did not maintain their improvement as much as did those who construed their changes as arising from their own efforts (Frank, 1976).

What are the implications of attribution research? Since in behavior therapy much improvement seems to be controlled by environmental forces, especially therapy relying on operant manipulation, it might be wise for behavior therapists to help their clients to feel more responsible. By encouraging an "I did it" attitude, perhaps by motivating them to practice new skills and to expose themselves to challenging situations, therapists may help their clients be less dependent on therapy and therapist and better maintain their treatment gains. Insight therapies have always emphasized the desirability of patients' assuming primary responsibility for their improvement. Behavior therapists have eventually realized that they must come to grips with the issue (Bandura, 1977; Mischel, 1977). On a more general level, the question of attributing improvement underscores the importance of cognitive processes in behavior therapy.

Some Basic Issues in Cognitive and Behavior Therapies

Cognitive and behavior therapies are expanding each year; with such a proliferation of activity, everyone concerned should remain aware of problems and issues that transcend particular experimental findings. The following considerations, many alluded to earlier, need to be kept clearly in mind.

Internal Behavior and Cognition

In Chapter 5, we demonstrated that the inference of intervening processes and other explanatory fictions is useful in interpreting data and generating fruitful hypotheses. Behavior therapists are often thought to hold only the radical behavioristic positions of Watson and Skinner, that it is not useful or legitimate to make inferences about internal processes of the organism.

The position we share with others (e.g., Bandura, 1986; Mahoney, 1974; Mischel, 1968) is that behavior therapy, as applied experimental psychology, is legitimately concerned with internal as well as external events, provided that the internal mediators are securely anchored to observable stimuli or responses. The cognitive therapies certainly illustrate this situation.

Unconscious Factors

With the growing interest in cognitive factors, cognitive therapists have begun to focus their assessments and interventions on internal mediators that lie outside the patient's awareness, that is, that are unconscious (Bowers & Meichenbaum, 1984; Mahoney, 1993). Ellis, for example, assumes that people are distressed by one or more beliefs he designates as irrational—even though a patient seldom states the problem in such terms. Rather, based on what the patient says and how the patient says it, and working from rational-emotive theory, Ellis may infer the operation of a belief such as "It is a dire necessity that I be perfect in everything I do." He then persuades the patient to accept the notion that this belief underlies the problems. Therapy is directed at altering that belief of which the patient may well have been unaware earlier. Although he tends to work more slowly and inductively than Ellis, Beck infers similar beliefs, which he called negative schemata or dysfunctional assumptions.

This is an interesting turn of events for an approach that developed in the 1950s out of a rejection of conceptualizations that utilized the notion of unconscious motivation and thought! And yet it is consistent with decades of research by experimental cognitive psychologists, who infer sets, beliefs, attitudes, and other abstract cognitive concepts of which the person is often unaware. To be sure, this does not make any of the cognitive therapies equivalent to psychoanalysis, but it does demonstrate the wisdom of some of Freud's clinical insights and is reflected in the kinds of rapprochements explored later.

Thus cognitive behavior therapists, not unlike their analytic counterparts, believe generally that there is more to the patient than immediately meets the eye (Goldfried & Davison, 1976). Guidano and Liotti (1983), for example, spoke of the "protective belt" behind which one must search for core beliefs, which themselves are generally related to one's idea of oneself, such as a negative self-image. According to Mahoney (1982, 1990), core, central cognitions may be extremely difficult to change, even when uncovered, because they stem from one's earlier developmental history. And well before the popularity of cognitive behavior therapy, George Kelly distinguished between "core constructs" and "peripheral constructs," the former relating to the person's basic sense of self or identity (Kelly, 1955).

Although changing core beliefs is not a simple matter for either patient or therapist, it is believed by many contemporary researchers to be essential to cognitive therapy if its positive effects are to be enduring. The subtlety in assessing variables that are not immediately apparent is similar to that of advanced accurate empathy, discussed in Chapter 18 (page 543), as can be seen from the following case example given by Safran et al. (1986):

> For example, a client who failed an exam . . . accessed the automatic thought: "I can't handle university." At this point the therapist could have challenged this belief or encouraged the client to examine evidence relevant to this belief. Instead she decided to engage in a process of vertical exploration. In response to the therapist's probes a constellation of automatic thoughts emerged that revolved around the client's beliefs that he was not smart enough. The client at this point spontaneously recalled two memories of situations in which he had felt humiliated and worthless because he felt he had "been stupid" at the time. As he recounted these memories he became visibly more emotional. Further exploration revealed that these feelings of intellectual inferiority and associated feelings of worthlessness cut across a number of problem situations for the client. It also emerged that he believed that his value as a person was completely dependent upon his intellectual performance. In this situation had the therapist intervened when the first automatic thought emerged, she may not have accessed the entire chain of self-evaluative cognitions and higher level constructs that underlay the client's distress (p. 515)

Broad-Spectrum Treatment

Our review of the cognitive and behavior therapies has necessarily been fragmented because we have dealt with separate techniques one at a time. In clinical practice, however, several procedures are usually employed at once or sequentially in an attempt to deal with all the important controlling variables; this approach is generally referred to as *broad-spectrum behavior therapy* (Lazarus, 1971). For example, a patient fearful of leaving home might well undergo in vivo desensitization by walking out the door and gradually engaging in activities that take him or her farther from that safe haven. Over the years, however, the person may also have built up a dependent relationship with his or her spouse. As the person becomes bolder in venturing forth, this change in behavior may disrupt the equilibrium of the relationship that the couple has worked out over the years (see page 143). To attend only to the fear of leaving home would be incomplete (Lazarus, 1965) and might even lead to replacement of the agoraphobia with another difficulty that would serve to keep the person at home—a problem frequently called symptom substitution.

In a related vein, therapists do not invariably focus only on the patient's complaint as stated during the first interview. A clinical graduate student was desensitizing an undergraduate for test anxiety. The client made good progress up the hierarchy of imagined situations but was not improving at all in the real world of test taking. The supervisor of the graduate student suggested that the therapist find out whether the client was studying for the tests. It turned out that he was not; worry about the health of his mother was markedly interfering with his attempts to study. Thus the goal of making the client nonchalant about taking tests was inappropriate, for he was approaching the tests themselves without adequate preparation. On the basis of additional assessment, the therapy shifted away from desensitization to a discussion of how the client could deal with his realistic fears about his mother's possible death.

Relationship Factors

A good relationship between client and therapist is important for many reasons and regardless of the particular theoretical orientation. As discussed in Chapter 4, it seems doubtful that clients will reveal deeply personal information if they do not trust or respect their therapists. Furthermore, since therapy can seldom be imposed on an unwilling client, a therapist must obtain the cooperation of the client if there is to be any possibility that techniques will have their desired effect. In desensitization, for example, a client could readily sabotage the best efforts of the therapist by not imagining a particular scene, by not signaling anxiety appropriately, and by not practicing relaxation. And in virtually all other cognitive and behavior therapy procedures clients are able to, and sometimes will, work against the therapist if relationship factors are neglected (Davison, 1973).

Flesh on the Theoretical Skeleton

Determining the most important controlling variables is related to another overlooked aspect of behavior therapy—indeed, of any therapy—namely, moving from a general principle to a concrete clinical intervention.

To illustrate, let us consider an early report in which undergraduates were trained to analyze the behavior of severely disturbed children in operant conditioning terms (Davison, 1964). The students were encouraged to *assume* that the important determinants of these children's behavior were the consequences of that behavior. Armed with M & M candies as reinforcers, these student-therapists attempted to bring the behavior of the severely disturbed children under their control. Eventually, one child appeared to be losing interest in earning the candies. Working within a framework that required an effective reinforcer, the therapist looked around for another incentive. Luckily, he noticed that each time the child passed a window, she would pause for a moment to look at her reflection. The therapist obtained a mirror and was subsequently able to make peeking into the mirror the reinforcer for desired behavior; the peeks into the mirror were used in the same *functional* way as the M & M candies. Thus, *although guided by a general principle, the therapist had to rely on improvisation and inventiveness as demanded by the clinical situation.*

An outsider can get the impression that devising therapy along behavioral lines is easy and straightforward, that the application of a general principle to a particular case is a simple matter. Although a given theoretical framework helps guide the clinician's thinking, it is by no means sufficient.

> The clinician in fact approaches his work with a given set, a framework for ordering the complex data that are his domain. But frameworks are insufficient. The clinician, like any other applied scientist, must fill out the theoretical skeleton. Individual cases present problems that always call for knowledge beyond basic psychological principles. (Lazarus & Davison, 1971, p. 203)

The preceding quotation from two behavior therapists is very similar to the following one from an article written by two experimental social psychologists.

> In any experiment, the investigator chooses a procedure which he intuitively feels is an empirical realization of his conceptual variable. All experimental procedures are "contrived" in the sense that they are invented. Indeed, it can be said that the art of experimentation rests primarily on the skill of the investigator to judge the procedure which is the most accurate realization of his conceptual variable and has the greatest impact and the most credibility for the subject. (Aronson & Carlsmith, 1968, p. 25)

Thus behavior therapists are faced with the same kinds of decision-making challenges that their experimental colleagues face. There are no easy solutions in dealing with human problems.

Psychoanalysis and Behavior Therapy—A Rapprochement?

Is contemporary psychoanalysis compatible with behavior therapy? This question has been discussed for many years, and few professionals are optimistic about a meaningful rapprochement, arguing that these two points of view are incompatible paradigms. But Paul Wachtel, in his work on just such an integration (1977, 1982), offered a scheme that, in our view, holds considerable promise at least for establishing a dialogue between psychoanalytically oriented therapists and behavior therapists.

As indicated in Chapter 18, ego analysts place much more emphasis on current ego functioning than did Freud. Sullivan, for example, suggested that patients will feel better about themselves and function more effectively if they focus on problems in their current interpersonal behavior. But even Sullivan appears to have been ambivalent about the wisdom of working directly on how people act and feel in the present if this might mean they would not recover memories of repressed infantile conflicts. Wachtel, however, suggests that the therapist *should* help the client change current behavior, not only so that he or she can feel better in the here and now but indeed so that the client can *change* those childlike fears from the past.

Wachtel bases his principal position on Horney (1939), Sullivan (1953), and Erikson (1950) and calls it "cyclical psychodynamics" (1982). He believes that people maintain repressed problems by their current behavior and the feedback it brings from their social relations. Although their problems were set in motion by past repressed events, people keep acting in ways that maintain them. For example, take a young man who has repressed his extreme rage at his mother for having mistreated his father years ago, when he was still a child. To control this rage, as a youngster he developed defenses that took the form of overpoliteness and deference to women. Today this solicitousness and unassertiveness encourage some women to take advantage of him, but he also misperceives situations in which women are genuinely nice to him. Misinterpreting their friendly overtures as condescending insults, he comes to resent women even more and retreats still further. In this fashion his submissiveness, originating in his "woolly mammoth" (page 42), his buried problem of long ago, creates personal problems in the present and revives his repressed rage. It is as though his adult ego is saying, unconsciously, "You see, women, like my mother, really are bitchy. They're not to be trusted. They're hurtful and sadistic." This present-day confirmation of his belief from childhood turns back upon the buried conflict and keeps it alive. The cycle continues, with the young man's own behavior and misconceptions confirming the nastiness of women.

The implications for therapy are to alter current behavioral patterns both for their own sake, which is the behavior therapist's credo, and for the purpose of uncovering the underlying psychodynamics. By pointing out that a direct alteration of behavior may help clients attain a more realistic understanding of their past repressed conflicts, traditionally the goal of psychoanalysis, Wachtel hopes to interest his analytic colleagues in the techniques employed by behavior therapists. He would probably give the deferential young man some assertion training, in hopes of breaking into the vicious cycle by changing his here-and-now relations with women. Once his belief that all women want to take advantage of him is repeatedly disconfirmed, the young man can begin to understand the repressed conflict of love–hate with his mother.

Similarly, Wachtel holds that behavior therapists can learn much from their analytic colleagues, especially concerning the *kinds* of problems people tend to develop. For example, psychoanalytic theory tells us that children have strong and usually ambivalent feelings about their parents and that, presumably, some of these are so unpleasant that they are repressed, or at least are difficult to focus on and talk about openly.

To a behavior therapist the deferential young man might initially appear fearful of heterosexual relationships. Taking these fears at face value, he or she would work to help the client reduce them, perhaps by a combination of desensitization, rational-emotive therapy, and social-skills training. But the behavior therapist will fail to explore the possibility, suggested by the psychoanalytic literature, that the young man is basically *angry* at women. Wachtel advises the behavior therapist to be sensitive to the childhood conflicts that analysts focus on and to question the young man about his relationship with his mother. His reply or manner may give a hint of resentment. The therapist will then *see* the deferential young man differently and hypothesize that he is not just fearful of women but angry at them as well, because he associates them with a mother who has been the object of both hate and love from early childhood. This additional information will presumably suggest a different behavioral intervention, for the anger must be dealt with.

Wachtel would also have the behavior therapist appreciate that reinforcers can be *subtle* and that, furthermore, a client may deny that he or she really wants something. And the client may well be unaware of this denial. In other words, therapists should be attuned to unconscious motivation, to the possibility that a person may be motivated or reinforced by a set of events that he or she is not conscious of for psychodynamic reasons.

Contemporary psychoanalytic thought may also help the behavior therapist become aware of the *meaning* that a particular intervention has for a client. Consider the case of a young woman with whom a behavior therapist decided to do assertion training. As role-playing procedures were described, the client stiffened in her chair and then began to sob. To proceed with the training without dealing with her reaction to the description of it would of course be insensitive and poor clinical practice. An awareness of psychoanalytic theories had sensitized the therapist to the possibility that assertion *symbolized* something to the client. The therapist gently encouraged the woman to talk freely, to free-associate about the idea of assertion training. She recalled a series of incidents from childhood in which her parents had criticized the way she acted with her friends, without providing support and constructive suggestions about other ways to behave. Without initially being aware of it herself, the client was reminded of this pain from the past when the therapist suggested that she learn more assertive ways of dealing with others. The psychologist was able to distinguish the current enterprise, assertion training, from the unhelpful and negative criticisms made in the past and thereby persuaded the young woman to try role-playing. The incident also pointed up the client's unresolved problems with her parents and with authority figures in general.

In a related vein, Wachtel argues that psychoanalysts are more likely than behavior therapists to consider the nonnormative or unusual concerns, wishes, and fears of their patients. Guided by the view that emotional problems derive from the repression of id conflicts, they consider psychological difficulties to be reflections of infantile wishes and fears, dark mysteries of primary process thinking. Behavior therapists tend to have a more straightforward, more prosaic, if you will, view of their patients' problems.

In our view, as clinical psychologists who have taught and practiced in a cognitive-behavioral framework for many years, the actual practice of experienced behavioral clinicians often reflects the kind of subtlety characteristic of psychodynamic clinicians like Wachtel. What is unclear to us, and we believe to Wachtel, is the degree to which sophisticated practice is derivable from the theories that constitute contemporary cognitive and behavior therapy. It is the disjunction between theory and practice that lies at the core of Wachtel's critical discussion of behavior therapy and the ways in which psychoanalysis might enrich both behavioral theory and practice. We turn now to some general issues in eclecticism and psychotherapy integration.

Eclecticism and Theoretical Integration in Psychotherapy

Wachtel's efforts at rapprochement are part of a long tradition in the field of psychotherapy. As reviewed by Garfield and Bergin (1986) and Arkowitz (1992), other efforts preceded his, and still others are developing. An early plea for behavior therapists and psychoanalysts to become conversant with each other's work came from a psychoanalyst, Judd Marmor (1971). And before him was the pioneering conceptual work of Dollard and Miller (1950), whose stimulus–response research and theorizing on anxiety attempted to explain psychoanalysis in learning theory terms. In addition, Jerome Frank (1971, 1973) and Sol Garfield (1974) articulated positions on the nature of effective psychotherapy that cut across doctrinaire lines. Other position statements, for example, those of Goldfried and Davison (1976), Davison (1977), and Goldfried (1980), were also part of the integrative Zeitgeist of the 1970s. There is even a new periodical, *Journal of Psychotherapy Integration,* devoted to the topic.

The Lazarus-Messer Debate

Some of the issues surrounding eclecticism and integration were recently explored in an article by two leading figures, Arnold Lazarus and Stanley Messer, colleagues at Rutgers University (Lazarus & Messer, 1991). The article is unusual in that it is set up in a point–counterpoint framework, mirroring an actual debate at the 1990 convention of the Society for the Exploration of Psychotherapy Integration, an organization founded in 1983 and noted for annual meetings that involve lively and spirited exchanges among theorists and clinicians who might in other times never have attended the same convention.

The core philosophical-epistemological question is one that we have addressed many times in this book, namely, whether one can make theory-free observations, that is, whether in our complex world, we can speak of objective facts outside a particular paradigm or theory. It is interesting that the answer one gives to this very abstract question about the nature of knowledge and reality influences how one views the challenge of integrating diverse forms of psychotherapy.

For many years Lazarus, trained as a behavior therapist by Wolpe in the late 1950s in South Africa, advocated what he called "technical eclecticism," a willingness to use whatever techniques work best for a particular patient or disorder, without regard to the theoretical approach from which they are drawn. As will become clear, though, the technique is fitted into the therapist's theoretical framework. He elaborated this view in his own approach to psychotherapy, multimodal therapy (cf. page 571). Lazarus argues not only that this empirically based eclecticism at the technique level will be of most benefit to the most patients, but that to attempt rapprochement or integration at the theoretical level—for example, seeking a way, as Wachtel does, to blend psychoanalytic and behavioral theory—is fruitless, a waste of time, and impossible. Indeed, recent moves to theoretical integration, instead of facilitating dialogue and rapprochement, are, in Lazarus's view, creating even more chaos.

Before getting into the particulars of the Lazarus–Messer debate, it will be useful to distin-

Arnold Lazarus, Rutgers psychologist and master clinician, who developed multimodal therapy.

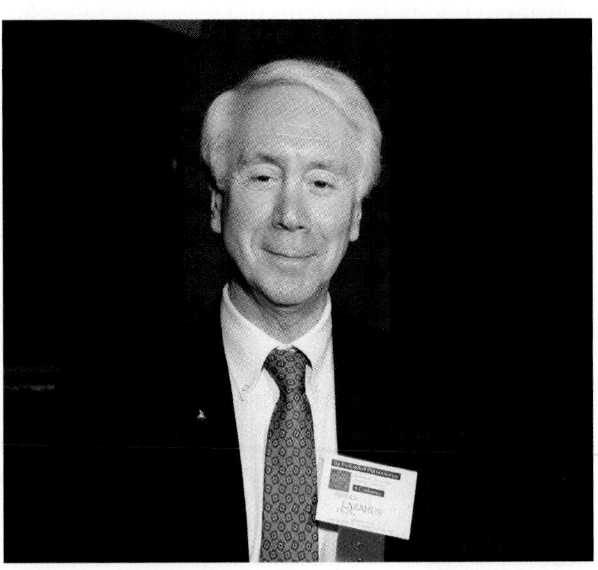

guish among three modes of psychotherapy integration (Arkowitz, 1989): technical eclecticism,[6] common factorism, and theoretical integration. In the first, exemplified in Lazarus's multimodal approach, the therapist works within a particular theoretical framework, for example, cognitive behavior therapy, but sometimes imports from other orientations techniques deemed effective *without subscribing to the theories that spawned them.* Use whatever works is the operating principle of the technical eclectic, but rationalize the use of a technique from one's own framework. For example, Lazarus sometimes uses the Gestalt empty chair as a method of behavioral rehearsal rather than as a way to help the patient reclaim disowned parts of his or her personality, which is how the technique is conceived of in Gestalt therapy.

A common factors approach (e.g., Frank, 1961, 1982; Goldfried, 1980, 1991; Schofield, 1964) seeks something that all therapy schools might share, for example, informing a patient how he or she affects others, a strategy that is employed by many different kinds of therapists and that is believed by many (e.g., Brady et al., 1980) to be an important component of effective psychotherapy.

The third approach, theoretical integration, tries to synthesize not only techniques but theories; Wachtel's efforts to justify and make sense of assertion training within a modified psychoanalytic framework is a prime example of an effort toward theoretical integration. The resulting theory is itself something different because of the blending of pschoanalytic and behavioral elements.

It is theoretical integration that Lazarus inveighs against. One reason is that most theories of psychotherapy are epistemologically incompatible. For example, the definition of a fact in psychoanalysis is different from the definition of a fact in behavior therapy. Different standards of evidence prevail. So, the argument here is that you cannot integrate two theories that do not share the same ways of defining reality.

But, Lazarus asks rhetorically, can one not use a "disembodied technique" (Strupp, 1989)? His answer is yes, one can, that is, one can borrow techniques without buying into the theories that gave rise to them. Thus, he uses the empty chair as one way to implement behavior rehearsal within his cognitive-behavioral framework. Lazarus believes that having the client imagine that a significant other, such as a parent, is in an empty chair opposite the client makes the role-play more vivid and realistic. There apparently is something about having the person talk to an empty chair that helps bring the parent into the consulting room, better perhaps than having the therapist pretend to be the client's parent. And, he argues further, one can employ the procedure without adopting the Gestalt conceptual framework in which it was developed.

Lazarus's technical eclecticism is not a mishmash based on personal preferences or ignorance, rather it is, he asserts, based solely and simply on *data,* on information about what works under certain conditions. And this information is for the most part theory-free: one can determine what is true or not true without subscribing to a particular theory. As he puts it: "Observations simply reflect empirical data without offering explanations. 'Adolescents tend to imitate the behavior of peers whom they respect,' is an observation. 'They do so unconsciously due to inadequate parental introjects,' is a theory" (Lazarus & Messer, 1991, p. 147).

In response, Messer suggests that Lazarus's dissatisfaction with theoretical integration stems in part from a belief that there is, lurking in the wings, an all-encompassing theory of psychotherapy waiting to be discovered and that, until this happy uncovering, it is best to eschew attempts to integrate theories in favor of using whatever techniques work (technical eclecticism). In contrast, Messer's view, sometimes referred to as a social constructionist one (cf. Davison, 1991; Gergen, 1982; Mahoney, 1991), sometimes as hermeneutic (cf. Messer, Sass, & Woolfolk, 1988), holds that we *invent* our theories—something Lazarus would not dispute—*and that we view the world through the prisms that our theories or paradigms provide*—a view that this textbook espouses and that Lazarus does not fully embrace. That is, there is no such thing as an objective observation, an objective fact; rather, our understanding of reality is only within the context of a particular theory or paradigm. As Messer put it, there is no such thing as an "immaculate perception."

This view leads Messer to criticize Lazarus's technical eclecticism. When Lazarus borrows a technique and uses it within his own cognitive-behavioral framework, that technique becomes

[6]As discussed in Chapter 2 (page 55), eclecticism per se refers to "a largely pragmatic approach in which the therapist uses whatever techniques he or she believes are likely to be effective, with little or no underlying theory to guide these choices" (Arkowitz, 1992, p. 262). This strategy is regarded with skepticism by many mental health professionals, including Lazarus and the authors of this book, for it lacks a rationale for when a therapist decides which technique to use and under what circumstances. Without theoretical guidelines to help the therapist conceptualize the client's problem and the processes of therapeutic change, eclecticism is equivalent to chaos, in which choices are made on whim, on the basis of what feels right, or for any number of other reasons that make for neither good science nor sound practice.

something different from what it was in its original theoretical framework. The Gestalt empty chair, for example, is different when Lazarus uses it than when Perls used it. Messer credits Lazarus for making creative use of this technique—but in so doing it becomes something else, something other than the Gestalt empty chair. Both in theory and in practice, the empty chair in Lazarus's hands is different from what it is in Gestalt therapy. In the latter, the technique is designed to put the client in better touch with unacknowledged feelings and conflicting parts of the self. In contrast, Lazarus uses it to help the client relate differently to a significant person in his or her life, a form of behavior rehearsal, a strategy aimed at improving how the person behaves toward another.

Now, consider Lazarus's criterion for importing a technique—it has to be demonstrably effective. Herein lies a serious problem, according to Messer, for any evidence that the Gestalt literature can provide on the effectiveness of the empty chair is not going to be relevant to the cognitive-behavioral context in which Lazarus works. Again, simply put, the empty chair that Lazarus uses is not the empty chair that the Gestalt therapist uses. To argue that he is using only empirically validated techniques, Lazarus will have to look for supporting evidence in experiments that evaluate the empty chair as a behavior rehearsal procedure, something Gestalt therapists have not bothered with (nor have behaviorally oriented researchers).

Messer goes on to critique Lazarus's assertion that "Adolescents tend to imitate the behavior of peers whom they respect" is an objective, verifiable, theory-free observation. No, says Messer, it is replete with theory, for adolescents may imitate their peers for a host of other reasons; that they do so out of respect is a theoretical explanation of their imitative behavior. Indeed, the very phrase "imitate the behavior of peers" is itself not a theory-free statement, for there are other ways to refer to such behavior.[7]

Messer concludes by suggesting a fourth mode of integration: evolutionary or assimilative integration (which we regard as equivalent to theoretical integration). By this he means that "Techniques and concepts from one therapy . . . find their way into another, and get incorporated within its slowly evolving theory and mode of practice" (Lazarus & Messer, 1991, p. 153). Like technical eclecticism, a technique is imported into a new framework, but in so doing, that framework begins to change as theoretical elements from the technique's framework are incorporated. In this way one's original theory evolves, becoming something different—presumably more comprehensive and useful. In our view, Wachtel's cyclical psychodynamics is an example, for it is a viewpoint that evolved from its psychoanalytic source by incorporating both techniques and ideas from behavior therapy. It is a blend of the two. As Messer wrote: "I would not claim, as does Lazarus, that I am merely importing an observation or technique shorn of excess theoretical baggage. Rather, I am incorporating an attitude, perspective, or approach that is transformed in its new context even while retaining something of value from its point of origin" (Lazarus & Messer, 1991, p. 153).

Arguments Against Premature Integration

As we contemplate efforts at theoretical integration, we have asked ourselves whether a grand, all-encompassing theory or approach is necessarily desirable or even possible. We believe not, and our own use of different paradigms in the study of both psychopathology and intervention aligns us more with the views of Garfield and Bergin:

> A comprehensive conception of how the body works does not demand that every system or organ of the body operate according to the same principles. Thus, our view of how the circulatory system works is quite different from our view of the nervous system. The forces and actions of the human heart operate according to the principles of fluid mechanics, whereas the principles of electrochemistry apply to the transmission of nerve impulses through the neuron; yet these two quite different processes occur in the same human body and are coordinated harmoniously despite their apparently disparate functions.
>
> Similarly, human personality may operate in accordance with a complex interaction of seemingly disparate processes that act together, though each differently and in its own sphere. Thus, it is conceivable that the same individual may suffer at one time from a repressed conflict, a conditioned response, an incongruent self-image, and irrational cognitions; and that each of these dysfunctions may operate in semi-independent systems of psychic action that are amenable to rather different interventions, each of which is compatible with the "system" to which it is being applied. Diagnosis and therapy might then become concerned with the locus of the disorder or

---

[7]In fairness to Lazarus, Messer's argument here is almost tantamount to saying that whenever we use language, we are not theory–neutral. "Imitative behavior" strikes us as free of theorizing as can reasonably be expected; it is certainly less theory-laden than something like "identify with," which assumes a psychodynamic process. But perhaps that is the essence of the constructionist thesis.

> with which portion or portions of the multisystem psyche is involved. (1986, p. 10)

Indeed, not all of those interested in psychotherapy integration agree with the overall notion that the more the blurring between conceptual frameworks, the better. In a recent article entitled "Disappearing Differences Do Not Always Reflect Healthy Integration," Haaga and Davison (1991) pointed out several ways in which Ellis's RET and Beck's CT have begun to merge. For example, Beck originally focused almost entirely on cognitive biases and how they might distort a person's analysis of a situation. Thus, a depressed person who complains that he or she has no friends is encouraged, like a scientist, to determine whether in fact this is true. In contrast, Ellis's sole emphasis was on the belief or assumption under which a person operates, for example, I must be perfect in everything I do." Nowadays, however, Beck devotes at least as much time talking about "dysfunctional schemata," which, as we have seen, can look a great deal like Ellis's "irrational beliefs." And Ellis does not ignore social realities, for even at the beginning (Ellis, 1962) he advocated teaching someone without social skills how better to interact with others, with the goal of improving relationships (rather than just encouraging the person to care little about turning people off).

From an integrative point of view, this might be seen as progress, but Haaga and Davison caution that it may be premature, that we may lose something by blurring such distinctions, especially if such integration is not based on research (and they argue that, in fact, it isn't). If one preserves the uniqueness of these two therapies, one might then construct a more integrative therapy that uses the particular strengths of each. For example, perhaps for certain kinds of people under certain kinds of circumstances, it is best to focus on changing social realities, while other circumstances might call for changing people's interpretations of an unchanging and perhaps unchangeable social reality. But to work in this direction requires at least two things: (1) holding on to at least some of the original distinctions between RET and CT, and, most importantly, (2) constructing or utilizing a superordinate theory that can subsume both RET and CT and specify when a particular aspect of one is suitable and when a feature of the other is appropriate. The intricacies of this go somewhat beyond our purposes; suffice it to say that science sometimes moves forward more readily when rapprochement among divergent theories is *not* encouraged.

SUMMARY

In this chapter we have reviewed theory and research in the cognitive and behavior therapies, which attempt to apply the methodologies and principles of experimental psychology to the alleviation of psychological distress.

Through counterconditioning a substitute desirable response is elicited in the presence of a stimulus that has evoked an undesired response. Systematic desensitization is believed by some to be effective because of counterconditioning.

In operant conditioning, desired responses are taught and undesired ones discouraged by applying the contingencies of reward and punishment. The token economy is a prime example of the clinical application of operant conditioning.

Modeling—helping the client to acquire new responses and unlearn old ones by observing models—is useful in eliminating fears and efficient in teaching new patterns of behavior.

Cognitive therapies, such as Ellis's Rational-Emotive Therapy and Beck's Cognitive Therapy, alter the thoughts that are believed to underlie emotional disorders. Self-control presents some interesting challenges to the behavioral paradigm: an active and conscious human being by autonomous and deliberate choice acts independently of environmental influences.

Behavioral medicine attempts by psychological procedures to alter bad living habits, distressed psychological states, and aberrant physiological processes, in order to prevent and to treat medical illnesses. Paradoxical therapy is a mode of intervention that directs patients not to change or even to make worse the problems for which they are seeking help. Several strategies are employed to maintain gains once a patient is no longer in regular contact with the therapist, such as eliminating sources of secondary gain and encouraging the patient to attribute improvement more to his or her own efforts than to the expertise of the therapist.

Several important issues in cognitive and behavior therapy are discussed, such as the role of mediational variables, unconscious influences, relationship factors, and the possibilities of integrating some parts of psychoanalytic theorizing into behavior therapy. Finally, issues of rapprochement are examined, with distinctions made among technical eclecticism, common factors, and theoretical integration as different ways of integrating diverse therapeutic approaches.

KEY TERMS

behavior therapy
systematic desensitization
aversion therapy
token economy
cognitive restructuring
rational-emotive therapy (RET)
cognitive therapy (CT)
social problem solving
metacognition
multimodal therapy
triadic reciprocality
behavioral medicine
health psychology
biofeedback

c h a p t e r t w e n t y

Group, Couples and Family Therapy, and Community Psychology

Group Therapy
- Insight-Oriented Group Therapy
- Behavior Therapy Groups
- Evaluation of Group Therapy

Couples and Family Therapy
- The Normality of Conflict
- From Individual to Conjoint Therapy
- The Essentials of Conjoint Therapy
- Special Considerations
- Evaluation of Couples and Family Therapy

Community Psychology
- The Focus: Prevention and Seeking
- Values and the Question of Where to Intervene
- Community Mental Health Centers
- Community Psychology in Action
- Evaluation of Community Psychology Work

Cultural and Racial Factors in Psychological Intervention
- African-Americans and Psychological Intervention
- Hispanics and Psychological Intervention
- Asian-Americans and Psychological Intervention
- Native Americans and Psychological Intervention
- Toward a More Complete Science of Behavior

Summary

A couple with a marriage of twenty years duration sought treatment for the male's problem of total inability to have an erection. This had been a problem for over nineteen of their twenty years of marriage. Successful intercourse had only taken place in the first few months of the marriage. The woman in this couple was also unable to reach an orgasm, and indeed had never had an orgasm from any form of stimulation, in her entire life. However, she reported that she greatly enjoyed sex and was extremely frustrated by her husband's inability to have an erection.

In treating this couple, through techniques [based on those of Masters and Johnson], very rapid progress was made. The husband very quickly began to have erections in response to his wife's manual stimulation of his genitals.

She also learned to have orgasm, first through her own masturbation and then through her husband's manual and oral stimulation of her genitals. By session 10 of weekly therapy, the couple was able to engage in normal intercourse with both of them having orgasm. Thus, the case was essentially "cured" within ten sessions.

However, at this point, something rather peculiar happened. Rather than continuing intercourse after this success, the couple discontinued all sexual activity for the next several weeks. Upon careful exploration by the therapist a rather interesting picture emerged. First, it became clear that the husband had a great need to remain distant and aloof from his wife. He had great fears of being overwhelmed and controlled by her, and found closeness to be very uncomfortable. He himself had had a rather disturbed relationship with his mother, with her being extremely controlling, manipulating, and intrusive in his life, well into his adulthood. For him, the inability to have an erection served to keep his wife distant from him, and to maintain his need for privacy, separateness, and autonomy in the relationship.

In exploring the situation with the wife, [the therapist found] in contrast to her overt statements . . . an extremely ambivalent attitude toward sex. She had been raised in a very anti-sexual family. While she claimed to have rejected these anti-sexual teachings in her own late adolescence and adulthood, in point of fact this rejection had occurred only at a superficial intellectual level. Emotionally, she still had a great deal of difficulty in accepting her sexual feelings. She had fears of being overwhelmed by uncontrollable sexual urges if she allowed herself to enjoy sex. Thus, her husband's erectile problems served to protect her from her own fears about sex. Furthermore, over the nineteen years of her husband being unable to attain an erection, she had come to have a very powerful position in the relationship. She very often reminded her husband that he owed her a lot because of her sexual frustration. Thus, she was essentially able to win all arguments with him, and to get him to do anything that she wanted.

For this couple, the rapid resolution of their sexual dysfunction threatened elements in both their own personalities, and in the way their relationship was structured. In exploring their inability to continue having intercourse, once they had succeeded, they came to realize the [link] between their sexual problems and the structure of their [marriage]. With several additional weeks of therapy focused on resolving these individual and relationship factors, they were able to resume sexual activity successfully. (LoPiccolo & Friedman, 1985, pp. 465–466)

In this chapter we review three means of therapeutic intervention. Although different from one another in many important ways, they are similar in that they make far more efficient use of professional time and are more economical than the one-to-one therapies reviewed in the preceding two chapters. As we will see, however, economy is not the primary reason that any of these is chosen. Rather, each treatment has developed from a particular rationale for providing effective help. In **group therapy** a professional treats a number of patients simultaneously; in **couples (marital) therapy** and **family therapy**, committed partners and sometimes children are seen together in conjoint sessions; and **community psychology** is oriented toward prevention and treats the problems of patients without removing them from their customary surroundings.

Group Therapy

Group therapy began in the early twentieth century, but its development accelerated in the 1930s, perhaps because of the Great Depression and the leadership of President Franklin Roosevelt, whose New Deal approach emphasized the utility of collective action. Short of money, people tried to find solutions in group endeavor. As psychotherapists experimented with therapy in groups, they discovered that, for many patients, it was as good as individual therapy (Wolf & Kutash, 1990).

Most group therapists regard their form of treatment as uniquely appropriate for accomplishing certain goals. For example, group members can learn vicariously when attention is focused on another participant. Social pressures, too, can be surprisingly strong in groups. If a therapist tells an individual client that his or her behavior seems hostile even when hostility is not intended, the message may be rejected; however, if three or four other people agree with the interpretation, the person may find it much more difficult to dismiss. In addition, many people derive comfort and support solely from the knowledge that others have problems similar to their own.

Many of the techniques employed in individual therapy have been, or can be, used for treating people in groups. Thus there are psychoanalytic groups (Slavson, 1950; Wolf, 1949), Gestalt groups (Perls, 1969), client-centered groups (Rogers, 1970), behavior therapy groups (Lazarus, 1968a; Paul & Shannon, 1966; Upper & Ross, 1980), and countless other kinds. Some researchers, for example, Bednar and Kaul (in press), argue that it is hazardous to build a group therapy on the basis of a theory of individual psychotherapy. Their reasoning is that extrapolation from a model of individual therapy overlooks the uniqueness of a group setting, for example, the complex interactions among people who are fellow patients, in contrast with the individual setting, where the only person the patient relates to is the therapist. They assert also that theorizing about individual therapy tends to be biased toward intrapsychic rather than interpersonal processes. These postulated differences between individual–intrapsychic and interpersonal approaches play a central role in couples and family therapy, which we turn to in the next section of this chapter.

Group therapies have been used with children and their parents, with adolescents, with patients suffering from a host of medical illnesses, with the elderly and their caregivers, with abusive parents, with delinquents, with homosexuals, and with hospitalized mental patients (Lubin, 1983). We examine a few group psychotherapies, in hopes of imparting some idea of the range of prevailing theories and procedures, and then review the evidence bearing on their effectiveness.

Insight-Oriented Group Therapy

Psychoanalytic Group Therapy

At the annual meeting of the American Group Psychotherapy Association in 1957, a discussion took place between the well-known psychoanalytic theoretician Lawrence Kubie and two pioneering group therapists who were working within a psychoanalytic framework, Foulkes and Grotjahn. As published a year later in the *International Journal of Group Psychotherapy*, Kubie asserted that psychoanalysis in groups could not be effective because the transference to the therapist would be diluted. Debating against this view were Foulkes and Grotjahn, whose group therapy psychoanalytic work derives from Alexander Wolf, regarded as having begun the practice of psychoanalysis in groups in 1938. Foulkes and Grotjahn's arguments are believed by some to have "dealt a blow to the invincibility of individual psychoanalysis to be the only really effective method of psychotherapy" (Sager, 1990, p. xi).[1] Over the past four decades, analytically oriented therapists have adapted some of the concepts and methods of individual psychoanalysis and psychodynamic therapy to the group setting.

Psychoanalytic group therapists employ such Freudian concepts and methods as transference, free association, dream analysis, resistance, the power of the unconscious, and the importance of past history, all in an effort to move patients toward an understanding of intrapsychic processes. Some therapists (e.g., Wolf & Kutash, 1990) concentrate on the psychodynamics of each individual group member, whereas others (e.g., Bion, 1959; Foulkes, 1964) conceive of the group itself as having a kind of collective set of psychodynamics, manifested in such things as a group transference to the therapist. Sometimes the therapist sees each of the group members for many sessions of individual psychoanalysis or psychoanalytically oriented therapy prior to group therapy. Interpretations of what members say are offered not only by the therapist but by other members of the group. What all such approaches have in common is the belief that increased self-understanding and deep emotional change can take place in the individual within the context of a group and that the group itself can facilitate these curative psychoanalytic processes.

---

[1]The reader should also bear in mind that during this same period of time individual psychotherapy was broadened to include the various behavioral and cognitive-behavioral approaches described in Chapter 19, as well as the several humanistic and existential approaches presented in Chapter 18.

Sensitivity Training and Encounter Groups

Aronson (1972) differentiated the **sensitivity training** or **T-group** from the more radical **encounter group**, which grew in popularity primarily on the West Coast at such places as the Esalen Institute, where Perls was in residence in the 1960s. T-groups tend to rely more on verbal procedures and to avoid the physical contact, touching exercises, and unrestrained expressions of emotion employed by many encounter groups. Aronson's distinction is not accepted by all workers, however. Rogers (1970) traced the development of encounter groups to his training of counselors at the University of Chicago in 1946, in which he emphasized personal growth and improved interpersonal communication. We agree with his judgment that T-groups and encounter groups are usually impossible to distinguish from each other today. Indeed, throughout the turbulent sixties, ideas from Gestalt therapy and other approaches were introduced into the actual functioning of T-groups as more and more people—including those who would be unlikely to carry a DSM diagnosis—sought to understand themselves better and to learn to relate openly and honestly to each other in an era when public attacks on perceived hypocrisies and the Establishment were becoming commonplace.

The T-group was originally conceived in 1947, and the National Training Laboratory was established through conferences on small-group dynamics held in Bethel, Maine. The impetus came from colleagues of Kurt Lewin, a famous social psychologist at MIT (Lubin, 1983). The original groups were comprised of people in industry, and the goal was to increase efficiency in business practices at the highest levels of management by making executives more aware of their impact on other people and of their own feelings about others. Over the past fifty years millions of people have participated in such groups, including no doubt some readers of this book. Attention has shifted in these years from group dynamics to individual growth and the attainment of one's full human potential.

The T-group is best viewed as educational; it was not designed for those who are seriously disturbed. Typically, members are encouraged to focus on their here-and-now relationships with one another. Individuals are often drawn to T-groups because, even though their lives are not full of problems, they feel that they are missing something, that they live without intensity and intimacy.

In the most general terms, T-groups and encounter groups provide a setting in which people are encouraged to behave in an unguarded, honest fashion. They are then helped to receive and give feedback, to see how they come across to and affect others, and to examine how they feel about their behavior and that of others. They are expected to become more aware and accepting of themselves and of other group members.

Levels of Communication Figure 20.1 is Aronson's schematic representation of a dyadic or two-person

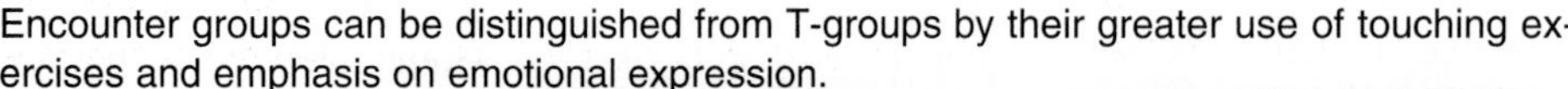
Encounter groups can be distinguished from T-groups by their greater use of touching exercises and emphasis on emotional expression.

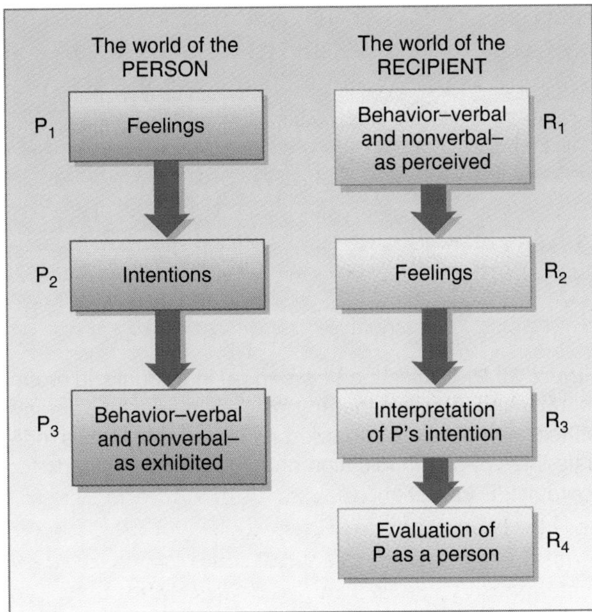

Figure 20.1 Schematic representation of a two-person interaction. The diagram illustrates the different levels of communication possible. After Aronson, 1972.

interaction. In our everyday lives we usually operate at level P_3, namely, behaving in some verbal or nonverbal way toward another person. Usually the recipient of our P_3 behavior responds at level R_4, evaluating us. There are obviously many points at which misjudgments can occur. For example, at level R_3 the recipient may misinterpret P's intention. Even though the person may feel warmly (P_1) toward his or her friend, the recipient, the person may have difficulty expressing warmth and therefore show sarcasm at P_3. The recipient then interprets P's intention as a wish to hurt (R_3), rather than as a desire to express warm feelings. Without the open discussion that is encouraged in a T-group, the recipient can reject (R_4) the person as a nasty individual and never come to understand that the person really feels warmly (P_1) but has just not learned to express those feelings (P_3) appropriately. A properly run T-group encourages the participants to break down their personal communications and reactions into all the various components so that they can examine their true feelings toward other persons and their perceptions of what they are receiving from them.

Experienced and competent group leaders watch for undue coercion and direct the stream of conversation away from an individual when they sense excessive probing into the person's private feelings. They make every effort not to impose their will and ideas on the other participants, but they are, of course, aware of the very powerful position they occupy in the group. It seems likely that some of the unfortunate abuses of encounter and T-groups can be attributed to the all-too-human tendency of some trainers to wield this power unwisely.

Variations Sensitivity and encounter groups may vary in a number of ways. Rogerian groups tend to operate according to individual client-centered therapy, outlined in Chapter 18; the leader tries to clarify the feelings of group members, on the assumption that growth can occur as people confront their emotions with honesty. The group leader—or facilitator—tends to be less active than in the T-groups Aronson describes. Some groups may meet for hours at a time, perhaps over a weekend, with little if any sleep allowed. Such marathons (Bach, 1966; Mintz, 1967; Stoller, 1968) rely on fatigue and extended exposure to a particular set of social conditions to weaken defenses and help the participants become more open and presumably more authentic. A particularly direct, and sometimes brutal, variation of encounter groups is the type of meeting pioneered at Synanon and other residential drug abuse treatment centers (page 321), where the assumption is made that vigorous and speedy stripping away of defenses and cop-outs is necessary to help substance abusers confront their problems and take responsibility for their lives (Casriel, 1971).

Synanon was among the earliest residential treatment centers for drug addicts. Direct and often brutal confrontation is used to help addicts honestly confront their problems.

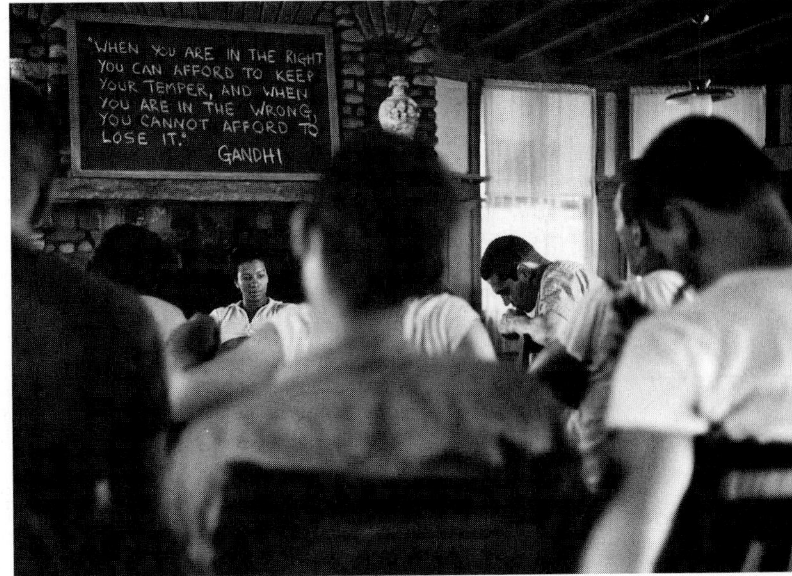

Behavior Therapy Groups

Individualized Behavior Therapy in Groups

Arnold Lazarus (1968a), a pioneer in group behavior therapy, pointed out that behavior therapists may, primarily for reasons of efficiency, choose to treat several people suffering from the same kind of problem by seeing them in a group rather than individually. The emphasis, as in one-to-one therapy, remains on interactions between the therapist and each individual patient or client (Figure 20.2a).[2]

Group desensitization (Lazarus, 1961) is a good example of this individualized approach. A single therapist can teach deep muscle relaxation and present a hierarchy to each member of the group simultaneously, thus saving therapist time. Fears handled in this manner include test anxiety (Nawas, Fishman, & Pucel, 1970), snake phobias (Ritter, 1968), anxiety about public speaking (Paul & Shannon, 1966), and social anxiety (Wright, 1976).

Groups using behavioral techniques to help individual members lose weight (Wollersheim, 1970) and stop smoking (Koenig & Masters, 1965) have also been successful, as have groups that reinforce conversational efforts by hospitalized chronic schizophrenics (Liberman, 1972). Whether this should be considered group therapy is open to question. The members of these special-purpose groups do seem to provide valuable encouragement and social support for one another, however.

Social-Skills Training Groups

Social skills are taught to groups of people who have similar deficits in relating to others, for example, job interview skills or conversational and dating skills; efforts are usually made to treat people with comparable levels of deficiency so that an appropriate pace can be maintained for all group members (Bartzokis, Liberman, & Hierholzer, 1990; Kelly, 1985). Participants rehearse together the skills they are learning and thus provide one another unique and appropriate help in changing behavior. Because members interact, the lines of communication are among all participants, not just between therapist and participant (Figure 20.2*b*). Groups of depressed people, for example, have learned social skills that are likely to bring them more reinforcement from others (Lewinsohn, Weinstein, & Alper, 1970; Teri & Lewinsohn, 1986); and for over ten years social-skills training groups have helped schizophrenic and mood-disordered patients cope with the interpersonal challenges they would face when discharged from the psychiatric division of the Brentwood Veteran's Administration Medical Center in Los Angeles (Liberman, DeRisi, & Mueser, 1989).

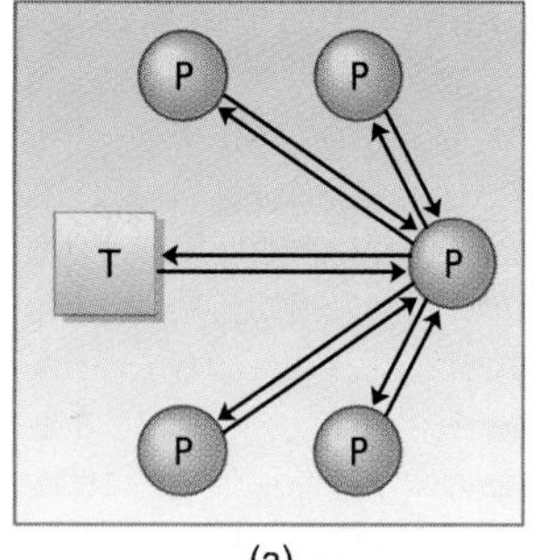

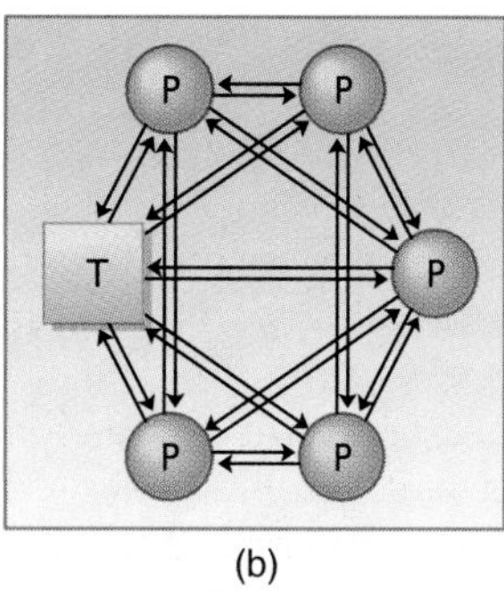

Figure 20.2 Distinction between (a) individualized group therapy and (b) group therapy in which interactions among all the members are regarded as important. Arrows indicate lines of communication and influences; T stands for therapist, P for patient.

Assertion Training Groups

A particularly important social skill is assertiveness (see page 572). Lazarus conducts assertion training groups composed of about ten people of the same sex. At the first meeting he describes the general goals of the therapy group, commenting particularly on the problems that unassertiveness can create for individuals in our society. He also suggests that the therapy group can provide a good setting for cooperative problem-solving. Like Rogers, he calls for honesty and acceptance within the group and prescribes constructive criticism and the diligent practice of new skills.[3] Members introduce themselves briefly, and the others are encouraged to comment on the manner of each person's presentation, especially if he or she was apologetic.

Members of the group are then given a situation that calls for an assertive response. The therapist

[2]Gestalt therapy groups generally operate in this fashion as well. The therapist works with one group member at a time; often this individual will sit in a particular chair, or on a particular pillow, referred to as the hot seat.

[3]Because assertion training involves awareness and encouragement of feelings, it should come as no surprise that commonalities have been noted between this kind of behavioral group and those run along humanistic lines (Lazarus, 1971). This is another sign of the rapprochement among therapy orientations discussed in Chapter 19 (page 588).

turns the situation into a skit and demonstrates being assertive. Then group members, in pairs or larger groupings, take turns playing out the skit. The therapist and other members tell the persons practicing assertiveness what they are doing right and doing wrong. Assertiveness is rehearsed again and again in this fashion. Of particular importance are assignments carried out by the members between sessions. People are encouraged to describe both successful and unsuccessful attempts at assertive behavior in their everyday activities, and they often role-play within the group to help them improve on their assertion in past or anticipated situations. A sensitive and skillful therapist can create an atmosphere in which group members begin to trust themselves to express criticism without fearing that they are hurting other people's feelings. Assertion groups may even be effective in reducing the compliant, withdrawn behavior of chronic schizophrenics (Bloomfield, 1973).

There are some similarities between Lazarus's assertion training groups and the sensitivity training groups described earlier, but an important difference is the attention Lazarus pays to between-session activities; people are trained within the group to make specific changes later, outside the group therapy setting. Although T-groups are similarly concerned with helping people change their everyday lives, much less systematic attention is paid to what clients do between group sessions.

In general, behavioral and cognitive-behavioral approaches utilize the uniqueness of the group setting. For example, Rose (1986) described problem-solving groups on college campuses in which members helped each other generate possible solutions to each other's life challenges. Some group leaders also do what can be termed "problem-solving the group," whereby group members are challenged to deal with a particular problem—such as a few people doing all the talking. The group process itself thus becomes material for the honing of problem-solving skills. This general approach has been followed for many years in sensitivity training and encounter groups as well.

Evaluation of Group Therapy

Like other therapies, group therapy has its share of glowing testimonials.

> I have known individuals for whom the encounter experience has meant almost miraculous change in the depth of their communication with spouse and children. Sometimes for the first time real feelings are shared. . . . I have seen teachers who have transformed their classroom . . . into a personal, caring, trusting, learning group, where students participate fully and openly in forming the curriculum and all the other aspects of their education. Tough business executives who described a particular business relationship as hopeless have gone home and changed it into a constructive one. (Rogers, 1970, p. 71)

Such observations, especially by a highly skilled and respected clinician, contribute to the faith many people have in encounter groups. Comments of this nature do not, however, satisfy most behavioral scientists.

Some critics have suggested that those who participate in T-groups learn only how to participate in T-groups. They are not able to transfer to real-life situations the insights and skills that have been acquired in a group (Houts & Serber, 1972). Transfer of learning is a difficult problem for, whether we like it or not, the real world is not set up to encourage openness and frankness. Those who are not operating by the rules of a T-group may be offended by the open and honest expression of feelings. Indeed, as Aronson reminds us, if someone insists that others be totally open when they do not want to be, he or she is being insensitive to their feelings and so really has *not* learned some of the essentials from what might have seemed a good T-group experience. This is not to say that T-group experiences can never transfer to the real world. Knowledge of how a person feels about others and comes across to them may be extremely useful in everyday activities, even though the overt behavior encouraged in a T-group or encounter group is not continued.

In three reviews in a widely cited handbook, Bednar and Kaul (1978, 1986, in press) found few studies of group therapy that met basic standards of psychological research, for example, random assignment of subjects to different treatments. Even when research designs are good, independent variables (page 120) are often described so vaguely that it is difficult to know what, in fact, was studied. To say, for example, that a group intervention was nondirective simply because the therapist was once trained in the Rogerian tradition is unsatisfactory, for it tells us precious little about what really went on in the group meetings. Still, several tentative conclusions can be drawn from these careful reviews of research as well as from the considered opinions of others:

1. In general, group therapies of different kinds appear to have beneficial effects on a wide variety of clients, and in some instances these fa-

vorable outcomes endure at several months' follow-up. However, there have seldom been appropriate attention-placebo controls for nonspecific factors. (This complaint should by now be familiar to the reader.)

2. Pregroup training, that is, teaching general skills about participating in group therapy and instilling positive attitudes toward the experience, can help people get more out of group therapy experiences.
3. Dependent people appear to do better in a highly structured group, whereas independent, better functioning individuals improve to a greater extent in groups that have less structure and offer more opportunity for self-expression.
4. Different factors are curative at different stages of group development. For example, Kivlighan and Mullison (1988) found that, in the earliest sessions, universality, the sense that one's problems are not unique to oneself, is important, whereas interpersonal learning, discovering how one does and can relate to others, has relatively greater influence in later sessions. Other factors believed to be significant include feelings of belonging and inculcation of hope (Yalom, 1985), and it is likely that factors differ depending on the needs and character of the group members. But of all factors believed to be active ingredients for positive change, probably none is as operative as group cohesiveness (though in our view findings would be more persuasive if the dependent measures relied less on self-report by the participants about how much benefit they had derived from the group).
5. Marathon groups may have no particular advantage over similarly constituted groups that meet for shorter periods of time; in fact, concentrating group hours in a few marathon sessions may accomplish less than spreading them over more sessions.
6. Casualties of therapy, people who become worse in the course of treatment, are very few, with most studies finding rates of less than 3 percent. Members who do become worse are usually particularly disturbed or lacking in self-esteem. Those responsible for selecting group members try to screen out people who might need more individual attention or for whom the stress of confrontation and open sharing of feelings with others might be too great. Particular styles of leadership, such as a challenging, authoritative attitude that pushes group members to deal with more feeling, especially anger, than they are ready for, may be harmful (Lieberman, Yalom, & Miles, 1973; see Focus Box 20.1).
7. No body of evidence supports the superiority of one kind of group therapy over another. Although one theoretical approach may be more suitable than another for treating a particular problem, research has only begun to address such questions.
8. It has long been assumed that progress in group therapy is facilitated by feedback, by candid comments made by one person to another about the feelings he or she arouses, the impressions made, "how you're comin' across." Evidence indicates that feedback is indeed useful, especially when negative feedback, "You sound imperious when you ask things of people," is accompanied by positive feedback. "I like the way you said that" (Jacobs et al., 1973).

Couples and Family Therapy

Many married couples who seek or who are referred for therapy to deal with problems in their relationship have children. Sometimes the problems that parents have with a child arise from conflicts in the marriage; other times a child's behavior creates distress in an otherwise well-functioning couple. The line between marital therapy and family therapy is often blurred, and professionals who specialize in working with couples often find themselves working with the children as well. For these reasons we have elected to discuss couples and family therapy together, distinguishing between the two when useful.

In addition, changing mores prompt us sometimes to use the term *couples therapy* rather than marital therapy because of the growing numbers of couples who live together in a committed relationship and are not married. These include both heterosexual and gay couples, and children are sometimes part of the therapeutic picture for both kinds of couples. There may, therefore, be couples or family therapy involving adult partners who are unmarried or of the same sex.

The Normality of Conflict

There is almost universal agreement among couples therapists and researchers, regardless of theoretical orientation, that conflict is inevitable in a marriage or in any other long-term relationship. The aura of

20.1 • Therapy, for Better or for Worse

In 1966 Bergin applied the term *deterioration effect* to the harm that can come to someone from therapy. Several reviews of the literature since his initial report (Bergin, 1971; Bergin & Lambert, 1978; Lambert, Bergin, & Collins, 1977; Strupp, Hadley, & Gomes-Schwartz, 1977) indicate an unpleasant fact of life; although individual psychotherapy benefits many people, some are hurt by the experience. Group therapy (Yalom & Lieberman, 1971) and couples and family treatment (Gurman, Kniskern, & Pinsoff, 1986) also have casualties. Risk of being harmed is of course not peculiar to psychological intervention. Patients have been made worse by a wide range of medical procedures as well, including electroconvulsive therapy (Elmore & Sugerman, 1975) and the prescription of psychoactive drugs (Shader & DiMascio, 1970), both of which aim at psychological change. Some people who do *not* seek treatment also deteriorate. Avoiding contact with a mental health professional—indeed, *any* health professional—is no guarantee against getting worse.

Several noted behavior therapists have examined the studies on which Bergin and others base their claim of a deterioration effect. They (Mays & Franks, 1980; Rachman & Wilson, 1980) suggest that the evidence is far weaker than assumed earlier. It is proving as difficult to show that therapy can sometimes harm as it has been to show that it can help. One problem is insufficient information on spontaneous deterioration, that is, on the rate at which people who receive no therapy at all become worse. We know that some disturbed and untreated people do get worse. But therapy outcome studies have thus far failed to assess this deterioration adequately. Thus certain people who deteriorate while in therapy may do so not because of the therapy itself, but because of factors outside the consulting room, beyond the control of the therapist. Even so, some patients clearly worsen during therapy, which raises serious empirical and ethical questions.

What are the factors that might be responsible for the deterioration effect? Highly disturbed people and those with great expectations and a need to improve are among those often harmed. Another factor is the therapist's failure to structure sessions properly, inadequately focusing on important issues and instead allowing the patient to ramble. Other therapist factors include failure to deal with the patient's negative attitudes toward therapy or the therapist, dealing inadequately with patient resistance, and timing interpretations poorly (Sachs, 1983). Indeed, there is evidence that just as there are therapists whose work is associated with a disproportionate number of therapy casualties, there are also therapists who seldom have patients get worse and who generally help their patients (Lambert et al., 1986).

The therapist will bear ultimate responsibility for harm to the client. Lieberman, Yalom, and Miles (1973) found casualties in encounter groups that were led by an "aggressive stimulator," by a challenging, authoritative person who insisted on self-disclosure and catharsis of group participants even when they were not willing or ready for it. Any therapy can be abused by a practitioner who follows it foolishly, without tailoring it to the needs of the client. Some clients, desperate for support, reassurance, and advice and lacking in interpersonal skills, may become worse if a client-centered therapist unflinchingly declines to provide some guidance. Other clients, already overly dependent on others, may not be able to make choices and grow if the behavior therapist does not recognize this as a need and, instead, takes total charge of their lives.

Any therapist or community worker can err when assessing the patient's problem, thereby embarking on treatment that cannot possibly help him or her. In addition, therapists, it must be remembered, are only human beings! Their training and experience do not qualify them as Superpeople in Mental Health. Their own needs and personal problems, even though they know they should not allow them to intrude, can blind them to the needs of the client and can otherwise reduce their ability and willingness to work on the client's behalf. Sadly, some therapists are unethical as well. A few go so far as to claim that clients (always the more attractive ones) can profit from a sexual encounter with the therapist; these workers sometimes initiate or permit sexual intimacies. Licensing laws and codes of ethics do not themselves ensure that therapists will always act wisely and humanely. Most do, and the vast majority of clients are *not* hurt by them. But the deterioration effect has been observed too often to be disregarded or underestimated.

the honeymoon passes when the couple makes unromantic decisions about where to live, where to seek employment, how to budget money, what kind of meals to prepare and the sharing of that responsibility, when to visit in-laws, if and when to have children and whether to experiment with novel sexual techniques. Now, in addition, couples have the changed nature of gender roles to negotiate. For example, if both spouses work, will their place of residence be determined by the husband's employment or by the wife's? These sources of conflict must be handled by any two people living together, whether they are married or not, whether they are of the opposite sex or not. Authorities agree that it is how couples deal with such inherent conflicts that determines the quality and duration of their cohabitation relationship (e.g., Schwartz & Schwartz, 1980).

A strategy some couples adopt, deliberately or unconsciously, is to avoid acknowledging disagreements and conflicts. Because they believe in the reality of the fairy-tale ending, "And they lived happily ever after," any sign that their own relationship is not going smoothly is so threatening that it must be ignored. Unfortunately, dissatisfaction and resentment usually develop and begin to take their toll as time goes by. Because the partners do not quarrel, they may appear to be a perfect couple to outside observers. But without opening the lines of communication, they may drift apart emotionally.

From Individual to Conjoint Therapy

The terms *family therapy* and *couples therapy* do not denote a set procedure. Although the focus is on at least two members of a family unit, how the therapist views the problem, what techniques are chosen to alleviate it, how often members are seen, and whether children and even grandparents are included are all variables of treatment.

Couples and family therapy share some theoretical frameworks with individual therapy. Psychoanalytic marital therapists, for example, focus on the way a person seeks or avoids a partner who resembles, to his or her unconscious, the opposite-sexed parent (Segraves, 1990). Frustrated and unsatisfied by his love-seeking attempts as a child, the adult man may unconsciously seek maternal nurturance from his wife and make excessive, even infantile, demands of her. Much of the discussion will center on the conflicts he is having with his wife and, presumably, the repressed striving for maternal love that underlies his immature ways of relating to her. These unconscious forces will be plumbed, with the wife assisting and possibly revealing some of her own unresolved yearnings for her father. Notice that the transference examined in analytic couples therapy is that between the two partners rather than between the client and the therapist. The overall goal is to help each partner see the other as he or she actually is rather than as a symbolic parent (Fitzgerald, 1973). Each partner can be seen separately by different therapists (Martin & Bird, 1953), separately by the same therapist (Greene, 1960), or conjointly by the same therapist (Ackerman, 1966).

Wachtel's interpersonal psychoanalytic views, discussed elsewhere in this book, have been applied to couples and family therapy (Wachtel & Wachtel, 1986). Because of their concern with interactions among people, the Wachtels bring families together in the consulting room so that interactions can be directly observed, commented upon to all family members, and hopefully altered by gentle prodding, encouragement, and reinforcement. Although this approach sounds similar to cognitive-behavioral methods, the difference lies in the assumptions made by the Wachtels of the importance of the client's unconscious wishes and fears, along the lines of the individual therapy that Wachtel (1977) advocates.

Ellis's rational-emotive therapy has also been applied to family conflict. Again, the perspective is individualistic or intrapsychic; the therapist assumes that something going on within one or both of the partners is causing the distress in the relationship. The wife, for example, may harbor the irrational belief that her husband must constantly adore her, that his devotion must never falter. She is likely then to overreact when at a social gathering he enjoys himself away from her side, talking to other men and women.

Early sex therapy treated a sexual problem of one or both partners directly, expecting that whatever other difficulties the couple might have—anger, resentment—would dissipate thereafter. This pattern undoubtedly holds for many sexually distressed couples. But, as mentioned in Chapter 13, the increasing popularity of sex therapy since the publication of Masters and Johnson's *Human Sexual Inadequacy* in 1970 has brought to the attention of sex therapists many troubled couples for whom the sexual problem is but one aspect of a more complex *system* (Friedman & Hogan, 1985; Heiman & Verhulst, 1990). Couples and family therapy looks for these systems. The case history that opened this chapter illustrates how a sexual dysfunction can serve a *useful* purpose in maintaining a couple's relationship and how its apparently successful treatment can actually worsen their overall connection and cut short their newfound sexual enjoyment.

Couples therapy deals with relationship problems. It can take a number of forms ranging from psychoanalytic to behavioral.

The Essentials of Conjoint Therapy

As an overall approach, family and couples therapy seems to have begun with the work of John Bell (1961; 1975), a psychologist working in the 1950s at the Mental Research Institute (MRI) in Palo Alto, California. In the past forty years an increasing number of mental health professionals have devoted their professional lives to this kind of work. During the 1960s the efforts of Virginia Satir (1967), a psychiatric social worker, and Donald Jackson, a psychiatrist, also at MRI, provided the field with fresh impetus.

The MRI people identify faulty communication patterns, uneasy relationships, and inflexibility. Members of the family come to realize how their behavior affects their relations with others. They then devote their energies to making specific changes. Few family therapists are concerned with past history, and none believes that working with only one member of the family can be fruitful. Whatever the clinical problem, the family therapist takes a **family systems approach**, a general view of etiology and treatment that focuses on the complex interrelationships within families; as such, treatment is viewed as most effective within this group context. The legacy of the MRI group is less a body of techniques than a general way of thinking about the complexities and constant interactive patterns in couples and family conflict.

Most couples therapy is conjoint, that is, the partners are *together* in sessions with a therapist. Initially, distressed couples do not react very positively toward each other, which is not surprising! Jacobson and Margolin (1979), two behavioral marital therapists, recommend attending to this problem as an initial step in helping a couple improve their marriage. One strategy is the "caring days" idea of Richard Stuart (1976). The wife agrees to devote herself to doing nice things for her husband on a given day, without expecting anything in return. The husband will do the same for her on another day. If successful, this strategy accomplishes at least two important things: first, it breaks the cycle of distance, suspicion, and aversive control of each other; and second, it shows the giving partner that he or she is able to affect the spouse in a positive way. This enhanced sense of positive control is achieved simply by pleasing the partner. The giving can later be more reciprocal; each partner may agree to please the other in certain specific ways, in anticipation of the partner's reciprocating. For example, one partner may agree to prepare dinner on Tuesdays, and on that day the other contracts to stop at the supermarket on the way home from work and do the weekly shopping. The improved atmosphere that develops as a consequence of each partner's doing nice things for the other and having nice things done for him or her in return helps each become motivated to please the other person on future occasions.

Behavioral couples therapists generally adopt Thibaut and Kelley's (1959) exchange theory of interaction. According to this view of human relationships, people value others if they receive a high ratio of benefits to costs, that is, if they see themselves getting at least as much from the other person as they have to expend. Furthermore, people are assumed to be more disposed to continue a given relationship if other alternatives are less attractive to them, promising fewer benefits and costing more. Therapists therefore try to encourage a mutual dispensing of rewards by partner A and partner B.

Behavioral marital or couples therapy has in common with other approaches a focus on enhancing communication skills between the partners, but the emphasis is more on increasing the ability of each partner to please the other, the core assumption being that "the relative rates of pleasant and unpleasant interactions determine the subjective quality of the relationship" (Wood & Jacobson, 1985). Indeed, this is claimed by such therapists to be more than an assumption, for they can point to data supporting the view that distressed couples differ from nondistressed ones in reporting lower frequencies of positive exchanges and higher frequencies of unsatisfying exchanges. Also, as Camper et al. (1988) found, spouses in distressed marriages view negative behavior from their partners as global and stable, whereas they construe positive partner behavior as less so. These and related findings suggest that

> distressed spouses are highly reactive to immediate or recent events in their relationship, while happy couples tend to maintain their satisfaction independently of recent events (Jacobson, Waldron, and Moore, 1980; Margolin, 1981). . . . They are also more likely to reciprocate negative or punishing behaviors initiated by their partners (Billings, 1979; Gottman, 1979; Margolin and Wampold, 1981). In contrast, nondistressed marriages are relatively resilient, even in the face of unpleasant events, and less vulnerable to the impact of negative interchange. While happy couples also respond to variability in the quality of day-to-day interactions, their degree of affective reactivity is much lower than that of distressed couples. (Wood & Jacobson, 1985, p. 345)

For these reasons, behavioral couples therapy concentrates on increasing positive exchanges, the hope being not only that short-term satisfaction will increase but also that a foundation will be laid for long-term trust and positive feelings, qualities that the aforementioned research shows to be characteristic of nondistressed relationships. Cognitive change is also seen as important, for couples often need training in problem-solving and encouragement to acknowledge when positive changes are occurring (distressed couples often *perceive* inaccurately the ratio of positive to negative exchanges, tending to overlook the former and fixate on the latter).

In all forms of couples therapy, each partner is trained to listen empathically to the other and to state clearly to the partner what he or she understands is being said and what the feelings behind the remarks are. One way to improve communication is to distinguish between the intent of a remark and its impact in a manner similar to Aronson's analysis of a two-person exchange (see page 597). Partner A, for example, may wish to be helpful by asking whether partner B would like him or her to get something from the store, but this question may have a negative impact if partner B would prefer partner A to stay home and help with a project. Partner A's intent, then, would be positive, but the question would affect partner B negatively. Research has shown that the communications of distressed and happy couples may not differ so much in intent as in impact. In one study Gottman and his colleagues (1976) found that both types of couples made the same number of positive statements to partners, but distressed spouses reported having *heard* fewer positive statements than satisfied spouses. Gottman proposed a technique for clarifying intent when two partners are in a heated argument. One partner calls "Stop action" and asks the other to indicate what he or she believes the first is trying to say. The feedback indicates immediately whether remarks are having the intended impact.

Couples and family therapy have made creative use of the good-quality videotape equipment now available. A couple can be given a problem to solve during part of a therapy session, such as where to go on vacation, and can be videotaped while they attempt to solve it. The ways in which they push forward their own wishes—or fail to—and the ways in which they accommodate the other's wishes—or fail to—are but one aspect of their communication that a therapist can glean from later viewing of the tape, often with the couple watching, too. Patterns of communication and miscommunication can be more readily discerned. The partners can agree to try out new ways of negotiating and new ways of dealing with conflictual issues (Margolin & Fernandez, 1985). Attempts are now being made to formally combine certain kinds of cognitive therapy with the communication training and behavioral contracting that have long characterized behavioral couples therapy (Baucom & Lester, 1986), as well as to recognize the cognitive elements that have been present for some time in the actual practices of those who call themselves behavioral couples therapists (Jacobson, 1991; Segraves, 1990).

Many operant behavior therapists follow Gerald Patterson's (1974a) practice of working with the parents to alter reinforcement of a child whose behavior is a problem. The child has few direct contacts with the therapist. An improvement in the child's behavior often reduces much distress between husband and wife. But sometimes a child's aberrant behavior can be traced to the marital distress; although the child may be the identified patient, his or her problems may better be regarded as reflecting marital conflict. In such instances family-marital therapists usually decide to intervene in the marital relationship, hoping that the child's difficulties will diminish if the parents learn to get along better. Unfortunately, there is little decisive information on where it is best to intervene. Some research done by K. D. O'Leary's Stony Brook group suggests that altering the child's problematic behavior can improve the marital relationship (Oltmanns, Broderick, & O'Leary, 1976); other research by the same group indicates that successful marital treatment has a favorable impact on children's problems (Turkewitz & O'Leary, 1977).

Special Considerations

The marital dysfunction treated by therapists is not all the same, as Margolin and Fernandez (1985) remind us. One couple may seek professional assistance when there is only dissatisfaction in their relationship, but another may wait until the crisis is so great that one or both partners have already consulted a divorce lawyer. There are, then, different *stages* of marital distress (Duck, 1984; Weiss & Cerreto, 1980), and different therapeutic approaches may be called for, depending on where the therapist judges the couple to be.

An interesting line of research has focused on individual problems in one of the partners and how such problems respond to conjoint therapy versus an intervention targeted to the individual problem. Noting that depression in at least one of the partners is often a part of a distressed couple's relationship and that relapse into depression is more likely if the formerly depressed partner is in a troubled marriage (Hooley & Teasdale, 1989), researchers at Stony Brook (Beach & O'Leary, 1986; O'Leary & Beach, 1990) and at the University of Washington (Jacobson, Holzworth-Munroe, & Schmaling, 1989; Jacobson et al., 1991) have studied behavioral marital therapy (BMT) as a treatment for depression. The findings indicate that Beck's individualized cognitive therapy for the depressed partner is no more effective than BMT in alleviating depression and that cognitive therapy is not as effective as BMT in enhancing marital satisfaction. Interestingly, in the Jacobson et al. (1991) study, which included couples in which one spouse was depressed but the marital relationship was *not* a problem, BMT did not have a beneficial impact on depression either right at the end of treatment or at six- and twelve-month follow-ups (Jacobson et al., in press). This suggests that someone who is depressed and is also in a troubled relationship might be helped as much by a systems-oriented approach to the relationship as by an individualized intervention—with the advantage of also deriving benefit for relationship problems. This research highlights the interpersonal nature of depression—a theme examined in Chapter 9 (page 238)—and, at the same time, the role of depression in a distressed intimate relationship. Moreover, the finding that individualized cognitive therapy does not improve a marriage in the same way that improvement in a marriage lifts depression points up both the limits of a nonsystems individualized therapy, such as cognitive therapy, as well as the strengths of a systems approach, such as BMT.

Evaluation of Couples and Family Therapy

A meta-analysis of twenty carefully selected outcome studies meeting stringent methodological standards concluded that, overall, family therapy has beneficial effects for many family problems (Hazelrigg, Cooper, & Borduin, 1987). Comprehensive reviews of the area by Gurman and Kniskern (1978), Gurman, Kniskern and Pinsoff (1986), and Jacobson and Addis (1993) reach the following conclusions about outcome and process in couples and family therapy:

1. Conjoint therapy for couples problems appears to be more successful than individual therapy with one partner. Indeed, the state of about 10 percent of patients seen individually for couples problems worsens.
2. The beneficial effects of behavioral couples therapy (BCT) have been demonstrated in more than two dozen studies in at least four countries (Hahlweg & Markman, 1988). Positive findings have also been reported on an experiential therapy (Greenberg & Johnson, 1988; Johnson & Greenberg, 1985) and an insight-oriented therapy (Snyder & Wills, 1989), although only a few such studies have been published.

   On the other hand, Jacobson and Addis (1993) also point out that almost all these positive findings are based on comparisons with no-treatment control groups, where deterioration often occurs, thus making it all the easier for *any* intervention to do better than no formal treatment at all. Also, although statistically significant, the outcomes are not always *clinically*

20.2 • Acceptance in Behavioral Couples Therapy

An interesting development in behavioral couples therapy (BCT) (a term that seems to be replacing behavioral marital therapy) is a growing appreciation of *acceptance* of the partner while trying to encourage and support change. Based on earlier work by Rogers (Chapter 18) and Ellis (Chapter 19) and on Marsha Linehan's (in press-a, in press-b) dialectical behavior therapy (page 280), Neil Jacobson (1992), in collaboration with Andrew Christensen (Jacobson & Christensen, in press), argues that behavior therapists have overlooked the importance of people in a committed relationship being able to accept their partner while at the same time hoping for and encouraging change.

The notion of acceptance, of course, has a time-honored history in clinical psychology and psychiatry, dating back at least to Sigmund Freud. As Jacobson indicates, the use of interpretation in psychoanalytic couples therapy (e.g., Scharff, in press) can lead to greater acceptance of displeasing behavior by attributing it to childhood wounds, thereby fostering sympathy for the partner who is behaving in negative ways.* But the concept assumes greater meaning in the work of Carl Rogers, whose client-centered therapy rests on the belief that "conditions of worth" should not be set for others, rather, that we should try to accept them—and ourselves—as worthy people deserving of respect regardless of our behavior at any point in time. Albert Ellis's rational-emotive approach also emphasizes acceptance by encouraging people to renounce many of the demands (shoulds) that they impose on themselves and on others.

In following up the results from an earlier outcome study (Jacobson, 1984), Jacobson noticed that after two years, of the two-thirds of couples who had benefited from BCT, one-third had relapsed (Jacobson, Schmaling, & Holtzworth-Munroe, 1987). Thus, although BCT was very effective for almost half the couples, it was *not* effective for the other half over an extended (two-year) period of time. This led to the question of what might be wrong or missing from BCT.

As mentioned earlier, predictors of poor outcome from BCT include being married for a long time, emotional disengagement, high severity of distress in the relationship, and rigidly held gender roles. It seemed to Jacobson and Christensen that a factor or theme common to these negative predictors might be low amenability to compromise with and accommodate to the other person. And since BCT requires compromise—by, for example, trying to meet the partner's wishes in exchange for certain reinforcers—it may not be surprising that the BCT approach works less well for people who cannot readily accommodate to the desires of their partners.

This should not be news to anyone who has tried to mediate in a marital problem or who has been in a distressed marriage. When a couple has been together for many years, there can be an accumulation of anger, hurt, resentment, and betrayal that makes it a challenge even to decide

*At the same time, such historical attributions can be used by the patient as an excuse not to change. Therapists such as Fritz Perls are inclined to see such explanations as cop-outs. Behavioral and cognitive therapists take a similar tack.

significant (Jacobson et al., 1984), an issue we touched on earlier (page 118). For example, across all studies, no more than half the treated couples were really happily married at the end of treatment (even if they had improved in a strictly statistical sense). Furthermore, few studies have much in the way of follow-up, and those that do—and they are behaviorally oriented—find frequent relapse (Jacobson, Schmaling, & Holtzworth-Munroe, 1987) and divorce (Snyder et al., 1991). One study found an extremely low divorce rate in couples treated with an insight-oriented couples therapy (Snyder & Wills, 1989; Snyder, Wills, & Grady-Fletcher, 1991). As Jacobson and Addis caution, these findings should temper premature enthusiasm for the efficacy of conjoint therapies, regardless of their theoretical bases.

3. Direct comparisons of different couples therapies have not shown clear superiority of one approach over another (Baucom & Hoffman, 1986). Jacobson and Addis's (1993) judgment is that the longer a given approach has been around, the less startlingly superior its results seem to be as compared with other approaches.
4. Reducing the level of expressed emotion in the

what restaurant to go to on a Friday evening. Good will is gone. Motives are constantly questioned; if a negative interpretation can be placed on a seemingly positive behavior, it will be. And if a behavior therapist asks the partners to do something nice for each other, the kind of couple Jacobson and Christensen are talking about will either not budge or, if they do make a specific change, will readily attribute it to the therapist's instruction, for example, "He doesn't *really* appreciate me for my good work at the office today, he's complimenting me only because Dr. Smith told him to." It is no accident that couples therapy sessions can be extraordinarily taxing for the therapist, and unusually boisterous and noisy. Another factor working against direct change attempts is reactance, the resistance people can feel when another person is trying to change them (Brehm, 1966; Davison, 1973). It seems to us that reactance will be especially high when the would-be influencer is held in contempt by the would-be influencee. Since behavior therapy is characterized by open attempts to change people, such direct influence attempts are unlikely to succeed when exchanges are encouraged between two partners who feel little affection and respect for each other.

With all this as context, what is acceptance in Jacobson and Christenson's terms? It refers to "a letting go of the struggle to change and in some cases even embracing those aspects of a partner which have . . . been precipitants of conflict . . . [it] implies that some conflicts cannot be resolved, and it attempts to turn areas of conflict into sources of intimacy and closeness" (Jacobson, 1992, p. 497).† Of course, as Jacobson points out, acceptance does imply change—but the change is in the partner who is giving up efforts to change the other! And, if reactance diminishes with acceptance, as indeed it might (see our earlier discussion of Shoham-Solomon's paradoxical therapy research on page 580), more change in the partner may come about by giving up on trying to effect the change!

†Some might say that this is the closest that psychologists come to defining love.

Jacobson's behavioral roots show, however, in his suggestions about how therapists can bring about change within the context of acceptance. He gives the example of a wife who found her husband's unavailability very objectionable. (Note: the assumption is that the man's unavailability was not due to such things as fooling around with other women. Jacobson is certainly attuned to the ethical and political dimensions of psychotherapy; cf. Jacobson, 1983, 1989.) In addition to the traditional BCT goal of helping them improve their intimacy with each other, he encouraged the woman to develop some independent interests so that she would not rely so much on her husband on those occasions when he could not be present.

Is acceptance tantamount to resignation, to accepting a status quo that keeps one or both partners in a destructive relationship, one that perhaps demeans one partner in order to satisfy the selfish demands of the other? Jacobson argues that acceptance is actually affirmative, holding out the promise of even greater intimacy. And as suggested here, some behavioral changes that were formerly—and unsuccessfully—worked toward in BCT by only direct change attempts might be facilitated by embedding such efforts within a context of acceptance. Ultimately, if acceptance should maintain or increase the distress for which the couple has sought help, there is no moral imperative for the partners to stay together.

families of schizophrenics discharged from the hospital and maintained on neuroleptics lowers relapse rates.

5. Although focused on the fearfulness of one partner, Barlow's exposure treatment, which involves encouragement and collaboration by the spouse, has proved effective in reducing agoraphobia (see Chapter 6, page 142) and has avoided the deterioration in the marital relationship that has sometimes been reported when the agoraphobic partner gets better (Himadi et al., 1986).
6. Not surprisingly, the results of couples therapy are generally better for younger couples and when no steps have yet been taken toward divorce.
7. Predictors of poor outcome include what Jacobson and Addis (1993) call "emotional disengagement," manifested by poor communication of feelings and by low frequency of sexual activity. Another sign of a poor prognosis in couples therapy is a relationship marked by rigidly held traditional gender roles, where the wife is very much oriented to affiliation and relationships and the husband is oriented primarily to work and autonomy (Jacobson, Follette, & Pa-

gel, 1986). Finally, depression in one of the partners does not bode well for couples therapy (even though, as just noted, behavioral couples therapy can have a positive impact on both a person's depression and on the relationship).

8. Efforts to prevent distress in couples suggest that brief training in communication skills can enhance future satisfaction with the relationship and even lower divorce rates when compared with no-intervention controls (Markman et al., 1988). Since couples therapy generally works better when people are younger and highly involved with each other, prevention efforts seem particularly sensible and promising.
9. Overall, most nonbehavioral approaches, such as the analytic and humanistic approaches, have not been subjected to as much controlled research as have behavioral and systems approaches, a probable reflection of the lesser research emphasis in these paradigms. Johnson and Greenberg (1985) did find superiority of a Gestalt therapy–based couples intervention that focused on uncovering unacknowledged feelings and needs as compared with the problem-solving component of behavioral couples therapy. As they speculated, it may be important for a couples intervention to work directly on increasing trust and sensitivity to one's own unmet needs and hidden fears as well as those fears and needs of one's partner. Indeed, more and more attention is being paid by behavioral couples therapists to the affective dimensions of conflict, yet another sign of the move toward rapprochement among contrasting therapeutic orientations (page 588). Another integrative direction is described in Focus Box 20.2.

Some studies have been conducted on **divorce mediation**, consultations occurring before a divorce has been obtained. An alternative to the usual adversarial process, mediation is conducted by a third party (a lawyer, counselor, or trained layperson) who strives for neutrality and whose goal is to help the distressed couple reach agreement on child custody and financial arrangements before involving their own respective lawyers. Mediation can help estranged couples continue functioning as parents even as they move toward divorce. Data indicate that mediation is associated with "(1) a higher rate of pretrial agreements; (2) a higher level of satisfaction with the agreements; (3) major reductions in the amount of litigation after final court orders; (4) an increase in joint custody agreements; and (5) . . . decrease in public expenses such as custody studies and court costs (Sprenkle and Storm, 1983)" (Gurman, Kniskern, & Pinsoff, 1986, p. 589).

Community Psychology

We have already described many examples of community psychology, for example, the prevention of cigarette smoking among young adolescents through school-based programs (page 326) and the prevention of HIV infection and AIDS through programs aimed at changing sexual practices among sexually active adults and adolescents (see page 383). We turn now to an examination of some general principles of community psychology and to a review of a number of noteworthy efforts.

The Focus: Prevention and Seeking

Community psychology's focus on prevention sets it apart from most of what we have studied so far. Gerald Caplan (1964), whose writings have had considerable impact, distinguishes three levels of prevention. **Tertiary prevention** is in many respects equivalent to the treatment of disorders already discussed. It also seeks to reduce the long-term consequences of having a disorder; for example, mental health workers help those who have recovered from mental illness to participate fully in the occupational and social life of the community. **Secondary prevention** consists of efforts to detect problems early, before they become serious, and to prevent their development into chronic disabilities. Quick and accurate assessment by people in the community—physicians, teachers, clergy, police officers, court officials, social workers—allows remedial procedures to begin early. Crisis-intervention work and twenty-four-hour emergency services are examples of secondary prevention.

Primary prevention tries to reduce the incidence of new cases of social and emotional problems in a population. Altering stressful and depriving conditions in the environment and strengthening individuals so that they can resist stress and cope with adversity are two means of primary prevention. Some examples of primary prevention measures include attention to overcrowding, poor housing, job discrimination, neighborhood recreation, school curricula, and neighborhood group work with children from broken homes. Genetic counseling, prenatal care for inner-city mothers, school lunches, and Meals on Wheels are also primary prevention measures.

Community psychologists concentrate their efforts on primary and secondary prevention. Not all primary and secondary prevention efforts, however, constitute community psychology. A clinical psychologist working individually in a private office with a healthy, fee-paying patient can be working at primary prevention of cardiovascular disease by encouraging the person to alter eating habits and life-style. This behavioral medicine approach would not be considered an instance of community psychology. Consider also the research of biologically oriented psychopathologists, like Mednick's high-risk research into possible somatic diatheses for schizophrenia (page 412). Such research clearly has primary prevention as a long-term goal, and yet it is seldom considered community psychology. (Perhaps it should be.) Thus, although primary prevention is an important feature of many community psychology efforts, other characteristics define the approach as well.

Nearly all the therapies reviewed thus far are administered by professional persons with advanced degrees who make themselves available by appointment in offices, clinics, and hospitals. They provide assistance to individuals who initiate the contact themselves or are referred by the courts. Such delivery of services has been referred to as in the *waiting mode* (Rappaport & Chinsky, 1974). In contrast, community psychology operates in the *seeking mode,* that is, those who are troubled or are likely one day to be so are sought out by community workers, some of whom are paraprofessionals supervised by psychologists, psychiatrists, or social workers. Mental health services are often provided outside of offices and clinics, in the schools, businesses, and factories of the person's own community.

Rappaport and Chinsky (1974) proposed that every type of mental health care has two components, the delivery and the conceptual. The delivery component relates to the difference between seeking and waiting, that is, the *attitude* about making services available. As noted, community psychology has a seeking orientation. The conceptual component, on the other hand, consists of the *theoretical* and *data-based underpinnings* of the services. Two examples are psychoanalytic and learning approaches. For example, a twenty-four-hour-a-day hot line in a suicide prevention center would be in the community psychology seeking mode. But what *specifically* the people answering the phones say and do when a call comes in depends on the conceptual mode. One worker might take a psychoanalytic approach; another might construe suicide threats in learning terms. Clearly, these two workers would treat the calls differently—but both would be delivering community psychology. Further, the question whether a particular conceptual orientation is more suited to one of the delivery modes than to the other is a separate, and crucial, issue, one that creates ongoing controversy among community psychologists and psychiatrists.

Values and the Question of Where to Intervene

In an effort to explain the essence of community psychology, Rappaport (1977) proposed that we view society as composed of four levels: the individual, the small group, the organization, and the institution. Therapists intervene at a given level, depending on their values and goals for people. For example, human problems may be seen as *individual in nature*, and treatment therefore focuses on changing the individual. This tertiary prevention is pursued in a number of ways—from behavior therapy to psychoanalysis to chemotherapy—but in all these modes of intervention society is considered good and people in need of adjustment to it. In contrast, human problems may be assumed to derive from *interpersonal difficulties*, such as conflicts within families, at work, and in other *small groups*. The therapist applies family and encounter therapy to help members of the group communicate better. The therapist does *not* try to change just the individual, because the problem is assumed to lie in group processes.

If the third level, that of *organizations*, is considered the problem, therapists have another view of human disorders. They blame the way units such as schools and prisons operate. To help a child who is failing in academic work, for example, therapists examine the school curriculum and how it is implemented by principals and teachers; they do *not* provide remedial tutoring for the pupil. Community psychology operates at this level and at the *institutional* level, which is closely related to it but is more abstract and all-inclusive. Institutions refer not to physical entities such as school buildings and prisons but to the basic values and ideologies that characterize a society, its religion, and its politics. For example, the community psychologist may assert that people are unhappy because of a lopsided distribution of wealth and power. Professional efforts would then be directed at political parties, the courts, legislatures, and the like, *not* to encourage them to function more efficiently but rather to shift their goals and basic assumptions so that they work toward a more equitable social distribution of wealth and power.

Rappaport's analysis makes it clear why some community workers tend to be impatient with individual and group therapy. They do not believe that problems lie with the individual or the group, and they even assert that by concentrating on these levels the therapist "blames the victim" (Ryan, 1971) and overlooks the real problems of organizations and institutions. For these reasons community psychologists work in the seeking mode and make no pretense, as some individual and group therapists do, of being politically and ethically neutral.

Why a shift to community activism in the treatment of mental disorders? For many years it was obvious how few people could avail themselves of psychotherapeutic services, which were usually very expensive, in short supply, and apparently geared to so-called YAVIS clients—individuals who are young, attractive, verbal, intelligent, and successful (Schofield, 1964). Eysenck (1952) questioned the effectiveness of most kinds of psychotherapy, finding treated patients' rates of improvement no better than the spontaneous remission rate. Although Eysenck's criticisms were compellingly rebutted by a number of scholars (e.g., Bergin, 1971), the idea took hold among mental health professionals that psychotherapy aimed at changing the individual might not be the best way to alleviate the psychological problems of the majority of people. Focus began to shift from repressions, conflicts, and neurotic fears to large-scale social problems, such as poverty, overcrowding, poor education, segregation, the alienation felt in large cities, and the impersonal nature of many aspects of present-day living.

The shift from intrapsychic factors to social factors probably reflected the Zeitgeist, or tenor of the times. The 1960s were a period of tremendous social upheaval and activism. Institutions of all kinds were challenged. Cities and college campuses erupted in riots, and a range of minority groups, from African-Americans to gays, charged racism and political repression. This social upheaval, which at times seemed to border on revolution, further encouraged looking at social institutions for causes of individual suffering. At the same time the Kennedy and Johnson administrations (1961–1968) lent the monetary clout of the federal government to a progressive liberalism. John Kennedy's New Frontier and Lyndon Johnson's Great Society programs poured tens of millions of dollars into attempts at bettering the human condition.

Community Mental Health Centers

The greatest single impetus to the community psychology movement was a practical one. In 1955 Congress authorized the Joint Commission on Mental Illness and Health to examine the state mental hospitals. On the basis of its six-year survey, the commission concluded that the care offered was largely custodial and that steps must be taken to provide effective treatment. Its 1961 report recommended that no additional large hospitals be built and that instead community mental health clinics be established. In 1963 President Kennedy sent a message to Congress calling for a "bold new approach," proposing the Community Mental Health Centers Act to provide comprehensive services in the community and to implement programs for the prevention and treatment of mental disturbances. The act was passed. For every 100,000 people a mental health center was to provide outpatient therapy, short-term inpatient care, day hospitalization for those able to go home at night, twenty-four-hour emergency services, and consultation and education to other agencies in the community.

Additional impetus came from the 1965 Swampscott Conference (Bennett et al., 1966), organized out of the growing dissatisfaction felt by many clinical psychologists with the inherent limitations of traditional delivery of mental health services and for what they perceived as the need for a new commitment to the promotion of human welfare on a broad scale. Though the political climate in the country in

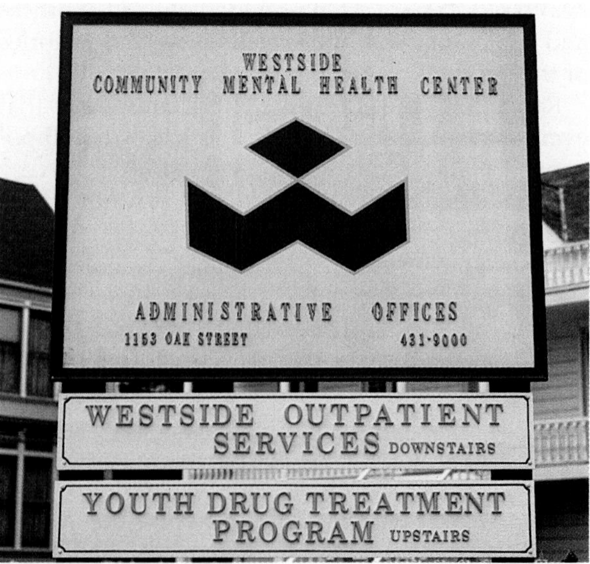

Community mental health centers were begun during the Kennedy administration in an attempt to shift the location of treatment away from large mental hospitals to smaller facilities in a person's own community.

the 1980s was not particularly supportive of community psychology and related efforts, five NIMH-sponsored Preventive Intervention Research Centers were operating in the late 1980s (Gesten & Jason, 1987).

The principal objective of a community mental health center is to provide outpatient mental health care in a person's own community and at a cost that is not beyond the means of most people. The increased availability of clinical services presumably means that fewer individuals require institutionalization and can, instead, remain with their families and friends and continue to work while receiving therapy locally several times a week. The community health center also provides short-term inpatient care, usually on a psychiatric ward of a community general hospital, again, where relatives and friends of patients may conveniently visit them. When it is needed, partial hospitalization, during the day or sometimes for the night, is usually available on a psychiatric ward. A twenty-four-hour walk-in crisis service offers emergency consultation around the clock and rap sessions for members of the community. In Chapter 12 we discussed rape crisis work, a service often run by community mental health centers.

Centers are staffed by psychiatrists, psychologists, social workers, and nurses, and sometimes by paraprofessionals who live in the neighborhood and can help bridge the gap between the middle- and upper-middle-class professionals and community members to whom mental health service is sometimes an alien concept. Paraprofessionals and volunteers can provide needed staffing within the limited budgets of the centers. A wide range of services is included under the rubrics of consultation and education. A principal one is to educate other community workers, teachers, clergy, and police, in the principles of preventive mental health and in how to extend help themselves (see Focus Box 20.3).

Community Psychology in Action

With the foregoing as historical and conceptual context, let us turn to a few noteworthy examples of community psychology as actually implemented. We focus on projects whose effectiveness has been evaluated empirically and on topics that will give a flavor for the scope of this field.

Suicide Prevention Centers and Telephone Crisis Services

Many suicide prevention centers are modeled after the Los Angeles Suicide Prevention Center, founded in 1958 by Farberow and Shneidman. There are at present more than 200 such centers in the United States. Staffed largely by nonprofessionals under the supervision of psychologists or psychiatrists, these centers attempt to provide twenty-four-hour consultation to people in suicidal crises. Usually the initial contact is made by telephone. The center's phone number is well publicized in the community. The worker tries to assess the likelihood that the caller will actually make a serious suicide attempt, and, most importantly, tries to establish personal contact and dissuade the caller from suicide.

The potential value of such community facilities rests in the fact that most suicides give warnings—cries for help—before taking their lives (see page 253). Ambivalence about living or dying is the hallmark of the suicidal state (Shneidman, 1976). Usually their pleas are directed first to relatives and friends, but many potential suicides are isolated from these sources of emotional support; a hot-line service may save the lives of such individuals.

Victims of suicide include survivors, especially if they are among the unfortunate 25 percent who were speaking to or in the presence of the person when the act was committed (Andress & Corey, 1978). Sometimes these survivors are therapists or

Peer support groups are important in helping the friends and family of someone who has committed suicide cope with its aftermath.

20.3 • Community Psychology and Community Mental Health—Related but Different

Although related, the community mental health movement and community psychology should be distinguished from each other. Community psychology is concerned predominantly with primary prevention, intervention where no dysfunctions are yet evident. Community psychology shows its concern for individuals by trying to alter social systems on the institutional level and by creating different and, it is hoped, better environments for people to live in, both to reduce the forces that are thought to bring maladaptions and to promote opportunities for individuals to realize their potential. Community psychology requires intervention with the entire range of social institutions, including the courts, police, schools, and city services and planning agencies. Political more than clinical skills are required for such work; in fact, relatively little time is spent dealing directly with the individuals affected by the larger social forces.

Community mental health, by contrast, provides more tertiary prevention in the form of care for the needy, troubled people who have traditionally been underserved by the mental health professions. Because community mental health delivers mental health services for needy individuals, its orientation is often as individualistic as traditional consulting room therapy of the kind discussed in Chapters 18 and 19. On the staffs of mental health centers are psychiatrists, clinical and counseling psychologists, and social workers who conduct individual or group therapy in offices at the center. The two movements are sometimes equated; the inclusion of community mental health in this discussion of community psychology reflects the relationship between these two forces in psychology today. Nonetheless, their differences are as important to appreciate as are their similarities.

hospital emergency room personnel. All are subject to strong feelings of guilt and self-recrimination, second-guessing what they might have done to prevent the suicide. Even dispassionate analysis does not invariably allay the guilt and anger. Grieving tends to last much longer than when deaths are not self-inflicted. For these many reasons, peer support groups exist to help survivors cope with the aftermath of a suicide. They provide social support, opportunities to ventilate feelings, constructive information, and referrals to professionals if that seems advisable (Fremouw et al., 1990).

It is exceedingly difficult to do controlled research on suicide. Indeed, a meta-analysis of five studies on the effectiveness of suicide prevention centers failed to demonstrate that rates decline after the implementation of services (Dew et al., 1987). Once again, we are left with little if any convincing evidence. Human lives are precious, however, and since many people who contact prevention centers weather a suicidal crisis successfully, there is at present no reason to discontinue these efforts.

The Use of Media and Mass Education to Change Harmful Life-styles

Cardiovascular diseases, such as high blood pressure and coronary heart disease, are responsible for more deaths in the United States than any other single group of illnesses. In many respects the life-style of an affluent, industrialized society increases risk of premature cardiovascular diseases. A group of researchers in the Stanford Heart Disease Prevention Program, led by Nathan Maccoby (Maccoby & Altman, 1988), a psychologist noted for his work in communications, have for several years been studying ways to educate large numbers of people about the desirability of altering their life-styles in order to reduce their risk of cardiovascular diseases. For the Three Communities Project they chose a media campaign and a direct, intensive instructional program (Maccoby et al., 1977; Maccoby & Alexander, 1980; Meyer et al., 1982).

Three towns in northern California were studied; Watsonville and Gilroy were the two experimental towns, and Tracy was the control town. For two years both experimental towns were bombarded by a mass media campaign to inform citizens about cardiovascular diseases. It consisted of television and radio spots, weekly newspaper columns, and newspaper advertisements and stories, all urging people to stop smoking, exercise more, and eat foods low in cholesterol. Posters in buses and in stores conveyed briefly and graphically such vital information as the desirability of eating fewer eggs, since the yolks are rich in cholesterol. In addition, a sample of Watsonville residents at high risk for heart disease received intensive instruction consisting of group sessions and individual home counseling over a ten-week period. The researchers wanted to examine whether information (e.g., how to select and prepare food low in fat and cholesterol) and exhortations to alter life-style delivered face-to-face might add to whatever positive benefits derived from the mass media campaign.

The control town, Tracy, had media services that were quite different from those of the two experimental towns. Tracy is separated from Watsonville and Gilroy by a range of low mountains and therefore has entirely separate local television stations. The inhabitants of Tracy were of course not imprisoned in their hometown for the duration of the two-year study, but for the most part they did not receive through their media the messages conveyed to the citizens of the two experimental towns. Because all three towns had a sizable Spanish-speaking population, all media messages were in Spanish as well as in English.

The findings reveal that citizens of Watsonville and Gilroy significantly increased their knowledge of cardiovascular risk factors; people in the control town did not gain in such knowledge. Egg consumption was reduced more in Watsonville and Gilroy than in Tracy, and clinically significant blood pressure decreases were observed in the two experimental towns, in contrast with small increases in the control town. The high-risk people of Watsonville who participated in the special, intensive instruction program reaped even greater benefits in lower egg consumption and blood pressure. Finally, the researchers considered the townspeople's overall measure of risk, a weighted average of the several known physical risk factors—high blood levels of cholesterol, smoking cigarettes, and not exercising enough. Not surprisingly, they found highly significant drops in risk in the people in the experimental towns, an important result since we know from previous research, the Framingham, Massachusetts, longitudinal study of risk factors in cardiovascular diseases (Truett, Cornfield, & Kannel, 1967), that elevated risk scores predict reasonably well the incidence of heart disease over a twelve-year period.

These positive findings led to a more ambitious and larger scale program called the Stanford Five City Project, which is extending face-to-face instructional programs to a variety of community settings such as schools, community colleges, hospitals, and work sites and involving many more people across a broader age range. Most importantly, the aim is to embed the education programs in existing community organizations so that at least some aspects are retained, the hope being that any beneficial effects will persist well after the researchers leave the scene (Altman, Flora, & Farquhar, 1986). Moreover, dependent measures will include actual illness and death from cardiovascular diseases. Begun in 1978 and continuing well into the 1990s, early results support the efficacy of the interventions in significantly reducing several risk factors, such as cigarette usage, cholesterol levels, and blood pressure (Farquhar et al., 1990; Jackson et al., 1991; Maccoby & Altman, 1988).

The work of the Stanford group and similar projects in Finland (Tuomilehto et al., 1986) and in South Africa (Farquhar et al., 1990) are important as community psychology efforts for they demonstrate that lay people can learn from properly designed and delivered mass media and other large-scale educational programs how to reduce their overall risk for cardiovascular diseases. The multiyear span of these studies is considerable and highly unusual as far as experiments in psychology are concerned! But in terms of the serious health problems that can develop through certain long-standing detrimental behavior patterns, five or ten or more years is not a very long time at all.

There is great potential for such community-based programs to reduce the incidence and seriousness of many medical illnesses beyond what is

Educational campaigns are designed to provide information to motivate people to change behaviors that put them at risk for illness.

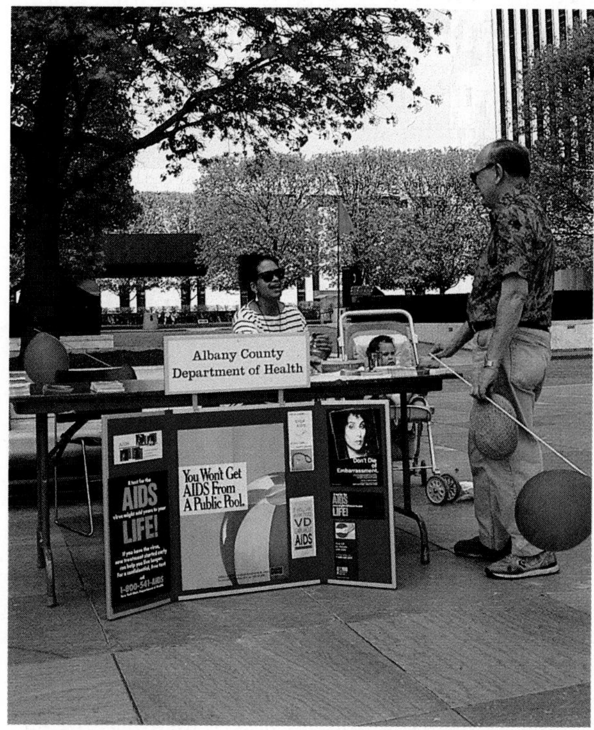

achievable by strictly medical practices, for it is increasingly accepted that people's physical health is primarily in their own hands and that changing lifestyle practices is often the best means of reducing the risk of illness (Bandura, 1986).

Behavioral Medicine at the Work Site

Some of the behavioral medicine approaches reviewed earlier (e.g., pages 574–578) are being followed in programs conducted by companies for their employees at the work site itself. Particular attention is being paid to reducing the risk of cardiovascular diseases by helping employees lose weight, exercise more and regularly, eat more nutritionally, and stop smoking. Stress management, originally a buzzword in industry, is also a frequent focus, with workers being trained in muscle relaxation, time management, and other procedures for handling the challenges of their work.

Results thus far are mixed, however. For example, though weight reduction and smoking cessation programs can be successful in the short term (e.g., Jeffrey, Forster, & Schmid, 1989), relapse and dropout rates as high as 75 percent are the rule rather than the exception. But if companies would offer encouragement to their workers, for instance, by lowering their health insurance premiums as a reward for weight loss and lower cholesterol, the effectiveness of these preventive work site efforts might be enhanced. All things considered, the same criticism can be applied to such programs as is properly directed at individual psychotherapy: as long as the person is exposed to factors outside the treatment environment that do not support the objectives of the program and that often even work against them, the success of such efforts is bound to be limited.

Halfway Houses and Aftercare

Some people function too well to remain in a mental hospital and yet do not function independently enough to live on their own or even within their own families. For such individuals there are halfway houses, an early example of which was Fairweather's "community lodge" (Fairweather et al., 1969). These are protected living units, typically located in large, formerly private residences. Here patients discharged from a mental hospital live, take their meals, and gradually return to ordinary community life by holding a part-time job or going to school. Living arrangements may be relatively unstructured; some houses set up money-making enterprises that help to train and support the residents. Depending on how well funded the halfway house is, the staff may include psychiatrists or clinical psychologists. The most important staff members are paraprofessionals, often graduate students in clinical psychology or social work who live in the house and act both as administrators and as friends to the residents. Group meetings, at which residents talk out their frustrations and learn to relate to others in honest and constructive ways, are often part of the routine.

The nation's requirements for effective halfway houses for ex-mental patients cannot be underestimated, especially in light of deinstitutionalization efforts that have seen tens of thousands of patients discharged from mental hospitals when thirty years ago they would have remained in the protected hospital setting. Although civil rights issues are very important in shielding mental patients from ill-advised and even harmful detention, discharge has all too often led to shabbily dressed former patients left to fend for themselves in the streets (see page 649) or else being rehospitalized in what has been

Corporate health programs are designed to lower work stress, improve health, and increase worker productivity.

called the revolving-door syndrome. Discharge is a desirable goal, but ex-patients often need follow-up community-based services, and these are scarce.

A model of what aftercare can be is provided by the Paul and Lentz (1977) comparative treatment study discussed in Chapter 19 (page 559). When patients were discharged from any of the three wards of the program, social-learning, milieu therapy, or routine hospital management, they usually went to live in nearby boarding homes. These homes, often converted motels, were staffed by workers who had been trained by the Paul–Lentz project to treat the ex-patients according to social-learning principles. The workers, some of whom had B.A. degrees, attended to the specific problems of the ex-patients, using rewards, including tokens, to encourage more independence and normal functioning. They positively reinforced appropriate behavior of the residents and did not attend much to bizarre behavior.

The staff knew at all times how a particular patient was doing, because assessment was careful and ongoing. The mental health center project—and this is of paramount importance—acted as consultant to these community boarding homes in order to help their staff work with the ex-patients in as effective a manner as possible. Some boarding homes for ex-mental patients are supported financially by the state as part of the mental health system, but only rarely have the procedures followed in these homes been carefully planned and monitored by professional mental health staff.

In spite of many practical problems, such as staff layoffs, the results were as positive as had been the impact of the social-learning ward program. The ex-patients seemed to benefit from the aftercare; more than 90 percent of the patients discharged from the social-learning ward were able to remain continuously in the community residences during the year-and-a-half follow-up period. Some had been living in the community residences for over five years. The revolving-door syndrome in this instance was halted. Finally, in a finding rather critical in these days of diminishing public funds, the social-learning program—the mental health center treatment combined with the aftercare—was much less expensive than the institutional care such patients usually receive.

Encouraging findings on milieu therapy community programs in nonhospital residential settings have also been reported by Mosher and his colleagues (Mosher & Burti, 1989; Mosher et al., 1986), who found results equivalent to those of a well-staffed inpatient unit. The patients were young adults experiencing their first psychotic episodes (and therefore very different from the chronic patients in the Paul–Lentz project). The hospital treatment relied heavily on psychotropic drugs, whereas the alternative setting employed Jones's therapeutic community principles reviewed earlier (page 559). The positive outcomes for the community-based program indicate that hospitalization may not even be necessary for some acutely disturbed patients.

Competence Enhancement and Family Problems

The negative effects that *nonsexual* child abuse has on perpetrators, the victim, and other family members render this problem one of considerable social and psychological importance. A number of preventive approaches have been studied (Rosenberg & Reppucci, 1985). One approach emphasizes competence enhancement, that is, instruction in parenting skills so that the various challenges of child rearing are more familiar and less daunting. If parents know what to expect in child development—that contrariness and selfishness are normal in two- and three-year-olds, for example—they may react less negatively when their children act in these ways. Also, learning ways to cope with their children's behavior and to control them in nonaversive ways may help parents to be less emotionally coercive and physically punitive. Some programs utilize live or videotaped skits that model assertive problem-solving (Gray, 1983, reported in Rosenberg & Reppucci, 1985). Results from several large-scale programs suggest positive attitudinal changes, but the actual impact on lessening child abuse has yet to be assessed.

Similarly indeterminate are the effects of community-wide media campaigns and hot lines available to parents under stress. Indications are that crisis services like hot lines are utilized less often to prevent child abuse than to report abuse or to seek referrals for handling abuse that has already occurred. Better validation exists for efforts directed at high-risk groups, families that are more likely than others to have child abuse and neglect problems, for example, teenage-mother and single-parent families. One such study (Olds, 1984, reported in Rosenberg & Reppucci, 1985) added regular visits by a nurse to other postnatal services during the baby's first two years of life. Special intervention included parent education and enhancement of social-support networks. Results indicated that nurse-visited mothers had fewer conflicts with their babies and punished them less. Most importantly, the frequency of child abuse and neglect was less, compared with controls.

Some efforts to reduce child *sexual* abuse focus on children themselves, such as instructing them in their rights to control access to their bodies and in assertive behaviors when adults talk to or touch them in discomfiting ways. Data are lacking on the effectiveness of such efforts, however, and there are anecdotal reports of negative effects of such open discussions, for example, nightmares. Documentation of results is clearly of paramount importance (Reppucci, 1987).

Children of divorced couples have also been attended to by community researchers. In their Children of Divorce Intervention Program, Pedro-Carroll and Cowen (1985) and Pedro-Carroll et al., (1986) had school-based groups of fourth- to sixth-graders discuss common concerns in a supportive group atmosphere and learn useful skills such as anger control. A subsequent program also involved some of the youngsters serving on an expert panel, fielding questions from peers about coping with their parents' divorce. Results generally demonstrated fewer classroom adjustment problems and lower anxiety levels as compared with control groups. Similar programs (e.g., Stolberg & Garrison, 1985) report encouraging findings. What remains unexamined, in these and in most other primary prevention studies, is the degree to which they truly reduce the incidence of psychopathology. This is a tall order indeed, but the aspirations and rhetoric of community psychologists have been ambitious and should perhaps be judged by the criteria they themselves have set.

Outreach for Children's Stress from the Persian Gulf War

The Persian Gulf campaign against Iraq's invasion of Kuwait, beginning in late July 1990 with the mobilization of allied forces (Desert Shield) and culminating in a short but intense war, principally from the air, in February 1991 (Desert Storm) appeared deceptively easy on service personnel. There were, after all, very few casualties on the allied side, very strong support from citizens around the world, and an engagement that overwhelmed Iraq with strategic, technological, and personnel superiority. And yet, mental health professionals recognized that those who were dispatched to the Middle East for this war would not be shielded from the stressors of wartime. Nor indeed would their families, especially their children, for whom the war was brought home in telecasts unique in their immediacy and vividness. Indeed, unlike the troops in Vietnam, the service personnel included many reservists, people well into their thirties and beyond and much more settled in civilian living; few of them—with good reason—ever expected to be called to active duty.

In response to the ominous situation in the Gulf, the American Psychological Association and the Kent State University Applied Psychology Center Task Force on War-Related Stress convened a group of trauma and intervention experts to discuss the nature of combat-related stress and to publish a general article for dissemination to psychologists (Hobfoll et al., 1991). The intent was to provide state-of-the-art information on the nature, prevention, and treatment of stress and posttraumatic stress disorder. Covering much of the material we reviewed earlier in Chapter 6, this task force had some especially useful things to say about the predicament of children, whose stress reactions to the dangers of war—especially when a parent is called up for duty thousands of miles away—can sometimes be overlooked or underestimated by adults. Their recommendations included the following:

1. Parents and teachers need to learn to listen empathically and nonjudgmentally to children's concerns.
2. They need also to provide reassurance without minimizing the children's worries. It is usually not a good idea to try to comfort a child by promising that nothing bad could possibly happen. A better tack is to point out the measures taken to maximize the safety of service personnel and of the world in general—something that could not have been easy during the earliest stages of the Persian Gulf campaign.
3. Adults must try their utmost not to burden children with their own concerns about the war. Sometimes children are stressed by seeing adult figures, especially parents, under strain. For this reason alone, adults would do well to seek professional assistance for their own emotional difficulties, so that they can better meet the needs of children in their charge.[4]
4. Adults should try to instill in children a sense of self-efficacy (Bandura, 1982), a belief that, although the road ahead is rough, they will be able to cope.
5. Like adults, children can benefit from being involved in helping behaviors, for example, writing letters to service personnel, sending little gifts, and so on.

[4]This raises a general issue for health providers, namely, does one always tell a patient the truth? In the present context, does the parent who remains at home serve the child's best interests by minimizing or even concealing extreme worry about the loved one in the war theater? At what point do such efforts to shield children become an unjustifiable and impractical deception?

The task force recommended that health professionals be proactive in disseminating information about war-related stress, through psychoeducational messages broadcast through the media and through schools, community groups, military organizations, and support groups. Via such community psychological outreach, the largest numbers of people can benefit from theory and research on the nature of posttraumatic stress and its prevention and amelioration.

Evaluation of Community Psychology Work

It has been suggested that the results of community psychology have not lived up to the rhetoric (Bernstein & Nietzel, 1980; Phares, 1992).

Primary Prevention

Nowhere are successes more notably lacking than in primary prevention, in keeping disorders from developing in the first place. One infrequently discussed reason for the limited effectiveness of primary prevention efforts may be that some of the problems community psychologists are trying to prevent are not readily amenable to environmental or social manipulation, for they have major genetic or biological components that are left untouched by the kinds of community-based interventions described in this chapter. As we saw in Chapter 14, for example, there is very strong evidence that schizophrenia has some kind of biological diathesis. Although an environmental preventive effort may conceivably reduce the amount of stress that a predisposed individual is subject to in normal daily living, it seems unlikely that any realistic social change will be able to keep stress levels low enough to prevent schizophrenic episodes from occurring or recurring in high-risk people. Family therapy for reducing expressed emotion (page 416) is a prototype of what might be necessary on a societal scale to have a positive impact on the recurrence of schizophrenic episodes. How practical is it, however, to apply such an approach on a broad scale?

Community Mental Health Centers

Problems of community mental health centers (CMHCs) were examined more than two decades ago in a rather controversial critique by Ralph Nader's Center for Study of Responsive Law (Holden, 1972). This report held that the centers are based on a good and commendable set of ideas but that the implementation has been rather poor. Often the problem is one of old wine in new bottles. Nader's group pointed out that centers are usually controlled by psychiatrists, whose training and outlook are tied to one-to-one therapy, typically along psychoanalytic lines; the fit between treatment and the problems of lower-income people who are the centers' primary clients is often poor. Indeed, a study conducted by Hollica and Milic (1986) in a Connecticut community mental health center indicated that assignment to psychotherapy was made more often for patients of higher social class, who had more education and better employment status. On the plus side was the finding that lower-class patients had indeed been able to obtain some access to outpatient therapy, so-called categorical treatment that focused on specific problems like alcohol and drug abuse. What this study did not address, of course, is who is better off in their respective treatment assignment.

Fewer than 800 of the 2000 community mental health centers envisioned by Congress and needed to provide care have been established. An earlier report from the President's Commission on Mental Health (1978) found that centers were not providing good services to underserved populations, such as the elderly and the chronically mentally ill. More recent data, however, suggest a positive change. For example, day treatment and partial hospitalization are on the rise, and child-oriented services show greater attention to specific pressing problems, such as prevention of child abuse (Jerrell & Larsen, 1986).

Political and Ethical Factors in Community Psychology

Enthusiasm for community psychology must unfortunately be tempered with awareness of social reality—the conditions of deprivation that community psychologists assume are important in producing and maintaining disordered behavior. To train an African-American youngster for a specific vocational slot can have a beneficial long-term outcome for the individual only to the extent that society at large provides the appropriate opportunity to use these skills. Those who work in community psychology are aware that racial and social prejudices play a central role in limiting the access of many minority groups to the rewards of the culture at large. Although efforts to improve the sociocultural milieu must of course continue if our society has any commitment to fostering social and mental well-being, programs may raise expectations that will only be dashed by the realities of the larger culture. This is the quandary of any mental health professional who ventures forth from the consulting room into the community.

Community psychology has as its goal the change of large systems and groups of people rather than treating individual problems. And it is in the seeking mode; psychologists take the initiative in serving people, rather than waiting for individuals in need to come to them. On the face of it, this is a tall order. What do we know about the principles that operate to produce change in societal values and institutions? When a community psychologist organizes a rent strike, for example, what is the best way of doing so, that is, of persuading the greatest number of tenants to work together in the joint effort? Will gentle persuasion be most effective, or does the situation call for harangues against the landlord? Further, if the community psychologist hopes to take actions that meet the wishes and needs of the community, how does he or she determine them? Recall from Chapters 3 and 4 the difficulties the psychologist has in assessing the needs of an individual client with whom there is extensive direct contact. How much more difficult, then, to assess the needs of thousands of people!

Community psychologists necessarily become social activists to some degree, which raises the danger that these well-meaning professionals may *impose* values and goals on their clients. John Kennedy's launching of the community mental health movement proclaimed that the federal government is rightfully concerned about improving the mental health of Americans. But what is mental health? Who is to decide? To what extent do the people being served by community psychologists have a say in how they are to be helped?

These are but a few of the nettlesome questions that must continually be posed if community psychology is to act responsibly and effectively. The focus of this field is on large-scale factors. Many people are involved; many lives, then, will be affected by decisions and actions. Questions of values and of effectiveness are inherent in any effort to alter the human condition, but they are of special importance when the clients themselves do not seek the intervention.

Cultural and Racial Factors in Psychological Intervention

As we close our three-chapter discussion of intervention, it will be useful to revisit the issue of cultural diversity that we have addressed several times already throughout this book. This is an issue of importance to highly heterogeneous countries, such as the United States and Canada, but it is of importance to other countries as well because most of our discussion of psychopathology and intervention is presented within the context and constraints of western European society. Despite our increasing understanding of biological factors in the nature of mental illness and how to prevent and treat many disorders, social circumstances are ignored only at great risk.

For a variety of historical and socioeconomic reasons, many minorities in the United States have had contact with the mental health system primarily through lower-cost agencies like community mental health centers, where the therapists they see are often paraprofessionals. Often these helpers come from the same backgrounds as those receiving services; these paraprofessionals have some training but not the credentials for mental health work. The prevailing belief is that these individuals will better know the life circumstance of those in need, and, most importantly, will be more acceptable to them. Extensive research on modeling provides some justification for these assumptions. Subjects in studies of learning through observation are found to acquire information more readily from models who are perceived as credible and relevant to them; similarity of age and background are important determinants of credibility and relevance (Rosenthal & Bandura, 1978). We can therefore expect that individuals unaccustomed to the standard middle-class fare of a professional office and formal appointments will find the activities and advice of helpers similar to themselves more acceptable.

It would be a mistake, however, to assume that services rendered by paraprofessionals are "good enough" for ethnic and racial minorities. Obviously many middle and upper-class minorities avail themselves of the services of mental health professionals, and all people are entitled to the best services available. Moreover, many of those who cannot afford professional help are white. As will become evident, the following discussion is as relevant to the traditional settings discussed in Chapters 18 and 19 as to the community-oriented work that is the subject of the present chapter. That minorities are overrepresented among the clientele of paraprofessionals and community psychology workers is an accident of history and discrimination.

A final caveat: our discussion of racial factors in intervention runs the risk of stereotyping because we will be reviewing generalizations that experts make about the way a *group* of people react to psychological assistance. No less than whites, people from minority groups are *individuals* who can differ as much from each other as their racial group differs from another racial group. Still, a consideration of group characteristics is important and is part of a developing specialty called minority mental health.

African-Americans and Psychological Intervention

Several studies have examined the effects of race on the counseling relationship. One review suggests that African-American clients prefer African-American counselors to white counselors, engage in more self-exploration with counselors of their own race, and in general feel more positively toward African-American than toward white helpers (Jackson, 1973). At the same time studies suggest that race differences are *not* insurmountable barriers to understanding between counselor and client. Therapists with considerable empathy are perceived as more helpful by clients, regardless of the racial mix.

African-Americans who have not fully accepted the values of white America generally react differently to whites than to other African-Americans: with African-Americans they are more open and spontaneous, whereas with whites they tend to be more guarded and less talkative (Gibbs, 1980; Ridley, 1984). Also, therapists need to accept the fact that virtually all African-Americans have encountered prejudice and racism, and many must often wrestle with their anger at a majority culture that is sometimes insensitive to and unappreciative of the emotional consequences of growing up as a feared, resented, and sometimes hated minority. On the other hand, as Greene (1985) cautions, therapists' sensitivity to social oppression should not translate into a paternalism that removes personal responsibility and individual empowerment from the African-American client.

Hispanics and Psychological Intervention

Findings about how Mexican Americans react to non-Hispanic therapists are mixed. However, with improved experimental designs in three interrelated studies, Lopez et al. (1991) recently found that Mexican Americans reported a clear preference for ethnically similar therapists, especially when the clinical problem related to ethnic concerns (e.g., a woman feeling pressure from Mexican parents to marry rather than have a career). Therapy with most Hispanics should appreciate their difficulty in expressing psychological concerns; men in particular may have great trouble expressing weakness and fear, which may be exacerbated by the growing independence of many Hispanic women as wage earners.

Asian-Americans and Psychological Intervention

It has already been noted that there is considerable variability within groups identified as Hispanic or as African-American. This is certainly the case with Asian-Americans, who comprise more than two dozen distinct subgroups (e.g., Filipino, Chinese, Japanese, Vietnamese) and who differ also on such dimensions as how well they speak English, whether they immigrated or came as refugees from war or terrorism in their homeland, and the degree to which they identify with their native land or that of their parents if they were born in the United States (Yoshioka et al., 1981, as cited in Sue & Sue, 1992). With this caveat in mind, it is fair to say that therapists should be aware of greater tendencies among these groups than among whites to be ashamed of emotional suffering and, coupled with a relative lack of assertiveness, to seek out professional help with great reluctance. Above all, the stereotype of Asian-Americans as having made it, as invariably being highly educated, earning good salaries, and being well adjusted emotionally, is belied by the facts. The discrimination suffered by Asians in this and many other countries appears to be as severe as that endured by other racial and ethnic minority groups (Sue & Sue, 1992).

There are many implications for how to conduct psychotherapy with Asian-Americans. Sue and Sue (1992) advise therapists to be sensitive to the personal losses that many Asian refugees have suffered and, especially in light of the great importance that family connections have for them, to the likelihood that they are very stressed from these losses. Another way to put this is to appreciate the role of posttraumatic stress in Asian-Americans who have come to this country as refugees. Therapists should also be aware that Asian-Americans have a tendency to "somaticize," that is, to experience and to talk about stress in physical terms, like headaches and fatigue. Next, their values are quite different from the Western values of the majority culture in our country. For example—and allowing for considerable individual variation—Asians respect structure and formality in interpersonal relationships, whereas a Western therapist is likely to favor informality and a less authoritarian attitude. Respect for authority may take the form of agreeing readily to what the therapist does and proposes—and perhaps, rather than discussing differences openly, just not showing up for the next session. Indeed, the very acceptability of psychotherapy as a way to handle stress is likely to be much lower among Asian-Americans, who tend to see emotional duress as something to be handled on one's own and through willpower (Kinzie, 1985). Asian-Americans may consider some areas off-limits for discussion with a therapist, for example, the nature of the marital relationship, and especially sex. Asian-Americans born in the United States are often caught between two cultures; one form that a resolution can take is to identify vigorously with majority values and denigrate anything Asian, a kind of racial self-hate. Others are torn by conflicting loyalties, experiencing (poorly expressed) rage at a discriminatory Western culture but at the same time questioning aspects of their Asian background. Finally, the therapist may have to be more directive and active than he or she otherwise might be, given the preference of many Asian-Americans for a structured approach over a reflective one (Atkinson, Maruyama, & Matsui, 1978).

Native Americans and Psychological Intervention

As with other minority groups, Native Americans are a highly heterogeneous group, with about 500 tribes residing in the United States. With due regard for individual differences, such as the degree to which the person is assimilated, some generalizations can be made that pertain to this discussion (Sue & Sue, 1992). Because Native American children are often looked after in the households of different relatives, the pattern of a child or young adult moving around in different households is not necessarily a sign of trouble. A youngster's avoidance of eye contact is a traditional sign of respect, but may be misconstrued by someone unfamiliar with the culture as quite the opposite and regarded as a problem to be remedied, as reported by Everett, Proctor, and Cartmell (1989). As with other minorities, conflicts about identification can be severe—young people can be torn between traditional values and those of the (decidedly more privileged) majority culture, which may underlie the high rates of truancy, substance abuse, and suicide among Native American young people (Red Horse, 1982). Indeed, drug abuse, especially alcoholism, is a widespread problem and should probably be considered a potential source of difficulty; because it frequently leads to child abuse, that problem, too, needs to be weighed when there is family conflict. A value placed on cooperativeness rather than competitiveness can be misinterpreted by a culturally unaware therapist as lack of motivation. The importance of family may make it advisable to conduct treatment in the home with family members present and an integral part of the intervention.

Toward a More Complete Science of Behavior

Regardless of whether the therapist has the same skin color or ethnicity as the client, it is important that the mental health professional be aware of and sensitive to the different value structures and life experiences of the client. The same can be said of the treatment of *any* client who is different from the therapist in ways that affect attitudes and behavior.

The study of ethnic or racial factors in psychological intervention, as well as their role in clinical assessment (page 102), can be seen in the broader context of the social and scientific importance of including such variables in the study of human behavior. The inclusion of diversity can enhance our scientific understanding of people (Betancourt & Lopez, in press; Rokeach, 1979). If membership in a particular subculture plays a role, for example, in how readily emotion is expressed, then neglecting culture as a variable may limit our understanding of the role of expressed emotion in psychopathology. And such a constraint will vitiate not only our data-based knowledge but our ability to meet our social responsibilities. Culture and values are increasingly recognized as key factors in how a society structures its science and makes its policy; our continuing sensitivity throughout this book to paradigms in science reflects this understanding. As we turn now to the final chapter, we will appreciate even more the complex interplay between scientific knowledge and the use to which that knowledge is put in affecting people's lives.

SUMMARY

Group therapy takes advantage of some special properties of the group itself. A group can exert strong social pressure for change. Members also benefit from sharing common concerns and aspirations. Sensitivity training and encounter groups enable people to learn how they affect others and are affected by them. Efforts are made to get behind the social facades that people present to the world, so that they may deal honestly and more effectively with one another. Controlled research on outcome and process in group therapy of all kinds is just beginning to be done.

In family therapy the problems of the identified patient are considered the manifestation of disturbances within the family unit. Family members learn how their behavior and attitudes affect one another, that flexibility and changing communication patterns can bring greater harmony. Marital or couples therapy helps unhappy couples resolve the conflicts inevitable in any ongoing relationship of two adults living together. One technique consists of caring days; one partner at a time concentrates on giving pleasure to the other, breaking the cycle of bitterness and hostility plaguing them. Couples therapists of all theoretical allegiances try to improve partners' communication of needs and wants to each other. An act may be well intentioned but have a negative impact. Talking openly about this problem appears to ease the tensions of many couples. Continuing research in family and couples therapies promises to elucidate the problems for which they are the most appropriate and the processes by which they bring relief.

Community psychology and the related community mental health movement try to prevent mental disorders from developing, to seek out troubled people, and to find the social conditions that may be causing or exacerbating human problems. Community workers must make their values explicit, for they are often fostering social change rather than helping individuals adjust to what some consider untenable social conditions. Deinstitutionalization, the policy of having former mental patients live, if at all possible, at home or in small residences, is part of this movement. Much work needs to be done, however, in designing and supplying adequate sheltered residences and care that will help them live in the community in an acceptable fashion. Primary prevention is difficult to institute, a reflection of our inadequate knowledge of how disordered behavior develops. More needs to be learned about how to determine the needs of a community or how to mobilize large groups of people for change.

Finally, as a capstone to the three chapters on intervention, we discussed a variety of considerations raised by the cultural and racial backgrounds of patients. Particular issues surround the treatment of African-Americans, Latinos, Asian-Americans, and Native Americans, including the kinds of problems these groups may have and the kinds of sensitivities clinicians should foster in themselves so that they can deal respectfully and effectively with patients from minority groups.

KEY TERMS

group therapy
couples (marital) therapy
community psychology
sensitivity training group (T-group)
encounter group
family systems approach
divorce mediation
tertiary prevention
secondary prevention
primary prevention

c h a p t e r t w e n t y - o n e

Legal and Ethical Issues

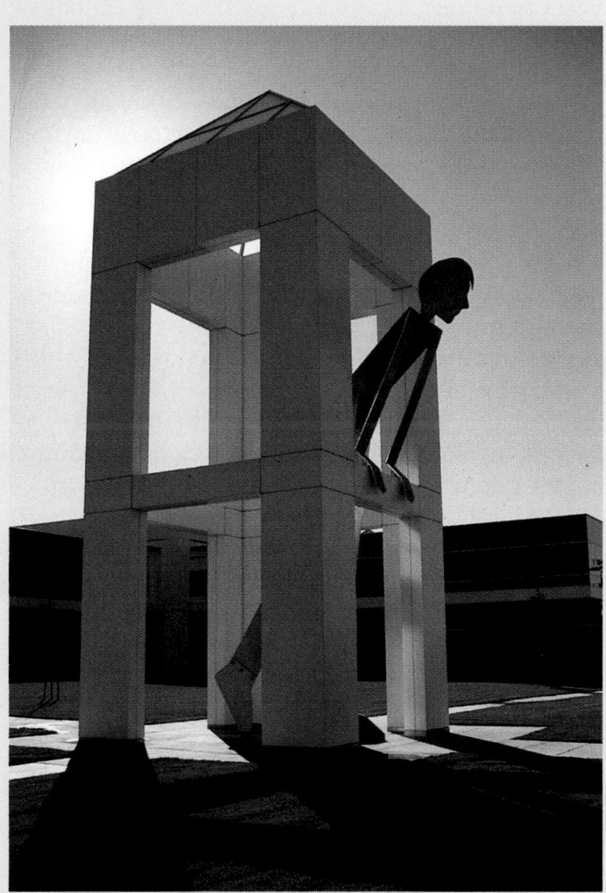

Amendment 1 Congress shall make no law respecting an establishment of religion, or prohibiting the free exercise thereof; or abridging the freedom of speech, or of the press; or the right of the people peaceably to assemble, and to petition the Government for a redress of grievances.

Amendment 4 The right of the people to be secure in their persons, houses, papers, and effects, against unreasonable searches and seizures, shall not be violated. . . .

Amendment 5 No person . . . shall be compelled in any criminal case to be a witness against himself, nor be deprived of life, liberty, or property, without due process of law. . . .

Amendment 6 In all criminal prosecutions, the accused shall enjoy the right to a speedy and public trial . . . ; to be confronted with the witnesses against him; to have compulsory process for obtaining witnesses in his favor, and to have the Assistance of Counsel for his defense.

Amendment 8 Excessive bail shall not be required, nor excessive fines imposed, nor cruel and unusual punishment inflicted.

Amendment 13 . . . Neither slavery nor involuntary servitude, except as a punishment for crime whereof the party shall have been duly convicted, shall exist within the United States, or any place subject to their jurisdiction. . . .

Amendment 14 . . . No State shall . . . deprive any person of life, liberty, or property, without due process of law; nor deny to any person within its jurisdiction the equal protection of the laws.

Amendment 15 . . . The right of citizens of the United States to vote shall not be denied or abridged by the United States or by any State on account of race, color, or previous condition of servitude.

These elegant statements describe and protect some of the rights of U.S. citizens and others residing in this country. Against what are these rights being protected? Be mindful of the circumstances under which most of these statements were issued. After the Constitutional Convention delegates had delineated the powers of government in 1787, the first Congress saw fit in 1789 to amend what they had framed and to set specific limits on the federal government. Amendments beyond the original ten have been added since that time. In particular, the Fourteenth Amendment is directed to the states, which, as will be seen, are playing increasingly important roles in the protection of the rights of mental patients. The philosophical ideal of American government has always been to allow citizens the maximum degree of liberty consistent with preserving order in the community at large.

We open our final chapter in this way because the legal and mental health systems collaborate continually, although often subtly, to deny a substantial proportion of our population their basic civil rights. With the best of intentions, judges, governing boards of hospitals, bar associations, and professional mental health groups have worked over the years to protect society at large from the actions of people regarded as mentally ill or mentally defective and considered dangerous to themselves or to others. But in so doing they have abrogated the rights of thousands of people in both criminal and civil commitment proceedings. The mentally ill who have broken the law, or who are alleged to have done so, are subject to **criminal commitment**, a procedure whereby a person is confined in a mental institution either for determination of competency to stand trial or after acquittal by reason of insanity. **Civil commitment** is a set of procedures by which a mentally ill and dangerous person who has not broken a law can be deprived of liberty and incarcerated in a mental hospital. In effect, both commitments remove individuals from the normal processes of the law. In this chapter we will look at both of these legal procedures in some depth. Then we will turn to an examination of some important ethical issues as they relate to therapy and research.

Criminal Commitment

We shall examine first the role of psychiatry and psychology in the criminal justice system. Almost as early as the concept of *mens rea*, or guilty mind, and the rule "No crime without an evil intent" had begun to be accepted in English common law, insanity had to be taken into consideration, for a disordered mind may be regarded as unable to formulate and carry out a criminal purpose (Morse, 1992). In other words, a disordered mind could not be a guilty mind; only a guilty mind can engender culpable actions. At first insanity was not a trial defense, but the English Crown sometimes granted pardons to people who had been convicted of homicide if they were judged completely and totally mad (A. A. Morris, 1968). By the reign of Edward I (1272–1307), the concept of insanity had begun to be argued in court and could lessen punishment. During the course of the fourteenth century it became the rule of law that a person proved to be wholly and continually mad could be defended against a criminal charge.

In today's courts judges and lawyers have called on psychiatrists, and recently clinical psychologists as well, for assistance in dealing with criminal acts thought to result from the accused's disordered mental state, not from free will. Are such emotionally disturbed perpetrators less criminally responsible than those who are not distraught but commit the same crimes? Should such individuals even be brought to trial for transgressions against society's laws? Although efforts to excuse or protect the accused through the insanity defense or by judging them incompetent to stand trial are undoubtedly well-intentioned, invoking these doctrines can often subject those accused to a greater denial of liberties than they would otherwise experience.

The Insanity Defense

The **insanity defense** is the legal argument that a defendant should not be held responsible for an illegal act if the conduct is attributable to mental illness that interferes with rationality or that results in some other excusing circumstance, such as not knowing right from wrong. A staggering amount of material has been written on the insanity defense, even though it is pleaded in only about 2 percent of all cases that reach trial and is rarely successful (N. Morris, 1968; Morse 1982b; Steadman, 1979). Alan A. Stone (1975), a professor of law and psychiatry at Harvard, proposed an intriguing reason for this great interest in finding certain people NGRI, not guilty by reason of insanity. Criminal law rests on the assumption that people have free will and that, if they do wrong, they have *chosen* to do so, are blameworthy, and should therefore be punished. Stone suggests that the insanity defense strengthens the concept of free will by pointing to the few people who constitute an exception because they do not have it, namely, those judged to be insane. These individuals are assumed to have less responsibility for their actions because of a mental defect, an inability to distinguish between right and wrong, or both. They lack the degree of free will that would justify holding them legally accountable for criminal acts. By exclusion, everyone else *has* free will! "The insanity defense is in every sense the exception that proves the rule. It allows the courts to treat every other defendant as someone who chose 'between good and evil' " (Stone, 1975, p. 222).

Landmark Cases and Laws

In modern Anglo-American criminal law, several court rulings and established principles bear on the problems of legal responsibility and mental illness. The so-called irresistible impulse concept was formulated in 1834 in a case in Ohio. It was decided that an insanity defense was legitimate if a pathological impulse or drive the person could not control had compelled that person to commit the criminal act. The irresistible impulse test was confirmed in two subsequent court cases, *Parsons* v. *State* and *Davis* v. *United States*.[1]

The second well-known concept, the M'Naghten rule, was announced in the aftermath of a murder trial in England in 1843. The defendant, Daniel M'Naghten, had meant to kill the British prime minister, Sir Robert Peel, but had instead mistaken the secretary for his employer. M'Naghten claimed that he had been instructed to kill Lord Peel by the "voice of God." The judges ruled that

> to establish a defence of insanity, it must be clearly proved that, at the time of the committing of the act, the party accused was labouring under such a defect of reason, from disease of the mind, as not to know the nature and quality of the act he was doing; or if he did know it, that he did not know he was doing what was wrong.

By the beginning of the twentieth century, this right–wrong test was being used in all the states except New Hampshire and in all federal courts. By the late 1980s it was the sole test in eighteen states, and in several others was applied in conjunction with irresistible impulse. However, early on a committee of the American Psychiatric Association expressed the view that understanding the difference between right and wrong was out of step with modern conceptions of insanity. It was in this context that a third important court decision was made.

Judge David Bazelon ruled in 1954, in the case of *Durham* v. *United States*,[2] that the "accused is not criminally responsible if his unlawful act was the product of mental disease or mental defect." Bazelon believed that by referring simply to mental illness he would leave the profession of psychiatry free to apply its full knowledge. It would no longer be limited to considering impulses or knowledge of right and wrong. Judge Bazelon purposely did not incorporate in what would be called the Durham test any particular symptoms of mental disorder that might later become obsolete. The psychiatrist

---

[1]*Parsons* v. *State*, 2 So. 854, 866–67 (Ala. 1887); *Davis* v. *United States*, 175 U.S. 373, 378 (1897).

[2]*Durham* v. *United States*, 214 F.2d 862, 876 (D.C. Cir. 1954).

was accorded great liberty to convey to the court his or her own evaluation of the accused's mental condition. Forcing the jury to rely to this extent on expert testimony did not prove workable courtroom practice, however. Since 1972 the Durham test has not been used in any jurisdiction, and Judge Bazelon withdrew his support for it, feeling that it allowed too much leeway to expert witnesses.

In 1962 the American Law Institute (ALI) proposed its own guidelines, which were intended to be more specific and informative to lay jurors than other tests.

> **1.** A person is not responsible for criminal conduct if at the time of such conduct as a result of mental disease or defect he lacks substantial capacity either to appreciate the criminality (wrongfulness) of his conduct or to conform his conduct to the requirements of law.
>
> **2.** As used in the Article, the terms "mental disease or defect" do not include an abnormality manifested only by repeated criminal or otherwise antisocial conduct. (The American Law Institute, 1962, p. 66)

The first of the ALI guidelines in a sense combines the M'Naghten rule and the irresistible impulse concept. The second ALI guideline concerns those who are repeatedly in trouble with the law; they are not to be deemed mentally ill only because they keep committing crimes. Indeed, the phrase "substantial capacity" in the first guideline is designed to limit an insanity defense to those with the most serious mental disorders. Until 1984 the ALI test was in use in more than half the states and in all federal courts. Some scholars, however, argue that words like *substantial* and *appreciate* introduce ambiguities that foster disagreements among both expert witnesses and jurors as to whether a defendant's state of mind is sufficiently disturbed to justify a verdict of not guilty by reason of insanity (Simon & Aaronson, 1988).

In the past several years there has been a fifth major effort in the United States to clarify the legal defense of insanity, strengthened by the controversy created by the NGRI verdict in the highly publicized trial of John Hinckley, Jr. for an assassination attempt against President Ronald Reagan. Judge Parker, who presided over the trial, received a flood of mail from outraged citizens that a would-be assassin of a U.S. president had not been held criminally responsible and had only been committed to an indefinite stay in a mental hospital until deemed mentally healthy enough for release. (As we write this in mid-1993, Hinckley has been incarcerated in St. Elizabeth's Hospital for over twelve years, but can be released whenever his mental health is deemed adequate.)

Because of the publicity of the trial and the public outrage at the NGRI verdict, the insanity defense became a target of vigorous and sometimes vituperative criticism from many quarters. As Judge Parker put it: "For many, the [Hinckley] defense was a clear manifestation of the failure of our criminal justice system to punish individuals who have clearly violated the law" (Simon & Aaronson, 1988, p. vii).

As a consequence of political pressures to get tough on criminals, Congress enacted in October 1984 the Insanity Defense Reform Act, addressing the insanity defense for the first time. This new law, which has been adopted in all federal courts, contains several provisions:

John Hinckley, President Reagan's assailant, wrote this letter to actress Jodie Foster expressing his dream of marrying her and becoming president.

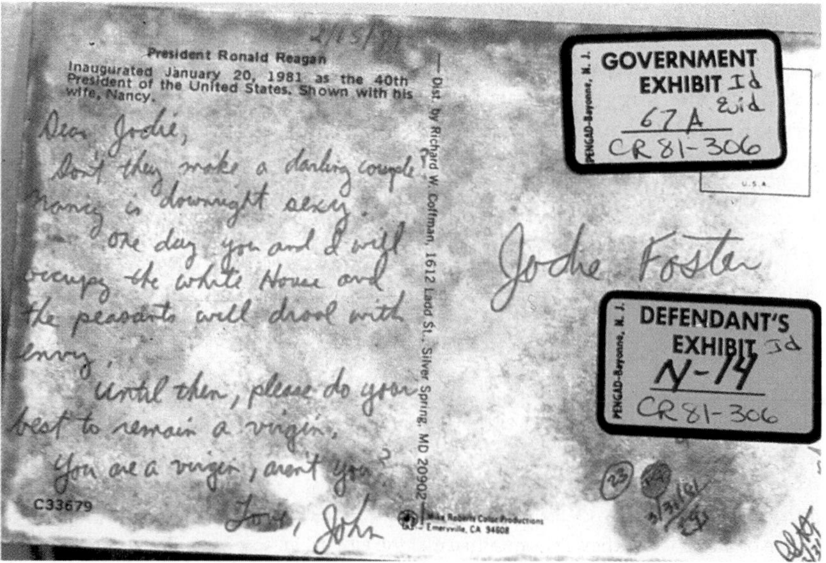

2/15/81

President Ronald Reagan
Inaugurated January 20, 1981 as the 40th President of the United States. Shown with his wife, Nancy.

Dear Jodie,
Don't they make a darling couple?
Nancy is downright sexy.
One day you and I will occupy the White House and the peasants will drool with envy.
Until then, please do your best to remain a virgin.
You are a virgin, aren't you?
Love, John

C33679

Dist. by Richard W. Coffman, 1612 Ladd St., Silver Spring, MD 20902

Jodie Foster

GOVERNMENT EXHIBIT Id 2id
67A
CR81-306

DEFENDANT'S EXHIBIT Id
N-14
CR81-306

1. It eliminates the irresistible impulse component of the ALI rules, which referred to inability of the person to conform to the requirements of the law as a result of a mental disease or defect. This volitional and behavioral aspect of the ALI guidelines had been strongly criticized because one could regard *any* criminal act as arising from an inability to stay within the limits of the law.
2. It changes the ALI's lack of "substantial capacity . . . to appreciate" to "unable to appreciate." This alteration in the cognitive component of the law is intended to tighten the grounds for an insanity defense.
3. The 1984 act also stipulates that the mental disease or defect be "severe," the intent being to exclude insanity defenses on the bases of nonpsychotic disorders, such as antisocial personality disorder. (The ALI guidelines were developed to impose similar restrictions by the use of the word *substantial* to describe incapacity; this apparently was not considered strong enough in the immediate aftermath of the Hinckley acquittal.) Also abolished by the act were defenses relying on "diminished capacity" or "diminished responsibility," based on such mitigating circumstances as extreme passion or "temporary insanity".
4. The Insanity Defense Reform Act of 1984 also shifts the burden of proof from the prosecution to the defense. Instead of the prosecution having to prove that the person was sane beyond a reasonable doubt at the time of the crime (the most stringent criterion, consistent with the constitutional requirement that people are considered innocent until proved guilty), the defense must prove that the defendant was not sane and must do so with "clear and convincing evidence" (a less stringent but still demanding standard of proof). The importance of this shift can be appreciated by keeping in mind that if the prosecution bears the burden of proof beyond a reasonable doubt, then the defense need only introduce a reasonable doubt to defeat the prosecution's efforts to prove sanity. The heavier burden that the 1984 Reform Act places on the defense is, like the other provisions, designed to make it more difficult to relieve a defendant of moral and legal responsibility.[3]
5. Finally, the new act responds to what many felt to be the most annoying possibility allowable under existing laws, namely, release from commitment after a shorter period of time than an ordinary sentence would have provided. If the person is judged to have recovered from mental illness, then instead of allowing release from the prison hospital, the period of incarceration can be extended to the maximum allowable for the actual crime.

Fourteen states have since supplemented the NGRI defense with what seems to be a compromise verdict, namely, guilty but mentally ill (GBMI). Initially adopted by Michigan in 1975, this principle allows an accused person to be found legally guilty of a crime—thus maximizing the chances of incarceration—but allows for psychiatric judgment of how to deal with the convicted person if he or she is considered to have been mentally ill when the act was committed. Thus, even a seriously ill person can be held morally and legally responsible, but can then be committed to a prison hospital or other suitable facility for psychiatric treatment rather than to a regular prison for punishment.

This trend reflects the uneasiness of the legal and mental health professions in excusing a person who, in Thomas Szasz's terms is *descriptively* responsible for a crime—that is, there is no disputing that he or she actually committed the act—without being held *ascriptively* responsible for it—that is, without having to suffer some sort of societal negative consequence for breaking the law (Focus Box 21.1). This legal modification avoids the irony of (1) determining that a person committed a crime, (2) determining that he or she is not to be held legally responsible because of insanity at the time of the crime—the NGRI defense—and then (3) by the time the person is to be criminally committed, he or she is judged to be no longer mentally ill, and (4) the person is *not* incarcerated (or is released after a confinement shorter than it would have been had the person been found guilty of the crime he or she committed).[4] A GBMI verdict allows the usual sentence to be imposed for being found guilty of a given crime, but also allows for the person to be treated for mental illness during incarceration.

So far, however, evidence does not indicate that the GBMI alternative per se results in appropriate

[3]According to Simon and Aaronson (1988), this provision arose in large measure from the inability of the prosecution to prove John Hinckley's sanity when he shot Reagan and three others. Several members of the jury testified after the trial to a subcommittee of the Senate Judiciary Committee that the judge's instructions on the burden of proof played a role in their verdict of NGRI. Even before the act, almost half the states required that the defendant must prove insanity, but only one, Arizona, had the "clear and convincing" standard. Since *Hinckley*, about two-thirds of the states now place the burden of proof on the defense, albeit with the least exacting of legal standards of proof, "by a preponderance of the evidence."

[4]Things can go the other way, however, as demonstrated in the case of *Jones* v. *United States* described shortly.

FOCUS 21.1 • Thomas S. Szasz and the Case Against Forensic Psychiatry and Psychology

His Polemic

> By codifying acts of violence as expressions of mental illness, we neatly rid ourselves of the task of dealing with criminal offenses as more or less rational goal-directed acts, no different in principle from other forms of conduct. (Szasz. 1963, p. 141)

This quotation from one of Thomas Szasz's most widely read books enunciates the basic theme of his argument against the weighty role that his own profession of psychiatry plays in the legal system. We have already mentioned Szasz's distinction between descriptive and ascriptive responsibility. To hold a person criminally responsible is to ascribe legal responsibility for an act for which the person is descriptively responsible. A given social group makes the judgment that the person who is descriptively responsible for a criminal act will receive criminal punishment. As Szasz points out, being criminally responsible is not an inherent trait that society uncovers. Rather, society at a given time and for a given criminal act decides that it will hold the perpetrator legally responsible and will punish him or her.

Szasz also suggests that mental illness began to be used as an explanation for criminal behavior when people acted in a way that was considered particularly irrational and threatening to society. According to Szasz, these exceptional cases all involved violence against people of high social rank. In shooting at Lord Onslow in 1724, a man named Arnold was believed to have as little understanding of his murderous act as "a wild beast." Another man, James Hadfield, was deemed deranged for attempting to assassinate King George III as he sat in a box at the Theatre Royal in 1800. And a third person, named Oxford, was regarded as insane for trying to kill Queen Victoria in 1840. The best-known case has already been mentioned, that of David M'Naghten (1943), who killed Sir Robert Peel's private secretary after mistaking him for Peel. In all these cases from English law, which forms the basis for U.S. law, people of low social rank openly attacked their superiors. Szasz believes that "the issue of insanity may have been raised in these trials in order to obscure the social problems which the crimes intended to dramatize" (1963, p. 128).

Other cases here and abroad, such as the assassinations of John and Robert Kennedy, South African prime minister Hendrik Verwoerd, Martin Luther King, Jr., and John Lennon, and the attempted assassinations of Ronald Reagan and Pope John Paul II, may to a degree reflect the social ills of the day. Moreover, events in the former Soviet Union provide examples of the role of politics in criminal and civil commitment. In *A Question of Madness*, the well-known Russian biochemist Zhores Medvedev (1972) told how So-

Noted psychiatrist, Thomas S. Szasz, argues strongly against the use of the insanity defense.

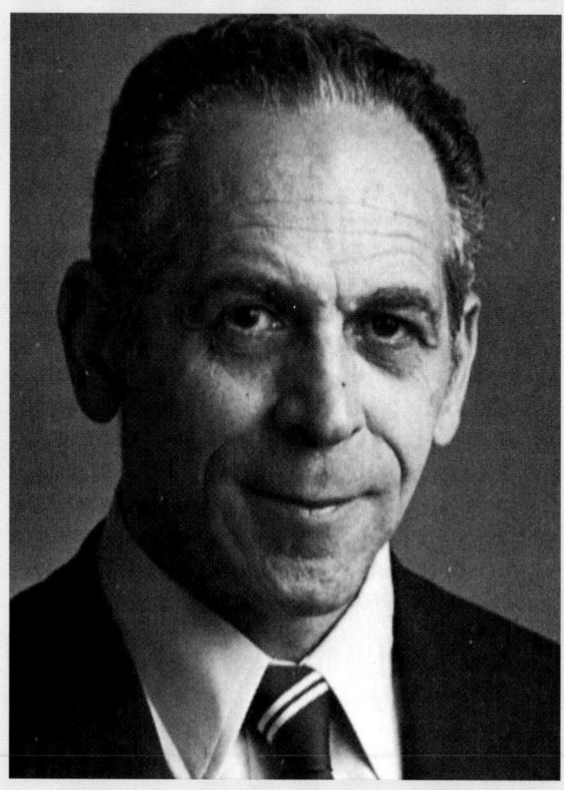

viet psychiatrists collaborated with the state in attempting to muzzle his criticism of the government. They diagnosed him as suffering from paranoid delusions, split personality, and other mental ailments that would make it dangerous for him to be at large in society.

But pleas of insanity are generally made in far more ordinary cases. Of course Szasz does not claim that all these pleas involve some sort of silent conspiracy of the establshment to cover up social problems. Szasz sets forth a polemic much broader in scope. His basic concern is with individual freedom, which includes the right to deviate from prevailing mores. Far from advocating that people be held *less* accountable for antisocial acts, he argues that legal responsibility be extended to *all*, even to those whose actions are so far beyond the limits of convention that some people explain their behavior in terms of mental illness. Szasz's overall lament is that

> instead of recognizing the deviant as an individual different from those who would judge him, but nonetheless worthy of their respect, he is first discredited as a self-responsible human being and then subjected to humiliating punishment defined and disguised as treatment. (1963, p. 108)

Evaluation of Szasz's Position

The Insanity Defense Reform Act of 1984 as well as changes in civil commitment to be described shortly, are consistent with the arguments that Szasz has put forward for the past thirty years. Indeed, these shifts in the direction of holding the mentally ill accountable for their actions and thereby more deserving of protection of their civil rights are probably due in large measure to his unrelenting attacks on the liaison between the law and the mental health professions.

However, Szasz has not gone uncriticized by those who sincerely believe that psychiatry and psychology should have an important role in deciding how to deal with people whose criminal acts seem attributable to mental illness. The abuses documented by Szasz should not blind us to the fact that—for whatever combination of biological and psychological reasons—some people are, at times, a danger to others and to themselves. Although Szasz and others object to mental illness as an explanation, it is difficult to deny that there is, indeed, madness in the world. People *do* occasionally imagine persecutors, whom they sometimes act against with force. Some people *do* hallucinate and on this basis may behave in a dangerous fashion. Our concern for the liberties of one individual has always been tempered with our concern for the rights of others.

But does it help a criminal acquitted by reason of insanity to be placed in a prison mental hospital with an indeterminate sentence, pending rehabilitation? The answer can surely not be an unqualified yes. Should such a person, then, be treated like any other convicted felon and be sent to a penitentiary? Considering the psychic damage that we know may occur in ordinary prisons, a yes to this question cannot be enthusiastic either. But a prison sentence is more often a finite term of incarceration. If we cannot demonstrate that people are rehabilitated in mental hospitals, perhaps it is just as well to rely on our prisons and on the efforts of penologists to improve these institutions and to find ways of helping inmates alter their behavior so that they will not be antisocial after release.

Stephen J. Morse, a University of Pennsylvania law professor and a leading theorist in forensics, has also written on the need to treat mentally ill people as responsible individuals and on the associated need to improve the prison system.

> If involuntary commitment is abolished, there may well be an increase in the processing of cases of relatively mild deviance through the criminal justice system and increased numbers of crazy persons may spend some time in unpleasant and often terrible jails. But, if crazy persons are almost always responsible for their behavior, and if incarceration in a jail is justified, there is no reason why they should not go to jail. This outcome is in fact more respectful of the dignity and autonomy of crazy persons than assuming that they are nonresponsible and must be "fixed."Jails and locked hospitals are both massive intrusions on liberty. The best response to the argument that jails are bad places, as they surely are for non-crazy and crazy inmates alike, is to clean them up. Using unjustified hospitalization—merely another form of incarceration that offers little if any of the benefits it promises—to avoid jails is not a sensible solution to the problems of criminal justice: it merely allows us to avoid those problems. (Morse, 1982a, p. 98)

psychiatric treatment for those convicted (Fentiman, 1985). The GBMI verdict is opposed by both the American Psychiatric Association and the American Bar Association and also lacks support from professionals outside the fourteen states that currently allow the verdict (Simon & Aaronson, 1988).

In general, applying the insanity defense requires applying an abstract principle to specific life situations. As in all aspects of the law, terms can be defined in a number of ways—by defendants, defense lawyers, prosecutors, judges, and, of course, by jurors—and testimony can be presented in diverse fashion, depending on the skill of the interrogators and the intelligence of the witnesses. Furthermore, because the defendant's mental condition *only at the time the crime was committed* is in question, retrospective, often speculative, judgment on the part of attorneys, judges, jurors, and psychiatrists is required. And disagreement between defense and prosecution psychiatrists and psychologists is the rule.

A final point should be emphasized. There is an important difference between insanity and mental illness or defect. A person can be diagnosed as mentally ill and yet be held responsible for a crime. *Insanity* is a legal, not a psychiatric or psychological concept. This distinction was made vivid by the February 15, 1992, conviction of Jeffrey Dahmer in Milwaukee, Wisconsin. He had been accused of and had admitted to butchering, cannibalizing, and having sex with the corpses of fifteen boys and young men. Pleading guilty but mentally ill, Dahmer's sanity was the sole focus of an unusual trial that had jurors listening to conflicting testimony from mental health experts about the defendant's state of mind during the serial killings to which he had confessed. They had to decide whether he had been suffering from a mental disease that prevented him from knowing right from wrong or from being able to control his action (note the blend of the ALI guidelines, M'Naghten, and irresistible impulse). Even though there was no disagreement that he was a sick man, diagnosable as having some sort of paraphilia, Dahmer was deemed sane and therefore legally responsible for the grisly murders. He was sentenced by the judge to fifteen consecutive life terms (Associated Press, 1992).

Insanity is a legal concept and differs from the psychological concept of mental illness. Jeffrey Dahmer, a serial killer and paraphiliac, seemed clearly psychopathological but was not judged insane because he was regarded as knowing right from wrong and able to control his behavior.

The Case of *Jones* v. *United States*

Case Description To illustrate the predicament that a person can get into by raising insanity as an excusing condition for a criminal act, we consider a Supreme Court case.[5] Michael Jones was arrested unarmed on September 19, 1975, for attempting to steal a jacket from a department store in Washington, D.C. He was charged the following day with attempted petty larceny, a misdemeanor punishable by a maximum prison sentence of one year. The court ordered that he be committed to St. Elizabeth's Hospital, a public mental hospital in Washington, D.C., for a determination of his competency to stand trial. On March 2, 1976, almost six months after the alleged crime, a hospital psychologist reported to the court that Jones was competent to stand trial, although he suffered from "schizophrenia, paranoid type." The psychologist also reported that the alleged crime itself was caused by Jones's condition, his paranoid schizophrenia. This is noteworthy because the psychologist was not asked to offer an opinion on the nature of the crime itself, only on whether Jones was competent to stand trial. Jones then decided to plead not guilty by reason of insanity. Ten days later, on March 12, the court found him not guilty by reason of insanity and formally committed him to St. Elizabeth's Hospital for treatment of his mental disorder.

[5] *Jones* v. *United States*, 463 U.S., 103 S.Ct., L. Ed. 2d, 51 U.S.L.W. 5041 (1983).

On May 25, 1976 a customary fifty-day hearing was held to determine whether Jones should remain in the hospital any longer. A psychologist from the hospital testified that, indeed, Jones still suffered from paranoid schizophrenia and was therefore still a danger to himself and to others. A second hearing was held on February 22, 1977, seventeen months after the commission of the crime and Jones's original commitment to St. Elizabeth's for determination of competency. The defendant demanded release since he had already been hospitalized longer than the one-year maximum sentence he would have served had he been found guilty of the theft of the jacket. The court denied the request and returned him to St. Elizabeth's.

The District of Columbia Court of Appeals agreed with the original court. Ultimately, in November 1982, more than seven years after his hospitalization, Jones's appeal to the Supreme Court was heard. On June 29, 1983, by a five-to-four decision, the Court affirmed the earlier decision: Jones was to remain at St. Elizabeth's.

The Decision of the Supreme Court The basic question that Jones took to the Supreme Court was whether someone "who was committed to a mental hospital upon being acquitted of a criminal offense by reason of insanity, must be released because he has been hospitalized for a period longer than he might have served in prison had he been convicted" (*Jones* v. *United States*, p. 700). Having already spent more time in the prison hospital than he would have served in prison had he been convicted, Jones believed that he should be released.

The Supreme Court, however, saw matters differently.

> An insanity acquittee is not entitled to his release merely because he has been hospitalized for a period longer than he could have been incarcerated if convicted. The length of a sentence for a particular criminal offense is based on a variety of considerations, including retribution, deterrence, and rehabilitation. However, *because an insanity acquittee was not convicted, he may not be punished.* The purpose of his commitment is to treat his mental illness and protect him and society from his potential dangerousness. There simply is no necessary correlation between the length of the acquittee's hypothetical criminal sentence and the length of time necessary for his recovery. (p. 700, emphasis added)[6]

> Where [the] accused has pleaded insanity as a defense to a crime, and the jury has found that the defendant was, in fact, insane at the time the crime was committed, it is just and reasonable . . . that the insanity, once established, should be presumed to continue and that the accused should automatically be confined for treatment until it can be shown that he has recovered. (S Rep No. 1170, 84th Cong, 1st Sess 13 (1955), as cited in *Jones* v. *United States*, p. 705)
>
> And because it is impossible to predict how long it will take for any given individual to recover—or indeed whether he ever will recover—Congress has chosen, as it has with respect to civil commitment, to leave the length of commitment interdeterminate, subject to periodic review of the patient's suitability for release. (p. 708)

The fact that Jones was acquitted means, said the Court, that he cannot be punished for the crime. For to be punished, the individual must be blameworthy. Jones's insanity left him legally blameless, for he could not possess *mens rea*, a guilty mind. His free will to have committed the theft was deemed to have been superseded by his disturbed mental state. This is the logic of the insanity defense. Furthermore, said the Court, since punishment cannot have any of its intended individual or societal effects on a mentally disturbed person—rehabilitation, deterrence, or retribution—it was irrelevant that Jones was being held longer than a normal prison sentence.

Critique of the Supreme Court Decision The burden of proof was on Jones, the acquittee, to prove that he was no longer mentally ill, or dangerous to society. This contrasts with the normal practice of justice in the United States, that a person's *accusers* have the burden of proving him or her guilty. And as we shall soon see, it differs as well from civil commitment, in which the government, not the person, bears the burden of proof; Jones was denied this civil right.

The Court was concerned about Jones's illness-produced dangerousness. What the Court said about "dangerousness" is therefore interesting. Jones argued in his petition to the Supreme Court that his theft of the jacket was not dangerous because his was not a violent crime. The Court stated, however, that for there to be violence in a criminal act, the act itself need not be dangerous. It cited a previous decision that a nonviolent theft of an article such as a watch may frequently result in violence through the efforts of the criminal to escape, or of the victim to protect his or her property, or of the police to apprehend the fleeing thief.[7]

[6]At the time, this absence of correlation between the criminal act and the length of incarceration could also work the other way, namely, "no matter how serious the act committed by the acquittee, he may be released within fifty days of his acquittal if he has recovered" (p. 708).

[7]*Overholser* v. *O'Beorne*, 112 App. D.C. 267, 302 F.2d 852, 861 (1961).

The dissenting justices of the Court commented that the longer someone like Jones had to remain in the hospital, the more difficult it would be for him to demonstrate that he was no longer a dangerous person nor mentally ill. Extended institutionalization would likely make it more difficult for him to afford medical experts other than those associated with the hospital and to behave like someone who was not mentally ill.

> The current [use of] psychotropic drugs . . . may render mental patients docile . . . , but it does not "cure" them or allow them to demonstrate that they would remain non-violent if they were not drugged. . . . At petitioner's May 1976 hearing, the Government relied on testimony [from hospital mental health experts] that petitioner was "not always responsive in a positive way to what goes on" and was "not a very active participant in the informal activities on the Ward" to support its contention that he had not recovered. (p. 716, n. 16)

The insanity defense remains a controversial and emotionally charged issue for a society that values the rule of law and civil rights for its citizens.

Competency to Stand Trial

The insanity defense concerns the accused's mental state *at the time of the crime.* A second issue, whether the person is competent to stand trial, concerns the defendant's mental condition *at the time of his or her trial.* It is obviously possible for a person to be judged competent to stand trial yet be acquitted by reason of insanity. By the same token, a person can be deemed incompetent to stand trial when no final courtrom consideration has yet been given to his or her criminal responsibility for the act in question.

Far greater numbers of people are committed to prison hospitals after being judged incompetent to stand trial than are tried and acquitted by reason of insanity. Our criminal justice system is so organized that the fitness of individuals to stand trial must be decided before it can be determined whether they are responsible for the crime of which they are accused.

With the Supreme Court case *Pate* v. *Robinson*[8] as precedent, the defense attorney, prosecutor, or judge may raise the question of mental illness whenever there is reason to believe that the accused's mental condition might interfere with his or her upcoming trial. Another way of stating this problem of competency is to say that the courts do not want a person to be brought to trial *in absentia* (although not present), which is a centuries-old principle of English common law. A disturbed person can, of course, be physically present; what is referred to here is his or her mental state. If after examination the person is deemed too mentally ill to participate meaningfully in a trial, the trial is routinely delayed. The accused is incarcerated in a prison hospital with the hope that means of restoring adequate mental functioning can be found. This happened to Jones, immediately after his arrest.

If a court fails to order a hearing when there is evidence that raises a reasonable doubt about competency to stand trial, or if it convicts a legally incompetent defendant, there is a violation of due process.[9] Once competency is questioned, there must be a preponderance of evidence that the defendant is competent to stand trial.[10] The test to be applied is whether the defendant shows sufficient ability to consult with his or her lawyer with a reasonable degree of understanding and whether he or she has a rational as well as a factual understanding of the proceedings.[11] The court has to consider evidence such as irrational behavior and any medical or psychological evidence that might bear on the defendant's competency.[12]

Being judged competent to stand trial can have severe consequences for the individual. Bail is automatically denied, even though it might be routinely granted if the question of incompetency had not been raised. The accused is usually kept in a facility for the criminally insane for the pretrial examination; these institutions are not the best of hospitals. During this period the accused is supposed to receive treatment to render him or her competent to stand trial.[13] In the meantime, the accused may well lose employment and undergo the trauma of being separated from family and friends and from familiar surroundings for months or even years, perhaps making his or her emotional condition even worse and thereby delaying the judgment of fitness to stand trial. In the past, some people languished in a prison hospital for many years, waiting to be found competent to stand trial.

A 1972 Supreme Court case, *Jackson* v. *Indiana*,[14] forced the states to a speedier determination of incompetency. The case concerned a mentally re-

---

[8] *Pate* v. *Robinson*, 383 U.S. 375 (1966).

[9] *United States* v. *White*, 887 F.2d 705 (6th Cir. 1989); *Wright* v. *Lockhart* 914 F.2d 1093, *cert. denied*, 111 S.Ct. 1089 (1991).

[10] *United States* v. *Frank* 956 F.2d 872, *cert. denied*, 113 S.Ct. 363 (1992); *United States* v. *Blohm*, 579 F.Supp. 495 (1983).

[11] *United States* v. *Frank*, op. cit.; *Wright* v. *Lockhart*, op. cit.

[12] *United States* v. *Hemsi*, 902 F.2d 293 (2nd Cir. 1990); *Balfour* v. *Haws* 892 F.2d 556 (7th Cir. 1989).

[13] *United States* v. *Sherman*, 912 F.2d 907 (7th Cir. 1990).

[14] *Jackson* v. *Indiana*, 406 U.S. 715 (1972).

tarded deaf-mute man who was deemed not only incompetent to stand trial but unlikely ever to become competent. The Court ruled that the length of pretrial confinement must be limited to the time it takes to determine whether treatment during this detainment is likely to render the defendant competent to stand trial. If the defendant is unlikely ever to become competent, the state should after this period either institute civil commitment proceedings or release the defendant. It has been suggested that lawyers participate with mental health professionals in making the competency determination, for a knowledgeable lawyer understands exactly what the defendant must be able to do to participate in the trial (Roesch & Golding, 1980). Legislation has been drafted in most states to define more precisely the minimal requirements for competency to stand trial, ending the latitude that has deprived thousands of people of their rights to due process (Amendment 14) and a speedy trial (Amendment 6). Fortunately, defendants today cannot be committed for determination of competency for a period longer than the maximum possible sentence they face.[15]

The era of modern medicine has also had an impact on the competency issue. The concept of "synthetic sanity"(Schwitzgebel & Schwitzgebel, 1980) was introduced: if a drug, such as Thorazine, temporarily produces a modicum of rationality in an otherwise deranged defendant, then, it has been argued, the trial may proceed. The likelihood that the defendant will again become incompetent to stand trial if and when the drug is withdrawn would not disqualify the person from going to court.[16] However, the individual rights of the defendant are to be protected against forcible medication, because there is no guarantee that such treatment would, in fact, render the person competent to stand trial and there is a chance that the drugs might even cause harm. A recent Supreme Court ruling[17] held that a criminal defendant could not be forced to take psychotropic medication in an effort to render him competent to stand trial. One of the Justices in fact expressed strong reservations that a drugged defendant could ever really get a fair trial. In general, the courts have responded to the existence of powerful psychoactive medications by requiring safeguards against their involuntary use, to ensure that the defendant's civil rights are protected, even when a drug might restore legal competency to stand trial.[18]

Finally, if the defendant wishes, the effects of the medication must be explained to the jury, lest—if the defendant is pleading NGRI—the jury conclude from his or her relatively calm and rational drug-produced demeanor that the defendant could not have been insane at the time of the crime.[19] This ruling relates to our earlier comment about the difficulty of concluding, from retrospective evidence, what a defendant's mental state was at the time of committing the crime, perhaps years earlier than the trial. This legal principle would seem to acknowledge that juries form their judgment of legal responsibility or insanity at least in part on how the defendant appears during the trial. If he or she seems too normal, they may be less likely to believe the crime to have been an act of a disturbed mental state than of free will. Focus Box 21.2 discusses the unusual challenge posed by multiple personality disorder in criminal commitments.

Civil Commitment

Civil commitment affects far greater numbers of people than criminal commitment. It is beyond the scope of this book to examine in detail the variety of state civil commitment laws and regulations. Each state has its own, and they are in almost constant flux. Our aim instead is to provide an overview that will give the reader a basic understanding of the issues and of the current directions of change.

In virtually all states, a person can be committed to a mental hospital against his or her will if a judgment is made that he or she is (1) mentally ill and (2) a danger to self—that is, unable to provide for the basic physical needs of food, clothing, and shelter—or a danger to others (Warren, 1982). At present, dangerousness to others is more often the second criterion, and recent court rulings point to *imminent* dangerousness as the principal criterion.[20] Such commitment is supposed to last for only as long as the person remains dangerous.[21]

Historically, governments have had the duty to protect their citizens from harm. We take for granted the right and duty of government to set limits on our freedom for the sake of protecting us. Few

[15]*United States* v. *DeBellis*, 649 F.2d 1 (1st Cir. 1981); *United States* v. *Moore* 467 N.W.2d 201 (1991).

[16]*State of Louisiana* v. *Hamptom*, 216 So.2d 311 (1969); *State of Tennessee* v. *Stacy*, No. 446 (Crim. App., Knoxville, Tenn., August 4, 1977); *United States* v. *Hayes*, 589 F.2d 811 (1979).

[17]*Riggins* v. *Nevada*, 112 S.Ct. 1810 (1992).

[18]*United States* v. *Waddell*, 687 F.Supp. 208 (1988).

[19]*States* v. *New Mexico* v. *Jojola*, 89 N.W., 489 (1976).

[20]*Suzuki* v. *Yuen*, 617 F.2d 173 (9th Cir. 1980).

[21]*United States* v. *DeBellis*, op. cit.

FOCUS 21.2 • Multiple Personality and the Insanity Defense

Imagine that as you are having a cup of coffee one morning, you hear pounding at the front door. You hurry to answer and find two police officers staring grimly at you. One of them asks, "Are you John Smith?" "Yes," you reply. "Well, sir, you are under arrest for grand theft and for the murder of Jane Doe." The officer then reads you your Miranda rights against self-incrimination, handcuffs you, and takes you to the police station, where you are allowed to call your lawyer.

This would be a scary situation for anybody, but what is particularly frightening and puzzling to you and your lawyer is that you have absolutely no recollection of having committed the crime that a detective later describes to you. You are aghast that you cannot account for the time period when the murder was committed—in fact, your memory is startlingly blank for that entire time. And, as if this were not Kafkaesque enough, the detective then shows you a videotape in which you are clearly firing a shotgun at a bank teller during a holdup. "Is that you in the videotape?" asks the detective. You confer with your lawyer, saying that it certainly looks like you, including the clothes, but you are advised not to admit anything one way or the other.

Let's move forward in time now to your trial some months later. Witnesses have come forward and identified you beyond a reasonable doubt. There is no one you know who can testify that you were somewhere other than at the bank on the afternoon of the robbery and the murder. And it is clear that the jury is going to find you, in Szasz's terms, descriptively responsible for the crimes. But did *you* murder the teller in the bank? You are able to assert honestly to yourself and to

The theme of Robert Louis Stevenson's *Dr. Jekyll and Mr. Hyde* was perhaps suggested by an actual case of multiple personality.

drivers, for example, question the limits imposed on them by traffic signals. We usually go along with the Food and Drug Administration when it bans uncontrolled use of drugs that cause cancer in laboratory animals, although some people, to be sure, feel they have the right to decide for themselves what risks to take with their own bodies. Government, then, has a long-established right to protect us both from ourselves—the *parens patriae* power of the state, and from others—the police power of the

the jury that you did not. And yet even you have been persuaded that the person in the videotape is you, and that that person committed the robbery and the murder.

Because of the strange nature of the case, your lawyer arranged prior to the trial to have you interviewed by a psychiatrist and a clinical psychologist, both of them well-known experts in forensics. Through extensive questioning, they have decided that you suffer from multiple personality disorder, and that the crimes were committed not by you, John Smith, but by your rather violent alter, Dick. Indeed, during one of the interviews, Dick emerged and boasted about the crime, even chuckling over the fact that you, John, would be imprisoned for it.

This fictional account is not as farfetched as you might think (recall our earlier discussion of multiple personality disorder in Chapter 7). In fact, mental health lawyers have for some time been concerned with such scenarios as they wrestle with various aspects of the insanity defense. But nearly all the people who successfully use this defense are diagnosable as schizophrenic (or more generally, psychotic), and MPD is regarded as a dissociative disorder (and used to be classified as one of the neuroses). Can MPD be an excusing condition for a criminal act? Should John Smith be held ascriptively responsible for a crime committed by his alter, Dick?

Consider the widely accepted legal principle that people accused of crimes should be punished only if they are blameworthy. The several court decisions and laws we have reviewed in this chapter all rest on this principle. In a recent exhaustive review of the MPD literature and of its forensic implications, Elyn Saks (1992) of the University of Southern California Law Center argues that MPD should be regarded as a special case in mental health law, that a new legal principle should be established, "irresponsibility by virtue of multiple personality disorder."

What we find intriguing about Saks's argument is that she devotes a major portion of it to defining personhood. *What is a person?* Is a person the body we inhabit? Well, most of the time our sense of who we are as a person does not conflict with the body we have come to know as our own, or rather, as *us*. But in MPD, there is a discrepancy—the body that committed the crimes at the bank was not the same as John Smith, for it was his alter, Dick, who readily admitted to them. Saks argues that, peculiar as it may sound, the law should be interested in the body only as a container for the person. It is the person who may or may not be blameworthy, not the body. Nearly all the time they are one and the same, but in the case of MPD, they are not. In a sense, Dick committed the murder by using John's body.

Is, then, John blameworthy? The person John did not commit the crime; indeed, he did not even know about it.* If the judge were to sentence John, or more specifically, the body in the courtroom who usually goes by that name, this would not be just, argues Saks, for John is descriptively innocent. To be sure, sending John to prison would punish Dick, for whenever he would emerge, he would find himself imprisoned. But what of John? Saks concludes that we cannot imprison him because he is not blameworthy. Rather, we must find him not guilty by reason of multiple personality disorder, and remand him for treatment of the disorder.

Saks reviews the literature, such as it is, on the treatment of MPD (cf. page 184) and concludes that it is effective enough so as not to violate the right to treatment by committing such a person to a mental hospital. She is optimistic about the effectiveness of therapy for MPD and believes that people like John–Dick can be integrated into one personality and then released to rejoin society. Indeed, Saks even goes so far as to argue that people with MPD who are judged dangerous but who have not committed a crime should be subject to civil commitment, even though this would be tantamount to preventive detention. In this way, she suggests, future crimes might be avoided.

*One might ask whether the situation would be different if John had co-consciousness of Dick, that is, if John were aware even during the criminal acts of what Dick was doing. Saks argues that this would not matter, unless it could be shown that John could have prevented Dick from his felonious behavior.

state. Civil commitment is one further exercise of these powers.

Specific commitment procedures are generally of two types, formal and informal. Formal or judicial commitment is by order of a court. It can be requested by any responsible citizen; usually the police, a relative, or a friend seeks the commitment. If the judge believes that there is a good reason to pursue the matter, he or she will order a mental health examination. The person has the right to object to these attempts to "certify" him or her, and a court hearing can be scheduled to allow the person to present evidence against commitment.

Informal, emergency commitment of the mentally ill can be accomplished without initially involving the courts. For example, a hospital administrative board may decide that a voluntary patient requesting discharge is too disturbed and dangerous to be released. They are able to detain the patient with a temporary, informal commitment order.

Any person acting wildly may be taken immediately to the state hospital by the police. Perhaps the most common informal commitment procedure is the 2PC or two physicians' certificate. In most states two physicians, not necessarily psychiatrists, can sign a certificate that will allow a person to be incarcerated for some period of time, ranging from twenty-four hours to as long as twenty days. Detainment beyond this period requires formal judicial commitment.

Problems in the Prediction of Dangerousness

Civil commitment is necessarily a form of preventive detention: the prediction is made that a person judged mentally ill may in the future behave in a dangerous manner and should therefore be detained. Ordinary prisoners, however, are released from penitentiaries even though statistics show that most will commit additional crimes. Moreover, conviction by a court of law and subsequent imprisonment are carried out only after a person has done some harm to others. Some may say it is like closing the barn door after the horses have thundered out. But our entire legal and constitutional system is organized to protect people from preventive detention. Even if witnesses have seen a person commit a serious crime, he or she is assumed innocent until proven guilty by the courts. The person who openly threatens to inflict harm on others, such as an individual who for an hour each day stands in the street and shouts threats to people in a nearby apartment house, is another matter. Does the state have to wait until the person acts on the threats? No. Here the civil commitment process can be brought into play, although the person must be deemed not only an imminent danger to others but mentally ill as well (Schwitzgebel & Schwitzgebel, 1980). Most mental health professionals, in agreement with lay people, would conclude that a person has to be psychotic to behave in this way.

The likelihood of committing a dangerous act is central to civil commitment, but is dangerousness easily predicted? Studies have examined how reliably mental health professionals predict that a person will commit a dangerous act (e.g., Kozol, Boucher, & Garofalo, 1972; Monahan, 1973, 1976; Stone, 1975); they were found to be poor at making this judgment. Some workers have even argued that civil commitment for the purposes of preventive detention should be abolished. Monahan (1978), however, carefully scrutinized these studies and concluded that the professional's ability to predict violence is still an open question. Most of the studies conformed to the following methodological pattern.

1. People were institutionalized for mental illness and for being a danger to the community.
2. While these people were in the hospital, some of them were again predicted to be violent if they were released into the community.
3. After a period of time, these people were released, thus putting together the conditions for a natural experiment.
4. Checks on the behavior of the released patients over the next several years did not reveal much dangerous behavior.

What is wrong with such research? Monahan points out that little if any consideration was given to changes that institutionalization itself might have effected. In the studies reviewed, the period of incarceration ranged from several months to fifteen years. Prolonged periods of enforced hospitalization might very well make patients more docile, if for no other reason than that they become that much older. Furthermore, the conditions in the open community where the predicted violence would occur can vary widely. We should not expect this kind of prediction to have great validity (Mischel, 1968).

These studies, which have occasioned such pessimism about predicting whether a patient is dangerous, are therefore flawed. Yet they have also been used in arguments against emergency commitment. The fact of the matter is that neither these studies nor any others have examined this specific issue! Monahan, however, has theorized that prediction of dangerousness is probably far easier and surer in true emergency situations than after extended periods of hospitalization. When an emergency commitment is sought, the person may appear out of control and be threatening violence in his or her own living room or, like the person in the street, shouting threats. He or she may also have been violent in the past—a good predictor of future violence—and victims and weapons may be on hand. A dangerous outburst seems imminent. Thus, unlike the danger to society predicted in the studies previously examined, the violence requiring an emergency commitment is expected almost immediately and in a known situation. Common sense tells us that such predictions of violence are likely to be very accurate. To test the validity of these expectations, we would have to leave alone half the people predicted to be immediately violent and later compare their behavior with that of persons hospitalized in such emergency circumstances. Such an experiment would be ethically irresponsible. Mental health professionals must apply logic and make the most prudent judgments possible.

There are indications in what Monahan (1984) has called a "second generation of violence" prediction that suggest greater accuracy in predicting dangerousness. A review of these studies led Litwack (1985) to delineate conditions under which the prediction of violence might be good enough to be relied on to make forensic decisions, whether involving mental patients or others. He suggested that violence prediction has been or will be best under the following conditions (note the role played by situational factors, sometimes in interaction with personality variables):

1. If a person has been repeatedly violent in the recent past, it is reasonable to predict that he or she will be violent in the near future unless there have been major changes in the person's attitudes or in the circumstances in which he or she has been violent. Thus, if a violent person is placed in a restrictive environment, such as a prison or high-security psychiatric hospital facility, he or she may well not be violent given the markedly changed environment.
2. If violence is in the person's distant past, if it was even just a single but a very serious act, and if that person has been incarcerated for a period of time, then violence can be expected on release if there is reason to believe that the person's predetention personality and physical abilities have not changed and if the person is going to return to the same environment in which he or she was previous violent.
3. Even with no history of violence, violence can be predicted if the person is judged to be on the brink of a violent act, for example, if the person previously described is pointing a loaded gun at an occupied building.

Although convincing data on the ability of mental health professionals to predict violence are very difficult to obtain, Litwack argues that at the very least such individuals have the tools to gather the kinds of information that seem useful in predicting violence, for example, interview procedures that can uncover violent intentions, as well as other assessment techniques that can determine whether a person still has personality characteristics that are believed to have contributed to violent behavior in the past.

The basic question is how good a prediction has to be to warrant interfering with someone's civil rights. Once again, there is a balancing act between individual liberty and the obligation of government to protect its citizens. Litwack makes the important point that different degrees of certainty are required for different legal and societal purposes. He points out, for example, that the Supreme Court case of *Addington* v. *Texas* (1979)[22] requires clear and convincing evidence of violence proneness and mental illness to justify *extended* civil commitment; presumably a lesser quality of evidence would be enough for short-term, emergency commitment. If confinement is to be relatively brief (e.g., a few days), the down-side risk for the individual detained would be only a few days' loss of freedom, whereas the possible benefit to society would be saving another from harm or from murder. This is a legal[23] and moral decision, not a psychological or psychiatric one (see also Focus Box 21.3).

Recent Trends for Greater Protection

The United States Constitution is a remarkable document. It lays down the basic duties of our elected federal officials and guarantees a set of civil rights. But there is often some distance between the abstract delineation of a civil right and its day-to-day implementation. Moreover, judges must *interpret* the Constitution as it bears on specific contemporary problems. Since nowhere in this cornerstone of our democracy is there specific mention of committed mental patients, lawyers and judges interpret various sections of the document to justify what they consider necessary in society's treatment of people whose mental health is in question.

In 1972 voluntary admissions to mental hospitals began to outnumber involuntary admissions. But a great number of people admitted to a state or county mental hospital are still there against their wishes. Moreover, it is impossible to know how

[22]*Addington* v. *Texas*, 99 S.Ct. 1804 (1979). The clear and convincing standard of proof, however, still protects the person less than would application of the criminal standard of beyond a reasonable doubt. The criminal standard—beyond a reasonable doubt—is referred to as the 90 percent standard. The clear and convincing standard is set at 75 percent certainty.

[23]*United States* v. *Sahhar*, 917 F.2d 1197, *cert. denied*, 111 S.Ct. 1591 (1991).

21.3 • The Tarasoff Case—The Duty to Warn and to Protect

The client's right to privileged communication—the legal right of a client to require that what goes on in therapy remain confidential—is an important protection, but as we shall see, it is not absolute. Society has long stipulated certain conditions in which confidentiality in a relationship should not be maintained because of the harm that can befall others. A famous California court ruling in 1974* described circumstances in which a therapist not only may but should breach the sanctity of a client's communication. First, what appear to be the facts in the case:

> In the fall of 1968, Prosenjit Poddar, a graduate student from India studying at the University of California at Berkeley, met Tatiana (Tanya) Tarasoff at a folk dancing class. They saw each other weekly during the fall, and on New Year's Eve she kissed him. Poddar interpreted this act as a sign of formal engagement (as it might have been in India, where he was a member of the Harijam or "untouchable caste"). [But] Tanya told him that she was involved with other men, and indicated that she did not wish to have an intimate relationship with him.
>
> Poddar was depressed as a result of the rebuff, but he saw Tanya a few times during the spring (occasionally tape recording their conversations in an effort to understand why she did not love him). Tanya left for Brazil in the summer, and Poddar at the urging of a friend went to the student health facility where a psychiatrist referred him to a psychologist for psychotherapy. When Tanya returned in October 1969, Poddar discontinued therapy. Based in part on Poddar's stated intention to purchase a gun, the psychologist notified the campus police, both orally and in writing, that Poddar was dangerous and should be taken to a community mental health center for psychiatric commitment.
>
> The campus police interviewed Poddar, who seemed rational and promised to stay away from Tanya. They released him and notified the health service. No further efforts at commitment were made because the supervising psychiatrist apparently decided that such was not needed and, as a matter of confidentiality, requested that the letter to the police as well as certain therapy records be destroyed.
>
> On October 27, Poddar went to Tanya's home armed with a pellet gun and a kitchen knife. She refused to speak to him. He shot her with the pellet gun. She ran from the house, was pursued, caught, and repeatedly and fatally stabbed. Poddar was found guilty of voluntary manslaughter rather than first- or second-degree murder. The defense established with the aid of the expert testimony of three psychiatrists, that Poddar's diminished mental capacity, paranoid schizophrenia, precluded the malice necessary for first- or second-degree murder. After his prison term, he returned to India, where, according to his own report, he is happily married. (Schwitzgebel & Schwitzgebel, 1980, p. 205)

Under the privileged communication statute of California (see page 653), the counseling center psychologist properly breached the confidentiality of the professional relationship and took steps to have Poddar civilly committed, for he judged him to be an imminent danger. Poddar had stated that he intended to purchase a gun, and by his other words and actions he had convinced the therapist that he was desperate enough to harm Tanya. What the psychologist did not do, and what the court decided he should have done, was to warn the likely victim, Tanya Tarasoff, that her former friend had bought a gun and might use it against her. Such a warning would have been consistent with previous court decisions requiring physicians to warn the public when they are treating people with contagious diseases and requiring mental institutions to warn others when a dangerous patient has escaped (Knapp & Vandecreek, 1982). Or, as stated by the California Supreme Court in *Tarasoff*: "Once a therapist does in fact determine, or under applicable professional standards reasonably should have determined, that a patient poses a serious danger of violence to others, he bears a duty to exercise reasonable care to protect the foreseeable victims of that danger."

A subsequent California court ruling† held by a bare majority that foreseeable victims include those in close relationship to the identifiable victim, in this instance the son of a woman who was shot by a patient. The mother was hurt by a shot-

***Tarasoff* v. *Regents of the University of California*, 529 P.2d 553 (Cal. 1974), *vacated, reheard in bank, and affirmed* 131 Cal. Rptr. 14, 551 P.2d 334 (1976). The 1976 California Supreme Court ruling was by a four-to-three majority.

†*Hedlund* v. *Superior Court of Orange County*, 194 Cal. Rptr. 805 (Cal. 1983).

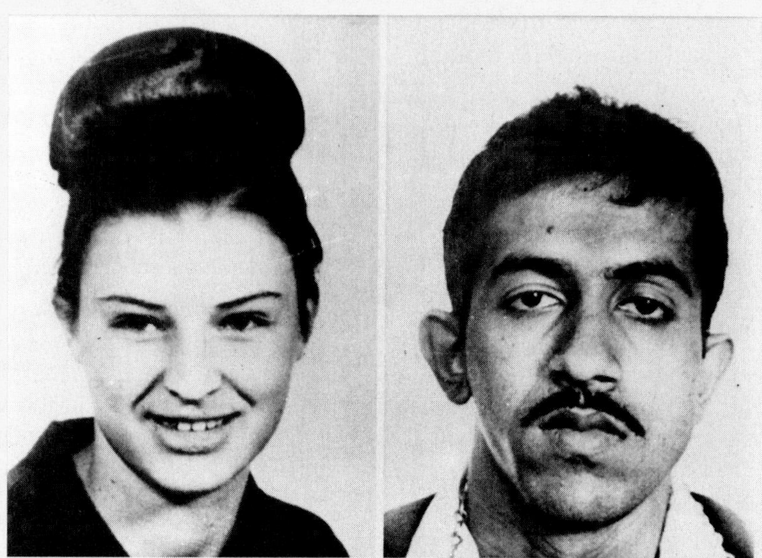

Prosenjit Poddar was convicted of manslaughter in the death of Tatiana Tarasoff. The court ruled that his therapist, who had become convinced Prosenjit might harm Tatiana, should have warned her of the impending danger.

gun fired by the dangerous patient, and her seven-year-old son was present when this happened. The boy later sued the psychologists for damages brought on by emotional trauma. Since a young child is likely to be in the company of his mother, the court concluded in *Hedlund* that the *Tarasoff* ruling extended to him.

The duty to warn and to protect principle may be having a profound impact on psychotherapists, some claim a chilling effect, for it imposes on them a new obligation. They argue that if clients are informed of this limitation to the confidentiality of what they say to their therapists—and professional ethics require therapists to provide this information—clients may become reluctant to express feelings of extreme anger to therapists, for fear therapists will notify the people at whom they are angry. Clients may become less open with their therapists, perhaps derive less benefit from therapy, and even become *more* likely to inflict harm on others for not having disclosed their fury as a first step toward controlling it. The welfare of the people whom the *Tarasoff* decision intends to protect may be endangered by the very ruling itself!

The *Tarasoff* ruling, now being applied in other states as well,[‡] requires clinicians, in deciding when to violate confidentiality, to use the very imperfect skill of predicting dangerousness. A survey of over 1200 psychologists and psychiatrists in California (Wise, 1978) indicated how the *Tarasoff* decision was affecting their thinking and practices. On the plus side, one-third reported consulting more often with colleagues concerning cases in which violence was an issue. This should have a good outcome, since input from other professionals may improve the solitary clinician's decision making, presumably to the benefit of the client. Consultation can also demonstrate that the clinician took extra steps to adhere to Tarasoff; this can reduce legal liability if the patient later harms someone (Monahan, 1993). On the minus side, about 20 percent of the respondents indicated that they avoided asking their clients ques-

[‡] *White* v. *United States* 780 F.2d 97 (D.C. Cir. 1986); *Soutear* v. *United States* 646 F.Supp. 524 (1986); *Dunkle* v. *Food Services East Inc.* 400 Pa. Super. 58, 582 A.2d. 1342 (1990); *People* v. *Clark* 50 Cal. 3d 583, 268 Cal. Rptr. 399, 789 P.2d 127 (1990).

tions about violence, an ostrichlike stance that may keep the clinician from obtaining important information and yet reduces his or her legal liability should the client harm another person. And a substantial number of therapists were keeping less detailed records, again in an effort to reduce legal liability.

A 1983 decision of a federal circuit court in California.[§] may alter some of these tactics of evasion. The court ruled that Veterans Administration psychiatrists should earlier have warned the murdered lover of an outpatient, Phillip Jablonski, that she was a foreseeable victim, even though the patient had never made an explicit threat against her to the therapists. The reasoning was that Jablonski, having previously raped and otherwise harmed his wife, would likely direct his continuing "violence . . . against women very close to him" (p. 392).

The court also found the hospital psychiatrists negligent in not obtaining Jablonski's earlier medical records. These records showed a history of harmful violent behavior that, together with the present threats his lover was complaining about, should have moved the hospital to institute emergency civil commitment. The court ruled that the failure to warn was a proximate or immediate cause of the woman's murder. Proper consideration of the medical records, said the judge, would have convinced the psychiatrists that Jablonski was a real danger to others and should be committed.

This broadening of the duty to warn now places mental health professionals in California in an even more difficult predicament, for the potentially violent patient need not even mention whom specifically he or she may harm. It is up to the therapist to deduce who are possible victims, based on what he or she can learn of the patient's past and present circumstances. Ironically, Jablonski's lover realized that she was in danger; she had moved out of the apartment she was sharing with him and had complained to her priest and to the Veterans Administration psychiatrists themselves that she feared for her safety. One of the psychiatrists had even advised her to leave Jablonski, at least while he was being evaluated at the medical center. But "when [the lover] responded 'I love him,' [the psychiatrist] did not warn her further because he believed she would not listen to him" (p. 393). The court found this warning "totally unspecific and inadequate under the circumstances" (p. 398).

[§]*Jablonski by Pahls* v. *United States*, 712 F.2d 391 (1983).

Tarasoff was extended by a Vermont State Supreme Court ruling, *Peck* v. *Counseling Service of Addison County,*[‖] which held that a mental health practitioner has a duty to warn a third party if there is a danger of *damage of property.* The case involved a twenty-nine-year-old male patient who, after a heated argument with his father, told his therapist that he wanted to get back at his father and indicated that he might do so by burning down his father's barn. He proceeded to do so. No people or animals were harmed in the arsonous conflagration; the barn housed no animals and was located 130 feet away from his parents' home. The court's conclusion that the therapist had a duty to warn was based on reasoning that arson is a violent act and therefore a lethal threat to people who may be in the vicinity of the fire. This can be seen as an extension of the *Hedlund* court decision as well; whereas *Hedlund* speaks of humans who may be at risk because of possible physical proximity to the endangered victim, *Peck* speaks of humans who could be harmed via threat to an inanimate object. Furthermore, since some chronic psychiatric patients have a history of fire setting (Geller & Bertsch, 1985), Stone (1986) predicts that there will be future lawsuits based on this Vermont decision.

As problematic as *Tarasoff* and associated rulings may be for the mental health professions, the situation may not be as bleak as it has appeared to many. When the original 1974 *Tarasoff* ruling was reaffirmed in 1976 by the California Supreme Court, the duty to warn was broadened to a duty to *protect* (see the earlier quotation from the 1976 decision), and it is this seemingly slight change that makes it possible for practitioners to adhere to *Tarasoff* without necessarily breaking confidentiality, that is, without having always to warn a potential victim. As Appelbaum (1985) pointed out, clinicians can undertake such preventive measures as increased frequency of sessions, initiation of or changes in psychotropic medication, and, in general, closer supervision of the patient. He suggested further that if such measures are judged reasonable, the therapist is unlikely to be held liable if the patient does ultimately harm somebody.

One strategy described by Appelbaum involved an eighteen-year-old patient who threatened during a session that he would beat up his landlady for not permitting her son to associate with him.

[‖]*Peck* v. *Counseling Service of Addison County,* 499 A.2d 422 (Vt. 1985).

On the basis of other information about the patient, the therapist determined that *Tarasoff* was relevant. He decided to involve the patient in the discussion, explaining his legal responsibility to protect a potential victim but also his reluctance to break therapeutic confidentiality. He presented to the patient the choice between hospitalization (the patient was indeed sometimes psychotic) and warning the landlady. The patient preferred to stay out of the hospital and said he would not object to the therapist calling the landlady. When this was done, the landlady told the therapist that the young man had threatened her previously and that she knew how to take care of herself. In other words, she did not take the threats literally. Appelbaum observed that the patient's threats seemed to be manipulative—he succeeded in once again issuing a verbal threat to his landlady, this time through his psychotherapist. But the psychotherapist succeeded in involving the patient in the decision making as well as preserving trust in the therapeutic relationship. As anxiety provoking as *Tarasoff* can be to clinicials, it does not call for therapists to reflexively pick up the phone to call a possible victim whenever a patient expresses a threat. Many other responsible options are available, e.g., directly asking the patient or relatives whether he or she has previously assaulted someone; taking care to obtain hospital records of a potentially dangerous patient (Monahan, 1993).

many of those who admit themselves voluntarily do so under threat of civil commitment. One survey (Gilboy & Schmidt, 1971) revealed that 40 percent of patients who had voluntarily admitted themselves to a mental hospital in Chicago had actually been threatened with commitment by the police officers who had brought them there. The issue of enforced mental hospitalization is still very much with us. Even though psychiatrists, psychologists, the courts, and hospital staff are growing more reluctant to commit, tens of thousands of mental patients are in hospitals against their will.

In a democratic society the most grievous wrong that can be suffered by a citizen is loss of liberty. The situation of mental patients is improving, however. The rights accorded to ordinary citizens, and even to criminals, are gradually being extended to those threatened with civil commitment and to those who have already been involuntarily hospitalized. It is no longer assumed that deprivation of liberty for purposes of mental health care is a reason to deny to the individual all other rights.

For example, a 1976 federal court decision in Wisconsin, *Lessard* v. *Schmidt*,[24] gives a person threatened with civil commitment the right to timely, written notice of the proceeding, opportunity for a hearing with counsel, the right to have the hearing decided by jury, Fifth Amendment protection against self-incrimination, and other similar procedural safeguards already accorded defendants in criminal actions, including being present at any hearing to decide the need for commitment.[25] Such protections are to be provided even under emergency commitment conditions.[26] As mentioned earlier, and as implemented in recent lower court rulings,[27] a 1979 Supreme Court decision, *Addington* v. *Texas*, further provides that the state must produce clear and convincing evidence that a person is mentally ill and dangerous before he or she can be involuntarily committed to a mental hospital. And in 1980 the Ninth Circuit Court of Appeals ruled that this danger must be imminent.[28] Clearly the intent is to restrict the state's power to curtail individual freedoms because of mental illness. Although protection of the rights of the mentally ill adds tremendously to the burden of both civil courts and state and county mental hospital staffs, it is a price a free society must pay.

> Given the record of past [criminal proceedings and] the tragic parody of legal commitment used to warehouse American citizens, it is . . . important that the individual feel sure that the [present] mental health system [in particular] cannot be so used and abused . . . for while the average citizen may have some confidence that if called by the Great Inquisitor in the middle of the night and charged with a given robbery, he may have an alibi or be able to prove his innocence, he may be far less certain of his capacity, under the press of fear, to instantly prove his sanity. (Stone, 1975, p 57)

Least Restrictive Alternative

Civil commitment rests on presumed dangerousness, a condition that may vary depending on the surrounding circumstances. Thus a person may be deemed dangerous if allowed to live in an apart-

[24]*Lessard* v. *Schmidt*, 349 F.Supp. 1078 (E.D. Wisc. 1972), *vacated and remanded on other grounds*, 94 S.Ct. 712 (1974), *reinstated* 413 F.Supp, 1318 (E.D. Wisc. 1976).

[25]*In Re: Lawaetz* 728 F.2d 225 (3rd Cir. 1984).

[26]*Doremus* v. *Farrell* 407 F.Supp. 509 (1975).

[27]*Dautremont* v. *Broadlawns Hospital*, 827 F.2d 291 (8th Cir. 1987).

[28]*Suzuki* v. *Yuen*, 617 F.2d 173 (1980).

ment, but not dangerous if living in a boarding home and taking prescribed psychoactive drugs every day under medical supervision. The least restrictive alternative to freedom is to be provided when treating disturbed people and protecting them from harming themselves and others. A number of court rulings require that only mental patients who cannot be adequately looked after in less restrictive homes be confined in hospitals.[29] Thus commitment is no longer necessarily in an institution; rather, a patient might well be required to reside in a supervised boarding home or in other sheltered quarters. In general terms, mental health professionals have to provide the treatment which restricts the patient's liberty to the least degree possible while still being workable.[30] Indeed, it is unconstitutional to confine a nondangerous mental patient who is capable of surviving on his or her own or with the help of willing and responsible family or friends.[31] Of course, this principle will have meaning only if society provides suitable residences and treatments.

In a thought-provoking analysis of how principles of civil commitment are actually implemented, Turkheimer and Parry (1992) conclude that the dangerousness criterion is less frequently followed in actual practice than a judgment of "grave disability." This latter, outmoded criterion is concerned with whether a patient might be unable to take care of himself or herself and would thus become a burden or a nuisance to society if not involuntarily institutionalized. This disability criterion is *not* supposed to be sufficient for civil commitment, yet it often is. The reason, argue the authors, is that judges, defense attorneys, and mental health professionals realize that there is a dearth of community alternatives to which certain patients can be referred (or even committed—for it is possible, as we have just seen, to execute what is called an outside commitment).

These least restrictive alternatives were supposed to be created when the deinstitutionalization movement took hold in the 1970s, but since the 1981 cessation of federal funding for community mental health centers and other nonhospital placements, society has been faced with a growing number of people, usually ex-mental patients, who are no longer dangerous and yet in need of more care than is available outside a hospital. A vivid example of what can happen is detailed in Focus Box 21.4. Turkheimer and Parry's argument is that awareness of the dearth of less restrictive alternatives leads to rather desultory protection of civil rights (e.g., attorneys not arguing vigorously against commitment) and to commitment of people even when they are not judged dangerous.

Civil commitment supposedly requires that the person is dangerous. But in actual practice the decision to commit can be based on a judgment of severe disability as in the case of some homeless persons.

Right to Treatment

Another aspect of civil commitment that has come to the attention of the courts is the so-called right to treatment, a principle first articulated by Birnbaum (1960). If a person is deprived of liberty because he or she is mentally ill and is a danger to self or others, is not the state required to provide treatment to alleviate these problems? Is it not unconstitutional (and even indecent) to incarcerate someone without afterward providing the help he or she is supposed to need? This important question has been the subject of several court cases.

The right to treatment has gained in legal status since the 1960s and was extended to all civilly committed patients in a landmark case, *Wyatt* v. *Stickney*.[32] In that case, an Alabama federal court ruled in 1972 that the only justification for the civil commitment of patients to a state mental hospital is treatment. As stated by Judge Frank Johnson, "to deprive any citizen of his or her liberty upon the altruistic theory that the confinement is for humane and therapeutic reasons and then fail to provide adequate treatment violates the very fundamentals of

[29] *Lake* v. *Cameron*, op. cit., and *Lessard* v. *Schmidt*, op. cit.
[30] *In Re: Tarpley*, 556 N.E.2d 71, superseded by 581 N.E.2d 1251 (1991).
[31] *Project Release* v. *Prevost*, 722 F.2d 960 (2nd Cir. 1983).

[32] *Wyatt* v. *Stickney*, 325 F.Supp. 781 (M.D. Ala. 1971), *enforced in* 334 F.Supp. 1341 (M.D. Ala. 1971), 344 F.Supp. 373, 379 (M.D. Ala. 1972), *aff'd sub nom Wyatt* v. *Anderholt*, 503 F.2d 1305 (5th Cir. 1974).

due process." Rather, committed mental patients "have a constitutional right to receive such individual treatment as will give each of them a realistic opportunity to be cured or to improve his or her mental condition." This ruling, upheld on appeal, is frequently cited as ensuring protection of people confined by civil commitment, at least to this extent: the state cannot simply put them away without meeting minimal standards of care. In fact, when mentally retarded patients (as opposed to those judged to be mentally ill) are released from an institution, health officials are not relieved of their constitutional duty to provide reasonable care and safety as well as appropriate training.[33]

The *Wyatt* ruling, although it applied only in Alabama, was significant, for in the past the courts had asserted that it was beyond their competence to pass judgment on the care given to mental patients. The courts had assumed that mental health professionals possess special and exclusive knowledge about psychopathology and its treatment. Repeated reports of abuses, however, gradually prodded the American judicial system to rule on what goes on within the walls of mental institutions. The *Wyatt* decision set forth very specific requirements, such as dayrooms of at least forty square feet; curtains or screens for privacy in multipatient bedrooms, to accommodate no more than five persons; a comfortable bed; one toilet per eight persons; the right to wear any clothing the patient wishes, provided it is not deemed dangerous; opportunities to interact with members of the opposite sex; and no physical restraints, except in emergency situations. And to provide care twenty-four hours a day, seven days a week, there should be, for every 250 patients, at least two psychiatrists, three additional physicians, twelve registered nurses, ninety attendants, four psychologists, and seven social workers. When the *Wyatt* action was taken, Alabama state mental facilities averaged one physician per 2000 patients, an extreme situation indeed.[34] The *Wyatt* requirements are still good law, and similar protections are extended to the mentally retarded as well.[35]

The trend of the *Wyatt* ruling, however, may have been weakened by a later Supreme Court decision, *Youngberg* v. *Romeo*,[36] regarding the treatment of a mentally retarded boy, Nicholas Romeo, who had been placed in physical restraints on occasion to keep him from hurting himself and others. Holding that the patient has a right to reasonable care and safety, the decision deferred to the professional judgment of the mental health professionals responsible for the boy: "courts must show deference to the judgment exercised by a qualified professional . . . the decision, if made by a professional, is presumptively valid" (pp. 322, 323). On the other hand, the aforementioned 1990 *Thomas S.* v. *Flaherty* decision held that professional judgment is not the final word when it comes to constitutional protections of mentally retarded patients in public mental hospitals. The situation seems to be in flux.

In a more celebrated case, *O'Connor* v. *Donaldson*,[37] which eventually found its way to the Supreme Court, a civilly committed mental patient sued two state hospital doctors for his release and for money damages, on the grounds that he had been incarcerated against his will for fourteen years without being treated and without being dangerous to himself or to others. In January 1957, at the age of forty-nine, Kenneth Donaldson had been com-

Kenneth Donaldson, displaying a copy of the Supreme Court opinion stating that nondangerous mental patients cannot be confined against their will under civil commitment.

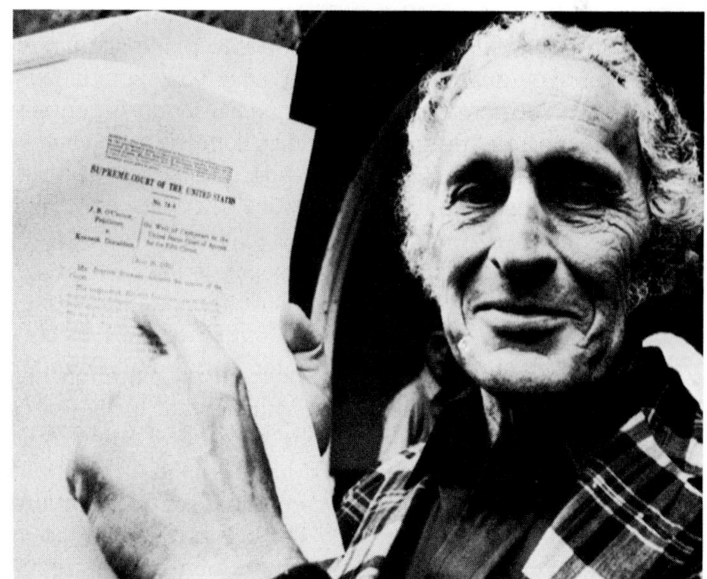

[33]*Thomas S.* v. *Flaherty*, 902 F.2d 250, *cert. denied*, 111 S.Ct. 373 (1990).

[34]Of course, the underlying assumption is that patients civilly committed to public mental hospitals will receive adequate care there. The evidence is weak, however. Even though the extremely negligent conditions that the *Wyatt* decision remedied in Alabama seldom hold today, it is questionable, argued Morse (1982c), whether forced hospitalization benefits patients. But public mental hospitals can provide, at the very least, shelter, food, protection, and custodial care, which many deinstitutionalized patients lack.

[35]*Feagley* v. *Waddill*, 868 F.2d 1437 (5th Cir. 1989).

[36]*Youngberg* v. *Romeo*, 102 S.Ct. 2462 (1982).

[37]*O'Connor* v. *Donaldson*, 95 S.Ct. 2486 (1975).

FOCUS 21.4 • The Strange Case of Billie Boggs

The conflict between individual civil rights and the responsibility of the government to care for its citizens was played out in an almost surreal way a few years ago in the case of Billie Boggs, a forty-year-old New York City homeless woman (Hornblower & Svoboda, 1987; Kasindorf, 1988). Her real name is Joyce Brown, and she achieved notoriety in 1987 when the sometime flamboyant and always forthright mayor, Edward Koch, concerned about the living conditions of his city's homeless, decided in October to round up those homeless who seemed to be mentally ill and to hospitalize them, even if they did not want it. Mayor Koch had come under intense political pressure to do something about homeless people freezing to death in the shadows of luxurious Manhattan skyscrapers. He had started Project HELP in 1982, but it was stymied by difficulties in getting mentally ill street people hospitalized. The incident that follows arose from a reinterpretation of case law that city attorneys told Koch would permit commitment if a person could be judged a danger to self or others "in the reasonably foreseeable future" rather than at the moment.

On a tour with other city officials, Koch came upon Ms. Brown lying near a heating grate with her jaw swollen, and, when told that she could not be committed, he said to one of the officials, "You're loony yourself." Brown was then taken involuntarily to Bellevue Hospital with the diagnosis of paranoid schizophrenia, based on such behavior as screaming and cursing at African-American men on the street ("Come suck my d--k, you black motherf----r"), lifting her skirt to expose her bare buttocks and shouting, "Kiss my black ass, you motherf-----g nigger," defecating in her clothes or on the pavement, tearing up and burning money, and talking to herself—in addition to living in the streets.

Billie Boggs, shown with her lawyers, was released after confinement in a mental hospital.

Brown's family background was a conventional middle-class one. She graduated from high school and worked for ten years as a secretary. Never married, she lived at home with her mother, who died in 1979. Brown had been a heavy user of cocaine and heroin since high school, and she ultimately lost her job in 1983 because of spotty attendance and bizarre behavior, like swearing at people for no reason. Her life began to come apart, and she began to hear voices and to talk

mitted to the Florida state hospital at Chattahoochee on petition by his father, who felt that his son was delusional. Donaldson was found at a brief court hearing before a county judge to be a paranoid schizophrenic and was committed for "care, maintenance, and treatment." The Florida statute then in effect allowed for such commitment on the usual grounds of mental illness and dangerousness. At that time, dangerousness could be defined as inability to manage property and to protect oneself from being taken advantage of by others.

In 1971, Donaldson sued Dr. O'Connor, the hospital superintendent, and Dr. Gumanis, a hospital psychiatrist, for release. Evidence presented at the trial in a U.S. district court in Florida indicated that the hospital staff could have released Donaldson at any time following a determination that he was not a dangerous person. Testimony made it clear that at no time during his hospitalization had Donaldson's conduct posed any real danger to others or to himself. In fact, just before his commitment in 1957, he had been earning a living and taking adequate care to herself. One day she went into a store with one of her sisters and, seeing a security guard, began for no reason to curse at him loudly. "It was 'Motherf----r this and motherf----r that' " reported a sister (Kasindorf, 1988, p. 38). She also developed the idea that she would marry a handsome, professional white man, and started to harass someone with phone calls about this. From time to time she lived with one or more of her four sisters and in 1985 was removed from a Newark, New Jersey, shelter because of disruptive behavior. She was seen by more than one psychiatrist, was prescribed Thorazine (which she refused to take), and had numerous mental health clinic contacts. During this time she became obsessed with Bill Boggs, the host of a local television talk show program, and tried to engage him in conversation when she visited the television station. Boggs reported that the conversations never made any sense to him. She thereafter adopted his name. Her sisters attempted more than once to commit her after trying valiantly to house her in their own homes or in apartments they found for her and partially paid for.

Five days after being picked up on Mayor Koch's orders, she appeared before a judge who would rule on whether she could be detained longer against her will. Brown was calm and articulate, explaining away much of her unusual behavior; for example, because the nearest public toilet was too far away to reach, she would sometimes defecate in her pants. Four city psychiatrists testified that she was mentally ill, but she was declared sane by three psychiatrists hired by American Civil Liberties Union attorneys, who had taken a civil rights interest in her. Indeed, when she testified on her own behalf, she was lucid, calm, and intelligent, a fact that her attorneys claimed showed that she was not mentally ill but that the city psychiatrists claimed was irrelevant in that mentally ill people are not necessarily retarded nor do they always appear disturbed.

Unable to obtain guidance from the diametrically opposed psychiatric testimony of the city and of the patient, the judge focused on Brown's in-court demeanor and determined that, even if she were mentally ill, she was neither malnourished, suicidal, nor dangerous to others. He declared further that, while living in the streets may be an "offense to aesthetic senses, freedom, constitutionally guaranteed, is the right of all, no less of those who are mentally ill . . . beggars can be choosers" (*Time*, 1988, p. 29).

She was, however, detained in Bellevue while the city contested the judge's ruling to release her. On several appeals, the ACLU and other civil rights–minded people claimed that all the mayor was concerned about was cleaning up the streets so that rich constituents would not be confronted with destitute homeless people. Koch and others claimed that the city had a responsibility to help the helpless. The public debate was loud and bitter, Brown's lawyers calling Koch a demagogue and Koch calling them loonies. During her enforced stay at Bellevue, Brown cooperated not at all with any treatment program and refused all psychotropic medication.

In January 1988 Brown was released from Bellevue and became a cause célèbre in the ongoing efforts of advocates for the homeless to force city and state government to provide adequate housing and, to the mentally ill, appropriate outpatient mental health services. She appeared on several local New York talk programs and even on CBS's "60 Minutes." Two weeks after a February 1988 appearance at the Harvard Law School Forum, where she was as big a hit as she had been on the television programs, she was back on the streets again, panhandling and swearing at African-Americans.

of himself (and immediately upon discharge he secured a job in hotel administration). Nonetheless, O'Connor had repeatedly refused the patient's requests for release, feeling it was his duty to determine whether a committed patient could adapt successfully outside the institution. His judgment was that Donaldson could not. In deciding the question of dangerousness on the basis of adjustment outside the institution, O'Connor continued to apply a more restrictive standard than that on which most state laws for commitment rested.

Several responsible people had attempted to obtain Donaldson's release by guaranteeing that they would look after him. For example, in 1963 a halfway house formally requested that Donaldson be released to its care, and between 1964 and 1968 a former college classmate made four separate attempts to have the patient released to his custody. O'Connor refused, saying that the patient could be released only to his parents, who by this time were quite old and infirm.

The evidence indicated that Donaldson received

only custodial care during his hospitalization. No treatment that could conceivably alleviate or cure his assumed mental illness was undertaken. The milieu therapy that O'Connor claimed Donaldson was undergoing consisted, in actuality, of being kept in a large room with sixty other patients, many of whom were under criminal commitment. Donaldson had been denied privileges to stroll around the hospital grounds or even to discuss his case with Dr. O'Connor. O'Connor also regarded as delusional Donaldson's expressed desire to write a book about his hospital experiences, which Donaldson did, in fact, do after his release. The book sold well.

The original trial and a subsequent appeal concluded that Donaldson was not dangerous and had been denied his constitutional right to treatment, based on the Fifth Amendment. Throughout this litigation Donaldson declared that he was neither dangerous nor mentally ill. *But*, went his claim, *even if* he were mentally ill, he should be released because he was not receiving treatment.

On appeal to the Supreme Court, it was ruled, on June 26, 1975, that "a State cannot constitutionally confine . . . a nondangerous individual who is capable of surviving safely in freedom by himself or with the help of willing and responsible family members or friends." In 1977 Donaldson ultimately settled for $20,000 from Dr. Gumanis and from the estate of Dr. O'Connor, who had died during the appeals process.

The Supreme Court decision on *O'Connor* v. *Donaldson* created a stir when it was issued and has given mental health professionals pause in detaining patients. Although this decision is often cited as yet another affirmation to the right to treatment, the Supreme Court did not, in fact, rule on the constitutionality of this doctrine. Indeed, Chief Justice Warren E. Burger issued some warnings about the right to treatment.

> Given the present state of medical knowledge regarding abnormal behavior and its treatment, few things would be more fraught with peril than [for] a State's power to protect the mentally ill [to depend on its ability to provide] such treatment as will give them a realistic opportunity to be cured. Nor can I accept the theory that a State may lawfully confine an individual thought to need treatment and justify that deprivation of liberty solely by providing such treatment. Our concepts of due process would not tolerate such a "trade off." (pp. 588–589)

The *Donaldson* decision did say that a committed patient's status must be periodically reviewed, for the grounds on which a patient was initially committed cannot be assumed to continue in effect forever. In other words, people can change while in a mental hospital and may no longer require confinement. This seems straightforward enough! And yet reminders seem still to be necessary, as appreciated by a 1986 court decision involving a mentally retarded woman who had spent her entire adult life in a state institution for the retarded after having been committed at age fifteen; during her twenty years of confinement she had never been given a hearing to reconsider the grounds for the original commitment.[38]

Right to Refuse Treatment

If a committed mental patient has the right to expect appropriate treatment, since the need for help has resulted in loss of freedom, does he or she have a right to *refuse* treatment, or a particular kind of treatment? The answer appears to be yes, for a right to obtain treatment does not oblige the patient to *accept* treatment (Schwitzgebel & Schwitzgebel, 1980). But there are qualifications. A state hospital may have adequate staff to provide up-to-date chemotherapy as well as group therapy but lack the professional resources to offer individual therapy. Suppose that a patient refuses the available modalities and insists on individual therapy. Would the patient later be able to sue the hospital for not offering the specific services requested? If the patient has the right to refuse certain forms of treatment, how far should the courts go in ensuring this right, remaining at the same time realistic about the state's ability to provide alternatives? When should the judgment of a professional override the wishes of a patient, especially one who is grossly psychotic? Are the patient's best interests always served if he or she can veto the plans of those responsible for care (Stone, 1975)?

Some court decisions illustrate the thorny issues that arise when the right to refuse treatment is debated. In a 1979 decision on some cases in which "unjustified polypharmacy" and "force or intimidation" had allegedly been applied, without due consideration for the serious negative side effects of drugs, the judge in a New Jersey federal district court concluded that drugs can actually inhibit recovery, that therefore, except in emergencies, even an involuntarily committed patient can refuse to take them, based on the rights of privacy (First Amendment) and due process (Fourteenth Amendment).[39] He ordered that there be advocates in each state mental hospital to help patients exercise the

[38] *Clark* v. *Cohen* 794 F.2d 79, 55 U.S.L.W. 2044 (1986).

[39] *Rennie* v. *Klein*, Civil Action No. 77-2624, Federal District Court of New Jersey, 14 September 1979.

right to refuse treatment and that there be posted in each hospital ward a listing of all the side effects of the drugs that might be given to patients. In a reconsideration of this case, however, the judge stated that the opinion of the health professional must take precedence over the right to refuse treatment when patients are a danger to themselves or to others, in other words, in emergency situations.[40]

Not surprisingly, the right of committed patients to refuse psychotropic drugs is hotly debated. Although somatic therapies like electroconvulsive therapy and psychosurgery have for some time been subject to judicial review and control, only recently has close attention been paid to drugs used with mental patients. Legal and ethical issues surrounding the use of psychotropic medication are important: the side effects of most neuroleptic drugs are often very aversive to the patient and sometimes harmful and irreversible, and they do not truly address all of the patient's psychosocial problems (see discussion of negative symptoms on page 414). Moreover, neuroleptic drugs are often the only kind of treatment a patient in a state hospital receives with any regularity.

The question of refusing medication continues to be the subject of lawsuits on behalf of both involuntary and voluntary mental hospital patients. Decisions on behalf of patients judged incompetent are frequently made by the hospital's professional staff. Although there is inconsistency among different jurisdictions and although the forensic picture is still developing, there appears to be a trend that even involuntarily committed mental patients have certain rights to refuse psychotropic medication, based on the constitutional protection of freedom from physical invasion, freedom of thought, and the right to privacy.[41] In an extension of the least restrictive treatment principle, *United States* v. *Charters* ruled that the government cannot force antipsychotic drugs on a person only on the supposition that at some future time he or she might become dangerous. Threat to the public safety has to be clear and imminent to justify the risks and restrictions that such medications pose, and it has to be shown that less intrusive intervention will not likely reduce imminent danger to others. In other words, forcible medication necessarily restricts liberty in addition to whatever physical risks it could bring; there has to be a very good reason to deprive even a committed mental patient of liberty and privacy via such intrusive measures.

The hands of mental health professionals are not tied, however. For example, it was ruled in a 1987 case that forcing a psychoactive drug on a former mental patient did not violate his constitutional rights because he had been threatening to assassinate the president of the United States, posed a threat to his own safety, and could be shown by clear and convincing evidence to be seriously mentally impaired.[42] Professional decisions, though, are subject to judicial review.[43]

Opponents of the right to refuse treatment are concerned that mental hospitals will revert to being warehouses of poorly treated patients. Psychiatrists fear that lawyers and judges will not accept that some people are too mentally deranged to be believed, too mentally disturbed to be able to make sound judgments about their treatment. When a patient is believed to be too psychotic to give informed consent about a treatment, mental health law sometimes invokes the doctrine of *substituted judgment*, the decision that the patient *would have made* if he or she had been able or competent to make a decision.[44] Obviously this principle creates problems as well as solves them.

Does civil commitment imply an incompetency that renders the patient incapable of forming reasonable opinions concerning therapies? The issue is similar to the problem in criminal commitment proceedings, when a judgment that the accused is mentally ill can deny him or her access to the courts. Stone believes that a civilly committed person may indeed be competent to refuse a given treatment, and recent legal opinion (e.g., *Rivers* v. *Katz*, 1986) supports him. The reasons one can commit (danger to self or others and being mentally ill) are not the same as those for forcing treatment on a person (e.g., to help the person be able one day to leave the hospital) (Clayton, 1988).

Law, Free Will, and Ethics

Mental health law construes voluntariness somewhat differently from the way many social scientists do. The latter group operates within paradigms that tend to assign less importance to the concept of free will than does the law, which rests utterly on that idea (Morse, 1992). As psychologists (who, moreover, are familiar with actual practices in mental hospitals), we are sensitive to the subtle coercion that can operate on hospitalized patients, even those

[40]*Rennie* v. *Klein*, 720 F.2d 266 (3d Cir. 1983).

[41]*United States* v. *Charters* 829 F.2d 479, 56 U.S.L.W. 2219 (1987); *United States* v. *Watson* 893 F.2d 970 (1990).

[42]*Dautremont* v. *Broadlawns Hospital*, op. cit.

[43]*United States* v. *Charters*, 863 F.2d 302, *cert. denied* 494 U.S. 1016 (1990).

[44]*Guardianship of Weedon* 565 N.E. 2d 432, 409 Mass. 196 (1991).

who entered voluntarily. A hospital patient is subject to strong persuasion and pressure to accept the treatment recommendations of professional staff. Although one could argue that this is as it should be, the fact remains, in our view, that even a "voluntary" and informed decision to take psychotropic medication or to participate in any other therapy regimen is often (maybe usually) less than free. The issue then is even more complicated and thorny than most mental health law thus far conceives—and the arguments of the legal profession do not lack for complexity and thorniness! Related questions of freedom of choice are discussed in Focus Box 21.5. (See page 656)

That we are dealing ultimately with an ethical issue is suggested by Clayton (1988):

> The most important force behind the notion of a patient's right to reject therapy is the recognition that the weighing of risks and benefits inherent in a decision to undergo or to defer treatment is value-laden. Personal preferences play a role in determining which risks are unacceptable and which benefits are desirable. For instance, the doctor's decision to treat an objecting patient with psychotropic drugs is a value judgment; it reflects the physician's view that freedom from psychosis outweighs the costs of overriding the patient's wishes and of exposing him or her to side effects. This means, at a minimum, that a physician and patient may not always agree on what constitutes the "best" therapy. . . . [Furthermore, the argument that the psychiatrist is acting only in the patient's best interests] assumes a general entitlement to intervene in another's best interest. Society, however, does not generally overrule an individual's decisions merely because they are not objectively self-regarding, to say nothing of not being in his or her best interest. People are permitted to engage in all sorts of dangerous activities, from hang-gliding to cigarette smoking. (pp. 19–20)

Rights to Treatment, to Refuse Treatment, and to Be Treated in the Least Restrictive Setting—Can They Be Reconciled?

We have reviewed several legal principles developed over the years that guide the courts and mental health professionals in meeting their constitutional obligations to civilly committed mental patients. Actions taken to implement one principle may conflict with another, however. The basic question is whether the right to be treated in the least restrictive residence can be reconciled with both the right to treatment and the right to refuse treatment. A creative proposal was put forth nearly twenty years ago by Paul and Lentz (1977) in their report on social-learning and milieu therapies on wards at a mental health center (see page 559 for a discussion of this report). They argued that under certain conditions a committed mental patient can and should be coerced into a particular therapy program, even if the patient states that he or she does not wish to participate. Further, these conditions would not, as *Rennie* v. *Klein* requires, have to be emergencies.

They proposed that some hospital treatments have minimal and others optimal goals, and that institutions should have the right and the duty to do whatever is reasonable to move patients toward minimal goals. Achievement of minimal goals—self-care, such as getting up in the morning, bathing, eating meals, and the like; being able to communicate with others on the most basic level; and not being violent or assaultive—will allow patients to move into a less restrictive residence. The elimination of symptomatic behavior would also be regarded as a minimal goal if the local community requires patients to conform, at least to some extent, to community standards.[45] Paul and Lentz argued further that if empirical evidence indicates that particular treatments do achieve minimal goals—as the social-learning program did in their study—patients might justifiably be forced to participate in them, even if they or their legal guardians do not give consent voluntarily. Protection of their interests would be the responsibility of an institutional review board, a group of professionals and lay people who would review all therapy and research activities for a given hospital. The board would decide *for* patients which therapy is likely to achieve minimal goals that would allow them to leave the hospital.

If the patient is determined to be operating above minimal levels, he or she should have the right to refuse treatments that have optimal goals, such as acquiring vocational skills, obtaining a high school diploma, and other luxury items that can enhance the quality of a patient's life. According to Paul and Lentz, these goals should not be considered so vital that the patient is forced into working toward them.

Deinstitutionalization, Civil Liberties, and Mental Health

The cumulative impact of court rulings such as *Wyatt* v. *Stickney* and *O'Connor* v. *Donaldson* was to put mental health professionals on notice that they must be more careful about keeping people in mental hospitals against their will, and that they must attend

[45]Many therapists are accused of forcing patients to conform to community standards that are themselves open to question. But the basic issue here is not whether mental patients wear clean pants with a belt to hold them up, but whether they wear pants at all.

more to the specific treatment needs of committed patients. Pressure was placed on state governments in particular to upgrade the quality of care in mental institutions. In view of the abuses that have been documented in hospital care, these are surely encouraging trends.

But the picture is not all that rosy. For judges to declare that patient care must meet certain minimal standards does not automatically translate into that praiseworthy goal. There is not an unlimited supply of money, and care of the mentally ill has never been one of government's high priorities. Nor is support of research in the social and behavioral sciences.

Over the past thirty years, many states have been embarked on a policy of deinstitutionalization, discharging as many patients as possible from mental hospitals and also discouraging admissions. As we have just seen, civil commitment is more difficult to achieve now than it was forty and more years ago, and even if committed, patients are able, with the help of civil rights–minded lawyers, to refuse much of the treatment made available to them in the hospital. At its peak in the 1950s, state mental hospitals housed almost half a million patients; by the late 1980s, the population had dropped to about 130,000. The maxim has become "Treat them in the community," the assumption being that virtually anything is preferable to institutionalization.

But what is this community that former mental patients are supposed to find more helpful to them on discharge? Facilities outside the hospitals are not prepared to cope with the influx of former mental patients. Some promising programs were described in Chapter 20, but these are very much the exception, not the rule. The state of affairs in many large metropolitan areas is an unrelenting social crisis, for hundreds of thousands of chronically ill mental patients have been released onto the street without sufficient job training and without community services to help them. It is doubtful even that deinstitutionalization has reduced the rate of chronic mental illness, and, as Gralnick (1987) has argued, the acutely ill are largely neglected because it is very difficult to commit them unless they are found to be a danger to themselves and to others, a condition that can take years to develop. By that time, Gralnick suggests, the problems may have become chronic and more difficult to deal with. The irony is that deinstitutionalization may be contributing to the very problem it was designed to alleviate, chronic mental illness.

Indeed, deinstitutionalization may be a misnomer. Transinstitutionalization may be more apt, for declines in the census of public mental hospitals have occasioned *increases* in the presence of mentally ill people in jails and prisons, nursing homes, and the mental health departments of nonpsychiatric hospitals (Kiesler, 1991), and these settings are by and large not equipped to handle the particular needs of mental patients. The oft-mentioned revolving door is seen in the increase in readmission rates from 25 percent before the deinstitutionalization movement to around 80 percent by the 1980s (Paul & Menditto, 1992).

Many discharged mental patients are eligible for benefits from the Veterans Administration and for Social Security Disability Insurance, but a large number are not receiving them. Homeless persons do not have fixed addresses and need assistance in establishing eligibility and residency for the purpose of receiving benefits. A study by the Community Service Society (Baxter & Hopper, 1981), an old and respected social agency in New York City, found them living in the streets, in train and bus terminals, in abandoned buildings, on subways, in cavernous steam tunnels running north from Grand Central Station in Manhattan, and some of them in shelters operated by public agencies, churches, and charitable organizations. The lives of these homeless are desperate.

> [In a train station at 11:00 P.M.] . . . the attendant goes off duty and women rise from separate niches and head for the bathroom. There they disrobe, and wash their clothes and bodies. Depending on the length of [the] line at the hand dryers, they wait to dry their clothes, put them in their bags or wear them wet. One woman cleans and wraps her ulcerated legs with paper towels every night. The most assertive claim toilet cubicles, line them with newspapers for privacy and warmth and sleep curled around the basin. Once they are taken, the rest sleep along the walls, one on a box directly beneath the hand dryer which she pushes for warm air. One of the women regularly cleans up the floors, sinks and toilets so that no traces of their uncustomary use remain. *(p. 77)*

No one knows how many of the homeless are deinstitutionalized mental patients. Those who are not homeless live marginal and unhealthful lives in nursing homes, jails, and rundown hotels. They are a visible part of the population, but their proportions may be diminishing with so many other people being dispossessed from their homes and apartments and losing their jobs. The very state of homelessness undoubtedly exacerbates the emotional suffering of former mental patients. Whatever their numbers, the mentally ill remain an especially defenseless segment of the homeless population.

The relationships between homelessness and mental health were enumerated and analyzed by a committee of the National Academy of Sciences (Committee on Health Care for Homeless People, 1988, as summarized in Leeper, 1988). It is estimated that 25 to 40 percent of the homeless are alcoholics, with similar proportions suffering from some form of serious mental illness, usually schizophrenia. Such problems are probably aggravated by their nomadic and dangerous existence; homeless people, especially women, are likely victims of violence and rape, even when living in shelters for the homeless (D'Ercole & Struening, 1990). Children, too, are among the homeless, a fact that the NAS committee terms "a national disgrace," for these youngsters are forced to live their formative years in chaotic and dangerous situations, with parents under severe stress. One committee member noted in an interview that "many children have developmental delays. I've seen two-year-olds who can't walk, six-month-olds who don't cuddle in your arms, and four-year-olds acting like mothers to one-year-olds because their mother isn't giving them the care they need" (Leeper, 1988, p. 8). That such children often drop out of school and suffer from anxiety, depression, and substance abuse, and are subject as well to physical and sexual abuse, should come as no surprise.

Do such appalling facts justify reversing the policy of deinstitutionalization? The NAS committee thinks not because, in their view, the problem lies with the failure of communities to provide suitable living and rehabilitation conditions, a theme sounded earlier in this book.

> [The] vulnerability [of former patients] . . . became clear in January 1982, when a sixty-one-year-old former psychiatric patient was found dead in a cardboard box on a New York City street. She had been living in the box for eight months after her entitlements were revoked for failure to appear for recertification. She had refused the efforts of various agencies to relocate her, and she died of hypothermia hours before a court order was obtained directing her removal to a hospital.
>
> This case led to the creation of Project HELP, the Homeless Emergency Liaison Project, which is a mobile, psychiatric outreach team that identifies homeless people in need of psychiatric aid, and has authority under State and local laws to involuntarily remove homeless people in danger to themselves to a hospital for help and evaluation. *(Committee on Government Operations, 1985, p. 5)*

Gralnick (1986) fears that schizophrenics will increasingly be seen as misfits, drug abusers, and panhandlers rather than as ill people in need of professional care. Jails, shelters, and church basements will be seen as appropriate places for them rather than mental wards. Indeed, a large-scale field study (Teplin, 1984) found that police officers were 20 percent more likely to arrest people if they were showing signs of mental disorder than if they were (merely) committing offenses for which arrest was an option. Furthermore, to the extent that treatment will be seen as an (outpatient) option, it will, Gralnick predicts, be biological and drug based because such treatment is cheaper, more straightforward, and does not require the close interpersonal relationship that is intrinsic to any psychotherapy. He also predicts that biological factors will be focused on *to the exclusion of* psychological factors.[46] This focus will interfere with achieving full understanding of serious mental illness, which he, along with most workers in the field (including the authors of this textbook), views as a complex interaction between biological diatheses and environmental stressors. Gralnick recommends, among other things, that the psychiatric hospital be restored to its previous position as the place of choice to treat and do research in schizophrenia and that research be more vigorously pursued in aftercare for patients who are discharged.

Ethical Dilemmas in Therapy and Research

In this textbook we have examined a variety of theories and a multitude of data focusing on *what is* and *what is thought to be.* Ethics and values, often embodied in our laws, are a different order of discussion. They concern *what ought to be,* having sometimes little to do with what is. It is extremely important to recognize the difference. Within a given scientific paradigm we are able to examine what we believe is reality. As the study of philosophy and ethics reveals, however, the statements that people have made for thousands of years about what *should* be are another matter. The Ten Commandments are such statements. They are prescriptions and proscriptions about human conduct. For example, the eighth commandment, "Thou shalt not steal," in no way describes human conduct, for stealing is not uncommon. It is, instead, a pronouncement of an

[46]He is not arguing that major advances are not being made in biological approaches to diagnosis, etiology, and treatment—one would have to be out of contact with reality to believe this. Rather, he is concerned that scientific advances will be *coupled to* a distancing from the personal plight of schizophrenics and lead to a scientifically unjustified and socially questionable neglect of their sad living situation in the era of what he and others regard as misguided deinstitutionalization.

ideal that people should aspire to. The integrity of an ethical code that proscribes stealing does not depend on any evidence concerning the percentage of people who steal. Morals and data are two separate realms of discourse.

The legal trends reviewed thus far in this chapter place limits on the activities of mental health professionals. These legal constraints are important, for laws are one of society's strongest means of forcing all of us to behave in certain ways. Psychologists and psychiatrists also have professional and ethical constraints. All professional groups promulgate shoulds and should nots, and by guidelines and mandates they limit to some degree what therapists and researchers may do with their patients, clients, and subjects. Courts as well have ruled on some of these questions. We examine now the ethics of making psychological inquiries and interventions into the lives of other human beings.

Ethical Restraints on Research

It is basic to science that what can be done is likely to be attempted. The most reprehensible ethical insensitivity is documented in the brutal experiments conducted by certain German physicians on concentration camp prisoners during the Third Reich. One experiment, for example, investigated how long people lived when their heads were bashed repeatedly with a heavy stick. Even if important information might be obtained from this kind of atrocity, which seems extremely doubtful, such actions cannot be allowed. The Nuremberg trials, conducted by the Allies following the war, brought these and other barbarisms to light and meted out severe punishment to some of the soldiers, physicians, and other Nazi officials who had engaged in or contributed to such actions, even when they claimed that they had merely been following orders.

It would be reassuring to be able to say that such gross violations of human decency take place only during incredible and cruel epochs such as the Third Reich, but unfortunately this is not the case. Spurred on by a blind enthusiasm for their work, researchers in the United States and other countries have sometimes dealt with human subjects in reproachable ways.[47]

Henry K. Beecher, a research professor at Harvard Medical School, surveyed medical research since 1945 and found that "many of the patients [used as subjects in experiments] never had the risk satisfactorily explained to them, and . . . further hundreds have not known that they were the subjects of an experiment although grave consequences have been suffered as the direct result" (1966, p. 1354). One experiment compared penicillin with a placebo as a treatment to prevent rheumatic fever. Even though penicillin had already been acknowledged as the drug of choice to give people with a streptococcal respiratory infection in order to protect them from later contracting rheumatic fever, placebos were administered to 109 service personnel without their knowledge or permission. More subjects received penicillin than received the placebo, but three members of the control group contracted serious illnesses—two had rheumatic fever and one acute nephritis, a kidney disease—compared with none of those who had received penicillin.

The training of scientists equips them splendidly to pose interesting questions, sometimes even important ones, and to design experiments that are as free as possible of confounds. They have no special qualifications, however, for deciding whether a particular line of inquiry that involves humankind *should* be followed. Society needs knowledge, and a scientist has a right in a democracy to seek that knowledge. The ordinary citizens employed as subjects in experiments must, however, be protected from unnecessary harm, risk, humiliation, and invasion of privacy.[48]

There are several international codes of ethics for the conduct of scientific research—the Nuremberg Code formulated in the aftermath of the Nazi war crime trials, the Declaration of Helsinki, and statements from the British Medical Research Council. Closer to home, in the early 1970s the Department of Health, Education and Welfare began to issue guidelines and regulations governing scientific research that employs human subjects. In addition, a blue-ribbon panel, the National Commission for the Protection of Human Subjects of Biomedical and Behavioral Research, conducted hearings and inquiries into restrictions that the federal government might impose on research performed with mental patients, prisoners, and children. And for several years now the proposals of behavioral researchers, many of whom conduct experiments related to psychopathology and therapy, have been reviewed for safety and general ethical propriety by human subjects committees and institutional review boards in

[47]Researchers who use animals in their experiments have also occasionally dealt with their subjects in gratuitously harsh fashion. The American Psychological Association has guidelines for handling laboratory animals that are intended to minimize their discomfort and danger. Strict standards have also been promulgated by the National Institutes of Health.

[48]This very statement is an ethical, not an empirical, one.

hospitals, universities, and research institutes. Such committees—and this is very significant—are composed not just of behavioral scientists but of citizens from the community, lawyers, students, and specialists in a variety of disciplines, such as professors of English, history, and comparative religion. They are able to block any research proposal or require questionable aspects to be modified if in their collective judgment the research will put participating subjects at too great risk.

Informed Consent

Participation in research brings up the all-important concept of **informed consent**. Just as committed mental patients are gaining some right to refuse treatment, so may anyone refuse to be a subject in an experiment. The investigator must provide enough information to enable subjects to judge whether they want to accept any risks, if there are any, that are inherent in being a participant. The prospective subjects must be legally capable of giving consent, and there must be no deceit or coercion in obtaining it. For example, an experimental psychologist might wish to determine whether imagery helps college students associate one word with another. One group of subjects will be asked to associate pairs of words in their minds by generating a fanciful image connecting the two, such as "a CAT riding on a BICYCLE." If a prospective subject decides that the experiment is likely to be boring, that subject may decline to participate and, in fact, may withdraw from the experiment at any time, without fear of penalty.

Paired-associates research like this is relatively innocuous, but what if the experiment poses real risks, such as ingesting a drug? Or what if the prospective subject is a committed mental patient, or a retarded child, unable to understand fully what is being asked? Such a subject may not feel free or even be able to refuse participation. And what of the rights of the researcher, which often are not as carefully considered as those of subjects, and of the cost to society of important research left undone? Will scientists become reluctant to undertake certain types of work because review committees make the process of obtaining informed consent unduly onerous and time-consuming?

It is in fact not easy to demonstrate that a researcher has obtained informed consent. Epstein and Lasagna (1969) found that only one-third of subjects volunteering for an experiment really understood what the experiment entailed. In a more elaborate study, Stuart (1978) discovered that most college students could not accurately describe a simple experiment, even though it had just been explained to them and they had agreed to participate. A signature on a consent form is no assurance that informed consent has really been obtained, which poses a challenge to investigators and members of review panels who are committed to upholding codes of ethics governing participation of human subjects in research. Similar problems have been found in clinical settings, where there is a question of whether psychiatric patients understand the nature of neuroleptic medication. Irwin et al. (1985) found that although most patients *said* they understood the benefits and side effects of their drugs, only a quarter of them actually did when queried specifically. The authors' conclusions are that simply reading information to hospitalized patients—especially the more disturbed ones—is no guarantee that they fully comprehend; therefore, *informed* consent cannot be said to have been obtained.

In general, however, there is increasing recognition of the fact that being judged mentally ill—more specifically, being diagnosed schizophrenic and being hospitalized—does not necessarily mean that one is not capable of giving informed consent (Appelbaum & Gutheil, 1991; Grisso, 1986). A recent experiment by Grisso and Applebaum (in press) found that, although schizophrenic patients on average were not as good as nonpsychiatric patients at understanding issues relating to treatment involving medication, there was a wide *range* of understanding among the schizophrenics. Some of them showed as good understanding as nonimpaired patients, pointing to the importance of examining each person individually for ability to give informed consent, rather than assuming that a person is unable to do so only by virtue of being hospitalized as a schizophrenic. Before a mental patient can give informed consent in New York state hospitals, for example, a licensed psychologist or psychiatrist must certify that the person is capable of doing so. Thus, although professional judgment is required, and may therefore be erroneous, there is the real possibility that being judged mentally ill will not *ipso facto* deny a patient the ability to give informed consent.

Confidentiality and Privileged Communication

When an individual consults a physician, a psychiatrist, or a clinical psychologist, he or she expects all that goes on in the session to remain confidential.

Nothing will be revealed to a third party, excepting only to other professionals and those intimately involved in the treatment, such as a nurse or medical secretary. The ethical codes of the various helping professions dictate this **confidentiality**.

A **privileged communication** is one between parties in a confidential relation that is protected by statute. The recipient cannot legally be compelled to disclose it as a witness. The right of privileged communication is a major exception to the access that courts have to evidence in judicial proceedings. Society believes that, in the long term, the interests of people are best served if communications to a spouse and to certain professionals remain off limits to the prying eyes and ears of the police, judges, and prosecutors. The privilege exists between such people as husband–wife, doctor–patient, pastor–penitent, attorney–client, and psychologist–client.

There are important limits to the client's right of privileged communication, however. For example, according to the current California psychology licensing law (similar elements are present in other state laws), this right is eliminated for any of the following reasons.

1. If the client is accused of a crime and has requested that a determination be made about his sanity.
2. If the client has accused the therapist of malpractice; the therapist, in other words, can divulge information about the therapy in order to defend himself or herself in any legal action initiated by the client.
3. If the client is under sixteen years old and the therapist has reason to believe that the child has been a victim of a crime, such as child abuse. In fact, the psychologist is *required* to report to the police or to a child welfare agency within thirty-six hours any suspicion he or she has that the child client has been physically abused, including being sexually molested.
4. If the client initiated therapy in hopes of evading the law for having committed a crime or for planning to do so.
5. If the therapist judges that the client is a danger to self or to others and if disclosure of information is necessary to ward off such danger (recall Focus Box 21.3).

Who is the Client?

Is it always clear to the clinician who the client is? In private therapy, when an adult pays a clinician a fee for help with a personal problem that has nothing to do with the legal system, the consulting individual is clearly the client. But an individual may be seen by a clinician for an evaluation of his or her competency to stand trial. Or the clinician may be hired by an individual's family to assist in civil commitment proceedings. Perhaps the clinician is employed by a state mental hospital as a regular staff member and sees a particular patient about problems in controlling aggressive impulses. It should be clear, although it is alarming how seldom it *is* clear, that in these instances the clinician is serving more than one client. In addition to the patient, he or she serves the family or the state, and it is incumbent on the mental health professional to inform the patient that this is so. This dual allegiance does not necessarily indicate that the patient's own interests will be sacrificed, but it does mean that discussions will not inevitably remain secret and that the clinician may in the future act in a way that displeases the individual.

Choice of Goals

Ideally the client sets the goals for therapy, but in practice it is naive to assume that some are not imposed by the therapist and even go against the wishes of the client. School systems often want to institute programs that will teach children to "be still, be quiet, be docile" (Winett & Winkler, 1972, p. 499). Many behavior therapists have assumed that young children *should* be compliant, not only because the teacher can then run a more orderly class but because children are assumed to learn better when they are so. But do we really know that the most efficient and most enjoyable learning takes place when children are forced to remain quietly in their seats? Some advocates of open classrooms believe that curiosity and initiative, even in the youngest elementary school child, are at least as important as the acquisition of academic skills. As is generally the case in psychology, evidence is less plentiful than are strongly held and vehemently defended opinions. But the issue is clear: any professionals consulted by a school system should be mindful of their own personal biases with respect to goals and should be prepared to work toward different ones if the parents and school personnel so wish. Any therapist of course retains the option of not working for a client whose goals and proposed means of attaining them are abhorrent in his or her view.

This question of goals is particularly complex in family and couples therapy (Margolin, 1982). If several people are clients simultaneously—inevitable in family treatment!—an intervention that benefits

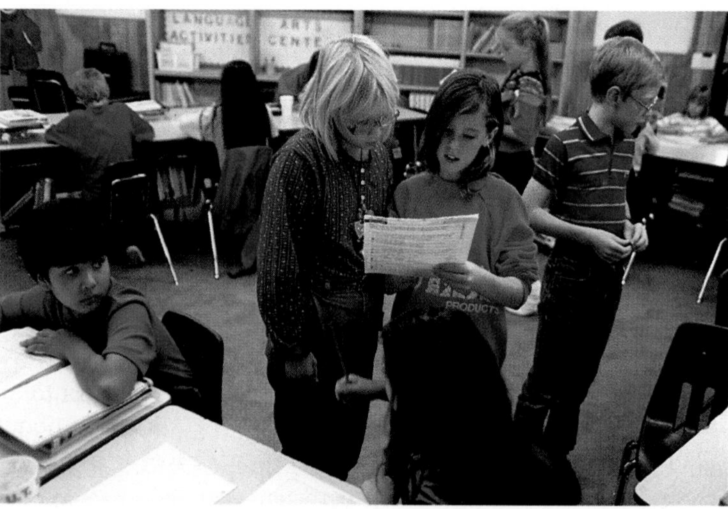

Which environment best fosters learning: (left) typical classroom or (right) "open" classroom.

one or more individuals may well work to the disadvantage of one or more of the others. This can happen if one partner in couples therapy really wants to end the relationship, but the other sees the therapy as a way to save it. People often do not openly express their real concerns and wishes at the very beginning of therapy; the therapist can already be deeply enmeshed in their lives before learning that the two partners have conflicting goals (Gurman & Kniskern, 1981).

Although the plight of people who voluntarily consult therapists is in no way as confining as that of institutionalized patients, they do operate with constraints on their freedom. The issue was addressed by Seymour Halleck (1971), a psychiatrist, who asserts that the neutrality of the therapist is a myth. In his opinion therapists influence their clients in ways that are subtle yet powerful.

> At first glance, a model of psychiatric [or psychological] practice based on the contention that people should just be helped to learn to do the things they want to do seems uncomplicated and desirable. But it is an unobtainable model. Unlike a technician, a psychiatrist [or psychologist] cannot avoid communicating and at times imposing his own values upon his patients. The patient usually has considerable difficulty in finding the way in which he would wish to change his behavior, but as he talks to the psychiatrist his wants and needs become clearer. In the very process of defining his needs in the presence of a figure who is viewed as wise and authoritarian, the patient is profoundly influenced. He ends up wanting some of the things the psychiatrist thinks he should want. (p. 19)

Psychologists agree, and research (e.g., Rosenthal, 1955) supports the contention that patients are indeed influenced by the values of their therapists. A person not only seeks out a therapist who suits his or her taste and meets what the person believes are his or her needs but also adopts some of the ideals, sometimes even the mannerisms, of the therapist. Most therapists are keenly aware of this modeling after themselves, which surely increases the already heavy responsibilities of their professional role. Perry London (1964, 1985), a leading writer on the ethics of therapeutic intervention, even suggested that therapists are contemporary society's secular priests, purveyors of values and ethics to help clients live "the good life" (see Focus Box 21.5).

Choice of Techniques

The end does not justify the means. Most of us take in this maxim with our mother's milk. It is said to be intrinsic to a free society. Over the past twenty years questions concerning behavioral techniques have been debated among professionals and have even been the subject of court rulings. Perhaps because the various insight therapies de-emphasize direct efforts to change behavior, they have seldom been scrutinized as behavior therapy has. The very concreteness, specificity, and directiveness of behavioral techniques have called attention to them, as has their alignment with experimental psychology. It is offensive to some to believe that our understanding of human beings could possibly be advanced by employing rats and pigeons as subject analogues.

Particular concern has been expressed about the ethics of inflicting pain for purposes of therapy. To some people the very term *behavior therapy* conjures up an image of the violent protagonist in Kubrick's *Clockwork Orange,* eyes popped open with a torturous apparatus, being made nauseous by a drug while scenes of violence flashed on a screen. Aversion therapy programs never really reach this level of coercion and drama, but certainly any such procedure entails making the patient uncomfortable, sometimes extremely so. Making patients vomit or cringe with pain from electric shock applied to the extremities are two aversion techniques worthy of their name. Can there be any circumstances that justify therapists inflicting pain on clients?

Before quickly exclaiming "No!" consider the following report.

The patient was a nine-month-old baby who had already been hospitalized three times for treatment of vomiting and chronic rumination (regurgitating food and rechewing it in the mouth). A number of diagnostic tests, including an EEG, plus surgery to remove a cyst on the right kidney, had revealed no organic basis for the problems, and several treatments, including a special diet, had been attempted without success. When referred to Lang and Melamed (1969), two behavior therapists, the child was in critical condition and was being fed by tubes leading from the nose directly into the stomach. The attending physician had stated that the infant's life was in imminent danger if the vomiting could not be halted.

Treatment consisted of delivering a series of one-second-long electric shocks to the infant's calf each time he showed signs of beginning to vomit. Sessions followed feeding and lasted under an hour. After just two sessions, shock was rarely required, for the infant learned quickly to stop vomiting in order to avoid the shock. By the sixth session he was able to fall asleep after eating. Nurses reported that the in-session inhibition of vomiting generalized as the infant progressively reduced his vomiting during the rest of the day and night. About two weeks later the mother began to assume some care of the hospitalized child, and shortly thereafter the patient was discharged with virtually complete elimination of the life-threatening pattern of behavior. Throughout the three weeks of treatment and observation, the child gained weight steadily. One month after discharge the child weighed twenty-one pounds and was rated as fully recovered by the attending physician. Five months later he weighed twenty-six pounds and was regarded as completely normal, both physically and psychologically.

The use of aversion therapy has been subject to an understandably high degree of regulation. An additional reason for administrative and judicial concern is that aversion techniques smack more of research than of standard therapy. The more established a therapeutic procedure, whether it be medical or psychological, the less likely it is to attract the attention of the courts or other governmental agencies. Paul and Lentz (1977) had a few very assaultive patients. Their account of administrative problems demonstrates that patients might be subject to more extreme procedures because special attention is paid to new techniques.

> Some consideration was given to the contingent use of mild electric shock. . . . However, early in the explorations of the necessary safeguards and review procedures to be followed before evaluating such methods, the department director telephoned to explain that aversion conditioning was a politically sensitive issue. Therefore, more than the usual proposal, preparation, documentation, and committee reviews would be required—to the extent that approval would probably take about eighteen months. Instead, it was suggested that convulsive shock (which can cause tissue damage) be employed since "ECT is an accepted medical treatment." With those alternatives, our choice was to abandon either use of shock. (p. 499)

Mindful that short-term application of electric shock can sometimes keep retarded and autistic children from their self-destructive acts, Martin (1975) proposed that

> the test should be that aversive therapy might be used where other therapy has not worked, where it can be administered to save the individual from immediate and continuing self-injury, when it allows freedom from physical restraints which would otherwise be continued, when it can be administered for only a few short instances and when its goal is to make other nonaversive therapy possible. Such an aversive program certainly requires consent from a guardian and immediate review of the results of each separate administration. (p. 77)[49]

Extra precautions such as these are necessary when treatment deliberately inflicts pain on a patient or client; they are especially necessary when the patient cannot realistically be expected to give informed consent. But should we be concerned only with physical pain? The anguish we suffer when a loved one dies is psychologically painful. It is perhaps more painful than an electric shock of 1500 microamperes. Who is to say? Since we allow that pain

[49]In addition to being humane, Martin's suggestions are consistent with an established legal principle that holds that therapy should begin with the technique that intrudes least on the patient's freedom and exposes him or her to the least possible risk (Morris, 1966).

FOCUS 21.5 • Not Can but Ought: An Opinion on the Treatment of Homosexuality

Several psychologists have argued that the social pressures on homosexuals to become heterosexual make it difficult to believe that the small minority of people who consult therapists for help in changing from same-sex to opposite-sex partners act with free choice (Begelman, 1975; Davison, 1974, 1976, 1991; Silverstein, 1972). Although most states have dropped their sodomy laws, which used to be enforced selectively against homosexual acts, there remains some legal pressure against homosexuality: a 1986 U.S. Supreme Court decision*, still valid, refused to find constitutional protection in the right to privacy for consensual adult homosexual activity and thereby upheld a Georgia law that prohibits oral–genital and anal–genital acts, even in private and between consenting adults. Silverstein's statement about the pressures homosexuals are under to want to become heterosexual was given in Chapter 12 (page 359). It has further been suggested that the mere availability of change-of-orientation programs serves to condone the prejudice against homosexuality. Clinicians work to develop procedures and study their effects only if they are concerned about the problem to be dealt with by their techniques. The therapy literature contains relatively little material on helping homosexuals develop as individuals without changing their sexual orientation, in contrast with the many articles and books on how best to discourage homosexual behavior and substitute for it heterosexual patterns. Aversion therapy used to be the most widely used behavioral technique (Davison & Wilson, 1973; Henkel & Lewis-Thomé, 1976). "What are we really saying to our clients when, on the one hand, we assure them that they are not abnormal and on the other hand, present them with an array of techniques, some of them painful, which are aimed at eliminating that set of feelings and behavior that we have just told them is okay?" (Davison, 1976, p. 161)

For these reasons it has been proposed that therapists not help homosexuals become heterosexual even when such treatment is requested. This is obviously a radical proposal, held probably by a small minority of clinicians, and it has evoked some strong reactions. Gay-activist groups are understandably pleased, considering the suggestion concrete support for the belief that homosexuality per se is not a mental disorder. But many psychologists and psychiatrists are concerned about limiting the choices available to people seeking therapy. Why should a therapist decide for potential clients which options should be available? Do not therapists have a responsibility to satisfy the needs expressed by their clients (Stur-

Bowers v. *Hardwick*, 106 S. Ct. 2841 (1986).

can be psychological, should we forbid a Gestalt therapist from making a patient cry by confronting the patient with feelings that have been avoided for years? Should we forbid a psychoanalyst from guiding a patient to an insight that will likely cause great anguish, all the more so for the conflict's having been repressed for years?

Concluding Comment

An underlying theme of this book concerns the nature of knowledge. How do we decide that we understand a phenomenon? The rules of science that govern our definition of and search for knowledge require theories that can be tested, experiments that can be replicated, and data that are public. But given the complexity of abnormal behavior and the vast areas of ignorance, far more extensive than the domains that have already been mapped by science as it is currently practiced, we have great respect for theoreticians and clinicians, those inventive souls who make suppositions, offer hypotheses, follow hunches—all based on rather flimsy data but holding some promise that scientific knowledge will be forthcoming.

This final chapter demonstrates again something emphasized at the very beginning of this book, namely, that the behavioral scientists and mental health professionals who conduct research and give treatment are only human beings. They suffer from the same foibles that sometimes plague nonspecialists. They occasionally act with a certainty their evidence does not justify, and they sometimes fail to anticipate the moral and legal consequences of the ways in which they conduct research and apply the gis & Adams, 1978)? A reply to this important criticism would be that therapists always decide what therapy they will offer when they refuse to take as clients people whose goals they disagree with. The request of a patient for a certain kind of treatment has never been sufficient justification for providing it (see Davison, 1978).

It has been asserted that continued research will help develop sex reorientation programs that are even more effective than those already available (Sturgis & Adams, 1978). To discourage such work would deprive today's homosexuals of promising therapies and tomorrow's homosexuals of improved treatments. This objection, however, is not relevant. The fact that we *can* do something does not indicate that we *should.* The proposal to deny sexual reorientation therapy is philosophical-ethical in nature, not empirical. The decision whether we should change sexual orientation will have to be made on moral grounds.

Will numbers of people be hurt by eliminating the sex reorientation option? Some have raised the specter of an upsurge in suicides among homosexuals if therapists refuse to help them switch. These are very serious concerns, but they overlook the possibility, some would say the fact, that far greater numbers of people have been hurt over the years by the availability of sex reorientation programs. As already argued, the existence of these treatments is consistent with societal prejudices and discrimination against homosexuals.

It is noteworthy that since 1975 there has been a dramatic reduction in the use of aversion therapy for changing homosexual orientation to heterosexual (Rosen & Beck, 1988) and a sharp decrease also in reports of other procedures for altering homosexuality. Other signs of increased acceptance of homosexuality as a life-style are the elimination of ego-dystonic homosexuality from the DSM and the establishment within the American Psychological Association of the Division of Lesbian and Gay Psychologists and the Committee on Lesbian and Gay Concerns on the Board of Social and Ethical Responsibility.

The proponents who wish to terminate change-of-orientation programs believe that much good can come of their proposal. Homosexuals would be helped to think better of themselves, and greater efforts could be directed toward the problems homosexuals have, rather than to the issue of homosexuality.

> It would be nice if an alcoholic homosexual, for example, could be helped to reduce his or her drinking without having his or her sexual orientation questioned. It would be nice if a homosexual fearful of interpersonal relationships, or incompetent in them, could be helped without the therapist assuming that homosexuality lies at the root of the problem. It would be nice if a nonorgasmic or impotent homosexual could be helped as a heterosexual would be rather than [being guided] to change-of-orientation regimens . . . the hope [is] that therapists will concentrate their efforts on such human problems rather than focusing on the most obvious "maladjustment"—loving members of one's own sex (Davison, 1978, p. 171).

tentative findings of their young discipline. When society acts with great certainty on the basis of expert scientific opinion, particularly when that opinion denies to an individual the rights and respect accorded others, it may be well to let Szasz (1963) remind us that Sir Thomas Browne, a distinguished British physician, testified in a British court of law in 1664 that witches did indeed exist, "as everyone knew."

The authors of this textbook hope that they have communicated in some measure their love for the subject matter and, more importantly, their commitment to the kind of questioning, doubting stance that wrests useful knowledge from nature and will yield more as new generations of scholars build upon the achievements of their predecessors.

SUMMARY

This final chapter deals with legal and ethical issues in treatment and research. Some civil liberties are rather routinely set aside when judgments are made by mental health professionals and the courts that mental illness has played a role in determining their behavior. Criminal commitment sends a person to a hospital either before a trial for an alleged crime, because the person is deemed incompetent to stand trial, or after an acquittal by reason of insanity, because a mental defect, the inability to know right from wrong, or both, are believed to have played a role in the person's committing a criminal act.

A person who is considered ill and dangerous to self and to others, though he or she has not broken a law, can be civilly committed to an institution. Recent court rulings have provided greater protection to all committed mental patients, particularly those under civil commitment: they have the right to written notification, to counsel, to a jury decision concerning their commitment, and to Fifth Amendment protection against self-incrimination; the right to the least restrictive treatment setting; the right to be treated; and, in most circumstances, the right to refuse treatment, particularly any procedure that entails considerable risk.

There are a number of moral issues in therapy and research: ethical restraints on research, the duty of scientists to obtain informed consent from prospective human subjects, the question whether a program is treatment or research, the right of clients to confidentiality, the setting of therapy goals, and the choice of techniques.

KEY TERMS

criminal commitment
civil commitment
insanity defense
informed consent
confidentiality
privileged communication

Glossary

abnormal behavior. Patterns of emotion, thought, and action deemed pathological for one or more of the following reasons: infrequent occurrence, violation of norms, personal distress, disability or dysfunction, and unexpectedness.

accurate empathic understanding. In client-centered therapy, an essential quality of the therapist, referring to the ability to see the world through the client's phenomenology as well as from perspectives of which the client may be only dimly aware.

acetylcholine. A *neurotransmitter*[1] of the central, somatomotor, and *parasympathetic nervous systems* and of the ganglia and the neuron–sweat gland junctions of the *sympathetic nervous system.*

acquaintance (date) rape. Forcible sex between two people who know each other, sometimes occurring on a date.

addiction. See *substance dependence.*

Addison's disease. An endocrine disorder produced by *cortisone* insufficiency and marked by weight loss, fatigue, and a darkening of the skin.

adrenal glands. Two small areas of tissue located just above the kidneys. The inner core of each gland, the medulla, secretes *epinephrine* and *norepinephrine;* the outer cortex secretes *cortisone* and other steroid hormones.

adrenaline. A hormone that is secreted by the *adrenal glands;* also called *epinephrine.*

adrenergic system. All the nerve cells for which *epinephrine* and *norepinephrine* (and more broadly, other *monoamines, dopamine,* and *serotonin*) are the transmitter substances, as opposed to the *cholinergic system,* which consists of the nerve cells activated by *acetylcholine.*

advanced accurate empathy. A form of *empathy* in which the therapist infers concerns and feelings that lie behind what the client is saying; it represents an *interpretation.* Compare with *primary empathy.*

affect. A subjective feeling or emotional tone often accompanied by bodily expressions noticeable to others.

affirming the consequent. An error in logic by which, if A causes B on one occasion, it is assumed that A is the cause when B is observed on any other occasion.

age effects. The consequences of being a given chronological age. Compare with *cohort effects.*

ageism. Prejudicial attitudes toward old people.

[1]Italicized words or variants of these terms are themselves defined elsewhere in the glossary.

agoraphobia. A cluster of fears centering on being in open spaces and leaving the home.

AIDS (acquired immunodeficiency syndrome). A fatal disease transmitted by transfer of the human immunodeficiency virus, usually during sexual relations or by using needles previously infected by an HIV-positive person; it compromises the person's immune system to such a degree that he or she ultimately dies from cancer or one of any number of infections.

alcoholism. A behavioral disorder in which consumption of alcoholic beverages is excessive and impairs health and social and occupational functioning; a physiological dependence on alcohol. See *substance dependence.*

alkaloid. An organic base found in seed plants, usually in mixture with a number of similar alkaloids. Alkaloids are the active chemicals that give many drugs their medicinal properties and other powerful physiological effects.

alogia. A *negative symptom* in schizophrenia, marked by blocking and poverty of speech content.

alpha rhythm. The dominant pattern (8 to 13 cps) of the *brain waves* of a resting but awake adult.

alternate form reliability. See *reliability.*

altruistic suicide. As defined by Durkheim, self-annihilation that the person feels will serve a social purpose, such as the self-immolations practiced by Buddhist monks during the Vietnam War.

Alzheimer's disease. A *dementia* involving a progressive atrophy of cortical tissue and marked by memory impairment, involuntary movements of limbs, occasional *convulsions,* intellectual deterioration, and psychotic behavior.

ambivalence. The simultaneous holding of strong positive and negative emotional attitudes toward the same situation or person.

American Law Institute guidelines. Rules proposing insanity to be a legitimate defense plea if, during criminal conduct, an individual could not judge right from wrong or control his or her behavior as required by law. Repetitive criminal acts are disavowed as a sole criterion. Compare *M'Naghten rule* and *irresistible impulse.*

amino acid. One of a large class of organic compounds, important as the building blocks of proteins.

amnesia. Total or partial loss of memory that can be associated with a *dissociative disorder,* brain damage, or *hypnosis.*

amniocentesis. A prenatal diagnostic technique in which

fluid drawn from the uterus is tested for birth defects, such as *Down syndrome* and Tay-Sachs disease.

amphetamines. A group of stimulating drugs that produce heightened levels of energy and, in large doses, nervousness, sleeplessness, and paranoid *delusions.*

anal personality. An adult who, when anal retentive, is found by psychoanalytic theory to be stingy and sometimes obsessively clean; when anal expulsive, to be aggressive. Such traits are assumed to be caused by *fixation* through either excessive or inadequate gratification of id impulses during the *anal stage* of psychosexual development.

anal stage. In psychoanalytic theory, the second *psychosexual stage,* occurring during the second year of life, during which the anus is considered to be the principal *erogenous* zone.

analgesia. An insensitivity to pain without loss of consciousness; sometimes found in *conversion disorder.*

analogue experiment. An experimental study of a phenomenon different from but related to the actual interests of the investigator.

analysand. A person being psychoanalyzed.

analysis of defenses. The study by a *psychoanalyst* of the ways in which a patient avoids troubling topics by the use of *defense mechanisms.*

analyst. See *psychoanalyst.*

analytical psychology. A variation of Freud's psychoanalysis introduced by Carl Jung and focusing less on biological drives and more on such factors as self-fulfillment, collective unconscious, and religious symbolism.

anesthesia. An impairment or loss of sensation, usually of touch but sometimes of the other senses, that is often part of *conversion disorder.*

anger-in theory. The view that *psychophysiological disorders,* such as *essential hypertension,* arise from a person not expressing anger or resentment.

angina pectoris. See *coronary heart disease.*

anhedonia. A *negative symptom* in schizophrenia in which the individual is unable to feel pleasure.

animal phobias. The fear and avoidance of small animals.

anomic suicide. As defined by Durkheim, self-annihilation triggered by a person's inability to cope with sudden and unfavorable change in a social situation.

anorexia nervosa. A disorder in which a person is unable to eat or to retain any food or suffers a prolonged and severe diminution of appetite. The individual has an intense fear of becoming obese, feels fat even when emaciated, and, refusing to maintain a minimal body weight, loses at least 25 percent of original weight.

anosmia. A *conversion disorder* marked by loss or impairment of the sense of smell.

anoxia. A deficiency in oxygen reaching the tissues that is severe enough to damage the brain permanently.

Antabuse (trade name for disulfiram). A drug that makes the drinking of alcohol produce nausea and other unpleasant effects.

antidepressant. A drug that alleviates *depression,* usually by energizing the patient and thus elevating mood.

antisocial personality. Also called a psychopath or a sociopath, a person with this disorder is superficially charming and a habitual liar, has no regard for others, shows no remorse after hurting others, has no shame for behaving in an outrageously objectionable manner, is unable to form relationships and take responsibility, and does not learn from punishment.

anxiety. An unpleasant feeling of fear and apprehension accompanied by increased psysiological arousal. In learning theory it is considered a drive that mediates between a threatening situation and avoidance behavior. Anxiety can be assessed by self-report, by measuring physiological arousal, and by observing overt behavior.

anxiety disorders. Disorders in which fear or tension is overriding and the primary disturbance: *phobic disorders, panic disorder, generalized anxiety disorder, obsessive-compulsive disorder;* and *posttraumatic stress disorder.* These disorders form a major category of DSM-IV and cover most of what used to be referred to as the *neuroses.*

anxiety neurosis. DSM-II term for what are now diagnosed as *panic disorder* and *generalized anxiety disorder.*

anxiolytics. Tranquilizers; drugs that reduce anxiety.

aphasia. The loss or impairment of the ability to use language because of lesions in the brain: **executive**, difficulties in speaking or writing the words intended; **receptive**, difficulties in understanding written or spoken language.

aphonia. A *conversion disorder* marked by a loss of voice.

apnea. Cessation of breathing for short periods of time, sometimes occurring during sleep.

applied behavior analysis. The study of the antecedent conditions and *reinforcement* contingencies that control behavior. See also *operant conditioning.*

aptitude test. A paper-and-pencil assessment of a person's intellectual functioning that is supposed to predict how he or she will perform at a later time; well-known examples include the Scholastic Aptitude Test and the Graduate Record Examination.

arousal. A state of activation, either behavioral or physiological.

ascriptive responsibility. The social judgment assigned to someone who has committed an illegal act and who, it is decided, should be punished for it. Contrast with *descriptive responsibility.*

asociality. A *negative symptom in schizophrenia* marked by inability to form close relationships and to feel intimacy.

assertion training. *Behavior therapy* procedures that attempt to help a person express more easily thoughts, wishes, beliefs, and legitimate feelings of resentment or approval.

asthma. A *psychophysiological disorder* characterized by narrowing of the airways and increased secretion of mucus, which often cause breathing to be extremely labored and wheezy.

asylums. Refuges established in western Europe in the fifteenth century to confine and provide for the mentally ill; the forerunners of the mental hospital.

attention-deficit hyperactivity disorder (ADHD). A disorder in children marked by difficulties in focusing adaptively on the task at hand and by inappropriate fidgeting and antisocial behavior.

attribution. The explanation a person has for his or her behavior.

aura. A signal or warning of an impending epileptic *convulsion,* taking the form of dizziness or an unusual sensory experience.

autistic disorder. An absorption in self or fantasy as a means of avoiding communication and escaping objective reality. In this *pervasive developmental disorder,* the child's world is one of profound aloneness.

automatic thoughts. In Beck's theory, the things people picture or tell themselves as they make their way in life.

autonomic lability. Tendency for the *autonomic nervous system* to be easily aroused.

autonomic nervous system (ANS). The division of the nervous system that regulates involuntary functions; innervates *endocrine glands, smooth muscle,* and heart muscle; and initiates the physiological changes that are part of expression of emotion. See *sympathetic* and *parasympathetic nervous system.*

aversion therapy. A *behavior therapy* procedure that pairs a noxious stimulus, such as a shock, with situations that are undesirably attractive to make the latter less appealing.

aversive conditioning. Process believed to underlie the effectiveness of *aversion therapy.*

aversive stimulus. A stimulus that elicits pain, fear, or avoidance.

avoidance conditioning. Learning to move away from a stimulus that has previously been paired with an *aversive stimulus* such as electric shock.

avoidance learning. An experimental procedure in which a neutral stimulus is paired with a noxious one so that the organism learns to avoid the previously neutral stimulus.

avoidant disorder. In childhood or adolescence, a persistent shrinking from strangers and from peers, despite a clear desire for affection, to the extent that social functioning is impaired, although relations with family members are warm.

avoidant personality. Individuals with an avoidant personality have poor self-esteem and thus are extremely sensitive to potential rejection and remain aloof, even though they very much desire affiliation and affection.

avolition. A *negative symptom* in *schizophrenia* in which the individual lacks interest and drive.

barbiturates. A class of synthetic *sedative* drugs that are addictive and in large doses can cause death by almost completely relaxing the diaphragm.

baseline. The state of a phenomenon before the *independent variable* is manipulated, providing a standard against which the effects of the variable can be measured.

behavior genetics. The study of individual differences in behavior that are attributable in part to differences in genetic makeup.

behavior modification. A term sometimes used interchangeably with *behavior therapy.*

behavior rehearsal. A *behavior therapy* technique in which a client practices new behavior in the consulting room, often aided by demonstrations and roleplay by the therapist.

behavior therapy. A branch of psychotherapy narrowly conceived as the application of *classical* and *operant conditioning* to the alteration of clinical problems, but more broadly conceived as applied experimental psychology in a clinical context.

behavioral assessment. A sampling of ongoing cognitions, feelings, and overt behavior in their situational context. Contrast with *projective test* and *personality inventory.*

behavioral medicine. An interdisciplinary field concerned with integrating knowledge from medicine and behavioral science in order to understand health and illness and to prevent as well as to treat *psychophysiological disorders* and other illnesses in which a person's psyche plays a role.

behavioral observation. A form of *behavioral assessment* that entails careful observation of a person's overt behavior in a particular situation.

behavioral pediatrics. A branch of *behavioral medicine* concerned with psychological aspects of childhood medical problems.

behaviorism. The school of psychology associated with John B. Watson, who proposed that observable behavior, not consciousness, is the proper subject matter of psychology. Currently, many who consider themselves behaviorists do use *mediational* concepts, provided they are firmly anchored to observables.

bell and pad. A *behavior therapy* technique for eliminating nocturnal *enuresis;* if the child wets, an electric circuit is closed and a bell sounds, waking the child.

beta rhythm. The dominant pattern (14 to 25 cps) of *brain waves* found in an alert adult responding to a stimulus. See also *alpha rhythm.*

bilateral ECT. *Electroconvulsive therapy* in which electrodes are placed on each side of the forehead and an electrical current is passed between them through both hemispheres of the brain.

bioenergetics. The therapy based on Wilhelm Reich's unorthodox analytic theory that all psychological distress is caused by problems in achieving full sexual satisfaction.

biofeedback. A term referring to procedures that provide an individual immediate information on even minute changes in muscle activity, skin temperature, heart rate, blood pressure, and other somatic functions. It is assumed that voluntary control over these bodily processes can be achieved through this knowledge, thereby ameliorating to some extent certain *psychophysiological disorders.*

biological paradigm. A broad theoretical view that holds that mental disorders are caused by some aberrant somatic process or defect.

bipolar disorder. A term applied to the disorder of people who experience episodes of both *mania* and *depression* or of mania alone.

bisexuality. Sexual desire or activity directed toward both men and women.

blocking. A disturbance associated with thought disorders in which a train of speech is interrupted by silence before an idea is fully expressed.

body dysmorphic disorder. Preoccupation with an imagined or exaggerated defect in appearance, for example, facial wrinkles or excess facial or body hair.

borderline personality. This impulsive and unpredictable person has an uncertain self-image, intense and unstable social relationships, and extreme swings of mood.

brain stem. The part of the brain connecting the spinal cord with the *cerebrum*. It contains the *pons* and *medulla oblongata* and functions as a neural relay station.

brain wave. The rhythmic fluctuations in voltage between parts of the brain produced by the spontaneous firings of its *neurons;* shown in an *electroencephalogram*.

brief reactive psychosis. A disorder in which a person has a sudden onset of *psychotic* symptoms—*incoherence, loose associations, delusions, hallucinations*—immediately after a severely disturbing event; the symptoms last more than a few hours but no more than two weeks. See *schizophreniform disorder*.

brief therapy. Time-limited psychotherapy, usually ego-analytic in orientation and lasting no more than twenty-five sessions.

Briquet's syndrone. See *somatization disorder*.

bulimia nervosa. Episodic uncontrollable eating binges, often followed by purging either by vomiting or by taking laxatives.

Cannabis sativa. See *marijuana*.

cardiovascular disorder. A medical problem involving the heart and blood circulation system, such as *hypertension* or *coronary heart disease*.

case study. The collection of historical or biographical information on a single individual, often including experiences in therapy.

castration. The surgical removal of the *testes*.

castration anxiety. The fear of having the genitals removed or injured.

CAT scan. Computerized axial tomography, a method of diagnosis employing X-rays taken from different angles and then analyzed by computer to produce a representation of the part of the body in cross section. Often used on the brain.

catatonic immobility. A fixity of posture, sometimes grotesque, maintained for long periods with accompanying muscular rigidity, trancelike state of consciousness, and *waxy flexibility*.

catatonic schizophrenia. A *psychosis* whose primary symptoms alternate between stuporous immobility and excited agitation.

catecholamines. *Monoamine* compounds, each having a catechol portion. Catecholamines known to be *neurotransmitters* of the central nervous system are *norepinephrine* and *dopamine;* another, *epinephrine*, is principally a hormone.

catechol-o-methyltransferase (COMT). An enzyme that deactivates *catecholamines* in the *synapse*.

categorical classification. An approach to assessment in which the basic decision is whether a person is or is not a member of a discrete grouping. Contrast with *dimensional classification*.

cathartic method. A therapeutic procedure introduced by Breuer and developed further by Freud in the late nineteenth century whereby a patient recalls and relives an earlier emotional catastrophe and reexperiences the tension and unhappiness, the goal being to relieve emotional suffering.

central nervous system. The part of the nervous system that in vertebrates consists of the brain and spinal cord and to which all sensory impulses are transmitted and from which motor impulses pass out; it also supervises and coordinates the activites of the entire nervous system.

cerebellum. An area of the hindbrain concerned with balance, posture, and motor coordination.

cerebral atherosclerosis. A chronic disease impairing intellectual and emotional life, caused by a reduction in the brain's blood supply through a buildup of fatty deposits in the arteries.

cerebral contusion. A bruising of neural tissue marked by swelling and hemorrhage and resulting in coma; it may permanently impair intellectual functioning.

cerebral cortex. The thin outer covering of each of the *cerebral hemispheres;* it is highly convoluted and composed of nerve cell bodies which constitute the *gray matter* of the brain.

cerebral hemisphere. Either of the two halves that make up the *cerebrum*.

cerebral hemorrhage. Bleeding onto brain tissue from a ruptured blood vessel.

cerebral thrombosis. The formation of a blood clot in a cerebral artery that blocks circulation in that area of brain tissue and causes paralysis, loss of sensory functions, and possibly death.

cerebrovascular disease. An illness that disrupts blood supply to the brain, such as a *stroke*.

cerebrum. The two-lobed structure extending from the *brain stem* and constituting the anterior part of the brain. The largest and most recently developed portion of the brain, it coordinates sensory and motor activities and is the seat of higher cognitive processes.

character disorder. The old term for *personality disorder*.

child sexual abuse. Sexual contact with a minor.

chlorpromazine. The generic term for one of the most widely prescribed antipsychotic drugs, sold under the name *Thorazine*.

cholinergic system. All the nerve cells for which *acetylcholine* is the transmitter substance, in contrast to the *adrenergic*.

choreiform. Pertaining to the involuntary, spasmodic, jerking movements of the limbs and head found in *Huntington's chorea* and other nervous disorders.

chromosomes. The threadlike bodies within the nucleus of the cell, composed primarily of DNA and bearing the genetic information of the organism.

chronic. Of lengthy duration or recurring frequently, often with progressing seriousness.

chronic brain syndrome. See *senile dementia.*

chronic schizophrenic. A *psychotic* patient who deteriorated over a long period of time and has been hospitalized for more than two years.

civil commitment. A procedure whereby a person can be legally certified as mentally ill and hospitalized, even against his or her will.

classical conditioning. A basic form of learning, sometimes referred to as Pavlovian conditioning, in which a neutral stimulus is repeatedly paired with another stimulus (called the unconditioned stimulus, UCS) that naturally elicits a certain desired response (called the unconditioned response, UCR). After repeated trials the neutral stimulus becomes a conditioned stimulus (CS) and evokes the same or similar response, now called the conditioned response (CR).

classificatory variables. The characteristics that subjects bring with them to scientific investigations, such as sex, age, and mental status; studied by *correlational* research and *mixed designs.*

client-centered therapy. A *humanistic-existential insight therapy,* developed by Carl Rogers, which emphasizes the importance of the therapist's understanding the client's subjective experiences and assisting him or her to gain more awareness of current motivations for behavior; the goal is not only to reduce anxieties but also to foster actualization of the client's potential.

clinical interview. General term for conversation between a clinician and a patient, aimed at determining diagnosis, history, causes for problems, and possible treatment options.

clinical psychologist. An individual who has earned a Ph.D. degree in psychology or a Psy.D. and whose training has included an internship in a mental hospital or clinic.

clinical psychology. The special area of psychology concerned with the study of psychopathology, its causes, prevention, and treatment.

clinician. A health professional authorized to provide services to people suffering from one or more pathologies.

clitoris. The small, heavily innervated structure located above the vaginal opening; the primary site of female responsiveness to sexual stimulation.

clonic phase. The stage of violent contortions and jerking of limbs in a *grand mal epileptic* attack.

clonidine. An antihypertensive drug that shows some promise in helping people wean themselves from *substance dependence.*

cocaine. A pain-reducing, stimulating, and addictive *alkaloid,* obtained from coca leaves, which increases mental powers, produces euphoria, heightens sexual desire, and in large doses causes *paranoia* and *hallucinations.*

cognition. The process of knowing; the thinking, judging, reasoning, and planning activities of the human mind. Behavior is now often explained as depending on the course these processes take.

cognitive paradigm. General view that people can best be understood by studying how they perceive and structure their experiences.

cognitive restructuring. Any *behavior therapy* procedure that attempts to alter the manner in which a client thinks about life so that he or she changes overt behavior and emotions.

cognitive therapy (CT). A *cognitive restructuring* therapy associated with the psychiatrist Aaron T. Beck, concerned with changing negative *schemata* and certain cognitive biases or distortions that influence a person to construe life in a depressing way.

cohort effects. The consequences of having been born in a given year and having grown up during a particular time period with its own unique pressures, problems, challenges, and opportunities. To be distinguished from *age effects.*

coitus. Sexual intercourse.

colic. A condition found in infants in which gas collects in the stomach and produces distress.

collective unconscious. Jung's concept that every human being has within him- or herself the wisdom, ideas, and strivings of those who have come before.

community mental health. The delivery of services to needy, underserved groups through centers that offer outpatient therapy, short-term inpatient care, day hospitalization, twenty-four-hour emergency services, and consultation and education to other community agencies, such as the police.

community psychology. An approach to therapy that emphasizes prevention and the seeking out of potential difficulties rather than waiting for troubled individuals to initiate consultation. The location for professional activities tends to be in the person's natural surroundings rather than in the therapist's office. See *prevention.*

comorbidity. The co-occurrence of two disorders, as when a person is both depressed and alcoholic.

competency to stand trial. A legal decision as to whether a person can participate meaningfully in his or her own defense.

compulsion. The irresistible impulse to repeat an irrational act over and over again.

concordance. As applied in *behavior genetics,* the similarity in psychiatric diagnosis or in other traits within a pair of twins.

concurrent (descriptive) validity. See *validity.*

concussion. A jarring injury to the brain produced by a blow to the head that usually involves a momentary loss of consciousness followed by transient disorientation and memory loss.

conditioned response (CR). See *classical conditioning.*

conditioned stimulus (CS). See *classical conditioning.*

conduct disorders. Patterns of extreme disobedience in youngsters, including theft, vandalism, lying, and early drug use; may be precursors of *antisocial personality disorder.*

confabulation. Filling in gaps in memory caused by brain dysfunction with made-up and often improbable stories that the subject accepts as true.

confidentiality. A principle observed by lawyers, doctors, pastors, psychologists, and psychiatrists that dictates that the goings-on in a professional and private relationship are not divulged to anyone else. See *privileged communication.*

conflict. A state of being torn between competing forces.

confounds. Variables whose effects are so intermixed that they cannot be measured separately, making the design of an *experiment* internally invalid and its results impossible to interpret.

congenital. Existing at or before birth but not acquired through heredity.

conjoint therapy. *Couples* or *family therapy* where partners are seen together and children are seen with their parents and possibly with an extended family.

construct. An entity inferred by a scientist to explain observed phenomena. See also *mediator.*

construct validity. The extent to which scores or ratings on an assessment instrument relate to other performance of subjects according to some theory or hypothesis.

contingency. A close relationship, especially of a causal nature, between two events, one of which regularly follows the other.

control group. The subjects in an *experiment* for whom the *independent variable* is not manipulated, thus forming a *baseline* against which the effects of the manipulation of the experimental group can be evaluated.

controlled drinking. A pattern of alcohol consumption that is moderate and avoids the extremes of total abstinence and of inebriation.

conversion disorder. A *somatoform disorder* in which sensory or muscular functions are impaired, usually suggesting neurological disease, even though the bodily organs themselves are sound; *anesthesias* and paralyses of limbs are examples.

convulsion. Violent and extensive twitching of the body caused by involuntary pathological muscle contractions.

convulsive therapy. See *electroconvulsive therapy.*

coronary heart disease (CHD). Angina pectoris, chest pains caused by insufficient supply of blood and thus oxygen to the heart; and myocardial infarction, or heart attack, in which the blood and oxygen supply is reduced so much that heart muscles are damaged.

corpus callosum. The large band of nerve fibers connecting the two *cerebral hemispheres.*

correlation coefficient. A statistic that measures the degree to which two variables are related.

correlation. The tendency for two variables to covary, e.g., height and weight.

correlational method. The research strategy used to establish whether two or more variables are related. Such relationships may be positive—as values for one variable increase, those for the other do also—or negative—as values for one variable increase, those for the other decrease.

cortisone. A hormone secreted by the adrenal cortices.

co-twin. In *behavior genetics* research using the *twin method,* the member of the pair who is tested later to determine whether he or she has the same diagnosis or trait discovered earlier in the birth partner, the *index case* (*proband*).

counseling psychologist. A doctoral level mental health professional whose training is similar to that of a *clinical psychologist,* though usually with less emphasis on research and serious *psychopathology.*

counterconditioning. Relearning achieved by eliciting a new response in the presence of a particular stimulus.

countertransference. Feelings that the *analyst* unconsciously directs to the *analysand,* stemming from his or her own emotional vulnerabilities and unresolved *conflicts.*

couples (marital) therapy. Any professional intervention that treats relationship problems of a couple.

covert sensitization. A form of *aversion therapy* in which the subject is told to imagine the undesirably attractive situations and activities at the same time that unpleasant feelings are also induced by imagery.

cretinism. A condition beginning in prenatal or early life characterized by *mental retardation* and physical deformities, caused by severe deficiency in the output of the *thyroid gland.*

criminal commitment. A procedure whereby a person is confined in a mental institution either for determination of *competency to stand trial* or after acquittal by reason of insanity.

critical period. A stage of early development in which an organism is susceptible to certain influences and during which important irreversible patterns of behavior are acquired. See *imprinting.*

cross-dependent. Acting on the same receptors, as *methadone* does with *heroin.* See *heroin substitutes.*

cross-sectional studies. Studies in which different age groups are compared at the same time. Compare with *longitudinal studies.*

crystallized intelligence. Semantic knowledge, such as grammatical structure and conceptual knowledge; tends to increase rather than decrease with age.

cultural-familial retardation. A mild backwardness in mental development with no indication of brain pathology but evidence of similar limitation in at least one of the parents or siblings.

cunnilingus. The oral stimulation of female genitalia.

Cushing's syndrome. An endocrine disorder usually affecting young women, produced by oversecretion of *cortisone* and marked by mood swings, irritability, agitation, and physical disfigurement.

cyclical psychodynamics. The reciprocal relations between current behavior and repressed conflicts, such that they mutually reinforce each other.

cyclothymic disorder. Swings between elation and depression not severe enough to warrant the diagnosis of *bipolar disorder.*

defect theorist. In the study of *mental retardation,* a person who believes that the cognitive processes of retardates are qualitatively different from those of normal individuals. Contrast with *developmental theorist.*

defense mechanisms. In psychoanalytic theory, reality-distorting strategies unconsciously adopted to protect the ego from anxiety.

delay of reward gradient. The learning theory term for the finding that rewards and punishments lose their effectiveness the further they are removed in time from the response in question.

delayed echolalia. See *echolalia.*

delirium. A state of great mental confusion in which consciousness is clouded, attention cannot be sustained, and the stream of thought and speech is incoherent. The person is probably disoriented, emotionally erratic, restless or lethargic, and often has *illusions, delusions,* and *hallucinations.*

delirium tremens (DTs). One of the *withdrawal symptoms* when a period of heavy alcohol consumption is terminated; marked by fever, sweating, trembling, cognitive impairment, and *hallucinations.*

delta rhythm. See *slow brain waves.*

delusions. Beliefs contrary to reality, firmly held in spite of evidence to the contrary; common in *paranoid disorders.* **of control,** belief that one is being manipulated by some external force such as radar, television, or a creature from outer space: **of grandeur,** belief that one is an especially important or powerful person: **of persecution,** belief that one is being plotted against or oppressed by others.

delusional (paranoid) disorders. See *paranoid disorder.*

delusional jealousy. The unfounded conviction that one's mate is unfaithful. The individual may collect small bits of "evidence" to justify the *delusion.*

dementia. Deterioration of mental faculties—of memory, judgment, abstract thought, control of impulses, intellectual ability—that impairs social and occupational functioning and eventually changes the personality.

dementia praecox. An older term for *schizophrenia,* chosen to describe what was believed to be an incurable and progressive deterioration of mental functioning beginning in adolescence.

demographic variable. A varying characteristic that is a vital or social statistic of an individual, sample group, or population, for example, age, sex, *socioeconomic status,* racial origin, education.

demonology. The doctrine that a person's abnormal behavior is caused by an autonomous evil spirit.

denial. *Defense mechanism* in which a thought, feeling, or action is disavowed by the person.

dependent personality. Lacking in self-confidence, people with a dependent personality passively allow others to run their lives and make no demands on them so as not to endanger these protective relationships.

dependent variable. In a psychological *experiment,* the behavior that is measured and is expected to change with manipulation of the *independent variable.*

depersonalization. An alteration in perception of the self in which the individual loses a sense of reality and feels estranged from the self and perhaps separated from the body. It may be a temporary reaction to stress and fatigue or part of *panic disorder, depersonalization disorder,* or *schizophrenia.*

depersonalization disorder. A *dissociative disorder* in which the individual feels unreal and estranged from the self and surroundings enough to disrupt functioning. People with this disorder may feel that their extremities have changed in size or that they are watching themselves from a distance.

depression. An emotional state marked by great sadness and apprehension, feelings of worthlessness and guilt, withdrawal from others, loss of sleep, appetite, sexual desire, loss of or interest and pleasure in usual activities, and either lethargy or agitation. Called *major depression* in DSM-IV and *unipolar depression* by others. It can be an associated symptom of other disorders.

derealization. Loss of the sense that the surroundings are real; present in several psychological disorders, such as *panic disorder, depersonalization disorder,* and *schizophrenia.*

descriptive responsibility. In legal proceedings, the judgment that the accused performed an illegal act. Contrast with *ascriptive responsibility.*

deterioration effect. In abnormal psychology, a harmful outcome from being in psychotherapy.

detoxification. The initial stage in weaning an addicted person from a drug; involves medical supervision of the sometimes painful *withdrawal.*

detumescence. The flow of blood out of the genital area.

developmental theorist. In the study of *mental retardation,* a person who believes that the cognitive development of retardates has simply been slower than that of normal individuals, and not qualitatively different. Contrast with *defect theorist.*

diagnosis. The determination that the set of symptoms or problems of a patient indicates a particular disorder.

dialectical behavior therapy. A therapeutic approach to *borderline personality* disorder that combines client-centered empathy and acceptance with behavioral problem solving, social-skills training, and limit setting.

diathesis. *Predisposition* toward a disease or abnormality.

diathesis–stress paradigm. As applied in psychopathology, a view that assumes that individuals predisposed toward a particular mental disorder will be particularly affected by stress and will then manifest abnormal behavior.

dichotic listening. An experimental procedure in which a subject hears two taped messages simultaneously through earphones, one in each ear, usually with the instruction to attend to only one of the messages.

diencephalon. The lower area of the forebrain, containing the *thalamus* and *hypothalamus.*

dimensional classification. An approach to assessment according to which a person is placed on a continuum. Contrast with *categorical classification.*

directionality problem. A difficulty in the *correlational method* of research whereby it is known that two variables are related, but it is unclear which is causing the other.

discriminative stimulus. An event that informs an organism that, if a particular response is made, reinforcement will follow.

disease. The medical concept that distinguishes an impairment of the normal state of the organism by its particular group of symptoms and its specific cause.

disease model. See *medical model.*

disorder of written expression. Difficulties writing without errors in spelling, grammar, or punctuation.

disorganized schizophrenia. *Schizophrenia* in which the person has rather diffuse and regressive symptoms; the individual is given to silliness, facial grimaces, and inconsequential rituals and has constantly changeable moods and poor hygiene. There are few significant remissions and eventually considerable deterioration. This form of *schizophrenia* was formerly called hebephrenia.

disorganized speech (thought disorder). Speech, found in schizophrenics, marked by problems in the organization of ideas and in speaking so that others can understand.

disorientation. A state of mental confusion with respect to time, place, identity of self, other persons, and objects.

displacement. A *defense mechanism* whereby an emotional response is unconsciously redirected from an object or concept perceived as dangerous to a substitute less threatening to the *ego*.

dissociation. A process whereby a group of mental processes is split off from the mainstream of consciousness, or behavior loses its relationship with the rest of the personality.

dissociative amnesia. A *dissociative disorder* in which the person suddenly becomes unable to recall important personal information to an extent that cannot be explained by ordinary forgetfulness.

dissociative disorders. Disorders in which the normal integration of consciousness, memory, or identity is suddenly and temporarily altered; *dissociative amnesia, dissociative fugue, multiple personality*, and *depersonalization disorder* are examples.

divorce mediation. A form of *marital therapy* in which a distressed couple is helped to collaborate on issues such as child custody outside the adversarial framework of a formal legal process.

dizygotic (DZ) twins. Birth partners who have developed from separate fertilized eggs and who are only 50 percent alike genetically, no more so than siblings born from different pregnancies; sometimes called fraternal twins.

dominant gene. One of a pair of *genes* that predominates over the other and determines that the *trait* it fosters will prevail in the *phenotype*.

dopamine. A *catecholamine* that is both a precursor of *norepinephrine* and itself a *neurotransmitter* of the central nervous system. Disturbances in certain of its tracts apparently figure in *schizophrenia* and *Parkinson's disease*.

double-bind theory. An interpersonal situation in which an individual is confronted, over long periods of time, by mutually inconsistent messages to which she or he must respond, formerly believed by some theorists to cause *schizophrenia*.

double-blind procedure. A method for reducing the biasing effects of the expectations of subject and experimenter; neither is allowed to know whether the *independent variable* of the *experiment* is being applied to the particular subject.

Down syndrome (trisomy 21). A form of *mental retardation* generally caused by an extra *chromosome*. The child's IQ is usually less than 50, and his or her physical characteristics are distinctive, most notably slanted eyes.

dream analysis. A key psychoanalytic technique in which the unconscious meanings of dream material are uncovered.

drive. A *construct* explaining the motivation of behavior, or an internal physiological tension impelling an organism to activity.

drug abuse. See *substance abuse*.

drug addiction. See *substance dependence*.

DSM-IV. The current Diagnostic and Statistical Manual of the American Psychiatric Association.

dualism. Philosophical doctrine, advanced most definitively by Descartes, that a human being is both mental and physical and that these two aspects are separate but interacting. Contrast with *monism*.

Durham decision. A 1954 U.S. court ruling that an accused person is not *ascriptively responsible* if his or her crime is judged attributable to mental disease or defect.

dysfunction. An impairment or disturbance in the functioning of an organ, organ system, behavior, or cognition.

dyslexia. A disturbance in the ability to read; a *learning disorder*.

dyspareunia. Painful or difficult sexual intercourse; the pain or difficulty is usually caused by infection or a physical injury, such as torn ligaments in the pelvic region.

dysthymic disorder. State of depression that is long lasting but not severe enough for the diagnosis of *major depression*.

echolalia. The immediate and sometimes pathological repetition of the words of others, often found in autistic children. In **delayed echolalia** this inappropriate echoing takes place hours or weeks later.

eclecticism. In psychology, the view that more is to be gained by employing concepts from various theoretical systems than by restricting oneself to a single theory.

Ecstasy. A relatively new *hallucinogen* that is chemically similar to *mescaline* and the *amphetamines*.

ego. In psychoanalytic theory, the predominantly conscious part of the personality, responsible for decision making and for dealing with reality.

ego analysis: An important set of modifications of classical *psychoanalysis*, based on a conception of the human being as having a stronger, more autonomous ego with gratifications independent of id satisfactions. Sometimes called ego psychology.

ego analysts. Those who practice *ego analysis*.

ego-alien. Foreign to the self, such as a *compulsion*.

ego-dystonic homosexuality. According to DSM-III, a disorder of people who are persistently dissatisfied with their *homosexuality* and wish instead to be attracted to members of the opposite sex.

egoistic suicide. As defined by Durkheim, self-annihilation committed because the individual feels extreme alienation from others and from society.

ejaculate. To expel semen, typically during male orgasm.

elective mutism. A pattern of continuously refusing to speak in almost all social situations, including school, even though the child understands spoken language and is able to speak.

Electra complex. See *Oedipus complex.*

electrocardiogram. A recording of the electrical activity of the heart, made with an *electrocardiograph.*

electroconvulsive therapy (ECT). A treatment that produces a *convulsion* by passing electric current through the brain. Though an unpleasant and occasionally dangerous procedure, it can be useful in alleviating profound *depression.*

electrodermal responding. A recording of the minute electrical activity of the sweat glands on the skin, allowing the inference of an emotional state; also referred to as the *galvanic skin response.*

electroencephalogram (EEG). A graphic recording of electrical activity of the brain, usually of the *cerebral cortex,* but sometimes of lower areas.

empathy. Awareness and understanding of another's feelings and thoughts. See *primary empathy* and *advanced accurate empathy.*

empty-chair technique. A *Gestalt therapy* procedure for helping the client become more aware of denied feelings; the client talks to important people or to feelings as though they were present and seated in a nearby vacant chair.

encephalitis. Inflammation of brain tissue caused by a number of agents, the most important being several viruses carried by insects.

encephalitis lethargica. Known as sleeping sickness, a form of encephalitis that occurred early in this century and was characterized by lethargy and prolonged periods of sleeping.

encopresis. A disorder in which, through faulty control of the sphincters, the person repeatedly defecates in his or her clothing after an age at which continence is expected.

encounter group. See *sensitivity training group.*

endocrine gland. Any of a number of ductless glands that release *hormones* directly into the blood or lymph. The secretions of some endocrine glands increase during emotional arousal.

endogenous. Attributable to internal causes.

endorphins. Opiates produced within the body; they may have an important role in the processes by which the body builds up *tolerance* to drugs and is distressed by the withdrawal.

enuresis. A disorder in which, through faulty control of the bladder, the person wets repeatedly during the night (nocturnal enuresis) or during the day after an age at which continence is expected.

enzyme. A complex protein produced by the cells to act as a catalyst in regulating metabolic activities.

epidemiology. The study of the frequency and distribution of illness in a population.

epilepsy. An altered state of consciousness accompanied by sudden changes in the usual rhythmical electrical activity of the brain. See also *grand mal, petit mal, Jacksonian,* and *psychomotor epilepsy.*

epinephrine. A hormone (a *catecholamine*) secreted by the medulla of the *adrenal gland;* its effects are similar, but not identical, to those of stimulating the *sympathetic* nerves. It causes an increase in blood pressure, inhibits peristaltic movements, and liberates glucose from the liver. Also called *adrenaline.*

ergot. See *LSD.*

erogenous. Capable of giving sexual pleasure when stimulated.

Eros (libido). Freud's term for the life-integrating instinct or force of the *id,* sometimes equated with sexual drive. Compare *Thanatos.*

essential hypertension. A *psychophysiological disorder* characterized by high blood pressure that cannot be traced to an organic cause. Over the years it causes enlargement and degeneration of small arteries, enlargement of the heart, and kidney damage.

estrogen. A female sex hormone produced especially in the ovaries that stimulates the development and maintenance of the secondary sex characteristics, such as breast enlargement.

etiological validity. See *validity.*

etiology. All the factors that contribute to the development of an illness or disorder.

eugenics. The field concerned with improving the hereditary qualities of the human race through social control of mating and reproduction.

***ex post facto* analysis.** In the *correlational method* of research, an attempt to reduce the *third-variable problem* by picking subjects who are matched on characteristics that may be *confounds.*

excess dopamine activity theory. The view that schizophrenia arises from a surfeit of the *neurotransmitter dopamine.*

excitement phase. As applied by Masters and Johnson, the first stage of sexual arousal that is initiated by any appropriate stimulus.

executive aphasia. See *aphasia.*

executive functioning. The *cognitive* capacity to plan how to do a task, how to devise strategies, and how to monitor one's performance.

exhibitionism. Marked preference for obtaining sexual gratification by exposing one's genitals to an unwilling observer.

existential analysis. See *existential therapy.*

existential therapy. An insight therapy that emphasizes choice and responsibility to define the meaning of one's life. In contrast with *humanistic therapy,* it tends to be less cheerful or sanguine in outlook, focusing more on the anxiety that is inherent to confronting one's ultimate aloneness in the world.

exogenous. Attributable to external causes.

exogenous depression. A profound sadness assumed to be caused by an environmental event.

exorcism. The casting out of evil spirits by ritualistic chanting or torture.

experiment. The most powerful research technique for determining causal relationships, requiring the manipulation of an *independent variable*, the measurement of a *dependent variable*, and the *random assignment* of subjects to the several different conditions being investigated.

experimental effect. A statistically significant difference between two groups experiencing different manipulations of the independent variable.

experimental hypothesis. What the investigator assumes will happen in a scientific investigation if certain conditions are met or particular variables are manipulated.

expressed emotion (EE). In the literature on *schizophrenia*, the amount of hostility and criticism directed from other people to the patient, usually within a family.

expressive language disorder. Difficulties expressing oneself in speech.

external validity. See *validity*.

extinction. The elimination of a classically *conditioned response* by the omission of the *unconditioned stimulus*. In *operant conditioning*, the elimination of the *conditioned response* by the omission of *reinforcement*.

extradural hematoma. Hemorrhage and swelling between the skull and dura mater when a *meningeal* artery is ruptured by a fractured bone of the skull.

factitious disorders. Disorders in which the individual's physical or psychological symptoms appear under voluntary control and are adopted merely to assume the role of a sick person. This goal is not voluntary, however, and implies a severe disturbance. Compare with *malingering*.

falsifiability. The extent to which a scientific assertion is amenable to systematic probes, any one of which could negate the scientist's expectations.

familiar. In witchcraft, a supernatural spirit often embodied in an animal and at the service of a person.

family interaction method. A procedure for studying family behavior by observing their interaction in a structured laboratory situation.

family method. A research strategy in *behavior genetics* in which the frequency of a *trait* or of abnormal behavior is determined in relatives who have varying percentages of shared genetic background.

family systems approach. A general approach to etiology and treatment that focuses on the complex interrelationships within families.

family therapy. A form of *group therapy* in which members of a family are helped to relate better to one another.

fear of performance. Being overly concerned with one's behavior during sexual contact with another, postulated by Masters and Johnson as a major factor causing sexual dysfunction.

fear-drive. In the Mowrer–Miller theory, an unpleasant internal state that impels avoidance. The necessity to reduce a fear-drive can form the basis for new learning.

fear-response. In the Mowrer–Miller theory, a response to a threatening or noxious situation that is covert and unobservable but that is assumed to function as a stimulus to produce measurable physiological changes in the body and observable overt behavior.

fellatio. Oral stimulation of the *penis*.

female orgasmic disorder. A recurrent and persistent delay or absence of orgasm in a woman during sexual activity adequate in focus, intensity, and duration; in many instances the woman may experience considerable sexual excitement nonetheless.

female sexual arousal disorder. Formally called frigidity, the inability of a female to reach or maintain the lubrication swelling stage of sexual excitement or the inability to enjoy a subjective sense of pleasure or excitement during sexual activity.

fetal alcohol syndrome. Retarded growth of the developing fetus and infant; cranial, facial, and limb anomalies and *mental retardation* caused by heavy consumption of alcohol by the mother during pregnancy.

fetishism. Reliance on an inanimate object for sexual arousal.

first-rank symptoms. In *schizophrenia*, specific *delusions* and *hallucinations* proposed by Schneider as particularly important for its more exact diagnosis.

fixation. In psychoanalytic theory, the arrest of *psychosexual* development at a particular stage through too much or too little gratification at that stage.

flashback. An unpredictable recurrence of *psychedelic* experiences from an earlier drug trip.

flat affect. A deviation in emotional response wherein virtually no emotion is expressed whatever the stimuli, emotional expressiveness is blunted, or a lack of expression and muscle tone is noted in the face.

flight of ideas. A symptom of *mania* that involves a rapid shift in conversation from one subject to another with only superficial associative connections.

flooding. A *behavior therapy* procedure in which a fearful person is exposed to what is frightening, in reality or in the imagination, for extended periods of time and without opportunity for escape.

fluid intelligence. Involves short-term memory, abstract thinking, creativity, and *reaction time*; tends to decline with age.

follow-up study. A research procedure whereby individuals observed in an earlier investigation are contacted at a later time for further study.

forced-choice item. A format of a *personality inventory* in which the response alternatives for each item are equated for *social desirability*.

forcible rape. The legal term for rape, to force sexual intercourse or other sexual activity on another person. Statutory rape is sexual intercourse between an adult male and someone who is under the age of consent, as fixed by local statute.

forensic psychiatry or psychology. The branch of psychiatry or psychology that deals with the legal questions raised by disordered behavior.

fragile X syndrome. Malformation (or even breakage) of the X chromosome associated with *moderate mental retardation*. Symptoms include large, underdeveloped ears, a long, thin face, a broad nasal root, and enlarged testicles in males; many individuals show attention deficits and hyperactivity.

free association. A key psychoanalytic procedure in which the *analysand* is encouraged to give free rein to his or her thoughts and feelings, verbalizing whatever comes into the mind without monitoring its content. The assumption is that, over time, hitherto *repressed* material will come forth for examination by the *analysand* and *analyst*.

freebase. The most potent part of *cocaine*, obtained by heating the drug with ether.

free-floating anxiety. Continual anxiety not attributable to any specific situation or reasonable danger. See *generalized anxiety disorder*.

frontal lobe. The forward or upper half of each *cerebral hemisphere*, in front of the central *sulcus*, active in reasoning and other higher mental processes.

fugue. See *dissociative fugue*.

functional psychosis. A condition in which thought, behavior, and emotion are disturbed without known pathological changes in tissues or the conditions of the brain.

functional social support. The quality of a person's relationships, for example, a good versus a distressed marriage. Contrast with *structural social support*.

galvanic skin response (GSR). A change in electric conductivity of the skin caused by an increase in activity of sweat glands when the *sympathetic nervous system* is active, in particular when the organism is anxious.

gay. A colloquial term for *homosexual*, now often adopted by homosexuals who have openly announced their sexual orientation.

gay liberation. The often militant movement seeking to achieve civil rights for homosexuals and recognition of the normality of *homosexuality*.

gender identity. The deeply ingrained sense a person has of being either a man or a woman.

gender identity disorders. Disorders in which there is a deeply felt incongruence between anatomic sex and the sensed gender; *transsexualism* and **gender identity disorder of childhood** are examples.

gene. An ultramicroscopic area of the *chromosome*, the gene is the smallest physical unit of the DNA molecule that carries a piece of hereditary information.

general adaptation syndrome (GAS). Hans Selye's model to describe the biological reaction of an organism to sustained and unrelenting stress; there are several stages, culminating in death in extreme circumstances.

general paresis. See *neurosyphilis*.

generalized anxiety disorder (GAD). One of the *anxiety disorders*, where anxiety is so chronic, persistent, and pervasive that it seems *free-floating*. The individual is jittery and strained, distractible and apprehensive that something bad is about to happen. A pounding heart, fast pulse and breathing, sweating, flushing, muscle aches, a lump in the throat, and an upset gastrointestinal tract are some of the bodily indications of this extreme anxiety.

genital stage. In psychoanalytic theory, the final *psychosexual stage* reached in adulthood, in which heterosexual interests predominate.

genotype. An individual's unobservable, physiological genetic constitution; the totality of *genes* possessed by an individual. Compare *phenotype*.

genuineness. In *client-centered therapy*, an essential quality of the therapist, referring to openness and authenticity.

germ theory [of disease]. The general view in medicine that disease is caused by infection of the body by minute organisms and viruses.

gerontology. The interdisciplinary study of aging and of the special problems of the elderly.

Gestalt therapy. A *humanistic therapy*, developed by Fritz Perls, that encourages clients to satisfy emerging needs so that their innate goodness can be expressed, to increase their awareness of unacknowledged feelings, and to reclaim parts of the personality that have been denied or disowned.

gestation period. The length of time, normally nine months in human beings, during which a fertilized egg develops into an infant ready to be born.

glans. The heavily innervated tip of the *penis*.

glove anesthesia. A *hysterical* lack of sensation in the part of the arm that would usually be covered by a glove.

grand mal epilepsy. The most severe form of *epilepsy*, involving loss of consciousness and violent *convulsions*.

grandiose delusions. Found in paranoid schizophrenia and other paranoid disorders, an exaggerated sense of one's importance, power, knowledge, or identity.

Graves' disease. An endocrine disorder resulting from oversecretion of the hormone thyroxin, in which metabolic processes are speeded up, producing apprehension, restlessness, and irritability.

gray matter. The neural tissue made up largely of nerve cell bodies that constitutes the cortex covering the *cerebral hemisphere*, the *nuclei* in lower brain areas, columns of the spinal cord, and the ganglia of the *autonomic nervous system*.

grimace. A distorted facial expression, often a symptom of *schizophrenia*.

group therapy. Method of treating psychological disorders whereby several persons are seen simultaneously by a single therapist.

gyrus. A ridge or convolution of the *cerebral cortex*.

habituation. In physiology, a process whereby an organism's response to the same stimulus temporarily lessens with repeated presentations.

halfway house. A homelike residence for people who are considered too disturbed to remain in their accustomed surroundings but do not require the total care of a mental institution.

hallucinations. Perceptions in any sensory modality without relevant and adequate external stimuli.

hallucinogen. A drug or chemical whose effects include *hallucinations*. Hallucinogenic drugs such as *LSD*, *psilocybin*, and *mescaline* are often called *psychedelic*.

hashish. The dried resin of the *Cannabis* plant, stronger in its effects than the dried leaves and stems that constitute *marijuana*.

health psychology. A branch of psychology dealing with the role of psychological factors in health and illness.

hebephrenia. See *disorganized schizophrenia*.

helplessness. A *construct* referring to the sense of having no control over important events; considered by many theorists to play a central role in *anxiety* and *depression*. See *learned helplessness theory*.

hermaphrodite. A person with parts of both male and female genitalia.

heroin. An extremely addictive *narcotic* drug derived from *morphine*.

heroin antagonists. Drugs, like naxolone, that prevent a heroin user from experiencing any high.

heroin substitutes. Narcotics, like *methadone*, that are *cross-dependent* with *heroin* and thereby replace it and the body's craving for it.

heterosexual. One who desires or engages in sexual relations with members of the opposite sex.

hidden observer. In hypnosis, the part of the self that is aware of things outside conscious awareness.

high-risk method. A research technique involving the intensive examination of people who have a high probability of later becoming abnormal.

histrionic personality. This person is overly dramatic and given to emotional excess, impatient with minor annoyances, immature, dependent on others, and often sexually seductive without taking responsibility for flirtations. Formerly called hysterical personality.

homophobia. Fear of *homosexuality*.

homosexuality. Sexual desire or activity directed toward a member of one's own sex.

homovanillic acid. A major metabolite of *dopamine*.

hormone. A chemical substance produced by an *endocrine gland* and released into the blood or lymph for the purpose of controlling the function of a distant organ or organ system. Metabolism, growth, and development of secondary sexual characteristics are among the functions so controlled.

humanistic and existential therapies. A generic term for insight psychotherapies that emphasize the individual's subjective experiences, free will, and ever-present ability to decide on a new life course.

humanistic therapy. An insight therapy that emphasizes freedom of choice, growth of human potential, the joys of being a human being, and the importance of the patient's phenomenology; sometimes called an experiential therapy. See also *existential therapy*.

Huntington's chorea. A fatal *presenile dementia*, passed on by a single *dominant gene*. The symptoms include spasmodic jerking of the limbs, psychotic behavior, and mental deterioration.

5-hydroxyindoleacetic acid (5-HIAA). The major metabolite of *serontonin* present in the cerebrospinal fluid.

hyperactivity. See *attention-deficit hyperactivity disorder*.

hyperkinesis. See *attention-deficit hyperactivity disorder*.

hypertension. Abnormally high arterial blood pressure, with or without known organic causes. See *essential hypertension*.

hyperventilation. Very rapid and deep breathing associated with high levels of anxiety; causes the level of carbon dioxide in blood to be lowered with possible loss of consciousness.

hypnosis. A trancelike state or behavior resembling sleep, characterized primarily by increased suggestibility and induced by suggestion.

hypoactive sexual desire disorder. The absence of or deficiency in sexual fantasies and urges.

hypochondriasis. A *somatoform disorder* in which the person, misinterpreting rather ordinary physical sensations, is preoccupied with fears of having a serious disease and is not dissuaded by medical opinion. Difficult to distinguish from *somatization disorder*.

hypomania. An above-normal elevation of mood, but not as extreme as *mania*.

hypothalamus. A collection of *nuclei* and fibers in the lower part of the *diencephalon* concerned with the regulation of many visceral processes, such as metabolism, temperature, water balance, and so on.

hysteria. A disorder, known to the ancient Greeks, in which a physical incapacity, a paralysis, an anesthesia, or an analgesia, is not due to a physiological dysfunction, for example, *glove anesthesia*; an older term for *conversion disorder*. In the late nineteenth century *dissociative disorders* were identified as such and considered hysterical states.

hysterical neurosis. The DSM-II category for *dissociative* and *somatoform disorders*.

id. In psychoanalytic theory, that part of the personality present at birth, composed of all the energy of the *psyche*, and expressed as biological urges that strive continually for gratification.

ideas of reference. *Delusional* thinking that reads personal significance into seemingly trivial remarks and activities of others and completely unrelated events.

identity crisis. A developmental period in adolescence marked by concerns about who one is and what one is going to do with his or her life.

idiographic [context]. In psychology, relating to investigative procedures that consider the unique characteristics of a single person, studying them in depth, as in the *case study*. Contrast with *nomothetic*.

idiot savant. An individual with a rare form of *mental retardation*, extraordinarily talented in one or a few limited areas of intellectual achievement.

illusion. A misperception of a real external stimulus, such as hearing the slapping of waves as footsteps.

imipramine. An *antidepressant* drug, one of the *tricyclic* group.

imprinting. The irreversible acquisition of behavior by a neonate of a social species during a *critical period* of development. The neonate is attracted to and mimics the first moving object seen, thereby acquiring specific patterns of behavior.

in absentia. Literally, "in one's absence." Courts are concerned that a person be able to participate personally and meaningfully in his or her own trial and not be tried *in absentia* because of a distracting mental disorder.

in vivo. As applied in psychology, taking place in a real-life situation.

inappropriate affect. Emotional responses that are out of context, such as laughter when hearing sad news.

incest. Sexual relations between close relatives, most often between daughter and father or between brother and sister.

incidence. In community studies of a particular disorder, the rate at which new cases occur in a given place at a given time. Compare with *prevalence.*

incoherence. In *schizophrenia,* an aspect of *thought disorder* wherein verbal expression is marked by disconnectedness, fragmented thoughts, jumbled phrases, and *neologisms.*

independent variable. In a psychological *experiment,* the factor, experience, or treatment that is under the control of the experimenter and that is expected to have an effect on the subjects as assessed by changes in the *dependent variable.*

index case (proband). The person who in a genetic investigation bears the diagnosis or *trait* in which the investigator is interested.

individual psychology. A variation of Freud's psychoanalysis introduced by Alfred Adler and focusing less on biological drives and more on such factors as people's conscious beliefs and goals for self-betterment.

indoleamines. *Monoamine* compounds, each containing an indole portion; indoleamines believed to act in neurotransmission are *serotonin* and tryptamine.

infectious disease. An illness caused when a microorganism, such as a bacterium or a virus, invades the body, multiplies, and attacks a specific organ or organ system; pneumonia is an example.

informed consent. The agreement of a person to serve as a research subject or to enter therapy after being told the possible outcomes, both benefits and risks.

inhibited male orgasm. A recurrent and persistent delay or absence of ejaculation after an adequate phase of sexual excitement.

insanity defense. The legal argument that a defendant should not be held *ascriptively responsible* for an illegal act if the conduct is attributable to mental illness.

insight therapy. A general term for any *psychotherapy* that assumes that people become disordered because they do not adequately understand what motivates them, especially when their needs and drives conflict.

instrumental learning. See *operant conditioning.*

intelligence quotient (IQ). A standardized measure indicating how far an individual's raw score on an *intelligence test* is from the average raw score of his or her chronological age group.

intelligence test. A standardized means of assessing a person's current mental ability, for example, the Stanford–Binet test and the Wechsler Adult Intelligence Scale.

internal validity. See *validity.*

interpersonal therapy. A psychodynamic psychotherapy that focuses on the patient's interactions with others and that directly teaches how better to relate to others.

interpretation. In *psychoanalysis,* a key procedure in which the *psychoanalyst* points out to the *analysand* where *resistance* exists and what certain dreams and verbalizations reveal about impulses repressed in the *unconscious;* more generally, any statement by a therapist that construes the client's problem in a new way.

interrater reliability. See *reliability.*

introjection. In psychoanalytic theory, the unconscious incorporation of the values, attitudes, and qualities of another person into the individual's own ego structure.

intromission. Insertion of the *penis* into the *vagina* or anus.

introspection. A procedure whereby trained subjects are asked to report on their conscious experiences. This was the principal method of study in early twentieth-century psychology.

involutional melancholia. A *mood disorder* characterized by profound sadness and often occurring in late middle age.

irrational beliefs. Self-defeating assumptions that are assumed by *rational-emotive* therapists to underlie psychological distress.

irresistible impulse. The term used in an 1834 Ohio court ruling on criminal responsibility that determined that an *insanity defense* can be established by proving that the accused had an uncontrollable urge to perform the act.

Korsakoff's psychosis. A chronic brain disorder associated with *Wernicke's disease* and marked by loss of recent memories and associated *confabulation,* and by additional lesions in the *thalamus.*

la belle indifférence. The blasé attitude people with *conversion disorder* have toward their symptoms.

labeling theory. The general view that serious psychopathology, like *schizophrenia,* is caused by society's reactions to unusual behavior.

labile. Easily moved or changed, quickly shifting from one emotion to another or easily aroused.

laceration. A jagged wound; in the brain, a tearing of tissue by an object entering the skull, often causing paralysis, change in personality, intellectual impairment, and even death.

language disorder. Difficulties understanding spoken language (receptive) or expressing thoughts verbally (expressive).

latency period. In psychoanalytic theory, the years between ages six and twelve during which *id* impulses play a minor role in motivation.

latent content. In dreams, the presumed true meaning hidden behind the *manifest content.*

law of effect. A principle of learning that holds that behavior is acquired by virtue of its consequences.

learned helplessness theory. An individual's passivity and sense of being unable to act and to control his or her life, acquired through unpleasant experiences and traumata in which efforts made were ineffective; according to Seligman, this brings on *depression.*

learning disabilities. General term for *learning disorders,* communication disorders, and *motor skills disorder.*

learning disorders. A set of developmental disorders encompassing *dyslexia, mathematics disorder,* and disorder of written expression, and characterized by failure to develop in a specific academic area to the degree expected by the child's intellectual level. Not diagnosed if the disorder is due to a sensory deficit.

learning paradigm. As applied in abnormal psychology, a set of assumptions that abnormal behavior is learned in the same way as other human behavior.

least restrictive alternative. The legal principle according to which a committed mental patient must be treated in a setting that imposes as few restrictions as possible on his or her freedom.

lesbian. Female *homosexual.*

lesion. Any localized abnormal structural change in organ or tissue caused by disease or injury.

libido. See *Eros.*

Life Change Unit (LCU) score. A score produced by totaling ratings of the stressfulness of recently experienced life events; high scores are found to be related to the contraction of a number of physical illnesses.

life-span developmental psychology. The study of changes in people as they grow from infancy to old age.

lifetime prevalence rates. The proportion of a sample that has ever had a disorder.

limbic system. The lower parts of the *cerebrum,* made up of primitive cortex; controls visceral and bodily changes associated with emotion and regulates drive-motivated behavior.

linkage analysis. A technique in genetic research whereby occurrence of a disorder in a family is evaluated alongside a known genetic marker.

lithium carbonate. A drug useful in treating both *mania* and *depression* in *bipolar disorder.*

lobotomy. A brain operation in which the nerve pathways between the *frontal lobes* of the brain and the *thalamus* and *hypothalamus* are cut in hopes of effecting beneficial behavioral change.

logotherapy. *Existential psychotherapy,* developed by Viktor Frankl, aimed at helping the demoralized client restore meaning to life by placing his or her suffering in a larger spiritual and philosophical context. The individual assumes responsibility for his or her existence and for pursuing a meaningful life.

longitudinal studies. Investigation that collects information on the same individuals repeatedly over time, perhaps over many years, in an effort to determine how phenomena change. Compare with *cross-sectional studies.*

loose associations (derailment). In *schizophrenia,* an aspect of *thought disorder* wherein the patient has difficulty sticking to one topic and drifts off on a train of associations evoked by an idea from the past.

LSD. *d*-lysergic acid diethylamide, a drug synthesized in 1938 and discovered to be a *hallucinogen* in 1943. It is derived from lysergic acid, the principal constituent of the *alkaloids* of ergot, a grain fungus that in earlier centuries brought on epidemics of spasmodic ergotism, a nervous disorder sometimes marked by *psychotic* symptoms.

Luria–Nebraska test. A battery of *neuropsychological tests* that can detect impairment in different parts of the brain.

magical thinking. The conviction of the individual that his or her thoughts, words, and actions may in some manner cause or prevent outcomes in a way that defies the normal laws of cause and effect.

mainstreaming. A policy of placing disabled children in regular classrooms; although special classes are provided as needed, the children share as much as possible in the opportunities and ambience afforded normal youngsters.

maintenance dose. An amount of a drug designed to enable a patient to continue to benefit from a therapeutically effective regimen of medication. It is often less than the dose required to bring about the positive change in the first place.

major (unipolar) depression. A disorder of individuals who have experienced episodes of *depression* but not of *mania.*

male erectile disorder. A recurrent and persistent inability to attain or maintain an erection until completion of sexual activity.

male orgasmic disorder. See *inhibited male orgasm.*

malingering. Faking a physical or psychological incapacity in order to avoid a responsibility or gain an end; the goal is readily recognized from the individual's circumstances. To be distinguished from *conversion disorder,* in which the incapacity is assumed to be beyond voluntary control.

malleus maleficarum ("the witches' hammer"). A manual written by two Dominican monks in the fifteenth century to provide rules for identifying and trying witches.

mammillary body. Either of two small rounded structures located in the *hypothalamus* and consisting of *nuclei.*

mania. An emotional state of intense but unfounded elation evidenced in talkativeness, *flight of ideas* and distractibility, grandiose plans, and spurts of purposeless activity.

manic-depressive illness, manic-depressive psychosis. Originally described by Kraepelin, a *mood disorder* characterized by alternating euphoria and profound sadness or by one of these moods. Called *bipolar disorder* in DSM-IV.

manifest content. The immediately apparent, conscious content of dreams. Compare with *latent content.*

marathon group. A group session run continuously for a day or even longer, typically for *sensitivity training,* the assumption being that defenses can be worn down by the physical and psychological fatigue generated through intensive and continuous group interaction.

marijuana. A drug derived from the dried and ground leaves and stems of the female hemp plant, *Cannabis sativa.*

marital therapy. See *couples therapy.*

masturbation. Self-stimulation of the genitals, typically to *orgasm.*

masochism. See *sexual masochism.*

mathematics disorder. Difficulties dealing with arithmetic symbols and operations.

mediational theory of learning. In psychology, the general view that certain stimuli do not directly initiate an overt response but activate an intervening process, which in turn initiates the response. It explains thinking, drives, emotions, and beliefs in terms of stimulus and response.

mediator. In psychology, an inferred state intervening between the observable stimulus and response, activated by the stimulus and in turn initiating the response; in more general terms, a thought, drive, emotion, or belief. Also called a *construct.*

medical (disease) model. As applied in abnormal psychology, a set of assumptions that conceptualizes abnormal behavior as similar to physical diseases.

medulla oblongata. An area in the *brain stem* through which nerve fiber tracts ascend to or descend from higher brain centers.

megalomania. A paranoid *delusion of grandeur* in which an individual believes that he or she is an important person or is carrying out great plans.

melancholia. A vernacular diagnosis of several millenniums' standing for profound sadness and depression. In *major depression* with melancholia the individual is unable to feel better even momentarily when something good happens, regularly feels worse in the morning and awakens early, and suffers a deepening of other symptoms of depression.

meninges. The three layers of nonneural tissue that envelop the brain and spinal cord. They are the dura mater, the arachnoid, and the pia mater.

meningitis. An inflammation of the *meninges* through infection, usually by a bacterium, or through irritation. **Meningococcal**, the epidemic form of the disease caused by *Neisseria meningitidis*, takes the lives of 10 percent who contract it and causes cerebral palsy, hearing loss, speech defects, and other forms of permanent brain damage in one of four who recover.

mental age. The numerical index of an individual's cognitive development determined by standardized *intelligence tests.*

mental retardation. Subnormal intellectual functioning associated with impairment in social adjustment and identified at an early age.

meprobamate. Generic term for *Miltown*, an *anxiolytic*, the first introduced and for a time one of the most widely used.

mescaline. A *hallucinogen* and *alkaloid* that is the active ingredient of *peyote.*

mesmerize. The first term for *hypnotize*, after Franz Anton Mesmer, an Austrian physician who in the late eighteenth century treated and cured hysterical or *conversion disorders* with what he considered the animal magnetism emanating from his body and permeating the universe.

meta-analysis. A quantitative method of analyzing and comparing various therapies by standardizing their results.

metabolism. The sum of the intracellular processes by which large molecules are broken down into smaller ones, releasing energy and wastes, and by which small molecules are built up into new living matter by consuming energy.

metacognition. The knowledge people have about the way they know their world, such as recognizing the usefulness of a map in finding one's way in a new city.

methadone. A synthetic addictive *heroin substitute* for treating *heroin* addicts that acts as a substitute for heroin by eliminating its effects and the craving for it.

methedrine. A very strong *amphetamine*, sometimes shot directly into the veins.

3-methoxy-4-hydroxyphenylethylene glycol (MHPG). A major metabolite of *norepinephrine.*

midbrain. The middle part of the brain that consists of a mass of nerve fiber tracts connecting the spinal cord and *pons*, *medulla*, and *cerebellum* to the *cerebral cortex.*

migraine headaches. Extremely debilitating headaches caused by sustained dilation of the extracranial arteries, the temporal artery in particular; the dilated arteries trigger pain-sensitive nerve fibers in the scalp.

mild mental retardation. A limitation in mental development measured on IQ tests at between 50–55 and 70; children with such a limitation are considered the educable mentally retarded and are placed in special classes.

milieu therapy. A treatment procedure that attempts to make the total environment and all personnel and patients of the hospital a *therapeutic community*, conducive to psychological improvement; the staff conveys to the patients the expectation that they can and will behave more normally and responsibly.

Miltown. The trade name for *meprobamate*, one of the principal *anxiolytics.*

minimal brain damage. The term sometimes applied to *hyperactive* children, reflecting the belief that at least some of these youngsters suffer from minor brain defects.

Minnesota Multiphasic Personality Inventory (MMPI). A lengthy *personality inventory* by which individuals are diagnosed through their true–false replies to groups of statements indicating states such as *anxiety*, *depression*, masculinity–femininity and *paranoia.*

mixed design. A research strategy in which both *classificatory* and experimental *variables* are used; assigning subjects from discrete populations to two experimental conditions is an example.

M'Naghten rule. A British court decision of 1843 that stated that an *insanity defense* can be established by proving that the defendant did not know what he or she was doing or did not realize that it was wrong.

model. A set of concepts from one domain applied to another by analogy. For example, in trying to understand the brain we may assume that it functions like a computer.

modeling. Learning by observing and imitating the behavior of others.

moderate mental retardation. A limitation in mental development measured on IQ tests between 35–40 and 50–55; children with this degree of retardation are often institutionalized, and their training is focused on self-care rather than on development of intellectual skills.

modified leucotomy. A surgical procedure that severs

an area near the *corpus callosum* to relieve *obsessive-compulsive disorder.*

mongolism. See *Down syndrome.*

monism. Philosophical doctrine that ultimate reality is a unitary organic whole and that therefore mental and physical are one and the same. Contrast with *dualism.*

monoamine. An organic compound containing nitrogen in one amino group (NH). Some of the known *neurotransmitters* of the central nervous system, called collectively brain amines, are *catecholamines* and *indoleamines,* which are monoamines.

monoamine oxidase (MAO). An enzyme that deactivates *catecholamines* and *indoleamines* within the presynaptic neuron, indoleamines in the *synapse.*

monoamine oxidase inhibitors. A group of *antidepressant* drugs that prevent the enzyme *monoamine oxidase* from deactivating *neurotransmitters* of the central nervous system.

monozygotic (MZ) twins. Genetically identical siblings who have developed from a single fertilized egg; sometimes called identical twins.

mood disorders. Disorders in which there are disabling disturbances in emotion.

moral anxiety. In psychoanalytic theory, the *ego*'s fear of punishment for failure to adhere to the *superego*'s standards of proper conduct.

moral treatment. A therapeutic regimen, introduced by Philippe Pinel during the French Revolution, whereby mental patients were released from their restraints and were treated with compassion and dignity rather than with contempt and denigration. *Milieu therapy* gives patients similar encouraging attention.

morbidity risk. The probability that an individual will develop a particular disorder.

morphine. An addictive narcotic *alkaloid* extracted from *opium,* used primarily as an analgesic and as a *sedative.*

motor skills disorder. A *learning disability* characterized by marked impairment in the development of motor coordination that is not accounted for by a physical disorder like cerebral palsy.

mourning work. In Freud's theory of *depression,* the recall by a depressed person of memories associated with a lost one, serving to separate the individual from the deceased.

multiaxial classification. Classification having several dimensions, each of which is employed in categorizing; the DSM-IV is an example.

multifactorial. Referring to the operation of several variables influencing in complex fashion the development or maintenance of a phenomenon.

multimodal therapy. A cognitive-behavioral therapy introduced by Arnold Lazarus which employs techniques from diverse approaches in an effort to help people make positive changes in their BASIC IB, or behavior, affects, sensations, images, cognitions, interpersonal relationships, and biological functioning.

multiple personality disorder (MPD). A very rare *dissociative disorder* in which two or more fairly distinct and separate personalities are present within the same individual, each of them with his or her own memories, relationships, and behavior patterns and only one of them dominant at any given time.

multiple-baseline design. An experimental design in which two behaviors of a single subject are selected for study and a treatment is applied to one of them. The behavior that is not treated serves as a baseline against which the effects of the treatment can be determined. This is a common design in operant research.

mutism. The inability or refusal to speak.

myocardial infarction. See *coronary heart disease.*

myxedema. An endocrine disorder of adults produced by thyroid deficiency in which metabolic processes are slowed and the patient becomes lethargic, slow-thinking, and depressed.

narcissistic personality. Extremely selfish and self-centered, people with a narcissistic personality have a grandiose view of their uniqueness, achievements, and talents and an insatiable craving for admiration and approval from others. They are exploitative to achieve their own goals and expect much more from others than they themselves are willing to give.

narcosynthesis. A psychiatric procedure originating during World War II in which a drug was employed to help stressed soldiers recall the battle traumata underlying their disorders.

narcotics. Addictive *sedative* drugs, for example, *morphine* and *heroin,* that in moderate doses relieve pain and induce sleep.

negative reinforcement. The strengthening of a tendency to exhibit desired behavior by virtue of the fact that previous responses in that situation have been rewarded by the removal of an aversive stimulus.

negative symptoms. Behavioral deficits in *schizophrenia* such as *flat affect* and *apathy.*

negative triad. In Beck's theory of depression, a person's baleful views of the self, the world, and the future; the triad is in a reciprocal causal relationship with pessimistic assumptions (*schemata*) and cognitive biases such as *selective abstraction.*

negativism. A tendency to behave in a manner opposite to the desires of others or to what is expected or requested.

neo-Freudian. A person who has contributed to the modification and extension of Freudian theory.

neologism. A word made up by the speaker that is usually meaningless to a listener.

neoplasm. See *tumor.*

nerve impulse. A change in the electric potential of a neuron; a wave of depolarization spreads along the neuron and causes the release of neurotransmitter.

neurodermatitis. A chronic (*psychophysiological*) disorder in which patches of skin become inflamed.

neuroleptics. Psychoactive drugs, such as *Thorazine,* that reduce *psychotic* symptoms but have side effects resembling symptoms of neurological diseases.

neurologist. A person who studies the nervous system, especially its structure, functions, and abnormalities.

neuron. A single nerve cell.

neuropsychological tests. Psychological tests, such as

the *Luria–Nebraska,* that can detect impairment in different parts of the brain.

neuropsychologist. A psychologist concerned with the relationships among cognition, affect, and behavior on the one hand, and brain function on the other.

neuroses. A large group of non-*psychotic* disorders characterized by unrealistic *anxiety* and other associated problems, for example, *phobic* avoidances, *obsessions,* and *compulsions.*

neurosyphilis (*general paresis*). Infection of the central nervous system by the spirochete *Treponema pallidum,* which destroys brain tissue; marked by eye disturbances, tremors, and disordered speech as well as severe intellectual deterioration and *psychotic* symptoms.

neurotic anxiety. In psychoanalytic theory, a fear of the consequences of expressing previously punished and repressed *id* impulses; more generally, unrealistic fear.

neurotransmitter. A chemical substance important in transferring a nerve impulse from one *neuron* to another.

niacin. One of the complex of B vitamins.

nicotine. The principal *alkaloid* of tobacco (its addicting agent).

Niemann-Pick disease. An inherited disorder of lipid (fat) metabolism that produces *mental retardation* and paralysis and brings early death.

nitrous oxide. A gas that, when inhaled, produces euphoria and sometimes giddiness.

nomenclature. A system or set of names or designations used in a particular discipline, such as the DSM-IV.

nomothetic [context]. Relating to the universal and to the formulation of general laws that explain a range of phenomena. Contrast with *idiographic.*

norepinephrine. A *catecholamine* that is a *neurotransmitter* of the central nervous system. Disturbances in its tracts apparently figure in *depression* and *mania.* It is also a neurotransmitter secreted at the nerve endings of the *sympathetic nervous system,* a hormone liberated with *epinephrine* in the adrenal medulla and similar to it in action, and a strong vasoconstrictor.

normal curve. As applied in psychology, the bell-shaped distribution of a measurable trait depicting most people in the middle and few at the extremes.

nosology. A systematic classification of diseases.

nuclear magnetic response imaging (NMR). A biological assessment that entails placing a person inside a large magnet that causes hydrogen atoms to move when force is turned on and then return to their original positions when force is turned off, producing an electromagnetic signal that a computer can translate into black-and-white pictures of living tissue.

nucleus. In anatomy, a mass of nerve cell bodies (*gray matter*) within the brain or spinal cord by which descending nerve fibers connect with ascending nerve fibers.

object choice. In the psychology of sex, the type of person or thing selected as a focus for sexual desire or activity.

objective (realistic) anxiety. In psychoanalytic theory, the *ego's* reaction to danger in the external world; realistic fear.

observer drift. The tendency of two raters of behavior to begin to agree with each other, achieving unusually high levels of *reliability;* their way of coding behavior differentiates their scores from those of another pair of raters. This is regarded as a threat to reliable and valid *behavioral assessment.*

obsession. An intrusive and recurring thought that seems irrational and uncontrollable to the person experiencing it.

obsessive-compulsive disorder (OCD). An *anxiety disorder* in which the mind is flooded with persistent and uncontrollable thoughts or the individual is compelled to repeat certain acts again and again, causing significant distress and interference with everyday functioning.

obsessive-compulsive personality. People who have inordinate difficulty making decisions, are overly concerned with details and efficiency, and relate poorly to others because they demand that things be done their way. They are unduly conventional, serious, formal, and stingy with their emotions.

occipital lobe. The posterior area of each *cerebral hemisphere,* situated behind the *parietal lobe* and above the *temporal lobes,* responsible for reception and analysis of visual information and for some visua memory.

Oedipus complex. In Freudian theory, the desire and conflict of the four-year-old male child who wants to possess his mother sexually and to eliminate the father rival. The threat of punishment from the father causes *repression* of these *id* impulses. Girls have a similar sexual desire for the father, which is repressed in analogous fashion and is called the *Electra complex.*

operant behavior. A response that is supposedly voluntary and operates on the environment, modifying it so that a reward or goal is attained.

operant conditioning. The acquisition or elimination of a response as a function of the environmental contingencies of *reward* and *punishment.*

operationism. A school of thought in science that holds that a given concept must be defined in terms of a single set of identifiable and repeatable operations that can be measured.

opium. The dried milky juice obtained from the immature fruit of the opium poppy. This addictive *narcotic* produces euphoria and drowsiness and reduces pain.

oral stage. In psychoanalytic theory, the first *psychosexual stage,* which extends into the second year; during it the mouth is the principal *erogenous* zone.

organismic variable. The physiological or psychological factor assumed to be operating "under the skin"; these variables are a focus of *behavioral assessment.*

orgasm (climax). The involuntary, intensely pleasurable, climactic phase in sexual arousal that lasts a number of seconds and usually involves muscular contractions and *ejaculation* in the male and similar contractions in the genitalia of the female.

orgasmic reorientation. A *behavior therapy* technique for altering classes of stimuli to which people are sexually attracted; individuals are confronted by a conventionally arousing stimulus while experiencing *orgasm* for another, undesirable reason.

outcome studies. Research on the effectiveness of *psychotherapy*. Contrast with *process studies*.

overcontrolled [behavior]. In reference to childhood disorders, problems that create distress for the child, such as *anxiety* and *social withdrawal*.

pain disorder. A *somatoform disorder* in which the person complains of severe and prolonged pain that is not explainable by organic pathology; it tends to be stress related or permits the patient to avoid an aversive activity or to gain attention and sympathy.

panic disorder. An *anxiety disorder* in which the individual has sudden and inexplicable attacks of jarring symptoms, such as difficulty breathing, heart palpitations, dizziness, trembling, terror, and feelings of impending doom. In DSM-IV, said to occur with or without *agoraphobia*.

paradigm. A set of basic assumptions that outline the universe of scientific inquiry, specifying both the concepts regarded as legitimate and the methods to be used in collecting and interpreting data.

paranoia. The general term for *delusions of persecution*, of *grandiosity*, or both; found in several pathological conditions, *paranoid disorders*, *paranoid schizophrenia*, and *paranoid personality* disorder. Can be produced as well by large doses of certain drugs, such as *cocaine* or alcohol.

paranoid disorder. A disorder in which the individual has persistent persecutory *delusions* or *delusional jealousy*—and is very often contentious but has no *thought disorder* or *hallucinations*.

paranoid personality. This person, expecting to be mistreated by others, becomes suspicious, secretive, jealous, and argumentative. He or she will not accept blame and appears cold and unemotional.

paranoid schizophrenia. A *psychosis* in which the patient has numerous systematized *delusions* as well as *hallucinations* and *ideas of reference*. He or she may also be agitated, angry, argumentative, and sometimes violent.

paraphilias. Sexual attraction to unusual objects and sexual activities unusual in nature.

paraphrenia. Term sometimes used to refer to *schizophrenia* in an older adult.

paraprofessional. In clinical psychology, an individual lacking a doctoral degree but trained to perform certain functions usually reserved for clinicians, for example, a college student trained and supervised by a behavioral therapist to shape the behavior of *autistic* children through contingent reinforcers.

parasympathetic nervous system. The division of the *autonomic nervous system* that is involved with maintenance; it controls many of the internal organs and is active primarily when the organism is not aroused.

paresthesia. *Conversion disorder* marked by a sensation of tingling or creeping on the skin.

parietal lobe. The middle division of each *cerebral hemisphere*, situated behind the central *sulcus* and above the lateral sulcus; the receiving center for sensations of the skin and of bodily positions.

Parkinson's disease. A *presenile dementia* characterized by uncontrollable and severe muscle tremors, a stiff gait, a masklike, expressionless face, and withdrawal.

pathology. The anatomical, physiological, and psychological deviations of a disease or disorder; the study of these abnormalities.

PCP. See *phencyclidine*.

Pearson product moment correlation coefficient (*r*). A statistic, ranging in value from −1.00 to +1.00; the most common means of denoting a *correlational* relationship. The sign indicates whether the relationship is positive or negative and the magnitude indicates the strength of the relationship.

pedophiles. People with a preference for obtaining sexual gratification through contact with youngsters defined legally as underage; pedophilia is a *paraphilia*.

penile plethysmograph. A device for detecting blood flow and thus for recording changes in size of the *penis*.

penis. The male organ of copulation.

perseveration. The persistent repetition of words and ideas, often found in *schizophrenia*.

personality disorders. A heterogeneous group of disorders, listed separately on axis II, regarded as long-standing, inflexible, and maladaptive personality traits that impair social and occupational functioning.

personality inventory. A self-report questionnaire by which an examinee indicates whether statements assessing habitual tendencies apply to him or her.

personality structure. See *trait*.

pervasive developmental disorders. Severe childhood problems marked by profound disturbances in social relations and oddities in behavior. *Autistic disorder* is one.

PET scan. Computer-assisted motion pictures of the living brain, created by analysis of radioactive particles from isotopes injected into the bloodstream.

petit mal epilepsy. A form of *epilepsy* involving a momentary alteration in consciousness, more frequent in children than adults.

peyote. A *hallucinogen* obtained from the root of the peyote cactus; the active ingredient is *mescaline*, an *alkaloid*.

phallic stage. In psychoanalytic theory, the third *psychosexual stage*, extending from ages three to six, during which maximal gratification is obtained from genital stimulation.

phencyclidine (PCP). Also known as angel dust, PeaCE Pill, zombie, and by other street names. This very powerful and hazardous drug causes profound disorientation, agitated and often violent behavior, and even seizures, coma, and death.

phenomenology. As applied in psychology, the philosophical view that the phenomena of subjective experience should be studied because behavior is considered to be determined by how people perceive themselves and the world, rather than by objectively described reality.

phenothiazine. The name for a group of drugs that relieve psychotic symptoms and are considered *neuroleptics;* their molecular structure, like that of the *tricyclic drugs,* consists of three fused rings.

phenotype. The totality of observable characteristics of a person. Compare with *genotype.*

phenylketonuria (PKU). A genetic disorder that, through a deficiency in a liver enzyme, phenylalanine hydroxylase, causes severe *mental retardation* unless phenylalanine can be largely restricted from the diet until the age of six.

phobia. An *anxiety disorder* in which there is intense fear and avoidance of specific objects and situations, recognized as irrational by the individuals.

phonological disorder. A *learning disability* in which some words sound like baby talk because the person is not able to make certain speech sounds.

physiology. The study of the functions and activities of living cells, tissues, and organs and of the physical and chemical phenomena involved.

Pick's disease. A *presenile dementia* involving diffuse atrophy of *frontal* and *temporal lobes* which impairs memory, concentration, and ability to think abstractly and eventually results in *psychosis* and death.

placebo. Any inactive therapy or chemical agent, or any attribute or component of such a therapy or chemical, that affects a person's behavior for reasons related to his or her expectation of change.

placebo effect. The action of a drug or psychological treatment that is not attributable to any specific operations of the agent. For example, a tranquilizer can reduce anxiety both because of its special biochemical action and because the recipient expects relief. See *placebo.*

plateau phase. According to Masters and Johnson, the second stage in sexual arousal, during which excitement and tension have reached a stable high level before *orgasm.*

play therapy. The use of play as a means of uncovering what is troubling a child and of establishing *rapport.*

pleasure principle. In psychoanalytic theory, the demanding manner by which the *id* operates, seeking immediate gratification of its needs.

plethysmograph. An instrument for determining and registering variations in the amount of blood present or passing through an organ.

polysubstance abuse. The misuse of more than one drug at a time, such as drinking heavily and taking cocaine.

pons. An area in the *brain stem* containing nerve fiber tracts which connect the *cerebellum* with the spinal cord and with motor areas of the *cerebrum.*

positive reinforcement. The strengthening of a tendency to behave by virtue of the fact that previous responses in that situation have been followed by presentation of a desired reward.

positive spikes. An EEG pattern recorded from the *temporal lobe* of the brain, with frequencies of 6 to 8 cps and 14 to 16 cps, that is often found in impulsive and aggressive people.

positive symptoms. In *schizophrenia,* behavioral excesses, such as *hallucinations* and bizarre behavior. Compare with *negative symptoms.*

posttraumatic stress disorder (PTSD). An *anxiety disorder* in which a particularly stressful event, such as military combat, rape, or a natural disaster, brings in its aftermath intrusive reexperiencings of the trauma, a numbing of responsiveness to the outside world, estrangement from others, a tendency to be easily startled, nightmares, recurrent dreams, and otherwise disturbed sleep.

poverty of content. Reduced informational content in speech, one of the *negative symptoms* of schizophrenia.

poverty of speech. Reduced amount of talking, one of the *negative symptoms* of schizophrenia.

predictive validity. See *validity.*

predisposition. An inclination or *diathesis* to respond in a certain way, either inborn or acquired; in abnormal psychology, a factor that lowers the ability to withstand stress and inclines the individual toward *pathology.*

prefrontal lobotomy. A surgical procedure that destroys the tracts connecting the *frontal lobes* to lower centers of the brain; once believed to be an effective treatment for *schizophrenia.*

premature ejaculation. Inability of the male to inhibit his *orgasm* long enough for mutually satisfying sexual relations.

premorbid adjustment. In research on *schizophrenia,* the social and sexual adjustment of the individual before the onset or diagnosis of the symptoms. Patients with good premorbid adjustment are those found to have been relatively normal earlier; those with poor premorbid adjustment had inadequate interpersonal and sexual relations.

preparedness. In *classical conditioning* theory, a biological *predisposition* to associate particular stimuli readily with the *unconditioned stimulus.*

presenile dementia. An often progressive mental deterioration occurring when the individual is in his or her forties or fifties.

prevalence. In *epidemiological* studies of a disorder, the percentage of a population that has it at a given time. Compare with *incidence.*

prevention. Primary, efforts in *community psychology* to reduce the incidence of new cases of psychological disorder by such means as altering stressful living conditions and genetic counseling; **secondary,** efforts to detect disorders early, so that they will not develop into full blown, perhaps chronic, disabilities; **tertiary,** efforts to reduce the long-term consequences of having a disorder, equivalent in most respects to therapy.

primary empathy. A form of *empathy* in which the therapist understands the content and feeling of what the client is saying and expressing from the client's *phenomenological* point of view. Compare with *advanced accurate empathy.*

primary narcissism. In psychoanalytic theory, the part of the *oral stage* of *psychosexual* development during which the *ego* has not yet differentiated from the *id.*

primary prevention. See *prevention.*

primary process. In psychoanalytic theory, one of the

id's means of reducing tension, by imagining what it desires.

privileged communication. The communication between parties in a confidential relation that is protected by statute. A spouse, doctor, lawyer, pastor, psychologist, or psychiatrist cannot be forced, except under unusual circumstances, to disclose such information.

proband. See *index case.*

process studies. Research on the mechanisms by which a therapy may bring improvement. Compare with *outcome studies.*

process-reactive dimension [of schizophrenia]. A dimension used to distinguish schizophrenics: process schizophrenics suffer long-term and gradual deterioration before the onset of their illness, whereas reactive schizophrenics have a better premorbid history and a more rapid onset of symptoms. See *premorbid adjustment.*

profound mental retardation. A limitation in mental development measured on IQ tests at less than 20–25; children with this degree of retardation require total supervision of all their activities.

progestins. Steroid progestational hormones that are the biological precursors of androgens, the male sex hormones.

prognosis. A prediction of the likely course and outcome of an illness. Compare with *diagnosis.*

projection. A *defense mechanism* whereby characteristics or desires unacceptable to the *ego* are attributed to someone else.

projective hypothesis. The notion that highly unstructured stimuli, as in the *Rorschach*, are necessary to bypass defenses in order to reveal unconscious motives and conflicts.

projective test. A psychological assessment device employing a set of standard but vague stimuli on the assumption that unstructured material will allow unconscious motivations and fears to be uncovered. The *Rorschach* series of inkblots is an example.

pronoun reversal. A speech problem in which the child refers to himself or herself as "he," "she," or "you" and uses "I" or "me" in referring to others; often found in the speech of children with *autistic disorder.*

pseudocommunity. An illusory world built up by a *paranoid* person, dominated by false beliefs that are not properly verified and shared by others.

psilocybin. A *psychedelic* drug extracted from the mushroom *Psilocybe mexicana.*

psyche. The soul, spirit, or mind as distinguished from the body. In psychoanalytic theory, it is the totality of the *id, ego,* and *superego,* including both conscious and unconscious components.

psychedelic. A drug that expands consciousness. See also *hallucinogen.*

psychiatric social worker. A mental health professional who holds a Master of Social Work (M.S.W.) degree.

psychiatrist. A physician (M.D.) who has taken specialized postdoctoral training, called a residency, in the diagnosis, treatment, and prevention of mental and emotional disorders.

psychoactive drugs. Chemical compounds having a psychological effect that alters mood or thought process. Valium is an example.

psychoanalysis. A term applied primarily to the therapy procedures pioneered by Freud, entailing *free association, dream analysis,* and *working through* the *transference neurosis.* More recently the term has come to encompass the numerous variations on basic Freudian therapy.

psychoanalyst (analyst). A therapist who has taken specialized postdoctoral training in psychoanalysis after earning either an M.D. or a Ph.D.

psychoanalytic (psychodynamic) paradigm. General view based on *psychoanalysis.*

psychodynamics. In psychoanalytic theory, the mental and emotional forces and processes that develop in early childhood and their effects on behavior and mental states.

psychogenesis. Development from psychological origins as distinguished from somatic origins. Contrast with *somatogenesis.*

psychological autopsy. The analysis of an individual's *suicide* through the examination of his or her letters and through interviews with friends and relatives in the hope of discovering why he or she committed suicide.

psychological deficit. The term used to indicate that performance of a pertinent psychological process is below that expected of a normal person.

psychological dependency. The term sometimes applied as the reason for *substance abuse;* the reliance on, not physiological addiction to, a drug because its effects make stressful situations more bearable.

psychological factor influencing a medical condition. An indication in DSM-IV that a physical illness is caused (in part) or exacerbated by psychological *stress.*

psychological tests. Standardized procedures designed to measure a subject's performance on a particular task or to assess his or her personality.

psychomotor epilepsy. A form of epileptic seizure in which the individual loses contact with the environment but appears conscious and performs some routine, repetitive act or engages in more complex activity.

psychopath. See *antisocial personality.*

psychopathologists. Mental health professionals who conduct research into the nature and development of mental and emotional disorders; their academic backgrounds can differ, some having been trained as experimental psychologists, others as psychiatrists, and still others as biochemists.

psychopathology. The field concerned with the nature and development of mental disorders.

psychopathy. See *antisocial personality.*

psychophysiological disorders. Disorders with physical symptoms that may involve actual tissue damage, usually in one organ system, and that are produced in part by continued mobilization of the *autonomic nervous system* under stress. Hives and ulcers are examples. No longer listed in DSM-IV in a separate category, such disorders are now diagnosed on axis I as psychological factor influencing a medical condition; on axis III the specific physical condition is given.

psychophysiology. The discipline concerned with the bodily changes that accompany psychological events.

psychosexual stages. In psychoanalytic theory, critical developmental phases that the individual passes through, each stage characterized by the body area providing maximal erotic gratification. The adult personality is formed by the pattern and intensity of instinctual gratification at each stage.

psychosexual trauma. As applied by Masters and Johnson, earlier frigntening or degrading sexual experience that is related to a present *sexual dysfunction.*

psychosis. A severe mental disorder in which thinking and emotion are so impaired that the individual is seriously out of contact with reality.

psychosomatic [disorder]. See *psychophysiological disorders.*

psychosurgery. Any surgical technique in which neural pathways in the brain are cut in order to change behavior. See *lobotomy.*

psychotherapy. A primarily verbal means of helping troubled individuals change their thoughts, feelings, and behavior to reduce distress and to achieve greater life satisfaction. See *insight therapy* and *behavior therapy.*

psychotic depression. A profound sadness and unjustified feelings of unworthiness in which there are also *delusions.*

punishment. In psychological experiments, any noxious stimulus imposed on the animal to reduce the probability that it will behave in an undesired way.

random assignment. A method of assigning subjects to groups in an *experiment* that gives each subject an equal chance of being in each group. The procedure helps to ensure that groups are comparable before the experimental manipulation begins.

rape. See *forcible rape.*

rapid-smoking treatment. A *behavior therapy* technique for reducing cigarette smoking in which the person is instructed to puff much more quickly than usual in an effort to make the whole experience an aversive one.

rapport. A close, trusting relationship, believed to be essential for effective psychotherapy.

rational-emotive therapy (RET). A *cognitive-restructuring behavior therapy* introduced by Albert Ellis and based on the assumption that much disordered behavior is rooted in absolutistic demands that people make upon themselves. The therapy aims to alter the unrealistic goals individuals set for themselves, such as, "I must be universally loved."

rationalization. A *defense mechanism* in which a plausible reason is unconsciously invented by the *ego* to protect itself from confronting the real reason for an action, thought, or emotion.

Raynaud's disease. A *psychophysiological disorder* in which capillaries, especially of the fingers and toes, are subject to spasm. It is characterized by cold, moist hands, is commonly accompanied by pain, and may progress to local gangrene.

reaction formation. A *defense mechanism* whereby an unconscious and unacceptable impulse or feeling that would cause anxiety is converted into its opposite so that it can become conscious and be expressed.

reaction time test. A procedure for determining the interval between the application of a stimulus and the beginning of the subject's response.

reactivity [of behavior]. The phenomenon whereby the object of observation is changed by the very fact that it is being observed.

reading disorder. See *dyslexia.*

reality principle. In psychoanalytic theory, the manner in which the *ego* delays gratification and otherwise deals with the environment in a planned, rational fashion.

receptive aphasia. See *aphasia.*

receptive language disorder. Difficulties understanding spoken language.

receptor. Proteins embedded in the membrane covering a neural cell that interact with one or more *neurotransmitters.*

recessive gene. A *gene* that must be paired with one identical to it in order to determine a *trait* in the *phenotype.*

recovery time. The period it takes for a physiological process to return to *baseline* after the body has responded to a stimulus.

refractory phase. The brief period after stimulation of a nerve, muscle, or other irritable element during which it is unresponsive to a second stimulus; or the period after intercourse during which the male cannot have another orgasm.

regression. A *defense mechanism* in which anxiety is avoided by retreating to the behavior patterns of a earlier *psychosexual stage.*

reinforcement. In *operant conditioning,* increasing the probability that a response will recur either by presenting a contingent positive event or by removing a negative one.

reliability. The extent to which a test, measurement, or classification system produces the same scientific observation each time it is applied. Some specific kinds of reliability include **test-retest**, the relationship between the scores that a person achieves when he or she takes the same test twice; **interrater**, the relationship between the judgments that at least two raters make independently about a phenomenon; **split half**, the relationship between two halves of an assessment instrument that have been determined to be equivalent; **alternate form**, the relationship between scores achieved by subjects when they complete two versions of a test that are judged to be equivalent.

repression. A *defense mechanism* whereby impulses and thoughts unacceptable to the *ego* are pushed into the *unconscious.*

residual schizophrenia. Diagnosis given to patients who have had one episode of schizophrenia but who presently show no psychotic symptoms, though signs of the symptoms do exist.

resistance. During *psychoanalysis,* the defensive tendency of the unconscious part of the *ego* to ward off from consciousness particularly threatening *repressed* material.

resistance to extinction. The tendency of a *conditioned response* to persist in the absence of any *reinforcement.*

resolution phase. The last stage in the sexual arousal cycle, during which sexual tensions abate.

response acquiescence. A yea-saying *response set,* or agreeing with a question regardless of its content.

response cost. An *operant conditioning punishment* procedure in which the misbehaving person is fined already earned reinforcers.

response deviation. A tendency to answer questionnaire items in an uncommon way, regardless of their content.

response hierarchy. The ordering of a series of responses according to the likelihood of their being elicited by a particular stimulus.

response prevention. A *behavior therapy* technique in which the person is discouraged from making an accustomed response; used primarily with *compulsive* rituals.

response set. The tendency of an individual to respond in a particular way to questions or statements on a test—for example, with a False—regardless of the content of each query or statement.

reticular formation. Network of *nuclei* and fibers in the central core of the *brain stem* that is important in arousing the cortex and maintaining alertness, in processing incoming sensory stimulation, and in adjusting spinal reflexes.

retrospective reports. Recollections by an individual of past events.

reversal (ABAB) design. An experimental design in which behavior is measured during a baseline period (A), during a period when a treatment is introduced (B), during the reinstatement of the conditions that prevailed in the baseline period (A), and finally during a reintroduction of the treatment (B). It is commonly used in operant research to isolate cause–effect relationships.

reward. Any satisfying event or stimulus that, by being contingent upon a response, increases the probability that the subject will so respond again.

Rh factor. A substance present in the red blood cells of most people. If the Rh factor is present in the blood of a fetus but not in that of the mother, her system produces antibodies that may enter the bloodstream of the fetus and indirectly damage the brain.

right to refuse treatment. A legal principle according to which a committed mental patient may decline to participate in unconventional or risky treatments.

right to treatment. A legal principle according to which a committed mental patient must be provided some minimal amount and quality of professional intervention, enough to afford a realistic opportunity for meaningful improvement.

risk factor. A condition or variable that, if present, increases the likelihood of developing a disorder.

role-playing. Teaching people to behave in a certain way by encouraging them to pretend that they are in a particular situation; helps people acquire complex behaviors in an efficient way. See also *behavior rehearsal.*

Rorschach Inkblot Test. A *projective test* in which the examinee is instructed to interpret a series of ten inkblots reproduced on cards.

Rosenthal effect. The tendency for results to conform to experimenters' expectations unless stringent safeguards are instituted to minimize human bias; named after Robert Rosenthal, who performed many of the original experiments revealing the problem.

rubella (German measles). An infectious disease that if contracted by the mother during the first three months of pregnancy has a high risk of causing *mental retardation* and physical deformity in the child.

sadism. See *sexual sadism.*

schema. A mental structure for organizing information about the world. Pl. schemata.

schizoaffective disorder. Diagnosis to be applied when it is difficult to determine whether a patient has an affective (mood) disorder or either *schizophreniform disorder* or *schizophrenia.*

schizoid personality. This person, emotionally aloof and indifferent to the praise, criticism, and feelings of others, is usually a loner with few, if any, close friends and with solitary interests.

schizophrenia. A group of *psychotic* disorders characterized by major disturbances in thought, emotion, and behavior; disordered thinking in which ideas are not logically related; faulty perception and attention; bizarre disturbances in motor activity; flat or inappropriate emotions; and reduced tolerance for stress of interpersonal relations. The patient withdraws from people and reality, often into a fantasy life of *delusions* and *hallucinations.* See *schizoaffective disorder, schizophreniform disorder,* and *brief reactive psychosis.*

schizophreniform disorder. Diagnosis for people who have all the symptoms of *schizophrenia,* except that the disorder lasts more than two weeks but less than six months. See *brief reactive psychosis.*

schizophrenogenic mother. A cold, dominant, conflict-inducing mother believed to cause *schizophrenia* in her child.

schizotypal personality. This eccentric individual has oddities of thought and perception (*magical thinking, illusions, depersonalization, derealization*), speaks digressively and with over-elaborations, and is usually socially isolated. Under stress he or she may appear *psychotic.*

school phobia. An acute, irrational dread of attending school, usually accompanied by somatic complaints. It is the most common *phobia* of childhood.

science. The pursuit of systematized knowledge through reliable observation.

secondary gain. Benefits that a person unconsciously obtains from a disability.

secondary prevention. See *prevention.*

secondary process. The reality-based decision-making and problem-solving activities of the *ego.* Compare with *primary process.*

secondhand smoke. The smoke from the burning end of a cigarette, containing higher concentrations of ammonia, carbon monoxide, nicotine, and tar than that inhaled by the smoker.

sedative. A drug that slows bodily activities, especially those of the central nervous system; it is used to reduce pain and tension and to induce relaxation and sleep.

selective abstraction. A cognitive bias in Beck's theory of depression whereby a person picks out from a complex situation only certain features and ignores aspects that could lead to a different conclusion.

selective mortality. A possible confound in *longitudinal studies*, whereby the less healthy people in a sample are more likely to drop out over time.

self-actualization. Fulfilling one's potential as an always growing human being; believed by *client-centered therapists* to be the master motive.

self-efficacy. In Bandura's theory, the belief that one can achieve certain goals.

self-instructional training. A cognitive-behavioral approach that tries to help people improve their overt behavior by changing the ways they silently talk to themselves.

self-monitoring. In *behavioral assessment*, a procedure whereby the individual observes and reports certain aspects of his or her own behavior, thoughts, or emotions.

self psychology. Kohut's variant of psychoanalysis, in which the focus is on the development of the person's self-worth from acceptance and nurturance by key figures in childhood.

semantic differential. A self-report inventory requiring the respondent to rate each concept, such as "mother," in one of seven positions between a number of polar adjectives, such as "clean–dirty," "strong–weak."

senile dementia. A disorder that can be brought on by progressive deterioration of the brain caused in part by aging; marked by memory impairment, inability to think abstractly, loss of standards and control of impulses, poor personal hygiene, great *disorientation*, and eventually obliviousness.

senile plaques. Small areas of tissue degeneration in the brain, made up of granular material and filaments.

sensate focus. A term applied to exercises prescribed at the beginning of the Masters and Johnson sex therapy program; partners are instructed to fondle each other to give pleasure but to refrain from intercourse, thus reducing anxiety about sexual performance.

sensitivity training group (T-group). A small group of people who spend a period of time together both for therapy and for educational purposes; participants are encouraged or forced to examine their interpersonal functioning and their often overlooked feelings about themselves and others.

sensory-awareness procedures. Techniques that help clients tune into their feelings and sensations, as in *sensate-focus* exercises, and to be open to new ways of experiencing and feeling.

separation anxiety disorder. A disorder in which the child feels intense fear and distress when away from someone on whom he or she is very dependent; it is said to be an important cause of *school phobia*.

serotonin. An *indoleamine* that is a *neurotransitter* of the central nervous system. Disturbances in its tracts apparently figure in *depression* and *mania*.

severe mental retardation. A limitation in mental development measured in IQ tests at between 20–25 and 35–40. Individuals so afflicted often cannot care for themselves, communicate only briefly, and are listless and inactive.

sex-reassignment surgery. An operation removing existing genitalia of a *transsexual* and constructing a substitute for the genitals of the opposite sex.

sexual aversion disorder. Avoidance of nearly all genital contact with other people.

sexual disorders. Disorders of sexual functioning including *gender identity disorders*, *paraphilias*, and *sexual dysfunctions*.

sexual dysfunctions. Dysfunctions in which the appetitive or psychophysiological changes of the normal sexual response cycle are inhibited.

sexual masochism. A marked preference for obtaining or increasing sexual gratification through subjection to pain.

sexual orientation disturbance. An earlier term for DSM-III's *ego-dystonic homosexuality*.

sexual sadism. A marked preference for obtaining or increasing sexual gratification by inflicting pain on another person.

sexual response cycle. The general pattern of sexual physical processes and feelings, building to an orgasm by stimulation and made up of five phases: interest, *excitement*, *plateau*, *orgasm*, and *resolution*.

sexual script. Rules people have for guiding their actions in sexual situations.

sexual value system. As applied by Masters and Johnson, the activities that an individual holds to be acceptable and necessary in a sexual relationship.

shaping. In *operant conditioning*, reinforcing responses that are successively closer approximations to the desired behavior.

shellshock. A term from World War I for what is now referred to as *posttraumatic stress disorder*; it was believed to be due to sudden atmospheric changes from nearby explosions.

sibling. One of two or more persons having the same parents.

significant difference. See *statistical significance*.

single-subject experimental design. A design for an experiment conducted with a single subject, for example, the *reversal* and *multiple-baseline designs* in operant research.

situational determinants. The environmental conditions that precede and follow a particular piece of behavior, a primary focus of *behavioral assessment*.

situational orgasmic dysfunction. Inability to have an *orgasm* in particular situations.

skeletal (voluntary) muscle. Muscle that clothes the skeleton of the vertebrate, is attached to bone, and is under voluntary control.

Skinner box. A laboratory apparatus in which an animal is placed for an *operant conditioning* experiment. It contains a lever or other device that the animal must manipulate to obtain a reward or avoid punishment.

sleeping sickness. See *encephalitis lethargica*.

slow brain wave. The *theta rhythm* (4 to 7 cps) usually recorded by an EEG from subcortical parts of the brain and the *delta rhythm* (less than 4 cps) normally recorded during deep sleep; sometimes recorded in awake psychopaths.

smooth (involuntary) muscle. Thin sheets of muscle cells associated with *viscera* and walls of blood vessels, performing functions not usually under direct voluntary control.

social desirability. In completion of *personality inventories*, the tendency of the responder to give what he or she considers the socially acceptable answer, whether or not it is accurate.

social phobia. A collection of fears linked to the presence of other people.

social problem-solving. A form of cognitive behavior therapy that has people construe their psychological difficulties as stemming from soluble problems in living and then teaches them how to generate useful solutions.

social selection theory. An attempt to explain the correlation between social class and *schizophrenia* by proposing that schizophrenics move downward in social status.

social-skills training. *Behavior therapy* procedures for teaching socially unknowledgeable individuals how to meet others, to talk to them and maintain eye contact, to give and receive criticism, to offer and accept compliments, to make requests and express feelings, and otherwise to improve their relations with other people. *Modeling* and *behavior rehearsal* are two such procedures.

social-withdrawal disorder. A disorder of extremely shy children who never warm up to new people both young and old, even after prolonged exposure to them. They have loving relations within the family, but they do not join in group play, and in crowded rooms they cling to their parents or hide.

socioeconomic status. A relative position in the community as determined by occupation, income, and amount of education.

sociogenic hypothesis. Generally, an idea that seeks causes in social conditions, for example, that being in a low social class can cause one to become *schizophrenic.*

sociopath. See *antisocial personality.*

sodomy. Originally, penetration of the male organ into the anus of another male; later broadened in English law to include heterosexual anal intercourse and by some U.S. state statutes to cover unconventional sex generally.

soma. The totality of an organism's physical makeup.

somatic nervous system. That part of the nervous system that controls muscles under voluntary control.

somatic-weakness. The vulnerability of a particular organ or organ system to psychological stress and thereby to a particular *psychophysiological disorder.*

somatization disorder (Briquet's syndrome). A *somatoform disorder* in which the person continually seeks medical help for recurrent and multiple physical symptoms that have no discoverable physical cause. The medical history is complicated and dramatically presented. Compare with *hypochondriasis.*

somatoform disorders. Disorders in which physical symptoms suggest a physical problem but have no known physiological cause; they are therefore believed to be linked to psychological conflicts and needs but not voluntarily assumed. Examples are *somatization disorder* (Briquet's syndrome), *conversion disorder, pain disorder, hypochondriasis.*

somatoform pain disorder. A *somatoform disorder* in which the person complains of severe and prolonged pain that is not explainable by organic pathology; it tends to be stress related or permits the patient to avoid an aversive activity or to gain attention and sympathy.

somatogenesis. Development from bodily origins as distinguished from psychological origins. Compare with *psychogenesis.*

SORC. An acronym for the four sets of variables that are the focus of *behavioral assessment*: *situational determinants, organismic variables,* (*overt*) *responses,* and *reinforcement contingencies.*

specific phobia. An unwarranted fear and avoidance of a specific object or circumstance, for example, fear of nonpoisonous snakes or fear of heights.

specific-reaction theory. The hypothesis that an individual develops a given *psychophysiological disorder* because of the innate tendency of the *autonomic nervous system* to respond in a particular way to stress, for example, by increasing heart rate or developing tension in the forehead.

spectator role. As applied by Masters and Johnson, a pattern of behavior in which the individual's focus on and concern with sexual performance impedes his or her natural sexual responses.

split–half reliability. See *reliability.*

stability-lability. A dimension of classifying the responsiveness of the *autonomic nervous system.* Labile individuals are those in whom a wide range of stimuli can elicit autonomic *arousal;* stable individuals are not so easily aroused.

standardization. The process of constructing an assessment procedure that has norms and meets the various psychometric criteria for *reliability* and *validity.*

state-dependent learning. The phenomenon whereby an organism shows the effects of learning that took place in a special condition, such as while intoxicated, better than in another condition.

state-dependent memory. The phenomenon whereby people are more able to remember an event if they are in the same state as when it occurred. If they are in a greatly different state when they try to remember—happy now, and sad then, for example—memory is poorer.

statistical significance. A magnitude of difference that has a low probability of having occurred by chance alone and is by convention regarded as important.

statutory rape. See *forcible rape.*

stepping-stone theory. The belief that the use of one kind of drug, such as *marijuana,* leads to the use of a more dangerous one, such as *cocaine.*

stimulant. A drug that increases alertness and motor activity and at the same time reduces fatigue, allowing an individual to remain awake for an extended period of time.

strategic processing. The use of *cognitive* strategies to solve problems; said to be defective in the *mentally retarded.*

stress. State of an organism subjected to a *stressor;* it can take the form of increased *autonomic* activity and, in the long term, cause the breakdown of an organ or development of a mental disorder.

stress management. A range of psychological procedures that help people control and reduce their *stress* or *anxiety.*

stressor. An event that occasions *stress* in an organism, for example, loss of a loved one.

stroke. A sudden loss of consciousness and control followed by paralysis; caused when a blood clot obstructs an artery or by hemorrhage into the brain when an artery ruptures.

structural social support. A person's network of social relationships, for example, number of friends. Contrast with *functional social support.*

subdural hematoma. Hemorrhage and swelling of the arachnoid torn by a fractured bone of the skull.

subintentioned death. A death that is believed to have been caused in some measure by the person's unconscious intentions.

substance abuse. The use of a drug to such an extent that the person is often intoxicated throughout the day and fails in important obligations and in attempts to abstain, but where there is no physiological dependence. See *psychological dependency.*

substance dependence. The abuse of a drug accompanied by a physiological dependence on it, made evident by *tolerance* and *withdrawal* symptoms; also called addiction.

substance-related disorders. Disorders in which drugs such as *alcohol* and *cocaine* are abused to such an extent that behavior becomes maladaptive; social and occupational functioning is impaired, and control or abstinence becomes impossible. Reliance on the drug may be either psychological, as in *substance abuse,* or physiological, as in *substance dependence,* or addiction.

successive approximations. Responses that closer and closer resemble the desired response in *operant conditioning.* See *shaping.*

suicide. The taking of one's own life intentionally.

suicide prevention centers. Based on the assumption that people are often ambivalent about taking their own lives, these centers are staffed primarily by paraprofessionals who are trained to be *empathic* and to encourage suicidal callers to consider nondestructive ways of dealing with what is bothering them.

sulcus (fissure). A shallow furrow in the *cerebral cortex* separating adjacent convolutions or *gyri.*

superego. In psychoanalytic theory, the part of the personality that acts as the conscience and reflects society's moral standards as learned from parents and teachers.

symbolic loss. In *psychoanalytic* theory, the unconscious interpretation by the *ego* of an event such as the rebuff of a loved one as a permanent rejection.

sympathetic nervous system. The division of the *autonomic nervous system* that acts on bodily systems—for example, speeding up the contractions of the blood vessels, slowing those of the intestines, and increasing the heartbeat—to prepare the organism for exertion, emotional stress, or extreme cold.

symptom. An observable physiological or psychological manifestation of a disease, often occurring in a patterned group to constitute a *syndrome.*

synapse. A small gap between two *neurons* where the nerve impulse passes from the axon of the first to the dendrites, cell body, or axon of the second.

syndrome. A group or pattern of *symptoms* that tend to occur together in a particular *disease.*

systematic desensitization. A major *behavior therapy* procedure that has a fearful person, while deeply relaxed, imagine a series of progressively more fearsome situations. The two responses of relaxation and fear are incompatible and fear is dispelled. This technique is useful for treating psychological problems in which *anxiety* is the principal difficulty.

systematic rational restructuring. A variant of *rational-emotive therapy* in which the client imagines a series of increasingly anxiety-provoking situations while attempting to reduce distress by talking about them to the self in a more realistic, defusing fashion.

systems perspective. A general viewpoint that holds that a phenomenon, for example, a child's conduct problem, is best understood in the broad context in which it occurs, for example, the child's family and school environments.

T-group. See *sensitivity training group.*

tachycardia. A racing of the heart, often associated with high levels of *anxiety.*

tarantism. Wild dancing mania, prevalent in thirteenth-century western Europe, supposedly incited by the bite of a tarantula.

tardive dyskinesia. A muscular disturbance of older patients who have taken *phenothiazines* for a very long time, marked by involuntary lip smacking and chin wagging.

Taylor Manifest Anxiety Scale. Fifty items drawn from the MMPI, used as a self-report questionnaire to assess *anxiety.*

temporal lobe. A large area of each *cerebral hemisphere* situated below the lateral *sulcus* and in front of the *occipital lobe;* contains primary auditory projection and association areas and general association areas.

tertiary prevention. See *prevention.*

testes. Male reproductive glands or gonads; the site where sperm develop and are stored.

testosterone. Male sex hormone secreted by the *testes* that is responsible for the development of sex characteristics such as enlargement of the testes and growth of facial hair.

test-retest reliability. See *reliability.*

tetrahydrocannabinol (THC). The major active chemical in *marijuana* and *hashish.*

thalamus. A major brain relay station consisting of two egg-shaped lobes located in the *diencephalon;* it receives impulses from all sensory areas except the olfactory and transmits them to the *cerebrum*.

Thanatos. In psychoanalytic theory, the death instinct; with *Eros*, the two basic instincts within the *id*.

Thematic Apperception Test (TAT). A *projective test* consisting of a set of black-and-white pictures reproduced on cards, each depicting a potentially emotion-laden situation. The examinee, presented with the cards one at a time, is instructed to make up a story about each situation.

theta rhythm. See *slow brain waves*.

theory. A formally stated and coherent set of propositions that purport to explain a range of phenomena, order them in a logical way, and suggest what additional information might be gleaned under certain conditions.

therapeutic community. A concept in mental health care that views the total environment as contributing to prevention or treatment.

thiamine. One of the complex of B vitamins.

third-variable problem. The difficulty in the *correlational method* of research whereby the relationship between two variables may be attributable to a third factor.

Thorazine. Trade name for *chlorpromazine*, one of the *neuroleptics* and a member of the *phenothiazine* group of drugs.

thought disorder. A symptom of *schizophrenia*, evidenced by problems such as *incoherence*, *loose associations*, and poverty of speech and poverty of content of speech.

thyroid gland. An endocrine structure whose two lobes are located on either side of the windpipe; it secretes thyroxin.

time-of-measurement effects. A possible confound in *longitudinal studies*, whereby conditions at a particular point in time can have a specific effect on a variable that is being studied over time.

time-out. An *operant conditioning* punishment procedure in which, after bad behavior, the person is temporarily removed from a setting where reinforcers can be obtained and placed in a less desirable setting, for example, in a boring room.

token economy. A *behavior therapy* procedure, based on *operant conditioning* principles, in which institutionalized patients are given scrip rewards, such as poker chips, for socially constructive behavior. The tokens themselves can be exchanged for desirable items and activities such as cigarettes and extra time away from the ward.

tolerance. A physiological process in which greater and greater amounts of an addictive drug are required to produce the same effect. See *substance dependence*.

tonic phase. The state of rigid muscular tension and suspended breathing in a *grand mal epileptic* attack.

trait. A somatic characteristic or an enduring *predisposition* to respond in a particular way, distinguishing one individual from another.

trance logic. A way of thinking during *hypnosis* that allows a person to entertain as real phenomena notions and images that are inherently contradictory, such as seeing two people in place of one.

tranquilizer. A drug that reduces anxiety and agitation, such as *Valium*. See *anxiolytics*.

transference. The venting of the *analysand*'s emotions, either positive or negative, by treating the *analyst* as the symbolic representative of someone important in the past. An example is the analysand's becoming angry with the analyst to release emotions actually felt toward his or her father.

transference neurosis. A crucial phase of *psychoanalysis* during which the *analysand* reacts emotionally toward the *analyst*, treating the analyst as a parent and reliving childhood experiences in his or her presence. It enables both analyst and analysand to examine hitherto *repressed* conflicts in the light of present-day reality.

transsexual. A person who believes he or she is opposite in sex to his or her biological endowment; often, sex-reassignment surgery is desired.

transvestitic fetishism. The practice of dressing in the clothing of the opposite sex, usually for the purpose of sexual arousal.

trauma. A severe physical injury or wound to the body caused by an external force, or a psychological shock having a lasting effect on mental life. Pl. traumata.

traumatic disease. An illness produced by external assault, such as poison, a blow, or stress; for example, a broken leg.

tremor. An involuntary quivering of voluntary muscle, usually limited to small musculature of particular areas.

triadic reciprocality. The influence of cognition and behavior on each other through the relationships among thinking, behavior, and the environment.

tricyclic drugs. A group of *antidepressants* with molecular structures characterized by three fused rings. Tricyclics are assumed to interfere with the reuptake of *norepinephrine* and *serotonin* by a *neuron* after it has fired.

trisomy. A condition wherein there are three rather than the usual pair of homologous *chromosomes* within the cell nucleus.

tumescence. The flow of blood into the genitals.

tumor (neoplasm). Abnormal growth that when located in the brain can either be malignant and directly destroy brain tissue or be benign and disrupt functioning by increasing intracranial pressure.

twin method. Research strategy in *behavior genetics* in which *concordance* rates of *monozygotic* and *dizygotic twins* are compared.

two-factor theory. Mowrer's theory of *avoidance learning* according to which (1) fear is attached to a neutral stimulus by pairing it with a noxious *unconditioned stimulus*, and (2) a person learns to escape the fear elicited by the *conditioned stimulus*, thereby avoiding the UCS. See *fear-drive*.

Type A behavior patterns. One of two contrasting psychological patterns revealed through studies seeking the cause of *coronary heart disease*. Type A people are competitive, rushed, hostile, and overcommitted to their work. Type As are believed to be at heightened risk for heart disease. Those who meet the other pattern,

Type B people are more relaxed and relatively free of pressure.

ultrasound. The use of controlled sound waves to visualize internal organs; circumvents the need for x-rays.

unconditional positive regard. According to Rogers, a crucial attitude for the *client-centered* therapist to adopt toward the client, who needs to feel complete acceptance as a person in order to evaluate the extent to which current behavior contributes to *self-actualization.*

unconditioned response (UCR). See *classical conditioning.*

unconditioned stimulus (UCS). See *classical conditioning.*

unconscious. A state of unawareness without sensation or thought. In psychoanalytic theory, it is the part of the personality, in particular the *id* impulses, or *id* energy, of which the *ego* is unaware.

undercontrolled [behavior]. In reference to childhood disorders, problem behavior of the child that creates trouble for others, such as disobedience and aggressiveness.

undifferentiated schizophrenia. Diagnosis given for patients whose psychotic symptoms do not fit a listed category, or that meet the criteria for more than one category.

unilateral ECT. *Electroconvulsive therapy* in which electrodes are placed on one side of the forehead so that current passes through only one brain hemisphere.

unipolar depression. A term applied to the disorder of individuals who have experienced episodes of *depression* but not of *mania;* referred to as *major depression* in DSM-IV.

vagina. The sheathlike female genital organ that leads from the uterus to the external opening.

vaginal barrel. The passageway of the vaginal canal leading from the external opening to the uterus.

vaginal orgasm. The sexual climax experienced through stimulation of the *vagina.*

vaginal plethysmograph. A device for recording the amount of blood in the walls of the *vagina* and thus for measuring arousal.

vaginismus. Painful, spasmodic contractions of the outer third of the *vaginal barrel* which make insertion of the *penis* impossible or extremely difficult.

validity. **internal,** the extent to which experimental results can be confidently attributed to the manipulation of the *independent variable;* **external,** the extent to which research results may be generalized to other populations and settings. As applied to psychiatric diagnoses, **concurrent,** the extent to which previously undiscovered features are found among patients with the same diagnosis; **predictive,** the extent to which predictions can be made about the future behavior of patients with the same diagnosis; **etiological,** the extent to which a disorder in a number of patients is found to have the same cause or causes. See also *construct validity.*

Valium. An anxiety-reducing drug, or *anxiolytic,* believed to be the most widely prescribed of those available to physicians.

variable. A characteristic or aspect in which people, objects, events, or conditions vary.

vasoconstriction. A narrowing of the space within the walls (lumen) of a blood vessel, implicated in diseases such as *hypertension.*

vicarious conditioning. Learning by observing the reactions of others to stimuli or by listening to what they say.

Vineland Adaptive Behavior Scale. An instrument for assessing how many age-appropriate, socially adaptive behaviors a child engages in.

viscera. The internal organs of the body located in the great cavity of the trunk proper.

vitamins. Various organic substances that are, as far as is known, essential to the nutrition of many animals, acting usually in minute quantities to regulate various metabolic processes.

voodoo death. The demise of a member of a primitive culture after breaking a tribal law or being cursed by the witch doctor.

voyeurism. Marked preference for obtaining sexual gratification by watching others in a state of undress or having sexual relations.

vulnerability schema. The schema of people who are socially anxious and who generally think about danger, harm, and unpleasant events that may come to them.

waxy flexibility. An aspect of *catatonic immobility* in which the patient's limbs can be moved into a variety of positions and maintained thereafter for unusually long periods of time.

Wernicke's disease. A chronic brain disorder produced by a deficiency of B-complex vitamins that is marked by confusion, drowsiness, partial paralysis of eye muscles, and unsteady gait and by lesions in the *pons, cerebellum,* and *mammillary bodies.* Chronic alcoholics are especially susceptible.

white matter. The neural tissue, particularly of the brain and spinal cord, consisting of tracts or bundles of myelinated (sheathed) nerve fibers.

withdrawal symptoms. Negative physiological and psychological reactions evidenced when a person suddenly stops taking an addictive drug; cramps, restlessness, and even death are examples. See *substance abuse.*

woolly mammoth. A metaphor for the way in which the repressed *conflicts* of *psychoanalytic* theory are encapsulated in the *unconscious,* making them inaccessible to examination and alteration; thus maintained, the conflicts cause disorders in adulthood.

working through. In *psychoanalysis,* the arduous, time-consuming process through which the *analysand* confronts repressed conflicts again and again and faces up to the validity of the *analyst's interpretations* until problems are satisfactorily solved.

Zeitgeist. The German word for the trends of thought and feeling of culture and taste of a particular time period.

zygote. The fertilized egg cell formed when the male sperm and female ovum unite.

References

Abel, G.G., Barlow, D.H., Blanchard, E.B., & Guild, D. (1977). The components of rapists' sexual arousal. *Archives of General Psychiatry, 34,* 895–903.

Abel, G.G., Becker, J.V., Murphy, W.D., & Flanagan, B. (1981). Identifying dangerous child molesters. In R. Stuart (Ed.), *Violent behavior: Social learning approaches to prediction, management, and treatment.* New York: Brunner.

Abel, G.G., Blanchard, E.B., & Barlow, D.H. (1981). Measurement of sexual arousal in several paraphilias: The effects of stimulus modality, instructional set, and stimulus content. *Behaviour Research and Therapy, 19,* 25–33.

Abel, G.G., Mittelman, M.S., & Becker, J.V. (1985). Sexual offenders: Results of assessment and recommendations for treatment. In M.H. Ben-Aron, S.J. Hucker, & C.D. Webster (Eds.), *Clinical criminology: The assessment and treatment of criminal behavior.* Toronto: M & M Graphics.

Abelin, T., Buehler, A., Mueller, P., Vesanen, K., & Imhof, P.R. (1989, January 7). Controlled trial of transdermal nicotine patch in tobacco withdrawal. *Lancet,* 7–10.

Abelin, T., Ehrsam, R., Buehler-Reichert, A., Imhof, P.R., Mueller, P., Thommen, A., & Vesanen, K. (1989). Effectiveness of a transdermal nicotine system in smoking cessation studies. *Methods and Findings in Experimental Clinical Pharmacology, 11,* 205–214.

Abrams, R., Swartz, C.M., & Vedak, C. (1991). Antidepressant effects of high-dose right unilateral electroconvulsive therapy. *Archives of General Psychiatry, 48,* 746–748.

Abramson, L.Y., Metalsky, G.I., & Alloy, L.B. (1989). Hopelessness depression: A theory-based subtype of depression. *Psychological Review, 96,* 358–372.

Abramson, L.Y., Seligman, M.E.P., & Teasdale, J.D. (1978). Learned helplessness in humans: Critique and reformulation. *Journal of Abnormal Psychology, 87,* 49–74.

Abramson, P.R., Parker, T., & Weisberg, S.R. (1988). Sexual expression of mentally retarded people: Educational and legal implications. *American Journal of Mental Retardation, 93,* 328–334.

Achenbach, T.M. (1982). *Developmental psychopathology* (2nd ed.). New York: Wiley.

Achenbach, T.M., & Edelbrock, C.S. (1978). The classification of child psychopathology: A review of empirical efforts. *Psychological Bulletin, 85,* 1275–1301.

Achenbach, T.M., & Edelbrock, C.S. (1983). *Manual for the child behavior checklist.* Burlington, VT: Author.

Ackerman, N.W. (1966). *Treating the troubled family.* New York: Basic Books.

Adams, E.H., & Durell, J. (1984). Cocaine: A growing public health problem. In J. Grabowski (Ed.), *Cocaine: Pharmacology, effects, and treatment of abuse.* Rockville, MD: NIDA.

Adams, K.M. (1980). In search of Luria's battery: A false start. *Journal of Consulting and Clinical Psychology, 48,* 511–516.

Adler, A. (1929). *Problems of neurosis.* New York: Harper & Row.

Adler, A. (1964). Compulsion neurosis. In H.L. Ansbacher & R.R. Ansbacher (Eds.), *Superiority and social interest.* Evanston, IL: Northwestern University Press.

Agras, W.S., Sylvester, D., & Oliveau, D. (1969). *The epidemiology of common fears and phobias.* Unpublished manuscript.

Akhter, S., Wig, N.N., Varma, V.K., Pershad, D., & Varma, S.K. (1975). A phenomenological analysis of symptoms in obsessive-compulsive neurosis. *British Journal of Psychiatry, 127,* 342–348.

Albee, G.W., Lane, E.A., & Reuter, J.M. (1964). Childhood intelligence of future schizophrenics and neighborhood peers. *Journal of Psychology, 58,* 141–144.

Aldrich, C.K., & Mendkoff, E. (1963). Relocation of the aged and disabled: A mortality study. *Journal of the American Geriatrics Society, 11,* 185–194.

Alexander, F. (1950). *Psychosomatic medicine.* New York: Norton.

Alexander, F., & French, T.M. (1946). *Psychoanalytic therapy.* New York: Ronald Press.

Alexander, P.C., & Lupfer, S.L. (1987) Family characteristics and long-term consequences associated with sexual abuse. *Archives of Sexual Behavior, 16,* 235–245.

Allderidge, P. (1979). Hospitals, mad houses, and asylums: Cycles in the care of the insane. *British Journal of Psychiatry, 134,* 321–324.

Allen, G.J., Chinsky, J.M., Larsen, S.W., Lockman, J.E., & Selinger, H.V. (1976). *Community psychology and the schools: A behaviorally oriented multilevel preventive approach.* Hillsdale, NJ: Erlbaum.

Allen, M.G. (1976). Twin studies of affective illness. *Archives of General Psychiatry, 33,* 1476–1478.

Allison, R.B. (1984). Difficulties diagnosing the multiple personality syndrome in a death penalty case. *International Journal of Clinical and Experimental Hypnosis, 32,* 102–117.

Alloy, L.B., & Abramson, L.Y. (1979). Judgment of contingency in depressed and nondepressed students: Sadder but wiser? *Journal of Experimental Psychology: General, 108,* 441–485.

Alloy, L.B., & Abramson L.Y. (1988). Depressive realism: Four theoretical perspectives. In L.B. Alloy (Ed.), *Cognitive processes in depression* (pp. 223–265). New York: Guilford.

Alloy, L.B., Kelly, K.A., Mineka, S., & Clements, C.M. (1990). Comorbidity in anxiety and depressive disorders: A helplessness/hopelessness perspective. In J.D. Maser & C.R. Cloninger (Eds.), *Comorbidity in anxiety and mood disorders.* Washington, DC: American Psychiatric Press.

Allport, G.W. (1937). *Personality: A psychological interpretation.* New York: Holt, Rinehart & Winston.

Allport, G.W. (1954). *The nature of prejudice.* Cambridge, Mass:, Addison-Wesley.

Allport, G.W. (1961). *Pattern and growth in personality.* New York: Holt, Rinehart & Winston.

Almada, S.J. et al. (1991). Neuroticism and cynicism and risk of death in middle aged men: The Western Electric study. *Psychosomatic Medicine, 53,* 165–175.

Altman, D.G., Flora, J.A., & Farquhar, J.W. (1986, August). *Institutionalizing community-based health promotion programs.* Paper presented at the annual meeting of the American Psychological Association, Washington, DC. As cited in Maccoby & Altman (1988).

Amaro, H. (1988). Considerations for prevention of HIV infection among Hispanic women. *Psychology of Women Quarterly, 12,* 429–443.

American Cancer Society.(1976). *Task force on tobacco and cancer—Target 5.* Report to the Board of Directors, American Cancer Society.

American Cancer Society. (1991). *Cancer facts and figures—1991.* Atlanta: Author.

American Heart Association. (1981). *Heart Facts.* Dallas: Author.

American Law Institute. (1962). *Model penal code: Proposed official draft.* Philadelphia: Author.

American Medical Association. (1987). *Report of the Council on Ethical and Judicial Affairs: Ethical issues involved in the growing AIDS crisis.* Chicago: Author.

American Psychiatric Association. *Diagnostic and statistical manual of mental disorders.* First edition, 1952; second edition, 1968; third edition, 1980; revised, 1987. Washington, DC: Author.

American Psychological Association Division 33. (1989). Guidelines on effective behavioral treatment for persons with mental retardation and developmental disabilities. *Psychology in Mental Retardation, 14,* 3–4.

Amoss, P.T., & Harrell, S. (1981). Introduction: An anthropological perspective on aging. In P.T. Amoss, & S. Harrell (Eds.), *Other ways of growing old* (pp. 1–24). Stanford, CA: Stanford University Press.

Anastasi, A. (1990). *Psychological testing.* (6th ed.). New York: Macmillan.

Anderson, B.J., & Wolf, F.M. (1986). Chronic physical illness and sexual behavior: Psychological issues. *Journal of Consulting and Clinical Psychology, 54,* 168–175.

Anderson, B.L. (1983). Primary orgasmic dysfunction: Diagnostic considerations and review of treatment. *Psychological Bulletin, 93,* 105–136.

Anderson, G.M., & Hoshino, Y. (1987). Neurochemical studies of autism. In D.J. Cohen, A.M. Donnellan, & R. Paul (Eds.), *Handbook of autism and pervasive developmental disorders* (pp. 166–191). New York: Wiley.

Anderson, L.P. (1991). Acculturative stress: A theory of relevance to black Americans. *Clinical Psychology Review, 11,* 685–702

Anderson, N.B., Lane, J.D., Taguchi, F., & Williams, R.B. (1989). Patterns of cardiovascular responses to stress as a function of race and parental hypertension in men. *Health Psychology, 8,* 525–540.

Andreasen, N.C. (1979). Thought, language, and communication disorders: II. Diagnostic significance. *Archives of General Psychiatry, 36,* 1325–1330.

Andreasen, N.C., Flaum, M., Swayze, V.W., Tyrrell, G., & Arndt, S. (1990). Positive and negative symptoms in schizophrenia: A critical reappraisal. *Archives of General Psychiatry, 47,* 615–621.

Andreasen, N.C., & Olsen, S.A. (1982). Negative versus positive schizophrenia. Definition and validation. *Archives of General Psychiatry, 39,* 789–794.

Andreasen, N.C., Olsen, S.A., Dennert, J. W., & Smith, M.R. (1982). Ventricular enlargement in schizophrenia: Relationship to positive and negative symptoms. *American Journal of Psychiatry, 139,* 297–302.

Andreasen, N.C., Rice, J., Endicott, J., Coryell, W., Grove, W.W., & Reich, T. (1987). Familial rates of affective disorder. *Archives of General Psychiatry, 44,* 461–472.

Andreasen, N.C., Swayze, V.W., Flaum, M. et al. (1990). Ventricular enlargement in schizophrenia evaluated with computed tomographic scanning: Effects of gender, age, and stage of illness. *Archives of General Psychiatry, 47,* 1008–1015.

Andress, V.R., & Corey, D.M. (1978). Survivor-victims: Who discovers or witnesses suicide? *Psychological Reports, 42,* 759–764.

Angier, N. (1990). Diagnosis of Alzheimer's is no matter of certainty. *The New York Times, 89,* p. A16.

Angrist, B., Lee, H.K., & Gershon, S. (1974). The antagonism of amphetamine-induced symptomatology by a neuroleptic. *American Journal of Psychiatry, 131,* 817–819.

Aniline, O., & Pitts, F.N., Jr. (1982). Phencyclidine (PCP): A review and perspectives. *CRC Critical Review of Toxicology, 10,* 145–177.

Anthony-Bergstone, C., Zarit, S.H., & Gatz, M. (1988). Symptoms of psychological distress among caregivers of dementia patients. *Psychology and Aging, 3,* 245–248.

Antoni, M.H., Schneiderman, N., Fletcher, M.A., Goldstein, D.A., Ironson, G., & Laperriere, A. (1990). Psychoneuroimmunology and HIV-1. *Journal of Consulting and Clinical Psychology, 58,* 38–49.

Appelbaum, P.S. (1985). *Tarasoff* and the clinician: Problems in fulfilling the duty to protect. *American Journal of Psychiatry, 142,* 425–429.

Appley, M., & Trumball, R. (1967). *Psychological Stress.* New York: Appleton-Century-Crofts.

Aragone, J., Cassady, J., & Drabman, R.S. (1975). Treating overweight children through parental training and contingency contracting. *Journal of Applied Behavior Analysis, 8,* 269–278.

Ard, B.N., Jr. (1977). Sex in lasting marriages: A longitudinal study. *Journal of Sex Research, 13,* 274–285.

Arieti, S. (1979). New views on the psychodynamics of phobias. *American Journal of Psychotherapy, 33,* 82–95.

Arkonac, O., & Guze, S.B. (1963). A family study of hysteria. *New England Journal of Medicine, 268,* 239–242.

Arkowitz, H. (1989). The role of theory in psychotherapy integration. *Journal of Integrative and Eclectic Psychotherapy, 8,* 8–16.

Arkowitz, H. (1992). Integrative theories of therapy. In D. Freedheim (Ed.), *The history of psychotherapy: A century of change.* Washington, DC: American Psychological Association.

Armor, D.J., Polich, J.M., & Stambul, H.B. (1978). *Alcoholism and treatment.* New York: Wiley.

Arndt, I.O., Dorozynsky, L., Woody, G.E., McLellan, A.T., & O'Brien, C.P. (1992). Desipramine treatment of cocaine dependence in methadone-maintained patients. *Archives of General Psychiatry, 49,* 888–893.

Arnetz, B.B., Wasserman, J., Petrini, B., Brenner, S.O., Levy, L., Eneroth, P., Salovaara, H., Lalovaara, L., Theorell, T., & Petterson, L.L. (1987). Immune function in unemployed women. *Psychosomatic Medicine, 49,* 3–12.

Aronson, E. (1972). *The social animal.* San Francisco: Freeman.

Aronson, E., & Carlsmith, J.R. (1968). Experimentation in social psychology. In G. Lindzey & E. Aronson (Eds.), *The handbook of social psychology: Vol 2. Research methods.* Menlo Park, CA: Addison-Wesley.

Ascher, L.M., & Turner, R.M. (1979). Paradoxical intention and insomnia: An experimental investigation. *Behaviour Research and Therapy, 17,* 408–411.

Atchley, R. (1980). Aging and suicide: Reflection of the quality of life. In S. Haynes & M. Feinleib (Eds.), *Proceedings of the Second Conference on the Epidemiology of Aging.* National Institute of Health, Washington, DC: U.S. Government Printing Office.

Atkeson, B.M., Calhoun, K.S., Resick, P.A., & Ellis, E.M. (1982). Victims of rape: Repeated assessment of depressive symptoms. *Journal of Consulting and Clinical Psychology, 50,* 96–102.

Atkinson, D.R., Maruyama, M., & Matsui, S. (1978). The effects of counselor race and counseling approach on Asian Americans' perception of counselor credibility and utility. *Journal of Counseling Psychology, 25,* 76–83.

Atkinson, D.R., Winzelberg, A., & Holland, A. (1985). Ethnicity, locus of control for family planning, and pregnancy counselor credibility. *Journal of Counseling Psychology, 32,* 417–421.

Atkinson, R.C., & Shiffrin, R.M. (1969). Human memory: A proposed system and its control processes. In K.W. Spence & J.T. Spence (Eds.), *The psychology of learning and motivation: Advances in research and theory* (Vol. 2). New York: Academic Press.

August, G.J., Stewart, M.A., & Tsai, L. (1981). The incidence of cognitive disabilities in siblings of autistic children. *British Journal of Psychiatry, 138,* 416–422.

Austin, L.S., Lydiard, R.B., Forey, M.D., & Zealberg, J.J. (1990). Panic and phobic disorders in patients with obsessive personality disorder. *Journal of Clinical Psychiatry, 51,* 456–458.

Axline, V.M. (1964). *Dibs: In search of self.* New York: Ballantine.

Ayllon, T., & Azrin, N.H. (1968). *The token economy: A motivational system for therapy and rehabilitation.* New York: Appleton-Century-Crofts.

Azrin, N.H. (1976). Improvements in the community-reinforcement approach to alcoholism. *Behaviour Research and Therapy, 14,* 339–348.

Azrin, N.H., Sisson, R.W., Meyers, R., & Godley, M. (1982). Alcoholism treatment by disulfiram and community reinforcement therapy. *Journal of Behaviour Therapy and Experimental Psychiatry, 13,* 105–112.

Azrin, N.H., Sneed, T.J., & Foxx, R.M. (1973). Dry bed: A rapid method of eliminating bedwetting (enuresis) of the retarded. *Behaviour Research and Therapy, 11,* 427–434.

Bach, G.R. (1966). The marathon group: Intensive practice of intimate interactions. *Psychological Reports, 181,* 995–1002.

Badian, N.A. (1983). Dyscalculia and nonverbal disorders of learning. In H.R. Myklebust (Ed.), *Progress in learning disabilities* (Vol. 5). New York: Grune & Stratton.

Baer, J.S., & Lichtenstein, E. (1988). Cognitive assessment. In D.M. Donovan, & G.A. Marlatt (Eds.), *Assessment of addictive behaviors* (pp. 189–213). New York: Guilford.

Baer, L. et al. (1990). Standardized assessment of personality disorders in obsessive compulsive disorder. *Archives of General Psychiatry, 47,* 826–831.

Baker, T., & Brandon, T.H. (1988). Behavioral treatment strategies. In *A report of the Surgeon General: The health consequences of smoking: Nicotine addiction.* Rockville, MD: U.S. Department of Health and Human Services.

Bakwin, H. (1973). The genetics of enuresis. In J. Kolvin, R.C. MacKeith, & S.R. Meadow (Eds.), *Enuresis and encopresis.* Philadelphia: Lippincott.

Ball, J.C., & Chambers, C.D. (Eds.). (1970). *The epidemiology of opiate addiction in the United States.* Springfield, IL: Charles C. Thomas.

Ballenger, J.C., Burrows, G.O., DuPont, R.L., Lesser, M., Noyes, R.C., Pecknold, J.C., Rifkin, A., & Swinson, R.P. (1988). Aprazolam in panic disorder and agoraphobia, results from multicenter trial. *Archives of General Psychiatry, 45,* 413–421.

Baller, W.R. (1975). *Bed-wetting: Origin and treatment.* Elmsford, NY: Pergamon.

Ball-Rokeach, S.J., Rokeach, M., & Grube, J.W. (1984). *The great American values test.* New York: Free Press.

Baltes, M.M. (1988). The etiology and maintenance of dependency in the elderly: Three phases of operant research. *Behavior Therapy, 19,* 301–319.

Bancroft, J.H. (1989). *Human sexuality and its problems* (2nd ed.). Edinburgh: Churchill Livingston.

Bancroft, J.H., Jones, G.H., & Pullan, B.R. (1966). A simple transducer for measuring penile erections, with comments on its use in the treatment of sexual disorders. *Behaviour Research and Therapy, 4,* 239–241.

Bancroft, J.H., & Bell, C. (1985). Simultaneous recording of penile diameter and penile arterial pulse during laboratory-based erotic stimulation in normal subjects. *Journal of Psychosomatic Research, 29,* 303–313.

Bandura, A. (1969). *Principles of behavior modification.* New York: Holt, Rinehart & Winston.

Bandura, A. (1973). *Aggression: A social learning analysis.* Englewood Cliffs, NJ: Prentice-Hall.

Bandura, A. (1977). Self-efficacy: Toward a unifying theory of behavioral change. *Psychological Review, 84,* 191–215.

Bandura, A. (1982). The psychology of chance encounters. *American Psychologist, 37,* 747–755.

Bandura, A. (1986). *Social foundations of thought and action: A social cognitive theory.* Englewood Cliffs, NJ: Prentice-Hall.

Bandura, A., Blanchard, E.B., & Ritter, B. (1969). Relative efficacy of desensitization and modeling approaches for inducing behavioral, affective, and attitudinal changes. *Journal of Personality and Social Psychology, 13,* 173–199.

Bandura, A., Grusec, J.E., & Menlove, F.L. (1967). Vicarious extinction of avoidance behavior. *Journal of Personality and Social Psychology, 5,* 16–23.

Bandura, A., Jeffrey, R.W., & Bachicha, D.L. (1974). Analysis of memory codes and cumulative rehearsal in observational learning. *Journal of Research in Personality, 7,* 295–305.

Bandura, A., & Menlove, F.L. (1968). Factors determining vicarious extinction of avoidance behavior through symbolic modeling. *Journal of Personality and Social Psychology, 8,* 99–108.

Bandura, A., & Perloff, B. (1967). Relative efficacy of self-monitored and externally imposed reinforcement systems. *Journal of Personality and Social Psychology, 7,* 111–116.

Bandura, A., & Rosenthal, T.L. (1966). Vicarious classical conditioning as a function of arousal level. *Journal of Personality and Social Psychology, 3,* 54–62.

Bandura, A., & Walters, R.H. (1959). *Adolescent aggression.* New York: Ronald Press.

Bandura, A., & Walters, R.H. (1963). *Social learning and personality development.* New York: Holt, Rinehart & Winston.

Banis, H.T., Varni, J.W., Wallander, J.L., Korsch, B.M., Jay, S.M., Adler, R., Garcia-Temple, E., & Negrete, V. (1988). Psychological and social adjustment of obese children and their families. *Child: Care, Health, and Development, 14,* 157–173.

Barabee, H.E., Marshall, W.L., & Lanthier, R. (1979). Deviant sexual arousal in rapists. *Behaviour Research and Therapy, 17,* 215–222.

Barabee, H.E., Marshall, W.L., Yates, E., & Lightfoot, L. (1983). Alcohol intoxication and deviant sexual arousal in male social drinkers. *Behaviour Research and Therapy, 21,* 365–373.

Barber, T.X., & Silver, M.J. (1968). Fact, fiction, and the experimenter bias effect. *Psychological Bulletin, Monograph Supplement, 70,* 1–29.

Barefoot, J.C. et al. (1991). Hostility patterns and health implications: Correlates of Cook-Medley hostility scale scores in a national survey. *Health Psychology, 10,* 18–24.

Barefoot, J.C., Dahlstrom, G., & Williams, R.B. (1983). Hostility, CHD incidence, and total mortality: A 25-year follow-up study of 255 physicians. *Psychosomatic Medicine, 45,* 59–63.

Barkley, R.A. (1981). *Hyperactive children: A handbook for diagnosis and treatment.* New York: Guilford.

Barkley, R.A. (1990). *Attention-deficit hyperactivity disorder: A handbook for diagnosis and treatment.* New York: Guilford.

Barkley, R.A., & Cunningham, C.E. (1979). The effects of methylphenidate on the mother–child interactions of hyperactive children. *Archives of General Psychiatry, 36,* 201–208.

Barkley, R.A., DuPaul, G.J., & McMurray, M.B. (1990). A comprehensive evaluation of attention deficit disorder with and without hyperactivity defined by research criteria. *Journal of Consulting and Clinical Psychology, 58,* 775–789.

Barkley, R.A., Fischer, M., Edelbrock, C.S., & Smallish, L. (1990). The adolescent outcome of hyperactive children diagnosed by research criteria: I. An 8 year prospective follow-up study. *Journal of the American Academy of Child and Adolescent Psychiatry, 29,* 546–557.

Barkley, R.A., Grodzinsky, G., & DuPaul, G.J. (1992). Frontal lobe functions in attention deficit disorder with and without hyperactivity: A review and research report. *Journal of Abnormal Child Psychology, 20,* 163–188.

Barkley, R.A., Karlsson, J., & Pollard, S. (1985). Effects of age on the mother-child interactions of hyperactive children. *Journal of Abnormal Child Psychology, 13,* 631–638.

Barlow, D.H. (1986). Causes of sexual dysfunction: The role of anxiety and cognitive interference. *Journal of Consulting and Clinical Psychology, 54,* 140–148.

Barlow, D.H. (1988). *Anxiety and its disorders: The nature and treatment of anxiety and panic.* New York: Guilford.

Barlow, D.H., Abel, G.G., & Blanchard, E.B. (1979). Gender identity change in transsexuals. *Archives of General Psychiatry, 36,* 1001–1007.

Barlow, D.H., Becker, R., Leitenberg, H., & Agras, W.S. (1970). A mechanical strain gauge for recording penile circumference. *Journal of Applied Behavior Analysis, 3,* 73–76.

Barlow, D.H., Blanchard, E.B., Vermilyea, J.A., Vermilyea, B.B., & DiNardo, P.A. (1986). Generalized anxiety and generalized anxiety disorder: Description and reconceptualization. *American Journal of Psychiatry, 143,* 40–44.

Barlow, D.H., Cohen, A.B., Waddell, M.T., Vermilyea, B.B., Klosko, J.S., Blanchard, E.B., & DiNardo, P.A. (1984). Panic and generalized anxiety disorders: Nature and treatment. *Behavior Therapy, 15,* 431–449.

Barlow, D.H., Reynolds, E.J., & Agras, W.S. (1973). Gender identity change in a transsexual. *Archives of General Psychiatry, 29,* 569–576.

Barlow, D.H., Sakheim, D.K., & Beck, J.G. (1983). Anxiety increases sexual arousal. *Journal of Abnormal Psychology, 92,* 49–54.

Barlow, D.H., & Waddell, M.T. (1985). Agoraphobia. In D.H. Barlow (Ed.), *Clinical handbook of psychological disorders.* New York: Guilford.

Baron, M., Gershon, E.S., Rudy, V., Jonas, W.Z., & Buchsbaum, M. (1975). Lithium carbonate response in depression. *Archives of General Psychiatry, 32,* 1107–1111.

Baron, M., Levitt, M., Gruen, R. et al. (1984). Platelet monoamine oxidase activity and genetic vulnerability to schizophrenia. *American Journal of Psychiatry, 141,* 836–842.

Baron, M., Risch, N., Levitt, M., & Gruen, R. (1985). Familial transmission of schizotypal and borderline personality disorders. *American Journal of Psychiatry, 142,* 927–934.

Baron, R.A., & Byrne, D. (1977). *Social psychology: Understanding human interaction* (2nd ed.). Boston: Allyn & Bacon.

Barr, C.E., Mednick, S.A., & Munk-Jorgensen, P. (1990). Exposure to influenza epidemics during gestation and adult schizophrenia: A 40-year study. *Archives of General Psychiatry, 47,* 869–874.

Barrett, C.L., Hampe, E., & Miller, L. (1978). Research on psychotherapy with children. In S.L. Garfield & A.E. Bergin (Eds.), *Handbook of psychotherapy and behavior change: An empirical analysis* (2nd ed.). New York: Wiley.

Bartlett, F. (1932). *Remembering.* Cambridge: Cambridge University Press.

Bartzokis, G., Liberman, R.P., & Hierholzer, R. (1990). Behavior therapy in groups. In I.L. Kutash & A. Wolf (Eds.), *The group psychotherapist's handbook: Contemporary theory and technique.* New York: Columbia University Press.

Basedow, H. (1925). *The Australian aboriginal.* London: Adelaide.

Basmajian, J.V. (1977). Learned control of single motor units. In G.E. Schwartz & J. Beatty (Eds.), *Biofeedback: Theory and research.* New York: Academic Press.

Bastani, B., Nash, J.F., & Meltzer, H.Y. (1990). Prolactin and cortisol responses to MK-212, a serotonin agonist, in obsessive compulsive disorder. *Archives of General Psychiatry, 47,* 833–839.

Bates, G.W. (1990). *Social anxiety and self-presentation: Conversational behaviours and articulated thoughts of heterosexually anxious males.* Unpublished doctoral dissertation, University of Melbourne, Australia.

Bates, G.W., Campbell, T.M., & Burgess, P.M. (1990). Assessment of articulated thoughts in social anxiety: Modification of the ATSS procedure. *British Journal of Clinical Psychology, 29,* 91–98.

Bateson, G., Jackson, D.D., Haley, J., & Weakland, J. (1956). Toward a theory of schizophrenia. *Behavioral Science, 1,* 251–264.

Baucom, D.H., & Hoffman, J.A. (1986). The effectiveness of marital therapy: Current status and application to the clinical setting. In N.S. Jacobson & A.S. Gurman (Eds.), *Clinical handbook of marital therapy* (pp. 597–620). New York: Guilford.

Baucom, D.H., & Lester, G.W. (1986). The usefulness of cognitive restructuring as an adjunct to behavioral marital therapy. *Behavior Therapy, 17,* 385–403.

Baumeister, A.A. (1984). Some methodological and conceptual issues in the study of cognitive processes with retarded people. In P.H. Brooks, R. Sperber, & C. McCauley (Eds.), *Learning and cognition in the mentally retarded.* Hillsdale, NJ: Erlbaum.

Baumeister, R.F. (1990). Suicide as escape from self. *Psychological Review, 97,* 90–113.

Baumgartner, G.R., & Rowen, R.C. (1987). Clonidine vs. chlordiazepoxide in the management of acute alcohol withdrawal. *Archives of Internal Medicine, 147,* 1223–1226.

Baxter, D.J., Marshall, W.L., Barabee, H.E., Davidson, P.R., & Malcolm, P.B. (1984). Deviant sexual behavior: Differentiating sex offenders by criminal and personal history, psychometric measures, and sexual response. *Criminal Justice and Behavior, 11,* 477–501.

Baxter, E., & Hopper, K. (1981). *Private lives/public places: Homeless adults on the streets of New York City.* New York: Community Service Society.

Baxter, L.R., Schwartz, J.M., Bergman, K.S., Szuba, M.P., Guze, B.H., Mazziotta, J.C., Alazraki, A., Selin, C.E., Ferng, H., Munford, P., & Phelps, M.E. (1992). Caudate glucose metabolic rate changes with both drug and behavior therapy for obsessive-compulsive disorder. *Archives of General Psychiatry, 49,* 681–689.

Beach, S.R.H., & O'Leary, K.D. (1986). The treatment of depression occurring in the context of marital discord. *Behavior Therapy, 17,* 43–49.

Beck, A.T. (1967). *Depression: Clinical, experimental and theoretical aspects.* New York: Harper & Row.

Beck, A.T. (1976). *Cognitive therapy and the emotional disorders.* New York: International Universities Press.

Beck, A.T. (1986a). Cognitive therapy: A sign of retrogression or progress. *The Behavior Therapist, 9,* 2–3.

Beck, A.T. (1986b). Hopelessness as a predictor of eventual suicide. In J.J. Mann & M. Stanley (Eds.), *Psychobiology of suicidal behavior.* New York: New York Academy of Sciences.

Beck, A.T. (1987). Cognitive models of depression. *Journal of Cognitive Psychotherapy: An International Quarterly, 1,* 5–37.

Beck, A.T., Brown, G., Berchick, R.J., Stewart, B.L., & Steer, R.A. (1990). Relationship between hopelessness and ultimate suicide: A replication with psychiatric outpatients. *American Journal of Psychiatry, 147,* 190–195.

Beck, A.T., Brown, G., Steer, R.A., Eidelson, J.I., & Riskind, J.H. (1987). Differentiating anxiety and depression: A test of the cognitive-content-specificity hypothesis. *Journal of Abnormal Psychology, 96,* 179–183.

Beck, A.T., & Emery, G. (1985). *Anxiety disorders and phobias: A cognitive perspective.* New York: Basic Books.

Beck, A.T., Kovacs, M., & Weissman, A. (1975). Hopelessness and suicidal behavior: An overview. *Journal of the American Medical Association, 234,* 1146–1149.

Beck, A.T., Kovacs, M., & Weissman, A. (1979). Assessment of suicidal ideation: The Scale for Suicide Ideation. *Journal of Consulting and Clinical Psychology, 47,* 343–352.

Beck, A.T., Rush, AJ., Shaw, B.F., & Emery, G. (1979). *Cognitive therapy of depression.* New York: Guilford.

Beck, A.T., Schuyler, D., & Herman, I. (1974). Development of suicidal intent scales. In A.T. Beck, H.L.P. Resnik, & D.J. Lettieri (Eds.), *The prediction of suicide.* Bowie, MD: Charles Press.

Beck, A.T., Steer, R.A., Kovacs, M., & Garrison, B. (1985). Hopelessness and eventual suicide: A 10-year prospective study of patients hospitalized with suicidal ideation. *American Journal of Psychiatry, 142,* 559–563.

Beck, A.T., & Ward, C.H. (1961). Dreams of depressed patients: Characteristic themes in manifest content. *Archives of General Psychiatry, 5,* 462–467.

Beck, A.T., Ward, C.H., Mendelson, M., Mock, J.E., & Erbaugh, J.K. (1962). Reliability of psychiatric diagnosis: II. A study of consistency of clinical judgments and ratings. *American Journal of Psychiatry, 119,* 351–357.

Beck, J.G., Barlow, D.H., Sakheim, D.K., & Abrahamson, DJ. (1984). *Sexual responding during anxiety: Clinical versus nonclinical patterns.* Paper presented at the 18th Annual Convention of the Association for Advancement of Behavior Therapy, Philadelphia. As cited in Barlow (1986).

Beck, M. (1979, November 12). Viet vets fight back. Newsweek, pp. 44–49.

Becker, J.V. (1988). Adolescent sex offenders. *The Behavior Therapist, 11,* 185–187.

Bedell, J.R., Archer, R.P., & Marlow, H.A. (1980). A description and evaluation of a problem-solving skills training program. In D. Upper & S.M. Ross (Eds.), *Behavioral group therapy: An annual review* (pp. 3–35). Champaign, IL: Research Press.

Bednar, R.L., & Kaul, T.J. (in press). Experiential group research: Can the canon fire? In A.E. Bergin & S.L. Garfield (Eds.), *Handbook of psychotherapy and behavior change* (4th ed.). New York: Wiley.

Beecher, H.K. (1966). Ethics and clinical research. *New England Journal of Medicine, 274,* 1354–1360.

Begelman, D.A. (1975). Ethical and legal issues of behavior modification. In M. Hersen, R. Eisler, & P.M. Miller (Eds.), *Progress in behavior modification.* New York: Academic Press.

Beidel, D.C. (1991). Social phobia and overanxious disorder in school-age children. *Journal of the American Academy of Child and Adolescent Psychiatry, 30,* 545–552.

Bell, J.E. (1961). *Family group therapy.* Washington, DC: U.S. Department of Health, Education, and Welfare.

Bellack, A.S., Hersen, M., & Turner, S.M. (1976). Generalization effects of social skills training in chronic schizophrenics: An experimental analysis. *Behavior Research and Therapy, 14,* 391–398.

Bell-Dolan, D.J., Last, C.G., & Strauss, C.C. (1990). Symptoms of anxiety disorders in normal children. *Journal of the American Academy of Child and Adolescent Psychiatry, 29,* 759–765.

Bem, D.J., & Allen, A. (1974). On predicting some of the people some of the time: The search for cross-situational consistencies in behavior. *Psychological Review, 81,* 506–520.

Bem, S.L. (1974). The measurement of psychological androgyny. *Journal of Consulting and Clinical Psychology, 42,* 155–162.

Bem, S.L. (1984). Gender schema theory and its implications for child development: Raising gender-aschematic children in a gender-schematic society. *Signs: Journal of Women in Culture and Society, 8,* 598–616.

Bemis, K.M. (1978). Current approaches to the etiology and treatment of anorexia nervosa. *Psychological Bulletin, 85,* 593–617.

Bender, L., & Blau, A. (1937). The reactions of children to sexual relations with adults. *American Journal of Orthopsychiatry, 7,* 500–518.

Bennett, C.C., Anderson, L.S., Cooper, S., Hassol, L., Klein, D.C., & Rosenblum, G. (Eds.). (1966). *Community psychology: A report of the Boston Conference on the education of psychologists for community mental health.* Boston: Boston University Press.

Bennett, I. (1960). *Delinquent and neurotic children.* London: Tavistock.

Bennett, W. (1980). The nicotine fix. *Harvard Magazine, 82,* 10–14.

Benowitz, N.L., & Jacob, P., III. (1984). Daily intake of nicotine during cigarette smoking. *Clinical Pharmacology Therapeutics, 35,* 499–504.

Ben-Porath, Y.S., & Butcher, J.N. (1989). The comparability of MMPI and MMPI-2 scales and profiles. *Psychological Assessment, 1,* 345–347.

Benson, H. (1975). *The relaxation response.* New York: Morrow.

Benson, H., Beary, J.F., & Carl, M.P. (1974). The relaxation response. *Psychiatry, 37,* 37.

Ben-Tovim, M.V., & Crisp, A.H. (1979). Personality and mental state within anorexia nervosa. *Journal of Psychosomatic Research, 23,* 321–325.

Berger, K.S., & Zarit, S.H. (1978). Late life paranoid states: Assessment and treatment. *American Journal of Orthopsychiatry, 48,* 528–537.

Bergin, A.E. (1971). The evaluation of therapeutic outcomes. In A.E. Bergin & S.L. Garfield (Eds.), *Handbook of psychotherapy and behavior change: An empirical analysis.* New York: Wiley.

Bergin, A.E., & Lambert, M.J. (1978). The evaluation of therapeutic outcomes. In S.L. Garfield & A.E. Bergin (Eds.), *Handbook of psychotherapy and behavior change: An empirical analysis* (2nd ed.). New York: Wiley.

Bergman, J.D., Dykens, E., Watson, M., Ort, S.I., & Leckman, J.F. (1987). Fragile-X syndrome: Variability of phenotypic expression. *Journal of the American Academy of Child and Adolescent Psychiatry, 26,* 463–467.

Berlin, F.S., & Meinecke, C.F. (1981). Treatment of sex offenders with antiandrogenic medication: Conceptualization, review of treatment modalities, and preliminary findings. *American Journal of Psychiatry, 138,* 601–607.

Berman, E.M., & Lief, H.I. (1976). Sex and the aging process. In W.W. Oaks, G.A. Melchiode, & I. Ficher (Eds.), *Sex and the life cycle.* New York: Grune & Stratton.

Bernstein, D.A., & Nietzel, M.T. (1980). *Introduction to clinical psychology.* New York: McGraw-Hill.

Berrettini, W.H., Goldin, L.R., Gelernter, J. et al. (1990). X-chromosome markers and manic-depressive illness: Rejection of linkage to Xq28 in nine bipolar pedigrees. *Archives of General Psychiatry, 47,* 366–373.

Berry, J.C. (1967). *Antecedents of schizophrenia, impulsive character and alcoholism in males.* Paper presented at the 75th Annual Convention of the American Psychological Association, Washington, DC.

Besdine, R.W. (1980). Geriatric medicine: An overview. In C. Eisodorfer (Ed.), *Annual review of gerontology and geriatrics.* New York: Springer.

Betancourt, H., & Lopez, S.R. (in press). The study of culture, ethnicity, and race in American psychology. *American Psychologist.*

Bettelheim, B. (1967). *The empty fortress.* New York: Free Press.

Bettelheim, B. (1969). *Children of the dream.* London: Collier-Macmillan.

Bettelheim, B. (1973). Bringing up children. *Ladies Homes Journal, 90,* 28.

Bettelheim, B. (1974). *A home for the heart.* New York: Knopf.

Beutler, L.E. (1979). Toward specific psychological therapies for specific conditions. *Journal of Consulting and Clinical Psychology, 47*, 882–897.

Beutler, L.E. (1983). *Eclectic psychotherapy: A systematic approach.* New York: Pergamon.

Beutler, L.E. (1990). Introduction to the special series on advances in psychotherapy research. *Journal of Consulting and Clinical Psychology, 58*, 263–264.

Beutler, L.E., Crago, M., & Arizmendi, T.G. (1986). Therapist variables in psychotherapy process and outcome. In S.L. Garfield & A.E. Bergin (Eds.), *Handbook of psychotherapy and behavior change* (3rd ed.). New York: Wiley.

Beutler, L.E., Scogin, F., Kirkish, P., Schretlen, D., Corbishley, A., Hamblin, D., Beutler, L., & Crago, M. (Eds.). (1991). *Psychotherapy research.* Washington, DC: American Psychological Association.

Beutler, L.E. (1991). Have all won and must all have prizes? Revisiting Luborsky et al.'s verdict. *Journal of Consulting and Clinical Psychology, 59*, 226–232.

Bieber, I., Dain, H.J., Dince, P.R., Drellich, M.G., Grand, H.C., Gundlach, R.H., Kremer, M.W., Rifkin, A.H., Wilbur, C.B., & Bieber, T.B. (1962). *Homosexuality: A psychoanalytical study.* New York: Random House.

Biederman, J., Rivinus, T.M., Herzog, D.B., Ferber, R.A., Harper, G.P., Orsulak, P.J., Harmatz, J.S., & Schildkraut, J.J. (1984). Platelet MAO activity in anorexia nervosa patients with and without a major depressive disorder. *American Journal of Psychiatry, 141*, 1244–1247.

Billings, A. (1979). Conflict resolution in distressed and nondistressed married couples. *Journal of Consulting and Clinical Psychology, 47*, 368–376.

Billings, A.G., Cronkite, R.C., & Moos, R.H. (1983). Social-environmental factors in unipolar depression: Comparisons of depressed patients and nondepressed controls. *Journal of Abnormal Psychology, 92*, 119–133.

Bion, W. (1959). *Experiences in groups.* New York: Basic Books.

Birbaumer, H. (1977). Biofeedback training: A critical review of its clinical applications and some possible future directions. *European Journal of Behavioral Analysis and Modification, 4*, 235–251.

Birnbaum, M. (1960). The right to treatment. *American Bar Association Journal, 46*, 499–505.

Birren, J.E., & Sloane, R.B. (Eds.). (1980). *Handbook of mental health and aging.* Englewood Cliffs, NJ: Prentice-Hall.

Bisette, G., Smith, W.H., Dole, K.C., Crain, B., Ghanbari, B., Miller, B., & Nemeroff, C.B. (1991). Alterations in Alzheimer's disease-associated protein in Alzheimer's disease frontal and temporal cortex. *Archives of General Psychiatry, 48*, 1009–1011.

Bitterman, M.E. (1975). Issues in the comparative psychology of learning. In R.B. Masterson, M.E. Bitterman, C.B.G. Campbell, & N. Hotten (Eds.), *The evolution of brain and behavior in vertebrates.* Hillsdale, NJ: Erlbaum.

Bjorkqvist, S.E. (1975). Clonidine in alcohol withdrawal. *Acta Psychiatrica Scandinavica, 52*, 256–263.

Blackburn, I.M., Eunson, K.M., & Bishop, S. (1986). A two-year naturalistic follow-up of depressed patients treated with cognitive therapy, pharmacotherapy, and a combination of both. *Journal of Affective Disorders, 10*, 67–75.

Blader, J.C., & Marshall, W.L. (1989). Is assessment of sexual arousal in rapists worthwhile? A critique of current methods and the development of a response compatibility approach. *Clinical Psychology Review, 9*, 569–587.

Blagg, N.R. & Yule, W. (1984). The behavioural treatment of school refusal: A comparative study. *Behaviour Research and Therapy, 22*, 119–127.

Blake, W. (1973). The influence of race on diagnosis. *Smith College Studies in Social Work, 43*, 184–192.

Blanchard, E.B., Andrasik, F., Neff, D.F., Arena, J.G., Ashles, T.A., Jurish, S.E., Pallmeyer, T.P., Saunders, N.L., & Teders, S.J. (1982). Biofeedback and relaxation training with three kinds of headache: Treatment effects and their prediction. *Journal of Consulting and Clinical Psychology, 50*, 562–575.

Blanchard, E.B., McCoy, G.C., Musso, A., Gerardi, M.A., Pallmeyer, T.P., Gerardi, R.J., Cotch, P.A., Siracusa, K., & Andrasik, F. (1986). A controlled comparison of thermal biofeedback and relaxation training in the treatment of essential hypertension: I. Short-term and long-term outcome. *Behavior Therapy, 17*, 563–579.

Blanchard, E.B., Miller, S.T., Abel, G.G., Haynes, M.R., & Wicker, R. (1979). Evaluation of biofeedback in the treatment of borderline essential hypertension. *Journal of Applied Behavior Analysis, 12*, 99–109.

Blanchard, E.B., Theobald, E.E., Williamson, D.A., Silver, B.V., & Brown, D.A. (1978). Temperature biofeedback in the treatment of migraine headaches: A controlled evaluation. *Archives of General Psychiatry, 35*, 581–588.

Bland, K., & Hallam, R. (1981). Relationship between response to graded exposure and marital satisfaction in agoraphobics. *Behaviour Research and Therapy, 19*, 335–338.

Blatt, B. (1966). The preparation of special educational personnel. *Review of Educational Research, 36*, 151–161.

Blau, Z.S., Oser, G.T., & Stephens, R.C. (1979). Aging, social class, and ethnicity: A comparison of Anglo, Black, and Mexican-American Texans. *Pacific Sociological Review, 22*, 501–525.

Blazer, D., Hughes, D., & George, L.K. (1987). Stressful life events and the onset of a generalized anxiety syndrome. *American Journal of Psychiatry, 144*, 1178–1183.

Blazer, D.G. (1982a). *Depression in late life.* St. Louis: Mosby.

Blazer, D.G. (1982b). Social support and mortality in an elderly community population. *American Journal of Epidemiology, 115*, 684–694.

Blazer, D.G., Bachar, J.R., & Manton, K.G. (1986). Suicide in late life: Review and commentary. *Journal of the American Geriatrics Society, 34*, 519–525.

Blazer, D.G., & Siegler, I.C. (1984). *A family approach to health care of the elderly.* Menlo Park, CA: Addison-Wesley.

Blazer, D.G., & Williams, C.D. (1980). Epidemiology of dysphoria and depression in the elderly population. *American Journal of Psychiatry, 137*, 439–444.

Blehar, M.C., & Rosenthal, N.E. (1989). Seasonal affective disorders and phototherapy: Report of a National Institute of Mental Health-sponsored workshop. *Archives of General Psychiatry, 46*, 469–474.

Blenker, M. (1967). Environmental change and the aging individual. *Gerontologist, 7*, 101–105.

Bleuler, E. (1923). *Lehrbuch der Psychiatrie* (4th ed.). Berlin: Springer.

Bliss, E.L. (1980). Multiple personalities: A report of 14 cases with implications for schizophrenia and hysteria. *Archives of General Psychiatry, 37*, 1388–1397.

Bliss, E.L. (1983). Multiple personalities, related disorders, and hypnosis. *American Journal of Clinical Hypnosis, 26*, 114–123.

Bliwise, D., Carskadon, M., Carey, E., & Dement, W. (1984). Longitudinal development of sleep-related respiratory disturbance in adult humans. *Journal of Gerontology, 39*, 290–293.

Block, A.P. (1990). Rape trauma syndrome as scientific expert testimony. *Archives of Sexual Behavior, 19*, 309–323.

Block, J. (1971). *Lives through time.* Berkeley, CA: Bancroft Books.

Bloomfield, H.H. (1973). Assertive training in an outpatient group of chronic schizophrenics: A preliminary report. *Behavior Therapy, 4*, 277–281.

Blowers, C., Cobb, J., & Mathews, A. (1987). Generalized anxiety: A controlled treatment study. *Behaviour Research and Therapy, 25*, 493–502.

Blumenthal, J.A., Williams, R.B., Kong, Y., Schanberg, S.M., & Thompson, I.W. (1978). Type A behavior and angiographically documented coronary disease. *Circulation, 58*, 634–639.

Bockhoven, J. (1963). *Moral treatment in American psychiatry*. New York: Springer.

Boesch, E. (1977). Authority and work attitude of Thais. In K. Wenk & K. Rosenburg (Eds.), *Thai in German eyes* (pp. 176–231). Bangkok: Kledthai.

Bohman, M., Cloninger R.C., Sigvardsson, S., & Knorring, A. von. (1982). Predisposition to criminality in Swedish adoptees: I. Genetic and environmental heterogeneity. *Archives of General Psychology, 39*, 1233–1241.

Boll, T.J. (1985). Developing issues in clinical neuropsychology. *Journal of Clinical and Experimental Neuropsychology, 7*, 473–485.

Boll, T.J., Heaton, R., & Reitan, R.M. (1974). Neuropsychological and emotional correlates of Huntington's chorea. *Journal of Nervous and Mental Disease, 158*, 61–69.

Bond, I.K., & Hutchinson, H.C. (1960). Application of reciprocal inhibition therapy to exhibitionism. *Canadian Medical Association Journal, 83*, 23–25.

Bonica, J.J. (1981). Pain research and therapy: Past and current status and future needs. In L. Ng & J.J. Bonica (Eds.), *Pain, discomfort, and humanitarian care.* New York: Elsevier.

Bootzin, R.R., & Engle-Friedman, M. (1987). Sleep disturbances. In L.L. Carstensen & B.A. Edelstein (Eds.), *Handbook of clinical gerontology.* New York: Pergamon.

Bootzin, R.R., Engle-Friedman, M., & Hazelwood, L. (1983). Sleep disorders and the elderly. In P.M. Lewinsohn & L. Teri (Eds.), *Clinical geropsychology: New directions in assessment and treatment.* New York: Pergamon.

Borgatta, E.F., Montgomery, R.J.Y., & Borgatta, M.L. (1982). Alcohol use and abuse, life crisis events, and the elderly. *Research on Aging, 4*, 378–408.

Borkovec, T.D., & Inz, J. (1990). The nature of worry in generalized anxiety disorder: A predominance of thought activity. *Behaviour Research and Therapy, 28*, 153–158.

Borkovec, T.D., & Mathews, A. (1988). Treatment of nonphobic anxiety disorders: A comparison of nondirective, cognitive and coping desensitization therapy. *Journal of Consulting and Clinical Psychology, 56*, 877–884.

Bornstein, P.E., Clayton, P.J., Halikas, J.A., & Robins, E. (1973). The depression of widowhood after thirteen months. *British Journal of Psychiatry, 122*, 561–566.

Bornstein, R.F., Leone, D.R., & Galley, D.J. (1987). The generalizability of subliminal mere exposure effects: Influence of stimuli perceived without awareness on social behavior. *Journal of Personality and Social Psychology, 53*, 1070–1079.

Boskind-Lodahl, M., & White, W.C. (1978). The definition and treatment of bulimarexia in college women—A pilot study. *Journal of American College Health Association, 27*, 84–97.

Boudewyns, P.A., Fry, T.J., & Nightingale, E.J. (1986). Token economy programs in VA medical centers: Where are they today? *The Behavior Therapist, 9*, 126–127.

Bourne, P.G. (1970). *Men, stress, and Vietnam.* Boston: Little, Brown.

Boverman, H., & French, A.P. (1979). Treatment of the depressed child. In A. French & I. Berlin (Eds.), *Depression in children and adolescents.* New York: Human Sciences Press.

Bower, G.H. (1981). Mood and memory. *American Psychologist, 36*, 129–148.

Bowers, J., Jorm, A.F., Henderson, S., & Harris, P. (1990). General practitioners' detection of depression and dementia in elderly patients. *The Medical Journal of Australia, 153*, 192–196.

Bowers, K.S., & Meichenbaum, D. (Eds.). (1984). *The Unconscious reconsidered.* New York: Praeger.

Bowers, M.B., Jr. (1974). Central dopamine turnover in schizophrenic syndromes. *Archives of General Psychiatry, 31*, 50–54.

Bowers, M.K., Brecher-Marer, S., Newton, B.W., Piotrowski, Z., Spyer, T.C., Taylor, W.S., & Watkins, J.G. (1971). Therapy of multiple personality. *International Journal of Clinical and Experimental Hypnosis, 19*, 57–65.

Boyle, M. (1991). *Schizophrenia: A scientific delusion?* NY: Routledge.

Bradley, L., & Bryant, P.E. (1985). *Rhyme and reason in reading and spelling.* Ann Arbor: University of Michigan Press.

Brady, J.P., Davison, G.C., DeWald, P.A., Egan, G., Fadiman, J., Frank, J.D., Gill, M.M., Hoffman, I., Kempler, W., Lazarus, A.A., Raimy, V., Rotter, J.B., & Strupp, H.H. (1980). Some views on effective principles of psychotherapy. *Cognitive Therapy and Research, 4*, 269–306.

Brand, F.N., Smith, R.T., & Brand, P.A. (1977). Effect of economic barriers to medical care on patients' noncompliance. *Public Health Reports, 92*, 72–78.

Brand, R.J., Rosenman, R.H., Jenkins, C.D., Sholtz, R.L., & Zyzanski, S.J. (in press). Comparison of coronary heart disease prediction in the Western Collaborative Group Study using the structured interview and the Jenkins Activity Survey assessments of coronary-prone Type A behavior pattern. *Journal of Chronic Diseases.*

Brandon, Y.H., Zelman, D.C., & Baker, T.B. (1987). Effects of maintenance sessions on smoking relapse: Delaying the inevitable? *Journal of Consulting and Clinical Psychology, 55*, 780–782.

Brandt, J., Buffers, N., Ryan, C., & Bayog, R. (1983). Cognitive loss and recovery in chronic alcohol abusers. *Archives of General Psychiatry, 40*, 435–442.

Bransford, J.D., & Johnson, M.K. (1973). Considerations of some problems of comprehension. In W.G. Chase (Ed.), *Visual information processing.* New York: Academic Press.

Brassier, R. (1987). Drug use in the geriatric patient. In L.L. Carstensen & B.A. Edelstein (Eds.), *Handbook of clinical gerontology.* New York: Pergamon.

Braswell, L., & Kendall, P.C. (1988). Cognitive-behavioral methods with children. In K.S. Dobson (Ed.), *Handbook of cognitive-behavioral therapies.* New York: Guilford.

Brecher, E.M., & the Editors of *Consumer Reports.* (1972). *Licit and illicit drugs,* Mount Vernon, NY: Consumers Union.

Breen, M.J. (1989). Cognitive and behavioral differences in ADHD boys and girls. *Journal of Child Psychology and Psychiatry, 30*, 711–716.

Brehm, J.W. (1966). *A theory of psychological reactance.* New York: Academic Press.

Brehm, S.S., & Brehm, J.W. (1981). *Psychological reactance: A theory of freedom and control.* New York: Academic Press.

Brehony, K.A., & Geller, E.S. (1981). Agoraphobia: Appraisal of research and a proposal for an integrative model. In M. Hersen, R.M. Eisler, & P.M. Miller (Eds.), *Progress in behavior modification* (Vol. 12). New York: Academic Press.

Breier, A., Charney, D.S., & Heninger, G.R. (1986). Agoraphobia with panic attacks. *Archives of General Psychiatry, 43*, 1029–1036.

Breier, A., Schreiber, J.L., Dyer, J., & Pickar, D. (1991). National Institute of Mental Health longitudinal study of chronic schizophrenia: Prognosis and predictors of outcome. *Archives of General Psychiatry, 48*, 239–246.

Brenner, J. (1973). *Mental illness and economics.* Cambridge, MA: Harvard University Press.

Bretschneider, J.G., & McCoy, N.L. (1988). Sexual interest and behavior in healthy 80 to 102-year-olds. *Archives of Sexual Behavior, 17*, 109–129.

Breuer, J., & Freud, S. (1982). *Studies in hysteria.* (J. Strachey, Trans. and Ed., (original work published 1895) with the collaboration of A. Freud). New York: Basic Books.

Brickel, C.M. (1984). The clinical use of pets with the aged. *Clinical Gerontologist, 2*, 72–75.

Brickman, A.S., McManus, M., Grapentine, W.L., & Alessi, N. (1984). Neuropsychological assessment of seriously delinquent adolescents. *Journal of the American Academy of Child Psychiatry, 23*, 453–457.

Bridge, T.B., & Wyatt, R.J. (1980). Paraphrenia: Paranoid states of late life. II. American research. *Journal of the American Geriatrics Society, 28*, 205–210.

Bridge, T.B., Cannon, H.E., & Wyatt, R.J. (1978). Burned-out schizophrenia: Evidence for age effects on schizophrenic symptomatology. *Journal of Gerontology, 33*, 835–839.

Bridger, W.H., & Mandel, I.J. (1965). Abolition of the PRE by instructions in GSR conditioning. *Journal of Experimental Psychology, 69*, 476–482.

Brodie, H.K.H., & Leff, M.J. (1971). Bipolar depression: A comparative study of patient characteristics. *American Journal of Psychiatry, 127*, 1086–1090.

Brooks, J., & Weinraub, M. (1976). A history of infant intelligence testing. In M. Lewis (Ed.), *Origins of intelligence: Infancy and early childhood.* New York: Plenum.

Broverman, J.K., Broverman, D.M., & Clarkson, F.E. (1970). Sexual stereotypes and clinical judgments of mental health. *Journal of Consulting and Clinical Psychology, 34*, 1–7.

Brown, G.L., & Goodwin, F.K. (1986). Cerebrospinal fluid correlates of suicide attempts and aggression. *Annals of the New York Academy of Science, 487*, 175–188.

Brown, G.W., & Birley, J.L.T. (1968). Crises and life changes and the onset of schizophrenia. *Journal of Health and Social Behavior, 9*, 203–214.

Brown, G.W., Bone, M., Dalison, B., & Wing, J.K. (1966). *Schizophrenia and social care.* London: Oxford University Press.

Brown, G.W., & Harris, T.O. (1978). *Social origins of depression.* London: Tavistock.

Brown, J., Henteleff, P., Barakat, S., & Rowe, C.J. (1986). Is it normal for terminally ill patients to desire death? *American Journal of Psychiatry, 143*, 208–211.

Brown, S.A., et al. (1990). Severity of psychosocial stress and outcome of alcoholism treatment. *Journal of Abnormal Psychology, 99*, 344–348.

Brownell, K.D., Hayes, S.C., & Barlow, D.H. (1977). Patterns of appropriate and deviant sexual arousal: The behavioral treatment of multiple sexual deviations. *Journal of Consulting and Clinical Psychology, 45*, 1144–1155.

Brownell, K.D., Stunkard, A.J., & Albaum, J.M. (1980). Evaluation and modification of exercise patterns in the natural environment. *American Journal of Psychiatry, 137*, 1540–1545.

Brownmiller, S. (1975). *Against our will: Men, women and rape.* New York: Simon & Schuster.

Bruch, H. (1980). Preconditions for the development of anorexia nervosa. *American Journal of Psychoanalysis, 40*, 169–172.

Bruch, H. (1981). Developmental considerations of anorexia nervosa and obesity. *Canadian Journal of Psychiatry, 26*, 212–217.

Bruck, M. (1987). The adult outcomes of children with learning disabilities. *Annals of Dyslexia, 37*, 252–263.

Bryant, R.A., & McConkey, K.M. (1989). Visual conversion disorder: A case analysis of the influence of visual information. *Journal of Abnormal Psychology, 98*, 326–329.

Buchsbaum, M.S., Kessler, R., King, A., Johnson, J., & Cappelletti, J. (1984). Simultaneous cerebral glucography with positron emission tomography and topographic electroencephalography. In G. Pfurtscheller, E.J. Jonkman, & F.H. Lopes da Silva (Eds.), *Brain ischemia: Quantitative EEG and imaging techniques.* Amsterdam: Elsevier.

Buglass, D., Clarke, J., Henderson, A.S., Kreitman, N., & Presley, A.S. (1977). A study of agoraphobic housewives. *Psychological Medicine, 7*, 73–86.

Bulfinch's mythology. (1979). New York: Avenel Books.

Bunney, W.E., Goodwin, F.K., & Murphy, D.L. (1972). The "Switch Process" in manic-depressive illness. *Archives of General Psychiatry, 27*, 312–317.

Bunney, W.E., Murphy, D.L., Goodwin, F.K., & Borge, G.F. (1970). The switch process from depression to mania: Relationship to drugs which alter brain amines. *Lancet, 1*, 1022.

Burgess, A.W., & Holmstrom, L.L. (1974). *Rape: Victim of crisis.* Bowie, MD: Robert J. Brady Company.

Burgess, I.S. et al. (1981). The degree of control exerted by phobic and nonphobic verbal stimuli over the recognition behaviour of phobic and non-phobic subjects. *Behaviour Research and Therapy, 19*, 233–243.

Burgio, L.D., Burgio, K.L., Engel, B.T., & Tice, L.M. (1986). Increasing distance and independence of ambulation in elderly nursing home residents. *Journal of Applied Behavior Analysis, 19*, 357–366.

Burnam, M.A., Stein, J.A., Golding, J.M., Siegel, J.M., Sorenson, S.B., Forsythe, A.B., & Telles, C.A. (1988). Sexual assault and mental disorders in a community population. *Journal of Consulting and Clinical Psychology, 56*, 843–850.

Burns, B., & Taub, C.A. (1990). Mental health services in general medical care and nursing homes. In B.S. Fogel, A. Furino, & G. Gottlieb (Eds.), *Protecting minds at risk* (pp. 63–84). Washington, DC: American Psychiatric Association.

Buss, A.H. (1966). *Psychopathology.* New York: Wiley.

Busse, E.W. (1976). Hypochondriasis in the elderly: A reaction to social stress. *Journal of the American Geriatrics Society, 24*, 145–149.

Busse, E.W., & Blazer, D.G. (1979). Disorders related to biological functioning. In E.W. Busse & D. Blazer (Eds.), *Handbook of geriatric psychiatry.* New York: Van Nostrand-Reinhold.

Butcher, J.N., Dahlstrom, W.G., Graham, J.R., Tellegen, A., & Kraemer, B. (1989). *Minnesota Multiphasic Personality Inventory-2: Manual for administration and scoring.* Minneapolis: University of Minnesota Press.

Butler, G., & Mathews, A. (1983). Cognitive processes in anxiety. *Advances in Behaviour Research and Therapy, 5*, 51–62.

Butler, R.N. (1963). The life review: An interpretation of reminiscence in the aged. *Psychiatry, 119*, 721–728.

Butler, R.N., & Lewis, M.I. (1982). *Aging and mental health: Positive psychosocial approaches* (3rd ed.). St. Louis: Mosby.

Butterfield, E.C., & Belmont, J.M. (1975). Assessing and improving the executive cognitive functions of mentally retarded people. In I. Bialer & M. Sternlicht (Eds.), *Psychological issues in mental retardation.* New York: Psychological Dimensions.

Butterfield, E.C., & Belmont, J.M. (1977). Assessing and improving the cognitive functions of mentally retarded people. In I. Bialer and M. Sternlicht (Eds.), *The psychology of mental retardation: Issues and approaches.* New York: Psychological Dimensions.

Cacioppo, J.T., Glass, C.R., & Merluzzi, T.V. (1979). Self-statements and self-evaluations: A cognitive-response analysis of heterosexual social anxiety. *Cognitive Therapy and Research, 3*, 249–262.

Caddy, G.R. (1983). Alcohol use and abuse. In B. Tabakoff, P.B. Sutker, & C.L. Randell (Eds.), *Medical and social aspects of alcohol use.* New York: Plenum.

Caddy, G.R. (1985). Cognitive behavior therapy in the treatment of multiple personality. *Behavior Modification, 9*, 267–292.

Cadoret, R.J. (1978). Evidence for genetic inheritance of primary affective disorder in adoptees. *American Journal of Psychiatry, 135*, 463–466.

Calhoun, J.B. (1970). Space and the strategy of life. *Ekistics, 29*, 425–437.

Calhoun, K.S. and Atkeson, B.M. *Treatment of rape victims.* Elmsford, NY: Pergamon Press.

Calhoun, K.S., Atkeson, B.M., & Resick, P.A. (1982). A longitudinal examination of fear reactions in victims of rape. *Journal of Counseling Psychology, 29*, 655–661.

Cameron, D.J., Thomas, R.I., Mulvhill, M., & Bronheim, H. (1987). Delirium: A test of the Diagnostic and Statistical Manual III criteria on medical inpatients. *Journal of the American Geriatrics Society, 35,* 1007–1010.

Cameron, N. (1959). The paranoid pseudocommunity revisited. *American Journal of Sociology, 65,* 52–58.

Cameron, N. (1963). *Personality development and psychopathology: A dynamic approach.* Boston: Houghton Mifflin.

Cameron, N., & Magaret, A. (1951). *Behavior pathology.* Boston: Houghton Mifflin.

Campbell, M. (1987). Drug treatment of infantile autism: The past decade. In H.Y. Meltzer (Ed.), *Psychopharmacology: The third generation of progress.* New York: Raven.

Campbell, M. (1988). Fenfluramine treatment of autism. *Journal of Child Psychology and Psychiatry, 29,* 1–10.

Campbell, M., Adams, P., Small, A.M., Perry, R., Curren, E., Tesch, L. McV., Lynch, N., & Pidhorodeckyj, C. (in press). The effects of fenfluramine on behavioral symptoms and learning: A double-blind and placebo controlled study. Cited in Campbell (1988).

Campbell, M., Anderson, L.T., Small, A.M., Locascio, J.J., Lynch, N.S., & Choroco, M.C. (1990). Naltrexone in autistic children: A double-blind and placebo controlled study. *Psychopharmacology Bulletin, 26,* 130–135.

Campbell, M., Overall, J.E., Small, A.M., Sokol, M.S., Spencer, E.K., Adams, P., Foltz, R.L., Monti, K.M., Perry, R., Nobler, M., & Roberts, E. (1989). Naltrexone in autistic children: An acute dose range tolerance trial. *Journal of the American Academy of Child and Adolescent Psychiatry, 28,* 200–206.

Campbell, M., Rosenbloom, S., Perry, R., George, A.E., Kercheff, I.I., Anderson, L., Small, A.M. & Jennings, S.J. (1982). Computerized axial tomography in young autistic children. *American Journal of Psychiatry, 139,* 510–512.

Campbell, S.B. (1990). *Behavioral problems in preschoolers: Clinical and developmental issues.* New York: Guilford.

Camper, P.M., Jacobson, N.S., Holtzworth-Munroe, A., & Schmaling, K.B. (1988). Causal attributions for interactional behaviors in married couples. *Cognitive Therapy and Research, 12,* 195–209.

Cangelosi, A., Gressard, C.F., & Mines, R. A. (1980). The effects of a rational thinking group on self-concepts in adolescents. *The School Counselor, 27,* 357–361.

Cannon, D.S., & Baker, T.B. (1981). Emetic and electric shock alcohol aversion therapy: Assessment of conditioning. *Journal of Consulting and Clinical Psychology, 49,* 20–23.

Cannon, D.S., Baker, T.B., Gino, A., & Nathan, P.E. (1986). Alcohol-aversion therapy: Relation between strength of aversion and abstinence. *Journal of Consulting and Clinical Psychology, 54,* 825–830.

Cannon, D.S., Baker, T.B., & Wehl, C.K. (1981). Emetic and electric shock alcohol aversion therapy: Six- and twelve-month follow-up. *Journal of Consulting and Clinical Psychology, 49,* 360–368.

Cannon, T.D., Mednick, S.A., & Parnas, J. (1990). Antecedents of predominantly negative and predominantly positive-symptom schizophrenia in a high-risk population. *Archives of General Psychiatry, 47,* 622–632.

Cannon, W.E. (1942). "Voodoo" death. *American Anthropologist, 44,* 169–182.

Cantor, N., Markus, H., Niedenthal, P., & Nurius, P. (1986). On motivation and the self-concept. In R.M. Sorrentino & E.T. Higgins (Eds.), *Handbook of motivation and cognition: Foundations of social behavior* (pp. 96–121). New York: Guilford.

Cantwell, D.P. (1983). Childhood depression: What do we know, where do we go? In S.B. Cruze, I.J. Baris & J.E. Barrett (Eds.), *Childhood psychopathology and development.* New York: Raven.

Cantwell, D.P., Baker, L., & Rutter, M. (1978). Family factors. In M. Rutter & E. Schopler (Eds.), *Autism: A reappraisal of concepts and treatment.* New York: Plenum.

Caplan, G. (1964). *Principles of preventive psychiatry.* New York: Basic Books.

Caporael, L. (1976). Ergotism: The satan loosed in Salem? *Science, 192,* 21–26.

Carey, G., & Gottesman, I.I. (1981). Twin and family studies of anxiety, phobic, and compulsive disorders. In D.F. Klein & J.G. Rabkin (Eds.), *Anxiety: New research and changing concepts.* New York: Raven.

Carone, B.J., Harrow, M., & Westermeyer, J.F. (1991). Posthospital course and outcome in schizophrenia. *Archives of General Psychiatry, 48,* 247–253.

Carpenter, W.T. (1986). Thoughts on the treatment of schizophrenia. *Schizophrenia Bulletin, 12,* 527–539.

Carpenter, W.T., Murphy, D.L., & Wyatt, R.J. (1975). Platelet monoamine oxidase activity in acute schizophrenia. *American Journal of Psychiatry, 132,* 438–441.

Carr, A.T. (1971). Compulsive neurosis: Two psychophysiological studies. *Bulletin of the British Psychological Society, 24,* 256–257.

Carr, A.T. (1974). Compulsive neurosis: A review of the literature. *Psychological Bulletin, 81,* 311–319.

Carr, E.G., Schreibman, L., & Lovaas, O.I. (1975). Control of echolalic speech in psychotic children. *Journal of Abnormal Child Psychology, 3,* 331–351.

Carroll, B.J. (1982). The dexamethasone suppression test for melancholia. *British Journal of Psychiatry, 140,* 292–304.

Carver, C.S., Scheier, M.F., & Weintraub, J.K. (1989). Assessing coping strategies: A theoretically based approach. *Journal of Personality and Social Psychology, 56,* 267–283.

Cashman, J.A. (1966). *The LSD story.* Greenwich, CT: Fawcett.

Casriel, D. (1971). The dynamics of Synanon. In R.W. Siroka, E.K. Siroka, & G.A. Schloss (Eds.), *Sensitivity training and group encounter.* New York: Grosser and Dunlap.

Cassell, S. (1965). Effect of brief puppet therapy upon the emotional responses of children undergoing cardiac catheterization. *Journal of Consulting Psychology, 29,* 1–8.

Casson, I.R., Siegel, O., Sham, R., Campbell, E.A., Tarlau, M., & DiDomenico, J. (1984). Brain damage in modern boxers. *Journal of the American Medical Association, 251,* 2263–2267.

Castaneda, R., & Galanter, M. (1988). Ethnic differences in drinking practices and cognitive impairment among detoxifying alcoholics. *Journal of Studies on Alcohol, 49,* 335–339.

Cautela, J.R. (1969). A classical conditioning approach to the development and modification of behavior in the aged. *The Gerontologist, 9,* 109–113.

Cautela, J.R. (1966). Behavior therapy and geriatrics. *Journal of Genetic Psychology, 108,* 9–17.

Cautela, J.R. (1966). Treatment of compulsive behavior by covert sensitization. *Psychological Record, 16,* 33–41.

Caven, R.S. (1973). Speculations on innovations to conventional marriage in old age. *The Gerontologist, 13,* 409–411.

Chambers, K.C. (1985). Sexual dimorphism as an index of hormonal influence on conditioned food aversions. *Annals of the New York Academy of Sciences, 443,* 110–125.

Chambers, K.C., Resko, J.A., & Phoenix, C. (1982). Correlations of diurnal changes in hormones with sexual behavior and age in male rhesus macques. *Neurobiology of Aging, 3,* 37–42.

Chambliss, C.A., & Murray, E.J. (1979). Efficacy attribution, locus of control, and weight loss. *Cognitive Therapy and Research, 3,* 349–353.

Chaney, E.F., O'Leary, M.R., & Marlatt, G.A. (1978). Skills training with alcoholics. *Journal of Consulting and Clinical Psychology, 46,* 1092–1104.

Chapman, L.J., & Chapman, J.P. (1969). Illusory correlation as an obstacle to the use of valid psychodiagnostic signs.

Journal of Abnormal Psychology, 74, 271–287.

Charlesworth, W.B. (1976). Human intelligence as adaptation. An ethological approach. In L.E. Resnick (Ed.), *The nature of intelligence.* Hillsdale, NJ: Erlbaum.

Charney, D.S., Heniger, C.R., & Breier, A. (1984). Noradrenergic function in pain attacks. *Archives of General Psychiatry, 41,* 751–763.

Charney, D.S., Heninger, G.R., & Kleber, H.D. (1986). The combined use of clonidine and naltrexone as a rapid, safe, and effective treatment of abrupt withdrawal from methadone. *American Journal of Psychiatry, 143,* 831–837.

Chassin, L., Presson, C., Sherman, S.J., McLaughlin, L., & Gioia, D. (1985). Psychosocial correlates of adolescent smokeless tobacco use. *Addictive Behaviors, 10,* 431–436.

Chelune, G.J., Ferguson, W., Koon, R., & Dickey, T.O. (1986). Frontal lobe disinhibition in attention deficit disorder. *Child Psychiatry and Human Development, 16,* 264–281.

Chemtob, C., Roitblat, H.C., Hamada, R.S., Carlson, J.G., & Twentyman, C.T. (1988). A cognitive action theory of post-traumatic stress disorder. *Journal of Anxiety Disorders, 2,* 253–275.

Chesney, M.A., Eagleston, J.R., & Rosenman, R.H. (1980). The Type A structured interview: A behavioral assessment in the rough. *Journal of Behavioral Assessment, 2,* 255–272.

Chesler, P. (1972). *Women and madness.* Garden City, NY: Doubleday.

Chiles, J., Miller, M.L., & Cox, G.B. (1980). Depression in an adolescent delinquent population. *Archives of General Psychiatry, 37,* 1179–1184.

Choosing death. (1991, August 26). *Newsweek,* pp. 42–46.

Christensen, A. (1983). Intervention. In H.H. Kelley, E. Berscheid, A. Christensen, J.H. Harvey, T.L. Huston, G. Levinger, E. McClintock, L.A. Peplau, & D.R. Peterson (Eds.), *Close relationships.* San Francisco: Freeman.

Christensen, A., & Nies, D.C. (1980). The Spouse Observation Checklist: Empirical analysis and critique. *American Journal of Family Therapy, 8,* 69–79.

Christensen, A., Sullaway, M., & King, C. (1982). *Dysfunctional interaction patterns and marital happiness.* Paper presented at the annual meeting of the Association for Advancement of Behavior Therapy, Los Angeles. As cited in Margolin, Michelli, & Jacobson (1988).

Christie, A.B. (1982). Changing patterns in mental illness in the elderly. *British Journal of Psychiatry, 140,* 154–159.

Churchill, D.W. (1969). Psychotic children and behavior modification. *American Journal of Psychiatry, 125,* 1585–1590.

Churchill, W. (1967). *Homosexual behavior among males: A cross-cultural and cross-species investigation.* Englewood Cliffs, NJ: Prentice-Hall.

Cimons, M. (1992, May 22). Record number of Americans stop smoking. *Los Angeles Times,* p. A4.

Clark, D.F. (1988). The validity of measures of cognition: A review of the literature. *Cognitive Therapy and Research, 12,* 1–20.

Clark, D.M. (1986). A cognitive approach to panic. *Behavior Research and Therapy, 24,* 461–470.

Clark, D.M., Salkovskis, P.M., & Chalkley, A.J. (1985). Respiratory control as a treatment for panic attacks. *Journal of Behavior Therapy and Experimental Psychiatry, 16,* 23–30.

Clark, J.V., & Arkowitz, H. (1975). Social anxiety and the self-evaluation of interpersonal performance. *Psychological Reports, 36,* 211–221.

Clark, W.B., & Cahalan, D. (1976). Changes in drinking behavior over a four-year span. *Addictive Behaviors, 1,* 251–259.

Clarke, K., & Greenberg, L. (1986). Differential effects of the gestalt two chair intervention and problem solving in resolving decisional conflict. *Journal of Counseling Psychology, 33,* 48–53.

Clausen, J.A., & Kohn, M.L. (1959). Relation of schizophrenia to the social structure of a small city. In B. Pasamanick (Ed.), *Epidemiology of mental disorder.* Washington, DC: American Association for the Advancement of Science.

Clayton, E.W. (1988). From Rogers to Rivers: The rights of the mentally ill to refuse medications. *American Journal of Law and Medicine, 13,* 7–52.

Clayton, P.J. (1973). The clinical morbidity of the first year of bereavement: A review. *Comparative Psychiatry, 14,* 151–157.

Clayton, P.J., Halikas, J.A., & Maurice, W.L. (1972). The depression of widowhood. *British Journal of Psychiatry, 129,* 532–538.

Clayton, V.P., & Birren, J.E. (1980). The development of wisdom across the life span: A reexamination of an ancient topic. In P.B. Baltes & O.G. Brim (Eds.), *Life-span development and behavior* (Vol. 3). New York: Academic Press.

Cleckley, H. (1976). *The mask of sanity* (5th ed.). St. Louis: Mosby.

Climko, R.P., Roehrich, H., Sweeney, D.R., & Al-Razi, J. (1987). Ecstasy: A review of MDMA and MDA. *International Journal of Psychiatry in Medicine, 16,* 359–372.

Clomipramine Collaborative Study Group. (1991). Clomipramine in the treatment of patients with obsessive-compulsive disorder. *Archives of General Psychiatry, 48,* 730–738.

Cloninger, R.C., Bohman, M., & Sigvardsson, S. (1981). Inheritance of alcohol abuse: Cross-fostering analysis of adopted men. *Archives of General Psychiatry, 38,* 861–868.

Cloninger, R.C., Martin, R.L., Guze, S.B., & Clayton, P.L. (1986). A prospective follow-up and family study of somatization in men and women. *American Journal of Psychigary, 143,* 713–714.

Cloninger, R.C., Reich, T., & Guze, S.B. (1975). The multifactorial model of disease transmission: II. Sex differences in the familial transmission of sociopathy (antisocial personality). *British Journal of Psychiatry, 127,* 11–22.

Cloninger, R.C., Sigvardsson, S., Bohman, M., & Knorring, A. von. (1982). Predisposition to petty criminality in Swedish adoptees: II. Cross-fostering analysis of gene-environment interaction. *Archives of General Psychiatry, 39,* 1242–1247.

Clum, A., & Knowles, S.L. (1991). Why do some people with panic disorders become avoidant? A review. *Clinical Psychology Review, 11,* 295–314.

Clunies-Ross, G.G. (1979). Accelerating the development of Down's syndrome infants and young children. *The Journal of Special Education, 13,* 169–177.

Coates, S., & Person, E.S. (1985). Extreme boyhood femininity: Isolated behavior or pervasive disorder? *Journal of the American Academy of Child Psychiatry, 24,* 702–709.

Coates, T.J. (1990). Strategies for modifying sexual behavior for primary and secondary prevention of HIV disease. *Journal of Consulting and Clinical Psychology, 58,* 57–69.

Coates, T.J., Kegeles, S., Stall, J.D., Lo, B., Morin, S., & McKusick, L. (1988). AIDS antibody testing: Will it stop the AIDS epidemic? Will it help persons infected with HIV? *American Psychologist, 43,* 859–864.

Coffey, C.E., Weiner, R.D., Djang, W.T., Figiel G.S., Soady, S.A.R., Patterson, L.J., Holt, P.D., Spritzer, C.E., & Wilkinson, W.E. (1991). Brain anatomic effects of electroconvulsive therapy: A prospective magnetic resonance imaging study. *Archives of General Psychiatry, 48,* 1009–1012.

Cohen, A.H. (1986). Preventing adults from becoming sexual molesters. *Child Abuse and Neglect, 10,* 559–562.

Cohen, D., Eisdorfer, C., Prinz, P., Breen, A., Davis, M., & Gadsby, A. (1983). Sleep disturbances in the institutionalized aged. *Journal of the American Geriatrics Society, 31,* 79–82.

Cohen, D.J., Solnit, A.J., & Wohlford, P. (1979). Mental health services in Head Start. In E. Zigier & J. Valentine (Eds.), *Project Head Start.* New York: Free Press.

Cohen, G.D. (1990). Psychopathology and mental health in the mature and elderly adult. In J.E. Birren, & K.W. Schaie (Eds.), *Handbook of the psychology of aging* Third edition (pp. 359–371). New York: Academic Press.

Cohen, L.J., & Roth, S. (1987). The psychological aftermath of rape: Long-term effects and individual differences in recovery. *Journal of Social and Clinical Psychology, 5*, 525–534.

Cohen, S. (1981). Adverse effects of marijuana: Selected issues. *Annals of the New York Academy of Science, 362*, 119–124.

Cohen, S. (1988). Psychosocial models of the role of social support in the etiology of physical disease. *Health Psychology, 7*, 269–297.

Cohen, S., Evans, G.W., Krantz, D.S., & Stokols, D. (1980). Physiological, motivational and cognitive effects of aircraft noise on children. *American Psychologist, 35*, 231–243.

Cohen, S., Tyrell, D.A.J., & Smith, A.P. (1991). Psychological stress and susceptibility to the common cold. *New England Journal of Medicine, 325*, 606–612.

Cohen, S., & Wills, T.A. (1985). Stress, social support, and the buffering process. *Psychological Bulletin, 98*, 310–357.

Cole, J.D. (1988). Where are those new antidepressants we were promised? *Archives of General Psychiatry, 45*, 193–194.

Collaborative study of children treated for phenylketonuria, preliminary report 8. (1975, February). R. Koch, principal investigator. Presented at the Eleventh General Medicine Conference, Stateline, NV.

Colletti, G., & Kopel, S.A. (1979). Maintaining behavior change: An investigation of three maintenance strategies and the relationship of self-attribution to the long-term reduction of cigarette smoking. *Journal of Consulting and Clinical Psychology, 47*, 614–617.

Colligan, R.C., & Offord, D.P. (1988). The risky use of MMPI hostility scale in assessing risk for coronary heart disease. *Psychosomatics, 29*, 188–196.

Collins, L.F., Maxwell, A.E., & Cameron, C. (1962). A factor analysis of some child psychiatric clinic data. *Journal of Mental Science, 108*, 274–285.

Combs, G., Jr., & Ludwig, A.M. (1982). Dissociative disorders. In J.H. Greist, J.W. Jefferson, & R.L. Spitzer (Eds.), *Treatment of mental disorders*. New York: Oxford University Press.

Comfort, A. (1980). Sexuality in later life. In J.E. Birren & R.B. Sloane (Eds.), *Handbook of mental health and aging*. Englewood Cliffs, NJ: Prentice-Hall.

Comfort, A. (1984). Sexuality and the elderly. In J.P. Abrahams & V. Crooks (Eds.), *Geriatric mental health*. Orlando, FL: Grune & Stratton.

Committee on Government Operations. (1985). *The federal response to the homeless crisis*. Washington, DC: U.S. Government Printing Office.

Committee on Health Care for Homeless People. (1988). *Homelessness, health, and human needs*. Washington, DC: National Academic Press.

Compton, D.R., Dewey, W.L., & Martin, B.R. (1990). Cannabis dependence and tolerance production. *Advances in Alcohol and Substance Abuse, 9*, 129–147.

Conger, J.J. (1951). The effects of alcohol on conflict behavior in the albino rat. *Quarterly Journal of Studies on Alcohol, 12*, 129.

Connelly, M. (1992, March 7). 3 found dead after inhaling laughing gas. *Los Angeles Times*, pp. A1, A23.

Conners, C.K. (1969). A teacher rating scale for use in drug studies with children. *American Journal of Psychiatry, 126*, 884–888.

Conners, F.A., Caruso, D.R., & Detterman, D.K. (1986). Computer-assisted instruction for the mentally retarded. In N.R. Ellis & N.W. Bray (Eds.), *International review of research in mental retardation* (Vol. 14). New York: Academic Press.

Conoley, C.W., Conoley, J.C., McConnell, J.A., & Kimzey, C.E. (1983). The effect of the ABCs of rational emotive therapy and the empty-chair technique of Gestalt therapy on anger reduction. *Psychotherapy: Theory, Research, and Practice, 20*, 112–117.

Cook, M. & Mineka, S. (1989). Observational conditioning of fear to fear-relevant versus fear-irrelevant stimuli in rhesus monkeys. *Journal of Abnormal Psychology, 98*, 448–459.

Cooper, A.F., Garside, R.F., & Kay, D.W.K. (1976). A comparison of deaf and non-deaf patients with paranoid and affective psychoses. *British Journal of Psychiatry, 129*, 532–538.

Cooper, A.F., Kay, D.W.K., Curry, A.R., Garside, R.F., & Roth, M. (1974). Hearing loss in paranoid and affective psychoses of the elderly. *Lancet, 2*, 851–854.

Cooper, A.F., & Porter, R. (1976). Visual acuity and ocular pathology in the paranoid and affective psychoses of later life. *Journal of Psychosomatic Research, 20*, 107–114.

Cooper, A.J. (1986). Progestogens in the treatment of male sex offenders: A review. *Canadian Journal of Psychiatry, 31*, 73–79.

Cooper, J.E., Kendell, R.E., Gurland, B.J., Sharpe, L., Copeland, J.R.M., & Simon, R. (1972). *Psychiatric diagnosis in New York and London*. London: Oxford University Press.

Coppen, A., Prange, A.J., Whybrow, P.C., & Noguera, R. (1972). Abnormalities in indoleamines in affective disorders. *Archives of General Psychiatry, 26*, 474–478.

Cornblatt, B., & Erlenmeyer-Kimling, L.E. (1985). Global attentional deviance in children at risk for schizophrenia: Specificity and predictive validity. *Journal of Abnormal Psychology, 94*, 470–486.

Costa, P.T., Jr., Zonderman, A.B., McCrae, R.R., Cornoni-Huntley, J., Locke, B.Z., & Barbano, H.E. (1987). Longitudinal analyses of psychological well-being in a national sample: Stability of mean levels. *Journal of Gerontology, 42*, 50–55.

Costello, E.J. (1989). Child psychiatric disorders and their correlates: A primary care pediatric sample. *Journal of the American Academy of Child and Adolescent Psychiatry, 28*, 851–855.

Cotton, D.J. (1988). The impact of AIDS on the medical care system. *Journal of the American Medical Association, 260*, 519–523.

Courchesne, E., Yeung-Courchesne, R., Press, G.A., Hesselink, J.R., & Jernigan, T.L. (1988). Hypoplasia of cerebellar vermal lobules VI and VII in autism. *New England Journal of Medicine, 318*, 1349–1354.

Covi, L., Lipman, R.S., Derogatis, L.R., Smith, J.E., & Pattison, J.H. (1974). Drugs and group psychotherapy in neurotic depression. *American Journal of Psychiatry, 131*, 191–197.

Cox, A., Rutter, M., Newman, S., & Bartak, L. (1975). A comparative study of infantile autism and specific developmental language disorders: II. Parental characteristics. *British Journal of Psychiatry, 126*, 146–159.

Cox, D.J., Freundlich, A., & Meyer, R.G. (1975). Differential effectiveness of electromyographic feedback, verbal relaxation instructions, and medication placebo with tension headaches. *Journal of Consulting and Clinical Psychology, 43*, 892–898.

Coyne, J.C. (1976). Depression and the response of others. *Journal of Abnormal Psychology, 85*, 186–193.

Coyne, J.C., & Gotlib, I.H. (1983). The role of cognition in depression: A critical appraisal. *Psychological Bulletin, 94*, 472–505.

Craft, M.J. (1969). The natural history of psychopathic disorder. *British Journal of Psychiatry, 115*, 39–44.

Craig, M.M., & Glick, S.J. (1963). Ten years' experience with the Glueck social prediction table. *Crime and Delinquency, 9*, 249–261.

Craighead, W.E., Evans, D.D., & Robins, C.J. (1992). Unipolar depression. In S.M.

Turner, K.S. Calhoun, & H.E. Adams (Eds.), *Handbook of clinical behavior therapy* (2nd ed., pp. 99–116). New York: Wiley.

Craske, M.G., Brown, A.T., & Barlow, D.H. (1991). Behavioral treatment of panic disorder: A two-year follow-up. *Behavior Therapy, 22,* 289–304.

Craske, M.G., Rapee, R.M., & Barlow, D.H. (1992). Cognitive-behavioral treatment of panic disorder, agoraphobia, and generalized anxiety disorder. In S.M. Turner, K.S. Calhoun, & H.E. Adams (Eds.), *Handbook of clinical behavior therapy* (2nd ed. pp. 39–65). New York: Wiley.

Creer, T.L. (1982). Asthma. *Journal of Consulting and Clinical Psychology, 50,* 912–921.

Creer, T.L., Renna, C.M., & Chai, H. (1982). The application of behavioral techniques to childhood asthma. In D.C. Russo & J.W. Varni (Eds.), *Behavioral pediatrics: Research and practice.* New York: Plenum.

Crisp, A.H. (1967). The possible significance of some behavioral correlates of weight and carbohydrate intake. *Journal of Psychosomatic Research, 11,* 117–131.

Crissey, M.S. (1975). Mental retardation. Past, present, and future. *American Psychologist, 30,* 800–808.

Crofton, J., Campbell, I.E., Cole, P.V., Friend, J.A.R., Oldham, P.D., Springett, V.H., Berry G., & Raw, M. (1983). Comparison of four methods of smoking withdrawal in patients with smoking related diseases: Report by a subcommittee of the Research Committee of the British Thoracic Society. *British Medical Journal, 286,* 595–597.

Cross, D.G., & Sharpley, C.F. (1981). The Locke-Wallace Marital Adjustment Test reconsidered: Some psychometric findings as regards its reliability and factorial validity. *Educational and Psychological Measurement, 41,* 1303–1306.

Crow, T.J. (1980). Molecular pathology of schizophrenia: More than one disease process? *British Medical Journal, 280,* 784–788.

Crowe, R.R. (1974). An adoption study of antisocial personality. *Archives of General Psychiatry, 31,* 785–791.

Crowe, R.R., Noyes, R., Pauls, D.L., & Slymen, D.J. (1983). A family study of panic disorder. *Archives of General Psychiatry, 40,* 1065–1069.

Crowe, R.R., Pauls, D.L., Slymen, D.J., & Noyes, R. (1980). A family study of anxiety neurosis: Morbidity risk in families of patients with and without mitral valve prolapse. *Archives of General Psychiatry, 37,* 77–79.

Crtryn, L., & McKnew, D.H. (1979). Affective disorders. In J. Noshpitz (Ed.), *Basic handbook of child psychiatry* (Vol. 2). New York: Basic Books.

Cunningham, P.J., & Mueller, C.D. (1991). Individuals with mental retardation in residential facilities: Findings from the 1987 National Medical Expenditure Survey. *American Journal on Mental Retardation, 96,* 109–117.

Dackis, C.A., & Gold, M.S. (1985). Pharmacological approaches to cocaine addiction. *Journal of Substance Abuse Treatment, 2,* 139–145.

D'Amicis, L., Goldberg, D., LoPiccolo, J., Friedman, J., & Davies, L. (1985). Clinical follow-up of couples treated for sexual dysfunction. *Archives of Sexual Behavior, 14,* 461–483.

Daneman, E.A. (1961). Imipramine in office management of depressive reactions (a double-blind study). *Diseases of the Nervous System, 22,* 213–217.

Dauphinais, P., & King, J. (1992). Psychological assessment with American Indian children. *Applied and Preventive Psychology, 1,* 97–110.

Davidson, J., Kudler, H., Smith, R., Mahorney, S.L., Lipper, S., Hammett, W.B., Saunders, W.B., & Kavenar, J.O. (1990). Treatment of posttraumatic stress disorder with amitriptyline and placebo. *Archives of General Psychiatry, 47,* 259–268.

Davidson, J.T.R., Giller, E.L., Zisook, S., & Overall, J.E. (1988). An efficacy study of isocarboxazid in depression and its relationship to depressive nosology. *Archives of General Psychiatry, 45,* 120–128.

Davidson, W.S., Redner, R., Blakely, C.H., Mitchell, C.M., & Emshoff, J.G. (1987). Diversion of juvenile offenders: An experimental comparison. *Journal of Consulting and Clinical Psychology, 55,* 68–75.

Davila, R., Manero, E., Zumarraga, M., et al. (1988). Plasma homovanillic acid as a predictor of response to neuroleptics. *Archives of General Psychiatry, 45,* 564–567.

Davis, J.M. (1978). Dopamine theory of schizophrenia: A two-factor theory. In L.C. Wynne, R.L. Cromwell, & S. Matthysse (Eds.), *The nature of schizophrenia.* New York: Wiley.

Davis, K.L., Kahn, R.S., Ko, G., & Davidson, M. (1991). Dopamine and schizophrenia: A review and reconceptualization. *American Journal of Psychiatry, 148,* 1474–1486.

Davison, G.C. (1964). A social learning therapy programme with an autistic child. *Behaviour Research and Therapy, 2,* 146–159.

Davison, G.C. (1966). Differential relaxation and cognitive restructuring in therapy with a "paranoid schizophrenic" or "paranoid state." *Proceedings of the 74th Annual Convention of the American Psychological Association.* Washington, DC: American Psychological Association.

Davison, G.C. (1968a). Elimination of a sadistic fantasy by a client-controlled counterconditioning technique. *Journal of Abnormal Psychology, 73,* 84–90.

Davison, G.C. (1968b). Systematic desensitization as a counterconditioning process. *Journal of Abnormal Psychology, 73,* 91–99.

Davison, G.C. (1973). Counter countrol in behavior modification. In L.A. Hamerlynck, L.C. Handy, & E.J. Mash (Eds.), *Behavior change: Methodology, concepts and practice.* Champaign, IL: Research Press.

Davison, G.C. (1974). *Homosexuality: The ethical challenge.* Presidential address to the Eighth Annual Convention of the Association for Advancement of Behavior Therapy, Chicago.

Davison, G.C. (1976). Homosexuality: The ethical challenge. *Journal of Consulting and Clinical Psychology, 44,* 157–162.

Davison, G.C. (1977). *Theory and practice in behavior therapy: An unconsummated marriage.* Paper presented at the annual meeting of the Association for Advancement of Behavior Therapy, Atlanta. Audiotape distributed by Biomonitoring Associates, Guilford Press, New York.

Davison, G.C. (1978). Not can but ought: The treatment of homosexuality. *Journal of Consulting and Clinical Psychology, 46,* 170–172.

Davison, G.C. (1980). And now for something completely different: Cognition and little r. In M.J. Mahoney (Ed.), *Psychotherapy process: Current issues and future directions.* New York: Plenum.

Davison, G.C. (1991). Constructionism and therapy for homosexuality. In J. Gonsiorek & J. Weinrich (Eds.), *Homosexuality: Research findings for public policy.* Newbury Park, CA: Sage.

Davison, G.C., & Darke, L. (1991). Managing pain. In R. Bjork & D. Druckman (Eds.), *In the mind's eye: Understanding the basis of human performance.* Washington, DC: National Academy Press.

Davison, G.C., Feldman, P.M., & Osborn, C.E. (1984). Articulated thoughts, irrational beliefs, and fear of negative evaluation. *Cognitive Therapy and Research, 8,* 349–362.

Davison, G.C., & Goldfried, M.R. (1973). Postdoctoral training in clinical behavior therapy. *Menninger Clinic Bulletin 17.*

Davison, G.C., Haaga, D.A., Rosenbaum, J., Dolezal, S.L., & Weinstein, K.A. (1991). Assessment of self-efficacy in articulated thoughts: "States of Mind" analysis and association with speech anxious behavior. *Journal of Cognitive Psychotherapy: An International Quarterly, 5,* 83–92.

Davison, G.C., & Neale, J.M. (1986). *Abnormal Psychology.* Fourth edition. New York: Wiley.

Davison, G.C., Robins, C., & Johnson, M.K. (1983). Articulated thoughts during simulated situations: A paradigm for studying cognition in emotion and behavior. *Cognitive Therapy and Research, 7,* 17–40.

Davison, G.C., & Thompson, R.F. (1988). Stress management. In D. Druckman & J.A. Swets (Eds.), *Enhancing human performance: Issues, theories, and techniques.* Washington, DC: National Academic Press.

Davison, G.C., Tsujimoto, R.N., & Glaros, A.G. (1973). Attribution and the maintenance of behavior change in failing asleep. *Journal of Abnormal Psychology, 82,* 124–133.

Davison, G.C., & Valins, S. (1969). Maintenance of self-attributed and drug-attributed behavior change. *Journal of Personality and Social Psychology, 11,* 25–33.

Davison, G.C., Williams, M.E., Nezami, E., Bice, T.L., & DeQuattro, V. (1991). Relaxation, reduction in angry articulated thoughts, and improvements in borderline essential hypertension and heart rate. *Journal of Behavioral Medicine, 14,* 453–468.

Davison, G.C., & Wilson, G.T. (1973). Attitudes of behavior therapists toward homosexuality. *Behavior Therapy, 4,* 686–696.

Davison, G.C., & Zighelboim, V. (1987). Irrational beliefs in the articulated thoughts of college students with social anxiety. *Journal of Rational-Emotive Therapy, 5,* 238–254.

Dawson, M.E., Schell, A.M., & Banis, H.T. (1986). Greater resistance to extinction of electrodermal responses conditioned to potentially phobic CSs: A noncognitive process? *Psychophysiology, 23,* 552–561.

Dekker, E., & Groen, J. (1956). Reproducible psychogenic attacks of asthma. *Journal of Psychosomatic Research, 1,* 58–67.

Dekker, E., Pelser, H.E., & Groen, J. (1957). Conditioning as a cause of asthmatic attacks. *Journal of Psychosomatic Research, 2,* 97–108.

Delgado, P.L., Charney, D.S., Price, L.H., Aghajanian, G.K., Landis, H., & Herringer, G.R. (1990). Serotonin function and the mechanism of antidepressant action: Reversal of antidepressant-induced remission by rapid depletion of plasma tryptophan. *Archives of General Psychiatry, 47,* 411–418.

deLint, J. (1978). Alcohol consumption and alcohol problems from an epidemiological perspective. *British Journal of Alcohol and Alcoholism, 17,* 109–116.

Dembroski, T.M., MacDougall, J.M., Costa, P.T., & Grandits, G.A. (1989). Components of hostility as predictors of sudden death and myocardial infarction in the Multiple Risk Factor Intervention Trial. *Psychosomatic Medicine, 51,* 514–522.

Dement, W.C., Laughton, E., & Carskadon, M.A. (1981). "White paper" on sleep and aging. *Journal of the American Geriatrics Society, 30,* 25–50.

DeMyer, M. (1975). The nature of the neuropsychological disability of autistic children. *Journal of Autism and Childhood Schizophrenia, 5,* 109–127.

Depue, R.A., & Monroe, S.M. (1978). Learned helplessness in the perspective of the depressive disorders: Conceptual and definitional issues. *Journal of Abnormal Psychology, 87,* 3–20.

D'Ercole, A., & Struening, E. (1990). Victimization among homeless women: Implications for service delivery. *Journal of Community Psychology, 18,* 141–152.

DeRubeis, R.J., Hollon, S.D., Evans, M.D., & Bemis, K.M. (1982). Can psychotherapies for depression be discriminated? A systematic investigation of cognitive therapy and interpersonal therapy. *Journal of Consulting and Clinical Psychology, 50,* 744–760.

Detterman, D.K. (1979). Memory in the mentally retarded. In N.R. Ellis (Ed.), *Handbook of mental deficiency, psychological theory and research* (2nd ed.). Hillsdale, NJ: Erlbaum.

Deutsch, A. (1949). *The mentally ill in America.* New York: Columbia University Press.

Devine, V., Adelson, R., Goldstein, J., Valins, S., & Davison, G.C. (1974). Controlled test of the analgesic and relaxant properties of nitrous oxide. *Journal of Dental Research, 53,* 486–490.

DeVries, H.A. (1975). Physiology of exercise and aging. In D.S. Woodruff & J.E. Birren (Eds.), *Aging: Scientific perspectives and social issues.* New York: Van Nostrand-Reinhold.

Dew, M.A., Bromet, E.J., Brent, D., & Greenhouse, J.B. (1987). A quantitative literature review of the effectiveness of suicide prevention centers. *Journal of Consulting and Clinical Psychology, 55,* 239–244.

Dewys, W.D., Begg, C., & Lavin, P.T. (1980). Prognostic effect of weight loss prior to chemotherapy in cancer patients. *American Journal of Medicine, 69,* 491–497.

Deykin, E.Y., Alpert, J.J., & McNamara, J.J. (1985). A pilot study of the effect of exposure to child abuse or neglect on adolescent suicidal behavior. *American Journal of Psychiatry, 142,* 1299–1303.

Diamond, S., Baldwin, R., & Diamond, R. (1963). *Inhibition and choice.* New York: Harper & Row.

Didion, J. (1979). *The white album.* New York: Simon & Schuster.

Dietz, P.E., Hazelwood, R.R., & Warren, J. (1990). The sexually sadistic criminal and his offenses. *Bulletin of the American Academy of Psychiatry and the Law, 18,* 163–178.

DiFranza, J.R., et al. (1991). RJR Nabisco's cartoon camel promotes Camel Cigarettes to children. *Journal of the American Medical Association, 266,* 3149–3153.

DiMascio, A., Weissman, M.M., Prusoff, B.A., Neu, C., Zwilling, M., & Klerman, G.L. (1979). Differential symptom reduction by drugs and psychotherapy in acute depression. *Archives of General Psychiatry, 36,* 1450–1456.

Dimsdale, J.E. (1988). A perspective on Type A behavior and coronary disease. *The New England Journal of Medicine, 318,* 110–112.

Dimsdale, J.E., Pierce, C., Schoenfeld, D., Brown, A., Zusman, R., & Graham, R. (1986). Suppressed anger and blood pressure: The effects of race, sex, social class, and age. *Psychosomatic Medicine, 48,* 430–436.

Dobson, K.S. (1989). A meta-analysis of the efficacy of cognitive therapy for depression. *Journal of Consulting and Clinical Psychology, 57,* 414–419.

Dobson, K.S., & Shaw, B.F. (1986). Cognitive assessment with major depressive disorders. *Cognitive Therapy and Research, 10,* 13–29.

Dodge, K.A. (in press). The structure and function of reactive and proactive aggression. In D.J. Pepler & K.H. Rubin (Eds.), *The development and treatment of childhood aggression.* Hillsdale, NJ: Erlbaum.

Dodge, K.A., & Coie, J.D. (1987). Social information-processing factors in reactive and proactive aggression in children's peer groups. *Journal of Personality and Social Psychology, 53,* 1146–1158.

Dodge, K.A., & Frame, C.L. (1982). Social cognitive biases and deficits in aggressive boys. *Child Development, 53,* 620–635.

Dodson, B. (1974). *Liberating masturbation.* New York: Bodysex Designs.

Dohrenwend, B.P., Levav, P.E., Schwartz, S., Naveh, G., Link, B.G., Skodol, A.E., & Stueve, A. (1992). Socioeconomic status and psychiatric disorders: The causation-selection issue. *Science, 255,* 946–952.

Dole, V., & Nyswander, M. (1966). Methadone maintenance: A report of two years' experience. In *Problems of drug dependence.* Washington, DC: National Academy of Science.

Dollard, J., & Miller, N.E. (1950). *Personality and psychotherapy.* New York: McGraw-Hill.

Doran, A.R., Pickar, D., Boronow, J. et al. (1985). CT scans in schizophrenics, medical and normal controls. Annual meeting of the American College of Neuropsychopharmamacology, Maui, HI.

Dowd, J.J., & Bengston, V.L. (1978). Aging in minority populations: An examination of the double jeopardy hypothesis. *Journal of Gerontology, 33,* 427–436.

Draguns, J.G. (1989). Normal and abnormal behavior in cross-cultural perspective: Specifying the nature of their relationships. In J.J. Berman (Ed.), *Nebraska symposium on motivation.* Lincoln, NE: University of Nebraska Press.

Drabman, R.S., Spitalnik, R., & O'Leary, K.D. (1973). Teaching self-control to disruptive children. *Journal of Abnormal Psychology, 82,* 10–16.

Drake, R.D., & Sederer, L.I. (1986). The adverse effects of intensive treatment of chronic schizophrenia. *Comprehensive Psychiatry, 27,* 313–326.

Duck, S. (1984). A perspective on the repair of personal relationships. In S. Duck (Ed.), *Personal relationships: 5. Repairing personal relationships.* New York: Academic Press.

Duggan, C.F., Lee, A.S., & Murray, R.M. (1991). Do different subtypes of hospitalized depressives have different long term outcomes? *Archives of General Psychiatry, 48,* 308–312.

Dunham, H.W. (1965). *Community and schizophrenia: An epidemiological analysis.* Detroit: Wayne State University Press.

DuPaul, G.J. (1991). Parent and teacher ratings of ADHD symptoms: Psychometric properties in a community-based sample. *Journal of Clinical Child Psychology, 20,* 245–253.

Dura, J.R., Stukenberg, K.W., & Kiecolt-Glaser, J.K. (1991). Anxiety and depressive disorders in adult children caring for demented parents. *Psychology and Aging, 6,* 467–473.

Durham, R.C., & Turvey, A.A. (1987). Cognitive therapy vs. behaviour therapy in the treatment of chronic general anxiety. *Behaviour Research and Therapy, 25,* 229–234.

Durkheim, E. (1951). *Suicide* (Trans.). J.A. Spaulding & G. Simpson, New York: Free Press. (Original work published 1897; 2nd ed., 1930).

Dweck, C.S. (1975). The role of expectation and attributions in the alleviation of learned helplessness. *Journal of Personality and Social Psychology, 31,* 674–685.

Dworkin, B.R., Filewich, R.J., Mier, N.E., & Craigmyle, N. (1979). Baroreceptor activation reduces reactivity to noxious stimulation: Implications for hypertension. *Science, 205,* 1299–1301.

Dworkin, R.H., & Lenzenwenger, M.F. (1984). Symptoms and the genetics of schizophrenia: Implications for diagnosis. *American Journal of Psychiatry, 141,* 1541–1546.

Dworkin, R.H., Lenzenwenger, M.F., & Moldin, S.O. (1987). Genetics and the phenomenology of schizophrenia. In P.D. Harvey and E.F. Walker (Eds.), *Positive and negative symptoms of psychosis.* Hillsdale, N.J.: Erlbaum.

Dye, C.J. (1978). Psychologist's role in the provision of mental health care for the elderly. *Professional Psychology, 9,* 38–49.

Dykman, B.M., Abramson, L.Y., Alloy, L.B., & Hartlage, S. (1989). Processing of ambiguous and unambiguous feedback by depressed and nondepressed college students: Schematic biases and their implications for depressive realism. *Journal of Personality and Social Psychology, 56,* 431–455.

Dykman, B.M., Horowitz, L.M., Abramson, L.Y., & Usher, M. (1991). Schematic and situational determinants of depressed and nondepressed students' interpretation of feedback. *Journal of Abnormal Psychology, 100,* 45–55.

Dysken, M.W. (1979). Clinical usefulness of sodium amobarbital interviewing. *Archives of General Psychiatry, 36,* 789–794.

D'Zurilla, T.J. (1986). *Problem-solving therapy: A social competence approach to clinical intervention.* New York: Springer.

D'Zurilla, T.J. (1990). Problem-solving training for effective stress management and prevention. *Journal of Cognitive Psychotherapy: An International Quarterly, 4,* 327–355.

D'Zurilla, T.J., & Goldfried, M.R. (1971). Problem-solving and behavior modification. *Journal of Abnormal Psychology, 78,* 107–126.

Eaton, W.W., & Keyl, P.M. (1990). Risk factors for the onset of diagnostic interview schedule/DSM-III agoraphobia in a prospective, population-based study. *Archives of General Psychiatry, 47,* 819–825.

Eaton, W.W., Kramer, M., Anthony, J.C., et al. (1989). The incidence of specific DIS/DSM-III mental disorders: Data from the NIMH Epidemiologic Catchment Area Programs. *Acta Psychiatrica Scandinavaca, 79,* 163–178.

Eckert, E.D., Goldberg, S.C., Halmi, K.A., Casper, R.C., & Davis, J.M. (1982). Depression in anorexia nervosa. *Psychological Medicine, 12,* 115–122.

Edmondson, E., Beden, J.R., & Gordon, R. (1984). In A. Gartner & F. Riessman (Eds.), *The self-help revolution.* New York: Human Sciences Press.

Edwards, G., Hensman, C., Hawker, A., & Williamson, V. (1967). Alcoholics Anonymous: The anatomy of a self-help group. *Social Psychiatry, 1,* 195–204.

Egan, G. (1975). *The skilled helper.* Monterey, CA: Brooks/Cole.

Egan, T. (1990). As memory and music faded, Alzheimer patient met death. *The New York Times, 89,* pp. A1, A16.

Egeland, J.A., Gerhard, D.S., Pauls, D.L., Sussex, J.N., Kidd, K.K., Allen, C.R., Hosterer, A.M., & Housman, D.E. (1987). Bipolar affective disorders linked to DNA markers on chromosome 11. *Nature, 325,* 783–787.

Ehlers, A., et al. (1988). Anxiety induced by false heart rate feedback in patients with panic disorder. *Behaviour Research and Therapy, 26,* 1–11.

Ehrhardt, A., & Money, J. (1967). Progestin-induced hermaphroditism: IQ and psychosexual identity in a study of ten girls. *Journal of Sex Research, 3,* 83–100.

Eidelson, R.J., & Epstein, N. (1982). Cognition and relationship maladjustment: Development of a measure of dysfunctional relationship belief. *Journal of Consulting and Clinical Psychology, 50,* 715–720.

Eiser, C., Eiser, R.J., Town, C., & Tripp, J. (1991). Discipline strategies and parental perceptions of preschool children with asthma. *British Journal of Medical Psychology, 64,* 45–53.

Eisler, R.M., & Blalock, J.A. (1991). Masculine gender role stress: Implications for the assessment of men. *Clinical Psychology Review, 11,* 45–60.

Ekstrand, M., & Coates, T.J. (in press). Maintenance of safer sexual behaviors and predictors of risky sex: The San Francisco Men's Health Study. *American Journal of Public Health.*

Elias, M., & Clabby, J.F. (1989). *Social decision making skills: A curriculum for the elementary grades.* Rockville, MD: Aspen Publishers.

Elkin, I., Parloff, M.B., Hadley, S.W., & Autry, J.H. (1985). NIMH Treatment of Depression Collaborative Research Program. *Archives of General Psychiatry, 42,* 305–316.

Elkin, I., Shea, T., Imber, S., Pilkonis, P., Sotsky, S., Glass, D., Watkins, J., Leber, W., & Collins, J. (1986). *NIMH Treatment of Depression Collaborative Research Program: Initial outcome findings.* Paper presented to the American Association for the Advancement of Science.

Elkin, I., Shea, M.T., Watkins, J.T., Imber, S.D., Sotsky, S.M., Collins, J.F., Glass, D.R., Pilkonis, P.A., Leber, W.R., Docherty, J.P., Fiester, S.J., & Parloff, M.B. (1989). NIMH Treatment of Depression Collaborative Research Program: I. General effectiveness of treatments. *Archives of General Psychiatry, 46,* 971–983.

Ellenberger, H.F. (1972). The story of "Anna O": A critical review with new data. *Journal of the History of the Behavior Sciences, 8,* 267–279.

Ellingson, R.J. (1954). Incidence of EEG abnormality among patients with mental disorders of apparently nonorganic origin: A criminal review. *American Journal of Psychiatry, 111*, 263–275.

Ellis, A. (1961). *The folklore of sex.* New York: Grove.

Ellis, A. (1962). *Reason and emotion in psychotherapy.* New York: Lyle Stuart.

Ellis, A. (1971). Rational-emotive treatment of impotence, frigidity, and other sexual problems. *Professional Psychology, 2*, 346–349.

Ellis, A. (1984). Rational-emotive therapy. In R.J. Corsini (Ed.), *Current psychotherapies* (3rd ed.). Itasca, IL: Peacock Press.

Ellis, H. (1906). *Studies in the psychology of sex.* New York: Random House.

Ellis, H. (1910). *Studies in the psychology of sex.* Philadelphia: FA Davis.

Ellis, N.R., Deacon, J.R., & Wooldridge, P.W. (1985). Structural memory deficits of mentally retarded persons. *American Journal of Mental Deficiency, 89*, 393–402.

Elmore, A.M. (1979). *A comparison of the psychophysiological and clinical response to biofeedback for temporal pulse amplitude reduction and biofeedback for increases in hand temperature in the treatment of migraine.* Unpublished doctoral dissertation, State University of New York at Stony Brook.

Elmore, A.M., & Tursky, B. (1978). The biofeedback hypothesis: An idea in search of a theory and method. In A.A. Sugerman & R.E. Tarter (Eds.), *Expanding dimensions of consciousness.* New York: Springer.

Elmore, A.M., & Tursky, B. (1981). A comparison of two psychophysiological approaches to the treatment of migraine. *Headache, 21*, 93–101.

Elmore, J.L., & Sugerman, A.A. (1975). Precipitation of psychosis during electroshock therapy. *Diseases of the Nervous System, 3*, 115–117.

Emerick, C., Lassen, D.L., & Edwards, M.T. (1977). Nonprofessional peers as therapeutic agents. In A.M. Razin, & A.S. Gurman (Eds.), *Effective psychotherapy: A handbook of research.* New York: Pergamon.

Emery, R.E. (1982). Interparental conflict and the children of discord and divorce. *Psychological Bulletin, 92*, 310–330.

Emery, R.E., & O'Leary, K.D. (1979). *Children's perceptions of marital discord and behavior problems of boys and girls.* Paper presented at the annual meeting of the Association for Advancement of Behavior Therapy, San Francisco.

Emmelkamp, P.M.G. (1986). Behavior therapy with adults. In S.L. Garfield & A.E. Bergin (Eds.), *Handbook of psychotherapy and behavior change* (3rd ed.). New York: Wiley.

Emmelkamp, P.M.G., Visser, S., & Hoekstra, R.J. (1988). Cognitive therapy versus exposure *in vivo* in the treatment of obsessive-compulsives. *Cognitive Therapy and Research, 12*, 103–114.

Emmons, R.A., & Diener, E. (1986). Situation selection as a moderator of response consistency and stability. *Journal of Personality and Social Psychology, 51*, 1013–1019.

Emory, L.E., Williams, D.H., Cole, C.M., Amparo, E.G., & Meyer, W.J. (1991). Anatomic variation of the corpus callosum in persons with gender dysphoria. *Archives of Sexual Behavior, 20*, 409–417.

Endicott, J., Nea, J., Fleiss, J., Cohen, J., Williams, J.B., & Simon, R. (1982). Diagnostic criteria for schizophrenia. Reliability and agreement between systems. *Archives of General Psychiatry, 39*, 884–889.

English, H.B. (1929). Three cases of the "conditioned fear response." *Journal of Abnormal and Social Psychology, 34*, 221–225.

Ennis, B., & Emery, R. (1978). *The rights of mental patients—An American Civil Liberties Union Handbook.* New York: Avon.

Ennis, B., & Siegel, L. (1973). *The rights of mental patients.* American Civil Liberties Union Handbook Series. New York: Avon.

Enright, J.B. (1970). An introduction to Gestalt techniques. In J. Fagan & I.L. Shepherd (Eds.), *Gestalt therapy now: Theory, techniques, applications.* Palo Alto, CA: Science and Behavior Books.

Epstein, L.C., & Lasagna, L. (1969). Obtaining informed consent. *Archives of Internal Medicine, 123*, 682–688.

Epstein, L.H., Beck, S., Figneroa, J., Farkas, G., Kazdin, A.E., Danema, D., & Becker, D. (1981). The effects of point economy and parent management on urine glucose and metabolic control in children with insulin dependent diabetes. *Journal of Applied Behavior Analysis, 14*, 365–375.

Epstein, L.H., Masek, B.J., & Marshall, W.R. (1978). A nutritionally based school program for control of eating in obese children. *Behavior Therapy, 9*, 766–788.

Epstein, L.H., Wing, R.R., Thompson, J.K., & Griffen, W. (1980). Attendance and fitness in aerobics exercise: The effects of contract and lottery procedures. *Behavior Modification, 4*, 465–479.

Epstein, S. (1979). The stability of behavior: On predicting most of the people much of the time. *Journal of Personality and Social Psychology, 37*, 1097–1126.

Erdberg, P., & Exner, J.E., Jr. (1984). Rorschach assessment. In G. Goldstein & M. Hersen (Eds.), *Handbook of psychological assessment.* New York: Pergamon.

Erikson, E.H. (1950). *Childhood and society.* New York: Norton.

Erikson, E.H. (1959). *Identity and the life cycle. Selected papers.* New York: International Universities Press.

Erikson, E.H. (1968). *Identity: Youth and crisis.* New York: W.W. Norton.

Erlenmeyer-Kimling, L.E., & Cornblatt, B. (1987). The New York high-risk project: A follow-up report. *Schizophrenia Bulletin, 13*, 451–461.

Ernst, F.A., Francis, R.A., Nevels, H., & Lemeh, C.A. (1991). Condemnation of homosexuality in the black community: A gender-specific phenomenon? *Archives of Sexual Behavior, 20*, 579–585.

Escobar, J.I., Burnam, M.A., Karno, M., et al. (1987). Somatization in the community. *Archives of General Psychiatry, 44*, 713–720.

Esler, J., Julius, S., Sweifler, A., Randall, O., Harburg, E., Gardiner, H., & DeQuattro, V. (1977). Mild high-renin essential hypertension: A neurogenic human hypertension. *New England Journal of Medicine, 296*, 405–411.

Etringer, B.D., Gregory, V.R., Lando, H.A. (1984). Influence of group cohesion on the behavioral treatment of smoking. *Journal of Consulting & Clinical Psychology, 52*, 1080–1086.

Evans, I.M. (1976). Classical conditioning. In M.P. Feldman & A. Broadhurst (Eds.), *Theoretical and experimental bases of the behaviour therapies.* New York: Wiley.

Evans, M.D., Hollon, S.D., DeRubeis, R.J., Piasecki, J.M., Grove, W.M., Garvey, M.J., & Tuason, V.B. (1992). Differential relapse following cognitive therapy, pharmacotherapy, and combined cognitive-pharmacotherapy for depression. *Archives of General Psychiatry, 49*, 802–808.

Evans, P.D., & Edgerton, N. (1990). Life events as predictors of the common cold. *British Journal of Medical Psychology.* Vol. 64. pp. 35–44.

Evans, R.B. (1969). Childhood parental relationships of homosexual men. *Journal of Consulting and Clinical Psychology, 33*, 129–135.

Evans, R.I., Rozelle, R.M., Maxwell, S.E., Raines, B.E., Dill, C.A., Guthrie, T.J., Henderson, A.H., & Hin, P.C. (1981). Social modelling films to deter smoking in adolescents: Results of a three-year field investigation. *Journal of Applied Psychology, 66*, 399–414.

Everett, F., Proctor, N., & Cartmell, B. (1989). Providing psychological services to American Indian children and families. In D.R. Atkinson, G. Morten, & D.W. Sue (Eds.), *Counseling American minorities* (3rd ed.). Dubuque, IA: W.C. Brown.

Exner, J.E. (1978). *The Rorschach: A comprehensive system. Vol.2. Current research and advanced interpretation.* New York: Wiley.

Exner, J.E., Jr. (1986). *The Rorschach: A com-*

prehensive system. Vol. 1. Basic foundations (2nd ed.). New York: Wiley.

Eysenck, H.J. (1952). The effects of psychotherapy: An evaluation. *Journal of Consulting Psychology, 16*, 319–324.

Eysenck, H.J. (1975). Crime as destiny. *New Behaviour, 9*, 46–49.

Fagan, J.F., & Singer, L.T. (1983). Infant recognition memory as a measure of intelligence. In L.P. Lipsitt (Ed.), *Advances in infancy research* (Vol. 2). Norwood, NJ: Ablex.

Fagerstrom, K.O. (1978). Measuring degree of physical dependence to tobacco smoking with reference to individualization of treatment. *Addictive Behaviors, 3*, 235–241.

Fairbank, J.A., & Brown, T.A. (1987). Current behavioral approaches to the treatment of posttraumatic stress disorder. *The Behavior Therapist, 3*, 57–64.

Fairbank, J.A., DeGood, D.E., & Jenkins, C.W. (1981). Behavioral treatment of a persistent post-traumatic startle response. *Journal of Behaviour Therapy and Experimental Psychiatry, 12*, 321–324.

Fairburn, C.G. (1980). Self-induced vomiting. *Journal of Psychosomatic Research, 24*, 193–197.

Fairburn, C.G., & Beglin, S.J. (1990). Studies of the epidemiology of bulimia nervosa. *The American Journal of Psychiatry, 147*, 401–408.

Fairburn, C.G., Kirk, J., O'Connor, M., & Cooper, P.J. (1986). A comparision of two psychological treatments for bulimia. *Behaviour Research and Therapy, 24*, 629–643.

Fairweather, G.W. (Ed.). (1964). *Social psychology in treating mental illness: An experimental approach.* New York: Wiley.

Fairweather, G.W., Sanders, D.H., Maynard, H., & Cressler, D.L. (1969). *Community life for the mentally ill: An alternative to institutional care.* Chicago: Aldine-Atherton.

Fallon, A.E., & Rozin, P. (1985). Sex differences in perceptions of desirable body shape. *Journal of Abnormal Psychology, 94*, 102–105.

Falloon, I.R.H., Boyd, J.L., McGill, C.W., Razani, J., Moss, H.B., & Gilderman, A.N. (1982). Family management in the prevention of exacerbation of schizophrenia: A controlled study. *New England Journal of Medicine, 306*, 1437–1440.

Falloon, I.R.H., Boyd, J.L., McGill, C.W., Williamson, M., Razani, J., Moss, H.B., Gilderman, A.M., & Simpson, G.M. (1985). Family management in the prevention of morbidity of schizophrenia. *Archives of General Psychiatry, 42*, 887–896.

Faraone, S.V., Kremen, W.S., & Tsuang, M.T. (1990). Genetic transmission of affective disorders: Quantitative models and linkage analysis. *Psychological Bulletin, 108*, 109–127.

Farina, A. (1976). *Abnormal psychology.* Englewood Cliffs, NJ: Prentice-Hall.

Farkas, G., & Rosen, R.C. (1976). The effects of alcohol on elicited male sexual response. *Studies in Alcohol, 37*, 265–272.

Farquhar, J.W., Fortmann, S.P., Flora, J.A., & Maccoby, N. (1990). Methods of communication to influence behaviour. In W. Holland, R. Detels, & G. Knox (Eds.), *Oxford textbook of public health* (2nd ed.). New York: Oxford University Press.

Farquhar, J.W., Fortmann, S.P., Flora, J.A., Taylor, B., Haskell, W.L., Williams, P.T., Maccoby, N., & Wood, P.D. (1990). Effects of communitywide education on cardiovascular disease risk factors: The Stanford Five-City Project. *Journal of the American Medical Association, 264*, 359–365.

Farris, E.J., Yeakel, E.H., & Medoff, H. (1945). Development of hypertension in emotional gray Norway rats after air blasting. *American Journal of Physiology, 144*, 331–333.

Favell, J.E., Azrin, N.H., Baumeister, A.A., Carr, E.G., Dorsey, M.F., Forehand, R., Foxx, R.M., Lovaas, O.I., Rincover, A., Risley, T.R., Romanczyk, R.G., Russo, D.C., Schroeder, S.R., & Solnick, J.V. (1982). The treatment of self-injurious behavior. *Behavior Therapy, 13*, 529–554.

Fawcett, J., Epstein, P., Fiester, S.J., Elkin, I., & Autry, J.H. (1987). Clinical Management—Imipramine/placebo administration manual: NIMH Treatment of Depression Collaborative Research Program. *Psychopharmacology Bulletin, 23*, 309–324.

Fedora, O., Reddon, J.R., & Yeudall, L.T. (1986). Stimuli eliciting sexual arousal in genital exhibitionists: A possible clinical application. *Archives of Sexual Behavior, 15*, 417–427.

Fein, D., Pennington, B., Markowitz, P., Braverman, M., & Waterhouse, L. (1986). Toward a neuropsychological model of infantile autism: Are the social deficits primary? *Journal of the American Academy of Child Psychiatry, 25*, 198–212.

Feingold, B.F. (1973). *Introduction to clinical allergy.* Springfield, IL: Charles C. Thomas.

Feingold, B.F. (1975). *Why your child is hyperactive.* New York: Random House.

Feinsilver, D.B., & Gunderson, J.G. (1972). Psychotherapy for schizophrenics—Is it indicated? *Schizophrenia Bulletin, 1*, 11–23.

Fenichel, O. (1945). *The psychoanalytic theory of neurosis.* New York: Norton.

Fenigstein, A. (1979). Self-consciousness, self-attention, and social interaction. *Journal of Personality and Social Psychology, 37*, 75–86.

Fenigstein, A., Scheier, M.F., & Buss, A.H. (1975). Public and private self-consciousness: Assessment and theory. *Journal of Consulting and Clinical Psychology, 43*, 522–527.

Fentiman, L.C. (1985). Guilty but mentally ill: The real verdict is guilty. *Boston College Law Review, 26*, 601–653.

Ferenczi, S. (1960). The further development of an active therapy in psychoanalysis. In J. Richman (Ed.), *Further contributions to the theory and technique of psychoanalysis.* London: Hogarth.

Fernando, C.K., & Basmajian, J.V. (1978). Biofeedback in physical medicine and rehabilitation. *Biofeedback and Self-regulation, 3*, 435–455.

Ferster, C.B. (1961). Positive reinforcement and behavioral deficits of autistic children. *Child Development, 32*, 437–456.

Ferster, C.B. (1965). Classification of behavioral pathology. In L. Krasner & L.P. Ullmann (Eds.), *Research in behavior modification.* New York: Holt, Rinehart & Winston.

Field, T., Goldberg, S., Stern, D., & Sostek, A. (Eds.). (1980). *High-risk infants and children: Adult and peer interactions.* New York: Academic Press.

Field, T., Sostek, A., Goldberg, J., & Shuman, M. (Eds.). (1979). *Infants born at risk.* New York: Spectrum.

Figley, C.R. (1978a). Introduction. In C.R. Figley (Ed.), *Stress disorders among Vietnam veterans.* New York: Brunner/Mazel.

Figley, C.R. (1978b). Psychosocial adjustment among Vietnam veterans: An overview of the research. In C.R. Figley (Ed.), *Stress disorders among Vietnam veterans.* New York: Brunner/Mazel.

Figley, C.R., & Leventman, S. (1980). Introduction: Estrangement and victimization. In C.R. Figley & S. Leventman (Eds.), *Strangers at home: Vietnam veterans since the war.* New York: Praeger.

Fillmore, K.M., & Caetano, R. (1980, May 22). *Epidemiology of occupational alcoholism.* Paper presented at the National Institute on Alcohol Abuse and Alcoholism's Workshop on Alcoholism in the Workplace, Reston, VA.

Finkelhor, D. (1979). *Sexually victimized children.* New York: Free Press.

Finkelhor, D. (1983). Removing the child—Prosecuting the offender in cases of sexual abuse: Evidence from the national reporting system for child abuse and neglect. *Child Abuse and Neglect, 7*, 195–205.

Finkelhor, D., & Araji, S. (1986). Explanations of pedophilia: A four-factor model. *Journal of Sex Research, 22*, 145–161.

Finn, S.E. (1982). Base rates, utilities, and DSM-III: Shortcomings of fixed-rule systems of psychodiagnosis. *Journal of Abnormal Psychology, 91*, 294–302.

Fiore, J., Becker, J., & Coppel, D.B. (1983). Social network interactions: A buffer or a stress? *American Journal of Community Psychology, 11*, 423–439.

Fiore, M.C., Novotny, T.F., Pierce, J.P., Giovino, G.A., Hatziandreu, E.J., Newcomb, P.A., Surawicz, T.S., & Davis, R.M. (1990). Methods used to quit smoking in the United States: Do cessation programs help? *Journal of the American Medical Association, 263*, 2760–2765.

Fischer, M. (1971). Psychoses in the offspring of schizophrenic monozygotic twins and their normal co-twins. *British Journal of Psychiatry, 118*, 43–52.

Fischetti, M., Curran, J.P., & Wessberg, H.W. (1977). Sense of timing. *Behavior Modification, 1*, 179–194.

Fishbain, D.A., & Goldberg, M. (1991). The misdiagnosis of conversion disorder in a psychiatric emergency service. *General Hospital Psychiatry, 13*, 177–181.

Fishman, D.B., Rodgers, F., & Franks, C.M. (Eds.). (1988). *Paradigms in behavior therapy: Present and promise* (pp. 254–293). New York: Springer.

Fitts, S.N., Gibson, P., Redding, C.A., & Deiter, P.J. (1989). Body dysmorphic disorder: Implications for its validity as a DSM-III-R clinical syndrome. *Psychological Reports, 64*, 655–658.

Fitzgerald, R.V. (1973). *Conjoint marital therapy.* New York: Jason Aronson.

Flemming, A.S., Rickards, L.D., Santos, J.F., & West, P.R. (1986). *Report on a survey of community mental health centers* (Vol. 3). Washington, DC: Action Committee to Implement the Mental Health Recommendations of the 1981 White House Conference on Aging. As cited in Roybal (1988).

Foa, E.B., Steketee, G.S., & Ozarow, B.J. (1985). Behavior therapy with obsessive-compulsives: From theory to treatment. In M. Mavissakalian, S.M. Turner, & L. Michelson (Eds.), *Obsessive-compulsive disorder: Psychological and pharmacological treatment.* New York: Plenum.

Foa, E.B., Feske, U., Murdock, T. B., Kozak, M.J. & McCarthy, P.R. (1991). Processing of threat-related information in rape victims. *Journal of Abnormal Psychology, 100*, 156–165.

Foa, E.B., & Kozak, M.J. (1986). Emotional processing of fear: Exposure to corrective information. *Psychological Bulletin, 99*, 20–35.

Foa, E.B., Kozak, M.J., Steketee, G.S., & McCarthy, P.R. (in press), Treatment of depressive and obsessive-compulsive symptoms in OCD by imipramine and behavior therapy. *British Journal of Clinical Psychology.*

Foa, E.B., Zinbarg, R., & Rothbaum, B.O. (in press). Uncontrollability and unpredictability in post-traumatic stress disorder: An animal model. *Psychological Bulletin.*

Fodor, I. (1978). Phobias in women: Therapeutic approaches. In *Helping women change: A guide for professional counseling.* New York: BMA Audio Cassette Program.

Folkman, S., Bernstein, L., & Lazarus, R.S. (1987). Stress processes and the misuse of drugs in older adults. *Psychology and Aging, 2*, 366–374.

Folkman, S., & Lazarus, R.S. (1985). If it changes it must be a process: Study of emotions and coping during 3 stages of college examination. *Journal of Personality and Social Psychology, 48*, 150–170.

Folks, D.G., Ford, C.V., & Regan, W.M. (1984). Conversion symptoms in a general hospital. *Psychosomatics, 25*, 285–295.

Folstein, M.F., Marshal, F., Bassett, S.S., et al. (1991). Dementia: A case ascertainment in a community survey. *Journals of Gerontology, 46*, 132–138.

Folstein, M.F., & McHugh, P.R. (1978). Dementia syndrome of depression. In R. Katzman, R.D. Terry, & K.L. Bick (Eds.), *Alzheimer's disease: Senile dementia and related disorders. Vol.7. Aging.* New York: Raven.

Folstein, S., & Rutter, M. (1978). A twin study of individuals with infantile autism. In M. Rutter & E. Schopler (Eds.), *Autism: A reappraisal of concepts and treatment.* New York: Plenum.

Ford, C., & Neale, J.M. (1985). Effects of a helplessness induction on judgments of control. *Journal of Personality and Social Psychology, 49*, 1330–1336

Ford, C.S., & Beach, F.A. (1951). *Patterns of sexual behavior.* New York: Harper.

Ford, C.V., & Folks, D.G. (1985). Conversion disorders: An overview. *Psychosomatics, 26*, 371–383.

Ford, C.V., & Sbordone, R.J. (1980). Attitudes of psychiatrists towards elderly patients. *American Journal of Psychiatry, 137*, 571–575.

Ford, D.H., & Urban, H.B. (1963). *Systems of psychotherapy: A comparative study.* New York: Wiley.

Fordney-Settlage, D.S. (1975). Heterosexual dysfunction: Evaluation of treatment procedures. *Archives of Sexual Behavior, 4*, 367–388.

Fordyce, W.E., Brockway, J.A., Bergman, J.A., & Spengler, D. (1986). Acute back pain: A control-group comparison of behavioral vs. traditional methods. *Journal of Behavioral Medicine, 9*, 127–140.

Foreyt, J.P. (1990). Behavioral medicine. In C.M. Franks, G.T. Wilson, P.C. Kendall, & J.P. Foreyt (Eds.). *Annual review of behavior: Theory and practice* (Vol. 12). New York: Guilford.

Forstein, M. (1988). Homophobia: An overview. *Psychiatric Annals, 18*, 33–36.

Forsythe, W.I., & Redmond, A. (1974). Eneuresis and spontaneous cure rate: Study of 1129 enuretics. *Archives of Disease in Childhood, 49*, 259–263.

Forth, A.E., & Hare, R.D. (1989). The contingent negative variation in psychopaths. *Psychophysiology, 26*, 676–682.

Foucault, M. (1965). *Madness and civilization.* New York: Random House.

Foulkes, S.H. (1964). *Therapeutic group analysis.* New York: International Universities Press.

Fox, R., Eldred, L.J., Fuchs, E.J., Kaslow, R.A., Visscher, B.R., Ho, M., Phair, J.P., & Polk, B.F. (1987). Clinical manifestations of acute infection with human immunodeficiency virus in a cohort of gay men. *AIDS, 1*, 35–38.

Foy, D.W., Carroll, E.M., & Donahoe, C.P., Jr. (in press). Etiological factors in the development of PTSD in clinical samples of combat veterans. *Journal of Consulting and Clinical Psychology.*

Foy, D.W., Resnick, H.S., Carroll, E.M., & Osato, S.S. (1990). Behavior therapy. In A.S. Bellack, & M. Hersen (Eds.), *Handbook of comparative treatments for adult disorders* (pp. 302–315). New York: Wiley.

Foy, D.W., Resnick, H.S., Sipprelle, R.C., & Carroll, E.M. (1987). Premilitary, military, and postmilitary factors in the development of combat-related posttraumatic stress disorder. *The Behavior Therapist, 10*, 3–9.

Foy, D.W., Sipprelle, R.C., Rueger, D.B., & Carroll, E.M. (1984). Etiology of posttraumatic stress disorder in Vietnam veterans: Analysis of premilitary, military, and combat exposure influences. *Journal of Consulting and Clinical Psychology, 52*, 79–87.

Frame, C., Matson, J.L., Sonis, W.A., Fialkov, M.J., & Kazdin, A.E. (1982). Behavioral treatment of depression in a prepubertal child. *Journal of Behaviour Therapy and Experimental Psychiatry, 3*, 239–243.

Frances, A. (1980). The DSM-III personality disorders section: A commentary. *American Journal of Psychiatry, 137*, 1050–1054.

Frank, E., Anderson, C., & Kupfer, D.J. (1976). Profiles of couples seeking sex therapy and marital therapy. *American Journal of Psychiatry, 133*, 559–562.

Frank, E., Anderson, C., & Rubenstein, D. (1978). Frequency of sexual dysfunctions in "normal" couples. *New England Journal of Medicine, 299*, 111–115.

Frank, E., Kupfer, D.J., Perel, J.M. et al. (1990). Three-year outcomes for maintenence therapies in recurrent depression. *Archives of General Psychiatry, 47*, 1093–1099.

Frank, J.D. (1961). *Persuasion and healing.* Baltimore: Johns Hopkins University Press.

Frank, J.D. (1971). Therapeutic factors in psychotherapy. *American Journal of Psychotherapy, 25*, 350–361.

Frank, J.D. (1973). *Persuasion and healing* (2nd ed.). Baltimore: Johns Hopkins University Press.

Frank, J.D. (1976). Psychotherapy and the sense of mastery. In R.L. Spitzer & D.F. Klein (Eds.), *Evaluation of psychotherapies: Behavioral therapies, drug therapies and their interactions.* Baltimore: Johns Hopkins University Press.

Frank, J.D. (1982). Therapeutic components shared by all psychotherapies. In J.H. Harvey, & M.M. Parks (Eds.), *The Master Lecture Series. Vol. 1. Psychotherapy research and behavior change* (pp. 73–122). Washington, DC: American Psychological Association.

Frank, J.B., Giller, E.L., Koster, T.R., & Dan, E. (1988). A randomized clinical trial of phenelzine and imipramine for post-traumatic stress disorder. *American Journal of Psychiatry, 145*, 1289–1291.

Frankl, V. (1959). *From death camp to existentialism.* Boston: Beacon.

Frankl, V. (1963). *Man's search for meaning.* New York: Washington Square.

Frankl, V. (1967). *Psychotherapy and existentialism.* New York: Simon & Schuster.

Franks, C.M. (1990). Behavior therapy: An overview. In C.M. Franks, G.T. Wilson, P.C. Kendall, & J.P. Foreyt (Eds.), *Review of behavior therapy: Theory and practice* (Vol. 12). New York: Guilford.

Frazier, P.A. (1990). Victim attributions and post-rape trauma. *Journal of Personality & Social Psychology, 59*, 298–304.

Freeman, B.J., & Ritvo, E.R. (1976). Cognitive assessment. In E.R. Ritvo, B.J. Freeman, E.M. Ornitz, & P.E. Tanguay (Eds.), *Autism: Diagnosis, current research and management.* New York: Spectrum.

Fremouw, W.J., Perczel, W.J., & Ellis, T.E. (1990). *Suicide risk: Assessment and response guidelines.* Elmsford, NY: Pergamon.

Freud, A. (1946a). *The ego and mechanisms of defense.* New York: International Universities Press.

Freud, A. (1946b). *The psychoanalytic treatment of children: Lectures and essays.* London: Imago.

Freud, A. (1966). *The ego and the mechanisms of defense.* New York: International Universities Press.

Freud, S. (1936). *The problem of anxiety.* New York: Norton. (Original work published 1926)

Freud, S. (1937). Analysis terminable and interminable. *International Journal of Psychoanalysis, 18*, 373–391.

Freud, S. (1938). Three contributions to the theory of sex. In A.A. Brill (Ed.), *The basic writings of Sigmund Freud.* New York; Modern Library. (Original work published 1905)

Freud, S. (1949). *A general introduction to psychoanalysis.* New York: Garden City Publishing.

Freud, S. (1917). Mourning and melancholia. In *Collected papers* (Vol. 4). London: Hogarth and the Institute of Psychoanalysis, 1950.

Freud, S. (1955). Lines of advance in psychoanalytic therapy. In *The complete psychological works of Sigmund Freud.* J. Strachey (Ed. and Trans.) London: Hogarth and the Institute of Psychoanalysis. (Original work published 1918)

Freud, S. (1956). Analysis of a phobia in a five-year-old boy. In *Collected works of Sigmund Freud* (Vol. 10). London: Hogarth. (Original work published 1909)

Freud, S. (1956). A case of paranoia running counter to the psychoanalytical theory of the disease. In *Collected papers* (Vol. 2). London: Hogarth. (Original work published 1915)

Freud, S. (1964). New introductory lectures in psychoanalysis. In J. Strachey (Ed. and Trans.), *The standard edition of the complete psychological works of Sigmund Freud* (Vol. 22, pp. 7–184). London: Hogarth. (Original work published 1933)

Freund, K., Watson, R., & Dickey, R. (1990). Does sexual abuse in childhood cause pedophilia: An exploratory study. *Archives of Sexual Behavior, 19*, 557-568.

Freund, K., Watson, R., Dickey, R., & Rienzo, D. (1991). Erotic gender differentiation in pedophilia. *Archives of Sexual Behavior, 20*, 555–566.

Friar, L.R., & Beatty, J. (1976). Migraine: Management by trained control of vasoconstriction. *Journal of Consulting and Clinical Psychology, 44*, 46–53.

Frick, P.J., Lahey, B.B., Hardagen, S., & Hynd, G.W. (1989). Conduct problems in boys: Relations to maternal personality, marital satisfaction, & socioeconomic status. *Journal of Clinical Child Psychology, 18*, 11–12.

Friedberg, C.K. (1966). *Diseases of the heart* (3rd ed.). Philadelphia: Saunders.

Friedman, J.M. (1978). Sexual adjustment of the postcoronary male. In J. LoPiccolo & L. LoPiccolo (Eds.), *Handbook of sex therapy.* New York: Plenum.

Friedman, J.M., & Hogan, D.R. (1985). Sexual dysfunction: Low sexual desire. In D.H. Barlow (Ed.), *Clinical handbook of psychological disorders.* New York: Guilford.

Friedman, M. (1969). *Pathogenesis of coronary artery disease.* New York: McGraw-Hill.

Friedman, M., Thoresen, C.E., Gill, J.J., Powell, L.H., Ulmer, D., Thompson, L., Price, V.A., Rabin, D.D., Breall, W.S., Dixon, T., Levy, R., & Bourg, E. (1984). Alteration of type A behavior and reduction in cardiac recurrences in post-myocardial infarction patients. *American Heart Journal, 108*, 237–248.

Friedman, M., Thoresen, C.E., Gill, J.J., Ulmer, D., Thompson, L., Powell, L., Price, A., Elek, S.R., Rabin, D.D., Breall, W.S., Piaget, G., Dixon, T., Bourg, E., Levy, R., & Tasto, D.I. (1982). Feasibility of altering type A behavior pattern after myocardial infarction. *Circulation, 66*, 83–92.

Friedman, M., & Ulmer, D. (1984). *Treating type A behavior and your heart.* New York: Fawcett Crest.

Fristoe, M., & Lloyd, L.L. (1979). Nonspeech communication. In N.R. Ellis (Ed.), *Handbook of mental deficiency, psychological theory and research* (2nd ed.). Hillsdale, NJ: Erlbaum.

Frith, U. (1989). *Autism: Explaining the enigma.* Cambridge, MA: Basil Blackwell.

Fromm-Reichmann, F. (1948). Notes on the development of treatment of schizophrenics by psychoanalytic psychotherapy, *Psychiatry, 11*, 263–273.

Fromm-Reichmann, F. (1952). Some aspects of psychoanalytic therapy with schizophrenics. In E. Brady & F.C. Redlich (Eds.), *Psychotherapy with schizophrenics.* New York: International Universities Press.

Frude, N. (1982). The sexual nature of sexual abuse: A review of the literature. *Child Abuse and Neglect, 6*, 211–223.

Fuller, R.K. (1988). Disulfiram treatment of alcoholism. In R.M. Rose & J.E. Barrett (Eds.), *Alcoholism: Treatment and Outcome.* New York: Raven.

Fuller, R.K., Branchey, L., Brightwell, D.R., Derman, R.M., Emrick, C.D., Iber, F.L., James, K.E., & Lacoursiere, R.B. (1986). Disulfiram treatment of alcoholism: A Veterans Administration cooperative study. *Journal of the American Medical Association, 256*, 1449–1455.

Furby, L., Weinrott, M.R., & Blacksbaw, L. (1989). Sex offender recidivism. A review. *Psychological Bulletin, 105*, 3–30.

Gabbay, F.H. (1992). Behavior genetic strategies in the study of emotion. *Psychological Science, 3*, 50–55.

Gagne, P. (1981). Treatment of sex offenders with medroxyprogesterone acetate. *American Journal of Psychiatry, 138*, 644–646.

Gagnon, J.H. (1977). *Human sexualities.* Chicago: Scott, Foresman.

Gagnon, J.H., & Davison, G.C. (1974). *Enhancement of sexual responsiveness in behavior therapy.* Paper presented at the 82nd Annual Convention of the American Psychological Association, New Orleans.

Gagnon, J.H., & Davison, G.C. (1976). Asylums, the token economy, and the metrics of mental life. *Behavior Therapy, 7,* 528–534.

Gagnon, J.H., & Simon, W. (1973). *Sexual conduct: The social origins of human sexuality.* Chicago: Aldine.

Gaines, J. (1974). The founder of Gestalt therapy: A sketch of Fritz Perls. *Psychology Today, 8,* 117–118.

Galaburda, A.M. (1989). Ordinary and extraordinary brain development: Anatomical variation in developmental dyslexia. *Annals of Dyslexia, 39,* 67–80.

Galanter, M., & Castaneda, R. (1985). Self-destructive behavior in the substance abuser. *Psychiatric Clinics of North America, 8,* 251–261.

Galanter, M., & Castaneda, R. (1990). Psychotherapy. In A.S. Bellack, & M. Hersen (Eds.), *Handbook of comparative treatments for adult disorders* (pp. 463–478). New York: Wiley.

Galin, D., Diamond, R., & Braff, D. (1977). Lateralization of conversion symptoms: More frequent on the left. *American Journal of Psychiatry, 134,* 578–580.

Gallagher, D., Breckenridge, J.N., Thompson, L.W., Dessonville, C., & Amaral, P. (1982). Similarities and differences between normal grief and depression in older adults. *Essence, 5,* 127–140.

Gallagher, D., & Thompson, L.W. (1982). *Elders' maintenance of treatment benefits following individual psychotherapy for depression: Results of a pilot study and preliminary data from an ongoing replication study.* Paper presented at the annual meeting of the American Psychological Association, Washington, DC.

Gallagher, D., & Thompson, L.W. (1983). Cognitive therapy for depression in the elderly. A promising model for treatment and research. In L.D. Breslau & M.R. Haug (Eds.), *Depression and aging: Causes, care and consequences.* New York: Springer.

Garber, J., Kriss, M.R., Koch, M., & Lindholm, L. (1988). Recurrent depression in adolescents: A follow-up study. *Journal of the American Academy of Child and Adolescent Psychiatry, 27,* 49–54.

Garcia, J., McGowan, B.K., & Green, K.F. (1972). Biological constraints on conditioning. In A.H. Black & W.F. Prokasy (Eds.), *Classical conditioning II: Current research and theory.* New York: Appleton-Century-Crofts.

Garfield, S.L., & Kurtz, R. (1974). A survey of clinical psychologists: Characteristics, activities, and orientations. *The Clinical Psychologist, 28,* 7–10.

Garfield, S.L. (1974). *Clinical psychology: The study of personality and behavior.* Chicago: Aldine.

Garfield, S.L. (1978). Research on client variables in psychotherapy. In S.L. Garfield, & A.E. Bergin (Eds.), *Handbook of psychotherapy and behavior change* (2nd ed.). New York: Wiley.

Garfield, S.L., & Bergin, A.E. (Eds.). (1986a). *Handbook of psychotherapy and behavior change* (3rd ed.). New York: Wiley.

Garfield, S.L., & Bergin, A.E. (1986b). Introduction and historical overview. In S.L. Garfield & A.E. Bergin (Eds.), *Handbook of psychotherapy and behavior change* (3rd ed.). New York: Wiley.

Garfinkel, P.E., & Garner, D.M. (1982). *Anorexia nervosa: A multidimensional perspective.* New York: Brunner/Mazel.

Garmezy, N. (1977). DSM-III: Never mind the psychologists—Is it good for the children? *The Clinical Psychologist, 31,* 3–4.

Garner, D.M., Fairburn, C.G., & Davis, R. (1987). Cognitive-behavioral treatment of bulimia nervosa. *Behavior Modification, 11,* 398–431.

Garner, D.M., Olmsted, M.P., & Polivy, J. (1984). Comparison between weight-preoccupied women and anorexia nervosa. *Psychosomatic Medicine, 46,* 255–266.

Gatchel, R.J., Baum, A., & Krantz, D.S. (1989). *An introduction to health psychology* (2nd ed.) New York: Random House.

Gatz, M., Bengtson, V.L., & Blum, M.J. (1990). Caregiving families. In J.E. Birren, & K.W. Schaie (Eds.), *Handbook of the psychology of aging* Third edition (pp. 404–426). New York: Academic Press.

Gatz, M., & Pearson, C.G. (1988). Ageism revised and the provision of psychological services. *American Psychologist, 43,* 184–188.

Gatz, M., Pearson, C., & Fuentes, M. (1984). Older women and mental health. In A.U. Rickel, M. Gerrard, & I. Iscoe (Eds.), *Social and psychological problems of women: Prevention and crisis intervention.* Washington, DC: Hemisphere.

Gatz, M., & Smyer, M.A. (1992). The mental health system and older adults in the 1990s. *American Psychologist, 47,* 741–751.

Gatz, M., Karel, M.J., & Wolkenstein, B. (1991). Survey of providers of psychological services to older adults. *Professional Psychology: Research and Practice, 5,* 413–415.

Gauthier, J., Bois, R., Allaire, D., & Drollet, M. (1981). Evaluation of skin temperature biofeedback training at two different sites for migraine. *Journal of Behavioral Medicine, 4,* 407–419.

Gauthier, Y., Fortin, C., Drapeau, P., Breton, J., Gosselin, J., Quintal, L., Weisnagel, J., & Lamarre, A. (1978). Follow-up study of 35 asthmatic preschool children. *Journal of the American Academy of Child Psychiatry, 17,* 679–694.

Gauthier, Y., Fortin, C., Drapeau, P., Breton, J., Gosselin, J., Quintal, L., Weisnagel, J., Tetreault, L., & Pinard, G. (1977). The mother-child relationship and the development of autonomy and self-assertion in young (14–30 months) asthmatic children. *Journal of the American Academy of Child Psychiatry, 16,* 109–131.

Gawin, F.H., & Kleber, H.D. (1986). Abstinence symptomatology and psychiatric diagnosis in cocaine abusers. *Archives of General Psychiatry, 43,* 107–113.

Gebhard, P.H., Gagnon, J.H., Pomeroy, W.B., & Christenson, C.V. (1965). *Sex offenders.* New York: Harper & Row.

Geer, J.H., Davison, G.C., & Gatchel, R.I. (1970). Reduction of stress in humans through nonveridical perceived control of aversive stimulation. *Journal of Personality and Social Psychology, 16,* 731–738.

Geer, J.H., Heiman, J., & Leitenberg, H. (1984). *Human sexuality.* Englewood Cliffs, NJ: Prentice-Hall.

Geller, E., Ritvo, E.R., Freeman, B.J., & Yuwifler, A. (1982). Preliminary observations on the effect of fenfluramine on blood serotonin and symptoms in three autistic boys. *New England Journal of Medicine, 307,* 165–169.

Geller, E., Yokota, A., Schroth, P., & Novak, P. (1984). Study of fenfluramine in outpatients with the syndrome of autism. *Journal of Pediatrics, 105,* 823–828.

Geller, J.L., & Bertisch, G. (1985). Firesetting behavior in the histories of a state hospital population. *American Journal of Psychiatry, 142,* 464–468.

Gendlin, E.T. (1962). *Experiencing and the creation of meaning: A philosophical and psychological approach to the subject.* New York: Free Press.

General Register Office. (1968). *A glossary of mental disorders.* London: Author.

Gentry, W.D., Chesney, A.P., Gary, H.G., Hall, R.P., & Hamburg, E. (1982). Habitual anger-coping styles: I. Effect of mean blood pressure and risk for essential hypertension. *Psychosomatic Medicine, 44,* 195–202.

Gentry, W.D., Chesney, A.P., Hall, R.P., & Hamburg, E. (1981). Effect of habitual anger-coping pattern on blood pressure in black/white, high/low stress area respondents. *Psychosomatic Medicine, 43,* 88.

George, L.K. (1980). *Role transitions in later life.* Monterey, CA: Brooks/Cole.

George, L.K., & Gwynther, L.P. (1985). *Support groups for caregivers of memory impaired elderly: Easing caregiver burden.* Paper presented at the NMHA Commission on the Prevention of Mental and Emotional Disability, Alexandria, VA. As cited in Gesten & Jason (1987).

George, L.K., & Weiler, S.J. (1981). Sexuality in middle and late life: The effects of age, cohort, and gender. *Archives of General Psychiatry, 38,* 919–923.

Gerber, L.M. (1983). Ethnicity still matters: Socio-demographic profiles of the ethnic elderly in Ontario. *Canadian Ethnic Studies, 15,* 60–80.

Gergen, K.J. (1982). *Toward transformation in social knowledge.* New York: Plenum.

Gerson, S.C., Plotkin, D.A., & Jarvik, L.F. (1988). Antidepressant drug studies, 1964 to 1986: Empirical evidence for aging patients. *Journal of Clinical Psychopharmacology, 8,* 311–322.

Gesten, E.L., & Jason, L.A. (1987). Social and community interventions. *Annual Review of Psychology, 38,* 427–460.

Ghoneim, M.M., & Mewaldt, S.P. (1990). Benzodiazepines and human memory: A review. *Anesthesiology, 72,* 926–938.

Giarretto, H. (1982). A comprehensive child sexual abuse treatment program. *Child Abuse and Neglect, 6,* 263–278.

Gibbons, D.C. (1975). *Delinquent behavior.* Englewood Cliffs, NJ: Prentice-Hall.

Gibbs, J. (Ed.). (1968). *Suicide.* New York: Harper & Row.

Gibbs, J.T. (1980). The interpersonal orientation in mental health consultation: Toward a model of ethnic variations in consultation. *American Journal of Orthopsychiatry, 45,* 430–445.

Gibson, D., & Harris, A. (1988). Aggregated early intervention effects for Down's syndrome persons: Patterning and longevity of benefits. *Journal of Mental Deficiency Research, 32,* 1–17.

Gilboy, J.A., & Schmidt, J.R. (1971). "Voluntary" hospitalization of the mentally ill. *Northwestern University Law Review, 66,* 429–439.

Gillberg, C., & Svendsen, P. (1983). Childhood psychosis and computed tomographic brain scan findings. *Journal of Autism and Developmental Disorders, 13,* 19–32.

Gim, R., Atkinson, D., & Kim, S. (1991). Asian-American acculturation, counselor ethnicity, and cultural sensitivity. *Journal of Counseling Psychology, 38,* 57–62.

Ginsburg, A.B., & Goldstein, S.G. (1974). Age bias in referral to psychological consultation. *Journal of Gerontology, 29,* 410–415.

Ginzburg, H.M. (1986). Naltrexone: Its clinical utility. In B. Stimmel (Ed.), *Advances in alcohol and substance abuse* (pp. 83–101). New York: Haworth.

Gittelman, R., Abikoff, H., Pollack, E., Klein, D., Katz, F., & Mattes, J. (1980). A controlled trial of behavior modification and methylphenidate in hyperactive children. In C. Whalen & B. Henker (Eds.), *Hyperactive children: The social ecology of identification and treatment* (pp. 221–246). New York: Academic Press.

Gittelman, R., Mannuzza, S., Shenker, R., & Bonagura, N. (1985). Hyperactive boys almost grown up. *Archives of General Psychiatry, 42,* 937–947.

Gladue, B.A. (1985). Neuroendocrine response to estrogen and sexual orientation. *Science, 230,* 961.

Glasner, P.D., & Kaslow, R.A. (1990). The epidemiology of Human Immunodeficiency Virus infection. *Journal of Consulting and Clinical Psychology, 58,* 13–21.

Glass, C.R., & Arnkoff, D.B. (1989). Behavioral assessment of social anxiety and social phobia. *Clinical Psychology Review, 9,* 75–90.

Glass, D.C. (1977). *Behavior patterns, stress, and coronary disease.* Hillsdale, NJ: Larry Erlbaum.

Glassman, A.H., & Roose, S.P. (1981). Delusional depression. *Archives of General Psychiatry, 38,* 424–427.

Glover, E. (1956). *On the early development of mind.* New York: International Universities Press.

Goffman, E. (1961). *Asylums: Essays on the social situation of mental patients and other inmates.* Chicago: Aldine.

Gold, M.S., Pottash, A.C., Sweeney, D.R., & Kleber, H.D. (1980). Opiate withdrawal using clonidine. *Journal of the American Medical Association, 243,* 343–346.

Gold, M.S., Redmond, D.E., Jr., & Kleber, H.D. (1978). Clonidine in opiate withdrawal. *Lancet, 1,* 929–930.

Goldberg, E.M., & Morrison, S.L. (1963). Schizophrenia and social class. *British Journal of Psychiatry, 109,* 785–802.

Golden, C.J. (1981a). The Luria-Nebraska Children's Battery: Theory and formulation. In G.W. Hynd & J.E. Obrzut (Eds.), *Neuropsychological assessment and the school-age child: Issues and procedures.* New York: Grune & Stratton.

Golden, C.J. (1981b). A standardized version of Luria's neuropsychological tests: A quantitative and qualitative approach to neuropsychological evaluation. In S.B. Filskov & T.J. Boil (Eds.), *Handbook of clinical neuropsychology.* New York: Wiley.

Golden, C.J., Hammeke, T., & Purisch, A. (1978). Diagnostic validity of a standardized neuropsychological battery derived from Luria's neuropsychological test. *Journal of Consulting and Clinical Psychology, 46,* 1258–1265.

Goldfried, M.R. (1980). Toward the delineation of therapeutic change principles. *American Psychologist, 35,* 991–999.

Goldfried, M.R. (Ed.). (1982). *Converging themes in the practice of psychotherapy.* New York: Springer.

Goldfried, M.R. (1991). Research issues in psychotherapy integration. *Journal of Psychotherapy Integration, 1,* 5–25.

Goldfried, M.R., & Davison, G.C. (1976). *Clinical behavior therapy.* New York: Holt, Rinehart & Winston.

Goldfried, M.R., Decenteceo, E.T., & Weinberg, L. (1974). Systematic rational restructuring as a self-control technique. *Behavior Therapy, 5,* 247–254.

Goldfried, M.R., & D'Zurillia, T.J. (1969). A behavioral-analytic model for assessing competence. In C.D. Speilberger (Ed.), *Current topics in clinical and community psychology* (Vol. 1). New York: Academic Press.

Goldfried, M.R., Greenberg, L.S., & Marmar, C. (1990). Individual psychotherapy: Process and outcome. *Annual Review of Psychology, 41,* 659–688.

Goldfried, M.R., Linehan, M., & Smith, J.L. (1978). Reduction of test anxiety through cognitive restructuring. *Journal of Consulting and Clinical Psychology, 46,* 32–39.

Goldfried, M.R., Padawer, W., & Robins, C. (1984). Social anxiety and the semantic structure of heterosocial interactions. *Journal of Abnormal Psychology, 93,* 87–97.

Goldfried, M.R., Stricker, G., & Weiner, I.B. (1971). *Rorschach handbook of clinical and research applications.* Englewood Cliffs, NJ: Prentice-Hall.

Golding, J.M., Smith, G.R., & Kashner, T.M. (1991). Does somatization disorder occur in men? Clinical characteristics of women and men with unexplained somatic symptoms. *Archives of General Psychiatry, 48,* 231–235.

Goldmeier, J. (1988). Pets or people: Another research note. *The Gerontologist, 26,* 203–206.

Goldstein, A. (1976). Opioid peptides (endorphins) in pituitary and brain. *Science, 193,* 1081–1086.

Goldstein, A.J. & Chambless, D.L. (1978). A reanalysis of agoraphobic behavior. *Behavior Therapy, 9,* 47–59.

Goldstein, H.S., Edelberg, R., & Meier, C.F. (1988). Relationship of resting heart rate and blood pressure to experienced anger and expressed anger. *Psychosomatic Medicine, 50,* 321–329.

Goldstein, M.J., & Rodnick, E. (1975). The family's contribution to the etiology of schizophrenia: Current status. *Schizophrenia Bulletin, 14,* 48–63.

Goldstein, M.J., & Link, B.G. (1988). Gender differences in the clinical expression of schizophrenia. *Journal of Psychiatric Research, 22,* 141–155.

Goldstein, S.E., & Birnbom, F. (1976). Hypochondriasis and the elderly. *Journal of the American Geriatrics Society, 24,* 150–154.

Gomes-Schwartz, B. (1978). Effective ingredients in psychotherapy: Prediction of outcome from process variables. *Journal of Consulting and Clinical Psychology, 46,* 1023–1035.

Gomez, F.C., Piedmont, R.L., & Fleming,

M.Z. (1992). Factor analysis of the Spanish version of the WAIS: The Escala de Inteligencia Wechsler para Adultos (EIWA). *Psychological Assessment, 4,* 317–321.

Gonnan, J.M., Fyer, M.R., Goetz, R., Askanazi, J., Leibowitz, M.R., Fyer, A.J., Kinney, J., & Klein, D.F. (1988). Ventilatory physiology of patients with panic disorder. *Archives of General Psychiatry, 45,* 53–60.

Goodman, R., & Stevenson, J. (1989). A twin study of hyperactivity: II. The aetiological role of genes, family relationships, and perinatal adversity. *Journal of Child Psychology and Psychiatry, 30,* 691–709.

Goodwin, D.W. (1979). Alcoholism and heredity: A review and hypothesis. *Archives of General Psychiatry, 36,* 57–61.

Goodwin, D.W. (1982). Substance induced and substance use disorders: Alcohol. In J.H. Griest, I.W. Jefferson, & R.L. Spitzer (Eds.), *Treatment of mental disorders.* New York: Oxford University Press.

Goodwin, D.W., Crane, J.B., & Guze, S.B. (1969). Alcoholic "blackouts": A review and clinical study of 100 alcoholics. *American Journal of Psychiatry, 26,* 191–198.

Goodwin, D.W., & Guze, S.B. (1984). *Psychiatric diagnosis* (3rd ed.). New York: Oxford University Press.

Goodwin, D.W., Schulsinger, F., Hermansen, L., Guze, S.B., & Winokur, G.A. (1973). Alcohol problems in adoptees raised apart from alcoholic biological parents. *Archives of General Psychiatry, 128,* 239–243.

Goodwin, D.W., Schulsinger, F., Knop, J., Mednick, S.A., & Guze, S.B. (1977). Psychopathology in adopted and non-adopted daughters of alcoholics. *Archives of General Psychiatry, 34,* 1005–1009.

Goodwin, F., & Jamison, K. (1990). *Manic-depressive illness.* New York: Oxford University Press.

Gorenstein, E.E. (1982). Frontal lobe functions in psychopaths. *Journal of Abnormal Psychology, 91,* 368–379.

Gorenstein, E.E. (1991). A cognitive perspective on antisocial personality. In P.A. Magaro (Ed.), *Cognitive bases of mental disorders.* Newbury Park, CA: Sage.

Gorenstein, E.E. & Newman, J.P. (1980). Disinhibitory psychopathology: A new perspective and a model for research. *Psychological Review, 87,* 301–315.

Gorman, J.M., Fyer, M.R., Goetz, R., Askanazi, J., Leibowitz, M.R., Fyer, A.J., Kinney, J., & Klein, D.F. (1988). Ventilatory physiology of patients with panic disorder. *Archives of General Psychiatry, 45,* 53–60.

Gorman, J.M., Levy, G.F., Liebowitz, M.R., McGrath, P., Appleby, I.L., Dillon, D.J., Davies, S.O., & Klein, D.F. (1983). Effect of acute beta-adrenergic blockade on lactate-induced panic. *Archives of General Psychiatry, 40,* 1079–1082.

Gorman-Smith, D., & Matson, J.L. (1985). A review of the treatment research for self-injurious and stereotyped responding. *Journal of Mental Deficiency Research, 29,* 295–308.

Gotlib, I.H. (1982). Self-reinforcement and depression in interpersonal interaction: The role of performance level. *Journal of Abnormal Psychology, 93,* 19–30.

Gotlib, I.H., & Asarnow, R.F. (1979). Interpersonal and impersonal problem-solving skills in mildly and clinically depressed students. *Journal of Consulting and Clinical Psychology, 47,* 86–95.

Gotlib, I.H., & Robinson, L.A. (1982). Responses to depressed individuals: Discrepancies between self-report and observer-rated behavior. *Journal of Abnormal Psychology, 91,* 231–240.

Gotlib, I.H., & Whiten, V.E. (in press). The interpersonal context of depression: Implications for theory and research. In D. Perlman & W. Jones (Eds.), *Advances in personal relationships.* Greenwich, CT: JAI Press.

Gottesman, I.I., McGuffin, P., & Farmer, A.E. (1987). Clinical genetics as clues to the "real" genetics of schizophrenia. *Schizophrenia Bulletin, 13,* 23–47.

Gottesman, I., & Shields, J. (1972). *Schizophrenia and genetics: A twin study vantage point.* New York: Academic Press.

Gottlieb, J. (1990). Mainstreaming and quality education. *American Journal on Mental Retardation, 95,* 16.

Gottman, I.M. (1979). *Marital interaction: Experimental investigations.* New York: Academic Press.

Gottman, I.M., & Levenson, R.W. (1986). Assessing the role of emotion in marriage. *Behavioral Assessment, 8,* 31–48.

Gottman, J.M., Markman, H., & Notarius, C. (1977). The topography of marital conflict: A sequential analysis of verbal and nonverbal behavior. *Journal of Marriage and the Family, 39,* 461–477.

Gottman, J., Notarius, C., Gonso, J., & Markman, H. (1976). *A couple's guide to communication.* Champaign, IL.: Research Press.

Gove, W.R. (1970). Societal reaction as an explanation of mental illness: An evaluation. *American Sociological Review, 35,* 873–884.

Gove, W.R., & Fain, T. (1973). The stigma of mental hospitalization. *Archives of General Psychiatry, 28,* 494–500.

Goyette, C.H., & Conners, C.K. (1977). *Food additives and hyperkinesis.* Paper presented at the 85th Annual Convention of the American Psychological Association.

Grabowski, J. (Ed.). (1984). *Cocaine: Pharmacology, effects, and treatment of abuse.* Rockville, MD: National Institute on Drug Abuse.

Graham, D.T. (1967). Health, disease and the mind–body problem: Linguistic parallelism. *Psychosomatic Medicine, 29,* 52–71.

Graham, J.R. (1988). *Establishing validity of the revised form of the MMPI.* Symposium presentation at the 96th Annual Convention of the American Psychological Association, Atlanta.

Graham, J.R. (1990). *MMPI-2: Assessing personality and psychopathology.* New York: Oxford University Press.

Graham, J.W., Johnson, C.A., Hansen, W.B., Flay, B.R., & Gee, M. (1990). Drug use prevention programs, gender, and ethnicity: Evaluation of three seventh-grade Project SMART cohorts. *Preventive Medicine, 19,* 305–313.

Graham, P.J., Rutter, M.L., Yule, W., & Pless, I.B. (1967). Childhood asthma: A psychosomatic disorder? Some epidemiological considerations. *British Journal of Preventive Medicine, 21,* 78–85.

Granick, A. (1986). Future of the chronic schizophrenic patient: Prediction and recommendation. *American Journal of Psychotherapy, 40,* 419–429.

Grant, I., & Heaton, R.K. (1990). Human Immunodeficiency Virus-1 (HIV-1) and the brain. *Journal of Consulting and Clinical Psychology, 58,* 13–21.

Gray, E.B. (1983). *Final report: Collaborative research of community and minority group action to prevent child abuse and neglect. Vol. III. Public awareness and education using the creative arts.* Chicago: National Committee for Prevention of Child Abuse.

Gray, J.A. (1971). *The psychology of fear and stress.* New York: McGraw-Hill.

Gray, J.A. (1982). *The neuropsychology of anxiety: An enquiry into the functions of the septo-hippocampal system.* Oxford: Oxford University Press.

Gray, J.A. (1987). *The psychology of fear and stress* (2nd Ed.). Cambridge: Cambridge University Press.

Green, R. (1969). Mythological, historical and cross-cultural aspects of transsexualism. In R. Green & J. Money (Eds.), *Transsexualism and sex reassignment.* Baltimore: Johns Hopkins University Press.

Green, R. (1974). *Sexual identity conflict in children and adults.* New York: Basic Books.

Green, R. (1976). One hundred ten feminine and masculine boys: Behavioral contrasts and demographic similarities. *Archives of Sexual Behavior, 5,* 425–446.

Green, R. (1985). Gender identity in childhood and later sexual orientation: Follow-up of 78 males. *American Journal of Psychiatry, 142,* 339–341.

Green, R., & Fleming, D.T. (1990). Transsexual surgery follow-up: Status in the 1990s. In J. Bancroft, C. Davis, & D. Weinstein (Eds.), *Annual review of sex research* (pp. 163–174).

Green, R., & Money, J. (1969). *Transsexualism and sex reassignment.* Baltimore: Johns Hopkins University Press.

Greenberg, L., Fine, S.B., Cohen, C., Larson, K., Michaelson-Baily, A., Rubinton, P., & Glick, I.D. (1988). An interdisciplinary psychoeducation program for schizophrenic patients and their families in an acute care setting. *Hospital and Community Psychiatry, 39,* 277–281.

Greenberg, L.S., & Safran, J. (1984). Integrating affect and cognition: A perspective on the process of therapeutic change. *Cognitive Therapy and Research, 8,* 559–578.

Greenberg, L.S., & Johnson, S.M. (1988). *Emotionally focussed couples therapy.* New York: Guilford.

Greenberg, L.S., & Rice, L.N. (1981). The specific effects of a gestalt intervention. *Psychotherapy: Theory, Research, and Practice, 18,* 31–37.

Greenblatt, D.J., & Shader, R.I. (1978). Pharmacotherapy of anxiety with benzodiazepines and beta-adrenergic blockers. In M.A. Lipton, A. DiMascio, & K.E. Kilham (Eds.), *Psychopharmacology: A generation of progress.* Ncw York: Raven.

Greenblatt, M., Solomon, M.H., Evans, A.S., & Brooks, G.W. (Eds.). (1965). *Drugs and social therapy in chronic schizophrenia.* Springfield, IL: Charles C. Thomas.

Greene, B.A. (1985). Considerations in the treatment of black patients by white therapists. *Psychotherapy, 22,* 115–122.

Greene, B.L. (1960). Marital disharmony: Concurrent analysis of husband and wife. *Diseases of the Nervous System, 21,* 1–6.

Greene, R.M. (1985). A study of the relationship between divorced mothers' attitude towards their ex-husbands, perceived supportive and coercive behavior in mother-son interactions, and aggressive behavior in boys. *Dissertation Abstracts International, 45,* 2039.

Greer, S., Morris, T., & Pettigale, K.W. (1979). Psychological response to breast cancer: Effect on outcome. *Lancet, 2,* 785–787.

Grings, W.W., & Dawson, M.E. (1978). *Emotions and bodily responses: A psychophysiological approach.* New York: Academic Press.

Grinker, R.R., & Spiegel, J.P. (1979). *War neuroses.* New York: Arno Press.

Grisso, T. (1986). *Evaluating competencies: Forensic assessments and instruments.* New York: Plenum.

Grisso, T., & Appelbaum, P.S. (in press). Mentally ill and non-mentally ill patients' abilities to understand informed consent disclosures for medication: Preliminary data. *Law and Human Behavior.*

Gross, M.D. (1984). Effects of sucrose on hyperkinetic children. *Pediatrics, 74,* 876–878.

Grossman, H.J. (Ed.). (1983). *Classification in mental retardation.* Washington, DC: American Association of Mental Deficiency.

Grosz, H.J., & Zimmerman, J. (1970). A second detailed case study of functional blindness: Further demonstration of the contribution of objective psychological laboratory data. *Behavior Therapy, 1,* 115–123.

Groth, N.A., & Burgess, A.W. (1977). Sexual dysfunction during rape. *New England Journal of Medicine, 297,* 764–766.

Groth, N.A., Hobson, W.F., & Guy, T.S. (1982). The child molester: Clinical observations. In J. Conte & D.A. Shore (Eds.), *Social work and child sexual abuse.* New York: Haworth.

Group for Advancement of Psychiatry. (1966). *Psychopathological disorders in childhood: Theoretical considerations and a proposed classification* (Report 62). New York: Mental Health Memorials Center.

Guess, D., Helmstetter, E., Turnbull, H.R. III, & Knowlton, S. (1986). *Use of aversive procedures with persons who are disabled: An historical review and critical analysis* (Monograph). Seattle: The Association for Persons with Severe Handicaps.

Guidano, V.F., & Liotti, G. (1983). *Cognitive processes and emotional disorders.* New York: Guilford.

Gunderson, J.G. (1986). Pharmacotherapy for patients with borderline personality disorder. *Archives of General Psychiatry, 43,* 698–700.

Gunderson, J.G., Kolb, J.E., & Austin, V. (1981). The diagnostic interview for borderline patients. *American Journal of Psychiatry,* lu, 896–903.

Guralnik, J.M., Yanagashita, M., & Schneider, E.L. (1988). Projecting the older population of the United States: Lessons from the past and prospects for the future. *The Milbank Quarterly, 66,* 283–308.

Gurland, B.J., & Cross, P.S. (1982). Epidemiology of psychopathology in old age. In L.F. Jarvik & G.W. Small (Eds.), *Psychiatric Clinics of North America.* Philadelphia: Saunders.

Gurland, B. (1991). Epidemiology of psychiatric disorders. In J. Sadavoy, & L.F. Jarvik (Eds.), *Comprehensive review of geriatric psychiatry* (pp. 25–40). Washington, DC: American Psychiatric Press.

Gurman, A.S., & Kniskern, D.P. (1978). Research on marital and family therapy: Progress, perspective, and prospect. In S.L. Garfield & A.E. Bergin (Eds.), *Handbook of psychotherapy and behavior change: An empirical analysis* (2nd ed.). New York: Wiley.

Gurman, A.S., & Kniskern, D.P. (1981). Family therapy outcome research: Knowns and unknowns. In A.S. Gurman & D.P. Kniskern (Eds.), *Handbook of family therapy.* New York: Brunner/Mazel.

Gurman, A.S., Kniskern, D.P., & Pinsoff, W.M. (1986). Research on the process and outcome of marital and family therapy. In S.L. Garfield & A.E. Bergin (Eds.), *Handbook of psychotherapy and behavior change* (3rd ed.). New York: Wiley.

Gustafson, Y., Berggren, D., Bucht, B., Norberf, A., Hansson, L.I., & Winblad, B. (1988). Acute confusional states in elderly patients treated for femoral neck fracture. *Journal of the American Geriatrics Society, 36,* 525–530.

Guze, S.B. (1967). The diagnosis of hysteria: What are we trying to do? *American Journal of Psychiatry, 12A,* 491–498.

Guze, S.B. (1976). *Criminality and psychiatric disorders.* New York: Oxford University Press.

Gwynther, L.P., & George, L.K. (1986). Caregivers for dementia patients: Complex determinants of well-being and burden. *The Gerontologist, 26,* 245–247.

Haaga, D.A. (1986). A review of the common principles approach to integration of psychotherapies. *Cognitive Therapy and Research, 10,* 527–538.

Haaga, D.A. (1987a). *Smoking schemata revealed in articulated thoughts predict early relapse from smoking cessation.* Paper presented at the 21st Annual Convention of the Association for Advancement of Behavior Therapy, Boston.

Haaga, D.A. (1987b). Treatment of the type A behavior pattern. *Clinical Psychology Review, 7,* 557–574.

Haaga, D.A. (1988a). *Cognitive aspects of the relapse prevention model in the prediction of smoking relapse.* Paper presented at the 22nd Annual Convention of the Association for Advancement of Behavior Therapy, New York.

Haaga, D.A. (1988b). *Cognitive assessment in the prediction of smoking relapse.* Unpublished doctoral dissertation, University of Southern California, Los Angeles.

Haaga, D.A.F. (1989). Articulated thoughts and endorsement procedures for cognitive assessment in the prediction of smoking relapse. *Psychological Assessment: A Journal of Consulting and Clinical Psychology, 1,* 112–117.

Haaga, D.A.F. (1990). Issues in relating self-efficacy to smoking relapse: Importance of an "Achilles' Heel" situation and of prior quitting experience. *Journal of Substance Abuse, 2,* 191–200.

Haaga, D.A., & Davison, G.C. (1986). Cognitive change methods. In A.P. Goldstein & F.H. Kanfer (Eds.), *Helping people change* (3rd ed.). Elmsford, NY: Pergamon.

Haaga, D.A., & Davison, G.C. (1989). Outcome studies of rational-emotive therapy. In M.E. Bernard & R. DiGiuseppe (Eds.), *Inside rational-emotive therapy.* New York: Academic Press.

Haaga, D.A.F., & Davison, G.C. (1991). Cognitive change methods. In F.H. Kanfer, & A.P. Goldstein (Eds.), *Helping people change: A textbook of methods* (4th ed.), Elmsford, NY: Pergamon.

Haaga, D.A.F., & Davison, G.C. (1992). Disappearing differences do not always reflect healthy integration: An analysis of cognitive therapy and rational-emotive therapy. *Journal of Psychotherapy Integration,* 1, 287–303.

Haaga, D.A.F., Dyck, M.J., & Ernst, D. (1991). Empirical status of cognitive theory of depression. *Psychological Bulletin, 110,* 215–236.

Haaga, D.A.F., & Stewart, B.L. (1992). Self-efficacy for recovery from a lapse after smoking cessation. *Journal of Consulting and Clinical Psychology, 60,* 24–28.

Haas, G.L., Glick, I.D., Clarkin, J.F., et al. (1990). Gender and schizophrenia outcome: A clinical trial of an outpatient intervention. *Schizophrenia Bulletin, 16,* 277–292.

Habot, B., & Libow, L.S. (1980). The interrelationship of mental and physical status and its assessment in the older adult: Mind–body interaction. In J.E. Birren & R.B. Sloane (Eds.), *Handbook of mental health and aging.* Englewood Cliffs, NJ: Prentice-Hall.

Hafner, R.J. (1982). Marital interaction in persisting obsessive-compulsive disorders. *Australian and New Zealand Journal of Psychiatry, 16,* 171–178.

Hafner, R.J., Gilchrist, P., Bowling, J., & Kalucy, R. (1981). The treatment of obsessional neurosis in a family setting. *Australian and New Zealand Journal of Psychiatry, 15,* 145–151.

Hahlweg, K., & Markman, H.J. (1988). The effectiveness of behavioral marital therapy: Empirical status of behavioral techniques in preventing and alleviating marital distress. *Journal of Consulting and Clinical Psychology, 56,* 440–447.

Haley, S.A. (1978). Treatment implications of post-combat stress response syndromes for mental health professionals. In C.R. Figley (Ed.), *Stress disorders among Vietnam veterans.* New York: Brunner/Mazel.

Haley, W.E., Levine, E.G., Brown, S.L., Berry, J.W., & Hughes, G.H. (1987). Psychological, social, and health consequences of caring for a relative with senile dementia. *Journal of the American Geriatrics Society, 35,* 405–411,

Hall, C.S., Lindzey, G., Loehlin, J.C., & Manosevitz, M. (1985). *Introduction to theories of personality.* New York: Wiley.

Hall, S.M., Tunstall, C., Rugg, D., Jones, R.T., & Benowitz, N. (1985). Nicotine gum and behavioral treatment in smoking. *Journal of Consulting and Clinical Psychology, 53,* 256–258.

Halleck, S.L. (1971). *The politics of therapy.* New York: Science House.

Hamilton, E.W., & Abramson, L.Y. (1983). Cognitive patterns and major depressive disorder: A longitudinal study in a hospital setting. *Journal of Abnormal Psychology, 92,* 173–184.

Hammen, C.L. (1980). Depression in college students: Beyond the Beck Depression Inventory. *Journal of Consulting and Clinical Psychology, 48,* 126–128.

Hammen, C.L. (1991). Generation of stress in the course of unipolar depression. *Journal of Abnormal Psychology,* 100, 555–561.

Hammen, C.L., & Cochran, S.D. (1981). Cognitive correlates of life stress and depression in college students. *Journal of Abnormal Psychology, 90,* 23–27.

Hammen, C.L., Ellicott, A., & Gitlin, M. (1989). Vulnerability to specific life events and prediction of course of disorder in unipolar depressed patients. *Canadian Journal of Behavioral Science, 21,* 377–388.

Hammen, C., Marks, T., Mayol, A., & deMayo, R. (1985). Depressive self-schemas, life stress, and vulnerability to depression. *Journal of Abnormal Psychology, 94,* 308–319.

Hampe, E., Noble, H., Miller, L.C., & Barrett, C.L. (1973). Phobic children one and two years posttreatment. *Journal of Abnormal Psychology, 82,* 446–453.

Hansen, W.B., & Graham, J.W. (1991). Preventing alcohol, marijuana, and cigarette use among adolescents: Peer pressure resistance training versus establishing conservative norms. *Preventive Medicine, 20,* 414–430.

Hansen, W.B., Johnson, C.A., Flay, B.R., Graham, J.W., & Sobel, J. (1988). Affective and social influence approaches to the prevention of multiple substance abuse among seventh grade students. *Preventive Medicine, 17,* 135–154.

Hanusa, B.H., & Schulz, R. (1977). Attributional mediators of teamed helplessness. *Journal of Personality and Social Psychology, 35,* 602–611.

Haracz, J.L. (1982). The dopamine hypothesis: An overview of studies with schizophrenic patients. *Schizophrenia Bulletin, 8,* 438–469.

Harburg, E., Erfurt, J.C., Hauenstein, L.S., Chape, C., Schull, W.J., & Schork, M.A. (1973). Socioecological stress, suppressed hostility, skin color, and black-white male blood pressure: Detroit. *Psychosomatic Medicine, 35,* 276–296.

Harburg, E., Gleiberman,L., Russell, M., & Cooper, M.L. (1991). Anger-coping styles and blood pressure in black and white males: Buffalo, New York. *Psychosomatic Medicine, 53,* 153–162.

Hare, E. (1969). *Triennial statistical report of the Royal Maudsley and Bethlem Hospitals.* London: Bethlem and Maudsley Hospitals.

Hare, R.D. (1970). *Psychopathy: Theory and research.* New York: Wiley.

Hare, R.D. (1978). Electrodermal and cardiovascular correlates of sociopathy. In R.D. Hare & D. Schalling (Eds.), *Psychopathic behaviour: Approaches to research.* New York: Wiley.

Hare, R.D. (1980). A research scale for the assessment of psychopathy in criminal populations. *Personality and Individual Differences, 1,* 111–119.

Hare, R.D. (1982). Psychopathy and physiological activity during anticipation of an aversive stimulus in a distraction paradigm. *Psychophysiology, 19,* 266–271.

Hare, R.D., Harpur, T.J., Hakstian, R.A. et al. (1990). The revised Psychopathy Checklist: Reliability and factor structure. *Psychological Assessment,* 2, 338–341.

Hare, R.D., Hart, S.D., & Harpur, T.J. (1991). Psychopathy and the DSM-IV criteria for antisocial personality disorder. *Journal of Abnormal Psychology, 100,* 391–398.

Hare, R.D., & Jutai, J.W. (1983). Psychopathy and electrocortical indices of perceptual processing during selective attention. *Psychophysiology, 20,* 146–151.

Harpur, T.J., & Hare, R.D. (1990). Psychopathy and attention. In J. Enns (Ed.), *The development of attention: Research and theory.* Amsterdam: New Holland.

Harrington, A., & Sutton-Simon, K. (1977). Rape. In A.P. Goldstein, P.J. Monti, T.J. Sardino, & D.J. Green (Eds)., *Police crisis intervention.* Kalamazoo, MI: Behaviordelia.

Harris, E.L., Noyes, R., Crowe, R.R., & Chaudhry, D.R. (1983). Family study of agoraphobia: Report of a pilot study. *Archives of General Psychiatry, 40,* 1061–1064.

Harris, K.R. (1986). The effects of cognitive-behavior modification on private speech and task performance during problem solving among learning disabled and normally achieving children. *Journal of Abnormal Child Psychology, 14,* 63–67.

Harris, L. (1987). *Inside America.* New York: Vintage Books.

Harris, M.J., & Jeste, D.V. (1988). Late-onset schizophrenia: A review. *Schizophrenia Bulletin, 14,* 39–55.

Harrison, E. (1992, February 6). "Dr. Death" arrested in 2 women's suicides. *Los Angeles Times,* p. A15.

Harrison, J., Chin, J., & Ficarrotto, T. (1989). Warning: Masculinity may be dangerous to your health. In M.S. Kimmel, & M.A. Messner (Eds.), *Men's lives* (pp. 296–309). New York: Macmillan.

Hart, S.D., & Hare, R.D. (1989). Discriminant validity of the Psychopathy Checklist in a forensic psychiatric population. *Psychological Assessment, 1,* 211–218.

Hartley, D.E., & Strupp, H.H. (1983). The therapeutic alliance: Its relationship to outcome in brief psychotherapy. In J. Masling (Ed.), *Empirical studies of psychoanalytical theories.* (Vol. 1). Hillsdale, NJ: Analytical Press.

Hartmann, H. (1958). *Ego psychology and the problem of adaptation.* New York: International Universities Press.

Hartsough, C.S., & Lamber, N.M. (1985). Medical factors in hyperactive and normal children: Prenatal, developmental, and health history findings. *American Journal of Orthopsychiatry, 55,* 190–201.

Harvey, J., Judge, C., & Wiener, S. (1977). Familial X-linked mental retardation with an X chromosome abnormality. *Journal of Medical Genetics, 14,* 45–50.

Harvey, P.D. (1987). Laboratory research: Its relevance to positive and negative symptoms. In P.D. Harvey and E.F. Walker (Eds.), *Positive and negative symptoms of psychosis.* Hillsdale, NJ: Erlbaum.

Hasin, D., Grant, B., Harford, T., Hilton, M., & Endicott, J. (1990). Multiple alcohol-related problems in the United States: On the rise? *Journal of Studies on Alcohol, 51,* 484–493.

Hastrup, J.L., Light, K.C., & Obrist, P.A. (1982). Parental hypertension and cardiovascular response to stress in healthy young adults. *Psychophysiology, 19,* 615–622.

Hathaway, S.R., & McKinley, J.C. (1943). *MMPI manual.* New York: Psychological Corporation.

Hay, D.P. (1991). Electroconvulsive therapy. In J. Sadavoy, L.W. Lazarus, & L.F. Jarvik (Eds.), *Comprehensive review of geriatric psychiatry* (pp. 469–485). Washington, D.C.: American Psychiatric Press.

Hayashi, K., Toyama, B., & Quay, H.C. (1976). A cross-cultural study concerned with differential behavioral classification: 1. The Behavior Checklist. *Japanese Journal of Criminal Psychology, 2,* 21–28.

Hayes, S.C. (1987). A contextual approach to therapeutic change. In N.S. Jacobson (Ed.), *Psychotherapists in clinical practice: Cognitive and behavioral perspectives* (pp. 327–387). New York: Guilford.

Haynes, S.N., & Horn, W.F. (1982). Reactivity in behavioral observation: A review. *Behavioral Assessment, 4,* 369–385.

Hays, P. (1976). Etiological factors in manic-depressive psychoses. *Archives of General Psychiatry, 33,* 1187–1188.

Hazelrigg, M.D., Cooper, H.M., & Borduin, C.M. (1987). Evaluating the effectiveness of family therapies: An integrative review and analysis. *Psychological Bulletin, 101,* 428–442.

Hearn, M.D. (1989). Hostility, coronary heart disease, and total mortality: A 33-year follow-up study of university students. *Journal of Behavioral Medicine, 12,* 105–121.

Hechtman, L., Weiss, G., & Perlman, T. (1984). Hyperactives as young adults: Past and current substance abuse and antisocial behavior. *American Journal of Orthopsychiatry, 54,* 415–425.

Heiman, J.R., & LoPiccolo, J. (1983). *Effectiveness of daily versus weekly therapy in the treatment of sexual dysfunction.* Unpublished manuscript, State University of New York at Stony Brook.

Heiman, J.R., & LoPiccolo, J. (1988). *Becoming orgasmic: A sexual and personal growth program for women* (2nd ed.). New York: Prentice-Hall.

Heiman, J.R., Rowland, D.L., Hatch, J.P., & Gladue, B.A. (1991). Psychophysiological and endocrine responses to sexual arousal in women. *Archives of Sexual Behavior, 20,* 171–186.

Heiman, J.R., & Verhulst, J. (1990). Sexual dysfunction and marriage. In F.D. Fincham, & T.N. Bradbury (Eds.), *The psychology of marriage: Basic issues and applications* (pp. 299–322). New York: Guilford.

Heiman, N.M. (1973). Postdoctoral training in community mental health. *Menninger Clinical Bulletin 17.*

Heimberg, R.G., Dodge, C.S., & Becker, R. (1987). Social phobia. In L. Michelson, & L.M. Ascher (Eds.), *Anxiety and stress disorders* (pp. 280–309). New York: Guilford.

Heisenberg, W. (1971). *Physics and beyond: Encounters and conversations.* New York: Harper & Row.

Heller, J. (1966). *Something happened.* New York: Knopf.

Heller, K.A., Holtzman, W.H., & Messick, S. (Eds.). (1982). *Placing children in special education: A strategy for equity.* Washington, DC: National Academy Press.

Helzer, J.E., Robins, L.N., & McEvoy, L. (1987). Post-traumatic stress disorder in the general population. *New England Journal of Medicine, 317,* 1630–1634.

Hembree, W.C., Nahas, G.G., & Huang, H.F.S. (1979). Changes in human spermatozoa associated with high dose marihuana smoking. In G.G. Nahas & W.D.M. Paton (Eds.), *Marihuana: Biological effects.* Elmsford, NY: Pergamon.

Hempel, C. (1958). The theoretician's dilemma. In H. Feigl, M. Scriven, & G. Maxwell (Eds.), *Minnesota studies in the philosophy of science* (Vol. 2). Minneapolis: University of Minnesota Press.

Hendin, H. (1982). *Suicide in America.* New York: Norton.

Heninger, G.R., Charney, D.S., & Menkes, D.B. (1983). Receptor sensitivity and the mechanism of action of antidepressant treatment. In P.J. Clayton & J.E. Barrett (Eds.), *Treatment of depression: Old controversies and new approaches.* New York: Raven.

Henkel, H., & Lewis-Thomé, J. (1976). *Verhaltenstherapie bei männlichen Homosexuellen.* Diplomarbeit der Studierenden der Psychologie. University of Marburg, Germany.

Hepler, R.S., & Frank, I.M. (1971). Marijuana smoking and intraocular pressure. *Journal of the American Medical Association, 217,* 1392.

Herbert, J. (1965). Personality factors and bronchial asthma. A study of South African Indian children. *Journal of Psychosomatic Research, 8,* 353–364.

Herbert, M. (1978). *Conduct disorders of childhood and adolescence.* New York: Wiley.

Herbert, M. (1982). Conduct disorders. In B.B. Lahey & A.E. Kazdin (Eds.), *Advances in clinical child psychology* (Vol. 5). New York: Plenum.

Herd, J.A. (1986). Neuroendocrine mechanisms in coronary heart disease. Cited in K.A. Matthews, S.M. Weiss, T. Detre, T.M. Dembroski, B.E Faulkner, S.B. Marruck, & R.B. Williams (Eds.), *Handbook of stress, reactivity, and cardiovascular disease.* New York: Wiley.

Hernandez-Peon, R., Chavez-Ibarra, G., & Aguilar-Figueron, E. (1963). Somatic evoked potentials in one case of hysterical anesthesia. *EEG and Clinical Neurophysiology, 15,* 889–892.

Hersen, M., & Barlow, D.H. (1976). *Single case experimental designs: Strategies for studying behavior change.* New York: Pergamon.

Hersen, M., & Bellack, A.S. (Eds.). (1981). *Behavioral assessment: A practical handbook* (2nd ed.). New York: Pergamon.

Hersen, M., & Bellack, A.S. (Eds.). (1988). *Behavioral assessment: A practical handbook* (3rd ed.). New York: Pergamon.

Hersen, M., Bellack, A.S., Himmelhoch, J.M., & Thase, M.E. (1984). Effects of social skill training, amitriptyline, and psychotherapy in unipolar depressed women. *Behavior Therapy, 15,* 21–40.

Hershberg, S.G., Carlson, G.A., Cantwell, D.P., & Strober, M. (1982). Anxiety and depressive disorders in psychiatrically ill disturbed children. *Journal of Clinical Psychiatry, 43,* 358–361.

Hester, R.K., & Miller, W.R. (1989). Self-control training. In R.K. Hester & W.R. Miller (Eds.), *Handbook of alcoholism treatment approaches: Effective alternatives* (pp. 141–149). New York: Pergamon.

Heston, L.L. (1966). Psychiatric disorders in foster home reared children of schizophrenic mothers. *British Journal of Psychiatry, 112,* 819–825.

Heston, L.L., & White, J.A. (1991). *The vanishing mind.* New York: Freeman.

Hewett, F.M. (1965). Teaching speech to an autistic child through operant conditioning. *American Journal of Orthopsychiatry, 33,* 927–936.

Heyd, D., & Bloch, S. (1981). The ethics of suicide. In S. Bloch & P. Chodoff (Eds.), *Psychiatric ethics.* New York: Oxford University Press.

Hibbert, G.A. (1984). Hyperventilation as a cause of panic attacks. *British Medical Journal, 288,* 263–264.

Higgins, G.F. (1978). Sexuality and the spinal cord injured patient. In J. LoPiccolo & L. LoPiccolo (Eds.), *Handbook of sex therapy.* New York: Plenum.

Hill, C.E., O'Grady, K.E., & Elkin, I. (1992). Applying the Collaborative Study Psychotherapy Rating Scale to rate therapist adherence to cognitive-behavior therapy, interpersonal therapy, and clinical management. *Journal of Consulting and Clinical Psychology, 60,* 73–79.

Hill, J.H., Liebert, R.M., & Mott, D.E.W. (1968). Vicarious extinction of avoidance behavior through films: An initial test. *Psychological Reports, 12,* 192.

Hill, S.Y. (1980). Introduction: The biological consequences. In *Alcoholism and alcohol abuse among women: Research issues.* Rockville, MD: National Institute on Alcohol Abuse and Alcoholism.

Hilterbrand, K. (1983). *Depression in anorexia nervosa.* Unpublished manuscript, University of Southern California, Los Angeles.

Himadi, W.G., Cerny, J.A., Barlow, D.H., Cohen, S., & O'Brien, G.T. (1986). The relationship of marital adjustment to agoraphobia treatment outcome. *Behaviour Research and Therapy, 24,* 107–115.

Hindman, J. (1988). Research disputes assumptions about child molesters. *NDAA Bulletin, 7,* 1–3.

Hinshaw, S.P. (1987). On the distinction between attentional deficits/hyperactivity and conduct problems/aggression in child psychopathology. *Psychological Bulletin, 101,* 443–463.

Hinshaw, S.P., Henker, B., & Whalen, C.K. (1984). Self-control in hyperactive boys in anger-inducing situations: Effects of cognitive-behavioral training and of methylphenidate. *Journal of Abnormal Child Psychology, 12,* 55–77.

Hinz, L.D., & Williamson, D.A. (1987). Bulimia and depression: A review of the affective variant hypothesis. *Psychological Bulletin, 102,* 150–158.

Hiroto, D.S., & Seligman, M.E.P. (1975). Generality of learned helplessness in man. *Journal of Personality and Social Psychology, 31,* 311–327.

Hirschfeld, R.A., & Cross, C.K. (1982). Epidemiology of affective disorders. *Archives of General Psychiatry, 39,* 35–46.

Hite, S. (1976). *The Hite Report: A nationwide study of female sexuality.* New York: Dell.

Ho, D., Rota, T., Schooley, R., Kaplan, J., Aren, J., Groopman, J., Resnick, L., Felsenstein, L., Andrews, C., & Hirsch, M. (1985). Isolation of HTLV-III from cerebrospinal fluid and neural tissues of patients with neurologic symptoms related to the acquired immune deficiency syndrome. *New England Journal of Medicine, 313,* 1493–1497.

Ho, D.D., Sarngadharan, M.G.,Resnick, L., Dimarzo-Veronese, F., Rota, T.R., & Hirsch, M.S. (1985). Primary Human T-Lymphotropic Virus Type III infection. *Annals of Internal Medicine, 103,* 880–883.

Hobbs, S.A., Beck, S.J., & Wansley, R.A. (1984). Pediatric behavioral medicine: Directions in treatment and prevention. In M. Hersen, R.M. Eisler, & P.M. Miller (Eds.), *Progress in behavior modification* (vol. 16). New York: Academic Press.

Hoberman, H.M., & Garfinkel, B.D. (1988). Completed suicide in children and adolescents. *Journal of the American Academy of Child and Adolescent Psychiatry, 27,* 689–695.

Hoberman, H.M., Lewinsohn, P.M., & Tilson, M. (1988). Group treatment of depression: Individual predictors of outcome. *Journal of Consulting and Clinical Psychology, 56,* 393–398.

Hobfoll, S.E., Spielberger, C.D., Breznitz, S., Figley, C., Folkman, S., Lepper-Green, B., Meichenbaum, D., Milgram, N.A., Sandler, I., Sarason, I., & van der Kolk, B. (1991). War-related stress: Addressing the stress of war and other traumatic events. *American Psychologist, 46,* 848–855.

Hoch, P.H., & Dunaiff, S.L. (1955). Pseudopsychopathic schizophrenia. In P.H. Hoch & J. Zubin (Eds.), *Psychiatry and the law.* New York: Grune & Stratton.

Hoch, P.H., & Polatin, P. (1949). Pseudoneurotic forms of schizophrenia. *Psychiatric Quarterly, 23,* 248–276.

Hodgson, R.J., & Rachman, S.J. (1972a). The effects of contamination and washing on obsessional patients. *Behaviour Research and Therapy, 10,* 111–117.

Hodgson, R.J., & Rachman, S.J. (1972b). The treatment of chronic obsessive-compulsive neurosis. *Behaviour Research and Therapy, 10,* 181–189.

Hoffman, M.L. (1970). Moral development. In P.H. Mussen (Ed.), *Carmichael's manual of child psychology.* London: Wiley.

Hogan, D. (1978). The effectiveness of sex therapy: A review of the literature. In J. LoPiccolo & L. LoPiccolo (Eds.), *Handbook of sex therapy.* New York: Plenum.

Hogarty, G.E., Anderson, C.M., Reiss, D.J., Kornblith, S.J., Greenwald, D.P., Javna, C.D., & Madonia, M.J. (1986). Family psychoeducation, social skills training, and maintenance chemotherapy in the aftercare treatment of schizophrenia: 1. One year effects of a controlled study on relapse and expressed emotion. *Archives of General Psychiatry, 43,* 633–642.

Hogarty, G.E., Anderson, C.M., Reiss, D.J., Kornblith, S.J., Greenwald, D.P., Ulrich, R.F., Carter, M., & The Environmental–Personal Indicators in the Course of Schizophrenia (EPICS) Research Group. (1991). Family psychoeducation, social skills training, and maintenance chemotherapy in the aftercare treatment of schizophrenia. *Archives of General Psychiatry, 48,* 340–347.

Hogarty, G.E., Goldberg, S.C., Schooler, N.R., Ulrich, R.F., & The Collaborative Study Group (1974). Drug and sociotherapy in the aftercare of schizophrenic patients: II. Two-year relapse rates. *Archives of General Psychiatry, 31,* 603–608.

Hokanson, J.E., & Burgess, M. (1962). The effects of three types of aggression on vascular processes. *Journal of Abnormal and Social Psychology, 65,* 446–449.

Hokanson, J.E., Burgess, M., & Cohen, M.F. (1963). Effects of displaced aggression on systolic blood pressure. *Journal of Abnormal and Social Psychology, 67,* 214–218.

Hokanson, J.E., Rubert, M.P., Welker, R.A., et al. (1989). Interpersonal concomitants and antecedents of depression among college students. *Journal of Abnormal Psychology, 98,* 209–217.

Hokanson, J.E., Willers, K.R., & Koropsak, E. (1968). Modification of autonomic responses during aggressive interchange. *Journal of Personality, 36,* 386–404.

Holden, C. (1972). Nader on mental health centers: A movement that got bogged down. *Science, 177,* 413–415.

Holder, H., Longabaugh, R., Miller, W.R., & Rubonis, A.V. (1991). The cost effectiveness of treatment for alcoholism: A first approximation. *Journal of Studies on Alcohol, 52,* 517–540.

Holinger, P.C. (1979). Violent deaths among the young: Recent trends in suicide, homicides, and accidents. *American Journal of Psychiatry, 136,* 1144–1147.

Holinger, P.C. (1987). *Violent deaths in the United States.* New York: Guilford.

Holland, B.F. (1988). Autonomy in long-term care: Background issues and a programmatic response. *The Gerontologist, 28* (Suppl.), 3–9.

Hollander, E., et al. (1992). Serotonergic function in obsessive-compulsive disorder: Behavioral and neuroendocrine responses to oral m-chlorophenylpiperazine and fenfluramine in patients and healthy volunteers. *Archives of General Psychiatry, 49,* 21–27.

Hollingshead, A.B., & Redlich, F.C. (1958). *Social class and mental illness: A community study.* New York: Wiley.

Hollon, S.D., & Beck, A.T. (1986). Cognitive and cognitive-behavioral therapies. In S.L. Garfield & A.E. Bergin (Eds.), *Handbook of psychotherapy and behavior change* (3rd ed.). New York: Wiley.

Hollon, S.D., DeRubeis, R.J., & Seligman, M.E.P. (1992). Cognitive therapy and the prevention of depression. *Applied and Preventive Psychology, 1,* 89–95.

Hollon, S.D., DeRubeis, R.J., Tuason, V.B., Weimer, M.J., Evans, M.D., & Garvey, M.J. (1989). *Cognitive therapy, pharmacotherapy, and combined cognitive-pharmacotherapy in the treatment of depression: I. Differential outcome.* Unpublished manuscript, Vanderbilt University, Nashville, TN.

Hollon, S.D., & Kendall, P.C. (1980). Cognitive self-statements in depression: Development of an automatic thoughts questionnaire. *Cognitive Therapy and Research, 4,* 383–395.

Holmes, T.H., & Rahe, R.H. (1967). The social readjustment rating scale. *Journal of Psychosomatic Research, 11,* 213–218.

Holmes, T.S., & Holmes, T.H. (1970). Short-term intrusions into the life style routine. *Journal of Psychosomatic Research, 14,* 121–132.

Holroyd, K., Penzien, D., Hursey, K., Tobin, D., Rogen, L., Holm, J., Marcille, P., Hall, J., & Chila, A. (1984). Change mechanisms in EMG biofeedback training: Cognitive changes underlying improvements in tension headache. *Journal of Consulting and Clinical Psychology, 52,* 1039–1053.

Holtzworth-Munroe, A., Jacobson, N.S., DeKlyen, M., & Whisman, M. (1989). Relationship between behavioral marital therapy outcome and process variables. *Journal of Consulting and Clinical Psychology, 57,* 658–662.

Honigfeld, G., & Howard, A. (1978). *Psychiatric drugs: A desk reference* (2nd ed.). New York: Academic Press.

Hooley, J.M. (1986). Expressed emotion and depression: Interactions between patients and high-versus-low-expressed emotion spouses. *Journal of Abnormal Psychology, 95,* 237–246.

Hooley, J.M., & Teasdale, J.D. (1989). Predictors of relapse in unipolar depressives: Expressed emotion, marital distress, and perceived criticism. *Journal of Abnormal Psychology, 98,* 229–235.

Hoon, E.F., & Hoon, P.W. (1978). Styles of sexual expression in women: Clinical implications of multivariate analyses. *Archives of Sexual Behavior, 7,* 105–116.

Hoon, P., Wincze, J., & Hoon, E. (1977). A test of reciprocal inhibition: Are anxiety and sexual arousal in women mutually inhibitory? *Journal of Abnormal Psychology, 86,* 65–74.

Horn, W.F., Wagner, A.E., & Ialongo, N. (1989). Sex differences in school-aged children with pervasive attention deficit hyperactivity disorder. *Journal of Abnormal Child Psychology, 17,* 109–125.

Hornblower, M., & Svoboda, W. (1987, November 23). Down and out—But determined: Does a mentally disturbed woman have the right to be homeless? *Time,* p. 29.

Horney, K. (1939). *New ways in psychoanalysis.* New York: International Universities Press.

Horney, K. (1942). *Self-analysis.* New York: Norton.

Horovitz, B. (1992, March 10). Cigarette ads under fire. *Los Angeles Times,* pp. D1, D6.

Horowitz, M.J. (1975). Intrusive and repetitive thoughts after experimental stress. *Archives of General Psychiatry, 32,* 223–228.

Horowitz, M.J. (1986). *Stress response syndromes.* Northvale, NJ: Aronson.

Horowitz, M.J. (1988). *Introduction to psychodynamics: A new synthesis.* New York: Basic Books.

Horowitz, M.J. (1990). Psychotherapy. In A.S. Bellack & M. Hersen (Eds.), *Handbook of comparative treatments for adult disorders* (pp. 289–301). New York: Wiley.

Horowitz, MJ., Marmar, C.R., Weiss, D.S., Kaltreider, N.B., & Wilner, N.R. (1986). Comprehensive analysis of change after brief dynamic psychotherapy. *American Journal of Psychiatry, 143,* 582–589.

Horwitz, L. (1974). *Clinical prediction in psychotherapy.* New York: Jason Aronson.

House, J.S., Landis, K.R., & Umberson, D. (1988). Social relationships and health. *Science, 241,* 540–544.

Houts, A.C. (1991). Nocturnal enuresis as a biobehavioral problem. *Behavior Therapy, 22,* 133–151.

Houts, P.S., & Serber, M. (Eds.). (1972). *After the turn-on, what? Learning perspectives on humanistic groups.* Champaign, IL: Research Press.

Howard, K.I., Orlinsky, D.E., Saunders, S.M., Bankoff, E., Davidson, C., & O'Mahoney, M. (1991). Northwestern University–University of Chicago Psychotherapy Research Program. In L. Beutler, & M. Crago (Eds.), *Psychotherapy research.* Washington, DC: American Psychological Association.

Hsu, L.K.G. (1980). Outcome of anorexia nervosa: A review of the literature (1954 to 1978). *Archives of General Psychiatry, 37,* 1041–1046.

Hsu, L.K.G. (1986). The treatment of anorexia nervosa. *American Journal of Psychiatry, 143,* 573–581.

Huesmann, L.R., Eron, L.D., Lefkowitz, M.M., & Walder, L.O. (1984). Stability of aggression over time and generations. *Developmental Psychology, 20,* 112–114.

Hugdahl, K., Fredrikson, M., & Ohman, A. (1977). Preparedness and arousability as determinants of electrodermal conditioning. *Behaviour Research and Therapy, 15,* 345–353.

Hughes, J.R., et al. (1991). Caffeine self-adminstration, withdrawal, and adverse effects among coffee drinkers. *Archives of General Psychiatry, 48,* 611–617.

Hughes, J.R. (1985). As cited in "Many factors account for failures with nicotine gum." In *Pharmacologic treatment of tobacco dependence.* Report from an International Congress, November 3–5, 1985, New York.

Hughes, J.R., Gust, S.W., Keenan, R.M., Fenwick, J.W., & Healey, M.L. (1989). Nicotine versus placebo gum in general medical practice. *Journal of the American Medical Association, 261,* 1300–1305.

Hughes, J.R., Gust, S.W., Skoog, K., Keenan, R.M., & Fenwick, J.W. (1991). Symptoms of tobacco withdrawal: A replication and extension. *Archives of General Psychiatry, 48,* 52–61.

Hughes, P.L., Wells, L.A., Cunningham, C.J., & Ilstrup, D.M. (1986). Treating bulimia with desipramine. *Archives of General Psychiatry, 43,* 182–186.

Hull, J.G. (1981). A self-awareness model of the causes and effects of alcohol consumption. *Journal of Abnormal Psychology, 90,* 586–600.

Hunt, G.M., & Azrin, N.H. (1973). A community-reinforcement approach to alcoholism. *Behaviour Research and Therapy, 11,* 91–104.

Hunt, W.A., & Bespalec, D.A. (1974). An evaluation of current methods of modifying smoking behavior. *Journal of Clinical Psychology, 30,* 431–438.

Hurst, J. (1992, March). Blowing smoke. *Los Angeles Times,* pp. A3, A29.

Hussian, R.A., & Lawrence, P.S. (1980). Social reinforcement of activity and problem-solving training in the treatment of depressed institutionalized elderly patients. *Cognitive Therapy and Research, 5,* 57–69.

Husted, J.R. (1975). Desensitization procedures in dealing with female sexual dysfunction. *The Counseling Psychologist, 5,* 30–37.

Hutchings, B., & Mednick, S.A. (1974). Registered criminality in the adoptive and biological parents of registered male adoptees. In S.A. Mednick, R. Schulsinger, J. Higgins, & B. Bell (Eds.), *Genetics, environment and psychopathology.* New York: Elsevier.

Hutt, C., Huff, S.J., Lee, D., & Ountsted, C. (1964). Arousal and childhood autism. *Nature, 204,* 908–909.

Huttenlocher, P.R. (1974). Dendritic development in neocortex of children with mental defect and infantile spasms. *Neurology, 24,* 203–210.

Hyland, M.E. (1990). The mood-peak flow relationship in adult asthmatics: A pilot study of individual differences and direction of causality. *British Journal of Medical Psychology, 63,* 379–384.

Imber, S.D., Elkin, I., Watkins, J.T., Collins, J.F., Shea, M.T., Leber, W.R., & Glass, D.R. (1990). Mode-specific effects among three treatments for depression. *Journal of Consulting and Clinical Psychology, 58,* 352–359.

Ingram, R.E., & Kendall, P.C. (1987). The cognitive side of anxiety. *Cognitive Therapy and Research, 11,* 523–536.

Innes, G., Millar, W.M., & Valentine, M. (1959). Emotion and blood pressure. *Journal of Mental Science, 105,* 840–851.

Insell, T.R. (1986). The neurobiology of anxiety. In B.F. Shaw, Z.V. Segal, T.M. Wallis, & F.E. Cashman (Eds.), *Anxiety disorders.* New York: Plenum.

Insell, T.R., Murphy, D.L., Cohen, R.M., Alterman, I., Itts, C., & Linnoila, M. (1983). Obsessive-compulsive disorders. A double-blind trial of clomipramine and clorgyline. *Archives of General Psychiatry, 40,* 605–612.

Insull, W. (Ed.). (1973). *Coronary risk handbook.* New York: American Heart Association.

Irwin, M., Lovitz, A., Marder, S.R., Mintz, J., Winslade, W.J., Van Putten, T., & Mills, M.J. (1985). Psychotic patients' understanding of informed consent. *American Journal of Psychiatry, 142,* 1351–1354.

Isen, A.M., Shaiken, T.F., Clark, M., & Karp, L. (1978). Affect, accessibility of material in memory, and behavior: A cognitive loop? *Journal of Personality and Social Psychology, 36,* 1–12.

Issidorides, M.R. (1979). Observations in chronic hashish users: Nuclear aberrations in blood and sperm and abnormal acrosomes in spermatozoa. In G.G. Nahas & W.D.M. Paton (Eds.), *Marihuana: Biological effects.* Elmsford, NY: Pergamon.

Istvan, J., & Matarazzo, J.D. (1984). Tobacco, alcohol and caffeine use: A review of their interrelationships. *Psychological Bulletin, 95,* 301–326.

Jackson, A.M. (1973). Psychotherapy: Factors associated with the race of the therapist. *Psychotherapy: Theory, Research, and Practice, 10,* 273–277.

Jackson, C., Winkleby, M.A., Flora, J.A., & Fortmann, S.P. (1991). Use of educational resources for cardiovascular risk reduction in the Stanford Five-City Project. *American Journal of Preventive Medicine, 7,* 82–88.

Jackson, J.L., Calhoun, K.S., Amick, A.E., Maddever, H.M., & Habif, V.L. (1990). Young adult women who report childhood intrafamilial sexual abuse: Subsequent adjustment. *Archives of Sexual Behavior, 19,* 211–221.

Jacobs, M., Jacobs, A., Gatz, M., & Schaible, T. (1973). Credibility and desirability of positive and negative structured feedback in groups. *Journal of Consulting and Clinical Psychology, 40,* 244–252.

Jacobson, A., & McKinney, W.T. (1982). Affective disorders. In J.H. Griest, J.W. Jefferson, & R.L. Spitzer (Eds.), *Treatment of mental disorders.* New York: Oxford University Press.

Jacobson, E. (1929). *Progressive relaxation.* Chicago: University of Chicago Press.

Jacobson, N.S. (1984). A component analysis of behavioral marital therapy: The relative effectiveness of behavior exchange and problem solving training. *Journal of Consulting and Clinical Psychology, 52,* 295–305.

Jacobson, N.S. (1991). Behavioral versus insight-oriented marital therapy: Labels can be misleading. *Journal of Consulting and Clinical Psychology, 59,* 142–145.

Jacobson, N.S. (1992). Behavioral couple therapy: A new beginning. *Behavior Therapy, 23,* 493–506.

Jacobson, N.S., & Addis, M.E. (1993). Research on couples and couple therapy: What do we know? Where are we going? *Journal of Consulting and Clinical Psychology, 61,* 85–93.

Jacobson, N.S., & Christensen, A. (in press). *Couple therapy: An integrative approach.* New York: Norton.

Jacobson, N.S., Dobson, K., Fruzzetti, A.E., Schmaling, K.B., & Salusky, S. (1991). Marital therapy as a treatment for depression. *Journal of Consulting and Clinical Psychology, 59,* 547–557.

Jacobson, N.S., Follette, W.C., & McDonald, D.W. (1982). Reactivity to positive and negative behavior in distressed and nondistressed married couples. *Journal of Consulting and Clinical Psychology, 50,* 706–714.

Jacobson, N.S., Follette, W.C., & Pagel, N. (1986). Predicting who will benefit from behavioral marital therapy. *Journal of Consulting and Clinical Psychology, 54,* 518–522.

Jacobson, N.S., Follette, W.C., Revenstorf, D., Baucom, D.H., Hahlweg, K., & Margolin, G. (1984). Variability of outcome and clinical significance of behavioral marital therapy: A reanalysis of outcome data. *Journal of Consulting and Clinical Psychology, 52,* 497–504.

Jacobson, N.S., Fruzzetti, A.E., Dobson, K., Whisman, M., & Hops, H. (in press). Couple therapy as a treatment for depression. II: The effects of relationship quality and therapy on depressive relapse. *Journal of Consulting and Clinical Psychology.*

Jacobson, N.S., Holzworth-Munroe, A., & Schmaling, K.B. (1989). Marital therapy and spouse involvement in the treatment of depression, agoraphobia, and alcoholism. *Journal of Consulting and Clinical Psychology, 57,* 5–10.

Jacobson, N.S., & Margolin, G. (1979). *Marital therapy: Strategies based on social learning.* New York: Brunner/Mazel.

Jacobson, N.S., McDonald, D.W., Follette, W.C., & Berley, R.A. (1985). Attributional process in distressed and nondistressed married couples. *Cognitive Therapy and Research, 9,* 35–50.

Jacobson, N.S., Schmaling, K.B., & Holtzworth-Munroe, A. (1987). Component analysis of behavioral marital therapy: Two-year follow-up and prediction of relapse. *Journal of Marital and Family Therapy, 13,* 187–195.

Jacobson, N.S., Waldron, H., & Moore, D. (1980). Toward a behavioral profile of marital distress. *Journal of Consulting and Clinical Psychology, 48,* 696–703.

Jaffe, J.H. (1985). Drug addiction and drug abuse. In *Goodman and Gilman's the pharmacological basis of therapeutic behavior.* New York: Macmillan Co.

James, N., & Chapman, J. (1975). A genetic study of bipolar affective disorder. *British Journal of Psychiatry, 126,* 449–456.

Jamison, K.R. (1979). Manic-depressive illness in the elderly. In O.J. Kaplan (Ed.), *Psychopathology of aging.* New York: Academic Press.

Jampole, L., & Weber, M.K. (1987). An assessment of the behavior of sexually abused and nonsexually abused children with anatomically correct dolls. *Child Abuse and Neglect, 11,* 187–192.

Jandorf, L., Deblinger, E., Neale, J.M., & Stone, A.A. (1986). Daily vs. major life events as predictors of symptom frequency. *Journal of General Psychology, 113,* 205–218.

Jarvik, L.F., Ruth, V., & Matsuyama, S. (1980). Organic brain syndrome and aging: A six-year follow-up of surviving twins. *Archives of General Psychiatry, 37,* 280–286.

Jarvik, M.E., & Schneider, N.G. (1984). Degree of addiction and effectiveness of nicotine gum therapy for smoking.

American Journal of Psychiatry, 141, 790–791.

Jarvis, MJ., Raw, M., Russell, M.A.H., & Feyerabend, C. (1982). Randomised controlled trial of nicotine chewing-gum. *British Medical Journal, 285,* 537–540.

Jary, M.L., & Stewart, M.A. (1985). Psychiatric disorder in the parents of adopted children with aggressive conduct disorder. *Neuropsychobiology, 13,* 7–11.

Jasinski, D.R., Johnson, R.E., & Kocher, T.R. (1985). Clonidine in morphine withdrawal. *Archives of General Psychiatry, 42,* 1063–1066.

Jasnoski, M.L., & Kugler, J. (1987). Relaxation, imagery, and neuroimmunomodulation. *Annals of the New York Academy of Sciences, 496,* 722–730.

Jasnow, N. (1982). *Effects of relaxation training and rational emotive therapy on anxiety reduction in sixth grade children.* Unpublished doctoral dissertation, Hofstra University, Hempstead, NY.

Jay, S.M., Elliott, C.H., Katz, E., & Siegel, S.E. (1987). Cognitive-behavioral and pharmacologic interventions for children's distress during painful medical procedures. *Journal of Consulting and Clinical Psychology, 55,* 860–865.

Jay, S.M., Elliott, C.H., Ozolins, M., & Olson, R.A. (1982). *Behavioral management of children's distress during painful medical procedures.* Paper presented at the annual meeting of the American Psychological Association, Washington, DC.

Jeans, R.F.I. (1976). An independently validated case of multiple personality. *Journal of Abnormal Psychology, 85,* 249–255.

Jeffrey, D.B. (1974). A comparison of the effects of external control and self-control on the modification and maintenance of weight. *Journal of Abnormal Psychology, 83,* 404–410.

Jeffrey, R.W., Forster, J.L., & Schmid, T.L. (1989). Worksite health promotion: Feasibility testing of repeated weight control and smoking cessation classes. *American Journal of Health Promotion, 3,* 11–16.

Jellinek, E.M. (1952). Phases of alcohol addiction. *Quarterly Journal of Studies on Alcohol, 13,* 673–684.

Jenike, M.A. (1986). Theories of etiology. In M.A. Jenike, L. Baer, & W.E. Minichiello (Eds.), *Obsessive-compulsive disorders.* Littleton, MA: PSG Publishing.

Jenike, M.A. (1990). Psychotherapy. In A.S. Bellack & M. Hersen (Eds.), *Handbook of comparative treatments for adult disorders* (pp. 245–255). New York: Wiley.

Jenike, M.A., et al. (1991). Cingulotomy for refractory obsessive-compulsive disorder: A long-term follow-up of 33 cases. *Archives of General Psychiatry, 48,* 548–557

Jenkins, C.D. (1971). Psychologic and social precursors of coronary disease. *New England Journal of Medicine, 284,* 244–255, 307–317.

Jenkins, C.D. (1976). Recent evidence supporting psychologic and social risk factors for coronary disease. *New England Journal of Medicine, 294,* 987–994, 1033–1038.

Jenkins, C.D., Rosenman, R.H., & Zyzanski, S.J. (1974). Prediction of clinical coronary heart disease by a test for the coronary-prone behavior pattern. *New England Journal of Medicine, 290,* 1271–1275.

Jenkins, C.D., Zyzanski, S.J., & Rosenman, R.H. (1978). Coronary-prone behavior: One pattern or several? *Psychosomatic Medicine, 40,* 25–43.

Jerrell, J.M., & Larsen, J.K. (1986). Community mental health centers in transition: Who is benefitting? *American Journal of Orthopsychiatry, 56,* 78–88.

Jerremalm, A., Jansson, L., & Ost, L. (1986). Cognitive and physiological reactivity and the effects of different behavioral methods in the treatment of social phobia. *Behaviour Research and Therapy, 24,* 171–180.

Johnson, D.R. (1987). The role of the creative arts therapist in the diagnosis and treatment of psychological trauma. *The Arts in Psychotherapy, 14,* 7–13.

Johnson, E.H. (1984). *Anger and anxiety as determinants of elevated blood pressure in adolescents.* Unpublished doctoral dissertation, University of South Florida.

Johnson, E.H., Nazzaro, P., & Gilbert, D.C. (1991). Cardiovascular reactivity to stress in black male offspring of hypertensive parents. *Psychosomatic Medicine, 53,* 420–432.

Johnson, J., Horvath, E., & Weissman, M.M. (1991). The validity of depression with psychotic features based on a community study. *Archives of General Psychiatry, 48,* 1075–1081.

Johnson, J., Weissman, M.M., & Klerman, G.L. (1990). Panic disorder and suicide attempts. *Archives of General Psychiatry, 47,* 805–808.

Johnson, S.M., & Greenberg, L.S. (1985). Differential effects of experiential and problem-solving interventions in resolving marital conflict. *Journal of Consulting and Clinical Psychology, 53,* 175–184.

Johnston, D.G., Troyer, I.E., & Whitsett, S.F. (1988). Clomipramine treatment of agoraphobic women. *Archives of General Psychiatry, 45,* 453–459.

Johnston, M.B., Whitman, T.L., & Johnson, M. (1980). Teaching addition and subtraction to mentally retarded children: A self-instructional program. *Applied Research in Mental Retardation, 1,* 141–160.

Joiner, T.E., Alfano, M.S., & Metalsky, G.I. (1992). When depression breeds contempt: Reassurance seeking, self-esteem, and rejection of depressed college students by their roommates. *Journal of Abnormal Psychology, 101,* 165–173.

Jones, E. (1955). *The life and work of Sigmund Freud* (Vol. 2). New York: Basic Books.

Jones, M. (1953). *The therapeutic community.* New York: Basic Books.

Jones, M.C. (1924). A laboratory study of fear: The case of Peter. *Pedagogical Seminary, 31,* 308–315.

Jones, M.C. (1968). Personality correlates and antecedents of drinking patterns in males. *Journal of Consulting and Clinical Psychology, 32,* 2–12.

Jones, R.T. (1977). Human effects. In R.C. Peterson (Ed.), *Marijuana research findings: 1976* (NIDA Research Monograph 14). Washington, DC: U.S. Government Printing Office.

Jones, R.T. (1980). Human effects: An overview. In *Marijuana research findings* Washington, DC: U.S. Government Printing Office.

Jones, R.T. (1983). Cannabis and health. *Annual Review of Medicine, 34,* 247–258.

Jones, R.T., & Benowitz, N. (1976). The 30-day trip—Clinical studies of cannabis tolerance and dependence. In M.C. Braude & S. Szara (Eds.), *Pharmacology of marijuana.* New York: Raven.

Josephs, R.A., & Steele, C.M. (1990). The two faces of alcohol myopia: Attentional mediation of psychological stress. *Journal of Abnormal Psychology, 99,* 115–126.

Judson, F.N., Cohn, D., & Douglas, J. (1989, June). *Fear of AIDS and incidence of gonorrhea, syphilis, and hepatitis B. 1982–1988.* Paper presented at the Fifth International Conference on AIDS, Montreal. As cited in Coates (1990).

Jutai, J.W., & Hare, R.D. (1983). Psychopathy and selective attention during performance of a complex perceptual-motor task. *Psychophysiology, 20,* 140–151.

Kahana, R.J. (1987). Geriatric psychotherapy: Beyond crisis management. In J. Sadavoy, & M. Leszcz (Eds.), *Treating the elderly with psychotherapy.* Madison, CT: International Universities Press.

Kahn, R.L., Zarit, S.H., Hilbert, N.M., & Niederebe, G. (1975). Memory complaint and impairment in the aged. *Archives of General Psychiatry, 32,* 1569–1573.

Kahn, R.L., Zarit, S.H., Hilbert, N.M., & Niederehe, G. (1975). Memory complaint and impairment in the aged: The effect of depression and altered brain function. *Archives of General Psychiatry, 32,* 1569–1573.

Kahneman, D. (1973). *Attention and effort.* Englewood Cliffs, NJ: Prentice-Hall.

Kaiser, F.E., Viosca, S.P., Morley, J.E., Mooradian, A.D., Davis, S.S., & Korenman, S.G. (1988). Impotence and aging:

Clinical and hormonal factors. *Journal of the American Geriatrics Society, 36,* 511–519.

Kalichman, S.C. (1991). Psychopathology and personality characteristics of criminal sexual offenders as a function of victim age. *Archives of Sexual Behavior, 20,* 187–198.

Kammen, D.P. van, Bunney, W.E., Docherty, J.P., Jimerson, D.C., Post, R.M., Sivis, S., Ebart, M., & Gillin, J.C. (1977). Amphetamine-induced catecholamine activation in schizophrenia and depression. *Advances in Biochemical Psychopharmacology, 16,* 655–659.

Kanas, N. (1986). Group therapy with schizophrenics: A review of controlled studies. *International Journal of Group Therapy, 36,* 339–351.

Kandel, D.B. (1984). Marijuana users in young adulthood. *Archives of General Psychiatry, 41,* 200–209.

Kandel, D.B., Davies, M., Karus, D., & Yamaguchi, K. (1986). The consequences in young adulthood of adolescent drug involvement. *Archives of General Psychiatry, 43,* 746–754.

Kandel, D.B., Murphy, D., & Karus, D. (1985). *National Institute on Drug Abuse Research Monograph Series 61.* Washington, DC: NIDA.

Kane, J., Honigfeld, G., Singer, J., Meltzer, H., et al. (1988). Clozapine for treatment resistant schizophrenics. *Archives of General Psychiatry, 45,* 789–796.

Kane, J.M., Woerner, M., Weinhold, P., Wegner, J., Kinon, B., & Bernstein, M. (1986). Incidence of tardive dyskinesia: Five-year data from a prospective study. *Psychopharmacology Bulletin, 20,* 387–389.

Kane, R.L., Parsons, D.A., & Goldstein, G. (1983). Statistical relationships and discriminative accuracy of the Halstead–Reitan, Luria–Nebraska, and Wechsler IQ scores in the identification of brain damage. *Journal of Clinical and Experimental Neuropsychology, 7,* 211–223.

Kanfer, F.H. (1979). Self-management: Strategies and tactics. In A.P. Goldstein & F.H. Kanfer (Eds.), *Maximizing treatment gains: Transfer enhancement in psychotherapy.* New York: Academic Press.

Kanfer, F.H., & Busenmeyer, J.R. (1982). The use of problem-solving and decision making in behavior therapy. *Clinical Psychology Review, 2,* 239–266.

Kanfer, F.H., & Phillips, J.S. (1970). *Learning foundations of behavior therapy.* New York: Wiley.

Kanner, L. (1943). Autistic disturbances of affective contact. *Nervous Child, 2,* 217–250.

Kanner, L. (1973). Follow-up of eleven autistic children originally reported in 1943. In L. Kanner (Ed.), *Childhood psychosis: Initial studies and new insights.* Washington, DC: Winston-Wiley.

Kanner, L., & Eisenberg, L. (1955). Notes on the follow-up studies of autistic children. In P. Hoch & J. Zubin (Eds.), *Psychopathology of childhood.* New York: Grune & Stratton.

Kanter, J., Lamb, R., & Loeper, G. (1987). Expressed emotions in families: A critical review. *Hospital and Community Psychiatry, 38,* 374–380.

Kanter, J.S., Zitrin, C.M., & Zeldis, S.M. (1980). Mitral valve prolapse syndrome in agoraphobic patients. *American Journal of Psychiatry, 137,* 467–469.

Kantorovich, N.V. (1930). An attempt at associative-reflex therapy in alcoholism. *Psychological Abstracts, 4,* 493.

Kaplan, A.S., & Woodside, D.B. (1987). Biological aspects of anorexia nervosa and bulimia nervosa. *Journal of Consulting and Clinical Psychology, 55,* 645–653.

Kaplan, H.S. (1974). *The new sex therapy.* New York: Brunner/Mazel.

Karacan, I., Thornby, J., Holzer, C.E., Warheit, G.J., Schwab, J.J., & Williams, R.L. (1976). Prevalence of sleep disturbance in a primarily urban Florida county. *Social Science Medicine, 10,* 239–244,

Karasu, T.B., Stein, S.P., & Charles, E.S. (1979). Age factors in the patient-therapist relationship. *Journal of Nervous and Mental Disease, 167,* 100–104.

Karrer, R., Nelson, M., & Galbraith, G.C. (1979). Psychophysiological research with the mentally retarded. In N.R. Ellis (Ed.), *Handbook of mental deficiency. Psychological theory and research* (2nd ed.). Hillsdale, NJ: Erlbaum.

Kashani, J.H., & Orvaschel, H. (1988). Anxiety disorders in mid-adolescence: A community sample. *American Journal of Psychiatry, 145,* 960–964.

Kasindorf, J. (1988, May 2). The real story of Billie Boggs: Was Koch right—Or the civil libertarians? *New York,* pages 36–44.

Kasl, S.V., & Cobb, S. (1970). Blood pressure changes in men undergoing job loss: A preliminary report. *Psychosomatic Medicine, 32,* 19–38.

Kaslow, F.W. (1981). Divorce and divorce therapy. In A.S. Gurman & D.P. Kniskern (Eds.), *Handbook of family therapy.* New York: Brunner/Mazel.

Kaslow, N.J., & Racusin, G.R. (1990). Childhood depression: Current status and future directions. In A.S. Bellack, M. Hersen, & A.E. Kazdin (Eds.), *International handbook of behavior modification and therapy* (2nd ed.). New York: Plenum.

Kasprowicz, A.L., Manuck, S.B., Malkoff, S., & Kranz, D.S. (1990). Individual differences in behaviorally evoked cardiovascular response: Temporal stability and hemodynamic patterning. *Psychophysiology, 27,* 605–619.

Kaszniak, A.W., Nussbaum, P.D., Berren, M.R., & Santiago, J. (1988). Amnesia as a consequence of male rape: A case report. *Journal of Abnormal Psychology, 97,* 100–104.

Katchadourian, H.A., & Lunde, D.T. (1972). *Fundamentals of human sexuality.* New York: Holt, Rinehart & Winston.

Katz, E.R. (1980). Illness impact and social reintegration. In J. Kellerman (Ed.), *Psychological aspects of childhood cancer.* Springfield, IL: Charles C. Thomas.

Katz, E.R., Kellerman, J., & Siegel, S.E. (1980). Behavioral distress in children with leukemia undergoing bone marrow aspirations. *Journal of Consulting and Clinical Psychology, 48,* 356–365.

Katz, R.C., Gipson, M.T., Kearl, A., & Kriskovich, M. (1989). Assessing sexual aversion in college students: The Sexual Aversion Scale. *Journal of Sex and Marital Therapy, 15,* 135–140.

Katz, S., & Kravetz, S. (1989). Facial plastic surgery for persons with Down syndrome: Research findings and their professional and social implications. *American Journal on Mental Retardation, 94,* 101–110.

Kaufmann, P.G., Jacob, R.G., Ewart, C.K., Chesney, M.A., Muenz, L.R., Doub, N., Mercer, W., & HIPP Investigators. (1988). Hypertension intervention pooling project. *Health Psychology, 7,* 209–224.

Kay, D.W.K., Cooper, A.F., Garside, R.F., & Roth, M. (1976). The differentiation of paranoid from affective psychoses by patient's premorbid characteristics. *British Journal of Psychiatry, 129,* 207–215.

Kazdin, A.E. (1985). *Treatment of antisocial behavior in children and adolescents.* Homewood, IL: Dorsey Press.

Kazdin, A.E. (1986). Research designs and methodology. In S.L. Garfield & A.E. Bergin (Eds.), *Handbook of psychotherapy and behavior change* (3rd ed.). New York: Wiley.

Kazdin, A.E., Bass, D., Siegel, T., & Thomas, C. (1989). Cognitive-behavioral therapy and relationship therapy in the treatment of children referred for antisocial behavior. *Journal of Consulting and Clinical Psychology, 57,* 522-535.

Keane, T.M., Fairbank, J.A., Caddell, J.M., & Zimering, R.T. (1989). Implosive (flooding) therapy reduces symptoms of PTSD in Vietnam combat veterans. *Behavior Therapy, 20,* 245–260.

Keane, T.M., Foy, D.W., Nunn, B., & Rychtarik, R.G. (1984). Spouse contracting to increase antabuse compliance in alcoholic veterans. *Journal of Clinical Psychology, 40,* 340–344.

Keane, T.M., Gerardi, R.J., Quinn, S.J., & Litz, B.T. (1992). Behavioral treatment of post-traumatic stress disorder. In S.M. Turner, K.S. Calhoun, & H.E. Adams (Eds.), *Handbook of clinical behavior therapy* 2nd ed., pp. 87–97. New York: Wiley.

Keane, T.M., Zimering, R.T., & Caddell, J. (1985). A behavioral formulation of post-traumatic stress disorder in Vietnam veterans. *The Behavior Therapist, 8,* 9–12.

Keefe, F.J., & Gil, K.M. (1986). Behavioral concepts in the analysis of chronic pain syndromes. *Journal of Consulting and Clinical Psychology, 54,* 776–783.

Keith, J. (1982). *Old people as people.* Boston: Little, Brown.

Keller, M.B., Shapiro, R.W., Lavori, P.W., & Wolpe, N. (1982). Relapse in major depressive disorder: Analysis with the life table. *Archives of General Psychiatry, 39,* 911–915.

Kellerman, J. (1989), *Silent partner.* New York: Bantam Books.

Kellerman, J., & Varni, J.W. (1982). Pediatric hematology/oncology. In D.C. Russo & J.W. Varni (Eds.), *Behavioral pediatrics: Research and practice.* New York: Plenum.

Kellner, R. (1982). Disorders of impulse control (not elsewhere classified). In J.H. Griest, J.W. Jefferson, & R.L. Spitzer *(Eds.), Treatment of mental disorders.* New York: Oxford University Press.

Kelly, G.A. (1955). *The psychology of personal constructs.* New York: Norton.

Kelly, H.S. (1992). *Aggressive symptoms in children with behavior and comorbid mood disorders.* Unpublished manuscript, State University of New York at Stony Brook.

Kelly, J.A. (1985). Group social skills training. *The Behavior Therapist, 8,* 93–95.

Kelly, J.A., & St. Lawrence, J.S. (1988a). *The AIDS health crisis: Psychological and social interventions.* New York: Plenum.

Kelly, J.A., & St. Lawrence, J.S. (1988b). AIDS prevention and treatment: Psychology's role in the health crisis. *Clinical Psychology Review, 8,* 255–284.

Kelly, J.A., St. Lawrence, J.S., Betts, R., Brasfield, T., & Hood, H. (1990). A skills training group intervention model to assist persons in reducing risk behaviors for HIV infection. *AIDS Education and Prevention, 2,* 24–35.

Kelly, J.A., St. Lawrence, J.S., Hood, H., & Brasfield, T. (1989). Behavioral intervention to reduce AIDS risk activities. *Journal of Consulting and Clinical Psychology, 57,* 60–67.

Kelly, J.A., St. Lawrence, J.S., Hood, H.V., Smith, S., Jr., & Cook, D. (1988). Nurses' attitudes towards AIDS. *The Journal of Continuing Education in Nursing, 19,* 78–83.

Kendall, P.C. (1990). Cognitive processes and procedures in behavior therapy. In C.M. Franks, G.T. Wilson, P.C. Kendall, & J.P. Foreyt (Eds.), *Review of behavior therapy: Theory and practice* (Vol. 12, pp. 103–137. New York: Guilford.

Kendall, P.C., & Braswell, L. (1985). *Cognitive-behavioral therapy for impulsive children.* New York: Guilford.

Kendall, P.C., & Hollon, S.D. (Eds.). (1981). *Assessment strategies for cognitive-behavioral interventions.* New York: Academic Press.

Kendall, P.C., & Ingram, R.E. (1989). Cognitive-behavioral perspectives: Theory and research on depression and anxiety. In P.C. Kendall, & D. Watson (Eds.), *Anxiety and depression: Distinctive and overlapping features* (pp. 27-54). New York: Academic Press.

Kendall, P.C., Reber, M., McLeer, S., Epps, J., & Ronan, K. (1990). Cognitive-behavioral treatment of conduct-disordered children. *Cognitive Therapy and Research, 14,* 279–297.

Kendall-Tackett, K.A., Williams, L.M., & Finkelhor, D. (1993). Impact of sexual abuse on children: A review and synthesis of recent empirical studies. *Psychological Bulletin, 113,* 164–180.

Kendell, R.E. (1975). *The role of diagnosis in psychiatry.* London: Blackwell.

Kendler, K.S., & Masterson, C. C., & Davis, K. L. (1985). Psychiatric illness in first degree relatives of patients with paranoid psychosis, schizophrenia and medical controls. *British Journal of Psychiatry,* 147, 524–531.

Kennedy, W.A. (1965). School phobia: Rapid treatment of 50 cases. *Journal of Abnormal Psychology, 70,* 285–289.

Kent, R.N., O'Leary, K.D., Diament, C., & Dietz, A. (1974). Expectation biases in observational evaluation of therapeutic change. *Journal of Consulting and Clinical Psychology, 42,* 774–780.

Kermis, M.D. (1986). The epidemiology of mental disorder in the elderly: A response to the Senate/AARP report. *Gerontologist, 26,* 482–487.

Kernberg, O.F. (1985). *Borderline conditions and pathological narcissism.* Northvale, NJ: Jason Aronson.

Kernberg, O.F. (1973). Summary and conclusion. In "Psychotherapy and psychoanalysis: Final report of the Menninger Foundation's Psychotherapy Research Project." *International Journal of Psychiatry, 11,* 62–77.

Kernberg, O.F. (1970). A psychoanalytic classification of character pathology. *Journal of the American Psychoanalytic Association, 18,* 800–822.

Kernberg, O.F., Burstein, E.D., Coyne, L., Applebaum, A., Horwitz, L., & Voth, H. (1972). Psychotherapy and psychoanalysis: Final report of the Menninger Foundation's Psychotherapy Research Project. *Bulletin of the Menninger Clinic, 36,* 1–276.

Kessel, N., & Grossman, G. (1961). Suicide in alcoholics. *British Medical Journal, 2,* 1671–1672.

Kessler, J. (1966). *Psychopathology of childhood.* Englewood Cliffs, NJ: Prentice-Hall.

Kessler, R.C., & Neighbors, H.W. (1986). A new perspective on the relationships among race, social class and psychological distress. *Journal of Health and Social Behavior, 27,* 107–115.

Kety, S.S. (1974). From rationalization to reason. *American Journal of Psychiatry, 131,* 957–963.

Kety, S.S., Rosenthal, D., Wender, P.H., & Schulsinger, F. (1968). The types and prevalence of mental illness in the biological and adoptive families of adopted schizophrenics. In D. Rosenthal & S.S. Kety (Eds.), *The transmission of schizophrenia.* Elmsford, NY: Pergamon.

Kety, S.S., Rosenthal, D., Wender, P.H., Schulsinger, F. & Jacobson, B. (1975). Mental illness in the biological and adoptive families of adopted individuals who have become schizophrenic: A preliminary report based on psychiatric interviews. In R.R. Fieve, D. Rosenthal, & H. Brill (Eds.), *Genetic research in psychiatry.* Baltimore: Johns Hopkins University Press.

Keuthen, N. (1980). *Subjective probability estimation and somatic structures in phobic individuals.* Unpublished manuscript, State University of New York at Stony Brook.

Kidder, T. (1978). Soldiers of misfortune. *The Atlantic Monthly, 241,* 41–52.

Kiecolt-Glaser, J.K., Fisher, L.D., Ogrocki, P., Stout, J.C., Speicher, C.E., & Glaser, R. (1987). Marital quality, marital disruption, and immune function. *Psychosomatic Medicine, 49,* 13- 34.

Kiecolt-Glaser, J.K., Garner, W., Speicher, C.E., Penn, G.M., Holliday, J., & Glaser, R. (1984). Psychosocial modifiers of immunocompetence in medical students. *Psychosomatic Medicine, 46,* 7–14.

Kiecolt-Glaser, J.K., & Glaser, R. (1987). Psychosocial moderators of immune function. *Annals of Behavioral Medicine, 9,* 16–20.

Kiecolt-Glaser, J., Dura, J.R., Speicher, C.E., & Trask, O. (1991). Spousal caregivers of dementia victims: Longitudinal changes in immunity and health. *Psychosomatic Medicine, 54,* 345–362.

Kiecolt-Glaser, J., Glaser, R., Strain, E., Stout, J.C., Tarr, K.L., Holliday, J.E., & Speicher, C.E. (1986). Modulation of cellular immunity in medical students. *Journal of Behavioral Medicine, 9,* 5–21.

Kiecolt-Glaser, J.K., Glaser, R., Williger, D.,

Stout, J., Messick, G., Sheppard, S., Ricker, D., Romischer, S.C., Briner, W., Bonnell, G., & Donnerberg, R. (1985). Psychosocial enhancement of immunocompetence in a geriatric population. *Health Psychology, 4,* 25–41.

Kiecolt-Glaser, J.K., Kennedy, S., Malkoff, S., Fisher, L., Speicher, D.E., & Glaser, R. (1988). Marital discord and immunity in males. *Psychosomatic Medicine, 50,* 213–229.

Kiesler, C.A. (1991). Changes in general hospital psychiatric care. *American Psychologist, 46,* 416–421.

Kihlstrom, J.F., Barnhardt, T.M. & Tataryn, D.J. (1992). The psychological unconscious: Found, lost, and regained. *American Psychologist, 47,* 788–791.

Kilhstrom, J.F. & Tataryn, D. J. (1991). Dissociative disorders. In P.B. Sutker, & H.E. Adams (Eds.), *Comprehensive handbook of psychopathology.* 2nd ed. New York: Plenum.

Killen, J.D., Fortmann, S.P., Newman, B., & Varady, A. (1990). Evaluation of a treatment approach combining nicotine gum with self-guided behavioral treatments for smoking relapse prevention. *Journal of Consulting and Clinical Psychology, 58,* 85–92.

Killen, J.D., Maccoby, N., & Taylor, C.B. (1984). Nicotine gum and self-regulation training in smoking relapse prevention. *Behavior Therapy, 15,* 234–248.

Kiloh, L.G. (1961). Pseudo-dementia. *Acta Psychiatrica Scandinavia, 37,* 336–351.

Kilpatrick, D.G., & Best, C.L. (1990, April). *Sexual assault victims: Data from a random national probability sample.* Paper presented at the annual convention of the Southeastern Psychological Association, Atlanta.

Kilpatrick, D.G., Best, C.L., Veronen, L.J., Amick, A.E., Villeponteaux, L.A., & Ruff, G.A. (1985). Mental health correlates of criminal victimization: A random community survey. *Journal of Consulting and Clinical Psychology, 53,* 866–873.

Kimble, G.A., Garmezy, N., & Zigler, E. (1980). *Principles of general psychology.* New York: Wiley.

Kimmel, D.C. (1979). Adjustments to aging among gay men. In B. Berzon & R. Leighton (Eds.), *Positively gay.* Millbrae, CA: Celestial Arts.

Kimura, D. (1983). Sex differences in cerebral organization for speech and praxic functions. *Canadian Journal of Psychology, 37,* 19–35.

King, M.B. (1990). Sneezing as a fetishistic stimulus. *Sexual and Marital Therapy, 5,* 69–72.

Kingsley, L.A., Kaslow, R., Rinaldo, C.R., Detre, K., Odaka, N., Van-Raden, M., Detels, R., Polk, B.F., Chmiel, J., Kelsey, S.F., Ostrow, D., & Visscher, B. (1987). Risk factors for seroconversion to human immunodeficiency virus among male homosexuals. *Lancet, 1,* 345–348.

Kinsey, A.C., Pomeroy, W.B., Main, C.E., & Gebbard, P.H. (1953). *Sexual behavior in the human female.* Philadelphia: Saunders.

Kinsey, A.C., Pomeroy, W.B., & Martin, C.E. (1948). *Sexual behavior in the human male.* Philadelphia: Saunders.

Kinsman, R.A., Spector, S.L., Shucard, D.W., & Luparello, T.J. (1974). Observations on patterns of subjective symptomatology of acute asthma. *Psychosomatic Medicine, 36,* 129–143.

Kinzie, J.D. (1985). Overview of clinical issues in the treatment of Southeast Asian refugees. In T.C. Owan (Ed.), *Southeast Asian mental health treatment, prevention services, training, and research.* Washington, DC: National Institute of Mental Health.

Kivlighan, D.M., & Mullison, D. (1988). Participants' perception of therapeutic factors in group counseling: The role of interpersonal style and stage of group development. *Small Group Development, 19,* 452–468.

Klee, G.D., & Weintraub, W. (1959). Paranoid reactions following lysergic acid diethylamide (LSD-25). In P.B. Bradley, P. Demicker, & C. Radonco-Thomas (Eds.), *Neuropsychopharmacology.* Amsterdam: Elsevier.

Kleeman, S.T. (1967). Psychiatric contributions in the treatment of asthma. *Annals of Allergy, 25,* 611–619.

Klein, D. (1992, April 1). The empty pot. *Los Angeles Times,* pp. A3, A14.

Klein, D.C., & Seligman, M.E.P. (1976). Reversal of performance deficits and perceptual deficits in learned helplessness and depression. *Journal of Abnormal Psychology, 85,* 11–26.

Klein, D.N., Taylor, E.B., Dickstein, S., & Harding, K. (1988). Primary early-onset dysthymia: Comparison with primary nonbipolar nonchronic major depression on demographic, clinical, familial, personality, and socioenvironmental characteristics and short-term outcome. *Journal of Abnormal Psychology, 97,* 387–398.

Klein, M. (1932). *The psychoanalysis of children.* London: Hogarth.

Kleinke, C.L., Staneski, R.A., & Mason, J.K. (1982). Sex differences in coping with depression. *Sex Roles, 8,* 877–889.

Klerman, G.L. (1972). Drug therapy of clinical depressions. *Journal of Psychiatric Research, 9,* 253–270.

Klerman, G.L. (1975). Drug therapy of clinical depressions—Current status and implications for research on neuropharmacology of the affective disorders. In D.F. Klein & R. Gittelman-Klein (Eds.), *Progress in psychiatric drug treatment.* New York: Brunner/Mazel.

Klerman, G.L. (1983). Problems in the definition and diagnosis of depression in the elderly. In M. Hauge & L. Breslau (Eds.), *Depression in the elderly: Causes, care, consequences.* New York: Springer.

Klerman, G.L. (1988). Depression and related disorders of mood (affective disorders). In A.M. Nicholi, Jr. (Ed.), *The new Harvard guide to psychiatry.* Cambridge, MA: Harvard University Press.

Klerman, G.L. (1990). Treatment of recurrent unipolar major depressive disorder. *Archives of General Psychiatry, 47,* 1158–1162.

Klerman, G.L., Weissman, M.M., Rounsaville, B.J., & Chevron, E.S. (1984). *Interpersonal psychotherapy of depression.* New York: Basic Books.

Kluft, R.P. (1984a). An introduction to multiple personality disorder. *Psychiatric Annals, 7,* 19–24.

Kluft, R.P. (1984b). Multiple personality in childhood. *Psychiatric Clinics of North America, 7,* 121–134.

Kluft, R.P. (1984c). Treatment of multiple personality disorder: A study of 33 cases. *Psychiatric Clinics of North America, 7,* 929.

Kluft, R.P. (1985a). The treatment of multiple personality disorder (MPD): Current concepts. In F.F. Flach (Ed.), *Directions in psychiatry.* New York: Hatherleigh.

Kluft, R.P. (1985b). Using hypnotic inquiry protocols to monitor treatment progress and stability in multiple personality disorder. *American Journal of Clinical Hypnosis, 28,* 63–75.

Kluger, J.M. (1969). Childhood asthma and the social milieu. *American Academy of Child Psychiatry, 8,* 353–366.

Knapp, P.H. (1969). The asthmatic and his environment. *Journal of Nervous and Mental Disease, 149,* 133–151.

Knapp, S., & Vandecreek, L. (1982). Tarasoff: Five years later. *Professional Psychology, 13,* 511–516.

Knaus, W., & Bokor, S. (1975). The effect of rational-emotive education lessons on anxiety and self-concept in sixth grade students. *Rational Living, 10,* 7–10.

Knight, B. (1983). An evaluation of a mobile geriatric team. In M.A. Smyer & M. Gatz (Eds.), *Mental health and aging: Programs and evaluations.* Beverly Hills, CA: Sage.

Knight, B. (1986). *Psychotherapy with older adults.* Beverly Hills, CA: Sage.

Knight, B.G., & Davison, G.C. (1992). Caregiver distress: Method variance, gender, and ethnicity. Research grant proposal to the National Institute of Mental Health.

Knight B. G., Kelly, M., & Gatz, M. (1992). Psychotherapy and the older adult. In D.K. Freedheim (Ed.), *History of psychotherapy: A century of change* (pp. 528–551). Washington, DC: American Psychological Association.

Knight, B.G., Lutzky, S.M., & Olshevski, J.L. (1992). A randomized comparison of stress reduction training to problem solving training for dementia caregivers: Processes and outcomes. Unpublished manuscript, University of Southern California.

Knight, B. (1989). *Outreach with the elderly: Community education, assessment, and therapy*. New York: New York University Press.

Knight, R.A., & Prentky, R.A. (1990). Classifying sexual offenders: The development and corroboration of taxonomic models. In W.L. Marshall, D.R. Laws, & H.E. Barabee (Eds.), *Handbook of sexual assault: Issues, theories, and treatment of the offender*. New York: Plenum.

Koegel, R.L., Schreibman, L., Britten, K.R., Burkey, J.C., & O'Neill, R.E. (1982). A comparison of parent training to direct child treatment. In R.L. Koegel, A. Rincover, & A.L. Egel (Eds.), *Educating and understanding autistic children*. San Diego, CA: College-Hill.

Koenig, K., & Masters, J. (1965). Experimental treatment of habitual smoking. *Behaviour Research and Therapy, 3*, 235–243.

Koenig, S., Gendelman, H., Orenstein, J., DeCanto, J.C., Pezeshkpour, G.H., Yougbluth, G., Janoffa, F., Aksamit, A., Main, M., & Fend, A. (1986). Detection of AIDS virus in macrophages in brain tissue from AIDS patients with encephalopathy. *Science, 233*, 1089–1093.

Koenigsberg, H.W., & Handley, R. (1986). Expressed emotion: From predictive index to clinical construct. *American Journal of Psychiatry, 143*, 1361–1373.

Kohn, M.L. (1968). Social class and schizophrenia: A critical review. In D. Rosenthal & S.S. Kety (Eds.), *The transmission of schizophrenia*. Elmsford, NY: Pergamon.

Kohut, H. (1966). Forms and transformations of narcissism. *Journal of the American Psychoanalytic Association, 14*, 243–272.

Kohut, H. (1971). *The analysis of the self.* New York: International Universities Press.

Kohut, H. (1977). *The restoration of the self.* New York: International Universities Press.

Kohut, H., & Wolf, E.S. (1978). The disorders of the self and their treatment: An outline. *International Journal of Psychoanalysis, 59*, 413–425.

Kolden, G.G. (1991). The generic model of psychotherapy: An empirical investigation of patterns of process and outcome relationships. *Psychotherapy Research, 1*, 62–73.

Kolvin I., McKeith, R.C., & Meadows, S.R. (1973). *Bladder control and enuresis*. Philadelphia: Lippincott.

Konig, P., & Godfrey, S. (1973). Prevalence of exercise-induced bronchial liability in families of children with asthma. *Archives of Diseases of Childhood, 48*, 518.

Korchin, S.J. (1976). *Modern clinical psychology*. New York: Basic Books.

Kornetsky, C. (1976). Hyporesponsivity of chronic schizophrenic patients to dextroamphetamine. *Archives of General Psychiatry, 33*, 1425–1428.

Koss, M.P. (1985). The hidden rape victim: Personality, attitudinal, and situational characteristics. *Psychology of Women Quarterly, 9*, 193–212.

Koss, M.P., & Butcher, J.N. (1986). Research on brief psychotherapy. In S.L. Garfield & A.E. Bergin (Eds.), *Handbook of psychotherapy and behavior change* (3rd ed.). New York: Wiley.

Koss, M.P., & Shiang, J. (in press). Research on brief psychotherapy. In A.E. Bergin, & S.L. Garfield (Eds.), *Handbook of psychotherapy and behavior change*. (4th ed). New York: Wiley.

Kosson, D.S. Smith, S.F., & Newman, J.P. (1990). Evaluating the construct validity of psychopathy in Black and white male inmates: Three preliminary studies. *Journal of Abnormal Psychology, 99*, 250–259.

Kosten, T.R., Mason, J.W., Giller, E.L., Ostroff, R., & Harkness, I. (1987). Sustained urinary norepinephrine and epinephrine elevation in posttraumatic stress disorder. *Psychoneuroendocrinology, 12*, 13–20.

Kosten, T.R., Morgan, C.M., Falcione, J., & Schottenfeld, R.S. (1992). Pharmacotherapy for cocaine-abusing methadone-maintained patients using amantadine or desipramine. *Archives of General Psychiatry, 49*, 894–898.

Kovacs, M., Feinberg, T.L., Crouse-Novack, M.A., Paulauskas, S.L., & Finkelstein, R. (1984). Depressive disorders in childhood: I. A longitudinal prospective study of characteristics and recovery. *Archives of General Psychiatry, 41*, 229–237.

Kovacs, M., Rush, AJ., Beck, A.T., & Hollon, S.D. (1981). Depressed outpatients treated with cognitive therapy or pharmacotherapy: A one-year follow-up. *Archives of General Psychiatry, 38*, 33–39.

Kowalik, D.L., & Gotlib, I.H. (1987). Depression and marital interaction: Concordance between intent and perception of communication. *Journal of Abnormal Psychology, 96*, 127–134.

Kowall, N.K., & Beal, M.F. (1988). Cortical somatostatin, neuropeptide Y, and NADPH diphorase neurons: Normal anatomy and alterations in Alzheimer's disease. *Annals of Neurology, 23*, 105–113.

Kozel, N.J., & Adams, E.H. (1986). Epidemiology of drug abuse: An overview. *Science, 234*, 970–974.

Kozel, N.J., Crider, R.A., & Adams, E.H. (1982). National surveillance of cocaine use and related health consequences. *Morbidity and Mortality Weekly Report 31, 20*, 265–273.

Kozlowski, L.T., Skinner, W., Kent, C., & Pope, M. (1989). Prospects for smoking treatment in individuals seeking treatment for alcohol and other drug problems. *Addictive Behaviors, 14*, 273–279.

Kozol, H., Boucher, R., & Garofalo, R. (1972). The diagnosis and treatment of dangerousness. *Crime and Delinquency, 18*, 37–92.

Kraepelin, E. (1981). *Clinical psychiatry*. (A.R. Diefendorf, Trans.), Delmar, NY: Scholars' Facsimiles and Reprints. (Original work published 1883).

Kramer, M. (1977). *Psychiatric services and the changing institutional scene 1950–1985*. Washington, DC: National Institute of Mental Health.

Krantz, S., & Hammen, C.L. (1979). Assessment of cognitive bias in depression. *Journal of Abnormal Psychology, 88*, 611–619.

Krech, D., Rosenzweig, M., & Bennett, E. (1966). Environmental impoverishment, social isolation, and changes in brain chemistry and anatomy. *Physiology and Behavior, 1*, 99–104.

Kringlen, E. (1970). Natural history of obsessional neurosis. *Seminars in Psychiatry, 2*, 403–419.

Kroll, P., Chamberlain, P., & Halpern, D. (1979). The diagnosis of Briquet's syndrome in a male population. *Journal of Nervous and Mental Disease*, 169, 171–174.

Krystal, J.H., Kosten, T.R., Southwick, S., Mason, J.W., Perry, B.D., & Giller, E.L. (1989). Neurobiological aspects of PTSD: Review of clinical and preclinical studies. *Behavior Therapy, 20*, 177–198.

Kucharski, L.T., White, R.M., & Schratz, M. (1979). Age bias, referral for psychological assistance and the private physician. *Journal of Gerontology, 34*, 423–428.

Kuhn, T.S. (1962). *The structure of scientific revolutions*. Chicago: University of Chicago Press.

Kundera, M. (1991). *Immortality*. New York: Grove Press.

Kunst-Wilson, W.R., & Zajonc, R.B. (1980). Affective discrimination of stimuli that cannot be recognized. *Science, 207,* 557–558.

Kuriansky, J.B., Deming, W.E., & Gurland, B.J. (1974). On trends in the diagnosis of schizophrenia. *American Journal of Psychiatry, 131,* 402–407.

Kutchinsky, B. (1970). *Studies on pornography and sex crimes in Denmark.* Copenhagen: New Social Science Monographs.

Lacey, J.I. (1967). Somatic response patterning and stress: Some revisions of activation theory. In M.H. Appley & R. Trumball (Eds.), *Psychological stress.* New York: McGraw-Hill.

Ladd, G.W. (1981). Effectiveness of a social learning method for enhancing children's social interaction and peer acceptance. *Child Development, 52,* 171–178.

La Greca, A.J., Akers, R.L., & Dwyer, J.W. (1988). Life events and alcohol behavior among older adults. *The Gerontologist, 28,* 552–558.

Lahey, B.B., Piacentini, J.C., McBurnett, K., Stone, P., Hartdagen, S., & Hynd, G. (1988). Psychopathology in the parents of children with conduct disorder and hyperactivity. *Journal of the American Academy of Child and Adolescent Psychiatry, 27,* 163–170.

Lambert, M.J., Bergin, A.E., & Collins, J.L. (1977). Therapist-induced deterioration in psychotherapy. In A.S. Gurman & A.M. Razin (Eds.), *Effective psychotherapy: A handbook of research.* Elmsford, New York: Pergamon.

Lambert, M.J., Shapiro, D.A., & Bergin, A.E. (1986). The effectiveness of psychotherapy. In S.L. Garfield & A.E. Bergin (Eds.), Handbook of psychotherapy and behavior change (3rd ed.). New York: Wiley.

Lando, H.A. (1977). Successful treatment of smokers with a broad-spectrum behavioral approach. *Journal of Consulting and Clinical Psychology, 45,* 361–366.

Lane, E.A., & Albee, G.W. (1965). Childhood intellectual differences between schizophrenic adults and their siblings. *American Journal of Orthopsychiatry, 35,* 747–753.

Lang, A.R., Goeckner, D.J., Adessor, V.J., & Marlatt, G.A. (1975). Effects of alcohol on aggression in male social drinkers. *Journal of Abnormal Psychology, 84,* 508–518.

Lang, A.R., & Marlatt, G.A. (1982). Problem drinking: A social learning perspective. In R.J. Gatchel, A. Baum, & J.E. Singer (Eds.), *Handbook of psychology and health.* Hillsdale, NJ: Erlbaum.

Lang, P.J. (1969). The mechanics of desensitization and the laboratory study of fear. In C.M. Franks (Ed.), *Behavior therapy: Appraisal and status.* New York: McGraw-Hill.

Lang, P.J., & Lazovik, A.D. (1963). Experimental desensitization of a phobia. *Journal of Abnormal and Social Psychology, 66,* 519–525.

Lang, P.J., & Melamed, B.G. (1969). Case report: Avoidance conditioning therapy of an infant with chronic ruminative vomiting. *Journal of Abnormal Psychology, 74,* 1–8.

Lang, R.A., Flor, H.P., & Frenzel, R.R. (1990). Sex hormone profiles in pedophilic and incestuous men. *Annals of Sex Research, 3,* 59–74.

Lange, A.J., & Jakubowski, P. (1976). *Responsible assertive behavior.* Champaign, IL: Research Press.

Langeluddeke, A. (1963). *Castration of sexual criminals.* Berlin: de Gruyter.

Langer, E.J. (1981). Old age: An artifact? In J. McGaugh & S. Kiesler (Eds.), *Aging: Biology and behavior.* New York: Academic Press.

Langer, E.J., & Abelson, R.P. (1974). A patient by any other name . . . : Clinician group difference in labelling bias. *Journal of Consulting and Clinical Psychology, 42,* 4–9.

Langer, E.J., & Rodin, J. (1976). The effects of choice and enhanced personal responsibility for the aged. *Journal of Personality and Social Psychology, 34,* 191–198.

Langevin, R., Paitich, D., & Russon, A.E. (1985). Are rapists sexually anomalous, aggressive, or both? In R. Langevin (Ed.), *Erotic preference, gender identity, and aggression in men: New research studies* (pp. 13–38). Hillsdale, NJ: Erlbaum.

Lanyon, R.I. (1986). Theory and treatment of child molestation. *Journal of Consulting and Clinical Psychology, 54,* 176–182.

LaRue, A., Dessonville, C., & Jarvik, L.F. (1985). Aging and mental disorders. In J.E. Birren & K.W. Schaie (Eds.), *Handbook of psychology of aging* (2nd ed.). New York: Van Nostrand-Reinhold.

Last, C.G., & Strauss, C.C. (1990). School refusal in anxiety-disordered children and adolescents. *Journal of the American Academy of Child & Adolescent Psychiatry, 29,* 31–35.

Lavelle, T.L., Metalsky, G.I., & Coyne, J.C. (1979). Learned helplessness, test anxiety, and acknowledgment of contingencies. *Journal of Abnormal Psychology, 88,* 381–387.

Lawler, B.A., Sunderland, T., Mellow, A.M., et al. (1989). Hyperresponsivity to the serotonin agonist m-chlorophenylpiperazine in Alzheimer's disease. *Archives of General Psychiatry, 46,* 542–548.

Laws, D.R., & Hohnen, M.L. (1978). Sexual response faking by pedophiles. *Criminal Justice and Behavior, 5,* 343–356.

Lawton, M.P. (1972). Schizophrenia forty-five years later. *Journal of Genetic Psychology, 121,* 133–143.

Lawton, M.P. (1979). Clinical geropsychology: Problems and prospects. In *Master lecture series on the psychology of aging.* Washington, DC: American Psychological Association.

Layne, C. (1986). Painful truths about depressives' cognitions. *Journal of Clinical Psychology, 39,* 848–853.

Lazar, I. (1979). Social services in Head Start. In E. Zigler & J. Valentine (Eds.), *Project Head Start.* New York: Free Press.

Lazarus, A.A. (1961). Group therapy of phobic disorders by systematic desensitization. *Journal of Abnormal and Social Psychology, 63,* 504–510.

Lazarus, A.A. (1965). Behavior therapy, incomplete treatment, and symptom substitution. *Journal of Nervous and Mental Disease, 140,* 80–86.

Lazarus, A.A. (1968a). Behavior therapy in groups. In G.M. Gazda (Ed.), *Basic approaches to group psychotherapy and counseling.* Springfield, IL: Charles C. Thomas.

Lazarus, A.A. (1968b). Learning theory and the treatment of depression. *Behavior Research and Therapy, 6,* 83–89.

Lazarus, A.A. (1971). *Behavior therapy and beyond.* New York: McGraw-Hill.

Lazarus, A.A. (1973). Multimodal behavior therapy: Treating the basic ID. *Journal of Nervous and Mental Disease, 156,* 404–411.

Lazarus, A.A. (1989). *The practice of multimodal therapy.* Baltimore: Johns Hopkins University Press.

Lazarus, A.A., & Davison, G.C. (1971). Clinical innovation in research and practice. In A.E. Bergin & S.L. Garfield (Eds.), *Handbook of psychotherapy and behavior change: An empirical analysis.* New York: Wiley.

Lazarus, A.A., & Messer, S.B. (1991). Does chaos prevail? An exchange on technical eclecticism and assimilative integration. *Journal of Psychotherapy Integration 1,* 143–158.

Lazarus, A.A., Davison, G.C., & Polefka, D. (1965). Classical and operant factors in the treatment of school phobia. *Journal of Abnormal Psychology, 70,* 225–229.

Lazarus, R.S. (1966). *Psychological stress and the coping process.* New York: McGraw-Hill.

Lazarus, R.S. (1984). Puzzles in the study of daily hassles. *Journal of Behavioral Medicine, 7,* 375–384.

Lazarus, R.S., & Cohen, J.P. (1977). Environmental stress. In I. Altman & J.F. Wohlwill (Eds.), *Human behavior and the environment: Current theory and research.* New York: Plenum.

Lazarus, R.S., & Folkman, S. (1984). *Stress, appraisal, and coping.* New York: Springer.

Lazovik, A.D., & Lang, P.J. (1960). A laboratory demonstration of systematic desensitization psychotherapy. *Journal of Psychological Studies, 11,* 238–247.

Leach, S., & Roy, S.S. (1986). Adverse drug reactions: An investigation on an acute geriatric ward. *Age and Ageing, 15* 241–246.

Lee, D., DeQuattro, V., Cox, T., Pyter, L., Foti, A., Allen, J., Barndt, R., Azen, S., & Davison, G.C. (1987). Neurohormonal mechanisms and left ventricular hypertrophy: Effects of hygienic therapy. *Journal of Human Hypertension, 1,* 147–151.

Lee, T., & Seeman, P. (1977). Dopamine receptors in normal and schizophrenic human brains. *Proceedings of the Society of Neurosciences, 3,* 443.

Lee, V.E., Brooks-Gunn, J., & Schnur, E. (1988). Does Head Start work? A 1-year follow-up comparison of disadvantaged children attending Head Start, no preschool, and other preschool programs. *Developmental Psychology, 24,* 210–222.

Leeper, P. (1988). Having a place to live is vital to good health. *News Report, 38,* 5–8.

Lehrer, P.M., & Woolfolk, R.L. (1982). Self-report assessment of anxiety: Somatic, cognitive, and behavioral modalities. *Behavioral Assessment, 4,* 167–177.

Lehrer, P.M., & Woolfolk, R.L. (1993) *Principles and practice of stress management.* Second edition. New York: Guilford.

Leiblum, S.R., & Rosen, R.C. (Eds.). (1988). *Sexual desire disorders.* New York: Guilford.

Lemieux, G., Davignon, A., & Genest, J. (1956). Depressive states during rauwolfia therapy for arterial hypertension. *Canadian Medical Association Journal, 74,* 522–526.

Lenane, M.C., et al. (1990). Psychiatric disorders in first degree relatives of children and adolescents with obsessive compulsive disorder. *Journal of the American Academy of Child and Adolescent Psychiatry, 29,* 407–412.

Leon, G.R., Gillum, B., Gillum, R., & Gouze, M. (1979). Personality stability and change over a 30-year period—Middle age to old age. *Journal of Consulting and Clinical Psychology, 47,* 517–524.

Lerer, B., Bleich, A., Kotler, M., Garb, R., Hertzberg, M., & Levin, B. (1987). Posttraumatic stress disorder in Israeli combat veterans. *Archives of General Psychiatry, 44,* 976–981.

Lesage, A., & Lamontagne, Y. (1985). Paradoxical intention and exposure *in vivo* in the treatment of psychogenic nausea: Report of two cases. *Behavioral Psychotherapy, 13,* 69–75.

Lesch, K.P. et al. (1991). 5-Hydroxytryptamine1A receptor responsivity in obsessive-compulsive disorder: Comparison of patients and controls. *Archives of General Psychiatry, 48,* 540–538.

Leuchter, A.F. (1985). Assessment and treatment of the late-onset psychoses. *Hospital and Community Psychiatry, 36,* 815–818.

Levenson, M. (1972). *Cognitive and perceptual factors in suicidal individuals.* Unpublished doctoral dissertation, University of Kansas, Lawrence, KS.

Levin, M., & Kaplan, T. (1992, September 6). Cigarettes for sale, 20 cents apiece. *Los Angeles Times,* pp. A1, A28, A29.

Levine, E.S., & Padilla, A.M. (1980). *Crossing cultures in therapy: Counseling for the Hispanic.* Monterey, CA: Brooks/Cole.

Levine, S.B., & Yost, M.A. (1976). Frequency of sexual dysfunction in a general gynecological clinic: An epidemiological approach. *Archives of Sexual Behavior, 5,* 229–238.

Levitsky, A., & Perls, F.S. (1970). The rules and games of Gestalt therapy. In J. Fagan & I.L. Shepherd (Eds.), *Gestalt therapy now: Theory, techniques, applications.* Palo Alto, CA: Science and Behavior Books.

Levy, S.M., Herberman, R.B., Whiteside, T., Sanzo, K., Lee, J., & Kirkwood, J. (1990). Perceived social support and tumor estrogen/progesterone receptor status as predictors of natural killer cell activity in breast cancer patients. *Psychosomatic Medicine, 52,* 73–85.

Lewinsohn, P.M. (1974). A behavioral approach to depression. In R.J. Friedman and M.M. Katz (Eds.), *The psychology of depression: Contemporary theory and research.* Washington, DC: Winston-Wiley.

Lewinsohn, P.M., & Libet, J.M. (1972). Pleasant events, activity schedules and depression. *Journal of Abnormal Psychology, 79,* 291–295.

Lewinsohn, P.M., Weinstein, M., & Alper, T. (1970). A behavioral approach to the group treatment of depressed persons: A methodological contribution. *Journal of Clinical Psychology, 26,* 525–532.

Lewinsohn, P.M., Mischef, W., Chapion, W., & Barton, R. (1980). Social competence and depression: The role of illusory self-perceptions. *Journal of Abnormal Psychology, 89,* 203–212.

Lewinsohn, P.M., Steimetz, J.L., Larsen, D.W., & Franklin, J. (1981). Depression related cognitions: Antecedent or consequences? *Journal of Abnormal Psychology, 90,* 213–219.

Ley, R. (1987). Panic disorder: A hyperventilation interpretation. In L. Michelson & L.M. Asher (Eds.), *Anxiety and stress disorders.* New York: Guilford.

Liberman, R.P. (1972). Reinforcement of social interaction in a group of chronic mental patients. In R. Rubin et al., *Advances in behavior therapy.* New York: Academic Press.

Liberman, R.P., DeRisi, W.J., & Mueser, K.T. (1989). *Social skills training for psychiatric patients.* Elmsford, NY: Pergamon Press.

Liberman, R.P., King, L.W., DeRisi, W.J., & McCann, M. (1975). *Personal effectiveness.* Champaign, IL: Research Press.

Liberman, R.P., Wheeler, E.G., & Kuehnel, J.M. (1983). Failures in behavioral marital therapy. In E.B. Foa & P.M.G. Emmelkamp (Eds.), *Failures in behavior therapy.* New York: Wiley.

Lieberman, J.A., Yunis, J., Egea, E., et al. (1990). HLA-B38, DR4, DQw3, and clozapine-induced agranulocytosis in Jewish patients with schizophrenia. *Archives of General Psychiatry, 47,* 945–948.

Lieberman, M.A. (1987). Effects of large group awareness training on participants' psychiatric status. *American Journal of Psychiatry, 144,* 460–464.

Lieberman, M.A., Yalom, J.D., & Miles, M.B. (1973). *Encounter groups: First facts.* New York: Basic Books.

Lieberman, M.A. & Videka-Sherman, L. (1986). The impact of self-help groups on the mental health of widows and widowers. *American Journal of Orthopsychiatry, 56,* 435–449.

Liebert, R.M., Neale, J.M., & Davidson, E.S. (1973). *The early window.* Elmsford, NY: Pergamon.

Liebson, I. (1967). Conversion reaction: A teaming theory approach. *Behaviour Research and Therapy, 7,* 217–218.

Lief, H.I. (1988). Foreword. In S.R. Leiblum & R.C. Rosen (Eds.), *Sexual desire disorders.* New York: Guilford.

Lifton, R.J. (1976). Advocacy and corruption in the healing profession. In N.L. Goldman & D.R. Segal (Eds.), *The social psychology of military service.* Beverly Hills, CA: Sage.

Light, K.C., Dolan, C.A., Davis, M.R., & Sherwood, A. (1992). Cardiovascular responses to an active coping challenge as predictors of blood pressure patterns 10 to 15 years later. *Psychosomatic Medicine, 54,* 217–230.

Lindemann, E. (1944). Symptomatology and management of acute grief. *American Journal of Psychiatry, 101,* 141–148.

Lindsay, W.R. (1986). Cognitive changes after social skills training with young mildly mentally handicapped adults. *Journal of Mental Deficiency Research, 30,* 81–88.

Linehan, M.M. (1985). The reasons for living inventory. In P. Keller & L. Ritt (Eds.), *Innovations in clinical practice: A sourcebook* (pp. 321–330). Sarasota, FL: Professional Resource Exchange.

Linehan, M.M. (1987). Dialectical behavior therapy for borderline personality disorder. *Bulletin of the Menninger Clinic, 51,* 261–276.

Linehan, M.M. (in press-b). *Behavioral skills training manual for treating borderline personality disorder.* New York: Guilford Press.

Linehan, M.M. (in press-a). *Cognitive behavioral treatment of borderline personality disorder: The dialectics of effective treatment.* New York: Guilford.

Linehan, M.M., Armstrong, H.E., Suarez, A., Allmon, D., & Heard, H.L. (1991). Cognitive-behavioral treatment of chronically parasuicidal borderline patients. *Archives of General Psychiatry, 48,* 1060–1064.

Linehan, M.M., Camper, P., Chiles, J.A., Strosahl, K., & Shearin, E.N. (1987). Interpersonal problem-solving and parasuicide. *Cognitive Therapy and Research, 11,* 1–12.

Linehan, M.M., Goodstein, J.L., Nielsen, S.L., & Chiles, J.A. (1983). Reasons for staying alive when you are thinking of killing yourself. *Journal of Consulting and Clinical Psychology, 51,* 276–286.

Linehan, M.M., Heard, H.L., & Armstrong, H.E. *Naturalistic follow-up of a behavioral treatment for chronically parasuicidal borderline patients.* Unpublished manuscript, University of Washington, 1992.

Linehan, M.M., & Shearin, E.N. (1988). Lethal stress: A social-behavioral model of suicidal behavior. In S. Fisher & J. Reason (Eds.), *Handbook of life stress, cognition, and health.* New York: Wiley.

Links, P.S., Steiner, M., Boiago, I., & Irwin, D. (1990). Lithium therapy for borderline patients: Preliminary findings. *Journal of Personality Disorders,* 4, 173–181.

Linn, M.W., Linn, B.S., & Jensen, J. (1984). Stressful events, dysphoric mood, and immune responsiveness. *Psychological Reports, 54,* 219–222.

Linton, H.B., & Langs, R.J. (1964). Empirical dimensions of LSD-25 reactions. *Archives of General Psychiatry, 10,* 469–485.

Linz, D.G., Donnerstein, E., & Penrod, S. (1988). Effects of long-term exposure to violent and sexually degrading depictions of women. *Journal of Personality and Social Psychology, 55,* 758–768.

Lion, J.R. (1978). Outpatient treatment of psychopaths. In W.H. Reid (Ed.), *The psychopath: A comprehensive study of antisocial disorders and behaviors.* New York: Brunner/Mazel.

Lipman, A. (1984). Homosexuals. In E.B. Palmore (Ed.), *Handbook on the aged in the United States.* Westport, CT: Greenwood Press.

Lipowski, Z.J. (1980). *Delirium: Acute brain failure in man.* Springfield, IL: Charles C. Thomas.

Lipowski, Z.J. (1983). Transient cognitive disorders (delirium and acute confusional states) in the elderly. *American Journal of Psychiatry, 140,* 1426–1436.

Liskow, B. (1982). Substance induced and substance use disorders: Barbiturates and similarly acting sedative hypnotics. In J.H. Greist, J.W. Jefferson, & R.L. Spitzer (Eds.), *Treatment of mental disorders.* New York: Oxford University Press.

Liston, E.H. (1982). Delirium in the aged. In L.E. Jarvik & G.W. Small (Eds.), *Psychiatric clinics of North America.* Philadelphia: Saunders.

Litwack, T.R. (1985). The prediction of violence. *The Clinical Psychologist, 38,* 87–90.

Livesley, W.J., Schroeder, M.L., & Jackson, D.N. (1990). Dependent personality and attachment problems. *Journal of Personality Disorders,* 4, 131–140.

Lloyd, L.L., & Karlan, G.R. (1984). Nonspeech communication symbols and systems: Where have we been and where are we going? *Journal of Mental Deficiency Research, 28,* 3–20.

Lobitz, W.C., & Post, R.D. (1979). Parameters of self-reinforcement and depression. *Journal of Abnormal Psychology, 88,* 33–41.

London, P. (1964). *The modes and morals of psychotherapy.* New York: Holt, Rinehart & Winston.

London, P. (1986). *The modes and morals of psychotherapy* (2nd ed.). New York: Hemisphere.

Loney, J., Langhorne, J.E., Jr., & Paternite, C.E. (1978). An empirical basis for subgrouping the hyperkinetic-minimal brain dysfunction syndrome. *Journal of Abnormal Psychology, 87,* 431–441.

Lopez, S.R. (1988). The empirical basis of ethnocultural and linguistic bias in mental health evaluations of Hispanics. *American Psychologist, 43,* 1095–1097.

Lopez, S.R. (1989). Patient variable biases in clinical judgment: Conceptual overview and methodological considerations. *Psychological Bulletin, 106,* 184–203.

Lopez, S.R., & Hernandez, P. (1986). How culture is considered in evaluations of psychopathology. *Journal of Nervous and Mental Disease, 176,* 598–606.

Lopez, S.R., Lopez, A.A., & Fong, K.T. (1991). Mexican Americans' initial preferences for counselors: The role of ethnic factors. *Journal of Counseling Psychology, 38,* 487–496.

Lopez, S., & Nunez, J.A. (1987). Cultural factors considered in selected diagnostic criteria and interview schedules. *Journal of Abnormal Psychology, 96,* 270–272.

Lopez, S.R., & Romero, A. (1988). Assessing the intellectual functioning of Spanish-speaking adults: Comparison of the EIWA and the WAIS. *Professional Psychology: Research and Practice, 19,* 263–270.

Lopez, S.R., & Taussig, I.M. (1991). Cognitive-intellectual functioning of Spanish-speaking impaired and nonimpaired elderly: Implications for culturally sensitive assessment. *Psychological Assessment: A Journal of Consulting and Clinical Psychology,* 3, 448–454.

LoPiccolo, J. (1977). Direct treatment of sexual dysfunction in the couple. In J. Money & H. Musaph (Eds.), *Handbook of sexology,* New York: Elsevier/North-Holland.

LoPiccolo, J. (1980). Low sexual desire. In S. Leiblum, & L. Pervin (Eds.), *Principles and practice of sex therapy.* New York: Guilford.

LoPiccolo, J. (1991). Counseling and therapy for sexual problems in the elderly. *Clinics in Geriatric Medicine, 7,* 161–179.

LoPiccolo, J. (1992a). Post-modern sex therapy for erectile failure. In R.C. Rosen & S.R. Leiblum (Eds.), *Erectile failure: Assessment and treatment.* New York: Guilford.

LoPiccolo, J. (1992b). Psychological evaluation of erectile failure. In R. Kirby, C. Carson, & G. Webster (Eds.), *Diagnosis and management of male erectile failure dysfunction.* Oxford: Butterworth-Heinemann.

LoPiccolo, J., & Friedman, J.M. (1985). Sex therapy: An integrated model. In S.J. Lynn & J.P. Garskee (Eds.), *Contemporary psychotherapies: Models and methods.* New York: Merrill.

LoPiccolo, J., & Friedman, J. (1988). Broad-spectrum treatment of low sexual desire: Integration of cognitive, behavioral, and systemic therapy. In S. Leiblum & R.C. Rosen (Eds.), *Sexual desire disorders.* New York: Guilford.

LoPiccolo, J., Heiman, J., Hogan, D., & Roberts, C. (1985). Effectiveness of single therapists vs. co-therapy teams in sex therapy. *Journal of Consulting and Clinical Psychology, 53,* 287–294.

LoPiccolo, J., & Hogan, D.R. (1979). Multidimensional treatment of sexual dysfunction. In O.F. Pomerleau & J.P. Brady (Eds.), *Behavioral medicine: Theory and practice.* Baltimore: Williams & Wilkins.

LoPiccolo, J., & Lobitz, W.C. (1972). The role of masturbation in the treatment of orgasmic dysfunction. *Archives of Sexual Behavior, 2,* 163–171.

LoPiccolo, J., & LoPiccolo, L. (1978) (Eds.), *Handbook of sex therapy.* New York: Plenum.

LoPiccolo, J., & Stock, W.E. (1986). Treatment of sexual dysfunction. *Journal of Consulting and Clinical Psychology, 54,* 158–167.

LoPiccolo, J., & Stock, W.E. (1987). Sexual function, dysfunction, and counseling in gynecological practice. In Z. Rosenwaks, F. Benjamin, & M.L. Stone (Eds.), *Gynecology*. New York: Macmillan.

Loranger, A., Oldham, J., Russakoff, L.M., & Susman, V. (1987). Structured interviews and borderline personality disorder. *Archives of General Psychiatry, 41*, 565–568.

Loranger, A.W., Oldham, J.M., & Tulis, E.H. (1983). Familial transmission of DSM-III borderline personality disorder. *Archives of General Psychiatry, 40*, 795–799.

Lostof, E.J. (1953). Intelligence, verbal fluency, and the Rorschach test. *Journal of Consulting Psychology, 17*, 21–24.

Lothstein, L.M. (1980). The postsurgical transsexual: Empirical and theoretical considerations. *Archives of Sexual Behavior, 9*, 547–564.

Lothstein, L.M. (1983). *Female-to-male transsexualism: Historical, clinical, and theoretical issues.* Boston: Routledge and Kegan Paul.

Lotter, V. (1966). Epidemiology of autistic conditions in young children: I. Prevalence. *Social Psychiatry, 1*, 124–137.

Lotter, V. (1974). Factors related to outcome in autistic children. *Journal of Autism and Childhood Schizophrenia, 4*, 263–277.

Lotter, V. (1978). Follow-up studies. In M. Rutter & E. Schopler (Eds.), *Autism: A reappraisal of concepts and treatment*. New York: Plenum.

Lovaas, O.I. (1987). Behavioral treatment and normal educational and intellectual functioning in young autistic children. *Journal of Consulting and Clinical Psychology, 55*, 3–9.

Lovaas, O.I., Berberich, J.P., Perloff, B.F., & Schaeffer, B. (1966). Acquisition of imitative speech by schizophrenic children. *Science, 151*, 705–707.

Lovaas, O.I., Freitag, G., Gold, V.J., & Kassoria, I.C. (1965). Experimental studies in childhood schizophrenia: Analysis of self-destructive behavior. *Journal of Experimental Child Psychology, 2*, 67–84.

Lovaas, O.I., Koegel, R., Simmons, J.Q., & Long, J.S. (1973). Some generalization and follow-up measures on autistic children in behavior therapy. *Journal of Applied Behavior Analysis, 6*, 131–166.

Lovaas, O.I., Litrownik, A., & Mann, R. (1971). Response latencies to auditory stimuli in autistic children engaged in self-stimulatory behavior. *Behaviour Research and Therapy, 9*, 39–49.

Lovaas, O.I., Newsom, C., & Hickman, C. (1987). Self-stimulatory behavior and perceptual reinforcement. *Journal of Applied Behavior Analysis, 20*, 45–68.

Lovaas, O.I., Schreibman, L., Koegel, R., & Rehm, R. (1971). Selective responding by autistic children to multiple sensory input. *Journal of Abnormal Psychology, 77*, 221–222.

Lowen, A. (1958). *The physical dynamics of character structure.* New York: Grune & Stratton.

Lowenthal, M.F., Berkman, P., & Associates (1967). *Aging and mental disorder in San Francisco.* San Francisco: Jossey-Bass.

Lubin, B. (1983). Group therapy. In I.B. Weiner (Ed.), *Clinical methods in psychology* (2nd ed.). New York: Wiley.

Luborsky, L., Barber, J.P., & Crits-Christoph, P. (1990). Theory-based research for understanding the process of dynamic psychotherapy. *Journal of Consulting and Clinical Psychology, 58*, 281–287.

Luborsky, L., Crits-Christoph, P., Melon, J., & Auerbach, A. (1988). *Who will benefit from psychotherapy: Predicting therapeutic outcomes.* New York: Basic Books.

Luborsky, L., & Spence, D.P. (1978). Quantitative research on psychoanalytic therapy. In S.L. Garfield & A.E. Bergin (Eds.), *Handbook of psychotherapy and behavior change: An empirical analysis* (2nd ed.). New York: Wiley.

Luepnitz, R.R., Randolph, D.L., & Gutsch, K.U. (1982). Race and socioeconomic status as confounding variables in the accurate diagnosis of alcoholism. *Journal of Clinical Psychology, 38*, 665–669.

Luthe, W., & Schultz, J.H. (1969). *Autogenic therapy: Vol. 1. Autogenic methods.* New York: Grune & Stratton.

Lykken, D.T. (1957). A study of anxiety in the sociopathic personality. *Journal of Abnormal and Social Psychology, 55*, 6–10.

Lyon, G.R., & Moats, L.C. (1988). Critical issues in the instruction of the learning disabled. *Journal of Consulting and Clinical Psychology, 56*, 830–835.

Lystad, M.M. (1957). Social mobility among selected groups of schizophrenics. *American Sociological Review, 22*, 288–292.

Maccoby, E.E., & Jacklin, C.N. (1974). *The psychology of sex differences.* Stanford, CA: Stanford University Press.

Maccoby, N., & Alexander, J. (1980). Use of media in lifestyle programs. In P.O. Davidson & S.M. Davidson (Eds.), *Behavioral medicine: Changing health lifestyles.* New York: Brunner/Mazel.

Maccoby, N., & Altman, D.G. (1988). Disease prevention in communities: The Stanford Heart Disease Prevention Program. In R.H. Price, E.L. Cowen, R.P. Lorion, & J. Ramos-McKay (Eds.), *14 ounces of prevention: A casebook for practitioners* (pp. 165–174). Washington, DC: American Psychological Association.

Maccoby, N., Farquhar, J.W., Wood, P.D., & Alexander, J. (1977). Reducing the risk of cardiovascular disease: Effects of a community-based campaign on knowledge and behavior. *Journal of Community Health, 3*, 100–114.

MacDonald, D.I. (1987, March). Testimony before the U.S. Senate of Representatives Committee on Appropriations, Subcommittee on the Departments of Labor, Health and Human Services, and Education, 100th Congress, 1st Session. Washington, DC: U.S. Government Printing Office. As cited in Roybal (1988).

Mackay, A.V.P., Iversen, L.L., Rossor, M., Spokes, E., Arregio, A., Crease, I., & Snyder, S.H. (1982). Increased brain dopamine and dopamine receptors in schizophrenia. *Archives of General Psychiatry, 39*, 991–997.

Macleod, C., & Hemsley, D.R. (1985). Visual feedback of vocal intensity in the treatment of hysterical aphonia. *Journal of Behaviour Therapy and Experimental Psychiatry, 4*, 347–353.

MacLeod, C., Mathews, A., & Tata, P. (1986). Attentional bias in emotional disorders. *Journal of Abnormal Psychology, 95*, 15–20.

Madonna, P.G., Van Scoyk, S., & Jones, D.B. (1991). Family interactions within incest and nonincest families. *American Journal of Psychiatry, 148*, 46–49.

Magenis, R.E., Overton, K.M., Chamberlin, J., Brady, T., & Lovrien, E. (1977). Paternal origin of the extra chromosome in Down's syndrome. *Human Genetics, 37*, 7–16.

Magraf, J., Ehlers, A., & Roth, W.T. (1986). Sodium lactate infusions and panic attacks: A review and critique. *Psychosomatic Medicine, 48*, 23–51.

Maher, B.A. (1966). *Principles of psychopathology: An experimental approach.* New York: McGraw-Hill.

Maher, B.A. (1974). *Journal of Consulting and Clinical Psychology, 42*, 1–3 [Editorial].

Mahoney, L.J. (1977). Early diagnosis of breast cancer: The breast self-examination problem. *Progress in Clinical and Biological Research, 12*, 203–206.

Mahoney, M.J. (1972). Research issues in self-management. *Behavior Therapy, 3*, 45–63.

Mahoney, M.J. (1974). *Cognition and behavior modification.* Cambridge, MA: Ballinger.

Mahoney, M.J. (1982). Psychotherapy and human change processes. In *Psychotherapy research and behavior change* (Vol. 1). Washington, DC: American Psychological Association.

Mahoney, M.J. (1991). *Human change processes: Notes on the facilitation of human development.* New York: Basic Books.

Mahoney, M.J. (1993). Theoretical developments in the cognitive psychotherapies. *Journal of Consulting and Clinical Psychology, 7*, 138–157.

Main, T.F. (1958). Perception and ego-function. *British Journal of Medical Psychology, 31*, 1–7.

Malamuth, N.M. (1981). Rape proclivity among males. *Journal of Social Issues, 37*, 138–157.

Malamuth, N.M., & Check, J.V.P. (1981). The effects of mass media exposure on acceptance of violence against women: A field experiment. *Journal of Research in Personality, 15*, 436–446.

Malamuth, N.M., & Check, J.V.P. (1983). Sexual arousal to rape depictions: Individual differences. *Journal of Abnormal Psychology, 92*, 55–67.

Malamuth, N.M., Feshbach, S., & Jaffe, Y. (1977). Sexual arousal and aggression: Recent experiments and theoretical issues. *Journal of Social Issues, 33*, 110–133.

Malamuth, N.M., Haber, S., & Feshbach, S. (1980). Testing hypotheses regarding rape: Exposure to sexual violence, sex differences, and the "normality" of rapists. *Journal of Research in Personality, 14*, 121–137.

Malgady, R.G., Rogler, L.H., & Constantino, G. (1987). Ethnocultural and linguistic bias in mental health evaluation of Hispanics. *American Psychologist, 42*, 228–234.

Malin, H., Coakley, J., Kaelber, C., Munch, N., & Houand, W. (1982). An epidemiologic perspective on alcohol abuse in the United States. In *Alcohol consumption and related problems*. National Institute of Alcohol Abuse and Alcoholism. Washington, DC: U.S. Government Printing Office.

Mandler, G. (1966). Anxiety. In D.L. Sills (Ed.), *International encyclopedia of the social sciences*. New York: Macmillan.

Mandler, G. (1972). Helplessness: Theory and research in anxiety. In C.D. Spielberger (Ed.), *Anxiety: Current trends in theory and research*. New York: Academic Press.

Manji, H.K., Hsiao, J.K., Risby, E.D., et al. (1991). The mechanisms of action of lithium: I. Effects on serotonergic and noradrenergic systems in normal subjects. *Archives of General Psychiatry, 48*, 505–512.

Mann, V.A., & Brady, S. (1988). Reading disability: The role of language deficiencies. *Journal of Consulting and Clinical Psychology, 56*, 811–816.

Mannello, T.A., & Seaman, F.J. (1979). *Prevalence, costs, and handling of drinking problems on seven railroads*. Washington, DC: University Research Corporation.

Manos, N., Vasilopoulou, E., & Sotiriou, M. (1987). DSM-III diagnoses of borderline disorder and depression. *Journal of Personality Disorders, 1*, 263–268.

Manson, S.M., Walker, R.D. & Kivlahan, D.R. (1987). Psychiatric assessment and treatment of American Indians and Alaskan natives. *Hospital and Community Psychiatry, 38*, 165–173.

Manton, K.G., Blazer, D.G., & Woodbury, M.A. (1987). Suicide in middle age and later life: Sex and race specific life table and cohort analyses. *Journal of Gerontology, 42*, 219–227.

Manuck, S.B., et al. (1989). Behaviorally elicited heart rate reactivity and atherosclerosis in female cynomolgus monkeys (*Macaca fascicularis*). *Psychosomatic Medicine, 51*, 306–318.

Manuck, S.B., Kaplan, J.R., & Clarkson, T.B. (1983). Behaviorally induced heart rate reactivity and atherosclerosis in cynomolgus monkeys. *Psychosomatic Medicine, 49*, 95–108.

Manuck, S.B., Kasprowicz, A.L., & Muldoon, M.F. (1990). Behaviorally-evoked cardiovascular reactivity and hypertension: Conceptual issues and potential associations. *Annals of Behavioral Medicine, 12*, 17–29.

Manuck, S.B., & Krantz, D.S. (1986). Psychophysiologic reactivity in coronary heart disease and essential hypertension. In K.A. Matthews, S.M. Weiss, T. Detre, T.M. Dembroski, B.F. Faulkner, S.B. Manuck, & R.B. Williams (Eds.), *Handbook of stress, reactivity, and cardiovascular disease*. New York: Wiley.

Marcus, J., Hans, S.L., Nagier, S., Auerbach, J.G., Mirsky, A.F., & Aubrey, A. (1987). Review of the NIMH Israeli Kibbutz-City and the Jerusalem infant development study. *Schizophrenia Bulletin, 13*, 425–438.

Margolin, G. (1978). The relationship among marital assessment procedures: A correlational study. *Journal of Consulting and Clinical Psychology, 46*, 1556–1558.

Margolin, G. (1981). Behavior exchange in happy and unhappy marriages: A family cycle perspective. *Behavior Therapy, 12*, 329–343.

Margolin, G. (1982). Ethical and legal considerations in marital and family therapy. *American Psychologist, 37*, 788–801.

Margolin, G., & Fernandez, V. (1985). Marital dysfunction. In M. Hersen & A.S. Bellack (Eds.), *Handbook of clinical behavior therapy with adults*. New York: Plenum.

Margolin, G., Michelli, J., & Jacobson, N.S. (1988). Assessment of marital dysfunction. In M. Hersen & A.S. Bellack (Eds.), *Behavioral assessment: A practical handbook* (3rd ed.). New York: Pergamon.

Margolin, G., & Wampold, B.F. (1981). Sequential analysis of conflict and accord in distressed and non-distressed marital partners. *Journal of Consulting and Clinical Psychology, 49*, 554–567.

Margolin, G., & Weiss, R.L. (1978). Comparative evaluation of therapeutic components associated with behavioral marital treatment. *Journal of Consulting and Clinical Psychology, 46*, 1476–1486.

Margolin, L. (1990). Gender and the stolen kiss: Social support of male and female to violate a partner's sexual consent in a noncoercive situation. *Archives of Sexual Behavior, 19*, 281–291.

Marijuana research findings. (1980). Washington, DC: U.S. Government Printing Office.

Marin, G. (1989). Prevention among Hispanics: Needs, risk behaviors, and cultural values. *Public Health Reports, 104*, 411–415.

Markman, H.J., Floyd, F.J., Stanley, S.M., & Storaasli, R.D. (1989). Prevention of marital distress: A longitudinal investigation. *Journal of Consulting and Clinical Psychology, 56*, 210–217.

Marks, I.M. (1969). *Fears and phobias*. New York: Academic Press.

Marks, I.M. (1981a). *Care and cure of neuroses: Theory and practice of behavioral psychotherapy*. New York: Wiley.

Marks, I.M. (1981b). Review of behavioral psychotherapy: 1. Obsessive-compulsive disorders. *American Journal of Psychiatry, 138*, 584–592.

Marks, I.M. (1983a). Are there anticompulsive or antiphobic drugs? Review of the evidence. *British Journal of Psychiatry, 143*, 338–347.

Marks, I.M. (1983b) Behavioral psychotherapy for anxiety disorders. *Psychiatric Clinibs of North America, 8*, 25–34.

Marks, I.M., & Gelder, M.G. (1967). Transvestism and fetishism: Clinical and psychological changes during faradic aversion. *British Journal of Psychiatry, 113*, 711–729.

Marks, I.M., Gelder, M.G., & Bancroft, J. (1970). Sexual deviants two years after electrical aversion. *British Journal of Psychiatry, 117*, 73–85.

Marlatt, G.A. (1983). The controlled drinking controversy: A commentary. *American Psychologist, 38*, 1097–1110.

Marlatt, G.A. (1985). Relapse prevention: Theoretical rationale and overview of the model. In G.A. Marlatt & J. Gordon (Eds.), *Relapse prevention: Maintenance strategies in addictive behavior change*. New York: Guilford.

Marlatt, G.A., Demming, B., & Reid, J.B. (1973). Loss of control drinking in alcoholics: An experimental analogue. *Journal of Abnormal Psychology, 81*, 233–241.

Marlatt, G.A., & Gordon, J.R. (Eds.). (1985). *Relapse prevention.* New York: Guilford.

Marmor, J. (1962). Psychoanalytic therapy as an educational process: Common denominators in the therapeutic approaches of different psychoanalytic schools. In J.H. Masserman (Ed.), *Science and psychoanalysis: Vol. 5. Psychoanalytic education.* New York: Grune & Stratton.

Marmor, J. (1971). Dynamic psychotherapy and behavior therapy: Are they irreconcilable? *Archives of General Psychiatry, 24,* 22–28.

Marshall, W.L., Barabee, H.E., & Christophe, D. (1986). Sexual offenders against female children: Sexual preferences for age of victims and type of behavior. *Canadian Journal of Behavioural Science, 18,* 424–439.

Marshall, W.L., Jones, R., Ward, T., Johnston, P., & Barabee, H.E. (1991). Treatment outcomes with sex offenders. *Clinical Psychology Review, 11,* 465–485.

Martin, B. (1961). The assessment of anxiety by physiological behavioral measures. *Psychological Bulletin, 58,* 234–255.

Martin, D., & Lyon, P. (1972). *Lesbian woman.* New York: Bantam.

Martin, P.A., & Bird, H.W. (1953). An approach to the psychotherapy of marriage partners—The stereoscopic technique. *Psychiatry, 16,* 123–127.

Martin, R. (1975). *Legal challenges to behavior modification: Trends in schools, corrections, and mental health.* Champaign, IL.: Research Press.

Maruish, M.E., Sawicki, R.F., Franzen, M.D., & Golden, C.J. (1984). Alpha coefficient reliabilities for the Luria–Nebraska Neuropsychological Battery summary and localization scales by diagnostic category. *The International Journal of Clinical Neuropsychology, 7,* 10–12.

Marziali, E. (1984). Prediction of outcome of brief psychotherapy from therapist interpretive interventions. *Archives of General Psychiatry, 41,* 301–304.

Masling, J. (1960). The influences of situational and interpersonal variables in projective testing. *Psychological Bulletin, 57,* 65–85.

Maslow, A.H. (1968). *Toward a psychology of being.* New York: Van Nostrand-Reinhold.

Masson, J.M. (1984). *The assault on truth: Freud's suppression of the seduction theory.* New York: Farrar, Strauss, Giroux.

Masters, W.H., & Johnson, V.E. (1966). *Human sexual response.* Boston: Little, Brown.

Masters, W.H., & Johnson, V.E. (1970). *Human sexual inadequacy.* Boston: Little, Brown.

Masters, W.H., Johnson, V.E., & Kolodny, R.C. (1988). *Human sexuality.* (3rd ed.). Boston: Little Brown.

Matarazzo, J.D. (1972). *Wechsler's measurement and appraisal of adult intelligence* (5th ed.). Baltimore: Williams & Wilkins.

Mateer, C.A., Polen, S.B., & Ojemann, G.A. (1982). Sexual variation in cortical localization of naming as determined by stimulation mapping. *The Behavioral and Brain Sciences, 5,* 310–311.

Mathe, A., & Knapp, P. (1971). Emotional and adrenal reactions of stress in bronchial asthma. *Psychosomatic Medicine, 33,* 323–329.

Matheny, A.P., Jr., Dolan, A.B., & Wilson, R.S. (1976). Twins with academic problems: Antecedent characteristics. *American Journal of Orthopsychiatry, 46,* 464–469.

Matsuyama, S.S., & Jarvik, L.F. (1989). Hypothesis: Microtubules, a net to Alzheimer disease. *Neurobiology, 86,* 8152–8156.

Matthews, K.A. (1978). Assessment and developmental antecedents of pattern A behavior in children. In T.M. Dembroski, S.M. Weiss, J.L. Shields, S.G. Haynes, & M. Feinleib (Eds.), *Coronary-prone behavior.* New York: Springer-Verlag.

Matthews, K.A. (1982). Psychological perspectives on the type A behavior pattern. *Psychological Bulletin, 91,* 293–323.

Matthews, K.A., et al. (1989). Menopause and risk factors in coronary heart disease. *New England Journal of Medicine, 321,* 641–646.

Matthews, K.A., Glass, D.C., Rosenman, R.H., & Bonner, R.W. (1977). Competitive drive, pattern A, and coronary heart disease: A further analysis of some data from the Western Collaborative Group Study. *Journal of Chronic Diseases, 30,* 489–498.

Matthews, K.A., & Rakaczky, C.J. (1987). Familial aspects of type A behavior and physiologic reactivity to stress. In T. Dembroski and T. Schmidt (Eds.), *Behavioral factors in coronary heart disease.* Heidelberg: Springer-Verlag.

Mattick, R.P., Peters, L., & Clarke, J.C. (1989). Exposure and cognitive restructuring for severe social phobia. *Behavior Therapy, 20,* 3–23.

Mavissikalian, M., Hammen, M.S., & Jones, B. (1990). DSM-III personality disorders in obsessive-compulsive disorder. *Comprehensive Psychiatry, 31,* 432–437.

Mays, D.T., & Franks, C.M. (1980). Getting worse: Psychotherapy or no treatment—The jury should still be out. *Professional Psychology, 11,* 78–92.

McAllister, T.W., & Price, T.R.P. (1982). Severe depressive pseudodementia with and without dementia. *American Journal of Psychiatry, 139,* 626–629.

McAnulty, R.D., & Adams, H.E. (1990). Patterns of sexual arousal of accused child molesters involved in custody disputes. *Archives of Sexual Behavior, 19,* 541–556.

McCarthy, B.W. (1986). A cognitive-behavioral approach to understanding and treating sexual trauma. *Journal of Sex and Marital Therapy, 12,* 322–329.

McCary, J.L. (1973). *Human sexuality* (2nd ed.). New York: Van Nostrand-Reinhold.

McClelland, D.C. (1976). *The achieving society.* New York: Irvington.

McConaghy, N. (1990). Sexual deviation. In A.S. Bellack, M. Hersen, & A.E. Kazdin (Eds.), *International handbook of behavior modification and therapy* (2nd ed., pp. 565–580). New York: Plenum.

McConaghy, N., Blaszczynski, A., & Kidson, W. (1988). Treatment of sex offenders with imaginal desensitization and/or medroxyprogesterone. *Acta Psychiatrica Scandinavica, 77,* 199–206.

McCord, W., & McCord, J. (1964). *The psychopath: An essay on the criminal mind.* New York: Van Nostrand-Reinhold.

McCrady, B.S. (1985). Alcoholism. In D.H. Barlow (Ed.), *Clinical handbook of psychological disorders.* New York: Guilford.

McCraine, E.W., Watkins, L.O., Brandsma, J.M., et al. (1986). Hostility, coronary heart disease (CHD) incidence, and total mortality: Lack of association in a 25-year follow-up study of 478 physicians. *Journal of Behavioral Medicine, 9,* 119–125.

McCutchan, J.A. (1990). Virology, immunology, and clinical course of HIV infection. *Journal of Consulting and Clinical Psychology, 58,* 5–12.

McFall, R.M., & Hammen, C.L. (1971). Motivation, structure, and self-monitoring: Role of nonspecific factors in smoking reduction. *Journal of Consulting and Clinical Psychology, 37,* 80–86.

McFall, R.M., & Lillesand, D.B. (1971). Behavior rehearsal with modeling and coaching in assertion training. *Journal of Abnormal Psychology, 77,* 313–323.

McGee, R., Feehan, M., Williams, S., Partridge, F., Silva, P.A., & Kelly, J. (1990). DSM-III disorders in a large sample of adolescents. *Journal of the American Academy of Child and Adolescent Psychiatry, 29,* 611–619.

McGee, R., & Williams, S. (1988). A longitudinal study of depression in nine-year-old children. *Journal of the American Academy of Child and Adolescent Psychiatry, 27,* 49–54.

McGee, R., Williams, S., & Silva, P. (1987). A comparison of girls and boys with teacher-identified problems of attention. *Journal of the American Academy of Child and Adolescent Psychiatry, 26,* 711–717.

McGhie, A., & Chapman, I.S. (1961). Disorders of attention and perception in early schizophrenia. *British Journal of Medical Psychology, 34,* 103–116.

McGlashan, T.M. (1983). The borderline syndrome: I. Testing three diagnostic systems. *Archives of General Psychiatry, 40,* 1311–1318.

McGue, M., Pickens, R.W., & Svikis, D.S. (1992). Sex and age effects on the inheritance of alcohol problems: A twin study. *Journal of Abnormal Psychology, 101,* 3–17.

McGuiness, D. (1981). Auditory and motor aspects of language development in males and females. In A. Ansara (Ed.), *Sex differences in dyslexia.* Towson, MD: The Orton Dyslexia Society.

McGuiness, D. (1985). *When children don't learn.* New York: Basic Books.

McGuire, R.J., Carlisle, J.M., & Young, B.G. (1965). Sexual deviations as conditioned behaviour: A hypothesis. *Behaviour Research and Therapy, 2,* 185–190.

McIntyre-Kingsolver, K., Lichtenstein, E., & Mermelstein, R.J. (1986). Spouse training in a multicomponent smoking-cessation program. *Behavior Therapy, 17,* 67–74.

McKeon, P., & Murray, R. (1987). Familial aspects of obsessive-compulsive neurosis. *British Journal of Psychiatry, 151,* 528–534.

McKnight, D.L., Nelson, R.O., Hayes, S.C., & Jarrett, R.B. (1984). Importance of treating individually assessed response classes in the amelioration of depression. *Behavior Therapy, 15,* 315–335.

McKusick, L., Coates, T.J., & Morin, S. (in press). Longitudinal predictors of unprotected anal intercourse among gay and bisexual men in San Francisco: The AIDS Behavioral Research Project. *American Journal of Public Health.*

McLarnon, L.D., & Kaloupek, D.G. (1988). Psychological investigation of genital herpes recurrence: Prospective assessment and cognitive-behavioral intervention for a chronic physical disorder. *Health Psychology, 7,* 231–249.

McMullen, S., & Rosen, R.C. (1979). Self-administered masturbation training in the treatment of primary orgasmic dysfunction. *Journal of Consulting and Clinical Psychology, 47,* 912–918.

McNally, R.J. (1987). Preparedness and phobias: A review. *Psychological Bulletin, 101,* 283–303.

McNally, R.J., & Reiss, S. (1982). The preparedness theory of phobias and human safety-signal conditioning. *Behaviour Research and Therapy, 20,* 153–159.

McNally, R.J., et al. (1990). Selective processing of threat cues in posttraumatic stress disorder. *Journal of Abnormal Psychology, 99,* 398–406.

McNeal, E.T., & Cimbolic, P. (1986). Antidepressants and biochemical theories of depression. *Psychological Bulletin, 99,* 361–374.

McNeil, E. (1967). *The quiet furies.* Englewood Cliffs, NJ: Prentice-Hall.

Medical Research Council Working Party on Mild to Moderate Hypertension. Adverse reactions to bendroflumethiazide and propanadol for the treatment of mild hypertension. *Lancet, 11,* 539.

Mednick, S.A., Gabrielli, W.F., & Hutchings, B. (1984). Genetic influences in criminal convictions: Evidence from an adoption cohort. *Science, 224,* 891–894.

Mednick, S.A., & Hutchings, B. (1978). Genetic and psychophysiological factors in psychopathic behaviour. In R.D. Hare & D. Schalling (Eds.), *Psychopathic behavior: Approaches to research.* New York: Wiley.

Mednick, S.A., Machon, R., Hottunen, M.O., & Bonett, D. (1988). Fetal viral infection and adult schizophrenia. *Archives of General Psychiatry, 45,* 189–192.

Mednick, S.A., & Schulsinger, F. (1968). Some premorbid characteristics related to breakdown in children with schizophrenic mothers. In D. Rosenthal & S.S. Kety (Eds.), *The transmission of schizophrenia.* Elmsford, NY: Pergamon.

Medvedev, Z. (1972). *A question of madness.* New York: Knopf.

Meehl, P.E. (1962). Schizotaxia, schizotypy, schizophrenia. *American Psychologist, 17,* 827–838.

Meehl, P.E. (1986). Diagnostic taxa as open concepts: Methodological and statistical questions about reliability and construct validity in the grand strategy of nosological revision. In T. Millon, & G.L. Klerman (Eds.). *Contemporary directions in psychopathology.* New York: Wiley.

Meichenbaum, D.H. (1971). Examination of model characteristics in reducing avoidance behavior. *Journal of Personality and Social Psychology, 17,* 298–307.

Meichenbaum, D.H. (1975). A self-instructional approach to stress management: A proposal for stress inoculation training. In I. Sarason & C.D. Spielberger (Eds.), *Stress and anxiety* (Vol. 2). New York: Wiley.

Meichenbaum, D.H., & Asarnow, J. (1979). Cognitive-behavioral modification and metacognitive development: Implications for the classroom. In P.C. Kendall & S.D. Hollon (Eds.), *Cognitive-behavioral interventions: Theory, research, and procedures.* New York: Academic Press.

Meichenbaum, D.H., & Goodman, J. (1969). Reflection-impulsivity and verbal control of motor behavior. *Child Development, 40,* 785–797.

Meichenbaum, D.H., & Goodman, J. (1971). Training impulsive children to talk to themselves. A means of developing self-control. *Journal of Abnormal Psychology, 77,* 115–126.

Meiselman, K.C. (1978). *Incest: A psychological study of causes and effects with treatment considerations.* San Francisco: Jossey-Bass.

Melamed, B.G., Hawes, R.R., Heiby, E., & Glick, J. (1975). Use of filmed modeling to reduce uncooperative behavior of children during dental treatment. *Journal of Dental Research, 54,* 797–801.

Melamed, B.G., & Siegel, L.J. (1975). Reduction of anxiety in children facing hospitalization and surgery by use of filmed modeling. *Journal of Consulting and Clinical Psychology, 43,* 511–521.

Mellinger, G.D., Balter, M.B., & Uhlenhuth, E.H. (1985). Insomnia and its treatment. *Archives of General Psychiatry, 42,* 225–232.

Mello, N.K., & Mendelson, J.H. (1970). Experimentally induced intoxication in alcoholics: A comparison between programmed and spontaneous drinking. *Journal of Pharmacology and Experimental Therapy, 173,* 101.

Mellor, C.S. (1970). First rank symptoms of schizophrenia. *British Journal of Psychiatry, 117,* 15–23.

Melman, A., & Rossman, B. (1989). *Penile vein ligation for corporal incompetence: An evaluation of short and long term results.* Paper presented at the 15th Annual Meeting of the International Academy of Sex Research, Princeton. As cited in Wincze & Carey (1991).

Meltzer, H.Y., Sachar, E.J., & Frantz, A.G. (1974). Serum prolactin levels in acutely psychotic patients: An indirect measurement of central dopaminergic activity. In E. Usdin (Ed.), *Neuropsychopharmacology of monoamines and their regulatory enzymes.* New York: Raven.

Mendels, J. (1970). *Concepts of depression.* New York: Wiley.

Mendels, J., & Cochrane, C. (1968). The nosology of depression: The endogenous-reactive concept. *American Journal of Psychiatry, 12,* 1–11.

Mendels, J., Fieve, A., Fitzgerand, R.G., Ramsey, T.A., & Stokes, J.W. (1972). Biogenic amine metabolites in cerebrospinal fluid of depressed and manic patients. *Science, 175,* 1380–1382.

Mendels, J., Stinnett, J.L., Burns, D., & Frazer, A. (1975). Amine precursors and depression. *Archives of General Psychiatry, 32,* 22–30.

Mendelson, J.H. (1964). Experimentally induced chronic intoxication and withdrawal in alcoholics. *Quarterly Journal of Studies on Alcohol* (Suppl. 2).

Mendelson, J.H., Rossi, A.M., & Meyer, R.E. (Eds.). (1974). *The use of marijuana: A psychological and physiological inquiry.* New York: Plenum.

Mendlewicz, J., & Rainer, J.D. (1977). Adoption study supporting genetic transmission in manic-depressive illness. *Nature, 268,* 327–329.

Messer, S.B., Sass, L.A., & Woolfolk, R.L. (Eds.). *Hermeneutics and psycological theory: Integrative perspectives on personality, psychotherapy and psychopathology.* New Brunswick, NJ: Rutgers University Press.

Metalsky, G.I., Abramson, L.V., Seligman, M.E.P., Semmel, A., & Peterson, C. (1982). Attributional styles and life events in the classroom: Vulnerability and invulnerability to depressive mood reactions. *Journal of Personality and Social Psychology, 43,* 612–617.

Metalsky, G.I., Haberstadt, L.J., & Abramson, L.Y. (1987). Vulnerability and invulnerability to depressive mood reactions: Toward a more powerful test of the diathesis–stress and causal mediation components of the reformulated theory of depression. *Journal of Personality and Social Psychology, 52,* 386–393.

Metzner, R., Litwin, G., & Weil, G.M. (1965). The relation of expectation and mood to psilocybin reactions. *Psychedelic Review, 5,* 3–39.

Meuwissen, I., & Over, R. (1992). Sexual arousal across phases of the human menstrual cycle. *Archives of Sexual Behavior, 21,* 101–119.

Meyer, A. (1917). The aims and meaning of psychiatric diagnosis. *American Journal of Insanity, 74,* 163–168.

Meyer, J.J. (1988). Impotence: Assessment in the private-practice office. *Postgraduate Medicine, 84,* 87–91.

Meyer, J.J., & Reter, D.J. (1979). Sex reassignment follow-up. *Archives of General Psychiatry, 36,* 1010–1015.

Meyer, R.E. (1988). Overview of the concept of alcoholism. In R.M. Rose & J.E. Barrett (Eds.), *Alcoholism: Origins and outcome.* New York: Raven.

Meyer, V. (1966). Modification of expectations in cases with obsessional rituals. *Behaviour Research and Therapy, 4,* 273–280.

Meyer, V., & Chesser, E.S. (1970). *Behavior therapy in clinical psychiatry.* Baltimore: Penguin.

Meyer-Bahlburg, H. (1979). Sex hormones and female homosexuality: A critical examination. *Archives of Sexual Behavior, 8,* 101–119.

Meyerowitz, B.E., & Chaiken, S. (1987). The effect of message framing on breast self-examination attitudes, intentions, and behavior. *Journal of Personality and Social Psychology, 52,* 500–510.

Michelson, L., Mavissakalian, M., & Marchione, K. (1985). Cognitive and behavioral treatments of agoraphobia: Clinical, behavioral, and psychophysiological treatments of agoraphobia. *Journal of Consulting and Clinical Psychology, 53,* 913–925.

Michelson, L., Sugai, D.P., Wood, R.P., & Kazdin, A.E. (1983). *Social skills assessment and training with children: An empirically based handbook.* New York: Plenum.

Miklich, D.R., Rewey, H.H., Weiss, J.H., & Kolton, S. (1973). A preliminary investigation of psychophysiological responses to stress among different subgroups of asthmatic children. *Journal of Psychosomatic Research, 17,* 1–8.

Miklowitz, D.J. (1985). *Family interaction and illness outcome in bipolar and schizophrenic patients.* Unpublished Ph.D. thesis, University of California at Los Angeles.

Miklulineen, M., & Solomon, Z. (1988). Attributional style and posttraumatic stress disorder. *Journal of Abnormal Psychology, 97,* 308–313.

Miles, L.E., & Dement, W.C. (1980). Sleep and aging. *Sleep, 3,* 119–220.

Milgram, N.A. (1973). Cognition and language in mental retardation: Directions and implications. In D.K. Routh (Ed.), *The experimental psychology of mental retardation.* Chicago: Aldine.

Miller, E. (1975). Impaired recall and the memory disturbance in presenile dementia. *British Journal of Social and Clinical Psychology, 14,* 73–79.

Miller, H.R. (1981). Psychiatric morbidity in elderly surgical patients. *British Journal of Psychiatry, LM,* 17–20.

Miller, N.E. (1948). Studies of fear as an acquirable drive: I. Fear as motivation and fear-reduction as reinforcement in the learning of new responses. *Journal of Experimental Psychology, 38,* 89–101.

Miller, N.E. (1959). Liberalization of basic S-R concepts: Extensions to conflict behavior, motivation, and social learning. In S. Koch (Ed.), *Psychology: A study of a science* (Vol. 2). New York: McGraw-Hill.

Miller, S.O. (1989). Optical differences in cases of multiple personality disorder. *Journal of Nervous and Mental Disease, 177,* 480–487.

Miller, W.R., Seligman, M.E.P., & Kurlander, H.M. (1975). Learned helplessness, depression, and anxiety. *Journal of Nervous and Mental Disease, 161,* 347–357.

Millon, T. (1981). *Disorders of personality: DSM III. Axis II.* New York: Wiley.

Milton, F., & Hafner, J. (1979). The outcome of behavior therapy for agoraphobia in relation to marital adjustment. *Archives of General Psychiatry, 36,* 807– 811.

Milton, O., & Wahler, R.G. (Eds.). (1969). *Behavior disorders: Perspectives and trends* (2nd ed.) Philadelphia: Lippincott.

Mineka, S. (1985). Animal models of anxiety-based disorders: Their usefulness and limitations. In A.H. Tuma & J.D. Maser (Eds.), *Anxiety and the anxiety disorders.* Hillsdale, NJ: Erlbaum.

Mineka, S. (1992). Evolutionary memories, emotional processing, and the emotional disorders. In D. Medin (Ed.), *The psychology of learning and motivation* (Vol. 28). New York: Academic Press.

Mineka, S., Davidson, M., Cook, M., & Keir, R. (1984). Observational conditioning of snake fear in rhesus monkeys. *Journal of Abnormal Psychology, 93,* 355–372.

Mineka, S., Gunnar, M., & Champoux, M. (1986). Control and early socioemotional development: Infant rhesus monkeys reared in controllable versus uncontrollable environments. *Child Development, 57,* 1241–1256.

Mintz, E. (1967). Time-extended marathon groups. *Psychotherapy, 4,* 65–70.

Mintz, J. (1983). Integrating research evidence. *Journal of Consulting and Clinical Psychology, 51,* 71–75.

Mintz, R.S. (1968). Psychotherapy of the suicidal patient. In H.L.P. Resnik (Ed.), *Suicidal behaviors.* Boston: Little, Brown.

Minuchin, S. (1974). *Families and family therapy.* Cambridge, MA: Harvard University Press.

Minuchin, S., Baker, L., Rosman, B.L., Liebman, R., Milman, L., & Todd, T.C. (1975). A conceptual model of psychosomatic illness in children: Family organization and family therapy. *Archives of General Psychiatry, 32,* 1031–1038.

Mirenda, P.L., Donnelflan, A.M., & Yoder, D.E. (1983). Gaze behavior: A new look at an old problem. *Journal of Autism and Developmental Disorders, 13,* 397–409.

Mirsky, A.F. (1987). Behavioral and psychophysiological markers of disordered attention. *Environmental Health Perspectives, 74,* 191–199.

Mischel, W. (1968). *Personality and assessment.* New York: Wiley.

Mischel, W. (1973). Toward a cognitive social learning reconceptualization of personality. *Psychological Review, 80,* 252–283.

Mischel, W. (1977). On the future of personality assessment. *American Psychologist, 32,* 246–254.

Mischel, W., & Peake, P.K. (1982). Beyond déjà vu in the search for cross-situational consistency. *Psychological Review, 89,* 730–755.

Mitchell, J., McCauley, E., Burke, P.M., & Moss, S.J. (1988). Phenomenology of depression in children and adolescents. *Journal of the American Academy of Child and Adolescent Psychiatry, 27,* 12–20.

Mitchell, J.E., Hatsukami, D., Eckert, E.D., & Pyle, R.L. (1985). Characteristics of 275 patients with bulimia. *American Journal of Psychiatry, 142,* 482–485.

Mitchell-Heggs, N., Kelly, D., & Richardson, A. (1976). Stereotactic limbic leucotomy—A follow-up at 16 months. *British Journal of Psychiatry, 128,* 226–240.

Modestin, J. (1987). Quality of interpersonal relationships: The most characteristic DSM-III BPD characteristic *Comprehensive Psychiatry, 28,* 397–402.

Moffatt, M.E.K., Kato, C., & Pless, I.B. (1987). Improvements in self-concept after treatment of nocturnal enuresis: Randomized controlled trial. *The Journal of Pediatrics, 110,* 647–652.

Mohr, D.C., Beutler, L.E. (1990). Erectile dysfunction: A review of diagnostic and treatment procedures. *Clinical Psychology Review, 10,* 123–150.

Mohr, J.W., Turner, R.E., & Jerry, M.B. (1964). *Pedophilia and exhibitionism.* Toronto: University of Toronto Press.

Mohs, R.C., Breftner, J.C.S., Silverman, J.M., & Davis, K.L. (1987). Alzheimer's disease: Morbid risk among first-degree relatives approximates 50% by 90 years of age. *Archives of General Psychiatry, 44,* 405–408.

Mollica, R.F., & Milic, M. (1986). Social class and psychiatric practice: A revision of the Hollingshead and Redlich model. *American Journal of Psychiatry, 143,* 12–17,

Money, J., Hampson, J.G., & Hampson, J.L. (1955). An examination of some basic sexual concepts: The evidence of human hermaphroditism. *Johns Hopkins Hospital Bulletin, 97,* 301–319.

Moniz, E. (1936). *Tentatives opératoires dans le traitement de certaines psychoses.* Paris: Masson.

Monahan, J. (1973). The psychiatrization of criminal behavior. *Hospital and Community Psychiatry, 24,* 105–107.

Monahan, J. (1976). The prevention of violence. In J. Monahan (Ed.), *Community mental health and the criminal justice system.* Elmsford, NY: Pergamon.

Monahan, J. (1977, April 30). Prisons: A wary verdict on rehabilitation. *Washington Post,* p. A13.

Monahan, J. (1978). Prediction research and the emergency commitment of dangerous mentally ill persons: A reconsideration. *American Journal of Psychiatry, 135,* 198–201.

Monahan, J. (1981). *The clinical prediction of violent behavior.* Rockville, MD: National Institution of Mental Health.

Monahan, J. (1984). The prediction of violent behavior: Toward a second generation of theory and policy. *American Journal of Psychiatry, 141,* 10–15.

Monahan, J., Caldeira, C., & Friedlander, H. (1979). The police and the mentally ill: A comparison of arrested and committed persons. *International Journal of Law and Psychiatry, 2,* 509–518.

Monahan, J. *Limiting Therapist Exposure to Tarasoff Liability: Guidelines to Risk Containment.* American Psychologist, 1993, Vol. 4, 242–250.

Moran, M. (1991). Psychological factors affecting pulmonary and rheumatological diseases: A review. *Psychosomatics, 32,* 14–23.

Morey, L.C. (1988). Personality disorders in DSM-III and DSM-IIIR: Convergence, coverage, and internal consistency. *American Journal of Psychiatry, 145,* 573–577.

Morey, L.C., & Ochoa, E.S. (1989). An investigation of adherence to diagnostic criteria: Clinical diagnosis of the DSM-III personality disorders. *Journal of Personality Disorders, 3,* 180–192.

Morin, C.M., & Azrin, N.H. (1988). Behavioral and cognitive treatments of geriatric insomnia. *Journal of Consulting and Clinical Psychology, 56,* 748–753.

Morokoff, P. (1985). Effects of sex guilt, repression, sexual "arousability," and sexual experience on female sexual arousal during erotica and fantasy. *Journal of Personality and Social Psychology, 49,* 177–187.

Morokoff, P.J. (1988). Sexuality in perimenopausal and postmenopausal women. *Psychology of Women Quarterly, 12,* 489–511.

Morris, A.A. (1968). Criminal insanity. *Washington Review, 43,* 583–622.

Morris, J. (1974). *Conundrum.* New York: Harcourt, Brace, Jovanovich.

Morris, J.B., & Beck, A.T. (1974). The efficacy of antidepressant drugs. *Archives of General Psychiatry, 30,* 667–674.

Morris, N. (1966). Impediments to legal reform. *University of Chicago Law Review, 33,* 627–656.

Morris, N. (1968). Psychiatry and the dangerous criminal. *Southern California Law Review, 41,* 514–547.

Morrow, J., & Nolen-Hoeksema, S. (1990). Effects of responses to depression on the remediation of depressive affect. *Journal of Personality and Social Psychology, 58,* 519–527.

Morse, S.J. (1978). Crazy behavior, morals, and science: An analysis of mental health law. *Southern California Law Review, 51,* 527–654.

Morse, S.J. (1979). Diminished capacity: A moral and legal conundrum. *International Journal of Law and Psychiatry, 2,* 271–298.

Morse, S.J. (1982a, June 23). In defense of the insanity defense. *Los Angeles Times.*

Morse, S.J. (1982b). Failed explanation and criminal responsibility: Experts and the unconscious. *Virginia Law Review, 678,* 971–1084.

Morse, S.J. (1982c). A preference for liberty: The case against involuntary commitment of the mentally disordered. *California Law Review, 70,* 54–106.

Morse, S.J. (1992). The "guilty mind": Mens rea. In D.K. Kagehiro & W.S. Laufer (Eds.), *Handbook of psychology and law* (pp. 207–229). New York: Springer-Verlag.

Moser, C., & Levitt, E.E. (1987). An exploratory-descriptive study of a sadomasochistically oriented sample. *The Journal of Sex Research, 23,* 322–337.

Moser, P.W. (1989, January). Double vision: Why do we never match up to our mind's ideal? *Self Magazine,* pp. 51–52.

Moses, J.A. (1983). Luria–Nebraska Neuropsychological Battery performance of brain dysfunctional patients with positive or negative findings on current neurological examination. *International Journal of Neuroscience, 22,* 135–146.

Moses, J.A., & Scheftt, B.K. (1984). Interrater reliability analyses of the Luria–Nebraska Neuropsychological Battery. *The International Journal of Clinical Neuropsychology, 7,* 31–38.

Mosher, L.R., & Burti, L. (1989). *Community mental health: Principles and practice.* New York: Norton.

Mosher, L.R., Kresky-Wolff, M., Mathews, S., & Menn, A. (1986). Milieu therapy in the 1980s: A comparison of two residential alternatives to hospitalization. *Bulletin of the Menninger Clinic, 50,* 257–268.

Moss, H.B. (1990). Pharmacotherapy. In A.S. Bellack & M. Hersen (Eds.), *Handbook of comparative treatments for adult disorders* (pp. 506–520). New York: Wiley.

Moss, H.B., & Procci, W.R. (1982). Sexual dysfunction associated with oral antihypertensive medication: A critical survey of the literature. *General Hospital Psychiatry, 4,* 121–129.

Mothersill, K.J., McDowell, I., & Rosser, R. (1988). Subject characteristics and long term post-program smoking cessation. *Addictive Behaviors, 13,* 29–36.

Mowrer, O.H. (1939). A stimulus-response analysis of anxiety and its role as a reinforcing agent. *Psychological Review, 46,* 553–565.

Mowrer, O.H. (1947). On the dual nature of learning—A reinterpretation of "conditioning" and "problem-solving." *Harvard Educational Review, 17,* 102–148.

Mowrer, O.H. (1950). *Learning theory and personality dynamics.* New York: Ronald Press.

Mowrer, O.H., & Mowrer, W.M. (1938). Enuresis: A method for its study and treatment. *American Journal of Orthopsychiatry, 8,* 436–459.

Mowrer, O.H. & Viek, P. (1948). An experimental analogue of fear from a sense of helplessness. *Journal of Abnormal and Social Psychology, 43,* 193–200.

Mrazek, D.A., et al. (1991). Early asthma onset: Consideration of parenting issues. *Journal of the American Academy of Child and Adolescent Psychiatry, 30,* 277–282.

Mrazek, F.J. (1984). Sexual abuse of children. In B. Lahey & A.E. Kazdin (Eds.), *Advances in child clinical psychology* (Vol. 6). New York: Plenum.

Mueller, P., Abelin, R., Ehrsam, P., Imhof, P.R., Howard, H., & Mauli, D. (1990). The use of transdermal nicotine in smoking cessation. *Lung,* (Suppl.), 445–453.

Mukherjee, S., Shukla, S., Woodle, J., Rosen, A.M. & Olarte, S. (1983). Misdiagnosis of schizophrenia in bipolar patients: A multiethnic comparison. *American Journal of Psychiatry, 140,* 1571–1574.

Mulick, J.A. (1990). The ideology and science of punishment in mental retardation. *American Journal of Mental Retardation, 95,* 142–156.

Muller, D., Roeder, F., & Orthner, H. (1973). Further results of stereotaxis in human hypothalamus in sexual deviations: First use of this operation in addiction to drugs. *Neurochirurgia, 16,* 113–126.

Mulligan, T., & Palguta, R.F. (1991). Sexual interest, activity, and satisfaction among male nursing home residents. *Archives of Sexual Behavior, 20,* 199–204.

Mulligan, T., Retchin, S.M., Chinchilli, V.M., & Bettinger, C.B. (1988). *Journal of the American Geriatrics Society, 36,* 520–524.

Munby, M., & Johnston, D.W. (1980). Agoraphobia: The long-term follow-up of behavioural treatment. *British Journal of Psychiatry, 137,* 418–427.

Munjack, D.J., & Kanno, P.H. (1979). Retarded ejaculation: A review. *Archives of Sexual Behavior, 8,* 139–150.

Murphy, J. (1976). Psychiatric labeling in cross-cultural perspective. *Science, 191,* 1019–1028.

Muscettola, G., Potter, W.Z., Pickar, D., & Goodwin, F.K. (1984). Urinary 3-methoxy-4-hydroxyphenyl glycol and major affective disorders. *Archives of General Psychiatry, 41,* 337–342.

Musetti, L., Perugi, G., Soriani, A., Rossi, V.M., Cassano, G.B., & Akiskal, H.S. (1989). Depression before and after age 65: A re-examination. *British Journal of Psychiatry, 155,* 330–336.

Muse, M. (1986). Stress-related, posttraumatic chronic pain syndrome: Behavioral treatment approach. *Pain, 25,* 389–394.

Myers, H.F. (1982). Stress, ethnicity, and social class: A model for research with black populations. In E. Jones & S. Korchin (Eds.), *Minority mental health.* New York: Holt, Rinehart & Winston.

Myers, J.K., & Weissman, M.M. (1980). Psychiatric disorders and their treatment. *Medical Care, 18,* 117–123.

Myers, J.K., Weissman, M.M. Tischler, G.L., Holzer, C.E., Leaf, P.J., Orvaschel, H.A., Anthony, J.C., Boyd, J.H., Burke, J.E., Kramer, M., & Stoltzman, R. (1984). Six-month prevalence of psychiatric disorders in three communities: 1980–1982. *Archives of General Psychiatry, 41,* 959–967.

Nastadt, G., Romanoski, A.J., Chahal, R., Merchant, A., Folstein, A.F., et al. (1990). An epidemiological study of narcissistic personality disorder. *Psychological Medicine, 20,* 413–422.

National Advisory Mental Health Council. (1990). *National plan for research on child and adolescent mental disorders.* Rockville, MD: National Institute of Mental Health.

National Cancer Institute. (1977). *The smoking digest: Progress report on a nation kicking the habit.* Washington, DC: U.S. Department of Health, Education and Welfare.

National Center for Health Statistics. (1979). *The National Nursing Home Survey: 1977 Summary for the United States* (Department of Health, Education and Welfare Publication No. PHS 79-1794). Hyattsville, MD: U.S. Department of Health and Human Services.

National Center for Health Statistics. (1985). *Vital statistics of the United States, 1980: Vol. II. Mortality, Part B.* Hyattsville, MD: U.S. Department of Health and Human Services.

National Center for Health Statistics. (1988). Advance report of final mortality statistics, 1986. *NCHS Monthly Vital Statistics Report, 37* (Suppl. 6).

National Center for Health Statistics (1989). *National nursing home survey* (DHHS Publication No. PHS 89-1758, Series 13, No. 97). Washington, DC: U.S. Government Printing Office.

National Commission on Testing and Public Policy. (1990). *From gatekeeper to gateway: Transforming testing in America.* Chestnut Hill, MA: Boston College.

National Council on Alcoholism. (1986). *Facts on alcoholism.* New York: Author.

National Institute on Alcohol Abuse and Alcoholism. (1983). *Special Report to the U.S. Congress on Alcohol and Health.* Washington, DC: U.S. Government Printing Office.

National Institute on Alcohol Abuse and Alcoholism. (1990). *Seventh special report to the U.S. Congress on alcohol and health* (DHHS Publication No. ADM 90-1656). Washington, DC: U.S. Government Printing Office.

National Institute on Drug Abuse. (1979). *National Survey on Drug Abuse.* Washington, DC: Author.

National Institute on Drug Abuse. (1982). *National Survey on Drug Abuse.* Washington, DC: Author.

National Institute on Drug Abuse. (1983a). *National Survey on Drug Abuse: Main Findings 1982* (DHHS Publication No. ADM 83-1263). Washington, DC: U.S. Government Printing Office.

National Institute on Drug Abuse. (1983b). *Population projections, based on the National Survey on Drug Abuse, 1982.* Rockville, MD: Author.

National Institute on Drug Abuse. (1988). *National household survey on drug abuse: Main findings 1985.* Washington, DC: Department of Health and Human Services.

National Institute on Drug Abuse. (1991). *National Household Survey on Drug Abuse: Population Estimates, 1991.* Washington, DC.

Navia, B.A., Cho, E., Petito, C.K., & Price, R.W. (1986). The AIDS dementia complex: II. Neuropathology. *Annals of Neurology, 19,* 525–535.

Nawas, M.M., Fishman, S.T., & Pucel, J.C. (1970). The standardized densensitization program applicable to group and individual treatment. *Behaviour Research and Therapy, 6,* 63–68.

Neale, J.M. (1971). Perceptual span in schizophrenia. *Journal of Abnormal Psychology, 77,* 196–204.

Neale, J.M., & Katahn, M. (1968). Anxiety, choice and stimulus uncertainty. *Journal of Personality, 36,* 238–245.

Neale, J.M., & Liebert, R.M. (1986). *Science and behavior: An introduction to methods of research* (3rd ed.). Englewood Cliffs, NJ: Prentice-Hall.

Neighbors, H., Jackson, J., Bowman, P., & Gunn, G. (1983). Stress, coping and black mental health: Preliminary findings from a national study. *Prevention in Human Services, 2,* 5–29.

Neisser, U. (1976). *Cognition and reality.* San Francisco: Freeman.

Nelson, J.C., & Bowers, M.B. (1978). Delusional unipolar depression. *Archives of General Psychiatry, 35,* 1321–1328.

Nelson, R.E., & Craighead, W.E. (1977). Selective recall of positive and negative feedback, self-control behaviors, and depression. *Journal of Abnormal Psychology, 86,* 379–388.

Nelson, R.O., Lipinski, D.P., & Black, J.L. (1976). The reactivity of adult retardates' self-monitoring: A comparison among behaviors of different valences, and a comparison with token reinforcement. *Psychological Record, 26,* 189–201.

Nemeroff, C.J., & Karoly, P. (1991). Operant methods. In F.H. Kanfer, & A.P.

Goldstein (Eds.), *Helping people change: A textbook of methods*. Fourth edition. Elmsford, NY: Pergamon Press.

Nemetz, G.H., Craig, K.D., & Reith, G. (1978). Treatment of female sexual dysfunction through symbolic modeling. *Journal of Consulting and Clinical Psychology, 46*, 62–73.

Nemiroff, R.A., & Colarusso, C.A. (1985). *The race against time: Psychotherapy and psychoanalysis in the second half of life.* New York: Plenum.

Nesselroade, J.R., & Labouvie, E.W. (1985). Experimental design in research on aging. In J.E. Birren, & K.W. Schaie (Eds.), *Handbook of the psychology of aging*. Second edition (pp. 35–60). New York: Van Nostrand Reinhold.

Nettelbeck, T. (1985). Inspection time and mild mental retardation. In N.R. Ellis & N.W. Bray (Eds.), *International review of research in mental retardation* (Vol. 13). New York: Academic Press.

Neugebauer, R. (1979). Mediaeval and early modern theories of mental illness. *Archives of General Psychiatry, 36*, 477–484.

Neuhaus, E.C. (1958). A personality study of asthmatic and cardiac children. *Psychosomatic Medicine, 20*, 181–186.

Neuringer, C. (1964). Rigid thinking in suicidal individuals. *Journal of Consulting Psychology, 28*, 54–58.

Newman, J.P., & Kosson, D.S. (1986). Passive avoidance learning in psychopathic and nonpsychopathic offenders. *Journal of Abnormal Psychology, 95*, 257–263.

Nezu, A.M. (1986). Efficacy of a social problem-solving therapy approach for unipolar depression. *Journal of Consulting and Clinical Psychology, 54*, 196–202.

Nicholson, R.A., & Berman, J.S. (1983). Is follow-up necessary in evaluating psychotherapy? *Psychological Bulletin, 93*, 261–278.

Nihira, K., Foster, R., Shenhaas, M., & Leland, H. (1975). *AAMD-Adaptive Behavior Scale.* Washington, DC: American Association on Mental Deficiency.

Nisbett, R.E., & Wilson, T.D. (1977). Telling more than we can know: Verbal reports on mental processes. *Psychological Review, 84*, 231–259.

Nocks, B.C., Learner, R.M., Blackman, D., & Brown, T.E. (1986). The effects of a community-based long term care project on nursing home utilization. *The Gerontologist, 26*, 150–157.

Nolen-Hoeksema, S. (1987). Sex differences in unipolar depression: Evidence and theory. *Psychological Bulletin, 101*, 259–282.

Nolen-Hoeksema, S. (1990). *Sex differences in depression.* Stanford, CA: Stanford University Press.

Nolen-Hoeksema, S. (1991). Responses to depression and their effects on the duration of depressive episodes. *Journal of Abnormal Psychology, 100*, 569–582.

Nolen-Hoeksema, S., & Morrow, J. (1991a). *The effects of rumination and distraction on naturally occurring depressed moods.* Manuscript submitted for publication, cited in Nolen-Hoeksema (1991).

Nolen-Hoeksema, S., & Morrow, J. (1991b). A prospective study of depression and distress following a natural disaster: The 1989 Loma Prieta earthquake. *Journal of Personality and Social Psychology, 61*, 115–121.

Nolen-Hoeksema, S., Morrow, J., & Frederickson, B.L. (1991). *The effects of response styles on the duration of depressed mood: A field study.* Manuscript submitted for publication. Cited in Nolen-Hoeksema (1991).

Norgaard, J.P. (1989a). Urodynamics in enuretics: I. Reservoir function. *Neurourology and Urodynamics, 8*, 199–211.

Norgaard, J.P. (1989b). Urodynamics in enuretics: II. A pressure/flow study. *Neurourology and Urodynamics, 8*, 213–217.

North, A.F. (1979). Health services in Head Start. In E. Zigler & J. Valentine (Eds.), *Project Head Start.* New York: Free Press.

Norton, G.R., Harrison, B., Hauch, J., & Rhodes, L. (1985). Characteristics of people with infrequent panic attacks. *Journal of Abnormal Psychology, 94*, 216–221.

Norton, J.P. (1982). *Expressed emotion, affective style, voice tone and communication deviance as predictors of offspring schizophrenia spectrum disorders.* Unpublished doctoral dissertation, University of California at Los Angeles.

Noshirvani, H.F., et al. (1991). Gender-divergent factors in obsessive-compulsive disorder. *British Journal of Psychiatry, 158*, 260–263.

Nowlan, R., & Cohen, S. (1977). Tolerance to marijuana: Heart rate and subjective "high." *Clinical Pharmacology Therapeutics, 22*, 550–556.

Noyes, R., Anderson, D.J., Ciancy, J., Crowe, R.R., Slyman, D.J., Ghoneim, M.M., & Hinrichs, J.V. (1984). Diazepam and propanolol in panic disorder and agoraphobia. *Archives of General Psychiatry, 41*, 287–292.

Noyes, R., Crowe, R.R., Harris, E.L., Hamra, B.J., McChesney, C.M., & Chandry, D.R. (1986). Relationship between panic disorder and agoraphobia: A family study. *Archives of General Psychiatry, 43*, 227–232.

Noyes, R., et al. (1990). Outcome of panic disorder: Relationship to diagnostic subtypes and comorbidity. *Archives of General Psychiatry, 47*, 809–818.

Nurnberg, H.G., Prudic, J., Fiori, M., & Freedman, E. (1984). Psychopathology complicating acquired immune deficiency syndrome (AIDS). *American Journal of Psychiatry, 141*, 95–96.

Nyth, A.L., Gottfries, C.G., Blennow, F., et al. (1991). Heterogeneity in the course of *Alzheimer's disease*: A differentiation of subgroups. *Dementia, 2*, 18–24.

Obler, M. (1973). Systematic desensitization in sexual disorders. *Journal of Behavior Therapy and Experimental Psychiatry, 4*, 93–101.

Obrist, P.A., Gaebelein, C.J., Teller, E.S., Langer, A.W., Grignolo, A., Light, K.C., & McCubbin, J.A. (1978). The relationship among heart rate, carotid *dP/dt*, and blood pressure in humans as a function of the type of stress. *Psychophysiology, 15*, 102–115.

Ochitil, H. (1982). Conversion disorder. In J.H. Greist, J.W. Jefferson, & R.L. Spitzer (Eds.), *Treatment of mental disorders.* New York: Oxford University Press.

O'Connor, D.W., Pollitt, P.A., Roth, M., Brook, P.B., & Reiss, B.B. (1990). Memory complaints and impairment in normal, depressed, and demented elderly persons identified in a community survey. *Archives of General Psychiatry, 47*, 224–227.

O'Conner, M.C. (1989). Aspects of differential performance by minorities on standardized tests: Linguistic and sociocultural factors. In B.R. Gifford (Ed.), *Test policy and test performance: Education, language, and culture* (pp. 129–181). Boston: Kluwer Academic Publishers.

O'Connor, R.D. (1969). Modification of social withdrawal through symbolic modeling. *Journal of Applied Behavior Analysis, 2*, 15–22.

O'Donohue, W.T. (1987). The sexual behavior and problems of the elderly. In L.L. Carstensen & B.A. Edelstein (Eds.), *Handbook of clinical gerontology.* New York: Pergamon.

Offord, D.R., Boyle, M.H., Szatmari, P., Rae-Grant, N.I., Links, P.S., Cadman, D.T., Byles, J.A., Crawford, J.W., Blum, H.M., Byrne, C., Thomas, H., & Woodward, C.A. (1987). Ontario Child Health Study: II. Six-month prevalence of disorder and rates of service utilization. *Archives of General Psychiatry, 44*, 832–836.

Ogata, S.N., Silk, K.R., Goodrich, S., et al. (1990). Childhood sexual and physical abuse in adult patients with borderline personality disorder. *American Journal of Psychiatry, 147*, 1008–1013.

Ogilvie, D.M., Stone, P.J., & Shneidman, E.S. (1983). A computer analysis of suicide notes. In E.S. Shneidman, N. Farberow, & R. Litman (Eds.), *The psychology of suicide* (pp. 249–256). New York: Jason Aronson.

Ogloff, J.R., & Wong, S. (1990). Electrodermal and cardiovascular evidence of a coping response in psychopaths. *Criminal Justice and Behavior, 17*, 231–245.

O'Hara, M.W., Hinrichs, J.V., Kohout, F.J., Wallace, R.B., & Lemke, J.H. (1986). Memory complaint and memory performance in the depressed elderly. *Psychology and Aging, 1*, 208–214.

Öhman, A., Erixon, G., & Loftberg, I. (1975). Phobias and preparedness: Phobic versus neutral pictures as conditional stimuli for human autonomic responses. *Journal of Abnormal Psychology, 34*, 41–45.

Olds, D.L. (1984). *Final report: Prenatal/early infancy project.* Washington, DC: Maternal and Child Health Research, National Institute of Health.

O'Leary, K.D. (1980). Pills or skills for hyperactive children. *Journal of Applied Behavior Analysis, 13*, 191–204.

O'Leary, K.D., & Beach, S.R.H. (1990). Marital therapy: A viable treatment for depression and marital discord. *American Journal of Psychiatry, 147*, 183-186.

O'Leary, K.D., & Emery, R.E. (1984). Marital discord and child behavior problems. In M.D. Levine & P. Satz (Eds.), *Middle childhood: Development and dysfunction* (pp. 345–364). Baltimore: University Park Press.

O'Leary, K.D., & O'Leary, S.G. (Eds.). (1977). *Classroom management* (2nd ed.). Elmsford, NY: Pergamon.

O'Leary, K.D., Pelham, W.E., Rosenbaum, A., & Price, G.H. (1976). Behavioral treatment of hyperkinetic children: An experimental evaluation of its usefulness. *Clinical Pediatrics, 15*, 510–515.

O'Leary, K.D., & Turkewitz, H. (1978). Marital therapy from a behavioral perspective. In T.J. Paolino, Jr., & B.S. McCrady (Eds.), *Marriage and marital therapy*. New York: Brunner/Mazel.

O'Leary, K.D., Turkewitz, H., & Taffel, S.I. (1973). Parent and therapist evaluation of behavior therapy in a child psychological clinic. *Journal of Consulting and Clinical Psychology, 41*, 289–293.

O'Leary, K.D., & Wilson, G.T. (1975). *Behavior therapy: Application and outcome.* Englewood Cliffs, NJ: PrenticeHall.

Oltmanns, T.F., Broderick, J.E., & O'Leary, K.D. (1976). *Marital adjustment and the efficacy of behavior therapy with children.* Paper presented at the Association for the Advancement of Behavior Therapy, New York.

Olweus, D. (1979). Stability of aggressive reaction in males: A review. *Psychological Bulletin, 86*, 852–875.

Omizo, M.M., Cubberly, W.E., & Omizo, S.A. (1985). The effects of rational-emotive education groups on self-concept and locus of control among learning disabled children. *The Exceptional Child, 32*, 13–19.

O'Neal, J.M. (1984). First person account: Finding myself and loving it. *Schizophrenia Bulletin, 10*, 109–110.

O'Reilly, K., Higgins, D.L., Galavottio, C., Sheridan, J., Wood, R., & Cohn, D. (1989, June). *Perceived community norms and risk reduction: Behavior change in a cohort of gay men.* Paper presented at the Fifth International Conference on AIDS, Montreal. As cited in Coates (1990).

Orleans, C.T., Schoenbach, V.J., Wagner, E.H., Quade, D., Salmon, M.A., Pearson, D.C., Fiedler, J., Porter, C.Q., & Kaplan, B.H. (1991). Self-help quit smoking interventions: Effects of self-help materials, social support instructions, and telephone counseling. *Journal of Consulting and Clinical Psychology, 59*, 439–448.

Orlinsky, D.E., & Howard, K.L. (1986). The psychological interior of psychotherapy: Explorations with therapy session reports. In L.S. Greenberg & W.M. Pinsof (Eds.), *The psychotherapeutic process: A research handbook.* New York: Guilford.

Orne, M.T., Dinges, D.F., & Orne, E.C. (1984). The differential diagnosis of multiple personality in the forensic court. *International Journal of Clinical and Experimental Hypnosis, 32*, 118–169.

Ornitz, E. (1973). Childhood autism: A review of the clinical and experimental literature. *California Medicine, 118*, 21–47.

Osgood, N.J. (1984). Suicides. In E.B. Palmore (Ed.), *Handbook on the aged in the United States.* Westport, CT: Greenwood Press.

Ost, L.G. (1987). Age of onset in different phobias. *Journal of Abnormal Psychology, 96*, 223–229.

Ost, L.G., Jerremalm, A., & Johansson, J. (1981). Individual response patterns and the effects of different behavioral methods in the treatment of social phobia. *Behaviour Research and Therapy, 19*, 1–16.

Overholser, J.C., & Beck, S. (1986). Multimethod assessment of rapists, child molesters, and three control groups on behavioral and psychological measures. *Journal of Consulting and Clinical Psychology, 54*, 682–687.

Ozer, E. (1986). *Health status of minority women.* Washington, DC: American Psychological Association.

Pahnke, W.N. (1963). *Drugs and mysticism.* Unpublished doctoral dissertation, Harvard University, Cambridge.

Paris, J. (1990). Completed suicide in borderline personality disorder. *Psychiatric Annals, 20*, 19–21.

Park, C.C. (1987). Growing out of autism. In E. Schopler & G.B. Mesibov (Eds.), *Autism in adolescents and adults.* New York: Plenum.

Parkes, C.M., & Brown, R.J. (1972). Health after bereavement: A controlled study of young Boston widowers. *Psychosomatic Medicine, 34*, 49–461.

Parks, C.V., Jr., & Hollon, S.D. (1988). Cognitive assessment. In A.S. Bellack, & M. Hersen (Eds.), *Behavioral assessment* (3rd ed.). Elmsford, NY: Pergamon.

Parsons, O.A. (1975). Brain damage in alcoholics: Altered states of consciousness. In M.M. Gross (Ed.), *Alcohol intoxication and withdrawal.* New York: Plenum.

Patel, C., Marmot, M.G., Terry, D.J., Carruthers, M., Hunt, B., & Patel, M. (1985). Trial of relaxation in reducing coronary risk: Four year follow-up. *British Medical Journal, 290*, 1103–1106.

Pato, M.T., Zohar-Kadouch, R., Zohar, J., & Murphy, D.L. (1988). Return of symptoms after desensitization of clomipramine and patients with obsessive-compulsive disorder. *American Journal of Psychiatry, 145*, 1521–1525.

Patterson, G.R. (1974a). A basis for identifying stimuli which control behaviors in natural settings. *Child Development, 45*, 900–911.

Patterson, G.R. (1974b). Interventions for boys with conduct problems: Multiple settings, treatments, and criteria. *Journal of Consulting and Clinical Psychology, 42*, 471–481.

Patterson, G.R. (1982). *Coercive family process.* Eugene, OR: Castalia.

Patterson, G.R. (1986). Performance models for antisocial boys. *American Psychologist, 41*, 432–444.

Patterson, G.R., Cobb, J.A., & Ray, R.S. (1973). A social engineering technology for retraining families of aggressive boys. In H.E. Adams & I.P. Unikel (Eds.), *Issues and trends in behavior therapy.* Springfield, IL: Charles C. Thomas.

Patterson, G.R., Ray, R.S., Shaw, D.A., & Cobb, J.A. (1969). *Manual for coding of family interactions.* New York: ASIS/NAPS, Microfiche Publications.

Patterson, G.R., & Reid, J.B. (1970). Reciprocity and coercion: Two facets of social systems. In C. Neuringer & J. Michael (Eds.), *Behavior modification in clinical psychology.* New York: Appleton-Century-Crofts.

Paul, G.L. (1966). *Insight vs. desensitization in psychotherapy.* Stanford, CA: Stanford University Press.

Paul, G.L. (1967). Insight versus desensitization in psychotherapy two years after termination. *Journal of Consulting Psychology, 31*, 333–348.

Paul, G.L. (1969). Chronic mental patient: Current status-future directions. *Psychological Bulletin, 71*, 81–94.

Paul, G.L., & Lentz, R.J. (1977). *Psychosocial treatment of chronic mental patients: Milieu versus social learning programs.* Cambridge, MA: Harvard University Press.

Paul, G.L., & Menditto, A.A. (1992). Effectiveness of inpatient treatment programs for mentally ill adults in public psychiatric facilities. *Applied and Preventive Psychology: Current Scientific Perspectives, 1*, 41–63.

Paul, G.L., & Shannon, D.T. (1966). Treatment of anxiety through systematic desensitization in therapy groups. *Journal of Abnormal Psychology, 71*, 124–135.

Paul, R. (1987). *Communication.* In D.J. Cohen, A.M. Donnellan & R. Paul (Eds.), *Handbook of Autism and Pervasive Developmental Disorders* (pp. 61–84). New York: Wiley.

Paulauskas, S.L., & Campbell, S.B.G. (1979). Social perspective-taking and teacher ratings of peer interaction in hyperactive boys. *Journal of Abnormal Child Psychology, 7*, 483–493.

Pavlov, I.P. (1928). *Lectures on conditioned reflexes.* New York: International Publishers.

Paykel, E.S. (1979). Recent life events in the development of the depressive disorders. In R.A. Depue (Ed.), *The psychobiology of the depressive disorders.* New York: Academic Press.

Peachey, J.E. (1986). The role of drugs in the treatment of opioid addicts. *Medical Journal of Australia, 145*, 395–399.

Pearlin, L.I., Mullan, J.T., Semple, S.J., & Skaff, M.M. (1990). Caregiving and the stress process: An overview of concepts and their measures. *Gerentologist, 30*, 583–594.

Pearson, C., & Gatz, M. (1982). Health and mental health in older adults: First steps in the study of a pedestrian complaint. *Rehabilitation Psychology, 27*, 37–50.

Peck, E. (1974). The relationship of disease and other stress to second language. *International Journal of Social Psychiatry, 20*, 128–133.

Pedro-Carroll, J.L., & Cowen, E.L. (1985). The children of divorce intervention program: An investigation of the efficacy of a school-based prevention program. *Journal of Consulting and Clinical Psychology, 53*, 603–611.

Pedro-Carroll, J.L., Cowen, E.L., Hightower, A.D., & Guare, J.C. (1986). Preventive intervention with latency-aged children of divorce: A replication study. *American Journal of Community Psychology, 14*, 277–290.

Pelham, W.E., McBurnett, K., Harper, G.W., Milich, R., Murphy, D.A., Clinton, J., & Thiele, C. (1990). Methylphenidate and baseball playing in ADHD children: Who's on first? *Journal of Consulting and Clinical Psychology, 58*, 130–133.

Pendery, M.L., Maltzman, I.M., & West, L.J. (1982). Controlled drinking by alcoholics? New findings and a reevaluation of a major affirmative study. *Science, 217*, 169–175.

Pennebaker, J., Kiecolt-Glaser, J.K., & Glaser, R. (1988). Disclosure of traumas and immune function: Health implications for psychotherapy. *Journal of Consulting and Clinical Psychology, 56*, 239–245.

Pennington, B.F., & Smith, S.D. (1988). Genetic influences on learning disabilities: An update. *Journal of Consulting and Clinical Psychology, 56*, 817–823.

Pentoney, P. (1966). Value change in psychotherapy. *Human Relations, 19*, 39–46.

Perley, M.J., & Guze, S.B. (1962). Hysteria—The stability and useful ness of clinical criteria. *New England Journal of Medicine, 266*, 421–426.

Perls, F.S. (1947). *Ego, hunger, and aggression.* New York: Vintage.

Perls, F.S. (1969). *Gestalt therapy verbatim.* Moab, UT: Real People Press.

Perls, F.S. (1970). Four lectures. In J. Fagan & I.L. Shepherd (Eds.), *Gestalt therapy now: Therapy, techniques, applications.* Palo Alto, CA: Science and Behavior Books.

Perls, F.S., Hefferline, R.F., & Goodman, P. (1951). *Gestalt therapy: Excitement and growth in the human personality.* New York: Julian Press.

Perris, L. (1969). The separation of bipolar (manic-depressive) from unipolar recurrent depressive psychoses. *Behavioral Neuropsychiatry, 1*, 17–25.

Peters, J.J. (1977). The Philadelphia rape victim project. In D. Chappell, R. Geis, & G. Geis. (Eds.), *Forcible rape: The crime, the victim, and the offender.* New York: Columbia University Press.

Peters, M. (1977). Hypertension and the nature of stress. *Science, 198*, 80.

Peterson, C., & Seligman, M.E.P. (1984). Causal explanations as a risk factor for depression: Theory and evidence. *Psychological Review, 91*, 347–374.

Pfeiffer, E. (1977). Psychopathology and social pathology. In J.E. Birren & K.W. Schaie (Eds.), *Handbook of psychology and aging.* New York: Van Nostrand-Reinhold.

Pfeiffer, E., & Busse, E.W. (1973). Mental disorders in later life—Affective disorders: Paranoid, neurotic and situational reactions. In E.W. Busse & E. Pfeiffer (Eds.), *Mental illness in later life.* Washington, DC: American Psychiatric Association.

Pfeiffer, E., Eisenstein, R.B., & Dabbs, G.E. (1967). Mental competency evaluation for the federal courts: 1. Methods and results. *Journal of Nervous and Mental Disease, 144*, 320–328.

Pfeiffer, E., Verwoerdt, A., & Wang, H.S. (1968). Sexual behavior in aged men and women: I. Observations on 254 community volunteers. *Archives of General Psychiatry, 19*, 753–758.

Pfeiffer, E., Verwoerdt, A., & Wang, H.H. (1969). The natural history of sexual behavior in a biologically advantaged group of aged individuals. *Journal of Gerontology, 24*, 193–198.

Phares, E.J. (1992). *Clinical psychology: Concepts, methods, and profession* (4th ed.). Pacific Grove, CA: Brooks/Cole.

Phares, E.J. (1979). *Clinical psychology: Concepts, methods, and professions.* Homewood, Ill.: Dorsey Press.

Phelps, L., Wallace, D., & Waigant, A. (1989, August). *Impact of sexual assault: Post assault behavior and health status.* Paper presented at the annual convention of the American Psychological Association, New Orleans. As cited in Calhoun & Atkeson (1991).

Phillips, D.P. (1974). The influence of suggestion on suicide: Substantive and theoretical implications of the Werther effect. *American Sociological Review, 39*, 340–354.

Phillips, D.P. (1977). Motor vehicle fatalities increase just after publicized suicide stories. *Science, 196*, 1464–1465.

Phillips, D.P. (1985). The found experiment: A new technique for assessing impact of mass media violence on real-world aggressive behavior. In G. Comstock (Ed)., *Public communication and behavior* (Vol.1). New York: Academic Press.

Phillips, L. (1953). Case history data and prognosis in schizophrenia. *Journal of Nervous and Mental Disease, 117*, 515–525.

Phillips, R.D. (1985). Whistling in the dark? A review of play therapy research. *Psychotherapy, 22*, 752–760.

Pierce, C.M. (1980). Enuresis. In H.I. Kaplan, A.H. Friedman, & B.J. Sadock (Eds.), *Comprehensive textbook of psychiatry*, (3rd ed.). Baltimore: Williams & Wilkins.

Pierce, C.M. (1985). Enuresis. In H.I. Kaplan & B.J. Sadock (Eds.), *Comprehensive textbook of psychiatry* (4th ed.). Baltimore Williams & Wilkins.

Pigott, T.A., et al. (1990). Controlled comparison of clomipramine and fluoxetine in the treatment of obsessive-compulsive disorder. *Archives of General Psychiatry, 47*, 926–932.

Pilowsky, I. (1970). Primary and secondary hypochondriasis. *Acta Psychiatrica Scandinavica, 46*, 273–285.

Pinel, P. (1962). *A treatise on insanity, 1801.* English (D.D. Davis, Trans.). New York: Hafner.

Pinkston, E., & Linsk, N. (1984). Behavioral family intervention with the impaired elderly. *The Gerontologist, 24*, 576–583.

Pirsig, R.M. (1974). *Zen and the art of motor-*

cycle maintenance: An inquiry into values. New York: Morrow.

Pitman, R.K., et al. (1990). Psychophysiologic responses to combat imagery of Vietnam veterans with post-traumatic stress disorder vs. other anxiety disorders. *Journal of Abnormal Psychology, 99,* 49–54.

Plotkin, D.A., Mintz, J., & Jarvik, L.F. (1985). Subjective memory complaints in geriatric depression. *American Journal of Psychiatry, 142,* 1103–1105.

Pokorny, A.D. (1968). Myths about suicide. In H.L.P. Resnik (Ed.), *Suicidal behaviors.* Boston: Little, Brown.

Poland, R.E., Rubin, R.T., Lesser, I.M., Lane, L.A., & Hart, P.J. (1987). Neuroendocrine aspects of primary endogenous depression. *Archives of General Psychiatry, 44,* 790–796.

Pollard,C.A., Pollard, H.J., & Corn, K.J. (1989). Panic onset and major events in the lives of agoraphobics: A test of contiguity. *Journal of Abnormal Psychology, 98,* 318–321.

Pope, H.G., & Hudson, J.I. (1984). *New hope for binge eaters: Advances in the understanding and treatment of bulimia.* New York: Harper & Row.

Pope, H.G., Jonas, J.M., Hudson, J.I., Cohen, B.M., & Gunderson, J.G. (1983). The validity of DSM-III borderline personality disorder. *Archives of General Psychiatry, 40,* 23–30.

Posner, M.I. (1988). Structures and functions of selective attention. In T. Boll & B. Bryant (Eds.), *Master lectures in clinical neuropsychology* (pp. 173–202). Washington, DC: American Psychological Association.

Post, F. (1975). Dementia, depression, and pseudodementia. In D.F. Benson & D. Blumer (Eds.), *Psychiatric aspects of neurologic disease.* New York: Grune & Stratton.

Post, F. (1978). The functional psychosis. In A.D. Isaacs & F. Post (Eds.), *Studies in geriatric psychiatry.* Chichester, England: Wiley.

Post, F. (1980). Paranoid, schizophrenia-like and schizophrenic states in the aged. In J.E. Birren & R.B. Sloane (Eds.), *Handbook of mental health and aging.* Englewood Cliffs, NJ: Prentice-Hall.

Post, F. (1987). Paranoid and schizophrenic disorders among the aging. In L.L. Carstensen & B.A. Edelstein (Eds.), *Handbook of clinical gerontology.* New York: Pergamon.

Poster, D.S., Penta, J.S., Bruno, S., & Macdonald, J.S. (1981). Delta 9-tetrahydrocannabinol in clinical oncology. *Journal of the American Medical Association, 245,* 2047–2051.

Potashnik, S., & Pruchno, R. (1988, November). *Spouse caregivers: Physical and mental health in perspective.* Paper presented at the meeting of the Gerontological Society of America, San Francisco.

Powell, L.H., Friedman, M., Thoresen, C.E., Gill, J.J., & Ulmer, D.K. (1984). Can the type A behavior pattern be altered after myocardial infarction? A second year report from the Recurrent Coronary Prevention Project. *Psychosomatic Medicine, 46,* 293–313.

Praderas, K., & MacDonald, M.L. (1986). Telephone conversational skills training with socially isolated impaired nursing home residents. *Journal of Applied Behavior Analysis, 19,* 337–348.

Premack, D. (1959). Toward empirical behavior laws: I. Positive reinforcement. *Psychological Review, 66,* 219–233.

President's Commission on Mental Health (1978). *Report to the President.* Washington, DC: Superintendent of Documents, U.S. Government Printing Office.

Price, L.H., Charney, D.S., Rubin, A.L., & Heninger, G.R. (1986). Alpha-2 adrenergic receptor function in depression. *Archives of General Psychiatry, 43,* 849–860.

Price, V.A. (1982). *Type A behavior pattern: A model for research and practice.* New York: Academic Press.

Prieto, S.L., Cole D.A., & Tageson, C.W. (1992). Depressive self-schemas in clinic and nonclinic children. *Cognitive Therapy & Research, 16,* 521–534.

Prinz, P., & Raskind, M. (1978). Aging and sleep disorders. In R. Williams & R. Karacan (Eds.), *Sleep disorders: Diagnosis and treatment.* New York: Wiley.

Prioleau, L., Murdock, M., & Brody, N. (1983). An analysis of psychotherapy versus placebo studies. *The Behavioral and Brain Sciences, 6,* 275–310.

Prochaska, J.O. (1984). *Systems of psychotherapy* (2nd ed.). Homewood, Ill: Dorsey Press.

Proctor, J.T. (1958). Hysteria in childhood. *American Journal of Orthopsychiatry, 28,* 394–407.

Psychosocial intervention and the natural history of cancer [Editorial]. (1989). *Lancet, 2,* 901–902.

Pu, T., Mohamed, E., Imam, K., & El-Roey, A.M. (1986). One hundred cases of hysteria in eastern Libya. *British Journal of Psychiatry, 148,* 606–609.

Puig-Antich, J. (1982). Major depression and conduct disorder in prepuberty. *Journal of the American Academy of Child and Adolescent Psychiatry, 21,* 118–128.

Puig-Antich, J., Lukens, E., Davies, M., Goetz, D., Brennan-Quattrock, J., & Todak, G. (1985). Psychosocial functioning in prepubertal major depressive disorders: 1. Interpersonal relationships during the depressive episode. *Archives of General Psychiatry, 42,* 500–507.

Puig-Antich, J., Perel, J.M., Lupatkin, W., Chambers, W.J., Tabrizi, M.A., King, J., Goetz, R., Davies, M., & Stiller, R.L. (1987). Imipramine in prepubertal major depressive disorders. *Archives of General Psychiatry, 44,* 81–89.

Puig-Antich, J., & Rabinovich, H. (1986). Relationship between affective and anxiety disorders in childhood. In R.G. Helman (Ed.), *Anxiety disorders of childhood.* New York: Guilford Press.

Purcell, K., & Weiss, J.H. (1970). Asthma. In C.G. Costello (Ed.), *Symptoms of psychopathology: A handbook.* New York: Wiley.

Purdie, F.R., Honigman, T.B., & Rosen, P. (1981). Acute organic brain syndrome: A view of 100 cases. *Annals of Emergency Medicine, 10,* 455–461.

Purpura, D.P. (1976). Discussants' comments. In T.D. Tjossem (Ed.), *Intervention strategies for high risk infants and young children.* Baltimore: University Park Press.

Putnam, F.W., Guroff, J.J., Silberman, E.K., Barban, L., & Post, R.M. (1986). The clinical phenomenology of multiple personality disorder: Review of 100 recent cases. *Journal of Clinical Psychiatry, 47,* 285–293.

Putnam, F.W., Post, R.M., & Guroff, J.J. (1983). *100 cases of multiple personality disorder.* Paper presented at the annual meeting of the American Psychiatric Association, New York.

Putnam, F.W., Zahn, T.P., & Post, R.M. (1990). Differential autonomic nervous system activity in multiple personality disorder. *Psychiatry Research, 31,* 251–260.

Quay, H.C. (1965). Psychopathic personality as pathological stimulus seeking. *American Journal of Psychiatry, 122,* 180–183.

Quay, H.C. (1964). Personality dimensions in delinquent males as inferred from the factor analysis of behavior ratings. *Journal of Research in Crime and Delinquency, 1,* 33–37.

Quay, H.C. (1979). Classification. In H.C. Quay & J.S. Werry (Eds.), *Psychopathological disorders of childhood* (2nd ed.). New York: Wiley.

Quay, H.C. (1986). Conduct disorders. In H.C. Quay & J.S. Werry (Eds.), *Psychopathological disorders of childhood* (3rd ed.). New York: Wiley.

Quay, H.C., & Parskeuopoulos, I.N. (1972, August). *Dimensions of problem behavior in elementary school children in Greece, Iran, and Finland.* Paper presented at the 20th International Congress of Psychology, Tokyo.

Quinsey, V.L., & Chaplin, T.C. (1982). Penile responses to nonsexual violence among rapists. *Criminal Justice and Behavior, 9,* 372–384.

Rabavilas, A., & Boulougouris, J. (1974). Physiological accompaniments of ruminations, flooding and thought-stopping in obsessional patients. *Behaviour Research and Therapy, 12,* 239–244.

Rabins, P.V., & Folstein, M.F. (1982). Delirium and dementia: Diagnostic criteria and fatality rates. *British Journal of Psychiatry, 140,* 149–153.

Rabkin, J.G. (1974). Public attitudes toward mental illness: A review of the literature. *Schizophrenia Bulletin,* 9–33.

Rachman, S.J. (1966). Sexual fetishism: An experimental analogue. *Psychological Record, 16,* 293–296.

Rachman, S.J., & Hodgson, R.J. (1980). *Obsessions and compulsions.* Englewood Cliffs, NJ: Prentice-Hall.

Rachman, S.J., & Wilson, G.T. (1980). *The effects of psychological therapy* (2nd ed.). Elmsford, NY: Pergamon.

Radloff, L. (1975). Sex differences in depression: The effects of occupation and marital status. *Sex Roles, 1,* 249–265.

Ragland, D.R., & Brand, R.J. (1988). Type A behavior and mortality from coronary heart disease. *The New England Journal of Medicine, 318,* 65–69.

Rahe, R.H., & Lind, E. (1971). Psychosocial factors and sudden cardiac death: A pilot study. *Journal of Psychosomatic Research, 15,* 19–24.

Raine, A., O'Brien, M., Chan, C.J., et al. (1990). Reward learning in adolescent psychopaths. *Journal of Abnormal Child Psychology, 18,* 451–463.

Rapaport, D. (1951). *The organization and pathology of thought.* New York: Columbia University Press.

Rapaport, K., & Burkhart, B.R. (1984). Personality and attitudinal characteristics of sexually coercive college males. *Journal of Abnormal Psychology, 93,* 216–221.

Rapee, R.M. (1991). Generalized anxiety disorder: A review of clinical features and theoretical concepts. *Clinical Psychology Review, 11,* 419–440.

Rapoport, J.L., Buchsbaum, M.S., Zahn, T.P., Weingartner, H., Ludlow, D., & Mikkelson, E.J. (1978). Dextroamphetamine: Cognitive and behavioral effects in normal prepubertal boys. *Science, 199,* 560–563.

Rapp, S.R., Parisi, S.A., & Walsh, D.A. (1988). Psychological dysfunction and physical health among elderly medical inpatients. *Journal of Consulting and Clinical Psychology, 56,* 851–855.

Rapp, S.R., Parisi, S.A., Walsh, D.A., & Wallace, C.E. (1988). Detecting depression in elderly medical impatients. *Journal of Consulting and Clinical Psychology, 56,* 509–513.

Rappaport, J. (1977). *Community psychology: Values, research, and action.* New York: Holt, Rinehart & Winston.

Rappaport, J. (1981). In praise of paradox: A social policy of empowerment over prevention. *American Journal of Community Psychology, 9,* 1–25.

Rappaport, J., & Chinsky, J.M. (1974). Models for delivery of service from a historical and conceptual perspective. *Professional Psychology, 5,* 42–50.

Raskin, F., & Rae, D.S. (1981). Psychiatric symptoms in the elderly. *Psychopharmacology Bulletin, 17,* 96–99.

Rather, B.C., Goldman, M.S., Roehrich,L., & Brannick, M. (1992). Empirical modeling of an alcohol expectancy memory network using multidimensional scaling. *Journal of Abnormal Psychology, 101,* 174–183.

Raymond, J., Rhoads, D., & Raymond, R. (1980). The relative impact of family and social involvement on Chicano mental health. *American Journal of Community Psychology, 5,* 557–569.

Raymond, J.G. (1979). *The transsexual empire: The making of the she-male.* Boston: Beacon.

Redfield, J., & Stone, A.A. (1979). Individual viewpoints of stressful life events. *Journal of Consulting and Clinical Psychology, 47,* 147–154.

Redfield, P.R., Wright, D.G., & Tramont, E.C. (1986). The Walter Reed staging classification for HTLV III/LAV infection. *New England Journal of Medicine, 314,* 131–132.

Red Horse, Y. (1982). A cultural network model: Perspectives for adolescent services and paraprofessional training. In S. Manson (Ed.), *New directions in prevention among American Indians and Alaskan Native communities.* Portland: Oregon Health Sciences University.

Redick, R.W., & Taube, C.A. (1980). Demography and mental health care of the aged. In J.E. Birren & R.B. Sloane (Eds.), *Handbook of mental health and aging.* Englewood Cliffs, NJ: Prentice-Hall.

Redmond, D.E. (1977). Alterations in the function of the nucleus locus coeruleus. In I. Hanin & E. Usdin (Eds.), *Animal models in psychiatry and neurology.* New York: Pergamon.

Reed, D., McGhee, D., Yano, K., & Feinleib, M. (1983). Social networks and coronary heart disease among Japanese men in Hawaii. *American Journal of Epidemiology, 119,* 356–370.

Reed, S.D., Katkin, E.S., & Goldband, S. (1986). Biofeedback and behavioral medicine. In F.H. Kanfer & A.P. Goldstein (Eds.), *Helping people change: A textbook of methods* (3rd ed.). Elmsford, NY: Pergamon.

Rees, L. (1964). The importance of psychological, allergic and infective factors in childhood asthma. *Journal of Psychosomatic Research, 7,* 253–262.

Regier, D.A., Boyd, J.H., Burke, J.D., Jr., Rae, D.S., Myers, J.K., Kramer, M., Robins, L.N., George, L.K., Karno, M., & Locke, B.Z. (1988). One-month prevalence of mental disorders in the United States. *Archives of General Psychiatry, 45,* 977–1986.

Rehm, L.P., Kaslow, N.J., & Rabin, A.S. (1987). Cognitive and behavioral targets in a self-control therapy program for depression. *Journal of Consulting and Clinical Psychology, 55,* 60–67.

Reich, J. (1987). Sex distribution of DSM-III personality disorders in psychiatric outpatients. *American Journal of Psychiatry, 144,* 485–488.

Reich, J. (1990). Comparison of males and females with DSM-III dependent personality disorder. *Psychiatry Research, 33,* 207–214.

Reid, E.C. (1910). Autopsychology of the manic-depressive. *Journal of Nervous and Mental Disease, 37,* 606–620.

Reifler, B.V., Larson, E., & Hanley, R. (1982). Coexistence of cognitive impairment and depression in geriatric outpatients. *American Journal of Psychiatry, 139,* 623–626.

Reiss, I.L., & Leik, R.K. (1989). Evaluating strategies to avoid AIDS: Number of partners vs. use of condoms. *The Journal of Sex Research, 26,* 411–433.

Rekers, G.A., & Lovaas, 0.I. (1974). Behavioral treatment of deviant sex role behaviors in a male child. *Journal of Applied Behavioral Analysis, 7,* 173–190.

Renshaw, D.C. (1988). Profile of 2376 patients treated at Loyola Sex Clinic between 1972 and 1987. *Sexual and Marital Therapy, 3,* 111–117.

Renvoize, E.B., & Beveridge, A.W. (1989). Mental illness and the late Victorians: A study of patients admitted to three asylums in York, 1880–1884. *Psychological Medicine, 19,* 19–28.

Reppucci, N.D. (1987). Prevention and ecology: Teen-age pregnancy, child sexual abuse, and organized youth sports. *American Journal of Community Psychology, 15,* 1–22.

Rescorla, R.A., & Solomon, R.L. (1967). Two-process learning theory: Relationships between Pavlovian conditioning and instrumental learning. *Psychological Review, 74,* 151–182.

Resick, P.A., Veronen, L.J., Calhoun, K.S., Kilpatrick, D.G., & Atkeson, B.M. (1986). Assessment of fear reactions in sexual assault victims: A factor-analytic study of the Veronen–Kilpatrick Modified Fear Survey. *Behavioral Assessment, 8,* 271–283.

Resnik, H.L.P. (Ed.). (1968). *Suicidal behaviors.* Boston: Little, Brown.

Review Panel on Coronary-Prone Behavior and Coronary Heart Disease (1981). Coronary-prone behavior and coronary heart disease: A critical review. *Circulation, 63,* 1199–1215.

Riccio, D., Richardson, R., & Ebner, D. (1984). Memory retrieval deficits based upon altered contextual cues: A paradox. *Psychological Bulletin, 96,* 152–165.

Rice, J., Reich, T., Andreasen, N.N., Endicott, J., Eerdewegh, M. Van, Fishman, R., Hirschfeld, R.M.A., & Klerman, G.L. (1987). The familial transmission of bipolar illness. *Archives of General Psychiatry, 44,* 451–460.

Richards, P., Berk, R.A., & Forster, B. (1979). *Crime as play—Delinquency in a middle class suburb.* Cambridge, MA: Ballinger.

Richardson, S.A., Katz, M., & Koller, H. (1986). Sex differences in number of children administratively classified as mildly mentally retarded: An epidemiological review. *American Journal of Mental Deficiency, 91,* 250–256.

Richardson, J.L., Dwyer, K.M., McGuigan, K., Hansen, W.B., Dent, C.W., Johnson, C.A., Sussman, S.Y., Brannon, B., & Flay, B. (1989). Substance use among eighth grade students who take care of themselves after school. *Pediatrics, 84,* 556–566.

Richter, C.P. (1957). On the phenomenon of sudden death in animals and man. *Psychosomatic Medicine, 19,* 191–198.

Ricks, D.M. (1972). *The beginning of vocal communication in infants and autistic children.* Unpublished doctoral dissertation. University of London.

Ridley, C.R. (1984). Clinical treatment of the nondisclosing black client. *American Psychologist, 39,* 1234–1244.

Rieder, R.O., Mann, L.S., Weinberger, D.R., Kammen, D.P. van, & Post, R.M. (1983). Computer tomographic scans in patients with schizophrenia, schizoaffective, and bipolar affective disorder. *Archives of General Psychiatry, 40,* 735–739.

Riessman, F. (1985). New dimensions in self-help. *Social Policy, 15,* 2–5.

Riggs, D. et al. (1991). Post-traumatic stress disorder following rape and nonsexual assault: A predictive model. Unpublished manuscript.

Rimland, B. (1964). *Infantile autism.* New York: Appleton-Century-Crofts.

Ritter, B. (1968). The group treatment of children's snake phobias, using vicarious and contact desensitization procedures. *Behaviour Research and Therapy, 6,* 1–6.

Rittig, S., Knudsen, U.B., Norgaard, J.P., Pedersen, E.B., & Djurhuus, J.C. (1989). Abnormal diurnal rhythm of plasma vasopressin and urinary output in patients with enuresis. *American Journal of Physiology, 256,* 664–671.

Ritvo, E.R., Freeman, B.J., Geller, E., & Yuwiler, A. (1983). Effects of fenfluramine on 14 outpatients with the syndrome of autism. *Journal of the American Academy of Child Psychiatry, 22,* 549–558.

Ritvo, E.R., Yuwiler, A., Geller, E., Ornitz, E.M., Saeger, K., & Plotkin, S. (1970). Increased blood serotonin and platelets in early infantile autism. *Archives of General Psychiatry, 23,* 556–572.

Roan, S. (1992, October 15). Giving up coffee tied to withdrawal symptoms. *Los Angeles Times,* p. A26.

Roberts, M.C., Wurtele, S.K., Boone, R.R., Ginther, L.J., & Elkins, P.D. (1981). Reduction of medical fears by use of modeling: A preventive application in a general population of children. *Journal of Pediatric Psychology, 6,* 293–300.

Robins, C.J., Block, P., & Peselow, E.D. (1989). Relations of sociotropic and autonomous personality characteristics to specific symptoms in depressed patients. *Journal of Abnormal Psychology, 98,* 86–88.

Robins, L.N. (1966). *Deviant children grown up.* Baltimore: Williams & Wilkins.

Robins, L.N. (1972). Follow-up studies of behavior disorders in children. In H.C. Quay & J.S. Werry (Eds.), *Psychopathological disorders of childhood.* New York: Wiley.

Robins, L.N. (1978). Sturdy childhood predictors of adult antisocial behavior: Replications from longitudinal studies. *Psychological Medicine, 8,* 611–622.

Robins, L.N., Helzer, J.E., Croughan, J., & Ratliff, K.S. (1981). National Institute of Mental Health: Diagnostic Interview Schedule. *Archives of General Psychiatry, 38,* 381–389.

Robins, L.N., Helzer, J.E., Przybec, T.R., & Regier, D.A. (1988). Alcohol disorders in the community: A report from the Epidemiologic Catchment Area. In R.M. Rose & J.E. Barrett (Eds.), *Alcoholism: Origins and Outcome.* NY: Raven, 1988.

Robins, L.N., Helzer, J.E., Weissman, M.M., Orvaschel, H., Gruenberg, E., Burke, J.D., & Reiger, D.A. (1984). Lifetime prevalence of specific psychiatric disorders in three sites. *Archives of General Psychiatry, 41,* 942–949.

Robinson, N.M., & Robinson, H.B. (1976). *The mentally retarded child* (2nd ed.). New York: McGraw-Hill.

Rodin, J. (1980). Managing the stress of aging: The control of control and coping. In H. Ursin & S. Levine (Eds.), *Coping and Health.* New York: Academic Press.

Rodin, J. (1983). Behavioral medicine: Beneficial effects of self-control training in aging. *International Review of Applied Psychology, 32,* 153–181.

Rodin, J. (1986). Aging and health: Effects of the sense of control. *Science, 233,* 1271–1276.

Rodin, J. & Ickovics, J.R. (1990). Women's health: Review and research agenda as we approach the 21st century. *American Psychologist, 45,* 1018–1034.

Rodin, J., & Langer, E.J. (1977). Long-term effects of a control-relevant intervention with the institutionalized aged. *Journal of Personality and Social Psychology, 35,* 897–902.

Rodin, J., McAvay, G., & Timko, C. (1988). A longitudinal study of depressed mood and sleep disturbances in elderly adults. *Journal of Gerontology: Psychological Sciences, 43,* 45–53.

Roesch, R., & Golding, S.L. (1980). *Competency to stand trial.* Urbana: University of Illinois Press.

Rogers, C.R. (1942). *Counseling and psychotherapy: New concepts in practice.* Boston: Houghton Mifflin.

Rogers, C.R. (1951). *Client-centered therapy.* Boston: Houghton Mifflin.

Rogers, C.R. (1961). *On becoming a person: A therapist's view of psychotherapy.* Boston: Houghton Mifflin.

Rogers, C.R. (1970). *Carl Rogers on encounter groups.* New York: Harper & Row.

Rogers, C.R., Gendlin, G.T., Kiesler, D.V., & Truax, C.B. (1967). *The therapeutic relationship and its impact: A study of psychotherapy with schizophrenics.* Madison: University of Wisconsin Press.

Rogler, L.H., & Hollingshead, A.B. (1985). *Trapped: Families and schizophrenia* (3rd ed.). Maplewood, NJ: Waterfront Press.

Rohde, P., Lewinsohn,P.M., & Seeley, J.R. (1991). Comorbidity of unipolar depression: II Comorbidity with other mental disorders in adolescents and adults. *Journal of Abnormal Psychology, 100,* 214–222.

Rokeach, M. (1973). *The nature of human values.* New York: Free Press.

Rokeach, M. (1979). Some unresolved issues in theories of beliefs, attitudes, and values. *Proceedings of the Nebraska Symposium on Motivation.* Lincoln: University of Nebraska Press.

Romanczyk, R.G., Diament, C., Goren, E.R., Trundeff, G., & Harris, S.L. (1975). Increasing isolate and social play in severely disturbed children: Intervention and postintervention effectiveness. *Journal of Autism and Childhood Schizophrenia, 43,* 730–739.

Romanczyk, R.G., Kent, R.N., Diament, C., & O'Leary, K.D. (1973). Measuring the reliability of observational data: A reactive process. *Journal of Applied Behavior Analysis, 6,* 175–184.

Romero, D. (1992, March 7). Two drugs crash the party scene. *Los Angeles Times,* pp. A1, A22–23.

Ronningstam, E. & Gunderson, J.G. (1990). Identifying criteria for narcissistic personality disorder. *American Journal of Psychiatry, 147*, 918–922.

Rooth, F.G. (1973). Exhibitionism, sexual violence, and pedophilia. *British Journal of Psychiatry, 122*, 705–710.

Rose, S.D. (1986). Group methods. In F.H. Kanfer & A.P. Goldstein (Eds.), *Helping people change: A textbook of methods* (3rd ed.). Elmsford, NY: Pergamon.

Rosen, E., Fox, R., & Gregory, I. (1972). *Abnormal psychology* (2nd ed.). Philadelphia: Saunders.

Rosen, J., & Bohon, S. (1990). Pharmacotherapy. In A.S. Bellack & M. Hersen (Eds.), *Handbook of comparative treatments for adult disorders* (pp. 316–326). New York: Wiley.

Rosen, J.C., & Leitenberg, H.C. (1985). Exposure plus response prevention treatment of bulimia. In D.M. Garner & P.E. Garfinkel (Eds.), *Handbook of psychotherapy for anorexia nervosa and bulimia.* New York: Guilford.

Rosen, J.N. (1964). A method of resolving acute catatonic excitement. *Psychiatric quarterly, 20*, 183–198.

Rosen, R.C., & Beck, J.G. (1988). *Patterns of sexual arousal: Psychophysiological processes and clinical applications.* New York: Guilford.

Rosen, R.C., & Hall, E. (1984). *Sexuality.* New York: Random House.

Rosen, R.C., & Rosen, L. (1981). *Human sexuality.* New York: Knopf.

Rosenbaum, M. (1980). The role of the term schizophrenia in the decline of diagnoses of multiple personality. *Archives of General Psychiatry, 37*, 1383–1385.

Rosenbaum, M. (1980). A schedule for assessing self-control behaviors: Preliminary findings. *Behavior Therapy, 11*, 109–121.

Rosenberg, M.S., & Reppucci, N.D. (1985). Primary prevention of child abuse. *Journal of Consulting and Clinical Psychology, 53*, 576–585.

Rosenblatt, R.A., & Spiegel, C. (1988, December 2). Half of state's nursing homes fall short in federal study. *Los Angeles Times*, pp. 3, 34.

Rosenman, R.H., Brand, R.J., Jenkins, C.D., Friedman, M., Straus, R., & Wurm, M. (1975). Coronary heart disease in the Western Collaborative Group Study: Final follow-up experience of $8\frac{1}{2}$ years. *Journal of the American Medical Association, 233*, 872–877.

Rosenman, R.H., Friedman, M., Straus, R., Wurm, M., Kositichek, R., Hahn, W., & Werthessen, N.T. (1964). A predictive study of coronary heart disease. *Journal of the American Medical Association, 189*, 103–110.

Rosenthal, D. (1955). Changes in some moral values following psychotherapy. *Journal of Consulting Psychology, 19*, 431–436.

Rosenthal, D. (1970). *Genetic theory and abnormal behavior.* New York: McGraw-Hill.

Rosenthal, N.E., Carpenter, C.J., James, S.P., Parry, B.L., Rogers, S.L.B., & Wehr, T.A. (1986). Seasonal affective disorder in children and adolescents. *American Journal of Psychiatry, 143*, 356–358.

Rosenthal, N.E., Sack, D.A., Carpenter, C.J., Parry, B.L., Mendelson, W.B., & Wehr, T.A. (1985). Antidepressant effects of light in seasonal affective disorder. *American Journal of Psychiatry, 142*, 163–170.

Rosenthal, R. (1966). *Experimenter bias in behavioral research.* New York: Appleton-Century-Crofts.

Rosenthal, T.L., & Bandura, A. (1978). Psychological modeling: Theory and practice. In S.L. Garfield & A.E. Bergin (Eds.), *Handbook of psychotherapy and behavior change: An empirical analysis* (2nd ed.). New York: Wiley.

Rosin, A.J., & Glatt, M.M. (1971). Alcohol excess in the elderly. *Quarterly Journal of Studies on Alcoholism, 32*, 53–59.

Rosman, B.L., Minuchin, S., & Liebman, R. (1975). Family lunch session: An introduction to family therapy in anorexia nervosa. *American Journal of Orthopsychiatry, 45*, 846–852.

Rosman, B.L., Minuchin, S., & Liebman, R. (1976). Input and outcome of family therapy of anorexia nervosa. In J.L. Claghorn (Ed.), *Successful psychotherapy.* New York: Brunner/Mazel.

Ross, A.O. (1981). *Psychological disorders of childhood: A behavioral approach to theory, research, and practice* (2nd ed.). New York: McGraw-Hill.

Ross, C.A. (1989). *Multiple personality disorder: Diagnosis, clinical features, and treatment.* New York: Wiley.

Ross, C.A. (1991). Epidemiology of multiple personality disorder and dissociation. *Psychiatric Clinics of North America*, 14, 503–517.

Ross, C.A., Miller, S.D., Reagor, P., et al. (1990). Structured interview data on 102 cases of multiple personality from four centers. *American Journal of Psychiatry, 147*, 596–600.

Ross, C.E., & Huber, J. (1985). Hardship and depression. *Journal of Health and Social Behavior, 75*, 668–670.

Ross, D.M., & Ross, S.A. (1973). Storage and utilization of previously formulated mediators in educable mentally retarded children. *Journal of Educational Psychology, 65*, 205–210.

Ross, D.M., & Ross, S.A. (1976). *Hyperactivity: Research, theory, and action.* New York: Wiley.

Ross, D.M., & Ross, S.A. (1982). *Hyperactivity: Research, theory, and action.* New York: Wiley.

Ross, J.L. (1977). Anorexia nervosa: An overview. *Bulletin of the Menninger Clinic, 41*, 418–436.

Rossiter, E.M., & Wilson, G.T. (1985). Cognitive restructuring and response prevention in the treatment of bulimia nervosa. *Behaviour Research and Therapy, 23*, 349–359.

Roth, D., & Rehm, L.P. (1980). Relationships among self-monitoring processes, memory, and depression. *Cognitive Therapy and Research, 4*, 149–157.

Roth, M. (1955). The natural history of mental disorder in old age. *Journal of Mental Science, 99*, 439–450.

Roth, M., & Kay, D.W.K. (1956). Affective disorder arising in the senium: II. Physical disability as an etiological factor. *Journal of Mental Science, 102*, 141–150.

Roth, S., & Kubal, L. (1975). The effects of noncontingent reinforcement on tasks of differing importance: Facilitation and learned helplessness effects. *Journal of Personality and Social Psychology, 32*, 680–691.

Rothbaum, B.O., & Foa, E.B. (1992). Exposure therapy for rape victims with post-traumatic stress disorder. *the Behavior Therapist, 15*, 219–222.

Rothbaum, B.O., & Foa, E.B. (in press). Cognitive-behavioral treatment of post-traumatic stress disorder. In P.A. Saigh (Ed.), *Posttraumatic stress disorder: A behavioral approach to assessment and treatment.* New York: Pergamon.

Rothbaum, B.O., et al. (in press). A prospective examination of post-traumatic stress disorder in rape victims. *Journal of Traumatic Stress.*

Rounsaville, B.J., Chevron, E.S., & Weissman, M.M. (1984). Specification of techniques in Interpersonal Psychotherapy. In J.B.W. Williams & R.L. Spitzer (Eds.), *Psychotherapy research: Where are we and where should we go?* New York: Guilford.

Rovner, B.W., Kafonek, S., Filipp, L., Lucas, M.J., & Folstein, M.F. (1986). Prevalence of mental illness in a community nursing home. *American Journal of Psychiatry, 143*, 1446–1449.

Roy, A. (1982). Suicide in chronic schizophrenics. *British Journal of Psychiatry, 141*, 171–177.

Roy, A., et al. (1991). Mental disorders among alcoholics: Relationship to age of onset and cerebrospinal fluid neuropeptides. *Archives of General Psychiatry, 48*, 423–427.

Roy, A., Everett, D., Pickar, D., & Paul, S.M. (1987). Platelet tritiated imipramine binding and serotonin uptake in depressed patients. *Archives of General Psychiatry, 44,* 320–327.

Roybal, E.R. (1988). Mental health and aging: The need for an expanded federal response. *American Psychologist, 43,* 189–194.

Ruberman, W., Weinblatt, E., Goldberg, J.D., & Chaudhary, B.S. (1984). Psychosocial influences on mortality after myocardial infarction. *New England Journal of Medicine, 311,* 552–559.

Ruch, L.O., & Leon, J.J. (1983). Sexual assault trauma and trauma change. *Women and Health, 8,* 5–21.

Runck, B. (1980). *Biofeedback—Issues in treatment assessment.* Rockville, MD: National Institute of Mental Health.

Runck, B. (1982). *Behavioral self-control: Issues in treatment assessment.* Rockville, MD: National Institute of Mental Health.

Runt, M.A.H., Merriman, R., Stapleton, J., & Taylor, W. (1983). Effect of nicotine chewing gum as an adjunct to general practitioners' advice against smoking. *British Medical Journal, 287,* 1782–1785.

Rush, A.J., Beck, A.T., Kovacs, M., & Hollon, S.D. (1977). Comparative efficacy of cognitive therapy and pharmacotherapy in the treatment of depressed outpatients. *Cognitive Therapy and Research, 1,* 17–39.

Rush, A.J., Beck, A.T., Kovacs, M., Weissenberger, J., & Hollon, S.D. (1982). Comparison of the effects of cognitive therapy on hopelessness and self-concept. *American Journal of Psychiatry, 139,* 862–866.

Russell, D.E.H. (1982). *Rape in marriage.* New York: Macmillan.

Russell, M.A.H., Feyeranbend, C., & Cole, P.V. (1976). Plasma nicotine levels after cigarette smoking and chewing nicotine gum. *British Medical Journal, 1,* 1043–1046.

Russo, D.C., & Varni, J.W. (1982). Behavioral pediatrics. In D.C. Russo & J.W. Varni (Eds.), *Behavioral pediatrics: Research and practice.* New York: Plenum.

Rutter, M. (1967). Psychotic disorders in early childhood. In A.J. Cooper (Ed.), Recent developments in schizophrenia. [Special Publication] *British Journal of Psychiatry.*

Rutter, M. (1971). Parent–child separation: Psychological effects on the children. *Journal of Child Psychology and Psychiatry, 12,* 233–260.

Rutter, M. (1979). Maternal deprivation, 1972–1978: New findings, new concepts, new approaches. *Child Development, 50,* 283–305.

Rutter, M. & Schopler, E. (1987). Autism and pervasive developmental disorders: Concepts and diagnostic issues. *Journal of Autism and Developmental Disorders, 17,* 159–186.

Rutter, M., Tizard, J., & Whitmore, K. (1970). *Education, health, and behavior.* London: Longmans.

Ryall, R. (1974). Delinquency: The problem for treatment. *Social Work Today, 15,* 98–104.

Ryan, G., Lane, S., Davis, J., & Isaac, C. (1987). Juvenile sex offenders: Development and correction. *Child Abuse and Neglect, 11,* 385–395.

Ryan, W. (1971). *Blaming the victim.* New York: Random House.

Rybstein-Blinchik, E. (1979). Effects of different cognitive strategies on chronic pain experience. *Journal of Behavioral Medicine, 2,* 93–101.

Sabin, J.E. (1975). Translating despair. *American Journal of Psychiatry, 132,* 197–199.

Sachs, J.S. (1983). Negative factors in brief psychotherapy: An empirical assessment. *Journal of Consulting and Clinical Psychology, 51,* 557–564.

Sackeim, H.A., Nordlie, J.W., & Gur, R.C. (1979). A model of hysterical and hypnotic blindness: Cognition, motivation and awareness. *Journal of Abnormal Psychology, 88,* 474–489.

Sacks, O. (1985). The twins. In *The man who mistook his wife for a hat and other clinical tales.* New York: Harper & Row.

Safer, D.J., & Krager, J.M. (1983). Trends in medication treatment of hyperactive school children. *Clinical Pediatrics, 22,* 500–504.

Safran, J.D., Vallis, T.M., Segal, Z.V., & Shaw, B.F. (1986). Assessment of core cognitive processes in cognitive therapy. *Cognitive Therapy and Research, 10,* 509–526.

Sager, C.J. (1990). Foreword. In I.L. Kutash & A. Wolf (Eds.), *The group psychotherapist's handbook: Contemporary theory and technique.* New York: Columbia University Press.

Sakel, M. (1938). The pharmacological shock treatment of schizophrenia. *Nervous and Mental Disease Monograph,* 62.

Salan, S.E., Zinberg, N.E., & Frei, E. (1975). Antiemetic effect of delta-9-THC in patients receiving cancer chemotherapy. *New England Journal of Medicine, 293,* 795–797.

Salovey, P., & Singer, J.A. (1991). Cognitive behavior modification. In F.H. Kanfer & A.P. Goldstein (Eds.), *Helping people change: A textbook of methods* (4th ed.), Elmsford, NY: Pergamon.

Salter, A. (1949). *Conditioned reflex therapy.* New York: Farrar, Straus.

Salzman, L. (1980). *Psychotherapy of the obsessive personality.* New York: Jason Aronson.

Salzman, L. (1985). Psychotherapeutic management of obsessive-compulsive patients. *American Journal of Psychotherapy, 39,* 323–330.

Salzman, L., & Thaler, F.H. (1981). Obsessive-compulsive disorders: A review of the literature. *American Journal of Psychiatry, 138,* 286–296.

Sanchez-Craig, M., & Wilkinson, D.A. (1987). Treating problem drinkers who are not severely dependent on alcohol. *Drugs and Society, 1,* 39–67.

Sanday, P.R. (1981). The socio-cultural context of rape: A cross- cultural study. *The Journal of Social Issues, 37,* 5–27.

Sanderson, W.C., Rapee, R.M., & Barlow, D.H. (1989). The influence of an illusion of control on panic attacks induced via inhalation of 5.5% carbon dioxide-enriched air. *Archives of General Psychiatry, 46,* 157–162.

Sanderson, W.C., et al. (1990). Syndrome comorbidity in patients diagnosed with a DSM-IIIR anxiety disorder. *Journal of Abnormal Psychology, 99,* 308–312.

Sandler, J. (1986). Aversion methods. In E.H. Kanfer & A.P. Goldstein (Eds.), *Helping people change: A textbook of methods* (3rd ed.). Elmsford, NY: Pergamon.

Sangsingkeo, P. (1969). Buddhism and some effects on the rearing of children in Thailand. In W. Caudhill & T.Y. Lin (Eds.), *Mental health research in Asia and the Pacific* (pp. 286–295). Honolulu: East-West Center Press.

Sarngadharan, M.G., Popovic, M.,Bruch, L., Schupbach, J., & Gallo, R.C. (1984). Antibodies reactive with human T-lymphotropic retroviruses (HTLV-III) in the serum of patients with AIDS. *Science, 224,* 506–508.

Sargent, J.D., Green, E.E., & Walters, E.D. (1972). Preliminary report on the use of autogenic feedback techniques in the treatment of migraine headaches. *Headache, 12,* 120–124.

Sargent, J.D., Green, E.E., & Walters, E.D. (1973). The age of autogenic feedback training in a pilot study of migraine and tension headaches. *Psychosomatic Medicine, 35,* 129–135.

Sartorius, N., Shapiro, R., & Jablonsky, A. (1974). The international pilot study of schizophrenia. *Schizophrenia Bulletin, 2,* 21–35.

Sassenrath, E.N., Chapman, L.F., & Goo, G.P. (1979). Reproduction in rhesus monkeys chronically exposed to moderate amounts of delta-9-tetrahydrocannabinol. In G.G. Nahas & W.D.M. Paton (Eds.), *Marihuana: Biological effects.* Elmsford, NY: Pergamon.

Saunders, E.A. (1991). Rorschach indicators of chronic childhood sexual abuse in female borderline patients. *Bulletin of the Menninger Clinic, 55,* 48–71,

Saunders, S.M., Howard, K.I., & Orlinsky, D.E. (1989). Therapeutic Bond Scales: Psychometric characteristics and relationship to treatment effectiveness. *Psychological Assessment: A Journal of Consulting and Clinical Psychology, 1,* 323–330.

Sayette, M.A., & Wilson, G.T. (1991). Intoxication and exposure to stress: Effects of temporal patterning. *Journal of Abnormal Psychology, 100,* 56–62.

Scarborough, H.S. (1990). Very early language deficits in dyslexic children. *Child Development, 61,* 128–174.

Scarlett, W. (1980). Social isolation from age-mates among nursery school children. *Journal of Child Psychology and Psychiatry, 21,* 231–240.

Schachter, D.L., Kihlstrom, J.F., Kihlstrom, L.C., & Berren, M.B. (1989). Autobiographical memory in a case of multiple personality disorder.*Journal of Abnormal Psychology, 98,* 508–514.

Schachter, S., & Latané, B. (1964). Crime, cognition, and the autonomic nervous system. In D. Levine (Ed.), *Nebraska symposium on motivation* (Vol. 12). Lincoln: University of Nebraska Press.

Schaie, K.W. (1965). A general model for the study of developmental problems. *Psychological Bulletin, 64* 92–107.

Schaie, K.W., & Hertzog, C. (1982). Longitudinal methods. In B.B. Wolman (Ed.), *Handbook of developmental psychology.* Englewood Cliffs, NJ: Prentice-Hall.

Scharff, J.S. (in press). Psychoanalytic marital therapy. In N.S. Jacobson & A.S. Gurman (Eds.), *Clinical handbook of couple therapy* (2nd ed.). New York: Guilford.

Schatzberg, A.F., & Colem, J.O. (1991). *Manual of clinical psychopharmacology.* Second edition. Washington, DC: American Psychiatric Press.

Schatzberg, A.F., Orsulak, P.J., Rosenbaum, A.H., Cole, J.O., & Scheerenberger, R.C. (1983). *A history of mental retardation.* Baltimore: P.H. Brookes.

Scheerer, M., Rothman, E., & Goldstein, K. (1945). A case of "idiot savant": An experimental study of personality organization. *Psychological Monographs, 58* (Whole No. 269).

Scheff, T.J. (1966). *Being mentally ill: A sociological theory.* Chicago: Aldine.

Schellenberg, G.D., Bird, T.D., Wijsman, E.M., Moore, D.K., Boehkne, E.M., Bryant, E.M., Lampe, T.H., Nochlin, D., Sumi, S.M., Deeb, S.S., Bayreuther, K., & Martin, G.M. (1988). Absence of linkage of chromosome 21q21 markers to familial Alzheimer's disease. *Science, 241,* 1507–1510.

Schinke, S.P., & Gilchrist, L.D. (1985). Preventing substance abuse with children and adolescents. *Journal of Consulting and Clinical Psychology, 53,* 596–602.

Schleifer, S.J., Keller, S.E., Camerino, M., Thornton, J.C., & Stein, M. (1983). Suppression of lymphocyte stimulation following bereavement. *Journal of the American Medical Association, 250,* 374–377.

Schlesier-Stropp, B. (1984). Bulimia: A review of the literature. *Psychological Bulletin, 95,* 247–257.

Schmauk, F.J. (1970). Punishment, arousal, and avoidance learning in sociopaths. *Journal of Abnormal Psychology, 76,* 443–453.

Schneider, K. (1959). *Clinical psychopathology.* New York: Grune & Stratton.

Schneider, N.G. (1987). Nicotine gum in smoking cessation: Rationale, efficacy, and proper use. *Comprehensive Therapy, 13,* 32–37.

Schneider, N.G., & Jarvik, M.E. (1984). Time course of smoking withdrawal symptoms as a function of nicotine replacement. *Psychopharmacology, 82,* 143–144.

Schneider, N.G., Jarvik, M.E., & Forsythe, A.B. (1984). Nicotine vs. placebo gum in the alleviation of withdrawal during smoking cessation. *Addictive Behaviors, 9,* 149–156.

Schneider, N.G., Jarvik, M.E., Forsythe, A.B., Read, L.L., Elliott M.L., & Schweiger, A. (1983). Nicotine gum in smoking cessation: A placebo-controlled, double-blind trial. *Addictive Behaviors, 8,* 253–261.

Schoenbach, V., Kaplan, B.H., Fredman, L., & Kleinaum, D.G. (1986) Social ties and mortality in Evans County, Georgia. *American Journal of Epidemiology, 123,* 577–591.

Schoeneman, T.J. (1977). The role of mental illness in the European witch-hunts of the sixteenth and seventeenth centuries: An assessment. *Journal of the History of the Behavioral Sciences, 13,* 337–351.

Schofield, W. (1964). *Psychotherapy: The purchase of friendship.* Englewood Cliffs, NJ: Prentice-Hall.

Schopler, E., Short, B. & Mesibov, G.B. (1989). Comments. *Journal of Consulting and Clinical Psychology, 157,* 162–167.

Schover, L.R. (1981). Unpublished research. As cited in Spector & Carey (1990).

Schuckit, M.A. (1983). The genetics of alcoholism. In B. Tabakoff, P.B. Sulker, & C.L. Randall (Eds.), *Medical and social aspects of alcohol use.* New York: Plenum.

Schuckit, M.A., & Gold, E.O. (1988). A simultaneous evaluation of multiple ethanol challenges to sons of alcoholics and controls. *Archives of General Psychiatry, 45,* 211–216.

Schuckit, M.A., & Moore, M.A. (1979). Drug problems in the elderly. In O.J. Kaplan (Ed.), *Psychopathology of aging.* New York: Academic Press.

Schuckit, M.A., & Rayses, V. (1979). Ethanol ingestion: Differences in blood acetaldehyde concentrations in relatives of alcoholics and controls. *Science, 203,* 54–55.

Schulsinger, F. (1972). Psychopathy: Heredity and environment. *International Journal of Mental Health, 1,* 190–206.

Schultz, R., & Brenner, G. (1977). Relocation of the aged: A review and theoretical analysis. *Journal of Gerontology, 32,* 323–333.

Schulz, R., & Williamson, G.M. (1991). A 2-year longitudinal study of depression among Alzheimer's caregivers. *Psychology and Aging, 6,* 569–578.

Schwab, J.J., Fennell, E.B., & Warheit, G.J. (1974). The epidemiology of psychosomatic disorders. *Psychosomatics, 15,* 88–93.

Schwartz, G.E. (1973). Biofeedback as therapy: Some theoretical and practical issues. *American Psychologist, 28,* 666–673.

Schwartz, G.E., & Weiss, S. (1977). What is behavioral medicine? *Psychosomatic Medicine, 36,* 377–381.

Schwartz, G.E., & Weiss, S.M. (1978). Behavioral medicine revisited: An amended definition. *Journal of Behavioral Medicine, 1,* 249–252.

Schwartz, M.S. (1946). The economic and spatial mobility of paranoid schizophrenics. Unpublished master's thesis, University of Chicago.

Schwartz, R., & Schwartz, L.J. (1980). *Becoming a couple.* Englewood Cliffs, NJ: Prentice-Hall.

Schwartz, R.M., & Gottman, J.M. (1976). Toward a task analysis of assertive behavior. *Journal of Consulting and Clinical Psychology, 44,* 910–920.

Schwartz, S.H., & Inbar-Saban, N. (1988). Value self-confrontation as a method to aid in weight loss. *Journal of Personality and Social Psychology, 54,* 396–404.

Schwarz, J.R. (1981). *The Hillside strangler: A murderer's mind.* New York: New American Library.

Schweizer, E., et al. (1990). Long-term therapeutic use of benzodiazapines: Effects of gradual taper. *Archives of General Psychiatry, 47,* 908–915.

Schwitzgebel, R.L., & Schwitzgebel, R.K. (1980). *Law and psychological practice.* New York: Wiley.

Scientific perspectives on cocaine abuse. (1987). *Pharmacologist, 29,* 20–27.

Seeman, T.E., & Syme, S.L. (1987). Social networks and coronary artery disease: A comparison of the structure and function of social relations as predictors of disease. *Psychosomatic Medicine, 49,* 381–406.

Segal, Z.V., & Shaw, B.F. (1988). Cognitive assessment: Issues and methods. In K.S.

Dobson (Ed.), *Handbook of cognitive-behavioral therapies* (pp. 39–81). New York: Guilford.

Segal, Z.V., Shaw, B.F., Vella, D.D., & Katz, R. (1992). Cognitive and life stress predictors of relapse in remitted unipolar depressed patients: Test of the congruency hypothesis. *Journal of Abnormal Psychology, 101,* 26–37.

Segovia-Riquelman, N., Varela, A., & Mardones, J. (1971). Appetite for alcohol. In Y. Israel & J. Mardones (Eds.), *Biological basis of alcoholism.* New York: Wiley.

Segraves, R.T. (1990). Theoretical orientations in the treatment of marital discord. In F.D. Fincham & T.N. Bradbury (Eds.), *The psychology of marriage: Basic issues and applications* (pp. 281–298). New York: Guilford.

Seiden, R.H. (1974). Suicide: Preventable death. *Public Affairs Report, 15,* 1–5.

Seidman, L.J. (1983). Schizophrenia and brain dysfunction: An integration of recent neurodiagnostic findings. *Psychological Bulletin, 94,* 195–238.

Seligman, L. (1990). *Selecting effective treatments: A comprehensive, systematic guide to treating adult mental disorders.* San Francisco: Jossey-Bass.

Seligman, M.E.P., & Binik, Y. (1977). The safety signal hypothesis. In H. Davis and H. Hurwitz (Eds.), *Operant-Pavlovian interactions.* Hillsdale, NJ: Erlbaum.

Seligman, M.E.P. (1971). Phobias and preparedness. *Behavior Therapy, 2,* 307–320.

Seligman, M.E.P. (1974). Depression and learned helplessness. In R.J. Friedman & M.M. Katz (Eds.), *The psychology of depression: Contemporary theory and research.* Washington, DC: Winston-Wiley.

Seligman, M.E.P. (1978). Comment and integration. *Journal of Abnormal Psychology, 87,* 165–179.

Seligman, M.E.P., Abramson, L.V., Semmel, A., & Von Beyer, C. (1979). Depressive attributional style. *Journal of Abnormal Psychology, 88,* 242–247.

Seligman, M.E.P., Castellon, C., Cacciola, J., Schulman, P., Luborsky, L., Ollove, M., & Downing, R. (1988). Explanatory style change during cognitive therapy for unipolar depression. *Journal of Abnormal Psychology, 97,* 13–18.

Seligman, M.E.P., & Hager, M. (Eds.). (1972). *Biological boundaries of learning.* New York: Appleton-Century-Crofts.

Selling, L.S. (1940). *Men against madness.* New York: Greenberg.

Seltzer, L.F. (1986). *Paradoxical strategies in psychotherapy: A comprehensive overview and guidebook.* New York: Wiley.

Selye, H. (1950). *The physiology and pathology of exposure to stress.* Montreal: Acta.

Serban, G., Conte, H.R., & Plutchik, R. (1987). Borderline and schizotypal personality disorders: Mutually exclusive or overlapping? *Journal of Personality Assessment, 5,* 15–22.

Settin, J.M. (1982). Clinical judgment in geropsychology practice. *Psychotherapy: Theory, Research and Practice, 19,* 397–404.

Shader, R.I., Caine, E.D., & Meyer, R.E. (1975). Treatment of dependence on barbiturates and sedative hypnotics. In R.I. Shader (Ed.), *Manual of psychiatric therapeutics: Practical psychopharmacology and psychiatry.* Boston: Little, Brown.

Shader, R.I., & DiMascio, A. (1970). *Psychotropic drug side-effects: Clinical and theoretical perspectives.* Baltimore: Williams & Wilkins.

Shaffer, D., Campbell, M., Cantwell, D., Bradley, S., Carlson, G., Cohen, D., Denckla, M., Frances, A., Garfinkel, B., Klein, R., Pincus, H., Spitzer, R.L., Volkmar, F., & Widiger, T. (1989). Child and adolescent psychiatric disorders in the DSM-IV: Issues facing the working group. *Journal of the American Academy of Child and Adolescent Psychiatry, 28,* 830–835.

Shapiro, D., & Surwit, R.S. (1979). Biofeedback. In O.E. Pomerleau & J.P. Brady (Eds.), *Behavioral medicine: Theory and practice.* Baltimore: Williams & Wilkins.

Shapiro, D., Tursky, B., & Schwartz, G.E. (1970). Control of blood pressure in man by operant conditioning. *Circulation Research, 26,* 127–132.

Shapiro, D.A., & Shapiro, D. (1983). Comparative therapy outcome research: Methodological implications of meta-analysis. *Journal of Consulting and Clinical Psychology, 51,* 42–53.

Shatan, C.F. (1978). Stress disorders among Vietnam veterans: The emotional content of combat continues. In C.R. Figley (Ed.), *Stress disorders among Vietnam veterans.* New York: Brunner/Mazel.

Shaw, B.F. (1977). Comparison of cognitive therapy and behavior therapy in the treatment of depression. *Journal of Consulting and Clinical Psychology, 45,* 543–551.

Shaw, B.F. (1984). Specification of the training and evaluation of cognitive therapists for outcome studies. In J.B.W. Williams & R.L. Spitzer (Eds.), *Psychotherapy research: Where are we and where should we go?* New York: Guilford.

Shea, M.T., Pilkonis, P.A., Beckham, E., Collins, J.F., Elkin, I., Sotsky, S.M., & Docherty, J.P. (1990). Personality disorders and treatment outcome in the NIMH Treatment of Depression Collaborative Research Program. *American Journal of Psychiatry, 147,* 711–718.

Shekelle, R.B., Honey, S.B., Neaton, J., Billings, J., Borlani, N., Gerace, T., Jacobs, D., Lasser, N., & Stander, J. (1983). Type A behavior pattern and coronary death in MRFIT. *American Heart Association Cardiovascular Disease Newsletter, 33,* 34.

Sher, K.J., Frost, R.O., Kushner, M., Crew, T.M., & Alexander, J.E. (1989). Memory deficits in compulsive checkers in a clinical sample. *Behaviour Research and Therapy, 27,* 65–69.

Sher, K.J., Frost, R.O., & Otto, R. (1983). Cognitive deficits in compulsive checkers: An exploratory study. *Behaviour Research and Therapy, 21,* 357–363.

Sher, K.J., & Levenson, R.W. (1982). Risk for alcoholism and individual differences in the stress-response-dampening effects of alcohol. *Journal of Abnormal Psychology, 91,* 350–367.

Sher, K.J., Walitzer, K.S., Wood, P.K., & Brent, E.F. (1991). Characteristics of children of alcoholics: Putative risk factors, substance use and abuse, and psychopathology. *Journal of Abnormal Psychology, 100,* 427–448.

Sherman, A.R. (1972). Real-life exposures as a primary therapeutic factor in the desensitization treatment of fear. *Journal of Abnormal Psychology, 79,* 19–28.

Sherwin, B.B., Gelfand, M.M., & Brender, W. (1985). Androgen enhances sexual motivation in females: A prospective, crossover study of sex steroid administration in the surgical menopause. *Psychosomatic Medicine, 47,* 339–351.

Shneidman, E.S. (1973). Suicide. In *Encyclopedia Britannica.* Chicago: Encyclopedia Britannica.

Shneidman, E.S. (1976). A psychological theory of suicide. *Psychiatric Annals, 6,* 51–66.

Shneidman, E.S. (1981). Suicide thoughts and reflections: 1960–1980. *Suicide and Life-Threatening Behavior, 11,* 197–360.

Shneidman, E.S. (1985). *Definition of suicide.* New York: Wiley.

Shneidman, E.S. (1987). A psychological approach to suicide. In G.R. VandenBos & B.K. Bryant (Eds.), *Cataclysms, crises, and catastrophes: Psychology in action.* Washington, DC: American Psychological Association.

Shneidman, E.S., & Farberow, N.L. (1970). A psychological approach to the study of suicide notes. In E.S. Shneidman, N.L. Farberow, & R.E. Litman (Eds.), *The psychology of suicide.* New York: Jason Aronson.

Shneidman, E.S., Farberow, N.L., & Litman, R.E. (Eds.). (1970). *The psychology of suicide.* New York: Jason Aronson.

Shoham-Salomon, V., Avner, R., & Neeman, R. (1989). You're changed if you do and changed if you don't: Mechanisms underlying paradoxical interventions. *Journal of Consulting and Clinical Psychology, 57,* 590–598.

Shoham-Salomon, V., & Rosenthal, R.

(1987). Paradoxical interventions: A meta-analysis. *Journal of Consulting and Clinical Psychology, 55,* 22–27.

Shontz, F.C., & Green, P. (1992). Trends in research on the Rorschach: Review and recommendations. *Applied and Preventive Psychology, 1,* 149–156.

Shopsin, B., Friedman, E., & Gershon, S. (1976). Parachlorophenylalanine reversal of tranylcypromine effects in depressed patients. *Archives of General Psychiatry, 33,* 811–819.

Shopsin, B., Gershon, S., Thompson, H., & Collins, P. (1975). Psychoactive drugs in mania. *Archives of General Psychiatry, 32,* 34–42.

Short, J.F., & Nye, F.I. (1958). Extent of unrecorded juvenile delinquency: Tentative conclusions. *Journal of Criminal Law, Criminology, and Police Science, 29,* 296–302.

Siegel, J.M., Sorenson, S.B., Golding, J.M., Burnam, M.A., & Stein, J.A. (1987). The prevalence of childhood sexual assault: The Los Angeles Epidemiological Catchment Area Project. *American Journal of Epidemiology, 126,* 1141–1153.

Siegel, R.K. (1982). Cocaine smoking. *Journal of Psychoactive Drugs, 14,* 277–359.

Siegler, I.C., & Costa, P.T., Jr. (1985). Health behavior relationships. In J.E. Birren & K.W. Schaie (Eds.), *Handbook of the psychology of aging* (2nd ed.). New York: Van Nostrand-Reinhold.

Siegler, I.C., George, L.K., & Okun, M.A. (1979). A cross-sequential analysis of adult personality. *Developmental Psychology, 15,* 350–351.

Siemens, A.J. (1980). Effects of cannabis in combination with ethanol and other drugs. *In Marijuana research findings: 1980.* Washington, DC: U.S. Government Printing Office.

Siever, L.J., Silverman, J.M., Horvath, T.B., et al. (1990). Increased morbid risk for schizophrenia-related disorders in relatives of schizotypal personality disordered patients. *Archives of General Psychiatry, 47,* 634–640.

Siever, L.J., & Uhde, T.W. (1984). New studies and perspectives on the noradrenergic receptor system in depression. *Biological Psychiatry, 19,* 131.

Sigman, M., Ungerer, J.A., Mundy, P., & Sherman, T. (1987). Cognition in autistic children. In D.J. Cohen, A.M. Donnellan, & R. Paul (Eds.), *Handbook of autism and pervasive developmental disorders* (pp. 103–120) New York: Wiley.

Silberman, E.K., Reus, V.I., Jimerson, D.C., et al. (1981). Heterogeneity of amphetamine response in depressed patients. *American Journal of Psychiatry, 118,* 1302–1307.

Silverman, K., Evans, S.M., Strain, E.C., & Griffiths, R.R. (1992). Withdrawal syndrome after the double-blind cessation of caffeine consumption. *New England Journal of Medicine, 327,* 1109–1114.

Silverstein, B., Feld, S., Kozlowki, L.T. (1980). The availability of low-nicotine cigarettes as a cause of cigarette smoking among teenage females. *Journal of Health & Social Behavior, 21,* 383–388.

Silverstein, C. (1972). *Behavior modification and the gay community.* Paper presented at the annual convention of the Association for Advancement of Behavior Therapy, New York.

Simeons, A.T.W. (1961). *Man's presumptuous brain: An evolutionary interpretation of psychosomatic disease.* New York: Dutton.

Simon, R.J., & Aaronson, D.E. (1988). *The insanity defense: A critical assessment of law and policy in the post-Hinckley era.* New York: Praeger.

Simons, A.D., Garfield, S.L., & Murphy, G.E. (1984). The process of change in cognitive therapy and pharmacotherapy for depression: Changes in mood and cognition. *Archives of General Psychiatry, 41,* 45–51.

Simons, A.D., Lustman, P.J., Wetzel, R.D., & Murphy, G.E. (1985). Predicting response to cognitive therapy of depression: The role of learned resourcefulness. *Cognitive Therapy and Research, 9,* 79–89.

Simons, A.D., Murphy, G.E., Levine, J.L., & Wetzel, R.D. (1985). Sustained improvement one year after cognitive and/or pharmacotherapy of depression. *Archives of General Psychiatry, 43,* 43–48.

Singer, J.L. (1984). The private personality. *Personality and Social Psychology Bulletin, 10,* 7–30.

Singer, M., & Wynne, L.C. (1963). Differentiating characteristics of the parents of childhood schizophrenics. *American Journal of Psychiatry, 120,* 234–243.

Sintchak, G.H., & Geer, J.H. (1975). A vaginal plethysmograph system. *Psychophysiology, 12,* 113–115.

Sisson, L.A., Van Hasselt, V.B., Hersen, M., & Awid, J.C. (in press). Tripartite behavioral intervention to reduce stereotypic and disruptive behaviors in young multihandicapped children. *Behavior Therapy.*

Sisson, R.W., & Azrin, N.H. (1989). The community-reinforcement approach. In R.K. Hester, & W.R. Miller (Eds.), *Handbook of alcoholism treatment approaches: Effective alternatives* (pp. 242–258). New York: Pergamon.

Sizemore, C.C., & Pittillo, E.S. (1977). *I'm Eve.* Garden City, NY: Doubleday.

Skinner, B.F. (1953). *Science and human behavior.* New York: Macmillan.

Sklar, L.A., & Anisman, H. (1979). Stress and coping factors influence tumor growth. *Science, 205,* 513–515.

Slater, E. (1961). The thirty-fifth Maudsley lecture: Hysteria 311. *Journal of Mental Science, 107,* 358–381.

Slater, E., & Glithero, E. (1965). A follow-up of patients diagnosed as suffering from hysteria. *Journal of Psychosomatic Research, 9,* 9–13.

Slater, E., & Shields, J. (1969). Genetic aspects of anxiety. In M.H. Lader (Ed.), *Studies of anxiety.* Ashford, England: Headley Brothers.

Slavson, S.R. (1950). *Analytic group psychotherapy with children, adolescents and adults.* New York: Columbia University Press.

Sloane, R.B. (1980). Organic brain syndrome. In J.E. Birren & R.B. Sloane (Eds.), *Handbook of mental health and aging.* Englewood Cliffs, NJ: Prentice-Hall.

Sloane, R.B., Staples, F.R., Cristol, A.H., Yorkston, N.J., & Whipple, K. (1975). *Psychoanalysis versus behavior therapy.* Cambridge, MA: Harvard University Press.

Small, G.W., & Jarvik, L.F. (1982). The dementia syndrome. *Lancet,* 1443–1446.

Small, G.W., Komanduri, R., Gitlin, M., & Jarvik, L.F. (1986). The influence of age on guilt expression in major depression. *International Journal of Geriatric Psychiatry, 1,* 121–126.

Small, G.W., Kuhl, D.E., Riege, W.H. et al. (1989). Cerebral glucose metabolic patterns in Alzheimer's disease: Effects of gender and age at dementia onset. *Archives of General Psychiatry, 46,* 527–533.

Small, J.C., Klapper, M.H., Milstein, V., et al. (1991). Carbamazine compared with lithium in the treatment of mania. *Archives of General Psychiatry, 48,* 915–921.

Smith, D.W., Bierman, E.L., & Robinson, N.M. (1978). *The biologic ages of man: From conception through old age.* Philadelphia: Saunders.

Smith, K.F., & Bengston, V.L. (1979). Positive consequences of institutionalization: Solidarity between elderly parents and their middle aged children. *The Gerontologist, 5,* 438–447.

Smith, M.L., Glass, G., & Miller, T. (1980). *The benefits of psychotherapy.* Baltimore: Johns Hopkins University Press.

Smith, P.B. (1975). Controlled studies of the outcome of sensitivity training. *Psychological Bulletin, 82,* 597–622.

Smith, S.S. & Newman, J.P. (1990). Alcohol and drug dependence in psychopathic and nonpsychopathic criminal offenders. *Journal of Abnormal Psychology, 99,* 430–439.

Smith, T., Snyder, C.R., & Perkins, S.C. (1983). Self-serving function of hypochondriacal complaints: Physical symptoms as self-handicapping strategies.

Journal of Personality and Social Psychology, 44, 787–797.

Smith, T.W. (1983). Change in irrational beliefs and the outcome of rational-emotive psychotherapy. *Journal of Consulting and Clinical Psychology, 51*, 156–157.

Smith, T.W., & Anderson, N.N. (1986). Models of personality and disease: An interactional approach to Type A behavior and cardiovascular risk. *Journal of Personality and Social Psychology, 50*, 1166–1173.

Smith, T.W., & Frohm, K.D. (1985). What's so unhealthy about hostility? Construct validity and psychosocial correlates of the Cook and Medley Ho scale. *Health Psychology, 4*, 503–520.

Smyer, M.A., Zarit, S.H., & Qualls, S.H. (1990). Psychological interventions with the aging individual. In J.E. Birren, & K.W. Schaie (Eds.), *Handbook of the psychology of aging* Third edition (pp. 375–403. New York: Academic Press.

Snyder, D.K., & Wills, R.M. (1989). Behavioral versus insight- oriented marital therapy: Effects of individual and interspousal functioning. *Journal of Consulting and Clinical Psychology, 57*, 39–46.

Snyder, D.K., Wills, R.M., & Grady-Fletcher, A. (1991). Long-term effectiveness of behavioral vs. insight-oriented marital therapy. *Journal of Consulting and Clinical Psychology, 59*, 138–141.

Snyder, M. (1983). The influence of individuals on situations: Implications for understanding the links between personality and social behavior. *Journal of Personality, 51*, 497–516.

Snyder, M., & White, E. (1982). Moods and memories: Elation, depression, and remembering the events of one's life. *Journal of Personality, 50*, 149–167.

Snyder, S.H. (1974). *Madness and the brain.* New York: McGraw-Hill.

Snyder, S.H., Banerjee, S.P., Yamamora, H.I., & Greenberg, D. (1974). Drugs, neurotransmitters, and schizophrenia. *Science, 184*, 1243–1253.

Sobell, L.C., Toneatto, A., & Sobell, M.B. (1990). Behavior therapy. In A.S. Bellack & M. Hersen (Eds.), *Handbook of comparative treatments for adult disorders* (pp. 479–505). New York: Wiley.

Sobell, M.B., & Sobell, L.C. (1976). Second-year treatment outcome of alcoholics treated by individualized behavior therapy: Results. *Behaviour Research and Therapy, 14*, 195–215.

Sobell, M.B., & Sobell, L.C. (1978). *Behavioral treatment of alcohol problems: Individualized therapy and controlled drinking.* New York: Plenum.

Sobell, M.B., & Sobell, L.C. (1987). Conceptual issues regarding goals in the treatment of alcohol problems. *Drugs and Society, 1*, 1–37.

Society of Behavioral Medicine. (1989). *By-laws of the Society of Behavioral Medicine.* Washington, DC: Author.

Solnick, R.L., & Corby, N. (1983). Human sexuality and aging. In D.S. Woodruff & J.E. Birren (Eds.), *Aging: Scientific perspectives and social issues* (2nd ed.). Monterey, CA: Brooks/Cole.

Soloff, P.H., et al. (1986). Paradoxical affects of amitriptyline on borderline patients. *American Journal of Psychiatry, 143*, 1603–1605.

Solomon, Z., Mikulincev, M., & Flum, H. (1988). Negative life events, coping response, and combat-related psychopathology: A prospective study. *Journal of Abnormal Psychology, 97*, 302–307.

Sonda, P., Mazo, R., & Chancellor, M.B. (1990). The role of yohimbine for the treatment of erectile impotence. *Journal of Sex and Marital Therapy, 16*, 15–21.

Soothill, K.L., & Gibbons, T.C.N. (1978). Recidivism of sexual offenders: A reappraisal. *British Journal of Criminology, 18*, 267–276.

Sorenson, S.B., & Brown, V.B. (1990). Interpersonal violence and crisis intervention on the college campus. *New Directions for Student Services, 49*, 57–66.

Sorenson, S.B., & Rutter, C.M. (1991). Transgenerational patterns of suicide attempts. *Journal of Consulting and Clinical Psychology, 59*, 861–866.

Sorotzin, B. (1984). Nocturnal enuresis: Current perspectives. *Clinical Psychology Review, 4*, 293–316.

Soueif, M.I. (1976). Some determinants of psychological deficits associated with chronic cannabis consumption. *Bulletin of Narcotics, 28*, 25–42.

Sourcebook of criminal justice statistics. (1983). Washington, DC: Bureau of Justice and Statistics.

Spadoni, A.J., & Smith, J.A. (1969). Milieu therapy in schizophrenia. *Archives of General Psychiatry, 20*, 547–557.

Spanier, G.B. (1976). Measuring dyadic adjustment: New scales for assessing the quality of marriage and similar dyads. *Journal of Marriage and the Family, 38*, 15–28.

Spanos, N.P., Weekes, J.R., & Bertrand, L.D. (1985). Multiple personality: A social psychological perspective. *Journal of Abnormal Psychology, 94*, 362–376.

Sparrow, S.S., Ballo, D.A., & Cicchetti, D.V. (1984). *Vineland Adaptive Behavior Scales.* Circle Pines, MI: American Guidance Service.

Special Report to the U.S. Congress on Alcohol and Health. (1983). Washington, DC: NIAA.

Spector, I.P., & Carey, M.P. (1990). Incidence and prevalence of the sexual dysfunctions: A critical review of the empirical literature. *Archives of Sexual Behavior, 19*, 389–408.

Spengler, A. (1977). Manifest sadomasochism of males: Results of an empirical study. *Archives of Sexual Behavior, 6*, 441–456 .

Spiegel, D. (1990). Can psychotherapy prolong cancer survival? *Psychosomatics, 31*, 361–366.

Spiegel, D., Bloom, J.R., Kraemer, H.C., & Gottheil, E. (1989). Effect of psychosocial treatment on survival of patients with metastatic breast cancer. *Lancet, 2*, 888–891.

Spiegel, D., Bloom, J.R., & Yalom, I. (1981). Group support for patients with metastatic cancer: A randomized prospective outcome study. *Archives of General Psychiatry, 38*, 527–534.

Spielberger, C.D. (1972). The nature and measurement of anxiety. In C.D. Spielberger (Ed.), *Anxiety: Current trends in theory and research.* New York: Academic Press.

Spielberger, C.D. (1988). *State-trait anger expression inventory: Professional manual.* Odessa, FL: Psychological Assessment Resources.

Spielberger, C.D., Johnson, E.H., Russell, S.F., Crane, R.J. & Worden, T.J. (1985). The experience and expression of anger. In M.A. Chesney & R.H. Rosenman (Eds.), *Anger and hostility in cardiovascular and behavioral disorders.* New York: Hemisphere.

Spiess, W.F.J., Geer, J.H., & O'Donohue, W.T. (1984). Premature ejaculation: Investigation of factors in ejaculatory latency. *Journal of Abnormal Psychology, 93*, 242–245.

Spinetta, J.J. (1980). Disease-related communication: How to tell. In J. Kenerman (Ed.), *Psychological aspects of childhood cancer.* Springfield, IL: Charles C. Thomas.

Spitzer, R.L., & Endicott, J. (1978). *Schedule for affective disorders and schizophrenia.* New York: New York State Psychiatric Institute, Biometrics Research Division.

Spitzer, R.L., Endicott, J., & Gibbon, M. (1979). Crossing the border into borderline personality and borderline schizophrenia. *Archives of General Psychiatry, 36*, 17–24.

Spitzer, R.L., Endicott, J., & Robins, E. (1977). *Research diagnostic criteria* (3rd ed.). New York: New York State Psychiatric Institute, Biometrics Research Division.

Spitzer, R.L., Skodol, A.E., Gibbon, M., & Williams, J.B.W. (1981) *DSM-III casebook.* Washington, DC: American Psychiatric Press.

Spitzer, R.L., & Williams, J.D.W. (1985). *Structured clinical interview for DSM-IIIR. Patient version.* New York: New York

State Psychiatric Institute, Biometrics Research Division.

Spitzer, R., & Williams, J.D.W. (1986). *Structured clinical interview for DSM-IIIR.* New York: New York State Psychiatric Institute, Biometrics Research Division.

Spivak, G., Platt, J., & Shure, M. (1976). *The problem-solving approach to adjustment.* San Francisco: Jossey-Bass.

Sprague, R.L., & Gadow, K.D. (1976). The role of the teacher in drug treatment. *School Review, 85,* 109–140.

Sprenkle, D.H., & Storm, C.L. (1983). Divorce therapy outcome research: A substantive and methodological review. *Journal of Marital and Family Therapy, 9,* 239–258.

Squires-Wheeler, E. Skodol, A.E., Friedman, D. & Erlenmeyer-Kimling, L. (1988). The specificity of DSM-III schizotypal personality traits. *Psychological Medicine, 18,* 757–765.

Srole, L., Langner, T.S., Michael, S.T., Opler, M.K., & Rennie, T.A.C. (1962). *Mental health in the metropolis: The midtown Manhattan study.* New York: McGraw-Hill.

Staats, A.W., & Staats, C.K. (1963). *Complex human behavior.* New York: Holt, Rinehart & Winston.

Stacy, A.W., Newcomb, M.D., & Bentler, P.M. (1991). Cognitive motivation and drug use: A 9-year longitudinal study. *Journal of Abnormal Psychology, 100,* 502–515.

Stacy, A.W., Sussman, S., Dent, C.W., Burton, D., & Flay, B.R. (1992). Moderators of peer social influence in adolescent smoking. *Personality and Social Psychology Bulletin, 18,* 163–172.

Stall, R.D., McKusick, L., Wiley, J., Coates, T., & Ostrow, D. (1986). Alcohol and drug use during sexual activity and compliance with safe sex guidelines for AIDS: The AIDS Behavioral Research Project. *Health Education Quarterly, 13,* 359–371.

Stampfer, M.J., Colditz, G.A., Willett, W.C., Speizer, F.E., & Hennekens, C.H. (1988). A prospective study of moderate alcohol consumption and risk of coronary disease and stroke in women. *New England Journal of Medicine, 319,* 267–273.

Stanton, A.H., & Schwartz, M.S. (1954). *The mental hospital.* New York: Basic Books.

Stanton, M.D., & Bardoni, A. (1972). Drug flashbacks: Reported frequency in a military population. *American Journal of Psychiatry,* 1B, 751–755.

Stanton, M.D., & Figley, C.R. (1978). Treating the Vietnam veteran within the family system. In C.R. Figley (Ed.), *Stress disorders among Vietnam veterans.* New York: Brunner/Mazel.

Starfield, B. (1972). Enuresis: Its pathogenesis and management. *Clinical Pediatrics, 11,* 343–350.

Stark, K.D., Kaslow, N.J., & Reynolds, W.M. (1987). A comparison of the relative efficacy of self-control therapy and a behavioral problem-solving therapy for depression in children. *Journal of Abnormal Child Psychology, 15,* 91–113.

Starr, B.D., & Weiner, M.B. (1981). *The Starr-Weiner report on sex and sexuality in the mature years.* New York: Stein & Day.

Steadman, H.J. (1979). *Beating a rap: Defendants found incompetent to stand trial.* Chicago: University of Chicago Press.

Steele, C.M., & Josephs, R.A. (1988). Drinking your troubles away: II An attention-allocation model of alcohol's effects on psychological stress. *Journal of Abnormal Psychology, 97,* 196–205.

Stenmark, D.E., & Dunn, V.K. (1982). Issues related to the training of geropsychologists. In J.F. Santos & G.R. VandenBos (Eds.), *Psychology and the older adult.* Washington, DC: American Psychological Association.

Stephens, B.J. (1985). Suicidal women and their relationships with husbands, boyfriends, and lovers. *Suicide and Life-Threatening Behavior, 15,* 77–89.

Stephens, J.H., & Kamp, M. (1962). On some aspects of hysteria: A clinical study. *Journal of Nervous and Mental Disease, 134,* 305–315.

Stern, D.B. (1977). Handedness and the lateral distribution of conversion reactions. *Journal of Nervous and Mental Disease, 164,* 122–128.

Stern, R.S., & Cobb, J.P. (1978). Phenomenology of obsessive-compulsive neurosis. *British Journal of Psychiatry, 132,* 233–234.

Steuer, J.L. (1982). Psychotherapy with older women: Ageism and sexism in traditional practice. *Psychotherapy: Theory, research and practice, 19,* 429–436.

Stevenson, J., & Jones, I.H. (1972). Behavior therapy technique for exhibitionism: A preliminary report. *Archives of General Psychiatry, 27,* 839–841.

Stolbach, L.L., Brandt, U.C., Borysenko, J.Z., Benson, H., Maurer, S.N., Lesserman, J., Albright, T.E., & Albright, N.L. (1988, April). *Benefits of a mind/body group program for cancer patients.* Paper presented at the annual meeting of the Society for Behavioral Medicine, Boston.

Stolberg, A.L., & Garrison, K.M. (1985). Evaluating a primary prevention program for children of divorce. *American Journal of Community Psychology, 13,* 111–124.

Stoller, F.H. (1968). Accelerated interaction: A time-limited approach based on the brief intensive group. *International Journal of Group Psychotherapy, 18,* 220–235.

Stone, A.A. (1975). *Mental health and law: A system in transition.* Rockville, MD: National Institute of Mental Health.

Stone, A.A. (1986). Vermont adopts *Tarasoff:* A real barn-burner. *American Journal of Psychiatry, 143,* 352–355.

Stone, A.A., Cox, D.S., Valdimarsdottir, H., Jandorf, L., & Neale, J.M. (1987). Evidence that secretory IgA antibody is associated with daily mood. *Journal of Personality and Social Psychology, 52,* 988–993.

Stone, A.A., & Neale, J.M. (1982). Development of a methodology for assessing daily experiences. In A. Baum and J. Singer (Eds.), *Environment and health.* Hillsdale, NJ: Erlbaum.

Stone, A.A., & Neale, J.M. (1984). The effects of "severe" daily events on mood. *Journal of Personality and Social Psychology, 46,* 137–144.

Stone, A.A., Reed, B.R., & Neale, J.M. (1987). Changes in daily event frequency precede episodes of physical symptoms. *Journal of Human Stress, 13,* 70–74.

Stone, G. (1982). *Health psychology,* a new journal for a new field. *Health Psychology, 1,* 1–6.

Stone, L.J., & Hokanson, J.E. (1967). Arousal reduction via self-punitive behavior. *Journal of Personality and Social Psychology, 12,* 72–79.

Stone, M.H. (1986). Exploratory psychotherapy in schizophrenia-spectrum patients: A reevaluation in the light of long-term follow-up of schizophrenic and borderline patients. *Bulletin of the Menninger Clinic, 50,* 287–306.

Stone, M.H. (1987) Psychotherapy of borderline patients in light of long-term follow-up. *Bulletin of the Menninger Clinic, 51,* 231–247.

Storandt, M. (1977). Age, ability level and methods of administering and scoring the WAIS. *Journal of Gerontology, 32,* 175–178.

Storandt, M. (1983). *Counseling and therapy with older adults.* Boston: Little, Brown.

Strauss, J.S., Carpenter, W., T., & Bartko, J.J. (1974). The diagnosis and understanding of schizophrenia: Part III. Speculations on the processes that underlie schizophrenic signs and symptoms. *Schizophrenia Bulletin, 1,* 61–69.

Strauss, R.P., Feuerstein, R., Mintzker, Y., Rand, Y., & Wexler, M. (1989). Ordinary faces? Down syndrome, facial surgery, active modification, and social perceptions. *American Journal on Mental Retardation, 94,* 115–118.

Stringer, A.Y., & Josef, N.C. (1983). Methylphenidate in the treatment of aggression in two patients with antisocial personality disorder. *American Journal of Psychiatry, 140*, 1365–1366.

Strong, R., Huang, J.S., Huang, S.S., et al. (1991). Degeneration of the cholinergic innervation of the locus ceruleus in *Alzheimer's disease. Brain Research, 542*, 23–28.

Strub, R.L., & Black, F.W. (1981). *Organic brain syndromes: An introduction to neurobehavioral disorders.* Philadelphia: F.A. Davis.

Strube, M.J. (1987). A self-appraisal model of the Type A behavior pattern. *Perspectives in personality, 2*, 201–250.

Strunin, L., & Hingson, R. (1987). Acquired immunodeficiency syndrome: Knowledge, beliefs, attitudes, and behaviors. *Pediatrics, 79*, 825–828.

Strupp, H.H. (1989). Psychotherapy: Can the practitioner learn from the researcher? *American Psychologist, 44*, 717–724.

Strupp, H.H., Hadley, S.W., & Gomes-Schwartz, B. (1977). *Psychotherapy for better or worse: An analysis of the problem of negative effects.* New York: Jason Aronson.

Stuart, F.M., Hammond, D.C., & Pett, M.A. (1987). Inhibited sexual desire in women. *Archives of Sexual Behavior, 16*, 91106.

Stuart, I.R., & Greer, J.G. (Eds.), (1984). *Victims of sexual aggression: Treatment of children, women and men.* New York: Van NostrandReinhold.

Stuart, R.B. (1976). An operant interpersonal program for couples. In D.H.L. Olson (Ed.), *Treating relationships.* Lake Mills, IA: Graphic Publishing Company.

Stuart, R.B. (1978). Protection of the right to informed consent to participate in research. *Behavior Therapy, 9*, 73–82.

Stuart, R.B. (1980). *Helping couples change: A social learning approach to marital therapy.* New York: Guilford.

Stunkard, A.J., & Rush, J. (1974). Dieting and depression reexamined: A critical review of reports of untoward responses during weight reduction for obesity. *Annals of Internal Medicine, 81*, 526–533.

Sturgis, E.T., & Adams, H.E. (1978). The right to treatment: Issues in the treatment of homosexuality. *Journal of Consulting and Clinical Psychology, 46*, 165–169.

Suddath, R.L., Christison, G.W., Torrey, E.F., et al. (1990). Anatomical abnormalities in the brains of monozygotic twins discordant for schizophrenia. *New England Journal of Medicine, 322*, 789–793.

Sue, D.W., & Sue, D. (1992). *Counseling the culturally different* (2nd ed.). New York: Wiley.

Sukhai, R.N., Mol, J., & Harris, A.S. (1989). Combined therapy of enuresis alarm and desmopressin in the treatment of nocturnal enuresis. *European Journal of Pediatrics, 148*, 465–467.

Sullivan, H.S. (1953). *The interpersonal theory of psychiatry.* New York: Norton.

Sullivan, H.S. (1929). Research in schizophrenia. *American Journal of Psychiatry, 9*, 553–567.

Suppes, T.,Baldessarini, R.J., Faedda, G.L., et al. (1991). Risk of recurrence following discontinuation of lithium treatment in bipolar disorder. *Archives of General Psychiatry, 48*, 1082–1087.

Surwit, R.S. (1982). Behavioral treatment of Raynaud's syndrome in peripheral vascular disease. *Journal of Consulting and Clinical Psychology, 50*, 922–932.

Sussman, S.S., et al. (1990). Peer-group association and adolescent tobacco use. *Journal of Abnormal Psychology, 99*, 349–352.

Sutcliffe, J.P., & Jones, J. (1962). Personal identiy, multiple personality, and hypnosis. *International Journal of Clinical and Experimental Hypnosis, 10*, 231–269.

Swartz, M., Blazer, D., George, L., & Landerman, R. (1986). Somatization disorder in a community population. *American Journal of Psychiatry, 143*, 1403–1408.

Swartz, M., Blazer, D., George, L., & Winfield, I. (1990). Estimating the prevalence of borderline personality in the community. *Journal of Personality Disorders, 1990*, 257–272.

Sweet, J.J., Carr , M.A., Rossini, E., & Kasper, C. (1986). Relationship between the Luria–Nebraska Neuropsychological Battery and the WISC-R: Further examination using Kaufman's factors. *International Journal of Clinical Neuropsychology, 8*, 177–180.

Swift, W.J., Andrews, D., & Barklage, N.E. (1986). The relationship between affective disorder and eating disorders: A review of the literature. *American Journal of Psychiatry, 143*, 290–299.

Syndulko, K. (1978). Electrocortical investigations of sociopathy. In R.D. Hare & D. Schalling (Eds.), *Psychopathic behaviour: Approaches to research.* New York: Wiley.

Szasz, T.S. (1960). The myth of mental illness. *American Psychologist, 15*, 113–118.

Szasz, T.S. (1963). *Law, liberty, and psychiatry.* New York: Macmillan.

Szasz, T.S. (Ed.). (1974). *The age of madness: The history of involuntary hospitalization.* New York: Jason Aronson.

Szasz, T. (1986). The case against suicide prevention. *American Psychologist, 41*, 806–812.

Szatmari, P., Offord, D.R., & Boyle, M.H. (1989). Ontario child health study: Prevalence of attention deficit disorder with hyperactivity. *Journal of Child Psychology and Psychiatry, 30*, 219–230.

Tallmadge, J., & Barkley, R.A. (1983). The interactions of hyperactive and normal boys with their mothers and fathers. *Journal of Abnormal Child Psychology, 11*, 565–579.

Tanzi, R.E., Gusella, F., Watkins, P.C., Bruns, G.A.P., St. George-Hyslop, P., Van Keunen, M.L., et al. (1987). Amyloid B protein gene: cDNA, mRNA distribution, and genetic linkage near the Alzheimer locus. *Science, 235*, 880–884.

Tashkin, D.P., Calvarese, B., & Simmons, M. (1978). Respiratory status of 75 chronic marijuana smokers: Comparison with matched controls. University of California at Los Angeles School of Medicine. (Abstract). *American Review of Respiratory Diseases, 117*, 261.

Tate, B.G., & Baroff, G.S. (1966). Aversive control of self-injurious behavior in a psychotic boy. *Behaviour Research and Therapy, 4*, 281–287.

Taylor, C.B. (1983). DSM-III and behavioral assessment. *Behavioral Assessment, 5*, 5–14.

Taylor, C.B., Ironson, G., & Burnett, K. (1990). Adult medical disorders. In A.S. Bellack, M. Hersen, & A.E. Kazdin (Eds.), *International handbook of behavior modification and therapy* (2nd ed.), New York: Plenum.

Taylor, J.A. (1953). A personality scale of manifest anxiety. *Journal of Abnormal and Social Psychology, 48*, 285–290.

Taylor, S.E., & Brown, J.D. (1988). Illusion and well-being: A social psychological perspective on mental health. *Psychological Bulletin, 103*, 193–210.

Teasdale, J.D., Fennell, M.J.V., Hibbert, G.A., & Amies, P.L. (1984). Cognitive therapy for major depressive disorder in primary care. *British Journal of Psychiatry, 44*, 400–406.

Telch, M.J., Lucas, J.A., & Nelson, P. (1989). Nonclinical panic in college students: An investigation of prevalence and symptomatology. *Journal of Abnormal Psychology, 98*, 300–306.

Telch, C.F., & Telch, M.J. (1986). Group coping skills instruction and supportive group therapy for cancer patients: A comparison of strategies. *Journal of Consulting and Clinical Psychology, 54*, 802–808.

Tennant, F., & Rawson, R.A. (1982). Cocaine and amphetamine dependence treated with desipramine. In *Problems of drug dependence.* Washington, DC: National Institute of Drug Abuse.

Teplin, L.A. (1984). Criminalizing mental disorder: The comparative arrest rate of the mentally ill. *American Psychologist, 29*, 794–803.

Teri, L., & Lewinsohn, P.M. (1986). Individual and group treatment of unipolar depression: Comparison of treatment outcome and identification of predictors of successful treatment outcome. *Behavior Therapy, 17*, 215–228.

Teri, L., & Reiffler, B.V. (1987). Depression and dementia. In L.L. Carstensen & B.A. Edelsein (Eds.), *Handbook of clinical gerontology.* New York: Pergamon.

Terman, L.W. (1916). *The measurement of intelligence.* Boston: Houghton Mifflin.

Thaker, G.K., Tamminga, C.A., Alphs, L.D., Lafferman, J., Ferraro, T.N., & Hare, T.A. (1987). β-aminobutyric acid abnormality in tardive dyskinesia. *Archives of General Psychiatry, 44*, 522–531.

Theodor, L.H., & Mandelcorn, M.S. (1973). Hysterical blindness: A case report and study using a modern psychophysical technique. *Journal of Abnormal Psychology, 82*, 552–553.

Thibaut, J.W., & Kelley, H.H. (1959). *The social psychology of groups.* New York: Wiley.

Thigpen, C.H., & Cleckley, H. (1954). *The three faces of Eve.* Kingsport, TN: Kingsport Press.

Thomas, S., Gilliam, A., & Iwrey, C. (1989). Knowledge about AIDS and reported risk behaviors among black college students. *Journal of American College Health, 31*, 61–66.

Thompson, G.O.B., Raab, G.M., Hepburn, W.S., Hunter, R., Fulton, M. & Laxen, D.P.H. (1989). Blood-lead levels and children's behaviour—Results from the Edinburgh lead study. *Journal of Child Psychology and Psychiatry, 30*, 515–528.

Thompson, L.W., Gallagher, D., & Breckenridge, J.S. (1987). Comparative effectiveness of psychotherapies for depressed elders. *Journal of Consulting and Clinical Psychology, 55*, 385–390.

Thoresen, C.E. (1990, June). *The recurrent coronary prevention project: Findings at $8\frac{1}{2}$ Years.* Invited paper, First International Congress of Behavioral Medicine, Uppsala, Sweden (as cited in Thoresen & Powell (1992).

Thoresen, C.E., Friedman, M., Powell, L.H., Gill, J.J., & Ulmer, D.K. (1985). Altering the type A behavior pattern in postinfarction patients. *Journal of Cardiopulmonary Rehabilitation, 5*, 258–266.

Thoresen, C.E., & Graff-Low, K. (1991). Women and the Type A behavior pattern: Review and commentary. In M. Strube (Ed.), *Type A behavior.* (pp. 117–133). Newberry Park, CA: Sage.

Thoresen, C.E., & Powell, L.H. (1992). Type A behavior pattern: New perspectives on theory, assessment, and intervention. *Journal of Consulting and Clinical Psychology, 60*, 595–604.

Thorndike, E.L. (1935). *The psychology of wants, interests and attitudes.* New York: Appleton-Century.

Thorndike, R.L., Hagen, E.P., & Sattler, J.M. (1986). *The Stanford–Binet Intelligence Scale: Fourth edition, guide for administering and scoring.* Chicago: Riverside Publishing Co.

Thyer, B.A., & Curtis, G.C. (1984). The effects of ethanol on phobic anxiety. *Behaviour Research and Therapy, 22*, 599–610.

Tiefer, L., Pedersen, B., & Melman, A. (1988). Psychosocial follow-up of penile prosthesis implant patients and partners. *Journal of Sex and Marital Therapy, 14*, 184–201.

Tienari, P., Sorri, A., Lahti, I., Naarala, M.N., Wahlberg, E., Moring, J., Pohjola, J., & Wynne, L.C. (1987). Genetic and psychosocial factors in schizophrenia: The Finnish adoptive family study. *Schizophrenia Bulletin, 13*, 477–484.

Tillich, P. (1952). *The courage to be.* New Haven, CT: Yale University Press.

Tippin, J., & Henn, F.A. (1982). Modified leucotomy in the treatment of intractable obsessional neurosis. *American Journal of Psychiatry, 139*, 1601–1603.

Tolber, N. (1986). Meta-analysis of 143 adolescent drug prevention programs: Quantitative outcome results of program participants compared to a control or comparison group. *Journal of Drug Issues, 16*, 537–568.

Tollefson, D.J. (1972). *The relationship between the occurrence of fractures and life crisis events.* Unpublished Master of Nursing thesis, University of Washington, Seattle.

Tomarken, A.J., Mineka, S., & Cook, M. (1989). Fear-relevant associations and covariation bias. *Journal of Abnormal Psychology, 98*, 381–394.

Torgersen, S. (1983). Genetic factors in anxiety disorders. *Archives of General Psychiatry, 40*, 1085–1089.

Torgersen, S. (1986). Genetics of somatoform disorder. *Archives of General Psychiatry, 43*, 502–505.

Tramontana, J., & Stimbert, V. (1970). Some techniques of behavior modification with an autistic child. *Psychological Reports, 27*, 498.

Treffert, D.A., McAndrew, J.B., & Dreifuerst, P. (1973). An inpatient treatment program and outcome for 57 autistic and schizophrenic children. *Journal of Autism and Childhood Schizophrenia, 3*, 138–153.

The Trials of Hypertension Prevention Collaborative Research Group. (1992). The effects of nonpharmacologic interventions on blood pressure of persons with high normal levels: Results of the Trials of Hypertension Prevention, Phase I. *Journal of the American Medical Association, 267*, 1213–1220.

Truett, J., Cornfield, J., & Kannel, W. (1967). Multivariate analysis of the risk of coronary heart disease in Framingham. *Journal of Chronic Disease, 20*, 511–524.

Trull, T.J., Widiger, T.A., & Frances, A. (1987). Covariation of criteria for avoidant, schizoid, and dependent personality disorders. *American Journal of Psychiatry, 144*, 767–771.

Tsoi, W.F. (1990). Developmental profile of 200 male and 100 female transsexuals in Singapore. *Archives of Sexual Behavior, 19*, 595–605.

Tucker, J.A., Vuchinich, R.E., & Downey, K.K. (1992). Substance abuse. In S.M. Turner, K.S. Calhoun, & H.E. Adams (Eds.), *Handbook of clinical behavior therapy* (pp. 203–223). New York: Wiley.

Tuckman, J., Kleiner, R.J., & Lavell, M. (1959). Emotional content of suicide notes. *American Journal of Psychiatry, 116*, 59–63.

Tuomilehto, J., Geboers, J., Salonen, J.T., Nissinen, A., Kuulasman, K., & Puska, P. (1986). Decline in cardiovascular mortality in North Karelia and other parts of Finland. *British Medical Journal, 293*, 1068–1071.

Turk, D.C., Meichenbaum, D.H., & Genest, M. (1983). *Pain and behavioral medicine: A cognitive behavioral perspective.* New York: Guilford.

Turk, D.C., Wack, J.T., & Kerns, R.D. (1985). An empirical examination of the "pain behavior" construct. *Journal of Behavioral Medicine, 8*, 119–130.

Turkat, I.D., & Maisto, S.A. (1985). Personality disorders: Application of the experimental method to the formulation and modification of personality disorders. In D.H. Barlow (Ed.), *Clinical handbook of psychological disorders.* New York: Guilford.

Turkewitz, H., & O'Leary, K.D. (1977). *A comparison of communication and behavioral marital therapy.* Paper presented at the Eleventh Annual Convention of the Association for Advancement of Behavior Therapy, Atlanta.

Turner, B.F., & Adams, C.G. (1988). Reported change in preferred sexual activity. *The Journal of Sex Research, 25*, 289–303.

Turner, B.F., & Turner, C.B. (1987). Percentages of elderly in psychotherapists' practices in the mid-1980s. *Adult Development and Aging Newsletter, 15*, 11–12.

Turner, C., Miller, H., & Moses, L. (Eds.). (1989). *AIDS, sexual behavior, and intravenous drug use.* Washington, DC: National Academy Press.

Turner, L.A., Althof, S.E., Levine, S.B., Risen, C.B., Bodner, D.R., Kursh, E.D., & Resnick, M.I. (1989). Self-injection of papaverine and phentolamine in the treatment of psychogenic impotence. *Journal of Sex and Marital Therapy, 15*, 163–176.

Turner, R.J., & Sternberg, M.P. (1978). Psychosocial factors in elderly patients admitted to a psychiatric hosital. *Age and aging, 7*, 171–177.

Turner, R.J., & Wagonfeld, M.O. (1967). Occupational mobility and schizophrenia. *American Sociological Review, 32*, 104–113.

Turner, R.M., & Ascher, L.M. (1979). Controlled comparison of progressive relaxation, stimulus control, and paradoxical intervention therapies for insomnia. *Journal of Consulting and Clinical Psychology, 47*, 500–508.

Turner, S.M., Beidel, D.C., & Townsley, R.M. (1992). Behavioral treatment of social phobia. In S.M. Turner, K.S. Calhoun, & H.E. Adams (Eds.), *Handbook of clinical behavior therapy*. 2nd ed., pp. 13–37. New York: Wiley.

Turner, S.M., et al. (1991). Social phobia: Axis I and II correlates. *Journal of Abnormal Psychology, 100*, 102–106.

Twentyman, C.T., & McFall, R.M. (1975). Behavioral training of social skills in shy males. *Journal of Consulting and Clinical Psychology, 43*, 384–395.

Uhl, G.R., Persico, A.M., & Smith, S.S. (1992). Current excitement with D2 dopamine receptor alleles in substance abuse. *Archives of General Psychiatry, 49*, 157–160.

Ullmann, L., & Krasner, L. (1975). *A psychological approach to abnormal behavior* (2nd ed.). Englewood Cliffs, NJ: Prentice-Hall.

Upper, D., & Ross, S.M. (Eds.). (1980). *Behavioral group therapy 1980: An annual review.* Champaign, IL: Research Press.

U.S. Bureau of the Census. (1986). *Statistical brief.* Washington, DC: U.S. Government Printing Office.

U.S. Bureau of the Census (1990). *Statistical abstract of the United States.* Washington, DC.

U.S. Department of Health and Human Services. (1982). Prevention in adulthood: Self-motivated quitting. *In Cancer: The health consequences of smoking, a report of the Surgeon General.* Washington, DC: U.S. Government Printing Office.

U.S. Department of Health and Human Services (1986). *Report of the secretary's task force on black and minority health* (Vols. 1–8). Washington, DC: Author.

U.S. Department of Health and Human Services. (1989). *Reducing the health consequences of smoking: 25 years of progress. A report of the Surgeon General, Executive summary* (DHHS Publication No. CDC 89–8411). Washington, DC: U.S. Government Printing Office.

U.S. Department of Health and Human Services, National Center for Health Statistics. (1990, August 30) *Monthly vital statistics.*

U.S. Public Health Service (1976). *Physicians' drug prescribing patterns in skilled nursing facilities.* Washington, DC: U.S. Department of Health, Education, and Welfare.

Vaillant, G.E. (1979). Natural history of male psychologic health: Effects of mental health on physical health. *New England Journal of Medicine, 301*, 1249–1254.

Vaillant, G.E. (1983). *The natural history of alcoholism: Causes, patterns, and paths to recovery.* Cambridge, MA: Harvard University Press.

Van der Kolk, B., Greenberg, M., Boyd, H., & Krystal, J.H. (1985). Inescapable shock, neurotransmitters, and addiction to trauma: Toward a psychobiology of posttraumatic stress. *Biological Psychiatry, 20*, 314–325.

van Egeren, L.F., & Madarasmi, S. (1987). A computerized diary for ambulatory blood pressure monitoring. In N. Schneiderman (Ed.), *Handbook on methods and measurements in cardiovascular behavioral medicine.* New York: Plenum.

vanKammen, D.P., Hommer, D.W., & Malas, K.L. (1987). Effects of pimozide on positive and negative symptoms in schizophrenic patients: Are negative symptoms state dependent? *Neuropsychobiology, 18*, 113–117.

VanKammen, W.B., Loeber, R., & Stouthamer-Loeber, M. (1991). Substance use and its relationship to conduct problems and delinquency in young boys. *Journal of Youth and Adolescence, 20*, 399–413.

Van Putten, T., May, P.R.A., Marder, S.R., & Wittman, L.A. (1981). Subjective response to antipsychotic drugs. *Archives of General Psychiatry, 38*, 187–190.

Vardaris, R.M., Weisz, D.J., Fazel, A., & Rawitch, A.B. (1976). Chronic administration of delta-9–tetrahydrocannabinol to pregnant rats: Studies of pup behavior and placental transfer. *Pharmacology and Biochemistry of Behavior, 4*, 249–254.

Varner, R.V., & Gaitz, C.M. (1982). Schizophrenic and paranoid disorders in the aged. In L.F. Jarvik & G.W. Small (Eds.), *Psychiatric clinics of North America.* Philadelphia: Saunders.

Varni, J.W. (1981). Self-regulation techniques in the management of chronic arthritic pain in hemophilia. *Behavior Therapy, 12*, 185–194.

Varni, J.W., & Bernstein, B.H. (1991). Evaluation and management of pain in children with rheumatoid diseases. *Pediatric Rheumatology, 17*, 985–1000.

Varni, J.W., & Dietrich, S.L. (1981). Behavioral pediatrics: Towards a reconceptualization. *Behavioral Medicine Update, 3*, 5–7.

Varni, J.W., & Wallander, J.L. (1984). Adherence to health-related regimens in pediatric chronic disorders. *Clinical Psychology Review, 4*, 585–596.

Vaughn, C.E., & Leff, J.P. (1976). The influence of family and social factors on the course of psychiatric illness. A comparison of schizophrenic and depressed neurotic patients. *British Journal of Psychiatry, 129*, 125–137.

Vaux, A. (1988). *Social support: Theory, research, and intervention.* New York: Praeger.

Velez, C.N., & Cohen, P. (1988). Suicidal behavior and ideation in a community sample of children: Maternal and youth reports. *Journal of the American Academy of Child and Adolescent Psychiatry, 27*, 349–356.

Ventura, J., Neuchterlein, K.H., Lukoff, D., & Hardesty, J.D. (1989). A prospective study of stressful life events and schizophrenic relapse. *Journal of Abnormal Psychology, 98*, 407–411.

Verbrugge, L.M. (1979). Female illness rates and illness behavior. *Women's Health, 4*, 61–79.

Videka-Sherman, L., & Lieberman, M. (1985). The effects of self-help and psychotherapy interventions on child loss: The limits of recovery. *American Journal of Orthopsychiatry, 55*, 70–82.

Viederman, M. (1986). Somatoform and factitious disorders. In A.M. Cooper, A.J. Frances, & M.H. Sacks (Eds.), *The personality disorders and neuroses.* Philadelphia: Lippincott.

Volkmar, F., & Cohen, D.J. (1985). The experience of infantile autism: A first-person account by Tony W. *Journal of Autism and Developmental Disorders, 15*, 47–54.

Von Felsinger, J.M., Lasagna, L., & Beecher, H.K. (1956). The response of normal men to lysergic acid derivatives. *Journal of Clinical and Experimental Psychopathology, 17*, 414–428.

von Krafft-Ebing, R. (1902). *Psychopathia sexualis.* Brooklyn, NY: Physicians and Surgeons Books.

Vygotsky, L.S. (1978). *Mind in society: The development of higher psyhological processes.* (M. Cole, V. John-Steiner, S. Scribner, & E. Souberman, Ed. and trans.). Cambridge, MA: Harvard University Press.

Wachtel, E.F., & Wachtel, P.L. (1986). *Family dynamics in individual psychotherapy: A guide to clinical strategies.* New York: Guilford.

Wachtel, P.L. (1973). Psychodynamics, behavior therapy, and the implacable experimenter: An inquiry into the consistency of personality. *Journal of Abnormal Psychology, 82*, 324–334.

Wachtel, P.L. (1977). *Psychoanalysis and behavior therapy: Toward an integration.* New York: Basic Books.

Wachtel, P.L. (1982). Vicious circles: The self and the rhetoric of emerging and unfolding. *Contemporary Psychoanalysis, 18,* 259–273.

Wadden, T.A. (1984). Relaxation therapy for essential hypertension: Specific or nonspecific effects. *Journal of Psychosomatic Research, 28,* 53–61.

Wahl, O.F. & Harrman, C.R. (1989). Family views of stigma. *Schizophrenia Bulletin, 15,* 131–139.

Wakefield, J. (1992). Disorder as dysfunction: A conceptual critique of DSM-III-R's definition of mental disorder. *Psychological Review, 99,* 232–247.

Walco, G.A., Varni, J.W., & Ilowite, N.T. (1992). Cognitive-behavioral pain management in children with juvenile rheumatoid arthritis. *Pediatrics, 89,* 1075–1079.

Waldron, I. (1976). Why do women live longer than men? *Journal of Human Stress, 2,* 1–13.

Waldron, I. (1978). The coronary-prone behavior pattern, blood pressure, employment and socioeconomic status in women. *Journal of Psychosomatic Research, 22,* 79–87.

Walen, S., Hauserman, N.M., & Lavin, P.J. (1977). *Clinical guide to behavior therapy.* Baltimore: William & Wilkins.

Wallace, C.J., Boone, S.E., Donahoe, C.P., & Foy, D.W. (1985). The chronically mentally disabled: Independent living skills training. In D.H. Barlow (Ed.), *Clinical handbook of psychological disorders.* New York: Guilford.

Wallace, C.J., & Liberman, R.P. (1985). Social skills training for patients with schizophrenia: A controlled clinical trial. *Psychiatry Research, 15,* 239–247.

Wallace, C.J., Nelson, C.J., Liberman, R.P., Aitchison, R.A., Lukoff, D., Elder, J.P., & Ferris, C. (1980). A review and critique of social skills training with schizophrenic patients. *Schizophrenia Bulletin, 6,* 42–63.

Walling, M., Anderson, B.L., & Johnson, S.R. (1990). Hormonal replacement therapy for postmenopausal women: A review of sexual outcomes and related gynecologic effects. *Archives of Sexual Behavior, 19,* 119–137.

Walsh, B.T., Stewart, J.W., Roose, S.P., Gladis, M., & Glassman, A.H. (1984). Treatment of bulimia with phenelzine. *Archives of General Psychiatry, 41,* 1105–1109.

Walsh, D.C., et al., (1991). A randomized trial of treatment for alcohol abusing workers. *New England Journal of Medicine, 325,* 775–782.

Ward, C.H., Beck, A.T., Mendelson, M., Mock, E., & Erbaugh, J.K. (1962). The psychiatric nomenclature: Reasons for diagnostic disagreement. *Archives of General Psychiatry, 7,* 198–205.

Warheit, G.J., Arey, S.A., & Swanson, E. (1976). Patterns of drug use: An epidemiologic overview. *Journal of Drug Issues, 6,* 223–237.

Warren, C.A.B. (1982). *The court as last resort: Mental illness and the law.* Chicago: University of Chicago Press.

Warren, N.C., & Rice, L.N. (1972). Structuring and stabilizing of psychotherapy for low prognosis clients. *Journal of Consulting and Clinical Psychology, 39,* 173–181.

Warren, R., Smith, G., & Velten, E. (1984). Rational-emotive therapy and the reduction of interpersonal anxiety in junior high school students. *Adolescence, 19,* 643–648

Warshaw, R. (1988). *I never called it rape.* New York: Harper & Row.

Washton, A.M., & Resnick, R.B. (1980). Clonidine for opiate detoxification: Outpatient clinical trials. *American Journal of Psychiatry, 137,* 1121–1122.

Waskow, I.E. (1984). Specification of the technique variable in the NIMH Treatment of Depression Collaborative Research Program. In J.B.W. Williams & R.L. Spitzer (Eds.), *Psychotherapy research: Where are we and where should we go?* New York: Guilford.

Watkins, J.G. (1984). The Bianchi (L.A. Hillside Strangler) case: Sociopath or multiple personality? *International Journal of Clinical and Experimental Hypnosis, 32,* 67–101.

Watson, D., & Pennebaker, J.W. (1989). Health complaints, stress, and distress: Exploring the central role of negative affectivity. *Psychological Review, 96,* 234–254.

Watson, G.C., & Buranen, C. (1979). The frequency and identification of false positive conversion reactions. *Journal of Nervous and Mental Disease, 167,* 243–247.

Watson, J.B. (1913). Psychology as the behaviorist views it. *Psychological Review, 20,* 158–177.

Watson, J.B., & Rayner, R. (1920). Conditioned emotional reactions. *Journal of Experimental Psychology, 3,* 1–14.

Watt, N.F. (1974). Childhood and adolescent roots of schizophrenia. In D. Ricks, A. Thomas, & M. Roll (Eds.), *Life history research in psychopathology* (Vol. 3). Minneapolis: University of Minnesota Press.

Watt, N.F., Stolorow, R.D., Lubensky, A.W., & McClelland, D.C. (1970). School adjustment and behavior of children hospitalized for schizophrenia as adults. *American Journal of Orthopsychiatry, 40,* 637–657.

Watts, F.N. (1986). Color naming of phobia-related words. *British Journal of Psychology, 77,* 97–108.

Watzlawick, P., Beavin, J., & Jackson, D.D. (1967). *Pragmatics of human communication: A study of interactional patterns, pathologies, and paradoxes.* New York: Norton.

Wechsler, D. (1968). *Escala de Inteligencia Wechsler para Adultos.* New York: Psychological Corporation.

Wechsler Intelligence Scale for Children— Third Edition (1991). San Antonio: The Psychological Corporation.

Weddington, W.W., Brown, B.S., Haertzen, M.H., et al. (1990). Changes in mood, craving, and sleep during short term abstinence reported by male cocaine addicts. *Archives of General Psychiatry, 47,* 861–868.

Weg, R.B. (Ed.). (1983). *Sexuality in the later years: Roles and behavior.* New York: Academic Press.

Wegner, D.M., Schneider, D.J., Carter, S.R., & White, T.L. (1987). Paradoxical effects of thought suppression. *Journal of Personality and Social Psychology, 53,* 5–13.

Wegner, D.M., Schneider, D.J., Knutson, B., & McMahon, S.R. (in press). Polluting the stream of consciousness: The effect of thought suppression on the mind's environment. *Cognitive Therapy and Research.*

Weicz, J.R., Suwanlert, S., Chaiyasit, W., & Walter, B.R. (1987). Over- and undercontrolled referral problems among children and adolescents from Thailand and the United States: The *wat* and *wai* of cultural differences. *Journal of Consulting and Clinical Psychology, 55,* 719–726.

Weidner, G., et al. (1987). The role of Type A behavior and hostility in an elevation of plasma lipids in adult women and men. *Psychosomatic Medicine, 49,* 136–146.

Weidner, G., & Collins, R.L. (in press). Gender, coping, and health. In H.W. Krohne (Ed.), *Attention and avoidance.* New York: Springer-Verlag.

Weidner, G., Friend, R., Ficarroto, T.J., & Mendell, N.R. (1989). Hostility and cardiovascular reactivity to stress in women and men. *Psychosomatic Medicine, 51,* 36–45.

Weinberg, G. (1972). *Society and the healthy homosexual.* New York: St. Martin's Press.

Weinberg, W.A., Rutman, J., Sullivan, L., Penick, E.C., & Dietz, S.G. (1973). Depression in children referred to an educational diagnostic center. *Journal of Pediatrics, 83,* 1065–1072.

Weinberger, D.R. (1987). Implications of normal brain development for the pathogenesis of schizophrenia. *Archives of General Psychiatry, 44,* 660–669.

Weinberger, D.R., Cannon-Spoor, H.E., Potkin, S.G., & Wyatt, R.J. (1980). Poor premorbid adjustment and CT scan abnormalities in chronic schizophrenia. *American Journal of Psychiatry, 137,* 1410–1413.

Weinberger, D.R., Wagner, R.L., & Wyatt, R.J. (1983). Neuropathological studies of schizophrenia: A selective review. *Schizophrenia Bulletin, 9,* 193–212.

Weiner, B. (1986). *An attributional theory of motivation and emotion.* Unpublished manuscript, University of California at Los Angeles.

Weiner, B., Frieze, L., Kukla, A., Reed, L., Rest, S., & Rosenbaum, R.M. (1971). *Perceiving the causes of success and failure.* New York: General Learning Press.

Weiner, H. (1977). *Psychobiology and human disease.* New York: Elsevier.

Weingartner, H., & Silverman, E. (1982). Models of cognitive impairment: Cognitive changes in depression. *Psychopharmacology Bulletin, 18,* 27–42.

Weinstein, K.A., Davison, G.C., DeQuattro, V., & Allen, J.W. (1986). *Type A behavior and cognitions: Is hostility the bad actor?* Paper presented at the 94th Annual Convention of the American Psychological Association, Washington, DC.

Weintraub, M., & Standish, R. (1983). Nabilone: An antiemetic for patients undergoing cancer chemotherapy. *Hospital Formulary, 18,* 1033–1035.

Weintraub, S., Liebert, D.E., & Neale, J.M. (1975). Teacher ratings of children vulnerable to psychopathology. *American Journal of Orthopsychiatry, 45,* 838–845.

Weintraub, S., Prinz, R., & Neale, J.M. (1978). Peer evaluations of the competence of children vulnerable to psychopathology. *Journal of Abnormal Child Psychology, 6,* 461–473.

Weiss, B., Weisz, J.R., & Bromfield, R. (1986). Performance of retarded and nonretarded persons on information-processing tasks: Further tests of the similar structure hypothesis. *Psychological Bulletin, 100,* 157–175.

Weiss, G. (1983). Long-term outcome: Findings, concepts, and practical implications. In M. Rutter (Ed.), *Developmental neuropsychiatry.* New York: Guilford.

Weiss, G., & Hechtman, L. (1986). *Hyperactive children grown up.* New York: Guilford.

Weiss, J., & Sampson, H. (1986). *The psychoanalytic process.* New York: Guilford.

Weiss, R., & Hardy, L.M. (1990). HIV infection and health policy. *Journal of Consulting and Clinical Psychology, 58,* 70–76.

Weiss, R.L. (1984). Cognitive and strategic interventions in behavioral marital therapy. In K. Hahlweg & N.S. Jacobson (Eds.), *Marital interaction: Analysis and modification.* New York: Guilford.

Weiss, R.L., & Cerreto, M.C. (1980). The Marital Status Inventory: Development of a measure of dissolution potential. *American Journal of Family Therapy, 8,* 80–85.

Weiss, R.L., Hops, H., & Patterson, G.R. (1973). A framework for conceptualizing marital conflict, a technology for altering it, some data for evaluating it. In L.A. Hamerlynck, L.C. Handy, & E.J. Mash (Eds.), *Behavior change: Methodology, concepts, and practice.* Champaign, IL: Research Press.

Weiss, R.L., & Perry, B.A. (1983). The Spouse Observation Checklist: Development and clinical applications. In E.E. Filsinger (Ed.), *Marriage and family assessment.* Beverly Hills, CA: Sage.

Weiss, R.L., & Wieder, G.B. (1982). Marital and family distress. In A.S. Bellack, M. Hersen, & A.E. Kazdin (Eds.), *International handbook of behavior modification.* New York: Plenum.

Weiss, S. (1986). Introduction and overview. In K.A. Matthews, S.J. Weiss, T. Detre, T.M. Dembroski, B. Falkner, S.B. Manuck, & R.B. Williams (Eds.), *Handbook of stress, reactivity, and cardiovascular disease.* New York: Wiley.

Weissberg, R.P., Gesten, E.L., Rapkin, B.D., Cowen, E.L., Davidson, E., deApodaca, R.F., & McKim, B.J. (1981). Evaluation of a social-problem-solving training program for suburban and inner-city third-grade children. *Journal of Consulting and Clinical Psychology, 49,* 251–261.

Weissman, A.N., & Beck, A.T. (1978). *Development and validation of the Dysfunctional Attitude Scale: A preliminary investigation.* Paper presented at the annual meeting of the American Educational Research Association, Toronto.

Weissman, M.M., Kidd, K.K., & Prusoff, B.A. (1982). Variability in rates of affective disorders in relatives of depressed and normal probands. *Archives of General Psychiatry, 39,* 1397–1403.

Weissman, M.M., Klerman, G.L., & Paykel, E.S. (1971). Clinical evaluation of hostility in depression. *American Journal of Psychiatry, 128,* 261–266.

Weissman, M.M., Klerman, G.L., Paykel, E.S., Prusoff, A., & Hanson, B. (1974). Treatment effects on the social adjustment of depressed patients. *Archives of General Psychiatry, 30,* 771–778.

Weissman, M.M., Klerman, G.L., Prusoff, B.A., Sholomskas, D., & Padian, N. (1981). Depressed outpatients. Results one year after treatment with drugs and/or interpersonal psychotherapy. *Archives of General Psychiatry, 38,* 51–56.

Weissman, M.M., Leaf, P.J., Tischler, G.L., et al. (1988). Affective disorders in five United States communities. *Psychological Medicine, 18,* 141–153.

Weissman, M.M., & Myers, J.K. (1978). Affective disorders in a U.S. urban community. *Archives of General Psychiatry, 35,* 1304–1310.

Weissman, M.M., Prusoff, B.A., DiMascio, A., New, C., Goklaney, M., & Klerman, G.L. (1979). The efficacy of drugs and psychotherapy in the treatment of acute depressive episodes. *American Journal of Psychiatry, 36,* 555–558.

Weisz, J.R., & Yeates, K.D. (1981). Cognitive development in retarded and nonretarded persons: Piagetian tests of the similar structure hypothesis. *Psychological Bulletin, 90,* 153–178.

Weitzenhoffer, A.M., & Hilgard, E.R. (1959). *Stanford hypnotic susceptibility scale, Forms A and B.* Palo Alto, CA: Consulting Psychologists Press.

Wells, C.E., & Duncan, G.W. (1980). *Neurology for psychiatrists.* Philadelphia: F.A. Davis Co.

Wender, P.H., Kety, S.S., Rosenthal, D., Schulsinger, F., Ortmann, J., & Lunde, I. (1986). Psychiatric disorders in the biological and adoptive families of adopted individuals with affective disorders. *Archives of General Psychiatry, 43,* 923–929.

Wenzlaff, R.M., Wegner, D.M., & Klein, S.B. (1991). The role of thought suppression in the bonding of thought and affect. *Journal of Personality and Social Psychology, 60,* 500–508.

Wester, P., Eriksson, S., Forsell, A., Puu, G., & Adolfsson, R. (1988). Monoamine metabolite concentrations and cholinesterase activities in cerebrospinal fluid of progressive dementia patents: Relation to clinical parameters. *Acta Neurologica Scandinavica, 77,* 12–21.

Whalen, C.K. (1983). Hyperactivity, learning problems, and the attention deficit disorders. In T.H. Ollendick & M. Hersen (Eds.), *Handbook of child psychopathology.* New York: Plenum.

Whalen, C.K., & Henker, B. (1985). The social worlds of hyperactive (ADDH) children. *Clinical Psychology Review, 5,* 447–478.

Whanger, A.D. (1973). Paranoid syndrome of the senium. In E. Eisdorfer & W.E. Fann (Eds.), *Psychopharmacology—Aging.* New York: Plenum.

Whitaker, A., Johnson, J., Shaffer, D., Rapoport, J.L., Kalikow, K., Walsh, B.T., Davies, M., Braiman S., & Dolinsky, A. (1990). Uncommon troubles in young people: Prevalence estimates of selected psychiatric disorders in a nonreferred adolescent population. *Archives of General Psychiatry, 47,* 487–496.

White, J., Davison, G.C., Haaga, D.A.F., & White, K. (1992). Articulated thoughts and cognitive distortion in depressed and nondepressed psychiatric patients. *Journal of Nervous and Mental Disease, 180,* 77–81.

White, K., & Cole, J.O. (1990). Pharmacotherapy. In A.S. Bellack & M. Hersen (Eds.), *Handbook of comparative treatments for adult disorders* (pp. 266–284). New York: Wiley.

White, P.F. (1986). Patient-controlled analgesia: A new approach to the management of postoperative pain. *Seminars in Anesthesia, 4,* 255–266.

White, W.C., & Boskind-White, M. (1981). An experiential-behavioral approach to the treatment of bulimarexia. *Psychotherapy: Theory, Research, and Practice, 18,* 501–507.

Whitehead, A. (1973). Verbal learning and memory in elderly depression. *British Journal of Psychiatry, 123,* 203–208.

Whitehead, W.E., Burgio, K.L., & Engel, B.T. (1985). Biofeedback treatment of fecal incontinence in geriatric patients. *Journal of the American Geriatrics Society, 33,* 320–324.

Whitehouse, P.J. (1991). Treatment of Alzheimer disease. *Alzheimer Disease and Associated Disorders, 5,* Suppl. 1, 532–536.

Whitlock, F.A. (1967). The aetiology of hysteria. *Acta Psychiatrica Scandinavica, 43,* 144–162.

Whitman, T.L. (1990). Self-regulation and mental retardation. *American Journal on Mental Retardation, 94,* 347–362.

Whittington, F.J. (1984). Addicts and alcoholics. In E.B. Palmore (Ed.), *Handbook on the aged in the United States.* Westport, CT: Greenwood Press.

Wickens, D.D., Allen, C.K., & Hill, F.A. (1963). Effects of instruction on extinction of the conditioned GSR. *Journal of Experimental Psychology, 66,* 235–240.

Widiger, T.A., Frances, A., Spitzer, R.L., & Williams, J.B.W. (1988). The DSM-III personality disorders: An overview. *American Journal of Psychiatry, 145,* 786–795.

Widiger, T.A., Frances, A., & Trull, T.J. (1987). A psychometric analysis of the social-interpersonal and cognitive-perceptual items for the schizotypal personality disorder. *Archives of General Psychiatry, 44,* 741–745.

Widiger, T.A., & Spitzer, R.L. (1991). Sex bias in the diagnosis of personality disorders: Conceptual and methodological issues. *Clinical Psychology Review, 11,* 1–22.

Wig, N.N., & Varma, V.K. (1977). Patterns of long-term heavy cannabis use in North India and its effects on cognitive functions. A preliminary report. *Drug and Alcohol Dependence, 2,* 211–219.

Wigdor, B., & Morris, G. (1977). A comparison of twenty-year medical histories of individuals with depressive and paranoid states. *Journal of Gerontology, 32,* 160–163.

Wiggins, J. (1968). Inconsistent socialization. *Psychological Reports, 23,* 303–336.

Wilder, A. (1980). *Opioid dependence: Mechanism and treatment.* New York: Plenum.

Wilkins, A.J., Jenkins, W.J., & Steiner, J.A. (1983). Efficacy of clonidine in treatment of alcohol withdrawal state. *Psychopharmacology, 81,* 78–80.

Wilkinson, D.A., Leigh, G.M., Cordingley, J., Martin, G.W., & Lei, H. (1987). Dimensions of multiple drug use and a typology of drug users. *British Journal of Addiction, 82,* 259–273.

Williams, D., & Anderson, L.P. (in press). The acculturative stress scale. In R.L. Jones (Ed.), *Handbook of tests and measurements for black populations.* Berkeley, CA: Cobb and Henry.

Williams, H., & McNicol, K.N. (1969). Prevalence, natural history and relationship of wheezy bronchitis and asthma in children: An epidemiological study. *British Medical Journal, 4,* 321–325.

Williams, J., & Maier, S. (1977). Transsituational immunization and therapy of learned helplessness in the rat. *Journal of Experimental Psychology: Animal Behaviour Processes, 3,* 240–252.

Williams, J.M., Little, M.M., Scates, S., & Blackman, N. (1987). Memory complaints and abilities among depressed older adults. *Journal of Consulting and Clinical Psychology, 55,* 595–598.

Williams, K., Goodman, M., & Green, R. (1985). Parent-child factors in gender role socialization in girls. *Journal of the American Academy of Child Psychiatry, 26,* 720–731.

Williams, L., Martin, G.L., McDonald, S., Hardy, L., & Lambert, L., Sr. (1975). Effects of a backscratch contingency of reinforcement for table serving on social interaction with severely retarded girls. *Behavior Therapy, 6,* 220–229.

Williams, L.S. (1984). The classic rape: When do victims report? *Social Problems, 31,* 459–467.

Williams, M.E., Davison, G.C., Nezami, E., & DeQuattro, V. (1992). Cognitions of type A and type B individuals in response to social criticism. *Cognitive Therapy and Research, 16,* 19–30.

Williams, R.B. (1987). Psychological factors in coronary artery disease: Epidemiological evidence. *Circulation, 76,* 117–123.

Williams, R.B., Barefoot, J.C., Haney, T.H., Harrell, F.E., Blumenthal, J., Pryor, D.B., & Peterson, B. (1986). *Type A behavior and angiographically documented coronary atherosclerosis in a sample of 2,289 patients.* Paper presented at the annual meeting of the Psychosomatic Society.

Williams, R.B., Haney, T.L., Lee, K.L., Kong, Y., Blumenthal, J.A., & Whalen, R.E. (1980). Type A behavior, hostility, and coronary atherosclerosis. *Psychosomatic Medicine, 42,* 539–549.

Williams, S.L., & Rappoport, A. (1983). Cognitive treatment in the natural environment for agoraphobics. *Behavior Therapy, 14,* 299–313.

Wilsnak, S.C. (1984). Drinking, sexuality, and sexual dysfunction in women. In S.C. Wilsnak & L.J. Beckman (Eds.), *Alcohol problems in women: Antecedents, consequences, and intervention* (pp. 189–227). New York: Guilford.

Wilson, G.T. (1987). Chemical aversion conditioning as a treatment for alcoholism: A re-analysis. *Behaviour Research and Therapy, 25,* 503–516.

Wilson, G.T., & Abrams, D. (1977). Effects of alcohol on social anxiety and physiological arousal: Cognitive versus pharmacological processes. *Cognitive Therapy and Research, 1,* 195–210.

Wilson, G.T. & Davison, G.C. (1969). Aversion techniques in behavior therapy: Some theoretical and metatheoretical considerations. *Journal of Consulting and Clinical Psychology, 33,* 327–329.

Wilson, G.T., & Davison, G.C. (1971). Processes of fear reduction in systematic desensitization. Animal studies. *Psychological Bulletin, 76,* 1–14.

Wilson, G.T., & Lawson, D.M. (1976). The effects of alcohol on sexual arousal in women. *Journal of Abnormal Psychology, 85,* 489–497.

Wilson, G.T., & O'Leary, K.D. (1980). *Principles of behavior therapy.* Englewood Cliffs, NJ: Prentice-Hall.

Wilson, G.T., & Rachman, S. (1983). Metaanalysis and the evaluations of psychotherapy outcome: Limitations and liabilities. *Journal of Consulting and Clinical Psychology, 51,* 54–64.

Wilson, G.T., Rossiter, E., Kleinfeld, E.I., & Lindholm, L. (1986). Cognitive-behavioral treatment of bulimia nervosa: A controlled evaluation. *Behaviour Research and Therapy, 24,* 277- 288.

Wilson, M.N. (1984). Mothers' and grandmothers' perception of parental behavior in three-generational black families. *Child Development, 55,* 1333-1339.

Wilson, T.D., Goldin, J.C., & Charbonneau-Powis, M. (1983). Comparative efficacy of behavioral and cognitive treatments of depression. *Cognitive Therapy and Research, 7,* 111–124.

Wilson, W.R. (1975). *Unobtrusive induction of positive attitudes.* Unpublished doctoral dissertation, University of Michigan.

Wincze, J.P., Bansal, S., & Malamud, M. (1986). The effects of medroxyprogesterone acetate on subjective arousal, arousal to erotic stimulation, and nocturnal penile tumescence in male sex offenders. *Archives of Sexual Behavior, 15,* 293–305.

Wincze, J.P., & Carey, M.P. (1991). *Sexual dysfunction: A guide for assessment and treatment.* New York: Guilford.

Winett, R.A., & Winkler, R.C. (1972). Current behavior modification in the classroom: Be still, be quiet, be docile. *Journal of Applied Behavior Analysis, 5,* 499–504.

Wing, L. (1976). Diagnosis, clinical description, and prognosis. In L. Wing (Ed.), *Early childhood autism: Clinical, educational, and social aspects.* New York: Pergamon.

Wing, L., & Attwood, A. (1987). Syndromes of autism and atypical development. In D.J. Cohen, A.M. Donnellan, & R. Paul (Eds.), *Handbook of autism and pervasive developmental disorders.* pp. (3–19) New York: Wiley.

Winick, C. (1962). Maturing out of narcotic addiction. *Bulletin on Narcotics, 14,* 1–7.

Winkler, R. (1977). What types of sex-role behavior should behavior modifiers promote? *Journal of Applied Behavior Analysis, 10,* 549–552.

Winters, K.C., & Neale, J.M. (1985). Mania and low self-esteem. *Journal of Abnormal Psychology, 94,* 282–290.

Winters, K.C., Weintraub, S., & Neale, J.M. (1981). Validity of MMPI code types in identifying DSM-III schizophrenics, unipolars and bipolars. *Journal of Consulting and Clinical Psychology, 49,* 486–487.

Wise, R.A., (1987). The neurobiology of craving: Implications for the understanding and treatment of addiction. *Journal of Abnormal Psychology, 97,* 118–132.

Wise, T. (1978). Where the public peril begins: A survey of psychotherapists to determine the effects of Tarasoff. *Stanford Law Review, 31,* 165–190.

Wolberg, L.R. (1954). *The technique of psychotherapy.* New York: Grune & Stratton.

Wolberg, L.R. (Ed.) (1965). *Short-term psychotherapy.* New York: Grune & Stratton.

Wold, D.A. (1968). *The adjustment of siblings to childhood leukemia.* Unpublished medical thesis, University of Washington, Seattle.

Wolf, A. (1949). The psychoanalysis of group. *American Journal of Psychotherapy, 3,* 16–50.

Wolf, A., & Kutash, I.L. (1990). Psychoanalysis in groups. In I.L. Kutash & A. Wolf (Eds.), *The group psychotherapist's handbook: Contemporary theory and technique.* New York: Columbia University Press.

Wolf, M., Bally, H., & Morris, R. (1986). Automaticity, retrieval processes, and reading: A longitudinal study in average and impaired readers. *Child Development, 57,* 988–1000.

Wolf, M., Risley, T., & Mees, H. (1964). Application of operant conditioning procedures to the behavior problems of an autistic child. *Behaviour Research and Therapy, 1,* 305–312.

Wolf, M.M. (1978). Social validity: The case for subjective measurement or how applied behavior analysis is finding its heart. *Journal of Applied Behavior Analysis, 11,* 203–214.

Wolfe, V.V. (1990). Sexual abuse of children. In A.S. Bellack, M. Hersen, & A.E. Kazdin (Eds.), *International handbook of behavior modification and therapy* (2nd ed., pp. 707–729). New York: Plenum Press.

Wolin, S.J. (1980). Introduction: Psychosocial consequences. In *Alcoholism and alcohol abuse among women: Research issues.* Rockville, MD.: National Institute on Alcohol Abuse and Alcoholism.

Wolitzky, D.L., & Eagle, M.N. (1990). Psychotherapy. In A.S. Bellack & M. Hersen (Eds.), *Handbook of comparative treatments for adult disorders* (pp. 123-143). New York: Wiley.

Wolpe, J. (1958). *Psychotherapy by reciprocal inhibition.* Stanford, Calif.: Stanford University Press.

Wolpe, J. (1980). Cognitive behavior and its role in psychotherapy: An integrative account. In M.J. Mahoney (Ed.), *Psychotherapy process: Current issues and future directions.* New York: Plenum.

Wolpe, J., & Rachman, S.J. (1960). Psychoanalytic "evidence," A critique based on Freud's case of Little Hans. *Journal of Nervous and Mental Disease, 131,* 135–147.

Wolraich, M., Milich, R., Stumbo, P., & Schultz, F. (1985). The effects of sucrose ingestion on the behavior of hyperactive boys. *Pediatrics, 106,* 675-682.

Wong, D.F., Wagner, H.N., Tune, L.E., Dannals, R.F., Pearlson, G.D., Links, J.M., *et al.* (1986). Positron emission tomography reveals elevated D2 dopamine receptors in drug-naive schizophrenics, *Science, 234,* 1558–1562.

Wood, D.L., Sheps, S.G., *et al.* (1984). Cold pressor test as a predictor of hypertension. *Hypertension, 6,* 301–306.

Wood, L.F., & Jacobson, N.S. (1985). Marital distress. In D.H. Barlow (Ed.), *Clinical handbook of psychological disorders.* New York: Guilford.

Woods, S.W., Chamey, D.S., Goodman, W.K., & Herringer, G.R. (1987). Carbon dioxide induced anxiety. *Archives of General Psychiatry, 44,* 365–375.

Workman, E.A., & La Via, M.F. (1987). T-lymphocyte polyclonal proliferation: Effects of stress and stress response style on medical students taking national board examinations. *Clinical Immunology and Immunopathology, 43,* 308–313.

World Health Organization. (1948). *Manual of the international statistical classification of diseases, injuries, and causes of death.* Geneva: Author.

Wortman, C.B., & Brehm, J.W. (1975). Responses to uncontrollable outcomes: An integration of the reactance theory and the learned helplessness model. In L. Berkowitz (Ed.), *Advances in social psychology.* New York: AcademicPress.

Wright, D.S. (1971). *The psychology of moral behavior.* Harmondsworth, England: Penguin.

Wright, J.C. (1976). A comparison of systematic desensitization and social skill acquisition in the modification of social fear. *Behavior Therapy, 7,* 205–210.

Wright, L.S. (1985). Suicidal thoughts and their relationship to family stress and personal problems among high school seniors and college undergraduates. *Adolescence, 20,* 575–580.

Wright, M.J., (1991). Identifying child sexual abuse using the Personality Inventory for Children. *Dissertation Abstracts International, 52,* 1744.

Wurmser, L. (1981). Psychodynamics of substance abuse. In J. Lowinson & P. Ruiz (Eds.), *Substance abuse: Clinical problems and perspectives.* Baltimore: Williams & Wilkins.

Wurtele, S.K., & Miller-Perrin, C.L. (1987). An evaluation of side-effects associated with participation in a child sexual abuse prevention program. *Journal of School Health, 57,* 228–231.

Yalom, I.D. (1980). *Existential psychotherapy.* New York: Basic Books.

Yalom, I.D. (1985). *The theory and practice of group psychotherapy* (3rd ed.). New York: Basic Books.

Yalom, I.D., Green, R., & Fisk, N. (1973). Prenatal exposure to female hormones: Effect on psychosexual development in boys. *Archives of General Psychiatry, 28,* 554–561.

Yoshioka, R.B., Tashima, N., Chew, M., & Murase, K. (1981). *Mental health services for Pacific/Asian Americans.* San Francisco: Pacific American Mental Health Project.

Young, G.C. (1965). The aetiology of enuresis in terms of learning theory. *Medical Officer, 113,* 19–22.

Yurchenco, H. (1970). *A mighty hard road: The Woody Guthrie story.* New York: McGraw-Hill.

Zakowski, S., Hall, M.H., & Baum, A. (1992). Stress, stress management, and the immune system. *Applied and Preventive Psychology, 1,* 1–13.

Zakowski, S.G., McAllister, C.G., Deal, M., & Baum, A. (in press). Stress, reactivity, and immune function. *Health Psychology.*

Zametkin, A.J., Nordahl, T.E., Gross, M., King, A.C., Semple, W.E., Rumsey, J., Hamburger, S., & Cohen, R.M. (1990). Cerebral glucose metabolism in adults with hyperactivity of childhood onset. *The New England Journal of Medicine, 20,* 1361-1366.

Zanarini, M.C., Gunderson, J.G., Frankenberg, F.R., & Chuncy, D.L. (1990). Discriminating borderline personality disorder from other Axis II disorders. *American Jounal of Psychiatry, 147,* 161–167.

Zanarini, M.C., Gunderson, J.G., Marino, M.F. et al. (1988). DSM-III disorders in the families of borderline outpatients. *Journal of Personality Disorders, 2,* 292–302.

Zane, M.D. (1984). Psychoanalysis and contextual analysis of phobias. *Journal of the American Academy of Psychoanalysis, 12,* 553–568.

Zarit, S.H. (1980). *Aging and mental disorders: Psychological approaches to assessment and treatment.* New York: Free Press.

Zarit, S.H. (1989). Issues and directions in family intervention research. In E. Light & B. Lebowitz (Eds.), *Alzheimer's Disease treatment and family stress.*

Zarit, S.H., Eiler, J., & Hassinger M. (1985). Clinical assessment. In J.E. Bifren & K.W. Schaie (Eds.), *Handbook of psychology of aging* (2nd ed.). New York: Van Nostrand-Reinhold.

Zarit, S.H., Todd, P.A., & Zarit, I.M. (1986). Subjective burden of husbands and wives as caregivers: A longitudinal study. *The Gerontologist, 26,* 260–266.

Zeaman, D., & Hanley, P. (1983). Stimulus preferences as structural features. In T.J. Tighe & B.E. Shepp (Eds.), *Perception, cognition, and development.* Hillsdale, NJ: Erlbaum.

Zeaman, D., & House, B.J. (1979). A review of attention theory. In N.R. Ellis (Ed.), *Handbook of mental deficiency, psychological theory and research* (2nd ed.). Hillsdale, NJ: Erlbaum.

Zeigob, L.E., Arnold, S., & Forehand, R. (1975). An examination of observer effects in parent–child interactions. *Child Development, 46,* 509–512.

Zeiss, A.M., Zeiss, R.A., & Dornbrand, L. (1988, November). *Assessing and treating sexual problems in older couples.* Paper presented at the meeting of the Gerontological Society of America, San Francisco.

Zerbin-Rüdin, E. (1972). Genetic research and the theory of schizophrenia. *International Journal of Mental Health, 1,* 42–62.

Ziegler, F.J., Imboden, J.B., & Meyer, E. (1960). Contemporary conversion reactions: A clinical study. *American Journal of Psychiatry, 116,* 901–910.

Zigler, E. (1967). Familial mental retardation: A continuing dilemma. *Science, 155,* 292–298.

Zigler, E., Hodapp, R.M., & Edison, M.R. (1990). From theory to practice in the care and education of mentally retarded individuals. *American Journal on Mental Retardation, 95,* 1–12.

Zilbergeld, B., & Evans, M. (1980). The inadequacy of Masters and Johnson. *Psychology Today, 14,* 28–43.

Zilboorg, G., & Henry, G.W. (1941). *A history of medical psychology.* New York: Norton.

Zillman, D., & Bryant, J. (1984). Effects of massive exposure to pornography. In N.M. Malamuth & E. Donnerstein (Eds.), *Pornography and sexual aggression.* New York: Academic Press.

Zimbardo, P.G., Andersen, S.M., & Kabat, L.G. (1981). Paranoia and deafness: An experimental investigation. *Science, 212,* 1529–1531.

Zimbardo, P.G., LaBerge, S., & Butler, L.D. (in press). Psychophysiological consequences of unexplained arousal: A posthypnotic suggestion paradigm. *Journal of Abnormal Psychology.*

Zimberg, S. (1978). Diagnosis and treatment of elderly alcoholics. *Alcoholism: Clinical and Experimental Research, 2,* 27–29.

Zimberg, S. (1987). Alcohol abuse among the elderly. In L.L. Carstebseb, & B.A. Edelstein (Eds.), *Handbook of clinical gerontology* (pp. 57–65). Elmsford, NY: Pergamon Press.

Zimmerman, M. (1988). Why are we rushing to publish DSM-IV? *Archives of General Psychiatry, 45,* 1135–1138.

Zimmerman, M., & Coryell, W. (1989). DSM-III personality disorder diagnoses in a nonpatient sample. *Archives of General Psychiatry, 46,* 682–689.

Zimmerman, M., Coryell, W., Pfohl, B., & Staid, D. (1986). The validity of four types of endogenous depression. *Archives of General Psychiatry, 43,* 234–245.

Zitrin, C.M., Klein, D.F, & Woerner, M.G. (1980). Treatment of agoraphobia with group exposure *in vivo* and imipramine. *Archives of General Psychiatry, 37,* 63–72.

Zitrin, C.M., Klein, D.F., Woerner, M.G., & Ross, D.C. (1983). Treatment of phobias: 1. Comparison of imipramine hydrochloride and placebo. *Archives of General Psychiatry, 40,* 125–138.

Zoccolillo, M. & Rogers, K. (1991). Characteristics and outcome of hospitalized adolescent girls with conduct disorder. *Journal of the American Academy of Child and Adolescent Psychiatry, 30,* 973–981.

Zohar, J., Insel, T.R., Zohar-Kadouch, R.C., Hill, J.Z., & Murphy, D.L. (1988). Serotenergic responsivity in obsessive-compulsive disorder. *Archives of General Psychiatry, 45,* 167–175.

Zucker, K.J., Finegan, J.K., Deering, R.W., & Bradley, S.J. (1984). Two subgroups of gender-problem children. *Archives of Sexual Behavior, 13,* 27–39.

Zuroff, D.C. (1986). Was Gordon Allport a trait theorist? *Journal of Personality and Social Psychology, 51,* 993–1000.

Quotation Credits

Permission was obtained for use of the following copyrighted material.

Page 25, figure 1.2: Langer, E. J., and Albelson, R. P. (1974). A look at how different theoretical orientations might affect the ways in which trained clinicians view the "adjustment" of a person. *Journal of Consulting and Clinical Psychology*, 42, 4–9. Copyright © 1974 by the American Psychological Association. Reprinted by permission.

Page 28, quotation: Yalom, I. D. (1980). *Existential psychotherapy*, 26. Copyright © 1980 by Yalom Family Trust. Reprinted by permission of Basic Books, a division of HarperCollins Publishers Inc.

Page 44, quotation: Watson, J. B. (1913). Psychology as the behaviorist views it. *Psychological Review*, 20, 158.

Page 55, quotation: Yalom, I. D. (1980). *Existential psychotherapy*, 4. Copyright © 1980 by Yalom Family Trust. Reprinted by permission of Basic Books, a division of HarperCollins Publishers Inc.

Page 61–62, table: DSM IV multiaxial classification system. *Diagnostic and Statistical Manual of Mental Disorders, Third Edition-Revised*. Copyright © 1944 by American Psychiatric Association. Reprinted by permission from a draft.

Page 70, table 3.3: Description of manic disorder in DSM-II versus DSM-IV. *Diagnostic and Statistical Manual of Mental Disorders, Third Edition-Revised*. Copyright © 1987 by American Psychiatric Association. Reprinted by permission.

Page 86, figure 4.1: Spitzer, R. L., & Williams, J. D. W. (1985). Patient version pertaining to obsessive-compulsive disorder. *Structural Clinical Interview for DSM-IIIR*. Reprinted by permission of New York State Psychiatric Institute, Biometrics Research Division.

Page 90, table 4.1: Hathaway, S. R., & McKinley, J. C. (1943). Typical clinical interpretations of items similar to those on the MMPI-Z. *MMPI Manual*. Revised 1989 Butcher et al.

Page 95, figure 4.3: Paul, G. L. (1966). Timed behavioral checklist for performance anxiety. *Insight vs. desensitization in psychotherapy*. Copyright © 1966 by the Board of Trustees of the Leland Stanford Junior University. Reprinted by permission of Stanford University Press.

Page 97, figure 4.4: Goldfried, M. R., & Davison, G. C. (1976). A behaviorally oriented intake report. *Clinical behavior therapy*. Reprinted by permission of Holt, Rinehart & Winston, Inc.

Page 112, figure 5.1: Miller, N. E. (1959). An illustration of the advantages of using anxiety as theoretical concept. In S. Koch (ed.), *Psychology: A study of a science* (Vol. 2), 278. Reprinted by permission of McGraw-Hill Book Company.

Page 116, table 5.1: Myers, J. K., Weissman, M. M., Tischler, G. L., Holzer, C. E., Leaf, P. J., Orraschel, H. A., Anthony, J. C., Boyd, J. H., Burke, J. E., Kramer, M., & Stoltzman, R. (1984). Life-time prevalence of several DSM-III diagnoses from the Myers et al. study. *Archives of General Psychiatry*, 41, 959–967. Reprinted by permission of Americal Medical Association.

Page 124, figure 5.4: Tate, B. G., & Baroff, G. S. (1966). Effects of a treatment for self-injurious behavior in an experiment with an ABAB single-subject design. *Behaviour Research and Therapy*, 4, 281–287. Reprinted by permission of Pergamon Press, Inc.

Page 140, quotation: Davison, G. C., & Zighelbom, V. (1987). Irrational beliefs in the articulated thoughts of college students with social anxiety. *Journal of Rational-Emotive Therapy*, 5, 238–254. Reprinted by permission of Human Sciences Press Inc.

Page 151, quotation: Akhter, S., Wig, N. N., Varma, V. K., Pershad, D., & Verma, S. K. (1975). A phenomenological analysis of symptoms in obsessive-compulsive neurosis. *British Journal of Psychiatry*, 127, 343–344. Reproduced by permission of The Royal College of Psychiatrists.

Page 168, figure 7.1: Netter, F. H., M. D. Adapted. Anesthesias in conversion disorder can be distinguished from true neurological dysfunctions. *The CIBA Collection of Medical Illustrations*, plates 5 and 6. Copyright © CIBA Pharmaceutical Company, Division of CIBA-GEIGY Corporation. Reprinted by permission.

Page 170, table 7.2: Perley, M. J., & Guze, S. B. (1962). Somatization disorder symptoms and their frequency as reported by a sample of patients. *New England Journal of Medicine*, 266, 421–426. Reprinted by permission of the New England Journal of Medicine.

Page 171, quotation: Arkonac, O., Guze, S. B. (1963). A family study of hysteria. *New England Journal of Medicine*, 268, 239–242. Reprinted by permission of the New England Journal of Medicine.

Page 189, quotation: Richter, C. P. (1957), Basedow (1925) cited in Richter (1957). *Psychosomatic Medicine*, 19, 191. © American Psychosomatic Society. Reprinted by permission of Williams & Wilkins.

Page 191, table 8.2: Schwab, J. J., Fennell, E. B., Warheit, G. J. (1974). Percentages of people reporting psychophysiological symptoms and conditions for the previous year. *Psychosomatics*, 15, 88–93. Reprinted by permission.

Page 192, table 8.3: Holmes, T. H., & Rahe, R. H. (1967). Social Readjustment Rating Scale, *Journal of Psychosomatic Research*, 11, 213–218. Reprinted by permission of Pergamon Press Ltd., Oxford, England.

Page 195, table 8.4: Williams, D., & Anderson, L. P. (1991). Sample items from Acculturative Stress Measure. The Acculturative stress scale. In R. L. Jones (Ed.), *Handbook of tests and measurements for black populations*. Reprinted by permission of Reginald L. Jones.

Page 196, figure 8.2: Stone, A. A., & Neale, J. M. (1982). Sample page from Stone & Neale's Assessment of Daily Experience scale.

In A. Baum, and J. Singer (Eds.), *Environment and health*. Reprinted by permission of authors and Laurence Erlbaum Associates Inc.

Page 197, figures 8.3 and 8.4: Stone, A. A., Reed, B. R., and Neale, J. M. (1987). Number of undesirable events for the ten days preceding an episode of respiratory infection. *Journal of Human Stress*, 13, 70–74. Copyright © 1987. Reprinted with permission of Helen Dwight Reid Educational Foundation. Published by Heldref Publications, 1319 18th Street, N.W., Washington, DC 20036-1802.

Page 204, quotation: Harburg, E., Erfurt, J. C., Hauenstein, L. S., Chape, C., Schull, W. J., Schork, M. A. (1973). Socioecological stress, suppressed hostility, skin color, and black-white male blood pressure: Detroit. *Psychosomatic Medicine*, 35, 280. © American Psychosomatic Society. Reprinted by permission of Williams & Wilkins.

Page 207, quotation: Rosenman, R. H., Friedman, M., Straus, R., Wurm, M., Kositichek, R., Hahn, W., & Werthessen, N. T. (1964). A predictive study of coronary heart disease. *Journal of the American Medical Association*, 189, 103–110. Reprinted by permission of American Medical Association.

Page 213, table 8.5: Rees, L. (1964). Relative importance of allergic, infective, and psychological factors in the etiology of asthma. *Journal of Psychosomatic Research*, 7, 253–262. Reprinted by permission.

Page 214, quotation: Kluger, J. M. (1969). Childhood asthma and the social milieu. *Journal of the American Academy of Child Psychiatry*, 8, 361. © American Academy of Child and Adolescent Psychiatry. Reprinted by permission of Williams & Wilkins.

Page 220, quotation: *The Lancet*, October 14, 1989. Reprinted by permission.

Page 221, quotation: Meyerowitz, B. E., & Chaiken, S. (1987). The effect of message framing on breast self-examination attitudes, intentions, and behavior. *Journal of Personality and Social Psychology*, 52, 504.

Page 226, quotation: Reid, E. C. (1910). Autopsychology of the manic-depressive. *Journal of Nervous and Mental Disease*, 37, 612–613. Copyright © 1910 Williams & Wilkins. Reprinted by permission.

Page 228, table 9.1: Depue, R. A., & Monroe, S. M. (1978). Learned helplessness in the perspective of the depressive disorders: Conceptual and definitional issues. *Journal of Abnormal Psychology*, 87, 3–20. Reprinted by permission.

Page 234, table 9.2: Beck, A. T. (1967). Sample items from the Beck Depression Inventory. *Depression: Clinical, experimental and theoretical aspects*. Reprinted by permission of author.

Page 249, table 9.4: Fremouw, W. I., Perczel, W. J., Ellis, T. E. (1990). Adapted from *Suicide risk: Assessment and response guidelines*, 24. Reprinted by permission of Simon & Schuster International.

Page 253, table 9.5: Shneidman, E. S. (1987). The ten commonalities of suicide. In G. R. Vandenbos & B. K. Bryant (Eds.), *Cataclysms, Crises and Catastrophes: Psychology in Action*, 167. Copyright © 1985 by E. S. Shneidman. Reprinted by permission of author.

Page 257, table 9.6: Linehan, M. (1981). Guidelines for treating suicidal clients. In H. Glazer, & J. Clarkin (Eds.), *Depression: Behavioral and Directive Intervention Strategies*, 229–294. Copyright © 1981 Garland Publishing Inc. Reprinted by permission of Garland Publishing Inc.

Page 264, table 10.1: Morey, L. C. (1988). Personality Disorder Diagnoses. *Journal of Abnormal Psychology*, 97, 319. Reprinted by permission of author.

Page 272, quotation: McNeill, E., (1967). The case of Dan in *The Quiet Furies*: Man and Disorder: 84, 85, 87. Copyright 1967. Adapted by permission of Prentice-Hall.

Page 277, figure 10.3: Schmauk, F. J., (1970). Punishment, arousal, and avoidance learning in sociopaths. *Journal of Abnormal Psychology*, 76, 443–453. Reprinted by permission.

Page 281, quotation: Linehan, M. M., (1992). Personal communication, 18 September and 16 November 1992. Reprinted by permission.

Page 286, table 11.1: Percent of the U. S. population reporting use of various drugs in the past month. *HHS News*, 19 December 1990. Reprinted by permission of National Institute of Drug Abuse.

Page 289, quotation: Rosen, E., Fox, R., & Gregory, I. (1972). Case history of long-term effects of prolonged alcohol abuse. *Abnormal psychology* (2nd ed). Reprinted by permission of W. B. Saunders Company.

Page 311, table 11.2: Steele, C. M., & Josephs, R. A. (1988). Drinking your troubles away II: An attention-allocation model of alcohol's effects on psychological stress. *Journal of Abnormal Psychology*, 97, 196–205. Reprinted by permission.

Page 313, table 11.3: Goodwin, D. W., Schulsinger, F., Hermansen, L., Guze, S. B., Winokur, G. A. (1973). The alcohol-related problems of offspring of alcoholics, adopted and raised by others, compared with those of controls. *Archives of General Psychiatry*, 28, 238–243. Reprinted by permission.

Page 316, table 11.4: *The Twelve Steps*. Reprinted with permission of Alcoholics Anonymous World Services, Inc.

Page 327, quotation: Hansen, W. B., Johnson, C. A., Flay, B. R., Graham, J. W., & Sobel, J. (1988). Affective and social influences approaches to the prevention of multiple substance abuse among seventh grade students. *Preventive Medicine*, 17, 135–154. Reprinted by permission of American Society Preventive Oncology.

Page 331, quotation: Rosen, R. C., & Rosen, L. (1981). Case study on William V. and his voyeuristic fantasies in *Human Sexuality*, 452–453. Reprinted by permission of McGraw-Hill Book Company.

Page 331, table 12.1: Sexual Disorders from *Diagnostic and Statistical Manual of Mental Disorders, Third Edition-Revised*. (1987). Reprinted by permission of American Psychiatric Association.

Page 334, quotation: Williams, K., Goodman, M., & Green, R. (1985). Parent-child factors in gender role socialization in girls. *Journal of the American Academy of Child Psychiatry*, 26, 722. Copyright © American Academy of Child and Adolescent Psychiatry. Reprinted by permission of Williams & Wilkins.

Page 337, quotation: Barlow, D. H., Reynolds, E. J., & Agras, W. S. (1973). Gender identity change in a transsexual. *Archives of General Psychiatry*, 29, 569–576. Reprinted by permission.

Page 359, quotation: Silverstein, C., (1972). *Behavior modification and the gay community*. Reprinted by permission of the author.

Page 373, figure 13.2: Masters, W. H., & Johnson, V. E. (1970). *Human sexual inadequacy*. Reprinted by permission of Masters & Johnson Institute.

Page 389, quotation: O'Neal, J. M., (1984). First person account: Finding myself and loving it. *Schizophrenia Bulletin*, 10, 109–110. Reprinted by permission of Center for Studies of Schizophrenia.

Page 390, quotation: McGhie, A., & Chapman, J. S. (1961). Disorders of attention and perception in early schizophrenia. *British Journal of Medical Psychology*, 34, 103–116. Reprinted by permission of British Psychological Society.

Page 392, quotation: Mellor, C. S., (1970). Catalogue of delusions of schizophrenics. *British Journal of Psychiatry*, 117, 15–23. Reprinted by permission of the Royal College of Psychiatrists.

Page 401, table 14.1: Gottesman, I. I., McGuffin, P., Farmer, A. E. (1987). Summary of major European family and twin studies of the genetics of schizophrenia. *Schizophrenia Bulletin*, 13, 23–47. Reprinted by permission.

Page 401, table 14.2: Gottesman, I., & Shields, J. (1972). Concordance in MZ and DZ twins as defined in three ways. *Schizophrenia and genetics: A twin study vantage point.* Academic Press.

Page 404, table 14.3: Heston, L. L. (1966). Subjects separated from their schizophrenic mothers in early infancy. *British Journal of Psychiatry*, 112, 819–825. Reproduced by permission of the Royal College of Psychiatrists.

Page 406, figure 14.1: Horn, A. S., Snyder, S. H. (1971). Chlorpromazine and dopamine: Conformational similarities that correlate with the anti-schizophrenic activity of phenothiazine drugs. *Proceedings of the National Academy of Science*, 68, 2325–2328. Reprinted by permission of S. H. Snyder.

Page 411, quotation: Bateson, G., Jackson, D. D., Haley, J., Weakland, J. (1956). Toward a theory of schizophrenia. *Behavioral Science*, 1, 251–264. Reprinted by permission of General Systems Science Foundation.

Page 411, table 14.4: Tienari, P., Sorri, A., Lahti, I., Naarala, M. N., Wahlberg, E., Moring, J., Pohjola, J., Wynne, L. C. (1987). Adjustment of adopted-away children of schizophrenic parents related to maladjustment of adoptive families. *Schizophrenia Bulletin*, 13, 477–484. Reprinted by permisison.

Page 417, quotation: Drake, R. D., & Sederer, L. I. (1986). The adverse effects of intensive treatment of chronic schizophrenia, *Comprehensive Psychiatry*, 27, 313–326. Reprinted by permission of American Psychopathological Association.

Page 429, quotation: Whalen, C. K. (1983). Hyperactivity, learning problems, and the attention deficit disorders. In T. H. Ollendick, & M. Hersen (Eds.), *Handbook of child psychopathology*, 151–153. Reprinted by permission of Carol Kupers Whalen.

Page 430, quotation: Oltmanns, T. F., Neale, J. M., Davison, G. C. (1991). *Case studies in Abnormal Psychology*, 3rd ed. Copyright © 1982, 1986, 1991 by John Wiley & Sons, Inc. Reprinted by permission of John Wiley & Sons, Inc.

Page 431, table: Barkley et al. (1990). Adapted from The adolescent outcome of hyperactive children diagnosed by research criteria, I: An 8 year prospective follow-up study. *Journal of the American Academy of Child.* Copyright © 1990 American Academy of Child Adolescent Psychology. Reprinted by permission.

Page 440, figure 15.1: Mowrer, H. O., Mowrer, W. M. (1938). Enuresis: A method for its study and treatment. *American Journal of Orthopsychiatry*, 8, 436–459. Copyright © 1938 by the American Orthopsychiatric Association, Inc. Reprinted with permission, from the American Journal of Orthopsychiatry.

Page 450, figure 15.2: Stunkard, A., Sorensen, T., & Schulsinger, F. (1980). Use of the Danish Adoption Register for the study of obesity and thinness. In S. Kety (Ed.), *The Genetics of Neurological and Psychiatric Disorders*, 119. Copyright © 1983 by Raven Press. Reprinted by permission of A. Stunkard.

Page 457–458, quotation: Grossman, H. J. (Ed). (1983). Case of mental retardation in *Classification in mental retardation.* Reprinted by permission of American Association of Mental Deficiency.

Page 458, table 16.1: Sparrow, S. S., Ballo, D. A., Cicchetti, D. V. (1984). Sample items from the *Vineland Adaptive Behavior Scales.* Copyright © 1984, 1985 American Guidance Service, Inc.

Page 478–479, quotation: Sacks, Oliver (1985). The twins. *The man who mistook his wife for a hat and other clinical tales*, 197–198, 199–200, 201–203. Reprinted by permission of John Farguharson Ltd.

Page 477, table 16.2: Volkmar, F. R., Cohen, D. J., Paul, R. (1986). Adapted from An evaluation of DSM-III criteria for infantile autism. *Journal of the American Academy of Child Psychiatry*, 25, 193. Copyright © 1986 American Academy of Child & Adolescent Psychiatry. Reprinted by permission.

Page 482–483, quotation: Volkmar, F., & Cohen, D. J. (1985). The experience of infantile autism: A first-person account, by Tony W. *Journal of Autism & Developmental Disorders*, 15, 47–54. Reprinted by permission.

Page 485–486, quotation: Park, C. C. (1987). Growing out of autism. In E. Schopler, & G. B. Mesibov (Eds.), *Autism in adolescents and adults.* Reprinted by permission. Plenum Publishing Corporation.

Page 490, quotation: Strub, R. L., & Black, F. W. (1981). *Organic brain syndromes: An introduction to neurobehavioral disorders*, 89–90. Reprinted by permission of F. A. Davis Co.

Page 496–497, quotation: Zarit, S. H. (1980). *Aging and mental disorders: Psychological approaches to assessment and treatment*, 179–180. Copyright © 1980 by the Free Press. Reprinted by permission.

Page 516, quotation: Rosenblatt, R. A., & Spiegel, C. (1988). Half of state's nursing homes fall short in federal study. *Los Angeles Times*, December 2, 1988, Part I, 3, 34. Copyright © 1988, Los Angeles Times. Reprinted with permission.

Page 538, table 18.1: Sloane, R. B., Staples, F. R., Cristol, A. H., Yorkston, N. J., Whipple, K. (1975). Characteristics of behavior therapy and analytically oriented psychotherapy in the Temple University study. *Psychoanalysis versus behavior therapy.* Copyright © 1975. Reprinted by permission of Harvard University Press.

Page 545, quotation: Yalom, I. D. (1980). *Existential psychotherapy*, 19. Copyright © 1980 by Yalom Family Trust. Reprinted by permission of Basic Books, a division of HarperCollins Publishers Inc.

Page 546, quotation: "Already Gone." (Tempchin, J., & Strandlund, R.), Copyright 1973. Jazzbird Music. All rights on behalf of Jazzbird Music administered by WB Music Corp. All rights reserved. Used by permission.

Page 548, quotation: Gaines, J. (1974). The founder of Gestalt therapy: Sketch of Fritz Perls. *Psychology Today*, 8, 117–118. Copyright © 1974 Sussex Publishers, Inc. Reprinted with permission from *Psychology Today* magazine.

Page 559, figure 19.1: Ayllon, T., & Azrin, N. H. Adapted from *The token economy: A motivational system for therapy and rehabilitation.* Reprinted by permission of Prentice-Hall, Inc. (1968)

Page 564, quotation: Goldfried, M. R., Davison, G. C. (1976). *Clinical Behavior Therapy*, 163–165. Reprinted by permission of Holt, Rinehart & Winston.

Page 585, quotation: Safran, J. D., Vallis, T. M., Segal, Z. V., & Shaw, B. F. (1986). Assessment of core cognitive processes in cognitive therapy. *Cognitive Therapy and Research*, 10, 575. Reprinted by permission.

Page 590: Lazarus, A. A., & Messner, S. B. (1991). Does chaos prevail? An exchange on technical eclecticism and assimilative integration. *Journal of Psychotherapy Integration.* Reprinted by permission of Plenum Publishing Corporation.

Page 594, quotation: LoPiccolo, J., & Friedman, J. M. (1985). In S. J. Lynn, & J. P. Garske (Eds.), *Contemporary psychotherapies: Models and methods.* Reprinted by permission.

Page 597, figure 20.1: Aronson, E. (1972). Schematic representation of a two-person interaction. *The social animal.* Copyright © 1972 by W. H. Freeman and Company. Reprinted by permission.

Page 629, quotation: Morse, S. J. (1982). A preference for liberty: The case against involuntary commitment of mentally disordered. *California Law Review, 70,* 98. Copyright © 1982 by California Law Review Inc. Reprinted by permission.

Page 648, quotation: Clayton, E. W. (1988). From Rogers to Rivers: The rights of the mentally ill to refuse medications. *American Journal of Law and Medicine, 13,* 19–20. Copyright © 1987 by American Society of Law & Medicine and Boston University School of Law. Reprinted by permission of American Society of Law & Medicine, Inc.

Page 649, quotation: Baxter, E., & Hopper, K. (1981). *Private lives/public places: Homeless adults on the streets of New York City.* Reprinted by permission of Community Service Society.

Page 638, quotation: Schwitzgebel, R. L., & Schwitzgebel, R. K. (1980). *Law and psychological practice.* Copyright © 1980 by John Wiley & Sons, Inc. Reprinted by permission of John Wiley & Sons, Inc.

Photo Credits

Chapter 1
Opener: Steven Hunt/The Image Bank. Page 6: David Burnett/Contact Stock Images. Page 7: Sipa Press. Page 8: John Ficara/Woodfin Camp & Associates. Page 9: Frank Siteman/Rainbow. Page 11: Topham/The Image Works. Page 12: Bettmann Archive. Page 13: Culver Pictures, Inc. Page 15, top: Bettmann Archive. Page 15, bottom: Bettmann Archive. Page 16: Bettmann Archive. Page 18: Historical Picture Services. Page 21: Eric Roth/The Picture Cube. Page 22, left: Jean-Loup Charmet/Photo Researchers. Page 22, right: Bettmann Archive. Page 23, left: Bettmann Archive. Page 23, right: Lucy Freeman Walker & Co., New York.

Chapter 2
Opener: Peter Angelo Simon/The Stock Market. Page 29: Dan McCoy/Rainbow. Page 34: Paul Meredith/Tony Stone World Wide. Page 35, left: Myrleen Ferguson/PhotoEdit. Page 35, right: Laura Dwight/Peter Arnold. Page 36: D. Chidester/The Image Works. Page 39: Courtesy The National Library of Medicine. Page 40, left: Courtesy Adler Consultation Center. Page 40, right: Courtesy Jon Erikson. Page 41: Bob Daemmrich/The Image Works. Page 42: Ellan Young/Photo Researchers. Page 44, top: Culver Pictures. Page 44, bottom: Culver Pictures. Page 45: Christopher Johnson/Stock, Boston. Page 49: Jerry Howard/Stock, Boston. Page 52, top: Institute for Rational-Emotive Therapy. Page 52, botton: Dan Miller/The New York Times.

Chapter 3
Opener: Orion FPG International. Page 63: Bob Daemmrich/Stock, Boston. Page 64: Arlene Collins/Monkmeyer Press Photo. Page 65, right: William Thompson/The Picture Cube. Page 65, left: Russ Kinne/COMSTOCK, Inc. Page 66: Ira Wyman/Sygma.

Chapter 4
Opener: Orion FPG International. Page 74: Steven E. Sutton/Duomo Photography, Inc. Page 78, top left: Dan McCoy/Rainbow. Page 78, top right: Dan McCoy/Rainbow. Page 78, bottom left: Dan McCoy/Rainbow. Page 78, bottom right: Dan McCoy/Rainbow. Page 79: Van Bucher/Photo Researchers. Page 80: Ulrike Welsch Photography. Page 82: Brian Seed/Tony Stone World Wide. Page 87, top: Courtesy Dr. Henri F. Ellenberger. Page 87, bottom: Will & Deni McIntyre/Photo Researchers. Page 88: Lew Merrim/Monkmeyer Press Photo. Page 89: Frida Leinwand/Monkmeyer Press Photo. Page 93: Lew Merrim/Monkmeyer Press Photo. Page 94: Jeff Isaac Greenberg/Photo Researchers. Page 99: Renata Hiller/Monkmeyer Press Photo. Page 100: Steve Shapiro/Sygma. Page 102: Gary Farr/Gamma Liaison. Page 105: Courtesy Columbia University Department of Psychology.

Chapter 5
Opener: Eric Meola/The Image Bank. Page 111: Peter Vandermark/Stock, Boston. Page 114: Geral Martineau/The Washington Post. Page 115: Rhoda Sidney/Monkmeyer Press Photo. Page 122: Martin Rogers/Woodfin Camp & Associates.

Chapter 6
Opener: Santi Visalli/The Image Bank. Page 133, bottom: M. Dwyer/Stock, Boston. Page 133, top: Harvey Stein. Page 137: Courtesy Dr. Susan Mineka. Page 139: James Balog/Black Star. Page 142: Courtesy of Dr. David H. Barlow/Center for Stress and Anxiety Disorders. Page 143: Mimi Forsyth/Monkmeyer Press Photo. Page 150: Courtesy New York Public Library, Astor, Lenox and Tilden Foundations. Page 151: Syndicated International/Photo Trends. Page 156: Paul Conklin/Monkmeyer Press Photo. Page 156: Peter Blakely/Woodfin Camp & Associates. Page 159: Arlene Collins/Monkmeyer Press Photo. Page 162: Bob Daemmrich/Stock, Boston.

Chapter 7
Opener: Bill Binzen/The Stock Market. Page 167: Schell/Mullaney Health Care Marketing. Page 168: Bettmann Archive. Page 170: Bob Pizarro/COMSTOCK, Inc. Page 174: Hank Morgan/Photo Researchers. Page 178: Bob Daemmrich/Stock, Boston. Page 179: Springer/Bettmann Archive. Page 182: COMSTOCK, Inc. Page 184: AP/World Wide Photos. Page 186: Phillipe Plailly/Photo Researchers.

Chapter 8
Opener: Don Carroll/The Image Bank. Page 193: Will McIntyre/Photo Researchers. Page 193: Chuch Fishman/Woodfin Camp & Associates. Page 197: Martha Cooper/Peter Arnold. Page 198: Sybil Shackman/Monkmeyer Press Photo. Page 203: Emily Stong/The Picture Cube. Page 204: Dorothy Littell Greco/Stock, Boston. Page 208: Simon Fraser/Photo Researchers. Page 210: Hattie

Young/Photo Researchers. Page 215: Dan McCoy/Rainbow.

Chapter 9

Opener: Bill Binzen/The Stock Market. Page 225: Everett Collection. Page 227: Everett Collection. Page 229: Griffin/The Image Works. Page 231: COMSTOCK, Inc. Page 238: Sybil Shackman/Monkmeyer Press Photo. Page 245: Will & Deni McIntyre/Photo Researchers. Page 249: Murray & Associates/Tony Stone World Wide. Page 254: Hazel Hankin/The New York Times Pictures. Page 255: Mark Antman/The Image Works. Page 257: Blake Discher/Sygma. Page 259: Bettmann Archive.

Chapter 10

Opener: Paul Biddle/The Image Bank. Page 267: Jerry Ohlinger's Movie Material Store. Page 268: Culver Pictures, Inc. Page 269: Russell Dian/Monkmeyer Press Photo. Page 271: Gamma Liaison. Page 278: Douglas Mason/Woodfin Camp & Associates. Page 280: Courtesy Marsha Linehan. Page 283: Bob Daemmrich/Tony Stone World Wide.

Chapter 11

Opener: G. & V. Chapman/The Image Bank. Page 287: Chuck Nacke/Picture Group. Page 288: Reuters/Bettmann Archive. Page 290: Gianni Tortoli/Photo Researchers. Page 291: Yoav Levy/Phototake. Page 293: Culver Pictures, Inc. Page 294: Steve Goldberg/Monkmeyer Press Photo. Page 295: Culver Pictures, Inc. Page 300, top: R. P. Kingston/The Picture Cube. Page 300, bottom: National Library of Medicine/Photo Researchers. Page 305: Bettmann Archive. Page 309: Eric Brissaud/Gamma Liaison. Page 310: Burk Ozzle/Actuality. Page 311: J. P. Laffont/Sygma. Page 315: Larry Mulvehill/Photo Researchers. Page 317: Courtesy Nathan Azrin. Page 320: John Giordano/Picture Group. Page 321: Mark Antman/The Image Works. Page 323: Grant LeDuc/Monkmeyer Press Photo. Page 327: Arnold J. Kaplan/The Picture Cube.

Chapter 12

Opener: Banus March/FPG International. Page 332: Kermani/Gamma Liaison. Page 333: Francene Keery/Stock, Boston. Page 335, left: Bettmann Archive. Page 335, right: Robin Laurence/NYT Photos. Page 340: Frank Fournier/Contact Press Images. Page 345: Jacques Chenet/Woodfin Camp & Associates. Page 347: Alon Reininger/Contact Press Images. Page 353: Everett Collection. Page 355: Rhoda Sidney/Monkmeyer Press Photo. Page 358: Chuch Nacke/Picture Group.

Chapter 13

Opener: FPG International, Icon Communications. Page 365, bottom left: Bettmann Archive. Page 365, top right: Bernard Gotfryd/Woodfin Camp & Associates. Page 365, bottom right: Ira Wyman/Sygma. Page 373: Everett Collection. Page 376: Sam C. Pierson, Jr./Photo Researchers. Page 383: Bob Daemmrich/The Image Works. Page 385: Jane Rossett/Sygma.

Chapter 14

Opener: Dick Reed/The Stock Market. Page 391: Courtesy of Mrs. Heidi Schneider. Page 393: Grunnitus/Monkmeyer Press Photo. Page 394, top: Radio Times Hulton Picture Library. Page 394, bottom: Bettmann Archive. Page 403: Kal Muller/Woodfin Camp & Associates. Page 409: Courtesy Daniel Weinberger, M.D., National Institute of Mental Health. Page 413: Courtesy Sarnoff Mednick. Page 414: Museum of Modern Art FilmStills Archive.

Chapter 15

Opener: James R. Levin/FPG International. Page 425: J. P. Laffont/Sygma. Page 431: Courtesy Dr. A. Zametkin, Department of Health and Human Services. Page 433: Lew Merrim/Monkmeyer Press Photo. Page 433: Doris De Witt/Tony Stone World Wide. Page 436: Mimi Forsyth/Monkmeyer Press Photo. Page 437, top left: Rick Kopstein/Monkmeyer Press Photo. Page 437, bottom right: Reuters/Bettmann Archive. Page 442: Simon Fraser/Photo Researchers. Page 444: Laura Dwight/Peter Arnold. Page 446: Frank Siteman/The Picture Cube. Page 447: M. Siluk/The Image Works. Page 449: Steve Schapiro/Sygma.

Chapter 16

Opener: Index Stock. Page 456: Hattie Young/Photo Researchers, Science Photo Library. Page 460: Stephen Frisch/Stock, Boston. Page 462: Greenlar/The Image Works. Page 463: /Everett Collection. Page 466, left: Kunkel/Phototake. Page 466, right: Kunkel/Phototake. Page 467: Will & Deni McIntyre/Photo Researchers. Page 469, top left: Hank Morgan/Rainbow. Page 469, bottom right: Jeff Albertson/Stock, Boston. Page 470: Culver Pictures, Inc. Page 471: Jacques Chenet/Woodfin Camp & Associates. Page 481: Glassman/The Image Works. Page 485: Alan Carey/The Image Works. Page 486: Susan Oliver Young/Courtesy of Ivar Lovaas.

Chapter 17

Opener: Index Stock. Page 492: Jackson Archives/The Image Works. Page 492: Bob Daemmrich/The Image Works. Page 495: Martin Rotker/Phototake. Page 497: Blair Seitz/Photo Researchers. Page 499: Ira Wyman/Sygma. Page 500: Freda Leinwand/Monkmeyer Press Photo. Page 506: Leonard Lessin/Peter Arnold. Page 509: Bob Daemmrich/Stock, Boston. Page 512: Frank Siteman/Monkmeyer Press Photo. Page 517: Charles Harbutt/Actuality. Page 517: Don & Pat Valenti/Tony Stone World Wide. Page 519: Charles Gupton/Stock, Boston.

Chapter 18

Opener: SUPERSTOCK. Page 530: Stacy Pickerell/Tony Stone World Wide. Page 530: Mark Antman/The Image Works. Page 535: Courtesy William Alanson White Psychiatric Foundation. Page 542: Michael Rougier, Life Magazine © Time, Inc. Page 546: Bernard Gotfryd. Page 547: Courtesy Dr. Rollo May. Page 548: Courtesy Gestalt Institute of Cleveland. Page 549: Peter Byron/Monkmeyer Press Photo.

Chapter 19

Opener: Andy Washnik/The Stock Market. Page 556: Courtesy of Public Relations Dept., Temple University Health Sciences Center. Page 558: Bob Daemmrich/The Image Works. Page 558: Courtesy Anthony Menditto, Ph. D. Page 564: Richard Hutchings/Photo Researchers. Page 575: Bob Daemmrich/Stock, Boston. Page 576: Peter Berndt, MD/Custom Medical Stock Photo. Page 577: Frank Siteman/Monkmeyer Press Photo. Page 583: Frank Siteman/Monkmeyer Press Photo. Page 588: Courtesy Dr. Arnold Lazarus.

Chapter 20

Opener: Mitchell Funk/The Image Bank. Page 596: Joe Sohm/Stock, Boston. Page 597: Charles Harbutt/Actuality. Page 603: Ann Chwatsky/Phototake. Page 610: Stephen Frisch/Stock, Boston. Page 611: Rob Nelson/Picture Group. Page 613: Froscher/The Image Works. Page 614: Hank Morgan/Rainbow.

Chapter 21

Opener: Robert A. Isaacs/Photo Researchers. Page 626: R. Mims/Sygma. Page 626: R. Mims/Sygma. Page 628: Courtesy Thomas Szasz/G. Szilasi Photography. Page 630: Sygma. Page 634: Wisconsin Center for Film and Theater Research. Page 639: AP/Wide World Photos. Page 642: Billy E. Barnes/Stock, Boston. Page 643: AP/Wide World Photos. Page 644: AP/Wide World Photos. Page 654: Larry Kolvoord/The Image Works. Page 654: Bill Bachmann/The Image Works.

Name Index

Subject Index

DSM-IV Classification: Axes I and II

Axis I

DISORDERS USUALLY FIRST DIAGNOSED IN INFANCY, CHILDHOOD, OR ADOLESCENCE

Mental Retardation
Mild Mental Retardation / Moderate Retardation / Severe Mental Retardation / Profound Mental Retardation
Learning Disorders (Academic Skills Disorders)
Reading Disorder (Developmental Reading Disorder) / Mathematics Disorder (Developmental Arithmetic Disorder) / Disorder of Written Expression (Developmental Expressive Writing Disorder)
Motor Skills Disorder
Developmental Coordination Disorder
Pervasive Developmental Disorders
Autistic Disorder / Rett's Disorder / Childhood Disintegrative Disorder / Asperger's Disorder
Disruptive Behavior and Attention-deficit Disorders
Attention-deficit/Hyperactivity Disorder / Oppositional Defiant Disorder / Conduct Disorder
Feeding and Eating Disorders of Infancy or Early Childhood
Pica / Rumination Disorder / Feeding Disorder of Infancy or Early Childhood
Tic Disorders
Tourette's Disorder / Chronic Motor or Vocal Tic Disorder / Transient Tic Disorder
Communication Disorders
Expressive Language Disorder (Developmental Expressive Language Disorder) / Mixed Receptive/Expressive Language Disorder (Developmental Receptive Language Disorder) / Phonological Disorder (Developmental Articulation Disorder) / Stuttering
Elimination Disorders
Encopresis / Enuresis
Other Disorders of Infancy, Childhood, or Adolescence
Separation Anxiety Disorder / Selective Mutism (Elective Mutism) / Reactive Attachment Disorder of Infancy or Early Childhood / Stereotypic Movement Disorder (Stereotypy/Habit Disorder)

DELIRIUM, DEMENTIA, AMNESTIC AND OTHER COGNITIVE DISORDERS

Deliria
Delirium Due to a General Medical Condition / Substance-induced Delirium / Delirium Due to Multiple Etiologies
Dementias
Dementia of the Alzheimer's Type; With Early Onset: if onset at age 65 or below; With Late Onset: if onset after age 65 / Vascular Dementia / Dementias Due to Other General Medical Conditions / Substance-induced Persisting Dementia / Dementia Due to Multiple Etiologies
Amnestic Disorders
Amnestic Disorder Due to a General Medical Condition / Substance-induced Persisting Amnestic Disorder (refer to specific substance for code)

SUBSTANCE RELATED DISORDERS

Alcohol Use Disorders
Amphetamine (or Related Substance) Use Disorders
Caffeine Use Disorders
Cannabis Use Disorders
Cocaine Use Disorders
Hallucinogen Use Disorders
Inhalant Use Disorders
Nicotine Use Disorders
Opioid Use Disorders
Phencyclidine (or Related Substance) Use Disorders
Sedative, Hypnotic, or Anxiolytic Substance Use Disorders
Polysubstance Use Disorder

SCHIZOPHRENIA AND OTHER PSYCHOTIC DISORDERS

Schizophrenia
Paranoid Type / Disorganized Type / Catatonic Type / Undifferentiated Type / Residual Type
Schizophreniform Disorder
Schizoaffective Disorder
Delusional Disorder
Brief Psychotic Disorder
Shared Psychotic Disorder (Folie à Deux)
Psychotic Disorder Due to a General Medical Condition
with delusions / with hallucinations / Substance-induced Psychotic Disorder

MOOD DISORDERS

Depressive Disorders
Major Depressive Disorder / Dysthymic Disorder
Bipolar Disorders
Bipolar I Disorder / Bipolar II Disorder (Recurrent Major Depressive Episodes with Hypomania) / Cyclothymic Disorder
Mood Disorder Due to a General Medical Condition
Substance-Induced Mood Disorder

ANXIETY DISORDERS

Panic Disorder
Without Agoraphobia / With Agoraphobia
Agoraphobia Without History of Panic Disorder
Specific Phobia (Simple Phobia)
Social Phobia (Social Anxiety Disorder)
Obsessive-Compulsive Disorder
Posttraumatic Stress Disorder
Acute Stress Disorder
Generalized Anxiety Disorder (includes Overanxious Disorder of Childhood)
Anxiety Disorder Due to a General Medical Condition
Substance-Induced Anxiety Disorder

SOMATOFORM DISORDERS

Somatization Disorder
Conversion Disorder
Hypochondriasis
Body Dysmorphic Disorder
Pain Disorder

FACTITIOUS DISORDERS

Factitious Disorder

DISSOCIATIVE DISORDERS

Dissociative Amnesia
Dissociative Fugue
Dissociative Identity Disorder (Multiple Personality Disorder)
Depersonalization Disorder

SEXUAL AND GENDER IDENTITY DISORDERS

Sexual Dysfunctions
Sexual Desire Disorders: Hypoactive Sexual Desire Disorder; Sexual Aversion Disorder / Sexual Arousal Disorders: Female Sexual Arousal Disorder; Male Erectile Disorder / Orgasm Disorders: Female Orgasmic Disorder (Inhibited Female Orgasm); Male Orgasmic Disorder (Inhibited Male Orgasm); Premature Ejaculation / Sexual Pain Disorders: Dyspareunia; Vaginismus / Sexual Dysfunctions Due to a General Medical Condition / Substance-induced Sexual Dysfunction

Paraphilias
Exhibitionism / Fetishism / Frotteurism / Pedophilia / Sexual Masochism / Sexual Sadism / Voyeurism / Transvestic Fetishism

Gender Identity Disorders
Gender Identity Disorder: in Children / in Adolescents and Adults (Transsexualism).

EATING DISORDERS

Anorexia Nervosa
Bulimia Nervosa

SLEEP DISORDERS

Primary Sleep Disorders
Dyssomnias: Primary Insomnia; Primary Hypersomnia; Narcolepsy; Breathing-Related Sleep Disorder; Circadian Rhythm Sleep Disorder (Sleep-Wake Schedule Disorder) / Parasomnias; Nightmare Disorder (Dream Anxiety Disorder); Sleep Terror Disorder; Sleepwalking Disorder / Sleep Disorders Related to Another Mental Disorder

Sleep Disorder Due to a General Medical Condition
Substance-induced Sleep Disorder

IMPULSE CONTROL DISORDERS NOT ELSEWHERE CLASSIFIED

Intermittent Explosive Disorder
Kleptomania
Pyromania
Pathological Gambling
Trichotillomania

ADJUSTMENT DISORDERS

Adjustment Disorder
With Anxiety
With Depressed Mood
With Disturbance of Conduct
With Mixed Disturbance of Emotions and Conduct
With Mixed Anxiety and Depressed Mood

Axis II

PERSONALITY DISORDERS

Paranoid Personality Disorder
Schizoid Personality Disorder
Schizotypal Personality Disorder
Antisocial Personality Disorder
Borderline Personality Disorder
Histrionic Personality Disorder
Narcissistic Personality Disorder
Avoidant Personality Disorder
Dependent Personality Disorder
Obsessive-Compulsive Personality Disorder

OTHER CONDITIONS THAT MAY BE A FOCUS OF CLINICAL ATTENTION

Psychological Factors Affecting Medical Condition
Medication-Induced Movement Disorders
Relational Problems
Relational Problem Related to A Mental Disorder or General Medical Condition / Parent-Child Relational Problem / Partner Relational Problem / Sibling Relational Problem

Problems Related to Abuse or Neglect
Physical Abuse of Child / Sexual Abuse of Child / Neglect of Child / Physical Abuse of Adult / Sexual Abuse of Adult

Additional Conditions That May Be a Focus of Clinical Attention
Bereavement / Borderline Intellectual Functioning / Academic Problem / Occupational Problem / Childhood or Adolescent Antisocial Behavior / Adult Antisocial Behavior / Malingering / Phase of Life Problem / Noncompliance with Treatment for a Mental Disorder / Identity Problem / Religious or Spiritual Problem / Acculturation Problem / Age-Associated Memory Decline